BUSINESS STUDIES for **A LEVEL**
THIRD EDITION

Ian Marcousé **Malcolm Surridge** **Andrew Gillespie**
Naomi Birchall **Marie Brewer** **Andrew Hammond**
Nigel Watson

Edited by Ian Marcousé

DYNAMIC LEARNING
Innovate · Motivate · Personalise

HODDER
EDUCATION
AN HACHETTE UK COMPANY

**SOUTHALL AND WEST
LONDON COLLEGE
LEARNING CENTRE**

Orders: please contact Bookpoint Ltd, 130 Milton Park, Abingdon, Oxon OX14 4SB. Telephone: (44) 01235 827720. Fax: (44) 01235 400454. Lines are open from 9.00 – 5.00, Monday to Saturday, with a 24-hour message answering service. You can also order through our website www.hoddereducation.co.uk.

British Library Cataloguing in Publication Data
A catalogue record for this title is available from the British Library

ISBN: 9780340966907

First Published 2008
Impression number   10 9 8 7 6 5 4
Year   2014 2013 2012 2011 2010 2009

Cover illustration © Oxford Designers & Illustrators
Typeset by Fakenham Photosetting Ltd, Fakenham Norfolk
Illustrations by Oxford Designers & Illustrators
Printed in Italy for Hodder Education, an Hachette UK company, 338 Euston Road, London NW1 3BH

Contents

Starting a business

Introduction to finance

Introduction to marketing

Introduction to people in organisations

Introduction to managing operations

Corporate objectives and strategies

Advanced accounting and finance

Advanced marketing

Advanced people in organisations

Advanced operations management

Advanced external influences

Managing change

Exam technique for A Level

Acknowledgements

Contributors

Ian Marcousé is Chair of Examiners for a major awarding body and an experienced teacher. He is Founding Editor of *Business Review* magazine and his previous books include *The Complete A-Z Business Studies Handbook*.

Malcolm Surridge is Chief Examiner for A Level Business Studies for a major awarding body and an experienced teacher and author.

Andrew Gillespie is Principal Examiner for A Level Business Studies for a major awarding body and an experienced teacher and author.

Naomi Birchall is an examiner for A Level Business Studies for a major examining board and an experienced teacher. She has developed a variety of resources for A Level, Applied A Level and GCSE Business Studies.

Marie Brewer is an Assistant Principal Examiner for A Level Business Studies for a major examining board and an established author and lecturer. She is also a co-author of *Business Studies for AS Revision Guide*.

Andrew Hammond is a Senior Examiner for a major examining board. He is Head of Business at Darrick Wood School and an experienced author.

Nigel Watson is Head of Business Studies and Economics at St Catherine's School and an established author.

Every effort has been made to trace and acknowledge ownership of copyright. The publishers will be glad to make suitable arrangements with any copyright holder whom it has not been possible to contact. The authors and publishers would like to thank the following for the use of photographs in this volume:

John Clark/EP, 1.2; © Richard Baker/Corbis, 1.3; © David J. Green/Alamy, 2.2; © Scott Hortop/Alamy, 7.1; © Robert Harding Picture Library Ltd/Alamy, 7.2; © Motoring Picture Library/Alamy,10.2; © Andy Rain/epa/Corbis, 16.2; Courtesy of Eggxactly, 16.3; © David J. Green/Alamy, 17.3; Nicholas Bailey/Rex Features,18.1; © PSL Images/Alamy, 21.3; © Ashley Cooper/Alamy, 22.1; © Jack Sullivan/Alamy, 22.2; © Transtock Inc./Alamy, 26.1; SAKKI/Rex Features, 26.2; Courtesy of FireAngel Limited, 27.5; © Mackie's of Scotland, 27.6; AP/PA Photos, 28.4; © Kay Nietfeld/dpa/Corbis, 32.1; Courtesy of The Cinnamon Club, Westminster, 32.3a & 32.3b; Jonathan Player/Rex Features, 33.1; Rex Features, 34.1; © Peter Treanor/Alamy, 39.1; © Scott Olson/Getty Images, 45.4; © Cephas Picture Library/Alamy, 47.2; Picture supplied by JCB, 49.1; © Rolf Haid/dpa/Corbis, 49.2; Patti the Architect, Inc/Malia Beving, 49.4; © WWD/Condé Nast/Corbis, 51.1; Nicholas Bailey/Rex Features, 52.3; William Philpott/AFP/Getty Images, 53.1; Leon Neal/AFP/Getty Images, 54.1; Courtesy of Reckitt Benckiser plc, 58.1; © Antony Nettle/Alamy, 59.1; © Tesco/AFP/Getty Images, 60.2; © UPPA/Photoshot, 62.1; Courtesy Heinz UK & Ireland, 62.3; © Paul Cooper/Rex Features, 63.1; © Martin Lee/Rex Features, 66.1; © Bettmann/CORBIS, 68.1; Fisher/Thatcher/Getty Images, 69.2; Time & Life Pictures/Getty Images, 71.1; Francis Dean/Rex Features, 71.2; Shaun Curry/AFP/Getty Images, 73.1; © The Boeing Company/Handout/epa/Corbis, 74.2; © Robert Stainforth/Alamy, 75.3; Eye Ubiquitous/Rex Features, 76.1; © Adrian Sherratt/Alamy, 77.2; AP/PA Photos, 79.1; Courtesy of John Smedley Ltd, 80.1; © 67photo/Alamy, 84.4; TopFoto/National News, 86.1; Courtesy of Texas Instruments, 87.1; Rex Features, 87.2; © Robert Harding Picture Library Ltd/Alamy, 87.3; © UK retail Alan King/Alamy, 88.2; Rex Features, 90.1; www.sainsbury.co.uk, 93.1; © JUPITERIMAGES/BrandX/Alamy, 101.1.

HODDER
EDUCATION
The Expert Choice

What does 'the expert choice' mean for you?

We work with more examiners and experts than any other publisher

- Because we work with more experts and examiners than any other publisher, the very latest curriculum requirements are built into this course and there is a perfect match between your course and the resources that you need to succeed. We make it easier for you to gain the skills and knowledge that you need for the best results.

- We have chosen the best team of experts – including the people that mark the exams – to give you the very best chance of success; look out for their advice throughout this book: this is content that you can trust.

Welcome to Dynamic Learning

Dynamic Learning is a simple and powerful way of integrating this text with digital resources to help you succeed, by bringing learning to life. Whatever your learning style, Dynamic Learning will help boost your understanding. And our Dynamic Learning content is updated online so your book will never be out of date.

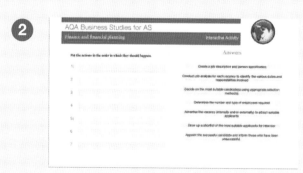

e direct contact with teachers and students than any other publisher

e talk with more than 100 000 students every year through our student onferences, run by Philip Allan Updates. We hear at first hand what you need to ake a success of your A-level studies and build what we learn into every new ourse. Learn more about our conferences at **www.philipallan.co.uk**

ur new materials are trialled in classrooms as we develop them, and the feedback uilt into every new book or resource that we publish. You can be part of that. If ou have comments that you would like to make about this book, please email us :: **feedback@hodder.co.uk**

e collaboration with Subject Associations than any other publisher

ubject Associations sit at the heart of education. We work closely with more ssociations than any other publisher. This means that our resources support the ost creative teaching and learning, using the skills of the best teachers in their eld to create resources for you.

e opportunities for your teachers to stay ahead than with any other publisher

hrough our Philip Allan Updates Conferences, we offer teachers access to ontinuing Professional Development. Our focused and practical conferences nsure that your teachers have access to the best presenters, teaching materials nd training resources. Our presenters include experienced teachers, Chief and rincipal Examiners, leading educationalists, authors and consultants. This course built on all of this expertise.

namic Learning Network Edition

oost your understanding through interactive activities on both Student Online and etwork editions.

etwork Edition gives easy access to the book's key charts and diagrams so that ou can use them in your studies.

ey business concepts are illustrated in more than 20 video clips featuring exciting oung entrepreneur Fraser Doherty and staff from First Direct in the Network dition.

ear examiners talk you through exam-style questions and answers in detail using ur unique 'Personal Tutor' software. You will see them build the answer that gets he best-possible marks and highlight common problems and errors.

etwork Edition gives access to easy-to-use PowerPoint presentations which how you what each chapter is going to deliver for you, and help you to check your nderstanding once you have worked through the section.

This book is supported by a free website at **www.dynamic-learning-student.co.uk**.
To access this website refer to the instructions printed on the inside front cover.

Copyright restrictions mean that some materials may not be accessible from within the Student Online edition.

u can find out more at **www.dynamic-learning.co.uk**

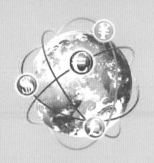

ENTERPRISE AND ENTREPRENEURS

DEFINITION

Enterprise is the combination of attitudes and skills that helps an individual turn an idea into reality. Many people think 'if only...', but do nothing about it; entrepreneurs show the enterprise to stop dreaming and get working.

1.1 Introduction

Most **entrepreneurs** see the opportunities that others see, but have the courage and initiative to act quickly. The past ten years have seen two clear trends: an increasing desire for travel, and more and more thrill-seeking, such as extreme sports. Many people could see that both trends pointed to a gap in the market for a new service: space tourism (i.e. individuals going into outer space – just for the fun of it). Richard Branson saw the same opportunity and started Virgin Galactic, which plans to charge £100,000 per trip. It hopes to make its first flight before 2010.

A successful entrepreneur needs the following characteristics:

● understanding of the market – to know what customers want, and to see how well or badly current companies are serving them

● initiative – showing the spark to seize the opportunities, without being intimidated by the thought 'Why is no one else doing this already?'; this requires self-confidence and the ability to cope with risk

● creativity may be a key factor, as in the case of Innocent Drinks – it took creative minds to design the style, tone and visual images that have made Innocent such a distinctive brand

● resilience and determination – to see things through if the going gets tough, backed by simple hard work

● passion – not just to make money, but to achieve something, such as to design a more efficient solar panel, or to transform rooms from shabby into bright and freshly painted

● persuasive abilities – entrepreneurs need to persuade others to do things like provide planning permission, supply goods on credit or work harder/faster to get things completed on time; they may also need to persuade staff to take a chance by joining a brand new, risky venture

● the ability to take **calculated risks**.

A-grade application

From sixth form to squillionaire

Aged 17, Andrew Michael turned an A-level project into an internet business start-up. In 2006 he sold the company, receiving a cheque for just over £46 million. His business was Fasthosts, which provides email and other services for small companies. It grew rapidly, earning a listing in *The Sunday Times* as the second-fastest-growing technology company in Britain.

Andrew's business was famous for the parties he threw for his staff. At different Christmases he hired Girls Aloud, The Darkness and The Sugababes. Now he's sad to have sold his business, but looking forward to a lifetime ambition of owning a helicopter.

1.2 Risk-taking

Business decisions are always about the future. Therefore they always involve uncertainty, because no one can be sure about the future. The oil giant BP's management had a wonderful reputation until a series of safety issues in America in 2005 and 2006 made its halo slip. Similarly, in 2005, phone companies such as 3 forecast huge growth from person-to-person video phoning, yet this has not happened.

Table 1.1 What makes an entrepreneur?

People who aren't entrepreneurs:	Bad entrepreneurs:	Good entrepreneurs:
are very cautious – never want to take any risks	ignore risks – assume that their own charisma/skill will guarantee success	take **calculated risks**, weighing up the potential risks and rewards
assume that things are the way they have to be	rush to bring in something new or make huge changes	launch new ideas in response to changing consumer tastes or attitudes
like to be sure of next month's pay cheque – and the one after . . . until retirement	trust that things will go as planned, spend freely at the start as they're sure the cash will start flowing tomorrow	accept that the early days of a new business may be very tough, so try to spend as little as possible

Good entrepreneurs consider what they think will happen, but also about what might happen differently. Someone opening a restaurant may expect 60 customers a day, each spending £25. In fact, one month after opening, there may just be 40 customers, spending £20 each. Receiving just £800 instead of £1500 may make it hard to survive financially; there may be a risk of closure. This possibility should have been foreseen so that plans could be made.

An entrepreneur looks at the risks, compares them with the possible rewards and makes a cool decision. If there's a good chance of making £1000 a week, but also a (small) chance of losing £500 a week, it is worth carrying on. Risk-takers accept that sometimes they will take a loss; that is part of business.

than they can get from a regular job. A recent NatWest survey of 1400 entrepreneurs (see Figure 1.1) named the top start-up motive as 'to gain more control and avoid being told what to do'. Just 6% said that they started their venture 'to make money'.

In some cases, starting a business can be hugely challenging, satisfying, absorbing and profitable. One example is Louisa Fletcher, who built a multi-million property empire, website and media career by her early thirties, having left school at 16. Yet some people kid themselves about enterprise. They assume it's more satisfying, glamorous and profitable than it often is. Many shopkeepers work very long hours for quite poor rewards. Many small builders speak bitterly about their experiences in dealings with customers, suppliers and

1.3 Motives for becoming an entrepreneur

Although 20% of entrepreneurs have money as their prime motive, most are looking for more. Typically they are looking for 'a challenge' or 'to prove myself'. In other words, people are looking for greater satisfaction

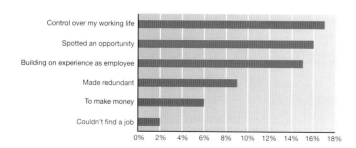

Figure 1.1 Key motivators for entrepreneurs
Source: Adapted from material published by NatWest Bank, IFF research, May 2007

Figure 1.2 Property entrepreneur Louisa Fletcher

employees; they feel it would be easier to just earn a wage. Furthermore, government figures show that 30% of new businesses fail within their first three years.

No wonder entrepreneurs need to have qualities such as resilience and the ability to take calculated risks.

Motives for becoming a social entrepreneur

Of course, not everyone is 'in it for the money' – some, known as **social entrepreneurs**, want to achieve something that is worth far more to them. In 1985, Farm Africa was set up as a charity by two men concerned about rural poverty in Kenya. It still does fine work, bringing fit goats to African villages. In 2004, Duncan Goose set up One Water, which uses the profits from selling bottled water to fund water projects in Africa. One Water has already financed more than 100 water wells.

Entrepreneurs such as these make use of their business skills in order to achieve their personal mission to make the world a better place. Duncan Goose was a well-paid advertising executive before starting One Water (and then spending two years without earning a penny for himself). Partly through his advertising skills, One Water's sales turnover has grown from £4000 to £4 million in three years.

Government support for enterprise

Novice entrepreneurs believe that the government will be behind them all the way. They will soon find out that life is not like that. Over 40% of those thinking about starting a business believe that they will get a grant; in fact only 2% get funding in this way (i.e. 1 new business in 50).

The government's main expenditure to support new business comes from the Business Link network. This offers advice for all those starting up; all new businesspeople are entitled to one free consultation with an expert nominated by Business Link. Unfortunately, the quality of the advice is said to be very variable. Some entrepreneurs speak highly of their **mentor**; others criticise that 'mine hadn't run a business in his life; he was just a banker'. The government's own research shows that just 7% of recent business start-ups have gone to Business Link for support.

Gordon Brown has long believed that the key support for enterprise is to encourage an 'enterprise culture'. In effect, create a spirit among young people that being enterprising is 'cool'. The argument runs that if lots of people want to start their own businesses, perhaps Britain will develop as dynamically as America – the heart of the enterprise culture.

Issues For Analysis

● Some people think that real entrepreneurs are born that way (i.e. they have the right skills, self-confidence and attitudes from birth). Others say that all the skills can be learnt – sometimes quite late in life. Research points clearly to the second argument – that the skills can be learnt.

● A second important issue is whether entrepreneurs tend to be school underachievers whose success comes from their reaction against their school 'failure'. Businesspeople such as Richard Branson and Louisa Fletcher were dyslexic, and did badly at school. Countering that, however, is any glance at Britain's 'Rich List'. Most of the business multi-millionaires came from wealthy families and had a good education.

Figure 1.3 Virgin founder Richard Branson

1.6 Enterprise and entrepreneurs
an evaluation

Perhaps the most important issue of all is whether the government does enough to help entrepreneurs. Business representatives like to suggest that 'red tape' (government regulation) makes it hard to start up. This is largely nonsense; Britain is one of the easiest, quickest and cheapest places in the world to start up a new firm. It comes as a shock to many, though, to find how little help there is out there. The government's huge spending on Business Link seems to achieve little. Perhaps it would be better to spend that money on the health service than to spend a lot in providing a small bit of help to just 7% of new firms.

Key terms

Calculated risks: risk decisions based on a careful comparison of the risks set against the rewards expected from a decision.

Entrepreneur: someone who makes a business idea happen, either through their own effort, or by organizing others to do the work.

Innovations: new ideas brought to the market.

Mentor: an experienced adviser, to be there when needed.

Social entrepreneurs: those who use their business skills to start an organisation with the goal of making the world a slightly better place.

Exercises

A. Revision questions

(25 marks; 25 minutes)

1 Why is 'initiative' an important quality in an entrepreneur? (2)

2 Section 1.1 lists the characteristics needed to be a successful entrepreneur. Which two items from this list seem of greatest importance to:
   (a) a new firm facing a collapse in demand due to flooding locally (2)
   (b) a 19-year-old entrepreneur wanting to start her own airline. (2)

3 Section 1.2 mentions a restaurant that expects 60 customers per day spending £25 each, but actually gets 40 customers spending £20. Calculate the shortfall in revenue that will result from these changes. (3)

4 Explain two actions the government could take to encourage more people to become entrepreneurs. (4)

5 Briefly explain one argument for and one against saying that entrepreneurs are born, not made. (5)

6 Having read this unit, explain briefly how successful or unsuccessful you think you would be as an entrepreneur. Take care to explain your reasoning. (7)

B. Revision exercises

B1 Data response

Travis Sporland is a surfer who believes he has come up with a revolutionary design for surfboards. His father was made redundant from a Devon boatyard two years ago, so Travis thinks they can start up a small manufacturing business together. The Travis surfboard is designed for children up to the age of 11. He believes the size of the world market may be as high as 1.5 million. Some of his forecasts about the business are at the foot of the page:

Questions

(20 marks; 20 minutes)

1 If you were asked to advise Travis, identify four questions you would like to ask him about his business plans. (8)

2 Explain your reasoning behind *one* of those questions. (3)

3 Discuss two main factors you think he should also consider before going ahead. (9)

Year 1 figures			
	UK market only (surfers under 11)	**US market only (surfers under 11)**	**Rest of the world (surfers under 11)**
Surfer population	22,000	580,000	460,000
Forecast year 1 sales	2,200	29,000	23,000
Surfboard selling price	£120	$200	$150

B2 Case study

Nearly Crusshed

In 1998, the same year that Innocent Drinks was launched, three men started Crussh, London's first smoothie bar. Whereas Innocent targeted the market for packaged soft drinks (and now has sales of over £100 million a year), Crussh would produce fresh smoothies or juices. James Learmond saw the need in London for drinks that were both delicious and healthy. He also saw that Starbucks had broken through various customer price ceilings. It was perfectly possible to get people to pay £2 or £3 for a drink.

James invested £100,000 to start the first Crussh bar, then needed further capital in 1999 to buy out his other founding shareholders. Worse came in 2001, when over-expansion plus an economic dip forced him to borrow £500,000 from the bank. Today James owns 40% of the business.

Current managing director Chris Fung points out that many of the early juice bar and smoothie start-ups went under because they could not cope with the seasonality of the business. In a typical July week in the City of London, Monday might be rainy, causing sales to be poor; Tuesday warm, creating strong sales; Wednesday hot, causing high demand, long queues and grumpy customers; and Thursday could see thunderstorms. Worse still, the winter months would see trade dry up. A profitable summer followed by a terrible winter can be very tough on **cash flow** for a new business.

Fortunately Crussh survived its early scares and by 2006 made £500,000 profit on sales of £5 million. By mid 2008 there were 21 Crussh smoothie bars in London, and plans in hand for spreading them throughout the country. This success has been built on a rethink of the **business model**. Handmade smoothies no longer form the bulk of the business. Chris Fung says that they 'capture the imagination' of consumers, who may then order an organic bread sandwich, a ham and pea soup or a cup of coffee. This is how sales have been adjusted to allow for the British weather. The Crussh start-up has become a great success, but don't suggest to James Learmond that it was easy.

Questions

(30 marks; 35 minutes)

1 Explain what is meant by the terms:
- cash flow (3)
- business model (3)

2 Crussh received no government support during its set-up phase. Should the government invest in the business now? Explain your answer. (6)

3 Discuss which of the qualities listed in Section 1.1 were important in James Learmond's case. (10)

4 a Why did Crussh change its product range over the period 1998–2007? (4)

4 b How did it do so? (4)

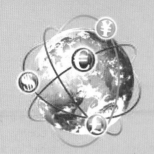

Unit 2 — IDENTIFYING BUSINESS OPPORTUNITIES

DEFINITION

Business opportunities must be spotted and acted upon before someone else gets there first.

2.1 Generating business ideas

At the heart of successful entrepreneurship is spotting a good business idea. This is usually based on a good understanding of consumer tastes and/or the needs of the retail trade. Both qualities were shown by Martyn Dawes, who spotted the opportunity for machines that could automatically make high-quality coffee. His Coffee Nation machines in motorway service stations (and, from 2007, Tesco Express stores) have made him a millionaire.

The main sources of business ideas are as follows.

- Observation: Martyn Dawes had seen similar machines in New York delis, and recognised their potential use in Britain.

- Brainstorming can be useful; this is where two or more people are encouraged to come up with ideas, without anyone criticising anyone else's ideas, no matter how bizarre; the appraisal process comes later.

- Thinking ahead: perhaps about the new opportunities that will arise if, say, the weather continues to get warmer (air conditioning; ice cream, etc.).

- Ideas from personal or business experience: for example, 'There are no ice cream parlours for miles around' or 'In my company we need quality sandwiches delivered at lunchtime.'

- **Innovations**: these may come from new science, such as Pilkington's self-cleaning glass (used in skyscrapers worldwide), or from clever reworkings of existing knowledge, such as James Seddon's 'Eggxactly' waterless egg cooker.

2.2 Spotting an opportunity

It would be easy to get gloomy and to think that all the great business ideas and opportunities have already gone: the hamburger chain, the fizzy cola, and so on. In fact this is completely wrong. Society changes constantly, with different attitudes or fads that mark out the generations. In the 1980s and 1990s most people went on 'package holidays' – trips to Spain run by big holiday companies. Today most people do things independently, giving opportunities for new discount airlines, independent hotels and small car hire companies. If people want a package holiday, it is more likely to be a specialist one, such as diving in Egypt; it will probably be run by a small, independent travel company.

The keys to spotting new business opportunities are to:

- think about changes to society, e.g. more concern about the body beautiful (cosmetic surgery, anti-ageing creams, fashion clothing, etc.)

- think about changes to the economy, e.g. if a downturn in America hits consumer confidence in Britain

- think about the local housing market, e.g. whether people are moving into or out of your area, and whether prices are moving up or down; many local business opportunities may rise or fall depending on these factors

- use the techniques outlined below – small budget research and careful market mapping.

2.3 Small budget research

Even before using market research (see Unit 22) good entrepreneurs take the time to gain a general understanding of the market. Someone thinking about buying into a Subway franchise for Huddersfield might:

● walk around the town, mapping where sandwich bars and other fast-food outlets are located (this is called **geographical mapping**)

● while they're at it, check on prices, special deals, student discounts, etc.

● ask Subway to arrange for them to spend a day at its franchise in a nearby town, to help understand the customer and the way the service is provided

● based on the knowledge gained from the above, produce a **market map** of fast food in Huddersfield; this will help identify whether Subway will have a **market niche** to itself.

Small budget research may also point towards new business opportunities. Buying *The Grocer* magazine provides many useful insights. Each week it highlights one consumer marketplace. For example, the 4 August 2007 issue highlighted that sales of dark chocolate have grown 12% to £67 million a year. This would be very helpful for a small chocolate-maker, who might decide to stretch beyond the usual milk chocolate products.

2.4 Market mapping

Market mapping is carried out in two stages:

1 identify the key features that characterise consumers within a market; examples in the market for women's clothes would be young/old and high fashion/ conservative

2 having identified the key characteristics, then every brand should be placed on a grid such as that shown in Figure 2.1; this will reveal where the competition is concentrated, and may reveal some gaps in the market.

Using this approach could help in identifying a product or market niche that has not yet been filled. In the market map shown in Figure 2.1 there appears to be an available niche for healthy eating for younger customers within the fast food sector. The market map points to this possibility; then it would be up to the entrepreneur to investigate further. In particular, the niche may be present, but too small to provide an opportunity for a profitable business.

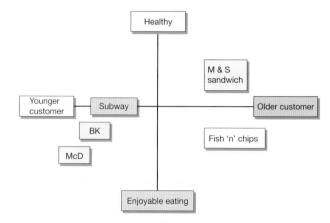

Figure 2.1 Market map: fast food

2.5 Franchises

Starting a new business with a new idea requires a huge amount of planning, skill, and perhaps luck, on the part of the businessperson. Government figures suggest that only 70% of new businesses will survive for three years. The reasons for this failure rate of nearly a third are easy to see:

● the business idea may not be good enough

● even a good idea can be copied by other firms rushing into the market

● a good idea can be wrecked if the product or service disappoints the customer (e.g. slow service, late delivery, inconsistent product or poorly trained staff).

Many of these problems can be avoided if the entrepreneur goes for a 'halfway house' towards running their own business: a franchise. NatWest Bank suggests that 93% of franchises survive their first three years (i.e. the failure rate is only 7%).

For example, if you start up an independent optician service, you have to:

● design and decorate a store that will create the right customer image

● create systems for staff training, stock control and accounting

● do your own advertising to bring in customers, and to make them willing to pay the high prices charged by opticians

Alternatively, you could start up your own, 100% independent limited company, and then sign up for a Specsavers franchise. This would mean, for example, access to the specially written Specsavers store management software. From a scan of a sold pair of glasses, the software ensures that all the necessary stock ordering and accounting actions are taken. The franchise owner (Specsavers) also provides full training for the **franchisee** (the entrepreneur), plus advice and supplier contacts for store decoration and display and, of course, the huge marketing support offered by a multi-million-pound TV advertising campaign. If you start up J. Bloggs Opticians, how many people will come through the doors? If you open up Specsavers, customers will trust the business from day one.

A-grade application

Specsavers

Specsavers was started by Doug and Mary Perkins in Guernsey in 1984. They opened branches in Devon and Cornwall, each run by a manager within their own Specsavers chain. In 1988, the company decided to speed up its growth by getting individuals to open their own Specsavers franchise outlets. Now the finance needed to open each new branch (approximately £140,000) would come from the franchisee, not Doug and Mary. Also, the founders would no longer have to manage each store on a day-to-day basis. Each franchisee has every incentive to run his/her store well, because all the outlet's revenues are kept locally – apart from the royalty rate of 5% that must be paid to Specsavers' head office. Doug and Mary also receive a start-up fee from each new franchisee, which is a sum of between £25,000 and £50,000 depending upon location.

   This approach has allowed Specsavers to develop into the third largest optician chain in the world, with more than 500 branches.

Founding a franchise

To start selling franchises in your own business becomes possible only when its success is clear and quite long-established. Fred deLuca, aged 17, borrowed $1000 in 1964 to open a sandwich shop. He built his business up to a chain of successful stores and then, in 1975, started offering franchises to others who wanted to buy into his Subway business. By 1995 there were 11,000 Subway outlets.

The franchise owner (also known as the **franchisor**) then needs to establish:

● a training programme, so that franchisees learn to do things 'the Subway way'

● a system of pricing that is profitable without putting off potential franchisees; usually the franchise rights are bought for £10,000–£100,000, then the franchisee must buy all store fittings and equipment via the franchise owner (this may cost £50,000–£250,000), and then buy all supplies from the franchise owner; on top of this, a 5% royalty is usually paid on all income and a fee of 3–5% to contribute towards the national advertising campaign

● a system of monitoring, so that poorly run franchises do not damage the reputation of the brand.

Becoming a franchisee

For those starting their first business, full independence means the freedom to make all decisions, including many mistakes. Buying into a franchise makes the start-up much safer. Instead of struggling to establish a local reputation, the business has a national reputation from day one (e.g. KFC, Subway and Specsavers). All marketing decisions will be handled by head office, not by the franchisee.

The franchisee will be an independent business, but working within the rules laid down by the franchise owner. These will cover the store decor, the staff uniforms, the product range, the product pricing and much else. Yet the franchisee will still have to manage: staff recruitment, training and motivation; stock ordering; quality control and management; effective customer service.

Pitfalls of running a franchise

It is important to be clear that really independent-minded people might hate to be franchisees; after all, they may want to start their own business to 'be their own boss'. A franchisee is the boss of the business, but without the normal freedoms of decision making. This could be very frustrating. It will also be important to choose the right franchise. On the fringes of franchising are some dubious businesses that sell the promises of training and advertising support, but supply very little after they have pocketed the franchise fee. As with anything in business, careful research is essential; better franchise operators are members of the British Franchise Association (the BFA). It should also be borne in mind that the franchise owner's slice of your income may make it difficult to make good profits from 'your' business.

Benefits of running a franchise

A young businessperson could treat being a franchisee as wonderful training towards becoming a full entrepreneur: 'Today I'll open a Subway; in five years I'll sell it and open my own restaurant.' Very few people have the range of skills required of the independent business owner. Who is expert at marketing, buying, store design, window display, staff management, sales, stock control and accounting? This is why the failure rate for new independent businesses is so much higher than for franchise businesses.

Due to the different failure rates, the attitude of bankers is very different when you seek finance for a franchise start-up. Ask NatWest for £50,000 to start J. Bloggs Sandwich Shop, and the door will quickly be closed; ask for £50,000 to help finance a Subway outlet and the response will be far more positive. Franchisees find finance easier and cheaper to get. The interest rate charged by a bank for a potential Subway franchisee will be lower than the rate it would charge to the founder of an independent business start-up.

Figure 2.2 Specsavers is a franchise with a national reputation

Issues For Analysis

● When thinking of a new business idea, it is important to not only think about its unique features and the response of customers, but also how easy it is to copy. Opening the first Polish restaurant in Luton may look like a licence to print money, but how will the business do when the second then the third Polish restaurants are opened down the road?

● Buying into a franchise can be seen as business-made-easy. The difficulties should not be underestimated, though. Above all else, most entrepreneurs gain most of their satisfaction from the challenge of creating and marketing a unique business idea. What they least look forward to is the

everyday slog of running a shop or managing semi-interested part-time staff. The life of a franchisee is a long way from the life of a full entrepreneur; it will only suit a certain type of person.

2.6 Identifying business opportunities
an evaluation

Every aspect of starting a business is challenging. If something looks easy it is probably only due to naivety on the part of the observer. Anyone who has started a successful business deserves respect. If their start-up seems to have been smooth, probe and question whether the whole story is being told. If it is, then the entrepreneur(s) were probably incredibly well organised, and perhaps a bit lucky. Most entrepreneurs are willing to accept that luck plays its part – for instance, in how intelligently competitors react to your start-up. Starting a business is fascinating precisely because not all the factors can be controlled – every start-up is a bit of a stab in the dark. Therefore, evaluative exam answers show an understanding that a struggling new business may actually have been quite well run by its founders. Business failure does not equal business incompetence.

> ### Key terms
>
> **Franchisee:** a person or company who has paid to become part of an established franchise business (such as Subway or Specsavers).
> **Franchisor:** the owner of the holding company and franchise (e.g. KFC).
> **Geographical mapping:** plotting on a map the locations of all the existing businesses in your market (i.e. to show where all your competitors are).
> **Innovations:** new ideas brought to the market.
> **Market map:** a grid plotting where each existing brand sits on scales based on two important features of a market (e.g. in the car market: luxury/economy and green/gas-guzzling).
> **Market niche:** a gap in the market (i.e. no one else is offering what you want to offer).

Exercises

A. Revision questions

(30 marks; 30 minutes)

1 Explain how 'observation' might help a business-minded person to come up with a great new idea for starting a firm. (3)

2 The UK population is growing older, with a rising proportion of over-sixties. Outline two business opportunities that might arise as the population gets older. (4)

3 Explain, in your own words, the purpose of geographical mapping. (3)

4 Identify three markets where age is a crucial factor in drawing up a market map. (3)

5 Examine two reasons why a successful, growing business might choose not to sell franchises in the business. (6)

6 Why are good franchise owners keen to inspect their franchisees regularly, even though they have no ownership stake in the franchisee businesses? (3)

7 Why should a potential franchisee be very careful to research fully the background of the franchise owner? (4)

8 Section 2.6 talks about the importance of luck in business start-ups; outline how bad luck might damage the start of a small bakery. (4)

B. Revision exercises

B1 Data response

Cara Phelps has worked in Sainsbury's Personnel Department for eight years and is getting bored. She owns her own flat in Leeds, has managed to save £18,000 and wants to start her own business. Her passion is shoes (she has 70 pairs!) so she wants to start a shoe shop. She has been eyeing a site close to Harvey Nichols, as she wants to target those willing to pay £50–£200 a pair. She was going to start up an independent shop, but her father has asked her to look at the franchise opportunities being offered by an upmarket London shoe shop.

Figure 2.3 presents a profile of Cara, drawn up by a friend who is a business consultant.

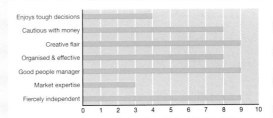

Figure 2.3 A profile of Cara Phelps

Questions

(25 marks; 25 minutes)

1 Outline two pieces of small budget research Cara should carry out before taking things any further with her upmarket shoe shop in Leeds. (6)

2a Outline one possible benefit to Cara of opting to become a franchisee. (3)

2b Outline one aspect of the London shoe shop franchise that Cara should examine more carefully before signing any agreements. (4)

3 Use the text and Figure 2.3 to discuss whether Cara is better suited to running a franchise or an independent shoe shop. (12)

B2 Data response

Why franchise?

After many years as a call centre manager, Malachy Miller looked into starting his own business. He quickly decided that franchising would be the right route for him: 'Unless you have an idea or product that will turn everything upside down then this is better than simply going it alone. . . Franchises allow you to minimise the risk and you're buying into something that's already there.'

When Mal went to a franchising exhibition in Birmingham he was impressed by the O'Brien's stand. This chain of 300 franchise sandwich bars has been going for over 15 years. The exhibition stand was being run by existing franchisees, who were very happy with their relationship with O'Brien's.

O'Brien's required an investment of £80,000, of which half had to be from Mal's own pocket. This would pay for all the shopfitting on new premises in Northampton. In addition to this initial outlay, O'Brien's takes 9% of the weekly turnover in fees and advertising support charges. As it can be hard to charge high prices for sandwiches, will there be enough profit for Mal to make a good living? By Googling 'O'Brien's' it soon becomes clear that quite a few are up for sale, including one in Glasgow on sale for £50,000. Should Mal proceed?

Not everyone has had good experiences with franchising. Mark Simmonds was a franchisee of the restaurant chain Pierre Victoire, when it went into liquidation. He has the following advice for potential franchisees.

- Don't rely on financial information given – get it checked out.
- Speak to other franchisees to validate the information given, especially profits.
- Make sure the revenue statistics are achievable.
- Validate start-up costs.
- Make sure the location's good if it's a food franchise.

Questions

(30 marks; 30 minutes)

1 Explain why Mal wanted to start a franchise, not an independent business. (4)

2 Examine why the views of the franchisees at the exhibition may not have been typical of those of all O'Brien's franchisees. (5)

3 Apart from the franchise fee, suggest three other business costs Mal would have to pay to run the sandwich shop. (3)

4 Consider the list of advice given by Mark Simmonds. Discuss which aspects of this would be especially useful for Mal. (9)

5 Recommend whether or not Mal should proceed with the O'Brien's franchise. Explain your thinking. (9)

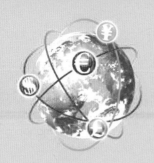

DEFINITION

'Demand' measures the level of interest customers have in buying a product. To be 'effective', that interest must be backed by the ability to pay. 'Supply' is the quantity of a product that producers are able to deliver within a specific time period (e.g. a week).

3.1 What makes a market?

The traditional market took place in a street or square. It was a place where buyers and sellers came together. Today the word 'market' usually means all the buyers and all the sellers across the country (e.g. 'the car market'). Such a market has a physical element (car showrooms, garages, and so on) and a virtual element, such as www.autocar.co.uk.

The common factor among all markets is that they rely on cash or credit to enable the sales to take place. In the case of the housing market, virtually no one pays in cash; the common currency is credit from a bank or building society. This, in turn, means debt for the buyer. Markets that rely a great deal on credit can collapse if credit becomes more difficult or more expensive to obtain.

Table 3.1 Examples of cash and credit markets

Cash markets	Credit markets
• Food and drink • Newspapers and magazines • Cinema, football and other leisure	• Cars • Houses • Carpets and furniture

Ideally, a market would be made up of lots of buyers and lots of sellers. The sellers would compete with each other, so that none could make an easy living by charging greedily. In a busy street market, if one seller is charging 20p extra per pound of potatoes, the buyers will go elsewhere. In effect the buyers will force the seller to cut the price back to the level charged by the competitors.

In a market with fierce competition, the rules are simple:

● high demand pulls prices up

● weak demand (not many customers) forces firms to cut prices

● if there's a supply shortage, prices tend to rise

● if supply is plentiful, prices will fall.

By no means all markets work in this way, however. The situation in the diamond market, for instance, is quite the opposite. The South African diamond giant De Beers has control over 50% of the world's diamonds. It uses this control to keep prices high (diamonds were quite cheap, readily available jewels until De Beers decided that 'Diamonds Are Forever'). With one company monopolising such a big slice of the world market, individual shops have to pay De Beers' prices if they want to have a full range of diamond-based jewellery.

A-grade application
Premier League tickets

On 5 April 2008 a ticket to the Premier League match at Fulham cost £5 for under-16s. Two weeks later it cost £20. Why the fourfold difference?

On 5 April the opposition was Sunderland, and the expectation of the Fulham ticket office was that it would be a struggle to sell the 26,000 tickets available. Two weeks' later, the visitors were Liverpool, and there was little doubt that the 26,000 seats could be sold. So, with low demand expected for the 5th, the price was cut sharply, whereas the in-demand Liverpool game led to high prices.

3.2 What should firms supply?

In some cases, this is an easy question to answer. When Fulham play Bolton, the 26,000 seats will provide more than enough supply. The ticket office will sell to whoever is willing to pay the price. The available supply will be 26,000; the demand may be around 20,000, leaving a surplus of 6000.

In other cases the supply may be harder to plan for. A farmer planting a field with apple trees knows that the first fruit crop will begin in two to five years' time, so the actual supply in three years' time is very uncertain. This is important because the big supermarket chains will deal only with suppliers who promise to deliver the right quantity at the right time.

Profit-focused firms will want to supply at the level that makes as a high a profit as possible. This is known as the profit-maximising point. In Table 3.2, that point occurs when the business supplies 40,000 units a week.

Table 3.2 Locating the profit-maximising point

Supply	Profit per unit	Total profit
10,000	£3.20	£32,000
20,000	£3.60	£72,000
30,000	£3.50	£105,000
40,000	**£3.20**	**£128,000**
50,000	£2.50	£125,000

There are several factors that affect the quantity of product a firm would want to supply:

● the operating costs, such as the cost of materials, the cost of rent, fuel, salaries, advertising, and so on; the higher the costs, the lower the incentive to supply – this is because, the higher the costs, the lower the profit per unit

● the price that can be reached within the marketplace – if the product is attractive enough to customers, they will be willing to pay a high price; this will result in higher potential profit per unit, in which case the business would be delighted to offer further supplies, if it is able to do so.

3 Physical constraints. Some businesses are not able to change one or more of the key factors determining supply. Between January 2004 and January 2008, the world price for copper rose from $2500 to $7500 per ton. A key factor was that the world's copper-mining companies struggled to increase supply, even though there was plenty of demand coming through from China. Quite simply, the mines were working flat out, and no new copper mines were discovered and opened during this time.

Drawing a supply curve

A **supply curve** can be drawn to show how supply increases when customers are willing to pay more for a product. In Figure 3.1, companies are willing to supply 20,000 tons when the price is $400. If the price were to rise further, to $600, suppliers would be delighted to offer 30,000 tons of supply.

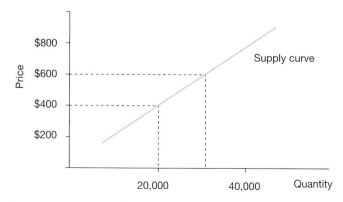

Figure 3.1 A supply curve

The supply curve is drawn on the assumption that suppliers can respond quickly to changes in demand. This would be possible if plenty of the product is kept in storage, or if the production process is speedy and flexible enough to be increased at will.

3.3 Factors affecting demand

Every business needs to learn about the key factors that affect the level of demand for its products. For producers of soft drinks and ice creams, nothing depresses demand more than a wet summer. A long, hot summer can treble the sales of Coke, Fruit Shoot and Walls Solero.

Important factors affecting demand are as follows.

- *Price:* the price set by the supplier is a crucial part of the consumer equation:

$$\frac{\text{quality}}{\text{price}} = \text{value for money}$$

  it should be remembered, though, that price also affects the image of quality, so it is as much a matter of psychology as maths.

- *Competitors' prices:* if the price of a direct substitute is set relatively low, the rival will probably steal market share from your own product. At the time of writing, Double Decker bars are on special offer at 29p; this will hit sales of comparable brands, such as the Mars bar, which is currently selling at 45–50p.

- *Fashion/taste:* what is fashionable at one time is often unfashionable soon afterwards; consumer trends such as anti-obesity or pro-organic can also fade in and out of importance; well-run businesses respond to changing consumer attitudes and desires.

- *The state of the economy:* if consumers fear that the future looks bleak, they will tend to save more and spend less, thereby causing the economic slowdown they feared. High interest rates and hikes in personal taxation are ways in which consumer spending may be forced downwards by people's lack of confidence in their future.

- *Other factors* may be hugely important in specific business circumstances, such as seasonality (toys, greetings cards, perfumes), the weather (beer, soft drinks, gloves) and marketing spending (e.g. the amount spent on advertising).

3.4 Drawing a demand curve

A **demand curve** can be drawn only after gathering evidence about the likely level of sales at different prices. If you had the rights to a one-off 'Evening with J. K. Rowling', in which Harry Potter's creator was to speak for the first time about 'Harry's greatest adventure', what would you charge for the tickets? Ideally, you would try to work out what the demand would be at different prices (see the demand curve in Figure 3.2). Then you could find out the cost of hiring different-sized venues, to create a supply curve. From that you'd be able to work out the most profitable combination of price and demand.

The graph in Figure 3.2 is based on (assumed) research findings that show:

Price	Demand for tickets (in Manchester)
£40	40,000
£50	38,000
£60	36,000
£70	34,000
£80	32,000

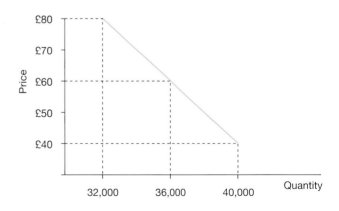

Figure 3.2 Demand curve for J. K. Rowling tickets

Once the curve has been drawn up, you can use it to work out, for instance, the right price to charge if you hire the City of Manchester Stadium, which would be able to seat 35,000 people for the evening show.

3.5 # Interaction of supply and demand

In the above example, if you found that there were three venues in Manchester capable of holding this level of audience (including Manchester United, which could easily take 40,000), you could draw a supply curve on the same graph as the demand curve (see Figure 3.3).

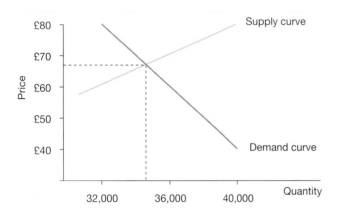

Figure 3.3 Supply and demand curves for J. K. Rowling in Manchester

The graph in Figure 3.3 shows that the most sensible outcome would be to hire the City of Manchester Stadium and price the tickets at £68 in order to fill the 35,000 seats. The price at which supply = demand is known as the **market price**.

The interaction of supply and demand is an important factor in many business decisions. In this case, the focus is on the price of tickets. In the wider world, the world oil price has an enormous effect on firms. This is also determined by supply and demand. In early 2008 the supply of oil was restricted by the difficulty of getting it safely out of the ground in major oil-producing countries such as Iraq. Meanwhile the demand for oil was kept

high by the booming, massive economies of China and India. As a result, the world oil price was $100 a barrel (more than three times the figure three years earlier). If, by 2012, the supply has risen and demand reduced, the figure may slip back to as low as $50 a barrel.

The impacts of different supply and demand conditions upon the price of oil (or any other commodity) are shown in Table 3.3.

3.6 # The benefits of market orientation

A well-run business is sensitive to demand. Its managers realise that demand is a complex, ever-changing factor. Running a hotel is a good example. Demand for hotel rooms is weakest on a Sunday night, so room rates are at their lowest. For city-centre hotels, Saturday night may

Table 3.4 Room rates at a Leeds hotel*, February 2008

	Executive room (for 2)
Wednesday 6 Feb	£140
Thursday 7 Feb	£140
Friday 8 Feb	£89
Saturday 9 Feb	£140
Sunday 10 Feb	£79
Monday 11 Feb	£115
Tuesday 12 Feb	£140

* Park Plaza, Leeds
Source: www.laterooms.com

Table 3.3 The impacts of different supply and demand conditions upon the price of a commodity

	The impact of supply upon price		
	Supply down	**Supply the same**	**Supply up**
Demand up	Price up sharply	Price up	Price unchanged
Demand stays the same	Price up	Price stays the same	Price down
Demand down	Price stays the same	Price down	Price down sharply

be a good night for bringing in wealthy nightclubbers, but business customers from Monday to Thursday are the biggest moneyspinners. Look at Table 3.4, which shows the room rates at a Leeds hotel in February 2008.

What these room prices show is a business that is well enough tuned in to its customers to know that the rates need to be different on different days. A really well-run hotel would also know that the breakfast service on a Sunday should be different from the fast-paced approach taken Monday–Friday.

Most businesses not only face daily sales variations but also seasonal ones. Carpet and furniture sales rise in the spring, as people see wear and tear more clearly in the spring sunshine. Swimwear and holiday sales peak in the summer, while businesses such as toys and perfumes can take 50% of their year's sales in the five weeks leading up to Christmas. Businesses that are close to their customers make sure that seasonal sales cause no surprise.

The key to meeting varying demand is to anticipate it by varying supply. The toy shop buys in extra supplies and hires extra, temporary staff in September; the stock is in place and the staff are trained comfortably before the Christmas rush. Cadbury starts making Creme Eggs for pre-Easter sale from summer the previous year, to ensure that plenty of stock is available for the amazing peak sales of this major UK brand.

Issues For Analysis

- It is essential to be able to analyse supply and demand in different circumstances and with application to different businesses or markets. It is not enough to simply memorise demand up, price up, and so on – understanding is the key. Therefore you must make sure to test yourself on the Section A and B questions in the Workbook.

- All businesses operate in a world where the forces of supply and demand provide pressure on business decisions. Nevertheless, some companies get close to the business ideal of dictating to the market instead of having market forces dictate to the business. For example, for 50 years Chanel has kept its 'No 5' brand as the 'must have' perfume among 20–50-year-old women. Its advertising creates the demand and its distribution policy controls supply, allowing Chanel No 5 to always be expensive and exclusive. In all these years, no other brand has come close to the image of Chanel No 5.

- In many other markets, competition is a central factor in every day's decisions. The publisher of the *Mirror* newspaper knows that tomorrow's sales of the newspaper would fall sharply if the *Sun* cuts its cover price to 10p. The sharp business analyst is the one who understands the circumstances of different businesses.

Building demand and managing supply

The cleverest judgements to be made in business come from the ability to separate what is from what might be. For 20 years the *Financial Times* (business) newspaper was priced at a small premium to the other 'quality' papers, *The Times* and the *Guardian*. Then, in 2007, the price went up 30p then another 20p until the *Financial Times* was twice the price of the others (£1.50 a day compared to 70p for *The Times*). Astonishingly, sales were virtually unaffected. A clever executive had spotted the opportunity to make a great deal more profit from the paper. Judgement as good as that is usually based upon market orientation (i.e. a really fine understanding of what customers think, feel and want). Good judgement is, of course, the same thing as good evaluation.

> ### Key terms
>
> **Demand curve:** a line showing the demand for a product at different prices (the higher the price, the lower the demand).
> **Market price:** the price of a commodity that has been established by the market (i.e. where supply = demand).
> **Supply curve:** a line showing the quantity of goods firms want to supply at different price levels (the higher the price, the more enthusiastic the supply).

Exercises

A. Revision questions

(35 marks; 35 minutes)

1 Choose one of the following terms, and explain what it means:
   (a) stock market
   (b) labour market
   (c) foreign exchange market. (4)

2 State the probable impact on price of:
   (a) falling demand, while supply remains unchanged
   (b) rising supply at a time when demand is unchanged
   (c) rising demand at a time of falling supply. (3)

3 When a shortage of Spice Girls tickets allows touts to charge £750 per ticket, only wealthy people can get to the concerts. Most people would not worry about this. But why might people be concerned about a high 'market price' if there was a shortage of water at a time of drought? (4)

4 Identify two possible physical constraints that might stop a railway company from completing engineering works on time. (2)

5a Draw a supply curve for Cadbury Creme Eggs, based on the following data:

(5)

Price	Supply
20p	0
25p	1m
30p	6m
35p	15m
40p	32m
45p	65m
50p	80m

5b Why might Cadbury be unwilling to supply any Creme Eggs at a price of 20p each? (2)

6 Use your knowledge of *one* of the following to explain the two factors you believe are the most important in determining the demand for:

(a) Birmingham City season tickets
(b) Vittel bottled water
(c) *OK!* magazine
(d) Kit-Kat four-finger pack. (3)

7 Suggest one way in which a business could try to estimate future demand for its brand new product. (3)

8 Look back at Figure 3.3 (Supply and demand curves for J. K. Rowling in Manchester) and answer the following questions.
   (a) Why is £68 the right price to charge for the tickets? (4)
   (b) What would be the effect of setting a price of £80 for the tickets? (5)

B. Revision exercises

B1 Data response

Kylie in demand

In February 2008 a London pop fan could have chosen three different concerts to take a loved one to. All were to take place in the 20,000-seater Millennium Stadium (O₂ Arena) and all the tickets were available on a well-known second-hand ticket website. The concerts were:

7 March 2008	Rihanna	Reserved seats	£93.50 each
17 May 2008	Girls Aloud	Reserved seats	£86.90 each
1 August 2008	Kylie	Reserved seats	£132.00 each

At first glance, the ticket prices seem to reflect differing demand for the three acts. In fact, though, the situation is more complicated. Kylie has six nights booked at the venue; therefore there is a supply of 120,000 seats in London in August. Rihanna has only one night, so the supply is 20,000, whereas Girls Aloud have two nights (i.e. 40,000 capacity).

What does this tell us about the fan base for each artist?

Questions

(30 marks; 30 minutes)

1 Explain why higher demand leads to higher prices. (4)

2 Examine the evidence and discuss whether Rihanna or Girls Aloud is the more popular act. (9)

3a Assuming all the Kylie seat capacity is sold at the price of £132 each, calculate the total revenue generated over her six days in London. (3)

3b If Kylie's managers decided to put on an extra two nights at the same venue in August, what might be the effect on the price of second-hand Kylie tickets for the other concerts? (5)

4 Discuss whether it should be illegal for websites to openly 're-sell' concert tickets at prices that may be much higher than the original price decided on by the artist. (9)

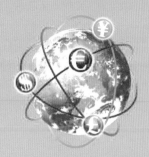

Unit 4

PROTECTING BUSINESS IDEAS

DEFINITION

An idea cannot be protected, but patents and copyright are methods of preventing others from copying an actual invention or piece of creative work.

4.1 Intellectual property

Intellectual property (IP) is the general term for assets that have been created by human ingenuity or creativity. These would include music, writing, photographs and engineering or other inventions. Around the world, governments are keen to protect IP because otherwise there would be no financial incentive to create anything. Why should J. K. Rowling spend years writing about Harry Potter if others could simply photocopy the books? She is protected by **copyright**. To get fully up-to-date information, go to www.ipo.gov.uk; this is the website of the Intellectual Property Office (IPO), formerly the Patent Office.

4.2 Patents

The August 2007 copy of the *Patents and Designs Journal* lists a series of **patent** applications that have now been granted. One is by a British inventor, Michael Reeves, for a 'Lightning Protected Golf Cart'. It is easy to see that, if this invention works (and can be produced at reasonable cost), it should sweep every other golf cart off the market.

The purpose of a patent is to provide a window of up to 20 years in which the work of an inventor cannot be copied by anyone else. The 20-year period starts from the moment the patent is applied for. The IPO itself admits that applications take at least two and a half years to process, and can take up to five years! In Michael Reeves's case, he probably has about 17 years after the patent has been granted to get his Lightning Protected Golf Cart to the market.

The patent system acts as an incentive to the inventor; nevertheless it can mean higher prices for the consumer. Mr Reeves might price his golf cart significantly higher

than rivals', just because it has the **monopoly power** that comes from the patent.

For a small firm, obtaining a patent can be expensive, perhaps costing between £1000 and £4000 for the UK alone. Then, if the product has worldwide potential, patent applications will be required in America, Japan, China, and so on. The total cost could be £50,000-plus. Worse may come later, if a competitor breaks the patent. This is because breaking a patent is not a criminal offence, so the police cannot be involved. It is a civil offence, so the patent owner has to sue the competitor. If a small firm is to take a giant, such as Nike, to court, there is a real risk that the cost of the court proceedings might ruin the minnow's finances.

Despite its shortcomings, the system of patents has proved an excellent way to give inventors the incentives

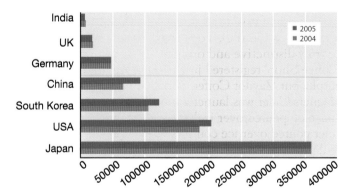

Figure 4.1 Patent applications by residents (top ten countries)
Source: WIPO database, 2007

they need. Figure 4.1 shows how patent applications are leaping ahead in China (up by 42% in 2005). It also shows Britain slipping back (down 7% in 2005) and the continuing dominance of Japan.

4.3 Copyright

Copyright applies to original written work such as books, newspaper articles, song lyrics, and so on. Unlike patents, it occurs automatically, so there is no need to spend time and money applying for it. Copyright in a literary work lasts for the lifetime of the author plus 70 years.

Clearly copyright is at the heart of industries such as publishing and music. Less obvious is that it is also at the heart of computing and the internet. The imaginative prices charged by Microsoft for its Office software are bound up in the copyright protection it enjoys. If Microsoft catches anyone breaking its copyright it will sue immediately. As with patents, it can be argued that this is crucial to the development of the industry. Whereas the cost of developing a PlayStation 1 game was said to be around £500,000 and PlayStation 2 around £5 million, today the cost of a PS3 game is more like £20 million. To justify such huge expenditure, the software producer needs to be confident that the game will sell millions of copies; being copied by millions will not pay the bills!

4.4 Trademarks

The IPO describes a **trademark** as 'any sign that can distinguish the goods and services of one trader from those of another'. It goes on to say that 'These signs can be words, logos, pictures, sounds, smells, colours...or any combination of these.' This makes a trademark a 'badge of origin', a way to spot one product or brand in a herd of competitors.

To have any force in law, a trademark must be registered at the IPO. To get registered, the mark must be truly distinctive and original. You would not get 'Coffee Shop' registered just because the font is bright purple, but 'Zaydor Coffee Shop' could be registered. Magners Cider was launched in 2005 with the brilliant image of 'poured over ice'; it asked whether advertising cider poured over ice could be trademarked, and was told no – something as common as pouring a drink over ice lacked distinctiveness.

The importance of trademarks becomes most obvious when you think of the iconic ones such as the Coca-Cola logo, the Lloyds Bank black horse, the Heinz Salad Cream label and Cadbury's 'glass and a half' (of milk).

Registering a trademark costs relatively little, perhaps £1000–£2000. It is not something that a small business would think much about until it starts to succeed. For a business such as Innocent Drinks, however, early registration of its trademarks was crucial to the company's success.

Issues For Analysis

- Consumers often ignore intellectual property. They will download music tracks without paying for them, or photocopy an article without paying the author. Many businesses rely hugely, though, on tightly regulated IP. The problem is that everyone can see the potential benefits of IP in the long term, but no one wants to pay higher prices in the short term.

- Business success relies on building a distinctive market position and consumer image. To cite a famous motor industry advertising campaign, BMW does not want its products called cars – they are 'the ultimate driving machine'. The more that patents, copyright and trademarks can help a firm achieve this, the more secure it will become compared to its rivals.

Protecting business ideas

Fifty years ago, most people bought products and services with little thought for who had made them. In today's brand- and fashion-conscious world, the logo on the back pocket of a pair of jeans can double its selling price, as can a tick on a pair of trainers (Nike even calls it a 'Swoosh' to try to differentiate it). With products and services making ever-greater appeals to our senses, trademarks become ever more important. The only time when trademarks matter less is when a firm has made a genuine technical breakthrough, perhaps from a patented product. If golfers want a Lightning Protected Golf Cart, they will quickly move away from the company that has supplied them in the past. IP is a huge business issue in the twenty-first century.

Key terms

Copyright: makes it unlawful for people to copy an author's original written work.
Monopoly power: the ability to charge high prices because you are the sole supplier of a product.
Patents: provide the inventor of a technical breakthrough with the ability to stop anyone copying the idea for up to 20 years.
Trademark: any sign that can distinguish the goods and services of one trader from those of another.

Exercises

A. Revision questions

(20 marks; 20 minutes)

1 Briefly explain why Michael Reeves should be able to build a very successful business based on the patent explained in Section 3.2. (4)

2 Explain why an entrepreneur may struggle if the success of a new business relies on a patented invention. (4)

3 Look at Figure 4.1 and identify:
   (a) two countries where the number of patents rose in 2005 (1)
   (b) two countries where the number of patent applications fell in 2005. (1)

4 Briefly explain why it might disappoint the British Government to see that the number of patent applications in Britain has been falling. (3)

5 For each of the following, identify whether the IP issue relates to patent, copyright or trademark:
   (a) Galaxy has designed a new pack for its Celebrations brand (1)
   (b) Burberry has come up with a new way to get solar power from a tartan cap, sufficient to keep an iPod powered all day long (1)
   (c) Lacoste has developed a new, completely distinctive scent for men (1)
   (d) you have just copied a tennis game from your friend's Wii console. (1)

6 Why may intellectual property be more important today than 50 years ago? Briefly explain your answer. (3)

B. Revision exercises

B1 Data response

In August 2006 James Seddon appeared on the TV show *Dragons' Den* to try to raise finance for his Eggxactly water-free egg boiler. Although Dragons Richard Farleigh and Peter Jones offered to invest £75,000, James decided against giving away 40% of his business. The cooker would use a flexible element to mould itself round eggs of different sizes. An electronic component would then calculate the right length of time needed to provide a soft- or hard-boiled egg. The electronics would even take into account the initial temperature of the egg (e.g. if taken straight from the fridge, a longer cooking time would be needed).

The technical issues involved were all innovations by James Seddon. Therefore he applied for a UK patent in late 2006. Once cash comes in from the launch of the product in Britain before Easter 2008, he will apply for patents in America, China and the rest of Europe. As James is financing the start-up himself, he could not easily find the cash to extend the patents until sales begin.

Questions

(20 marks; 20 minutes)

1 Explain in your own words the meaning of the word patent. (3)

2 Examine the likely reasons why James Seddon applied for a patent on the technical innovations within the Eggxactly product. (7)

3 Discuss whether James is likely to lose out as a result of waiting over a year before applying for patents in the rest of the world. (10)

B2 Data response

In its fourth annual Digital Music Survey, research consultancy Entertainment Media Research found that just under half of the 1700 people it questioned were illegally downloading music tracks. This was a third more than in 2006 and 40% more than in 2005. Legal downloading was found to be in decline.

Young people were found to be the worst culprits, with twice as many 18 to 24 year olds admitting to illegally downloading music as those aged between 25 and 34. The price of legal downloads was cited as the key factor for this, after 84% of those questioned said that older digital downloads should be cheaper to buy than new releases.

John Enser, head of music at law firm Olswang, agreed. He said: 'As illegal downloading hits an all-time high and consumers' fear of prosecution falls, the music industry must look for more ways to encourage the public to download music legally.'

However, music industry association the BPI disagreed with the research, claiming that both legal and illegal downloads had risen within the past year as a result of a 25% growth in broadband penetration.

A spokesman for the BPI told Computeractive: 'Consumers must also understand that by downloading songs free they are denying an artist money and rights, which could cause the industry to collapse.'

Questions

(25 marks; 25 minutes)

1 Explain whether the above issue is about breaking copyright or trademark law. (4)

2 Outline two possible reasons why 18–24 year olds may be the 'worst culprits'. (4)

3 Discuss whether John Enser is right to urge the music industry to cut its prices for officially downloaded music. (8)

4 Evaluate whether young people are likely to listen to the appeal by the BPI spokesman against 'downloading songs free'. (9)

Unit 5 DEVELOPING BUSINESS PLANS

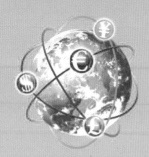

5.1 Purpose

Starting a business is quite complex, as it requires a lot of different tasks to come together in a coordinated way at the right time. For example, if you are opening your first restaurant, all the following tasks must have been completed on the day before your opening night: building work, decoration, kitchen equipment bought and fitted, staff hired and trained, menu chosen and printed, wines chosen and delivered, and wine list printed, food supplies bought, tills and credit card-reading equipment in place, and so on. For this to work without a clear plan is asking for the impossible. A business plan, then, seems essential for start-up success, yet most entrepreneurs treat a business plan as something banks ask for (i.e. something for others, not for themselves).

Government figures show that, on average, new business entrepreneurs are white, male, in their mid-thirties and have a university degree. As a consequence, many have built up the capital to start up without needing any external finance. Therefore they do not *need* a full business plan. As a result, the same government figures show that most businesses start up without a formal plan.

For a young entrepreneur, this would be virtually impossible. The need to find the capital to start up would make it crucial to have a plan persuasive enough to obtain funding. For most, that is the sole purpose of the plan: to obtain capital. This is a pity, because a good plan can act as the 'satnav to success', steering the novice businessperson towards her/his goals.

5.2 The contents of a good plan

A good plan should be persuasive to an outside investor and useful to the entrepreneur. It should explain what makes the business special and help the entrepreneur to keep sight of what s/he is trying to achieve. Despite this, it is clear that a business that needs capital will concentrate mainly on the outside investor. This might be a bank or (less likely) a 'dragon' type of investor, who will buy an ownership stake in the business. A bank's main concern is that the start-up will be a safe investment, whereas a 'dragon' is mainly interested in the upside potential (i.e. the chance of making a huge profit).

The heart of the business plan should be based around **competitive advantage**. This means identifying the features of your own product/service that will make it succeed against competitors. This might be based on a unique idea, a better product/service or the protection provided by a patent or copyright.

Every business plan should contain the following sections.

1 **Executive summary**: this should be short, but compelling enough to persuade the busy banker to want to read on. It should say who you are, what the customer's pain is and how you will relieve it, why your team is ideal for the task, how much capital you need for the start-up, and how much you are putting in yourself.

2 Details of the product/service: explain it from the customer's point of view – for example, with smoothies, not 'we'll crush fruit and put it in bottles', but 'it'll provide busy people with two portions of fruit in an enjoyable, unmessy way'. If others already

offer the service, you must explain what is different about your idea.

3 The market: focus on market trends rather than market size (i.e. whether the market is growing and, if so, how rapidly). Also there is a need to provide a brief analysis of key competitors.

4 Marketing plan: how do you plan to communicate to the customers you are targeting? How expensive will this be? Within this section should be an explanation of and justification for the prices you plan to set, plus a forecast of likely sales per month for the first two years.

5 Organisational plan: to explain who will be in the team and how they will be managed and organised; CVs should be provided for all key managers.

6 Operational plan: how the product/service will be produced and delivered. This might involve production in China, in which case you will need already to have made contacts with willing suppliers.

7 Financial plan: the heart of this will be a cash flow forecast (i.e. a prediction of monthly cash out and cash in from the start of the business until at least two years after the firm has started trading). This will give an idea of the bank balances over the start-up period, and therefore the financing needs.

8 Conclusion: this will include some idea of the longer-term plans for the business, including any 'exit strategy' (e.g. plan to sell the business within five years).

Benefits and problems of business plans

The key thing to remember is that the business plan is only as good as the information inside. As much of this will have to be estimated or guessed, it is clear that no one should treat a business plan as a factual document. It may help steer the business in the right general direction, but it may be an exaggeration to see it as a 'satnav'.

Sources of information and guidance

Government agencies

In addition to Business Link (see Unit 1), there are two other government agencies that might be helpful.

1 Regional Development Agencies, such as the North-West RDA. These agencies set priorities for their local areas, try to attract overseas investment (e.g. Toyota opening a new factory), and provide advice and help for new firms starting up. As with Business Link, most entrepreneurs question how valuable their advice really is.

2 BERR, the Department for Business, Enterprise and Regulatory Reform (formerly the DTI). This department runs the Small Firms Loan Guarantee Scheme, which encourages high-street banks to lend to high-risk small firms. If the firm collapses, the government guarantees to pick up the bill. Any firm using this way to borrow capital will have to pay an extra 2% interest per year on the loan. Up to £250,000 can be borrowed in this way.

Table 5.1 The business plan: benefits and problems

Benefits	Problems
Forces the entrepreneur to think carefully about every aspect of the start-up, which should increase the chances of success	Making a forecast (e.g. of sales) doesn't make it happen; entrepreneurs sometimes confuse the plan with reality; poor sales can come as a terrible shock
May make the entrepreneur realise that s/he lacks the skills needed for part of the plan, and therefore try harder to employ an expert or buy in advice	Problems arise if the plan is too rigid; it is better to make it flexible, so that you are prepared for what to do if sales are poor (or unexpectedly high)
If the plan is well received by investors, they may compete to offer attractive terms for obtaining capital	Plans based on high sales will include lots of staff to meet the demand; risks are lower if the business starts with a low-cost/low-sales expectation
Many entrepreneurs have the whole plan in their head, not on paper; if illness or accident strikes, others will only be able to keep things going with a paper plan	Business success is often about people, not paper; an over-focus on a perfect plan may mean too little time is spent visiting suppliers or talking to shoppers

The Loan Guarantee Scheme is meant to help new entrepreneurs. Yet the Independent Banking Advisory Service warns that banks offering these loans are less supportive of the borrower than normal.

Banks

Banks claim to provide great help to new small businesses, but rarely do. The only thing they are all keen to help with is to provide a business plan toolkit. After all, they want you to open your business banking account with them. Just Google 'banks business plan' and you'll be able to choose from at least six options from the different major banks. New firms need a bank account, so banks are essential; it would be wrong to think, though, that small-scale entrepreneurs spend hours talking things through with their bank adviser or manager.

Accountants

For those with no business knowledge it might be helpful to get cash flow and profit forecasts checked by an accountant. For those who have taken a course in Business Studies, this would be an unnecessary expense. The only aspect of a business start-up that an accountant would be invaluable for is advice on tax issues. Should the business buy a van or lease it? Should the business start as a limited company or sole trader? These are technical questions that an accountant will know more about than you ever will.

Small business advisers

Entrepreneurs are usually put in touch with these via the government service Business Link. Especially for a young person it is invaluable to have a mentor – someone to turn to when the unexpected happens. Say you have opened a phone shop in the High Street and a Carphone Warehouse opens next door six weeks later – it would be ideal to talk about what to do with a more experienced businessperson. The problem is that good people will not come cheap.

The Prince's Trust

The Prince's Trust works with unemployed or disadvantaged people up to the age of 30. It can lend up to £4000 to a new business start-up, but probably more important is that the Trust insists that you regularly attend sessions with a (free) mentor. Due to the royal connections of the Trust, these mentors are often quite high-powered businesspeople, whose advice is invaluable. To find out more, go to www.princes-trust.org.uk.

Issues For Analysis

- Even if there's no point in having a business plan, it may still be valuable to have prepared one. For most, the plan is likely to gather dust after it has served its purpose of raising finance. That may well be right, because the key thing is preparing it, not having it. Putting the plan together forces the entrepreneur to think about every aspect of the business and perhaps start to see a few cracks. Solutions may be put in place now, before the business actually starts up. When the business starts, the figures in the plan will probably soon look silly – too high or way too low.

5.5 Developing business plans
an evaluation

To start a great new business requires a great idea based on a strong understanding of the customer and the competition. Then the entrepreneur needs to have the personal qualities to build strong relationships with suppliers, retail buyers and staff. If drawing up a business plan helps in that process, that's fine. The worry is that getting your head buried in paper plans may divert you from the important tasks. Business plans can help get investment from outsiders and may help prevent a disorganised entrepreneur from making too many mistakes, but it is no substitute for having strong enterprise skills.

> **Key terms**
>
> **Competitive advantage:** features of your product/service that make it stronger in the marketplace than your competitors.
> **Executive summary:** brief highlights of a report, placed at the front, so that top executives can glance at the main points without having to read the whole thing.

Exercises

A. Revision questions

(30 marks; 30 minutes)

1 Explain in your own words the meaning of the term 'business plan'. (3)

2 Why may young entrepreneurs need a business plan more than middle-aged ones? Briefly explain your answer. (3)

3 Some people think that a business plan aimed at 'dragon' investors should be different from one aimed at bankers. Outline two ways in which a plan aimed at investors might be different from one aimed at a banker. (4)

4 Why might an entrepreneur find it easier to write a business plan for a second business start-up than for his/her first? (4)

5 Re-read the list of benefits and problems in Table 5.1 and decide whether the following entrepreneurs should take time to write out a full business plan. Explain your reasons.
   (a) A 30 year old, previously a teacher, who needs to borrow a small sum to help finance the launch of a nightclub. (3)
   (b) A 50 year old, previously an accountant, who can personally finance the start-up of a business producing digital radios. (3)

6 How might Business Link help someone draw up a good business plan? (3)

7 If you were to open your own business after finishing your A-levels, do you think you would complete a business plan? Explain your answer with reference to your own strengths and weaknesses. (7)

B. Revision exercises

B1 Data response

Extract from business plan for opening a Thai restaurant in Swindon

Section 3.3 Cash flow forecast for first 12 months

Refer to Figure 5.1 below.

Section 3.4 Financing requirement

The business will need £80,000 of start-up capital. The directors are investing £40,000 of their own funds, so we wish to borrow £40,000. As shown in the cash flow table, we will be able to repay the sum in full by the end of the first year of trading.

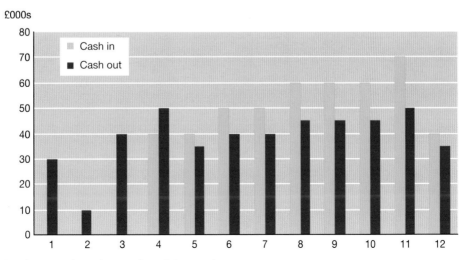

Figure 5.1 Cash in and cash out, first 12 months

Questions

(20 marks; 20 minutes)

1 Look carefully at the graph for the first four months of the life of the business. Are the directors borrowing the right sum of money? Explain your answer. (4)

2 If the cash flow forecast proves correct, are the directors right to say that the £40,000 can be repaid by the end of the first year? Explain your answer. (4)

3 Discuss why a banker might be concerned to read 'As shown in the cash flow table, we will be able to repay the sum in full. . .'. (7)

4 Explain why the directors might be wise to borrow rather more capital than they believe they will need to finance the first year of the business. (5)

B2 Data response

The chocolate therapy plan

It's an almost irresistible combination: relaxation, pampering and calorie-free chocolate. That's what is being offered to customers of a brand new business aimed at smoothing away the stresses of everyday life for the women of the Black Country.

Chocolate therapy is the signature treatment offered by Judith Morgan, who recently launched her holistic therapy business, Bodessa, inside Petra's Hair and Beauty Salon at Hayley Green in Halesowen. After a hitch in supplies of the manufactured gel-based facial mask had disrupted the business's first few weeks, Judith set about manufacturing her own Bodessa version of chocolate therapy.

Opening Bodessa is the culmination of 18 months of planning after Judith made a bold career change having spent 25 years in the catering industry. She has been encouraged by her husband, Brett, a graphic designer, who has produced some of her literature and designed her logo, and by Business Link West Midlands, who led her through the start-up process.

Judith's adviser acted as a sounding board for the new business, offering impartial advice, support and guidance to help Judith and Brett develop Bodessa. The adviser also helped Judith prepare the business plan that gave her a sound footing in starting the venture.

Judith added: 'The business plan advice was great. It allowed my husband and I to put together a plan that was very realistic, not just for the bank manager to be impressed with.'

Business Link West Midlands adviser, Bob Howard, said: 'As long as a company requires help they can come back to us. They know there's someone here for them who can keep giving them relevant information, perhaps guidance on training and maybe advice on gaining access to new finance to help them progress the business.'

Source: *Express & Star*, Wolverhampton 13 August 2007

Questions

(20 marks; 20 minutes)

1 Explain how Judith's start-up might have been helped by the business plan. (5)

2 Outline one feature of the start-up that raises questions about the effectiveness of this business plan. (3)

3 Examine two features of the start-up that might have been less effective without the help of Business Link West Midlands. (6)

4 From the evidence available, how likely is it that Judith's business will succeed? (6)

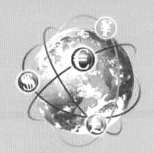

CHOOSING THE RIGHT LEGAL STRUCTURE

DEFINITION

The legal structure of a business is crucial in determining how serious the financial impact is on the owners, if things go wrong. It also has an impact on the taxation levels to be paid by the business and its owners.

Businesses with unlimited liability

Unlimited liability means that the finances of the business are treated as inseparable from the finances of the business owner(s). So if the business loses £1 million, the people owed money (the **creditors**) can get the courts to force the individual owners to pay up. If that means selling their houses, cars etc., so be it. If the owner(s) cannot pay, they can be made personally **bankrupt**. Two types of business organisation have unlimited liability: sole traders and partnerships.

Sole traders

A **sole trader** is an individual who owns and operates his or her own business. Although there may be one or two employees, this person makes the final decisions about the running of the business. A sole trader is the only one who benefits financially from success, but must face the burden of any failure. In the eyes of the law the individual and the business are the same. This means that the owner has unlimited liability for any debts that result from running the firm. If a sole trader cannot pay his/her bills, the courts can allow personal assets to be seized by creditors in order to meet outstanding debts. For example, the family home or car may be sold. If insufficient funds can be raised in this way the person will be declared bankrupt.

Despite the financial dangers involved, the sole trader is the most common form of legal structure adopted by UK businesses. In some areas of the economy this kind of business dominates, particularly where little finance is required to set up and run the business and customers demand a personal service. Examples include trades such as builders and plumbers, and many independent shopkeepers.

There are no formal rules to follow when establishing a sole trader, or administrative costs to pay. Complete confidentiality can be maintained because accounts are not published. As a result many business start-ups adopt this structure.

The main disadvantages facing a sole trader are the limited sources of finance available, long hours of work involved (including the difficulty of taking a holiday) and concern with respect to running the business during periods of ill health.

Partnerships

Partnerships exist when two or more people start a business without forming a company. Like a sole trader, the individuals have unlimited liability for any debts run up by the business. Because people are working together but are unlimitedly liable for any debts, it is vital that the partners trust each other. As a result this legal structure is often found in the professions, such as medicine and law. If the partners fail to draw up a formal document, the 1890 Partnership Act sets out a series of rules that govern issues such as the distribution of profits.

The main difference between a sole trader and a partnership is the number of owners. The key advantages and disadvantages in forming a partnership are outlined below.

Advantages

● *Additional skills:* a new partner may have abilities that the sole trader does not possess. These can help to strengthen the business, perhaps allowing new products or services to be offered, or improving the quality of existing provision.

- *More capital:* a number of people together can inject more finance into the business than one person alone. This, plus the extra skills, makes expansion easier.

- *Shared strain:* the new partner will help to share the worry of running the business, as well as taking on a share of the workload. This should help to reduce stress and allow holidays to be taken.

Disadvantages

- *Sharing profit:* the financial benefits derived from running the business will have to be divided up between the partners according to the partnership agreement made on formation. This can easily lead to disagreements about 'fair' distribution of workload and profits.

- *Loss of control:* multiple ownership means that no individual can force an action on the business; decision making must be shared.

- *Unlimited liability:* it is one thing to be unlimitedly liable for your own mistakes (a sole trader), but far more worrying, surely, to have unlimited liability for the mistakes of your partners. This problem hit many investors in the Lloyds insurance market in the 1990s. Certain partnerships (called syndicates) lost millions of pounds from huge insurance claims. Some investors lost their life savings.

A-grade application

Yan Wu and Taurean Carter began an informal partnership selling jewellery. She bought and he sold. From small beginnings they built up a £120,000 a year business by year 3. Then they decided to open their first shop, and took the opportunity to go from 50/50 partners to 50%-50% shareholders. They had decided that they wanted the protection of limited liability status.

6.2 Businesses with limited liability

Limited liability means that the legal duty to pay debts run up by a business stays with the business itself, not its owner/shareholders. If a company has £1 million of debts that it lacks the cash to repay, the courts can force the business to sell all its assets (cars, computers, etc.). If there is still not enough money, the company is closed down, but the owner/shareholders have no personal liability for the remaining debts.

To gain the benefits of limited liability, the business must go through a legal process to become a company. The process of **incorporation** creates a separate legal identity for the organisation. In the eyes of the law the owners of the business and the company itself are now two different things. The business can take legal action against others and have legal action taken against it. Each owner is protected by limited liability, and their investment in the business is represented by the size of their shareholding. Limited liability sounds unfairly weighted towards the shareholders, but it encourages individuals to put forward capital because the financial risk is limited to the amount they invest.

In order to gain separate legal status a company must be registered with the **Registrar of Companies**. The following two key documents must be completed.

1 The Memorandum of Association, which governs the relationship between the company and the outside world. This includes the company name, the object of the company (often recorded simply as 'as the owners see fit'), limitation of liability and the size of the authorised share capital.

2 The Articles of Association, which outline the internal management of the company. This includes the rights of shareholders, the role of directors and frequency of shareholder meetings.

The key advantages and disadvantages that result from forming a limited company are as follows.

Advantages

- Shareholders experience the benefits of limited liability, including the confidence to expand.

- A limited company is able to gain access to a wider range of borrowing opportunities than a sole trader or partnership. This makes funding the growth of the business potentially easier.

Disadvantages

- Limited companies must make financial information available publicly at Companies House. Small firms are not required to make full disclosure of their company accounts, but they have to reveal more than would be the case for a sole trader or partnership.

- Limited companies have to follow more, and more expensive, rules than unlimited liability businesses (e.g. audited accounts and holding an annual general meeting of shareholders); these things add several thousand pounds to annual overhead costs.

A-grade application

One Water

In 2003, Duncan Goose quit his job and founded One Water. He wanted to finance water projects in Africa from profits made selling bottled water in Britain. The particular water project was 'Playpumps': children's roundabouts plumbed in to freshly dug water wells. As the kids play, each rotation of the roundabout brings up a litre of fresh, clean water.

Duncan thought of forming a charity, but soon realised that the regulations governing charities force them to be inefficient. So, for £125 he founded a limited company, Global Ethics Ltd. This enabled him to set the rules – for instance, that the shareholders receive no dividends and the directors receive no fees. But, of course, it ensured that he and other volunteers who put time into One Water are protected should something go wrong and big debts build up.

6.3 Private limited companies

A small business can be started up as a sole trader, a partnership or as a private limited company. For a private limited company, the start-up capital will often be £100, which can be wholly owned by the entrepreneur, or other people can be brought in as investors. The shares of a private limited company can not be bought and sold without the agreement of the other directors. This means the company can not be listed on the stock market. As a result it is possible to maintain close control over the way the business is run. This form of business is often run by a family or small group of friends. It may be very profit focused or, like Global Ethics Ltd, have wholly different objectives than maximising profit.

A legal requirement for private companies is that they must state 'Ltd' after the company name. This warns those dealing with the business that the firm is relatively small and has limited liability. Remember, limited liability protects shareholders from business debts, so there is a risk that 'cowboy' businesspeople might start a company, run it into the ground, then walk away from its debts. Therefore the cheques of a Ltd company are not as secure as ones from an unlimited liability business. This is why many petrol stations have notices saying 'No company cheques allowed.'

6.4 Public limited companies

When a private limited company expands to the point of having share capital of more than £50,000, it can convert to a public limited company. This means it can be floated on the stock market, which allows any member of the general public to buy shares. This increases the company's access to share capital, which enables it to expand considerably. The term 'plc' will appear after the company name (e.g. Marks & Spencer plc, Tesco plc).

The principal differences between private and public limited companies are:

- a public company can raise capital from the general public, while a private limited company is prohibited from doing so

- the minimum capital requirement of a public company is £50,000. There is no minimum for a private limited company

- public companies must publish far more detailed accounts than private limited companies.

Almost every large business is a plc. Yet the process of converting from a private to a public company can be difficult. Usually, successful small firms grow steadily,

Table 6.1 When should a business start up as a sole trader and when as a private limited company?

Sole trader	Private limited company
When the entrepreneur has no intention of expanding, e.g. just wants to run one restaurant in Warwick	When the entrepreneur has ambitions to expand quickly and therefore needs it to be easier to raise extra finance
When there is no need for substantial bank borrowing, i.e. start-up costs are low	When large borrowings mean significant chances of large losses if things go wrong
When the business will be small enough to mean that one person can make all the big decisions	When the business may require others to make decisions, e.g. when the entrepreneur is on holiday or unwell

perhaps at a rate of 10 or 15% a year. Even that pace of growth causes problems, but good managers can cope. The problem of floating onto the stock market is that it provides a sudden, huge injection of cash. This sounds great, but it forces the firm to try to grow more quickly, otherwise the new shareholders will say 'What are you doing with our cash?' (see 'Application' on Sports Direct).

A-grade application

Sports Direct

On 28 February 2007, Mike Ashley made over £900 million when he floated Sports Direct onto the London stock market. Ashley had owned 100% of Sports Direct, and sold 43% of his shares at 300p a share. Within a few months City analysts were troubled by the way Ashley seemed too keen to spend his money. He bought 3% of the shares in Adidas, then made a takeover bid for Newcastle United. He also seemed desperate to spend the money raised by Sports Direct, as it went on a shopping spree including Blacks Leisure, Field & Trek and the Everlast boxing equipment company. With so much going on, it seemed that no one was paying enough attention to the company's trading position. Revenues and profits dropped back and, within six months of the float, the shares had halved in value.

Other problems with public limited companies

- When a firm becomes a plc, it becomes hard to hold on to any objective other than profit. This is because City analysts and business journalists criticise heavily any business that is not making more money this year than last. This pressure may have been the underlying problem that led BP to underspend on safety measures in America, leading to the deaths of 15 of its workers at a refinery in Texas in 2005.

- The extent to which any one individual, or group, can maintain control of an organisation is severely limited by the sale of its shares on the stock exchange. For example, a family may find its influence on a business diminished when a listing is obtained. In turn, this means that publicly quoted companies are always vulnerable to a takeover bid. In 2007 the Sainsbury family, with just a 25% stake in the family business, nearly lost the family grocer to a multi-billion-pound takeover bid.

- Shareholders are the owners of public limited companies, but they do not make decisions on a day-to-day basis. Many have little detailed knowledge of the firm's operations; nor can they know the directors who, theoretically, they vote on to and off the board. In fact, it is usually the chairman and chief executive who run the show. They have control, though the shareholders supposedly have the power. This situation is known as the 'divorce of ownership and control', and it may lead the directors to pursue the interests of their own careers and bank balances rather than the best interests of the business and its staff.

- A separate problem that may be caused by the divorce of ownership and control is 'short-termism'. In private companies, where shareholders and directors are usually family members, the desire is to build a successful business to hand over to the next generation. This is how the great retail firms such as Sainsbury's and Marks & Spencer built themselves up. In plcs, the lack of concern about the long-term future of the shareholders may lead directors to focus too much on the short term. Much research has shown that British managements are more likely than others to focus upon short-term issues, possibly to the neglect of long-term investment in research and development (R&D) or staff training.

6.5 Other forms of business organisation

Cooperatives

These can be worker-owned, such as John Lewis/Waitrose, or customer owned, such as the retail Coop. Cooperatives have the potential to offer a more united cause for the workforce than the profit of shareholders. Workers at John Lewis can enjoy annual bonuses of 20% of their salary as their share of the company's profits. The Coop has been less successful, though its focus on ethical trading has made it more relevant to today's shoppers.

Not-for-profit organisations

Mutual businesses

Mutual businesses, including many building societies and mutual life assurance businesses, have no shareholders and no owners. They exist solely for the best interests of their members (i.e. customers). In the 1980s and 1990s traditional mutual societies such as Abbey National and the Halifax turned into private companies. Nationwide now says it is 'proud to be different', as it is still a true building society (i.e. it has no shareholders pressuring for profits).

Charities

Many important organisations have charitable status; these include pressure groups such as Greenpeace and Friends of the Earth. They also include conventional charities such as Oxfam and Save The Children Fund. Charitable status ensures that those who fund the charity are not liable for any debts. It also provides significant tax benefits.

Issues For Analysis

When analysing which type of organisation is the most suitable for a business, consider the following factors.

- The financial risks involved: manufacturing businesses require heavy investment in plant and equipment before anything is available for sale. Therefore a great deal of capital is put at risk. This suggests limited liability is essential. Some service businesses such as tax advisers or dry cleaners require relatively little capital outlay. If the owner intends to finance the start-up without any borrowings, there is no need to seek limited liability.

- The image you wish to portray: although cautious businesses may refuse company cheques, most people think 'M. Staton Ltd' sounds more established and professional than 'Mervin Staton'. In the same vein, a small software production company called TIB Ltd changed its name to TIB plc. It rightly thought that this sounds bigger and more impressive. What's in a name? Ask Coca-Cola . . .

- An organisation considering a move to public company status and a stock market listing has far bigger issues to consider. It must weigh the benefits to be gained, particularly in terms of raising additional finance, against the costs incurred and the loss of control. Many business questions can be analysed fruitfully by considering the short versus the long term. Private (family) versus public (stock market investor) ownership is a classic case in point.

Choosing the right legal structure

Business organisation is a dry, technical subject. It does contain some important business themes, however; three are particularly valuable sources of evaluative comment.

1 The existence of limited liability has had huge effects on business. Some have been unarguably beneficial. How could firms become really big if the owners felt threatened by equally big debts? Limited liability helps firms take reasonable business risks; it also, however, gives scope for dubious business practices. Start a firm, live a great lifestyle, then go into liquidation leaving the customers/creditors out of pocket. Then start again. All too often this is the story told by programmes such as the BBC's *Watchdog*. Companies Acts try to make this harder to do, but it still happens. Such unethical behaviour is why government intervention to protect the consumer can always be justified.

2 Bill Gates and Richard Branson are worth billions of dollars (at the time of writing!). How can such wealth be justified for people who do not save lives (doctors) or help build them (teachers)? The answer lies in the risks involved in business. For every Richard Branson there are hundreds of thousands of small entrepreneurs who sunk their life savings into a business and saw those savings sink. Sadly, there are thousands every year who end up personally bankrupt. In other words, in a business world in which risk is ever present, rewards for success should be accepted.

3 Short-termism is a curse for effective business decision making. There is no proof that a stock exchange listing leads to short-termism, only the suspicion that in many cases it does. Of course, massive companies, such as Unilever, Nestlé and Shell, are likely to be above the pressures for short-term performance. In many other cases, though, it seems that British company directors focus too much on the short-term share price. Could this be because their huge bonuses depend on how the share price is? Worries about shareholder pressures or takeover bids may distract managers from building a long-term business in the way that companies such as BMW and Toyota have done.

Key terms

Bankrupt: when an individual is unable to meet personal liabilities, some or all of which can be as a consequence of business activities.
Creditors: those owed money by a business (e.g. suppliers and bankers).
Incorporation: establishing a business as a separate legal entity from its owners, and therefore giving the owners limited liability.
Limited liability: owners are not liable for the debts of the business; they can lose no more than the sum they invested.
Registrar of Companies: the government department that can allow firms to become incorporated; located at Companies House, where Articles of Association, Memorandums of Association and the annual accounts of limited companies are available for public scrutiny.
Sole trader: a one-person business with unlimited liability.
Unlimited liability: owners are liable for any debts incurred by the business, even if this requires them to sell all their assets and possessions and become personally bankrupt.

Exercises

A. Revision questions

(30 marks; 30 minutes)

1 Explain two differences between a sole trader and a partnership. (4)

2 In your own words, explain the importance of establishing a separate legal entity to separate the business from the individual owner. (4)

3 You can start a business today. All you have to do is tell the Inland Revenue (the taxman). Outline two risks of starting in this way. (4)

4 Briefly discuss whether each of the following businesses should start as a sole trader, a partnership or a private limited company:
  (a) a clothes shop started by Claire Wells with £40,000 of her own money plus £10,000 from the bank; it is located close to her home in Wrexham (3)
  (b) a builders started by Jim Barton and Lee Clark, who plan to become the number one for loft extensions in Sheffield; they've each invested £15,000 and are borrowing £30,000 from the bank. (3)

5 Explain the possible risks to a growing business of making the jump from a private limited company to 'going public', then floating its shares on the stock market. (5)

6 In what way may the type of business organisation affect the image of the business? (2)

7 Identify two types of businesses that are 'not-for-profit'. (2)

8 Outline one reason why a cooperative such as Waitrose might provide better customer service than a plc such as Tesco. (3)

B. Revision exercises

B1 Data response

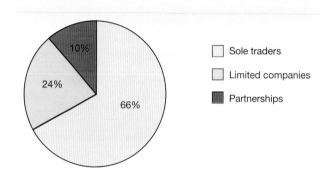

Figure 6.1 UK small business organisations (total = 3,600,000)
Source: Fraser, S. (2005). Finance for Small and Medium Sized Enterprises: The United Kingdom Survey of SME Finances, 2004.

Questions

(20 marks; 25 minutes)

1 a Calculate the number of sole traders in the UK; then calculate the number of limited companies. (3)

  b Explain two possible reasons why there are so many more sole traders than companies. (6)

2 What proportion of British businesses operate with unlimited liability? (1)

3 Dr Fraser's research also shows that one in five businesses is principally owned by a woman, and that 93% are owned by white and 7% by non-white ethnicity.

  a Examine two possible reasons why women are so much less likely to own a business than men. (6)

  b The % figures for non-white business ownership are slightly below the number of non-whites in the population (between 8 and 9%). Outline two reasons that might explain this. (4)

B2 Data response

In April 2007 Bernice Armstrong opened Devoted 2 Vintage in Hemel Hempstead, just north of London. She believed there was a gap locally for an independent shop buying and selling vintage clothes. Her own love of vintage clothes made her keen to start, and gave her insight both into sources of supply and distinguishing desirable clothes from ones that should go to charity shops.

In 2007 celebrity magazines were full of swirly 1960s clothes, so Bernice made every effort to focus on 1960s originals, for example by Mary Quant, inventor of the mini skirt. Her price range was from £10–£100, making the clothes affordable for all. By late summer 2007 Bernice was focusing her efforts on developing an online vintage clothing store.

To follow up this story, go to www.devoted2vintage.co.uk

Questions

(20 marks; 25 minutes)

1 a The name of the business is Devoted 2 Vintage. Does that suggest it's a sole trader or a private limited company? (1)

1 b Bearing in mind your answer to 1a, outline two factors Bernice should remember about the legal structure of the business she is running. (6)

2 As Bernice expands the business to develop online, should she consider changing the legal structure of the business? If so, why and how? (6)

3 Discuss how well Bernice has done so far in setting up her first business. (7)

C. Essay questions

(40 marks each)

1 Paddy Klein and Ed Caporn have started up a food manufacturing business. It specialises in posh cooking sauces. Discuss which type of business organisation they should use in order to set up the business.

2 After some research using Google, discuss whether Mike Ashley was right to float Sports Direct on the stock market.

LOCATION FACTORS FOR A BUSINESS START-UP

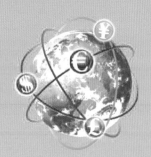

Location decisions are about where to site the company's buildings (e.g. its factory, head office and/or its shops).

7.1 Where to locate?

A business cliché in the hotel and catering industries is: 'What are the three most important factors to success? Location, location, location.' Many shop owners would say the same thing. The problem is that because everybody knows the importance of location, good locations are incredibly expensive and very hard to come by. The location a small business start-up would most like will already have been taken by Starbucks, Topshop, O_2 and the like. The high cost of good locations applies across the world, but especially in the UK.

This is a question that a new business will have to consider carefully as location could influence its chance of success. There are several factors that will influence a firm's choice of location. The quantitative ones take into account the financially related factors, whereas the qualitative ones are concerned with the non-financial influences, such as the family links that may attract the owner to a particular area. This unit focuses on the different factors and shows how the importance of these will vary according to the type of business involved.

7.2 Quantitative factors

Cost of land

If a firm chooses a high-cost location it may find that the prices it has to charge to help cover the costs may increase, and this may make the firm less price competitive. This is why firms for which a competitive selling price is vital in achieving sales will search for the **least-cost location**.

Space

Although a new firm will not be concerned with expansion in the early years, if it is successful it may need to increase the scale of its operations in the long term; this will be cheaper and less disruptive if the firm has the opportunity to extend its existing premises rather than relocating to larger premises.

Accessibility of supplies

Whether a firm needs to be close to its suppliers will depend upon whether it is using large materials that are costly to transport. A firm that uses bulky materials, often to produce smaller end products, will be better situated near its suppliers as this will be more cost effective. These firms are referred to as **bulk decreasing**. A firm that also relies on regular deliveries or employs a **just-in-time** system will also benefit from being close to

Figure 7.1 Topshop and other high-profile businesses occupy prime locations

its suppliers. On the other hand, firms like soft drinks companies would be described as **bulk increasing** as their products gain weight throughout the production process through the addition of water, so they would be more likely to locate nearer the market. Today, the bulk decreasing theory applies less for two reasons: first, better transport links mean that the costs of transportation has fallen, thus firms are not under as much pressure to locate near their suppliers; second, the growth of the service sector has meant that firms locate nearer the consumer.

Labour

The skills and size of workforce required will be dependent upon the nature of the business. If a firm needs a large workforce it will have to ensure that it locates in an area that is accessible or close to populated areas that can supply the required labour. Locating in an area with high employment may create recruitment difficulties, which may constrain a firm's chance of success, especially as it grows.

Market

For service industries such as retailers, locating close to their market is the most important factor. Customers do not expect to travel miles for hairdressers, restaurants or shops. However, there are an increasing number of service industries that sell via the internet; such firms are able to operate from cheap out-of-town locations as customers will not need to visit.

Infrastructure

Infrastructure describes the provision of all services in an area, including its transport links, telecommunication systems, health services and educational institutions. For many firms, however, it is the transport links that represent a key influence on their choice of location. In order for a firm to organise its operations smoothly it must be able to access its suppliers and its market quickly and cost effectively. This is not always possible if transport links are poor. Remember, however, even when an area has high-quality infrastructure, it may be so popular with businesses that the resulting congestion may reduce accessibility. Think of the M25 at any time of the year!

Government intervention

Financial incentives offered by government in an attempt to help areas with high unemployment may affect a firm's choice of location. However, there are restrictions on the types of firms that can attract this funding and it is unlikely that a new firm will meet the criteria necessary to attract funding.

7.3 Qualitative factors

In addition to the quantitative factors, some owners of businesses may choose their locations for purely personal reasons. Anita Roddick, founder of the Body Shop, set up her firm in Brighton because that is where she and her family lived. Other firms locate in areas due to the high quality of life and beauty that the area provides.

Figure 7.2 Brighton, home of The Body Shop founder, Anita Roddick

Which factor is the most important?

This will depend on the nature of the business. The factor that may attract one firm may not attract another. Some new businesses may select their location purely on the grounds of personal preference, whereas others may select the least-cost location. Table 7.1 shows that different factors will be important to different types of firm.

Table 7.1 Which location factor is the most important?

Nature of the business	Factors that will be most important	Examples
Service businesses	If the customer needs to visit the business to purchase the product, then proximity to the market will be crucial; in addition to this, the image of a location and its surroundings will also play a role	Gap Lush Costa Coffee
Manufacturing businesses	Most manufacturers will be concerned with proximity to suppliers or the size of land required for their operations; this means that many manufacturing firms may locate in out-of-town sites that provide the opportunity for expansion in the future	Bath Ales Brewery Car component suppliers HBPO and Intier Automotive have set up close to the newly expanded BMW Mini factory in Oxford
Method of distribution	As highlighted in the text, many firms do not come into direct contact with their customers as they sell via the internet and use distribution firms to deliver their products; such firms will not need to consider the proximity of their market or the image and appearance of their premises; however, high-quality transport links will be extremely important	The Natural Company Amazon Luxtowe Farms pick-your-own strawberries
Labour-intensive or capital-intensive businesses	If the firm relies heavily on labour in the production of its products then its labour costs will represent a high proportion of its costs; this may lead it to locate in areas where the cost of living is cheaper and there is a plentiful supply of labour, as this will help to reduce its labour costs	In 2007 Cadbury moved chocolate production from Keynsham (near Bristol) to Poland Call centre jobs in Glasgow, such as the new Lloyds TSB national call centre

7.4 Changes in the location factors

As a business becomes established the factors that influence its location may change. For example, a newly formed business may select a location near to the owner's residence, but as a firm becomes established and starts to grow it may find that it needs to extend and requires larger premises. In the long term, a successful firm may encounter increasing competition; this may mean that it needs to lower its prices, which may result in it looking for the least-cost location.

Technology and choice of location

The role of technology has had a major influence on a firm's choice of location. Technology, and the ease of communication that it facilitates, has enabled some firms to become more **footloose**. This means that they are not tied to any location and can operate anywhere without considering any of the influences previously discussed. Today, even relatively small firms switch their production sites around the country or around the world. Electrical goods manufacturer Dyson moved its factories from Wiltshire to Malaysia. James Dyson says this has cut costs and led to improved production quality.

Issues For Analysis

● You demonstrate the skill of analysis every time you use theory or business logic to develop a solution to a business problem. Good analysis acknowledges that short-term solutions may have long-term implications. For example, if a firm chooses a location because it attracts government finance this may be a good decision in the short term, but it may not be the best location in the long term if the firm needs to expand its premises or gain access to a wider geographical market.

7.5 Location factors for a business start-up
an evaluation

You demonstrate the skill of evaluation when you make judgements based on assessing and weighing up different evidence. Good evaluation is also demonstrated when you assess the quality, reliability and relevance of the evidence. For example, it is important to remember that new start-ups do not have access to the same financial resources as well-established firms, and they are also more likely to focus on a smaller and more local market. Therefore influences such as national transport links may not be as important in their choice of location as the cost of rent. It is therefore critical that you demonstrate your evaluation skills in relation to location by recognising that the factors that sway new entrepreneurs in the real world are not always those that

influence well-established firms. Many new businesses start out in spare rooms, garages and garden sheds until success enables them to expand their operations and locate in other places. Furthermore, it is also important to distinguish between theory and practice. For example, in theory we assume that all service businesses want to locate near to their market, whereas in practice, proximity to the market may be important but not vital. This is because an increasing number of firms' contact with the marketplace is made via telephones and the internet, using call centres.

Key terms

Bulk decreasing/bulk increasing: a firm that uses large, bulky materials to produce smaller end products/a firm that uses low-volume materials to produce larger end products.

Footloose: a firm that is not tied to a particular location as it relies on technology and communication links.

Infrastructure: the network of utilities, such as transport links, telecommunications systems, health and education services.

Just-in-time: a manufacturing system that aims to minimise the costs of holding stocks of raw materials, components and work in progress by producing goods in response to a definite order; it requires efficient ordering and delivery systems.

Labour intensive/capital intensive: a process in which labour costs represent a high proportion of the total costs; small firms and firms in the service sectors are likely to be labour intensive; by contrast, a capital-intensive process relies more on machinery in the production of its products.

Least-cost location: a site that allows a firm to minimise its costs.

Exercises

A. Revision questions

(30 marks; 30 minutes)

1 Explain what is meant by the 'quantitative' factors that may influence a firm's choice of location. (3)

2 Describe one factor that would be important to a manufacturing firm but not a retail firm when choosing a location. (2)

3 Explain why a firm relying on mail order may not locate in a high-rent area. (2)

4 How might the use of just-in-time production influence the location of a business? (3)

5 State two factors that would influence the location of a firm that employs a labour-intensive process. (2)

6 How may selecting the least-cost location improve a firm's competitive ability? (4)

7 Explain two reasons why a firm may decide to choose a location near to its supplier. (4)

8 Identify two qualitative factors that may influence a firm's choice of location. (2)

9 Explain how a cheap location for a new service industry may represent a 'false economy'. (4)

10 What is meant by the term footloose? Identify two factors that may prevent a business from being footloose. (4)

B. Revision exercises

B1 Activity

Choosing the right location for a pizza takeaway

Leona and Seun want to open a Domino's pizza franchise outlet in a medium-sized town in Bedfordshire. It will do pizza to take away or for delivery. After some weeks of research, they have narrowed down their choice to two locations (see table). Which should they go for?

Profiles of two locations

	Martin Way	Dame Alice Street
Road details	Busy main road from town to M1; near big housing estate	Busy high street near station; next to Primark
Accommodation	3-bed flat above premises in good order; access from back of shop; rental value up to £100 p.w.	2 flats, each with 2 beds; separate access from street; rental value £200 p.w. each
Leasehold details	Lease 15 years; price £55,000	Lease 12 years; price £220,000
Rent per year	£12,500 p.a.	£68,000 p.a.
Parking	Plenty at the back of premises	NCP car park 200 m away

Questions

1 Discuss the pros and cons of each location, bearing in mind the type of business.

2 Write a three-slide presentation on:

- strengths of the Martin Way location

- strengths of the Dame Alice Street location

- which you recommend and why.

B2 Data response

John Michaels set up a business producing wind-up radios 14 months ago. He produces the radios in his garage and sells them via a national mail-order company specialising in organic, 'green' products. Since starting up his business, the sales of his radios have increased by 18%. He is now considering renting a small industrial unit, which would enable him to increase the number of radios he could produce.

Questions

(20 marks; 20 minutes)

1 What factors should John take into account before moving his production to the industrial unit? (6)

2 Explain how John's profits could be affected by his decision to move to the industrial unit. (4)

3 What are the benefits of selling the radios via a mail-order company? (5)

4 What qualitative factors may be behind John's decision to relocate production from the garage to the industrial unit? (5)

EMPLOYING PEOPLE

8.1 Introduction: taking on new staff

Many entrepreneurs are obliged to take on a variety of jobs when they start out in business. Not only are they responsible for decision making and creative input, they are also required to carry out all the day-to-day activities needed to keep the business going. However, as the business expands, this approach may act as an obstacle to further growth. Most entrepreneurs will have an area of expertise that led them into business in the first place, but they will almost certainly lack some of the skills needed to run a business successfully. In addition, working around the clock may be necessary initially but, in the long term, can lead to stress and poor decision making. Eventually, any ambitious entrepreneur will have to employ new staff.

8.2 Factors to consider

Recruitment can be an expensive process, and has to be considered in relation to the wider objectives of the firm. Therefore, before spending time and money hiring staff, there are a number of factors to think about.

The business should start by identifying what skills, qualities and experience are required in order to allow it to continue to operate successfully. This will require a clear understanding of the exact nature of the firm's product and the market in which it operates. A detailed analysis of the marketplace usually forms a major part of a firm's business plan (see Unit 5).

The next step would be to pinpoint current skill strengths and weaknesses, so that gaps in expertise can be filled. For example, trying to get the books to balance

without the financial skills required to do so can use up a great deal of time. This could be spent more profitably promoting products, dealing with customers and managing suppliers.

Another factor to consider is the length of time that workers are likely to be needed. For instance, additional staff may be taken on in order to respond to an increasing workload. Is this increase likely to be temporary or permanent? How many extra hours of work will be needed each week? Once a business has developed a clear understanding of its workforce needs, it will be in a position to choose from a number of employment options.

8.3 Employment options

The firm may wish to consider a number of possible options before deciding on the best way of taking on

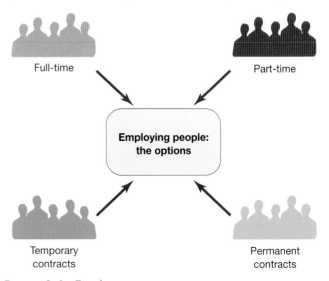

Figure 8.1 Employment options

additional workers (see Figure 8.1). This should help to ensure that the extra help can be acquired without creating unaffordable labour costs.

Part-time vs full-time employees

Employer surveys generally classify jobs as being part-time if the contracted period of work is equal to or less than 30 hours per week. Approximately 7.4 million, or 25%, of employees are currently employed on a part-time basis within the UK. Employing part-time rather than **full-time employees** can offer a business a number of benefits.

● It can be a more efficient way of meeting labour requirements, especially for small businesses, by keeping costs down when there is no need for full-time cover.

● Employing part-timers can also help to increase the degree of workforce flexibility, allowing firms to cater for predicable fluctuations in demand.

● Offering part-time contracts to staff may also help to improve the quality and productivity of the workforce. It may attract more applicants for job vacancies, including women with small children. The option of working part-time may also lead to a more motivated workforce, reduced absenteeism and labour turnover.

However, relying too heavily on **part-time employees** may mean additional induction, training and administration costs for a firm. It may also lead to a deterioration in communication, if staff see very little of each other, making it difficult to coordinate activities.

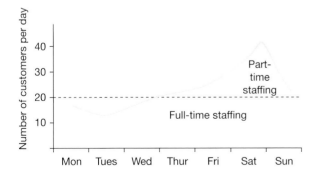

Figure 8.2 Full-time vs part-time staffing

Temporary vs permanent employees

A **temporary employee** is employed for a limited period of time by a business. Such workers are often hired on fixed-term contracts (i.e. a **contract of employment**

based on a definite period of time, such as three months). Employment is terminated once the contract expires and no notice is required from the employer, although the contract can be ended sooner if either side does give notice. The advantages of employing staff on a temporary basis include the following.

● A more flexible workforce can be created to cope with changes in demand over certain periods of time. For example, a retailer might choose to recruit sales assistants on a temporary basis to help deal with increased demand and maintain customer service standards over the Christmas sales period.

● Temporary workers can be used to cover for **permanent employees** – for instance, during maternity/paternity leave or secondment to another area of the business.

● Employing workers on fixed-term contracts allows even small businesses to gain access to highly specialised skills, such as IT or marketing, without having to bear the costs of having to permanently hire what are likely to be expensive employees.

The level of commitment of temporary employees to the business is, however, likely to be much lower than that of workers on permanent contracts. Lack of job security may mean that workers move to permanent jobs elsewhere as and when such positions arise, resulting in increased labour turnover. This, in turn, could lead to higher recruitment costs and lower productivity while new workers familiarise themselves with their duties.

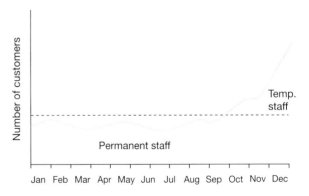

Figure 8.3 Permanent vs temporary staff

Using employment agency staff

One possibility for businesses looking to hire staff on a temporary basis is to use an **employment agency**. Although the workers supplied carry out duties within the business, they are paid by the agency. This means that the business has a contract with the agency, rather than individual workers, and pays a fee for its services.

Agency staff are often used to cover for short-term holiday or sickness absence, or in situations where there is a high labour turnover, such as in the hotel and catering industries. The main advantage to a business of using agency workers is that the agency is the employer; this makes the agency responsible for the recruitment and administration functions involved in employing staff. This is very useful if the job is something like a security guard or an office cleaner. Topshop wants to be good at selling attractive, fashionable clothes; it does not want its store managers worrying about recruiting new cleaners.

8.5 External advisers, consultants and contractors

A business in need of expert skills over a specific period of time may decide to use a business adviser, consultant or contractor. These individuals or organisations provide agreed services, such as accountancy or human resources functions, for a set time and fee.

Advisers, consultants and contractors can provide a cost-effective means of completing one-off projects or accessing skills and expertise to improve the performance of the business. They avoid the need for the potentially costly recruitment and training of permanent workers who may be under-utilised, especially in small firms. However, consultants and advisers can be very expensive, and their frequent or lengthy use may actually end up costing the business more than taking on permanent employees. These 'outsiders' may also fail to understand the special character of an individual business, and may lack commitment to its long-term success.

8.6 Legal responsibilities

Regardless of whether workers are employed on a full- or part-time, temporary or permanent basis, firms must be aware of the responsibilities involved in taking on additional staff. Employers have a number of obligations,

including the need to provide a safe and secure environment, to treat workers fairly and avoid discrimination. All workers must be given a written statement of the terms and conditions of their contract of employment, and have a number of legal entitlements, including:

- the right to receive the **National Minimum Wage.**

  In October 2008 the rates were set at:

  Over 21 £5.73 per hour

  18–21 £4.77 per hour

  16–17 £3.53 per hour

- minimum levels of rest breaks

- paid holidays and statutory sick pay.

Employers are required to register with HM Revenue & Customs (HMRC) and establish a payroll in order to deduct income tax and National Insurance contributions from employees' pay.

Part-time and fixed-term employees have the same employment rights as their full-time colleagues. This means that, by law, employers must treat staff in the same way, regardless of the basis for their employment. Therefore part-time staff should receive, pro rata, the same terms and conditions, including rates of pay, holidays and access to training, promotion and redundancy. Failure to treat staff fairly could result in an employee making a complaint to an **employment tribunal**, potentially leading to the firm having to pay compensation.

A-grade application
The employer and the law

The fear of legal action from employees has discouraged nearly one-third of small firms in the UK from taking on additional staff, according to recent research. The survey, carried out in 2005 by Sage HR Advice, also confirmed that 19% of respondents had considered giving up their business as a direct result of employment legislation.

Source: Adapted from www.startups.co.uk

Issues For Analysis

Opportunities for analysis using this topic are likely to focus on the following areas:

- the reasons for and against a small business expanding its workforce

- the advantages and/or disadvantages to a firm of employing staff on a part-time or full-time basis

- the benefits and drawbacks of employing staff on a temporary or full-time basis

- the suitability of using consultants or contractors to a firm in given circumstances.

8.7 Employing people
an evaluation

Taking on extra workers is one of the hardest decisions that an entrepreneur is likely to face. This is the point in the firm's development where the individual is forced to admit that s/he can't do everything. There may also be a reluctance to hand over some control to others – people who may have different opinions and challenge the way the business is run. Employing someone with strongly opposing views is likely to lead to conflict and, unless everyone is heading in the same direction, the business will not move forward. However, a successful firm requires a range of skills and experience. Refusing to bring in additional support and expertise can seriously damage the potential of the business to continue to survive and thrive.

Key terms

Contract of employment: a legal document setting out the terms and conditions of an individual's job. These include the responsibilities of the employee, rates of pay, working hours, holiday entitlement, etc.

Employment agency: an organisation that supplies workers with particular skills, on a short- or long-term basis, to other businesses, in return for a fee.

Employment tribunal: an informal courtroom where legal disputes between employees and employers are settled.

Full-time employees: staff who are under contract to work the normal basic full-time hours of a business.

National Minimum Wage: the lowest hourly wage rate that an employer can legally pay to an employee.

Part-time employees: staff who are contracted to work for anything less than what is considered the normal basic full-time hours of a business.

Permanent employees: workers with a contract of employment with a business that is open-ended (i.e. there is no time given at which the contract is due to end).

Temporary employees: employees on fixed-term contracts of employment, either for a predetermined time or until a specific task or set of tasks is completed.

Exercises

A. Revision questions

(40 marks; 40 minutes)

1 Outline three reasons why a small business may need to take on additional staff. (6)

2 Suggest two reasons why the owner of a small business might be reluctant to employ more staff. (2)

3 Explain why a business should consider any plans to expand the workforce in relation to its wider objectives. (4)

4 Examine two advantages of employing part-time staff to a small, expanding business. (6)

5 Suggest two reasons why an over-reliance on part-time staff could, in fact, increase the costs of a business. (4)

6 Briefly explain what is meant by a fixed-term contract. (2)

7 Analyse the main advantages and disadvantages of using temporary workers for a domestic cleaning business. (6)

8 Suggest one suitable method of dealing with the following staff shortages:
   (a) providing cover for a receptionist on two weeks' holiday (1)
   (b) providing extra sales assistance at a delicatessen on Saturdays (1)
   (c) providing additional waiters and kitchen staff at a restaurant over the busy Christmas period. (1)

9 Suggest one benefit and one drawback to a small business of using consultants to provide specialist skills. (4)

10 Briefly explain the main risks for a small business from failing to adhere to legislation regarding the employment of workers. (3)

B. Revision exercises

B1 Activity

The Gourmet Chocolate Pizza Company

Helen Ellis took the decision to set up her own business in 2006. Her job as a part-time administrator had come to an end after the company employing her had closed down. Supported by her family, and keen to continue to work from her Nottingham home, Helen surfed the internet, looking for inspiration. She came across the concept of chocolate pizzas from an American website and was confident that, by putting her own twist on the idea, she had a successful venture on her hands. The result was a range of chocolate-based pizzas, covered with a mouth-watering selection of toppings.

Working from home for 18 months had proved to Helen that she had many of the skills and qualities required to run her own business: hard working and dedicated, with good organisational skills and an ability to deal with suppliers and the general public. Helen decided to pay a professional designer in order to get the business's website up and running quickly, and carried out her own research to see how other similar businesses marketed themselves.

Despite putting in a lot of hours, including evenings and weekends, and receiving a great deal of unpaid help from her mother, the increasing workload meant that, although Helen was managing to meet the orders, she was unable to cope with all the other jobs involved in growing the business as well. In particular, the need for additional production staff to help box up the pizzas persuaded Helen to hire an extra worker. Her search focused on finding someone who was flexible and reliable, could show initiative and shared a similar approach to the business. After taking advice on employment terms and conditions, the new employee was hired on a six-month contract initially before being appointed on a permanent basis.

According to Helen, 'employing another member of staff was the best thing I did . . . a bit daunting, but one of those things you need to do to push the business forward, so really you take a deep breath and do it.'

Source: Gourmet Chocolate Pizza Company

Questions

(20 marks; 25 minutes)

1 Outline three qualities possessed by Helen Ellis that helped her establish her business. (6)

2 Describe one advantage and one disadvantage to Helen's business of employing new staff. (6)

3 Examine the benefits of appointing a new member of staff on a temporary contract initially. (8)

B2 Activity

Using short-term contractors at System Associates

System Associates is an award-winning internet technologies company that provides integrated software services. It has clients in both the private and public sector, including HM Treasury, the British Library and the National College of School Leadership. The company, located in Berkshire, employs 25 permanent employees, performing a range of functions, from consultants and developers to project managers and support staff. When System Associates won a major contract for London Connects, a London-based e-government agency, its workforce was operating at full capacity. The skills required to complete the project were of a very high level, so the decision was made to employ a team of content editors on short-term contracts.

According to managing director, David Macken, short-term contractors offered the company both labour flexibility and the ability to access specialist skills when they were needed. An internet recruitment service provided a shortlist of candidates. Interviews and references were then used to assess whether the contractors really had the skills they claimed and to ensure successful candidates would fit in with the existing team. The four contractors who were selected were issued with written agreements, covering terms and conditions, project schedules, deadlines and fees. The agreements also specified a one-day notice period, to allow the swift dismissal of anyone failing to meet expectations. Although the contractors were expected to 'hit the ground running', they were given induction training and included in company meetings and social events, to encourage them to integrate into the existing team. The project worked so well that two of the contractors were invited to join the company on a permanent basis.

Source: Business Link

Questions

(25 marks; 30 minutes)

1 Briefly explain how contracted workers differ from employees. (6)

2 Analyse two benefits to a small company like Systems Associates of using contractors. (7)

3 Assess the impact of continuing to increase the size of the workforce on the long-term success of Systems Associates. (12)

C. Essay questions

(40 marks each)

1 'People are the main assets of a business.' Discuss this statement in the context of a small business.'

2 To what extent should new businesses be concerned about taking on staff?

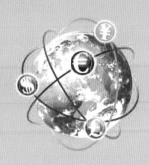

OPPORTUNITY COST AND TRADE-OFFS

Opportunity cost is the cost of missing out on the next best alternative when making a decision. For example, the opportunity cost of not going to university may be to risk missing out on massive extra lifetime earnings (in general, graduates are much better paid than non-graduates). Similarly, trade-offs look at what you have to give up in order to get what you want most. They may not easily be expressed as a 'cost' (i.e. it may not be possible to quantify them).

9.1 Introduction to opportunity cost

This concept will be useful throughout the A-level Business Studies course. It is at the heart of every business decision, from small to multinational companies. It can best be explained with reference to football club management. In 2007 new manager Lawrie Sanchez was given a budget of £25 million to buy new players for Fulham FC. In theory, he could have spent it on Owen Hargreaves (£17 million) plus most of the left leg of Carlos Tevez. Instead he spent it on nine players, largely from lower leagues or from Premiership reserve sides. The cost of these players was £25 million. The opportunity cost was missing out on Hargreaves and part of Tevez. The £25 million could only be spent once, so it was vital to spend it wisely (unfortunately he failed to do this and was sacked in December 2007).

Every business faces the same issue: limited resources mean that hiring a marketing manager leaves less money to spend on a marketing campaign! For a start-up business, lots of money spent on a flash opening party means less money to pay for staff training.

For a new business the two most important resources are money and time. Both have an opportunity cost. Time spent by an entrepreneur creating a pretty website might mean too little time recruiting and training staff, or too little time sitting back to reflect on priorities. The same issue arises with money: it can only be spent once.

It follows that every business decision has an opportunity cost, measured in time, money, and often both. The same is true in other walks of life. A prime minister focused on foreign adventures may lose sight of the key issues affecting people at home. A chancellor who spends an extra £10 billion on education may have to cut back on the NHS.

For a new business start-up, the most important opportunity cost issues are as follows.

- Don't tie up too much capital in stock, as this cash could be used more productively elsewhere in the business.

- Don't overstretch yourself – good decisions take time, so make sure you are not doing too much yourself.

- Take care over every decision that uses up cash; at the start of a business it's hard to get more of it, but more is always needed.

9.2 Opportunity costs in developing a business idea

Personal opportunity costs

Starting your first business is likely to be tough. Long hours and highly pressured decisions may cause stress, but the biggest problems are beyond psychology. A difficult cash flow position is quite normal, yet places a huge strain on the business and its owner(s).

If it's a first business, the owner will probably have come from a background as a salary earner, possibly a very well-paid one. So the first opportunity cost is missing out on the opportunity to earn a regular income. As it might take six months or more to get a business going, this is a long period of financial hardship.

Then comes the investment spending itself, such as the outlay on a lease, on building work, on fixtures and fittings, on machinery and then on the human resources (staff) to make everything work with a human face. All this is using money that could otherwise be used on the proprietor's house, holidays, and so on. The personal opportunity costs add up massively.

Business writers often use the term 'stakeholders', which means all those with a stake in the success or failure of a business. Usually, the key groups are those within the business ('internal stakeholders'), such as staff, managers and directors, and outside groups ('external stakeholders'), such as suppliers, customers, bankers and shareholders. In the case of a business start-up, however, there is a whole extra consideration – the wear and tear on the family. Starting a business is a hugely time-consuming and wholly absorbing activity. The restaurant owner might easily spend 80 hours a week on site in the early days, then take further paperwork home. An American business psychologist has said that, 'even when you are home, you're still thinking about the business – it's easy for a spouse to feel neglected, even jealous'.

Despite this, research by a US investment business has shown that, although 32% of new entrepreneurs said that the experience had caused marriage difficulties, 42% of chief executives in fast-growing new firms said that the pressures and exhilarations made their marriages stronger.

The opportunity costs of developing one business idea as opposed to another

When 30-year-old Mike Clare opened his first Sofabed Centre in 1985 he could raise only £16,000 of capital, even though his estimates showed that £20,000–25,000 was needed. Fortunately, hard work plus a great first month's sales brought in the cash he needed to get the business going properly. Back then, no bank would lend him a penny. Now, the renamed Dreams is Britain's biggest bed retailer, with 150 outlets and a sales turnover of more than £160 million. Mike Clare remains the main shareholder and the boss.

The fact is, though, that it would have been impossible for Mike to have chosen to launch two different businesses at the same time – he had to choose one. Fortunately, he chose wisely.

Given the need to focus on the opportunity, the main circumstance in which opportunity cost arises is when an entrepreneur has two ideas. One should be chosen and one rejected. This is possible if the entrepreneur is

ruthless. After evaluating the two options carefully, the weaker of the two should be stopped completely. The reason is simple: opening one business is tough enough; two would be impossible.

In the lead-up to Mike Clare's first store opening, he was organising public relations events (to get coverage in the local paper), helping with the building work, wrangling with suppliers over credit terms and making decisions about pricing and display. When the store opened, he spent 18 hours a day there 'doing everything'. When the first store took £30,000 in month 1, he also started looking for a second location. It was open in November 1985, six months after the first. Quite clearly, there was no possibility of starting more than one business at a time!

Deciding between opportunities

Successful businesspeople are the ones who can make successful decisions. The three founders of Innocent Drinks wanted to start a business together, but had no idea what type of business to start. All friends at university, they had already run nightclub events together, and two ran an annual music festival in west London. They could have developed their skills as showmen into a successful festival business, but stumbled upon the idea of a business making all-fruit smoothies. On finding an investor, in 1999, who could help turn their dream into a reality, they left their salaried jobs, gave up their other business opportunities and concentrated on building the (now massively successful) Innocent brand.

When deciding between business start-up opportunities, certain factors are crucial.

● *Estimating the potential sales that could be achieved by each idea:* this is hugely difficult, both in the short term and – even more – in the longer term. Innocent's first-year sales were £0.4 million. Who could have guessed that, eight years later, its sales would be more than 300 times greater? Yet estimates must be made, either by the use of market research, or by using the expertise of the entrepreneur. For instance, Mike Clare of Dreams had previously worked as an area manager for a furniture retailer, so he had a reasonable idea about what the sales might be. Inside knowledge is, of course, hard to beat.

● *Considering carefully the cash requirements of each idea:* the Innocent trio were very lucky to American investor who put £250,000 of the business in return for a 20% sta probably get at least £100 million for he decides to sell, providing a return of 39,900% on his investment!). Some new businesses are very hungry for cash (such as setting up a new restaurant in London, which costs over £1 million); other new business ideas (such as a new website) can be started from a back bedroom, keeping initial costs very low.

● *Deciding whether the time is right:* Innocent's 1999 launch fitted wonderfully with a time of luxury spending plus growing concern about diet. In the same year, a small business started in west London focusing on customising cars: 'souping up' the engines to make the cars go faster and give the engines a 'throaty roar'. As rising fuel prices became a greater concern, the business was squeezed out. Five years before, it might have made good money, but no longer.

● *Deciding whether the skills needed fit your own set of skills:* running a restaurant requires a mix of organisation, discipline and meticulous attention to detail – is that you? Or are you better suited to running an online business that can be handled in a relaxed way behind the scenes?

A-grade application
Cobra Beer

Cobra Beer has become the standard lager to be found in Indian restaurants throughout the UK. Its origins date back to when owner/founder Karan Bilimoria came from India to study at a British university. He found British lagers too gassy for comfort. After completing his degree, Karan and a family friend spent their time importing items from India to Britain, such as polo sticks, towels and silk jackets. They were planning to start importing seafood and visited a supplier that also had a small, privately owned brewery. Karan (now Lord) Bilimoria explained the less gassy style of beer that he wanted, and the brewery helped out.

The pair of friends had very little money, but managed to get a £7000 overdraft to pay for the first beer imports to Britain. To keep focused, they decided to drop all their other import businesses. Today Cobra Beer has annual sales of over £100 million. Lord Bilimoria's stake in the business is worth well over £50 million (he bought out his friend's stake along the way). Several times over, Lord Bilimoria made the right decision.

Source: D. Lester (2007) *How They Started*. Crimson Publishing.

9.4 Trade-offs

In business there are many occasions when one factor has to be traded off against another. An entrepreneur might get huge help at the start from friends, yet realise that these same friends lack the professionalism to help the business grow. The needs of the business may have to be traded off against the friendships. Can a softie be a real business success? Probably not – some inner toughness is clearly important.

Other trade-offs might include:

● when starting in the first place, trading off the start-up against a year's international travel (perhaps with friends); or trading the start-up against going to university

● trading off the aspects of the business you most enjoy doing against those that prove most profitable for the business; the chef/owner may love cooking, yet find the business works far better when s/he has the time to mix with the customers, motivate the waiting staff and negotiate hard with suppliers

● trading off time today and time tomorrow; the entrepreneur's ambition may be to 'retire by the time I'm 40'; that may sound great in the long term but, in the short term, her/his spouse and children may see little of them.

Overall, the key to success will be to be clear about what you and your family want from the business. It might be to become outrageously rich, no matter what, or – more likely – to find a balance between the freedom and independence of running your own business and the need to find time for the family. Books on business success assume that success can be measured only in £millions. Many people running their own small businesses would tell a different story – the independence alone may be the key to their personal satisfaction.

Exercises

A. Revision questions

(20 marks; 20 minutes)

1 Explain in your own words why time is an important aspect of opportunity cost. (3)

2 Give two ways of measuring the opportunity cost to you of doing this homework. (2)

3 Outline one opportunity cost to a restaurant chef/owner of opening a second restaurant. (3)

4 Explain the trade-offs that may exist in the following business situations. Choose the two contexts you feel most comfortable with.
   (a) Levi's pushes its workers to produce more pairs of jeans per hour.
   (b) A chocolate producer, short of cash, must decide whether to cut its advertising spending or cut back on its research and development into new product ideas.
   (c) A football manager decides to double the number of training sessions per week.
   (d) A celebrity magazine must decide whether or not to run photos that will generate huge publicity, but probably make the celeb unwilling to cooperate with the magazine in future. (6)

5 Re-read the A-grade application on Cobra Beer. Outline the trade-offs involved in Karan Bilimoria's decision to start his beer business. (6)

B. Revision exercises

B1 Data response

James Sutton had a job as a marketing manager, paying £55,000 a year. His career prospects looked very good, yet he handed in his notice to start up his own online business. He knew that it would take him away from 9–5 work and towards the dedication of 8 am until 9 pm. If he took on a member of staff, the wage bill would rise by £16,000.

Questions

(10 marks; 15 minutes)

1 Outline three opportunity cost issues within this short passage. (6)

2 Outline the possible impact on James of the increase in the workload. (4)

B2 Data response

In 2002 a cooperative agreement between coffee farmers in 250 Ugandan villages broke down. It had taken years to put together, but disagreements made it collapse. The prize for a successful cooperative was to produce organic coffee beans grown to Fairtrade standards for partners such as Cafédirect. This would ensure getting significantly higher prices for the raw coffee beans and also much better credit terms (being paid quickly to help with cash flow).

Over the next two years countless hours of work were put into forming a new cooperative. In early 2004 the new 'Gumutindo' coffee cooperative was Fairtrade certified. Over 3000 farmers are now part of Gumutindo. They receive a guaranteed price of $1.26 per pound of coffee beans, whereas the world price has been under $0.80 for the last six years. The extra (and stable) income should help the farmers, of whom only 25% have running water and 79% live in mud huts with iron sheet roofing. In future, the Fairtrade organisation will support the cooperative in starting up its own production plant – converting the raw coffee into packs of coffee ready for sale.
Source: www.fairtrade.org.uk

Questions

(25 marks; 30 minutes)

1 What would be the opportunity cost of the farmers who put 'countless hours of work into forming a new cooperative'? (4)

2 Outline one risk for the farmers and one risk for the Fairtrade organisation in forming a new cooperative with high guaranteed prices for coffee beans. (6)

3 Some commentators have suggested that Waitrose should make all its coffee 'Fairtrade', therefore getting rid of brands such as Nescafé Gold Blend. Outline the trade-offs Waitrose management would have to consider before making any such decision. (6)

4 Discuss whether producing coffee ready for sale would definitely increase the income levels of the 3000 members of the cooperative. (9)

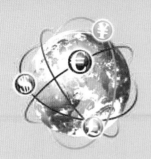

ECONOMIC FACTORS AFFECTING BUSINESS START-UP

DEFINITION

Economic factors deal with the economy as a whole (sometimes known as the 'macro' economy). These include interest rates and exchange rates, either of which could affect the success of a new small business start-up.

10.1 What is 'the economy'?

Each of us goes about our business in our own way. A teacher gets a monthly salary paid directly into the bank, and draws out the cash needed to buy the shopping, buy petrol and give the kids some pocket money. The kids may spend this on chocolate, Coke and Walkers crisps.

Although, as individuals, we 'do our own thing', the actions and decisions taken by millions of people and businesses make up 'the economy'. Collectively, everyone's spending on chocolate adds up to £3000 million. This, in turn, provides the income for chocolate producers and shopkeepers, who employ tens of thousands of staff.

If the value of all the spending on all the products bought in the UK is added together, it comes to an annual figure of over £1 trillion (a million million). So the spending on chocolate makes up just 0.3% of all the spending on all the goods sold in Britain in a year. All this spending provides the vast revenues companies need in order to pay for Britain's 28 million workers, and they still need enough profit to pay for business growth.

The key thing to remember about all this is that the economy is intertwined. Cadbury is successful only if families have enough cash to be able to buy chocolate bars. So, if there was a big cutback in consumer spending, perhaps because of a spread in economic gloom from America to Britain, many firms would struggle, including Cadbury.

When times are bad, almost every business suffers; this, in turn, can lead to job losses. When the economy is recovering, things get better for almost all firms.

10.2 Current economic climate

Business thrives on confidence. Confident consumers are willing to dip into their savings for a holiday, or to borrow to buy a new carpet or car. Confident investors are willing to put more money into businesses in return for shares. And the companies themselves will spend to invest in their future: new factory buildings, new machinery and new computer systems. All this spending can create an upsurge in economic activity.

The reverse also applies: gloom can spread doom. Therefore the **economic climate** is important. The sections that follow give an idea of the factors that help to create an economic climate either of optimism or pessimism. These factors include:

- changes in interest rates
- changes in the exchange rate
- the consequences for business of unemployment and inflation
- the effect of government spending or taxation.

10.3 Changes in interest rates

The interest rate is the price charged by a bank per year for lending money or for providing credit. Individual banks decide for themselves about the rate they will charge on their credit cards or for the overdrafts they provide. But they are usually influenced by the interest rate that the Bank of England charges the banks for

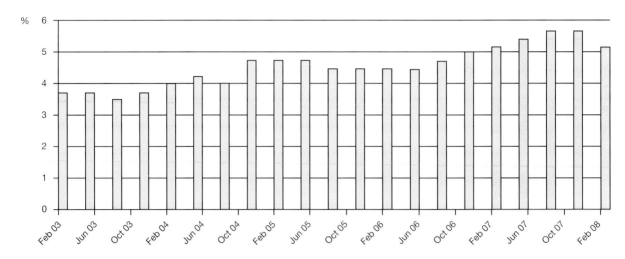

Figure 10.1 UK bank interest rates, 2003–08
Source: www.bankofengland.co.uk

borrowing money: the bank rate. This is set each month by a committee of the Bank of England.

The Bank of England committee is asked to set interest rates at a level which should ensure that UK prices rise by around 2% a year. If the committee members decide that the economy is growing so strongly that prices may rise faster than 2%, it will increase interest rates. Then people will feel worried about borrowing more (because of the higher repayment cost) and may cut their spending. This should help discourage firms from increasing their prices.

For firms, the level of interest rates is very important because:

● it affects **consumer demand**, especially for goods bought on credit, such as houses and cars; the higher the rate of interest, the lower the sales that can be expected

● the interest charges affect the total operating costs (i.e. the higher the interest rate, the higher the costs of running an overdraft, and therefore the lower the profit)

● the higher the rate of interest, the less attractive it is for a firm to invest money into the future of the business; therefore there is a risk of falling demand for items such as lorries, computers and factory machinery.

If interest rates fall, the opposite effects occur, to the benefit of both companies and the economy as a whole.

10.4 Exchange rates

In Britain goods and services are sold in our currency: the pound (£). In America goods and services are sold in dollars ($). The **exchange rate** measures the quantity of foreign currency that can be bought with one unit of domestic currency. Movements in the exchange rate can dramatically affect profitability because the exchange rate affects both the price of imported and exported goods.

The pound's rate of exchange against the US dollar is determined by the supply and demand for the pound on international currency markets. Exchange rates affect firms in different ways.

The impacts of a high exchange rate
On firms with large export markets

UK firms that sell a high proportion of their output overseas will prefer a low exchange rate (i.e. a weak pound). Why is this so? The best way of explaining is via a numerical example.

America is an important export market for Morgan Cars. Morgan charges its UK customers £18,000 for a basic two-seater Roadster.

To achieve the same profit margin in America, Morgan has to charge a price in US dollars that will convert into £18,000. At the beginning of 2007 the exchange rate against the US dollar was £1 = $1.90. To obtain £18,000 from the exported car, Morgan had to charge its American customers:

£18,000 × $1.90 = $34,200

Figure 10.2 A Morgan Roadster

By November 2007 the exchange rate had gone up to £1 = $2.10. To generate the same £18,000 of export revenue per car sold, Morgan had to charge its American customers:

£18,000 × $2.10 = $37,800

In other words, Morgan had to increase the price of its car in America by $3600 in order to maintain the current profit made on each car sold. That price increase would, of course, be off-putting to car buyers. So sales would be likely to fall.

On firms that import most of their raw materials or stock

Firms such as Tesco, which import much of their stock, will prefer a high exchange rate. A high exchange rate reduces the cost of buying goods from abroad. For example, Jack Daniel's whiskey is a popular product with Tesco's British consumers. However, Tesco has to import this product from the American firm that produces it. If the price of a case of Jack Daniel's is $50, the price paid by Tesco will be as follows.

If the exchange rate is £1 = $1.90, the case will cost Tesco $50/1.90 = £26.30.

However, if the exchange rate goes up to £1 = $2.10 the same case of Jack Daniel's will now cost Tesco £23.80 ($50/2.10 = £23.80). A high exchange rate will benefit Tesco because it will now be able to make more profit on each bottle of Jack Daniel's that it sells to UK customers.

The impacts of a low exchange rate

The impacts of a weak exchange rate are the reverse of the impacts of a strong exchange rate. Firms such as Morgan that were damaged by a strong currency find life easier when the exchange rate falls. A weak pound makes their exports seem cheaper to foreign consumers, so Morgan should be able to sell more of its cars in America.

On the other hand, firms such as Tesco will be damaged by a low exchange rate because it will now cost them more in pounds to buy in their imported stock. If Tesco reacts to the falling exchange rate by raising its prices the company could lose customers. If Tesco does nothing it will make less profit on each unit of imported stock sold.

10.5 The consequences for business of unemployment and inflation

Unemployment

Unemployment is created when the number of jobs (the demand for labour) falls in comparison to the number of people looking for work (the supply of labour). Therefore there are just two things to consider: the demand for labour and the supply.

The demand for labour in Britain is mainly affected by two things.

1 *The demand for goods in general and therefore the number of jobs available:* if the economy is booming, firms need plenty of full-time, part-time and seasonal staff, so there are plenty of jobs around. In an economic downturn, jobs are far less plentiful. In America, the growth in the number of jobs available increased by 95,000 a month during 2007, but fell by 17,000 in January 2008 as the economy slowed down.

2 *The demand for jobs in Britain compared with overseas:* in 2007 Cadbury switched chocolate production from Britain to Poland; many banks have switched their call centres from Britain to India. In fact, the number of jobs available in Britain reached record levels by early 2008, so the fear of 'outsourcing' is exaggerated.

The supply of labour in Britain is affected by two things:

1 demographic factors affecting the number of people of working age (roughly 27 million) plus the number of EU migrants available within the workforce (approximately 1 million)

2 the willingness of employable people to look for work, which may be weighed down by benefits such as free rent for those out of work, but is boosted by

rising minimum wage rates, which help to provide a better financial incentive to work; over the ten years to 2007 the number of people employed in Britain grew by 2 million.

In the long term, the above are key factors. In the short term the main single factor is likely to be the number of jobs on offer. Firms squeezed hard by an economic downturn will stop recruiting and may start to look for redundancies, to cut back on the workforce. This could push unemployment up sharply. In the past, as much as 20% of the workforce has been unemployed in Britain. In such an event, the impact on people's lives is very severe, especially if the unemployment lasts for several years, as in the 'recessions' of the early 1980s and 1990s.

What is inflation?

Inflation measures the percentage annual rise in the average price level. It reduces the internal purchasing power of money. For consumers, inflation increases the cost of living. The impacts of inflation on a firm's finances are mixed. There are some advantages created by inflation but there are also disadvantages created too.

Advantages of inflation to a business

1 Inflation can boost the recorded profitability of a business. For example, suppose that firm X made the following profit this year:

Total revenue	£100m
Total cost	£80m
Profit	£20m

During the following year inflation is 10%. Even if the firm's sales volume remains unchanged, its revenue can be increased. Inflation encourages the firm to increase its prices by 10%. It is also likely that the firm's costs will also rise by 10%. If the above turns out to be true, the firm's profit for the year will increase by £2 million.

Total revenue	£110m
Total cost	£88m
Profit	£22m

The firm could also claim that it had achieved a £10 million increase in revenue during the year. However, the increase is merely an illusion created by inflation. The firm still sold the same amount of product as it did the year before. There has been no increase in sales in **real terms** (taking into account the effects of inflation). Inflation has made the business look more profitable simply because it has made the revenue and cost figures larger.

2 Firms with large loans also benefit from inflation because inflation erodes the real value of the money owed. Firms with high borrowings typically find that the fixed repayments on their long-term borrowings become more easily covered by rising income and profits (after five years of inflation the repayments on a £1 million loan no longer seem so difficult to repay, because the business is enjoying higher revenues).

Disadvantages of inflation to a business

1 Inflation can damage profitability, especially for firms that have fixed-price contracts that take a long time to complete. For example, a local building company might agree a £5 million price for an extension to a local private school, which is expected to take three years to finish. If inflation is higher than expected, profit might be wiped out by the unexpectedly high cost increases created by the unexpectedly high rates of inflation.

2 Inflation can also harm a firm's cash position because it pushes up the price of new assets that need to be bought, such as machinery. This can penalise manufacturers such as Ford that need to replace their machinery regularly in order to stay internationally competitive.

3 If costs in Britain are rising faster than prices elsewhere, UK companies will find that they are losing their ability to compete effectively with foreign firms. In late 2007 the Indian firm Tata Motors brought out a new car priced at £1250. That would hardly pay the labour costs if the car was produced in Britain.

10.6 The effect of government spending or taxation

In addition to economic change, businesses can be affected by economic policy decisions taken by government. If worried about sharply rising prices, a government could decide to increase income tax. This would take spending power out of the pockets of consumers, softening the upward pressure on prices, but cutting demand for the products and services produced by businesses. What might be right for the economy as a whole could be damaging for individual businesses.

Why would any government take actions that could damage businesses and therefore threaten jobs? The answer is simple: because ministers may believe that short-term pain may be necessary for long-term gain. This might be correct, but it will be no consolation to any business squeezed out of business by an unexpected tax rise.

The other main weapon government can use to achieve its policy goals is to change the level of government (known as 'public') spending. At present, just over 40% of the British economy comes from public spending. Private consumers (you and me) do most of the rest. The government spends huge sums on the health service, defence, roads and much else. If the government was concerned about rising prices, it could consider cutting back on its own spending. This would reduce the income of businesses involved in education, road-building, and so on. They, in turn, might have to make redundancies, thereby dampening down consumer spending, which should help to keep prices from rising so sharply.

It follows, therefore, that sensible businesspeople keep an eye on government activity. Years ago, the government announced its tax and spending plans in the Spring Budget, which was always kept secret until the government announced it. Today, an 'Autumn Statement' announces, six months in advance, the government's public spending plans. This ensures that firms can anticipate the tax decisions that will be announced in the spring.

Table 10.1 shows how a government could use its power over taxation and spending to tackle different economic problems.

Issues For Analysis

The key to successful analysis of the effect of economic factors on business is to keep things simple. The best way to do this is to make a clear, direct link between the economic factor and the business featured in the exam question. Beware of drifting away towards complicated sequences of: 'this affects this, which affects that, which has a knock-on effect on that', and so on. For example:

- higher interest rates hit demand for goods bought on credit, such as cars and houses

- a rising £ will hit XXX Co, because it exports to 15 countries and will now face pressure to increase its overseas selling prices

- rising inflation may damage the XXX Co's competitiveness, by forcing the company to increase its prices.

Good analysis will take the answer quickly from the economics to the business reality.

Table 10.1 The impact of a change in spending and taxation

	Government spending up	Government spending down	Government puts taxes up	Government puts taxes down
To help reduce the level of unemployment	Extra spending on road-building, NHS and other services with big workforce			Reduce income tax to enable families to keep and spend more of the money they earn
To cut the growth rate when it's rising too fast		Cut the spending on health, education and defence, to take a bit of spending from the economy	Increase Income Tax to force people to think harder and more carefully about what they buy	
To improve the competitiveness of British firms	Extra spending on education			Cut company taxation (Corporation Tax)
To cut the rate of imports, especially of consumer goods		Cut benefits (e.g. state pension) to cut people's ability to buy imports	Increase VAT on all goods other than food and drink	

10.7 Economic factors affecting business start-up
an evaluation

Judging the importance of different economic factors is made much easier if you have a full grasp of the business context (i.e. what the firm does, how it does it, what its strengths and weaknesses are, and so on). For example, a 20% increase in the £'s value would cause serious problems for the UK car industry (as most UK-produced cars are exported), but would make little difference to a small corner shop.

As is true in every other part of the course, good judgement comes from breadth of experience. This can be helped by watching business TV, and reading *Business Review* and the A-grade application entries in this textbook.

Key terms

Consumer demand: the levels of spending by consumers in general (i.e. not just the demand from one consumer).

Economic climate: the atmosphere surrounding the economy (e.g. gloom and doom or optimism and boom).

Exchange rate: the price of a currency, measured by the amount of a foreign currency it will buy (e.g. £1 = $1.90).

Real terms: changes in £s totals (e.g. for household income) after allowing for the distorting effect of inflation.

Recession: a downturn in sales and production that occurs across most parts of the economy, perhaps leading to six months of continuous economic decline.

Exercises

A. Revision questions

(20 marks; 20 minutes)

1 Explain why a fall in spending in London might have a knock-on effect on the economy in Bradford, Plymouth, Norwich or anywhere else in the country. (3)

2 Explain how a business such as Alton Towers might be affected by a recession in America. (4)

3 Identify whether the Bank of England should raise or cut interest rates in the following circumstances:
   (a) a sharp recession has hit the UK economy
   (b) inflation is predicted to rise by 3% over the coming months
   (c) house prices have risen by 16% in each of the last two years. (1)

4 A British detective agency has been hired by a French woman to tail a man. The fee is €500 per week. After four weeks the sum of €2000 is due to be paid, but the rate for the £ against the € has fallen from 1.45 to 1.25.
   (a) What sum will the detective agency receive in £s for this four weeks' work? (3)
   (b) What might stop the firm from simply putting the € price up? (4)

5 Outline why an economic downturn might affect the level of unemployment. (5)

B. Revision exercises

B1 Data response

Is confidence enough?

In February 2008 the economic news in America was grim. Employment and the stock market were falling and the service sector (70% of the economy) was reporting a sharp slowdown. Yet although company chief executives reported 'concern at the prospect of a darkening economic picture', few admitted to seeing any problem with their own business or industry. Procter & Gamble, the world's largest household goods firm, reported no switch to own-label products. Consumers were still willing to pay the price premiums for brands such as Pampers and Gillette. Data for January 2008 showed that small firms were still taking on more staff and awarding pay rises. No sign of recession there, then.

Yet, according to an article in the prestigious *Harvard Business Review*, research over a 20-year period shows that, 'As evidence gathers that a downturn is likely, executives often continue to radiate confidence about the future. They don't want to frighten the troops [staff], which will only make matters worse … Some contend that their industries are safe. Others believe that their own company's ability to weather a downturn is superior to that of competitors.'

Chief executives could point to the interest rate cut from 4.25 to 3% as a clear sign that things were looking up. But financial analysts worried that optimism was 'preventing companies from planning for a downturn'.

Source: adapted from the Financial Times, 13 February 2008.

Questions

(20 marks; 25 minutes)

1 Explain why the experience of Procter & Gamble might not be typical of all firms. (4)

2a Explain why chief executives might want to 'radiate confidence about the future'. (4)

2b Outline two possible disadvantages to a business of excessive confidence on the part of a chief executive. (4)

3 The chief executives were pinning their hopes on the impact of the 1.25% cut in interest rates. Choose two of the following businesses, then analyse the effect of the fall in interest rates on each, in turn.
   (a) Procter & Gamble
   (b) Coca-Cola
   (c) A small building firm
   (d) Gucci, supplier of luxury clothes and accessories (8)

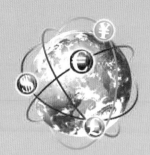

Unit 11

ASSESSING BUSINESS START-UPS

DEFINITION

Assessing means weighing up (i.e. making a judgement). This assessment should mirror the ways in which entrepreneurs need to decide: should I go ahead or not?

11.1 Introduction

Social entrepreneur Duncan Goose had, by mid-2007, established One Water as a £1.5 million brand. It was funding the building of a new water pump in Africa every ten days, and he was able to focus the six staff on his primary objective: one new water pump built every day.

Yet he was already looking ahead to his second project, One Condom. This would fund HIV/AIDS projects from profits made selling condoms in the UK. Vending machines at universities would be his first target. But launching a new idea takes time and money – and he was short of both. If One Condom drained Duncan's energies and those of his staff, what might be the effect on One Water? Duncan had to make a careful assessment of whether or not to start up One Condom.

Although he could see the reasons against, Duncan decided to go ahead. His objective in giving up a comfortable job and salary to start One was to make the world a better place. How could he stop now? The opportunity was there for building on One Water's success, so it would seem wrong to stop. The risks of failure only made it more of a challenge. Duncan made an assessment of the risks, costs and benefits of starting One Condom, but was motivated mainly by his personality. He wanted the challenge.

How should one assess whether or not a business start-up is worthwhile? There are four issues to consider:

1 the business objectives

2 the business plan

3 the risks involved

4 the possible causes and consequences of failure.

11.2 Summarising start-up objectives

There are three main types of objective when starting a business: financial, personal and social.

Financial

Some entrepreneurs are consciously setting out to get rich. They may be hoping to make enough money to retire by the age of 45, or even 25. For them, the ideal is to start up and build a business so that it can be sold or **floated** on the stock market. Either way, they will turn hard work into capital – lots of it. Mike Ashley started Sports Direct as a teenager and floated it in February 2007, aged 42. He sold 43% of the business for more than £900 million, keeping the remaining 57% of the shares. He then used his personal cash to buy Newcastle United FC.

The other financial goal is not to get rich, but simply to make a living. People who open a small grocery or sweetshop want to earn enough for the family, but may not be especially ambitious. Their financial goals may be no more than to make £25,000–£40,000 a year from the business.

Personal

Many people start up their own business because they want to prove that they can succeed. Perhaps they are disappointed with their own career and feel: 'this'll show them', or they are trying to prove something to themselves.

Among the key personal goals are to:

● be my own boss

- show what I can do

- get out of a boring career

- be able to build something

- avoid later regrets (if failing to take advantage of a business opportunity)

- build something for my family.

Social

As in the case of Duncan Goose, some people are true **social entrepreneurs**. The way they achieve their personal goals is through an enterprise that has a purpose other than profit-making. Yet it would be wise to be sceptical. For every one person who is a true social entrepreneur, there are probably ten who cover their financial ambitions in 'green' or charitable clothing. If 'carbon neutral' is a message that sells, many will adopt the slogan as a way to boost profit. Despite this, the fact that true social entrepreneurs exist means that it would be simplistic to suggest that all business start-ups are about making money.

Assessing start-up objectives

The success of a new organisation can be measured only in relation to the objectives of its founder. A London pizza business called Pizza Euforia started five years ago with the ambition of creating a chain of 20 restaurants within three years. Today there are two outlets, one of which is barely breaking even. Clearly this is no success. Yet government statistics show that restaurant start-ups have one of the lowest survival rates of all businesses: 40% fail within three years. So Pizza Euforia failed in relation to the founder's objectives, but not compared to national data.

The reason for setting an objective is to give a target to strive for (i.e. to provide motivation). The clearer the objective the better, such as the One Water objective of building one water pump per day. Some new firms start with no clear objective. The entrepreneur may just be looking for survival in year one 'and then let's see where we get to'. Woolly objectives such as this may interfere with the firm's progress. The problem will be most acute if the business employs several staff. Ideally, every staff member would treat every customer as precious – the future of the business. This would be easier to establish if everyone had a clear sense of purpose and direction.

Assessing the strengths and weaknesses of a business plan

There are two issues to consider here. A business plan is a detailed look at why and how a business idea could become successful. To raise capital from investors, there is an earlier stage that must be mastered: the **business model**.

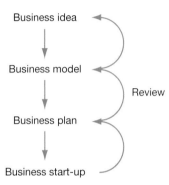

Figure 11.1 Developing the business from idea to start-up

Investors want the business idea summed up briefly, so that they can try to picture how the business can succeed. Examples include the following.

- *Chocolate:* a chain of high-street outlets offering varieties of hot chocolate, chocolate shakes, chocolate ice creams and chocolate bars; mainly takeaway but with bar stools for eating in; start with one outlet, build to four or five then use franchising for further growth.

- *Eggxactly:* patent-protected waterless cookers for the perfect 'boiled' egg selling for around £30; start by manufacturing in Britain and selling direct on the internet; once the business has built up, distribute more product to retailers, moving production to China when sales volumes are high enough

A good business model must have the potential to become profitable and – for venture capital investors – have significant growth prospects.

The business plan should develop the business model into a working document. It should show what needs to be done, by when and at what cost. A strong business plan will not necessarily be very long, but it will cover all the key aspects of the specific business being looked at. For example, a business plan for Eggxactly will need to set out the following points.

● The track record of the manufacturer chosen to supply the products, and whether there is a back-up company in case of supply problems.

● The relationship between internet orders and supply. Will there be a big warehouse of stock or will each item be produced, packed and posted per order?

● The supply cost per machine. What gross profit will that generate compared with the £30 selling price?

● The method used to attract customers to the website. If a marketing campaign is needed, how big is the budget and how will it be spent?

● How a Chinese supplier will be selected and monitored. Will there be an Eggxactly employee in China permanently to carry out quality checks?

These and many other issues must be tackled fully. If an important aspect of the business seems poorly thought through, investors may look elsewhere.

11.5 ## Why start-ups can be risky

The future is uncertain, therefore every business decision is risky. Latest research shows that only one in seven new products is a success, and these products are the high-profile ones from companies such as L'Oréal and Cadbury – launched in a blaze of publicity. Table 11.1 shows how old the Cadbury product portfolio is. Between these years of success have come countless new product flops – most forgotten by now. So, if big companies with big market research and advertising budgets struggle, how can a small business start-up be anything other than risky?

The risks come from all directions; all are based on uncertainty. A small business cannot know how high or low sales will be; nor can it know for certain what all its costs will be. Hiring staff may prove far harder than expected, and keeping good staff may be the hardest thing of all. The big risk at the start is that teething troubles may hit the cash position of the business, forcing it to close. Figure 11.2 shows what might happen

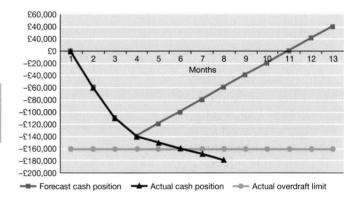

Figure 11.2 Cash flow crisis for new restaurant

Table 11.1 Cadbury brands: successes and flops

Cadbury's big sellers		Cadbury's flops	
Brand	Launch date	Brand	Launch date
Cadbury's Dairy Milk	1905	Cadbury's Strollers	1995
Cadbury's Milk Tray	1915	Fuse Bar	1996
Cadbury's Flake	1920	Cadbury's Marble	1998
Crunchie Bar	1929	Cadbury Spira	1999
Cadbury's Fudge	1949	Cadbury's Brunchbar	2001
Cadbury's Creme Egg	1971	Dream with Strawberries	2004
Double Decker	1976	Double Decker with Nuts	2005
Cadbury's Heroes	1999	Melts	2006

to a restaurant with a set-up cost of £140,000 that has fewer customers than forecast in its first year. Instead of making profits in the months after opening, it is losing money. Its bank could close it down at any time after month six.

11.6 Why start-ups may fail

There are three main types of reason for start-up failure:

- poor analysis of the market (i.e. the opportunity did not exist)

- right idea, but poor execution of the plan (i.e. put into practice badly)

- right idea, but bad luck (e.g. fierce competitor opens nearby or something unexpected happens).

Poor market analysis

China Fang opened in Cheshire in 2006. Its location was on a busy main road in a beautiful corner building. There was a side-road for parking and enough room for a kitchen and a restaurant seating 40 people. It opened to good customer numbers as local residents were curious to try it. There were no other restaurants nearby, just a pizza takeaway. Early customers were very pleased with the quality of the food and service, though they found the prices 'a little high'. All seemed well set, but after a month or two customer numbers steadily fell away. The problem was that locals preferred to go into the town centre, where there was a bit of a buzz in the evenings. A visit to China Fang was too low-key and quiet. It was a good restaurant in the wrong location. The restaurant closed in mid-2007.

Right idea, wrong execution

A good business idea might be poorly carried out. There are an enormous number of mistakes that can be made, including:

- poor staff recruitment and/or training and/or supervision – staff may enjoy joking with each other in a way that irritates or insults customers

- faulty purchasing – a young entrepreneur may set up a stylish clothes shop but prove poor at selecting and buying stock from suppliers such as the fashion houses (i.e. right shop, wrong stock)

- too desperate – any business needs to establish itself and the process is hard to rush; over-hasty buy-one-drink-get-one-free offers can make a bar busy without building brand loyalty; when another bar makes a better promotional offer, the customers desert the first one

- failure to control cash flow – the business operation may be going well, but if the finances are poorly managed, the bank may close down a business with a great future.

Right idea, bad luck

You might come up with a well-considered plan for a new cinema in a town that doesn't have one. You spend £15,000 on the research into whether this would be a worthwhile project and you're sure it's a winner. Then, just as you sign the papers to buy a good site, you hear that someone has the same idea, but is a month ahead of you. You could carry on and fight it out, or pull out altogether; either way you have been unlucky. The worst outcome would be to carry on the fight but end up with a failed business.

An entrepreneur should respond to bad luck with undimmed confidence and the determination to try again. Unfortunately, it may not be that easy. Established hoteliers Barry Hancox and Andrew Riley opened Russell's – a restaurant and hotel – in Worcestershire having borrowed 80% of the £1.5 million set-up costs from the bank. An entrepreneur with a business start-up failure to his/her name would have no chance of borrowing so much. Worse still, losses made from one failure – however unlucky – make it harder to find the personal capital to start again.

A-grade application

Chef David Everitt-Matthias opened Le Champignon Sauvage in Cheltenham in 1987. The year after the business opened, interest rates in Britain hit 15% and the restaurant takings slumped. Quite simply, 'lots of our customers went bust'. David suffered nearly two years with the business close to closure. He survived, and has since faced foot and mouth disease and flooding, but the business is well enough established to cope. It is now a successful Michelin two-star restaurant (i.e. more highly rated than many of Gordon Ramsay's restaurants), but bad luck nearly stopped it in its tracks.

Issues For Analysis

When tackling the issue of business start-up in an exam, bear in mind the following points.

- Awareness of risk and potential failure is a thoroughly good thing; fear of failure could easily become a serious problem; the good entrepreneur tries to anticipate possible problems and allow for them in the cash flow forecast – but doesn't treat possible problems as impossible hurdles.

- Therefore a good business plan will be based on realistic objectives and will allow for real life proving tougher than expected; every new business should press for a generous overdraft limit from the bank – to give a satisfactory cushion if things get tough.

- Despite the risks, the personal and financial rewards from entrepreneurship can be massive. How else would a fan on the terraces be able to end up buying Newcastle United? A Saturday Lottery win would hardly buy a player!

11.7 Assessing business start-ups
an evaluation

Every new business is unique, as each one depends upon the personality, character and motives of the founder, plus the specific market, competitive and economic context. Timing is another vital factor, in which luck plays a particularly important part. An ice cream parlour opening in May one year may be blessed with a hot summer; opening the following year, it may be cursed with rain and gloom.

It is because of these factors that it is hard to be sure whether a business plan will succeed or not. Whenever assessing a business start-up, it is very unwise to sound too certain about whether it will succeed or fail.

Key terms

Business model: the precise way in which profit will be generated from a specific business idea.

Floated: making a public company's shares widely available for purchase on the stock market.

Social entrepreneurs: strictly speaking, this should mean people who start up an organisation in pursuit of purely social objectives; but some profit-seekers dress themselves in social or environmental clothing.

Exercises

A. Revision questions

(23 marks; 25 minutes)

1 Outline two entrepreneurial qualities shown by Duncan Goose. (2)

2 Explain in your own words why it is wise to have doubts about some of the businesses that call themselves 'social enterprises'. (4)

3 Outline two ways to assess whether a business start-up has been a success. (4)

4 Explain why potential investors would want to hear about the business model before reading a business plan. (5)

5 Outline two possible reasons why an established firm such as Cadbury can achieve no better than a one in seven success rate when launching new products. (4)

6 Look again at Figure 11.2. If the entrepreneur had thought hard about the risks of starting a new restaurant, how might s/he have done things differently? Outline two points. (6)

B. Revision exercises

B1 Data response

In March 2007 two former dinner ladies won a contract to run a café in London's Regent's Park. They promised to provide good food, with no chips, and keep the café open for 364 days a year. Their start-up costs were £24,000, shared between them and an old friend who contributed £8000 in exchange for 20% of the share capital.

They started well, with takings as expected in April and May, but they knew the big period of the year was June–August. More than half the year's revenue should come in these three months. By June they already knew that the difference in takings between a sunny day and a rainy day was as much as tenfold (i.e. they might only get 20 customers on a bad day compared with 200 on a good one).

Then came the wettest summer on record. In a year of awful flooding in Hull, Sheffield and Tewkesbury, Regent's Park also suffered. The dinner ladies were relying on the summer to build up a strong cash position to get through the winter. That did not happen. At the time of writing it is not clear whether they will get through their first winter or not.

Questions

(20 marks; 25 minutes)

1 Assess whether the dinner ladies showed poor market analysis, good analysis but poor execution, or bad luck. Explain your answer. (6)

2a If the cash position for the winter looks worrying, examine two forms of finance that would be appropriate in this case, and could be arranged before the winter starts. (8)

2b Explain which form of finance would be more suitable, and why. (6)

B2 Data response

In 2004 22-year-old Jamie Murray-Wells used the last of his student loan to start a business: Glasses Direct. Puzzled that two pieces of glass and some plastic frames could cost £250 in a high-street optician, Jamie researched into the industry with care. When he approached manufacturers, he was greeted with suspicion; they worried that he might jeopardise their profits. But eventually he persuaded them to supply him. In September 2004 he started selling pairs of glasses over the internet for £15 a pair. Although he had no money for advertising, journalists were keen to write about his story, so he had terrific free PR (public relations). In the first year he sold 22,000 pairs, generating revenues of more than £300,000. By 2006 sales were heading towards £3 million, helped by a growing reputation for great customer service from the 17 staff.

From the start Jamie made it clear that he wanted to 'get very big very fast'. He realised that this would require outside finance. Since 2004 his family had helped provide the capital to grow; now it was time for serious investment by a venture capital fund. It took until July 2007 to achieve the right package. Two venture capital companies invested £2.9 million with the intention of using the capital on marketing – to make Glasses Direct a household name. It is not clear what percentage of the shares have been retained by Jamie and his family, but it is believed to be around 50%.

Questions

(25 marks; 30 minutes)

1a Identify the business objective at Glasses Direct. (1)

1b Explain why this objective may have helped encourage staff to provide 'great customer service'. (5)

2 Look at the six personal objectives listed in Section 11.2. Outline which one of them you believe was most important for Jamie when starting Glasses Direct. (5)

3 Glasses Direct seems to have enjoyed a relatively untroubled start-up. Outline two risks that the company faced, even though things turned out well. (6)

4 As Glasses Direct was growing satisfactorily, discuss whether Jamie was right to sell around 50% of the shares in exchange for the £2.9 million of fresh capital. (8)

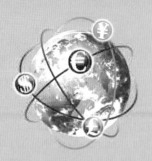
INTRODUCTION TO FINANCE

DEFINITION

Finance has two main aspects: it can provide the numbers that help managers to make better decisions, and it can count what is happening and what has happened. Here the focus is on finance for decision making.

12.1 The financial basics

Of the 60% of new restaurants that close within three years, almost all die because the business has run out of cash. As the crisis point starts to draw near, the staff will notice irate suppliers 'dropping by' to demand payment. Key supplies may not arrive, as the suppliers get increasingly tough about payment. So it's crucial to keep cash spending under tight control.

The main underlying problem is that people get starry-eyed about the process of business start-up. They start to believe their own publicity, and assume that their restaurant is going to be hot from day one, or their nightclub is going to be cool. The consequence of this is that too much of the start-up capital is tied up in fixed assets such as interior design and equipment. Far too little is left for the day-to-day running of the business – the working capital.

The problem is an obvious one. To be an entrepreneur you have to be an optimist; but optimists don't look for the downside. They expect business to be fantastic from week one, ignoring the evidence that most businesses find it hard to establish a loyal base of customers at the start. For most new businesses it is wise to set aside half the start-up capital as working capital. That will be the money used in the early weeks of operation, to pay the wages, pay the rent and pay upfront when suspicious suppliers demand to be paid with cash, not credit. Once the weekly takings are high enough, the money coming in will pay for all the costs that have to be paid out, but that may take time.

Look at Table 12.1: among small business start-ups in south London, this was how long it took until weekly cash in started to beat weekly cash outflows.

12.2 Working capital

The key, then, is to keep on top of the working capital. The top priority is to keep an everyday check on costs, credit transactions and cash payments. This can be hard if you have several people working for you. Each might expect to be given the authority to make a decision such as to buy a pizza oven from supplier X rather than supplier Y. But if lots of people are spending your money, it will be virtually impossible to keep track of everything.

Table 12.1 *Small business start-ups in south London: weeks until cash drain ceased*

Type of business	Location	Weeks until cash drain ceased
Barber	Near tube station	26 (i.e. 6 months)
Pizza restaurant	Residential area	10 weeks
Sports trophy shop	Local shopping street	156 (i.e. 3 years) (that was 15 years ago, so it was worth it)
Sweet shop	High street	6 weeks

New entrepreneurs often choose one person to be the 'moneybags', the person with sole control over spending. Clever entrepreneurs make sure to give the job to someone else. Then even the business owner has to work at justifying why exactly he wants gold washbasin taps instead of ordinary ones, or brand new kitchen equipment instead of second-hand.

In addition to keeping a check on a firm's day-to-day finance – its **working capital** – managers need to:

● identify the costs involved in making a product; this can be the first step in deciding the selling price

● work out how many products they need to sell to make a profit

● find out how much capital they will need in the coming months, and then decide on the best way to obtain this extra finance

● keep tight control over the way in which the firm's money is spent.

12.3 Key financial concerns for new business start-ups

The starting point is to work out three things.

1 How much it will cost to get from a business idea to opening its doors on the first day (i.e. the start-up costs). For a new clothes shop this will include a huge range of items (see the A-grade application) and might come to a figure such as £40,000.

2 How much the running costs will be (i.e. the costs week by week when the business is operating fully). These will come in two parts: the costs that will be fixed, no matter whether business is going well or badly, such as the rent, heating and lighting and staff salaries; in addition, there will be costs that vary in line with sales, such as the cost of purchasing the items you are selling (the dress sold for £40 may cost you £20 to buy from the dress designer). Every entrepreneur needs a solid understanding of the firm's **fixed costs** and **variable costs**. (Fuller coverage of this topic is provided in Unit 13.)

3 How much revenue can you expect from the customers you serve? Broadly this is a simple calculation of customers served x the amount they spend. Although the calculation is simple, it is very hard to anticipate what the figures will be. When the Glade Flameless Candle was launched in late 2007 at

the price of £9.99 (!), who could know how many would be sold? Market research could help in making a sales forecast, but as only one in five new products proves a success, four out of every five new products must come with an incorrect sales forecast (no one would launch a new product that was forecast to flop, so presumably there was a faulty forecast). In the case of Glade, not even the price element of the calculation would have proved accurate, as by February 2008 the greedy launch price had fallen to £4.99 in many shops. For new small businesses the problem is always the same: how can we forecast the number of loyal customers we can expect? This issue is tackled in Unit 64.

A-grade application
A costly start-up

Raza and Sujagan opened a new grocery shop on a busy Wimbledon road in December 2007. It was an unusually big shop as they were buying a lease from a furniture business that had closed down. The four-year lease cost £25,000 to purchase, and there were additional monthly payments of £1500. The fixtures and fittings (fridges, shelving, lighting, and so on) cost £32,000, and building and decorating added a further £9000. Two tills plus a scanning system and a CCTV security system added a further £8000. Because the shop floor space was so big, stocking the shop was very expensive, requiring a further investment of £28,000.

Once it was operating fully, it proved to be that, on average, for every £1 taken through the till, 72p had to be paid to suppliers. In other words, they were making 28p in the £ of profit (though that is before paying the monthly bills). Those monthly bills, including the £1500 to the landlord, came to £4800.

Wretchedly, in early January as Raza opened the shop at 6 o'clock one morning, a bulldozer was their first warning that a 20-week roadworks operation was to start right outside the shop. By mid-February, the shop was still taking nowhere near the amount needed to pay the £4800 of monthly fixed costs, let alone provide some profit.

Having worked out these three things, a business can use them in different ways.

● *To calculate the profit level that can be expected:* it is wise to do this at three different sales levels, based on what you believe to be the worst case (e.g. only ten customers a day), the best case (fully booked at 50 a day) and a midway point such as 30 a day; this is wiser than simply looking at one forecast sales level.

To estimate the cash inflows and outflows (i.e. to work out, month by month, what the firm's bank balance will look like in the future): this might identify, for example, that a new toy shop's cash position in early autumn looks very bleak, as lots of money is paid out on stock, but cash is not yet coming in from Christmas shoppers. Careful forecasting of cash flows can identify problems such as this, and enable the business to make the necessary arrangements (e.g. a temporary bank overdraft). Cash flow is covered in Unit 15.

To estimate how much finance the business needs to raise.

12.4 Raising finance

When a business is operating fully and successfully, cash coming in from customers will provide all the finance necessary for effective operation. Until then, raising finance is an important issue, especially for young entrepreneurs with little personal capital. Table 12.2 lists the sources of finance available to firms.

Table 12.2 Sources of business finance

Short term (under 1 year)	
Bank overdraft	Allowing the firm's bank account to go into the red up to an agreed limit Flexible and easy to arrange but interest charges are high
Trade credit	Suppliers agree to accept cash payment at a given date in the future Failure to pay on time can present problems for future orders
Medium term (2–4 years)	
Bank term loan	Banks lend sums of capital, often at a fixed rate of interest, to be repaid over fixed period Makes financial planning easy but interest rates can be high, particularly for small firms
Leasing	Firms sign a contract to pay a rental fee to the owner of an asset in return for the use of that asset over a period of 2–4 years (usually) Expensive, but avoids large cash outflows when buying new assets
Long term (5+ years)	
Owners' savings	Most small businesses are set up with the owners' savings They are 'interest free' but will be lost if the business fails Banks will not provide a loan or overdraft unless the owners are sharing the financial risk
Sale of shares	Private and public limited companies can sell shares in the ownership of the company In return, shareholders gain a say in how the firm is run, and are entitled to a share of profits
Reinvested profits	Profits are the most important source of long-term finance This form of finance is good because there are no interest payments to be made
Venture capital loans	These specialist providers of risk capital can provide large sums The finance is usually partly loan capital and partly share capital
Government loans	Although much paperwork is involved and only some firms are eligible, national government and the EU do offer grants and loans for firms Less than 3% of business finance stems from this source

A-grade application

Financing Bebo

Michael and Xochi Birch were internet entrepreneurs who started with no financial capital at all. In their spare time they launched three websites in the period 2000–2002: Lemonlink, Babysittingcircle and FriendlyWills. All flopped. But they showed their persistence by trying a fourth, Birthdayalarm (which emails you a one-week warning of your family/friends' birthdays), which took off like a rocket. This gave them the confidence and finance to start their first social network in 2005, which they called Ringo. Within three months it had 500,000 subscribers and they sold the business.

Now with some serious capital of their own, later in 2005 they launched Bebo. This took off to the point that, within a year, Bebo had 25 million users and had become the number one social networking site in the UK and Ireland. The site had been able to succeed against competition from MySpace, owned by the multinational News Corporation (owners of the *Sun* and Sky TV). By early 2008 there were 11 million Bebo users in Britain alone, many attracted by the innovative soap operas and TV-style dramas made especially for Bebo, such as *KateModern*. Facebook was Britain's number one site by then, but with Bebo close behind.

So how was Bebo's growth financed? Although the Birches financed the start-up from their own capital, by May 2006 they felt the need for some extra finance. They sold shares in the business for $15 million to Benchmark Capital, a London-based venture capital company. If Benchmark received the rumoured 18% of Bebo's shares, it will have made a very clever investment, as by February 2008 Bebo was suggested by *The Times* to be worth 'more than' $1000 million. This would make the Benchmark shares worth over $180 million – and Michael and Xochi Birch extraordinarily rich!

Key terms

Fixed costs: those that do not change as the number of sales change (e.g. rent or salaries).
Variable costs: those that change in line with the amount of business (e.g. the cost of buying raw materials).
Working capital: the finance available for the day-to-day running of the business.

Issues For Analysis

● The difference between cash and profit can lead to excellent analytical comment. Without cash, bills go unpaid and stocks are not bought. So it is possible for profitable firms to run out of cash and go out of business. In examinations, many students treat cash flow and profit as if they are the same thing. Distinguishing clearly between the two is a helpful starting point for strong analysis of a financial issue. This is covered fully in Unit 19.

● Also important is to place any financial question firmly in the context of the business. Are its founders novice investors or experienced and well advised? Is it largely dependent on just one product or customer? Is its marketplace fast-moving and fiercely competitive?

12.5 Introduction to finance
an evaluation

Reliability is a key issue when looking at any financial statement. Management accounts, such as cash flow forecasts, are predictions. In other words, they are not statements of fact but educated guesses. This means that they should be used only as a guideline. Questions need to be asked, such as who drew up the figures, do they have an interest in making the accounts point in a particular direction? For example, have forecasts been produced to try to persuade outsiders to invest, or are they produced by managers for their own use? In the first case, it may be that the desire to squeeze finance out of a bank or venture capital firm encourages an excessively optimistic set of forecasts.

A second key point to remember is how finance fits into the big picture of Business Studies. Feel the weight of this book. There are several units dedicated to finance, but many more covering other areas of business activity. Accounts are good at dealing with financial, quantitative information, but qualitative factors may be more important, such as whether the business is building strong customer loyalty. Today's high sales may collapse tomorrow if they are based only on special offers, not on customer loyalty.

Exercises

A. Revision questions

(30 marks; 30 minutes)

1 Outline two possible reasons why a newly started restaurant might run out of cash. (4)

2 Explain what is meant by working capital. (3)

3 Give two examples of situations in which a small bakery business might use:
   (a) short-term
   (b) medium-term
   (c) long-term sources of finance. (6)

4 Re-read the A-grade application 'A costly start-up'.
   (a) Calculate the founders' total start-up costs. (2)
   (b) Outline one factor that may have made the business struggle, even without the bad luck of the roadworks. (2)

5 Explain one advantage and one disadvantage to a firm of having large sums of cash for a long period of time. (4)

6 Re-read the A-grade application 'Financing Bebo'.
   (a) What % profit would Benchmark Capital receive if its shares were bought for $180 million? (3)
   (b) Were the Birches wise or unwise to have sold an 18% stake in the business for $15 million? Examine one reason for and one reason against their decision to sell for that sum. (6)

B. Revision exercises

B1 Data response

Starting up Moneysupermarket.com
Moneysupermarket.com was started in 1999 by 32-year-old Simon Nixon. The site was designed to provide people with up-to-date, easy-to-compare information on, for example, the interest charges on different credit cards. The start-up costs were 'around £100,000', all of which came from the sale of an earlier online business. Nixon's earlier experience made sure that he pursued a 'no frills' policy to his start-up, focusing most of the start-up capital on public relations (PR). He employed a City of London PR firm that made sure to contact financial journalists

regularly. The journalists came to use the site as an easy source of data, referencing all their articles to 'Source: Moneysupermarket.com'. Spreading the name in this way encouraged increasing usage by ordinary customers, providing a hit rate of 50,000 customers a month by the end of its first year.

Nixon built the business up steadily, launching Travelsupermarket.com in 2004. By 2006, he could for the first time afford to run a TV advertising campaign. Since then, the firm's spending on TV has escalated hugely, as it brought huge additional numbers of customers and income. In the first half of 2007, visitors to the group's websites rose by 58%, helping sales revenue to rise from £48 million to £78 million. So although the advertising spending rose from £2.7 to £9.8 million between 2006 and 2007, overall operating profits went up by £14 million.

Although Nixon managed to build the business largely through internal finance (reinvested profit), by 2007 he decided to sell up by floating the shares on the London stock market. On 31 July 2007, shares in Moneysupermarket.com were floated at 170p. This netted Nixon over £100 million in cash, though he still retains over 50% of the shares in the business he started. It now has the cash to be able to finance a growth future, not only in Britain but overseas.

Questions

(25 marks; 30 minutes)

1 Explain why Simon Nixon was able to limit the start-up costs of Moneysupermarket.com to £100,000. (3)

2 Outline two ways in which Nixon might have been helped in the Moneysupermarket.com story by the fact that he could finance the whole thing without outside sources of finance. (4)

3a Calculate the % increase in sales revenue between the first half of 2006 and the first half of 2007. (3)

3b Consider what factors may have led to this sales increase. (6)

4 In 2007 Nixon became fabulously rich. Discuss whether the entrepreneurial skills he showed justified becoming that rich. (9)

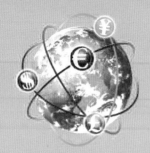

CALCULATING REVENUE, COSTS AND PROFIT

DEFINITION

Revenue is the value of total sales made by a business within a period (usually one year). Costs are the expenses incurred by a firm in producing and selling its products; this is likely to include expenditure on wages and raw materials. Profit is the difference that arises when a firm's sales revenue exceeds its total costs.

13.1 Business revenues

The revenue, or income, received by a firm as a result of trading activities is a critical factor in its success. When starting up, businesses may expect relatively low revenues for several reasons:

● their product is not well known

● they are unlikely to be able to produce large quantities of output

● it is difficult to charge a high price for a product that is not established on the market.

Entrepreneurs start their financial planning by assessing the income, or revenue, they are likely to receive during the coming financial year. Businesses calculate their revenue through use of the following formula:

Sales revenue = volume of goods sold × average selling price

You can see that there are two key elements that comprise sales revenue: the quantity of goods that are sold and the prices at which they are sold. A firm seeking to increase its revenue can plan to sell more or aim to sell at a higher price. Some firms may maintain high prices even though this policy depresses sales. Such companies, often selling fashion and high-technology products, believe that this approach results in higher revenue and, ultimately, higher profits.

To sustain high revenues from relatively few sales, a business has to be confident that consumers will be willing to pay a high price for the product, and that direct competition will not appear – at least in the short term. This is possible only if the start-up business has a product or service that is really special and different – unique even. An additional advantage of a low-output

strategy is that it keeps down the cost of producing the goods or services; this is important in the early stages of running an enterprise.

A-grade application

Weather hits company's revenue

The Traditional Pasty and Pie Company is a 'trailer retailer', selling its products at shows and events around the UK. The company's pies and pasties are made from fresh ingredients and then frozen. The frozen products are then cooked on the day for customers, and sold along with organic coffee.

The poor weather experienced in the summer of 2007 hit this company hard. Sales at events in the sporting and social calendar, such as Cowes Week, Goodwood and the Grand National, were down.

The co-owner of the company, Robin West, explains that for the first three days of a show you are trying to cover your costs: 'When you get to the last day, you go into profit mode. There are times when you won't manage it. It is as simple as that.' Racecourses charge retailers such as the Traditional Pasty and Pie Company a flat fee of between £1000 and £2000 for a small pitch during a prestigious meeting, while some music festivals ask five times that amount. If sales are down, these fixed costs can overwhelm revenues received.

Source: adapted from *BBC News*, 3 September 2007 (http://news.bbc.co.uk/1/hi/business/6958134.stm)

The other way to boost revenue is to charge a low price in an attempt to sell as many products as possible. In some markets this may lead to high revenues and profits. Firms following this approach are likely to be operating in markets where the goods are fairly similar and consumers do not exhibit strong preferences for any brand. This is true of the market for young holidaymakers in Ibiza or Benidorm. Price competition is fierce as businesses seek to maximise their sales and revenue (see Figure 13.1).

Some businesses adopt a revenue-orientated approach for different reasons. If the company experiences circumstances where few of its costs vary with the level of its output, then it will seek to maximise revenue. Because its costs are not sensitive to the level of its sales, maximising sales will result in maximum profits. This is the position for the operators of both theme parks and football clubs. Whereas making and selling a Mercedes creates revenue but also a lot of costs, the theme park's costs are largely **fixed costs**. Attracting extra customers on a day adds few costs. Similarly Fulham FC has the same costs whether its stadium is full or half empty. So when playing a less attractive team, prices for children are set at just £5.

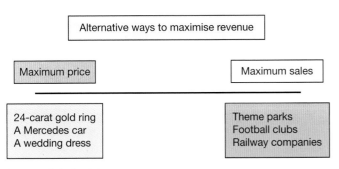

Figure 13.1 Alternative ways to maximise revenue

The new venture

Paul Merrills has achieved his lifetime ambition of opening a restaurant specialising in French cuisine in south London. Paul is a highly regarded and experienced restaurateur and wants to create a unique atmosphere in his new venture. How would you advise him to maximise his revenue in these circumstances?

You will have realised from the analysis so far that price, cost and volume are all important elements of a firm's planning and success. Each of these factors affects the others, and all of them together determine the profitability of a business.

If a business cannot control its costs then it will be unable to sell its products at a low price. In turn, this will mean a low sales volume. This will mean that overhead costs, such as the rent of a factory, will be spread over a low output, causing further pressure on costs of production.

It is to the costs of production that we now turn our attention.

13.2 The costs of production

Costs are a critical element of the information necessary to manage a business successfully. Managers need to be aware of the costs of all aspects of their business for a number of reasons.

● They need to know the cost of production to assess whether it is profitable to supply the market at the current price.

● They need to know actual costs to allow comparisons with their forecasted (or budgeted) costs of production. This will allow them to make judgements concerning the cost-efficiency of various parts of the business.

Fixed and variable costs

This is an important classification of the costs encountered by businesses. This classification has a number of uses. For example, it is the basis of calculating break-even, which is covered in a later unit.

Fixed costs

Fixed costs are any costs that do not vary directly with the level of output. These costs are linked to time rather than to level of business activity. Fixed costs exist even if a business is not producing any goods or services. An example of a fixed cost is rent, which can be calculated monthly or annually, but will not vary whether the office or factory is used intensively to produce goods or services or is hardly utilised at all.

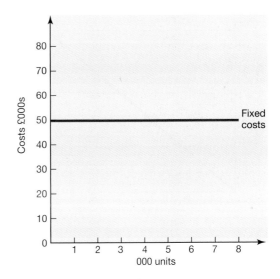

Figure 13.2 Fixed costs of £50,000

If a manufacturer can double output from within the same factory, the amount of rent will not alter – thus it is a fixed cost. In the same way, a seaside hotel has mortgage and salary costs during the winter, even though it may have very few guests. Given that fixed costs are inevitable, it is vital that managers work hard at bringing in customers, in order to keep the fixed costs covered.

In Figure 13.2, you can see that the firm faces fixed costs of £50,000 irrespective of the level of output. How much would the fixed costs per unit of production be if production were (a) 1000 units a year and (b) 8000 units a year? What might be the implications of this distinction for the managers of the business?

Other examples of fixed costs include the uniform business rate, management salaries, interest charges and depreciation.

In the long term, fixed costs can alter. The manufacturer referred to earlier may decide to increase output significantly; this may require renting additional factory space and negotiating loans for additional capital equipment. Thus rent will rise as may interest payments. We can see that, in the long term, fixed costs may alter, but that in the short term they are – as their name suggests – fixed!

Variable costs

Variable costs are those costs that vary directly with the level of output. They represent payments made for the use of inputs such as **piece-rate labour**, fuel and raw materials. If our manufacturer doubled output then these costs would double. A doubling of the sales of Innocent Strawberry Smoothies would require twice the purchasing of strawberries and bananas. There would also be extra costs for the packaging, the wage bill and the energy required to fuel the production line.

The graph in Figure 13.3 shows a firm with variable costs of £8 per unit of production. This means that variable costs rise steadily with, and proportionately to, the level of output. Thus a 10% rise in output will increase **total variable costs** by the same percentage.

However, it is not always the case that variable costs rise in proportion to output. Many small businesses discover that, as they expand, variable costs do not rise as quickly as output. A key reason for this is that, as the business becomes larger, it is able to negotiate better prices with suppliers. Its suppliers are likely to agree to sell at lower unit prices when the business places larger orders.

A-grade application
An unusual way to pay costs

Sellaband is a music website created by Johan Vosmeijer, Pim Betist and Dagmar Heijmans in August 2006 to assist bands in paying the costs of recording a professional album. It is located in Amsterdam, in the Netherlands, and was set up with the intention of helping amateur groups establish themselves.

Artists have to produce a profile of themselves, including three tracks for fans to hear. If the fans are sufficiently impressed they will buy 'parts' for $10 and become 'believers'. Any band that is able to sell 5000 parts raises $50,000 to pay for their own producer, studio and equipment to record and promote their album. In return for their investment, 'believers' are given a limited-edition copy of the album, a share of advertising revenue from the free download section of the site and revenue from the sales of the CD.

By summer 2007 over $700,000 had been invested into Sellaband and four bands had received $50,000, allowing them to pay the costs of recording an album. It remains to be seen whether this proves to be a good investment for their 'believers'.

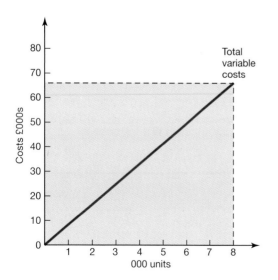

Figure 13.3 Variable costs of £8 per unit

Table 13.1 *Some costs are easy to classify, some are hard*

Variable costs	Fixed costs	Hard to classify
Raw materials	Rent	Delivery costs
Packaging	Heating and lighting	Electricity
Piece-rate labour	Salaries	Machine maintenance costs
Commission % on sales	Interest charges	Energy

Total costs

When added together, fixed and variable costs give the **total costs** for a business. This is, of course, a very important element in the calculation of the profits earned by a business.

The relationship between fixed, variable and total costs is straightforward to calculate but has some important implications for a business. If a business has relatively high fixed costs as a proportion of total costs, then it is likely to seek to maximise its sales to ensure that the fixed costs are spread across as many units of output as possible. In this way the impact of high fixed costs is lessened. For small businesses, it is often variable costs that are high – for example, high food costs at a restaurant. This may make them push their prices up to a level that makes customers reluctant to use them regularly. This can be the start of a slippery slope downwards for the business.

13.3 Profits

Having considered revenues and costs it is now appropriate to focus on a prime motive for businesses: profit. Profit is a comparison of revenues and costs. This comparison determines whether or not an enterprise makes any profit. As we saw at the beginning of this unit the key formula is:

Profit = total revenue − total costs

However, it is worth remembering that some businesses are not established with the objective of making profits. Not-for-profit businesses, also known as social enterprises, operate with other objectives. For example, Katie Alcott from Bristol received an entrepreneurship award in 2007 for her social enterprise Frank Water. Katie's business sells bottled spring water in the UK, and uses the proceeds to provide clean, safe water for villages in India and Africa. Her aim is to support others, not to make a profit.

Calculating profits

Although the profit formula is simple (revenue − costs), it is easy to make mistakes when calculating the figures. The problems rarely come from calculating revenue; the hard part is getting total costs right. The following example may help.

> Gwen and John's pasta restaurant charges £10 for three courses and has an average of 800 customers per week. The variable costs are £4 per customer and the restaurant has fixed costs of £3400 per week. To calculate profit:
>
> 1 calculate revenue: price × no. of customers
> £10 × 800 = £8000
> 2 calculate total costs: fixed costs + total variable costs (no. of customers x variable costs per meal)
> £3400 + (800 × £4 = £3200)
> 3 calculate profit: total revenue − total costs
> £8000 − (£3,400 + £3200) = £1400 per week

See the Workbook section for exercises that will allow you to practise this very important skill.

The types of profit

Although profit is always revenue minus costs, there are different profit figures that are used. Managers frequently refer to operating profit. This is the amount remaining once all fixed and variable costs have been deducted from total revenue, but before tax has been paid.

Perhaps a more important measure is profit after tax, since this is the profit that the business can decide how to allocate. The most important uses to which these profits can be put are:

● payments to the owners of the business, to partners or to shareholders in the form of dividends

● reinvestment into the business to purchase capital items such as property and machinery.

A-grade application

Reducing costs gives business a chance of profits

A Scottish tourist attraction has been saved from closure due to increasing losses. The Hydroponicum in Wester Ross is famous for growing plants without any soil and for producing tropical plants such as bananas in the cool Scottish climate. The business has attracted up to 10,000 visitors a year, but had fallen on hard times. As a result it had been put up for sale and bought by a local company.

The new owners have agreed to lease the business back to three former Hydroponicum employees who hope to be able to make the business profitable again. The three new directors of the Hydroponicum have agreed to work without pay while putting a new business plan into action. The three directors plan to reduce costs by restricting opening hours, reducing staffing levels and limiting the menu offered by the Hydroponicum's café.

Source: adapted from BBC News, 8 May 2007
(http://news.bbc.co.uk/1/hi/scotland/highlands_and_islands/663
5599.stm)

13.4 The importance of profit

Undeniably profits are important to the majority of businesses. Profits are usually assessed in relation to some yardstick – for example, the amount invested or sales revenue. We will consider how to measure profits in relation to other variables in Unit 18.

Profits are important for the following reasons:

● they provide a measure of the success of a business (important for a new business)

● they are the best source of capital for investment in the growth of the business (e.g. to finance new store openings or to pay for new product development)

● they act as a magnet to attract further funds from investors enticed by the possibility of high returns on their investment.

However, it is not uncommon for a new business to fail to make profits in the first months – or even years – of trading. The need to generate profits becomes more important as time passes. A business ultimately needs to make profits to reward its owners for putting money into the enterprise.

13.5 Contribution

Revenue and profits are important concepts, but it is also helpful to understand 'contribution'. Each time Waterstone's sells one of these books, it receives £19.99 from the customer. But the book costs it £11.99 to buy from the publisher. So although its revenue per book is £19.99, the real value to Waterstone's of selling the book is the £8 difference between the selling price and the purchase cost. This difference is known as contribution (per unit of sale). It's not 'profit' because the £8 surplus has not taken into account the fixed operating costs of running the bookshop and running the whole Waterstone's business. So the £8 has to make a contribution to covering the fixed costs. Only when this, and all its other sales, have covered the total fixed costs of the business can Waterstone's make a profit.

This enables profit to be calculated using contribution (helpful because it's quicker to do). If you multiply the contribution per sale by the number being sold, you get a figure for total contribution – for example, £8 a book times, let's say, 100 books being sold = £800. If you take away from that figure the fixed costs, you get the profit.

This may seem complicated, but it really isn't.

1 To calculate the contribution per sale, use the formula:

Selling price – Variable cost per unit = **Contribution per unit**

Book example: £19.99 − £11.99 = £8

2 To calculate the profit made from selling books, use the formula:

(Contribution per unit × Number sold) − Fixed costs = Profit

Book example: (£8 × 100) − £500 = £300

Contribution is used in many of the techniques for financial analysis and decision making. The key to remembering it is to tell yourself that:

Contribution is the amount each sale contributes towards the fixed costs of running the business. Once the fixed costs are covered, all extra contribution is profit.

Issues For Analysis

● Forecasting costs and revenues can be tricky for an entrepreneur starting a new business. It is not possible to look back at trading records for guidance and therefore the likelihood of inaccuracy is greater. At this stage of a business's history all cost and revenue figures are forecasts and therefore not necessarily correct. It is possible that entrepreneurs will underestimate fixed and variable costs and overestimate revenues, thereby suggesting higher profits (or lower losses) than proves to be the case.

● A key element with respect to the revenues earned by a business is the relationship between the price charged and the volume of sales achieved. Choosing the right price is an exercise requiring considerable judgement on the part of the entrepreneur. Simply raising price will not necessarily provide more revenue for a business. If a 10% price rise causes customer numbers to fall by 15%, the business will have lower revenues than it started with. Factors influencing consumers' decisions will include the quality of the products in question and how strong the competition is.

● You might like to consider circumstances in which firms might earn higher revenue by raising prices, and when the opposite could be true. Do you think a firm could earn more revenue by *lowering* its price?

may result in small profits initially, while the business builds a reputation. Profits may become a more important measure of success in the longer term.

An assessment of the true worth of a business's performance as measured by its profits would also take account of the general state of the economy: are businesses in general prospering or is it a time of recession? They would also take into account any unusual circumstances such as, for example, the business being subject to the emergence of a new competitor.

Key terms

Contribution per unit: the difference between the selling price and the variable costs.
Fixed costs: do not vary as output (or sales) vary.
Piece-rate labour: paying workers per item they make (i.e. with no regular pay).
Total costs: all the costs of producing a specific output level (i.e. fixed costs + total variable costs).
Total variable costs: all the variable costs of producing a specific output level (i.e. variable costs per unit x the number of units sold).
Variable costs: the costs that vary as output varies (can also be known as unit variable costs).

Calculating revenue, costs and profit

One important issue for evaluation in relation to costs, revenues and profits for a new enterprise is to judge the likely accuracy of the forecast figures and the degree of reliance that can be placed upon them. This is an important judgement for a number of stakeholders who may have an interest in the new business. Investors will obviously look closely at any forecast figures before committing money to the enterprise and suppliers will want to be assured of payment before agreeing to supply any raw materials.

It is also worth thinking about whether profits are the best measure of success for a new business. A successful first year of trading may see an enterprise gain a customer base and repeat orders by supplying at competitive costs. This

Exercises

A. Revision questions

(40 marks, 40 minutes)

1 Why might revenue be relatively low when a product is newly introduced to the market? (3)

2 State two circumstances in which a company may be able to charge high prices for a new product. (2)

3 For what reasons might a firm seek to maximise its sales revenue? (3)

4 If a business sells 4000 units of Brand X at £4 each and 2000 units of Brand Y at £3 each, what's its total revenue? (4)

5 Outline two reasons why firms have to know the costs they incur in production. (4)

6 Distinguish, with the aid of examples, between fixed and variable costs. (4)

7 Explain why fixed costs can alter only in the long term. (3)

8 Give two reasons why profits are important to businesses. (2)

9 Outline one advantage and one disadvantage that may result from a business deciding to lower the proportion of profits it distributes to its owners. (2)

10 State two purposes for which a business's profits might be used. (2)

11 Giovanni's Pizzas are priced at £8 and have variable costs of £2 each. The pizza restaurant has weekly fixed costs of £2100. On average there are 500 customers a week.
   (a) Calculate the contribution per pizza. (2)
   (b) Calculate the total contribution from selling 500 pizzas. (2)
   (c) Calculate the weekly profit made by the restaurant. (2)

12 Outline two ways in which a sweetshop could increase the contribution it makes per customer. (5)

B. Revision exercises

B1 Calculation practice questions

(30 marks; 30 minutes)

1 During the summer weeks, Devon Ice Cream has average sales of 4000 units a week. Each ice cream sells for £1 and has variable costs of 25p. Fixed costs are £800.
   (a) Calculate the total costs for the business in the summer weeks. (3)
   (b) Calculate Devon Ice Cream's weekly profit in the summer. (3)

2a If a firm sells 200 widgets at £3.20 and 40 squidgets at £4, what is its total revenue? (3)

2b Each widget costs £1.20 to make, while each squidget costs £1.50. What are the total variable costs? (3)

2c If fixed costs are £300, what profit is the business making? (3)

3 'Last week our sales revenue was £12,000, which was great. Our price is £2 a unit, which I think is a bit too cheap.'
   (a) How many unit sales were made last week? (2)
   (b) If a price rise to £2.25 cuts sales to 5600 units, calculate the change in the firm's revenue. (4)

4 BYQ Co has sales of 4000 units a month, a price of £4, fixed costs of £9000 and variable costs of £1. Calculate its profit. (4)

5 At full capacity output of 24,000 units, a firm's costs are as follows:

managers' salaries	£48,000
materials	£12,000
rent and rates	£24,000
piece-rate labour	£36,000

   (a) What are the firm's total costs at 20,000 units? (4)
   (b) What profit will be made at 20,000 units if the selling price is £6? (1)

B2 Case study

Cleaning up

Mary Ruffett saw the building of a large new housing estate across the road from her home as an opportunity, not an eyesore. The estate contained 500 new homes and was nearing completion with only a few houses left to sell. Most were large detached houses and Mary had noticed that there were no window cleaners offering their services on the estate. Although she had no experience as an entrepreneur or a window cleaner, Mary was interested.

Mary did some sums and researched local window cleaners in the *Yellow Pages* – there was only one listed. She could take out a loan to purchase a van, a ladder and the other equipment needed. She estimated that this would cost her £350 each month to repay. Her variable costs per house cleaned would be minimal – she estimated 50p per house. The tricky bit was the price to charge – eventually she estimated £4 per household. Limited research among the new occupants of the estate suggested that she might be able to clean the windows of 125 houses each month. At a price of £5 per household she forecast that she would have 100 customers monthly.

Questions

(25 marks; 30 minutes)

1 Which of Mary's two prices would provide her with the higher monthly revenue? (3)

2 Calculate Mary's monthly profits (or losses) in each case. (6)

3 Analyse two possible reasons why Mary's financial forecasts might not prove to be accurate. (7)

4 Analyse the case for and against Mary charging £5 per household for her window-cleaning service. (9)

B3 Case study

Chalfont Computer Services Ltd

Robert has decided to give up his job with BT and to work for himself offering computer services to local people. He has paid off his mortgage and owns his house outright, so feels this is the time to take a risk. Robert has no experience of running a business, but is skilled in repairing computers and solving software problems. In the past Robert has repaired computers belonging to friends and family, and is aware of the costs involved in providing this service. He believes that with the increase in internet usage there will be plenty of demand for his services. Robert has spoken to a few people in his local pub and this has confirmed his opinion. Robert needs to raise £10,000 to purchase equipment for his business and to pay for a new vehicle, and intends to ask his bank for a loan.

The work Robert has already done allows him to forecast that the average revenue from each customer will be £40, while the variable costs will be £15. His monthly fixed costs will be £1000. Robert estimates that he will have the following number of customers:

Month	Number of customers
January	40
February	50
March	60
April	82

Questions

(25 marks; 30 minutes)

1 What is meant by the term 'variable costs'? (2)

2 Calculate Robert's forecast profits for his first three months' trading. (5)

3 Robert estimates that if he cut his prices by 10% he would have 20% more customers each month. Calculate the outcome of these changes and whether this would benefit Robert. (8)

4 Examine the case for and against a bank lending Robert £10,000 on the basis of his forecast profits. (10)

C. Essay questions

(40 marks each)

1 Discuss whether a new ethnic restaurant, trading in a very competitive market, should aim to maximise its revenue, rather than its profits, during its first year of trading.

2 For all new enterprises it is vital to sell at the right price – this is the most important determinant of profits. Discuss whether this view is always correct.

3 The newly opened Bolton Bakery is the first upmarket baker in the town. The owners expect to make a £50,00 profit in their first year. Evaluate the factors that might stop them from achieving this.

14 Unit

BREAK-EVEN ANALYSIS

DEFINITION

Break-even analysis compares a firm's revenue with its fixed and variable costs to identify the minimum level of sales needed to cover costs. This can be shown on a graph known as a **break-even chart**.

14.1 Introduction

The starting point for financial management is to know how much goods or services cost to produce. This was covered in detail in Unit 13. Businesses also benefit from knowing how many products they have to produce and sell in order to cover all their costs. This is particularly important for new businesses with limited experience of their markets. It is also of value for established businesses that plan to produce a new product.

Look at Table 14.1, which shows the forecast revenue and cost figures for My Thai, a restaurant business that is planning to open its first outlet in two months' time.

You can easily identify that £15,000 is the sales revenue that My Thai must achieve each week to break even. Note what happens to its profits if sales are lower – or higher.

To calculate the break-even revenue we need information on both costs and prices. A change in costs or in the firm's pricing will change the level of sales at which the firm breaks even.

Break-even can be calculated and shown on a graph. The calculation of break-even is simpler and quicker than drawing break-even charts.

Table 14.1 Forecast revenue and cost figures for My Thai

Number of customers (per week)	Sales income (£ per week)	Total costs (£ per week)	Profit per week (£s)
0	0	9000	−9000
250	5000	11000	−6000
500	10000	13000	−3000
750	15000	15000	0
1000	20000	17000	+3000
1250	25000	19000	+6000

14.2 Calculating break-even revenue

Calculating the break-even sales level requires:

● the selling price of the product

● its **fixed costs**

● its variable costs per unit.

The break-even sales level can be calculated in two stages, as follows.

First, what is the **contribution** made per £ of sales? That is, out of every £1 how much does My Thai have to pay out in variable costs (ingredients, breakages, and so on)? In this case the answer is 40p in the £. Therefore the remaining 60p is the contribution.

Second, divide the fixed operating costs by the contribution per £ of sales. This tells you the sales revenue level needed to break even (i.e. to cover all your costs). Any sales made above that level will generate profit.

Break-even sales formula:

$$\frac{\text{Fixed costs}}{\text{Contribution per £}} = \text{Break-even sales revenue}$$

For My Thai: $\dfrac{£9000}{60p} = £15,000$

As we have seen, break-even sales revenue can be calculated using the simple equation above. There is far more to be learned, though, than simply the break-even position. It is hugely helpful to be able to see the

possible profits or losses at many different levels of customer demand. This can be achieved through the use of break-even charts.

A-grade application

Break-even point

Some exams ask for a calculation of the 'break-even point'. This uses the same logic as above, though the formula is slightly different. The break-even point is a useful calculation for a business that produces only one product. The calculation is based on the number of units sold, rather than on the revenue generated by customers.

Taking the same figures from the My Thai example used above, the information needed is:

1 the selling price (for My Thai the average sum spent by customers was £20, so that is the price of a meal)
2 the variable cost per meal (40p in the £, i.e. 40p × £20 = £8)
3 the contribution per meal: £12 (£20 − £8)
4 the fixed costs of the business: £9000

$$\text{Formula:} \ \frac{\text{Fixed costs}}{\text{Contribution per unit (per meal)}} =$$

$$\frac{£9000}{£12} = 750 \text{ customers}$$

For extra practice, try this example:
Depex Ltd sells widgets at a price of £6 each. The variable costs are £2 and fixed costs are £6000 per month. Calculate the break-even point.
Check that you can calculate the answer: 1500 units.

Example: Berry & Hall Ltd
Berry & Hall Ltd are manufacturers of confectionery. The company is planning to launch a new line called Aromatics – a distinctive sweet with a very strong fragrance. The company intends to sell these sweets for £1 a kilogram. The variable cost of production per kilogram is forecast at 60 pence and the fixed costs associated with this product are estimated to be £50,000 a year. The company's maximum output of Aromatics will be 250,000 kg per year.

14.3 Break-even charts

A break-even chart is a graph showing a business's revenues and costs at all possible levels of demand or output. The break-even chart is constructed on a graph by first drawing the horizontal axis to represent the number of customers (or number of sales in units) for the business in question. The vertical axis represents costs and revenues in £s.

First, put scales on the axes. The output scale has a range from zero to the company's maximum output – this will be 250,000 kg. The vertical axis records values of costs and revenues. Since revenue is usually the higher figure we simply multiply the maximum output by the selling price and then place values on the axis up to this figure. In this case it will have a maximum value on the axis of £250,000 (£1 × 250,000).

Having drawn the axes and placed scales upon them, the first line we enter is fixed costs. Since this value does not change with output it is simply a horizontal line drawn at £50,000.

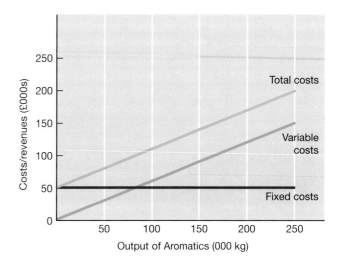

Figure 14.2 Fixed, variable and total costs for Aromatics

Finally, sales revenue must be added. For the maximum level of output calculate the sales revenue and mark this on the chart. In the case of Aromatics the maximum output per year is 250,000 kg; multiplied by the selling price this gives £250,000 each year. If Berry & Hall do not produce and sell any Aromatics it will not have any sales revenue. Thus zero output results in zero income. A straight diagonal line from zero to £250,000 represents the sales revenue for Aromatics (see Figure 14.3).

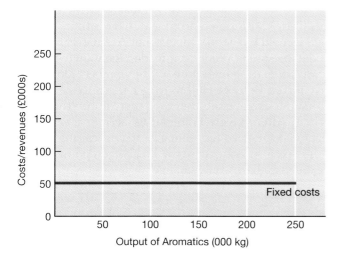

Figure 14.1 Fixed costs for Aromatics

These costs cover rent and rates for the factory that will be used to produce Aromatics and also interest paid on loans taken out by Berry & Hall Ltd to establish production of the new sweet.

Next, add on variable costs to arrive at total costs. The difference between total costs and fixed costs is variable costs. Total costs start from the left hand of the fixed costs line and rise diagonally. To see where they rise to, calculate the total cost at the maximum output level. In the case of Aromatics this is 250,000 kg per year. The total cost is fixed costs (£50,000) plus variable costs of producing 250,000 kg (£0.60 × 250,000 = £150,000). The total cost at this level of output is £50,000 + £150,000 = £200,000.

This point can now be marked on the chart (i.e. £200,000) at an output level of 250,000 kg. This can be joined by a straight line to total costs at zero output: £50,000. This is illustrated in Figure 14.2.

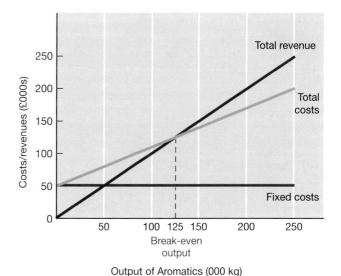

Figure 14.3 Break-even output for Aromatics

This brings together costs and revenues for Aromatics. A line drawn across from the point where total costs and sales revenue cross shows the break-even revenue. A line down to the horizontal axis shows the break-even output. For Aromatics, it is 125,000 kg per year.

14.4 Using break-even charts

Various pieces of information can be taken from break-even charts, such as that shown in Figure 14.3. As well as the level of break-even output, it also shows the level of profits or losses at every possible level of revenue. Many conclusions can be reached, such as those noted below.

● Any number of sales lower than 125,000 kg per year will mean the product is making a loss. The amount of the loss is indicated by the vertical distance between the total cost and the total revenue line. For example, at an output level of 90,000 units per year Aromatics would make a loss of £14,000 for Berry & Hall Ltd. This is because sales are worth £90,000 but costs are £104,000 (£54,000 + £50,000).

● Sales in excess of 125,000 kg of Aromatics per year will earn the company a profit. If the company produces and sells 150,000 kg of Aromatics annually it will earn a profit of £20,000. At this level of output total revenue is £150,000 and total costs are £130,000. This is shown on the chart by the vertical distance between the total revenue line (which is now the higher) and the total cost line.

● The **margin of safety**: one feature of a break-even chart is that it can show the margin of safety. This is the amount by which demand can fall before the firm starts making a loss. It is the difference between current sales and the break-even point. If annual sales of Aromatics were 175,000 kg, with a break-even output of 125,000 kg, then the margin of safety would be 50,000 kg:

Margin of safety = 175,000 − 125,000 = 50,000 kg

That is, output could fall by 50,000 units before Berry & Hall incurred a loss from its new product. The higher the margin of safety the less likely it is that a loss-making situation will develop. The margin of safety is illustrated in Figure 14.4.

14.5 Break-even analysis in a changing environment

The application of break-even analysis to the planned production of Aromatics shows how the technique operates. But it assumed a very stable (and therefore unrealistic) business environment. Competitors might have reacted to the introduction of Aromatics by producing similar products if it was a genuinely new idea or was generating high profits. This competition may have forced Berry & Hall to reduce the price of Aromatics even before they are entered onto the market. Alternatively, competitors' actions may have generated the need for more advertising, raising Berry & Hall's costs. In either case the break-even point and the break-even chart would change.

Suppose that Berry & Hall did have to carry out additional advertising for the launch of Aromatics and that this advertising cost £15,000 over the first year. What impact would this have upon the break-even point and the break-even chart? The extra costs would require a higher output (and income) to break even. The rise in marketing costs can be regarded as a fixed cost because this cost must be borne whatever the level of output. This is shown in Figure 14.5.

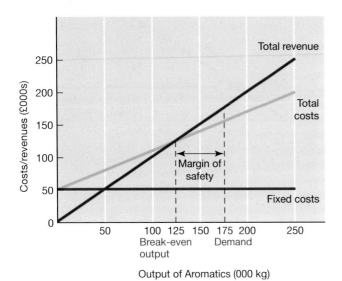

Figure 14.4 Margin of safety

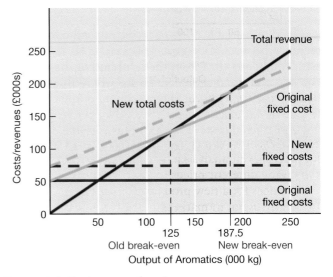

Figure 14.5 A rise in fixed costs

The break-even chart shows the increased fixed cost and total cost lines, which create a higher break-even output. This also has the effect of reducing the level of profit (or increasing the loss) made at any level of output. Any factor leading to a fall in fixed costs will have the opposite effects.

Other external factors can impact upon the break-even level of output and associated profits. If the cost of materials decline, then the variable cost and total cost will be lower. The total cost line will rise less steeply, leading to a lower break-even point of higher profits (lower losses) at any given level of output. The curve pivots (rather than making a parallel move) because at lower levels of output the saving from lower variable costs is proportionately reduced.

If costs remain unchanged and prices fall then this will result in a higher break-even level of production. Lower prices mean that more has to be produced and sold before a profit-making position can be reached. Conversely, a rise in price will result in a lower level of production necessary for break-even to be attained. Figure 14.6 illustrates the impact of a fall in the market price of a product.

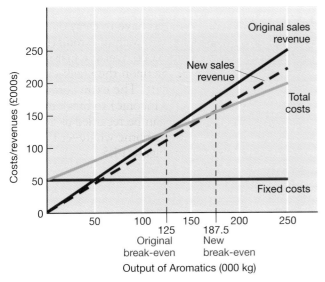

Figure 14.6 The effects of a fall in price

Figure 14.6 shows the effects of a fall in prices. When using break-even analysis a business may draw several charts using different prices to assess the impact of various prices for a new product. This approach is particularly useful in markets where prices may be volatile.

Summary of the changes to the break-even chart that the examiner can ask for.

1 Prices can go up or down. If a price is increased, the revenue line starts in the same place but rises more steeply.
2 Fixed costs can rise or fall, so you might have to draw a new horizontal line. But remember that a change to fixed costs will also affect the total cost line.
3 Variable costs can rise or fall. An increase will make the variable cost line rise more steeply, though it will still start at the same point – at the fixed cost line. A change in variable costs will change the total costs line as well.

Note that each of these three changes will alter the break-even revenue and break-even point.

14.6 The value of break-even analysis

Strengths

Break-even analysis is simple to understand, and useful – particularly for small and newly established businesses, where the managers may not be able to employ more sophisticated techniques. Businesses can use break-even to:

● estimate the future level of output they will need to produce and sell in order to meet given objectives in terms of profits

● assess the impact of planned price changes upon profit, and the level of output needed to break even

● assess how changes in fixed and/or **variable costs** may affect profits, and the level of output necessary to break even

● take decisions on whether to produce their own products or components, or whether to purchase from external sources

● support applications for loans from banks and other financial institutions – the use of the technique may indicate good business sense as well as provide a forecast of profitability.

Weaknesses

● The model assumes that costs increase constantly and that firms do not benefit from bulk buying. If, for example, a firm negotiates lower prices for purchasing larger quantities of raw materials then its total cost line will no longer be straight. It will in fact level out at higher outputs.

- Similarly, break-even analysis assumes the firm sells all its output at a single price. In reality firms frequently offer discounts for bulk purchases.

- A major flaw in the technique is that it assumes that all output is sold. This may well not be true and, if so, would result in an inaccurate break-even estimate. In times of low demand, a firm may have difficulty in selling all that it produces.

- Break-even analysis is only as good as the data on which it is based: poor-quality data can result in inaccurate conclusions being drawn.

A-grade application
Newquay airport targets break-even point

Managers at Newquay airport in Cornwall have announced plans to expand its passenger capacity ahead of schedule. The airport enlarged its existing terminal in 2005, which allowed it to handle 400,000 passengers each year, well short of its break-even level of 750,000 passengers annually. However, managers recognised that further expansion was essential to make the airport profitable and had drawn up a long-term plan to increase passenger numbers and make the airport profitable.

Rising demand for air travel to Cornwall brought about by competitive prices and the rising popularity of the region as a tourist destination has forced the airport's managers to bring their expansion plans forward, however. Several airlines, including bmibaby, have increased flights to Newquay in response to increasing demand from surfers and other tourists. Cornwall County Council has approved plans to build a new terminal south of the runway, which should allow the airport to exceed its break-even figure of 750,000 passengers each year.

A-grade application
Recently launched carbon-neutral food market closes

A £1.5 million carbon-neutral food market in Devon has gone into administration just three months after it started trading. Foodeaze was a food market with associated restaurants, operating with the objective of sustainability. The business, based in Exeter, sold locally produced products and ran its delivery vehicles on bio-diesel. The closure of the market has resulted in the loss of 60 jobs.

Foodeaze owner Nick Hess said it could not compete with the new £220 million Princesshay retail development in Exeter. Mr Hess said the development had a huge impact on Foodeaze's sales and its financial position. He said that, within five weeks of opening, they were close to their break-even point, but then the opening of the new retail development had a bigger impact than originally forecast.

'We put a percentage into our business plan for the effect we thought it was going to have but unfortunately it was far greater than we actually forecast,' he said. 'The new development is stunning and I'm not criticising it – it's just unfortunately one of those things of bad timing.'

Source: adapted from BBC News (www. http://news.bbc.co.uk/1/hi/england/devon/6660947.stm)

Table 14.2 How changes in business circumstances affect the break-even chart

	Cause	**Effect**
Internal factors	Extra launch advertising	Fixed costs rise, so total costs rise and break-even point rises
	Planned price increase	Revenue rises more steeply; break-even point falls
	Using more machinery (and less labour) in production	Fixed costs rise while variable costs fall; uncertain effect on break-even point
External factors	Fall in demand	Break-even point is not affected, though margin of safety is reduced
	Competitors' actions force price cut	Revenue rises less steeply; break-even point rises
	Fuel costs rise	Variable and total cost lines rise more steeply; break-even point rises

Issues For Analysis

● Analytical issues in relation to break-even centre upon the effective use of break-even charts. It is important to appreciate how changes in the business environment might affect the break-even position of a business. Any analysis of break-even should recognise that changes in revenues or costs will impact upon the level of break-even output.

● As an example, you should be able to state whether, in the following circumstances, break-even output will rise or fall:
  – wage negotiations result in a 4% pay rise
  – the business rate levied upon a firm's premises is increased
  – the market price for the business's product increases
  – a change in the price of oil means that fuel prices fall by 5%.

● A break-even chart shows the level of profit or loss at any level of output. If the business's circumstances change it is important to be able to quantify the extent to which profitability changes at any level of output.

14.7 Break-even analysis
an evaluation

There is a risk in exams of assuming that break-even charts tell you 'facts'. Break-even analysis seems simple to conduct and understand. It appears to be cheap and quick to carry out. That assumes, of course, that the business knows all its costs and can break them down into variable and fixed. Tesco certainly can, but not every business is as well managed. Football clubs such as Leeds United, Brentford and Darlington have hit financial problems partly because of ignorance of their financial circumstances. Similarly, few

NHS hospitals could say with confidence how much it costs to provide a heart transplant.

Break-even analysis is of particular value when a business is first established. Having to work out the fixed and variable costs will help the managers make better decisions – for example, on pricing. It also shows profit and loss at various levels of output, particularly when presented in the form of a chart. Indeed it may be that financial institutions will require this sort of financial information before lending any money to someone aspiring to run a business.

As long as the figures are accurate, break-even becomes especially useful when changes occur, such as rising raw material costs. The technique can allow for changing revenues and costs, and gives a valuable guide to potential profitability.

Key terms

Break-even chart: a line graph showing total revenues and total costs at all possible levels of output or demand from zero to maximum capacity.
Contribution: total revenue less variable costs. The calculation of contribution is useful for businesses which are responsible for a range of products.
Fixed costs: fixed costs are any costs which do not vary directly with the level of output, for example, rent & rates.
Margin of safety: the amount by which current output exceeds the level of output necessary to break-even.
Variable costs: variable costs are those costs which vary directly with the level of output. They represent payments made for the use of inputs such as raw materials, packaging and piece-rate labour.

Key formulae

Break-even output: $\dfrac{\text{fixed costs}}{\text{contribution per unit}}$

Contribution per unit: selling price – variable costs per unit
Margin of safety: sales volume – break-even output
Total contribution: contribution per unit × unit sales

Exercises

A. Revision questions

(30 marks; 30 minutes)

1 What is meant by the term 'break-even revenue'? (2)

2 State three reasons why a business might conduct a break-even analysis. (3)

3 List the information necessary to construct a break-even chart. (4)

4 How would you calculate the contribution made by each unit of production that is sold? (2)

5 A business sells its products for £10 each and the variable cost of producing a single unit is £6. Its monthly fixed costs are £18,000.
  (a) Calculate how much revenue it needs to break even. (3)
  (b) Calculate how many units it must sell to break even each month. (3)

6 Explain why the variable cost and total revenue lines start at the origin of a break-even chart. (3)

7 What point on a break-even chart actually illustrates break-even output? (1)

8 Explain how, using a break-even chart, you would illustrate the amount of profit or loss made at any given level of output. (3)

9 Why might a business wish to calculate its margin of safety? (3)

10 A business is currently producing 200,000 units of output annually, and its break-even output is 120,000 units. What is its margin of safety? (3)

B. Revision exercises

B1 Data response

Paul Jarvis is an entrepreneur and about to open his first hotel. He has forecast the following costs and revenues:
- maximum number of customers per month 800
- monthly fixed costs £10,000
- average revenue per customer £110
- typical variable costs per customer £90

Some secondary market research has suggested that Paul's prices may be too low. He is considering charging higher prices, though he is nervous about the impact this might have on his forecast sales. Paul has found his break-even chart useful during the planning of his new business, but is concerned that it might be misleading too.

Questions

(45 marks; 60 minutes)

1a Construct the break-even chart for Paul's planned business. (9)

1b State, and show on the graph, the profit or loss made at a monthly sales level of 600 customers. (4)

1c State, and show on the graph, the margin of safety at that level of output. (4)

2 Paul's market research shows that, in his first month of trading, he can expect 450 customers at his hotel.

  (a) If Paul's research is correct, calculate the level of profit or loss he will make. (5)

  (b) Illustrate this level of output on your graph and show the profit or loss. (3)

3 Paul has decided to increase his prices to give an average revenue per customer of £120.

  (a) Draw the new total revenue line on your break-even chart to show the effect of this change. (3)

(b) Mark on your diagram the new break-even point. (1)

(c) Calculate Paul's new break-even number of customers to confirm the result shown on your chart. (6)

4 Paul is worried that his break-even chart may be 'misleading'. Do you agree with him? Justify your view. (10)

B2 Data response

The Successful T-Shirt Company

Shelley has recently launched the Successful T-Shirt Company. It sells a small range of fashion T-shirts. The shirts are available in a range of colours and all bear the company's logo, which is becoming increasingly desirable for young, fashion-conscious people.

The shirts are sold to retailers for £35 each. They cost £16.50 to manufacture and the salesperson receives £2.50 commission for each item sold to retailers. The distribution cost for each shirt is £1.00 and current sales are 1000 per month. The fixed costs of production are £11,250 per month.

The company is considering expanding its range of T-shirts and has approached its bank for a loan. The bank has requested the company draw up a business plan, including a cash-flow forecast and break-even chart.

Questions

(30 marks; 40 minutes)

1 What is a break-even chart? (4)

2 Calculate the following:
   (a) the variable cost of producing 1000 T-shirts
   (b) the contribution earned through the sale of one T-shirt. (6)

3 Shelley has decided to manufacture the shirts in Poland. As a result, the variable cost per T-shirt (including commission and distribution costs) will fall to £15 per T-shirt. However, fixed costs will rise to £12,000.

   (a) Calculate the new level of break-even for Shelly's T shirts.
   (b) Calculate the margin of safety if sales are 1000 T shirts per month. (10)

4 Should Shelley rely on break-even analysis when taking business decisions? Justify your view. (10)

C. Essay questions

(40 marks each)

1 'Break-even is the most vital part of a business plan for a new enterprise.' Do you agree with this statement? Justify your view.

2 'Break-even analysis is of limited value to a start-up business because it ignores the market.' To what extent do you agree with this statement?

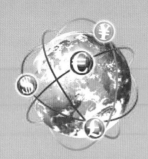

Unit 15

CASH FLOW MANAGEMENT AND FORECASTING

DEFINITION

Cash flow is the flow of money into and out of a business in a given time period. Cash flow forecasting is estimating the flow of cash in the future.

15.1 The importance of cash flow management

Managing cash flow is one of the most important aspects of financial management. Without adequate availability of cash from day to day, even a company with high sales could fail. As bills become due there has to be the cash available to pay. If a company cannot pay its bills, suppliers will refuse to deliver and staff will start looking for other jobs. Cash flow problems are the most common reason for business failure. This is particularly true for new businesses. It is estimated that 70% of businesses that collapse in their first year fail because of cash flow problems.

Businesses need to continually review their current and future cash position. In order to be prepared and to understand future cash needs, businesses construct a **cash flow forecast**. This sets out the expected flows of cash into and out of the business for each month. In textbooks cash flows are normally shown for six months but they can be done for any period of time. Most firms want to look 12 months ahead, so the cash flow forecast is constantly updated.

A-grade application

A bit of a steal

In 2007, a year when Premier League clubs spent more than £500 million on transfers, Fulham were pleased to get David Healy for just over £1 million. As the highest-scoring striker in the European Nations Cup qualifiers, why would Leeds sell him for such a modest fee? Healy's 32 international goals included winning strikes against England and Spain.

Part of the reason was that Healy was desperate to leave, quite simply because he was not getting paid. By mid-July, Leeds United's players had still not been paid their June wages. Cash flow problems can quickly spread throughout a business.

15.2 Who needs to use a cash flow forecast?

All businesses can benefit from using cash flow forecasts, but they are particularly useful for business start-ups. A carefully planned cash flow forecast will help ensure that the business has enough finance to keep afloat during the early months. This is the most difficult period for a business as sales may be slow. There will be little income but bills still need to be paid.

Existing businesses also need to be aware of their cash position. In many cases there are seasonal factors that make cash hard to manage. A seaside hotel has, every year, to cope with winter months when there will almost certainly be **negative cash flow** – in other words, cash out will be higher than cash in. A cash flow forecast will help to ensure that the business plans for future cash needs and can cope if unexpected events happen. If a business is growing, cash flow forecasts can be particularly useful. They enable the business to ensure that any growth is backed by sufficient funding.

15.3 Preparing a cash flow forecast

To prepare a cash flow forecast businesses need to estimate all the money coming into and out of the business, month by month. These flows of money are then set onto a grid showing the cash movements in each month.

Cash in

In this example (Table 15.1) the business is a new start-up. The business will receive an injection of capital of

Table 15.1 Cash inflow example

Month (cash inflow, £s)	March	April	May	June	July	August
Capital	30000					
Sales			7000	10000	13000	15000
Total inflow	**30000**	**0**	**7000**	**10000**	**13000**	**15000**

£30,000. This will be received in March. The business will start production in April and will receive cash only when sales start in May. Cash inflows are expected to increase each month until reaching a maximum of £15,000 in August.

It is important that the income from sales is shown when the cash is received not when the sale is made.

Outflow (see Table 15.2)

In March the firm will buy machinery for £23,000. Materials will cost £6000 each month. The first delivery in April must be paid for on delivery. After that the supplier will give the firm two months' credit so the next payments do not need to be made until July. Rent for the building costs £2000 per month, but the owner requires two months' rent in advance. Wages are estimated to be £2000 per month and there are other expenses of £1000 per month.

When these figures have been entered into the grid the total expenditure can be calculated.

The cash flow forecast can now be completed by calculating the following.

● *Monthly balance:* this is cash inflow for the month minus cash outflow. It shows each month if there is a positive or a negative movement of cash. In this case inflow is greater than outflow, except in April. When outflow is greater than inflow the monthly balance will be negative. This is shown in brackets to indicate that it is a minus figure.

● *Opening and closing balance:* this is like a bank statement. It shows what cash the business has at the beginning of the month (opening balance) and what the cash position is at the end of the month (closing balance). The closing balance is the opening balance plus the monthly balance (e.g. for August, the month starts with £1000 in the bank, another £4000 flows in during the month, so the month closes with a bank balance of £5000).

The closing balance shows the business its expected net cash position each month.

The completed cash flow forecast will be as shown in Table 15.3.

Table 15.2 Cash outflow example

Month (cash outflow, £s)	March	April	May	June	July	August
Equipment	23000					
Materials	0	6000			6000	6000
Rent	4000	2000	2000	2000	2000	2000
Wages		2000	2000	2000	2000	2000
Other expenses		1000	1000	1000	1000	1000
Total outflow	**27000**	**11000**	**5000**	**5000**	**11000**	**11000**

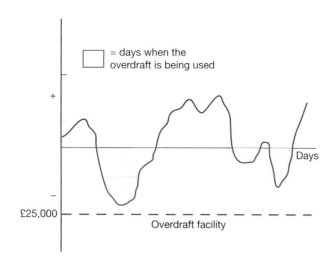

Figure 15.1 Daily cash balances for a firm with a £25,000 overdraft

This shows that there is a negative cash balance for the months of April, May and June. Only in July does the business start having a positive cash flow. As there is no such thing as negative money this cash flow forecast shows the business that it must take action if it is to avoid problems in the early months. The easiest remedy for a cash flow problem such as this is a bank **overdraft**.

15.4 Benefits of cash flow forecasts

A cash flow forecast will enable a business to do the following things.

● Anticipate the timing and amounts of any cash shortages: in the example above, the business can see from the cash flow forecast whether it has sufficient

Table 15.3 Cash flow forecast for Visible Engineering Ltd

Month (£s)	March	April	May	June	July	August
Cash inflow						
Capital	30000					
Sales			7000	10000	13000	15000
Total inflow	**30000**	**0**	**7000**	**10000**	**13000**	**15000**
Outflow						
Equipment	23000					
Materials	0	6000			6000	6000
Rent	4000	2000	2000	2000	2000	2000
Wages		2000	2000	2000	2000	2000
Other expenses		1000	1000	1000	1000	1000
Total outflow	**27000**	**11000**	**5000**	**5000**	**11000**	**11000**
Monthly balance	3000	(11000)	2000	5000	2000	4000
Opening balance	0	3000	(8000)	(6000)	(1000)	1000
Closing balance	**3000**	**(8000)**	**(6000)**	**(1000)**	**1000**	**5000**

cash. In fact this business does not have enough cash for three months (April, May and June). Unless it makes some changes the business will not be able to make some of its payments. It will not be able to pay wages or the rent. This would mean that, although the business looks cash rich in the longer term – by July it has a positive cash flow – it might not survive.

● Arrange financial cover for any anticipated shortages of cash: having information about when the business will have a cash shortage means that the business can take measures to ensure that it has cash available. In the example above, the business needs to find additional finance for the three months when it has a cash shortage.

● Review the timings and amounts of receipts and payments.

● Obtain loans (if the problems are long term) or overdrafts (if the problems are short term).

If a firm wants to take out a loan, the bank will always request a cash flow forecast. Banks do this in order to ensure that the business:

● has enough cash to enable it to survive

● is able to pay the interest on the loan

● will be able to repay the loan

● is aware of the need for cash flow management.

How reliable are cash flow forecasts?

In order to prepare a cash flow forecast, businesses need to make assumptions about the future – although they may be able to make some use of actual figures, such as the monthly rent agreed with the landlord.

When looking at cash flow forecasts it is useful for the firm to be aware that the figures are estimates and to build in some safety margins. Companies should ask themselves what would happen if:

● sales are lower than expected

● the customer does not pay up on time

● prices of materials are higher than expected.

Using spreadsheets enables companies to look at some of these possibilities. With the use of spreadsheets it is possible to adjust both the timings and amounts. This enables a business to evaluate the most likely and the worst-case situations. The business also needs to be aware that the figures are based on current assumptions about the market and the economic climate. If changes are detected look at how these will affect the cash flow position.

A-grade application

Kwik Save

Fresh evidence of the cash crisis facing discount grocery chain Kwik Save emerged this weekend – only days after it announced the closure of 79 stores. *The Sunday Times* disclosed last week that dairy group Arla had stopped supplying Kwik Save with milk because of 'payment problems'. And now British Bakeries – part of Premier Foods, with brands such as Hovis and Mothers Pride – has halted bread deliveries to Kwik Save.

Premier said it could not comment on commercial agreements. But reliable sources confirmed that British Bakeries has stopped supplying Kwik Save. As with Arla, 'payment problems' were alleged to be the reason.

Some Kwik Save stores have not received any cigarettes for months. And there is said to have been disruption to the chain's supplies of chilled and frozen goods.

Kwik Save approached Costcutter last month, hoping to secure access to a number of brands for which it had been impossible to negotiate terms with manufacturers. But Costcutter said it would not start supplying unless it could secure payment upfront.

Restructuring experts at accountancy firm KPMG have been called in to see if there is a way that Kwik Save can be saved from closure. The retailer closed 79 of its 226 stores last Tuesday. It is estimated that 800 people lost their jobs.

Source: Sunday Times, 3 June 2007

15.5 Managing the day-to-day finances

Even when the high set-up costs have been completed, new businesses can be shocked by the amount of capital needed to run the business day by day. To operate, the business needs money to buy stock, to pay wages and the day-to-day bills such as electricity and telephone bills. If the bills cannot be paid on time there are serious consequences. In the worst situation the business may fail.

The cash cycle

Managing the day-to-day finances is a continuous process. When a business starts up it takes time to generate income. Money to pay for stock and the running costs will need to be found from the initial capital invested in the business. As the business cycle gets going, income from customers will be available to pay for expenditure. The firm needs to ensure that there is always enough cash to meet daily requirements. If the business is expanding, extra care needs to be taken (see Figure 15.2).

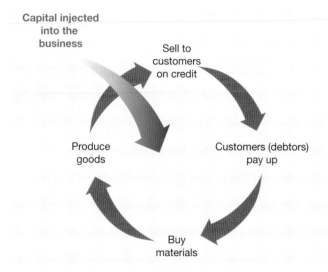

Figure 15.2 The cash cycle

Each business will have its own distinct cycle. Businesses may also suffer unexpected shocks and need the cash to be able to cope with these.

Problems caused by insufficient cash flow

- *With suppliers:* a firm with too little cash will struggle to pay its bills on time. It may resort to delaying payments. Unpaid suppliers may refuse credit for a future order.

- *Banks are quick to sense a cash flow crisis* – and equally quick to reduce the bank's risk by calling in any overdrafts. As they can insist on being repaid within 24 hours, the speed of repayment can put firms in terrible difficulties.

- *Opportunities may be missed:* the business may not be able to buy supplies in bulk. This removes the advantage of lower prices. Even more importantly, it may have to refuse a large order because it cannot finance the extra cash requirement.

In the longer term, shortage of cash means insufficient funds are available for development. The business will

not be able to grow as rapidly as rivals. This may make it hard for it to stay competitive.

15.6 Improving cash flow into the business

The business can improve the flow of cash into the business in several ways, as outlined below.

- *Getting goods to the market in the shortest possible time:* the sooner goods reach the customer the sooner payment is received. Production and distribution should be as efficient as possible.

- *Getting paid as quickly as possible:* the ideal arrangement is to get paid cash on delivery. Most business, though, works on credit. Even worse, it's interest-free credit, so the customer has little incentive to pay up quickly. Early payment should be encouraged by offering incentives such as discounts for early payment.

- *Controlling debtors:* confusingly this is known as credit control. If customers do not pay on time this will obviously mean that the cash does not come into the business when expected. Businesses can reduce the likelihood of non- or late payment by ensuring the debtor is creditworthy before granting credit (by getting a bank reference).

- *Factoring:* it may be possible to speed up payments by **factoring** money owed to the business. The company is able to receive 80% of the amount due within 24 hours of an invoice being presented. The factor then collects the money from the customer when the credit period is over, and pays the seller the remaining 20% less the factoring fees. These depend on the length of time before the payment is due, the credit rating of the creditor and current rates of interest. The fees are usually no more than 5% of the total value of the sale.

15.7 Reducing cash outflows from the business

The other way of improving cash flow is to manage the outflow of cash from the business. This can be done in the ways described below.

- *Obtaining maximum possible credit for purchases:* delaying payment of bills will keep cash in the business for longer.

- *Controlling costs:* this can be done by keeping administrative and production costs to a minimum.

Efficient production reduces costs. Savings may be possible by upgrading machinery to replace labour. This will benefit the firm's profit as well as its cash flow.

● *Keeping stocks of raw materials to a minimum:* good stock management, such as a just-in-time system, means that the business is not paying for stocks before it needs them for production. Controlling stock losses means that less is spent on replacements for lost or damaged stock.

Keeping cash in the business

Cash flow can also be improved by keeping cash in the business. Minimising short-term spending on new equipment keeps cash in the business. Things that the business can do include the following.

● *Lease rather than buy equipment:* this increases expenses but conserves capital.

● *Renting rather than buying buildings:* this also allows capital to remain in the business.

● *Postponing expenditure:* for example, on new company cars

15.8 Finding additional funding to cover cash shortages

If the business is unable to keep a healthy cash flow by internal management it may need to look outside to cover cash shortages. This can be done by the following means.

● *Using an overdraft:* an overdraft is arranged with a bank. It allows the business to overdraw up to an agreed limit negotiated in advance. Overdrafts usually incur interest rates as high as 6% over base rate. However, an overdraft ensures the firm borrows money only on the days it really needs it. It is a very flexible form of borrowing. This makes it suitable for small or short-term shortages of cash. Although it should only be used to fund short-term problems, a recent study of firms in Bristol found that 70% of small firms had a permanent overdraft. A risky aspect of an overdraft is that the bank can withdraw the facility at any time and demand instant repayment. So when a firm needs it most, such as in a recession, it may not be available.

Table 15.4 Ways to improve cash flow

Measure	**Result**	**Drawbacks**
Discounting prices	Increases sales Reduces stock Generates cash	May undermine pricing structure May leave low stocks for future activity
Reduce purchases	Cuts down expenditure	May leave business without means to continue
Negotiate more credit	Allows time to pay	May tarnish credit reputation
Delay payment of bill	Retains cash	Will tarnish credit reputation
Credit control – chase debtors	Gets payments in and sooner	May upset customers
Negotiate additional finance	Provides cash	Interest payments add to expenditure Has to be repaid
Factor debts	Generates cash A proportion of the income is guaranteed	Reduces income from sales Costs can be high
Selling assets	Releases cash	Assets are no longer available
Sale and leaseback	Releases cash Asset is still available	Increases costs – lease has to be paid Company no longer owns asset

- *Taking out a short-term loan:* this incurs a lower rate of interest than an overdraft. Although less flexible than an overdraft, short-term loans offer more security and may have fixed interest charges (whereas on an overdraft they are variable).

- *Sale and leaseback of assets:* if a business has fixed assets it may be possible to negotiate a **sale and leaseback** arrangement. This will release capital and give an immediate inflow of cash. The equipment will be paid for through a leasing arrangement. This will be a regular and ongoing cost that must be budgeted for.

A-grade application
Tesco's sale and leaseback

In March 2007 Tesco raised £570 million from a sale and leaseback on 21 of its biggest shops. The 20-year deal will help provide the finance for Tesco's ambitious plans to open 400 more overseas stores in the coming year. These include its Fresh & Easy shops in America, plus Tesco outlets in China and Russia. Tesco said the deal would 'release funding for future growth'. Tesco has property worth more than £20 billion, so why not use it to finance its expansion?

Issues For Analysis

When answering a question on cash flow management and forecasting, it is important to understand that the figures are only the starting point for analysis and decision making. Consideration needs to be given to the following aspects.

- The validity of the figures – who constructed the forecast? Are the figures reliable and unbiased?

- What the figures show (i.e. a careful analysis of the position month by month).

- The need to take full account of the circumstances of the business. If sales are to a foreign country, payment may not be certain and, even if it arrives, changes in currency values may make cash inflows worth fewer pounds than forecast.

- The differences between cash flow and profitability.

- Especially for small firms, cash flow is the equivalent of blood circulating round the body. If the cash dries up, the firm dies. When looking at how the firm can

improve its cash flow, consideration must be given to the type of firm and its market situation. There is no point suggesting that the firm should demand cash payment if it is supplying large businesses in a highly competitive market.

- When looking at solutions to cash flow problems it is important to consider what is causing the problem and how long it might go on for. There is a lot of difference between a problem caused by poor payment and one that is caused by poor sales.

15.9 Cash flow management and forecasting
an evaluation

There is no doubt that cash flow management is a vital ingredient in the success of any small business. For a new business, cash flow forecasting helps to answer key questions:

- Is the venture viable?

- How much capital is needed?

- Which are the most dangerous months?

For an existing business the cash flow forecast identifies the amount and timing of any cash flow problems in the future. It is also useful for evaluating new orders or ventures.

Nevertheless, completing a cash flow forecast does not guarantee survival. Consideration needs to be given to its usefulness and limitations. It must be remembered that cash flow forecasts are based on estimates. These estimates are not just amounts but also timings. The firm must be aware that actual figures can differ wildly from estimates – especially for a new, inexperienced firm. When preparing cash flow forecasts, managers need to ask themselves 'What if?' A huge mistake is to only look at one forecast. Far better to look at **best case** and **worst case** possibilities. Spreadsheets allow for easy manipulation of data, making it easy to see the impact of single and multiple changes to the forecast figures. This should help to reduce the risks. However, it does not guarantee results. Having completed a cash flow forecast and taken the necessary steps to ensure financing also does not guarantee success. The firm needs to be continually aware of the economic and market climate and its current cash position.

Improving cash flow will often uncover problems elsewhere in the business. Perhaps the reason there is poor stock control is that the person in charge is demotivated. In this respect managing cash flow is an integrated activity involving each aspect of the company. Efficient production keeps costs to a minimum and turns raw inputs into finished goods in the shortest possible time. Effective management of stock can have considerable impact on cash needs. Effective marketing ensures that the goods are sold and that demand is correctly estimated. This avoids wasted production. Cash then flows in from sales.

A business with plenty of cash flowing in and out is a healthy business.

Key terms

Best case: an optimistic estimate of the best possible outcome (e.g. if sales prove much higher than expected).

Cash flow forecast: estimating future monthly cash inflows and outflows, to find out the net cash flow.

Factoring: obtaining part-payment from a factoring company of the amount owed. The factoring company will then collect the debt and pass over the balance of the payment.

Negative cash flow: when cash outflows are greater than cash inflows.

Overdraft: short-term borrowing from a bank; the business borrows only as much as it needs to cover its daily cash shortfall.

Sale and leaseback: a contract that, at the same time, sells the freehold to a piece of property and buys back the leasehold.

Worst case: a pessimistic estimate, assuming the worst possible outcome (e.g. sales are very disappointing).

Exercises

A. Revision questions

(50 marks; 50 minutes)

1 What is meant by 'cash flow'? (2)

2 Why is it important to manage cash flow? (4)

3 What is a cash flow forecast? (3)

4 Explain two limitations of cash flow forecasts. (4)

5 Give two reasons why a bank manager might want to see a cash flow forecast before giving a loan to a new business. (2)

6 How might a firm benefit from delaying its cash outflows? (3)

7 What problems might a firm face if its cash flow forecast proved unreliable? (3)

8 How might a firm benefit from constructing its cash flow forecasts on a computer spreadsheet? (4)

9 Outline the probable cash cycle for a small sandwich shop. (4)

10 Explain why 'good management of cash flow starts with good forecasting'. (3)

11 Outline two problems that might arise if a firm is operating with very poor cash flow? (4)

12 How might a small producer of shelf fittings benefit from factoring? (4)

13 Outline three ways in which a business can improve its cash flow situation. (6)

14 What internal factors could affect a firm's cash flow? (4)

B. Revision exercises

B1 Cash flow

(20 marks; 20 minutes)

A business is to be started up on 1 January next year with £40,000 of share capital. It will be opening a designer clothes shop. During January it plans to spend £45,000 on start-up costs (buying a lease, buying equipment, decorating, etc.). On 1 February it will open its doors and gain sales over the next five months of: £12,000, £16,000, £20,000, £25,000 and £24,000 respectively. Each month it must pay £10,000 in fixed overheads (salaries, heat, light, telephone, etc.) and its variable costs will amount to half the revenue.

Complete the cash flow table below to find out:

1 the company's forecast cash position at the end of June (18)

2 the maximum level of overdraft the owners will need to negotiate with the bank before starting up. (2)

Cash flow table (all figures in £000s)

	Jan	Feb	Mar	Apr	May	June
Cash at start						
Cash in						
Cash out						
Net cash flow						
Opening balance						
Closing balance						

B2 Data response

Merlin Construction has planning permission to convert an old office block into four flats. The directors managed to borrow £130,000 from the bank in January. They used £100,000 to buy the building that month. The work will start in January and take nine months to complete. The plan is to build and sell the two upstairs flats in June and then complete the ground-floor flats. These will be sold in September. The flats should sell for £60,000 each. Materials are estimated to cost about £10,000 a month with one month's credit. Wages and salaries will be £4000 a month. Interest charges will be £1000 a month. Other expenses will be £1000 a month.

Questions

(30 marks; 35 minutes)

1 Construct a cash flow forecast for the business for January to September. (10)

2 Outline two significant features of this cash flow forecast. (6)

3 Discuss two possible courses of action. (8)

4 Examine two ways in which the cash flow forecast might be unreliable. (6)

B3 Data response

Danielle and Kamil chose to open a jewellery shop because she loves the products and he knows how to get them: cheaply from India. They opened their first shop in May and in the period until August managed to break even. That was fine because they knew that jewellery shops make 50% of the year's takings in the run-up to Christmas. So both were confident that the first year was going well. Despite help from an uncle who has been in the jewellery business for 35 years, Kamil has not quite finished this cash flow forecast for the next six months:

Questions

(25 marks; 25 minutes)

1 Explain two problems Kamil may have had in drawing up this cash flow forecast for D&K Jewellers. (6)

2 Complete the job for Kamil by working out the missing figures a–t. (10)

3 What would you recommend that Danielle and Kamil do about this forecast? Explain the reasons behind your answer. (9)

Cash flow forecast for D&K Jewellers (B3)

Month (£s)	September	October	November	December	January	February
Cash inflow						
From cash sales	12000	16000	20000	80000	6000	5000
From credit sales	5000	6000	10000	14000	50000	2000
Total cash in	17000	22000	a	b	c	d
Cash outflow						
Security costs	3000	3000	3000	4000	3000	3000
Buying jewellery stocks	10000	25000	55000	5000	0	2000
Rent	9000	0	0	9000	0	0
Wages	8000	8000	8000	8000	8000	8000
Other expenses	1000	1000	1000	1000	1000	1000
Total outflow	31000	37000	67000	27000	12000	14000
Monthly balance	(14000)	e	f	g	h	i
Opening balance	8000	j	k	l	m	n
Closing balance	o	p	q	r	s	t

B4 Case study

Hatta Lighting

Hatta Lighting plc makes component parts for the car industry. It started out making bulbs but now also supplies a range of electrical and electronic components. The company started as a family-run business, but expansion has meant that five years ago it became a public limited company. During the last two years its performance has been mediocre and dividends paid to shareholders have been falling. The share price has also fallen. One of the largest shareholders has decided that change is necessary and has managed to exert enough pressure to replace the established chairman. The new chairman has a strong financial background but has been involved in the retailing industry for many years. He has asked the management team to produce some information. The team has come up with the information in Figure 15.3.

After examining these figures the new chairman is very concerned about the cash flow situation of the company. Several large debts totalling £500,000 are due to be paid shortly. The firm does not have sufficient cash available to pay these. He sees this as being the most urgent issue facing the company and has arranged an urgent meeting of all the managers. He has asked each of the three department heads (marketing, finance and production) to come up with ideas to solve the problem.

Questions

(45 marks; 60 minutes)

1 What might be the reasons for the increase in the stock of finished goods and materials? (6)

2 Consider what suggestions the production director might make. Explain your reasoning. (10)

3 The finance director sees slow payment as his major problem. Examine the ways in which the firm might tackle this problem. (10)

4 Outline the contribution the marketing department might make to help improve the cash flow situation. (9)

5 Apart from tackling the issue of slow payment, consider what other short-term measures the firm might take to overcome the immediate cash crisis. (10)

	Last year	This year	Industry average
Stock turnover materials	44 days	48 days	40 days
Stock of finished goods	£780,000	£910,000	£700,000
Average days before payment	38	54	42
Working capital at year end	£560,000	£380,000	Not available

Figure 15.3

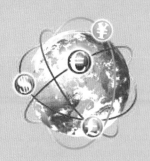

SOURCES OF FINANCE

All businesses need money. Where the money comes from is known as 'sources of finance'.

16.1 The need for finance

Starting up

New businesses starting up need money to invest in long-term assets such as buildings and equipment. They also need cash to purchase materials, pay wages, and to pay the day-to-day bills such as water and electricity. Inexperienced entrepreneurs often underestimate the capital needed for the everyday running of the business. Generally, for every £1000 required to establish the business, another £1000 is needed for day-to-day needs.

Growing

Once the business is established there will be income from sales. If this is greater than the operating costs the business will be making a profit. This should be kept in the business and used to help the business to grow. Later on, the owners can draw money out of the business, but at this stage as much as possible should be left in. Even so, there may not be enough to allow the business to grow as fast as it would like to. It may need to find additional finance and this will probably be from external sources.

Other situations

Businesses may also need finance in other circumstances. They may have a cash flow problem caused by changes in market conditions. A major customer may refuse to pay for the goods, causing a huge gap in cash inflows. Or there may be a large order, requiring the purchase of additional raw materials. In all these cases businesses will need to find additional funding.

16.2 Internal and external sources of finance

Finance for business comes from two main sources:

1 inside the business – known as 'internal sources of finance'

2 outside the business – known as 'external sources of finance'.

Internal sources

● Existing capital can be made to stretch further. The business may be able to negotiate to pay its bills later or work at getting cash in earlier from customers; the average small firm waits 75 days to be paid (i.e. two and a half months); if that period of time could be halved, it would provide a huge boost to cash flow.

● Nothing soothes a difficult cash situation better than profit. It is also the best (and most common) way to finance investment into a firm's future. Research shows that over 60% of business investment comes from reinvested profit.

External sources

If the business is unable to generate sufficient funds from internal sources then it may need to look to external sources. There are two sources of external capital: loan capital and **share capital**.

Loan capital

The most usual way is through borrowing from a bank. This may be in the form of a bank loan or an overdraft. A loan is usually for a set period of time. It may be short term (one or two years), medium term (three to five years) or long term (more than five years). The loan can either be repaid in instalments over time or at the end of the loan period. The bank will charge interest on the loan. This can be fixed or variable. The bank will demand **collateral** to provide security in case the loan cannot be repaid.

An overdraft is a very short-term loan. It is a facility that allows the business to be 'overdrawn'. This means that the account is allowed to go 'into the red'. The length of time that this runs for will have to be negotiated. The interest charges on overdrafts are usually much higher than on loans.

Share capital

Alternatively, if the business is a limited company it may look for additional share capital. This could come from private investors or **venture capital** funds. Venture capital providers are interested in investing in businesses with dynamic growth prospects. They are willing to take a risk on a business that may fail, or may do spectacularly well. They believe that if they make ten investments, five can flop, and four do OK as long as one does fantastically. Peter Theil, the original investor in Facebook, probably turned his $0.5 million investment into $200 million or more (i.e. made a profit of 39,900%!).

Once it has become a **public limited company (plc)**, the firm may consider floating on the stock exchange. For smaller businesses this will usually be on the Alternative Investment Market (AIM).

A-grade application

Financing growth

How do rapidly growing small firms finance their growth? By venture capital? By loans? To find an answer to this question, Hamish Stevenson from Templeton College, Oxford, looked at 100 of the fastest-growing UK firms. One of these is R Frazier, a firm that recycles computers. Its sales grew from £294,000 to £7,400,000 in just three years. In common with the majority of the firms, R Frazier's early growth was self-funded – in other words, from reinvested profits and trade credit. 'These are the real entrepreneurs,' says Stevenson. 'They grab money where they can. It is fly-by-the-seat-of-their-pants finance.' The 54 firms that used this method were doing so 'through default not by design', according to the research. In other words, they had no alternative.

Twenty-one of the firms received external finance from share capital: 15 from venture capital houses and 6 from business angels. Just ten used long-term bank debt. Having survived, even thrived, through these hectic early years, as many as 40 of the firms are looking at, or in the process of, floating their firms on the London **stock market**. This would secure the finance for the next stage of growth.

16.3 How much finance can the business obtain?

The type and amount of finance that is available will depend on several factors. These are as follows.

- *The type of business:* a sole trader will be limited to the capital the owner can put into the business plus any money he or she is able to borrow. A limited company will be able to raise share capital. In order to become a plc it will need to have share capital of £50,000+ and a track record of success. This will make borrowing easier.

- *The stage of development of the business:* a new business will find it much harder to raise finance than an established firm. As the business develops it is easier to persuade outsiders to invest in the business. It is also easier to obtain loans as the firm has assets to offer as security.

- *The state of the economy:* when the economy is booming, business confidence will be high. It will be easy to raise finance both from borrowing and from investors. It will be more difficult for businesses to find investors when interest rates are high. They will invest their money in more secure accounts such as building societies. Higher interest rates will also put up the cost of borrowing. This will make it more expensive for the business to borrow.

16.4 Advantages and disadvantages of sources of finance

Internal sources
Reinvested profit
The profit generated by the business will provide a return for the investors in the business and can be ploughed back into the business to help it to grow. The advantage of reinvested profit is that it does not have an associated cost. Unlike loans it does not have to be repaid, and there are no interest charges. The disadvantage is that it may be limited so will constrain the rate of business expansion.

Cash squeezed out of day-to-day finances
By cutting stocks, chasing up customers or delaying payments to suppliers, cash can be generated. This has the advantage of reducing the amount that needs to be borrowed. However, this is a very short-term solution and if the cash is taken from working capital for a purpose such as buying fixed assets, the firm may find itself short of day-to-day finance.

Sale of assets

An established business has assets. These can be sold to raise cash. The business loses the asset but has the use of the cash. It makes good business sense for businesses to dispose of underused assets. They can finance development without extra borrowing. If the asset is needed, it may be possible to sell it, but immediately lease it back. In this way the business has use of the money and the asset. This is known as sale and leaseback.

External sources

Bank overdrafts

This is the commonest form of borrowing for small businesses. The bank allows the firm to overdraw up to an agreed level. This has the advantages that the firm needs to borrow only when and as much as it needs. It is, however, an expensive way of borrowing, and the bank can insist on being repaid within 24 hours.

Trade credit

This is the simplest form of external financing. The business obtains goods or services from another business, but does not pay for these immediately. The average credit period is two months. It is a good way of boosting day-to-day finances. A disadvantage might be that other businesses may be reluctant to trade with the business if they do not get paid in good time.

Venture capital

This is a way of getting outside investment for businesses that are unable to raise finance through the stock markets or loans. Venture capitalists invest in smaller, riskier companies. To compensate for the risks, venture capital providers usually require a substantial part of the ownership of the company. They are also likely to want to contribute to the running of the business. This dilutes the owner's control but brings in new experience and knowledge. The term 'dragon' became a well-known term for a venture capital provider thanks to the BBC TV series *Dragons' Den*.

Debenture

This is a form of very long-term loan capital. It is the business equivalent of a mortgage, often lasting for 25 years and always secured against a specific property asset. So, if a firm defaults on its debenture payments it could lose the head office building or whatever piece of property the loan is secured against. For the lender, a debenture has much greater security than any other form of business capital. Therefore the lender is willing to charge lower rates of interest than an ordinary bank loan or overdraft. This may make a debenture attractive to the borrower.

16.5 Finance should be adequate and appropriate

Having adequate funding means ensuring the business has sufficient access to finance to meet its current and future needs. This is a major issue for new firms and for those that are expanding rapidly. When a business expands without a sufficient finance this is known as **overtrading**.

Appropriate financing means matching the type of finance to its use. A distinction is made in company financing between short- and long-term finance (see Figure 16.1). Short-term finance is usually considered to be for less than one year; medium-term finance is for one to five years; long-term finance is for longer than five years.

Short-term finance should not be used to finance long-term projects. Using short-term finance such as overdrafts puts continual pressure on the company's cash position. An overdraft should only be used to cope with ups and downs in cash flows. By its very nature, growth is a long-term activity, so appropriate long-term finance should be sought to fund it.

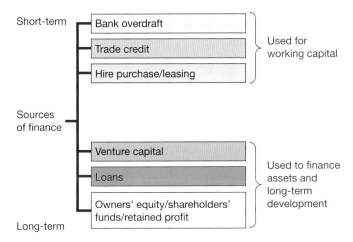

Figure 16.1 Short- and long-term sources of finance

A-grade application

Northern Rock

In September 2007 Northern Rock became the first British bank in 150 years to suffer a 'run on the bank', as savers feared for the bank's solvency. Northern Rock had expanded rapidly, financing its long-term growth with short-term finance; when the finance dried up, the bank collapsed. The business proved to have neither adequate nor appropriate finance. This was especially ironic given that banks are supposed to advise individuals and businesses on financial management. The crisis was averted only when the Bank of England guaranteed that no customers would lose their money.

Figure 16.2 Queues outside Northern Rock

Issues For Analysis

When analysing or suggesting appropriate sources of finance, ask yourself the following questions.

- *Why is the business seeking finance?* The key here is to ensure that the finance is suitable for the business in its particular circumstances. A new business will have very different needs from a growing business. Remember, the finance should be adequate and appropriate.

- *Is the business stable or risky?* If risky, the form of financing should be as safe as possible. Remember that financial institutions are unlikely to lend to risky or unproven enterprises.

- *What is the owner's attitude to sharing the business?* If the owners are reluctant to lose control of the business it is not a good idea to suggest raising finance by selling more shares. Financing growth by borrowing may be more appropriate.

16.6 Sources of finance and evaluation

Finding finance may involve balancing conflicting interests. Internal sources of finance may be too limited to provide opportunities for business development. Obtaining external finance increases the money available, but has its downsides. Borrowing too much can be risky. Raising extra share capital dilutes the control held by existing shareholders.

Having adequate and appropriate finance at each stage in the firm's development will ensure it stays healthy. Decisions about where to obtain the finance will be a matter of considering the business objectives, the stage of development of the business and the reasons for the funding requirement.

A well-run business plans ahead for its financing needs. To run out of cash (as with Northern Rock) suggests management incompetence.

Key terms

Collateral: an asset used as security for a loan. It can be sold by a lender if the borrower fails to pay back a loan.
Overtrading: when a firm expands without adequate and appropriate funding.
Public limited company (plc): a company with limited liability, and shares that are available to the public. Its shares can be quoted on the stock market.
Share capital: business finance that has no guarantee of repayment or of annual income, but gains a share of the control of the business and its potential profits.
Stock market: a market for buying and selling company shares. It supervises the issuing of shares by companies. It is also a second-hand market for stocks and shares.
Venture capital: high-risk capital invested in a combination of loans and shares, usually in a small, dynamic business.

Exercises

A. Revision questions

(30 marks; 30 minutes)

1 Describe the problem caused to a company if a major customer refuses to pay a big bill. (3)

2 Why do banks demand collateral before they agree to provide a loan? (2)

3 Outline two ways in which businesses can raise money from internal sources. (4)

4 What information might a bank manager want when considering a loan to a business? (4)

5 Read the 'Application' report on Northern Rock. Explain the two mistakes made by the bank. (4)

6 Outline two sources of finance that can be used for long-term business development. (4)

7 Explain why a new business might find it difficult to get external funding for its development. (5)

8 Outline one advantage and one disadvantage of using an overdraft. (4)

B. Revision exercises

B1 Activity

Dragons' Den

The BBC TV series *Dragons' Den* is the *X-Factor* for entrepreneurs: a talent contest in which entrepreneurs present their ideas to a panel of super-wealthy investors. The five 'dragons' sit sternly, with piles of cash in front of them, while someone climbs the stairs into the den, then nervously makes a presentation. Fewer than one in twenty get the investment they seek. Just occasionally, though, contestants walk away with £150,000 or £200,000 of cash investment into their business.

In August 2006 James Seddon came to the den to demonstrate his invention for a better way to cook 'boiled' eggs. Instead of a pan of boiling water, Eggxactly works like a sandwich toaster to cook an egg for the exact time you want. A soft-boiled (runny yolk) egg might take three minutes, while a hard-boiled egg takes four. Seddon has a patent pending on his invention (i.e. he has applied for one and is waiting for it to be granted). If accepted, it will provide 20 years' protection from rivals.

Computer software expert Seddon stood up to give his sales pitch, explaining the benefits of the product, then flicked a switch on the machine to start his demonstration. Four minutes later he opened up the Eggxactly to reveal nothing. He had forgotten to put an egg in! The 'dragons' are impatient with time-wasters, so this was not much help. He then put an egg in, re-set the machine and they chatted until, four minutes later, he took out the egg, broke into it and runny egg went everywhere. It was uncooked.

Figure 16.3 The Eggxactly

Despite this incompetence, the investors were so impressed with the man (his intelligence and confidence) and the idea that two of them agreed to invest £75,000 to help Seddon get Eggxactly to market. For their money, the two investors were each to take a 20% share in the business. This could prove a bargain given that one of them, Richard Farleigh, suggested that the device could 'sell zillions'.

Questions

(25 marks; 30 minutes)

1 If your £75,000 was at stake, what research would you carry out before investing in James Seddon's Eggxactly? Explain your reasoning. (8)

2 Outline the risks being taken on by the investors of £75,000. Are they wise? (6)

3 The £75,000 investment was share capital in exchange for 40% of James Seddon's business. Discuss whether James Seddon should accept the offer or turn it down. (11)

B2 Data response

Mayday Printers

Mayday Printers specialises in last-minute printing for firms. Its major selling point is that it will turn a job around within 24 hours, provided the artwork is ready. Mayday is able to charge a premium for this service and is seldom short of work. The firm does, however, need to be extremely flexible. This means having a flexible workforce and very reliable machines. It has had to turn away several large jobs lately because of a lack of machinery, and now the managers are considering buying an additional large printer. Although they know that this will not be used at full capacity they are worried that turning away business will damage their reputation and lead to a loss of business in future. The company is in good financial health with a strong cash flow, though the cash position can be strained sometimes when there is a rush of work. To complete an order Mayday might have to pay bonus wages to staff, often before payment is received.

The finance director has come up with two proposals that he will present to the next board meeting. The first is to buy a new printer and to fund the purchase with a bank loan. The printer will cost £100,000, so he suggests taking out a loan for that amount. The loan will be at bank rate plus 8% and will be for ten years. The bank rate is currently 4%.

The alternative proposal is to rent this new machine. He has found a company that will do this. The cost of the rental, including a maintenance contract, would be £1500 per month. The marketing department expects to pick up at least five additional contracts during the first year. These should generate at least £20,000 of revenue, but, just as importantly, will protect the company's reputation and existing business.

Question

(20 marks; 30 minutes)

1 Prepare a report for the board, outlining the advantages and disadvantages of each proposal. End your report with a clear recommendation. (20)

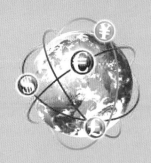

BUDGETS AND BUDGETING

A budget is a target for costs or revenue that a firm or department must aim to reach over a given period of time.

17.1 Introduction

Budgeting is the process of setting targets, covering all aspects of costs and revenues. It is a method for turning a firm's strategy into reality. Nothing can be done in business without money; budgets tell individual managers how much they can spend to achieve their objectives. For instance, a football manager might be given a transfer expenditure budget of £20 million to buy players. With the budget in place, the transfer dealing can get under way.

A budgeting system shows how much can be spent, and gives managers a way to check whether they are on track. Most firms use a system of budgetary control as a means of supervision. The process is as follows:

1 Make a judgement of the likely sales revenues for the coming year.

2 Set a cost ceiling that allows for an acceptable level of profit.

3 This budget for the whole company's costs is then broken down by division, department or by cost centre.

4 The budget may then be broken down further so that each manager has a budget and therefore some spending power.

In a business start-up, the budget should provide enough spending power to finance vital needs such as building work, decoration, recruiting and paying staff, and marketing. If a manager overspends in one area, s/he knows that it is essential to cut back elsewhere. A good manager gets the best possible value from the budgeted sum.

17.2 What is budgeting for?

● To ensure that no department or individual spends more than the company expects, thereby preventing unpleasant surprises.

● To provide a yardstick against which a manager's success or failure can be measured (and rewarded). For example, a store manager may have to meet a monthly sales budget of £25,000 at a maximum operating cost of £18,000. As long as the budget holder believes this target is possible, the attempt to achieve it will be motivating. The company can then provide bonuses for achieving or beating the profit target.

● To enable spending power to be **delegated** to local managers who are in a better position to know how best to use the firm's money. This should improve and speed up the decision-making process – and help motivate the local budget holders. Management expert Peter Drucker refers to 'management by self-control'. He regards this as the ideal approach. Managers should have clear targets, clear budgets and the power to decide how to achieve them. Then they will try everything they can to succeed.

● Budgeting can motivate the staff in a department. If budget figures are used as a clear basis for assessing their performance it becomes clear to staff what they must achieve in order to be considered successful.

17.3 Budgets as a means of delegating spending power

Once a business grows beyond a simple one-person operation, there will be times that the boss is not around to authorise spending money – even small amounts like ordering a little extra stock or paying the window cleaner. To make sure the business can run smoothly, the boss needs to find a way to give staff the power to make spending decisions themselves. However, the boss will want to ensure that these decisions are not going to bankrupt the firm. Budgets can be used to allow employees to decide what money to spend within the limits specified by the budget. If an entrepreneur who has successfully opened a beauty salon wants to open a second branch, s/he will need to appoint a manager of the second branch. The entrepreneur can then agree budget targets for the income and expenditure of the second branch, knowing that the manager will be working hard to hit the budget targets.

The budgets for costs should help to avoid any unexpected financial surprises – since the manager would be expected to discuss any budget overspend with the entrepreneur before they are incurred. The manager can run the shop on a day-to-day basis, spending whatever money needs to be spent without checking with the boss all the time, yet the boss will be happy that the costs of the second branch are being controlled within the limits set by the budget.

This principle applies to huge multinational companies as well as businesses that have just started growing. In a huge firm, there will be many more budget holders and many more separate budgets, however the concept is the same, as shown in the simple example in Figure 17.1.

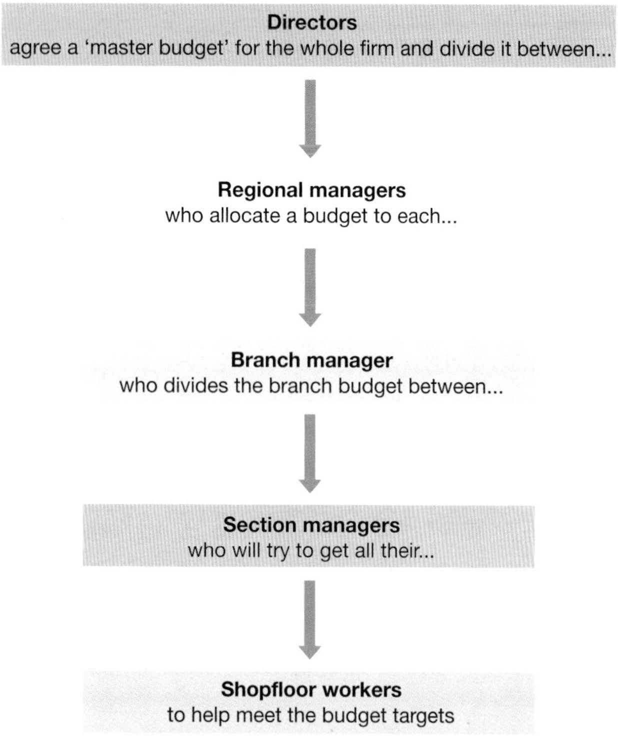

17.4 Budgets as a method of monitoring business performance

With budgets in place for each department, the management has **criteria** against which success can be measured. Budget holders will try to exceed revenue budgets or stay under cost targets. The implication, of course, is that budgeted figures will be compared with what actually happens to make a judgement on performance. It is this process of comparison that allows budgets to be used as a method of monitoring business performance.

17.5 Types of budget

Income budget

The **income budget** sets a minimum target for the desired revenue level to be achieved over a period of time. If a manager knows, halfway through the year, that sales figures have not been strong enough to achieve the target, s/he might decide to run a price promotion or a 'buy one get one free' (BOGOF) offer. When buying a new car it is clever to wait for the last day of the month, as showroom managers are often trying desperately to achieve their monthly sales target: their incentive may be a salary bonus or a monthly prize such as a trip to the Caribbean for the month's top-performing sales manager; your incentive is a cheaper car!

Expenditure budget

The **expenditure budget** sets a maximum target for costs – for example, the manager of the Derby McDonald's may have a staff budget of £2100 for the month of November. Spending beyond an expenditure budget occasionally will be tolerated, but a manager who

Directors
agree a 'master budget' for the whole firm and divide it between...

↓

Regional managers
who allocate a budget to each...

↓

Branch manager
who divides the branch budget between...

↓

Section managers
who will try to get all their...

↓

Shopfloor workers
to help meet the budget targets

Figure 17.1 Budget holders

persistently overspends is likely to get a stern talking-to. An intelligent boss will also question expenditure underspending (e.g. not spending the budget for safety training) as this may cause major problems later on.

A-grade application

The BP disaster

On 23 March 2005 a huge explosion at BP's Texas oil refinery killed 15 people and injured more than 180; most were its own staff. The refinery, America's third biggest, had suffered safety problems before. In 2004 two workers died when scalded by super-heated water that escaped from a high-pressure pipe and, in a separate incident, BP was fined $63,000 for safety breaches at the plant.

After an inquiry, the chairwoman of the US Chemical Safety Board (CSB) reported that 'BP implemented a 25% cut on fixed costs from 1998 to 2000 that adversely impacted maintenance expenditures at the refinery'. The report stated that 'BP's global management' (i.e. British Head Office) 'was aware of problems with maintenance spending and infrastructure well before March 2005', yet they did nothing about it. The chairwoman delivered the final critique thus:

Every successful corporation must contain its costs. But at an ageing facility like Texas City, it is not responsible to cut budgets related to safety and maintenance without thoroughly examining the impact on the risk of a catastrophic accident.

BP confirmed that its own internal investigation had findings 'generally consistent with those of the CSB'.

Source: adapted from Topical Cases, January 2007 (www.a-zbusinesstraining.com)

Profit budget

The **profit budget** is a function of the previous two budgets. The higher the income budget and the lower the expenditure, the higher the profit. Senior managers should look with care at how a profit budget has been met or beaten. For example, the profit achievement may have been a result of cost-cutting that threatens health and safety. Of course, managers are supposed to meet their profit targets, but there is more to running a business successfully than simply getting the numbers right.

17.6 Setting budgets

Setting budgets is not an easy job. How do you decide exactly what level of sales are likely next year, especially for new businesses with no previous trading to rely on? Furthermore, how can you plan for costs if the cost of your raw materials tends to fluctuate? Most firms treat last year's budget figures as the main determinant of this year's budget. Minor adjustments will be made for inflation and other foreseeable changes. Given the firm's past experience, budget-setting should be quite quick and quite accurate.

For start-ups, setting budgets will be a much tougher job. The entrepreneur will need to rely on:

- a 'guesstimate' of likely sales in the early months of the start-up

- the entrepreneur's expertise and experience, which will be better if the entrepreneur has worked in the industry before

- the entrepreneur's instinct, based on market understanding

- a significant level of market research.

A-grade application

Budgeting helps but is not easy for start-ups

Stanford University research into 78 business start-ups showed that firms with budgeting systems were more likely to survive and experience significant growth rates. They reported that budgeting systems allowed senior staff access to the information needed when making decisions. However, they acknowledged the difficulties in setting budgets for new start-ups. They point out that, for a new company, predicting the future is hugely unpredictable and setting 12-month budgets is likely to be unrealistic.

An alternative approach is zero budgeting. This sets each department's budget at zero and demands that budget holders, in setting their budget, justify every pound they ask for. This helps to avoid the common phenomenon of budgets creeping upwards each year.

The only serious drawback to **zero budgeting** is that it takes a long time to find good reasons to justify why you need a budget of £150,000 instead of £110,000. As it is so time consuming for managers, it is sensible to use zero budgeting every four to five years, rather than every year. Figure 17.2 shows the benefits of this approach.

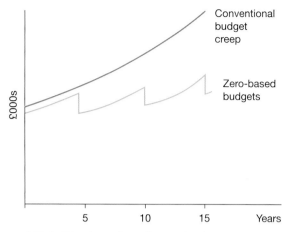

Figure 17.2 The benefits of zero budgeting

The best criteria for setting budgets are:

● to relate the budget directly to the business objective; if a company wants to increase sales and market share, the best method might be to increase the advertising budget and thereby boost demand

● to involve as many people as possible in the process; people will be more committed to reaching the targets if they have had a say in how the budget was set.

Simple budget statements

A simple example of a budget statement might look like that shown in Table 17.1.

This information is only of value if it proves possible for a manager to believe that these figures are achievable. Only then will s/he be motivated to try to turn the budgets into reality.

17.7 Problems in setting budgets

The main problem is that individual managers want as much spending power as possible (a high budget). This will help them do their job successfully and more enjoyably (e.g. a big expense account). The bosses, though, want to keep costs as low as possible among junior managers (i.e. to set low budgets). A senior Cadbury's manager might feel sure that an advertising budget of £2 million will be enough for Creme Eggs this year. Yet the brand manager for Creme Eggs may have a convincing argument for why £3.5 million is needed. (And no one knows the 'right' figure.)

The main problems in setting budgets occur when:

● a new firm or new manager lacks experience in knowing what things really cost

● a senior manager is too arrogant to listen to his/her

A-grade application

Chessington World of Adventures

In April 2007 Chessington World of Adventures opened for its summer season. The newly appointed merchandise manager (in charge of all non-food sales) was given his sales budget for the year, which had been set 6% higher than for 2006. He thought it was quite ambitious, but a sunny April brought in the crowds so the sales target started to look reasonable. The period May–August, though, saw some of the wettest months on record, washing his budget targets away. As a wet day at Chessington can cut crowds by 75%, there was nothing he could do. Do budgets have a purpose in a business such as this?

Table 17.1 Example of a budget statement

	January	**February**	**March**
Income	25000	28000	30000
Variable costs	10000	12000	13000
Fixed costs	10000	10000	11000
Total expenditure	20000	22000	24000
Profit	5000	6000	6000

Table 17.2 Adverse or favourable variance?

Variable	Budget	Actual	Variance	
Sales of X	150	160	10	Favourable
Sales of Y	150	145	5	Adverse
Material costs	100	90	10	Favourable
Labour costs	100	105	5	Adverse

staff, and just sets a budget without discussion (successful budgets should be agreed, not set)

- the type of business makes it hard to set budgets in a meaningful way (meaning that managers struggle to take them seriously); see the Application box.

Budgetary variances

Variance is the amount by which the actual result differs from the budgeted figure. It is usually measured each month, by comparing the actual outcome with the budgeted one. It is important to note that variances are referred to as adverse or favourable – not positive or negative. A **favourable variance** is one that leads to higher than expected profit (revenue up or costs down). An **adverse variance** is one that reduces profit, such as costs being higher than the budgeted level. Table 17.2 shows when variances are adverse or favourable.

The value of regular variance statements is that they provide an early warning. If a product's sales are slipping below budget, managers can respond by increasing marketing support or by cutting back on production

plans. In an ideal world, slippage could be noted in March, a new strategy put into place by May and a recovery in sales achieved by September. Clearly, no firm wishes to wait until the end-of-year profit and loss account to find out that things went badly. An early warning can lead to an early solution.

Figure 17.3 Cadbury Creme Egg

Issues For Analysis

- Especially relevant to a small business owner will be deciding whether designing and implementing a budgeting system will cost more in terms of time and money than it might save. In other words, s/he must decide on the opportunity costs involved. In the often chaotic world of a small business start-up, it is easy to see how time spent talking to customers and suppliers would be more valuable. It is harder to appreciate how time spent in front of a computer spreadsheet estimating revenues and costs will help to enhance profit and the chances of survival.

● Variances are the key to analysing budgets. Once a variance between budgeted and actual figures has been identified, the analysis can begin. The important step is to ask why that variance occurred. Does the person responsible know the reason? Is it a one-off, or does this same person offer a different excuse each month for poor performance?

● Variance analysis is a means of identifying symptoms. It is down to the user of the variance figures to make a diagnosis as to the exact nature of any problem, and then to suggest the most appropriate cure.

17.8 Setting budgets
an evaluation

The sophistication of budgeting systems is usually directly linked to the size of a business. Huge multinationals have incredibly complex budgeting systems. For a small business start-up, any budgeting system is likely to be far more simplistic. Most will rely on a rough breakdown of how the start-up budget is to be divided between the competing demands. There is, however, no doubt that budgeting provides a more effective system of controlling a business's finances than no system at all.

Budgets are a management tool. The way in which they are used can tell you a lot about a firm's culture. Firms with a culture of bossy management will tend to use a tightly controlled budgetary system. Managers will have budgets imposed upon them and variances will be watched closely by supervisors. Organisations with a more open culture will use budgeting as an aid to discussion and empowerment.

Whatever the culture, if a manager is to be held accountable for meeting a budget, s/he must be given influence over setting it, and control over reaching it. Although budgets are set for future time periods, analysis of actual against budgeted performance can take place only after the event. This is true of all financial monitoring and leads to doubts as to its effectiveness as a planning tool. Other measures may be far more reliable in predicting future performance – market research indicating growing levels of customer complaints, for instance, may well be more useful in predicting future performance.

Key terms

Adverse variance: a difference between budgeted and actual figures that is damaging to the firm's profit (e.g. costs up or revenue down).

Criteria: yardsticks against which success (or the lack of it) can be measured.

Delegated: passing authority down the hierarchy.

Expenditure budget: setting a maximum figure on what a department or manager can spend over a period of time; this is to control costs.

Favourable variance: a difference between budgeted and actual figures that boosts a firm's profit (e.g. revenue up or costs down).

Income budget: setting a minimum figure for the revenue to be generated by a product, a department or a manager.

Profit budget: setting a minimum figure for the profit to be achieved over a period of time.

Zero budgeting: setting all future budgets at £0, to force managers to have to justify the spending levels they say they need in future.

Exercises

Budget statement for question A7

	January	February	March	April
Income	4200	4500	4000	
Variable costs	1800		2000	1800
Fixed costs	1200	1600		1600
Total costs		3600	4100	
Profit				600

A. Revision questions

(45 marks; 45 minutes)

1 Explain the meaning of the term 'budgeting'. (2)

2 List three advantages that a budgeting system brings to a company. (3)

3 Why is it valuable to have a yardstick against which performance can be measured? (3)

4 What are the advantages of a zero-based budgeting system? (3)

5 Briefly explain how most companies actually set next year's budgets. (3)

6 Why should budget holders have a say in the setting of their budgets? (4)

7 Complete the budget statement at the top of the page by filling in the gaps. (8)

8 How might a firm respond to an increasingly adverse variance in labour costs? (4)

9 Explain what is meant by a 'favourable cost variance'. (3)

10 Look at the following table, then answer these questions.
   (a) Calculate the budgeted and actual profit figures for May and June. (2)
   (b) Identify the following:
      (i)   a month with a favourable revenue variance
      (ii) a month with an adverse fixed cost variance
      (iii) a month with an adverse variable cost variance

	May		June	
	Budgeted	**Actual**	**Budgeted**	**Actual**
Revenue	3500	3200	4000	4200
Variable costs	1000	900	1200	1500
Fixed costs	1200	1200	1300	1100
Total costs	2200	2100	2500	2600
Profit				

(iv) a month with a favourable fixed cost variance

(v) a month with an adverse total cost variance

(vi) a month with an adverse revenue variance

(vii) a month with a favourable total cost variance

(viii) a month with an adverse variable cost variance

(ix) a month with an adverse profit variance

(x) a month with a favourable profit variance. (10)

B. Revision exercises

B1 Data response

The partnership began in the Atlantic Ocean. Kurt and Brian were both windsurfing fanatics and got to know each other one winter in the Canary Isles. Looking for a way to fund ever more expensive winter watersports trips, they pooled their savings to buy the lease on a flooded former gravel pit back in the UK. The location, just outside London, gave them access to a large market of affluent watersports enthusiasts. KB Wetsports could provide this market with their fix of windsurfing, dinghy sailing or kayaking. In addition to the fees for use of the lake and tuition fees for beginners, a shop would also feature at the centre, selling specialist watersport supplies that were hard to find inland. Both Kurt and Brian had studied management at university and knew that budgeting would be important. They could use it to control expenses and to motivate their small team of staff. They drew up the budget statement below:

Questions

(30 marks; 30 minutes)

1 Complete the budget statement by filling in the gaps. (4)

2 Adjust the budget to show the effect of a 50% increase in shop sales in the third quarter and a 25% increase in wages in quarter 4. (4)

3 Explain why a budgeting system might help KB Wetsports to:
   (a) control expenses (6)
   (b) motivate staff (6)

4 To what extent is budget-setting a crucial element of a successful small business start-up such as KB Wetsports? (10)

Budget statement for Exercise B1

	Jan–Mar	Apr–Jun	Jul–Sep	Oct–Dec
Shop sales	200	3000	5000	2000
Lake fees	0	22000	25000	2800
Stock	2500	1000	2500	1000
Wages	1000	5000	5000	1000
Overheads	1000	4000	6000	4000
Profit				

B2 Data analysis

	January			February		
	B	**A**	**V**	**B**	**A**	**V**
Sales revenue	140*	150	10	180	175	?
Materials	70	80	(10)	90	95	?
Other direct costs	30	35	(5)	40	40	0
Overheads	20	20	0	25	22	?
Profit	20	15	(5)	?	18	?

*All figures in £000s

Questions

(20 marks; 20 minutes)

1 What are the five numbers missing from the variance analysis above. (5)

2 Examine one financial strength and two weaknesses in this data, from the company's viewpoint. (9)

3 How might a manager set about improving the accuracy of a sales budget? (6)

B3 Data response

Budget data for Clinton & Collins Ltd (£000s)

	January		February		March		April	
	B	**A**	**B**	**A**	**B**	**A**	**B**	**A**
Sales revenue	160	144	180	156	208	168	240	188
Materials	40	38	48	44	52	48	58	54
Labour	52	48	60	54	66	62	72	68
Overheads	76	76	76	78	76	80	76	80
Profit	(8)	(18)	(4)	(20)	14	(22)	34	(14)

Questions

(25 marks; 25 minutes)

1 Use the data to explain why February's profits were worse than expected. (5)

2 Why might Clinton & Collins Ltd have chosen to set monthly budgets? (5)

3 Explain how the firm might have set these budgets. (4)

4 The directors of Clinton & Collins Ltd knew that the recession was causing problems for the firm but were unsure as to whether things were improving or worsening. To what extent does the data suggest an improvement? (11)

B2 Data response

Cutting work trip hotel costs

According to new research, UK organisations are overspending by £1.3 billion every year on unnecessarily extravagant business trips. Nearly half of all organisations fail to produce an official business travel policy. Therefore many employees admit to booking what they want and 88% claim not to be influenced by cost.

Stephen Alambritis, chief spokesman of the Federation of Small Businesses, comments: 'Business owners understand the importance of face-to-face meetings and consider personal contact with customers an essential part of generating new sales. But well-run firms control the cost of business travel, setting budgets for both transport and accommodation. Controlling costs across the business underpins future growth and success.'

The findings were alarming – UK businesses simply don't maintain financial control over employee business trips.

The wastage facts
- Nearly half (48%) of all organisations never set a business trip budget. This figure rises to 59% when relating to small to medium businesses.
- Over 40% of employees make their own individual business trip arrangements and claim that they can spend what they like on trips.
- An overwhelming 88% say they aren't influenced by cost.
- Almost a third (30%) of 18–29 year olds exploit business trips as perks.
- Only 12% of employees believe their organisations are interested in cost-cutting.

This clear lack of control has left employees free to squander up to £1.3 billion of their employer's money every year.

Source: Adapted from "Cutting work trip hotel costs", www.workingbalance.co.uk

Questions

(20 marks; 25 minutes)

1 Identify and explain three pieces of evidence from the text that demonstrate the problems for firms that operate without a budget. (9)

2 Explain how a small business might benefit from setting expenditure budgets for its business travel. (5)

3 Outline two problems a business might have in setting a travel budget. (6)

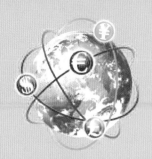

MEASURING AND INCREASING PROFIT

18.1 Measuring performance

The performance of organisations may be measured in many ways, such as:

- sales or sales growth
- market share
- the job satisfaction of its employees
- its track record on environmental issues
- customer satisfaction.

The most appropriate measure(s) will depend on the nature of the organisation; a hospital may look at the number of successful operations, a university may measure the number and class of the degrees of its students, and a sports club may measure the number of matches played and won. However, one of the most common measures of success for organisations is net profit.

Net profit measures the profit left after all the operating costs of the business have been deducted. These costs may include the costs of producing and marketing the products, as well as fixed costs (such as rent). Net profit is the lifeblood of the organisation, because unless the business makes a profit, it cannot finance growth. In a growing economy, with new opportunities arising all the time, a business that cannot grow is condemned to a slow death. The perfect example of this is Woolworths. In its 2007 financial year it made a net profit that was less than 1% of its sales. In other words, of every £1 taken through a Woolworths till, less than 1p was the company's net profit. Can Woolworths survive with such meagre rewards?

Net profit and net profit margin

The net profit of a business is an absolute number that is measured in value terms. For example, a business might earn a net profit of £10,000. Is this a good level of profit or not? To find out, the profit is measured in relation to the total value of sales. This is known as the net profit margin:

$$\text{Net profit margin} = \frac{\text{net profit} \times 100}{\text{sales}}$$

For example, if the net profit is £10,000 and the sales are £50,000 the net profit margin is:

$$\frac{£10,000}{£50,000} \times 100 = 20\%$$

This means that 20% of the firm's revenue is actually profit (i.e. of every £1 of sales, 20p is net profit). Notice that the net profit margin is a percentage.

A-grade application

In 2007 Cadbury Schweppes warned its investors not to expect any improvement in profit margins in the immediate future. At the time, profit margins were around 10%. Investment in the company had increased costs (especially the launch of Trident chewing gum) and, in addition to this, dairy prices had increased. The company later announced the closure of a UK factory and the loss of 700 jobs. Production was to be switched to Poland, where production was cheaper.

What is a good net profit margin?

The typical net profit margin in an industry will vary from one sector to another. The food retail market, for example, is a very competitive market and the profit per sale (i.e. the profit margin) is likely to be quite low (e.g. 5%). However, provided you can sell a high volume of items your overall net profits can still be high. You may make relatively little profit per can of beans, but provided you sell a lot of beans your overall profits may still be high.

In the case of luxury items such as Ted Baker clothes or Rolex watches the profit margin is likely to be much higher. However, although the profit per sale is relatively high this does not automatically mean the profits are high – that depends on how many items you sell.

18.3 The return on capital

Profitability measures profit in relation to some other variable. As we have seen, the net profit margin measures profit in relation to sales. We might also want to measure the net profit in relation to the amount invested in a project. The money invested is often called 'capital'.

If, for example, a business invests £20,000 into a project and this generates a profit of £5000 then the return on the capital invested (known as **return on capital**) is 25%:

$$\text{Return on capital} = \frac{\text{net profit} \times 100}{\text{capital invested}} =$$

$$\frac{£5000 \times 100}{£20,000} = 25\%$$

The return on capital is an important indicator of the success of a project or business. Imagine a business proposal is expected to earn a return on capital of 25% – this is very good compared to the return you are likely to get if you invest your money into a bank. The opportunity cost (i.e. the return you could get elsewhere) is probably lower than 25%, which makes the project attractive.

If, however, you expected to invest £20,000 and generate profits of only £500:

$$\text{Return on capital} = \frac{\text{net profit} \times 100}{\text{capital invested}}$$

$$\frac{£500 \times 100}{£20,000} = 2.5\%$$

In this case, the return on capital is only 2.5% and you would probably expect to earn more if you saved your money in a bank instead.

18.4 Return on capital and the net profit margin

Obviously the return on capital is linked to the net profit margin. The overall returns will depend on how many units are sold and on the profit per sale (the net profit margin).

If the firm can sell the same amount of products but with a higher profit margin the overall return on capital will increase. Alternatively, if the net profit margin remains the same but more units are sold this will also boost the overall return on capital.

18.5 Methods of improving profits

To increase profits a business must:

1 increase revenue

2 decrease costs

3 do a combination of 1 and 2.

To increase revenue a business may want to consider its marketing mix. Changes to the product may mean that it becomes more appealing to customers. Better distribution may make it more available. Changes to promotion may make customers more aware of its benefits. However, the business needs to be careful that rising costs do not swallow up the rise in sales revenues.

To reduce costs a business may examine many of the functional areas (such as marketing, operations, people and finance):

● Could the firm continue with fewer staff?

● Could money be saved by switching suppliers?

● Do the firm's sales really benefit from sponsoring the opera?

● Are there ways of reducing wastage?

Essentially, a business should look for ways of making the product more efficiently (e.g. with better technology) by using fewer inputs or paying less for the inputs being used. However, a business must be careful that when it reduces costs, the quality of service is not reduced. After all, this might lead to a fall in sales and revenue. Cutting staff in your coffee shop may cut costs but if long queues form it may also reduce the number of customers and your income. Managers must weigh up the consequences of any decision to reduce costs.

18.6 Methods of increasing profit margins

To increase net profits in relation to sales a business could do the following.

● *Increase its price:* this would boost the profit per sale, but the danger is that the sales overall may fall so much that the overall profits of the business are reduced. (Notice the important difference again between the net profit margin and the overall level of profits – you could make a high level of profit on one can of beans relative to its price but if you only sell one can your total profits are not that impressive!). The impact of any price increase will depend on the price elasticity of demand. Price elasticity is covered in Chapter 29. It is a way of measuring how sharply demand changes when the price of a product is changed. The more price elastic demand is, the greater the fall in demand will be, and the less likely it is that a firm will want to put up its prices. On the other hand, a price-elastic demand may mean it is worth cutting price. Although less profit may be made per item (there is a lower profit margin) the overall profits may increase due to the boost in sales.

● *Cut costs:* if this can be done without damaging the quality in any significant way then this clearly makes sense. Better bargaining to get the supply prices down, or better ways of producing may lead to high profits per sale. However, as we saw above, the business needs to be careful that reducing costs does not lead to a deterioration of the service or quality of the product, as this may damage sales.

A-grade application
Prudential

In 2007 the Prudential insurance company announced a 15% profit increase at the same time as announcing plans to cut its costs. The company also increased its dividend at the same time by 5%.

Prudential said that the targets would be achieved through a combination of internal cost-cutting and an expansion of its offshore and outsourcing operations, with around 3000 customer service and other jobs in the UK expected to be affected by the plans. The announcement of job cuts at the same time as higher profits highlights the pressure on managers to keep increasing profit.

18.7 Profits and the functions of business

As we can see, the profits and the profitability of a business depend on all the different functions of the business. The operations management may determine how much can be produced and sold. Human resources management may affect how many people need to be employed and the costs of staff. Marketing decisions will affect the sales and revenue earned. To boost profits you may consider each and every one of these functions to look for ways of increasing revenue and/or cutting costs.

Table 18.1 Net profit margins from selected 2007 company accounts

	Net profit	**Sales**	**% net profit margin**
Tesco	£2653 million	£46611 million	5.7%
Sainsbury's	£477 million	£17151 million	2.8%
Woolworths	£16 million	£2740 million	0.58%
Ted Baker*	£7 million	£66 million	10.6%

* Half-year only

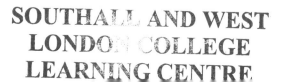

A-grade application

Jessops

In 2007 the photographic retailer Jessops warned that it would miss its profit targets after a shortage of digital cameras over Christmas. Production problems at Canon and Nikon (which account for around 80% of the market) created a worldwide shortage and meant Jessops could not meet demand. In this case it was not the firm's own problems but those of its suppliers that caused the profit shortfall.

Issues For Analysis

Many organisations survive without profit, but largely because of government or private charity. This unit is largely about business organisations that need profit to survive and, especially, to grow. If a business is as unprofitable as Woolworths it is hard to understand how it survives.

In exams there are various questions to ask yourself about a loss-making firm:

● What has caused the losses: **internal reasons** or external ones? Internal ones would include poor decision making.

● What may be the downsides to any new approach? Will staff cutbacks cost more from damaged morale than they provide from lower wage costs?

● Finally, what is the timescale of the decision making? Is the business forced to take action immediately to boost profit, or can it wait to see if today's poor circumstances ease off.

18.8 Measuring and increasing profit

A difficulty with questions about poor profits is that many suggestions made in exams are too obvious. As shown in Table 18.1, Sainsbury's has only half the profit margin of Tesco. But is it worth pointing out to Sainsbury's that it could look for bulk-buying discounts on its supplies? Of course not. A good exam answer will show the maturity to see that Sainsbury's managers will already be doing all they can to tackle the problem.

Key terms

Internal reasons: these come within the control of the management (e.g. the quality of the materials used in production).
Return on capital: profit as a percentage of the capital a firm invests in a project.

Figure 18.1 Long queues may turn away customers

18.9 Workbook

Exercises

A. Revision questions

(30 marks; 30 minutes)

1 What is meant by 'net profit'? (2)

2 What is meant by 'revenue'? (2)

3 Does an increase in price necessarily increase revenue? (3)

4 How can revenue increase without an increase in cash inflows? (3)

5 Is profitability measured in pounds or percentages? (1)

6 What is the equation for the net profit margin? (2)

7 How can the profit margin increase and yet the return on capital fall? (4)

8 Explain two ways of increasing profits. (6)

9 Why might cutting costs end up reducing profits? (3)

10 In what ways do the different functions of a business affect its profits? (4)

B. Revision exercises

B1 Data response

SOFA-SOGOOD Ltd is a retailer of sofas. It had been experiencing a very slow summer. Revenues had been falling but costs had been pushed up by pay increases, higher rent costs and higher interest payments on debts. As a result, net profits had fallen by 20% on last year. Renis, the managing director, was very disappointed that revenue had fallen because he had cut prices by 5% and had expected customer numbers to increase sharply. Once it became clear that this discounting policy was not working, he imposed a pay freeze on everyone in the company and a policy of non-recruitment. If any staff member left, s/he would not be replaced.

Questions

(30 marks; 30 minutes)

1 Distinguish between revenue, costs and net profit. (3)

2 Explain why a fall in price might not have led to an increase in revenue. (5)

3 Apart from the methods mentioned in the text, analyse two other actions SOFA-SOGOOD might take to improve its profitability. (8)

4 Discuss the advantages and disadvantages to the business of the staffing cost-saving actions taken by Renis. (14)

B2 Data response

Farmoor College

Farmoor College is a private sixth form based in London that charges students to study for their A-levels. The fees are £15,000 a year. The college is proud of its small classes (average size five students) and its excellent examination results. This year it has 200 students studying with it, which is about its present capacity in terms of the number of classrooms available. The college has a core of key staff but employs other teachers and support staff depending on the levels of demand in any year. The college's net profit margin is 12% and the capital invested in the business is £15 million.

Questions

(40 marks; 40 minutes)

1 Calculate the likely net profits for the college this year. (3)

2 Calculate the college's likely return on capital this year. Comment on your findings. (4)

3 Outline two costs the college is likely to have. (4)

4 Explain one factor that might cause a change in demand for the college. (4)

5 Explain how the net profit of the college might be used. (5)

6 Analyse how you might measure the performance of the college apart from looking at its financial results. (8)

7 Discuss the ways in which the college might increase its profits. (12)

C. Essay questions

(40 marks each)

1 Discuss how best to improve profitability at one of the following businesses:
— Newcastle United F.C.
— Tesco Plc
— HMV Stores

2 Your family opened a Mercedes car showroom last June. You employ 15 staff and although sales have risen to £200,000 a month, the business is barely profitable. Discuss whether the business should focus on boosting revenue or cutting costs in order to boost profit.

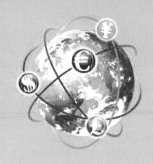

CASH FLOW VS PROFIT

19.1 Introduction

A year ago, a busy bar in Wimbledon closed down. Regulars were surprised – shocked even – that such a successful business had failed. The business *was* operating profitably, but the owners had become too excited by their success. Their investment into two new bars elsewhere in London had drained too much cash from the business, and the bank had panicked over the mounting debts. It forced the business to close. A profitable business had run out of cash.

To understand how cash differs from profit, the key is to master profit. On the face of it, profit is easy: total revenue *minus* total costs. Common sense tells you that revenue = money in and costs = money out. Unfortunately that's far too much of a simplification.

19.2 Distinguishing revenue from cash inflow

Revenue is *not* the same as money in. Revenue is the value of sales made over a specified period: a day, a month or a year. For example, the takings at a clothing store last Saturday = £450 of cash sales, £2450 on credit cards and £600 on store cards (i.e. £3500 in total) (see Figure 19.1). Note that the cash inflow for the day is just £450 (i.e. that revenue is not the same as 'cash in').

Whereas revenue comes from just one source (customers), cash inflow can come from many sources. It is not limited to trading. Selling an old warehouse for £600,000 does not generate revenue, but it does bring in cash. Similarly, taking out a bank loan could not be classed as revenue, but it does put cash into your bank current account.

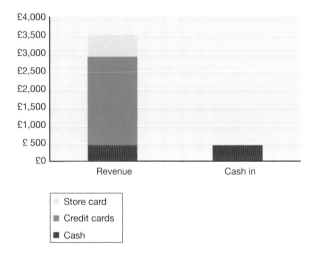

Figure 19.1 Saturday takings at the clothing outlet

Table 19.1 Differences between cash inflows and revenue

Financial item	Cash inflow	Revenue
Cash sales made to customers	✓	✓
Credit sales made to customers	✗	✓
Capital raised from share sales	✓	✗
Charge rent on flat upstairs	✓	✓
Take out a £20,000 bank loan	✓	✗
Carry out a sale and leaseback	✓	✗

So, cash inflows *can* be part of the revenue, but they do not have to be. Therefore cash and revenue are not the same.

19.3 Distinguishing costs from cash outflow

The same distinction applies to costs and cash outflows. There are many reasons why a firm might pay out cash. Paying the business costs is only one of them. For example, the firm may pay out **dividends** to its shareholders, or it may repay a bank loan, or it may buy a piece of land as an investment.

In the case of the Wimbledon bar mentioned above, the £200,000 annual profit gave the owners the confidence to buy leases on two new premises. They put together a business plan for expansion and received a £90,000 bank loan plus an £80,000 overdraft facility from a high-street bank. They then hired architects and builders to turn the premises into attractive bars. Unfortunately, building hitches added to costs while delaying the opening times. The first of the new bars opened without any marketing support (there was no spare cash) and with the second of the bars still draining the business of cash, the bank demanded to have its overdraft repaid. As there was no way to repay the overdraft, the business went into liquidation.

So, a profitable business may run out of cash, simply because it expands too ambitiously, perhaps unluckily. There are other reasons, outlined below, why a profitable business might run into **negative cash flow**.

Seasonal factors

A firm that is generating sufficient revenue to cover its costs over a 12-month period might still hit short-term cash flow problems. This is a particularly difficult problem for new small firms. A new bicycle shop opens in the spring and may enjoy an excellent first six months' trading. The owners may get quite excited at the good profit level, buy a new van and have a much-needed holiday. They would have expected the winter half-year to be pretty poor for bike sales, but may be shocked by the level of decline. By February they may run out of cash and be unable to pay their staff. If only they had known the pattern of demand the owners could have saved money in the first half of the year; but a fundamentally profitable business may close down due to a cash flow crisis.

Problems with credit periods

If a firm gives credit periods to its customers, there is risk from a serious delay to a credit payment. For example, a builder who has put a great deal of money into renovating a large house finds that the client keeps delaying the final payment. The more serious the builder's cash flow problems become, the stronger the position of the client. So a profitable business may be thrown into a cash crisis that could threaten its survival.

Table 19.2 *Differences between cash outflows and costs*

Financial item	Cash outflow	Costs
Cash payments to suppliers	✓	✓
Purchases from suppliers on credit	✗	✓
Paying out wages	✓	✓
Repayment of bank loans	✓	✗
Tax bill received but not yet paid	✗	✓
Buying freehold property*	✓	✗
Paying the electricity bill	✓	✓

* Because a £500,000 property is worth £500,000, an accountant would not treat it as a cost

19.4 Cash-rich firms can be unprofitable

It is also possible for a cash-rich business to be unprofitable. This has given rise to several business scandals in the past. A classic situation is as follows. A new insurance company is started up, and builds up a customer base through extensive TV advertising. New customers pay in their insurance premiums, which helps to pay for the advertising and a rapid build-up of staff. As extra customers join, the business finds itself awash with cash. In fact, because there are few, if any, insurance pay-outs yet, the business may be barely profitable (i.e. it may be operating at no more than its true break-even point). Yet because the cash inflows arrive before the cash outflows, the business is cash-rich. An honest and well-run business will be aware of this, and make sure to save the cash rather than spend it.

Table 19.3 Cash flow forecast for new beauty salon *

	1	2	3	4	5	6	7	8
Cash at start	0	(20)	(40)	(60)	(64)	(64)	(59)	(51)
Cash in	0	0	0	10	15	20	25	25
Cash out	20	20	20	14	15	15	17	17
Net cash	(20)	(20)	(20)	(4)	(0)	5	8	8
Cumulative cash**	(20)	(40)	(60)	(64)	(64)	(59)	(51)	(43)

* All figures in £000s
** This is the firm's bank balance at the end of each month

There have been many cases, though, where the proprietors have paid out large sums (to themselves, perhaps) and later been unable to pay out to the policy holders. The legal protection provided by limited liability can ensure that the owners enjoy pay-outs from 'profits' that prove an illusion.

19.5 What does all this imply for managers?

The key is to appreciate that cash flow and profit are different aspects of the same thing. Cash flow and profit are linked, but they are not the same. Good financial planning requires an estimate of the likely profitability of a course of action. It then requires a careful forecast of the flows of cash in and out of the business. Profitability shows the long-term value of a financial decision; cash flow shows the short-term impact of that decision on the firm's bank balance.

Cash vs profit: an example

Trish decides to open a beauty salon. She estimates that annual fixed overheads will be £120,000 and annual revenues £300,000, offset by variable costs at 20% of revenue (i.e. £60,000). In other words, annual profit should be: £300,000 − (£160,000 + £60,000) = £80,000.

The start-up costs of opening the salon are expected to be £60,000, so the business will be profitable from year one.

However, there are some important cash flow issues to consider: first, how long will it take before the salon opens its doors (and cash starts flowing in); second, will the business *really* start at a revenue level equivalent to £300,000 per year (£25,000 per month), or will it take many months before sales rise to a satisfactory level?

Table 19.3 shows the cash flow position of the business, assuming that it takes three months to prepare the beauty salon (building work, decoration, and so on) and that it will take four months before regular custom has built up fully. The forecast is for the first eight months.

As you can see, even after eight months the business still has a serious cash flow problem. If the figures remain the same, it will be another six months before cumulative cash flow (the bank account) becomes positive. So the 'profitable' first year (and any accountant would confirm that the year is profitable) ends in the red.

The reason for this is simple: the cash investment to set up the business all takes place at the start, before the salon can generate a penny of cash inflow. The cash flow problem occurs because the cash outflow happens before the cash inflows arrive. Therefore the bank must be kept informed so that it is willing to keep the business afloat. Unless the overdraft requirements are clear, and predicted, the bank manager may lose faith and demand all loans to be repaid.

Issues For Analysis

● A key difference between cash flow and profit is *time*. Starting a vineyard may prove hugely profitable – eventually. But experts warn that it takes ten years to recover the initial costs of starting up (i.e. cash flow will be negative for ten years). Cash flow measures today's money in and money out; profit is a more long-term calculation.

● The other key factor is the type of business. Most new business start-ups are vulnerable to cash flow problems, but which are in the toughest position? It is hardest by far for manufacturers, especially if they have an innovative new product. They have to spend months, perhaps years, developing the product, then building, equipping and staffing a factory. Only then (after all that cash outflow) can they start producing a product and start to sell it into retailers. Even when they have made a sale and delivered the goods, many retailers take 60 days to pay their bills. The impact on cash flow is awful, even for a product that later proves to be highly profitable.

19.6 Cash flow vs profit
an evaluation

Especially for small firms, every significant decision needs to be assessed in terms of cash flow as well as profit. The cash flow forecast predicts the impact on the bank balance, and may show the need for extra overdraft facilities to be negotiated. Or, if the firm's cash position is already weak, it may be safer to postpone the proposal.

Yet cash flow is no substitute for calculating profit. A cash-rich business idea (such as insurance) may inevitably lead to **insolvency** if the business is not profitable. Getting cash inflows at the start seems great, but will turn into a nightmare if the cash outflows eventually start flooding in.

Remember, then, that cash flow and profit are not the same. Cash flow measures the short term, and profit shows the longer-term financial result of a decision. Clever managers look at both before they proceed.

Key terms

Dividends: annual payments to shareholders from the profits made by the company; the equivalent of the interest paid to those who lend money.
Insolvency: inability to pay the bills, forcing closure.
Negative cash flow: when cash outflows outweigh cash inflows.
Sale and leaseback: selling the freehold to a piece of property then simultaneously leasing it back, perhaps for a period of 20 years. The owner gives up tomorrow's valuable asset in exchange for cash today.

Exercises

A. Revision questions

(25 marks; 25 minutes)

1 Explain in your own words why cash inflow is not the same thing as revenue. (3)

2 Look again at Table 19.1. Explain why taking out a £20,000 bank loan generates cash inflow but not revenue. (3)

3 Give two reasons why a profitable business might run out of cash when it expands too rapidly. (2)

4 Look again at Table 19.2. Explain why 'purchases from suppliers on credit' is treated as a cost, yet not as a cash outflow. (3)

5 Identify and briefly explain whether each of the following business start-ups would be cash-rich or cash-poor in the early years of the business:
(a) a pension fund, in which people save money in return for later pay-outs (2)
(b) building a hotel (2)
(c) starting a vineyard (grapes only pickable after three to five years). (2)

6 Look again at Table 19.3. Use it and the accompanying text to explain why the cash flow of the beauty salon differs from its profit. (4)

7 Why is it important for a small business to look both at profit and cash flow? (4)

B. Revision exercises

B1 Data response

On 23 August 2007 the former boss of a £1 billion insurance company broke down in tears at Southwark Crown Court. Michael Bright led the stock market flotation of Independent Insurance in 1986. Rapidly expanding the business, the company's market value soared to £1 billion in 2000. It had 500,000 personal policy holders and 40,000 business customers. A year later the business was bust, after underestimating the cost of claims and overseas expansion. About 1000 employees were out of work. Serious Fraud Office investigators were called in to examine the collapse. It was six years, though, before the case against three leading executives was brought to trial.

Source: *Guardian*, 24 August 2007

Questions

(15 marks; 20 minutes)

1 Outline three groups of people (stakeholders) who would have lost out in the collapse of Independent Insurance. (6)

2 Explain how a fast-growing insurance business could be cash-rich, yet unprofitable. (9)

B2 Data response

Investment dragon Peter Jones on cash and profit

Managing your cash in a focused manner is fundamental to survival, let alone success. Businesses are more likely to fail because they run out of cash – not because they're unable to generate a profit. You can have a lorryload of orders with the promise of untold profits in the pipeline, but if you don't have the cash to make and sell your products in the first place, and you are unable to pay your immediate bills, your business will fold.

Cash flow is a common hurdle for small and start-up enterprises. For that reason, it is important to *strengthen cash flow* from the outset.

● *Monitor profit* and *avoid over-commitment*. One common mistake entrepreneurs make is that they see a 'run rate' of business and immediately start to incur costs. They'll rent an office, take on new lease commitments, buy a new car. These monthly payments can result in losing sight of the real cash that's generated through the business.

● *Grow the business organically and keep costs down*, especially if you can't access bank finance. Focus on keeping costs to a bare minimum. Forget the office; work from home.

Forget the car; use public transport. Grow the business, grow a pot of cash and then invest in the business. Using that money to reinvest is vital.

● *Reinvest profits wisely*

– Understand what your start-up and ongoing costs are. Be realistic. It is better to overestimate expenditure and time and underestimate revenue than fall short of revenue and overspend.

– Evaluate and monitor profit continually.

– Reinvest your profit. That way, you'll scale the business far quicker than if you use the profit to rent another office building or buy a car. It's how you spend the profit that's important. Entrepreneurs always spend profit on the business. Successful entrepreneurs invest that profit on the right areas to maximise growth and enhance existing offerings.

Source: www.peterjones.tv

Questions
(20 marks; 25 minutes)

1 Explain why, in the first paragraph, Peter Jones seems to be suggesting that cash flow is more important than profit for a small business. (4)

2 By 'run rate' Peter Jones means the revenue generated by the business once it is up and running. Why does he think an entrepreneur should wait before spending at this rate? (5)

3 Growing 'organically' means from within (i.e. not rushing to buy up other businesses). Organic growth is usually at a slow enough pace to cope with cash flow pressures. Examine why rapid growth can cause big cash flow problems. (6)

4 Explain why it's 'better to overestimate expenditure and time and underestimate revenue'. (5)

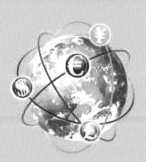
MANAGING WORKING CAPITAL

DEFINITION

Working capital is the finance available for the day-to-day running of the business.

20.1 What is working capital?

All businesses need money; it is required for the purchase of machinery and equipment. This expenditure on fixed assets is known as capital expenditure. The business also needs money to buy materials or stock and to pay wages and the day-to-day bills such as electricity and telephone bills. This money is known as working capital.

Managing working capital is about ensuring that the cash available is sufficient to meet the cash requirements at any one time. If the bills cannot be paid on time there are serious consequences. In the worst situation the business may fail. Insufficient working capital is the commonest cause of business failure. Managing working capital is therefore a vital business activity.

20.2 The working capital cycle

Managing working capital is a continuous process. When a business starts up it takes time to generate income. Money to pay for stock and the running costs will need to be found from the initial capital invested in the business. As the business cycle gets going, income from customers will be available to pay for expenditure. The firm needs to ensure that there is always sufficient cash to meet daily requirements. If the business is expanding or takes on a special order, extra care needs to be taken. Sufficient funds are needed to pay for the additional expenditure until the revenue arrives. This continuous process is shown in Figure 20.1, which also shows why working capital is sometimes referred to as circulating capital.

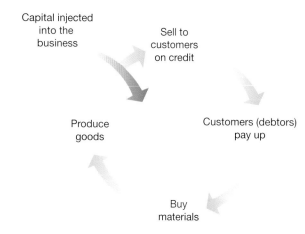

Figure 20.1 The working capital cycle

As can be seen from Figure 20.1, managing working capital is about two things:

1 ensuring the business has enough finance to meet its needs

2 keeping cash moving rapidly through the cycle, so there's enough to meet future orders.

Each business will have its own distinct cycle. Businesses will also be subject to unexpected events and need to be able to cope with these. Therefore it is helpful to have a generous overdraft limit, which can be drawn upon when needed.

Examples of unexpected events include:

● a major customer gets into financial difficulties and is therefore unable to pay its bills on time

● the cost of materials shoots ahead, as with the doubling in the price of rice in January to April 2008.

20.3 Problems caused by insufficient working capital

With suppliers

A firm with too little working capital will struggle to pay its bills on time. It has no spare cash. It may resort to delaying payments. It may need to borrow more money. Delaying payment means that suppliers are not paid on time. They may reduce the **credit period** or refuse credit for a future order.

With banks

If the business is resorting to borrowing it will have the additional cost of interest charges. If the bank is concerned about the financial situation it may impose higher charges. The business will find it more difficult to get loans. Any lender will want to be assured that the company is managing its working capital effectively.

Opportunities may be missed

The business may not be able to buy supplies in bulk. This removes the advantage of lower bulk buying prices. Even more importantly, it may have to refuse a large order because it cannot finance the extra working capital requirement.

In the longer term, shortage of cash means that no funds are available for development. The business will not be able to grow. In extreme cases creditors may ask for the business to be declared insolvent. A sole trader or partnership will be declared bankrupt. Most creditors will take this action only if they feel that there is little hope of being paid. They will look at the future prospects and past performance of the business.

20.4 How much working capital do businesses need?

The working capital requirement varies from business to business. It depends on the following factors.

The length of the business process

There are huge variations in the length of the **working capital cycle** for different businesses. A fruit stall market trader buys supplies for cash from a wholesaler in the morning and sells everything (for cash) by late afternoon; the cycle takes less than a day. By contrast, a small construction firm building four houses may take a year between starting the project and having cash paid by a new home owner.

The amount of stock the firm holds

Self-evidently, 'stock' is the fundamental part of every clothes shop and every supermarket; without stocked shelves, there would be no business. So every shop needs to have a great deal of working capital invested in stock. Nevertheless, some shops carry more stock than they need, often due to poor buying (too many size 16 dresses, or too much ice cream during the winter). For these shops, incompetence is leading them to tie up more money in working capital than is necessary.

The credit given to customers

Most shops get paid very promptly by their customers. Many pay in cash and even credit card payments come through within three or four days (from the credit card companies). By contrast, manufacturers usually have to give long credit periods of perhaps 60 days. This means that they have to wait for 60 days, and even then may find they have to chase payment if a customer has not paid on time. The longer the credit period you give to customers, the more working capital your business will need. As capital is always costly (and has a high opportunity cost), this is damaging to the firm's profitability.

The credit given for purchases of materials or stock

Most businesses obtain credit for their purchases. The length of time allowed before payment depends on:

- how established the firm is – an established firm can negotiate longer credit than a new firm
- its credit record – a firm with a good record of paying can negotiate longer credit
- the size of the order – larger orders may get longer credit
- regular orders – regular customers expect longer credit than occasional customers.

The business needs to take into account both the timing and the amounts involved when working out its working capital requirements. It also needs to include an allowance for uncertainty. An extra 10% on top of the expected cash requirement would be the very minimum required. For a new small firm such as a new restaurant, though, a bigger safety net can be wise. It can take months for word to spread sufficiently to push a business above its break-even point.

Figure 20.2 shows the need for **contingency finance** – in other words, financial back-up to allow for the unexpected. June 2007 was the wettest in 100 years, with Hull the worst-hit town; more than 10,000 homes had to be evacuated. Think about the double hit that would have been inflicted on small businesses in the flooded areas. Completely unpredictably they could have faced sales revenue down by, perhaps, 30% as residents moved away to temporary accommodation. For a new business with little cash in the bank, the position would have threatened its survival. Figure 20.2 shows the role of contingency finance such as an agreed overdraft facility.

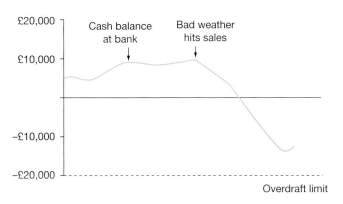

Figure 20.2 The need for contingency finance

Can a business have too much working capital?

In America and Britain it is thought important that a business should not have too much working capital. The term 'too much' implies that the capital would be wasted. In some ways this is true. There is no point in having too much capital tied up in stock or giving too much credit to customers. There is a problem, though, in defining what 'too much' actually means.

Japanese and German firms have always tended to adopt a very cautious approach to their finances. In the period 2003–07, City of London analysts questioned why firms such as Toyota had $billions of cash lying idle in their accounts. Why so much working capital? In fact, this level of caution proves hugely helpful when uncertainty strikes, as in early 2008, when the US economy looked to be heading for recession.

It should always be remembered that, whereas you can have too much stock or too many debtors, you can never have too much cash!

A-grade application
General Motors

For 80 years, General Motors has been the world's biggest car manufacturer. In 2008 that is due to change: the Japanese company Toyota will take over. In 2003 a London newspaper poked fun at the cautious finances of Japanese firms such as Toyota. It suggested that they 'had no idea how to look after their shareholders'. The complaint was that Toyota held nearly £8000 million of cash in its accounts. The newspaper journalist saw the money as a wasted asset; Toyota saw it as a form of contingency finance.

In February 2008 General Motors announced a record £19 billion loss (that's more than 15 times the annual revenues of Real Madrid, Manchester United, Barcelona, Chelsea and Arsenal Football Clubs put together!). At the same time Toyota announced profits of £12 billion for the 12 months of 2007. Toyota's cash kitty had enabled the business to invest in successful new cars such as the hybrid Prius. You can never have too much cash!

How should a business manage its working capital?

Intelligent working capital management is centred on the following aspects.

● *Controlling the cash you use:* for example, minimising stock levels, keeping customer credit as low as possible (without pushing customers away) and trying to get as much credit from suppliers as you can. It is also important to get goods to the market in the shortest possible time. The sooner goods reach the customer the sooner payment is received. Production and distribution should be as efficient as possible.

● *Minimising spending on fixed assets:* this keeps cash in the business. The business must balance its need for cash and its need for fixed assets. A compromise is to lease rather than buy equipment. This increases expenses but conserves capital.

● *Planning ahead by estimating the amount of cash needed next month and beyond:* in this way cash shortfalls can be anticipated and planned for. If the next two months look tricky, perhaps that purchase of the boss's new BMW should be delayed for a while.

● *Thinking carefully about possible long-term solutions to short-term working capital issues:* this is what Michael Dell did when he set up his hugely successful Dell Computers (see the A-grade application).

A-grade application
Dell Computers

Dell, the computer manufacturer, has an enviable record of success. One factor in this success is careful management of stock. Dell produces computers to the customer specification after the order has been placed. At the assembly plant it has stocks of component parts; it does not keep stocks of finished machines. After the order is received the computer is constructed. It is then shipped to a distribution centre. Here it meets up with its various peripherals. These items – such as monitors and keyboards – are not held in stock but are delivered to the distribution centres directly from the suppliers.

Minimising its investment in working capital in this way helped Dell to finance its incredible growth between 1990 and 2005. It has also helped the company avoid the problems of holding stocks of computers when a change in technology slashes the value of yesterday's model.

Issues For Analysis

To analyse working capital management in a business case study or data response question it is important to remember:

● that, for small firms especially, the working capital cycle is the equivalent of blood circulating around the body – if the cash dries up, the firm dies

● the problems caused by too little or too much working capital.

It would be nice if there was a perfect, 'right' level of working capital, but there isn't – so the key issue is: can the firm fund the short-term actions it would like to take? Is it safely in a position to pay its bills? And is its working capital position improving or worsening?

20.7 Management of working capital
an evaluation

Managing working capital is very important for every business. As in many other areas of business it is about getting the balance right. Too much may be wasteful – too little can be disastrous. Businesses need to consider working capital requirements right from the outset. Most new businesses underestimate their working capital needs. Typically, firms allow only £20 of working capital for every £100 of fixed capital (assets). Accountants usually advise a £50:£50 ratio.

Managing working capital is not just about managing cash flow. The timing and amounts of cash flow are important, but working capital management goes beyond that. It is about managing the whole business. In this respect it is an integrated activity. It involves each aspect of the company. Efficient production keeps costs to a minimum and turns raw inputs into finished goods in the shortest possible time. Effective management of stock can have considerable impact on working capital requirements. Effective marketing ensures that the goods are sold and that demand is correctly estimated. This avoids wasted production. Cash then flows in from sales. Efficient distribution gets the goods to the customer quickly. The accounting department can help to control costs. Effective credit control improves cash flow. Each of these can reduce the need for cash and or ensure that cash is available to the business.

Key terms

Contingency finance: planning how to cope if there are extra, unexpected financial requirements.
Credit period: the length of time allowed for payment.
Working capital cycle: how long it takes for a complete cycle from cash out (buying stock) to cash back in from a customer payment. It might be one day (e.g. for a fruit and veg stall) or one year (e.g. a house builder).

Exercises

A. Revision questions

(40 marks; 40 minutes)

1 What is working capital? (3)

2 What is capital expenditure? (3)

3 What is working capital used for? Give two examples. (5)

4 What problems might arise if a firm is operating with very low working capital? (4)

5 Why might a business be unable to get a loan or overdraft if it has working capital difficulties? (4)

6 On 1 February, JG Co received an order for £20,000 worth of office furniture. Between 15 February and 20 March the company spent £11,000 on materials and labour. Between 20 March and 31 March a further £4000 was contributed to fixed costs such as quality control. The finished order was delivered on 1 April, together with an invoice requiring payment in 60 days. On 1 June, the payment of £20,000 was received. How long is JG Co's working capital cycle? (3)

7 Explain two factors that influence the amount of working capital required by a firm. (4)

8 Outline three ways in which a business can improve its working capital situation. (6)

9 How does better stock management help a firm to control its working capital requirements? (5)

10 List three ways in which stock levels can be reduced. (3)

B. Revision exercises

B1 Data response

Life and death

Managing cash flow effectively is really a matter of life and death for a new business. Government figures show that small businesses are owed as much as £17 billion from customers at any one time, and that 10,000 UK businesses fail each year because of late payment from customers.

Ironically, one of the reasons for cash-flow problems is that small, growing businesses can find themselves 'overtrading' (i.e. sales may be strong, but the company lacks the cash to buy more stock or pay its bills).

A previous client of mine was worth over £1 million, yet was at the end of its bank overdraft limit simply because one customer was too large for its business. It used all its working capital supplying this one customer! In addition, though the client was paying its own bills immediately, it wasn't being firm about collecting money from its own customers.

To put the situation right, the firm first had to walk away from its large customer and focus on smaller ones, and then actively chase late payments. Chasing invoices is perfectly acceptable, and in fact some businesses will never pay until chased! Finally, the company also negotiated better terms with its own suppliers.

I recommend a number of important cash flow rules:

- make payment terms a central part of the contract, and enforce them
- invoice as soon as possible
- chase invoices the moment they become due
- walk away from bad payers
- do a cash-flow forecast and re-forecast regularly – at least every month
- cash cheques as soon as you receive them.

Source: adapted from an article by Jeff Maplin at www.startups.co.uk

Questions

(20 marks; 25 minutes)

1 Why might late payment from customers be such a serious matter? (3)

2 Explain the difficulties that may arise for a business that uses 'all its working capital supplying' one customer.

3 Outline one advantage and one involved in chasing late pay

4 Sum up what you see a themes that come th cash flow rules'

B2 Data response

Land of Leather

Land of Leather has seen no respite from its post-Christmas sales slump, with trading throughout January proving just as disappointing. The sofa retailer announced this morning that trading was 'unchanged' since 4 January, when it reported that sales were significantly below expectations – a warning that sparked alarm across the furniture sector.

This month is a key time for the company, as it makes a quarter of its sales between Boxing Day and 31 January. Shares in the company fell 6% in early trading, to 60p, and analysts warned investors to be cautious even though the shares have fallen 80% over the last year.

'Land of Leather continues to disappoint,' said Kevin Lapwood of Seymour Pierce. 'Any hopes of a pick-up over the sale period were not realised.'

On 4 January, Land of Leather said that underlying sales over the first nine days of the post-Christmas sales had fallen by a quarter, a decline it blamed partly on the credit crunch. Today it reported that sales during the rest of January were down 15.4% on a year ago, as the slowdown in consumer spending deters people from making 'big ticket' purchases.

Like-for-like sales over the last 26 weeks are also down 16.5%, with total sales 4.2% lower despite an expansion programme that has added around 20 stores in the last 18 months.

Data from Land of Leather published accounts, 29 July 2007

Stock	£15.3 million
Money owed by customers	£8.7 million
Cash	£25.5 million

Guardian, 31 January 2008; Land of ...pany accounts, 2007

(20 marks; 25 minutes)

...lain why the ...pointment is so
(3)

...had £25 million

of cash. How may that cash total have been affected by the situation outlined in the article?
(4)

3 With sales down by between 15 and 25% since last year, what might be the effect on Land of Leather's total stock holdings? (4)

4 Thinking about the difficult position the business faces in January 2008, outline three ways you would recommend of improving Land of Leather's working capital position. (9)

C. Essay questions

(40 marks each)

1 Managing working capital is vital for the future of any business. Discuss.

2 In periods of economic downturn it is even more important to control working capital in the business. Do you agree with this statement?

3 To what extent do you agree with the following statement? 'Managing working capital is not just the business of the finance department, it is the responsibility of everyone in the business'.

EFFECTIVE MARKETING OBJECTIVES AND STRATEGY

DEFINITION

Effective marketing achieves the firm's sales and profit targets by convincing customers to buy the firm's products again and again.

21.1 Marketing objectives

A marketing objective is a marketing target or goal that an organisation hopes to achieve, such as to boost market share from 9% to 12% within two years. Marketing objectives steer the direction of the business. Operating a business without knowing what your objectives are is like driving a car without knowing where you want to go. Some businesses achieve a degree of success despite the fact that they choose not to set marketing objectives, stumbling across a successful business model by accident. But why rely on chance? If firms set marketing objectives the probability of success increases because decision making will be more focused.

Marketing objectives should be compatible with a business's overall company objective; they cannot be set in isolation by the marketing department. Achieving its marketing objectives will help a firm to achieve its company-wide objective. For example, boosting market share from 9% to 12% will help the business achieve its overall objective of growth.

To be effective, marketing objectives should be quantifiable and measurable. Targets should also be set within a time frame. An example of a marketing objective that fits this criterion, which Nestlé might set, could be: 'To achieve a 9% increase in the sales of Kit-Kat by the end of next year.'

Examples of marketing objectives

Increasing sales

A car manufacturer, such as BMW, might set the following marketing objective: 'To increase the number of BMW 3 Series cars sold in China from 50,000 to 70,000 over the next 12 months.' Setting sales volume targets can be particularly important in industries such as car manufacturing because of the high fixed costs

associated with operating in this market. If sales volume can be increased, the high fixed costs of operating will be spread across a greater number of units of output, reducing fixed costs per unit. Lower unit costs will help BMW to widen its profit margins. Higher profit margins will give BMW the opportunity to increase its research and development budgets, increasing the likelihood of success for BMW's next generation of new car models.

Nike has benefited from a slightly different way of looking at sales volume. In 1996, chairman Phil Knight set Nike's sights on being the number one supplier of football boots and kit. At the time, Nike was a minor player in the football sector of the sportswear business compared with adidas. Nike's approach has clearly paid off. In 1994, it generated just $40 million from football; by 2006 Nike set, and then subsequently beat, a sales target for its football division of $1500 million!

To enhance, or reposition, a brand's image

Although some brands stay fresh for generations (Marmite is over 100 years old) others become jaded due to changes in consumer tastes and lifestyles. At this point the firms need to act and take measures to refresh the brand image in order to keep the product relevant to the target market. A clear objective must be set:

- What brand attributes do we want to create?

- What do we want the brand to stand for?

Repositioning occurs when a firm aims to change a brand's image, so that the brand appeals to a new target market. Kellogg's wanted to reposition Cornflakes as sales had been sliding for years. At the time consumers thought that Cornflakes were just one among many breakfast cereals. The company wanted consumers to rethink the brand as being a quick and healthy snack food to be eaten at any time of the day as a meal substitute that would help aid weight loss. In the longer term, repositioning should help to boost sales. When repositioning a brand it is important to have a clear objective: 'Who is our new target market?', 'How old are they?', 'Which social class do they belong to?', 'What is their lifestyle?', and so on.

A-grade application

Marketing objectives in the non-profit sector

Charities such as Oxfam and Save the Children need marketing to keep their brands alive and donations coming in. Typical marketing objectives that a charity might set could include the following.

- *Raise brand awareness:* brand awareness is the percentage of the market that know of your brand (i.e. can recognise it from a list of brand names, or can quote it unaided). Raising brand awareness could be a very important marketing objective for a smaller charity that is yet unknown. If a greater percentage of the general public is aware of a charity's existence, and its activities, donations may increase, enabling the charity to expand its work.
- *Brand loyalty:* brand loyalty exists when consumers repeat-purchase your brand rather than swapping and switching between brands. A charity might set a marketing objective to improve brand loyalty. If existing donors can be persuaded to set up a direct debt to the charity then its cash flow will improve.
- *Corporate image:* a scandal-hit charity might set a marketing objective of trying to improve its reputation in order to protect its income stream from donors.

21.2 Effective marketing strategy

Marketing strategy is the medium- to long-term plan for how to achieve your marketing objectives. The process of thinking it through requires rather more, though, than simply writing down a plan. In his book *Even More Offensive Marketing*, Hugh Davidson says that effective marketing strategy requires POISE (see Table 21.1).

It is easy to see that Nintendo showed all these features in its brilliant development and marketing of the Wii games console. While Sony and Microsoft focused on even better and faster graphics for the core shoot 'em up gamer market, Nintendo led the market towards a huge number of new users. The Wii was a huge risk because it was really innovative, but its huge followers among older people (busily 'brain training'), young children (playing

Table 21.1 POISE

P	Profitable	A proper balance between the firm's need for profit and the customer's need for value
O	Offensive	Get on the attack, leading the market, taking risks, and force competitors to be followers
I	Integrated	The marketing approach must flow through the whole company, from directors to telephonists
S	Strategic	Probing analysis of the market and your competitors leading to a winning strategy
E	Effectively executed	Strong and disciplined teamwork in carrying the strategy through effectively

Source: adapted from H. Davidson (1997) *Even More Offensive Marketing.* Penguin Books

Nintendogs) and young families (using the interactive facility) are all testimony to Nintendo's market leadership. On 24 January 2008, Nintendo announced that its profits had doubled in 2007, thanks to a 75% increase in sales. POISE is clearly profitable.

The most effective marketing strategies are not necessarily the most obvious ones. Unit 25 shows how firms think their strategies through using the marketing mix – carefully combining the four main marketing levers: product, price, promotion and place. Later on in this unit we focus on the underlying issues that must be planned with care, before a strategy can be put into action. These are:

- identifying the target market
- market segmentation
- market orientation
- identifying the right brand image.

21.3 What is effective marketing?

The term 'marketing' is widely misunderstood by people who have not studied business and management. Many people think that 'marketing' is just another interchangeable term for selling, advertising and other forms of promotion (e.g. sponsorship). Some people even think that marketing is about persuading consumers to buy or use a product they do not want. So, if marketing isn't just about designing glitzy advertising, or aggressive high-pressure 'selling', what is it?

Marketing is the business function that aims to identify, influence and then satisfy consumer wants profitably. Effective marketing starts with identifying an opportunity, just as Nintendo did with its DS console. Instead of assuming that all consoles had to target players of shoot 'em up games, Nintendo identified other opportunities among girls (*Nintendogs*) and older people (*Brain Trainer*).

In many small businesses the owner will come into regular contact with customers. This allows the owner to hear first-hand the needs and wants of the target market. In large businesses, formal market research is undertaken because head office managers cannot feel sure that they know what customers think and want. Once consumer wants have been identified, products and services will need to be designed to match consumer preferences. Finally, a launch marketing mix must be decided. This involves decisions such as setting price, choosing an appropriate distribution channel and setting a promotional strategy.

21.4 Why is effective marketing important?

Consumers tend to be quite rational. They will seek out fairly priced products that satisfy their needs. In a competitive market firms stand or fall according to their ability to satisfy the needs of the consumer. Generally, firms that fail will lack customer loyalty and be punished automatically by the market. These firms will lose market share and profit. Firms with products and services that offer genuine consumer benefits will attract revenue and profit.

Consumer tastes do not tend to stay the same for very long. Therefore, a key aspect of effective marketing is the ability to respond, quickly, to any change in consumer tastes. Firms that fail to adapt their business model, at a time when consumer tastes are changing, are normally forced out of business. In recent years retail chains such as KwikSave, Unwins and the Gadget Shop have collapsed.

A-grade application

Fopp

In June 2007 the music retailer Fopp announced that it was closing down all 105 of its UK stores. The management of Fopp had failed to react fast enough to a change in consumer preferences for buying music. In the last five years there has been a growing trend towards purchasing music via internet downloads. Fopp tried to respond by lowering its prices. Unfortunately for Fopp, this tactic failed to generate the revenues required by the company to break even, proving that low prices alone cannot save a business from closure, especially if consumers no longer wish to purchase the product that the business concerned sells.

Figure 21.1 The Fopp logo
The Fopp logo® is a registered trademark of Fopp Entertainment Limited and reproduced here by their kind authorisation

21.5 Key elements in effective marketing strategy

Identifying the target market

When a business creates a new market (as Richard Branson is attempting currently with space tourism) it can aim its product at everyone who can afford the product. Some time later competitors will arrive, and usually focus on one segment of the market. In space tourism, perhaps some firms will focus on thrill-seekers, while others target wealthy, older travellers seeking a super-safe, luxury version of the same thrill.

To succeed at marketing you need to know and understand the customers within your target market:

what do they *really* want from your product? The satisfaction of using/having the product, or the satisfaction of showing it off to friends? What are their interests and lifestyle?

Having a clear idea of the age, sex, personality and lifestyle of the target market enables the business to do the following things.

● *Focus market research by interviewing only those who make up the target market:* this should make the findings far more reliable. If the target market is clearly defined, the firm's market research budget can be spent with greater effect. Quota sampling could be used instead of a wide random sample; only those that meet the specific criteria for the target market will be interviewed, saving the firm time and money.

● *Focus advertising spending on the people most likely to buy the product:* one national TV commercial can cost £500,000; it will reach millions of people, but how many are really in the target market? Men do not need to know that 'Maybe it's Maybelline'. A product targeting young women would be advertised far more cost-effectively in magazines such as *More* or *Look*.

Market segmentation

Most markets are not made up of identikit consumers who all want exactly the same product. In practice, consumer preferences can vary greatly. Firms that market their products effectively in this situation produce a range of products, each targeted at specific market segments.

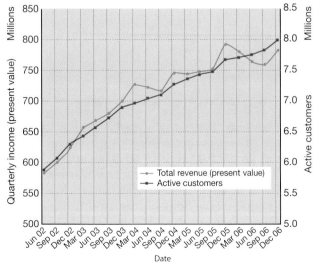

Figure 21.2 BSkyB subscription income

A good example of a company that has used market segmentation to great effect is British Sky Broadcasting (BSkyB); in 2007 the company made a pre-tax profit of close to £800 million.

Before Sky joined the market, the choice of what to watch on TV was limited. The BBC, ITV and Channel 4 tried in vain to produce a range of programmes in an attempt 'to be all things to all men'. Today Sky offers subscribers a choice of over 800 different channels. Among the target segments are kids, sports fans (men), ethnic minorities and fans of different music types – e.g. MTV Base and Performance (classical music). The output of each channel is carefully matched to a particular consumer interest or hobby. Many of these channels attract additional charges, which has helped BSkyB to increase its monthly income (see Figure 21.2).

Market-orientated marketing

Effective marketing is usually based around an approach that is market-orientated rather than production-orientated. In a market-orientated business managers take into account the needs of the consumer before making any decision. They put the customer at the heart of the decision-making process.

Some firms still use a production-orientated approach to marketing. Production orientation leads managers to focus on what the firm does best; internal efficiency comes before consumer preferences. The production-orientated approach to marketing may lead the business towards the following approaches.

● *The hard sell:* employing a large salesforce to go out and convince consumers that they should buy your product. Individualised sales targets, low basic salaries and high rates of commission ensure that sales staff will be 'motivated' to hit their targets, ensuring that the firm sells the products that it has already produced.

● *Cutting costs and prices:* if a production-orientated firm's products are not selling very well, managers tend to respond to this crisis by cutting costs. If costs can be cut, retail prices can also be cut without any loss of profit margin.

On the other hand, there are some weaknesses in market orientation. The death of Rover Cars (once one of the world's biggest car producers) was partly due to this. Rover management seemed convinced that customers could be attracted by marketing gimmicks such as 'special edition' cars or cars with angular steering wheels. A greater focus on the quality and reliability of the product would have been far more effective. The ideal approach is that of a firm such as BMW, which is

Figure 21.3 The clothing retailer Gap

hugely proud of its products, but always makes sure that it understands what its customers really want from them.

A coherent brand image

Firms that market their products successfully use the marketing mix in an integrated manner to create a coherent and attractive brand image that appeals to the target market. Marketing success depends upon getting all four marketing mix decisions right. A good product that is properly priced and promoted will still fail if distribution is poor. Firms use the marketing mix to create an attractive and coherent brand image for each of the products that they sell. Creating the right brand image is important. If the brand image created by the marketing mix appeals to the target market there should be an increased chance that the product will succeed.

The most important thing to remember is that all four elements of the mix must be coordinated. If the marketing mix is not coordinated mixed product messages will be sent out to the target market. This could create confusion, leading to disappointing sales. The key, then, is to think through the brand image that you want to create *before* making any other decisions on your product, how you might want to price it, promote it and distribute it.

Marketing is everyone's job

Many Japanese firms do not have a marketing department. Firms that adopt this approach believe that every employee has a part to play in marketing their business. Marketing should not be the preserve of a specialised marketing department – it is everyone's responsibility. To be successful the management has to create the right culture. Every member of staff must see their role as to better serve the needs and wants of the consumer.

21.6 Short-termist marketing = ineffective marketing

Short-termism describes a business philosophy whereby a firm pursues strategies that might boost profit in the short run, even if these strategies damage the firm's long-run profitability. Some examples of short-termist marketing strategies are given below.

High prices designed to exploit consumer loyalty or a dominant market position

In the short run, firms that operate in a market where there is little competition might be tempted to raise their prices to boost revenues and profits. In recent years both Manchester United and Chelsea have tried to exploit the loyalty of football fans by raising ticket prices. In the short run this can work; however, in the longer term fans may rebel against the price increases and drift away from the game completely. There are signs that this has already started to happen. For example, in September 2007 Chelsea sold fewer than 25,000 tickets for a Champions League game.

A decision to exploit consumers by charging high prices is definitely not a good example of effective marketing. High prices can also encourage new competitors to join the industry.

Short-run sales-driven marketing

Some managers believe that their employees can only be motivated to work hard if they are set targets that are linked to bonuses and other performance-related payments. An over-reliance on targets and performance-related pay can create a ruthless and dishonest culture that can affect a firm's marketing. For example, in 2007 a BBC investigation suggested that staff at a high-street bank were encouraged by their supervisors to lie to the bank's customers in order to hit their personal sales targets. Mis-selling inappropriate financial products to customers can improve a bank's profitability in the short run; however, if the unethical marketing practices are exposed, the resulting wave of bad publicity may hit demand for the firm's products.

Issues For Analysis

- Weak exam answers present marketing as a set of simple tools: the 4Ps. In fact, effective marketing is remarkably difficult, even for the biggest and best companies. An October 2007 survey by *The Grocer* magazine placed Coca-Cola as Britain's most valuable brand. Yet Coca-Cola has been responsible for some dreadful new product flops in this country recently, including Dasani water, Coke Blak (coffee-flavoured Coke!) and Vanilla Coke. Good exam answers acknowledge that marketing is difficult because it is based on judgements about the future: future competition, future consumer tastes and future consumer attitudes.

- Achieving success depends on devising a genuinely new type of product that meets an actual consumer need or desire. Apple's iPhone did exactly that, as did Innocent Drinks when they made smoothies an everyday drink for wealthy young adults.

21.7 An introduction to effective marketing

an evaluation

To judge the likely effectiveness of a firm's marketing plans requires a full understanding of the market. Therefore, just as the marketing manager must research into the market, so you must take care to study the evidence available within the case material. An exam question based on Cadbury might lead to very different answers to the same question based on Mars or Nestlé – even though they all make chocolate. Good judgement comes from good application to the market and to the company.

Exercises

A. Revision questions

(35 marks; 35 minutes)

1 In your own words, explain the meaning of the term 'marketing'? (3)

2 Explain why some firms choose not to carry out market research. (3)

3 Outline what you believe to have been the marketing objective of two of the following businesses:
  (a) Apple when it launched the iPhone in 2007
  (b) L'Oréal in its marketing of hair-care products
  (c) Cadbury in its 2008 relaunch of its Crunchie bar
  (d) Marks & Spencer in its 'This is not just food. It's M&S Food' advertising. (6)

4 Why do you think most firms decide to review their marketing strategy at fairly regular intervals? (3)

5 What is meant by the phrase 'target market'? (2)

6 Outline two reasons why it is important for firms to be able to identify their target market. (4)

7a Distinguish between a production-orientated and a market-orientated approach to marketing. (3)

7b Outline whether a production-orientated or market-orientated approach would be better for *one* of the following companies:
  (a) Manchester United FC
  (b) easyJet
  (c) Topshop. (3)

8 Explain how market segmentation has helped companies such as BSkyB to improve their profitability. (4)

9 What are the marketing advantages of not having a specialised marketing department? (4)

B. Revision exercises

B1 Discussion point

The role of chance/luck

Effective marketing usually comes about as a result of careful planning and market-orientated decision making. However, in some cases, firms stumble across a successful marketing strategy by chance. Morgan cars is a conservatively run private business. The production methods used by the company have hardly changed at all in 40 years. Cars are still made largely by hand. Morgan's best-selling cars are based on designs that have not been changed for decades. In most industries this approach would be a recipe for disaster. Fortunately for Morgan, the cars continue to sell well within a tiny niche comprised of customers that want to purchase a hand-built British sports car, built in the Brooklands tradition. Morgan has not deliberately engineered its niche market position, it has just happened accidentally – it has just been fortunate.

Questions

1 From your reading of the text, is it really true that all Morgan's success is down to luck?

2 What marketing problems might the business face if it attempts to expand?

B2 Case study

Wimbledon Quality Cars

Wimbledon Quality Cars (WQC) sells second-hand cars. The business was set up five years ago when the economy was still booming. The owner of the business, Roger Raymond, believes that most businesses over-complicate their marketing. According to Roger, 'marketing is just a set of tools to sell more products, in my case, cars'. The marketing mix of WQC could be summarised as follows.

● *Price:* according to Roger, the bulk of second-hand car buyers are interested in only one

21.8 Workbook

thing – low prices. Most of the cars sold by WQC are sold for less than £2000 – an important psychological pricing point.

- *Promotion:* Roger spends £300 per week advertising his cars in the south London press. He also employs two salesmen, Andy and John, who are paid a basic wage of £200 per week and a flat rate commission of £250 per car sold.

- *Product:* Roger believes that the bulk of his customers are not fussy about the make or model of car that they buy. 'Most of my punters want a cheap runaround. The majority of them don't know a good car from a death trap. In our market quality always comes second to a low price.' Roger buys most of his cars from car auctions.

- *Place:* WQC has an old, run-down car showroom, just opposite Wimbledon dog track.

Last year WQC enjoyed its most profitable year yet: sales were up 40% on the previous year. Unfortunately, events took a dramatic turn for the worse last month. To Roger's horror WQC was the subject of a TV documentary investigating sharp practice in the second-hand car market. The programme alleged that WQC sold cars that were not roadworthy. The implication was that Roger was happy to put the profits of WQC before his customers' safety. Ex-customers of WQC claimed that they had been tricked into buying poor-quality cars by WQC salesmen who failed to disclose faults with the cars.

Questions

(30 marks; 35 minutes)

1 According to Roger, 'Marketing is just a set of tools to sell more products.' Explain the possible drawbacks of this approach. (7)

2 How would you describe WQC's marketing philosophy? Is it production orientated or is it market orientated? (7)

3 Using the example of WQC, explain why an unethical approach towards marketing can often yield profitable results in the short-term. (8)

4 Outline two internal and two external factors that might affect the effectiveness of WQC's marketing? (8)

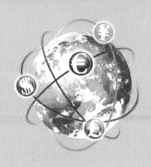
MARKET RESEARCH

Market research gathers information about consumers, competitors and distributors within a firm's target market. It is a way of identifying consumers' buying habits and attitudes to current and future products. Market research data can be numerical (e.g. 'What proportion of 16–24 year olds buy the *Sun* newspaper every day?') or psychological (e.g. 'Why do they buy the *Sun*?').

22.1 Conducting start-up market research

Where do you start? What do you need to know first? And how do you find it out?

The starting point is to discover the marketing fundamentals: how big is the market you are thinking about (market size), what is its future potential and what are the market shares of the existing companies and brands?

Market size means the value of the sales made annually by all the firms within a market. For example, in 2007 the UK market for yoghurts and pot desserts was worth £1736 million. Market potential can be measured by the annual rate of growth. In the case of yoghurt, this has been at a rate of 6% per year, by value. This implies that, by 2012, the potential market size will be over £2323 million.

When looking at a completely new market, these statistics will not be available. So research may be needed into other indicators. For example, the producer of an innovative new fishing rod would find out the number of people who go fishing regularly.

Market shares are also of crucial importance when investigating a market, as they indicate the relative strength of the firms within the market. In 2007, 27% of the yoghurt market was held by Müller, making it the leading brand by far. A benefit it received for its strong market share was a distribution level of almost 100% – nearly every grocery store stocked Müller. If one firm dominates, it may be very difficult to break into the market.

So how can firms find out this type of information? The starting point is **secondary research**: unearthing data that already exists.

Figure 22.1 Supermarket shelves stocked with Müller yoghurt

22.2 Methods of secondary research

The internet

These days most people start by 'Googling' the topic. This can provide invaluable information, though online providers of market research information will want to charge for the service. With luck, Google will identify a relevant article that can provide useful information.

Figure 22.2 Internet search engine Google

Trade press

All the above data about the yoghurt market came from an article in the magazine *The Grocer*. Every major market is served by one or more magazines written for people who work within that trade. Spending £1.75 on an issue of *The Grocer* provides lots of statistical and other information. Many trade magazines are available for reference in bigger public libraries.

Government-produced data

The government-funded National Statistics produces valuable reports, such as the *Annual Abstract of Statistics* and *Economic Trends*. These provide data on population trends and forecasts (e.g. for someone starting a hair and beauty salon, to find how many 16–20-year-old women there will be in 2012).

Having obtained background data, further research is likely to be tailored specifically to the company's needs, such as carrying out a survey among 16–20-year-old women about their favourite haircare brands. This type of first-hand research gathers primary data.

22.3 Methods of primary research

The process of gathering information directly from people within your target market is known as **primary research** (or field research). When carried out by market research companies it is expensive, but there is much that firms can do for themselves.

For a company that is already up and running, a regular survey of customer satisfaction is an important way of measuring the quality of customer service. When investigating a new market, there are various measures that can be taken by a small firm with a limited budget. Here are some examples.

● *Retailer research:* the people closest to a market are those who serve customers directly – the retailers. They are likely to know the up-and-coming brands, the degree of brand loyalty, the importance of price and packaging – all crucial information.

● *Observation:* when starting up a service business in which location is an all-important factor, it is invaluable to measure the rate of pedestrian (and possibly traffic) flow past your potential site compared to that of rivals. A sweet shop or a dry cleaners near a busy bus stop may generate twice the sales of a rival 50 yards down the road.

For a large company, primary research will be used extensively in new product development. For example, if we consider the possibility of launching Orange Chocolate Buttons, the development stages – plus research – would probably be those shown in Table 22.2.

Table 22.1 The pros and cons of primary and secondary research

	Secondary research	**Primary research**
Pros	● often obtained without cost ● good overview of a market ● usually based on actual sales figures, or research on large samples	● can aim questions directly at your research objectives ● latest information from the marketplace ● can assess the psychology of the customer
Cons	● data may not be updated regularly ● not tailored to your own needs ● expensive to buy reports on many different marketplaces	● expensive: £10,000+ per survey ● risk of questionnaire and interviewer bias ● research findings may only be usable if comparable **backdata** exists

Table 22.2 Orange Chocolate Buttons launch: likely development stages

Development stage	Primary research
1 The product idea (probably one of several)	1 Group discussions among regular chocolate buyers – some young, some old
2 Product test (testing different recipes – different sweetness, 'orangeyness', etc.)	2 A taste test on 200+ chocolate buyers (on street corners, or in a hall)
3 Brand name research (testing several different names, and perhaps logos)	3 Quantitative research using a questionnaire on a sample of 200+
4 Packaging research	4 As 3
5 Advertising research	5 Group discussions run by psychologists to discover which advertisement has the strongest effect on product image and recall
6 Total proposition test: testing the level of purchase interest, to help make sales forecasts	6 Quantitative research using a questionnaire and product samples on at least 200+ consumers

A-grade application
The Toyota MR2

When Toyota launched its MR2 sports car, sales were higher than expected. The only exception was France, where they were very poor. The Japanese Head Office asked the executives of Toyota France to look into this. Why had it been such a flop? Eventually the executives admitted that they should have carried out market research into the brand name MR2 prior to the launch. Pronounced 'Em-Er-Deux' in France, the car sounded like the French word 'merdre' (crap).

22.4 Qualitative research

Qualitative research is in-depth research into the motivations behind the attitudes and buying habits of consumers. It does not produce statistics such as '52% of chocolate buyers like orange chocolate'; instead it gives clues as to *why* they like it (e.g. is it really because it's orange, or because it's different/a change?). Qualitative research is usually conducted by psychologists, who learn to interpret the way people say things as well as what they say.

Qualitative research takes two main forms, as described below.

1 *Group discussions (also known as focus groups)*: free-ranging discussions led by psychologists among groups of six to eight consumers. The group leader will have a list of topics that need discussion, but will be free to follow up any point made by a group member. Among the advantages of group discussions are: it may reveal a problem or opportunity the company had not anticipated; it reveals consumer psychology, such as the importance of image and peer pressure.

A-grade application
Researching Häagen-Dazs

Group discussions were used prior to the UK launch of Häagen-Dazs. Groups of men and women were each given a half-litre tub of Häagen-Dazs and asked questions about when, how and with whom they would like to eat it. Respondents spoke about sharing a spoon with their partner, feeding each other and 'mellowing out' in front of a video. This led to a breakthrough in food advertising: Häagen-Dazs was advertised as a sensual pleasure to be shared. Its huge success when launched has become recognised as a success for qualitative research.

2 *Depth interviews*: informal, in-depth interviews between a psychologist and a consumer. They have the same function as group discussions, but avoid the risk that group opinion will be swayed by one influential person.

Table 22.3 Typical research questions to be answered by qualitative and quantitative research

Qualitative research	Quantitative research
<ul><li>Why do people *really* buy Nikes?</li><li>Who in the household *really* decides which brand of shampoo is bought?</li><li>What mood makes you feel like buying Häagen-Dazs ice cream?</li><li>When you buy your children Frosties, how do you feel?</li></ul>	<ul><li>Which pack design do you prefer?</li><li>Have you heard of any of the following brands: Ariel, Daz, Persil...etc.?</li><li>How likely are you to buy this product regularly?</li><li>How many newspapers have you bought in the past seven days?</li></ul>

22.5 Quantitative research

Quantitative research asks pre-set questions on a large enough sample of people to provide statistically valid data. Questionnaires can answer factual questions such as 'How many 16–20 year olds have heard of Chanel No 5?' There are three key aspects to quantitative research:

1 sampling (i.e. ensuring that the research results are typical of the whole population, though only a sample of the population has been interviewed)

2 writing a questionnaire that is unbiased and meets the research objectives

3 assessing the validity of the results.

Sampling
The two main concerns in sampling are how to choose the right people for interview (**sampling method**) and deciding how large a number to interview (**sample size**). There are three main sampling methods.

Random sample
This involves selecting respondents to ensure that everyone in the population has an equal chance of being interviewed. This sounds easy, but is not. If an interviewer goes to a street corner one morning and asks passers-by for an interview, the resulting sample will be biased towards those who are not in work, who do not own a car and have time on their hands (the busy ones will refuse to be interviewed). As a result the sample will not be representative. So achieving a truly random sample requires careful thought.

Research companies use the following method.

- Pick names at random from the electoral register (e.g. every 50th name).

- Send an interviewer to the address given in the register.

- If the person is out, visit up to twice more before giving up (this is to maximise the chances of catching those who lead busy social lives and are therefore rarely at home).

This method is effective, but slow and expensive.

Quota sample
This is selecting interviewees in proportion to the consumer profile within your target market. Table 22.4 gives an example.

Table 22.4 Quota sampling: an example

Adult		
	Chocolate buyers	Respondent quota (sample: 200)
Men	40%	80
Women	60%	120
16–24	38%	76
25–34	21%	42
35–44	16%	32
45+	25%	50

This method allows interviewers to head for busy street corners, interviewing whoever comes along. As long as they end up achieving the correct quota, they can interview when and where they want to. As this is a relatively cheap and effective way of sampling, it is the one used most commonly by market research companies.

Stratified sample

This involves interviewing only those with a key characteristic required for the sample. For example, the producers of Olay might decide only to interview women aged 30–45, the potential buyers of the future. Within this stratum/section of the population, individuals could be found at random (hence *stratified random* sample) or by setting quotas based on factors such as social class and region.

Sample size

Having decided which sampling method should be used, the next consideration is how many interviews should be conducted: 10, 100, 1000? The most high-profile surveys conducted in Britain are opinion polls (e.g. asking people how they will vote in a general election). These quota samples of between 1000 and 1500 respondents are considered large enough to reflect the opinions of an electorate of 45 million. How is this possible?

Of course, if you interviewed only ten people, the chances are slim that the views of this sample will match those of the whole population. Of these ten, seven may say they would definitely buy Orange Chocolate Buttons. If you asked another ten, however, only three may say the same. A sample of ten is so small that chance variations make the results meaningless. In other words, a researcher can have no statistical confidence in the findings from a sample of ten.

A sample of 100 is far more meaningful. It is not enough to feel confident about marginal decisions (e.g. 53% like the red pack design, 47% like the blue one), but is quite enough if the result is clear-cut (e.g. 65% like the name 'Spark'; 35% prefer 'Valencia'). Many major product launches have proceeded following research on as low a sample as 100.

With a sample of 1000 a high level of confidence is possible. Even small differences would be statistically significant with such a large sample. So why doesn't everyone use samples of 1000? The answer is money. Hiring a market research agency to undertake a survey on 100 people would cost approximately £10,000. A sample of 1000 people would cost three times that amount – good value if you can afford it, but not everyone can. As shown in the earlier example of launching Orange Chocolate Buttons, a company might require six surveys before launching a new product. So the spending on research alone might reach £180,000 if samples of 1000 were used.

Writing a questionnaire

Quantitative research is expensive and its results may influence major decisions such as whether to launch a new product. So a mistake in writing the questionnaire may prove very costly. For instance, the wording may influence respondents to sound more positive about a new product than they really feel. What are the key features of a good questionnaire?

- Clearly defined research objectives. What exactly do you need to find out?
- Ensure that questions do not point towards a particular answer.
- Ensure that the meaning of each question is clear, perhaps by testing (piloting) questions before putting them into fieldwork.
- Mainly use closed questions (i.e. ones with a limited number of pre-set answers that the respondent must tick); only in this way can you ensure quantifiable results.
- It is useful, though, to include a few open questions, to allow respondents to write a sentence or two, providing more depth of understanding.
- Ensure that the questionnaire finishes by asking for full demographic and usership details (i.e. the respondent's sex, age, occupation – and therefore social class – and buying habits). This allows more detailed analysis of sub-groups within the sample.

22.6 Other important considerations in primary research

Response rate

If a company sends out 2000 questionnaires and only 200 people send back a response, the following questions must be asked: 'Are those who respond typical of those who do not respond? Or is there a **bias** built into the findings as a consequence of the low response rate?'

Face-to-face versus self-completion

In the past, most surveys were conducted by interviewers who asked the questions face-to-face. This had drawbacks such as cost and the risk of bias (a bubbly young interviewer may generate more positive responses). Clear benefits, however, included a high response rate and the assurance that the interviewer could help to explain an unclear question. Today, self-completion questionnaires are increasingly common.

22.7 Market research today

Market research is increasingly influenced by technology. Instead of standing on windy street corners, interviewers are more likely to be sitting in a telephone booth in an office. There are also more and more internet opinion polls, in which a pop-up questionnaire appears on the screen. For instance, someone looking at the Amazon.com shopping site might be asked to answer questions about book buying.

An even stronger trend is towards database-driven research. Instead of finding the right people by trial and error, client firms supply research companies with database information on current or ex-customers. Retailers such as Tesco and Sainsbury's have millions of customer names on their databases, gained from customers' membership of loyalty card schemes such as Tesco's Clubcard. Shoppers are grouped into categories such as regular/irregular shoppers, petrol buyers, disposable nappy buyers, and so on. If Tesco wants to survey customer satisfaction with its baby products section, it knows exactly who should be contacted.

The future of market research is clearly bound up in technology. The basics will remain crucial, however: the avoidance of bias in the wording of questions, large enough sample sizes to provide valid data, and intelligent analysis of the research findings.

22.8 Test marketing

This a step beyond market research, because it means trying out a new product idea in a limited area of the country. For example, when Sunny Delight was tested in north-east England, it was distributed in all the main supermarkets and small shops – but just around Newcastle. The advantage of test marketing is that it is a much more realistic test of how shoppers will respond to a new product over a period of time. Market research will often provide a snapshot, but a six-week test market finds out what shoppers actually do with their own money. Will they try Sunny Delight? And, even more importantly, would they buy it again – and again?

The benefits from this are potentially huge. As the test market will provide more accurate data than any market research exercise, the company can benefit from:

- more accurate sales forecasts for when the products are launched nationally, enabling the business to establish the right amount of production capacity

- the ability to identify a weak link – for example, Tropicana Smoothies were launched in 2008 after test marketing; the final line-up of five blends (Blackberry & Blueberry, and so on) was changed because one of the five sold very weakly in test.

There are serious disadvantages to test marketing, however, including the following.

- It enables your competitors to see what you're doing and how strong sales appear to be; after Cadbury had trialled its Wispa (bubbly) chocolate bar, rival Aero slashed its prices at the time of the Wispa national launch, to make it harder for the Wispa product to get established.

- Test marketing is far more expensive than market research, as it requires large-scale production, with all the related costs. If the product flops, a lot more money will be lost than if it had flopped in market research. Test marketing will also take much longer than research, so an impatient manager might prefer to rush the new product into its national launch.

Issues For Analysis

When developing an argument in answer to an exam question, market research offers the following main lines of analysis:

- the key role of market research in market orientation (i.e. basing decisions upon the consumer's, rather than the producer's, needs or opinions)

- the need for a questioning approach to data – when presented with a research finding one needs to know: was the sample size large enough, who paid for the research; businesspeople learn to ask questions about every 'fact' shown by research

- the importance of market knowledge – large, established firms have a huge advantage over newer, smaller firms because of their knowledge of consumer attitudes and behaviour, built up from years of market research surveys

Market research

In large firms, it is rare for any significant marketing decision to be made without market research. Even an apparently minor change to a pack design will be carried out only after testing in research. Is this overkill? Surely marketing executives are employed to make judgements, not merely do what surveys tell them?

The first issue here is the strong desire to make business decisions as scientifically as possible. In other words, to act on evidence, not on feelings. Quantitative research, especially, fits in with the desire to act on science not hunch. Yet this can be criticised, such as by John Scully, former head of Apple Computers, who once said 'No great marketing decision has ever been made on the basis of quantitative data.' He was pointing out that true innovations, such as Apple's iPod, were the product of creativity and hunch, not science.

The second issue concerns management culture. In some firms, mistakes lead to inquests, blame and even dismissal. This makes managers keen to find a let-out. When the new product flops, the manager can point an accusing finger at the positive research results: 'It wasn't my fault. We need a new research agency.' In other firms, mistakes are seen as an inevitable part of learning. For every Sinclair C5 (unresearched flop) there may be an iPod (unresearched moneyspinner). In firms with a positive, risk-taking approach to business, qualitative insights are likely to be preferred to quantitative data.

Key terms

Backdata: keeping records of the results from past research to provide a comparison with the latest results.
Bias: a factor that causes research findings to be unrepresentative of the whole population (e.g. bubbly interviewers or misleading survey questions).
Primary research: finding out information first-hand (e.g. Coca-Cola designing a questionnaire to obtain information from people who regularly buy diet products).
Secondary research: finding out information that has already been gathered (e.g. the government's estimates of the number of 14–16 year olds in Wales).
Sample size: the number of people interviewed; this should be large enough to give confidence that the findings are representative of the whole population.
Sampling method: the approach chosen to select the right people to be part of the research sample (e.g. random, quota or stratified).

Exercises

A. Revision questions

(40 marks; 40 minutes)

1 State three ways in which a cosmetics firm could use market research. (3)

2 Outline three reasons why market research information may prove inaccurate. (6)

3 Distinguish between primary and secondary research. (3)

4 What advantages are there in using secondary research rather than primary? (3)

5 Which is the most commonly used sampling method? Why may it be the most commonly used? (4)

6 State three key factors to take into account when writing a questionnaire. (3)

7 Explain two aspects of marketing in which consumer psychology is important. (4)

8 Outline the pros and cons of using a large sample size. (4)

9 Identify three possible sources of bias in primary market research. (3)

10 Why may street interviewing become less common in the future? (3)

11 At present, five out of every six new products flop in the marketplace. Most have had market research; few have been test marketed. Should large firms use test marketing more often? (4)

B. Revision exercises

B1 Market research assignment

Hampton is a medium-sized producer of health foods. Its new company strategy is to break into the £400 million market for breakfast cereals. It has thought up three new product ideas that it wishes to test in research before further development takes place. These are as follows.

1 *Cracker:* an extra-crunchy mix of oats and almonds.

2 *Fizzz:* crunchy oats that fizz in milk.

3 *St James:* a luxury mix of oats, cashews and pecan nuts.

The research objectives are to identify the most popular of the three, in terms of product trial *and* regular usage; to identify price expectations for each; to find what people like and dislike about each idea and each brand name; and to be able to analyse the findings in relation to consumers' demographic profile and current usage patterns.

Questions

(30 marks; 30 minutes)

1 Write a questionnaire based upon the above details, bearing in mind the advice given in Section 22.5. (12)

2 Explain which sampling method you would use and why. (6)

3 Interview six to eight people using your questionnaire, then write a 200-word commentary on its strengths and weaknesses. (12)

B2 Data response

Each year more than £1000 million is spent on pet food in the UK. All the growth within the market has been for luxury pet foods and healthier products. Seeing these trends, in early 2008 Town & Country Petfoods launched 'HiLife Just Desserts', a range of pudding treats for dogs. They contain Omega-3 but no added sugar and therefore have no more than 100 calories per tin.

Sales began well, especially of the Apple & Cranberry version. Now sales have flattened out at around £1 million a year and the company thinks it is time to launch some new flavours. Three weeks ago it commissioned some primary research that was carried out using an online survey linked to pet care websites. The sample size was 150.

The main findings were as follows.

1 Have you ever bought your dog a pet food pudding?

EVER BOUGHT:	Never	Just once	Yes in past, but no longer	Yes, still do
	61%	13%	12%	14%

2 Which of these flavours might you buy for your dog?

MIGHT TRY:

	Never	Might try	Might buy monthly	Might buy once a week
Muesli yoghurt	61%	19%	15%	5%
Rhubarb crumble	43%	33%	22%	2%
Apples and custard	52%	34%	12%	2%

The marketing director is a bit disappointed that none of the new product ideas has done brilliantly, but we're happy that there's one clear winner. She plans a short qualitative research exercise among existing HiLife customers, and hopes to launch two new flavours in time for the annual Crufts' Dog Show in three months' time.

Questions

(20 marks; 30 minutes)

1 Outline whether the sample size of 150 was appropriate in this case. (4)

2 Examine the marketing director's conclusion that 'none of the new product ideas has done brilliantly, but we're happy that there's one clear winner'. (7)

3a Explain one method of qualitative research that could be used in this case. (3)

3b Analyse two ways in which qualitative research might help the marketing director. (6)

C. Essay questions

(40 marks each)

1 'Market research is like an insurance policy. You pay a premium to reduce your marketing risks.' To what extent do you believe this statement to be true?

2 After ten years of rising sales, demand for Shredded Wheat has been slipping. Discuss how the marketing manager might make use of market research to analyse why this has happened and help decide the strategy needed to return Shredded Wheat to sales growth.

3 Steve Jobs, boss of Apple, once said that he ignored market research in the early stages of the iPod. He believes that research is useful in relation to existing products, but does not work with innovative new products.

(a) Why may this be?

(b) How could research be used to best effect for assessing new innovations?

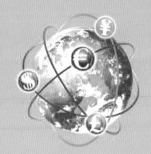

UNDERSTANDING MARKETS

DEFINITION

A market is where buyers meet sellers; examples include eBay or Smithfield meat market. The key elements within every market are its size (how much is spent by customers in a year), the extent to which it can be subdivided (e.g. the confectionery market into chocolate, sugar-based sweets and chewing gum), and the extent to which the market is dominated by one or two companies or brands.

23.1 Types of market

Local vs national

Most new small firms know and care little about the size of the national market. If you have just bought an ice cream van that you intend to operate in Chichester, it doesn't matter whether the size of the UK market for ice cream is £500 million or £600 million a year. Your concern is the level of demand and the level of competition locally. And you will probably be delighted if you achieve annual sales of £0.1 million (£100,000).

In the case of the market for ice cream in Chichester there are several things to consider.

● How do locals buy ice cream at the moment? (Multipacks from supermarkets? Individual cones from ice cream stalls or vans?)

● How many tourists come to the city? Do they come all year round? What type of ice cream do they buy? Where do they buy it?

● How much competition is there, what do competitors offer and charge at the moment? Are there gaps in the market that you can move into?

Other firms are focused more on the national market. For example, Klein Caporn is a small food company that started in 2005. It produces high-quality, high-priced ready-to-eat meals. It started by targeting small grocers, but soon found that the sales volumes were too low to cover its costs. A sales breakthrough in Waitrose supermarkets was followed in 2007 by acceptance by Sainsbury's. This enables the company to deliver to just two warehouses, cutting the business costs dramatically; then Waitrose and Sainsbury's distribute to their local shops. So Klein Caporn has a national presence even though sales remain well below 1% of the market for ready meals.

To deal on the national level, Klein Caporn has to deal professionally with the supermarket buyers, and produce eye-catching packaging that can compete effectively with that of national and multinational competitors.

Physical and electronic (virtual)

All markets used to be physical. The London Stock Exchange was a place where buyers met sellers and face-to-face agreements took place. Similarly, auctions were physical, with bidders having to catch the eye of the auctioneer.

Today an increasing number of markets are electronic. The stock market exists only on computer screens, and the likes of eBay are transforming auction and other markets worldwide.

From a business point of view the key factors about electronic markets (e.g. for finding hotel rooms or flights) are that:

● they are fiercely price competitive, so the companies supplying services have huge pressure to keep their costs as low as possible

● they do not rely on physical location (e.g. a business can easily be run from a bedroom, such as selling PS1 computer games)

● the market is easy and quite cheap to enter, so new competitors can arrive at any time

● they provide a 'long tail' of competitive, profitable small businesses, able to carve their own little niche in markets; this is very difficult to achieve in the high street, where rents are so high that only big firms can afford them.

23.2 Factors determining demand

Demand is the desire of consumers to buy a product or service, when backed by the ability to pay. It is also known as 'effective demand' (i.e. only when the customer has the money is demand effective). Several factors determine the demand for a specific product/service.

Price

This affects demand in three ways.

1 You may want an £80,000 Mercedes convertible, but you cannot afford it (i.e. the price puts it beyond your income level); the higher the price, the more people there are who cannot afford to buy.

2 The higher the price, the less good value the item will seem compared with other ways of spending the money (e.g. a Chelsea home ticket costing £48 is the equivalent of going to the cinema six to eight times, so is it worth it?); the higher the price of an item, the more there will be people who say 'It's not worth it.'

3 It should be remembered that the price tag put on an item gives a message about its 'value' (i.e. a ring priced at 99p will inevitably be seen as 'cheap', whether or not it is value for money), so although lower prices should boost sales, firms must beware of ruining their image for quality.

Incomes

The British economy grows at about 2.5% a year. This means that average income levels double every 30 years. Broadly, when your kids are about 16–18 years old, you are likely to be twice as well off as your parents are today. Economic growth means we all get richer over time (and lazier, and fatter, and spend more time in traffic jams).

The demand for most products and services grows as the economy grows. Goods like cars and cinema tickets are **normal goods**, for which demand rises broadly in line with incomes. In some cases it grows even faster (e.g. if the economy grows by 3% in a year, the amount spent on foreign holidays can easily rise by 6%). This type of product is known as a **luxury good**.

Still other goods behave differently, with sales falling when people are better off. These products are known as **inferior goods**. In their case, rising incomes mean falling sales. For example, the richer we get, the more Tropicana fruit juice we buy and the less Tesco orange squash. As orange squash is an inferior good, a couple of years of economic struggle (and perhaps more people out of work) would mean sales would increase as people switch from expensive Tropicana to cheap squash.

Actions of competitors

Demand for British Airways' Heathrow–New York flights does not only depend on their price and the incomes of consumers. It also depends on the actions of BA's rivals. If Virgin Atlantic is running a brilliant advertising campaign, demand for BA flights might fall as customers switch to Virgin. Or if American Airlines pushes its prices up, people might switch to BA.

The firm's own marketing activities

Following the same logic, if British Airways is running a new advertising campaign, perhaps based on improved customer service, it may enjoy increased sales. In effect its sales will rise if it can persuade customers to switch from Virgin and American Airlines to BA. One firm's sales increase usually means reduced sales elsewhere.

Seasonal factors

Most firms experience significant variations in sales through the year. Some markets boom in the summer and slump in the winter, such as ice cream, soft drinks, lager and seaside hotels. Others boom at Christmas, such as sales of perfume, liqueurs, greetings cards and toys. Other products that have less obvious reasons for seasonal variations in demand include cars, cat food, carpets, furniture, TVs and newspapers. The variation is caused by patterns of customer behaviour; nothing can be done about that. A well-run business makes sure it understands and can predict seasonal variations in demand, and then has a plan for coping.

23.3 Market size and trends

Market size is the measurement of all the sales by all the companies within a marketplace. It can be measured in two ways: by volume and by value. Volume measures the quantity of goods purchased – perhaps in tons, in packs or in units. Market size by value is the amount spent by customers on the volume sold. So the difference between volume and value is the price paid per unit.

Take, for example, the figures for the UK take-home fruit juice market shown in Table 23.1.

Table 23.1 UK take-home fruit juice market

2007 market by value	£987 million
2007 market by volume	936 million litres
Average price per serving	105.4 pence (£987/936)

Source: The Grocer, 5 May 2007

Market size matters because it is the basis for calculating market share (i.e. the proportion of the total market held by one company or brand). This, in turn, is essential for evaluating the success or failure of a firm's marketing activities. Market size is also the reference point for calculating trends. Is the market size growing or declining? A growth market is far more likely to provide opportunities for new products to be launched or new distribution initiatives to be successful.

Recent figures and forecasts for the car market in China help show the importance of market trends. Ten years ago the UK car market was four times bigger than China's. In 2006 China accelerated past Britain. And look at the forecasts for the coming years in Table 23.2.

By 2020 China will be the world's biggest car market. Clearly these figures show that success in China will be far more important to car firms than success in Britain.

Table 23.2 Sales of automobiles (actual and forecast)

Year	China	Britain
2005	2,400,000	2,450,000
2006	2,800,000	2,350,000
2007	3,800,000	2,450,000
2010 (forecast)	6,500,000	2,500,000
2020 (forecast)	20,000,000	2,600,000

Source: Forecasts by industry experts

23.4 Market share

Market share is the proportion of the total market held by one company or product. It can be measured by volume, but is more often looked at by value. Market share is taken by most firms as the key test of the success of the year's marketing activities. Total sales are affected by factors such as economic growth, but market share only measures a firm's ability to win or lose against its competitors. As shown in Table 23.3, rising market share can also lead to the producer's ideal of market leadership or market dominance. Magnum has market leadership among ice cream brands. Walkers has market dominance among crisps and snacks. The position of Pampers is stronger still, with its only rival (Huggies) far behind.

Table 23.3 Brands with the highest UK market share

Leading brand in its market	Sales of leading brand	Market size (by value)	Market share	Share of nearest competitor
Walkers Crisps*	£417 million	£1900 million	21.9%	7.6%
Cadbury's Dairy Milk	£370 million	£2928 million	12.6%	6.2%
Pampers	£256 million	£419 million	61.1%	18.7%
Actimel	£103 million	£250 million	41.2%	14.4%
Magnum Ice Cream	£71 million	£399 million	17.8%	8.0%

*Not including Sensations, Potato Heads or other Walkers brands
Source: The Grocer, 15 December 2007, quoting from IRI Infoscan

There are many advantages to a business in having the top-selling brand (the brand leader). Obviously, sales are higher than anyone else's, but also:

- the brand leader gets the highest distribution level, often without needing to make much effort to achieve it; even a tiny corner shop stocks Whiskas as well as a Happy Shopper own-label cat food; success breeds success

- brand leaders are able to offer lower discount terms to retailers than the number two or three brands in a market; this means higher revenues and profit margins per unit sold

- the strength of a brand-leading name such Walls Magnum makes it much easier to obtain distribution and consumer trial for new products based on that brand name.

23.5 Market segmentation

Most markets can be subdivided in several different ways. If you go to WHSmith and look at the magazine racks, you will see the process in action. There are magazines for men and (many more) for women. Within the women's section there are kids' magazines, teen mags, young adult mags, middle-aged mags and some for the elderly. Then there are magazines that target different interests and hobbies, from football to computer consoles to gardening.

Market segmentation is the acknowledgement by companies that customers are not all the same. 'The market' can be broken down into smaller sections in which customers share common characteristics – from the same age group to a shared love of Manchester United. Successful segmentation can increase customer satisfaction (if you love shopping and celebs, how wonderful that *Look* magazine is for you!) and provide scope for increasing company profits. After all, customers may be willing to pay a higher price for a magazine focused purely on the subjects they love, instead of buying a general magazine in which most of the articles stay unread.

The keys to successful market segmentation are as follows.

- Research into the different types of customer within a marketplace (e.g. different age groups, gender, region, personality types).

- See if they have common tastes/habits, (e.g. younger readers may be more focused on fashion and celebrities than older ones).

- Devise a product designed not for the whole market, but for a particular segment; this might achieve only a 1% market share, but if the total market is big enough, that might be highly profitable.

Issues For Analysis

The key to analysis is precision. Terms such as inferior goods and normal goods have to be understood so well that you spot where they are relevant and are able to use them to develop your answer. Every student would recognise that a Mercedes sports car is a luxury product. Few could continue by saying that its sales will therefore grow especially fast when times are good, but may slump when the economy is struggling.

To analyse the market that a business is operating in, make sure to consider the market size, trends and share, the degree of segmentation, the factors determining demand, and the type of market (e.g. local versus national). This is a powerful combination of concepts that should provide a lot of scope for analytic answers.

23.6 Understanding markets

When England flopped out of the European Championships in November 2007, the shares in Sports Direct plc fell by 20%. Not only was its retail business going to suffer from a collapse in sales of England shirts, but the company also had a 29.9% share stake in Umbro, England's kit-maker. Share buyers reasoned that a slump in the market for England shirts would shrink the size of the market for sports leisurewear. Well-run businesses try to make sure that they can benefit from opportunities, but avoid being too badly hit by slumps. They understand their market – from customers through to competitors.

Key terms

Inferior goods: products that people turn to when they are hard up, and turn away from when they are better off (e.g. Tesco Value Baked Beans instead of Heinz).

Luxury goods: Products that people buy much more of when they feel better off (e.g. jewellery, sports cars and holidays at posh hotels).

Normal goods: Products or services (e.g. travel and fast food) for which sales change broadly in line with the economy (i.e. economy grows 3%, sales rise 3%).

23.7 Workbook

Exercises

A. Revision questions

(35 marks; 35 minutes)

1 Outline three features of the market for fast food near to where you live. (6)

2 Section 23.2 lists five factors determining the demand for a product: price, incomes, actions of competitors, marketing activities and seasonality. Identify which two of these would most heavily affect sales of:
(a) strawberries
(b) easyJet tickets to Barcelona
(c) tickets to see Newcastle United
(d) DFS furniture. (8)

3 Explain in your own words the difference between market size by volume and market size by value. (2)

4a Toyota's share of the UK car market is about 6%. If it continues with that share, how many UK car sales would that amount to in 2020; and how many would there be in China in 2020, assuming the same market share? (4)

4b Outline two ways Toyota might respond to that sales difference. (4)

5 Why might a shoe shop focusing on 'Little Feat' be able to charge higher prices per pair than a general shoe shop? (2)

6 Explain in your own words how the market for shoes could be segmented. (3)

7 Look at Table 23.3. Discuss which business should be happier with its market position: Walkers or Pampers. (6)

B. Revision exercises

B1 Data response

In late August 2007 entertainment retailer ChoicesUK called in the receivers. It was unable to continue trading after losing money consistently during 2007. As many as 1700 jobs were threatened at ChoicesUK's 200 branches.

This came on top of the collapse of Fopp music retailers earlier in the year. At the same time, industry giant HMV suffered a halving of its profits. The reason was the same – the collapse in the total market for CDs and DVDs, compounded by a switch to buying online or downloading. The UK CD market, for example, fell by 10% in the first half of 2007.

Questions

(15 marks; 15 minutes)

1 Outline two reasons why a whole market may shrink in size, as happened to CD sales in the first half of 2007. (4)

2 ChoicesUK collapsed as the market declined. Explain two ways in which it might have set about boosting its market share (to combat the decline in the market as a whole). (6)

3 In the past, more than half the annual sales of ChoicesUK have taken place in the three months before Christmas. Should the directors have kept the business going a few months more? (5)

B2 Data response

Lidl and Aldi: winning grocery wars

Discount grocers are the big winners in 2007, TNS Worldpanel figures show (see Figure 23.1 on page 157). The grocery market grew by 4% year-on-year in the 12 weeks to 16 July 2007. Tesco, Sainsbury's and Asda all grew slightly faster than the total market, while Somerfield sales actually fell by 6%. Lidl and Aldi bucked the trend, with sales growth of 13% and 11% respectively. Iceland also performed well, growing by 12%. Perhaps these three low-cost grocers benefited from the collapse of Kwik-Save.

The changes leave Tesco as the market leader with 31.5% (unchanged on 2006), while Asda's share grew from 16.6% to 16.7% and Sainsbury's from 16% to 16.2%. Morrisons suffered a fall in market share, from 11.3% to 11.1%. A decline of 0.2% may seem trivial, but as the value of the UK grocery market is £128.2 billion a year, 0.2% market share represents sales of £256.4 million!

Questions

(30 marks; 35 minutes)

1a What was the grocery market size and market growth in 2007? (2)

1b Identify three possible reasons why sales at Somerfield fell in 2007. (3)

2a Show the workings to calculate that a 0.2% share of the UK grocery market equals £256.4 million. (3)

2b Use the figures and the bar chart to work out the value of the UK 2007 sales of Lidl. (2)

2c Examine two *possible* reasons why Lidl enjoyed the biggest sales growth within the grocery market in 2007. (6)

3a Outline two ways in which Tesco may benefit from being the grocery market leader. (4)

3b Ten years ago, Sainsbury's was the UK grocery market leader. Discuss whether it could return to that position within the next ten years. (10)

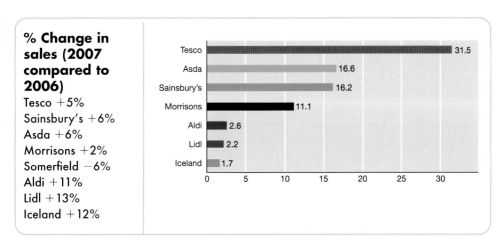

% Change in sales (2007 compared to 2006)
Tesco +5%
Sainsbury's +6%
Asda +6%
Morrisons +2%
Somerfield −6%
Aldi +11%
Lidl +13%
Iceland +12%

Figure 23.1 UK grocery market share 2007
Source: TNS Worldpanel and Nielsen, quoted in *The Grocer*, 28 July 2007

NICHE VERSUS MASS MARKETING

Unit 24

DEFINITION

Mass marketing means devising products with mass appeal and promoting them to all types of customer. Niche marketing is tailoring a product to a particular type of customer.

24.1 Mass marketing

Mass marketing is the attempt to create products or services that have universal appeal. Rather than targeting a specific type of customer, mass marketing aims the product at the whole market. The intention is that everyone should be a consumer of the product. Coca-Cola is a good example of a firm that uses mass-marketing techniques. The company aims its product at young and old alike. Its goal has always been to be the market leader, and it still is today. The ultimate prize of mass marketing is the creation of **generic brands**. These are brands that are so totally associated with the product that customers treat the brand name as if it were a product category; examples include 'Hoover' (vacuum cleaner) and 'Bacardi' (white rum).

As shown above, when mass marketing is carried out successfully it can be highly profitable. Firms such as

Ryanair set out to be high-volume, mass-market operators and achieve handsome profits. However, it is important to note that mass marketing does not have to go hand in hand with low prices. For example, Calvin Klein, producer of 'cK one', took the decision to target its fragrance at the mass market. By taking the unusual step of aiming its fragrance at both men and women the target market was doubled at a stroke. The decision to attract the mass market was also evident in terms of distribution policy. Calvin Klein decided to sell the fragrance through music stores as well as the more traditional distribution outlets of boutiques and department stores. By doing this, Calvin Klein increased the chance of trial purchase from those who might not have considered buying fragrances before. The company's mass-marketing strategy was vindicated by phenomenal sales and profitability. A highly effective advertising campaign featuring the supermodel Kate Moss provided the necessary **product differentiation** to sell high sales volumes without the need to cut prices.

24.2 Niche marketing

A niche market is a very small segment of a much larger market. Niche marketing involves identifying the needs of the consumers that make up the niche. A specialised product or service is then designed to meet the distinctive needs of these consumers. Niche-market products tend to sell in relatively low volumes. As a result the price of a niche-market product is usually higher than the mass-market alternative. Niche-market operators often distribute their products through specialist retailers, or directly to the consumer via the internet.

An entrepreneur wanting to set up a niche-market business must first identify a group of people who share a taste for a product or service, which is currently unsatisfied. A product or a service must then be

Mass marketing → Leads to → High sales → Which leads to → Mass production → Which leads to → Lower costs and higher profits →

Figure 24.1 Mass marketing

designed that is capable of meeting this unsatisfied need. To stand a good chance of success the new niche product will need to be superior to the mass-market equivalent that is currently available. Finally, the niche must be large enough to support a profitable business. Many new niche-market businesses fail because the revenue generated from their niche-market business is not high enough to cover the costs of operating.

A good example is a small neighbourhood restaurant called Bajou, which tried, unsuccessfully, to make a business out of selling Cajun food in south Croydon. At the weekend the restaurant was never completely empty, proving that a gap in the market did exist. Unfortunately, this gap in the market was not large enough to cover the overheads of running a restaurant. The restaurant was never full enough to operate above a break-even level. Six months after Bajou opened it was forced to close down. In niche markets entrepreneurs must manage their overhead costs with care if the business is to operate above its break-even point.

Small niche operators lack the **economies of scale** required to compete on price with larger, established operators. Instead, the small firm could try to find a small, profitable niche. The amount of profit generated by this niche needs to be high enough for the small firm, but too trivial for the big business. In Birmingham's city centre, Rubicon Exotic is a profitable line of soft drinks, but with a market share of less than 1% Coca-Cola will not crash this party. The profit generated is enough to satisfy the requirements of Rubicon Drinks, with its low overheads. Small niche-market businesses survive on the basis that they occupy a relatively unimportant, low-profit market niche. Larger firms operating in the mass market are happy to ignore the niche businesses because they pose no threat.

Niche market businesses sell specialised, differentiated products that are designed to appeal to their very specific target market. Firms selling niche-market products can exploit the low price sensitivity created by product differentiation by raising price. Total revenue will rise after the price increase because, in percentage terms, the fall in sales volume will be less than the price increase.

Successful niche marketing in practice

Until recently catalogue retailing has suffered from a downmarket image. Operators such as Argos based their success on selling mass-market products at budget prices. However, in the last few years, internet retailing has seen a host of new niche-market players entering the market. Companies such as Nordic Kids sell a highly differentiated range of niche-market, premium-quality designer clothes that are not available on the high street. In this case the niche market is affluent middle-class parents seeking, according to the company's website (http://www.nordickids.co.uk/), 'effortless Scandinavian cool'.

24.3 Are niche markets safe havens for small businesses?

In the past, many large companies stuck to mass markets and ignored small market gaps and the small companies that filled them. To fill lots of small niches would require lots of short production runs (e.g. 90 minutes on the printing press producing the Hartlepool FC fanzine, and 60 minutes producing the Darlington one). This has always been expensive, because it takes a long time to re-set machinery.

This has changed due to technology. As production lines are increasingly set up by computer, they can be re-set almost instantly. So large firms can build the sales volumes they need by producing a large variety of low-volume, niche-market products. Small-scale producers are coming under threat from larger companies that have begun to target their niches.

Fortunately, small firms are often quicker on their feet, so when a large firm lumbers towards the market, the

A-grade application

Flares

A good example of a successful business that uses the niche marketing approach is the Flares nightclub chain. Flares targets a niche market comprised, mostly, of ageing clubbers in their forties that want a 1970s retro night out. Each Flares nightclub tends to be quite small, so even relatively few customers will make the club look reassuringly busy. This small capacity also helps to reduce overheads, decreasing the number of customers required each week to break even. The interior design of a typical Flares nightclub is deliberately garish – an exaggerated version of what a typical nightclub looked like in the 1970s, complete with features such as mirror balls and an underlit glass dance floor. The music policy of a typical Flares nightclub holds no surprises either: 1970s funk and other kitsch retro classics such as ABBA, which are likely to appeal to the ageing clubber.

Source:http://www.flaresbars.co.uk/

smaller one may still be able to win the competitive war. When the multi-billion-dollar PepsiCo bought the smoothie business PJ's, Innocent Drinks thought that the market might become very difficult for it. In fact Innocent kept its market share rising within the small smoothie niche of the soft drinks market.

Issues For Analysis

● It is useful to analyse niche marketing in relation to **price elasticity**. Niche-market products are invariably designed to meet the needs of customers looking for something different. This means that buyers of niche-market goods are likely to be less price-sensitive than consumers of mass-market brands. This is especially true for the first brand to open up a niche market. Consumers may regard the originator of the market segment as 'the real thing'. An example would be Marmite, in the relatively tiny market for savoury spreads (most people prefer sweet things on their toast, such as honey or jam). This allows Marmite to charge extraordinarily high prices such as £4 for a jar the same size and weight as a £1 jar of honey.

● Fundamentally there are two approaches to making profit. The first is to be a high-volume, low-profit-margin operator, such as Ryanair. The second is to charge higher prices and be a low-volume, high-profit-margin business, such as Marmite. This is the route taken by those who adopt niche marketing tactics.

24.4 Niche versus mass marketing
an evaluation

Which is better? Mass or niche marketing? The answer is that it depends. In the bulk ice cream market, large packs of vanilla ice cream have become so cheap that little profit can be made. Better by far, then, to be in a separate niche, whether regional (Mackie's Scottish ice cream) or upmarket, such as Rocombe Farm or Häagen-Dazs. The latter can charge ten times as much per litre as the mass-market own-label bulk packs.

Yet would a film company prefer to be selling a critic's favourite or a blockbuster, smash hit? The latter, of course. In other words, the mass-market is great, if you can succeed there. Businesses such as Heinz, Kellogg's and even Chanel show that mass marketing can be successful and profitable in the long term.

Key terms

Economies of scale: factors that cause costs per unit to fall when a firm operates at a higher level of production.
Generic brands: brands that are so well known that customers say the brand name when they mean the product (e.g. 'I'll hoover the floor').
Price elasticity: the responsiveness of demand to a change in price.
Product differentiation: the extent to which consumers perceive your brand as being different from others.

Exercises

A. Revision questions

(20 marks; 20 minutes)

1 Identify three advantages of niche marketing over mass marketing. (3)

2 Give three reasons why a large firm may wish to enter a niche market. (3)

3 Why may small firms be better at spotting and then reacting to new niche-market opportunities? (3)

4 Give two reasons why average prices in niche markets tend to be higher than those charged in most mass markets. (2)

5 Outline two reasons why information technology has made niche marketing a more viable option for large firms. (4)

6 Explain why it is important for a large firm to be flexible if it is to successfully operate in niche markets. (2)

7 In your own words, explain why the price elasticity of niche-market products may be lower than for products in the mass market. (3)

B. Revision exercises

B1 Data response

The return of mass marketing

For many years, car manufacturers such as Toyota and Nissan have sought out market niches in an attempt to improve profitability. Cars such as the Toyota Prius, a hybrid electric-powered vehicle, are not intended to sell in high volumes. Instead, niche-market cars sell for high prices, delivering a higher profit margin per car than more conventional mass-market models.

However, in the last couple of years, there are signs that car manufacturers have sought a return to conventional mass marketing, particularly in Asia where rapid rates of economic growth have created a growing middle class. At present both the Indian and the Chinese car markets are unsaturated. For example, in India, car ownership is only 7 per 1000, whereas in the USA and the UK the corresponding figure is 477 and 373 respectively. Income per head, while increasing rapidly, is still low by American and European standards, and so far this has limited the demand for new cars in India.

Now car manufacturers have spotted a gap in the market for a basic, low-cost car. The first company to fill this gap in the market was the Indian car manufacturer, Tata Motors. It sells its basic 'People's car' for less than 100,000 rupees (£1500). Multinationals such as Renault and General Motors are now opening their own Indian factories to produce similar mass-market cars sold at ultra-low prices. The challenge for these producers will be to manufacture the cars cheaply enough to make the low prices profitable.

Environmentalists have expressed their concerns that these new cheap cars will add to the problem of global warming and climate change. This year, Tata Motors expects to sell a quarter of a million new cars in India.

Questions

(40 marks; 45 minutes)

1a What is a niche-market product? (2)

1b Explain why the Toyota Prius is a good example of a niche-market product. (2)

2 Explain two reasons why the Indian car market has grown. (4)

3a What is a mass-market product? (2)

3b Explain why the 'People's car' is a good example of a mass-market product. (4)

4 Analyse two advantages and two disadvantages for European car manufacturers, such as Renault, of mass marketing £2000 cars in India. (8)

5 £2000 cars can be profitably made in India. Explain why UK consumers are unlikely to benefit from similar low prices. (4)

6 Discuss whether companies such as Tata Motors should take into account the concerns of environmentalists when making their business decisions. (14)

B2 Data response

Winter melon tea

Mass-market soft drinks such as Coca-Cola and Pepsi are very popular in countries such as Hong Kong and Singapore. In an attempt to survive against the imported competition, local producers of soft drinks have managed to establish a flourishing niche market for traditional Asian drinks sold in 33 cl cans. Sales of these niche-market products have been rising, but from a very low level.

Consumers that make up this niche market are encouraged to believe, through advertising, that traditional drinks such as winter melon tea and grass jelly drink are healthier than their mass-market alternatives. Other firms use economic nationalism to sell their drinks, using slogans such as 'Asian heritage' in their advertising.

However, producers of traditional drinks could now become a victim of their own success.

Foreign multinationals have noticed the rapid growth of this market niche, and in response, they have launched their own range of traditional drinks.

Questions

(30 marks; 35 minutes)

1a What is a niche-market product? (2)

1b Explain why Asian traditional drinks are examples of niche-market products. (3)

2 Explain two ways in which the producers of traditional drinks, such as winter melon tea and grass jelly drink, created product differentiation.

(4)

3 Niche-market products are normally more expensive than most mass-market products. Using the example of traditional Asian drinks, explain why this is usually so. (7)

4 Discuss whether the local producers of Asian traditional drinks will be able to survive in the long term given that their products now have to compete against me-too brands produced by foreign multinationals such as Coca-Cola and Pepsi. (14)

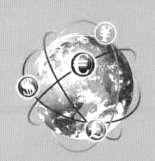

DESIGNING AN EFFECTIVE MARKETING MIX

DEFINITION

The marketing mix is the balance between the four main elements needed to carry out the marketing strategy. It consists of the '4Ps': product, price, promotion and place.

25.1 Components of the marketing mix

When working out how to market a product successfully, there are four main variables to consider (the **marketing mix**).

1   *Product:* the business must find a way to make the product (or service) both appealing and distinctive; to do this, it needs to understand fully both its customers and its competitors. No product will have long-term success unless this stage is completed successfully.

2   *Price:* having identified the right product to appeal to its target market, the business must set the right price. The 'right' price for a Versace handbag might be £1,200 – it is a great mistake to think that low prices or special discounts are the path to business success.

3   *Promotion:* marketing managers must identify the right way to create the right image for the product and present it to the right target audience. This might be achieved best by national TV advertising, but specific markets can be reached at far lower cost by more careful targeting (e.g. advertising lawnmowers in magazines such as *Amateur Gardening*). 'Promotion' includes both media advertising (TV, press, cinema, radio) and other forms of promotion (e.g. special offers, public relations, direct mail and online).

4   *Place:* for products, 'place' is how to get your product to the place where customers can be persuaded to buy; this might be through a vending machine or on a supermarket shelf, or positioned just by the till at a newsagent (the prime position for purchases bought on impulse); for service businesses, place may be online, or in the location of a retail outlet (e.g. Tesco Direct and Tesco stores).

The units that follow this one deal with each of these factors in turn.

A-grade application

Both McVitie's Jaffa Cakes and Burton's Jammie Dodgers are well-known biscuit brands, but the former is distributed in 90% of retail outlets, whereas the latter is in only 64%. Clearly this restricts sales of Jammie Dodgers, because few customers would make a special journey to find them. Both companies have a similar view of the right outlets for their products (e.g. supermarkets, corner shops, garages, canteens and cafés), so why may Burton's be losing out to McVitie's in this particular race? Possible reasons include:

● Jaffa Cakes have higher consumer demand, therefore retail outlets are more willing to stock the product
● Jammie Dodgers may have more direct competitors; high product differentiation may make Jaffa Cakes more of a 'must stock' line
● if Jaffa Cakes have more advertising support, retailers know customers will ask for the product by name while the advertising campaign is running
● McVitie's has a much larger market share, therefore the company is in a stronger position to cross-sell (i.e. persuade a shopkeeper to buy a range of McVitie's brands).

25.2 How is the marketing mix used?

The marketing mix can be used by a new business to develop ideas about how and where to market a product or service. A very small business start-up may look no further than leaflets to be handed out or posted in neighbouring front doors. In a larger business, a senior manager is likely to set a maximum budget, then the individual marketing managers will look at each of the ingredients in the mix. They then decide what marketing actions need to be taken under each of the '4P' headings. If marketing activity is to be effective, each ingredient needs to be considered.

For each market situation managers are trying to set the ideal combination of the ingredients based on a balance between cost and effectiveness. The ingredients need to work with each other. A good product poorly priced may fail. If the product is not available following an advertising campaign the expenditure is wasted. A successful mix is the one that succeeds in putting the strategy into practice (Figure 25.1).

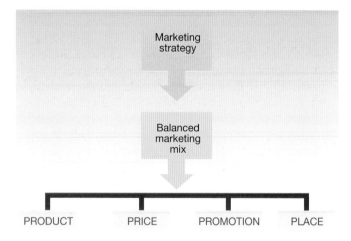

Figure 25.1 A balanced marketing mix

For each market situation there will be a different mix

The focus of the marketing mix will vary according to the market in which the firm is operating. Careful market research should reveal the attitudes and tastes of the target market. An important issue will be whether the goods are:

- regular purchases
- impulse purchases
- emergency purchases.

Impulse purchases (such as chocolate brands) are interesting because they require strong branding, great distribution and display, and eye-catching packaging. In other words, the mix focuses on place and promotion. Price is much less important and the quality of the product may not be hugely important.

Table 25.1 Different types of purchasing and the marketing mix

Type of purchasing	Most important elements of the mix
Regular purchases	Product, promotion and price
Impulse purchases	Place and promotion (including packaging)
Emergency purchases	Place and product

Within each market there may be many different segments

The differences in customers and buying habits result in many 'markets within markets'; these are known as market segments. Each segment will require its own marketing mix. The fashion industry is an example. At one end, cheap, cheerful with mass availability is the key; at the other end exclusivity, quality workmanship and a famous brand name are important.

The ingredients are not equally important

In most cases the product is the vital ingredient. No amount of marketing effort will make a poor product succeed. When selling to other businesses, reliability and quality will probably be far more important than brand image. However, a good product without good support may also fail. The balance will vary. In a price-sensitive market, pricing will be important. This is seen in the petrol market. If one company reduces its price the others follow rapidly.

Influences on the marketing mix

Finance

Every marketing director is attempting to achieve the best mix of marketing factors to enable the marketing strategy to be a success. S/he must decide how big a budget is needed to market the product successfully, and then how to divide the budget between the 4Ps. If £1 million is available, should it all be put into a TV advertising campaign, or should half the budget be kept for offering special discounts to retailers who stock the product for the first time?

If the budget is big enough, the company will be able to do all the things it wants. Yet even Cadbury, with a £12 million **marketing budget** for its Dairy Milk brand, cannot do everything. This is not surprising, given that a single week of strong TV advertising nationally would cost more than £1 million.

If the budget is very tight, the business may have to be clever about setting the right marketing mix. Small, upmarket food producer Klein Caporn started in 2005 with a strategy based on advertising in classy magazines, and distribution through small, independent food shops. After 12 months it became clear that this would never be profitable because of the costs of delivery to lots of small shops. So bosses Paddy Klein and Ed Caporn changed approach, cutting their price level and targeting the main supermarkets. Waitrose provided

distribution in its London stores and then, in 2007, the company made a breakthrough into Sainsbury's outlets nationally. They also changed their promotional strategy, hiring a public relations company to get them features in the press instead of spending on advertising. The new approach is working well.

Technology

As shown above in the YouTube example, clever firms need to keep up with modern customers. Years ago, a peak-time advertisement on ITV could reach 33% of the population. Now it would reach only 15%, and less than 10% of the key market of 15–24 year olds. Fewer and fewer families sit together through a night's television: grannies are on Google, while the 15–24 year olds may be in their bedroom on Facebook, playing *Halo 3* or swapping digital files with WiFi-connected friends.* Tesco showed the sharpness of its management in going into online sales and delivery in the 1990s. It left rivals such as Morrisons and Asda trailing. Long-term success in marketing requires that firms keep up with changes in technology.

Market research

If finance and technology are important to a successful marketing mix, market research is vital. Note that this does not have to be formal research (questionnaires, group discussions, and so on). All firms are in daily contact with their customers, but it is usually only small firms that can capture this information. If a Pizza Hut customer complains that a pizza is too greasy, the head office manager for pizza supplies is very unlikely to ever hear the bad news. At a small Italian restaurant, the chef should hear straight away and think hard about whether the dough has too much oil in it.

Medium-sized and large firms need primary research to keep the senior managers in touch with the customers they rarely see. Small firms should constantly be listening to what customers say – in praise or in criticism. There is no better form of market research, because getting the product right is the key to all marketing success.

A-grade application

A 2007/08 YouTube sensation in America is Will It Blend. It features the geeky-looking chief executive of a small US producer of food blenders. Although any other advertiser would show fruit being blended, Tom Dickson shows the machine's power to blend anything. Word had already spread about his clips blending an American football, a long-handled paddle and a set of golf balls. Then came his biggest hit: blending a brand new iPhone. This received 2 million hits (and rising). People go to the site for the fun of seeing the demonstration, but go away convinced that this is quite some machine. Dickson's company, Blendtec, claims a 650% increase in its online sales as a result of its YouTube campaign. The cost has been close to zero, as Dickson produces the clips himself, then just uploads them.

* By definition this sentence will be out of date by the time you read it.

25.4 Where does the marketing mix fit into marketing planning?

In **marketing planning**, the marketing mix should follow on from the **marketing strategy**. Managers need an excellent understanding of the market if they are to mix the ingredients effectively.

● Statistical analysis should highlight trends. Investigation will reveal the reasons for them.

● Market research should provide:
 – an understanding of the product's place in the market, the market segments and target customers
 – customers' views on the product
 – reasons for the success or failure of the product
 – an understanding of competitive activity.

● The marketing strategy should follow from this analysis. The marketing mix will put the strategy into practice (see Figure 25.2).

Figure 25.2 Where do the 4Ps fit into marketing planning?

25.5 Adapting the mix to product trial vs repeat purchase

When starting a business or launching a new product, most managers focus on product trial, i.e. getting people to buy your product for the first time. This may be a massive challenge. Some markets are hugely crowded with competent existing brands, so it may be hard to stand out.

It is tempting to draw customers in by using an extreme approach, such as a very low 'trial price' or by using an especially garish TV advertisement. The launch advertising for the household cleaner Cillit Bang won polls for the most annoying advertisement of the year, yet 25% of householders bought the brand, making it a huge success. Unfortunately it has been much less successful at achieving repeat purchase, so the brand's sales have fallen away since its 2004 launch. Low trial prices can also cause problems. Cadbury launched the brand Time Out as a rival to Kit-Kat. To achieve high trial it was heavily discounted, with prices as low as 15p per pack. This achieved high sales volumes, but made it harder to persuade customers to buy it regularly when the discount prices had ceased.

The best mix for achieving high product trial is:

● to have a *product* that people can immediately see is for them (i.e. no need for a long or hard sell because the product is innovative and relevant, such as Coke cans with a resealable lid)

● to be displayed prominently in the right *places* for impulse purchase, such as the cash till

● to be backed by advertising *promotion* that creates interest (i.e. is intriguing – it makes you want to look further)

● to have a *price* that is affordable but not 'cheap'.

The best mix for achieving high rates of repeat purchase is:

● the *product* quality must be really impressive, beating the expectations created by the advertising ('Wow, that's good!'); simply being good will probably not be enough to persuade the buyer to change his/her regular purchasing habits ('Oh, I just need some Galaxy')

● the *price* must go on being affordable, though it may be possible to increase it slightly once people have become brand loyal; *Look* magazine launched in February 2007 with a cover price of £1.30 – by early 2008 the price had risen to £1.40

● advertising and other forms of *promotion* must be lively enough to keep shopkeepers happy to stock the product; this forces suppliers to pay for special retail promotions from time to time, such as 'buy one, get one free'; in the long term, though, brand loyalty is best encouraged by consistently high-quality branding and advertising – over the years, BMW and Coca-Cola have been hard to beat

● *place* must never be taken for granted; in May 2007 posh pie manufacturer Square Pie thought it was heading for a massive future when Sainsbury's gave it shelf space in 71 stores – five months later it was withdrawn due to low sales; Square Pie's founder had underestimated the cost and effort that was needed to create the customer demand to shift the stock off the shelves.

Issues For Analysis

When answering questions on the marketing mix consideration should be given to the following points.

● How well the mix is matched to the strategy; only if every aspect of the mix is coordinated and focused will it be effective.

● The relative importance of the ingredients in the marketing mix. Although the product is likely to be the most important element of the mix, every case is different. Taste tests show Coca-Cola to be no better than Pepsi; yet Coke outsells its rival by up to 20 times – in nearly every country in the world.

● How each of the mix ingredients can be used to achieve effective marketing. The mix elements must be tailored to each case. One product may require (and afford) national television advertising. In another case, small-scale local advertising might be supported by below-the-line activity to increase distribution. There is never a single answer to a question about the marketing mix. The best approach depends on the product, its competitive situation, the objectives and the marketing budget.

Designing an effective marketing mix

The concept of the marketing mix has remained unchanged since it was first introduced in the 1950s. It has proved to be a useful marketing tool. However many believe that there are strong arguments for adding a fifth ingredient – people. Many also feel that it should not be presented as a list of equally important parts but that the mix should be seen with the product at the core, supported by the other ingredients.

With the growing importance of customer service and of good sales staff, it is legitimate to extend the marketing mix to include people. A customer who feels the salesperson is rude or lacks knowledge will go elsewhere. The type of people employed, and their attitude, can be used to build the company's image. Disney employees have to be smart, without facial hair, and be 'upbeat'. Particularly in service businesses, people matter. Good exam answers do not simply repeat a theory, they show a willingness to criticise it. It is worth remembering that not everyone agrees that the mix should have only 4Ps.

Although the 4Ps are presented as a list there is no doubt that in almost every case the product is the most important ingredient. A successful marketing mix should be matched to the marketing strategy. And that strategy is rooted in how well the product is matched to the segment of the market being targeted.

> **Key terms**
>
> **Marketing budget:** the sum of money provided for marketing a product/service during a period of time (usually a year).
> **Marketing mix:** the elements involved in putting a marketing strategy into practice; these are product, price, promotion and place.
> **Marketing planning:** producing a schedule of marketing activities based on decisions about the marketing mix. This will show when, what and how much will be spent on a product's advertising, promotions and distribution over the coming year.
> **Marketing strategy:** the medium- to long-term plan for meeting the firm's marketing objectives.

Exercises

A. Revision questions

(30 marks; 30 minutes)

1 Briefly outline each of the four ingredients of the marketing mix. (8)

2 Pick the marketing mix factor (the 'P') you think is of most importance in marketing any *two* of the following brands. Give a brief explanation of why you chose that factor.
  (a) The *Sun* newspaper
  (b) The iPod
  (c) Cadbury's Creme Eggs
  (d) A top-of-the-range BMW (6)

3 Outline how the marketing mix for Mars bars may affect their level of impulse sales in a small corner shop. (4)

4 What is meant by a market segment? (3)

5 Explain why new products are so important to businesses. (3)

6 List three different ways of promoting a product. (3)

7 Explain why it might be difficult for a new, small firm to get distribution in a supermarket chain such as Sainsbury's. (3)

B. Revision exercises

B1 Case study

The launch of *Look* magazine

The UK already had 30 women's weekly magazines. Yet 5 February 2007 saw the launch of another weekly: *Look*. The front cover of the preview issue featured pictures of Posh, Kate, Lindsay and Angelina (plus Brad), as well as an insert shouting 'Just In At Primark!' Fewer than one in eight new magazines becomes successful – how could *Look* be lucky?

Owners IPC Magazines invested £18 million in 18 months of planning for the launch, including £9 million to spend on marketing. *Look*'s editorial staff of 40 was higher than some national newspapers such as the *Daily Star*. This

expensive commitment to a high-quality product was to help meet a sales target of 250,000 copies a week within 12 months.

Editor Ali Hall was very clear about her target audience: a 24-year-old woman, keen on celebrities, even keener on shopping, and with a Saturday high-street ritual of Topshop, H&M, Primark and Dorothy Perkins. *Look* would be about youth, celebrities and style – not brands. At the heart of the product was the promise to give readers the quickest insights into what's hot and what's not. Sections include 'High Street's Hottest' and 'High Street Spy'. The latter tracks down what celebs are wearing and where to buy it (or the high-street imitation).

For £9 million of marketing spend, IPC launched a huge promotional programme, giving away 1.2 million free copies at supermarkets and shopping malls such as Bluewater and the Trafford Centre. There was also a big launch TV campaign. IPC is a major magazine publisher, so it knew there would be no problem getting distribution and prominent display in newsagents up and down the country.

A key decision was overpricing. Unlike celeb magazines such as *Heat* and *OK!*, *Look* is produced on high-quality glossy paper. It looks as good as rival *Grazia* and monthlies such as *Marie Claire*. Despite the expensive glossy paper, *Look* was priced at £1.30, significantly below *Grazia*'s £1.80. This was probably essential as the sales target of 250,000 would require *Look* to outsell the established *Grazia* (175,000 copies a week).

IPC's determination to succeed with *Look* appeared promising one year on: 12 months after launch sales had grown to an average of 305,000 a week and the price had been slipped up to £1.40.

Questions

(25 marks; 30 minutes)

1 Outline the way in which IPC segmented the market in its plans for the new *Look* magazine. (3)

2 Explain two possible reasons why seven out of

eight newly launched magazines prove to be flops. (4)

3 Identify and explain the approach to pricing taken by IPC in its launch of *Look*. (3)

4 Outline *Look*'s marketing mix. (6)

5 Using the evidence in the case plus any other information available to you, discuss why *Look* proved to be such a success. (9)

B2 Case study

The battle for customers

A leading UK supermarket chain is considering expanding into India. It sees this as a relatively untapped market. The home market is saturated, and price wars and loyalty cards have reduced profit margins. In the UK the supermarkets have been blamed for the disappearance of the corner shop. In India the situation is very different. A recent survey by an Indian market research firm concluded that small grocery shops will continue to dominate the food retailing market for the foreseeable future. Several firms, which have been lured to India by its rapid economic growth and over 1 billion mouths to feed, have not been successful in their attempts to establish supermarkets in India's largest cities. Neither of the two main contenders have managed to break even since opening in the early 1990s. They are continuing to expand and hoping that, eventually, economies of scale will permit lower prices and hopefully improve their standing and their profitability.

These new supermarkets have faced several problems.

- The local stores do not stock as many brands as the supermarkets, but they will stock an item if a customer wants it. If they do not have what the customer wants they will get it.

- The local stores offer a free delivery service and allow customers credit.

- The supermarkets cannot match the cost base of the local store. The poor infrastructure makes operational costs (such as transport and delivery) very expensive.

- Government laws limiting urban development mean that property prices are high. The smaller stores have often been in the family for generations, and so the initial cost of the site has long since been forgotten.

To try to gain customers, one of the supermarket chains has introduced promotions such as coupons, and has advertised in local newspapers. Another has teamed up with local manufacturers. It obtains staples such as lentils and rice locally. These are then packaged and branded by local manufacturers. This has helped to lower prices for customers and improve margins. A recent entrant into the market is trying to stay ahead of the competition. It has invested in air-conditioning and additional telephone lines to ensure that customers do not have to wait when they call.

The UK chain has looked at the existing market in India and feels it can succeed. However, the managers know they will do this only after a struggle to change customer attitudes.

Questions

(30 marks; 35 minutes)

1 What is meant by 'the home market is saturated'? (2)

2 What are the marketing implications for a business in a saturated market? (6)

3 Why might expansion allow economies of scale? (4)

4 What problems might a British retailer have in marketing its service in India? (6)

5 Using the marketing mix, analyse the existing market and evaluate the UK firm's chances of success. (12)

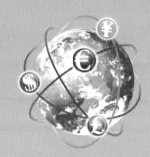

PRODUCT AND PRODUCT DIFFERENTIATION

A product is a good or service that is bought and sold within a market. Products are developed so that they satisfy a specific consumer need or want that has been targeted by the business.

26.1 What's in a product: actual and psychological benefits

Successful products are normally bought by consumers for more than one reason. Products such as Coca-Cola and Stella Artois deliver both physical and psychological consumer benefits. Both products taste good, delivering a fairly obvious physical benefit for the consumer. In addition, both brands also offer consumers psychological benefits: both products have brand images that consumers want to buy into.

Figure 26.1 An Alfa Romeo sports car

A-grade application

Alfa Romeo

Highly successful products deliver both physical and psychological benefits that are valued by consumers.

Alfa Romeo is an Italian-based producer of distinctively designed sports cars. Alfa has a very strong brand image that it communicates clearly to the middle-aged men that make up the bulk of its target market. The psychological benefits of owning an Alfa include: beautiful, distinctive design; the company's motor sports heritage; and the fact that the car is Italian.

In the 1980s and 1990s Alfa Romeo performed badly in quality and reliability surveys compared to other car manufacturers. However, despite these weaknesses the company managed to sell enough cars to survive. During this period the product sold on an emotional basis to a hard-core group of Alfa enthusiasts. They loved the company's designs and the brand's cult status. The consumers that made up this niche market were prepared to overlook the product's physical deficiencies.

The key to having a good product is achieving consumer satisfaction. A restaurant can improve the quality of its product in many ways. The most obvious method would be to improve the quality of food sold. Purchasing new superior tables and chairs could also improve the 'product'. However, the restaurant's product could also be improved by providing waiting staff with better training so that customer service improves. For service-sector businesses, such as hotels, a major element of the 'product' is the staff. Motivating employees so that they provide high standards of customer care is vital in terms of producing a high-quality product.

26.2 Influences on the development of new products

Technology

Technological advances can provide firms with opportunities to produce new products that offer consumers new benefits. According to 'Moore's law' computer speed and capacity doubles every two years.

Advances in computer technology have enabled firms to develop new and improved mobile phones and laptop computers that offer consumers new features. These new features enable the firm that was first to the market with these new products to steal market share away from its rivals.

Rapid technological advances in computing have major implications for computer and mobile phone producers. Product life cycles are very short in both markets. As a consequence, component suppliers face tremendous timescale pressures to launch new components before they become technologically obsolete. Even a delay of just a month could be the difference between a successful new product and a failed launch.

A-grade application
Mercedes-Benz technology at your service

Sleeping at the wheel is one of the major causes of road fatalities. To combat this problem Mercedes-Benz is trying to develop the technology necessary to detect driver fatigue. Teams of engineers, computer scientists and psychologists at Mercedes are working on the idea of installing an infra-red camera directed at the driver's eye. If eye-blink frequency drops below a critical level, indicating the onset of sleep, an audible alarm will sound inside the car to re-awaken the driver.

Competitors' actions

Firms operating in competitive markets may try to emulate a successful new product produced by one of their rivals by launching their own 'me-too' version of the successful new product. A me-too is a new brand that is largely an imitation of an existing product. Me-toos normally sell at a price discount compared to the original product.

The entrepreneurial skills of managers and owners

Most firms use market research findings to help them identify profitable new gaps in the market. Once these gaps in the market have been found, firms will then try to design new products that possess the characteristics required by the target market. Entrepreneurs need to be good at spotting gaps in the market; they also need to develop systems within their business that enable it to react first to changes in market trends.

Entrepreneurial managers can launch their new products quickly enough to benefit from '**first-mover advantage**'.

Firms that can launch their new products before their rivals have the opportunity to charge premium prices until competition arrives. In most markets **brand loyalty** tends to be established at a very early stage. Businesses run by managers with weaker entrepreneurial skills, which launched their new products late will probably find it very difficult to gain a foothold in the market.

A-grade application
Zara's fast fashion revolution

Zara is one of Europe's fastest-growing fashion retailers. The company has based its success on fast fashion. The aim of this strategy is to launch new lines of cheap clothing that replicate exclusive designs, shown just a week earlier at major fashion shows. To make this strategy possible, the founder of Zara, Amancio Ortega, used lean production techniques first developed by the car maker Toyota to reduce new product development times.

26.3 Product differentiation and USPs

Product differentiation is the degree to which consumers perceive that your brand is different from its competitors. A highly differentiated product is one that is viewed as having unique features, such as Marmite or the iPhone. A highly differentiated product may have substitutes. However, if differentiation is strong enough, consumers won't even bother looking at these other brands when making their purchasing decisions. The substitutes available are *not acceptable* to the consumer. A product's point of differentiation is often described as a **unique selling point** (USP).

Creating product differentiation

Product differentiation can be created in two ways.

1 Actual differentiation that creates genuine product advantages that benefit the consumer in some way. Actual product differentiation can be created by:
   - a unique design that is aesthetically pleasing to the eye (e.g. Scandinavian furniture from IKEA)
   - a unique product function (e.g. a mobile phone with a new feature)
   - a unique taste (e.g. Dr Pepper)
   - ergonomic factors (e.g. a product that is easier to use than its rivals)
   - superior performance (e.g. a Dyson vacuum cleaner).

2 Imagined differentiation. This type of differentiation involves creating differences that exist only in the mind of the consumer. A product can be differentiated by psychological factors despite the fact that the product is not physically different from a similar product produced by the competition. Imaginary product differentiation can be created via persuasive advertising, celebrity endorsements and sponsorship. When a product is consumed it is not just the product itself that is consumed – buyers also enjoy 'consuming' the brand's image too. Many people are prepared to pay a price premium for a product that has a brand image that appeals to them.

Issues For Analysis

When developing an argument in answer to an exam question, product differentiation offers the following main lines of analysis.

- Firms operating in competitive markets need to sell products that have strong USPs if they are to hold on to market share.

- Product differentiation reduces consumer price sensitivity. The brand loyalty created by the differentiation means that prices can be increased without having to worry about a substantial fall in sales volume. Total revenue should rise when prices are increased because highly differentiated products tend to be price inelastic.

- Product differentiation boosts value-added because it makes premium prices possible.

26.4 Product and product differentiation
an evaluation

Product differentiation is rarely permanent. Changes in consumer tastes and technological advances can make a product's point of differentiation ineffective. Can the idea be easily copied? Is there patent protection?

Which is more effective, imagined differentiation or actual differentiation? It could be argued that imagined differentiation, created by persuasive advertising, might be more long-lasting than actual differentiation because it might be harder for a me-too to replicate a brand's distinctive personality. Magners' original differentiation was relatively weak. Competitors quickly realised that they could also package their premium ciders in pint bottles, promoting the brand to be drunk over ice. If Magners is to hold on to its market share it must identify a new USP.

Globalisation has increased the availability of products to consumers. As a result firms now face increased competitive pressure. In order to survive, firms must continually develop new, ever more powerful USPs for their products. Will small firms with modest research and development resources be able to compete against their larger rivals?

Key terms

Brand loyalty: the desire by customers to stick with one brand; perhaps to always buy that brand (e.g. always buying Galaxy instead of Cadbury's).

First-mover advantage: the benefits of being the first business into a new market sector (as Coca-Cola once was – in 1886!).

Unique selling point: one feature that makes a product different from all its rivals (e.g. Bounty – the only mass-market chocolate bar featuring coconut).

Exercises

A. Revision questions

(40 marks; 40 minutes)

1 Outline two reasons that might explain the success of products such as Coca-Cola and Stella Artois. (4)

2 Analyse how training might be used to improve the quality of the product produced by a service-sector business such as a supermarket. (3)

3 Explain how technological advances can influence the direction of new product development. (3)

4 What is first-mover advantage? State two benefits firms receive if they can achieve first-mover advantage. (4)

5 What is a me-too product and why do some firms choose to launch them? (4)

6 Explain the meaning of the term product differentiation, using your own example. (4)

7 Outline two ways in which a clothes shop might differentiate itself from its competitors. (6)

8 Explain two benefits a firm can gain from selling a differentiated product. (4)

9 Why is it particularly helpful to have a product that is differentiated by a USP? (4)

10 Outline two examples of USPs in current products or services you buy. (4)

B. Revision exercises

B1 Data response

San Paulo is a highly successful Brazilian company that runs over 2000 coffee bars across South America. The idea for the business came ten years ago when the founder of the business, Roberto Carlos, visited Italy for a family holiday. During his holiday Carlos was impressed by the décor and ambience of the traditionally styled Italian coffee shops that he visited.

On his return to Brazil, Carlos decided to set up his own Italian-styled coffee bar. To ensure authenticity and a strong unique selling point, Carlos imported all the fixtures and fittings for his café from Italy. The business was an overnight success. At the time nothing like it existed in his home town of Campo Grande, and the business quickly expanded by opening up new franchised outlets in other cities across Brazil and Argentina. Over time, trading conditions have become tougher as new competitors have entered the market. Most of these competitors have sought to replicate San Paulo's original unique selling point: classic Italian interior design. Today, San Paulo is still the market leader; a significant percentage of customers see San Paulo as being the original coffee bar of its type. However, in an attempt to grow market share Carlos recently took the decision to reduce San Paulo's price premium.

The company now has plans to enter the UK market. The first bar will be set up in Croydon. The management of San Paulo believe that they will have to charge their UK consumers substantially more than their South American customers to overcome higher European wages and rents. The UK coffee bar market is extremely competitive. Will San Paulo be able to survive against companies such as Costa, Caffè Nero and Starbucks?

Questions

(25 marks; 30 minutes)

1a Define the term 'unique selling point'. (2)

1b Identify the original unique selling point that made San Paulo a successful business in South America. (2)

2 Using the data in the case as a starting point, discuss whether constant innovation is required to maintain product differentiation. (12)

3 You have been hired to manage the new bar in Croydon. Despite your concerns about the strength of the competition locally, your English boss wants you to charge high prices. Outline three ways that could be used to create the high product differentiation required for your coffee bar. (9)

26.5 Workbook

B2   Data response

Absolut vodka

Absolut vodka was developed by the Swedish state-owned monopoly provider of strong alcohol, Systembolaget, in the late 1970s. The government's goal was to create a premium-priced product that would sell well in America. Blind product tests showed that consumers were not able to tell the difference between one brand of vodka and another. The challenge, then, was to create a consumer preference for Absolut vodka where there was no real difference.

To create the product differentiation required, the advertising agency appointed to market Absolut had to create a unique image for the brand that would appeal to consumers. The first step was to create a distinctive award-winning bottle that reflected the brand's Scandinavian origins. The second step was more controversial. A brand heritage for Absolut was required to convince American consumers that the brand was authentic. Advertisements claimed that the brand was over 400 years old. Unfortunately, this was not true: Absolut was first sold in Sweden in 1879 and, for many years, the brand had been withdrawn and was unavailable for sale. Production of Absolut only restarted in 1979, just before the brand's relaunch. Less controversially, differentiation was also built up by the decision to use world-famous artists such as Andy Warhol to promote the brand. In America the company also sponsored arts and cultural events to enhance the image of the brand. The strategy worked. Today, Absolut holds over 30% of the American vodka market.

Figure 26.2 Effective branding has helped Absolut to gain 30% of the American vodka market

Questions

(30 marks; 35 minutes)

1 What is a premium-priced product? (2)

2 Explain why product differentiation can create premium prices. (6)

3 Outline two factors that might influence the direction of new product development in the alcoholic drinks industry. (6)

4 Analyse two ways in which product differentiation was created for the Absolut brand. (6)

5 Discuss the ethics of the marketing of Absolut vodka. (10)

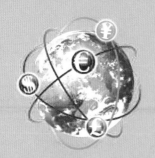
PRODUCT LIFE CYCLE AND PORTFOLIO ANALYSIS

DEFINITION

The product life cycle is the theory that all products follow a similar pattern over time, of development, introduction, growth, maturity and decline.

27.1 What is the product life cycle?

The product life cycle shows the sales of a product over time. When a new product is first launched sales will usually be slow. This is because the product is not yet known or proven in the market. Retailers may be reluctant to stock the product because it means giving up valuable shelf space to products that may or may not sell. This involves a high risk. Customers may also be hesitant – many may want to wait until someone else has tried it before they purchase it themselves.

If the product does succeed, then its sales will grow and it enters the growth phase of the product life cycle. However, at some point sales are likely to stabilise; this is known as the maturity phase. This slowing down of the growth of sales might be because competitors have introduced similar products or because the market has now become saturated. Once most households have bought a dishwasher, for example, sales are likely to be relatively slow. This is because new purchases will mainly involve people who are updating their machine, rather than new buyers.

At some point sales are likely to decline. This may be because new technology means the product has become outdated. An example is the way CD sales have fallen due to the rise of downloading. A decline in sales may also be because competitors have launched a more successful model or you have improved your own product – for example, the PlayStation 3 (PS3) replacing the PS2.

The five key stages of a product's life cycle are known as: development, introduction, growth, maturity and decline. These can be illustrated on a product life cycle diagram. The typical stages in a product's life are shown in Figure 27.1.

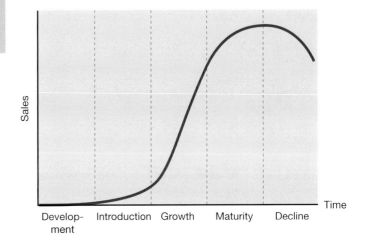

Figure 27.1 The product life cycle

Do remember that many products never make it as far as being launched. Many would-be entrepreneurs have what they think are great ideas. Unfortunately, it turns out they are not financially viable or they cannot find a way of successfully getting them to market. Just think how many ideas are rejected each series on the BBC TV show *Dragons' Den*, because the investors do not think demand is going to be high enough.

Even well-established firms will find that many of their new ideas do not prove commercially viable. Cadbury's rejects twenty new product ideas for every one that reaches the market. Apple's iPod may have been a great success but its internet software Cyberdog lasted about a year, and its first phone – launched with Motorola in 2005 and called the ROKR – was a flop. Thousands of products are taken out of production each year because they fail to hit their initial sales targets and have not reached the growth stage of the life cycle.

Table 27.1 Examples of how the marketing mix may vary at different stages of the product life cycle

	Development	**Introduction**	**Growth**	**Maturity**	**Decline**
Sales	Zero	Low	Increasing	Growth is slowing	Falling
Costs per unit	High; there is investment in product development but only a few prototypes and test products being produced	High, because sales are relatively low but launch costs are high and overheads are being spread over a few units	Falling as overheads are spread over more units	Falling as sales are still growing	Still likely to be low as development costs have been covered and reduced promotional costs are needed to raise awareness
Product	Prototypes	Likely to be basic	May be modified given initial customer feedback; range may be increased	Depends – may focus on core products and remove ones in the range not selling well; may diversify and extend brand to new items	Focus on most profitable items
Promotion	As development is nearly finished it may be used to alert customers of the launch	Mainly to raise awareness	Building loyalty	May focus on highlighting the differences with competitors' products	
Distribution	Early discussions with retailers will help in finalising the product packaging	May be limited as distributors wait to see customers' reactions	May be increasing as more distributors willing to stock it and product is rolled out to more markets	May focus on key outlets and more profitable channels	Lower budgets to keep costs down
Price	Not needed	Depends on pricing approach, e.g. a high price if skimming is adopted (if demand is high and not sensitive to price); a low price if penetration is adopted to gain market share	Depends on demand conditions and strategy adopted; e.g. with a skimming strategy the price may now be lowered to target more segments	May have to drop to maintain competitiveness	Likely to discount to maintain sales

27.2 What use is the product life cycle?

The product life cycle model helps managers plan their marketing activities. Marketing managers will need to adjust their marketing mix at different stages of the product life cycle, as outlined on page 176.

- In the introduction phase the promotion may focus on making customers aware that a new product exists; in the maturity phase it may focus more on highlighting the difference between your product and competitors that have arrived since.

- At the beginning of the life cycle, a technologically advanced product may be launched with a high price (think of the iPhone); over time the price may fall as newer models are being launched. By considering the requirements of each stage of the life cycle, marketing managers may adjust their marketing activities accordingly.

A-grade application
Energy-efficient light bulbs

The lighting industry is now working on a third generation of energy-efficient light bulbs, designed to last a lifetime. Already in use outdoors and in some shops and galleries, these light-emitting diodes (LEDs) have bulbs with a lifespan of up to 100 years. Since October 2006 the front of Buckingham Palace has been lit up with LED bulbs.

Although some energy-efficient bulbs already exist, and are growing in popularity, LEDs for the home are still at the development phase of the product life cycle. They are expected to be on sale in the next four years. A typical light bulb lasts up to one year and costs around 20 pence. The LED will cost over £4. In America, General Electric, the world's biggest bulb manufacturer, is closing seven of its fifty-four factories and warehouses. It is forecasting a downturn in demand for conventional bulbs as people switch to energy-efficient versions.

Managers know that the length of the phases of the life cycle cannot easily be predicted. They will vary from one product to another and this means the marketing mix will need to be altered at different times. For example, a product may be a fad and therefore the overall life of the product will be quite short. Many fashions are popular only for one season and some films

are popular only for a matter of weeks. Other products have very long life cycles. The first manufactured cigarettes went on sale in Britain in 1873. By chance, sales hit their peak (120,000 million!) exactly 100 years later. Since 1973 sales have gently declined. They now stand at 70,000 million.

It is also important to distinguish between the life cycle of a product category and the life cycle of a particular brand. Sales of wine are growing, but a brand that was once the biggest seller (Hirondelle) has virtually disappeared as wine buyers have become more sophisticated. Similarly, confectionery is a mature market but particular brands are at different stages in their life cycles: Mars bars are in maturity while Trident chewing gum is in its growth stage.

27.3 The product life cycle and capacity

When considering the future sales of the business, managers will need to link their forecasts to their plans for the firm's capacity. The capacity of an organisation is the maximum it can produce given its existing resources. If managers choose a capacity level that is relatively low this means that a sudden increase in sales (e.g. if the product enters the growth phase quickly) may mean customers have to be turned away. This happened to the Nintendo Wii in 2007/08, to the delight of rival Sony. On the other hand, if the chosen capacity level is high, if the product is not successful the business will have invested in facilities that are not required; this is inefficient and expensive. Trying to match the capacity of the business to the likely sales is a difficult challenge for managers.

A-grade application
Magners

In 2006 Magners cider was sold in England for the first time. Supported by heavy investment in promotion it was an incredible success. Sales grew 225% in one year and it was clearly in the growth phase of the product life cycle. In fact, the success of Magners prompted an interest in all kinds of cider, and total market sales grew 23% to 965 million pints in 2006. The growth of Magners led its managers to invest £135 million to increase capacity. Unfortunately, however, sales in 2007 were hit by bad weather and the entry of competitor brands.

27.4 Cash flow and the product life cycle

In the development phase before a product is launched, cash flow will be negative. The firm will be spending money on research and development, market research and production planning, but no revenue is yet being generated. Prototypes and models are being made (Dyson produced 5000 prototypes of the Dyson vacuum cleaner before launching it) but income is zero. The business may also decide to test-market the product, which again costs money.

Once the product is on sale cash should begin to come in. However, at this stage, sales are likely to be low and the firm will still be promoting the product heavily to generate awareness. Overall cash flow may continue to be negative for some time. In many cases, the cash flow will not become a positive figure until some way into the growth stage of the life cycle. It may only be at that stage that the firm reaches operational break-even. Cash flow should then continue to improve until the decline stage, when the volume of sales and the amount of cash coming in begin to fall.

It is important, therefore, for firms to manage their cash flow effectively during the life cycle, and to plan ahead. Although a product may prove successful in the long term it may also cause the firm severe cash flow problems in the short term unless its finances are properly managed. Careful budgeting is important at this stage, to avoid overspending.

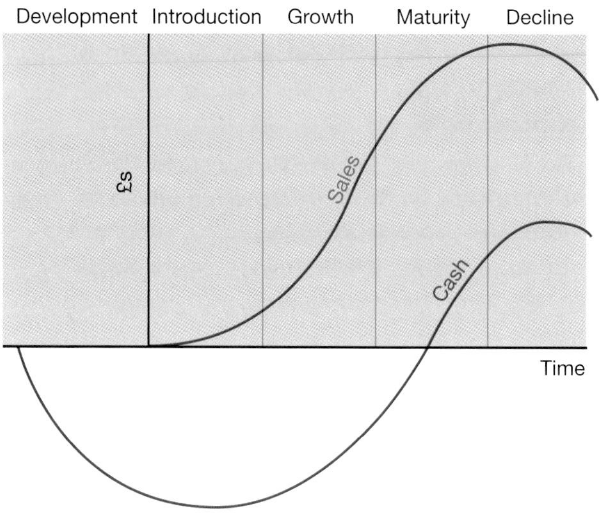

A-grade application
Ocado

Ocado is an online grocer that is in partnership with the supermarket Waitrose. Ocado was established in 2001 and, within its first six years, had gained sales of £300 million a year. Even so, it was still not making a profit because of the huge costs of establishing the business. For example, Ocado invested in an enormous central warehouse where the products are stocked and packed. This is the size of seven football pitches and six storeys high. By 2007 the warehouse was still operating at 35% capacity. However, the managers of Ocado remain positive about the future of the business. They are anticipating annual growth of up to 30% and believe they will start to make a profit in the coming year.

27.5 Extension strategies

The aim of an **extension strategy** is to prevent a decline in the product's sales. There are various means by which this can be achieved, as noted below.

- By *targeting a new segment of the market*: when sales of Johnson & Johnson's baby products started to fall, the company repositioned the product and aimed it at adults. Alternatively, a new geographic market may be targeted, e.g. China.

- By *developing new uses for the product*: the basic technology in hot-air paint strippers, for example, is no different from that in a hairdryer.

Figure 27.2 The product life cycle and cash flow

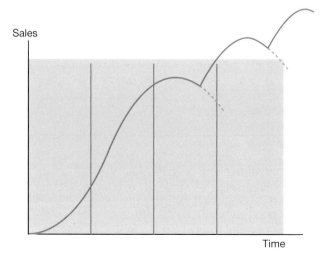

Figure 27.3 The effect of extension strategies

● *By increasing the usage of a product:* Actimel's 'challenge' was for consumers to eat one pot a day for a fortnight – a wonderful way to encourage increased consumption.

The continued success of products such as Coca-Cola and Kellogg's cornflakes is not just due to luck; it is down to sophisticated marketing techniques, which have managed to maintain sales over many years despite fierce competition. The Kellogg's logo is regularly updated, new pack sizes are often introduced, and various competitions and offers are used on a regular basis to keep sales high. The company has also tried to increase the number of students and adults eating its products. It has run advertising campaigns to encourage people to eat the product throughout the day as well as in the morning.

Given the fact that developing a product can involve high costs and that there is a high failure rate of new products, it is not surprising that if a product is successful managers will try to prolong its sales for as long as it is profitable. Who would have thought, in the 1880s, that a frothy drink would still be a huge seller more than 125 years later? Clever Coke.

27.6 Is a decline in sales inevitable?

In the standard product life cycle model it seems as if a decline in sales is inevitable. This may be true in some situations. For example, developments in technology may make some products obsolete. On the other hand, the decline in sales may be the result of poor marketing. Effective extension strategies may ensure that a product's sales are maintained. The long-term success of products and services such as Monopoly and Kit-Kat shows that sales can be maintained over a very long period of time. Creative marketing can avoid the decline phase for a substantial period of time – but only if the product is good enough to keep buyers coming back for more.

One of the reasons for sales decline may be that some managers assume the product will fail at some point and so do not make enough effort to save it. This is known as 'determinism': managers think sales will decline and so sales do fall because of inadequate marketing support. Instead of adapting their marketing strategy to find new ways of selling the product, they let it decline because they assume it cannot be saved.

It is important to remember that a life cycle graph only shows what has happened – it is not a prediction of the future. Top marketing managers try to influence the future, not just let it happen. They try to shape the product life cycle not let it shape their success.

27.7 The product portfolio

Product **portfolio analysis** examines the existing position of a firm's products. This allows the firm to consider its existing position and plan what to do next. There are several different methods of portfolio analysis. One of the best known was developed by the Boston Consulting Group, a management consultancy; it is known as the Boston Matrix.

The Boston Matrix shows the market share of each of the firm's products and the rate of growth of the markets in which they operate. By highlighting the position of each product in terms of market share and market growth, a business can analyse its existing situation and decide what to do next and where to direct its marketing efforts. This model has four categories, as described below.

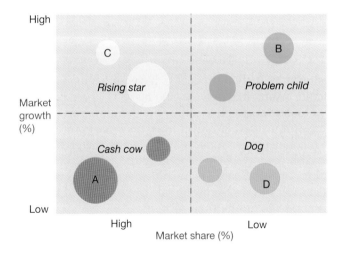

Figure 27.4 Product portfolio: the Boston Matrix

Cash cow: a high share of a slow-growing market

In Figure 27.4, product A has a high market share of a low-growth market. The size of the circle depends on the turnover of the product. This type of product is known as a **cash cow**. An example of a cash cow might be Heinz Baked Beans. The overall market for baked beans is mature and therefore slow growing. Within this market, the Heinz brand has a market share of more than 50%. This type of product generates high profits and cash for the company because sales are relatively high, while the promotional cost per unit is quite low.

Consumers are already aware of the brand, which reduces some of the need for promotion. High and stable sales keep the cost per unit relatively low. Heinz can therefore 'milk' cash from baked beans to invest in newer products such as Heinz Organic Ketchup.

Problem child: a low share of a fast-growing market

Product B, by comparison, is in a high-growth market but has a low market share. This type of product is known as a **problem child** (also called a 'question mark'). A problem child may well provide high profits in the future; the market itself is attractive because it is growing fast and the product could provide high returns if it manages to gain a greater market share. However, the success of such products is by no means certain and that is why they are like problem children – they may grow and prosper or things may go wrong. These products usually need a relatively high level of investment to promote them, get them distributed and keep them going. A new Heinz recipe might be in this position.

Rising star: a high share of a growing market

Rising stars such as product C have a high market share and are selling in a fast-growing market. These products are obviously attractive – they are doing well in a successful market. However, they may need protecting from competitors' products. Once again, the profits of the cash cows can be used to keep the sales growing. Heinz Organic Soups are in this category. They are very successful, with fast-growing sales, but still need heavy promotion to ensure their success.

Dogs: a low share of a stable or declining market

The fourth category of products are known as **dogs**. These products (like product D in Figure 27.4) have a low share of a low-growth market. They hold little appeal for a firm unless they can be revived. The product or brand will be killed off once its sales slip below the break-even point.

The purpose of product portfolio analysis

Product portfolio analysis aims to examine the existing position of the firm's products. Once this has been done

the managers can plan what to do next. Typically this will involve four strategies:

1 *building* – this involves investment in promotion and distribution to boost sales; this is often used with problem children (question marks)

2 *holding* – this involves marketing spending to maintain sales; this is used with rising star products

3 *milking* – this means taking whatever profits you can without much more new investment; this is often used with cash cow products

4 *divesting* – this involves selling off the product and is common with dogs or problem children.

The various strategies chosen will depend on the firm's portfolio of products. If most of the firm's products are cash cows, for example, it needs to be developing new products for future growth. If, however, the majority are problem children then it is in quite a high-risk situation; it needs to try to ensure some products do become stars. If it has too many dogs then it needs to be investing in product development or acquiring new brands.

Issues For Analysis

When analysing the importance of the product life cycle and portfolio model it might be useful to consider the following points.

- Portfolio analysis examines the position of all the firm's products, and helps managers decide what to do with each of them (e.g. invest more or milk them).

- The models do not in themselves tell the firm what to do; managers must interpret their findings and decide on the most effective course of action.

- Managers must avoid letting these models become self-fulfilling (e.g. deciding the product is in decline and so letting its sales fall).

- Product life cycles are generally becoming shorter due to the rapid developments in technology and the increasing levels of competition in most markets.

- As well as the life cycle for a particular product it can be useful to study the life cycle of a category of products (e.g. examining the life of Flora margarine and the life cycle for the whole margarine market).

Both the product life cycle and product portfolio analysis are marketing tools to help firms with their marketing planning. By analysing their existing situation they can identify what needs to be done with the marketing mix to fulfil their objectives. However, like all planning tools, simply being able to examine the present position does not in itself guarantee success. Firms still have to be able to select the right strategy and implement it successfully.

27.8 Product life cycle and portfolio analysis
an evaluation

The product life cycle model and portfolio analysis are important in assessing the firm's current position within the market. They make up an important step in the planning process. However, simply gathering data does not in itself guarantee success. A manager has to interpret the information effectively and then make the right decision. The models show where a business is at the moment; the difficult decisions relate to where the business will be in the future.

Product portfolio analysis is especially useful for larger businesses with many products. It helps a manager look critically at the firm's product range. Then decisions can be made on how the firm's marketing spending should be divided up between different products. By contrast, the product life cycle is of more help to a small firm with one or two products. A company called Filofax made a fortune in the 1990s marketing a paper-based 'personal organiser'. When people switched to electronic products such as the BlackBerry, Filofax wasted years (and many millions) persisting with its paper product. The business needed to acknowledge when a life cycle decline was unstoppable.

Key terms

Cash cow: a product that has a high share of a low-growth market.

Dog: a product that has a low share of a low-growth market.

Extension strategy: marketing activities used to prevent sales from declining.

Portfolio analysis: an analysis of the market position of the firm's existing products; it is used as part of the marketing planning process.

Problem child: a product that has a small share of a fast-growing market.

Rising star: a product that has a high share of a fast-growing market.

Exercises

A. Revision questions

(35 marks; 35 minutes)

1 Identify the different stages of the product life cycle. Give an example of one product or service you consider to be at each stage of the life cycle. (4)

2 Explain what is meant by an 'extension strategy'. (4)

3 Outline the likely relationship between cash flow and the different stages of the life cycle. (4)

4 How is it possible for products such as the Barbie doll to apparently defy the decline phase of the product cycle? (6)

5 What is meant by 'product portfolio analysis'? (3)

6 Distinguish between a cash cow and a rising star in the Boston Matrix. (4)

7 Explain how the Boston Matrix could be used by a business such as Cadbury. (4)

8 Firms should never take decline (or growth) for granted. Therefore they should never take success (or failure) for granted. Explain why this advice is important if firms are to make the best use of product life cycle theory. (6)

B. Revision exercises

B1 Data response

Fire Angel

Sam Tate and his partner have developed an innovative smoke detector called Fire Angel. This product is placed in a light fitting and its energy supply is automatically recharged when the light is turned on. This way the danger of your smoke detector failing to work because of flat batteries should be reduced and, because it recharges itself, customers don't need to buy new batteries. Fire Angel is now stocked in around 6000 stores.

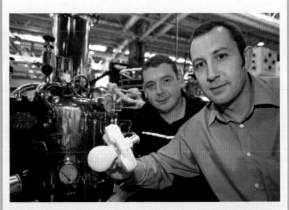

Figure 27.5 Fire Angel smoke detector

Before launching Fire Angel Sam did lots of market research. He spoke to the Fire Brigade and the government office responsible for fire safety, to ensure that there was a need for this sort of product, and to estimate the market size and market growth. He then interviewed people in the street to see what they thought, as well as analysing competitors' products. He also examined different ways of getting the product to market and eventually decided that selling through the supermarkets was the key to achieving a high volume of sales.

The average price of smoke detectors is between £5 and £10 but Sam felt he could charge a premium price because his product does not need a battery and lasts for up to ten years, so he set the price of the Fire Angel at £20. He felt it was better to go in with a higher price than a lower one because it is more difficult to lower the price than increase it later on. It took three years to get the Fire Angel from the idea stage to the launch stage; most of this time was spent on design and testing, but it did take many months to convince some of the retailers to stock it.

Source: adapted from Business Link

Questions

(30 marks; 35 minutes)

1 What is meant by 'market growth'? (2)

2 Outline the unique selling point of the Fire Angel, and explain how this can benefit the business. (6)

3 Analyse the possible benefits to Sam of undertaking market research before launching the Fire Angel. (7)

4 Explain why Sam might have had cash flow problems in the first few years of his business. (6)

5 At the moment the Fire Angel is still in its growth phase. Discuss the ways in which the marketing mix of the Fire Angel might change as it enters the maturity phase. (9)

B2   Data response

Mackie's ice cream

Figure 27.6 The Mackie family

Mackie's is a maker of luxury ice cream, based in Scotland.

All Mackie's ice cream is made at its farm in Aberdeenshire. Its production chain includes the wind that provides the business with renewable energy, its own crops that feed its cattle, and its own cows that produce the milk and cream for the ice cream. 'It's a real plough to plate – or cow to cone story,' says the company.

Mackie's employs 70 people and produces over 7 million litres of luxury ice cream a year.

Mackie's ice cream is well established as the brand leader in the luxury ice cream market in Scotland, has an increasing market share in England, and is being exported to Seoul (South Korea) and Norway.

The Mackie family have been farming at Westertown farm since the turn of the century, but it was only in 1986 that they started pilot trials for an ice cream. In 1993 some of the farm's facilities were converted to a modern ice cream dairy capable of producing more than 10 million litres a year. In 1996 the New Product Development Kitchen was added. In 2006 production machinery was added to raise capacity in the ice cream dairy to 6000 litres per hour. It sells through shops, restaurants and ice cream parlours.

Its luxury ice cream products include: Raspberry, Honeycomb, Strawberry and Cream, Chocolate Mint, and Absolutely Chocolate. These are available in a variety of sizes. It also produces 100%-fruit frozen smoothies, sorbets and organic ice cream.

Source: http://www.mackies.co.uk/

Questions

(30 marks; 35 minutes)

1 What is meant by the term 'market share'? (2)

2 Explain the factors that Mackie's might have considered before expanding its capacity. (5)

3 Explain how the promotion of a new Mackie's ice cream might vary at different stages in its life cycle. (5)

4 Examine the possible benefits to Mackie's of having a portfolio of products. (8)

5 Consider whether new product development is likely to be essential for success in the ice cream market. (10)

28 Unit

PRICING

DEFINITION

Price is the amount paid by the customer for a good or service.

28.1 How important are decisions about price?

Price is one of the main links between the customer (demand) and the producer (supply). It gives messages to consumers about product quality and is fundamental to a firm's revenues and profit margins. As part of the marketing mix it is fundamental to most consumer buying decisions. The importance of price to the customer will depend on several factors, as discussed below.

Customer sensitivity to price

Consumers have an idea of the correct price for a product (see Figure 28.1). They balance price with other considerations. These include:

- the quality of the product – products seen as having higher quality can carry a price premium; this may be real or perceived quality

- how much they want it – all purchases are personal; customers will pay more for goods they need or want

- their income – customers buy products within their income range; consumers with more disposable income are less concerned about price; uncertainty about future income will have the same effect as lower income; if interest rates are high, hard-pressed home-buyers will be much more sensitive to price; they need to save money and so they check prices more carefully and avoid high-priced items.

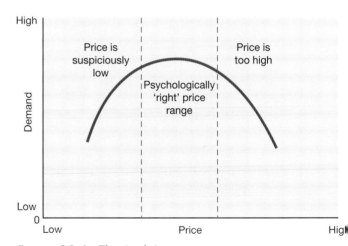

Figure 28.1 The 'right' price

Table 28.1 Price sensitivity in practice

Products, services and brands that are highly price sensitive	Products, services and brands that are not very price sensitive
No-frills air travel	Business-class air travel
Fiat and Ford cars	BMW and Mercedes cars
Children's white school shirts	Pampers disposable nappies
Monday-night cinema tickets	Saturday-night cinema tickets

The level of competitive activity

The fiercer the competition in a market, the more important price becomes. Customers have more choice, so they take more care to buy the best-value item, whereas a business with a strong **monopoly** position is able to charge higher prices.

The availability of the product

If the product is readily available consumers are more price conscious. They know they can go elsewhere and find the same product – perhaps cheaper. Scarcity removes some of the barriers to price. This is why perfume companies such as Chanel try to keep their products out of supermarkets and stores like Superdrug – they want to avoid shops price-cutting brands such as Chanel No 5.

28.2 Price determines business revenue

Pricing is important to the business. Unlike the other ingredients in the marketing mix it is related directly to revenue through the formula: revenue = price × units sold. If the price is not right the business could:

- lose customers – if the price is too high, sales may slump and therefore revenue will be lost; it will depend on the **price elasticity** of the product (see Unit 29); if goods remain unsold, costs of production will not be recovered

- lose revenue – if the price is too low, sales may be high, but not high enough to compensate for the low revenue per unit.

Pricing involves a balance between being competitive and being profitable.

28.3 How do businesses decide what price to charge?

At certain times during a product's life cycle pricing is especially important. Incorrect pricing when the product is launched could cause the product to fail. At other stages in the product's life, pricing may be used to revive interest in the brand.

There are two basic pricing decisions: pricing a new product and managing prices throughout the product life. Both decisions require a good understanding of the market – consumers and competitors.

Pricing decisions require an understanding of costs. These costs must include purchasing, manufacturing, distribution, administration and marketing. Cost information should be available from the company's management accounting systems.

The lowest price a firm can consider charging is set by costs. Except as a temporary promotional tactic (a loss leader), businesses must charge more for the product than the variable cost. This ensures that every product sold contributes towards the fixed costs of the business.

The market determines the highest price that can be charged. The price that is charged will need to take account of the company objectives. The right price will be the one that achieves the objectives.

There are several ways that businesses obtain market information:

- market research can provide consumer reactions to possible price changes

- competitive research tells the company about other products and prices

- analysis of sales patterns shows how the market reacts to price and economic changes

- sales staff can report on customer reactions to prices.

When making changes to product prices the business needs to understand the relationship between price changes and demand. Demand for some products is more sensitive to price changes than for others. Price

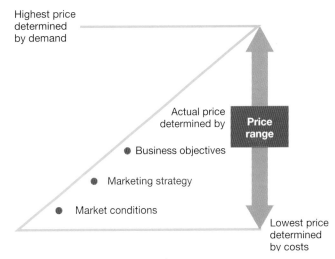

Figure 28.2 Determining the price

elasticity of demand measures how sensitive demand is to price changes. If demand for a product is sensitive to price changes an increase in price could cut total revenue.

28.4 Pricing strategies

A pricing strategy is a company's plan for setting its prices over the medium to long term. In other words it is *not* about deals such as 'This week's special: 40% off!' Short-term offers are known as tactics. Medium- to long-term plans are called strategies.

For new products, firms must choose between two main pricing strategies:

1 skimming, i.e. pricing high

2 penetration, i.e. pricing low to achieve high sales volume

Skimming is used when the product is innovative. As the product is new there will be no competition. The price can therefore be set at a high level. Customers interested in the new product will pay this high price. The business recovers some of the development costs, making sure that enthusiasts who *really* want the product pay the high price they expect to pay. For example, the first DVD players came onto the UK market at a price of around £1000. Firms use the initial

sales period to assess the market reaction. If sales become stagnant the price can be lowered to attract customers who were unwilling to pay the initial price. The price can also be lowered if competitors enter the market.

Penetration pricing is used when launching a product into a market where there are similar products. The price is set lower to gain market share. Once the product is established the price can be increased. It is hoped that high levels of initial sales will recover development costs and lead to lower average costs as the business benefits from bulk-buying benefits.

Pricing strategies for existing products.

For existing products the key is to be clear about where your brand stands in the market. Pricing strategy on the latest Mercedes sports car will be based on the confidence of the company in the strength of its brand name. Mercedes will not worry what Ford or Mazda charge for a sports car, nor even the prices of its BMW or Lexus rivals. The Merc will be a 'price leader': where it sets prices, others will follow. Weaker brands, such as Chrysler or Fiat, are the followers. They are 'price takers' (i.e. they have to take the lead set by the strong brands, usually pricing their own products at a lower level).

Table 28.2 Advantages and disadvantages of price skimming and price penetration

	Price skimming	**Price penetration**
Advantages	High prices for a new item such as the iPhone help establish the product as a must-have item	Low-priced new products may attract high sales volumes, which make it very hard for a competitor to break into the market
	Early adopters of a product usually want exclusivity and are willing to pay high prices, so skimming makes sense for them and for the supplier	High sales volumes help to cut production costs per unit, as the producer can buy in bulk and therefore get purchasing costs down
	Innovation can be expensive, so it makes sense to charge high prices to recover the investment cost	Achieving high sales volumes ensures that shops will provide high distribution levels and good in-store displays
Disadvantages	Some customers may be put off totally by 'rip-off pricing' at the start of a product's life	Pricing low may affect the brand image, making the product appear 'cheap'
	When the firm decides to cut its prices its image may suffer	It may be hard to gain distribution in more upmarket retail outlets, due to mass-market pricing
	Buyers who bought early (at high prices) may be annoyed that prices fell soon afterwards	Pricing on the basis of value for money can cause customers (and therefore competitors) to be very **price sensitive**

Price leader

This is where the price is set above the market level. This is possible when the company has strong brands or there is little effective competition. In Britain the accepted price of chewing gum is set by Wrigley's, which has a 90% market share. Other brands have little choice but to charge at or below the level set by Wrigley's.

Price taker

This is when the price is set at the market level or at a discount to the market. This happens in highly competitive markets or in markets where one brand dominates. When Branston Baked Beans were launched in 2006, they were priced at 41p, compared to the 44p charged by the price leader, Heinz.

Choosing a pricing strategy

The choice of pricing strategy will depend on the competitive environment. Figure 28.3 shows how the choice of pricing strategy will vary according to the level of competition.

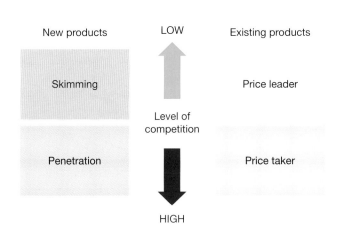

Figure 28.3 Factors affecting choice of pricing strategy

28.5 Pricing tactics

Whichever strategy has been selected, there are tactics that should also be considered. They can be part of normal pricing or used as one element in the firm's promotional tactics. They include the following.

● *Loss leaders*: prices are set deliberately low – so low that the firm may make a loss on every unit sold. The idea is to encourage customers to buy other products or **complementary goods** that generate profit. Supermarkets commonly use this approach. At Christmas they may attract custom by selling tree lights for 49p – confident that shoppers will end up with a full trolley of other goods. Children's sticker albums may also be offered very cheaply – but the packs of stickers to go inside are often expensive.

● *Psychological pricing*: prices are set at a level that seems lower to the customer. Without thinking about it, customers see a price of £9.99 as quite significantly lower than £10.50. The loss of 51p per item is more than made up for by higher sales.

● *Special offer pricing*: for example, buy one get one free; or offers made for a short period or to clear stocks.

Issues For Analysis

When answering a question on pricing it is important to understand the following points.

● *The relationship between price and demand*: in other words, a change in price will almost always affect the demand for a product.

● *The role of pricing as one part of the overall marketing mix*: the price should match the image suggested by the product design, advertising, branding and distribution outlets; an expensive-looking perfume displayed in Harrods would have its image undermined if it were priced at £9.99.

● *The influence of price upon profitability*: many products have profit margins of only 20%; therefore a 10% price cut will halve profit per unit. It would take a huge increase in demand to compensate.

● *The factors influencing pricing*: for example, cost, customer psychology and competitors.

28.6 Pricing

an evaluation

Economists think of price as a neutral factor within a marketplace. Its impact upon demand can be measured, predicted and captured in the concept of price elasticity (see Unit 29). Many businesses would disagree – especially those selling consumer goods and services. The reason is that consumer psychology can be heavily influenced by price. A '3p off' flash makes people reach for the Mars bars, but if they are half price people wonder whether they are old stock or have suffered in the sun – they are *too* cheap.

When deciding on the price of a brand new product, marketing managers have many options. Pricing high might generate too few sales to keep retailers happy to stock the product. Yet pricing too low carries even more dangers. Large companies know there are no safe livings to be made selling cheap jeans, cheap cosmetics or cheap perfumes.

If there is a key to successful pricing, it is to keep it in line with the overall marketing strategy. When Häagen-Dazs launched in the UK at prices more than double those of its competitors, many predicted failure. In fact the pricing was in line with the image of adult, luxury indulgence and Häagen-Dazs soon outsold all other premium ice creams. The worst pricing approach would be to develop an attractively packaged, well-made product and then sell it at a discount to the leading brands. In research, people would welcome it, but deep down they would not trust the product quality. Because psychology is so important to successful pricing, many firms use qualitative research, rather than quantitative, to obtain the necessary psychological insights.

Key terms

Complementary goods: products bought in conjunction with each other, such as bacon and eggs, or Gillette shavers and Gillette razors.
Early adopters: consumers with the wealth and the personality to want to be the first to get a new gadget or piece of equipment; they may be the first to wear new fashion clothes, and the first to get the new (and expensive) computer game.
Monopoly: a market dominated by one supplier.
Price elasticity: a measurement of the extent to which a product's demand changes when its price is changed.
Price sensitive: when customer demand for a product reacts sharply to a price change (i.e. the product is highly price elastic).

Exercises

A. Revision questions

(35 marks; 35 minutes)

1 Explain why price 'is fundamental to a firm's revenues'. (3)

2 Look at Figure 28.1. Outline two factors that would affect the 'psychologically right price range' for a new Nokia phone. (4)

3 Explain how the actions of Nike might affect the footwear prices set by Adidas. (3)

4 Look at Table 28.1, on the price sensitivity of products, brands and services. Think of two more examples of highly price sensitive and two examples of not-very-price-sensitive products, services or brands. (4)

5 Explain the difference between pricing strategy and pricing tactics. (3)

6 For each of the following, decide whether the pricing strategy should be skimming or penetration. Briefly explain your reasoning.
   (a) Richard Branson's Virgin group launches the world's first space tourism service (you are launched in a rocket, spend time weightless in space, watch the world go round, then come back to earth). (4)
   (b) Kellogg's launches a new range of sliced breads for families in a hurry. (4)
   (c) The first Google phone is launched (called G-Fone) with free, instant WiFi access to Google. (4)

7 Is a cash cow likely to be a price maker or a price taker? Explain your reasoning. (3)

8 Identify three circumstances in which a business might decide to use special offer pricing. (3)

B. Revision exercises

B1 Data response

On 24 September 2007, Tesco Pricecheck provided the following information on the prices of shampoo brands. Study the table on page 190 then answer the questions that follow.

Questions

(25 marks; 30 minutes)

1 Briefly explain why it might be fair to describe Elvive Anti-Dandruff shampoo as a price-taker. (3)

2 Neutrogena shampoo is priced at nearly 100 times the level of supermarket budget shampoos (per ml). Explain why customers might be willing to pay such a high price. (6)

3 Examine the position of the long-established brand Pantene Pro-V within the UK market for shampoo. What pricing strategy does it seem to be using and why might it be able to use this approach? (7)

4 Discuss whether dogs should have 'better' shampoo than kids. (9)

Product description	Tesco price	Sainsbury's price	Asda price
Neutrogena Shampoo 250 ml	£6.15	£6.15	£6.15
Pantene Pro-V Express 250 ml	£2.98	£2.97	£2.97
Head & Shoulders 250 ml	£2.39	£1.89	N.A.
Elvive Anti-Dandruff 250 ml	£1.96	£1.96	£1.97
Herbal Essences 250 ml	£1.99	£1.99	N.A.
Own-label Kids' Shampoo 250 ml	£0.38	£0.59	£0.38
Own-label Budget Shampoo 1000 ml	£0.28	£0.28	£0.28
Bob Martin Dog Shampoo 300 ml	£3.35	£3.35	£3.35

N.A. = Not available; Own-label means the supermarket's own brand.

B2 Data response

Figure 28.4 $100 laptop

The $100 laptop

Computer enthusiasts in the developed world will soon be able to get their hands on the so-called '$100 laptop'

The organisation behind the project has launched the 'give one, get one' scheme, which will allow US residents to purchase two laptops for $399 (£198). One laptop will be sent to the buyer while a child in the developing world will receive the second machine. The G1G1 scheme, as it is known, will offer the laptops for just two weeks, starting on 12 November.

Price hike

The XO laptop has been developed to be used by children and is as low cost, durable and simple to use as possible. It packs several

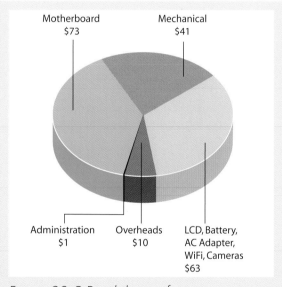

Figure 28.5 Breakdown of costs

innovations, including a sunlight readable display so that it can be used outside. It has no moving parts, can be powered by solar, foot-pump or pull-string powered chargers, and is housed in a waterproof case.

The machine's price has recently increased from $176 (£88) to $188 (£93), although the eventual aim is to sell the machines for $100 (£50).

Governments can buy the green and white machines in lots of 250,000. In July, hardware suppliers were given the green light to ramp-up production of all the components needed to build the low-cost machines. The decision suggested that the organisation had met or surpassed the three million orders it needed to make production viable. The names of the governments that have purchased the first lots of machines have not been released.

Early adopter

The first countries to receive the donated laptops will be Cambodia, Afghanistan, Rwanda and Haiti. Other least developed countries (LDCs), as defined by the UN, will be able to bid to join the scheme. The laptops will go on sale for two weeks through the xogiving.org website. They will only be available for two weeks to ensure OLPC can meet demand and so that machines are not diverted away from countries that have already placed orders.

Source: Adapted from bbc.co.uk

Questions

(30 marks; 35 minutes)

1 Describe the objectives behind the pricing of the XO laptop. (4)

2a Compare the 'breakdown of costs' pie chart in Figure 28.5 to the text to work out the recent profit per unit made on selling the XO laptop. (3)

2b Given that level of profit, how could the company hope 'to sell the machines for $100'? (4)

3a Explain what is meant by an 'early adopter'? (3)

3b Why may early adopters be important to a business? (4)

4 Some people see the XO laptop as a brave, charitable idea; others see it purely as a clever form of penetration pricing strategy. To what extent can you agree with either view? (12)

PRICE ELASTICITY OF DEMAND

DEFINITION

Price elasticity measures the extent to which demand for a product changes when its price is changed.

29.1 Introduction

When a company increases the price of a product, it expects to lose some sales. Some customers will switch to a rival supplier; others may decide they do not want (or cannot afford) the product at all. Economists use the term 'the law of demand' to suggest that, almost invariably:

Price up ———————➤ Demand down

Price down ———————➤ Demand up

Price elasticity looks beyond the law of demand to ask the more subtle questions 'When the price goes up, by how much do sales fall?', 'Do they collapse or do they fall only slightly?'

Elasticity measures the extent to which price changes affect demand.

29.2 Price elasticity of demand

In the short term, the most important factor affecting demand is price. When the price of the *Guardian* newspaper increased from 70p to 80p in 2007 sales fell by 8%, whereas a 30p increase in the price of the *Financial Times* newspaper in the same year cut sales by just 1.5%. Readers of the *Guardian* proved much more price sensitive than readers of the *Financial Times*. Therefore the owners of the *Financial Times* could feel delighted with their pricing decision. Selling 1.5% fewer papers but receiving 30% more for each one sold meant that revenue rose by more than a quarter.

The crucial question is *how much* will demand change when the price is changed? This question can be answered by calculating the price elasticity of demand.

Price elasticity is not about whether demand changes when price changes, it is about the degree of change. Consequently, price elasticity is a unit of measurement rather than being a thing in itself.

A price cut will not cause price elasticity to fall; instead the price elasticity figure explains the effect the price cut is likely to have on demand. Will demand rise by 1%, 5% or 25% following the price cut? The answer can be known only by referring to the product's price elasticity of demand. Price elasticity measures the *responsiveness* of demand to a change in price.

Some products are far more price sensitive than others. Following a 5% increase in price the demand for some products may fall greatly, say by more than 20%. The demand for another type of product may fall by less than 1%.

Price elasticity can be calculated using the formula shown below:

$$\text{Price elasticity} = \frac{\%\ \text{change in quantity demanded}}{\%\ \text{change in price}}$$

Price elasticity measures the percentage effect on demand of each 1% change in price. So if a 10% increase in price led demand to fall by 20%, the price elasticity would be 2. Strictly speaking, price elasticities are always negative, because price up pushes demand down, and price down pushes demand up. For example:

$$\frac{-20\%}{+10\%} = -2$$

The figure of −2 indicates that, for every 1% change in price, demand is likely to change by 2%. All price elasticities are negative. This is because there is a negative **correlation** between price and quantity demanded. In the short term, a price cut will always boost sales and a price rise will always cut sales.

29.3 Determinants of price elasticity

Why do some products, services or brands have low price elasticity and some high elasticity? Why is the price elasticity of Branston Baked Beans higher than that of Heinz Baked Beans? Or the price elasticity of the *Financial Times* as low as 0.05 while the elasticity of *Look* magazine is as high as 2.0 (i.e. 40 times higher)?

The main determinants of price elasticity are as follows.

- *The degree of product differentiation*: that is, the extent to which customers view the product as being distinctive compared with rivals. *Look* may be an excellent magazine, but it is offering the same mix of fashion, shopping and celebs as many other magazines aimed at young women. So if the cover price is increased, it is easy for readers to switch to an alternative, whereas readers of the *Financial Times* have nowhere else to go. Therefore the higher the product differentiation the lower the price elasticity.

- *The availability of substitutes*: customers may see Tango and Fanta as very similar orange drinks. In a supermarket they might buy the cheaper of the two. At a cinema, though, only Fanta may be available. At a train station vending machine, almost certainly Fanta will be the only orange drink. This is because it is a Coca-Cola brand and the distribution strength of Coke places Fanta where Tango never goes. When Fanta is on its own, its price elasticity is much lower; therefore the brand owner (Coke) can push the price up without losing too many customers.

- *Branding and brand loyalty*: products with low price elasticity are those that consumers buy without thinking about the price tag. Some reach for Coca-Cola without checking its price compared to that of Pepsi, or buy a Harley-Davidson motorcycle even though a Honda superbike may be £4000 cheaper. Strong brand names with strong brand images create customers who buy out of loyalty. Note that some strong brands create very little loyalty, such as BP; when buying petrol, drivers buy the cheapest they can, therefore the price elasticity of retail petrol brands such as BP is very high.

- *Actual or perceived necessity*: If a product is regarded as essential it is likely to be price inelastic. A commuter has to pay the railway company the price of a season ticket (however resentfully).

29.4 The significance of price elasticity

Being able to estimate a product's price elasticity is a hugely valuable aid to marketing decision making. When Wigan FC was promoted to the Premiership, its managers assumed that the attractions of Arsenal, Manchester United and the rest would make it easy to push up the price of match tickets. In fact ticket sales proved much worse than expected, forcing the club to cut its prices halfway through the 2006/2007 season. A firm that knows its price elasticity can make better decisions than one that is in ignorance.

Data on a product's price elasticity can be used for two purposes, as outlined below.

Sales forecasting

A firm considering a price rise will want to know the effect the price change is likely to have on demand. Producing a sales forecast will make possible accurate production, personnel and purchasing decisions. For example, when Sony cut the price of its PS2 by 25%, from £200 to £150, sales rose by 20%. The price elasticity of the PS2 proved to be:

$$\frac{-20\%}{+25\%} = -0.8$$

Sony could then use that knowledge to predict the likely impact of future price changes. Another price cut of 10% could lead to a sales increase of 8% ($-10\% \times -0.8 = +8\%$). This is valuable information to know. Before implementing the price cut the company could make sure to produce an extra 8% more stock to cope with the extra orders.

Pricing strategy

There are many external factors that determine a product's demand, and therefore its profitability. For example, a soft drinks manufacturer can do nothing about a wet, cold summer that hammers sales and profits. However, the price the firm decides to charge *is* within its control, and it can be a crucial factor in determining demand and profitability. Price elasticity information can be used in conjunction with internal cost data to forecast the implications of a price change on revenue.

Example

A second-hand car dealer currently sells 60 cars each

year. Currently he charges his customers £2500 per car. This means the business has a revenue of:

Total revenue = £2500 × 60 = £150,000

From past experience the salesman believes the price elasticity of his cars is approximately 0.75. The dealer is thinking about increasing his prices to £3000 per car, an increase of 20%. Using the price elasticity information a quick calculation would reveal the impact on revenue:

Percentage change in demand $= +20\% \times -0.75$
$= -15\%$

A 15% fall in demand on the existing sales volume of 60 cars per year will produce a fall in demand of nine cars per year. So demand will fall to 51 cars per year after the price increase. On the basis of these figures the new revenue would be:

Total revenue $= $ new price × new sales volume
$= £3\,000 \times 51$ cars
$= £153\,000$

So, even though the price rise cuts sales to 51 cars, the revenue actually increases. Obviously, in this case, the car dealer should change his pricing strategy. However, this is all based on two assumptions:

1 that the price elasticity of the cars actually proves to be −0.75

2 other factors that could also affect demand remain unchanged following the price increase.

29.5 Classifying price elasticity

Price-elastic products

A **price-elastic product** is one with a price elasticity of more than 1. This means that the percentage change in demand is greater than the percentage change in price that created it. For example, if a firm increased prices by 5% and as a result demand fell by 15%, price elasticity would be:

$$\frac{-15\%}{+5\%} \times 100 = -3$$

For instance, for every 1% change in price, there will be a 3% change in demand. The higher the price elasticity figure, the more price elastic the product. Cutting price on a price-elastic product will boost total revenue. This is because the extra revenue gained from the increased sales volume more than offsets the revenue lost from the price cut. On the other hand, a price increase on a price-elastic product will lead to a fall in total revenue.

It is important to note that price cutting can damage brand image. Customers often associate high prices with high quality. In addition, a price-cutting decision is usually difficult to reverse due to consumer resistance to price increases. Finally, the actions of the competition must also be taken into account. If your price cut prompts a price war the much needed gains in sales volume might not arise.

Price-inelastic products

Price-inelastic products have price elasticities below 1. This means the percentage change in demand is less than the percentage change in price. In other words, price changes have hardly any effect on demand – perhaps because consumers feel they *must* have the product or brand in question: the stunning dress, the trendiest designer label or – less interestingly – gas for central heating. Customers feel they must have it, either because it really is a necessity, or because it is fashionable. Firms with price-inelastic products will be tempted to push the prices up. A price increase will boost revenue because the price rise creates a relatively small fall in sales volume. This means the majority of customers will continue to purchase the brand but at a higher, revenue-boosting price.

29.6 Problems measuring price elasticity

What is the price elasticity of KitKat? Naturally, owners Nestlé would like to know, so that the right pricing decisions can be made. Therefore the company will do all it can to work out the price elasticity figure for this £100 million-plus brand. But how? All a firm can do is to work out what the price elasticity has been in the past, because it can only be calculated using past data. For example, if demand fell by 8% on the last occasion the price of KitKat was pushed up by 10%, the calculation is that the price elasticity was −0.8 (−8%/+10%).

Yet if that was a year ago, will the same be true today? Competition today may be a bit fiercer, making the price elasticity a bit higher. And today's consumer may be that much more sensitive about eating fatty foods, making a price rise a reason to stop buying KitKats altogether.

The price elasticity of a brand is a complex combination of its fashionability, the number of direct competitors it faces and the loyalty of its existing customers. All these things can change over time, causing the elasticity to go up or down. It is also possible that elasticity changes over a product's life cycle. It may be highly price elastic at the start, when people are suspicious of a new product. In its growth phase it may become trendy, making it less sensitive to price. In its decline phase people may keep buying the product only if the price is attractive, making it price elastic again.

In conclusion, it is unwise to talk about a product's price elasticity as if it is a fact. Firms make decisions using their assumptions or estimates about the price elasticity of their products. These assumptions are usually based on data that may now be out of date.

29.7 Strategies to reduce price elasticity

All businesses prefer to sell price-inelastic products. Charging more for a price-inelastic product guarantees an increase in short-term profit. If a firm has price-elastic products it will always feel vulnerable, as a rise in costs may be impossible to pass on to customers. And if a firm is tempted to cut the price of a price-elastic product, sales will probably rise so sharply that competitors will be forced to respond. A **price war** may result.

It is important to realise that the price elasticity of a brand is not set in stone. Price elasticity is not an **external constraint**. The most important influence on a brand's price elasticity is substitutability. If consumers have other brands available that they think deliver the same benefits, price elasticity will be high. So, to make a brand price inelastic, the firm has to find ways of reducing the number of substitutes available (or acceptable). How can this be done?

Increasing product differentiation

Product differentiation is the degree to which consumers perceive that a product is different (and preferably better) than its rivals. Some products are truly different from others, such as Britain's only business newspaper, the *Financial Times*. Others are successfully differentiated by image, such as Versace Jeans or the iPhone. The purchasers of highly differentiated products like Versace Jeans often remain brand loyal despite price rises. The reason for this low price elasticity is that wearing Versace Jeans makes a statement about the wearer, even if the cloth itself is no different from that used by Levi's or Wrangler.

Predatory pricing

Predatory pricing is a deliberate attempt to force a competitor out of a market by charging a low, loss-making price. Once the competitor has been forced out of the market, the consumer has one less source of supply. The reduction in the number of substitutes available to the customer allows the predator to raise prices successfully. If there are no cheaper substitutes available the customer is forced to pay the higher prices or go without. The same effect can be achieved by takeover bids (e.g. the purchase by Morrisons of Safeway food stores).

Issues For Analysis

In examinations, elasticity of demand is a key discriminator between good and weak candidates. Really weak candidates never bring the concept into their answers at all. Better candidates apply it, but imprecisely. Top-grade students see where it is relevant and show a clear understanding of the concept and its implications. Here are two ways to use price elasticity for business analysis.

● Whenever answering any question about pricing, elasticity is a vital factor. Even if a firm faces severe cost increases, a price rise will be very risky if its products have a high price elasticity. Pricing decisions must always start with careful consideration of price elasticity.

● People naturally assume that marketing (especially advertising) is always about trying to increase sales. In fact, most firms are far more interested in their image; a glance at any commercial break will confirm this. Companies focus upon their image because that is the way to differentiate themselves from others. That, in turn, is the way to reduce price elasticity and therefore give the company stronger control over its pricing.

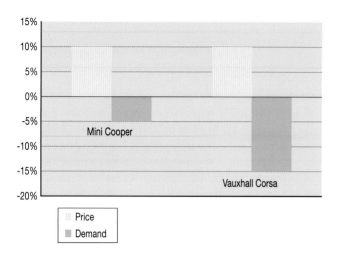

Figure 29.1 The impact of a 10% price rise on sales

29.8 Price elasticity of demand

an evaluation

For examiners, elasticity is a convenient concept. It is hard to understand, but very easy to write exam questions on! But how useful is it in the real world? Would the average marketing director know the price elasticities of his or her products?

In many cases the answer is no. Examiners and textbooks exaggerate the precision that is possible with such a concept. Figure 29.1 shows the impact on sales of a 10% price rise in two models of car. The Mini Cooper's price elasticity is – 0.5 while the Corsa is – 1.5. But just because those figures were true in the past, will they still be in the future? Price elasticities change over time, as competition changes and consumer tastes change.

Even though elasticities can vary over time, certain features tend to remain constant. Strong brands such as Apple and Coca-Cola have relatively low price elasticity. This gives them the power over market pricing that ensures strong profitability year after year. For less established firms, these brands are the role models: everyone wants to be the Coca-Cola of their own market or market niche.

Key terms

Correlation: the relationship between one variable and another.
External constraint: something outside the firm's control that can prevent it achieving its objectives.
Predatory pricing: pricing low with the deliberate intention of driving a competitor out of business.
Price-elastic product: a product that is highly price sensitive, so price elasticity is above 1.
Price-inelastic product: a product that is not very price sensitive, so price elasticity is below 1.
Price war: when two or more companies battle for market share by slashing prices, perhaps selling at or below cost.

Exercises

A. Revision questions

(40 marks; 40 minutes)

1a If a product's sales have fallen by 21% following a price rise from £2 to £2.07, what is its price elasticity? (4)

1b Is the product price elastic or price inelastic? (1)

2 Outline two ways in which Nestlé might try to reduce the price elasticity of its Aero chocolate bars. (4)

3 A firm selling 20,000 units at £8 is considering a 4% price increase. It believes its price elasticity is −0.5.
(a) What will be the effect upon revenue? (5)
(b) Give two reasons why the revenue may prove to be different from the firm's expectations. (2)

4 Explain three ways a firm could make use of information about the price elasticity of its brands. (6)

5 Identify three external factors that could increase the price elasticity of a brand of chocolate. (3)

6 A firm has a sales target of 60,000 units per month. Current sales are 50,000 per month at a price of £1.50. If its products have a price elasticity of −2, what price should the firm charge to meet the target sales volume? (4)

7 Why is price elasticity always negative? (2)

8 Explain why the manager of a product with a price elasticity of −2 may be reluctant to cut the price. (4)

9 Explain the importance of substitutability in determining a product's price elasticity (3)

10 Give two reasons why BMW cars have low price elasticity. (2)

B. Revision exercises

B1 Data response

A firm selling Manchester United pillow cases for £10 currently generates an annual turnover of £500,000. Variable costs average at £4 per unit and total annual fixed costs are £100,000. The marketing director is just about to impose a price increase of 10%.

Questions

(20 marks; 25 minutes)

1 Given that the price elasticity of the product is believed to be −0.4, calculate:
(a) the old and the new sales volume (3)
(b) the new revenue (3)
(c) the expected change in profit following the price increase. (6)

2 If the firm started producing mass-market white pillow cases, would their price elasticity be higher or lower than the Manchester United ones? Why is that? (8)

B2 Data response

The iPhone

The date 9 November 2007 was going to be an important one for Apple geeks. It saw the UK launch of the iPhone. Already a sensation in the States, with sales of more than one million units, it was the most eagerly awaited product launch in years. The appeal was simple: the best-looking phone ever, with the easiest user interface.

But what price should Apple charge for the phone, and how should it distribute it? To help keep competition down, it struck a deal to make O_2 – Britain's largest mobile operator – its exclusive British network for the handset. Apple knew from the outset that it could not take UK sales for granted. Nokia and Sony Ericsson are both bigger brands here than in the USA, so competition would be fiercer. Even more important, perhaps, would be the missing power:

by late 2007 more than 20% of UK phones were on the powerful 3G connection, making internet access fast and easy. The iPod was a more backward 2.5G.

A marketing analyst was quoted in the *Financial Times* as saying: 'On November 8th there will be iGeeks waiting outside the Apple store on Regent Street [London] with their sleeping bags and cups of coffee... There will be a big surge of interest in the beginning but, after that, there will be some difficulty in sustaining demand in the face of some very credible competition.

Apple decided to price the iPhone at £269. On top of this, users would have to sign up to an 18-month contract with a minimum payment of £35 a month, making the whole commitment a

whopping £899. This compared with a 3G Sony Walkman phone priced at £120 or a Samsung Slimline 3G, available for nothing as a contract upgrade.

Source: various, including the *Financial Times*, 19 September 2007

Questions

(20 marks; 25 minutes)

1 Explain the likely logic behind Apple's decision to sign an exclusive deal with the O_2 network. (6)

2 Use your understanding of price elasticity to discuss whether or not Apple was right to price the iPhone in this way. (14)

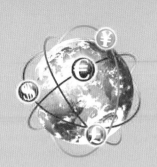

DEFINITION

Place is about availability (i.e. how to get the product to the right place for customers to make their purchases). It includes the physical place, availability and visibility. Promotion is the part of the marketing mix that focuses on persuading people to buy the product or service.

> I know that half the money I spend on advertising is wasted, but I can never find out which half. *Lord Leverhulme, British industrialist*

30.1 Introduction

The word 'place' can be unhelpful, because it suggests that manufacturers can place their products where they like (e.g. at the entrance of a Tesco store). The real world is not like that. Obtaining distribution at Tesco stores is a dream for most small producers – and a very hard dream to turn into reality. For new firms in particular, place is the toughest of the 4Ps.

Persuading retailers to stock a product is never easy. For the retailer, the key issues are opportunity cost and risk. As shelf space is limited, stocking a particular chocolate bar probably means scrapping another. Which one? What revenue will be lost? Will one or two customers be upset? ('What! No Coffee Walnut Whips any more?') The other consideration is risk. A new, low-cal chocolate bar endorsed by a supermodel may be a slimmer's delight, but high initial sales may then flop, leaving the shopkeeper with boxes of slow-moving stock.

30.2 Choosing appropriate distributors

When a new business wants to launch its first product, a key question to consider is the distribution channel – in other words, how the product passes from producer to consumer. Sold directly, as with pick-your-own

strawberries? Or via a wholesaler, then a retailer, as with newspapers bought from your local shop? This decision will affect every aspect of the business in the future, but especially its profit.

In 2008 entrepreneur James Seddon will launch his Eggxactly egg cooker in the UK. Since his appearance on the BBC TV series *Dragons' Den*, retailers such as John Lewis have made clear their interest in stocking the product at launch. But James has decided to start by selling purely from his own website. His reasoning is that this will transform his cash flow position. Instead of getting 50,000 machines produced in China (with the cash to be paid in advance) he could get them made in England in response to orders. This way, the customer cash is received before he has to pay out to get the machines made. This would solve another problem: instead of having to guess how many red and how many blue ones to make, he would respond to customer orders.

Manufacturers must decide on the right outlets for their own product. If Chanel chooses to launch a new perfume, 'Keira', backed by Keira Knightley, priced at £49.99 a bottle, controlling distribution would be vital. The company will want it sold in a smart location where elegant sales staff can persuade customers of its wonderful scent and gorgeous packaging. If Superdrug or Woolworths want to stock the brand Chanel will try hard to find reasons to say no.

Yet the control is often not in the hands of the producer, but of the retailer. If you came up with a wonderful idea for a brand new ice cream, how would you get distribution for it? The freezers in corner shops are usually owned by Walls and Mars, so they frown upon independent products being stocked in 'their' space. Offering a third freezer free would be hugely expensive, leading to impossibly high costs per unit, especially if you had only one product line to sell.

Furthermore, shopkeepers would lack the floor space to be willing to accept your 'free' gift. To the retailer, every foot of shop floor space has an actual cost (the rental value) and an opportunity cost (the cost of missing out on the profits that could be generated by selling other goods). In effect, then, your brand new ice cream is likely to stay on the drawing board, because obtaining distribution will be too large a **barrier to entry** to this market.

30.3 Distribution channels

There are three main channels of distribution.

1 *Traditional*: small producers find it hard to achieve distribution in big chains such as B&Q or Sainsbury's, so they usually sell to wholesalers who, in turn, sell to small independent shops. The profit mark-up applied by the 'middleman' adds to the final retail price, but there is no way that a small producer can afford to deliver individually to lots of small shops.

A-grade application

Tesco Online

In the first half of 2007, Tesco Online enjoyed a 29% rise in its sales revenue. This compared with a 12% rise for Tesco stores. This repeats a growth pattern typical within the company in the last few years. Interestingly, Online is more profitable for Tesco than its normal shop business. The figures in Table 30.1 show that Tesco Online gives higher net profit margins than the traditional business. No wonder Tesco has extended its internet business by launching Tesco Direct, which will deliver Tesco clothes and other non-food items direct to the consumer's door.

Table 30.1 Tesco stores vs Tesco Online, 26 weeks to 26 August 2007

	Tesco plc	**Tesco.com**
Sales	£22700m	£554m
Operating (net) profit	£1090m	£33.8m
Net profit margin	4.8%	6.1%

Source: Tesco plc, 2007 interim report and accounts

2 *Modern*: Tesco, B&Q and WHSmith do not buy from a wholesaler. They buy direct from producers and then organise their own distribution to their outlets. Their huge selling power gives them huge buying power. Therefore they are able to negotiate the highest discounts from the producers.

3 *Direct (i.e. the producer selling directly to the consumer)*: manufacturers can do this through mail order or – far more likely today – through a website. This ensures that the producer keeps 100% of the product's selling price. Often a manufacturer receives only half the shop selling price of an item, after the retailer and the wholesaler have taken their cut. So the benefit of the direct distribution channel is that the producer's higher profits can finance more spending on advertising or on new product development.

30.4 How does a small firm obtain good distribution?

To obtain distribution for the first time, a small firm producing organic biscuits would have to take the following steps.

● Announce, display and hand out free samples of the product at a trade exhibition, and/or use direct mail to send advertising messages and product samples to trade buyers. (But does it have a good mailing list? McVitie's will know every key decision maker in the grocery retail trade.)

● Advertise in the trade press (e.g. *The Grocer* magazine). The advertisement will show the attractiveness of the packaging and will emphasise the market gap that has been identified, the generous trade profit margins available, the heavy consumer advertising support and the package of point-of-sale (POS) display materials that are being provided to increase the level of **impulse purchasing** within the store.

● Identify and agree distribution and sales targets for each area of the country, and type of outlet. A major company such as McVitie's is likely to be confident of achieving distribution targets as high as 80%. A new small firm may find it very difficult to gain distribution at 15% of stores. Having set distribution targets, it should send sales representatives to visit each of the main wholesale and retail buyers. A possible way to break into major multiples is to agree on an exclusive arrangement (e.g. that the new product will be stocked only at Tesco for its first six months). This gives the retailer the possibility of a worthwhile benefit: Tesco scores a minor triumph in its competitive battle against Sainsbury's and the others.

- it is easier to persuade retailers to put the products in their stores
- other products can be promoted using the same brand name.

30.5 What is promotion?

Promotion is a general term that covers all the marketing activity that focuses on letting the customer know about a product and persuading them to buy that product. It is not just about advertising. The different elements of promotion can be grouped into two broad categories: those that stimulate short-term sales and those that build sales for the long term.

30.6 Types of promotion for building long-term sales

These include those described below.

Branding

One of the best forms of promotion is branding. Branding is the process of creating a distinctive and lasting identity in the minds of consumers. Establishing a brand can take considerable time and marketing effort, but once a product brand is established it becomes its own means of promotion. The brand name is recognised and this makes it more likely that the customer will buy the product for the first time. If the experience is satisfactory the customer is very likely to continue to choose the brand. Once established, branding has many advantages, such as:

- it enables the business to reduce the amount spent on promotion
- customers are more likely to purchase the product again (repeat purchases)

A-grade application

Activia

In 2007 a £12 million marketing campaign saw Activia yoghurt's share of 'Active Health' yoghurts rise to 75%. The brand's sales grew by 440% in the period 2002–2007. Danone spent most of the marketing budget on TV advertising, assuring women that Activia would fight 'that bloated feeling'. The huge marketing push made it impossible for competitors to keep up. The once powerful Benecol brand saw its market share fall from 5.8% in 2006 to just 3.2% in 2007, while Müller Vitality slipped from 19.2% to 16.0%. Somehow, the Activia message hit home. There may not really be that many women worried about feeling bloated, but Danone persuaded them that Activia would be better for you than ordinary yoghurt.

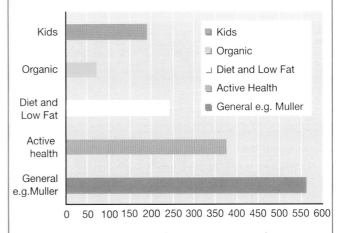

Figure 30.1 Sectors in the £1440m yoghurt market, 2007

Table 30.2 Examples of persuasive advertising

Company	Slogan	Meaning
Tesco	'Every little helps'	We understand your needs and we try to help (we're not just a great big, greedy business)
L'Oréal	'Because you're worth it'	Go on, spoil yourself; you can afford that bit extra, so buy our products, not our competitors'
Innocent Drinks	'Nothing, but nothing, but fruit'	Our products are pure (whereas others are not)

Persuasive advertising

Persuasive advertising is designed to create a distinctive image. A good example is BMW, which has spent decades persuading us that it produces not a car but a 'Driving Machine'. Advertising of this kind has also helped create clear consumer images for firms such as Tesco and L'Oréal (see Table 30.2).

Public relations

This is the attempt to affect consumers' image of a product without spending on media advertising. It includes making contacts with journalists to try to get favourable mentions or articles about your product. It would also include activities such as sponsorship of sport or the arts. The London Olympic Games in 2012 has Lloyds TSB as one of its main sponsors. This allows the business to advertise and use its logo alongside the Olympic logo.

30.7 Types of promotion for boosting short-term sales

These include those described below.

Sales promotions

These range from on-pack competitions to in-store offers such as buy one get one free (BOGOF). These can be very effective at boosting sales, but there are risks involved, such as: customers may stock up at (in effect) half price, then not need to buy more items in the weeks following the offer; special offers may undermine the brand image (what would it say to consumers if Apple started offering 'buy one iPhone get one free'?). These risks are worthwhile only if the promotion succeeds in attracting brand new customers, who come for the offer and then stay loyal after the offer has ended (which is asking a lot).

Direct selling

Potential customers are approached directly. At one time this would be done by door-to-door salesmen. Nowadays the main mechanism for direct selling is telesales. Both approaches are expensive, because one-to-one selling implies high labour costs. A TV advertisement sounds expensive at, perhaps, £100,000. But that money would buy you an audience of 5 million people. Therefore the cost per person is £100,000/5m = £0.02 (i.e. 2p). Just think how much more expensive it would be to pay someone to travel to you and spend time selling a product to you personally (2 hours @ £8 an hour + £4 travel costs = £20, and that's the absolute minimum). Therefore direct selling is affordable only if there are huge financial rewards to the seller (e.g. selling financial products or double glazing).

Merchandising

This requires staff to visit shops to ensure that a brand's display looks eye-catching and tidy. Merchandisers may set up 'dump bin' displays at the end of shopping aisles, perhaps featuring a newly launched product. The shop will charge rent for the space, but the extra sales can more than make up for this. Merchandisers may also offer shoppers free product samples, to encourage them to make their first trial purchase.

30.8 Promotional activity needs to fit in with marketing strategy

The type of promotion used and the level of promotional activity will vary not only from company to company and product to product but also in terms of the marketing strategy being followed. Different forms of promotion will achieve different purposes. Much will depend on what the business is trying to achieve (Table 30.3).

The correct **promotional mix** will be achieved only if the business has clear marketing objectives. Once the objectives and strategy are determined it is much easier for the business to develop an effective promotional campaign.

Table 30.3 *Marketing strategies and types of promotion*

Marketing strategy	Promotion needs to:
Launching a new product	• be informative • reach the target customers
Differentiating the product	• identify the special features of the product • persuade customers that it is different/better than rival products
Extending the life of an existing product	• reinforce the reasons for customers choosing it • highlight any new features • attract new customers
Increasing market share	• attract new customers • reinforce buying in existing customers
Building brand identity	• increase awareness of the company/product name • create customer recognition and loyalty

Table 30.4 *Advantages and disadvantages of various promotion methods*

	Advantages	Disadvantages
Advertising (e.g. on TV)	Reaches a large audience Increases prestige of the product/company Can be targeted to viewing groups	Very expensive Can be too broad-based to reach target customers
Direct selling	With good research enables the customer to be targeted directly	Can get a reputation as a nuisance caller Unless properly researched can be difficult to target
Direct marketing	With good research can be cost-effective	Wide coverage often produces only small response
Merchandising	Good product displays can increase the rate of impulse purchase, and can build brand awareness	Expensive as it relies on personal calling by sales staff
Sales promotions (such as buy one get one free)	Increases sales immediately and, possibly, dramatically	Customers may have bought anyway
Public relations (PR)	Gets the company name seen	Hard to measure effectiveness

Issues For Analysis

For exam purposes there are two key factors to consider about 'place'.

- A successful business must find where customers want to buy the product, then get it stocked at that place. If the product is ready-to-eat popcorn, the place must be the cinema; if it's unpopped corn, the place must be in the grocery store. Naive businesspeople try to get their product stocked everywhere, without thinking about the high costs of delivery, advertising materials and ongoing customer service. Today's customers value convenience highly, so the right product must be available in the right place at the right time. Clever firms look for appropriate outlets, not simply as many as possible.

- Anyone can have a brilliant new idea; anyone can decide on the price and the name of this new product – but getting shops to take a chance on a newcomer is more of a problem. Many new small manufacturers have been defeated by the costs, the slowness and the difficulty of obtaining product distribution. Therefore 'place' (sometimes called 'the silent P') is a critical part of the marketing mix.

There are also two key factors to bear in mind about promotion.

- Analysis should consider the different promotional methods that are available but should concentrate on those that are suitable for the particular business. There is no point suggesting that a new small business should look at advertising on TV or consider promoting a major sporting event.

- The single best form of analysis, though, is to consider promotion in relation to the timescale of the firm's objectives. If it wants to build a brand for the long term, it can do damage by using short-term tactics such as price promotions. Carefully targeted advertising designed to build the 'right' image is the key – 'right' being the image that best suits the customers being targeted. Over-60s may respond very well to secure, warm images, whereas the 16–25 age group may want images based on fun and celebrity.

30.9 Promotion and place
an evaluation

Place is of particular importance in Business Studies because it can represent a major barrier to entry, especially for new small firms. The practical constraint on the amount of shop floor space makes it hard for new products to gain acceptance, unless they are genuinely innovative. Therefore existing producers of branded goods can get quite complacent, with little serious threat from new competition. Famously, in the nineteenth century Ralph Waldo Emerson said that 'If a man can make a better mousetrap, though he builds his house in the woods the world will make a beaten path to his door.' In other words, if the product is good enough, customers will come and find you. In a modern competitive world, though, the vast majority of products are not *that* exciting or different from others. So it is crucial to provide customers with convenient access to your products and/or shelf space in an eye-catching location. Getting products into the right place should not be taken for granted.

Promotion is generally considered to be a good thing for businesses to do. But is it? How do they know if it is money well spent? It is very hard to measure the effect of promotion. If the business is using a mix of promotional methods it is very difficult to separate the effect of one from the other.

> **Key terms**
>
> **Barrier to entry:** factors that make it hard for new firms to break into an existing market (e.g. strong brand loyalty to the current market leaders).
> **Impulse purchasing:** buying in unplanned way (e.g. going to a shop to buy a paper, but coming out with a Mars bar and a Diet Coke).
> **Promotional mix:** the combination of promotional methods used by a business in marketing its products.

Exercises

A. Revision questions

(45 marks; 45 minutes)

1 Outline the meaning of the term 'place'. (2)

2 Explain in your own words why it may be that 'place is the toughest of the 4Ps'. (3)

3 Outline what you think are appropriate distribution channels for:
   (a) a new magazine aimed at 12–15-year-old boys (2)
   (b) a new adventure holiday company focusing on wealthy 19–32 year olds. (3)

4 Retailers such as WHSmith charge manufacturers a rent on prime store space such as the shelving near to the cash tills.
   (a) How might a firm work out whether it is worthwhile to pay the extra? (3)
   (b) Why might new small firms find it hard to pay rents such as these? (4)

5 Explain in your own words what is meant by the phrase 'a better mousetrap'. (3)

6 Outline three reasons for the success of direct distribution over the internet in recent years. (5)

7 Why is promotion an important element of the marketing mix? (3)

8 Outline one advantage and one disadvantage of TV advertising. (4)

9 Explain what form of promotion you think would work best for marketing:
   (a) a new football game for the PS3 (3)
   (b) a small, family-focused seaside hotel (3)
   (c) organic cosmetics for women. (3)

10 Explain why promotion is essential for new businesses. (4)

B. Revision exercises

B1 Data response

Getting distribution right

Secondary data can be hugely helpful to new companies looking for distribution of their first products. A company launching the first 'Kitten Milk' product has to decide where to focus its efforts. Where does cat food sell? Is it in pet shops, in corner shops or in supermarkets? Desk research company BMRB reports that, whereas 65% of dog owners shops for pet food at supermarkets, 81% of cat owners do the same. A different source (TNS, 52 weeks ending 12 August 2007) puts the cat food market size at £829 million. TNS also shows that the market is rising in value by around 2.5% a year.

Further secondary data (reported in *The Grocer*, 19 May 2007) shows that pet food shoppers spend only 80% of the amount they intend to when they go to a shop. This is because poor distribution stops them finding what they want. And 50% of shoppers will not return to the same store after being let down twice by poor availability.

Questions

(20 marks; 25 minutes)

1 State the meaning of the term 'market size'. (2)

2a The Year 1 sales target for Kitten Milk is £5 million. What share of the total market for cat food would that represent? (3)

2b Explain why it might be hard to persuade retailers to stock a product with that level of market share. (6)

3 The marketing manager for Kitten Milk is planning to focus distribution efforts on getting the brand placed in pet shops. Discuss whether this seems wise. (9)

B2 Data response

Green & Black's second bite

In 2005 organic chocolate-maker Green & Black's launched two varieties of biscuit. In 2007 it withdrew the products after accepting that they had flopped. Due into Asda in January 2008 is the replacement product line-up, including two new biscuits and two cereal bars. The cereal bars will come in packs of three, priced at £2.49. They feature unusual combinations such as Almond, Cherry and Apricot. The intention is to catch the key trends towards indulgence, organic and health. The company also intends to launch seasonal biscuit varieties in selected supermarkets.

Green & Black's is targeting sales of £7 million for the first year. To achieve this, the 2008 marketing campaign will include merchandising and product sampling in-store. The sampling will be to encourage product trial, with the company hoping that the quality of the product ensures high levels of repeat purchase.

Source: *The Grocer*, 20 October 2007

Questions

(30 marks; 30 minutes)

1 Outline two possible explanations of why the 2005 biscuit launches failed. (6)

2 Explain how the sales of the new biscuit varieties could be helped by a programme of in-store merchandising. (5)

3 Discuss whether 'sampling in-store' is likely to be a sufficiently powerful form of promotion for the new biscuit range. (12)

4 Outline the other aspects of the marketing mix being used by Green & Black's. (7)

B3 Data response

An arm's length from desire

From its origins in America in 1886, Coca-Cola has been a marketing phenomenon. It was the world's first truly global brand; it virtually invented the red, jolly Christmas Santa, and its bottle design (1919) was the first great piece of packaging design.

Yet a 1950 *Time* magazine article quoted another piece of marketing genius: 'Always within an arm's length of desire.' The marketing experts at Atlanta (home of Coca-Cola) realised nearly 60 years ago that sales of Coca-Cola were limited mainly by availability. Especially on a hot day, a cold Coke would be desired by almost anyone who had it an arm's length away. This led the company to develop a distribution strategy based on maximum availability, maximum in-store visibility and therefore maximum impulse purchase.

From then on, Coca-Cola targeted four main types of distribution:

1 in supermarkets and grocers
2 in any kiosk in a location based on entertainment (e.g. a bowling alley or a cinema)
3 in any canteen, bar or restaurant
4 in a vending machine near you; automatic vending proved one of the most valuable ways of building the market until worries about healthy eating saw them banned in schools in 2005 and 2006; a vending machine is the ultimate barrier to entry.

Overall, though, the Coca-Cola approach to distribution set out in 1950 what most companies still try to do today.

Questions

(25 marks; 30 minutes)

1 Explain how a vending machine can be a 'barrier to entry' to new competitors. (5)

2 Explain what the text means by the difference between 'maximum availability' and 'maximum visibility'. (5)

3 Explain why 'an arm's length from desire' might be less important for a business that does not rely upon impulse purchase. (7)

4 From all that you know about today's Coke, Diet Coke and Coke Zero, discuss whether Coca-Cola's distribution strategy was at the core of the firm's marketing success. (8)

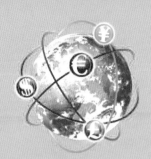
THE MARKETING MIX AND SOCIAL TRENDS

31.1 Introduction

How do some brands thrive over generations while others come, look promising, but then fade away? Remember Strollers (chocolate flop), the McHotel (the McD's hotel flop) and Virgin Cola (it would wipe out Coke, according to Richard Branson)? In the meantime, some brands keep on going, such as Heinz Tomato Ketchup (born 1888), Marmite (born 1902) and Maltesers (born 1932).

One of the hardest things in business is to distinguish a fad from a trend. In 2003 and 2004 sales of potatoes and bread fell significantly due to the impact of the 'Atkins diet' on sales of foods containing carbohydrate. Nestlé – worried about the possible impact on chocolate sales –

rushed to launch 'low carb' versions of Rolo, Kit-Kat and other brands. The time lags in getting from the drawing board to the market meant that the launch of these products coincided with the fading of the fad. Both sank without trace.

When Innocent Drinks began in 1999, it was far from clear that there was a long-term business to be built on small bottles of crushed fruit selling for £2 apiece. Yet the business happened to tap into a social trend that was sustained for the following ten years: the desire for food that is convenient, tasty and allows you to tell yourself that it's good for you. Hence the array of processed foods from Activia to Omega-3 fish fingers – all designed to tap into a social trend.

A-grade application

Selling soya

Research shows that 20% of UK adults believe they have a food allergy. The British Health Foundation says the correct figure is under 2%. So the widespread marketing of products such as soya 'milk' on health grounds is very dubious. Sales of soya substitutes for milk grew between 10% and 20% a year between 2003 and 2007, creating a market worth more than £100 million. This is marvellous for market leader Alpro, with its 65% market share. Whether it is making people healthier is more doubtful, though, as even the chairman of a major supplier can only suggest that the sales increases are of 'products perceived to offer health benefits for a broader market'. In other words, people who do not need a milk substitute are buying (expensive) soya for their families for no good reason.

31.2 The marketing mix and social trends – clever or too clever?

For more than ten years there has been rising social concern about environmental problems, especially that of global warming. It is now widely accepted that increases in greenhouse gases such as carbon dioxide are causing the planet to warm up year by year. This might cause a melting of polar ice caps, a rise in the sea level and therefore the flooding of large areas of low-lying land around the world. At the same time, warmer temperatures will lead to significant increases in the world's desert areas. The widespread acceptance of these views has put certain industries in the firing line, notably the oil and car industries.

The oil giant BP (British Petroleum) responded to this concern in 2000 by rebranding the business as BP – Beyond Petroleum. The logo changed to a bright green and yellow sunburst, and the company's advertising emphasised its new, greener thinking. Even today its website proclaims: 'Beyond Petroleum is a summation of our brand promise and values … It is both our philosophical ideal and a practical description of our work.' The brand promise is expanded to embrace 'the responsibility to produce and consume energy in ways that respect human rights and natural environments'.

Yet chief executive Lord Browne presided over a business that was eventually humiliated by its failure to live up to its promises. In March 2005 a giant explosion at BP's Texas oil refinery killed 15 people. A US government report eventually blamed BP for cutbacks in safety spending at the refinery. The chairwoman of the report blamed the explosion on 'ageing infrastructure, overzealous cost-cutting, inadequate design and risk blindness'. What about the human rights of the 15 dead?

In January 2006, BP was fined $1.42 million for safety violations at its Prudhoe Bay oilfield in Alaska. Two months later a hole in an oil pipeline leaked more than 1.2 million litres of oil in Alaska, creating an environmental 'catastrophe'. It later emerged that BP had failed to maintain the pipeline properly. Specifically, it had not invested in a 'pipeline crawler' that automatically checks for cracks. In the summer of 2006 it was forced to close down the whole oilfield because of safety concerns. Both these fiascos showed the hollowness of BP's boasts. Remarkably, BP's image seems little affected in Britain, but in America serious long-term damage has been done to the credibility of the brand.

Source: *Topical Cases, A–Z Business Training*, January 2007

31.3 Environmental trends and the marketing mix

In 2007, £1500 million was spent on organic food, marking a rise of 70% since 2002. This was a sign that people were starting to take seriously long-held concerns about animal welfare plus the need to eat purer food. Many businesses were at the heart of this development, including multiple retailers Waitrose and the Co-op, plus independents such as Planet Organic. Waitrose started stocking organic fruit and vegetables in 1983, even though they represented only 1% of sales. By 1995 the figure had risen to 4% but it was still not really profitable. Waitrose saw organic foods as a way to differentiate its stores from those of many of its rivals. So the business persisted, even though organics were loss-makers for years. Today, organic Christmas turkeys

are a huge moneyspinner for Waitrose – a fair reward for a 25-year commitment.

Other environmental factors affecting shoppers, and therefore being taken seriously by food manufacturers and retailers, are described below.

Recyclable packaging

Waste materials can be disposed of in one of only three ways: burn them, bury them or reuse them. Burning them directly increases greenhouse gas emissions and burying them is not only destructive of the environment, but can also cause air pollution. The ideal solution is therefore recycling, meaning to reuse as much as possible of the original materials. There are simple solutions to this that shoppers seem uninterested in – for instance, getting milk from a milkman who collects, washes and refills glass milk bottles; people are sufficiently ill-focused to make a fuss about recycled plastic when there's a much better solution available.

Nevertheless, individual businesses cannot concern themselves with re-educating the public – their duty is to attract custom. Innocent Drinks is now proud to proclaim a world first, in that all its bottles are now made from recycled plastic. At the same time, they have asked their supplier to make them slightly thinner, saving 20% on the weight of the plastic – cheaper for Innocent, and better for all of us. Innocent's website promotes this move enthusiastically, seeing it as a matter of great interest to many of its customers.

Food miles

The term **food miles** is used to criticise shoppers who buy food thoughtlessly. Britain grows wonderful cherries, but the eating season is early summer, so for nine months of the year there are no fresh British cherries. Campaigners criticise supermarkets for flying in supplies of cherries from California or Spain, pointing out the impact on CO_2 emissions of all the 'food miles' concerned.

When an issue such as this is raised, clever marketers can sometimes seize opportunities to build it into their marketing mix. So, in 2007, Walkers started advertising that all its potato supplies were British (Gary Lineker ended up in the mud to demonstrate this). From a marketing point of view, that was very clever. It made Walkers seem socially responsible. Did it make the planet a better place to live? Well, only if Walkers changed its buying practices to stop buying from abroad. It probably was already buying almost entirely from British farmers, making it an easy claim to make.

Sourcing sustainable materials

Sustainability means that the purchase you make will not affect long-term supplies of the product, because it is automatically replenished. For example, although cod is an endangered fish, with a serious risk that supplies will dry up, there are plenty of supplies of other fish available, such as pollock. In August 2007, Birds Eye gave in to pressure to reduce the amount of cod in its fish fingers, using pollock instead. Pollock and chips, anyone?

Other environmental factors

At the time of writing, another key environmental concern was the 'carbon footprint' created by products. This is a measurement of all the CO_2 emitted by the materials used, delivery miles, manufacturing and office costs (especially energy) involved in producing, packing and delivering a product. Walkers has carried out a detailed analysis of the carbon emissions involved in producing a single, standard pack of its Cheese & Onion crisps. It has worked out that each 35 g pack generates 75 g of carbon! (Source: www.walkerscarbonfootprint.co.uk)

An intelligently run business will try to avoid being the butt of media jokes about pollution. Walkers is clearly being very clever in keeping one step ahead of its rivals. Nevertheless, if a competitor was able to claim a 50 g carbon footprint for the same-sized pack of crisps, there may be an interesting new form of competition in future.

31.4 Online retailing and the marketing mix

Traditionally, location was a key factor for retailers. For online retailers that is clearly not a concern. Yet there are many other potential pitfalls. James Murray-Wells started Glasses Direct in June 2004 at the age of 21, just after completing a degree. He would be offering pairs of glasses for £15 instead of the £150 paid in the high street.

James designed the website himself, but – with no money and no publicity – sales in the first month averaged just one or two pairs a day. All he could afford was to get some leaflets printed. This is often a weak form of advertising, but with his incredibly strong offer (£15 instead of £150) his leaflets proved highly effective. He took a train from Bristol, handing out flyers to people who would be stuck on a train with nothing else to do but read them. Within days sales started coming through from people living in Bristol. Shortly afterwards came emails of thanks, with people clearly surprised that the specs were every bit as good as those available on the high street. By the end of the summer, word of mouth had spread and the first articles started appearing in papers. Orders were up to 100 pairs a day and the business was booming. By 2006 turnover hit £3 million and rising.

In this case an outstanding price offer combined with a good product, good service and a small investment in advertising to create a highly successful mix. In effect, it was the original idea (high-street glasses at non-rip-off prices) that was the key. In other cases this will not work, because the offer has to be similar to the competition. If you are selling skateboards online, your prices will not be much different to those of other suppliers. This will make it much more important to identify a winning marketing strategy.

Here are some that work well.

- *The saturation approach*, as used by Moneysupermarket.com to make sure that everyone thinks of you first; the downside, of course, is the huge cost of the TV advertising.

- *Google search optimisation* – that is, design your website so that it comes very high on the list when people are Googling for something you want to sell. This takes time and a bit of money, but is much, much cheaper than a multi-million-pound advertising campaign.

- *Build a website people will talk about* – some good examples are those of Innocent Drinks and Ted Baker. A fun website can provide strong support to a brand image, and get the brand written about in the media, which provides extra, free promotion.

31.5 Retailer purchasing power

By 2008 four retailers controlled more than 75% of Britain's grocery market, with Tesco alone accounting for more than 30%. As the pie charts in Figure 31.2 show, Britain's shopping habits have been transformed in the ten years to 2008. The four majors (Tesco,

Sainsbury's, Asda and Morrisons) all make sure that their marketing and advertising messages emphasise their wish to help the customer. Tesco's slogan 'Every Little Helps' may prove to have been Britain's most successful advertising slogan ever.

Yet there are many critics who feel that the supermarkets hide some questionable practices behind their slogans. In February 2008 the Competition Commission announced that suppliers to supermarkets would be able to complain (confidentially) to an independent 'ombudsman' if they were unhappy about their treatment. The concern was that farmer suppliers to the supermarkets can be forced to accept terms that make it impossible to operate profitably without cutting corners. If Tesco decides to run a promotion of '2 chickens for £5', it may be the birds that suffer for the customer's (and Tesco's) benefit.

The supermarkets retort that an ombudsman will add more bureaucracy without affecting customers or suppliers. This may well be true, as the only long-term solution is for customers to show the shops that they really care about where products come from and how they were made or grown. The reality is that many shoppers like to have it both ways: to sound shocked about poor conditions at the supplier end, yet still pick up a £1.99 chicken and a £3 school shirt on the way to the checkout.

Issues For Analysis

● The key is to analyse the real intent of the company. Is there a true commitment to a social purpose (the environment, or people's health, or to poorly paid staff working for suppliers) or is the motivation purely to cash in on a trend? Some people might argue that it doesn't matter – that, as long as companies are doing the 'right thing', it doesn't matter about their motives. The BP example shows, however, that just because a company says the right things it does not mean that it is really doing them.

● Analytically, it is easiest to see why companies such as Innocent Drinks will almost always be trying to align their marketing mix to the right social purpose. This is because Innocent's brand image is entirely associated with 'being innocent/good', and its brand image and company image are inseparable. The situation is more complex for a business such as Walkers (owned by PepsiCo). There is no doubt that the business has tried hard to act with social responsibility in relation to this key brand. The saturated fat content of the crisps has been reduced, yet potato crisps are unarguably bad for a population suffering rising obesity. For example, the Walkers brand Wotsits proudly proclaims 'NOW 25% less fat', yet the product still contains 33 g of fat per 100 g of crisps – about half the daily recommended allowance for an adult woman. Poor Walkers cannot escape questions about whether its packaging and promotion are really responsible.

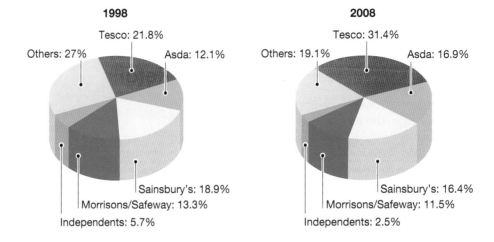

Figure 31.1 Comparing the grocery market, 1998–2008
Source: TNS Worldpanel

The marketing mix and social trends

The most important judgement concerns the extent to which firms can be relied upon to act responsibly in their marketing. The government has doubts, as it tries to put pressure on firms to conform to rules such as pack labelling in relation to diet, or the way firms act in relation to the threat of global warming. If companies are left to their own devices, they might act responsibly (to avoid bad publicity) but might do the absolute minimum. A well-run business will probably see the opportunity to motivate staff and customers by taking a forward-looking approach to social obligations. Then, if the business has done all it can to minimise any environmental or health damage caused by its products, it can honestly build its marketing mix on a positive social message.

Key terms

Food miles: a calculation of how much travelling is involved in making and delivering a product (e.g. raspberries flown 2000 miles from Israel, then driven 300 miles to a supermarket).

Sustainability: whether the supply source can be continued indefinitely into the future (if not, it is unsustainable).

Exercises

A. Revision questions

(40 marks; 40 minutes)

1 Outline two possible reasons why Maltesers is still selling successfully over 75 years after the brand's birth. (4)

2 Explain why it's important to distinguish between a trend and a fad. (4)

3 Re-read the A-grade application feature 'Selling soya'. Why does the writer question 'whether [soya] is making people healthier'? (3)

4 Re-read section 31.2 and consider whether BP's Lord Browne was right to rebrand British Petroleum as Beyond Petroleum. (5)

5a In February 2008, Cadbury announced the launch of a range of Easter eggs that would not have any outer packaging (they would just be sold in a foil wrapper). Outline one advantage and one disadvantage of this. (4)

5b Do you think this approach will be successful for Cadbury? Explain your reasoning. (5)

6 Explain whether you believe these businesses are pursuing a profitable marketing approach or a good social purpose. Choose two from the following:
   a) HSBC bank running a 'January sale', based on linking its products to improving the environment
   b) B&Q deciding (in January 2008) to stop selling outdoor patio heaters
   c) Coca-Cola sponsoring the London Marathon. (4)

7 Should shoppers see it as their personal responsibility to think about how a shop is able to sell a new suit for £25 or a chicken for £1.99? (6)

8 Identify what you believe to be the most important social trend today. Then explain how it applies to one of the following firms:
   a) Asda
   b) Wall's (ice cream)
   c) Nike
(5)

B. Revision exercises

B1 Data response

Green watchdog urges store reform

An over-arching policy on supermarkets is needed if the government is to meet targets on obesity, waste and climate change, an independent report has said.

A report by the Sustainable Development Commission (SDC) suggests the food chain contributes around one-fifth of total UK greenhouse gas emissions when the impact of fertilisers, transport, processing and rotting waste is taken into account. It also quotes from a study that claims food is a family's biggest source of greenhouse gas emissions. And the SDC blames stores for exacerbating global poverty and promoting unhealthy lifestyles.

Professor Tim Lang, the report's main author, told BBC News: 'When we go shopping, I don't think we really recognise the enormous impact our food is having on the environment. It … has an impact on our health, the energy use, how we get there – everything that matters is actually happening beyond our control, but government's got to get grip of that.'

The report follows the publication on Friday of the Competition Commission's review of British supermarkets. It has recommended measures to stop chains restricting who can buy land they have sold off and the creation of an ombudsman to resolve disputes between supermarkets and their suppliers.

Jane Milne from the British Retail Consortium said: 'There is a lot happening among all the major supermarkets in helping address healthy eating, in meeting the climate change challenge, in dealing with waste and all of these issues. But in order for all of that to happen we need some help from government as well.'

Points of tension

The SDC acknowledges that supermarkets have moved towards producing healthier meals with lower fat and salt, but complains that they still promote two-for-one offers on junk food like doughnuts. This may be helpful to people with large families on low incomes but it also encourages people to overeat or to throw food away. (see data below)

It says a policy to 'aim purely for quantity of supply or cheapness at all costs would be hopelessly inadequate'.

Source: adapted from bbc.co.uk

Questions

(35 marks; 40 minutes)

1a Outline briefly what is meant by the phrase 'greenhouse gas emissions'. (3)

1b To what extent are these the responsibility of supermarkets such as Tesco? (6)

2a What evidence is provided in the article in support of the view that supermarkets are to blame for 'promoting unhealthy lifestyles'? (5)

2b Discuss whether it is right to say that 'people with large families on low incomes' are helped by two-for-one offers in the way described in the article. (9)

3 A supermarket might respond to this report by pointing out that all it is trying to do is provide choice and an efficient service to its customers. Discuss whether this is a justified response to the Sustainable Development Commission's report. (12)

Impact of food

- 5.2m tonnes food-related packaging generated each year in the UK
- 6.7m tonnes food waste created each year by UK homes
- Agriculture globally consumes 70% of all fresh water for human use
- Proportion of men classified as obese has increased from 13% to 22%
- Economic cost of obesity to the UK economy estimated at £10bn a year

Source: Sustainable Development Commission

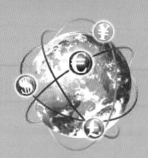

MARKETING AND COMPETITIVENESS

32.1 Introduction: what is a competitive market?

In the past, markets were physical places where buyers and sellers met in person to exchange goods. Street markets are still like that. Today, some buyers and sellers never meet each other, a good example being eBay.

Some markets are more competitive than others. In general, a competitive market could be described as one where there is intense rivalry between producers of a similar good or service. The number of firms operating within a market influences the intensity of competition; the more firms there are, the greater the level of competition. However, the respective size of the firms operating in the market should also be taken into account. A market consisting of 50 firms may not be particularly competitive, if, for instance, one of the firms holds a 60% market share and the 40% is shared between the other 49. Similarly, a market composed of just four firms could be quite competitive because the firms operating within this market are of a fairly similar size.

Consumers enjoy competitive markets. However, the reverse is true for the firms that operate in these markets. In competitive markets, prices and profit margins tend to be squeezed. As a result, firms operating in competitive markets try hard to minimise competition, perhaps by creating a unique selling point (**USP**) or using **predatory pricing**.

It could be argued that marketing is vital no matter what the level of competition is within the market. Firms that fail to produce goods and services that satisfy the needs of the consumers that make up their target market will find it hard to succeed in the long term. Ultimately, consumers will not choose to waste their hard-earned cash on products that fail to meet their needs.

32.2 The degree of competition within a market

One dominant business

Some markets are dominated by one large business. Economists use the word 'monopoly' to describe a market where there is a single supplier, and therefore no competition. In practice pure textbook monopolies rarely exist; even Microsoft does not have a 100% share of the office software market (though it does have a 90% share).

Monopolies are bad for consumers. They restrict choice, and tend to drive prices upwards. For that reason most governments regulate against monopolies and near monopolies that exploit consumers by abusing their dominant market position. The UK government's definition of a monopoly is somewhat looser. According to the Competition Commission, a monopoly is a firm that has a market share of 25% and above.

Deciding whether or not a firm has a monopoly is a far from straightforward task. First of all, the market itself has to be accurately defined – for example, Camelot has been granted a monopoly to run the National Lottery; however, it could be argued that Camelot does not have a dominant market position because there are other forms of gambling, such as horse racing and the football pools, available to consumers in the UK. Second, national market share figures should not be used in isolation because some firms enjoy local monopolies. In 2007 the Competition Commission accused Tesco of abusing its market position in towns such as Inverness and Slough by occupying sites previously occupied by its rivals. In both towns, consumers had to travel more than 15 minutes by car to reach another supermarket chain.

Firms implement their marketing strategy through the marketing mix. In markets dominated by a single large business, firms do not need to spend heavily on promotion because consumers are, to a degree, captive. Prices can be pushed upwards and the product element of the marketing mix should be focused on creating innovations that make it harder for new entrants to break in to the market. Apple spends millions of dollars on research and development in order to produce cutting-edge products such as the iPod Touch (see Figure 32.1). Apple is still the market leader in MP3s with a 60%-plus share of the massive US market. To ensure that Apple maintains its dominant market position new product launches are patented to prevent me-too imitations from being launched by the competition.

Figure 32.1 Apple's cutting-edge iPod Touch

Competition amongst a few giants

The UK supermarket industry is a good example of a market that is dominated by a handful of very large companies. Economists call markets like this **oligopolistic**. The rivalry that exists within such markets can be intense. Firms know that any gains in market share will be at the expense of their rivals. The actions taken by one firm affect the profits made by the other firms that compete within the same market.

In markets made up of a few giants, firms tend to focus on **non-price competition** when designing the marketing mix. Firms in these markets tend to be reluctant to compete by cutting price. They fear that the other firms in the industry will respond by cutting their prices too, creating a costly price war where no firm wins.

The fiercely competitive market

Fiercely competitive markets tend to be fragmented, made up of hundreds of relatively small firms, each of which competes actively against the others. In some of these markets competition is amplified by the fact that firms sell near identical products, called commodities. Commodities are products such as flour, sugar or blank DVDs that are hard to differentiate. Rivalry in commodity markets tends to be intense. In markets such as this firms have to manage their production costs very carefully because the retail price is the most important factor in determining whether the firm's product sells or not. If a firm cannot cut its costs it will not be able to cut its prices without cutting into profit margins. Without price cuts market share is likely to be lost.

In fiercely competitive markets firms will try, where possible, to create product differentiation. For example, the restaurant market in Croydon, Surrey, is extremely competitive. There are over 70 outlets within a two-mile radius of the town centre. To survive without having to compete solely on price, firms in markets like this must find new innovations regularly because points of differentiation are quickly copied.

Very little competition			Extremely competitive
Monopoly	Oligopoly	Competition between many firms	Competition between commodity products

Figure 32.2 Scale of market competition

Determinants of competitiveness

The key to competitiveness is customer satisfaction. If consumers are satisfied with quality and value for money, the firm concerned should be competitive. Competitive firms find it easier to hold on to, or even gain, market share. Competitiveness is a function of internal factors that are within the firm's control, and external factors, which are not.

Efficiency

Ryanair is a highly efficient company that manages its costs very effectively. The company's business model focuses on cost minimisation, by:

● avoiding airports that have high take-off and landing

charges; instead, Ryanair prefers flying from secondary airports, some of which actually pay it for using them

● operating only one type of aircraft – the Boeing 737; staff employed to pilot or service Ryanair's aircraft need only be trained on one plane, minimising staff training and stock holding costs (for plane components)

● cutting out free food, drinks and newspapers; passengers that wish to consume these items have to pay for them; charging for food and drink has converted a cost into an important source of revenue.

Cost-efficient businesses such as Ryanair can charge lower prices than their less efficient rivals, yet make the same or more profit per unit supplied. In highly competitive commodity markets, such as low-cost air travel, price cutting is a highly effective way of gaining market share.

Design

Some firms are highly competitive because they sell products that have been differentiated by their design. In countries such as the UK, where wage rates are relatively high, manufacturers cannot compete on price alone. Production costs are too high compared with rivals in countries where wage rates are lower. By using design as a USP, British manufacturers can compete on quality rather than price, making them less vulnerable to competition from China and India. Good-looking design can add value to a product. For example, the BMW Mini relies upon its retro 1960s styling to command its price premium within the small car market.

Brand image

In many markets brand image is crucial. The results of blind tests indicate that, in many cases, consumers are unable to tell the difference between supermarket own-label products and premium-priced brands. Clever branding and advertising may be the only thing ensuring that Stella Artois carries on outselling Tesco's Premium Lager.

External factors

Competitiveness is also partially determined by external factors that are beyond the firm's control. The going wage rate in a country is an excellent example of an external factor that is beyond any single firm's control. High wages tend to drive up costs, making a firm less

competitive. On average, factory workers in the USA get paid somewhere in the region of $15–$30 per hour. In China the corresponding figure is less than $1 per hour. Firms try to improve their competitiveness by making internal changes to help compensate for factors, such as labour costs, that are beyond their control. European car manufacturers such as VW and Mercedes have decided to close down some of their European factories and reopen them in low-cost countries such as China in an attempt to improve their competitiveness.

32.4 Methods of improving competitiveness

Training

Some firms aim to improve their efficiency by increasing the amount they spend on staff training. Well-trained staff create the following competitive advantages.

● *Lower costs:* training tends to increase the productivity of labour because trained staff can work faster and make fewer mistakes; if output per worker increases, unit labour costs will tend to fall.

● *Improved product quality:* trained staff know what they are doing, improving the build quality of the finished product, which could give the firm concerned a competitive advantage in the market.

● *Better customer service:* effective training can dramatically improve customer service; for example, in some supermarkets untrained staff are still sent straight to the checkouts to learn how to use the till on the job; this can lead to queues and irritated customers.

Management

The quality of management has an important impact on the competitiveness of a business. For many years newspapers blamed British workers for the decline of UK car producers such as Rover. Yet, today, the Nissan plant in Sunderland is the most productive car factory in Europe. This implies that British management methods were at fault, as the Nissan plant's workforce is British. Improving the quality of management within an organisation is notoriously difficult, requiring a change in an organisation's culture.

Modernisation and investment

Some firms try to improve their competitiveness by purchasing new machinery and technology designed to improve efficiency. For example, a car manufacturer could drive down unit costs by replacing labour with the latest CAM (computer-aided manufacturing) technology. It is hoped that the new machinery will boost efficiency by driving up productivity, while at the same time reducing the firm's wage bill.

32.5 Competitive advantage

Research shows that 60% of new restaurants close within two years of opening up. They have failed to establish themselves in the market. Either the owners identified a market niche wrongly, or the restaurant itself failed to match customers' expectations. The business has failed to secure a **competitive advantage** (i.e. an area of strength that matters to customers but cannot easily be matched by rivals). Examples of competitive advantages include:

- customers' trust in Marks & Spencer's food

- Walls ice cream's exceptionally powerful distribution position

- Primark's ability to produce a constant stream of new, fashionable stock

- Toyota's technical superiority with the 'green car', the hybrid Prius.

There are many potential sources of competitive advantage, including well-run operations (high-quality manufacture, quality of service, quality of design) plus marketing advantages such as a distinctive brand image or exceptionally loyal customers. Many of these advantages will help to produce value added (i.e. will spread further the gap between a firm's selling price and its cost of bought-in goods and services).

Marketing and competitiveness

Competitiveness is a much wider issue than marketing. It is affected by the quality of the design and build of the products, and by the enthusiasm of the staff. These are clearly operations and personnel issues. Nevertheless marketing is at the heart of competitiveness for many firms. Mars knows how to produce Galaxy chocolate, so the key to the firm's success next year is how well the brand can be marketed. The managers must understand the customers, and then have the wisdom and the creativity to find a way to make the product stand out.

Key terms

Competitive advantage: an area of strength that matters to customers but cannot easily be copied by competitors.

Non-price competition: rivalry based on factors other than price (e.g. advertising, sales promotions or 'new improved' products).

Oligopolistic: a market in which a few large companies have a dominant share (e.g. the UK chocolate market with a 70% share divided between Cadbury, Nestlé and Mars).

Predatory pricing: when a large company sets prices low with the deliberate intention of driving a weaker rival out of business.

USP: a point of genuine difference that makes one product stand out from the crowd (e.g. the Toyota Prius 'hybrid synergy drive').

Exercises

A. Revision questions

(35 marks; 35 minutes)

1 What is a competitive market? (2)

2 Explain how the marketing mix of Virgin Trains might be affected by a decision by government to allow other train operating companies to compete on Virgin's routes. (4)

3 Describe the main features of an oligopolistic market. (3)

4a What is a price war and . . . (3)

4b why are they rare? (3)

5 Explain why product differentiation becomes more important as competition within a market increases. (3)

6 Identify four factors that could be used to identify whether or not a business is competitive. (4)

7 How might the size of an organisation affect its efficiency? (3)

8 Why might a firm that is struggling to be competitive increase its training budget? (3)

9 Explain how the quality of management can impact upon an organisation's efficiency. (4)

10 Apart from market research, how might a firm achieve its goal of attempting to get closer to the consumer? (3)

B. Revision exercises

B1 Data response

At the beginning of the 1960s Indian food was a niche market business: there were just 500 Indian restaurants in the whole of the UK. As the table below illustrates, in the two decades that followed, the UK Indian restaurant market grew at a spectacular rate. In more recent times the market has continued to grow, however the rate of growth has declined. Today, the Indian restaurant market is firmly established. The industry is one of Britain's largest, employing over 60,000 people.

Number of Indian restaurants in UK

Year	No. of restaurants	Market growth rate (%)
1960	500	–
1970	1200	140
1980	3000	150
1990	5100	70
2000	7940	56
2004	8750	10

The Indian restaurant market is extremely decentralised. The market is made up of thousands of small, independent operators. In most British high streets there are several Indian restaurants that compete aggressively against one another. Indian food is very popular: over 23 million portions of Indian food are sold in restaurants each year. In the 1960s and 1970s, the growing affluence and cosmopolitan nature of the British public boosted takings at most Indian restaurants. Indian restauranteurs began to make serious money from the industry. Most owners chose to use some of the profit made to upgrade their facilities. Gradually the Indian restaurant scene became more sophisticated (e.g. luxurious-looking tables, chairs and tablecloths, piped Indian music, air conditioning, dinner-jacketed waiters and flock wallpaper). Some 30 years ago Indian restaurants tended to look the same. Most had fairly similar menus too. As a result Indian restaurants were forced into competing against each other on price. Unfortunately, intense price competition led to falling profit margins. Indian restauranteurs began to realise the importance of product differentiation as a competitive weapon. The first real attempt to create differentiation occurred in the early 1960s when a handful of forward-looking Indian restaurants, such as the Gaylord in Mortimer Street, London, imported tandoors. A tandoor is a special type of oven made from clay that gives the food cooked inside it a distinctive taste. Restaurants using tandoor ovens found that they could charge slightly higher prices without emptying their restaurants. Today, Indian restaurants use a variety of tactics to compete including those listed below.

- *Décor and design:* in recent times several now famous London-based Indian restaurants, such as the Cinnamon Club, opened in 2001 at a cost of £2.6 million in the Old Westminster Library, ditched the old-style traditional Indian restaurant décor (including the flock wallpaper!) in favour of a more upmarket-looking modern minimalistic interior design style. This change inspired many other Indian restaurants up and down the land to upgrade their fixtures and fittings in the hope that they too could charge Cinnamon Club-style premium prices (e.g. smoked rack of lamb with Rajasthani corn sauce and pilau rice for £22.00).

- *Exotic-sounding premium-priced menu items:* for example, Seabass Kaylilan prepared with fenugreek and tamarind.

Other restaurants have adopted a different approach. For example, the Khyber in Croydon has tried to win customers by emphasising its authenticity. The restaurant's website informs the reader that the Khyber won the Carlton TV London Indian Restaurant award in 1997 and that 'Our success is based on more traditional recipes.' The slogan 'It's just how mum would cook it back home' also features prominently on its internet menu. It also offers:

- balti cooking, including the super-sized big-as-your-table Nan breads!

- a prestigious imported German lager on draught, or a selection of fine wines

- flying in celebrated curry chefs from the Indian subcontinent for a limited period to cook up special food for a Curry Festival – the equivalent of a nightclub flying in a celebrity DJ.

Questions

(35 marks; 40 minutes)

1 Using the table, explain what has happened to the degree of competition within the UK Indian restaurant market over the last 50 years. (6)

2 Giving your reasons, discuss whether the Indian restaurant market in the UK is an example of a fiercely competitive market. (6)

3a Explain how efficiency might affect the competitiveness of an Indian restaurant. (4)

3b How might an Indian restaurant set about improving its efficiency? (4)

4 Identify and explain three internal factors that might affect the competitiveness of an Indian restaurant. (6)

5 Product differentiation is essential if an Indian restaurant is to survive in the long run. Discuss. (9)

Figure 32.3 The Cinnamon Club's bar and food

B2 Case study

Tesco's £9 toaster.

The prices of consumer electronics, such as toasters, satellite TV set-top boxes and MP3 players, have tumbled in recent years. Supermarket chains such as Tesco now sell DVD players that previously cost hundreds of pounds for under £10. So, why have the prices of these goods fallen? In part, the price falls reflect the falling price of the components that go into consumer electronics. Low prices also reflect the fact that there is now more competition in the market. In the past, consumers typically bought items such as TVs and computers from specialist retailers such as Currys. Today, the situation is somewhat different: in addition to these specialist retailers, consumers can now buy electrical goods over the internet and from supermarkets. Some industry analysts also believe that some of the supermarket chains are using set-top boxes and DVD players as loss leaders.

In today's ultra-competitive environment, manufacturers of consumer electronics face intense pressure from retailers to cut costs so that retail prices can be cut without any loss of profit margin. To cut prices without compromising product quality, manufacturers such as the Dutch giant Philips have transferred production from the Netherlands to low-cost locations such as China.

Questions

(35 marks; 40 minutes)

1 Describe three characteristics of a highly competitive market. (6)

2 Why has the market for consumer electronics become more competitive? (4)

3 Explain three factors that would affect the competitiveness of a manufacturer of consumer electronics. (6)

4 What is a loss leader and why do supermarkets use this tactic? (4)

5 How might the degree of competition impact upon the marketing mix used by a Chinese manufacturer of own-label toasters? (5)

6 In today's increasingly competitive market for consumer electronics, firms must constantly cut costs and prices if they are to survive. Discuss. (10)

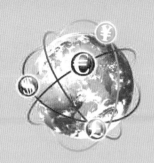

PRODUCTIVITY AND PERFORMANCE

33.1 Productivity: what is it?

Productivity is a measurement of a firm's efficiency. It measures output in relation to inputs. A firm can increase its efficiency by producing more with the same inputs or by producing the same amount with fewer inputs.

The most common measure is **labour productivity**. This measures the amount a worker produces over a given time. For example, an employee might make ten pairs of jeans in an hour. Measuring productivity is relatively easy in manufacturing, where the number of goods can be counted. In the service sector, however, it is not always possible to measure anything tangible. Productivity in services can be measured in some cases: number of customers served; number of patients seen; sales per employee. But how can the productivity of a receptionist be measured?

A-grade application
The US car industry

Each year the *Harbour Report* provides feedback on the productivity of the US car industry. Published on 1 June 2007, most of the figures shown in Table 33.1 are for 2005. Productivity is shown not as output of cars per person, but in terms of the time taken to produce each car; the lower the figure the better.

In its report, Harbour says that 'Toyota is the best in the industry. It is not a matter of spending more than competitors, but of effective *kaizen* improvement activities and the flexibility that comes with well-coordinated engineering.' The report also suggests that the highest-productivity factories are increasingly the highest-quality plants as well. It seems that well-managed staff will succeed at both together.

Source: *Harbour Report*, 2007 (reported on API newswire)

Table 33.1 US car industry productivity

	Manufacturing hours per vehicle 2005	Production hours per engine 2006	Stamping hours per engine** 2006	Capacity utilisation 2005	Profit per car 2005
General Motors	33.19	3.44	3+	90%	($1436)*
Ford	35.82	4+	3+	79%	($5243)*
DaimlerChrysler	33.71	4+	2.64	94–106%	($1072)*
Toyota	29.40	2.85	1.42	94–106%	$1200+
Nissan	32.51	4+	2.11	94–106%	$1200+
Honda	28.46	3.34	3+	91%	$1200+

* Loss made per vehicle sold
** Time taken to press metal into engine parts

Figure 33.1 A Toyota car plant

When considering a firm's efficiency it is important to distinguish between productivity and total output. By hiring more employees the firm may increase its total output, but does this necessarily mean that the output per employee has gone up? Similarly, it is possible to have less total output with higher productivity because of a fall in the number of workers. Imagine, for example, 20 employees producing 40 tables a week in a furniture company. Their productivity on average is two tables per week. If five employees make fifteen tables the overall output has fallen, but the output per worker has risen. This situation of falling output but rising productivity happened in many manufacturing companies in the UK in the early 1990s. Faced with high interest rates, high exchange rates and a recession many companies were forced to rationalise their organisations. This led to high levels of redundancy, and extra work for those who still had a job. The result was that there were fewer people working but at the same time there was often higher output per person.

33.2 Why does productivity matter?

Output per employee is a very important measure of a firm's performance. It has a direct impact on the cost of producing a unit. If productivity increases then, assuming wages are unchanged, the labour cost per unit will fall. Imagine that in one factory employees make five pairs of shoes a day, but in another they make ten pairs a day; assuming that the wage rate is the same, this means the labour cost of a pair of shoes will be halved in the second factory (see Table 33.2). With lower labour costs, this firm is likely to be in a better competitive position.

By increasing productivity a firm can improve its competitiveness. It can either sell its products at a lower price or keep the price as it was and enjoy a higher profit margin. This is why firms continually monitor their productivity relative to that of their competitors and, where possible, try to increase it. However, they need to make sure that quality does not suffer in the rush to produce more. It may be necessary to set both productivity and quality targets.

33.3 How to increase productivity

Increase investment in modern equipment

With modern, sophisticated machines and better production processes, output per worker should improve. Many modern factories have very few production workers; mechanisation and automation are everywhere. However, firms face financial constraints and should be cautious about assuming that mechanisation guarantees higher profits.

Table 33.2 Shoe factory productivity and wage costs

	Daily wage rate	**Productivity rate (per day)**	**Wage cost per pair**
Factory 1	£50	5	£10
Factory 2	£50	10	£5

Many managers call for new technology when in fact more output can be squeezed out of the existing equipment. It may prove more efficient to run the machines for longer, spend more on careful maintenance to prevent breakdowns and discuss how to improve working practices. Firms can often achieve significant productivity gains without new equipment. This is the reason for the success of the **kaizen** approach taken by many firms. Important benefits can be achieved from what seem like relatively small changes to the way the firm operates rather than large-scale investment in technology.

Improve the ability level of those at work

To increase productivity a firm may need to introduce more training for its employees. A skilled and well-trained workforce is likely to produce more and make fewer mistakes. Employees should be able to complete the task more quickly and will not need as much supervision or advice. They will be able to solve their own work-related problems and may be in a better position to contribute ideas on how to increase productivity further.

However, firms are often reluctant to invest in training because employees may leave and work for another firm once they have gained more skills. Training also involves higher costs in the short run, which the business may not be able to afford, and the actual training period may cause disruptions to the normal flow of work. There is also a danger that the training will not provide sufficient gains to justify the initial investment, so any spending in this area needs to be properly costed and researched. Simply training people for the sake of it is obviously of limited value. However, in general UK firms do not have a particularly good record in training and more investment here could probably have a significant effect on the UK's productivity levels.

It should also be remembered that elaborate training may not be necessary for a firm that recruits the right people. Great care must be taken in the selection process to find staff with the right skills and attitudes. A firm with a good reputation locally will find it much easier to pick the best people. This is why many firms take great care over their relations with the local community.

Improve employee motivation

Professor Herzberg once said that most people's idea of a fair day's work was less than half of what they could give if they wanted to. The key to success, he felt, was to create the circumstances in which people wanted to give all they could to the job. His suggestions on how to provide job enrichment are detailed in Unit 26.

There is no doubt that motivation matters. A motivated salesforce may achieve twice the sales level of an unmotivated one. A motivated computer technician may correct twice the computer faults of an unmotivated one. And, in both cases, overall business performance will be affected.

A-grade application
Motivation on the pitch

When Fulham Football Club appointed a new groundsman, few people even noticed. The fans had always been proud of the pitch, but newly appointed Frank Boahene was not impressed. He thought the pitch needed a dramatic improvement before the August start to the new season. With no time to re-seed the pitch, he decided the best way to strengthen the grass was to cut it three times a day! First thing in the morning and last thing in the afternoon was not a problem, but he also chose to 'pop back' from his home in Reading (an hour's drive) to do the third cut at 11 o'clock at night. That's motivation!

The role of management

The management's style and ability can have a significant impact on motivation and on how effectively resources are used. Good managers can bring about substantial productivity gains through well-organised work, the effective management of people and the coordination of resources. Bad managers can lead to wastage, inefficiency and low productivity.

Perhaps the key management role is to identify increasing productivity as a permanent objective. For example, Japanese bulldozer company Komatsu set a target of a 10% productivity increase every year, until the world-leading American producer Caterpillar had been overtaken. In many firms, productivity is not a direct target – the focus, day by day, is on production, not productivity. After all, it is production that ensures customer orders are fulfilled. An operations manager, faced with a 10% increase in orders, may simply ask the workforce to do overtime. The work gets done; the workforce is happy to earn extra money; and it's all rather easy to do. It's harder by far to reorganise the workplace to make production more effective. Managers whose main focus is on the short term, therefore, think of production not productivity.

Issues For Analysis

When answering a case study or essay question, it might be useful to consider the following points:

● productivity is an important determinant of a firm's ability to compete in this country or overseas because it can have a significant impact on unit costs

● high productivity does not in itself guarantee that a firm is competitive – it also depends on other factors such as the cost of materials, product quality, product design, good marketing and external factors such as the exchange rate

● the productivity within an industry will depend on a combination of factors, such as training, capital equipment and production techniques; the main single factor is the quality of management.

33.4 Productivity and performance
an evaluation

Greater labour productivity can lead to greater efficiency and higher profitability. This is because, all other things being equal, it lowers the labour cost per unit. However, productivity is only one factor that contributes to a firm's success. A firm must also ensure it produces a good-quality product, that it is marketed effectively and that costs are controlled. There is little point increasing productivity by 20% if at the same time you pay your staff 30% more. Similarly, there is no point producing more if there is no actual demand. Higher productivity, therefore, contributes to better performance but needs to be accompanied by effective decision making throughout the firm.

The importance of productivity to a firm depends primarily on the level of value added involved. Top-price perfumes, such as those produced by Chanel, have huge profit margins. Production costs are a tiny proportion of the selling price. Therefore a 10% productivity increase might have only a marginal effect on profit, and virtually none on the competitiveness of the brand. For mass-market products in competitive markets, high productivity is likely to be essential for survival. A 5% cost advantage might make all the difference. Therefore, when judging an appropriate recommendation for solving a business problem, a judgement is required as to whether boosting productivity is a top priority for the business concerned.

Key terms

Capacity: total output that could be produced with existing resources.

Kaizen: a Japanese term meaning 'continuous improvement'; regular, small increases in productivity may achieve more (and be less disruptive) than major changes to working methods.

Labour productivity: output per worker.

Exercises

A. Revision questions

(40 marks; 40 minutes)

1 What is meant by the term 'productivity'? (3)

2 Why may it be hard to measure the productivity of staff who work in service industries? (4)

3 How does productivity relate to labour costs per unit? (4)

4 Explain how a firm might be able to increase its employees' productivity. (4)

5 How can increased investment in machinery help to boost productivity? (3)

6 Identify two factors that help and two factors that limit your productivity as a student. (4)

7 Outline the likely effect of increased motivation on the productivity of a teacher. (5)

8 Look at the table below and calculate the change in productivity at BDQ Co since last year. (4)

	Output	Number of staff
Last year	32,000	50
This year	30,000	40

9 Explain how motivation and productivity might be linked. (4)

10 Explain how productivity can be linked to unit labour costs. (5)

B. Revision exercises

B1 Case study

Going Potty

Farah Stewart was trying to explain to the employees at her ceramics factory, FS Ltd, the need to boost productivity. Relations between Farah and her staff had not been good in recent years. The company was not doing well and she blamed the workers: 'On average you work eight hours a day at £8 an hour and produce around 160 pots each. Meanwhile, at Frandon I am told they produce 280 pots a day. Can't you see that this makes it cheaper for them and if things go on like this we'll be out of business? You need to work much harder to get our unit costs down! I know you are expecting to get a pay rise this year, but I cannot afford it until you produce more; then we'll think about it.'

Jeff Battersby, the spokesperson for the employees, was clearly annoyed by Farah's tone: 'First, Ms Stewart, have you ever considered that if you paid us more we might produce more for you? I'm not surprised productivity is higher at Frandon – they get about £80 a day. There's no point demanding more work from us if you are not willing to pay for it. We're not slaves you know. If you paid us £10 an hour like Frandon, I reckon we could increase productivity by 50%. However, that's not the only issue: they've got better equipment – it's not our fault if the kilns don't work half the time and take an age to heat up. Sort out the equipment and our pay and you'll soon see productivity improve. Why not *ask* us next time instead of jumping to conclusions?'

Questions

(60 marks; 75 minutes)

1a FS Ltd employs 50 pot makers, while Frandon Ltd employs 30 people in production. Calculate the total output for each of the two companies. (4)

1b With reference to FS Ltd and Frandon Ltd, explain the difference between 'total output' and 'productivity'. (6)

2a Calculate the average labour cost per pot at FS Ltd if employees are paid £8 an hour and their daily output is 160 pots each. (4)

2b What is the wage cost per pot at Frandon (assume an eight-hour day)? (3)

2c Analyse the short- and long-term benefits to Frandon of its lower labour costs per unit. (12)

2d Jeff Battersby claims that if the employees at FS Ltd were paid £10 an hour their productivity would increase 50%. What would the unit wage cost be then? (5)

3 Would you recommend Farah increases the pay of her employees to £10 an hour? Justify your answer. (12)

4 Discuss the possible gains from involving employees in discussions about how to improve productivity. (14)

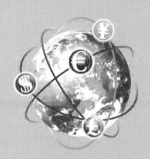

MOTIVATION IN THEORY

DEFINITION

One key theorist (Professor Herzberg) believes motivation occurs when people do something because they *want* to do it; others think of motivation as the desire to achieve a result. The difference between these two definitions is important and should become clear in this unit.

34.1 Introduction

A recent study by the Hay Group found that just 15% of UK workers consider themselves 'highly motivated'. As many as 25% say they're 'coasting' and 8% admit to being 'completely demotivated'. In the same survey, employees felt they could be 45% more productive if they were doing a job they loved, and 28% more productive with better training. Poor management is part of the problem, as 28% say they would be more productive with a better boss.

The Hay Group calculates that if the under-performance was tackled successfully, the value of UK output would rise by more than £350 billion a year. So motivation matters. This is why it merits a unit to itself – and why many consider motivation theory to be the most important topic within Business Studies.

34.2 F. W. Taylor and Scientific Management

Although there were earlier pioneers, the starting point for the study of motivation is F. W. Taylor (1856–1917). As with most of the other influential writers on this subject, Taylor was American. His influence over the twentieth-century world has been massive. Much business practice in America, Europe, Japan and the former Communist countries is still rooted in his writing and work.

A recent biography of Taylor is titled *The One Best Way*; this sums up neatly Taylor's approach to management. He saw it as management's task to decide exactly how every task should be completed, then to devise the tools needed to enable the worker to achieve the task as efficiently as possible. This method is evident today in every McDonald's in the world. Fries are cooked at 175 degrees for exactly three minutes, then a buzzer tells employees to take them out and salt them. Throughout every McDonald's is a series of dedicated, purpose-built machines for producing milkshakes, toasting buns, squirting chocolate sauce, and much else. Today, 100 years after his most active period working in industry, F. W. Taylor would feel very much at home ordering a Big Mac.

So, what was Taylor's view of the underlying motivations of people at work? How did he make sure that the employees worked effectively at following 'the one best way' laid down by managers?

Taylor believed that people work for only one reason: money. He saw it as the task of the manager to devise a system that would maximise efficiency. This would generate the profit to enable the worker to be paid a higher wage. Taylor's view of human nature was that of 'economic man'. In other words people were motivated only by the economic motive of self-interest. Therefore a manager could best motivate a worker by offering an incentive (a 'carrot') or a threat (the 'stick'). Taylor can be seen as a manipulator, or even a bully, but he believed his methods were in the best interests of the employees themselves.

Taylor's influence stemmed less from his theories than his activities. He was a trained engineer who acted as a very early management consultant. His methods were as follows:

- observe workers at work, recording and timing what they do, when they do it and how long they take over it (this became known as time and motion study)

- identify the most efficient workers and see how they achieve greater efficiency

- break the task down into small component parts that can be done quickly and repeatedly

- devise equipment specifically to speed up tasks

- set out exactly how the work should be done in future; 'each employee', Taylor wrote, 'should receive every day clear-cut, definite instructions as to what he is to do and how he is to do it, and these instructions should be exactly carried out, whether they are right or wrong'

- devise a pay scheme to reward those who complete or beat tough output targets, but that penalises those who cannot or will not achieve the **productivity** Taylor believed was possible; this pay scheme was called **piece rate** – no work, no pay.

As an engineer, Taylor was interested in practical outcomes, not in psychology. There is no reason to suppose he thought greatly about the issue of motivation. The effect of his ideas was profound, though. Long before the publication of his 1911 book *The Principles of Scientific Management*, Taylor had spread his managerial practices of careful measurement, monitoring and – above all else – control. Before Taylor, skilled workers chose their own ways of working and had varied, demanding jobs. After Taylor, workers were far more likely to have limited, repetitive tasks; and to be forced to work at the pace set by a manager or consultant engineer.

Among those influenced by Taylor was Henry Ford. His Model T was the world's first mass-produced motor car. By 1911 the Ford factory in Detroit, USA, was already applying Taylor's principles of high **division of labour**, purpose-built machinery and rigid management control. When Ford introduced the conveyor belt in 1913, he achieved the ultimate Taylorite idea: men's pace of work dictated by a mechanical conveyor belt, the speed of which was set by management.

Eventually workers rebelled against being treated like machines. **Trades union** membership thrived in factories run on Taylorite lines, as workers wanted to organise against the suffocating lives they were leading at work. Fortunately, in many western countries further developments in motivation theory pointed to new, more people-friendly approaches.

Figure 34.1 Ford Model T, the first mass-produced motor car

34.3 Elton Mayo and the Human Relations Approach

Elton Mayo (1880–1949) was a medical student who became an academic with a particular interest in people in organisations. Although an Australian, he moved to America in 1923. Early in his career, his methods were heavily influenced by F. W. Taylor. An early investigation of a spinning mill in Pennsylvania identified one department with labour turnover of 250% compared to 6% elsewhere in the factory. His Taylorite solution was to prescribe work breaks. These had the desired effect.

Mayo moved on to work at the Hawthorne plant of Western Electric Company in Chicago. His investigations there are known as the Hawthorne Experiments.

He was called in to Hawthorne to try to explain the findings of a previous test into the effects of lighting upon productivity levels. The lighting conditions for one work group had been varied, while those for another had been held constant. The surprise was that whatever was done to the lighting, production rose in *both* groups. This proved that there was more to motivation and efficiency than purely economic motives.

Between 1927 and 1932 Mayo conducted a series of experiments at Hawthorne. The first is known as the Relay Assembly Test. Six volunteer female assembly staff were separated from their workmates. A series of experiments was carried out. The results were recorded and discussed with the women. Every 12 weeks a new working method was tried. The alternatives included:

- different bonus methods, such as individual versus group bonuses

- different rest periods

- different refreshments

- different work layout.

Before every change, the researchers discussed the new method fully with the operators. Almost without exception productivity increased with every change. At the end, the group returned to the original method (48-hour, 6-day week with no breaks) and output went up to its highest level yet! Not only that, but the women claimed they felt less tired than they had at the start.

The experiments had started rather slowly, with some resistance from the operatives. Progress became much more marked when one member of the group retired. She was replaced by a younger woman who quickly became the unofficial leader of the group.

Mayo's conclusions

● The women gained satisfaction from their freedom and control over their working environment.

● 'What actually happened was that six individuals became a team and the team gave itself wholeheartedly and spontaneously to cooperation in the experiment' (Mayo, 1949).

● Group norms (expectations of one another) are crucial and may be influenced more by informal than official group leaders.

● Communication between workers and managers influences morale and output.

● Workers are affected by the degree of interest shown in them by their managers; the influence of this upon motivation is known as 'the Hawthorne effect'.

The consequences of Mayo's work were enormous. He influenced many researchers and writers, effectively opening up the fields of industrial psychology and industrial sociology. Many academics followed Mayo's approach in what became known as the Human Relations school of management.

Businesses also responded to the implications of Mayo's work for company profitability and success. If teamwork, communications and managerial involvement were that important, firms reasoned that they needed an organisational structure to cope. In Taylor's era, the key

person was the engineer. The winners from Mayo's work were personnel departments. They grew throughout America and Britain in the 1930s, 1940s and 1950s as companies tried to achieve the Hawthorne effect.

34.4 Maslow and the hierarchy of needs

Abraham Maslow (1908–70) was an American psychologist, whose great contribution to motivation theory was the 'hierarchy of needs'. Maslow believed that everyone has the same needs – all of which can be organised as a hierarchy. At the base of the hierarchy are physical needs such as food, shelter and warmth. When unsatisfied, these are the individual's primary motivations. When employees earn enough to satisfy these needs, however, their motivating power withers away. Maslow said that 'It is quite true that humans live by bread alone – when there is no bread. But what happens to their desires when there *is* bread?' Instead of physical needs, people become motivated to achieve needs such as security and stability, which Maslow called the safety needs. In full, Maslow's hierarchy consisted of the elements listed in Table 34.1.

Ever since Maslow first put his theory forward (in 1940) writers have argued about its implications. Among the key issues raised by Maslow are the following.

● Do all humans have the same set of needs? Or are there some people who need no more from a job than money?

● Do different people have different degrees of need – for example, are some highly motivated by the need for power, while others are satisfied by social factors?

Table 34.1 *Maslow's hierarchy of needs: implications for business*

Maslow's levels of human need	Business implications
physical needs, e.g. food, shelter and warmth	pay levels and working conditions
safety needs, e.g. security, a safe structured environment, stability, freedom from anxiety	job security, a clear job role/description, clear lines of accountability (only one boss)
social needs, e.g. belonging, friendship, contact	team working, communications, social facilities
esteem needs, e.g. strength, self-respect, confidence, status and recognition	status, recognition for achievement, power, trust
self-actualisation, e.g. self-fulfilment; 'to become everything that one is capable of becoming,' wrote Maslow	scope to develop new skills and meet new challenges, and to develop one's full potential

If so, the successful manager would be one who can understand and attempt to meet the differing needs of her/his staff.

● Can anyone's needs ever be said to be fully satisfied? The reason the hierarchy diagram (Figure 34.1) has an open top is to suggest that the human desire for achievement is limitless.

Maslow's work had a huge influence on the writers who followed him, especially McGregor and Herzberg. The hierarchy of needs is also used by academics in many subjects beyond Business Studies, notably Psychology and Sociology.

Figure 34.2 Maslow's hierarchy of needs

advancement – the last three being of greater importance for a lasting change of attitudes.' He pointed out that each of these factors concerned the job itself, rather than issues such as pay or status. Herzberg called these five factors 'the motivators'.

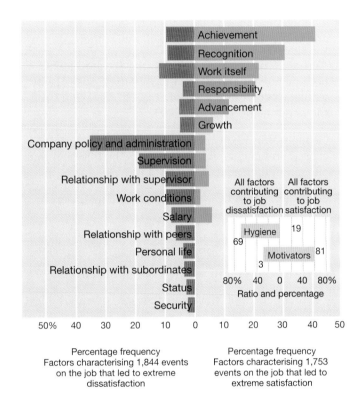

Figure 34.3 Comparison of satisfiers and dissatisfiers

34.5 Herzberg's two factor theory

The key test of a theory is its analytic usefulness. On this criterion, the work of Professor Fred Herzberg (1923–2000) is the strongest by far.

The theory stems from research conducted in the 1950s into factors affecting workers' **job satisfaction** and dissatisfaction. It was carried out on 200 accountants and engineers in Pennsylvania, USA. Despite the limited nature of this sample, Herzberg's conclusions remain influential to this day.

Herzberg asked employees to describe recent events that had given rise to exceptionally good feelings about their jobs, then probed for the reasons why. 'Five factors stand out as strong determiners of job satisfaction,' Herzberg wrote in 1966, 'achievement, recognition for achievement, the work itself, responsibility and

The researchers went on to ask about events giving rise to exceptionally bad feelings about their jobs. This revealed a separate set of five causes. Herzberg stated that 'the major dissatisfiers were company policy and administration, supervision, salary, interpersonal relations and working conditions'. He concluded that the common theme was factors that 'surround the job', rather than the job itself. The name he gave these dissatisfiers was '**hygiene factors**'; this was because fulfilling them would prevent dissatisfaction, rather than causing positive motivation. Careful hygiene prevents disease; care to fulfil hygiene factors prevents job dissatisfaction.

To summarise: motivators have the power to create positive job satisfaction, but little downward potential; hygiene factors will cause job dissatisfaction unless they are provided for, but do not motivate. Importantly, Herzberg saw pay as a hygiene factor, not a motivator. So a feeling of being underpaid could lead to a grievance; but high pay would soon be taken for

Table 34.2 *Herzberg's two factor theory*

Motivators (can create positive satisfaction)	Hygiene factors (can create job dissatisfaction)
Achievement	Company policy and administration (the rules, paperwork and red tape)
Recognition for achievement	Supervision (especially being over-supervised)
Meaningful, interesting work	Pay
Responsibility	Interpersonal relations (with supervisor, peers, or even customers)
Advancement (psychological, not just a promotion)	Working conditions

granted. This motivator/hygiene factor theory is known as the 'two factor theory' (see Table 34.2).

Movement and motivation

Herzberg was keen to distinguish between movement and motivation. Movement occurs when somebody does something; motivation is when they *want* to do something. This distinction is essential to a full understanding of Herzberg's theory. He did not doubt that financial incentives could be used to boost productivity: 'If you bully or bribe people, they'll give you better than average performance.' His worries about 'bribes' (carrots) were that they would never stimulate people to give of their best; people would do just enough to achieve the bonus. Furthermore, bribing people to work harder at a task they found unsatisfying would build up resentments, which might backfire on the employer.

Herzberg advised against payment methods such as piece rate. They would achieve movement, but by reinforcing worker behaviour, would make them inflexible and resistant to change. The salaried, motivated employee would work hard, care about quality and think about – even welcome – improved working methods.

Job enrichment

The reason why Herzberg's work has had such an impact on businesses is because he not only analysed motivation, he also had a method for improving it. The method is job enrichment, which he defined as 'giving people the opportunity to use their ability'. He suggested that, for a job to be considered enriched, it would have to contain the following.

● *A complete unit of work:* not just a small repetitive fragment of a job, but a full challenging task; Herzberg heaped scorn upon the 'idiot jobs' that resulted from Taylor's views on the merits of high division of labour.

● *Direct feedback:* wherever possible, a job should enable the worker to judge immediately the quality of what s/he has done; direct feedback gives the painter or the actor (or the teacher) the satisfaction of knowing exactly how well they have performed. Herzberg disliked systems that pass quality inspection off onto a supervisor: 'a man must always be held responsible for his own quality'. Worst of all, he felt, was annual appraisal, in which feedback is too long delayed.

● *Direct communication:* for people to feel committed, in control and to gain direct feedback, they should communicate directly – avoiding the delays of communicating via a supervisor or a 'contact person'. In itself, it is hard to see the importance of this. For a student of Business Studies, it leads to an important conclusion: that communications and motivation are interrelated.

Conclusion

Herzberg's original research has been followed up in many different countries, including Japan, Africa and Russia. An article he wrote on the subject in the *Harvard Business Review* in 1968 (called 'Just one more time, how do you motivate employees') has sold more than one million reprinted copies. His main insight was to show that unless the job itself was interesting, there was no way to make working life satisfying. This led companies such as Volvo in Sweden and Toyota in

Table 34.3 Key quotes from Professor Herzberg

On the two factor theory	'Motivators and hygiene factors are equally important, but for different reasons'
On movement	'If you do something because you want a house or a Jaguar, that's movement. It's not motivation'
The risks of giving bonuses	'A reward once given becomes a right'
The importance of training	'The more a person can do, the more you can motivate them'
The importance of always treating staff fairly	'A remembered pain can lead to revenge psychology... They'll get back at you some day when you need them'
On communication	'In industry, there's too much communication. And of course its passive... But if people are doing idiot jobs they really don't give a damn'
On participation	'When participation is suggested in terms of control over overall goals, it is usually a sham'

Japan to rethink their factory layouts. Instead of individual workers doing simple, repetitive tasks, the drive was to provide more complete units of work. Workers were grouped into teams, focusing on significant parts of the manufacturing process, such as assembling and fitting the gearbox, and then checking the quality of their work. Job enrichment indeed.

34.6 Motivation in theory
an evaluation

Most managers assume they understand human motivation, but they have never studied it. As a result they may underestimate the potential within their own staff, or unthinkingly cause resentments that fester.

The process of managing people takes place in every part of every organisation. By contrast, few would need to know the financial concept of 'gearing' in their working lives. So lack of knowledge of motivation theory is particularly unfortunate – and has exceptionally widespread effects. In some cases, ignorance leads managers to ignore motivation altogether; they tell themselves that control and organisation are their only concerns. Other managers may see motivation as important, but fail to understand its subtleties.

For these reasons, there is a case for saying that the concepts within this unit are the most important in the whole subject.

Issues For Analysis

● In an exam context, the starting point is to select the most appropriate theory to answer a question. If a case study context suggested poor relations between management and workforce, Elton Mayo's would be very suitable. If motivation was weak, Herzberg's theory provides a comprehensive analysis.

● When applying a theory, the analysis is strengthened by using a questioning approach. Herzberg's theory is admirable, but it is not perfect. It provides insights, but not necessarily answers – and certainly not blueprints. A job enrichment programme might be highly effective in one situation, but a disappointment in another.

● This leads on to another key factor: the success of any new policies will depend hugely on the history of trust – or lack of it – in the workplace. Successful change in the factors involved in motivation may be very difficult and slow to achieve. There are no magic solutions.

● Accordingly, when a firm faces a crisis, changes in factors relating to motivation will rarely provide an answer. A crisis must be solved in the short term, but human motivation requires long-term strategies.

Key terms

Division of labour: subdividing a task into a number of activities, enabling workers to specialise and therefore become very efficient at completing what may be a small, repetitive task.

Hygiene factors: 'everything that surrounds what you do in the job', such as pay, working conditions and social status – all potential causes of dissatisfaction, according to Herzberg.

Job satisfaction: the sense of well-being and achievement that stems from a satisfying job.

Piece rate: paying workers per piece they produce (e.g. £2 per pair of jeans made).

Productivity: output per person (i.e. a measure of efficiency).

Trades union: an organisation that represents the interests of staff at the workplace.

Further reading

Herzberg, F. (1959) *The Motivation to Work*. Wiley International.

Maslow, A. H. (1987) *Motivation and Personality*. HarperCollins (1st edn 1954).

Mayo, E. (1975) *The Social Problems of Industrial Civilisation*. Routledge (1st edn 1949).

Exercises

A. Revision questions

(35 marks; 35 minutes)

1 Which features of the organisation of a McDonald's could be described as Taylorite? (3)

2 Explain the meaning of the term 'economic man'. (3)

3 Explain how workers in a bakery might be affected by a change from salary to piece rate. (3)

4 Give a brief outline of Mayo's research methods at the Hawthorne plant. (4)

5 How may 'group norms' affect productivity at a workplace? (3)

6 Explain the meaning of the term 'the Hawthorne effect'. (2)

7 Which two levels of Maslow's hierarchy could be called 'the lower-order needs'? (2)

8 Describe in your own words why Maslow organised the needs into a hierarchy. (3)

9 State three business implications of Maslow's work on human needs. (3)

10 Herzberg believes pay does not motivate, but it is important. Why? (3)

11 How do motivators differ from hygiene factors? (3)

12 What is job enrichment? How is it achieved? (3)

B. Revision exercises

B1 Data response

Look back at Figure 34.2. It shows the results of Herzberg's research into the factors that cause positive job satisfaction and those that cause job dissatisfaction. The length of the bars shows the percentage of responses.

Questions

(20 marks; 25 minutes)

1 Which of the factors had the least effect on satisfaction or dissatisfaction? (1)

2 One of Herzberg's objectives was to question whether good human relations were as important in job satisfaction as claimed by Elton Mayo. Do you think he succeeded? (6)

3 Herzberg found that responsibility had the longest-lasting effects on job satisfaction. Why may this be the case? (5)

4 Discuss which of the factors is the most important motivator. (8)

B2 Case study

Tania was delighted to get the bakery job and looked forward to her first shift. It would be tiring after a day at college, but £52 for eight hours on a Friday would guarantee good Saturday nights in future.

On arrival, she was surprised to be put straight to work, with no more than a mumbled 'You'll be working packing machine B.' Fortunately, she was able to watch the previous shift worker before clocking-off time, and could get the hang of what was clearly a very simple task. As the 18.00 bell rang, the workers streamed out, but not many had yet turned up from Tania's shift. The conveyor belt started to roll again at 18.16.

As the evening wore on, machinery breakdowns provided the only, welcome, relief from the tedium and discomfort of Tania's job. Each time a breakdown occurred, a ringing alarm bell was drowned out by a huge cheer from the staff. A few joyful moments followed, with dough fights breaking out. Tania started to feel quite old as she looked at some of her workmates.

At the 22.00 meal break, Tania was made to feel welcome. She enjoyed hearing the sharp, funny comments made about the shift managers. One was dubbed 'Noman' because he was fat, wore a white coat and never agreed to anything. Another was called 'Turkey' because he strutted around, but if anything went wrong, got into a flap. It was clear that both saw themselves as bosses. They were not there to help or to encourage, only to blame.

Was the bakery always like this, Tania wondered? Or was it simply that these two managers were poor?

Questions

(25 marks; 30 minutes)

1 Analyse the working lives of the shift workers at the bakery, using Herzberg's two factor theory. (8)

2 If a managerial follower of Taylor's methods came into the factory, how might s/he try to improve the productivity level? (7)

3 Later on in this (true) story, Tania read in the local paper that the factory was closing. The reason given was 'lower labour productivity than at our other bakeries'. The newspaper grumbled about the poor attitudes of local workers. Consider the extent to which there is some justification in this view. (10)

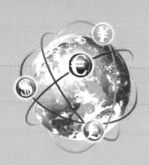

MOTIVATION IN PRACTICE

Unit 35

DEFINITION

Assessing how firms try to motivate their staff and how successful these actions appear to be. In this context, companies take 'motivation' to mean enthusiastic pursuit of the objectives or tasks set out by the firm.

35.1 Introduction

There are four main variables that influence the **motivation** of staff in practice:

1 the financial reward systems

2 job design

3 empowering the employees

4 working in teams.

All four will be analysed with reference to the theories outlined in Unit 34.

Motivation: famous sayings

'The worst mistake a boss can make is not to say well done.' *John Ashcroft, British executive*

'Motivation is everything. You can do the work of two people, but you can't be two people. Instead, you have to inspire the next guy down the line and get him to inspire his people.' *Lee Iacocca, successful boss of Chrysler Motors*

'I have never found anybody yet who went to work happily on a Monday that had not been paid on a Friday.' *Tom Farmer, Kwik-Fit founder*

'Motivating people over a short period is not very difficult. A crisis will often do just that, or a carefully planned special event. Motivating people over a longer period of time, however, is far more difficult. It is also far more important in today's business environment.' *John Kotter, management thinker*

'My best friend is the one who brings out the best in me.' *Henry Ford, founder of Ford Motors*

35.2 Financial reward systems

Piecework

Piecework means working in return for a payment per unit produced. The payment itself is known as piece rate. Pieceworkers receive no basic or shift pay, so there is no sick pay, holiday pay or company pension.

Piecework is used extensively in small-scale manufacturing – for example, of jeans or jewellery. Its attraction for managers is that it makes supervision virtually unnecessary. All the manager need do is operate a quality control system that ensures the finished product is worth paying for. Day by day, the workers can be relied upon to work fast enough to earn a living (or a good) wage.

Piecework has several disadvantages to firms, however:

● scrap levels may be high, if workers are focused entirely on speed of output

● there is an incentive to provide acceptable quality, but not the best possible quality

● workers will work hardest when they want higher earnings (probably before Christmas and before their summer holiday); this may not coincide at all with seasonal patterns of customer demand

● worst of all is the problem of change; Herzberg pointed out that 'the worst way to motivate people is piece rate…it reinforces behaviour'; focusing people on maximising their earnings by repeating a task makes them very reluctant to produce something different or in a different way (they worry that they will lose out financially).

Performance-related pay

Performance-related pay (PRP) is a financial reward to staff whose work is considered above average. It is used for employees whose work achievements cannot be assessed simply through numerical measures (such as units produced or sold). PRP awards are usually made after an appraisal process has evaluated the performance of staff during the year.

On the face of it, PRP is a highly attractive system for encouraging staff to work towards the organisation's objectives. The usual method is:

1 establish targets for each member of staff/management at an appraisal interview

2 at the end of the year, discuss the individual's achievements against those targets

3 those with outstanding achievements are given a Merit 1 pay rise or bonus worth perhaps 6% of salary; others receive between 0% and 6%.

Despite the enthusiasm they have shown for it, employers have rarely been able to provide evidence of the benefits of PRP. Indeed the Institute of Personnel and Development concluded in a report that:

> It was not unusual to find that organisations which had introduced merit pay some years ago were less certain now of its continued value … it was time to move on to something more closely reflecting team achievement and how the organisation as a whole was faring.

This pointed to a fundamental problem with PRP: rewarding individuals does nothing to promote teamwork. Furthermore it might create unhealthy rivalry between managers – each going for the same Merit 1 spot.

Other problems for PRP systems include the following.

● *Perceived fairness/unfairness:* staff often suspect that those awarded the maximum are being rewarded not for performance but out of favouritism; this may damage working relations and team spirit.

● *Whether they have a sound basis in human psychology:* without question Professor Herzberg would be very critical of any attempt to influence work behaviour by financial incentives; a London School of Economics study of Inland Revenue staff found that only 12% believed that PRP had raised motivation at work, while 76% said it had not; Herzberg would approve of the researchers' conclusion that 'The current system has not succeeded in motivating staff to any significant degree, and may well have done the reverse.'

As the last point illustrates, a key assumption behind PRP is that the chance to be paid a bit more than other employees will result in a change in individual behaviour, in increased motivation to work. A survey for the government publication *Employment in Britain* found that 'pay incentives were thought important for hard work by fewer than one in five, and for quality standards by fewer than one in ten.

So why do firms continue to pursue PRP systems? There are two possible reasons:

1 to make it easier for managers to manage/control their staff (using a carrot instead of a stick)

2 to reduce the influence of collective bargaining and therefore trades unions.

A-grade application
The greatest benefit?

In early 2007, *Human Resources* magazine asked a research company to analyse the impact of different benefits on employees 'engagement level' (i.e. their level of commitment and satisfaction at work). The most successful benefit proved to be home working (i.e. allowing staff to work at home for one day a week). Profit-related pay proved to have a very small benefit. The engagement level of staff without profit-related pay was 66.9%; with profit-related pay it was 69.3%. This increase of 2.4% compares with an increase of 8.4% when employees have the benefit of home working.

Despite this evidence, a spokesperson for John Lewis pointed out that the business had just paid out £155 million to its 'partners', giving a profit share worth 18% of annual salary. He made it clear that John Lewis staff 'don't take it for granted'.

Profit sharing

A different approach to financial incentives is to provide staff with a share of the firm's annual profit. This puts staff in the same position as shareholders as, in effect, they are paid an annual dividend. This offers clear psychological benefits, as outlined below.

● Staff can come to see profit positively. Before, they may have regarded it as an unfair way of diverting pay from their own pockets to those of shareholders.

● Herzberg and other theorists warn that financial incentives distort behaviour. For example, if you pay a striker £500 per goal, wave goodbye to passing in the penalty area. Profit sharing, however, is more of a financial reward than an incentive. It may encourage

Table 35.1 *The pros and cons of profit sharing*

Pros	Cons
Encourages staff to think about the whole business, not just their own job	If the employee share is only a small proportion of annual profit, the payouts may be meaninglessly small
Encourages thinking about cost saving as well as revenue raising	Large payouts, though, may either hit shareholder dividends or reduce the investment capital for long-term expansion
Focus on profit may make it easier for staff to accept changes in working practices (i.e. it may lessen resistance to change)	Because no single individual can have much impact on overall profits, there may be no incentive effect

people to work harder or smarter, but should not stop them working as a team.

● If paid to staff in the form of free shares, the employees may develop a strong sense of identity with the company and its fortunes.

Profit sharing can represent a substantial bonus on top of regular earnings. For instance, the John Lewis Partnership pays an annual bonus that can be worth over 20% of an employee's earnings, typically around £2000. In other cases, such as Tesco, the profit share amounts to no more than £100 or so. At such a low level it is clearly more of a thank you than a serious incentive.

Fringe benefits

These are forms of reward other than income. Some managers have generous expense accounts; many have company cars. Usually all maintenance and running costs are paid by the company. In some cases, even petrol for private mileage can be charged to the employer. Other fringe benefits include:

● membership of clubs or leisure centres

● low-interest-rate loans or mortgages

● discounts on the company's products, such as the British Airways' staff perk of air fares at 90% off.

In all cases, fringe benefits are offered to encourage staff loyalty and to improve human relations.

35.3 Job design

Herzberg's theory emphasised the importance of job design. He wanted employers to create jobs with the maximum scope to be motivating. For example, when Jose Mourinho became Chelsea manager, he was allowed the independence and authority to buy and sell players

as he thought best. He had full power over the tactics and the budget for running the team. Two years later, club owner Abramovic had brought in a managing director and a director of football to restrict the manager's powers. Players were bought against Mourinho's wishes. The result was Mourinho's evident job dissatisfaction during the 2006/07 season. His job had been redesigned in the worst way possible. Instead of being empowered to show what he could do, Mourinho was being held back by his bosses.

Job design is the thought process of deciding what tasks each employee must do, what equipment they will have, what decision-making power they will have and whether they are working alone or in a team. F. W. Taylor believed that management should design jobs to be simple, repetitive and easily monitored. Today, the term job design usually refers to job enrichment or job enlargement.

Job enrichment

Professor Herzberg defines job enrichment as 'giving people the opportunity to use their ability'. A full explanation of his theory is outlined in Unit 34.

How can job enrichment be put into practice? The key thing is to realise the enormity of the task. It is not cheap, quick or easy to enrich the job of the production line worker or the supermarket checkout operator. The first thought might be to add more variety to the work. The supermarket operator might switch between the checkout, shelf-stacking and working in the warehouse. Known as job rotation, this approach reduces repetition but still provides the employee with little challenge. Herzberg's definition of job enrichment implies giving people 'a range of responsibilities and activities'. Job rotation only provides a range of activities. To provide job enrichment, workers must have a complete unit of work (not a repetitive fragment), responsibility for quality and for self-checking, and be given the opportunity to show their abilities.

Full job enrichment requires a radical approach. Take a conventional car assembly line, for example. As shown in Figure 35.1, workers each have a single task they carry out on their own. One fits the left-hand front door to a car shell that is slowly moving past on a conveyor belt – every 22 seconds. Another worker fits right-hand front doors, and so on. Job enrichment can be achieved only by rethinking the production line completely.

Figure 35.1 Traditional production line

Figure 35.2 shows how a car assembly line could be reorganised to provide a more enriched job. Instead of working in isolation, people work in groups on a significant part of the assembly process. An empty car shell comes along the conveyor belt and turns in to the Interior Group Area. Six workers fit carpets, glove boxes, the dashboard and much else. They check the quality of their own work, then put a rather impressive-looking vehicle back on the conveyor belt. Not only does the teamwork element help meet the social needs of the workforce, but there are also knock-on effects.

Figure 35.2 Enriched 'teamworking' line

The workers can be given a time slot to discuss their work and how to improve it. When new equipment is needed, they can be given a budget and told to get out to meet potential suppliers. In other words, they can become managers of their own work area.

Such a major step would be expensive. Rebuilding a production line might cost millions of pounds and be highly disruptive in the short term. There would also be the worry that team working might make the job more satisfying, yet still be less productive than the boring but practical system of high **division of labour**.

Job enlargement

Job enlargement is a general term for anything that increases the scope of a job. There are three ways in which it comes about.

1 *Job rotation:* increasing a worker's activities by switching between tasks of a similar level of difficulty. This does not increase the challenge, but may reduce the boredom of a job.

2 *Job loading:* increasing workload, often as a result of redundancies. It may mean having to do more of the same, but often entails one or two extra activities that have to be taken on.

3 *Job enrichment:* this enlargement of the scope of the job involves extra responsibilities and challenges, as well as extra activities/workload.

Of these, only job enrichment is likely to provide long-term job satisfaction. Employers may like to use the term job enrichment, but often they are really carrying out job rotation or job loading.

35.4 Empowerment

Empowerment is a modern term for delegation. There is only one difference between the two. The empowered worker not only has the authority to manage a task, but also some scope to decide what that task should be. An IKEA store manager has power delegated to him/her, but head office rules may be so rigid that the manager has little scope for individual judgement. An empowered store manager would be one who could choose a range of stock suited to local customers, or a staffing policy that differs from the national store policy.

Empowerment means having more power and control over your working life, having the scope to make significant decisions about how to allocate your time and how to move forward. It is a practical application of the theories of Mayo and Herzberg. It may lead to greater risks being taken, but can also lead to opportunities being identified and exploited. Above all else, it should aid motivation.

The only major worry about empowerment in recent years has come from the financial services industry. A trader called Nick Leeson carried out a series of reckless trades that lost hundreds of millions of pounds and brought about the collapse of Barings Bank. In the credit squeeze of 2007, a series of other speculative failures emerged. In most cases, a fundamental problem was that the company bosses did not understand fully the risks that were being taken. Empowerment is highly dangerous in a situation of ignorance.

35.5 Team working

Team working is the attempt to maximise staff satisfaction and involvement by organising employees into relatively small teams. These teams may be functional (the 'drive-thru crew' at a McDonald's) or geographic. The key features of such teams are that they should be:

● multi-skilled, so that everyone can do everyone else's job

● working together to meet shared objectives, such as to serve every customer within a minute or produce a gearbox with **zero defects**

● encouraged to think of the future as well as the present, in a spirit of *kaizen* (**continuous improvement**).

From a theoretical point of view, team working fits in well with Mayo's findings on the importance of group working and **group norms**. It can also be traced back to Maslow's emphasis on social needs. In practical terms, modern managers like team working because of the flexibility it implies. If worker A is absent, there are plenty of others used to dealing with the job. Therefore there is no disruption. Team working also gives scope for motivating influences such as job enrichment and quality circles.

Professor Charles Handy suggests in his book *Inside Organisations* (BBC Books, 1990) that 'a good team is a great place to be, exciting, stimulating, supportive, successful. A bad team is horrible, a sort of human prison.' It is true that the business will not benefit if the group norms within the team discourage effort. Nevertheless, team working has proved successful in many companies in recent years. Companies such as Rolls-Royce, Trebor, Rover and Komatsu have reported major improvements in absenteeism and labour turnover, and significant shifts in workforce attitudes.

A-grade application

Motivation at the RNLI

How do you motivate 4500 unpaid staff? Especially when you require them to put you before everything else, including family? This is the task of Ali Peck, human resources director for the RNLI, the Royal National Lifeboat Institution. If a boat capsizes in stormy weather, the lifeboatmen must stop whatever they are doing, put out to sea, and risk their own lives to save someone else's; 2006 saw a record number of rescues.

Peck's task is made more difficult because the 230 lifeboat stations are, of course, dotted around the coast. So the only way to bring people together is through training. Every lifeboatman has to go through a retraining programme every three to five years. This takes place at a purpose-built college. This is also where new volunteers are trained. Peck explains that the RNLI spends 50% more per head on training than any comparable organisation. It is crucial, because if the volunteers drifted away from the job, the organisation would fold. In the case of the RNLI, the staff motivations come from the teamwork and from a real sense of personal achievement and pride. The lifeboatmen certainly aren't in it for the money.

Issues For Analysis

The key ways to analyse motivation in practice are as follows.

- To select and apply the relevant motivation theory to the method being considered: good analysis of methods such as Performance Related Pay or job rotation require a critical eye.

- To question the publicly stated motives of the organisation or manager concerned: businesses can be very loose in their use of words such as motivation or empowerment. They can be euphemisms for tougher targets and greater pressure. If the recent history of a firm makes employees sceptical of the goodwill of managers, students should be equally questioning.

- As John Kotter has said, 'Motivating people over a short period is not very difficult.' The key test of a new approach to motivation is over a two- to five-year period, not the early months of a new initiative. So always consider the timescale.

35.6 Motivation in practice
an evaluation

There are many aspects of business studies that point solely towards money. How profitable is this price or that? What is the forecast net cash flow for April? And so on. In such circumstances it is understandable that human implications may be forgotten. Setting a high price for an AIDS cure may be profitable, but life-threatening to those who cannot afford the medicine. April's positive cash flow might be achieved only by sacking temporary staff.

When covering motivation in practice, there is little excuse for ignoring the implications for people. Exaggerated commissions or performance-related pay can lead sales staff to oversell goods or services, which may cause customers huge difficulties later on, such as cosmetic surgery or questionable investments. Also, within the workplace, serious problems can arise: bullying to 'motivate' staff into working harder, or creating a culture of overwork which leads to stress.

Fortunately, there are many businesses in which the management of motivation is treated with respect – companies which know that quick fixes are not the answer. Successful motivation in the long term is a result of careful job design, employee training and development, honesty and trust. It may be possible to supplement this with an attractive financial reward scheme, but money will never be a substitute for motivation.

Key terms

Division of labour: subdividing a job into small, repetitive fragments of work.

Group norms: the types of behaviour and attitude seen as normal within a group.

***Kaizen* (continuous improvement):** moving productivity and product quality forward in regular, small steps.

Motivation: to professor Herzberg, it means doing something because you want to do it; most business leaders think of it as prompting people to work hard.

Zero defects: production that is right first time, therefore requiring no reworking; this saves time and money.

Exercises

A. Revision questions

(40 marks; 40 minutes)

1 'Job design is the key to motivation.' Outline one reason why this might be true, and one reason why it might not. (4)

2 Look at the famous saying by Lee Iacocca on page 236. Explain in your own words what he meant by this. (3)

3 How *should* a manager deal with a mistake made by a junior employee? (4)

4 State three reasons why job enrichment should improve staff motivation. (3)

5 Distinguish between job rotation and job enrichment. (4)

6 How does 'empowerment' differ from 'delegation'? (4)

7 Identify three advantages to an employee of working in a team. (3)

8 State two advantages and two disadvantages of offering staff performance-related pay. (4)

9 What might be the implications of providing a profit share to senior managers but not to the workforce generally? (5)

10 What problems might result from a manager bullying staff to 'motivate' them? (6)

B. Revision exercises

B1 Data response

Gambling on people

Procter & Gamble is the world's biggest advertiser and one of America's most respected companies. It is the company behind such brands as Fairy Liquid, Ariel, Crest, Max Factor, Head & Shoulders, Vidal Sassoon, Pringles, Sunny Delight and hundreds more. Behind its marketing success lies an exceptionally strong company culture and an advanced approach to the management of its people.

Procter & Gamble (P&G) was an early advocate of motivating staff by empowerment and job enrichment. Dave Swanson was the principal architect of the organisational design of the system. Swanson joined P&G in the early 1950s after studying at the Manchester Institute of Technology (MIT). While at MIT he had been inspired by the lectures of Professor Douglas McGregor. McGregor attacked the theory of command-and-control management, advocating empowerment. When Swanson had the opportunity to design a new detergent plant in Augusta, Georgia, he enlisted McGregor's help.

Processes were put in place to make communications and control flow up, down and sideways in a very easy, uninhibited way. They emphasised knowledge of the business and learning new skills for all employees of the plant. The objective was to push the Augusta plant to be as unstructured as possible: 'We were trying to take away the rule book and substitute principle for mandate . . . We wanted people to reach for responsibility,' Swanson said. They did. Factory productivity went up 30% and the system was expanded to other P&G plants.

In his book *What America Does Right*, Robert Waterman describes P&G as a pioneer in pushing leadership, responsibility and decision making down to the plant floor.

Source: C. Decker P&G99. HarperCollins

Questions

(30 marks; 35 minutes)

1 How might motivation be affected by 'taking away the rule book'? (6)

2 Explain the importance to staff motivation of freely flowing, accurate communication. (6)

3 Explain how the views of McGregor were put into practice by P&G's Dave Swanson. (8)

4 In this case, high motivation boosted productivity by 30%. Discuss whether increased motivation need always result in increased productivity. (10)

B2 Activity

Write a questionnaire for self-completion by full-time employees. Your research objectives are to discover:

- whether there are any policies in place for encouraging workplace involvement/consultation

- whether job enrichment or job rotation measures exist (and what their effect is)

- how your respondents would describe the workplace culture

- whether there are any financial bonuses available, such as piece rate or performance-related pay, and what is their effect on motivation

- how highly motivated they feel themselves to be

- how highly motivated they believe their colleagues are.

This questionnaire should be conducted with at least ten respondents. It is preferable for the questionnaire to be conducted face-to-face, but if that is not possible, self-completion is acceptable.

When the research is completed, analyse the results carefully and write a summary of them in report form.

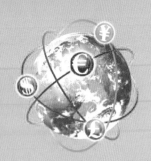

LEADERSHIP AND MANAGEMENT STYLES

DEFINITION

Management involves getting things done through other people. Leadership, at its best, means inspiring staff to achieve demanding goals. According to Peter Drucker, a manager does things right; a leader does the right thing.

36.1 Introduction to leadership styles

The way in which managers deal with their employees is known as their management style. For example, some managers are quite strict with workers. They always expect deadlines to be met and targets to be hit. Others are more relaxed and understanding. If there is a good reason why a particular task has not been completed by the deadline, they will be willing to accept this and give the employee more time. Although the way in which everyone manages will vary slightly from individual to individual, their styles can be categorised under three headings: autocratic, democratic and paternalistic.

Autocratic managers are authoritarian: they tell employees what to do and do not listen much to what workers themselves have to say. Autocratic managers

know what they want doing and how they want it done. They tend to use one-way, top-down communication. They give orders to workers and do not want much feedback. **Democratic managers**, by comparison, like to involve their workers in decisions. They tend to listen to employees' ideas and ensure people contribute to the discussion. Communication by democratic managers tends to be two-way. Managers put forward an idea and employees give their opinion. A democratic manager would regularly delegate decision-making power to junior staff.

The delegation of authority, which is at the heart of democratic leadership, can be approached in one of two main ways.

1 Management by objectives, in which the leader agrees clear goals with staff, provides the necessary resources, and allows day-to-day decisions to be made by the staff in question; this approach was advocated by management guru Peter Drucker and by Douglas

Table 36.1 *Assumptions and approaches of the three types of leader*

	Democratic	**Paternalistic**	**Autocratic**
Style derived from:	belief in Maslow's higher-order needs or in Herzberg's motivators	Mayo's work on human relations and Maslow's lower- and middle-order needs	a Taylorite view of staff
Approach to staff	Delegation of authority	Consultation with staff	Orders must be obeyed
Approach to staff remuneration	Salary, perhaps plus employee shareholdings	Salary plus extensive fringe benefits	Payment by results, e.g. piece rate
Approach to human resource management	Recruitment and training based on attitudes and teamwork	Emphasis on training and appraisal for personal development	Recruitment and training based on skills; appraisal linked to pay

McGregor (see below) in his support for what he called the Theory Y approach to management.

2   Laissez-faire, meaning let it be; this occurs when managers are so busy, or so lazy, that they do not take the time to ensure that junior staff know what to do or how to do it. Some people might respond very well to the freedom to decide on how to spend their working lives; others may become frustrated. It is said that Bill Gates, in the early days of Microsoft, hired brilliant students and told them no more than to create brilliant software. Was this a laissez-faire style or management by objectives? Clearly the dividing line can be narrow.

A **paternalistic manager** thinks and acts like a father. He or she tries to do what is best for their staff/children. There may be consultation to find out the views of the employees, but decisions are made by the head of the 'family'. This type of manager believes employees need direction but thinks it is important that they are supported and cared for properly. Paternalistic managers are interested in the security and social needs of staff. They are interested in how workers feel and whether they are happy in their work. Nevertheless it is quite an autocratic approach.

36.2 McGregor's Theory X and Y

In the 1950s Douglas McGregor undertook a survey of managers in America and identified two styles of management, which he labelled Theory X and Theory Y (see Table 36.2). Theory X managers tend to distrust their subordinates; they believe employees do not really enjoy their work and that they need to be controlled. In McGregor's own words, many managers believe that 'The average human being has an inherent dislike of work and will avoid it if he can.' Note that McGregor is not putting this forward as a theory about workers, but about managers. In other words, Theory X is about the view managers have of their workforce.

Theory Y managers, by comparison, believe that employees do enjoy work and that they want to contribute ideas and effort. A Theory Y manager is, therefore, more likely to involve employees in decisions and give them greater responsibility. The managerial assumptions identified by McGregor as Theory Y included:

'Commitment to objectives is a function of the rewards associated with their achievement.'

'The average human being learns, under proper conditions, not only to accept but to seek responsibility.'

'The capacity to exercise a relatively high degree of imagination, ingenuity and creativity in the solution of organizational problems is widely, not narrowly, distributed in the population.'

McGregor, D. (1987) *The Human Side of Enterprise*. Penguin Books (first published 1960).

It is clear that Theory Y managers would be inclined to adopt a democratic leadership style. Their natural approach would be to delegate authority to meet specific objectives.

Table 36.2 *Theory X vs Theory Y managers*

Theory X managers believe:	**Theory Y managers believe:**
employees dislike work and will avoid it if they can	putting some effort into work is as natural as play or rest; employees want to work
employees prefer to be directed, want to avoid responsibility and have little ambition	employees want responsibility provided there are appropriate rewards
employees need to be controlled and coerced	employees are generally quite creative

The Theory X approach is likely to be self-fulfilling. If you believe people are lazy, they will probably stop trying. Similarly, if you believe workers dislike responsibility, and fail to give them a chance to develop, they will probably stop showing interest in their work. They will end up focusing purely on their wage packet because of the way you treat them.

In his book *The Human Side of Enterprise* McGregor drew upon the work of Maslow and Herzberg. It need be no surprise that there are common features to the theories of these three writers. McGregor's unique contribution was to set issues of industrial psychology firmly in the context of the management of organisations. So whereas Herzberg's was a theory of motivation, McGregor's concerned styles of management (and thereby leadership).

So, which is the 'right' approach? Clearly a Theory Y manager would be more pleasant and probably more interesting to work for. A Theory X approach can work, however, and is especially likely to succeed in a business employing many part-time, perhaps student workers, or in a situation where a business faces a crisis.

A-grade application
Liverpool Football Club

On 19 February 2008, Liverpool manager Rafa Benitez was under intense pressure. A bright start to the season had descended into patchy league form and an embarrassing FA cup defeat to Barnsley. Now it was make or break, with a Champions League game against the mighty Inter Milan. A defeat would surely lead to a Benitez resignation; a victory would give a small amount of breathing space (until the second leg, at least).

Among Liverpool supporters there had always been faith in Benitez, and criticism of the club's American owners, but this match would be a huge test of leadership. Could he inspire the players to give everything for him and for the club?

Unlike the Premiership's best managers, Wenger and Ferguson, Benitez had always seemed rather distant. Wenger and Ferguson practise a management style that is simultaneously paternalistic and autocratic. Benitez seemed only autocratic, making decisions on team selection that baffled everyone, yet never feeling the need to explain.

Cometh the hour, cometh the man?

(Ninety minutes after this was written, Liverpool had won 2–0 and Rafa was the hero.)

36.3 Charismatic leadership

Gordon Brown is a highly intelligent man, whose leadership of the British economy between 1997 and 2006 was brilliant. Yet he has no charisma – people are not inspired by him; they do not even warm to him. He therefore has an enormous difficulty in communicating his ideas in a way that makes people want to follow his lead. There is a strong case for saying, therefore, that personal charisma is an important quality in a leader.

Yet it is important to remember that some charismatic historical leaders have led people to disaster, such as Napoleon and Hitler. Perhaps some charisma is good, but too much is dangerous. In recent times in business, the most charismatic leader was BP's Lord Browne. On 25 July 2006, the *Guardian* ran a leader article that began 'Lord Browne, the chief executive of the BP group, is the nearest thing British business has to a rock star.' The paper went on to describe Richard Branson as a 'mere pygmy' compared with the leader of 'one of the

world's largest companies'. The *Guardian* also said that 'the 96,000 people employed by BP around the world all have cause to admire Lord Browne's achievements'. Within six months Lord Browne had resigned from BP in a personal scandal. Those looking back today at Lord Browne's leadership are largely critical, especially of the company's approach to safety and the environment.

A-grade application
Leadership: famous sayings

'As for the best leaders, the people do not notice their existence. The next best, the people honour and praise. The next, the people fear; and the next, the people hate ... When the best leader's work is done the people say, "We did it ourselves."' *Lao-Tsu, quoted in Townsend, R., and Joseph, M., Further up the Organisation*

'... the capacity to create a compelling vision and translate it into action and sustain it'. *Warren Bennis*

'Leadership is a potent combination of strategy and character. But if you must be without one, be without the strategy.' *General Norman Schwarzkopf, US soldier*

'You do not lead by hitting people over the head – that's assault, not leadership.' *Dwight Eisenhower, US President*

Source: Stuart Crainer (1997) *The Ultimate Book of Business Quotations*, Capstone Publishing

36.4 What is the best style of leadership?

Each style of management can work well in different situations. If there is a crisis, for example, people often look for a strong leader to tell them what to do. Imagine that sales have unexpectedly fallen by 50%, causing uncertainty, even panic, within the organisation. The management needs to quickly take control and put a plan into action. An autocratic style might work well at this moment. In a stable situation where employees are trained and able to do their work successfully a more democratic leadership style might be more appropriate. It is often said that countries elect very different types of leaders when there is a threat of war or economic instability than when the country is doing well. Similarly, think about how people react when they are learning to drive. For the first few lessons they are uncertain what to do and are grateful to be told. Once they have passed their test and have driven for several years they will no doubt resent anyone telling them how to drive better!

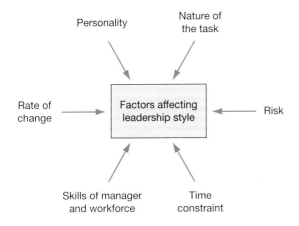

Figure 36.1 Factors affecting leadership style

The best style of management at any moment will depend on an enormous range of factors such as the personalities and abilities of the manager, and the workers, and the nature of the task. Imagine a confident manager who knows her job well but is faced with an unusually difficult problem. If the staff are well trained and capable, the manager would probably ask for ideas on what to do next. If, however, the manager was faced with a fairly routine problem she would probably just tell the employees what to do because there would be no need for discussion.

A manager's style should, therefore, change according to the particular situation and the people involved. It will also vary with the time and degree of risk involved. If a decision has to be made urgently and involves a high degree of risk, the manager is likely to be quite autocratic. If there is plenty of time to discuss matters and only a low chance of it going wrong, the style may well be more democratic.

Does the style of management matter?

The way in which a manager deals with his or her colleagues can have a real impact on their motivation and how effectively they work. An experienced workforce, which is used to being involved in decisions, may resent a manager who always tries to tell them what to do. This might lead to a reduction in the quality of their work, a fall in productivity and an increase in labour turnover. If, however, these employees were involved in decision making , the firm could gain from better ideas and a more highly motivated workforce. This does not mean that everyone wants to be involved, or indeed that it is appropriate – employees may lack the necessary training or experience. Therefore a democratic approach might simply mean that it takes longer for management to reach the decision it was going to make anyway.

What is the most common style of management?

The style of management people adopt depends on many factors, such as their personality, the particular circumstances at the time and the culture of the organisation. Although we have discussed three main styles, the actual approach of most managers is usually a combination of all of them, depending on the task or the nature of the situation. If an order has to be completed by tomorrow and time is short, for example, most managers are likely to be autocratic to make sure it gets done. If, however, there is plenty of time available the manager may be more democratic. No one is completely autocratic or completely democratic, it is simply a question of degree. However, some managers do tend to be more autocratic than others. This often depends on their own experiences (What was their boss like? What worked well when they were being trained?) and their personality (Do they like to be in control of everything? Are they willing to delegate? Do they value the opinions of others?).

In general, the move has been towards a more democratic style of management in the UK in recent years. This is probably because employees expect more from work than they did in the past. They are better educated, have a higher basic standard of living and want more than just money in return for their efforts. Having satisfied their lower-level needs they are now looking to satisfy their higher-level needs. The growth of democratic management and greater participation has also increased with the move towards lean production and the emphasis on techniques such as total quality management (TQM). These methods of production require much more involvement on the part of employees than in the past. Employees are given control over their own quality, given the authority to make decisions over the scheduling of work and are expected to contribute ideas on how to improve the way they are working. This approach requires much more trust in employees than was common many years ago. It has to be matched with a more democratic leadership style.

Issues For Analysis

Management style can have a significant impact on the way people work. By adopting the right approach employees are likely to be more motivated and show greater commitment. Therefore effective analysis of leadership should be rooted in the theories of writers such as Mayo and Herzberg.

● The 'correct' management style will depend on factors such as the task, the people involved and the amount of risk. There is no one style that is always appropriate. Therefore the context of the business case is always relevant.

● It may not be easy for managers to change their style. There may be situations in which managers should be more democratic; this does not necessarily mean they will be. Effective management training could be a useful way to persuade managers to be flexible.

● There is some debate about the extent to which you can train people to become effective managers or leaders. One extreme view is that good managers and leaders are born that way – if this is true, companies have to put their resources into finding the right sort of person. It is more likely that a good leader is the result of a combination of training and personal characteristics.

Leadership and management styles
an evaluation

All firms are seeking effective managers. Good managers make effective use of the firm's resources and motivate staff; they provide vision and direction, and are therefore a key element of business success. Look at any successful company and you will usually find a strong management team. The problem is knowing what it is that makes a good manager and what is the 'best' management style. Even if we thought we knew the best style, can we train anyone to adopt this approach, or does it depend on their personality? There are, of course, no easy answers to such questions. The 'right' style of management will depend on the particular circumstances and the nature of the task, and while it is possible to help someone develop a particular style it will also depend on the individual's personality. As employees have benefited from a higher standard of living in the UK, and have higher expectations of work, managers have generally had to adopt a more democratic style in order to motivate people. However, there are plenty of autocratic managers who also succeed.

> ## Key terms
>
> **Autocratic manager:** autocratic managers keep most of the authority to themselves; they do not delegate much or share information with employees. Autocratic, or authoritarian, managers tend to tell employees what to do.
> **Democratic manager:** democratic managers take the views of their subordinates into account when making decisions. Managers discuss what needs to be done and employees are involved in the decision.
> **Paternalistic manager:** a paternalistic manager believes he or she knows what is best for employees. Paternalistic managers tend to tell employees what to do, but will often explain their decisions. They are also concerned about the social needs of employees.

Exercises

A. Revision questions

(40 marks; 40 minutes)

1 Distinguish between autocratic and paternalistic management. (4)

2 Identify two features of democratic management. (2)

3 Outline one advantage and one disadvantage of an autocratic management approach. (4)

4 Distinguish between McGregor's Theory X and Theory Y. (4)

5 Why is it 'clear that Theory Y managers would be inclined to adopt a democratic leadership style.' (4)

6 Is there one correct leadership style for running a football team or a supermarket chain? (4)

7 Explain why autocratic managers may be more use in a crisis than democratic ones. (4)

8 Explain a circumstance in which an authoritarian approach to leadership may be desirable. (4)

9 Many managers claim to have a democratic style of leadership. Often, their subordinates disagree. Outline two ways of checking the actual leadership style of a particular manager. (4)

10 Analyse the leadership style adopted by your teacher/tutor. (6)

B. Revision exercises

B1 Data response

Leading Tesco's rise

Terry Leahy became Tesco's Chief Executive in 1997. Since then he has hardly put a foot wrong. An article in *Management Today* (February 2004) probed him on his approach to leadership.

When you meet Leahy, you're not confronted with some huge presence ... Blink and you would miss him.

What's his leadership style? 'I spend a lot of my time working on how I manage ...'. He meets with his executive committee every Monday and Wednesday morning for two hours, but what makes Leahy different is the extraordinary degree to which he chats with junior staff and absorbs their views, and the attention he pays to customers.

In Leahy's Tesco, the two – staff and customer – have become blurred. Tesco, he says, has always prided itself on being an 'egalitarian organisation'. It's a philosophy he's scrupulously followed. 'There are only six levels between me and a check-out assistant.' Every member of staff has the opportunity to train and rise up the ladder. This year, 10,000 Tesco staff will undergo training to move upwards.

'There's no officer class at Tesco, we don't have a graduate elite intake, there's no fast-track.' So speaks the chief who followed a girlfriend to London, got a casual job stacking shelves in the local Tesco and never left. There can't be a store he hasn't visited, a job he doesn't know.

The people he started out with back then in 1979 are his friends still today, many of them at senior levels in the business. 'I must have spoken to thousands of staff – I've grown up with many of them,' he says.

In June, he went to a store in Royston and mucked in as a general assistant. Come on, this sort of thing – it's all for show, isn't it? 'Not at all, I enjoy it, I find it very satisfying. I'm learning as well. I want a better understanding of how these jobs are done.' Leahy makes all his senior staff do it. Last year, 1000 store managers worked in other stores and 1000 staff from head office did the same.'

Questions

(25 marks; 30 minutes)

1 Analyse how Terry Leahy's approach compares with that of a charismatic leader. (6)

2 Explain which leadership style is closest to (Sir) Terry Leahy's leadership of Tesco. (8)

3 Discuss whether it is a good use of senior managers' time to spend a day working on the shop floor. (11)

B2 Assignment

An investigation into a leader

1 Arrange to interview an employee. Preferably this person should be a full-timer who has worked for at least a year. The employee could be a manager but should not be a director.

2 Your objective is to gain a full understanding of the leadership style prevailing at the employee's workplace, and the style employed by the individual's own manager.

3 Devise your own series of questions in advance, but make sure to include the following themes.

(a) How open are communications within the business?

(b) Are staff encouraged to apply a questioning or critical approach?

(c) Are there any forums for discussion or debate on important policy issues affecting staff?

(d) What does the organisational hierarchy look like? Where is your employee on that diagram? How powerful or powerless does s/he feel?

(e) How exactly does the employee's boss treat him or her? Is there delegation? Consultation? How effective is communication between the two of them?

Write at least 600 words summarising your findings and drawing conclusions about how well the experience conforms to the leadership theory dealt with in this unit.

C. Essay questions

(40 marks each)

1 'A good leader can always turn an ineffective business into a successful one.' To what extent can good management make a difference to the success of a firm?

2 'Management is no longer about leading others; it is about working with them.' Critically assess this view.

3 Consider the view that autocratic management has no place in today's business world.

4 'Good managers are born, not made.' Discuss this view.

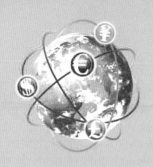

ORGANISATIONAL STRUCTURE

DEFINITION

Organisational structure is the formal and systematic way the management of a business is organised. When presented as a diagram, it shows the departmental functions and who is answerable to whom.

37.1 Introduction

As organisations became larger and more complex, early management thinkers such as F. W. Taylor and H. Fayol considered how to structure an organisation. Both saw the function of organisations as converting inputs – such as money, materials, machines and people – into output(s). Therefore, designing an organisation was like designing a machine, the objective being to maximise efficiency. Early managers wanted to be told the best way to manage and the organisational structure that would work best.

Taylor and Fayol based their thoughts largely on the way an army is organised. The key features of the hierarchy would be:

● to break the organisation up into divisions with a common purpose – in business, this was usually the **business functions** (marketing, finance, and so on)

● every individual would answer to one person – their **line manager**

● no manager would be overloaded with too many subordinates, so the **span of control** was kept low

● to achieve low spans of control, it was necessary to have many management layers (see Table 37.1).

Table 37.1 Management layers

Military	Business
Captain	Senior manager
Lieutenant	Manager
Sergeant	Team leader
Corporal	Supervisor
Foot-soldier	Shop-floor worker

37.2 The growing business

In the early stages of a new business, there are often only one or two people involved. When the business is so small the day-to-day tasks are carried out by the owner(s). It is not necessary to have a formal organisation structure, as communication and coordination will be carried out on an informal, face-to-face basis. However, as the business grows and more people become involved, the firm will need to develop a more formal organisational structure. This will show the roles, responsibilities and relationships of each member of the firm. This is often illustrated through an organisational chart; this is a diagram that shows the links between people and departments within the firm. It also shows communication flows/channels, lines of authority and layers of hierarchy. Each of these terms will be explained later in the unit.

Consider the example in the box.

Case study: Crazy Beetles

Sara developed a small, but successful, business refurbishing old camper vans. The firm, called Crazy Beetles, started out on a very small scale but Sara soon discovered that there was a growing market for her services. The increasing demand led to her employing James as he had in-depth knowledge of the second-hand camper van market. Between them they did the buying, restoring, advertising and selling of the revamped vans. However, as the business grew, they needed to expand the workforce and this called for a more formal organisational structure. They decided to divide their business into three areas, as follows.

1 The *operations department* was involved in sourcing and buying old vans that needed revamping and then carrying out the necessary repairs and improvements. This was headed by Luke, who was a trained mechanic. Luke was responsible for five workers in his

department; one of the workers, Pete, had two people in his section: Jon and Will.

2 The second department focused on *marketing* the finished product. This department advertised the vans and organised events to promote the company's name and services. Martha was in charge of this department as her business degree and additional experience equipped her with the skills and knowledge required. She had three subordinates (people she managed) in her department.

3 The final department was run by Steve, an accountant, who was responsible for managing the firm's *finances*. He had two financial assistants. The three department heads – Luke, Martha and Steve – were answerable to James, who dealt with the day-to-day issues; he, in turn, was answerable to Sara, who focused on the long-term plans for the business.

When reading this short case study, it is easy to become confused about the different roles and responsibilities adopted by those involved in the business. An organisational chart illustrates these more clearly and enables those within the firm and outside the firm to identify, more easily, who does what and who answers to whom. Figure 37.1 is a representation of the roles and responsibilities at Crazy Beetles.

37.3 The roles and relationships

This section describes the different roles and relationships within organisations and illustrates these with reference to Figure 37.1.

Roles

This describes the different tasks that the individuals are responsible for. At this point it is important to define responsibility, authority and accountability. Responsibility means carrying the burden of blame, even if an error is made by a subordinate. After all, if Alex Ferguson plays his reserve goalkeeper in a football match, it is Ferguson who will be blamed if the keeper lets in a soft goal. Authority means having the power to make a decision or carry out a task. However, if Martha delegated authority to Cathy to carry out a particular task, Martha would still retain the overall responsibility for that task. This shows how important it is for a manager to consider carefully to whom they delegate tasks. Accountability is the extent to which an individual is held responsible for her/his decisions and actions.

Directors

Members of 'the board' (i.e. the board of directors), who handle the most senior appointments and set out the main aims and objectives of the business. There are two types of director.

1 Executive directors are appointed to the board because they head up important divisions or departments (e.g. the marketing director).

2 Non-executive directors are part-time directors from outside the business; their job is to take an independent view of the shareholders' best interests.

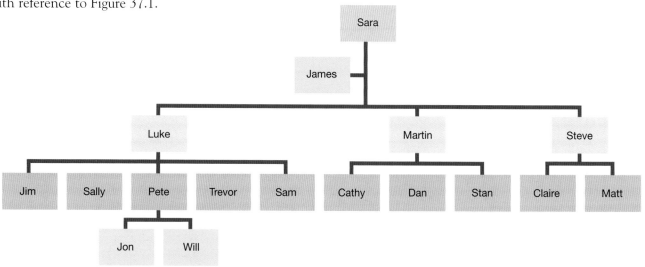

Figure 37.1 Crazy Beetles: roles and responsibilities

Manager

Person responsible for organising others to carry out tasks. A line manager is the person immediately above someone in the organisational chart. For example, Sian's line manager is Martha.

Team leader

This role will usually arise in firms that organise themselves in a **matrix management** structure. This is where the firm allocates its workers to project teams rather than departments, and a team leader will manage the workers involved in a particular project. Project teams will be made up of people with different skills – for example, in a typical team there will be financial, marketing and operations specialists. This will enable them to make integrated decisions for the project. Building and engineering firms usually adopt this matrix approach in which the team leader is responsible for the management of the tasks and people involved.

37.4 Other key terms

Levels of hierarchy

These show the number of different supervisory and management levels between the bottom of the chart and the top of the hierarchy. In Crazy Beetles there are four levels of hierarchy.

Span of control

This describes the number of people directly under the supervision of a manager. Luke has the biggest span of control as he has four workers directly under him. If managers have very wide spans of control, they are directly responsible for many staff, in which case they may find that there are communication problems or the workers may feel that they are not being given enough guidance. The ideal span of control will depend upon the nature of the tasks, and the skills and attitude of the workforce and manager. (Table 37.2 lists the advantages and disadvantages of a narrow span of control.)

Chain of command

This shows the reporting system from the top of the hierarchy to the bottom (i.e. the route through which information travels throughout the organisation). In an organisation with several levels of hierarchy the chain of command will be longer; this could create a gap between workers at the bottom of the organisation and managers at the top. If information has to travel via several people there is also a chance that it may become distorted.

Centralisation and decentralisation

This describes the extent to which decision-making power and authority is delegated within an organisation. A centralised structure is one in which decision-making power and control remains in the hands of the top management levels. A decentralised structure delegates decision-making power to workers lower down the organisation. Many organisations will use a combination of these approaches depending upon the nature of the decision involved. For example, in many schools and colleges, the decisions concerning which resources to

Table 37.2 Advantages and disadvantages of a narrow span of control

Advantages	Disadvantages
Allows close management supervision – vital if staff are inexperienced, labour turnover is high or if the task is critical (e.g. manufacturing aircraft engines)	Workers may feel over-supervised and therefore not trusted; this may cause better staff to leave, in search of more personal responsibility
Communications may be excellent within the small, immediate team (e.g. the boss and three staff)	Communications may suffer within the business as a whole, as a narrow span means more layers of hierarchy, which makes vertical communications harder
Many layers of hierarchy mean many rungs on the career ladder (i.e. promotion chances arise regularly – though each promotion may mean only a slightly different job)	The narrow span usually leads to restricted scope for initiative and experiment; the boss is always looking over your shoulder; this will alienate enterprising staff

use will be decentralised (i.e. taken by teachers as opposed to the senior management team). Other decisions, concerning future changes in subjects being offered, may be centralised – that is, taken by senior managers.

Communication flows

As firms grow, their organisational structure becomes more complex. Spans of control increase as more staff are hired, then get reduced when the business introduces a new layer of management. Staff love the extra promotion opportunities, but hate the disruption to their job role and, perhaps, status.

When these changes happen there can be severe effects on communication flows. A small team may be used to informal communication at every morning's coffee break and every Friday evening's drink after work. As more staff get taken on it may be necessary to have formal department meetings with notes ('minutes') taken. This may make the team weaker and the communication less effective.

The introduction of more layers of hierarchy is also problematic. Vertical communication becomes slower and less effective, especially if messages are conveyed verbally. Worst of all is that messages may possibly make it from the bottom to the top of the organisation, but rarely does the feedback follow on. So a policeman who wants to complain about racism in his/her station may never hear the outcome of the complaint.

A recent CIPD survey showed that just 55% of employees believed they were being kept informed about what the company was doing. 65% felt they were being given enough information to do their jobs effectively, implying that 35% were not! The survey went on to discover the three most effective communication channels:

1 Team briefings, 64%

2 Email, 59%

3 Intranet 38%

It is striking that none of these involves any real discussion between people. There is no way of telling whether that's how people like it, or perhaps they just don't see the opportunity for discussion.

Delegation

Delegation means passing authority down the hierarchy of a business, thereby spreading power down towards shop-floor staff. Effective delegation can be hugely motivating, turning time-clock-watching staff into enthusiasts who come in early on Mondays. The key is to make sure that staff take pride in the responsibility they are able to show and the trust that is shown in them. The key is for a manager to delegate meaningful tasks, rather than simply offloading the difficult or dull jobs. Among the many business benefits from delegation are:

● can motivate staff

● makes it easier in future to identify staff with the qualities needed for promotion

● allows the boss the opportunity to spend time planning and thinking, rather than doing.

A-grade application
Green Communication

Duncan Green is the managing director of a property-management company, Green Locations Ltd. He says: "I started my business from scratch and was used to being the main decision maker . . . The company had reached a critical stage and I realised I needed to offload some work. Now, with my good managers, everything runs smoothly and I'm happy to give some of them full autonomy."

"Communication with employees about tasks they're taking on is important. But this means explaining what you need, rather than telling them how to do it. My employees might do something differently to the way I would, but provided they carry out tasks ethically and get the same or a better result, that's fine."

"I've had a very positive response. My working day tends to be less stressful now, because there's less on my plate. I have a bit more thinking time, while my employees enjoy having more responsibility and with it a greater sense of achievement … Have trust in your employees and make the most of the skills that they have. Your delegating will improve their skills and they will become more motivated and productive."

Source: www.hie.co.uk

37.5 Recent changes in organisation structures

In the past, some firms had very tall hierarchical structures, which meant many layers of management, often with quite narrow spans of control. This made them expensive to run because of the management salaries that had to be paid. Tall structures also resulted in longer chains of command, which could have a negative impact on communication. More recently, companies have liked to announce that they are becoming flatter – meaning fewer layers of management, with each manager having a wider span of control. Although some managers dislike this increased responsibility, their workers may thrive under the increased independence that is gained. Furthermore, the firm will have reduced overhead costs, which should mean greater efficiency.

Why is organisational structure so important?

As a firm grows, more people become involved. To ensure that the different tasks are fulfilled it is vital that every person is clear about what their role involves and who they are answerable to. Poor organisational structures will lack coordination and the following problems could result:

- poor communication leading to mistakes
- duplication of tasks
- tasks being overlooked
- different departments failing to work together effectively.

In the longer term, these problems will create a substandard service, and this will have an impact on the firm's sales, revenue and profit. As a firm expands, it must ensure that its organisation structure accommodates the growth.

Issues For Analysis

- When discussing the topic of organisation structure, it is important to recognise that the structures are not static and they should adapt to the environment in which they operate. If more people enter the firm, then changes should take place, and this may have an impact on the roles and relationships of the existing workers.

- The key to a top exam answer is to think about the match between the structure and the type of organisation. When Google started up, it had virtually no structure – brilliant people were hired and told to do brilliant things; the structure was deliberately loose. Today Google is a vast business, needing a tighter structure, but probably not so tight as to strangle innovation.

37.6 Organisational structure
an evaluation

There is no 'ideal' organisational structure or span of control. What works for one business may fail in another, even if both are the same size. In exams there will usually be hints about whether the structure is working. A flat hierarchy may be at the heart of an innovative business, or there may be signs that staff lack direction and morale. A tall hierarchy may be at the centre of a focused, career-orientated workforce, or it may be bureaucratic and incapable of a quick decision. The judgement is yours.

Key terms

Line manager: a manager responsible for meeting specific business targets, and responsible for specific staff.
Matrix management: where staff work in project teams in addition to their responsibilities within their own department; therefore staff can be answerable to more than one boss.
Span of control: the number of staff who are answerable directly to a manager.

Exercises

A. Revision questions

(30 marks; 30 minutes)

1 What is meant by the chain of command? (2)

2 Define span of control. (2)

3 Some theorists believe that the ideal span of control is between three and six. To what extent do you agree with this? (5)

4 Explain two implications of a firm having too wide a span of control. (4)

5 Explain what an organisational chart shows. (4)

6 Why is it important for a growing firm to think carefully about its organisational structure? (4)

7 State three possible problems for a business with many levels of hierarchy. (3)

8 What is meant by the term 'accountable'? (2)

9 What do you think would be the right organisational structure for a hospital? Explain your answer. (4)

B. Revision exercises

B1 Data response

These following questions are based on the organisation structure of Crazy Beetles, featured in this unit.

Questions

(25 marks; 30 minutes)

1 Describe the chain of command that Sara would use if she needed to discuss overtime with Pete. (3)

2 What symptoms would indicate that James' span of control was too wide? (5)

3 Explain the usefulness of this chart for a new member of staff. (2)

4 How might Crazy Beetles use a matrix management approach? (5)

5 To what extent would Sara benefit if she introduced a more decentralised approach? (10)

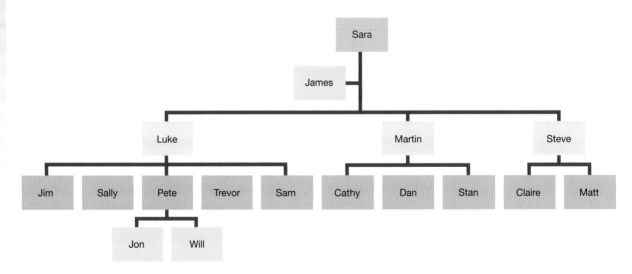

Figure 37.1 Crazy Beetles: roles and responsibilities

B2 Data response

Chicken Little

Peter (known as 'Paxo') Little set up his free-range chicken farm in the early 1990s. At the time it was an unusual move, especially on the grand scale envisaged by Paxo. His farm had the capacity to produce 250,000 chickens every 45 days, making 4 million birds a year. Since then the business has grown enormously, to a turnover of £25 million today.

But Paxo is getting concerned that his business is not as efficient as it used to be. As Managing Director, he finds that he rarely hears from junior staff; not even the quality manager's five staff, who used to see him regularly. As he said recently to the Operations Director, 'the communication flows seem like treacle today, whereas they used to be like wildfire'.

Fortunately, the boom in demand for free-range and organic produce has helped the business. So even though the team spirit seems to have slipped away, profits have never been higher.

Unfortunately the Marketing Director keeps talking about rumours that a huge Dutch farming business is about to set up poultry farms in Britain. That might set the cat among the chickens.

Questions

(25 marks; 30 minutes)

1 a) What is the Managing Director's span of control? (1)

1 b) Comment on the strength and weaknesses of this organisational structure. (6)

1 c) How important does Human Resources seem within this business? (3)

2 Explain why vertical communications may not be as effective today as they used to be in the past at Chicken Little. (5)

3 Discuss the ways in which the Factory Manager might benefit or suffer from the organisational structure shown in the diagram. (10)

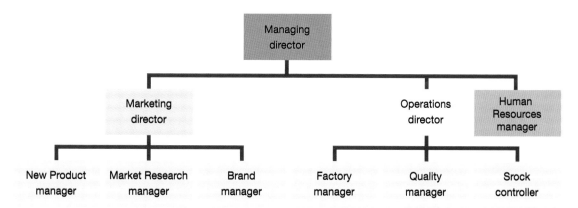

Figure 37.2 Organisational structure at 'Chicken Little' Farms

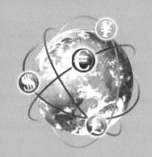

RECRUITMENT AND TRAINING

DEFINITION

Recruitment (and selection) is concerned with filling job vacancies that may arise within a business. The process involves a number of activities, including defining the job, attracting suitable candidates and selecting those best suited to fill it. Training is a provision of work-related education, where employees learn new skills or develop the skills they already possess.

38.1 The need for effective recruitment

Every service business relies on its staff to present the face of the organisation to the customer. It can be a gloomy, perhaps bored, face – or it can be lively and smiling. Many factors are involved in this stark difference, but it certainly helps if you recruit bright, enthusiastic staff in the first place.

In 2006, Marks & Spencer recruited over 20,000 new customer service assistants. A further 19,000 temporary staff were taken on between November and December to help meet seasonal demand. The company employs 40 people in its recruitment centre at its head office in London, and others in stores nationwide.

Despite the significant costs involved, businesses like Marks & Spencer recognise the importance of committing sufficient resources to recruitment. Ensuring that the right number and type of workers are available when they are needed is vital if company objectives are to be achieved.

38.2 The recruitment process

The recruitment process may be triggered by a number of events. For example, an existing employee may have chosen to leave their job, perhaps as a result of retirement

A-grade application
Wanted: high-fliers

The rapid growth of low-cost airlines has forced Ryanair and easyJet to compete fiercely for the scarcest resource: qualified pilots. To attract them, this is what each airline was offering in August 2007:

Table 38.1 Packages for pilots

	easyJet	**Ryanair**
Annual salary:	£73,792	'Up to £100,000'
Days off a year	137 days	162 days
Extra remuneration	7% pension contribution	Share option scheme
Extra attraction	Share options	Home every night

Source: easyjet.com, ryanair.com

or after finding employment elsewhere. At this point, it would be worth analysing the vacant job role – do all the responsibilities associated with the vacant job still need to be carried out, or are some redundant? Could the remaining duties be reorganised among existing employees? Alternatively, additional workers may need to be recruited in order to support a firm's expansion strategies, or employees with new skills may be required to help develop new products or new markets.

Once the firm has established its human resources requirements, the next step is to consider the nature of the work and workers required in order to draw up a **job description** and a **person specification**.

A job description relates directly to the nature of the position itself, rather than the person required to fill it. Typically, a job description would contain the following information:

● the title of the post

● details of the main duties and tasks involved

● the person to whom the job holder reports, and any employees for whom the job holder is responsible.

A person specification identifies the abilities, qualifications and qualities required of the job holder in order to carry out the job successfully. The main features of a person specification include:

● any educational or professional qualifications required

● necessary skills or experience

● suitable personality or character (e.g. ability to work under pressure or as part of a team).

A-grade application

Recruitment at easyJet

A major growth industry of recent years has been budget airlines; easyJet, for example, needed to hire 1300 more cabin staff in 2007. The airline's 'people director', Mike Campbell, worked out this number after allowing for its 90% retention level. In other words, every year 90% of staff stay, meaning that 10% leave. easyJet needs enough new recruits to cover its 10% level of labour turnover, plus extras to allow for the 13 new routes it is opening up in 2007.

Campbell said, in June 2007: 'We need more cabin crew so we need to retain the crew we have. It meant that last year we asked cabin crew what made their jobs less enjoyable. The first thing they said was that their uniform was uncomfortable, so we let them design their own.'

Both documents have an important influence on both recruitment and selection – not only can they be used to draw up job adverts, but also to assess the suitability of candidates' applications; they may also form the basis of any interview questions.

38.3 Internal recruitment

A business may choose to fill a vacancy internally (i.e. from the existing workforce). This could be done either by redeploying or promoting a worker from elsewhere in the business. Although **internal recruitment** can have a number of benefits, it also has a number of disadvantages and is obviously of no use when a business needs to expand its workforce in order to respond to an increase in demand.

Table 38.2 *Internal recruitment: advantages and disadvantages*

Advantages	**Disadvantages**
It is likely to be quicker and cheaper than external recruitment	Existing workers may not have the skills required, especially if the business wants to develop new products or markets
Greater variety and promotion opportunities may motivate employees	Relying on existing employees may lead to a stagnation of ideas and approaches within the business
It avoids the need (and cost) of induction training	
The firm will already be aware of the employee's skills and attitude to work	It may create a vacancy elsewhere, postponing external recruitment rather than avoiding it

38.4 Recruiting external candidates

Firms can choose from a range of methods to attract external candidates to fill a job vacancy (**external recruitment**). Such methods include the following.

● *Media advertising*: placing job adverts in newspapers or specialist magazines, on the radio, TV or by using dedicated employment websites such as www.jobstoday.co.uk.

● *Jobcentres*: government-run organisations that offer a free service to firms, and tend to focus on vacancies for skilled and semi-skilled manual and administrative jobs.

- *Commercial recruitment agencies:* such as Alfred Marks or Reed, which take on a number of human resources functions, including recruitment, on behalf of firms in return for a fee.

- *Executive search consultants:* paid to directly approach individuals – usually those in relatively senior positions (known as poaching or headhunting).

In addition, many businesses have careers pages on their own websites, which are used to advertise vacancies.

The choice of recruitment method or methods used by a business will depend on a number of factors, including:

- the cost of the recruitment method

- the size of the recruitment budget

- the location and characteristics of the likely candidates.

Table 38.3 External recruitment: advantages and disadvantages

Advantages	Disadvantages
It should result in a wider range of candidates than internal recruitment	It can be an expensive and time-consuming process, using up valuable resources
Candidates may already have the skills required to carry out the job in question, avoiding the need for (and cost of) training	It can have a demotivating effect on members of the existing workforce, who may have missed out on promotion

38.5 Selecting the best candidate

Once a number of suitable candidates have applied for the vacancy, the selection process can begin. This will involve choosing the applicant who most closely matches the criteria set out in the person specification for the job. A number of **selection techniques** exist, including the following.

- *Interviews:* still the most frequently used selection technique, interviews may consist of one interviewer

or a panel. Interviews are relatively cheap to conduct and allow a wide variety of information to be obtained by both sides, but are often susceptible to interviewer bias or prejudice and are, therefore, considered to be an unreliable indicator on their own of how well a candidate will carry out the job in question.

- *Testing and profiling:* aptitude tests measure the level of ability of a candidate (e.g. the level of IT skills), whereas psychometric profiling examines personality and attitudes (e.g. whether the candidate works well under pressure or is an effective team player). Profiling is commonly used as part of management and sales consultancy recruitment, but it is questionable as to whether recruiting a 'personality type' for a particular job is desirable – recruiting a wider range may lead to a more interesting and creative environment.

- *Assessment centres:* these allow for more in-depth assessment of a candidate's suitability by subjecting them to 'real-life' role plays and simulations, often over a number of days. Although assessment centres are considered to be an effective selection method, they can be expensive, and tend, therefore, to be reserved for filling more senior, management positions.

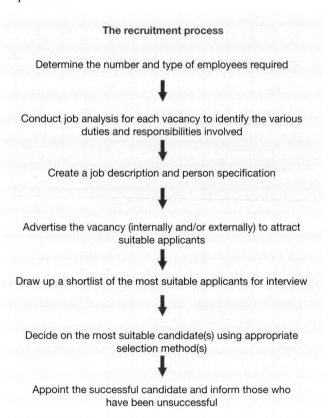

The recruitment process

Determine the number and type of employees required

↓

Conduct job analysis for each vacancy to identify the various duties and responsibilities involved

↓

Create a job description and person specification

↓

Advertise the vacancy (internally and/or externally) to attract suitable applicants

↓

Draw up a shortlist of the most suitable applicants for interview

↓

Decide on the most suitable candidate(s) using appropriate selection method(s)

↓

Appoint the successful candidate and inform those who have been unsuccessful

Figure 38.1 The recruitment process

Although a firm can be certain that the right person has been recruited only once he or she starts work, effective recruitment and selection will reduce the risk involved. There are a number of methods that can be used to evaluate the process, including calculating the cost and time involved in filling a vacancy, the percentage of candidates who actually accept job offers and the rate of retention of staff once employed.

A-grade application

Put off by poor recruitment procedures

Many graduates are put off taking up job opportunities with organisations as a result of poor recruitment processes, according to the results of research by Reed, one of the UK's leading recruitment firms. The survey, carried out in 2006, found that more than two-thirds of the 2500 graduates questioned had walked away from potential employers because of poor practices, including 'advertised jobs changing or no longer being available', 'lack of feedback' and 'long delays before being called for final interviews'. Over two-thirds complained that they had not been contacted at all by an organisation after submitting a job application.

Source: Adapted from 'Bad recruitment methods alienate graduates', 11 August 2006 (http://managementissues.com/2006/8/24/research/bad-recruilment-methods-alienote-granduates.asp) Management Issues

38.6 Training

The purpose of training is to help employees to develop existing skills or gain new ones. Types of training include the following.

Induction training

Induction training aims to make newly appointed workers fully productive as soon as possible by familiarising them with the key aspects of the business. Induction would typically include:

- information on important policies and procedures, such as health and safety

- a tour of the organisation and an introduction to colleagues

- details of employment (e.g. payment arrangements, holiday entitlement) and basic duties.

On-the-job training

On-the-job training is where employees are not required to leave their workplace but actually receive instruction while still carrying out their job. This means that workers can receive training while remaining productive to some extent. Common methods include mentoring, coaching and job rotation.

Off-the-job training

Off-the-job training is where employees leave their workplace in order to receive instruction. This may involve using training facilities within the firm (e.g. seminar rooms) or those provided by another organisation, such as a university, college or private training agency. Although this will inevitably involve a temporary loss of production, it should allow the trainee to concentrate fully on learning, and perhaps allow access to more experienced instructors than those available within the workplace.

Table 38.4 Training: benefits and costs

Benefits	Costs
It increases the level and range of skills available to the business, leading to improvements in productivity and quality	It can be expensive, both in terms of providing the training itself and also the cost of evaluating its effectiveness
It increases the degree of flexibility within a business, allowing it to respond quickly to changes in technology or demand	Production may be disrupted while training is taking place, leading to lost output
It can lead to a more motivated workforce by creating opportunities for development and promotion	Newly trained workers may be persuaded to leave and take up new jobs elsewhere (known as poaching), meaning that the benefits of training are enjoyed by other businesses

Labour market failure

Like any market, the labour market is made up of supply (labour services provided by those who wish to work) and demand (firms in need of workers to produce goods or provide services). An efficient labour market would require firms to provide training for their workers in order to improve their skills and knowledge. However, the danger of poaching may create a general disincentive for firms to invest in training, for fear that the short-term costs and disruption of training may not be recouped if newly trained employees are enticed to work elsewhere (**labour market failure**). In such circumstances, the government may become involved in training provision, in order to ensure the economy remains competitive.

Training and the government

The UK government uses a number of methods to support and encourage firms to train their workers, including the following.

- *Modern Apprenticeships*: structured programmes aimed at improving the level of technical skills within the workforce. Apprentices receive a combination of on-the-job training within a firm participating in the scheme and off-the-job training, usually by day-release to a local college, over a period of at least 12 months.

- *The New Deal*: aims to give unemployed people the opportunity to gain work experience and new skills to improve their employment opportunities. Candidates are screened and matched to suitable vacancies and, in some cases, financial help is provided in the form of subsidies and grants to the employer.

- *Investors In People*: promotes training by setting out a set of criteria, or 'standards', for firms to work towards. Those who do are allowed to display the Investors In People logo and are likely to enjoy a number of benefits, including improved quality, a reduction in costs and enhanced employee motivation.

A-grade application

Skills development 'in your hands'

In July 2007, the UK government launched an advertising campaign to encourage people to upgrade their skills. The three-year initiative, entitled 'Our future, it's in our hands', was designed to create a culture or desire to learn among the UK workforce. The campaign was seen as a response to the Leitch Report, published in December 2006. The report demanded a radical change in training within the UK in order to plug the skills gap and stop Britain from lagging behind its international competitors. The report claimed that 5 million adults have insufficient literacy skills and over 17 million lack basic numeracy skills. The report also claimed that one-third of employers provide no training at all for their staff.

Source: Adapted from www.bbc.co.uk/news

Issues For Analysis

Successful small businesses will make huge efforts to get their recruitment and training right, as one 'bad apple' can poison morale in a small office. When Google started, they put candidates through up to seven rounds of interviews before deciding on appointments. Yet why should the entrepreneur with the flair to think up a new business idea also be good at hiring and training staff? So it is always sensible to question whether the boss's recruitment skills are sufficient, and to marvel at any entrepreneur who has these among so many other necessary skills. Perhaps the ideal start-up was that of Innocent Drinks, with three ex-University friends having different skills yet a shared attitude to the business.

Opportunities for analysis are likely to focus on the following areas:

- the advantages and/or disadvantages of a firm using internal or external recruitment to fill job vacancies

- the suitability of recruitment and/or selection methods used in a given situation

- the costs and benefits involved in training

- the relevance of a particular training programme in terms of meeting the needs of both the employer and the employee.

38.7 Recruitment and training
an evaluation

Recruitment and training are key aspects of human resources management (HRM), and the importance of effective HR strategies in helping a firm – however large or small – to achieve its objectives cannot be overstated. 'Having the right person with the right skills in the right job at the right time' will allow a business to maintain or improve its competitiveness – having the wrong person is likely to lead to a deterioration in performance and an increase in costs. Many organisations continue to view training in particular as an avoidable expense, choosing to cut training budgets when under pressure to cut costs, or to poach employees already equipped with the necessary skills from other firms. New employees can bring a number of benefits, including fresh ideas and approaches to work. However, such an approach may fail to weigh up the possible long-term impact on the quality and motivation of the workforce, and the implications of this for productivity and competitiveness.

Key terms

External recruitment: where a job vacancy is filled by appointing a candidate from outside the business.

Induction training: familiarises newly appointed workers with key aspects of their jobs and their employer, such as health and safety policies, holiday entitlement and payment arrangements. The aim is to make employees fully productive as soon as possible.

Internal recruitment: where a job vacancy is filled by appointing someone from the existing workforce.

Job description: a document that outlines the duties and responsibilities associated with a particular job role.

Labour market failure: in the context of training, this refers to the reluctance of employers to invest in training for fear that staff, once trained, will be poached by other firms attempting to avoid training costs. If sufficient firms are discouraged from training employees, overall skill levels within the workforce will fall, leading to a loss of competitiveness for the economy as a whole.

Off-the-job training: where employees leave their normal place of work in order to receive instruction, either within the firm or by using an external organisation such as a college or university.

On-the-job training: where employees acquire or develop skills without leaving their usual workplace, perhaps by being guided through an activity by a more experienced member of staff.

Person specification: a document that outlines the qualifications, skills and other qualities needed to carry out a particular job successfully.

Selection techniques: the processes used by an organisation to choose the most appropriate candidate for a job, such as interviewing or testing.

Exercises

A. Revision questions

(40 marks; 40 minutes)

1 Outline two reasons why a business might need to recruit new employees. (4)

2 Briefly explain the difference between a job description and a person specification. (4)

3 Outline two factors that would influence the method of recruitment used by a business. (4)

4 Suggest two reasons why internal recruitment may not be a suitable means of filling vacancies for a rapidly expanding business. (2)

5 Outline one advantage and one disadvantage of external recruitment. (4)

6 Examine one suitable method for recruiting applicants to the following job roles:
  (a) caretaker for a local school (3)
  (b) a temporary sales assistant for a high-street retailer over the Christmas period (3)
  (c) a marketing director for a multinational company. (3)

7 Examine one advantage and one disadvantage of using interviewing as a method of selecting candidates for a job vacancy. (4)

8 Suggest two methods that a firm could use to evaluate the effectiveness of its recruitment and selection procedure. (2)

9 Outline two reasons why a firm should provide induction training for newly recruited employees. (2)

10 Briefly explain why market failure might lead to a skills gap in the UK labour market. (5)

B. Revision exercises

B1 Data response

Performance-based recruitment at O_2

Mobile phone company O_2 has developed a new approach to hiring staff, based on candidates' performance profiles rather than on skills and competency. The recruitment model, developed for the business by consultancy firm Ferguson McKenzie, involves an interview that assesses between four and six accomplishments in the candidate's career. Potential recruits also have their 'tactical' skills and behaviour compared to a 'talent assessment matrix', which rates their likelihood of success in the job role. The new recruitment model was initially piloted at O_2's call centre in Glasgow, where it was used to hire 500 new staff. It was also used to take on 20 sales advisers in four different areas of the company's UK retail operations.

O_2's UK resourcing manager, Fiona Davidson, said that the new technique allowed recruitment assessors to 'probe more and have more meaningful dialogue with candidates'. According to her, the new model provided a better assessment of applicants' motivation and work ethic, as well as guaranteeing a more consistent approach across the selection process. When the model is eventually deployed across O_2's UK retail and customer service divisions, it will fill between 2500 and 3000 job vacancies each year.

Source: 'O_2 hires on performance', 23 August 2001, *People Management* Magazine

Questions

(25 marks; 30 minutes)

1 Outline three 'tactical' skills that an employee would need to successfully carry out the role of a customer services adviser at O_2. (6)

2 Analyse two ways in which O_2 could assess the effectiveness of the new recruitment model. (8)

3 Assess the importance of effective recruitment and selection for a company like O_2. (11)

B2 Data response

Solving skills shortages at Mulberry

Mulberry is a leading manufacturer of luxury handbags and leather goods, based in the south-west of England. Its reputation depends to a great extent on maintaining a highly skilled workforce, trained to handle valuable materials and use a variety of leatherworking techniques, such as cutting and stitching. These techniques are complicated to teach, requiring lengthy training periods before workers can become productive.

With an ageing workforce and a chronic shortage of workers with the appropriate manufacturing skills across the UK textile industry generally, Mulberry was faced with a dilemma: if it recruited and trained workers in-house it would not qualify for the public funding available for employees undertaking recognised qualifications. However, the courses offered by external training providers were too general and, therefore, failed to address the company's specific training needs.

The company's solution was to set up a partnership with Bridgewater College, a further education institution with a reputation for supporting local employers. The collaboration resulted in a new two-year apprenticeship qualification, designed precisely to meet Mulberry's training needs. Apprentices spend the majority of their time at the company's industrial plant in Somerset, training 'on the job' and learning a range of techniques. The apprentices also spend half a day each week at the college, learning about the leather industry and developing skills such as teamwork and communication. The scheme allows Mulberry to control the content of the training and, because the scheme is recognised by the relevant awarding bodies, the company receives £2500 of public funds for each apprentice trained.

Source: *Skillfast UK*

Questions

(25 marks; 30 minutes)

1 Briefly explain, using examples, the difference between on-the-job and off-the-job training. (4)

2 Analyse one benefit and one drawback to a company such as Mulberry of its new apprenticeship scheme. (8)

3 To what extent do you agree that the reputation, and therefore success, of UK manufacturers like Mulberry depends on maintaining a highly skilled workforce? (13)

C. Essay questions

(40 marks each)

1 Stamford Software Solutions, a medium-sized IT company based in the south-east of England, needs to recruit a new sales manager. Consider how the company should go about doing this.

2 According to the Leitch Report, UK employers spend an estimated £33 billion in total each year on training, yet one-third of employers provide no training at all. Evaluate the main consequences for firms that choose not to train their staff.

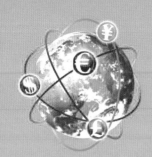

MEASURING THE EFFECTIVENESS OF THE WORKFORCE

DEFINITION

Staff costs are usually between 25% and 50% of a firm's total costs. For this reason, firms try to measure the performance of their people objectively (i.e. in an unbiased way). Calculations such as staff productivity can be used to measure the success of initiatives such as new methods of working or payment.

39.1 The need to measure performance

Managers require an objective, unbiased way to measure the performance of personnel. The firm needs to be able to see whether:

● the workforce is fully motivated

● the workforce is as productive as it could be

● the personnel policies of the business are helping the business to meet its goals.

It is not possible to measure these things directly. How, for example, can the level of motivation of workers be measured accurately? Instead, a series of indicators are used which, when analysed, can show the firm whether its personnel policies are contributing as much to the firm as they should.

There are two main performance indicators used to measure the effectiveness of a personnel department. These are:

1 labour productivity

2 labour turnover.

39.2 Labour productivity

Calculating labour productivity

Labour productivity is often seen as the single most important measure of how well a firm's workers are doing. It compares the number of workers with the output that they are producing. It is expressed through the formula:

$$\frac{\text{output per period}}{\text{number of employees per period}}$$

For example, if a window cleaner employs ten people and in a day will normally clean the windows of 150 houses, then the productivity is:

$$\frac{150}{10} = 15 \text{ houses per worker per day}$$

At its simplest, the higher the productivity of the workforce, the better it is performing. Any increase in the productivity figure suggests an improvement in efficiency. The importance of productivity lies in its impact on labour costs per unit. For example, the productivity of AES Cleaning is 15 houses per worker per day; MS Cleaning achieves only 10. Assuming a daily rate of pay of £45, the labour cost per house is £3 for AES but £4.50 for MS Cleaning. Higher productivity leads to lower labour costs per unit – and therefore greater competitiveness, both here and against international rivals.

Productivity is covered in more detail in Unit 33. The key thing for the present unit is to remember that productivity is just one way to measure staff performance. There are others, including labour turnover.

39.3 Labour turnover

Measuring labour turnover

Labour turnover is a measure of the rate of change of a firm's workforce. It is measured by the ratio:

$$\frac{\text{number of staff leaving the firm per year}}{\text{average number of staff}} \times 100$$

So a firm that has seen 5 people leave out of its staff of 50 has a labour turnover of:

$$\frac{5}{50} \times 100 = 10\%$$

As with all these figures, it would be a mistake to take one figure in isolation. It would be better to look at how the figure has changed over a number of years, and to look for the reasons why the turnover rate is as it is.

Causes of labour turnover

If the rate of labour turnover is increasing, it may be a sign of dissatisfaction within the workforce. If so, the possible causes could be either internal to the firm or external.

Internal causes of an increasing rate of labour turnover could include the following.

- A poor recruitment and selection procedure, which may appoint the wrong person to the wrong post. If this happens, then eventually the misplaced workers will wish to leave to find a job more suited to their particular interests or talents.

- Ineffective motivation or leadership, leading to workers lacking commitment to this particular firm.

Liz McGivern joined the RCH luxury hotel chain just after the 2001 terrorist attack on New York. Business was soon down by 20% as American tourists disappeared. Yet she noticed a shocking detail about RCH; its labour turnover was 80%. This would be poor for any hotel, but luxury hotels have to offer good service, which would always be tricky if new, inexperienced staff were dealing with guests. Nothing could be done about nervous flyers, but the high labour turnover was inexcusable.

Liz carried out some internal research which revealed high levels of staff dissatisfaction due to poor management and strained internal relationships. Her solution was to implement a company-wide training programme focusing on improved customer service. The cost per person was in the order of £1000 so, with a staff of more than 500, this was a substantial investment by the directors. Fortunately it went well, resulting in improved repeat business from guests and a fall in labour turnover to 29%. Even more importantly for the business, the revenue received per room rose by 11% at a time when the market trend was towards falling room rates.

Source: www.people1st.co.uk

They will feel no sense of loyalty to or ownership of the business, and will tend to look outside the firm for promotions or new career opportunities, rather than looking for new ways in which they could contribute to 'their' firm.

- Wage levels that are lower than those being earned by similar workers in other local firms: if wage rates are not competitive, workers will feel dissatisfied with their position; they may look elsewhere to find a better reward for doing a similar job.

External causes of an increasing rate of labour turnover could include the following.

- More local vacancies arising, perhaps due to the setting up or expansion of other firms in the area.

- Better transport links, making a wider geographical area accessible for workers. New public transport systems such as Manchester's network of trams or Newcastle's Metro links enable workers to take employment that was previously out of their reach.

Consequences of high labour turnover

A high rate of labour turnover can have both negative and positive effects on a firm. The negative aspects would be:

- the cost of recruitment of replacements

- the cost of retraining replacements

Figure 39.1 Transport links affect worker turnover

- the time taken for new recruits to settle into the business and adopt the firm's **culture**

- the loss of productivity while the new workers adjust.

On the positive side, labour turnover can benefit the business in several ways:

- new workers can bring new ideas and enthusiasm to the firm

- workers with specific skills can be employed rather than having to train up existing workers from scratch

- new ways of solving problems can be seen by workers with a different perspective, whereas existing workers may rely on tried and trusted techniques that have worked in the past.

On balance, then, there is a need for firms to achieve the *right* level of labour turnover, rather than aiming for the lowest possible level.

39.4 Evaluating the success of personnel management

Productivity and labour turnover data provide the firm with a commentary on its performance. Poor productivity and high labour turnover might be a commentary on poor management in the workplace. For the most effective comparisons, good managers analyse the figures to identify:

- changes over time (this year versus last)

- how the firm is performing compared to other similar firms

- performance against targets, such as a 20% improvement on last year.

Each of these comparisons will tell the firm how it is performing in relation to a yardstick. This will indicate to the firm where it is performing well and where it may have a problem. The firm must then investigate carefully the reasons for its performance before it can judge how well its personnel function is operating.

For example, labour productivity may have fallen over the past 12 months. Closer investigation may show that this fall is due to the time taken to train staff on new machinery installed at the start of the year. Figures may show that productivity in the last six months was actually higher than at any time in the past, and the firm can be confident that future productivity will continue to increase. In this case, an apparent problem is actually masking an improvement for the firm.

39.5 Downsides of personnel management: redundancy and dismissal

Redundancy occurs when a job is no longer needed, therefore the business has no further need for the person doing the job. For instance, an automated voice recognition system might do away with the job of a telephonist. A well-run business will have anticipated this situation, and discussed with the telephonist what to do next. Retrain, perhaps, as a personal assistant or as a telephone salesperson? Or perhaps the telephonist would rather take the opportunity to leave. A redundancy package for a 32 year old who has spent ten years at the firm would probably be no more than the government minimum figure of ten weeks' pay. This might amount to £3000–3500, which may do no more than tide the person over until a new job emerges.

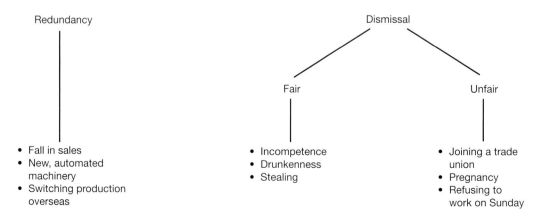

Figure 39.2 Possible causes of redundancy and dismissal

Statutory redundancy pay amounts to:

- for each year's employment for a worker aged 18 to 21 – half a week's pay

- for each year's employment for a worker aged 22 to 40 – one week's pay

- for each year's employment for a worker aged 41 to 65 – one and a half weeks' pay.

Clearly, then, if a struggling business needs to make people redundant, selecting young adults to leave will be the cheapest option by far.

Dismissal concerns the person, not the job. The business has decided (rightly or wrongly) that everyone will be better off without that person. By implication, s/he should never have been employed in the first place, so the recruitment staff ought to discuss how or why this happened. Dismissal will always be unpleasant, but may sometimes be essential. Football managers Arsene Wenger and Alex Ferguson both needed to clear boozy players out of their dressing rooms before they achieved real success. One incompetent member of a team can spoil the atmosphere (and, perhaps, the bonuses) for many.

Dismissal can be 'fair' or 'unfair'. It is 'fair' if the member of staff has had two verbal warnings about poor performance, followed by a written warning. If s/he fails to improve, dismissal is legally 'fair'. It is 'unfair' if dismissal is due to reasons that include:

- joining a trades union

- becoming pregnant

- refusing to work on Sundays.

Overall, a good leader would ensure that staff take great care over recruitment, to ensure that there are no 'rotten apples'. Then the personnel staff should work together to ensure that redundancies and dismissals are kept to the absolute minimum.

Issues For Analysis

There are several important business issues relating to personnel performance indicators.

- Business success comes from being the best and staying the best. This is always hard, but is the only way to be sure of staying at the top. Football managers might say all that counts is what happens on the pitch, but lateness or absence from training is often a good indicator of problems to come. Every manager should be alert to early warning signs, find out the reasons and tackle them straightaway.

- Personnel issues are considered 'soft' by some employers. Who cares about labour turnover or health issues, they say, as long as the job gets done and profits are high? This may be true in the short term; for firms pursuing long-term growth, however, the quality and involvement of staff is crucial. So morale matters – as do absence and lateness.

39.6 Measuring the effectiveness of the workforce
an evaluation

Performance ratios such as labour turnover raise questions – they do not supply answers. Follow-up staff surveys or chats may be needed to discover the underlying problems. Figures such as these give the firm an indication of what issues need to be addressed if the firm is to improve its position in the future, but this must be taken within the context of the business as a whole. A high labour turnover figure may have been the result of a deliberate policy to bring in younger members of staff who may be more adaptable to a changing situation at the factory.

Measures of personnel effectiveness are merely indicators for a firm to see where it may be facing problems. The measures may indicate poor performance, or reflect the short-term effect of a change in business strategy.

It must be remembered that these figures are all looking to the past. They tell the firm what has happened to its workforce. Although this has a strong element of objectivity, it is not as valuable as an indication of how the indicators may look in the future.

> **Key terms**
>
> **Culture:** the accepted attitudes and behaviours of people within a workplace.
> **Labour productivity:** output per person.
> **Labour turnover:** the rate at which people leave their jobs and need to be replaced.

Exercises

A. Revision questions

(20 marks; 20 minutes)

1 Define the following terms:
   (a) labour productivity
   (b) labour turnover. (4)

2 Why might an increase in labour productivity help a firm to reduce its costs per unit? (3)

3 In what ways might a hotel business benefit if labour turnover rose from 2% to 15% per year? (4)

4 Some fast food outlets have labour turnover as high as 100% per year. What might be the effects of this on the firm? (4)

5 How might a firm know if its personnel strategy was working effectively? (5)

B. Revision exercises

B1 Data response

A firm has the following data on its personnel function:

	Year 1	Year 2
Output	50,000	55,000
Average no. of workers	250	220
No. of staff leaving the firm	12	8
Working days per worker – possible	230	230
Average no. of staff absent	4	3

Questions

(15 marks; 15 minutes)

1 Calculate the following ratios for both years:
   (a) labour productivity
   (b) labour turnover. (5)

2 Explain what questions these figures might raise in the minds of the firm's management. (10)

B2 Data response

Monitoring personnel performance at Best Motors

James West, the new personnel officer at Best Motors, manufacturer of the world-famous handmade sports cars of the same name, sat down at his desk and considered the figures in front of him. He would need to report on the existing position of the business to Elizabeth Best, the chief executive, on Friday.

James knew the company operated for 50 weeks of the year (closing down only for the annual works holiday), and that all employees worked full-time, five days each week. He opened his briefcase and got out a calculator. 'The first thing to do is determine the key human resource indicators,' he thought to himself as he got to work (see page 271).

Questions

(25 marks; 30 minutes)

1 Calculate labour turnover and labour productivity at Best Motors for all five years. (10)

2 Using your results, evaluate the effectiveness of Best Motors' personnel management. (8)

3 What additional information would you seek in order to help James gain a better understanding of how staff have been managed at Best Motors? Explain your reasoning. (7)

Personnel performance at Best Motors (B2)

	4 YEARS AGO	3 YEARS AGO	2 YEARS AGO	LAST YEAR	THIS YEAR
NUMBER OF LEAVERS	3	2	4	6	7
WORKING DAYS LOST TO ABSENCE	124	102	145	169	204
TOTAL OUTPUT	780	803	805	790	811
NUMBER OF SHOP FLOOR ACCIDENTS	5	3	7	2	4
AVERAGE NUMBER OF EMPLOYEES	23	25	25	24	26

B3 Case study

Turner's Butchers is a chain of three shops in a large town in the north of England. The shops are all supplied with prepared and packaged produce from Turner's Farm, owned by the same family.

The management is particularly concerned at present by the differing performance of the three shops. In particular, they feel there may be a problem with the personnel management in the chain. The concerns were highlighted recently in a report looking at various indicators of personnel effectiveness. The key section of the report is shown below:

Questions

(30 marks; 45 minutes)

1 Briefly outline your observations on each of the three shops in terms of their personnel management. (12)

2 Give possible reasons for the factors you described in answer to question 1. (9)

3 Taking the business as a whole, make justified recommendations as to how any problems could be tackled by the management. (9)

Workforce performance data per shop (B3)

	Grayton Road	St John's Precinct	Lark Hill
Staff (full-time)	8	6	7
Labour turnover	25%	150%	0
Absence rate	5%	12%	1%
Sales per employee (£000s)	14	15	18

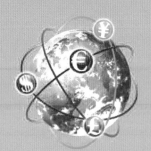

DEFINITION

Operations management turns a customer order into a delivery.

40.1 Introduction

Operations management is the central business function of creating the product or service and delivering it to the customer (i.e. meeting the customer requirement). Operations management at Ford means designing the cars and the machinery for making them, ordering the supplies, manufacturing the products, delivering them to the car showrooms and handling customer service issues such as warranty claims. Marketing creates the demand; operations management creates the supply to meet the demand. To achieve this, it requires human and financial resources.

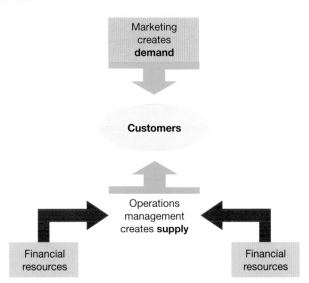

Figure 40.1 *The central role of operations management*

The importance of operations management is especially clear in the car industry. Rover Cars once commanded more than a 50% share of the British car market. Its cars were well designed but poorly made. In 2005 the business ceased to exist as a British producer. In the years of Rover's decline, Toyota moved from being

outside the top 20 world car producers to its current position as number one. Toyota has never been famous for producing stylish cars, but their quality and reliability have built its reputation worldwide. Toyota's business success has been built not on marketing but on operations management. This success has brought it annual profits of around £10 billion – more than the rest of the world's car makers put together.

40.2 What is operations management?

Step 1: design

The process starts by designing a product or service to meet the needs or desires of a particular type of customer (see Table 40.1 for examples). The key at this, and every other, stage is to be clear about the customer and his/her requirements. If an airline's target customer is a student, the design of the plane interior must be simple, economical and effective – to help keep costs low enough to provide the low prices the student traveller wants.

Step 2: establishing the supply chain

In a manufacturing process, the heart of the operation will be the factory. This is where a collection of materials and parts will be turned into a finished product. In the case of a car, literally thousands of parts are involved in making each vehicle. Components that may cost little to produce, such as metal fixings for seat belts, all combine to turn £4000 worth of parts into a car worth £10,000.

This does not mean, though, that the car maker receives £6000 of profit for every car sold; £6000 of value has been added to the components, but at what cost? The most obvious cost is labour (i.e. the staff needed to

Table 40.1 Examples of designs that aim to meet customer requirements

Market	Type of customer	Customer needs or wants	Outline operational design
Hotels	Busy traveller and busy worker	Low-cost but comfortable hotel room in city centre	Well-located building with small but very well-equipped rooms; all food and drink from vending machines
Car market	Family with young children	A car to make family journeys more pleasant	Spacious car with good entertainment (seat-back monitors, etc.) and a small refrigerated drinks unit
Mortgages	University students	Students wanting to buy a flat on a joint mortgage – to stop relying on landlords	Flexible, low-cost mortgage, which is easy to get into and out of; available online to students with limited financial histories

organise and run the factory). This will typically cost about 20–25% of the value of the output. Then come other things that are a clear waste of money for the business such as those listed below.

● *Production line errors leading to 'wastage'*: if a car reaches the end of the production line and, when tested, fails to start, labour time is wasted finding the fault, and more time and components involved in correcting the problem. Modern companies try to eliminate all activities that waste time, but taking too little care over quality can never make sense for any company that wants to build a long-term future.

● *Breakdowns, perhaps due to faulty maintenance, or just due to wear and tear*: a well-run business uses preventative maintenance – checking machinery and replacing worn parts before a breakdown occurs.

Having established a well-run factory, the business can establish the other key parts of the **supply chain**, as indicated in Figure 40.2.

Step 3: working with suppliers

Very few businesses produce 100% of a product or service. Almost all use suppliers. In some cases suppliers may do most of the operational work. Companies that 'bottle' Coca-Cola buy in: the aluminium cans, already printed with the can design; the water; the carbon dioxide used to create the fizz; and the secret Coke syrup (sent from the Coca-Cola factory in America). They may also get a distribution company such as Exel to make all the deliveries to wholesale and retail customers. So what does the Coca-Cola bottler actually do? Well, not a huge amount, clearly. But it must still be responsible for the coordination of all the suppliers and the quality of their work. If Waitrose ordered a container load of Coke Zero to reach its Bracknell depot at 10.00 on a Tuesday morning, did it turn up on time? If not, why not?

For many companies, working with suppliers is a key to success. A homemade ice cream parlour may do all the production operations on-site, but still relies on suppliers of: fresh fruit, fresh milk and cream; grocery items such as sugar; wafer biscuits and cones; paper cups and plastic spoons, and so on. To run the parlour

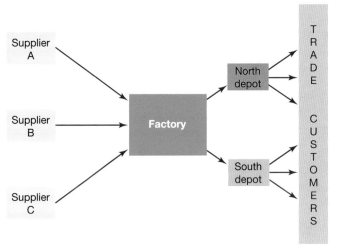

Figure 40.2 The supply chain: from supplier to customer

successfully all the operations have to be carried out successfully. If you have run out of cones, the best ice creams can remain unsold.

A company must therefore select suppliers that can deliver the right goods reliably; and must negotiate low enough prices for the supplies to make it possible to run the business economically.

Step 4: managing quality

Quality is not easy to define. It is a combination of real factors plus psychological ones. A haircut may be carried out very expertly, yet the customer may go away and cry! A less expert hairdresser may produce a technically worse cut, yet the effect may be just what the customer wants. In this case, providing quality means providing what the customer wants (i.e. delivering customer satisfaction).

Yet what if the customer wants the 'wrong' thing? The traveller may only care about getting to work on time, yet if the train company has safety concerns, the train should be slowed down or stopped. The traveller may get to work, cursing the train company's poor-quality service – but in reality the company has done the right thing.

Ten years ago few shoppers worried about healthy eating, so McDonald's and others made their money 'supersizing' their customers. Were the companies providing a high-quality service? Perhaps not.

Effective operations management requires certain quality objectives, though:

- the product/service must do what the customer has been promised
- it must arrive on time, in good condition
- it must last at least as long as the customer expects
- customer service should be effective (e.g. phones answered quickly)
- after-sales service should also be effective (e.g. speedy repair if something goes wrong).

These are the basics; on top of these should come the psychological factors that can mean a huge amount (e.g.

service with a warm smile, with staff showing warmth towards the customers). Modern business theory suggests that, to stand out, a company needs to achieve 'customer delight' not just customer satisfaction. The easiest way to delight a customer is to be genuinely welcoming; a fake smile is worse than none at all.

Step 5: using technology effectively

Twenty years ago it required a room full of computers to do what a laptop can do today. In ten years there will probably be more computing power in a mobile phone than today's PC. At a time of dramatic change, some firms have come unstuck when upgrading their whole IT system; still more have struggled to make the best use of the internet.

Within the operations department of a business, the key requirement has been to find software that will satisfactorily manage the day-to-day process, from supplies through to delivery. For example, if fashion retailer Zara of Spain suddenly orders 4000 'Glastonbury' jackets from your clothing factory, you need instantly to know:

- how many metres of cloth to order from your suppliers, and how many metres of lining
- how many buttons and zips to order
- when is the earliest date that all the above can be received, and therefore the job can begin
- how many hours of machine time will be needed
- how much overtime will be needed from staff, if the factory is already busy
- how many extra delivery vehicles will be needed and when
- when Zara can expect delivery of all 4000 items to its Spanish headquarters.

This should all be available at the touch of a button using **enterprise resource planning** (ERP) software. This software has all the details of the business operation and provides not only the planning but will also monitor on a day-to-day basis whether things are working to schedule.

Issues For Analysis

There are several concepts within operations management that are perfect for analysis:

- the idea that the heart of every business is the interface between marketing (demand) and operations (supply); and that operations relies on human and financial resources; only if all these departments work in harmony can the operation succeed

- success in managing operations requires a true understanding of what the customer really wants: a car to get from A to B, or an 'ultimate driving machine' to impress the neighbours?

- A well-run operation should be able to capture all its key information in the form of an ERP software package; in fact, most firms who buy this software find that they lack much of the information they need; without accurate data it can be 'garbage in, garbage out'. Exactly this problem happened with Sony in its much-delayed development of the PS3.

Introduction to operations management

Every business is different, especially in the status given to operations staff. In Toyota or BMW, top engineers are the stars of the business and the operations department will be at the heart of all major decisions. In a business such as Innocent Drinks, the marketing people lead the business, with the operations changing to suit the market. Usually the importance and power of operations staff will reflect the needs and history of the business. In some cases, though, career politics will have intervened. A company that should be based on strong operations may actually be dominated by marketing and finance people. In which case, key decisions about the future may be taken wrongly. The A-grade student not only analyses the precise circumstances of the business, s/he is also willing to make a judgement on whether the business is being run well or badly.

Key terms

Enterprise resource planning (ERP): logs all of a firm's costs, working methods and resources (machinery, labour, stocks of materials) within a piece of software; this provides a model of the business that can be used to answer questions such as 'When do we need to start working to get stocks made in time for delivery before Christmas?'

Supply chain: the whole path from suppliers of raw materials through production and storage on to customer delivery.

Exercises

A. Revision questions

(25 marks; 25 minutes)

1 Why may the quality of product design be less important for some businesses than others? (3)

2 Explain two key elements of operations management for:
   (a) a children's shoe shop (4)
   (b) a new, all-business-class airline. (4)

3 Choose one of the examples in Table 40.1 and outline one strength and one weakness of that business idea. (4)

4 Identify three ways in which staff might be at fault in production line errors that cause wastage. (3)

5 Examine the possible effects on a firm such as Coca-Cola of being unreliable in delivering to a big customer such as Waitrose. (5)

6 Outline one possible benefit to a business from 'delighting' rather than 'satisfying' its customers. (2)

B. Revision exercises

B1 Data response

Lean, green, efficient operations

Recent years have been great for Toyota, largely due to one car: the Prius. It is the car beloved of Hollywood stars due to its green technology – part electric, part petrol engine. The car has sold 'only' a million units, but its impact has been much greater. It has made the Toyota brand stand out in the crowded mass market in America, and helped Toyota challenge for the position of the world's number one car maker in 2007. Without doubt it is the world's richest, with more than £8000 million of cash in its bank account. Now Citroën wants to muscle in on Toyota's green success.

Of course, it is not enough to simply copy a rival. Citroën decided to tackle the main weakness of the Prius: its price. As it has two engines (one electric, one petrol), its production costs are higher, forcing it to be priced at

£2000–£3000 more than comparable cars. Citroën's new car is called the C-Cactus and it will be priced at the level of the comparable Citroën C4 model. This is because the C-Cactus has been made with dramatically fewer parts than a normal car. The car's interior, for example, has half the usual number of 400 separate components. That saves time and money in building the car. The C-Cactus therefore is less costly on parts and much less costly on labour than the C4.

Citroën's designers have questioned the need for every component in the car. Where possible they have cut back and simplified – but without risking passenger comfort. The car doors have two parts instead of the twelve on a normal car. The dashboard has gone, with most controls on a touch-screen indicator in front of the driver.

According to Citroën, the C-Cactus will not only drink less fuel, it will also use fewer labour hours. There is no doubting that it is designed to be lean and efficient; the only worry is whether customers will accept the very different look and feel of the car. It certainly won't have the luxury touches some car buyers expect.

Source: www.scoop.co.nz

Questions

(30 marks; 35 minutes)

1a Outline two features of the C-Cactus that might prove appealing to car buyers. (6)

1b Outline one reason why buyers of large family cars may not buy the C-Cactus. (4)

2a On average, Prius cars have sold for £12,000. How much revenue, therefore, has the brand generated for Toyota? (3)

2b Product development on the Prius took eight years and cost an estimated £850 million. Was it worth it? Explain your answer. (5)

3 This unit sets out five important elements of operations management. Discuss which one of the five proved the most important in the development of the C-Cactus. (12)

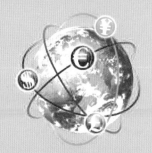

INVENTION, INNOVATION AND DESIGN

41.1 Introduction

At the heart of any business is the product it sells. That product is the key to success. Invention, innovation and design are the processes by which interesting, new or unique products enter markets. As illustrated by the business example in the A-grade application, inventions can increase the total value of a market, or can lead to the birth of totally new markets.

A-grade application

How inventions can affect the market

For over 20 years, scuba divers were kept under water by the same type of 'open' oxygen system. They breathed in from their oxygen tank and breathed out through a tube that sent a stream of air bubbles to the surface. With the technology unchanged, suppliers' market shares were also stable. In recent years, however, closed 'Rebreather' systems have been developed and marketed.

Exhaled oxygen is recycled, enabling the diver to stay under water for two to three times as long. The system also avoids the streams of bubbles, which might frighten away the fish or whales the diver is trying to observe.

Although the cost of around £2500 is far more than that of open diving equipment, Rebreathers have sold well in places like Florida and the Bahamas. This new technology has added value, changed market share and increased total spending within the marketplace.

41.2 Invention

The very activity of inventing new products is somewhat hit and miss. Many new products have been invented by accident. The Post-it note was the result of the discovery of a seemingly useless glue, which wasn't very sticky. Apple's iPod was largely the **invention** of company outsiders, but Apple added key design features and saw the need to link it with the music distribution system it called iTunes. When it made its press debut in 2001, the iPod wasn't particularly well received. It was the public that saw the big opportunity, not the press 'experts'. Other products have been invented in order to fulfil a particular purpose, such as stairlifts for the elderly and disabled.

Invention is not limited to products (**product invention**). Production processes have been invented that have led to great competitive advantages (**process invention**). The glass manufacturer Pilkington plc developed the self-cleaning glass process (branded and patented as Pilkington Activ). This has a coating that breaks down dirt particles so that they do not stick to the glass (and therefore are washed away by normal rainfall). This has earned the firm significant sums in licensing revenues from foreign manufacturers.

Although many inventions come from company research programmes, there is still a place for the lone inventor. An individual may come up with an idea that can be produced and marketed under licence by a larger firm with greater facilities. Or the inventor may set up his/her own firm, if the product idea is good enough and sufficient capital can be raised. James Dyson, inventor of the cyclonic vacuum cleaner, had his idea rejected by many major manufacturers, so he set up his own business in order to manufacture his revolutionary new cleaner. Within four years, the firm had grown so that it

Table 41.1 Product and process invention

Type of invention	Description	Examples
Product invention	Devising a new type or category of product, i.e. opening up a new market	• the Blu-Ray HD DVD • digital radios
Process invention	Devising a new way of producing or manufacturing (which may allow new products to be made, or improve the efficiency of making existing products)	• real fruit smoothies

employed 600 staff, claimed a 26% share of the UK market and was estimated to be worth between £100 and £250 million.

Having come up with an invention, a vital step is to patent it. This means registering with the Patent Office that the new technical process is a genuine step forward from previous patents. If a patent is granted, no other firm has the legal right to use your new process for at least 20 years. This provides a long period in which the inventor enjoys exclusive rights to sell the new product/process. This allows the inventor to gain high

rewards from selling at a high price due to the product's uniqueness. Dyson cleaners, for example, sell at more than twice the price of most other vacuums.

41.3 Innovation

As with invention, **innovation** can be based on products or processes. However, successful innovation requires business skill in addition to inventive talent. The inventive idea must be honed into a marketable product. Meanwhile the method of production must be developed and finance found. Successful innovation is vital for the long-term survival of a firm. Innovation allows the firm to update its product portfolio by replacing products at the end of their life cycle.

It is particularly important to continue to innovate in markets where competition is strong, product life cycles

A-grade application
Plug-In

Toyota's 1990s development of 'hybrid synergy drive' has become one of the biggest innovation success stories in business history. Not only had Prius sales amounted to more than £15,000 million by early 2008, but also the car had transformed the whole company image. In the huge US market, 'Toyota' means environmentally responsible (and technically advanced).

The only weakness of the Prius is that, unless the driver goes on long journeys, the battery is not charged up enough to operate as an electric car in town. So although the car is great for someone who drives 30 miles to work (in town), it is less effective for someone who crawls 2 miles to work in heavy traffic.

So, in autumn 2007 Toyota announced a Plug-In Prius. It will have the same petrol plus electric engine, but with the additional feature of having a plug-in facility to boost the electric battery at night or during the day. This will enable the car to use its electric motor for a much higher percentage of each journey, and therefore allow the car to have zero pollution emissions much more often. For the Toyota Prius user, this extra boost to the car's social responsibility is an extra reason to purchase.

A-grade application
The robot vacuum

In 2002 iRobot – a company formed in 1990 by three MIT research scientists – launched the Roomba vacuuming robot. Between then and 2008 more than 2 million have been sold worldwide, at prices of around £200. The Roomba lives on a recharging pod, gets itself up, can clean up to four rooms, then finds its way back to its pod and settles down to recharge its batteries. If you have a cat or dog (so that pet hair is a constant problem) a daily clean by Roomba is ideal. And what a present for older relatives who may struggle to keep their homes clean.

The latest Roomba can be programmed for the week, telling it when to clean. iRobot is soon to launch a 'Wash and Go' version that will wash and dry a kitchen floor!

low and the rate of innovation is high. Computer manufacturers seek to launch a new innovation every few months, in an attempt to gain a competitive advantage over rivals. In industries such as this, innovation is essential for survival. A computer firm selling three-year-old technology is unlikely to be able to add much value or sell high volumes.

Radical innovations such as the robot cleaner described in the A-grade application are rare. In most markets, the term 'innovation' means nothing so dramatic. In the salad cream market, the first squeezable bottle was called an innovation by Heinz. Breweries were equally thrilled to announce the first 'widget' canned beer. The reason is that, in large, established markets, quite small product innovations can have a major impact on market share. Coca-Cola hopes that its 2008 innovation of a resealable drink can will give it an extra edge over its rivals.

41.4 Design

The design of a product is not just about its appearance and shape. It is also about the product's function, quality and durability. Designers work to a design brief, which tells them the criteria for looks, cost and quality. All must be considered in designing the finished product. Larger firms may have their own design teams on the payroll. Smaller firms may rely on design consultants to turn a product idea or requirement into a finished product.

A useful way to consider design is through the design mix. As Figure 41.1 indicates, every designer must consider the following three factors.

Aesthetics
Chanel No. 5
BMW
Own-label lemonade
Function (& quality)
Economic manufacture

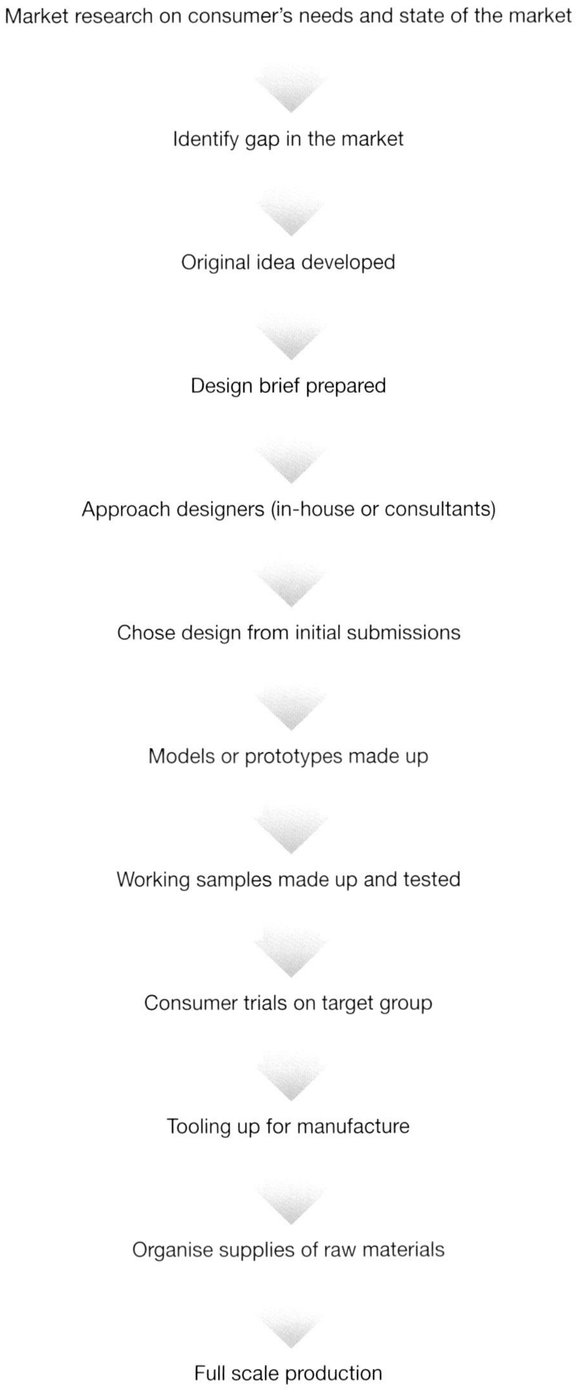

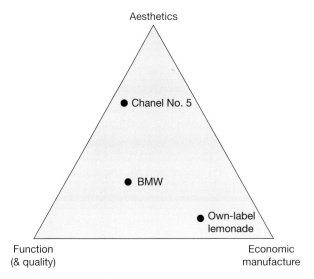

Figure 41.1 The design mix

1. *Aesthetics:* the look, feel, smell or taste (i.e. the appeal to the senses).
2. *Function:* does it work? Is it reliable? Is it strong enough or light enough for the customer's purpose?
3. *Economic manufacture:* is the design simple enough for it to be made quickly and efficiently?

Market research on consumer's needs and state of the market
Identify gap in the market
Original idea developed
Design brief prepared
Approach designers (in-house or consultants)
Chose design from initial submissions
Models or prototypes made up
Working samples made up and tested
Consumer trials on target group
Tooling up for manufacture
Organise supplies of raw materials
Full scale production

Figure 41.2 The design process

A-grade application
Designing the Post-It

Offices throughout the world are likely to have three brand names in common. Intel-based computers, Microsoft software and …. Post-It Notes. These yellow pads of sticky paper have made $multi-millions for the American company 3M. They were invented by 3M employee Art Fry in the 1960s. He had been shown a 'failed' development of a glue – it simply didn't stick well. He realised that the glue's 'problem' was that it stayed quite sticky for a long time, instead of being very sticky at one time. He tried it on pads of paper, found that yellow had the most impact – and the Post-It Note was born. The Post-It was an innovation that stemmed from a research and development programme.

In some cases, all three factors will be of equal importance. In most, there will be a clear priority. As Figure 41.1 shows, with own-label lemonade, cheap production would be the overwhelming priority. Therefore cheap design, using low-cost materials that are easy to manufacture, will be required. For BMW, design for function would be important, as would the car's appearance. Firms decide on their design priorities after careful market research to identify the purchasing motivations of existing and potential customers.

41.5 Invention and innovation in business

Invention and innovation in marketing

Many would argue that the most important element of the marketing mix is the product itself. Successful product development keeps a firm one step ahead of the competition. This usually means keeping one step ahead in pricing as well. Whether you are introducing a new drug, such as Viagra, or a new football management computer game, you have the opportunity to charge a premium price. Innovative new products are also very likely to get good distribution. Sainsbury's is very reluctant to find space on its shelves for just another ('me-too') cola or toothpaste, but if the new product is truly innovative, the space will be found.

Invention and innovation in finance

Invention, innovation and design all require significant amounts of long-term investment. Innovation takes time, and that time is spent by highly paid researchers. The result is that firms who are unwilling to accept long payback periods are unlikely to be innovators. Short-termist companies are far more likely to copy other firms' successes. In fact, much of the money spent by firms on invention and innovation provides no direct payback. Ideas are researched and developed before discovering that they will not succeed in the marketplace. The result is that innovation is something of a hit-and-miss process. There are no guaranteed rewards, but the possibility of a brand new, market-changing product. It is these successes that can radically alter the competitive conditions within a marketplace, allowing an innovative company to claim a dominant position.

Invention and innovation in people

Inventors are sometimes caricatured as 'mad scientists' working alone in laboratories with bubbling test tubes. This is far from the truth. For many years, firms have realised that teamwork provides many of the most successful innovations. As a result, research teams are encouraged to share their breakthroughs on a regular basis in the hope that the team can put their ideas together to create a successful product. These research teams are often created by taking specialists in various different fields of operation, from different departments within an organisation. This means that a team may consist of several scientists, an accountant, a production specialist and someone from the marketing department. This blend of expertise will enable the team to identify cost-effective, marketable new ideas that can be produced by the company, without the need for the new idea to be passed around the different departments within an organisation.

Invention and innovation in operations management

As previously mentioned, invention and innovation are not limited to finished products. New production processes can be invented or developed. These can lead to more efficient, cheaper or higher-quality production. Furthermore, new products often need new machinery and processes to be developed for their manufacture. Returning to the Post-it Note – its lack of successful imitators is because no other firm has been able to replicate successfully 3M's machine for sticking the glued pad together. Design is also important in production. The process needs to be clearly thought through so that every machine and activity has a logical place in the production system.

Issues For Analysis

- Invention should not be confused with innovation. The British have a proud record as inventors. The hovercraft, television, penicillin and many more products were British inventions. In recent years, however, there has been less success in this country with innovation. The Japanese have been the great innovators in electronics, the Americans in computers and the Swiss in watches. British firms have failed to invest sufficiently to develop ranges of really innovative new products.

- Major innovation can completely change a firm's competitive environment. The market shares of leading companies may change little for years – then an innovation comes along that changes everything. The firm that has not prepared for such change can be swept aside. This may happen to book shops that do not establish a major presence on the internet.

- Good management means looking ahead, not only to the next hill but the one after that. Anticipation makes change manageable. It may even ensure that your own firm becomes market leader due to far-sightedness of your own innovation. In turn, that would ensure high product differentiation and allow relatively high prices to be charged.

- Innovation can happen in management procedures, attitudes and styles. A management that is progressive and adventurous might well find that an empowered workforce is generating the new ideas that seemed lacking before. It would not be wise to assume that invention and innovation is all about scientists and engineering. It is about people.

Invention, innovation and design

The fundamental theme for evaluating any question involving design, invention and innovation is the contrast between long- and short-term thinking. Invention and innovation are clearly long-term activities. It could be argued that design is the same. Part of the brilliance of Mercedes engineering is that, although the cars develop year by year, there are design themes that keep a Mercedes completely recognisable. Companies whose objective is short-term profit maximisation are unlikely to spend heavily on invention, innovation or design. The key is to take a long-term view, then stick to it. This is what Pilkington did with its self-cleaning glass, which took ten years to perfect. The Toyota Prius took more than ten years to become profitable. As a past Guinness advertisement once said: 'Good things come to those who wait.'

Key terms

Innovation: bringing a profitable new product or process to life.
Invention: drawing up a new way of making a product or process.
Process invention: devising a new way of making things (production process).
Product invention: devising a new product to make.

Exercises

A. Revision questions

(40 marks; 45 minutes)

1 Distinguish between innovation and invention. (3)

2 Why is it important to reduce the time taken to develop new ideas? (4)

3 Distinguish between product and process innovation. (3)

4 Why is it 'vital' to patent an invention? (3)

5 What marketing advantages does good design bring to a firm? (4)

6 Where, on Figure 41.1 might you plot the following.
  (a) An iPhone (3)
  (b) The packaging of a Cadbury £4 Easter egg (3)
  Briefly explain your answers.

7 Why might product-orientated firms produce more inventions than market-orientated ones? (4)

8 How are the concepts of short-termism and innovation linked? (4)

9 Many businesses are concerned at the fall in the number of students taking science A-levels. How might this affect firms in the long term? (5)

10 What effect would a lack of innovation have on a company's product portfolio? (4)

B. Revision exercises

B1 Data response

Tide Coldwater

Procter & Gamble (P&G) is the world's biggest household products company. Its company website says that 'Innovation is the company's lifeblood'. If so, it has worked well, as P&G's annual sales in 2007 were $76.5 billion and profits exceeded $15 billion. In 2005, it launched the innovative Tide Coldwater in America after a long development phase that

had been conducted in strict secrecy. Tide had long been America's top-selling detergent, and now P&G wanted to persuade US customers that clothes could be washed perfectly well in cold water. The prize for P&G could be increased market share, and at slightly higher prices. After all, cold-water washing would save the householder money, so therefore the product would be worth more (i.e. it would have higher value added). P&G would not miss the opportunity to increase its profit margins.

The biggest prize, though, would be the huge goodwill that P&G could enjoy by basking in the warm, green glow of social responsibility. According to the company, 85% of the energy used when washing clothes comes from the water temperature (as opposed to the production of the detergent). As 7 million US households use Tide Coldwater, the energy saving represents millions of tonnes of carbon emissions per year.

Questions

(35 marks; 40 minutes)

1 Outline the market research that P&G would have needed to do before launching an innovative product such as Tide Coldwater. (8)

2a Calculate the % profit margin being made by P&G in 2007. (2)

2b In 2001, the company's profit margin was 10.9%. Examine two possible actions the management may have taken to increase the margins over recent years. (6)

3 Explain the possible impact on P&G's marketing managers of the company's proud boast that 'Innovation is the company's lifeblood'. (5)

4 Explain why the development of a product as ordinary as a detergent might be kept so secret. (6)

5 Examine the possible benefits to P&G of the environmental 'green glow' involved in the launch of Tide Coldwater. (8)

C. Essay questions

(40 marks each)

1 To what extent does an innovative product guarantee success?

2 'Any business has two, and only two, basic functions. Marketing and innovation.' Discuss whether there is value in this statement by Peter Drucker.

3 'Luck is the most important factor in successful innovation.' Discuss the validity of this statement.

4 Spending on research and development is wasted money since many firms find success through copying other firms' products. Discuss this statement.

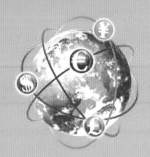

42 Unit

CUSTOMER SERVICE

DEFINITION

Customer service describes the range of actions taken by a business when interacting with its customers. Effective customer service will meet or surpass the expectations that customers have of the business.

42.1 Introduction

The biggest question in relation to this topic is whether firms try to provide good service to their customers or whether 'customer service' is a label used to describe actions that keep customers at arms' length from the organisation, e.g. call centres. Is providing a service a genuine part of the company's attitudes and **culture**?

42.2 How is customer service delivered?

Face to face

The most immediate, most powerful situation in which customer service is seen is in direct, face-to-face dealings with customers. Retailers must focus clearly on how shop staff interact with their customers. This is a situation with which you are likely to be highly familiar, perhaps from both sides. Here, the face of the employee is the face of the company to the customer.

Telephone

Much of customer service activity now happens in call centres. From finding out the price of a train from Leeds to Plymouth, to making an insurance claim following a car crash, the telephone is a key factor in customer service. Call centres are thought to be cost efficient, partly because they can be located in Birmingham, Belfast or Bangalore. It is highly questionable, though, as to whether they deliver 'customer service'. Most customers want to talk to an individual, not someone who is reading a script.

A-grade application
Customer service at home

Companies looking for a less controversial alternative to basing call centres in Asia may have found an answer in a concept known as home-shoring. An alternative to 'off-shoring' where customer service is provided from a call centre in another country, 'home-shoring' bases customer service assistants in their own homes. Research evidence seems to suggest that this boosts productivity and increases the level of service provided. The *Guardian* reports that all 1000 reservations staff at US airline JetBlue work at home. The customer complaint level is, amazingly, just one per 300,000 passengers, while staff turnover is just 3.5%, way below that experienced in a traditional call centre.

Source: Adapted from Guardian, 15 October 2005

Internet

Many online booking systems have eliminated direct human contact from customer service. Behind the scenes, though, the attitudes within the business remain all-important. You may book a bargain flight online, ticking the box for same-day delivery of the tickets. If the business fails to deliver the tickets on time, you are not going on holiday. Will the tickets arrive? Only if the faceless staff do their jobs on time. As customers, we have to trust that an online service will soon fail if it cannot meet its promises.

42.3 Methods of meeting customer expectations

To meet customer expectations, a business needs to follow a four-stage process as illustrated in Figure 42.1.

Identify customer expectations

↓

Agree how to meet customer expectations

↓

Train all staff to be able to provide the customer service level
the firm is aiming to achieve

↓

Monitor customer service and look for improvements

Figure 42.1 Meeting customer expectations

Market research

In order to find out what customers expect, market research will be used. This is likely to be a mixture of quantitative and qualitative research. The qualitative research is designed to probe selected key customers to find what level of support and service they expect from the firm. Such detailed qualitative research will probably enable the firm to gain a clear understanding of the range of expectations that different customers may have. With these identified, quantitative research can be used to assess how many customers expect certain features of customer service. An example may be using research to identify 'acceptable' queuing times when ringing a call centre.

Decision-time

Decisions will need to be made, based on the results of research into customers' expectations, of just what level of service the firm will aim to provide. If money were no object, any firm could provide exquisite customer service. We can only imagine the level of service available from James Bond's Savile Row tailor or Victoria Beckham's Beverly Hills hairstylist. Alternatively, a firm may decide to take a low-cost approach to customer service, perhaps outsourcing enquiries and technical problems to reduce costs. The costs and benefits of spending on customer service will be weighed. For those companies that value their reputation highly, the benefits may outweigh the costs, while for those that rely on low prices to shift their products, they may cut corners on customer service to protect their profit margin.

Training

Staff training can begin once the firm has decided on its customer service policies and practices. Note, however, that firms will have varying levels of commitment to training for staff. Some firms may offer staff just 30 minutes' informal training in customer service. They cannot expect their policies to be implemented as effectively as the firm that sends all new staff to a training centre for a full day's training. In America, McDonald's began a programme of getting staff to work with **zero training**. This was just at the start of the period when the firm's sales and profits collapsed in the period 2002–2005. The zero training approach disappeared when new managers decided that McDonald's needed more customer training, not less. At McDonald's, and everywhere else, the cost involved in improving the level of customer service must be set against the cost of not doing so.

Quality

As discussed in Unit 31, firms looking to ensure the quality of anything that they do, face a choice between quality control and quality assurance.

Quality control methods for customer service involve spotting defective service. The problem here is that poor customer service can be spotted only once it has been delivered, and this means at least one unhappy customer. Anyone who has rung a call centre is likely to have heard an announcement that 'Your call may be recorded for quality control purposes.' Those working in the retail sector are at the mercy of '**mystery shoppers**', who are paid to visit stores and report back on the customer service provided. Other methods of quality control involve planned or unannounced management checks.

Quality assurance is the attempt to introduce systems to ensure that quality errors cannot occur. Therefore quality assuring customer service systems must involve staff training. Given the key role of staff in meeting customer expectations, they will need to be 100% clear on how to deal with any situation they may face. The problem is that staff can start to see themselves, not the customers, as the focal point of the business. Management may keep saying 'the customer is king' or 'the customer is always right', but the staff don't really believe it.

Quality standards

Companies can apply for quality standards certification to show the rest of the world that they are serious about the quality of what they do. The basic **ISO 9000** certification series covers customer service in organisations for which the skill is relevant. However, for customer service specialists, there are customer service-specific standards:

Table 42.1 *Quality control vs quality assurance*

Quality control	Quality assurance
'Your call may be recorded for quality purposes'	Thorough, ongoing training in customer service
Mystery shoppers	Customer service is a key feature of company culture
Management checks	Clear systems, set out in writing, about how to deal with each type of customer complaint

- ISO 10002 – a customer complaint handling standard

- the BSI runs the CCA Standard – a special quality standard for call centres

- Charter Mark – administered by the government, this is a customer service standard for public- and voluntary-sector organisations, along with firms that provide a public service in the passenger train and bus, water, gas and electricity supply industries.

42.4 Monitoring and improving customer service

With a customer service system in place, the final step is to fight complacency. Systems designed to monitor the effectiveness of customer service must be used in order to ensure that standards do not slip and that the quality systems being used for customer service continue to produce the required results. However, in a spirit of continually trying to improve, most firms will monitor their own customer service standards relative to those of their rivals. Innovations in customer service are likely to be copied fairly quickly in most markets. This is why major changes to customer service, such as the use of the internet in the banking industry, tend to become common features of the industry in such a short time.

Benefits of good customer service

There is no doubt that good customer service has positive effects on a business, not just in terms of keeping customers from jumping to rival firms.

- *Brand loyalty:* good customer service tends to bring repeat custom. As customers feel positive about the experience they have had with a business, they are more likely to return to that firm for future purchases. Hanging on to existing customers is crucial for any sensible business, since attracting new customers from rivals tends to rely on expensive promotional tools, such as advertising and special offers.

- *Word-of-mouth promotion:* good customer service can actually generate free promotion as happy customers tell their friends. Anecdote suggests that word-of-mouth promotion is the most effective promotional tool available to a business. This is because you are more likely to believe your friends than a company's marketing department.

- *Increased efficiency:* since good customer service is likely to include better advice to customers, firms are less likely to sell inappropriate products or services that fail to meet customer needs. This should mean fewer complaints and therefore a reduced need for 'second phase' customer service back-up, such as customer complaint lines or product returns.

A-grade application
The best and worst. . .

The UK Customer Service Institute regularly publishes the results of its survey of customer service in the UK. This provides data on the best- and worst-performing sectors when it comes to customer service. It also highlights prime examples of excellent customer service. In the 2007 survey, perhaps unsurprisingly, the Ambulance Service came out on top; however, they were closely followed by John Lewis (including Waitrose), clear leaders in customer service within the retail sector. Meanwhile, the UK's worst-performing sector for customer service was local government, closely followed by utility companies (gas, water, electricity).

Source: http://www.ukcsi.com/Results.aspx

Issues For Analysis

- With so much customer service being provided by phone, call centres feature high in the customer service agenda. NatWest Bank is just one of many companies now stating clearly in its promotional literature that it uses only UK call centres. Why should it use UK call centres when the cost is far higher than for those located in India, and the staff in a UK call centre will be less qualified than their Indian counterparts? Customer service could be argued to be more qualitative than quantitative. Perceptions of customers are probably more important than the service they actually receive; the link between this area of operations management and the marketing department is strong.

- Some companies, notably DIY chain B&Q, believe that some types of people are better at customer service than others. Many major retailers use students and school-leavers as a huge portion of their shop-floor staff. However, B&Q feels that students and school-leavers are naturally less polite than older members of staff. The result is that B&Q actively encourages retired and semi-retired people to apply for positions in its stores, since it believes that these staff can provide the most effective customer service.

Customer service

Good customer service is unlikely to be provided by unmotivated staff. Although systems for ensuring customer service – such as market research, training and quality control systems – do help to improve customer service, it is the staff that will be the vital determinant. The message for businesses is therefore one that stresses the need to look after all staff. Often, a business may pay particular attention to motivating its managers, at the cost of ignoring the needs of staff lower down the organisation's hierarchy. However, in the majority of businesses, the front-line providers of customer service are the staff at the lowest level of the hierarchy who actually deal with customers. No matter how motivated the store management team, an unmotivated supermarket checkout assistant may well be the main determinant of a customer's shopping experience.

> ### Key terms
>
> **Culture:** within a business, this means 'the way we do things round here' (i.e. the attitudes and behaviours of staff within an organisation).
> **ISO 9000:** the International Standards Organisation (ISO) has a quality assurance certification system called ISO 9000.
> **Mystery shoppers:** employed to test customer service by visiting a shop or sales outlet unannounced, and therefore have the same experience as customers.
> **Zero training:** the opposite of customer service, in that it implies that staff need neither skills nor positive attitudes to work for the business.

Exercises

A. Revision questions

(35 marks; 35 minutes)

1 List three methods of meeting customer expectations. (3)

2 Explain how the use of a mystery shopper can help to maintain standards of customer service. (4)

3 Briefly explain how the following businesses might benefit from providing excellent customer service:
(a) a café
(b) a manufacturer of washing machines
(c) a bank. (9)

4 For a business that you use regularly where you feel customer service could be better, briefly explain:
(a) your own customer expectations
(b) how the business could identify what your expectations are
(c) how the business could try to meet your expectations. (9)

5 Explain why a small local plumber might benefit from offering better customer service than all her local rivals. (4)

6 Explain two benefits that an electricity supplier such as npower might find as a result of gaining a customer service quality standard such as the Charter Mark. (6)

B. Revision exercises

B1 Data response

The chiropractor

Brian Lima runs a hugely successful chain of chiropractors. A chiropractor is a specialist in spinal manipulation, who can relieve all sorts of physical complaints by working on the spine. Brian has always prided himself on operating to the very finest standards, not only in terms of the skills of his professional chiropractors, but also in terms of the level of customer service offered within each practice. Waiting rooms are decorated to the very highest standards, and equipped with all manner of calming and soothing accessories, including spacious and well-stocked fish tanks, along with soothing mood music. Receptionists are recruited very carefully to ensure that they are able to offer the levels of service his customers expect, while training for all staff focuses on meeting customers' expectations. A meticulously collated customer database allows his firm to provide relevant information to all customers and previous customers, who are also regularly contacted to conduct a customer satisfaction survey twice each year, while all staff are proud of having achieved the ISO quality standard for customer complaint handling – although a minuscule complaint level means that there is plenty of time to deal with any problems that do arise.

Questions

(20 marks; 25 minutes)

1a Briefly explain how Brian's business seeks to identify customer expectations. (2)

1b Explain two features of Brian's business that you consider may be vital elements of good customer service for medical practitioners. (4)

2 Explain how Brian's business attempts to monitor and improve customer service levels within the business. (6)

3 Analyse two possible benefits to Brian of providing the highest levels of customer service. (8)

B2 Data response

Twinkle.com

Twinkle.com is an internet service provider, aiming for the top end of the market in a marketplace that has experienced enormous growth over the past ten years. Twinkle knows the importance of customer service, but has experienced a number of problems over the past year. Its management is disappointed in this because this year it has spent more than ever before on a promotional campaign to recruit new customers. Disappointed with the results produced by its online and telephone customer service teams, Twinkle.com has called in a consultant to improve customer service levels who has gathered the data shown in the table below.

Questions

(30 marks; 35 minutes)

1 Briefly explain how the table shows evidence of poor customer service. (3)

2 Identify and explain a possible cause of poor customer service performance suggested by the table above. (4)

3 Analyse two other possible causes of poor customer service within the business. (6)

4 Analyse the reasons why customer service may be especially important for an ISP (internet service provider). (8)

5 To what extent can an external consultant help to improve the customer service levels offered by a firm such as Twinkle.com? (9)

	Quarter 1 (Jan–Mar)	Quarter 2 (Apr–Jun)	Quarter 3 (Jul–Sep)	Quarter 4 (Oct–Dec)
Complaints per month	864	967	932	902
% of complaints dealt with within 24 hours	28	24	29	34
Customer service training expenditure (£000s)	12	12	12	10
Overall customer service rating from monthly customer survey	6	5	5	4
Increase/decrease in total customer numbers	+3%	+2%	−3%	−12%

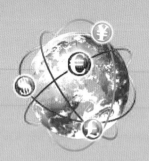

EFFECTIVE QUALITY MANAGEMENT

DEFINITION

Quality management means providing what the customer wants at the right time, with the right level of quality and consistency, and therefore yielding high customer satisfaction.

43.1 What is quality?

W. Edwards Deming, the American quality guru, said that 'quality is defined by the customer'. The customer may insist on certain specifications, or demand exceptional levels of customer comfort. Another definition of quality is 'fit for use'. Although hard to define, there is no doubt that customers are very aware of quality. Their perception of quality is a key part of the buying decision.

Customers will accept some **trade-off** between price and quality. There is, however, a minimum level of quality that is acceptable. The customer wants the product to work (be fit for use), regardless of the price. If the customers think that the quality is below a minimum level they will not buy the product. Above the minimum level of acceptable quality, customers will expect to get more as they pay more.

The importance of quality is related to the level of **competitiveness** in the market. When competition is fierce, the quality of the product can tip the balance in the customer's decision making. Dell is a hugely successful computer manufacturer, which sells directly to customers through the internet or newspaper advertising. Its mission statement is: 'Customers must have a quality experience and be pleased not just satisfied.'

For all customers, quality is about satisfying their expectations. The customer will take into account the total buying experience. Customer service and after-sales service may be as important as the product itself. The way the product is sold, even *where* it is sold, all contribute to the customer's feelings about the quality of the product.

Quality is a moving target. A quality standard that is acceptable today may not be in the future. Customer expectations of quality are constantly changing. As quality improves, customer demands also increase.

Quality:

- is satisfying (preferably beating) customer expectations
- applies to services as well as products
- involves the whole business process, not just the manufacturing of the product
- is an ever-rising target.

A-grade application
Mattel

Mattel, the world's largest toy maker, had a quality disaster in 2007. It was forced to withdraw millions of toys from the market at an eventual cost of £20 million.

Mattel first said that the problem was that toys made in China had unacceptable levels of lead in the paint. Then they said loose parts could be a danger to children. The world's media used the story to condemn China for poor quality standards. The American press went to town on this. Business media said it highlighted the difficulty of controlling quality when large businesses outsource manufacturing. At first Mattel said it would implement plans for additional checking and shift production away from subcontractors, i.e. back to its own factories. The company said it hoped that these moves would restore public confidence in its products.

Some weeks later Mattel faced the further embarrassment of admitting that "The vast majority of these products that we recalled were the result of a flaw in Mattel's design, not through a manufacturing flaw in Chinese manufacturers" (Thomas Debrowski, Mattel's Vice President for Worldwide Operations). Mattel had managed to make themselves look foolish twice over.

Quality defined by customer specifications

Where the customer is in a powerful position, quality is directly defined by the customer. Many firms lay down minimum standards for their suppliers. Large businesses, such as supermarkets and chain stores, are able to insist on quality standards. They have the buying power to force their suppliers to conform. For many years, Marks & Spencer has worked with suppliers to ensure that standards are met. Other large purchasers, such as government departments and local authorities, are also able to insist on high standards for supplies. As new roads and motorways are built, their surface is checked to ensure its quality. If the surface does not conform to the required standards the contractor will have to re-lay the area.

Other firms, and in particular local and central government agencies, will insist that their suppliers have obtained ISO 9000 (see box). This ensures that suppliers are operating within a quality framework.

A-grade application

ISO 9000

ISO 9000 is an international standard for quality systems. It is a British standard that is recognised worldwide. Companies that are registered can display the BSI symbol. In order to register, companies have to document their business procedures, prepare a quality manual and assess their quality management systems. They are assessed by an independent assessor. After obtaining the award, businesses are visited at regular intervals to ensure compliance. It is necessary that everyone in the organisation follows the processes outlined in the quality manual. Firms who have registered say that this has provided a range of benefits to the business. These include:

- less waste
- cost savings
- fewer mistakes
- increased efficiency
- improved competitiveness
- increased customer satisfaction
- increased profits
- most important of all is that ISO 9000 reasures the customer that quality standards have been established professionally.

Why is quality management important?

Quality is an important competitive issue. Where the consumer has choice, quality is vital. For a new business, effective quality management may mean the difference between success and failure. If the product or service cannot get a good reputation the business will not last long.

A reputation for good quality brings marketing advantages. A good-quality product will:

- generate a high level of repeat purchase, and therefore a longer product life cycle
- allow brand building and cross-marketing
- allow a price premium (this is often greater than any added costs of quality improvements; in other words, quality adds value – it generates additional profit)
- make products easier to place (retailers are more likely to stock products with a good reputation).

A-grade application

Cadbury fined £1 million over chocolate that made people ill

In spring 2006, 42 people became ill with salmonella food poisoning after eating Cadbury's chocolate. In June 2006 the company withdrew a million bars of its chocolate from sale. Later, the company was prosecuted for breaking food safety regulations. In 2007 it was fined £500,000 for putting unsafe chocolate on sale, and a further £500,000 for offences related to poor hygiene conditions at its Marlbrook factory.

The court case revealed that, in 2003, the company had decided to change its quality control standards. Before that, it would destroy any chocolate that tested positive for any level of salmonella cells – there was a **zero defects** policy. This led to a lot of wastage.

The change in policy allowed for a very low level of salmonella cells, assuming there would be no health risk. But the court was told that there is no such thing as a safe level for salmonella and that it could survive in chocolate for years.

The company apologised for what had happened and said 'We have spent over £20 million in changing our procedures to prevent this ever happening again.'

Source: Adapted from material which appeared on bbc.co.uk and in Scotsman, 14 July 2007

Table 43.1 Implications of poor product or service quality

Marketing costs	Business costs
Loss of sales	Scrapping of unsuitable goods
Loss of reputation	Reworking of unsatisfactory goods – costs of labour and materials
May have to price-discount	Lower prices for 'seconds'
May impact on other products in range	Handling complaints/warranty claims
Retailers may be unwilling to stock goods	Loss of consumer goodwill and repeat purchase

43.4 How can firms detect quality problems?

The ideal is to detect quality problems before they reach the customer. This can be done by:

- inspection of finished goods before sale – this has been the traditional method; it may be all goods or only a sample

- self-inspection of work by operatives – this is being used more as businesses recognise that quality needs to be 'everyone's business'

- statistical analysis within the production process – this can be used to ensure that specifications stay within certain limits; for example, Mars might set a target weight for 100 g bags of Maltesers of between 96 and 104 g (see Figure 43.1); only if the weight slips outside this range will an alarm indicator be triggered to warn that the specifications are not being met; staff could then stop the production line and readjust the machine to ensure that the correct weight is being given.

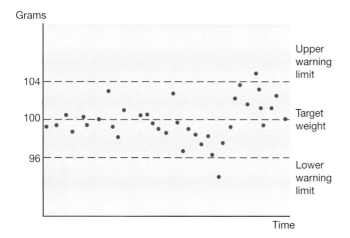

Figure 43.1 Actual weight of 100 g bags of Maltesers coming off the production line

Quality quotes

'Reducing the cost of quality is in fact an opportunity to increase profits without raising sales, buying new equipment, or hiring new people.' *Philip Crosby, American quality guru*

'Quality is remembered long after the price is forgotten.' *Gucci slogan*

'The only job security anybody has in this company comes from quality, productivity and satisfied customers.' *Lee Iacocca, successful boss of Chrysler Motors*

'Good management techniques are enduring. Quality control, for instance, was treated as a fad here, but it's been part of the Japanese business philosophy for decades. That's why they laugh at us.' *Peter Senge, US business author*

'Quality has to be caused, not controlled.' *Philip Crosby*

'Quality is our best assurance of customer allegiance, our strongest defence against foreign competition, and the only path to sustained growth and earnings.' *Jack Welch, General Electric chief*

How do businesses manage quality?

This depends on the size of the business. A small new business will be able to inspect every item and ensure that each customer is satisfied. As the business grows, keeping checks on quality needs to be more systematic. In large manufacturing businesses, quality control has traditionally been the responsibility of the production department. Most quality control processes were concentrated in the factory. These were intended to prevent faults leaving the factory. Today, firms are more likely to see quality as having product and service aspects.

There are four stages to quality management that apply to all businesses. These are prevention, detection, correction and improvement.

Prevention

This tries to avoid problems occurring. It requires thought and care at every stage:

● in the initial product design, to 'build in' quality

● in purchasing raw materials and components (i.e. not just trying to buy the cheapest supplies, but caring about quality)

● designing the factory layout to minimise production errors

● ensuring that all staff feel empowered to care about quality; at Toyota car plants, any factory worker with a quality concern can pull an alarm (*jidoka*) chord that stops the whole assembly line; this shows how seriously management takes quality.

Detection

This ensures that quality problems are spotted before they reach the customer. This has been the traditional emphasis of quality control. The use of electronic scanning has given firms better tools to detect faults.

Correction

This is not just about correcting faults. It is also about discovering why there is a problem. Once the problem is identified steps can be taken to ensure it does not recur.

Improvement

Customer expectations of quality are always changing. It is important that businesses seek to improve quality. Therefore staff need to be encouraged to put forward ways in which their jobs can be done better; the Japanese term *kaizen* (meaning continuous improvement) has become common in British manufacturing.

Programmes for managing quality

As the importance of quality for both marketing and cost control has been recognised, there has been a growth in initiatives to control and improve quality. Techniques for quality control, such as inspection and statistical control, continue. They have been supplemented by other policies aimed at controlling and improving quality. These include total quality management, quality control and quality assurance.

Total quality management

Total quality management (TQM) was introduced by American business guru W. Edwards Deming in the early 1980s. He worked with Japanese firms, and his techniques are said to be one of the reasons for the success of Japanese businesses. TQM is not a management tool: it is a philosophy. It is a way of looking at quality issues. It requires commitment from the whole organisation, not just the quality control department. The business considers quality in every part of the business process – from design right through to sales. TQM is about building-in rather than inspecting-out. It should draw closely on the Japanese experience with *kaizen*, set out on page 294.

Quality control

Quality control (QC) is the traditional way to manage quality, and is based on inspection. Workers get on with the task of producing as many units as possible, and quality control inspectors check that the output meets minimum acceptable standards. This might be done by checking every product – for example, starting up a newly built car and driving it from the production line to a storage area. Or it might be done by checking every 200th KitKat coming off the end of the factory's production line. If one KitKat is faulty, inspectors will check others from the same batch and – if concerned – may scrap the whole batch. The problem with this system is that faulty products can slip through, and it

Table 43.2 Pros and cons of TQM, QC and QA

	TQM	QC	QA
Pros	Should become deeply rooted into the company culture (e.g. product safety at a producer of baby car seats) Once all staff think about quality, it should show through from design to manufacture and after-sales service (e.g. at Lexus or BMW)	Can be used to guarantee that no defective item will leave the factory Requires little staff training, therefore suits a business with unskilled or temporary staff (as ordinary workers needn't worry about quality)	Makes sure the company has a quality system for every stage in the production process Customers like the reassurance provided by a badge such as 'ISO 9000'; they believe they will get a higher-quality service and may therefore be willing to pay more
Cons	Especially at first, staff sceptical of management initiatives may treat TQM as 'hot air'; it lacks the clear, concrete programme of QC or QA To get TQM into the culture of a business may be expensive, as it would require extensive training among all staff (e.g. all British Airways staff flying economy from Heathrow to New York)	Leaving quality for the inspectors to sort out may mean poor quality is built in to the product (e.g. clothes with seams that soon unpick) QC can be trusted when 100% of output is tested, but not when it is based on sampling; Ford used to test just 1 in 7 of its new cars; that led to quality problems	QA does not promise a high-quality product, only a high-quality, reliable process; this process may churn out OK products reliably QA may encourage complacency; it suggests quality has been sorted, whereas rising customer requirements mean quality should keep moving ahead

stops staff from producing the best quality: all they need focus on is 'good enough' to pass the checks. TQM is therefore a superior approach.

Quality assurance

Quality assurance (QA) is a system that assures customers that detailed systems are in place to govern quality at every stage in production. It would start with the quality-checking process for newly arrived raw materials and components. This includes schemes such as ISO 9000. Companies have to have in place a documented quality assurance system. This should be an effective quality system that operates throughout the company, and involves suppliers and subcontractors. The main criticism of QA is that it is a paper-based system and therefore encourages staff to tick boxes rather than care about quality.

43.7 Other quality initiatives

Continuous improvement (kaizen)

This is a system where the whole organisation is committed to making changes on a continual basis. The Japanese call it *kaizen*. It is an approach to doing business that looks for continual improvement in the quality of products, services, people and processes. In 1991 a book was published in Japan about Toyota, called *40 Years; 20 Million Ideas*. This alerted western business to the amazing ability of the Japanese car companies to get suggestions for improvement from their factory employees.

Six Sigma

A programme developed by America's General Electric Company, which aims to have fewer defective products than 1 per 300,000. To achieve this, staff are trained to become 'Green Belt' or 'Black Belt' quality experts. Although gimmicky, this has been followed widely by other companies.

Quality circles

A quality circle is a group of employees who meet together regularly for the purpose of identifying problems and recommending adjustments to the working processes. This is done to improve the product or process. It is used to address known quality issues such as defective products. It can also be useful for identifying better practices that may improve quality. In addition, it has the advantage of improving staff morale through employee involvement. It takes advantage of the knowledge of operators.

Zero defects

The aim is to produce goods and services with no faults or problems. This is vital in industries such as passenger aircraft production or the manufacture of surgical equipment.

Benchmarking

Benchmarking is a process of comparing a business with other businesses. Having identified the best, businesses attempt to bring their performance up to the level of the best, by adopting its practices.

Most of these initiatives rely on employee involvement. In addition to quality improvements and cost reductions, most businesses find that the initiatives in themselves deliver benefits. These include better working practices, improved employee motivation, increased focus on tasks and the development of team working.

Is quality expensive or free?

The traditional belief was that high quality was costly: in terms of materials, labour, training and checking systems. Therefore managements should beware of building too much quality into a product (the term given to this was 'over-engineered'). The alternative approach, put forward by the American writer Philip Crosby, is that 'quality is free'. The latter view suggests that getting things **right first time** can save a huge amount of time and money.

- The time required to make it work – quality initiatives take time. Workers may be away from their jobs while attending training or quality groups.

- Short-term versus long-term viewpoints – there may be a conflict between short-term costs and longer-term results. Shareholders may want returns today, but often quality initiatives require a long-term view. The investment will be a current cost. The benefits, however, may take some time to show. They may also be difficult to measure.

If quality control is to be effective it must balance the costs against the advantages; 100% quality is possible but it may make the product so expensive that it cannot be sold.

Issues For Analysis

When looking at quality issues in an exam question, the following are issues that need to be considered.

- The importance of quality to the business: this will depend on the type of business, the type of product or the service. It will also depend on the market in which the business is operating.

- Whether the firm has adopted the right approach to quality management: perhaps a firm using quality assurance should switch to TQM.

- Quality issues are often closely interwoven with other parts of the business. The role of the employee in quality control is an important issue. Interlinked with this are the changes in management styles and philosophies that come with many of the quality initiatives.

Remember that quality is not just about manufacturing, it is about the whole experience of contact with the business. A poor call centre could just as easily lose a sale as a faulty product.

Effective quality management

In recent years there has been a change in the emphasis on quality. The quality business has itself grown. The management section of any book shop will reveal several titles dedicated to quality management. The growth of initiatives such as TQM and continuous improvement goes on. The number of worldwide registrations for ISO 9000 increases by more than 25% a year. Not all of these are from British businesses – there has been a rapid rise in overseas registrations. With an increase in the international awareness of quality, British businesses will have to ensure that they continue to be competitive.

This growth in emphasis on quality has undoubtedly brought benefits to business. Increased quality brings rewards in the marketplace. Companies have also found that the initiatives, especially where they are people-based, have brought other advantages: changes in working practices have improved motivation and efficiency, and have reduced waste and costs.

This change in emphasis has not been without problems. The shift to a focus on the customer and the role of the employee could result in additional costs. Unless this results in increased profits, shareholders may feel that they are losing out. Some businesses have found that changing cultures is not easy. Resistance from workers and management has often caused problems.

Key terms

Benchmarking: comparing a firm's performance with best practice in the industry.

Competitiveness: the ability of a firm to beat its competitors (e.g. Galaxy is a highly competitive brand in the chocolate market).

Right first time: avoiding mistakes and therefore achieving high quality with no wastage of time or materials.

Trade-off: accepting less of one thing to achieve more of another (e.g. slightly lower quality in exchange for cheapness).

Zero defects: eliminating quality defects by getting things right first time.

Exercises

A. Revision questions

(35 marks; 35 minutes)

1 State two reasons why quality management is important. (2)

2 How important is quality to the consumer? (3)

3 Suggest two criteria customers might use to judge quality at:
(a) a budget-priced hotel chain (2)
(b) a Tesco supermarket (2)
(c) a McDonald's. (2)

4 Why has there been an increase in awareness of the importance of improving the quality of products? (3)

5 Give two marketing advantages that come from a quality reputation. (2)

6 What costs are involved if the firm has quality problems? (3)

7 Explain what is meant by the Gucci slogan shown among the 'Quality quotes' on page 292. (4)

8 What is total quality management? (4)

9 Outline two benefits of adopting quality circles to a clothing chain such as Topshop. (4)

10 Outline two additional costs that might be incurred in order to improve quality. (4)

B. Revision exercises

B1 Data response

Trac Parts

Trac Parts is a major manufacturer of parts for farm and construction machinery. It has been operating from a new centralised warehouse for four years. This year the company applied for ISO 9000. It gained accreditation. The main reason for applying was that several large customers had indicated that they would only deal with ISO 9000 companies when negotiating new contracts. The warehouse manager has been pleasantly surprised by the operational performance figures since accreditation:

- orders completed on time up from 75% to 84%
- errors in completing orders reduced by 40%
- average time from order receipt to dispatch reduced by two days.

Questions

(25 marks; 30 minutes)

1 What is ISO 9000? (3)

2 Why might a business want to become ISO 9000 approved? (4)

3 Examine the benefits to Trac Parts of the performance improvements identified in the text. (6)

4 In order to be accepted by ISO 9000, the firm will have had to introduce procedures to ensure that levels of quality are maintained. Using the four stages of quality control (prevention, detection, correction and improvement) examine the actions it might have taken. (12)

B2 Case study

Manufacturing defects – producer comparisons: PcNow

PcNow is a small computer manufacturer based in the East Midlands. It tailor-makes computers and accessories based on customers' own specifications. Although business grew steadily initially, it is now worried about falling sales. It believes it is losing sales to Japanese and American companies that have set up manufacturing facilities in Europe, as well as to other European and UK-based firms. An industry survey has produced data on industry levels of production defects. It has added its own figures and produced the chart shown below.

The firm realises that survival depends upon addressing the quality problems. It has decided to employ a quality manager, Cara Davenport, to address the issues. Her first suggestion is to get together workers from each department to discuss the problems and issues. Following a survey of the factory she has also suggested that the layout of the production facilities should be changed. This will be an expensive exercise, and management is reluctant to make the changes as they will require production to stop for a week and there will need to be investment in new equipment. The firm's weak cash flow position makes it hard for the owners to accept new capital spending. The other area that Cara has identified is a problem with one particular component. She has suggested that a new supplier should be found, or that she should work with the existing supplier to improve the quality of the component.

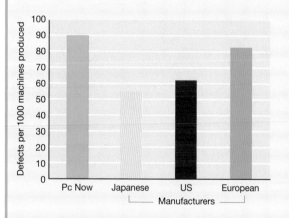

Figure 43.2 Manufacturing defects – producer comparisons

Questions

(40 marks; 50 minutes)

1a What does the chart show? (2)

1b What further data would help to make the bar chart more useful? (4)

2 From the case study, identify two reasons for the quality problems experienced by PcNow. (2)

3 What are the marketing implications for PcNow of the data in the bar chart? (8)

4 Outline the advantages PcNow might get from the discussion group formed to discuss the quality problems. (8)

5 How might Cara convince the firm's management to change the layout of the production facilities? (6)

6 Once these changes have been made, the firm needs to ensure that quality is maintained and improved. Discuss the implications for the firm of implementing a total quality management initiative. (10)

C. Essay questions

(40 marks each)

1 'Quality control is about building quality in, not inspecting it out.' Discuss.

2 Consider whether quality management is solely a matter for the production department.

3 To what extent is quality a major competitive issue in service businesses?

WORKING WITH SUPPLIERS

DEFINITION

Suppliers are other businesses that provide products or services to a firm. The relationship with suppliers is likely to have a critical impact on a firm. Operational success demands high-quality supplies delivered on time in the right quantities.

44.1 Key factors to consider when choosing suppliers

Cost

Cheaper supplies mean higher profit margins. The incentive to find a cheap supplier is huge for any firm; therefore, the price charged by a supplier will be a key factor in the relationship between a firm and its suppliers. Large businesses may be able to almost dictate prices to their suppliers. This is because the quantities they purchase may account for the whole output of the supplier, giving a huge amount of power to the buyer. However, for small businesses with limited purchasing power, the supplier may have the upper hand.

As a result of this, small businesses may be advised to shop around, looking for the cheapest supplier they can find. However, this may not always be the most sensible course of action – there are other important factors to consider when choosing suppliers.

Quality

There is frequently a trade-off between the price charged by suppliers and the quality of their offering. The cheapest supplier may be one with a poor reputation for the quality of its products or service. Choosing to use a supplier with quality problems is likely to lead to operational problems. Poor-quality supplies can lead to machinery breakdowns, along with poor-quality output. This can lead to problems with customer complaints, guarantee claims or reputation. Choosing the cheapest supplier may sow the seeds of long-term problems for a business.

Reliability

Supplies at the right price and of a high quality may be of little use if they arrive late. It is important that a supplier can offer reliability to a business. Failure to deliver on time can stop a manufacturing process or leave shop shelves empty. Suppliers' reliability will be easy to assess once a business has started working with them. However, a new business or a business sourcing new supplies may need to rely on word-of-mouth reputation to inform its choice. Larger firms may be able to impose certain penalties on suppliers who prove unreliable but, again, small businesses will be in a weaker position if trying to threaten a supplier.

Frequency

Depending on the type of business and the production system it uses, frequent deliveries may be needed from suppliers. Firms selling fresh produce will need to ensure that they are using suppliers that can supply and deliver frequently – probably a new batch each day. Similarly, a firm that uses a **just-in-time (JIT)** production system will need very frequent deliveries to feed its production system without it having to hold stock (Honda, for example, requires hourly deliveries of parts to its Japanese car factories). For firms such as these, it makes sense to look for a local supplier – they are far more likely to be willing to deliver with a greater level of frequency.

Flexibility

In a similar way to ensuring the right frequency of supplies, many firms will need to find a supplier with the capacity to cope with widely varying orders. Businesses selling products with erratic demand patterns, caused by changes in the weather or fashion, will need to find themselves suppliers that can meet their ever-changing needs. Probably the most common scenario is to ensure that suppliers have the spare capacity available to cope with sudden rush orders. In addition, some firms will need to find suppliers that can supply at the right time – perhaps night-time deliveries are needed for firms in congested town centres, or in areas where lorries are banned during the day. A key to supplier flexibility is a short **lead time** (i.e. there should not be too long a period between placing an order and receiving a delivery).

Payment terms

Most business transactions are on credit, not for cash. If Tesco wants to order 2000 cases of Heinz Beans, the bill is unlikely to be paid until 30 or more days after the goods have been delivered. This gives time for the goods to be sold, providing the cash to make it easy to pay the bill. Small business start-ups will struggle to get the same terms. A newly opened corner shop will not be given credit by Heinz. The supplier will want to be paid in cash until the new business has shown that it can survive and pay its bills. So a new small firm has to pay up front, placing extra strain on its cash flow. This should not be a problem as long as it has been anticipated (i.e. built in to its start-up cash flow forecast).

A-grade application

Going the extra mile(s) for quality

The Flying Fortress play centre in Sussex chose a supplier based on quality of product. The main feature of this indoor play centre for children is a huge aircraft-shaped climbing frame, supplied by a Canadian firm. Since the centre opened in 2005 it has proved hugely popular. This success was thanks to a supplier willing to provide a quality service as well as a quality product. The frame was constructed in Canada and transported to Britain. It proved a struggle to construct, threatening the big launch day for the play centre. The problem was solved when the supplier flew in more staff, who worked through the night to ensure the centrepiece was ready on time.

Source: http://www.flying-fortress.co.uk/home.htm

44.2 The role of suppliers in improving performance

Some businesses enjoy telling their shareholders how tough they are with their suppliers – after all, the lower the supply cost, the higher the profit. Many firms encourage competition between rival suppliers by threatening to go elsewhere if the terms are not what they want. This approach has been important in building the hugely profitable business of many high-street stores, which find cheap goods by negotiating toughly in Cambodia, China or the Philippines.

An alternative approach was followed in the past by Marks & Spencer, and today by car firms such as Toyota and Honda. These companies build long-term relationships with their suppliers, with the aim of working with, rather than against, them. There are many potential benefits from this approach, as discussed below.

A-grade application

'It's not just food...'

Following three months of falling food sales at the end of 2007, Marks & Spencer launched 'Project Genesis' in February 2008. Suppliers were informed that they would all have to cut 2% off their unit prices, and increase their 'contribution to marketing and advertising expenditure' from 0.5% to 1.5%. All at a time when food cost inflation was the highest it had been for years.

Many suppliers complained, but one took drastic action. In May Northern Foods announced that it would withdraw from its annual contract to provide £45 million of Italian ready meals to M&S. It preferred to close its Fenland factory with the loss of 730 jobs that to accept Marks & Spencer's new terms.

Another supplier was reported in *The Grocer* as saying: 'M&S is a third of my business but Project Genocide (sic) has set it back 10 to 15 years with suppliers and it's been extremely disruptive to our business...We will not support (product) development with M&S. If I were a shareholder I'd say it's destroying long-term value.'

Marks & Spencer itself claimed that most of its suppliers were happy with Project Genesis and that tough negotiations were part and parcel of business life. The risk, clearly, is that today's 2% will be the cost of long-term reluctance by suppliers to give their best, most innovative ideas to M&S. If so, Project Genesis will have been very short-sighted.

Working together on new product development

Developing new products involves many considerations. One of these will be how the product is to be manufactured, what materials will be used and what properties will be needed. Meanwhile, launching a new product will require careful production planning to ensure that consumers can get hold of the new product that the marketing department has told them about. The result is that suppliers have a major part to play in developing and launching new products. Many firms have recognised the importance of this and work hand in hand with their suppliers from the very earliest stages of developing a new product.

Flexibility

A strong relationship with a supplier should mean it is willing to make special deliveries if a business is running low on stock. A strong relationship may also allow some flexibility on payment. A toy shop may be struggling for cash in the months leading up to Christmas, so a trusting supplier may accept a delay in payment. This could be the lifeline required for the small firm. However, no supplier is likely to be able to sustain this generosity for a long period.

Sharing information to improve the efficiency of the supply chain

Large businesses with sophisticated IT systems have direct links between their cash tills and their suppliers. Cadbury knows at any hour of the day how many Creme Eggs are selling at Tesco. This enables Cadbury to plan its production levels (e.g. pushing up output if sales are proving brighter than expected). The supermarket can even allow Cadbury to make the decisions on how much stock to produce and deliver on the basis of the information it is receiving.

Small grocers use the same laser scanning software at their tills, but it would be rare for a small business to have a direct electronic link with a supplier. This means the shopkeeper has to make the purchasing decisions, or go to a wholesaler to buy the goods, which is much less efficient than the electronic systems of the big companies.

Issues For Analysis

- Although firms are likely to try to build a long-term relationship with their suppliers, there will be times when a business will consider changing supplier. This is an issue that has a number of aspects that need consideration, in addition to the standard factors covered earlier. There will be an existing relationship with the current supplier and this may bring advantages that would not be available with a brand new supplier. Meanwhile, the cliché that 'the grass is always greener on the other side' may be a factor in the motive for changing.

- When analysing any choice between suppliers, be sure to consider the consequences of the differences between them. Failure to consider consequences will lose analysis marks. Think through the consequences in your answers with lines of argument such as 'poor-quality materials may lead to poor-quality output, which could lead to customer disappointment, which will hit reputation, probably damaging future sales'.

A-grade application
Why do it yourself if suppliers can help?

Wickes is a DIY retailer that has worked hard to develop closer relations with its suppliers. The company invested in improved IT systems to enable better transfer of information between retail outlets and suppliers. Store-level sales and stock data are sent daily to suppliers to allow them to improve their production planning, ensuring the right amount is available to be delivered to each Wickes store. The system has also enhanced the role played by suppliers in the planning and development of new own-brand products for the stores. In the future, the group is hoping to move towards a system where store stock levels are actually monitored and managed by the suppliers themselves.

44.3 Working with suppliers
an evaluation

Evaluative themes relating to suppliers will centre on judgements that firms make as to which supplier to choose. This unit has covered a range of factors that need to be considered, but effective evaluation will, as always, come from a willingness to appreciate which factors are most important for the particular business being considered. A retailer that sells high volumes of cheap products at low prices may be right to compromise on quality to use the cheapest suppliers. The reverse would be the case for a firm with a luxury image or targeting socially conscious consumers. Take some time before putting pen to paper to work out which factors will be most important for the firm mentioned in the question.

Another judgement that should improve your answers is who has the most power in the relationship between company and supplier. Larger firms tend to have more power – indeed there are concerns over the way Britain's huge supermarket chains treat small farmers. However, size may not be the only factor to consider. A supplier with a patent on a particular component will need to be dealt with even if it fails to prove 100% reliable. Evaluation will shine through if a candidate judges effectively where power lies in the specific business relationship featured in an exam question.

Key terms

Just-in-time (JIT): ordering supplies so that they arrive 'just in time' (i.e. just when they are needed); this means operating without reserves of materials or components held 'just in case' they are needed.

Lead time: the time the supplier takes between receiving an order and delivering the goods.

44.4 Workbook

Exercises

A. Revision questions

(30 marks; 30 minutes)

1 Explain why the cheapest supplier may not be the best choice. (4)

2 Identify two businesses for which daily deliveries may be absolutely crucial. (2)

3 Briefly explain two problems that may arise when a firm uses a supplier with poor levels of quality. (4)

4 Describe why attractive credit terms from a supplier will be particularly useful for a new business. (4)

5 Outline two reasons why a firm might choose to change its supplier of an existing component. (4)

6 Examine one benefit a mobile phone shop might receive from encouraging several suppliers to compete with each other for every month's order of components. (4)

7 What benefits might the mobile phone shop miss out on by not building a long-term relationship with its suppliers? (4)

8 Describe how a car manufacturer such as Ford might benefit from including its component suppliers in the development process when designing a new car. (4)

B. Revision exercises

B1 Data response

Doll's Choice

KMH Ltd is a small manufacturer of children's toys. Having developed a brand new child's doll, it is considering which supplier to use for the plastic used in moulding the doll (see table). Having started up only 12 months ago, the firm has done well and is eagerly anticipating the Christmas rush that will begin soon. The management hopes that the new doll will be a best-seller this Christmas.

Supplier	A	B	C
Price per unit (£s)	3.20	3.50	3.65
Reject rate (per 000 products delivered)	28	18	5
Credit terms (days)	0	60	30
Lead time (days)	7	1	4

Questions

(20 marks; 25 minutes)

1 Which supplier offers the best:
  (a) quality
  (b) lead time
  (c) credit terms (3)

2 Explain why lead time is important. (5)

3 Which supplier should the firm choose, and why? (12)

B2 Data response

Crepe Heaven

Carla Turner set up Crepe Heaven in early 2007. As the only creperie in her local area, she attracted some attention with the launch of her small café specialising in French pancakes. Business was more brisk than she had expected and she often found herself popping out to the local supermarket to buy extra ingredients halfway through the day. The supermarket was more expensive than her catering suppliers, but Carla found it hard to predict sales in the early months of the business. Her stock of eggs, milk and fruit for fillings had a very limited life and the last thing she wanted to do was buy ingredients she would have to throw away.

Having been trading successfully for six months, Carla had an encouraging letter from the catering supplier she had been using, telling her that it was now willing to make an afternoon

44.4 Workbook

delivery if she needed extra supplies. This lowered her running costs – just what was needed as the interest payments on her bank loan were now biting hard into her cash flow. She also realised that she would need a second crepe-making machine if she was to make sure that waiting times during busy periods were kept to a minimum. She contacted the French supplier of her first machine, to be told that it would be two months before they could deliver and install the model she wanted. Furthermore she would have to pay cash on delivery – something she could ill afford.

Shopping around on the internet, she found a supplier in America who could deliver in a week. This was great news as she knew that some customers took one look at her peak-period queues and headed off to other cafés in the area. She was also grateful that the supplier was willing to accept a small deposit on order followed by 60 days' interest-free credit. This seemed perfect and she placed her order immediately.

The delivery went smoothly, though she had some trouble installing the new machine as it was rather different to her existing one. Worse was to come some months later, as the new machine started smoking when in use for more than a couple of hours. The American supplier was unhelpful, insisting that the fault must have been due to Carla failing to install the machine properly. The next few months were tough for Carla, as she struggled to get her money back from the US supplier. Fortunately, the shop remained popular and within six months she replaced the second machine with one from her original supplier.

Questions

(30 marks; 35 minutes)

1 Explain why Carla tended to under-order ingredient supplies in the early days of the business. (5)

2 Explain which two factors may have been most important to Carla when originally choosing her ingredient supplier. (6)

3 Analyse the benefits to Carla of choosing the American supplier for her second crepe machine. (8)

4 To what extent does the case study support the view that building a long-term relationship with a supplier is a better approach than shopping around for 'the best deal'? (11)

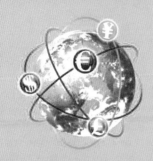

Unit 45

STOCK CONTROL

DEFINITION

Stock control is the management process that makes sure stock is ordered, delivered and handled in the best possible way. An efficient stock control system will balance the need to meet customer demand against the cost of holding stock.

45.1 Purchasing

Manufacturing businesses rely on stocks being bought in from other firms. These stocks can either be in the form of raw materials or components. They are part of the inputs that manufacturing firms process into outputs.

The purchasing function acts as a service to the rest of the business. Its main objective is to meet the needs of those running the internal operations of the business. In a factory, inefficient purchasing may lead (in the extreme) to a shutdown if key materials or components have not turned up when needed. In a retail store, poor purchasing could mean empty shelves or an over-full stockroom. In order to avoid this, the purchasing function of a business will try to ensure that:

- a sufficient quantity of stocks is available at all times ...

- ... but not so many as to represent a waste of resources

- stocks are of the right quality

- stocks are available where they are needed in the factory

- the price paid for stocks is as competitive as possible

- good relationships are built up with suppliers.

When purchasing stocks, a business must ask a range of questions about potential suppliers. The main thing that the buyer must be convinced of is that the supplier can meet its requirements on quality and on price.

- Quality can be checked through samples and/or a visit to the supplier's factory to inspect methods and conditions. If the supplier has achieved its ISO 9000

certificate this means it has an effective quality assurance system.

- The price may be negotiated, especially if the buyer is purchasing in bulk or is a regular customer. A lower price may be agreed, or longer credit periods established.

In addition, the buyer will have to consider other questions before deciding which supplier to use, such as:

- Will the supplier be consistent, supplying the quantity and quality needed on time, every time?

- Is the financial position of the firm sufficiently safe to guarantee as far as is possible its future survival?

- If the needs of the buyer change, can the supplier change quickly to meet demand?

- Can the supplier expand if the buyer's demand grows?

In the past, firms tended to focus on short-term buying decisions based on the lowest quoted price. Today's supplies might be from XZ Ltd; tomorrow's from PQ & Co. Companies such as Waitrose and Toyota took a different approach. They aimed to form an effective and lasting partnership with suppliers. In this way both businesses benefit from the relationship. More and more British companies are following this lead.

The purchasing department will need to take a strategic decision on how best to operate. Key questions will consider:

- whether the firm should place large orders occasionally, or small orders frequently

- whether the firm should accept lower-quality stocks at a lower cost

- whether the firm should rely on one supplier or use several.

45.2 Types of stock

Manufacturing firms hold three types of stock. These are:

- *raw materials and components* – these are the stocks the business has purchased from outside suppliers; they will be held by the firm until it is ready to process them into its finished output

- *work in progress* – at any given moment, a manufacturing firm will have some items it has started to process, but that are incomplete; this may be because they are presently moving through the production process; it may be because the firm stores unfinished goods to give it some flexibility to meet consumer demand

- *finished goods* – once a product is complete, the firm may keep possession of it for some time; this could be because it sells goods in large batches or no buyer has yet come in for the product; for producers of seasonal goods, such as toys, most of the year's production may be building stock in preparation for the pre-Christmas sales rush – this process is known as producing for stock, or stockpiling.

The firm's costs increase if it holds more stock. However, this needs to be set against the **opportunity cost** of keeping too little stock, such as not being able to meet customer demand. One theory is that a firm should try to keep as little stock as possible at all times. This system, known as just-in-time, is looked at in Unit 46.

The firm must keep control of all the different types of stock to ensure that it runs at peak efficiency.

45.3 Stock management

Stock management is the way a firm controls the stock within the business. If the purchasing function has been efficient, the business will receive the right quantity and quality of stock at the right time. However, once the stocks are inside the firm, they must be handled and used correctly. This is to make sure they are still in peak condition when they come to be used in the production process.

Stock rotation

Wherever possible, a firm will want to use its oldest stock first. This means that stocks do not deteriorate, go past their sell-by date or become obsolete. Stock can become obsolete if new specifications are used or if the product of which they were a part is no longer manufactured. By using a system of **stock rotation**, the firm will ensure that the risks of stock going out of date are minimised. Supermarkets, for example, should always put new stock at the back of the shelf to encourage shoppers to take the older stock first. The principle behind stock rotation is first-in-first-out (FIFO). This is to avoid a situation in which new stock is used first, leaving older stock to become unusable at the back of a shelf or a warehouse.

Stock wastage

This is the loss of stock in either a production or service process. Any wastage is a cost to the firm as it has paid for stock it will not use.

In a manufacturing process, the main causes of stock wastage are:

- materials being wasted, such as scraps of cloth being thrown away as offcuts from a dress maker; this can be minimised by careful planning – perhaps helped by computer-aided design (CAD) software

- the reworking of items that were not done correctly first time – good training and a highly motivated staff are the best ways to avoid this

- defective products that can not be put right, which will often be sold off as seconds or damaged goods.

For a retailer, the main causes of stock wastage will be:

- products becoming damaged due to improper handling or storage

- stealing from the shop, whether by customers or staff

- products such as food passing their sell-by dates.

In all these cases, sound management and administrative techniques could reduce or even eliminate the problem of stock wastage. Any wastage is a cost to the firm, and procedures need to be set up to prevent such losses.

However, it is important that the cost of the processes set up is not more than the money being saved by them. Cost-effective measures are needed to maximise the returns to the firm.

45.4 Stock control charts

One way in which a firm analyses its stock situation is by using stock control charts. These line graphs look at the level of stock in the firm over time. Managers will be able to see from these charts how stock levels have changed during the period, and will be able to note any unusual events with which they may need to be concerned.

A typical stock control graph will look like that shown in Figure 45.1. On this chart there are four lines, which represent the levels described below.

● *Stock levels:* this line shows how stock levels have changed over this time period. As the stock is used up, the level of stock gradually falls from left to right. When a delivery is made, however, the stock level leaps upwards in a vertical line. The greater the rise in the vertical line, the more stock has been delivered.

● *Maximum stock level:* this shows the largest amount that the firm is either willing or able to hold in stock. It may show the physical size of the warehouse and be the maximum because no more can be taken in. It may also, however, be set by management on the basis that (a) it is the most that can be used by the production process, (b) it is the most that can be kept to ensure sell-by dates are not missed, or (c) it is sufficient, given the time between deliveries and the rate of usage.

● *Re-order level:* this is a 'trigger' quantity. When stocks fall to this level a new order will be sent in to the supplier. The re-order level is reached some time before the delivery (shown by the vertical part of the stock level line). This is because the supplier will need some 'lead time' to process the order and make the delivery.

● *Minimum stock level:* this is also known as the **buffer stock**. The firm will want to keep a certain minimum level of stock for reasons of safety – it will have something to fall back on if an order does not arrive on time or if stock is used up particularly quickly, perhaps due to a sudden increase in demand.

Diagrams such as this, showing a neat and regular pattern to stock holding, will not happen in reality. Orders may arrive late and may not always be of the correct quantity. The rate of usage is unlikely to be constant. The slope of the stock level line may be steeper, showing more stock being used than normal, or shallower, showing a slower use of stock.

However, as a basis for analysing stock levels over time, stock control charts such as these give managers a clear picture of how things have changed, and shows them what questions need to be asked. For example, they may show that stocks are constantly arriving late. Managers would then know to ask if suppliers were taking longer than the agreed lead time, or if orders were not being placed when the re-order level of stock was reached.

Figure 45.2 shows a more realistic stock control graph. It is based on actual sales of Nestlé Lion Bars at a newsagent in south-west London over a three-month period.

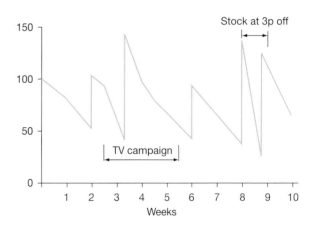

Figure 45.2 Weekly sales of Lion Bars at one newsagent

45.5 The costs of stock

The initial cost of purchasing stock is only one of the costs associated with a firm's stock holding (**stock holding costs**). A firm can hold too much or too little stock. Both cases will add to the costs of the firm.

Too much stock can lead to:

● *opportunity cost* – holding the firm's wealth in the

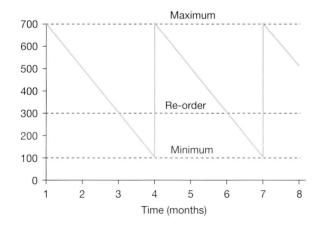

Figure 45.1 Stock control chart

form of stock prevents it using its capital in other ways, such as investing in new machinery or research and development on a new product; by missing out on such opportunities the firm may put itself at a disadvantage compared with competitors

● *cash flow problems* – holding the firm's wealth as stock may cause problems if it proves slow moving; there may be insufficient cash to pay suppliers

● *increased storage costs* – as well as the physical space needed to hold the stock, there may be increases in associated costs such as labour within the warehouse, heating and lighting or refrigeration; stocks need to be insured against fire and theft, the cost of which will increase as more stocks are held

● *increased finance costs* – if the capital needs to be borrowed, the cost of that capital (the interest rate) will be a significant added annual overhead

● *increased stock wastage* – the more stock is held, the greater the risk of it going out of date or deteriorating in condition.

This does not, however, mean that the business is free to carry very low stocks. Unless it can confidently run just-in-time systems (see below) the firm may well face increased costs from holding too little stock as well. These could include the following.

● Workers and machines standing idle as there are not enough materials or components to allow the process to operate. This costs the business in lost output and wages being paid for no work. It could also cost the business at a later date if extra overtime is needed to make up for the production lost.

● Lost orders, as customers needing a specific delivery date that cannot be met will go elsewhere.

● Orders not being fulfilled on time, leading to worsening relations with customers. This could lead to future orders being lost as customers turn to more reliable suppliers. The firm may also have to pay customers financial compensation for missing delivery dates.

● The loss of the firm's reputation and any goodwill it has been able to build up with its customers.

The total cost of stocks to the firm will therefore be a combination of these factors. As the level of stock grows, the costs of holding that stock will increase, but the costs of not holding stock will decrease. The cost of holding stock will therefore look like Figure 45.3.

For a firm, the optimum level of stock to hold will be where the total costs of holding stock are the lowest.

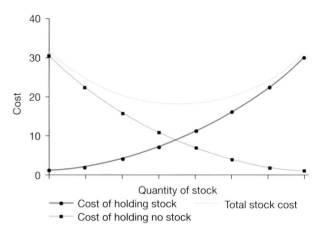

Figure 45.3 Cost of stockholding

A further consideration to the quantity of stocks being held is how much stock to order at any one time. Large orders need only be made a few times to keep sufficient stock levels, while smaller orders will mean that they have to be placed more regularly. The arguments for both of these are shown in Table 45.1.

Table 45.1 Large vs smaller orders

Advantages of many smaller orders	Advantages of few large orders
Less storage space needed	Economies from buying in bulk
More flexible to changing needs	Avoids chance of running out of stock
Less stock wastage	Prevents machines and workers standing idle

45.6 IT and stock control

Stock control is all about the efficient handling of information about current and required stocks. Information technology (IT) can handle large quantities of data quickly and easily. Therefore the use of IT can make the task of stock control both easier and more accurate.

Most businesses will hold records of their stock on large databases. Stock control systems exist that allow these databases to be updated instantaneously as stock leaves the warehouse or goes through the checkout.

Traditionally, the systems that achieved this were barcode scanners, which read the details of the stock coming in or going out. Today there is a big switch to RFID (radio frequency identification) systems, which allow the stock to be traced to exactly where it is being held within a warehouse. Either way, the data can be held on the warehouse computer system to keep an accurate, up-to-the-second picture of how much stock is held at any given time. The need to re-order stock can be identified by the system, and the order sent automatically from the warehouse IT system to the supplier's IT system. This largely does away with the need for human involvement in the stock control process.

Stock control systems such as these add to the ability of managers to analyse stock movements. They should make it possible for more accurate decisions to be made on what stock to hold and in what quantities. Supermarkets, for example, make much use of IT as the basis for decisions about stocks. Through electronic data interchange (EDI) links, manufacturers can even see the sales level of their products at supermarket checkouts. This enables them to anticipate the orders the supermarkets will soon be placing. Without such instant information, strategies such as just-in-time would be very difficult.

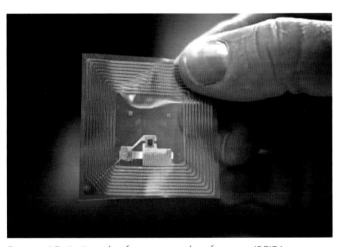

Figure 45.4 A radio frequency identification (RFID) tag

45.7 Just-in-time

Just-in-time (JIT) is a system of stock control that has become popular in UK firms over the last couple of decades. The basis of the system is that the costs of holding stock should be unacceptable to a firm, so the level of stock held ought to be as small as possible. In other words, JIT is the attempt to operate with a zero buffer stock. At the same time, a system must be developed so that the costs and risks of running out of stock are avoided by the firm.

A firm adopting the JIT system will attempt to do this by developing a close working relationship with

suppliers. By involving suppliers closely with the business, and by demonstrating the benefits to both the supplier and purchaser, it should be possible for both parties to work together for the common good.

The supplier will be required under the JIT system to make frequent deliveries to the purchaser as and when goods are needed. A delivery that arrives too early is as much a cost to the purchaser as a delivery arriving late. The purchaser will have to be certain that the deliveries will be made just in time for the goods to be used.

The advantages and disadvantages of a JIT system are listed in Table 45.2.

Establishing a JIT system is not something that can or should be achieved overnight. The risks of running out of stock are too great. Figure 45.4 shows how a firm might set out to achieve a JIT system in a carefully planned way. The diagram shows five phases, after which the firm would intend to keep going with phases six, seven and thereafter, until it could get as close as possible to zero buffer stock. The five phases are as follows.

A-grade application
RFID at Marks & Spencer

Marks & Spencer (M&S) began the phased rollout of item-level radio frequency identification (RFID) tags in 2007 following more than a year of extensive testing of the technology. The retailer planned to increase the number of stores that tag individual clothing items – including men's suits and women's casual wear – from 42 to 120 by Spring 2008.

James Stafford, head of clothing RFID at M&S, said the company would also expand the number of clothing departments using the technology from 6 to 13 to improve efficiency and customer service. 'Stock accuracy has improved, and stores and customers have commented on the more consistent availability of sizes in the pilot departments,' he said.

The retailer began tagging clothing, including men's suits, trousers and jackets, and women's suits, casual trousers and skirts, in 2006. Last year it extended the trial to include its autumn and winter range, bringing the total number of tags used to more than 35 million. The tags allow staff to carry out stocktaking more efficiently by passing an RFID reader over goods to determine what products need to be replaced. This has led to improved sales through greater product availability.

AMR Research analyst Nigel Montgomery said the full rollout will provide M&S with a significant competitive advantage.

Source: Adopted from an article by Dave Friedlos, *Computing*, 16 November 2006

Table 45.2 The advantages and disadvantages of using a JIT system

> ## Advantages of using JIT
> - Improves the firm's liquidity
> - The costs of holding stocks are reduced
> - Storage space can be converted to a more productive use
> - Stock wastage and stock rotation become lesser issues for management
> - Response times to changing demands are speeded up as new components can be ordered instantly
>
> ## Disadvantages of using JIT
> - Any break in supply causes immediate problems for the purchaser
> - The costs of processing orders may be increased
> - The purchaser's reputation is placed in the hands of the external supplier

1 The firm orders 20,000 units of stock to arrive every third week.

2 Suppliers are asked to move to weekly deliveries, therefore only one-third of the quantity is ordered.

3 As phase two has proved successful, there is no longer any need for such a high buffer stock. Stock levels are allowed to fall to a new, lower level.

4 With phase three complete, the firm now moves to deliveries twice a week. Therefore the order level is halved.

5 The suppliers have proved reliable enough to allow the buffer to be cut again …

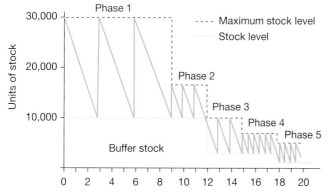

Figure 45.5 Step-by-step progress towards JIT stock control

Issues For Analysis

- Stock is an important issue for some firms; a vital one for others. Greengrocers with small turnovers cannot survive, because slow-moving stock means poor-quality fruit and vegetables. For many firms, poor stock control leads to increased theft, rising costs and a threat to survival.

- As with many aspects of management, there is no single answer to the question of how best to manage a firm's stock. Different-sized firms in different industries will have widely different stock control needs. JIT may be ideal in one context but inappropriate elsewhere.

- The use of IT as a means of stock control has, until recently, been restricted mainly to large firms needing to control masses of stock in different locations. While the applications are being made available in forms suitable for smaller firms now, it is questionable whether or not such firms are able to use the technology efficiently.

- How will the arrival of internet marketing (home shopping) affect decisions by retailers about stock levels? Will they feel they have to make greater efforts to ensure they have exactly the right size/colour combination for every customer? In other words, should they increase the breadth and depth of their stock levels?

45.8 Stock control

an evaluation

Stock control is at the heart of many business operations. For retailers such as Zara, Topshop and Primark, the desire for a constant flow of new, fashion-orientated stock means huge pressure to clear away 'old' stock (which may be only four weeks old). Therefore a JIT approach is ideal, with little or no buffer stock. In some cases it is quite helpful commercially to run out of stock, if it means that, next Saturday, shoppers come earlier to make sure they can get the must-have item. The only thing that will not work is to go to a clothes shop and see tired, over-fingered stock that's so last year.

To make a just-in-time approach work requires close collaboration between purchasers and suppliers. The purchasing firm needs to bring the supplier into discussions on product development. Advice may be needed on components and materials as well as to gain the supplier's commitment to the new project. This Japanese way of doing business has taken off in Britain, making it much easier to provide customers with what they need.

Yet there are still firms that believe mass production plus high stock levels is the only way to be efficient. If that's what Cadbury says about making chocolate – even the highly seasonal Creme Egg – it would be arrogant to argue. So it is always important to keep an open mind about what is right for a specific company. There are few right answers in business – only answers that are right with application to particular circumstances.

Key terms

Buffer stock: the desired minimum stock level held by a firm just in case something goes wrong.
Opportunity cost: the cost of missing out on the next best alternative when making a decision (or when committing resources).
Stock holding costs: the overheads resulting from the stock levels held by a firm.
Stock rotation: the administrative and physical processes to ensure that older stock is used first.

Exercises

A. Revision questions

(35 marks; 35 minutes)

1 Why may it be important to maintain good relationships with suppliers? (3)

2 State the three main categories of stock. (3)

3 What is meant by 'internal customers'? (3)

4 How would stock rotation help a firm manage its resources better? (4)

5 Sketch a typical stock control chart. (6)

6 State three costs associated with holding too much stock. (3)

7 Give three costs associated with running out of stock. (3)

8 What is meant by just-in-time stock control? (4)

9 Explain the meaning of the phrase in the text 'The purchaser's reputation is placed in the hands of the external supplier.' (3)

10 Why is stock control of particular importance to a greengrocer? (3)

B. Revision exercises

B1 Revision activities

(35 marks; 40 minutes)

1 A firm sells 40,000 units a month. It receives monthly deliveries. Its maximum stock level is 50,000 and minimum (buffer) stock is 10,000. After two months (eight weeks) it decides to switch to monthly deliveries.
   (a) Sketch a 12-week stock control graph to illustrate this situation. Assume the firm starts the first week with 50,000 units of stock. (10)
   (b) What short-term problems may the firm face in switching to weekly deliveries? (6)
   (c) Consider the long-term benefits that may result from the change. (9)

2 Sketch a graph to show the impact upon stock levels of a downturn in demand for a product for which a company has a non-cancellable fixed order from its suppliers. Fully label the graph to explain *what* happens *when*. (10)

B2 Data response

Ann Brennan established a bakery in Wigan in the early 1990s. Although the firm is profitable, Ann is considering the introduction of modern techniques to help the company develop. In particular, she wishes to introduce information technology to improve communications between her five shops and the central bakery, and to help her manage her stock of raw materials more effectively.

Stocks of raw materials at the business are currently purchased in response to usage. For example, the bakery uses on average 500 kilos of flour per week. The most Ann wishes to hold at any time is 2000 kilos. She would be worried if the stock fell below 500 kilos. An order takes one week to arrive, so Ann always re-orders when her stock falls to 1000 kilos.

Questions

(30 marks; 35 minutes)

1 What is meant by the following terms?
   (a) Re-order level
   (b) Buffer stock
   (c) Lead time (6)

2a Draw a stock control graph for flour at Brennan's Bakery over a six-week period. (6)

2b Draw a second graph showing the situation if twice the normal amount of flour was used in the fourth week. (6)

3 How might information technology be used to improve communication between Ann's shops and between the bakery and its suppliers? (6)

4 Assess the effect of a 'stock-out' on Brennan's Bakery. (6)

B3 Data response

Is JIT always the best option?

Executives at mattress maker Sealy Corp. learned the hard way in 2005 how much a natural disaster could disrupt a supply chain. That's when hurricanes Katrina and Rita battered the Gulf Coast and caused major damage to petrochemical processing facilities that supply Sealy with a raw material called TDI, which is used to manufacture the foam found in most of Sealy's bedding products.

This was bad news for a company that takes pride in its just-in-time (JIT) operations. In its company statement, Sealy notes that most bedding orders are shipped to warehouses within 72 hours of receipt. With a foam shortage at hand, the company issued a notice in October 2005 acknowledging that production delays were imminent.

Similar stories were reported shortly after the September 11th terrorist attacks in 2001, and doomsday predictions of health epidemics, war and more hurricanes continue to keep many manufacturers on their toes.

But, for the most part, analysts and manufacturers contend the benefits of JIT outweigh the risks. Research published in the *IndustryWeek*/Manufacturing Performance Institute 2006 Census of Manufacturers supports Adelberg's contention, with 43.4% of 758 manufacturers responding, saying they use JIT supplier deliveries to manage stock levels.

Preparing for the unpredictable

The typical approach manufacturers take when preparing for the unexpected is to carry some safety stock of the top-selling items. Adding buffer stock may stray somewhat from pure JIT, but it provides manufacturers with some leeway if something goes wrong.

Some manufacturers, like Toyota, don't have to worry too much about delivery problems during crisis situations because their suppliers are nearby. Toyota opened a Tundra plant in San Antonio last autumn in an industrial park that houses 21 of its suppliers.

Understanding demand

Aside from acts of nature and war, manufacturers who want to be successful with JIT need to

prepare for demand spikes.* Both Nintendo and Sony Corp. had out-of-stock issues with their popular video game systems after the past holiday season. 'Just-in-time is OK, but if all of a sudden there is a surge in demand, you may not have the flexibility available to meet the demand,' says one noted business analyst.

* A demand spike is a sudden, unexpected upsurge in demand.

Source: adapted from *IndustryWeek*, 1 June 2007

Questions

(30 marks; 35 minutes)

1 Examine two possible impacts upon Sealy beds of its October 2005 warning to customers of production delays. (6)

2 If less than half of US manufacturers were using JIT in 2006, how might the majority have been managing their stock ordering and management? (5)

3a Explain the meaning of the term 'buffer stock'. (4)

3b Explain one benefit to a business from operating JIT with a zero buffer stock level. (5)

4 Discuss whether a JIT approach to stock management is appropriate to a business with demand 'spikes', such as Nintendo. (10)

C. Essay questions

(40 marks each)

1 'The use of information technology makes stock control an automatic function, requiring little input from human beings.' Assess this statement.

2 Evaluate whether a medium-sized retailer such as Next would be wise to move to just-in-time stock control.

3 Assess the view that, with today's information technology, no firm ought to experience stock control problems.

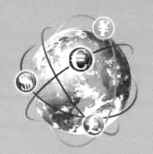

LEAN MANAGEMENT

Lean management is a philosophy that aims to produce more using less, by eliminating all forms of waste ('waste' being defined as anything that does not add value to the final product).

46.1 Introduction

The rise of the Japanese approach to production has been unstoppable in recent years. **Just-in-time** (JIT) and *kaizen* have been widely written about, but the underlying philosophy has sometimes been overlooked. The total approach has been termed 'lean production', though its ideas have been spread more generally to include service businesses as well, hence the term lean management (or lean thinking). It is based upon a combined focus by management and workers on minimising the use of the key business resources: materials, manpower, capital, floor space and time. The main components of lean management are:

● just-in-time (JIT)

● total quality management (TQM)

● time-based management.

Toyota and the origins of lean production

In most industries, new ideas and methods tend to emerge during a period of crisis when old ideas no longer seem to work. The motor industry is no different. The inspiration came from Eiji Toyoda's three-month visit to Ford's Rouge plant in Detroit in 1950. Eiji's family had set up the Toyota Motor Company in 1937. Now, in Japan's situation of desperate shortages after the Second World War, he hoped to learn from Ford. On his return, Eiji reported that the mass production system at the Rouge plant was riddled with *muda* (the Japanese term for wasted effort, materials and time). By analysing the weaknesses of mass production, Toyota was the first company to develop lean production.

Toyota realised that mass production could only be fully economic if identical products could be produced continuously. Yet Henry Ford's statement that 'they can have any colour they want ... as long as it's black' was no longer acceptable to customers. Mass production was also very wasteful, as poor-quality production led to a high reject rate at the end of the production line.

Toyota's solution was to design machines that could be used for many different operations – flexible production. Mass producers took a whole day to change a stamping machine from producing one part to making another. Toyota eventually reduced this time to just three minutes, and so simplified the process that factory line workers could do it without any help from engineers! This carried with it the advantage of flexibility. If buying habits changed in the USA, Ford could not react quickly, because each production line was dedicated to producing a particular product in a particular way. Toyota's multi-purpose machines could adapt quickly to a surge of demand for, for example, open-top cars or right-hand-drive models.

By a process of continuous refinement, Toyota developed the approach to:

● maximise the input from staff

● focus attention upon the quality of supplies and production

● minimise wasted resources in stock through just-in-time.

By the 1990s, the company was able to turn the spotlight onto product development – to shorten the time between product conception and product launch.

46.2 The benefits of lean production

Lean production:

- creates higher levels of labour productivity, therefore it uses less labour

- requires less stock, less factory space and less capital equipment than a mass producer of comparable size; the lean producer therefore has substantial cost advantages over the mass producer

- creates substantial marketing advantages – first, it results in far fewer defects, improving quality and reliability for the customer; second, lean production requires half the engineering hours to develop a new product; this means that the lean producer can develop a vast range of products a mass producer cannot afford to match.

A-grade application
General Motors fighting back?

In 1998 it took the American car maker General Motors 50% more hours than Toyota to make a car. This poor productivity caused General Motors to make a loss on every car it sold. To survive, General Motors had to close the productivity gap with Toyota.

In 2006 General Motors announced that it had reduced the productivity gap with Toyota to just under 14%. How did it achieve this turnaround? The main change that brought success was to find more reliable suppliers, even if they were slightly more expensive than existing suppliers. General Motors recognised that a failed delivery can lead to stoppages on the production line, which in turn holds back productivity.

46.3 The components of lean management

Lean people management

Lean producers reject the waste of human talent involved in narrow, repetitive jobs. They believe in empowerment, team working and job enrichment. Problem solving is not just left to specialist engineers. Employees are trained in preventative maintenance, to spot when a fault is developing and correct it before the production line has to stop. If a problem does emerge on

the line, they are trained to solve it without needing an engineer or a supervisor. Teams meet regularly to discuss ways in which their sections could be run more smoothly.

A-grade application
A need for lean thinking in the NHS

A combination of an ageing population and the rising cost of health equipment and drugs has caused spending on the NHS to soar in recent years. In 2006 the NHS budget was in deficit to the tune of £512 million. The government wants to reduce NHS spending without adversely affecting health care outcomes. To achieve this goal the managers appointed to run the NHS must find ways of reducing wastage.

A key component of lean management is tapping into the ideas of the real experts: the shop floor employees. The managers running Britain's hospitals must be prepared to delegate. First, doctors and nurses should be asked to assess current working practices to identify bottlenecks and inefficiencies. For example, if complementary machinery and equipment are located in different parts of a hospital, doctors and nurses will have to waste some of their valuable time walking from one part of the building to another. The time wasted could have been used more productively to treat patients. Second, doctors and nurses should be asked to identify bureaucratic activities that are currently carried out that consume scarce resources but add no value to the quality of health care given. Once identified, these bureaucratic activities should be stopped straight away. The financial and physical resources freed up can then be redeployed within the NHS more productively. Result: NHS performance improves, but at no extra cost to the taxpayer.

Lean approach to quality

In a mass production system, quality control is a specialised job that takes place at the end of the line. In a lean system, each team is responsible for checking the quality of its own work. If a fault is spotted, every worker has the power to stop the assembly line. This policy prevents errors being passed on, to be corrected only once the fault has been found at the end of the line. The lean approach, therefore, is self-checking at every production stage so that quality failures at the end (or with customers) become extremely rare.

One way to achieve lean quality is **total quality management** (TQM). This attempts to achieve a culture of quality throughout the organisation, so that the primary objective of all employees is to achieve quality the first time around without the need for any reworking. To achieve total quality, managers must 'make quality the number one, non-negotiable priority, and actively seek and listen to the views of employees on how to improve quality' (Roger Trapp, in the *Independent*).

Lean design

As consumers become more demanding and technology advances, car design has become highly complex. This threatens to boost costs and development times. Lean producers combat this by simultaneous engineering. This means integrating the development functions so that separate design and engineering stages are tackled at the same time. This speeds up development times, which cuts costs and reduces the risk of early obsolescence. Whereas US and European car manufacturers take over 60 months (five years!) from conception to launch of a new car model, the Japanese take 40+ months. Crucial to lean design and development is the principle of empowerment. Consequently, team members feel a greater pressure to make the right decision because it is more likely to hold.

Lean component supply

The approach to component supply varies greatly from company to company. Mass producers tend to have rather distant relationships with suppliers, often based on minimising the delivery cost per unit. They may buy from several sources to keep up the competitive pressure. The supplier, in turn, may be secretive about costs and profit margins to prevent the buyer from pressing for still lower prices. Lean producers work in partnership with their suppliers or, more often, with a single supplier. They keep the supplier fully informed of new product developments, encouraging ideas and technical advice. This means that by the time the assembly line starts running, errors have been ironed out so there are very few running changes or failures. Both parties are also likely to share financial and sales information electronically. This encourages an atmosphere of trust and common purpose, and aids planning.

46.4 Just-in-time

Lean producers run with minimal buffer stocks, relying on daily or hourly deliveries from trusted suppliers. As there is no safety net, a faulty shipment of components could bring an entire factory to a halt. Mass producers

rely on stockpiles, **just-in-case**. Lean producers insist on zero defects, whereas mass producers are happy with a quality standard that is 'good enough'.

The just-in-time (JIT) system of manufacturing is perhaps the best-known element of lean production. JIT aims to minimise the costs of holding unnecessary stocks of raw materials, components, work in progress and finished products. The principle that underpins JIT is that production should be 'pulled through' rather than 'pushed through'. This means that production should be for specific customer orders, so that the production cycle starts only once a customer has placed an order with the producer.

Summary of the just-in-time approach

● No buffer stocks of any type are held.

● Production is to order.

● Stock is ordered only when it is needed, just in time.

● Zero defects are essential as no stock safety net exists.

● No 'spare' workers are employed.

● Staff are multi-skilled and capable of filling in for absent colleagues.

● It is used by lean producers.

Summary of the just-in-case approach

● Stocks of raw materials, components, work in progress and finished products are held by the producer.

● Production is frequently stockpiled as manufacturers often seek economies of scale even at a time when sales are falling.

● Stock is ordered less frequently because the average order size tends to be large in order to take advantage of bulk-buying discounts.

● The incentive to achieve zero defects is less strong as stocks at every stage of production are held just in case of mistakes.

Capital and interest waste

Holding stock creates both actual and opportunity costs. The actual costs are the costs of paying for somewhere to keep the stock. The opportunity cost is the interest that could have been received had the capital tied up in stock been available to invest elsewhere.

Defect waste

By holding very little stock, firms no longer have a safety net. Consequently quality must improve – ideally to achieve zero defects. Firms must tackle quality problems at source, changing production methods or suppliers where necessary.

Overproduction waste

Mass producers set production levels on the basis of sales forecasts derived from quantitative market research findings. These forecasts may prove wrong. This can lead to heavy price discounting in order to clear surplus stock. By producing to order this wastage is avoidable.

46.5 Time-based management

Time-based management involves managing time in the same way most companies manage costs, quality or stock. Time-based manufacturers try to shorten rather than lengthen production runs in order to reduce costs and to increase levels of customer satisfaction. To do this manufacturers invest in flexible capital – machines that can make more than one model. Training must also be seen as a priority because staff have to be multi-skilled. This enables the firm to produce a variety of models without a cost penalty – something that mass producers using a high division of labour with inflexible capital thought impossible.

Time-based management creates four benefits.

1   By reducing lead and set-up times, productivity improves, creating a cost advantage.

2   Shortening lead times cuts customer response times, increasing consumer satisfaction as customers receive their orders sooner.

3   Lower stock holding costs – short lead and set-up times make firms more responsive to changes in the market. Consequently there should be less need for long production runs and stockpiles of finished products. If demand does suddenly increase, production can simply be quickly restarted.

4   An ability to offer the consumer a more varied product range without losing cost-reducing economies of scale. Time-based management therefore makes market segmentation a much cheaper strategy to operate.

A-grade application
Time-based management

When, in 2002, Christian Dior featured a glamorous embroidered Afghan coat on the catwalk, Zara had its own version in its shops within a fortnight. It was able to design, manufacture and distribute the coat to its shops throughout Europe within just 14 days – and sell it for just £95. If a style doesn't succeed within a week, it is withdrawn. No style stays on the shop floor for more than four weeks. The immediate result is obvious. Fashion- and price-conscious women flock to Zara.

Less obviously, Zara benefits from a vital secondary factor. In Spain, Zara's home country, an average high-street clothes store expects its regular customers to visit three times a year. That goes up to 17 for Zara. As the stock is constantly changing, the store is constantly worth visiting. It took Zara's owner 40 years to build his business fortune from £18 million in 1963 to £6 billion by 2002. Time well spent.

Issues For Analysis

- Lean thinking seeks to eliminate waste of all forms. By adopting lean techniques, firms should therefore become more efficient. By reducing waste, unit costs will be reduced. This makes it possible for lean producers to offer lower prices without any sacrifice of profit margin, or to offer higher product specifications for the same price as rivals. Consequently, lean production techniques can have an impact on firms' marketing strategies.

- Lean new product development techniques are increasingly decisive in a highly competitive world where product life cycles are becoming shorter. In this environment, reducing design lead times is vital. For a product to be considered innovative it must be launched quickly. If competitors beat you to it, your product will be seen as just another 'me too'.

- The attempt to achieve lean production can be expensive. Some firms have invested heavily in 'flexible' computer-aided manufacturing equipment. True lean production depends upon people rather than machines.

46.6 Lean production
an evaluation

Some of the arguments put forward above could be criticised for being too black and white (mass production = terrible; lean production = wonderful). The reality of business is often to do with shades of grey, with some lean producers having their own weaknesses. Some trends are unarguable, however. When people first started writing about the Toyota production system, Toyota was an also-ran compared with the giant US car producers Ford and General Motors. Today Toyota is the world's number one car maker.

However, there is a downside. By definition, lean thinking involves the elimination of waste. This waste could be over-manning. So by switching to a leaner system the consequence could be redundancies. Lean management in this context becomes little more than a fig leaf that a ruthless manager may wish to hide behind when seeking to justify controversial staffing decisions.

Key terms

Just-in-case: keeping buffer stocks of materials and components just in case something goes wrong.
Just-in-time: producing with minimum stock levels so every process must be completed just in time for the process that follows.
Kaizen: continuous improvement (i.e. encouraging all staff to regularly come up with ideas to improve efficiency and quality).
Total quality management: a passion for quality that starts at the top, then spreads throughout the organisation.

Exercises

A. Revision questions

(35 marks; 35 minutes)

1 State the three components of lean production. (3)

2 Outline three problems of mass production. (3)

3 Distinguish between just-in-time and just-in-case. (4)

4 What advantages are there in using time-based management? (4)

5 Why is it important to reduce machine set-up times? (3)

6 What are the opportunity costs of holding too much stock? (4)

7 Outline possible sources of waste in any organisation with which you are familiar. (Your school? Your part-time employer?) (4)

8 What is reworking and why does it add to costs? (5)

9 Why might it be important to be first to the market with a new product idea? (5)

B. Revision exercises

B1 Data response

Lean manufacturing in Plymouth

Who wouldn't want to double their revenues in four years? It sounds like any company's dream. But success sets its own challenges, as Kawasaki Precision Machinery (UK) is well aware.

Plymouth-based Kawasaki Precision Machinery (KPM) manufactures and sells hydraulic components – pumps, motors and control valves – for markets in Europe, India, the Middle East, South Africa and Australasia, and it has seen turnover increase from £30 million to nearly £60 million in recent years. Such a dramatic increase in business has inevitably created its own pressures. General Manager Steve Cardew says, 'We've needed to increase the capacity of the plant significantly. Space on the site has also come under pressure, and at present we have to store some goods off-site. But we're now focusing on reducing stocks, which will enable us to free up floor space and make better use of what's available.'

The investment he refers to has been significant and sustained. In fact, the company has been buying in new capital equipment at the rate of some £2 million a year. It has also found it necessary to increase the size of its workforce, which now stands at around 300. But this has involved an approach that goes beyond simply raising the headcount. 'There have been difficulties,' comments Cardew, 'given our geographical location. Getting the right skills hasn't been easy, so we've developed a substantial in-house training and upskilling programme. But we've also taken the opportunity to bring in some new people who already have the skills and knowledge we're looking for. In practice, that particularly means people with experience in the automotive industry, who can bring with them an understanding of lean manufacturing.'

It's a policy that can only sustain the impetus of a lean journey that's already well under way. The continuous improvement philosophy is at the heart of KPM's aspirations to become world class. It's necessary, too, to look beyond a company to its sources of supply, and that's a topic that also engages his attention. 'All our processes are only as good as the weakest link in the supply chain, and we have to be conscious of that. A lot of our raw materials are castings and forgings, but many foundries – especially those in the UK – now have a reduced capacity.'

It's clear that there will be no relenting in the quest for improvement. 'We're now in a period of growth,' Cardew concedes, 'but there has to come a time when our currently robust main markets stop growing, and we must be sure that we'll be competitive then. We can't afford to wait around until the demand decreases; we have to be realistic and increase our efficiency now.'

Source: adapted from www.themanufacturer.com, February 2008

Questions

(30 marks; 40 minutes)

1 Outline two possible pressures for a lean producer such as KPM of 'a dramatic increase in business'. (6)

2 Outline two elements of lean management being used by KPM. (4)

3 Would you recommend that KPM should move to JIT production and stock control? Justify and explain your reasoning. (8)

4 Discuss whether KPM is in a strong or weak position if there is a change to a position of 'demand decreases'. (12)

C. Essay questions

(40 marks each)

1 Discuss the difficulties and dilemmas faced by managers who are considering a switch to lean methods of production.

2 In some companies, lean production is viewed as just being another in a long line of management fads. In others it is embraced with enthusiasm by the staff. Why may this be so?

3 Why do some firms seem far better than others in terms of their ability to successfully implement lean production techniques?

4 Discuss the benefits, and the possible disadvantages, of lean production methods being utilised by an aircraft manufacturer. How might the balance between the benefits and the possible disadvantages change in the long term?

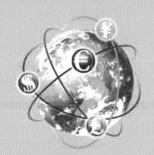

CAPACITY UTILISATION AND CAPITAL INTENSITY

DEFINITION

Capacity utilisation is the proportion of maximum possible output that is currently being used. A football stadium is at full capacity when all the seats are filled. A company producing 1500 units a week when the factory is capable of 2000 units has a capacity utilisation of 75%.

47.1 Operational targets

To run a successful operation such as Primark requires brilliant organisation and clear targets. The role of the targets is to help all staff aim at the same goal. The target at a hotdog stand outside a concert venue is to serve as many people as possible as quickly as possible, before and after the show. To achieve this the stallholder will plan ahead, cooking the sausages in advance and getting the onions ready. The most efficient stallholder will almost always make more money than the best cook. It is all down to clear targets and clear objectives.

There are three main targets focused on by operations managers:

1 quality targets (e.g. to have no more than 1 in 100 customers demand a refund)

2 capacity utilisation targets (e.g. that the factory should be working at 85–95% of its maximum possible capacity)

3 unit costs (e.g. keeping the average cost per unit at below £1.99, in order to keep the selling price below £2.99).

47.2 How is capacity utilisation measured?

Capacity utilisation is measured using the formula:

$$\frac{\text{current output}}{\text{maximum possible output}} \times 100$$

What does capacity depend upon? The amount a firm can make is determined by the quantity of buildings, machinery and labour it has available. Maximum capacity is achieved when the firm is making full use of all the buildings, machinery and labour available. The firm is said to be working at full capacity, or 100% capacity utilisation.

For a service business the same logic applies, though it is much harder to identify a precise figure. This is because it may take a different time to serve each customer. In a shop or a bank branch, demand may exceed capacity at certain times of the day, in which case queues will form. At other times the staff may have little to do. A service business wishing to stay cost-competitive will measure demand at different times of the day and then schedule the staffing level to match the capacity utilisation.

Many service businesses cope with fluctuating demand by employing temporary or part-time staff. These employees provide a far greater degree of flexibility to employers. Part-time hours can be increased, or extra temporary staff can be employed to increase capacity easily. If demand falls, temporary staff can be laid off without redundancy payments, or part-time staff can have their hours reduced, thus reducing capacity easily and cheaply. Many businesses like this flexibility as it limits wastage on staff costs. However, the situation may not be as appealing for employees, who have fewer rights than their full-time salaried predecessors. Figure 47.1 shows how flexible staffing (C) can reduce the wastage implied by having under-used full-time staff (A).

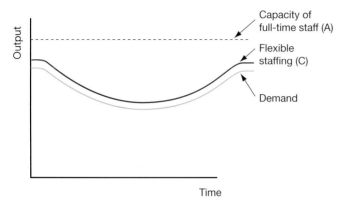

Figure 47.1 How flexible staffing (C) can reduce the wastage implied by having under-used full-time staff (A)

The reason why capacity utilisation is so important is that it has an inverse (opposite) effect upon fixed costs per unit. In other words, when utilisation is high, fixed costs are spread over many units. This cuts the cost per unit, which enables the producer either to cut prices to boost demand further, or to enjoy large profit margins. If utilisation is low, fixed costs per unit become punishingly high. This problem was faced in 2007 by airline start-up Silverjet, which found its £12.8 million of revenue swamped by £31 million of costs.

The ideal level of capacity utilisation, therefore, is at or near 100%. This spreads fixed costs as thinly as possible, boosting profit margins. There are two key concerns about operating at maximum capacity for long, however. These are:

47.3 Fixed costs and capacity

It is vital to understand clearly the relationship between fixed costs and capacity utilisation. Fixed costs are fixed in relation to output. This means that whether capacity utilisation is 50% or 100%, fixed costs will not change. The implication of this is clear. If a football club invests in a huge, expensive playing staff (whose salaries are a fixed cost), but matches are played to a half-empty stadium, the fixed costs will become a huge burden. This is because the very fact that fixed costs do not change *in total* as output changes means that they do change *per unit* of output/demand. A half-empty stadium means that the fixed costs per unit are double the level at maximum capacity (see Table 47.1).

When the stadium capacity utilisation is at 50%, then, £10 of the ticket price is needed for the players' wages alone. The many other fixed and variable costs of running a football club would be on top of this, of course.

A-grade application

Gordon Ramsay: footballer, chef, TV personality. . .and business guru?

In his TV series *Ramsay's Kitchen Nightmares*, the renowned chef spent a lot of time swearing and criticising chefs for the way they cooked. The series placed Gordon at a failing restaurant for a week. His task was to wave a magic wand and turn it into a profitable business. In almost every episode of the series, Ramsay identified each restaurant's failure to use anything near its full capacity. Commonly, he suggested the introduction of a simple lunchtime menu to boost trade during the day, in addition to speeding up service in the evenings to ensure that every table would see at least two sittings in the main evening session. Ramsay's advice, delivered in his own inimitable way, was simply a call to push capacity utilisation higher in order to spread each restaurant's fixed costs over more units of output (customers). The advice usually worked.

Table 47.1 Fixed costs and capacity

	Full stadium	Half-empty stadium
	50,000 fans	25,000 fans
Weekly salary bill (fixed costs)	£250,000	£250,000
Salary fixed cost per fan	£5	£10
	(£250,000/50,000)	(£250,000/25,000)

1 the risk that if demand rises further, you will have to turn it away, enabling your competitors to benefit

2 the risk that you will struggle to service the machinery and train/retrain staff; this may prove costly in the long term, and will increase the chances of production breakdowns in the short term.

The production ideal, therefore, is a capacity utilisation of around 90%.

47.4 How to get towards full capacity

If a firm's capacity utilisation is an unsatisfactory 45%, how could it be increased to a more acceptable level of around 90%? There are two possible approaches, as discussed below.

Increase demand (in this case, double it!)

Demand for existing products could be boosted by extra promotional spending, price cutting or – more

A-grade application

Odeon: filling seats with anyone it can

Odeon is acutely aware of the dangers of having capacity empty during quiet times. In an attempt to increase capacity utilisation during the day and on quieter evenings, Odeon has introduced a number of specialised film showings, catering for groups who are more likely to visit the cinema during 'quiet periods':

● Odeon kids – Saturday and Sunday mornings and every day during school holidays
● Senior screen – mid-morning showings of traditional and modern classics for 'mature guests', with free tea and coffee
● Odeon Newbies – for parents with babies, mid-morning showings with volume quieter than usual and lights higher than usual, to try to create a calming environment for babies and parents
● Director's Chair – showing foreign-language, independent and art-house films for serious film buffs, one quiet evening per week.

Even with reduced ticket prices for some of these options, each seat sold is still making a contribution to covering fixed costs as capacity utilisation edges higher for the cinema chain.

fundamentally – devising a new strategy to reposition the products into growth sectors. If supermarket own-label products are flourishing, perhaps offer to produce under the Tesco or Sainsbury's banner. If doubling of sales is needed, it is unlikely that existing products will provide the whole answer. The other approach is to launch new products. This could be highly effective, but implies long-term planning and investment.

Cut capacity

If your current factory and labour force is capable of producing 10,000 units a week, but there is demand for only 4500, there will be a great temptation to cut capacity to 5000. This might be done by cutting out the night shift (i.e. making those workers redundant). This would avoid the disruption and inflexibility caused by the alternative, which is to move to smaller premises. Moving will enable all fixed costs to be cut (rent, rates, salaries, and so on), but may look silly if, six months later, demand has recovered to 6000 units when your new factory capacity is only 5000.

How to select the best option

A key factor in deciding whether to cut capacity or boost demand is the underlying cause of the low utilisation. It may be the result of a known temporary demand shortfall, such as a seasonal low point in the toy business. Or it may be due to an economic recession, which (on past experience) may hit demand for around 18–24 months. Either way, it might prove a mistake in the long run to cut capacity. Nevertheless, if a firm faces huge short-term losses from its excess fixed costs, it may have to forget the future and concentrate on short-term survival.

47.5 Why and how to change capacity

Firms may find themselves with **excess capacity** if demand for their products slows down. Unless the reduction in demand is just a short-term glitch, a firm will seek to find ways to reduce its maximum capacity. This process is commonly called **rationalisation** – it means reorganising in order to boost efficiency. The three main elements of rationalising are as follows.

1 Closing down and selling off a factory or part of a factory if the space will not be needed in the foreseeable future. Alternatively, the firm may decide to lease out factory space to other companies on a short-term basis. This will enable it to get the extra space back if demand improves.

2 Machinery can be sold off second-hand or for scrap. A more flexible solution is to rent machinery rather than buy it outright in the first place. This would enable the firm to return machinery in times when capacity needs to be reduced.

3 Redundancy is the obvious answer for a firm with too large a workforce. As this can prove expensive, firms may **redeploy** their employees to other jobs. This may be difficult for the employee, who feels pushed towards a job s/he had never wanted. Many firms with excess labour will cut down the length of time worked by employees, perhaps by shortening shifts.

47.6 Dealing with non-standard orders

Firms organise their operations around the amount they expect to sell in coming months. For a brand such as Marmite, which has sold quite steadily for more than 100 years, the factory can be set up to mass produce Marmite around the clock. Sales of the brand are not especially seasonal, and change little year on year. So an automated production line can be set up, requiring a minimum of labour and therefore minimal costs.

Figure 47.2 A brand such as Marmite may use subcontracting to deal with non-standard orders

A problem arises, though, when a non-standard order arrives. Perhaps China, not known for its Marmite eating, is influenced by a TV programme into deciding that it loves, rather than hates, the taste. So Chinese shops suddenly put through a series of huge orders to the UK Marmite factory. How can it cope if it is already being run at a high capacity utilisation?

The answer may lie in subcontracting. In other words, the main Marmite factory may have a permanent arrangement with a food-processing factory that it will supply Marmite, when ordered, within an agreed lead time. So, the extra order can be accepted, the product delivered within, perhaps, two weeks and the customer will be happy. The subcontracted production will have to be checked extra carefully for quality, but that is not difficult. Marmite itself will probably make less profit from subcontracted production than when using its own factory, yet it will still work out far better than permanently running an under-utilised factory just in case an extra order comes along.

47.7 Capital and labour intensity

A further factor affecting production efficiency concerns the balance struck by the business between capital- and labour-intensive production. Measuring up a bride-to-be and then making a wedding dress by hand is the ultimate in labour-intensive production. However hard the dressmaker works, his/her productivity will be very low. This is because so little can be mechanised or automated. By contrast, a dress designer for Topshop may be able to order 10,000 identical size 10 dresses to be distributed across the Topshop stores. This batch of 10,000 can be produced largely by machine (i.e. through capital- rather than labour-intensive production).

The importance of this topic is that it points to a huge opportunity for small firms. In almost every industry there is scope for some labour-intensive production. This is because there are always some people who want – and can afford – an entirely individual product. In addition, there are businesses where labour-intensive production is inevitable, such as plumbing, advertising (creating and producing commercials), legal advice and running a school. Starting a new car manufacturing firm will be massively expensive and make you compete head-on with huge firms. Starting a new advertising agency has neither problem.

Labour-intensive production:

● means that labour costs form a high percentage of total costs

● has low financial **barriers to entry**, because it is cheap to start up production

● makes it necessary for management to focus on the cost of labour (making it especially attractive to switch production to a low-cost country such as Cambodia)

- has the advantage of being highly flexible, making it possible for a small firm to operate successfully without direct competition from a large one.

Capital-intensive production:

- has a large percentage of its total costs tied up in the fixed costs of purchasing and operating machinery

- has high financial barriers to entry

- may be able to keep producing in a high-cost country, because labour costs are such a small proportion of the total costs (e.g. mass production of Coca-Cola or Heinz Beans)

- can be inflexible, both in terms of switching from one product to another, and in the ability to tailor a product to an individual customer.

Capital intensity in the service sector

The issue of labour versus capital intensity also matters in service industries such as banking or retailing. Many service-sector jobs need people – to provide the human face of customer service. Yet whereas, in the past, banking was an entirely face-to-face service business, with all transactions taking place in a bank branch, today it is much more capital intensive. Hole-in-the-wall cash machines dispense money with virtually zero labour cost; the cost is in the machines and in renting the space they fill. If you try to phone your local Barclays, you will end up talking to a call centre where a highly structured, monitored service creates a half-human-half-machine version of service. In a recent YouGov survey, only 4% of customers said they had received a good service from a call centre. Despite this, the desire to cut labour costs presses firms to pursue more capital-intensive approaches within the 'service' sector.

So, which approach is better: labour-intensive or capital-intensive production? The answer is that it depends on the business circumstances. Clearly, if the opportunity exists to set up a highly automated, online auction service (eBay), why not do so? In this case users love how intelligently the automated systems provide them with the information they want and the opportunities the system provides. eBay provides terrific customer service through a highly capital-intensive system (though, of course, a lot of highly intelligent people have put the software systems together). Despite this, customers often love to have personal service, from a chatty receptionist or from a small clothes shop that will adjust a dress to make it fit better.

Issues For Analysis

When developing an argument in answer to a case study or essay question, the following lines of analysis should be considered.

- The time frame of the question: is spare capacity caused by a short-term fall in demand or is there a longer-term downward trend? Only if the demand decline is a long-term trend should capacity be cut. It must be remembered, though, that it is always hard to be sure of these things. In the early 1990s, falling attendance at football matches meant that when clubs such as Manchester United and Newcastle rebuilt their stadiums, they cut the crowd capacity. Looking back, with Arsenal playing in the new Emirates stadium and Liverpool's new, bigger Anfield being built, it is easy to say they were wrong. At the time they made what seemed the right decision. So consider the timescale, but be careful of sounding too definite about the 'right' solution.

- The link between capacity utilisation, fixed costs per unit and profitability: if dealing with a question about how to improve profitability, increasing capacity utilisation could well be a valid solution. If profits are poor, be sure to ask what capacity utilisation is at present.

- Modern production theory praises systems such as just-in-time, **flexible specialisation** and lean production: successful management of all three of these approaches is likely to mean capacity utilisation that is well below 100%. This is because all these approaches require flexible responses to customer requirements/orders. In turn, this requires spare capacity. Can lean production yield enough other benefits to compensate for the poor capacity utilisation?

Highly labour intensive				Highly capital intensive
Building a McLaren racing car	Small batches of Versace suits	Producing Big Macs	Producing Honda Accords	24 hour production of Heinz Beans

Figure 47.3 Labour- vs capital-intensive production

47.8 Capacity utilisation

an evaluation

Most firms will aim to operate close to full capacity, but probably not at 100%. A small amount of spare capacity is accepted as necessary, bringing a certain degree of flexibility in case of need. In this way, sudden surges of demand can be coped with in the short run by increasing output, or **downtime** can be used for maintenance. Spare capacity can be a good thing, particularly in small doses.

Firms operating close to full capacity are those that may be considering investing in new premises or machinery. Building new factories takes time, as well as huge quantities of money. Can the firm afford to wait 18 months for its capacity to be expanded? Perhaps the firm would be better served subcontracting certain areas of its work to other companies, thus freeing capacity.

Capacity utilisation also raises the difficult issue of cutting capacity by rationalisation and, often, redundancy. This incorporates many issues of human resource management, motivation and social responsibility. There are fewer more important tests of the skills and far-sightedness of senior managers.

When tackling case studies, it is important that you take a step back from any that deal with such a situation, to consider the cause and the effect. Is excess capacity the problem or an indicator of another problem, such as declining market share? By showing the broader picture in this way you can also show the skill of evaluation.

Key terms

Barriers to entry: factors that make it hard for new companies to enter a market.

Downtime: any period when machinery is not being used in production; some downtime is necessary for maintenance, but too much may suggest incompetence.

Excess capacity: when there is more capacity than justified by current demand (i.e. utilisation is low).

Flexible specialisation: a production system based upon batches of goods aimed at many market niches, instead of mass production/mass market.

Rationalisation: reorganising in order to increase efficiency. This often implies cutting capacity to increase the percentage utilisation.

Exercises

A. Revision questions

(30 marks; 30 minutes)

1 What is meant by the phrase '100% capacity utilisation'? (3)

2 At what level of capacity utilisation will fixed costs per unit be lowest for any firm? Briefly explain your answer. (4)

3 What formula is used to calculate the capacity utilisation of a firm? (2)

4 How can a firm increase its capacity utilisation without increasing output? (3)

5 If a firm is currently selling 11,000 units per month and this represents a capacity utilisation of 55%, what is its maximum capacity? (4)

6 Use the following information to calculate profit per week at 50%, 75% and 100% capacity utilisation.

Maximum capacity	800 units per week
Variable cost per unit	£1800
Total fixed cost per week	£1.5 million
Selling price	£4300

(9)

7 Briefly explain the dangers of operating at 100% capacity utilisation for any extended period of time. (5)

B. Revision exercises

B1 Data response

R. Sivyer & Co was founded 50 years ago. It has a successful history of manufacturing high-quality bicycle chains, which are supplied direct to retailers. In recent years, orders from retail customers have fallen, meaning that the firm is now manufacturing and selling only 12,000 chains per month.

The following cost information has been made available:

Materials cost per unit	80p
Shop floor worker's salary	£10,000 p.a.
Salary paid to other staff	£12,000 p.a.
Manager's salary	£32,000 p.a.
Maximum capacity	20,000 units per month
General overheads	£40,000 per month
Current selling price	£5.80
Number of managers currently employed	3
Number of shop floor staff currently employed	10
Number of other staff currently employed	4

The finance manager has called the other two managers to a meeting to discuss the firm's future. She puts forward two alternative courses of action:

1 make four shop floor and two other staff redundant, thus cutting the firm's fixed costs, and reducing maximum capacity to 12,000 units per month

2 sign a contract to supply a large bicycle manufacturer with a fixed quantity of 8000 chains per month at £5.80 each for the next four years; breaking the contract will lead to heavy financial penalties.

Questions

(30 marks; 35 minutes)

1 What is the firm's current monthly profit? (5)

2 Calculate the monthly profit that would result from each of the two options. (10)

3 Explain the advantages and disadvantages of each option. (10)

4 State which of the two options you would choose, and list any other information you would need before making the final decision. (5)

B2 Data response

Out of the red and into success

Steven Carragher had decided to set up a specialist sports goods store shortly after injury cut short his football career. With limited business experience, but plenty of local contacts, he bought a ten-year lease on a large high-street shop with plenty of floor space, along with storage on the two floors above the shop. He felt confident that business would be brisk as there were few specialised sports stores in Cheshire at the time. He blew most of his budget in preparing for the start-up, paying for the lease, a refit, staff training and plenty of stock to fill his stock rooms. With a little left over for a launch marketing campaign, he was optimistic on opening day. The first week was busy, with plenty of people coming in but few actually buying. By the end of the first month's trading, the picture had turned decidedly negative, with revenues failing to cover running costs and the store far from break-even.

Steven's old colleague Robbie knew a little about business and he pointed out that Steven was trying to run a small business in the sort of premises that a major chain store would expect to use. Robbie's solution had two main features:

1 turn the top floor of the building into a three-bedroom flat that could be rented out to cover 50% of the rent that Steven was paying

2 divide the shop in two, renting half the shop space to another retailer to help Steven cover the rent and bills.

When the two met again in 12 months, Steven paid for lunch. With both the flat and smaller shop unit rented out, he was now covering the costs of his shop comfortably. Meanwhile, Steven had set up an online ordering service that was proving to be highly successful.

Questions

(25 marks; 30 minutes)

1 Using the concept of capacity utilisation, analyse why Steven's business had initially failed to cover its costs. (6)

2a Explain why Robbie's ideas were always likely to improve Steven's profit. (4)

2b What crucial assumptions did Robbie make when offering his advice. (3)

3 Steven had few other options as a result of the length of his lease on the property. Use this case as a starting point to discuss why flexibility is vital in a small business start-up. (12)

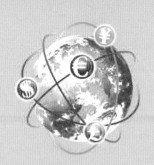

MAKING OPERATIONAL DECISIONS

DEFINITION

Operations management is the engine room of the business that turns plans into delivered products or services. Operational decisions are therefore the key to the success of the business day by day.

48.1 Operational targets

The starting point for every operations manager is to obtain a plausible forecast of demand (i.e. how many products will be needed and when). This enables

A-grade application

Getting the sums right

Before the iPhone was launched in 2007, many financial analysts made forecasts of the likely level of sales. As can be seen from Table 48.1, the variations were extraordinarily wide, from 0.25 million to 1.7 million. This shows that getting operational targets correct is especially difficult when a new product is being launched.

In fact, Apple later reported that the actual sales volume was 1,120,000 in the period up to the end of September 2007, so Piper Jaffray & Co produced a brilliant forecast.

operational targets to be set. When the iPhone was launched in America in 2007, Apple ensured that it had stockpiled enough units to meet sales of 300,000 phones in the first day and a half. Often the launch of new products such as this gets bogged down with inadequate supplies and frustrated customers. A well-run organisation will do all it can to avoid this.

Setting targets can be helpful in any business context. They give staff something to work towards and give the firm something against which to check its actual performance. Achieving these targets is the fundamental indicator of successful operations management. Targets are the key to most operational decisions.

Different firms will have different operational targets, including:

- unit costs
- quality
- capacity utilisation.

Table 48.1 Apple iPhone: sales forecasts

	Sales to Sept 2007	Sales in year to Sept 2008
American Technology Research	250,000	–
Bear Stearns Ltd	650,000	–
Credit Suisse	1,700,000	12,300,000
Pacific Crest Securities	800,000	4,800,000
Piper Jaffray & Co	1,200,000	8,000,000
UBS AG	950,000	8,100,000
Apple Innovation Blog	1,500,000	10,500,000

Source: analysts' research reports, reported at Bloomberg.com

Unit costs

The cost of one unit of output is a raw measure of the efficiency of a firm's operations. Unit cost is calculated by dividing the total cost of production for a period by the number of units produced, as shown below:

$$\frac{\text{Total cost}}{\text{Total output}} = \text{unit cost}$$

For example:

$$\frac{\text{Total cost for March}}{\text{Total output for March}} = \frac{£64,000}{32,000 \text{ units}} = £2 \text{ per unit}$$

Unit costs can be reduced in one of three ways: by cutting variable costs, perhaps by running the business with lower wastage levels; by cutting fixed costs; or by increasing sales volumes so that the firm's existing fixed costs are spread over more units of sale.

If a firm can lower its unit costs it can make a decision between two attractive alternatives:

1   cut the selling price to boost customer demand; if the product is **highly price elastic**, this would probably be the most attractive choice

2   keep the selling price constant, but make a **higher profit margin** on each unit sold; that would be the sensible approach if the product's price elasticity was low.

Such a desirable choice explains why so much management energy is focused on trying to reduce unit costs through increases in efficiency. However, unit costs themselves are not the only operational target that a business will set itself.

Capacity utilisation

Since a high level of capacity utilisation means that fixed costs are spread across more units of output, ensuring that a firm's capacity is nearly fully used all the time is an excellent way of keeping unit costs low. Therefore many firms will set themselves targets for capacity utilisation. Though operating at 100% capacity utilisation will bring the lowest unit costs, most capacity utilisation targets will be set just below that level. This is to allow for time to carry out routine maintenance, space to accept special orders, or just a slight margin for error in case of breakdowns.

Quality

The race to produce output as quickly as possible and reduce labour costs per unit can lead to mistakes.

Setting targets for unit costs and capacity utilisation is risky unless targets for quality levels are also taken seriously. As was discussed in Unit 43, poor-quality output has a number of negative consequences. Errors in products will lead to higher unit costs as a result of wasted materials or correcting the faults. This will slow production rates as a result of needing to correct the mistakes.

48.2 ## Matching production to demand

Many factors can cause sales levels to fluctuate, including:

● fashion

● temperature and weather

● marketing activity

● competitors' actions.

Some of these are predictable and others are unpredictable. Sales forecasting can help in production planning, especially for predictable changes in demand. However, the fundamental issue is the same for most businesses: how to organise their operations to cope with varying levels of demand for their products or services.

The issue of matching production to demand considers a firm's ability to make sure that whenever customers want to buy, there is something to supply them with. A factory manufacturing lawnmowers may be an ideal illustration. Sales are likely to follow a monthly pattern, as shown in Figure 48.1. Every springtime there will be a sales peak as people decide to replace their old lawnmowers – unused all winter.

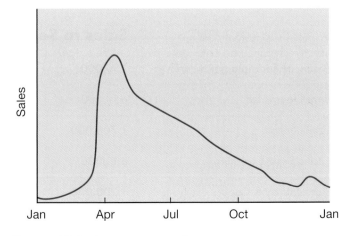

Figure 48.1 Lawnmower sales

The question facing the firm is, how should production be spread through the year. Figure 48.2 offers two alternative extremes: option A is where the firm maintains a constant production level throughout the year; option B shows a scenario where the firm exactly matches monthly production with monthly demand.

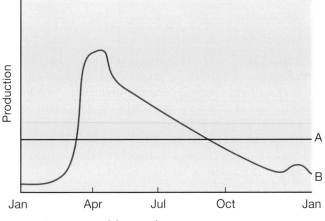

Figure 48.2 Possible production

There are a number of issues raised by each option.

Key issues (and some possible solutions)

Option A is to hold production constant. Surprisingly, this is how Cadbury's produces its Creme Eggs, even though sales only really take place in the lead-up to Easter. This approach offers the easiest solution in terms of planning, since it largely ignores demand fluctuations, and keeps production at a stable level. This has clear benefits: high capacity utilisation and maintaining a skilled and loyal workforce. Yet it implies that production in May will have to be stockpiled for more than six months before being sold in the run-up to the following Easter.

The cost involved in keeping stock will be huge. It is not just the physical costs of keeping stock, such as space for storage and the people whose job it is to organise the storage facilities – many businesses will find that stock becomes worthless over time. Food manufacturers may be forced to throw out stock that has passed its sell-by date, while fashion-related manufacturers and retailers do not want to find themselves heavily discounting last season's stock in a desperate attempt to empty their stock rooms. Service providers such as hairdressers face an even greater problem in that they cannot keep stock. If the salon is capable of dealing with 50 customers every day, but this demand level occurs only on Friday and Saturday, costs per customer will be unnecessarily high. Stylists are at

work, being paid, but cannot generate revenue when there are no customers.

The result is that many firms look towards option B: tailoring staffing and capacity levels to cope with expected demand. To achieve this, firms need to find ways to operate more flexibly; in particular, they need staff to be more flexible. The main ways to achieve this are through:

● overtime

● hiring temporary and part-time staff

● subcontracting.

Overtime

Paying staff extra to work longer hours than their contracts state may be a way of coping with busy periods. Of course, this requires staff who are willing to work overtime. Furthermore, staff generally expect a higher rate of pay if they are working overtime – pushing up labour costs.

A-grade application

Bovine overtime

The hot summer of 2006 saw Scottish ice cream maker Mackie's struggling to cope with a huge surge in demand for its ice cream. Staff at the company worked overtime, some up to an extra six hours per day, in order to maintain the increased production levels required to meet demand. This was only possible as a result of overtime being worked by the company's own cows. They were milked more often – up to four times a day during their busy period – something that the cows rather enjoy. The cows also illustrate how a company can cope with excess capacity: in quieter ice cream periods, Mackie's sells the cows' milk to other firms for other uses.

Hiring temporary and part-time staff

Temporary and part-time staff give extra flexibility to an employer. Temporary staff can be hired on fixed-term contracts designed to last only as long as the expected busy period. Most tourist attractions keep very few full-time staff, relying instead on an army of summer temps to run their attractions. Part-time staff can be hired with contracts that include flexible working hours, offering employers the chance to call them in during busy periods to work longer shifts. This is a phenomenon common among students working in retail over the Christmas period. Through the use of temporary or part-time staff, a company can reduce its fixed salary costs, thus reducing the break-even point to a level that is sustainable during quiet periods.

However, there are drawbacks. Motivating and communicating with temporary staff and part-timers can be much harder than with a stable workforce of full-timers. Quality and customer service issues may arise that have a damaging effect on a firm's reputation.

Subcontracting

Subcontracting is the term used to describe a situation where one firm is doing the work of another. A company struggling to cope with a rush of demand may subcontract its excess work to another. This depends on a good relationship with another company, and is also reliant on the other company having the capacity to cope with the order. On the other hand, a firm that finds its capacity is under-used may try to win work from other businesses looking to subcontract some of their work. This practice can be found not just in the manufacturing sector but in the service sector too. An insurance company whose call centres are overwhelmed with work may look to subcontract some of its claims to other call centres. Similarly, busy builders often subcontract some of their work to other building companies.

48.3 Other types of operational decision

Rationalisation

Longer-term reductions in demand may require long-term solutions to matching production with demand. Firms which find that sales have fallen due to changes in technology may choose **rationalisation** (i.e. to increase efficiency by permanently reducing overall capacity). This may be done by closing entire branches or factories, or simply shedding staff across the whole firm. At the time of writing, the BBC faces staff unrest, having announced that the workforce will be cut by some 3000 over the coming years. Rationalisation programmes must be handled carefully to minimise damage to the morale of the remaining staff and to minimise bad external publicity. Redundancies are never popular, but voluntary redundancy is a more attractive proposition than compulsory redundancy; however, neither is as pain-free as using **natural wastage** to rationalise.

Stock management

The issues already covered show the importance of managing stocks effectively. Stocks of finished goods waiting to be sold may be seen as a buffer against sudden surges in demand. However, keeping too much stock is a dangerously expensive habit. The balancing of stock levels is one of the major issues facing operations managers. Meanwhile, stock of raw materials and components presents similar problems. A lack of production inputs may force production to grind to a halt, while too much stock may lead to wasted materials or space.

Non-standard orders

Sometimes firms will be approached by customers with special orders at a different price to their regular selling price. A customer with special requirements, such as a different design or a very short delivery date, may offer a price above the norm. In other cases customers may try to buy special orders at specially low prices. Retailers such as Lidl and Tchibo sell cheaply to the public because of their skill at buying cheaply.

High-price special orders

Example: an Airbus super-jumbo bought and kitted out for Prince bin Talal of Saudi Arabia.

In a case study such as this, the order is likely to look profitable at first glance. However, the special nature of the order is such that it will be more expensive to produce. This will mean that unit costs are going to be higher. Perhaps overtime or subcontracting will be necessary to meet a tight order deadline or to adjust the standard design to meet the customer's needs. In these cases, extra costs must be factored into any calculation of the possible profit from the order.

Low-price special orders

Example: TK Maxx offers to buy 10,000 of last season's Ted Baker t-shirts for £5 each.

There are several reasons why a firm may consider accepting an order at lower than the usual selling price. The key is whether a firm has enough under-used capacity to meet the order and if the order will generate a positive contribution per unit. If the firm is already breaking even, a low-price order that generates a positive contribution per unit will generate extra profit. A further reason to accept the order is the possibility that it could lead to a new customer becoming a regular if he/she is happy with the quality and delivery of the order.

Issues For Analysis

- Whenever operational targets are missed, managers will want to know why. In these cases it is vital that you show a clear understanding of cause and effect. There will clearly be links between the three major target variables of unit cost, quality and capacity utilisation. Good analytic arguments will show a clear understanding of which events have caused which consequences. For example, an answer could suggest that unit costs have risen as a result of operating at a lower than anticipated level of capacity. This may have been the result of a fall in demand caused by a poor reputation, caused by poor quality levels last month.

- It is useful to experiment by taking each of the three target variables as a starting point, then thinking through the impact on the other two. For example, if capacity utilisation falls, what is the impact on unit costs and what might be the effect on quality? Or, what if quality performance falls?

- Another major analytical theme is likely to be an awareness of the arguments for and against keeping a stable production level month by month, as opposed to attempting to exactly match production with demand. Logically constructed arguments on both sides of this question are likely to lead to effective judgements when asked to evaluate.

Making operational decisions

Operations decisions are at the very heart of any business. Efficiency is king – without it, no firm will last long. Few customers are willing to wait for an unavailable product, while few firms have the financial resources to indefinitely fund inefficient stock-holding. The magical formula for matching production to demand does not exist. Instead, it is important to show an awareness that the forecasting skills and experience of operations managers will need to go hand in hand to ensure that a business is operationally efficient.

Key terms

Highly price elastic: when customers are so focused on price that a small price change can cause a big switch in customer demand (e.g. price up 5%, sales down 20%).

Higher profit margin: a wider gap between price and unit cost; if sales volumes stay the same, this must increase total profit.

Natural wastage: the 'natural' annual fall in staff levels caused by employees retiring, moving away or finding better jobs elsewhere.

Operational targets: the numerical goals set by management at the start of the year (e.g. output of 220,000 units with a quality wastage rate of no more than 1%).

Rationalisation: reorganising in order to increase efficiency; this usually leads to redundancies.

Exercises

A. Revision questions

(35 marks; 35 minutes)

1 Briefly explain what is meant by capacity utilisation. (2)

2 Explain why a high level of capacity usage makes cost per unit fall. (2)

3 Calculate the unit cost for a firm that manufactured 23,000 units with total costs of £11,500. (3)

4 Explain why quality targets may suffer if management is concerned only with meeting unit cost targets. (4)

5 Explain what is meant by the term rationalisation. (2)

6 Explain two methods that could be used to improve the level of capacity utilisation in a clothing factory. (4)

7 Explain two possible drawbacks to a farmer of relying on temporary staff when picking strawberries. (4)

8 Explain two benefits to a farmer of using temporary staff to pick strawberries. (4)

9 Explain two reasons why a company might agree to provide a customer with a special order at a selling price lower than its average unit cost. (4)

10 Outline three possible reasons why a cake manufacturer may try to closely match production with demand in order to reduce stock levels to a minimum. (6)

B. Revision exercises

B1 Data response

Hotel Torres is a part of the Hoteles Benitez group of hotels in Spain. For hotels, the main operational target is occupancy rates: the percentage of rooms that are occupied at any time. The chain's head office is assessing last year's performance at each branch and is particularly interested in the data shown below relating to the Hotel Torres in Barcelona.

Questions

(20 marks; 20 minutes)

1 Explain what the table reveals about Hotel Torres's operational efficiency during the year. (4)

2 Use the data in the table to explain the possible link between room occupancy performance and cost per guest. (6)

3 Analyse the benefits that the hotel might gain by setting targets for occupancy rates and cost per guest. (6)

4 Briefly explain two possible reasons why Hotel Torres failed to meet its targets. (4)

Hotel Torres data (B1)

	Quarter 1	Quarter 2	Quarter 3	Quarter 4
Average occupancy rate (%)	53	66	84	62
Target occupancy rate (%)	55	70	90	75
Group average occupancy rate (%)	58	72	90	75
Cost per guest (euros)	64	58	50	60
Target cost per guest (euros)	62	55	40	55

B2   Data response

DWS Ltd is a toy manufacturer, operating in the UK from a factory in the north-east. Having been running for 20 years, DWS is used to the particular problems posed by operating in such a seasonal industry. With 70% of sales being made in November and December, the managers have experience of battling to match production to demand. Their problem is intensified by the short product life cycles involved in manufacturing toys designed to tie in with the latest television and films. The table below shows units sold, output and maximum capacity month by month for last year.

The firm uses a range of methods to boost its maximum capacity during busy periods. These include overtime, temporary staff and subcontracting work to another trusted local manufacturer.

DWS has been approached by a major UK greetings card retailer, which is looking for a manufacturer of stuffed toys themed around various holidays, including Valentine's Day, Easter and Halloween. The initial contract would cover a 12-month period and would mean that sales levels would treble in January, March and October. The firm would pay a price equivalent to 5% above the variable cost of each unit of output.

Questions

(35 marks; 45 minutes)

1a Draw a graph to show units sold, output and maximum capacity. (6)

1b Shade the areas on the graph that represent under-use of capacity. (2)

2 Analyse the problems that DWS might experience by maintaining a consistent level of production all year round in order to avoid using overtime, temporary staff and subcontracting. (9)

3 Describe the pros and cons of two possible methods of increasing maximum capacity in the three affected months. (6)

4 Discuss whether DWS should accept this special order. (12)

	Sales (units)	Output (units)	Maximum capacity (units)
January	10,000	5,000	20,000
February	10,000	10,000	20,000
March	15,000	15,000	20,000
April	15,000	15,000	20,000
May	20,000	20,000	20,000
June	20,000	20,000	20,000
July	20,000	20,000	40,000
August	30,000	30,000	40,000
September	60,000	100,000	120,000
October	100,000	280,000	300,000
November	380,000	300,000	300,000
December	320,000	300,000	300,000

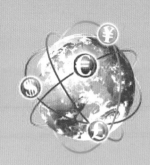

USING TECHNOLOGY IN OPERATIONS

DEFINITION

Technology means the computer hardware and software used to automate systems, and to handle, analyse and communicate business data.

49.1 Introduction

Information technology (IT) applications in business are various and rapidly changing. Often, though, the changes are to processing speed and business jargon – the essential tasks remain the same. In recent years, the most important business IT innovation has been the emergence of the internet. This will be covered relatively briefly, because the pace of change means that magazine articles will provide a more up-to-date understanding of the internet's business potential than is possible here.

Key applications of technology are:

● automated stock control systems

● computer-aided design (CAD)

● robotics

● information technology, including electronic data interchange (EDI) and the internet

● database management (the software behind efficient delivery systems such as Tesco Home Delivery).

49.2 Automated stock control systems

Modern stock control systems are based on laser scanning of bar-coded information. This ensures the computer knows the exact quantity of each product/size/colour that has come into the stockroom. In retail outlets, a laser scanning till is then used to record

Table 49.1 An example of aged stock analysis

Garment	Received (days ago)	Number received	In stock today
Green *Fabrice* dress, size 8	285	2	1
Blue *Channelle* dress, size 14	241	1	1
Red *Channelle* dress, size 8	241	2	2
Red *Grigio* jacket, size 10	235	4	3
Black *Grigio* dress, size 8	205	3	2
Black *Fabrice* dress, size 12	192	2	1
Blue *Florentine* suit, size 8	179	1	1

exactly what has been sold. This allows the store's computer to keep up-to-date records of current stocks of every item. This data can enable a buyer to decide how much extra to order, or an electronic link with the supplier can re-order automatically (see the section on EDI, below).

All this information will be held in the form of a database. This makes it easy for the firm to carry out an aged stock analysis: the computer provides a printout showing the stock in order of age. Table 49.1 shows a list of stock in a clothes shop, with the oldest first. It enables the manager to make informed decisions about what to do now and in the future. In this case:

● big price reductions seem to be called for on the first five items – they have been around too long

● there should be fewer orders in future for size 8 dresses.

49.3 Design technology

Computer-aided design (CAD) has been around for more than 20 years, but is now affordable and hugely powerful. Before CAD, product designers, engineers and architects drew their designs by hand. A CAD system works digitally, allowing designs to be saved, changed and reworked without starting from scratch. Even better, CAD can show a 3D version of a drawing and rotate to show the back and sides.

For multinationals such as Sony, a product designed in Tokyo can be sent electronically to Sony offices in

America and Europe, for local designers to tweak the work to make it better suited to local tastes. And when work is behind schedule, designers in Tokyo can pass a design on to London at the end of the Japanese working day, then the design is sent on to America. The time differences mean that 24-hour working can be kept up.

Figure 49.1 The record-breaking JCB Dieselmax

The benefits of CAD systems to successful design are that:

● the data generated by a CAD system can be linked to computer-aided manufacturing (CAM) to provide integrated, highly accurate production

A-grade application

JCB

In August 2006 the British firm JCB gained worldwide publicity for breaking the diesel vehicle land speed record in the JCB Dieselmax. It reached speeds of 328 miles an hour, more than 100 miles an hour faster than the previous record. JCB gave praise publicly for the contribution made by a sophisticated CAD system made by UGS. It enabled the JCB team to take early design ideas right through to rigorous virtual safety testing of 3D models. The same software then helped in building real models and gave the technical details for the manufacture of the real vehicle. JCB praised the 'integrity and accuracy of the (CAD) data [which] was something we relied on heavily throughout the development phases'.

Source: Adapted from 'World record breaking JCB Diesal max owes success to UGS NX CAD' 23 August 2006, www.mcsolutions.co.uk

Figure 49.2 Guggenheim Museum, Bilbao, designed by Frank Gehry

- they are hugely beneficial for businesses that are constantly required to provide designs that are unique, yet based on common principles (e.g. designing a new bridge, car or office block)

- CAD improves the productivity of designers and also helps them to be more ambitious; the extraordinary buildings of Frank Gehry could not have been produced without CAD (because only computers could calculate whether the unusual structure would fall down in a high wind). See Figure 49.2.

49.4 Robotics

Industrial robots are fundamental to the car industry worldwide, and are becoming increasingly important in the production of electrical goods such as TVs and computers. Nevertheless, it remains a bit of a surprise that robots have not become a more powerful force in industry. Thirty years ago, people assumed that few workers would be left in factories – the robots were coming. In Britain today there are fewer than 50 robots per 10,000 workers. Even in Japan (with more than 40% of the world's robots) the figure is only 350 robots per 10,000 manufacturing workers.

The surprise is the greater when you look at the graph in Figure 49.3. Robot prices have fallen since 1990 by about 50%, yet their quality, efficiency and speed have risen. So robots are now a bit of a bargain!

Industrial robots have important advantages over human labour. They are programmed to do the same thing over and over again, so repetitive tasks can be completed

with 100% consistency. This can be vital – for example, in the production of components for aircraft engines, or in the production of heart pacemakers. Robots are also likely to prove cheaper than people, as long as the business is able to use them effectively (e.g. for 20 hours a day).

Yet robots are clearly not a magic solution, or else they would have taken over. They are inflexible, so they cannot easily switch jobs in the way that people can; and they have rarely proved as reliable as they perhaps should be.

A-grade application
Toshiba robots

Three Toshiba robots are used at a pet food factory in Bremen, northern Germany. The company has made substantial investment in factory automation in order to improve productivity. Toshiba Machine robots now package birdseed sticks at a rate of 90 per minute. Where once there were seven people working on the application across three shifts, now three Toshiba Machine TH350 robots achieve the same results. The people have been redeployed across the plant.

The robots are part of a production line that manufactures birdseed sticks that are like a fat-based lollypop, embedded with nuts and seeds. The sticks are fed down three conveyors, each with a ceiling-mounted robot at its end. As this happens, the boxes are fed down another conveyor. A robot gripper then picks up the seed sticks and transfers them into boxes on a moving conveyor. Ceiling-mounted SCARA robots make the best use of the available work area.

49.5 Communication with customers

There are two main ways firms communicate electronically with their customers. The first is a website – for example, easyJet receives over 95% of its bookings in this way. The second is through careful database management. A database is a store of information that can be rearranged and sorted in numerous ways. For example, if you had a database of all your friends, classmates and work colleagues, you might like to:

- sort them by birthday, so that you never missed the chance of a party invitation

- sort them by activity, so that you could rustle up a football or hockey team when needed

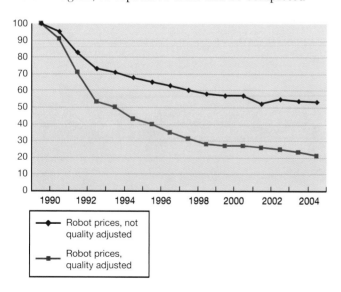

Figure 49.3 Price index of industrial robots, 1990–2005
Source: Adapted from 'Antomated Valve Fitting' 23 August 2007
http://tmrobolics.co.uk

- sort them by location, to give you a mailing list for organising a school reunion.

For businesses, the ability to store information on thousands, perhaps millions, of customers is invaluable. In order to maximise the speed and flexibility of a database, every type of information needs to be held in a different 'field'. Field 1 may be the surname, field 3 the address, field 7 the age, and so on. This enables the data to be sorted, or picked out, in different ways. If you have a new product aiming at the over-40s, those aged 40 and over can be picked out and a mailing list produced in seconds.

To obtain this data, businesses use various approaches:

- asking customers to fill in their name and address when purchasing goods

- recording the information on product warranty cards

- supplying 'loyalty' cards, such as Tesco's Clubcard

- buying databases from companies that specialise in gathering data.

If building a database, firms are legally required to register it with the Data Protection Registrar. The Data Protection Act 1984 gives people the right to see their personal file – for example, one held by a bank on a customer's creditworthiness.

Marketing and database management

Mailing lists have existed for decades. American Express, *Reader's Digest* and many others have built their business through well-targeted direct mail (sometimes referred to as 'junk mail'). They achieved this through the use of large, expensive mainframe computers. Nowadays even the smallest firm can afford a computer and some database software. Customers can be sorted into regular, light and occasional users, and be sent an appropriate mailshot. Each letter can be personalised (e.g. 'Dear Miss Hendrick. . .') and is therefore better suited to building a relationship with the customer. Alternatively, telephone sales staff can make direct contact to check on customer satisfaction and inquire whether any extra services are required.

The pursuit of an up-to-date, detailed database has reached its high point with supermarket loyalty cards. A Tesco Clubcard application form requires the customer to state details such as address, number of children, job and income. These details can be related to their lifestyle by recording what they buy and how much they

spend. If Tesco then wants to promote wine costing more than £8 per bottle, it can invite to an in-store tasting all those who have spent over £6 on a bottle of wine over the past six months. Having an accurate database minimises the waste, and therefore the cost, of such mailings. This makes them a more attractive proposition when compared to other advertising media.

These are all ways in which technology can cut costs, reduce waste, improve customer service quality and increase productivity.

49.6 Communication with suppliers

Electronic data interchange (EDI)

EDI is a permanent link between computers on different sites, enabling specified types of data to be exchanged. By establishing an EDI link, firms can ensure that the latest information is available instantly to other branches of their business, or even to other businesses. For example, Heinz's link with Tesco enables it to see how sales of soups are going this week. If chicken soup sales have pushed ahead 20% (perhaps because they were featured on a TV programme), production increases can be planned even before the Tesco head office phones through with a large order. This makes a just-in-time operation far more feasible.

Of course, Tesco does not want Heinz to have access to all its computer files, so the EDI link covers only specified data. Heinz might allow Tesco access to its stock levels and production plans in exchange for Tesco's daily sales data. This cooperation can help ensure that shelves are rarely empty.

EDI used to be for large companies only. Today, however, the availability of low-cost internet-based EDI means that any small supplier can keep this direct link with a retail customer. Sainsbury's, for example, set up JSnet for its smaller suppliers.

Electronic point of sale (EPOS)

EPOS equipment is at the heart of data collection by retailers. Laser scanning systems gather data from bar codes, which allow the computer to record exactly what has been bought and at what price. This forms the basis of the stock control system and also the recording of sales revenues. As with other aspects of IT, rapid falls in the cost of EPOS systems make them increasingly affordable for small shops.

Issues For Analysis

Information technology provides a series of tools that can be used to help businesses operate more effectively. This raises many issues for analysis, a couple of which are discussed below.

- Will electronic shopping mean shops are on the way out? The answer is probably no. But internet shopping will put new competitive pressures on high streets and shopping centres. If this book could be ordered in minutes on the internet and arrive in three days' time, would it make sense to go and look for it in a bookshop where it might not be in stock? Retailers are going to have to think very hard about whether they are offering the level of personal service that makes a visit worthwhile.

- Most managers and staff accept that new technology is necessary for businesses to keep up with their competitors. Yes, there are often problems when the time comes to update technology. Staff may worry that suggested 'improvements' are excuses for making people redundant. Managers need to be sensitive to people's fears, and win them over by honesty and openness.

49.7 Using technology in operations

an evaluation

Years ago the managers at Guinness thought change management was a technical question. When a change was needed, such as a new distribution system, they hired consultants, whose main focus was to establish effective information and communications technology (ICT) links. Time after time they were disappointed by the results. Improvements began only when they realised that the key variable was not the technology but the people. Not only were results better if staff were consulted fully, but also the new systems were successful only if staff applied them with enthusiasm and confidence.

Technology is only a set of tools. It can form the basis of a major competitive advantage, as with easyJet's initiative with internet bookings. More often, though, the successful application of IT relies on good understanding of customer and staff needs and wants. This suggests that good management of information technology is no different from good management generally.

Figure 49.4 Complex design files are effortlessly portable on iPhone's high-res widescreen display

Exercises

A. Revision questions

1 A database could be used by an aircraft manufacturer such as Boeing to record the supplier and batch number of every part used on every aircraft. How might this information be used? (3)

2 State two benefits of good database management in achieving efficient stock control. (2)

3 Read the A-grade application on JCB Dieselmax. Identify two benefits of 'virtual safety testing'. (2)

4 Look at Figure 49.3. Explain one possible implication for:
 (a) a UK factory owner feeling under pressure from competition from China (3)
 (b) a UK worker, with few qualifications or skills, thinking of taking a job in a factory. (3)

5 Explain one benefit and one drawback of computer-aided manufacture (CAM). (4)

6 From your reading of the whole unit, outline three ways in which technology can lead to improved quality. (6)

7 How significant might internet retailing become for each of the following types of business:
 (a) a music shop specialising in 1960s classic pop and rock (2)
 (b) a builders' merchant (selling bricks, cement, etc.) (2)
 (c) a mail-order clothing firm? (2)

8 From your reading of the whole unit, explain two ways in which technology can reduce waste within a business. (6)

B. Revision exercises

B1 Data response

Robots

Recently TM Robotics (Europe) Ltd worked with a major UK manufacturer to fit three Toshiba robots as part of an automated system to increase its output of valves.

The managers had to consider: the cost of the robots; the cost of installation and maintenance; the training required for key staff to manage the operation. All of this has to be weighed up against the cost of a manual alternative. One must also bear in mind potential downtime if the automated system is replacing an existing manual one.

The key factors in the success of the automation process were accuracy and flexibility. Accuracy was provided by the $+/-0.02$ mm repeatability of the Toshiba robot, and flexibility allowed the system to cope with 240 different product variants, all consisting of at least five component pieces.

One of the key factors in the installation process was ensuring a quick changeover period between different product variants, in order to minimise downtime. This is where a manual process can be advantageous – the worker simply finishing a batch of one product type and collecting the components for another, with no long changeover period required. Careful design ensured that the average changeover time was just 15 minutes, giving an impressive operating efficiency of 90%.

The total cycle time for the three robots to assemble the fitting is just 7.8 seconds, 4.2 seconds faster then the manual method. Furthermore, the automation has the obvious advantage of constant running. It doesn't slow down when it's tired, it doesn't take coffee breaks and never takes long lunches. Faster production time and constant output mean that the robot quickly pays for itself.

Source: adapted from www.tmrobotics.co.uk

Questions

(30 marks; 35 minutes)

1a Explain in your own words the meaning of 'downtime'. (3)

1b Why may firms be keen to minimise downtime? (4)

2 Examine the importance to this 'major UK manufacturer' of the accuracy and flexibility of these three robots. (6)

3a Calculate the % increase in production speed now that the robots are producing rather than people. (3)

3b Analyse two ways in which the manufacturer can benefit from the extra speed. (6)

4 Using the information in the case and your own knowledge, discuss two ways in which human workers may be more valuable than robots. (8)

B2 Data response

An architect and her iPhone

Patti the Architect, a small architectural firm based in Florida, is turning Apple's iPhone into a productivity-boosting mobile resource for construction-site communications.

With the Apple iPhone, architect Patricia 'Patti' Stough and her staff can now easily access their full library of design and construction documents on the move. The firm designs all its projects in CAD on high-performance Mac hardware, making the files effortlessly portable and displayable on iPhone's high-res widescreen display.

This mobility enables the firm to more easily communicate design intentions to customers on the site, as well as consult more effectively with builders, subcontractors and regulatory inspectors. And even if they had forgotten a document, they can easily retrieve it wirelessly via iPhone's Wi-Fi.

With a slight tap or pinch of their fingers, users can easily zoom in and out of drawings and 3D high-resolution photos on iPhone, drilling down to the finest of details or panning out for a big picture view via iPhone's revolutionary touchscreen interface. 'The days of hauling scrolls of paper drawings to job sites only to discover I

forgot a critical document are over,' says Stough. 'I can now carry even the largest, most complex and detailed CAD models in the palm of my hand. The ability to bring 3D digital drawings on site is a huge advantage, enabling me to better communicate and coordinate with everyone involved in the project.'

Patti the Architect is an award-winning architectural firm that specialises in beachfront townhouses, hotels, churches, schools, offices, retail additions and commercial interior renovations. Stough says that the huge productivity gains of designing in and working with 3D virtual building models are further enhanced through the mobility of iPhone.

Source: adapted from www.architosh.com, 14 August 2007

Questions

(25 marks; 30 minutes)

1 Outline three benefits of the CAD system to this architectural business. (6)

2 Explain how the iPhone-linked CAD has reduced time wastage for the business. (4)

3 Examine Patti Stough's suggestion that having CAD on the iPhone leads to 'huge productivity gains'. (6)

4 To what extent is the portable CAD system likely to improve Patti's customer service? (9)

C. Essay questions

(40 marks each)

1 Information technology is reducing the need to meet people face to face. Discuss the implications of this for running a successful business.

2 If industrial robots get cheap enough, they may replace almost all unskilled factory workers in the future. Discuss the benefits and costs of this to society.

3 'Internet retailing will mean the death of the high street.' Discuss.

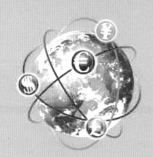

CORPORATE OBJECTIVES AND STRATEGY

DEFINITION

Corporate objectives are the company-wide goals that need to be achieved to keep the business on track to achieve its aims. Ideally they should be SMART (i.e. Specific, Measurable, Ambitious, Realistic and Timebound). Corporate strategy would provide a medium- to long-term plan for meeting the objectives.

50.1 Introduction

The key to success in understanding business is to see that every business is different. Even among public limited companies, the personality of the boss and the circumstances of the business can divide firms that seem to be in very similar positions. In UK supermarket retailing, the objectives of Tesco are completely different from the objectives of Sainsbury's. Similarly the objectives of Ryanair are wholly different from the objectives of British Airways. Then come the other types of business, from sole traders and private limited companies through to social enterprises and employee cooperatives.

Broadly, there is a clear distinction to be drawn between public companies (plcs) and every other type of business organisation. This is because only plcs have shareholders who have no connection with the business other than that they own its shares. A 30 year old who decides to buy £2000 worth of easyJet shares cares about only two things: the share price and the level of annual payments (dividends) paid out by the business. These are known as **shareholder value**. They are determined by two factors: the annual profits made by the business currently and investors' expectations of the business's future. If people think the growth prospects are terrific, the shares will be highly rated and therefore highly priced. A minority of share buyers may care about the social or environmental record of the business, but most care only about shareholder value.

A-grade application

On 3 June 2007 Russell Hardy was forced to quit his job as chief executive of Blacks Leisure plc (owners of the Millets retail chain). *The Times* reported that 'the 45 year old was leaving by mutual agreement and with immediate effect'. His departure followed Hardy's recent announcement of a plunge in annual profits at Blacks. Underlying profits had fallen from £22 million to just £100,000, forcing the shareholders' dividend to be cut by 75%. It is likely that the directors forced Hardy out because they were worried about the attitude of Blacks' biggest shareholder, Mike Ashley. Mr Ashley owns 29% of Blacks shares, as well as the bulk of the shares in Sports Direct and Newcastle United FC.

As shown in the case of Blacks Leisure, the plc shareholders' desire for rising profits puts a huge amount of pressure on the directors. Therefore there will always be many plc managements that place profit at the centrepiece of their corporate objectives.

For organisations other than plcs, there are many possible alternative objectives. There will be fishing shops that open up because individuals with a love of the sport have it as a lifetime ambition. The profits may not be great, but the satisfaction may be terrific. There will also be companies that start up with the intention of running a social enterprise. One well-known example is Duncan Goose, who founded Global Ethics Ltd in order to channel profit from selling bottled water into digging water wells in Africa.

50.2 Corporate objectives for plcs

- *Maximising shareholder value* (see Figure 50.1) is increasingly presented by the board of directors of large companies as the modern equivalent of profit maximisation. Share prices reflect the present value of the dividends the company is expected to pay out in the future. As a result this objective means taking actions that maximise the price of the organisation's shares on the stock market.

- *Growth* in the size of the firm: the managers of a business may choose to take decisions with the objective of making the organisation larger; the motivation behind this goal could be the natural desire to see the business achieve its full potential – it may also help defend the firm from hostile takeover bids. If your firm is the biggest, who could be big enough to take you over? Being number one in a marketplace is a version of the growth objective. It has been at the centre of the long-running battle between Nike and Adidas – both want to be the world's top provider of sportswear.

- *Diversification* in order to spread risk: in other words, to reduce dependence on one product or market. By 2000, Tesco boss Terry Leahy could see that there was little further growth to be gained in Britain, once Tesco's share of supermarket sales had gone beyond 25%. So he started on a huge overseas expansion, which culminated in the announcement of a £250 million a year investment between 2007 and 2011 in building Tesco 'fresh&easy' stores in America. This would help Tesco keep growing, but would also

A-grade application

In 2006 Adidas completed a £2 billion takeover of American sportswear rival Reebok. Herbert Hainer, boss of the German giant Adidas, said that the deal 'represents a major strategic milestone for our group'. The real purpose was to bring Adidas closer to its long-term goal of overtaking Nike as the world's biggest sportswear business. Mr Hainer went on to say, 'This is a once-in-a-lifetime opportunity to combine two of the most respected and well-known companies in the worldwide sporting goods industry.'

reduce its dependence on the UK market. A severe recession in Britain will not be something to fear if Tesco has profitable businesses worldwide. A firm may also diversify if it has a key product in the decline phase of the product life cycle – for example, cigarette manufacturers.

However, although diversification is one way of spreading risk and therefore reducing it, strategy expert Igor Ansoff has long warned how difficult it is to achieve successful diversification. In other words, diversifying is risky to do, yet reduces business risk if it can be achieved successfully. The risks involved in attempting to diversify come from two main sources.

1 First, the business will not understand the customers in a new market as well as in an existing one, such as Tesco attempting to succeed in America or China.

2 Second, the marketing strengths of an existing brand name and existing distribution channels may no longer apply. For instance, Heinz once decided to

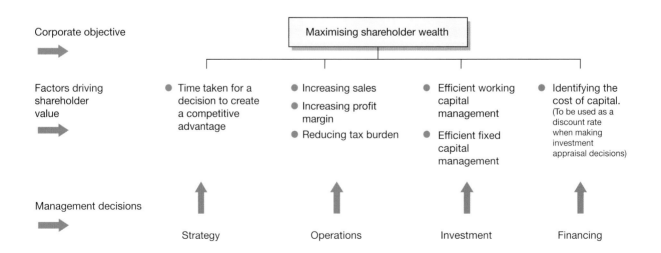

Figure 50.1 Maximising shareholder value
Source: Adapted from 'Shareholder Value' by Richard Barfield published in Accountancy October 1991

launch a vinegar-based household cleaning product. Consumers rejected this diversification because Heinz lacked credibility as a provider of anything other than food.

A-grade application

Why is Cadbury the master of the UK chocolate market, yet a bit player in UK biscuits and ice cream, and similarly small in the French, German and US chocolate markets? Within its core UK market, the name Cadbury means tradition, quality, social acceptability and a particular taste that most know and love. From Cadbury's point of view, the UK market is where it has virtually guaranteed high levels of distribution and in-store display, a full understanding of the different likes and dislikes of consumers, and a workforce steeped in market knowledge. There have been very occasional strategic lapses, such as when high cocoa prices in the 1970s led Cadbury to make its Dairy Milk bars thinner, opening up a new opportunity for the rival Yorkie bar to be launched. Overall, though, Cadbury can feel secure in its core market expertise and strength.

When straying from this market, however, different rules apply. In the ice cream market the Cadbury name means nothing other than reassurance about chocolate coating, and distribution becomes a weakness because it is virtually impossible to match Walls' promise to meet any retailer's order within 24 hours (even during a heatwave). Worst of all, though, is that Cadbury does not know whether to target Crunchie ice cream at adults or children, because it does not really understand the consumer.

50.3 Corporate objectives any business might adopt

Any business has certain objectives that may become fundamental to the operation. For new businesses, and for any that are struggling in the marketplace, the key one is survival. If things are going reasonably well, so that survival is not in doubt, a business might aim to increase its growth rate or its profitability. If these are also going well, the directors may look beyond the immediate financial needs to the 'market standing' of the business (see Figure 50.2).

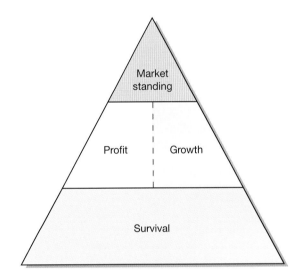

Figure 50.2 Pyramid of business objectives

Conclusions on objectives for plcs

Some academics argue that plc bosses have two sets of objectives. The first is based on profit 'satisficing' – in other words, achieving 'enough' profit rather than the maximum amount. A chief executive may be able to see how to get profit up by 30% in the coming year, but may worry that short-term profit gains will hit the longer-term security of the business. Therefore the boss makes decisions that can boost profit by 15% (enough to keep the shareholders happy) leaving scope for more profit growth in the coming years. Having found a way to keep the shareholders quiet, the directors can then decide on other objectives, such as to diversify.

Finally there is the possibility of a business organisation that has no commercial drivers, other than to generate the funds to achieve a social objective. Such an approach is rare, because many of the firms proclaiming their social or 'green' credentials are simply cashing in on a consumer concern. Even though non-profit motives are unusual, good answers show an understanding that businesses have many different objectives.

Market standing

For firms that already have a profitable, growing business and reasonable insulation from operational risks, the final piece in the corporate jigsaw is to establish an image that helps add value to the product range, and gives the consumer the confidence to assume the best in the company, not the worst. When Barclays announced the closure of hundreds of rural bank branches, the media and the general public queued up to condemn the company's greed and its lack of concern for its social responsibilities. Yet Black & Decker was able to announce 1000 redundancies in north-east England with hardly a murmur from the national media.

To have high market standing, the public needs to believe that the business operates as a force for good, whether through its products, its employment practices or its positive approach to its social responsibilities. All these things can be managed, as long as the commitment and the resources are available. For instance, the voluntary use of social and environmental audits can be the basis for building a reputation for ethical trading.

To have *really* high market standing, though, more is needed than just clever management of public relations. Apple is a company that most people *believe* in. If an Apple product is priced at £400, consumers assume that it costs around that amount to make and is therefore worth it. The brand embodies key images of the latest technology, the most creative designs and a business that is helping make life better for us all. Apple doesn't just have good management, it has an aura that makes it stand out.

Not-for-profit motives

Years ago people would have thought that social objectives imply charity work rather than business activity. Yet running a charity can be a bureaucratic nightmare, as the rules and regulations are highly restrictive. Therefore a quicker way to do some good in the world is to start a social enterprise (i.e. a business with a social rather than financial objective). In the case of One Water, its objective for 2008/2009 is 'to build one new Playpump per day'. This would require the business to generate about £2.5 million a year of net profit, which would be an incredible achievement for a business that started only in 2005.

Other businesses might see their task as to improve what people eat, to improve how children learn or to build better houses (Housing Associations are not-for-profit housing 'businesses').

50.4 Corporate strategy

The managers of a business should develop a medium-to long-term plan about how to achieve the objectives they have established. This is the organisation's corporate strategy (see Figure 50.3). It sets out the actions that will be taken in order to achieve the goals,

Figure 50.3 Corporate strategy

and the implications for the firm's human, financial and production resources. The key to success when forming a strategy of this kind is relating the firm's strengths to the opportunities that exist in the marketplace.

This analysis can take place at each level of the business, allowing a series of strategies to be formed in order to achieve the goals already established. A hierarchy of strategies can be produced for the whole organisation in a similar manner to the approach adopted when setting objectives.

● Corporate strategy deals with the major issues such as what industry, or industries, the business should compete in, in order to achieve corporate objectives. Managers must identify industries where the long-term profit prospects are likely to be favourable. In 2007, for example, Whitbread decided to pull out of the health club market by selling its David Lloyd Leisure subsidiary. It used the money to pay off some debt (to reduce gearing) and put the remainder behind its fast-growing Costa Coffee chain, in particular, setting up 200 Costa Coffees in China.

● Business unit (or divisional) strategy should address the issue of *how* the organisation will compete in the industry selected by corporate strategy. This will involve selecting a position in the marketplace to distinguish the firm from its competitors – in the case of Costa Coffee in China, how to differentiate the business from Starbucks.

● Functional (or department) strategy is developed in order to identify how best to achieve the objectives or targets set by the senior managers.

If a strategy is to achieve the objectives set, it must match the firm's strengths to its competitive

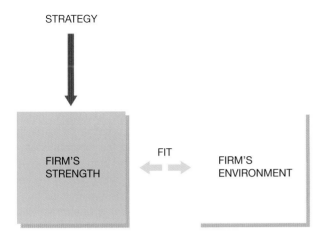

STRATEGY

FIRM'S
STRENGTH

FIT

FIRM'S
ENVIRONMENT

Figure 50.4 If a strategy is to achieve the objectives set, it must match the firm's strengths to its competitive environment

environment (see Figure 50.4). Whitbread decided that the market for health clubs in the UK was getting saturated and fierce competition was forcing clubs to cut prices, so it would be better to put its money behind the rapidly growing Costa chain and David Lloyd had to go.

As a company develops over time its employees acquire knowledge and skills. This 'organisational learning' represents what the firm as a whole is good at doing, or its 'core capabilities'. The key products or services produced by the business will reflect these strengths. The 2007 launch of the iPhone represented Apple's innovative abilities as a result of its research and development programme and design expertise.

Core capabilities need not be limited to a particular market. Marks & Spencer's move into financial services was based on a reputation for reliability and quality. This had built up over many years by its operation in the clothing and food markets. Corporate strategy can be shaped by identifying new opportunities to apply the existing strengths of the organisation.

Michael Porter, in his book *Competitive Advantage: Creating and Sustaining Superior Performance*, develops a method by which an organisation can analyse the competitive environment within which it operates in order to create strategic policy. He suggests that firms need to analyse five factors within an industry in order to understand the marketplace (see Figure 50.5). This will help managers understand how fierce or how favourable the competitive environment is. Each of Porter's **'five forces'** provides information that can be used to help devise an appropriate business strategy.

Porter believes that the overall strength or weakness of a firm's position depends on the following five factors.

1 *The intensity of rivalry with direct competitors.* In the 10 minutes' walk between South Wimbledon tube station and the Merton Park Metro stop there are five men's hairdressers. None stands out, and all charge between £6 and £8 for a haircut. Elsewhere in London the price is more likely to be £15, but the intensity of rivalry here keeps prices down – and makes it impossible for any of the five to make a great living out of their business.

2 *The threat of new entrants.* In the case of the hairdressers, there is nothing to prevent someone else opening a sixth shop. The barriers to entry are very low, as all you need is perhaps £10,000 to decorate and equip an existing retail outlet. In other cases, the barrier to entry is huge. For example, who today could set up an internet bookshop to rival Amazon? The millions of pounds needed to build the infrastructure (depots, etc.) would need to be matched by a fortune in advertising to wean people away from the tried and trusted Amazon. So there is very little threat to Amazon, even though it is now a hugely profitable business.

3 *The threat of new substitutes.* In the 1870s margarine, invented in France, was launched into the American market as a cheap alternative to butter. Sales were poor until it was discovered that adding artificial yellow colourings made consumers far more likely to buy it (margarine is naturally white). Farmers found sales of milk hit hard (butter is just churned milk) so they protested against margarine. Today margarine has a large share of the 'butter' market round the world. New substitutes can be bad news for producers.

4 *Bargaining power with suppliers.* The buying manager responsible for buying all of Tesco's biscuits has

Figure 50.5 Porter's 'five forces' framework
Source: Porter (1998)

power over the sales of 25–30% of all the biscuits made in the UK. Therefore Tesco has a huge amount of buying power. If a supplier wants to strike a special deal with Sainsbury's, perhaps only selling a new biscuit brand through Sainsbury's stores, Tesco will put a stop to that with one phone call. In contrast, a small corner shop has virtually no buying power (i.e. no leverage it can use to try to get a better deal for itself).

5 *Bargaining with customers.* When a small firm speaks to a big customer (e.g. the NHS, for medicines, or Hertz Rentals, for new cars), the minnow is likely to be very gentle. Only if the supplier is really huge would it be able to talk on level terms with the customer.

Porter's five forces help you analyse whether a business is in a strong or weak position overall.

Issues For Analysis

Does every business really need to write down its objectives and strategies? It may not be necessary, but it would always be useful. The fact is that running a large organisation is difficult, partly because staff who are one person among 70,000 (John Lewis) or 250,000 (Tesco) find it hard to be clear on what the business is trying to achieve overall. Writing down the objectives can help overcome this difficulty.

When analysing a business case study it is important to ask yourself the following questions.

● Do the objectives fit with the aims or mission of the business?

● Are the objectives clear and do they seem feasible (achievable)?

● Does everyone know and agree with these objectives (or are they a matter of dispute among staff or even among directors)?

● Are the strategies logical in relation to the objectives?

● Are the strategies achievable given the available resources (the right people; enough money; enough capacity)?

Armed with these questions it should be possible to analyse, and perhaps criticise, the corporate objectives and strategy.

50.5 Corporate objectives and strategy
an evaluation

The main judgements to be made are in relation to the analysis mentioned above (especially whether the strategy fits the objectives) plus the key issue of the external context. In other words, the corporate objectives and strategy must not only be right for the business, but also right for the year in question. If the economy is incredibly buoyant, as in 2006, ambitious corporate objectives might seem very wise. The exact same objectives in 2008 might be questionable, given widespread uncertainty over house prices and the creditworthiness of banks.

Judgements must always be subtle, so it is important to read with care about the external situation of the business. Examiners love to include phrases such as 'a fiercely competitive market' or 'a saturated market', and you need to pick up the messages. It is worth remembering that very few businesses can risk complacency about their market and their competition. A former chief executive of the giant computer business Intel, Andy Grove, once said 'only the paranoid survive'. Many other business leaders have loved to quote that to their own staff.

Key terms

Five forces: the five pressures on the business that Michael Porter says affect its success in the marketplace: near competitors; market accessibility to new entrants; possibility of substitutes; power of suppliers; power of customers.

Shareholder value: the value to investors of owning a company's shares. This is a function of the share price (up or down) plus the level of dividend payouts. Both are a function of the firm's profits plus the expectations of the company's future prospects.

Further reading

Barfield, R. (1991) Shareholder value. *Accountancy*, October.

Porter, M.E. (1998) *Competitive Advantage: Creating and Sustaining Superior Performance.* Simon & Schuster.

Exercises

A. Revision questions

(40 marks; 40 minutes)

1a List four possible corporate objectives. (4)

1b Explain the extent to which each is focused on the short or long run. (8)

2 Explain why every leader of a public limited company must think hard about the objective of maximising shareholder value. (4)

3 Increasingly, chief executives gain huge rewards from bonus payments linked to the price of their company's shares. Outline how this might affect their approach to shareholder value. (5)

4 Explain the benefits Tesco is receiving from its corporate objective of diversification. (4)

5 What is meant by the term 'satisficing'? (2)

6a List the five factors Porter suggests determine an industry's competitive environment. (5)

6b Explain why the price of a haircut is so cheap between South Wimbledon and Merton Park stations. (3)

7 Explain why it may be true to say that 'diversification is a risky way to reduce risk'. (5)

B. Revision exercises

B1 Data response

Fizzy orange turns sour

In 2007 retail sales of Tango fell by 27%, from £38 million to £28 million. Tango, produced by the soft drinks producer Britvic, has a tough time competing with the Coca-Cola brand Fanta. In 2007, Fanta sales were £124 million.

Both brands have been suffering from the recent trend towards 'healthy' drinks. People see fizzy drinks as in some way less healthy than still ones. So even Fanta has struggled, with its 2007 sales down by 2% on the previous year. Orange fizz has also suffered from the growth of fresh orange juice, notably the powerful (Pepsi-owned) brand

Tropicana. In 2007 Tropicana sales grew 12.5% to £238 million.

Britvic products may also suffer from a struggle for credibility when in negotiation with the major retail chains. Now that the 'big four' supermarkets have a market share of around 65% of all grocery sales, it can be hard to get distribution for minor brands such as Tango. If the brand's sales continue to decline, it may become harder for Britvic to achieve the purchasing economies of scale necessary for a profitable brand.

Source: Britvic Soft Drinks Report 2007; Nielsen data quoted in The Grocer, 15 December 2007

Questions

(20 marks; 25 minutes)

1 Use Porter's five forces to analyse Britvic's position with its Tango brand. (10)

2 To what extent does the five forces approach seem to offer a fully rounded analysis of the competitive position of Tango? (10)

B2 Case study

Objectives and strategy at Toyota – world number one

Extracts from the Toyota Annual Report (to shareholders) 2007

'In the two years since I became Toyota's President, I have reasserted the importance of building a solid foundation for sustainable growth. Given that the source of our growth is innovation, we will invest efficiently in research and development to continue building vehicles that meet customer needs. In securing our foundation, we intend to steadily tackle three key areas: quality, cost competitiveness and personnel training.

'Toyota's tradition and strength stem from carrying out these clear steps in an honest, steadfast and uncompromising manner.'

From 'An Interview with the President' (also in the

Annual Report):

'I expect that competition in the global automotive industry will become even more fierce, especially in the areas of environmental technologies and cost-competitiveness.'

'Since my appointment as President, I have consistently impressed upon everyone at Toyota that without quality improvement there cannot be growth. I believe that rather than … volume-related results we should take pride in quality – or the extent to which the vehicles we build meet the needs of our customers.'

'In the medium-term we are targeting group vehicle sales of about 9.8 million units in 2008. In 2006 group vehicle sales totalled 8.81 million units and we project sales of 9.34 million in 2007. We aim to steadily grow sales worldwide by continuing to bring new products to market that meet the needs of customers.'

Source: the above statements are from Mr Watanabe, President of Toyota, July 2007

Questions

(30 marks; 40 minutes)

1 Identify and explain two corporate objectives set by the Toyota President. (6)

2 Examine the strategy being put forward for one of those two objectives. (5)

3 If Toyota can achieve its target of 9.8 million cars in 2008, it will be the world's biggest car producer by quite a margin.
   (a) How may it benefit from this position? (4)
   (b) Use that and all the other information provided above to analyse Toyota's position using Porter's five forces. (5)

4 Discuss whether Mr Watanabe believes that technological development or human resource development is the more important for the future of Toyota. (10)

C. Essay questions

(40 marks each)

1 Discuss whether 'corporate' objectives can mean much in a company as big and as complex as Tesco plc.

2 The management expert Peter Drucker believes that it is a mistake for a business to focus upon a single objective. To what extent do you support him in this view?

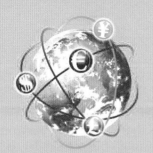
CORPORATE AIMS, MISSION AND CULTURE

51.1 Introduction

Some children as young as 10 or 11 seem very clear about what they want from life. They are determined to become a doctor or a vet. The clarity of their aim makes them work hard at school, choose science subjects and overcome any setbacks (a duff maths teacher, perhaps). So whereas most GCSE/A-level students drift from one day to the next, these individuals are focused: they have their eyes on their prize. This is the potentially huge benefit that can stem from clear aims.

Indeed, you could say that some of these focused students are driven by a sense of mission. Their aim is not just to get the label of 'doctor' but also to make a contribution to making the world a better place. The drive shown by these students will be the most impressive of all.

For new small businesses there can also be a powerful sense of mission. A chef may open his/her own restaurant, driven largely by the desire to win a Michelin star (the *Michelin Guide* to restaurants is the world's most prestigious). In Gordon Ramsay style, the approach to achieving this may prove to be ruthless or even fanatical. Yet such a person is far more likely to achieve their aim than one who opens a restaurant thinking, 'It would be nice to get a star; let's see whether it happens.'

In marketplaces where competition is fierce, passionate and determined businesses are always more likely to succeed than those that are drifting. This has always been one of the secrets to the success of *The Sun* newspaper. Its owner and editors have always believed passionately that its mix of fun and sport works because it gives people what they want. Their view is that newspapers should not 'preach' to their readers. The

Figure 51.1 Michelin-star chef Gordon Ramsay

Daily Mirror used to be Britain's number one paper, but it has drifted back to number three, out-fought and out-thought by *The Sun*.

From the clear sense of mission at *The Sun* has come its workplace culture. This is cut-throat and ruthless, with the drive to get the best stories and the best scoops. It has also led to many headlines that are on the borderline between acceptable and disgraceful.

To switch examples, consider the position of the John Lewis Partnership. This employee-owned business (Waitrose and John Lewis stores) has a mission statement that reads: 'Our purpose is the happiness of all our members (employees) through their worthwhile, satisfying employment in a successful business.' By putting its staff first, John Lewis makes clear how different it is from most businesses. The culture of the organisation fits in with this, as it is famously based on respect for each other, for customers, but above all for the institution that is John Lewis (one of the world's biggest employee-owned businesses).

To achieve a high grade at this subject, full understanding of this chapter is critical, because aims, mission and culture are fundamental to business success, and therefore exam success.

51.2 Aims

Aims are the generalised statement of where the business is heading. Possible examples include:

- 'to become a profitable business with a long-term future' (Hodges Sports, an independent sports shop started in January 2008)

- 'to become a football league club' (AFC Wimbledon, currently in the Isthmian League)

- 'to diversify away from dependence on Britain' (the implicit aim of Tesco in the past ten years).

One of the stated aims of the McDonald's fast food chain is to provide 'friendly service in a relaxed, safe and consistent restaurant environment'. The success of the organisation depends upon turning this aim into practice. In order for this to be achieved, employees must understand and share the aim. When a customer enters a McDonald's restaurant anywhere in the world they know what to expect. The organisation has the ability to reproduce the same 'relaxed, safe and consistent' atmosphere with different staff, in different locations. This has built the company's reputation. This corporate aim is effective because it recognises what lies at the heart of the organisation's success.

But do aims need to be written down? Many businesses do not write down their aims or even spend time trying to define them. This is particularly true of small organisations where employees know each other and understand their shared purpose. Even when an aim is unstated it may be possible to identify it by looking at the actions taken by a firm over time. Staff in a small firm may work together to achieve a common aim with a level of commitment that may not exist in a large firm that sets out its aims in writing.

Whether stated or unstated, corporate aims act as a basis upon which to form goals or objectives for the organisation (see Unit 50). These are the targets that must be achieved if the aims are to be realised. The success or failure of each individual decision within the firm can be judged by the extent to which it meets the business objectives. This allows the delegation of authority within the organisation, while at the same time maintaining coordination.

51.3 Mission statements

A **mission statement** is an attempt to put corporate aims into words that inspire. The mission statement of Wal-Mart, the world's biggest retailer, is 'to give ordinary folk the chance to buy the same thing as rich people'. Shop floor staff are more likely to be motivated by a mission statement of this kind than by the desire to maximise profit.

It is hoped that, by summarising clearly the long-term direction of the organisation, a focus is provided that helps to inspire employees to greater effort and ensure the departments work together. Without this common purpose each area of a firm may have different aims and choose to move in conflicting directions.

A-grade application

Examples of mission statements

- *Pret A Manger:* 'Pret creates handmade natural food avoiding the obscure chemical additives and preservatives common to so much of the prepared and "fast" food on the market today'
- *3M:* 'To solve unsolved problems innovatively'
- *Body Shop:* 'Tirelessly work to narrow the gap between principle and practice, whilst making fun, passion and care part of our daily lives'
- *Coca-Cola:* 'To refresh the world – in body, mind and spirit'
- *James Dyson:* 'Long-term business success based on newly invented, innovatively designed products'
- *Nike:* 'To bring innovation and inspiration to every athlete* in the world' (*If you have a body you are an athlete)

It is also important to note that not every company has a written mission statement. The bosses of Innocent Drinks have always been clear that they and their staff 'live the mission' and therefore do not need to write it down. Marks & Spencer plc has stopped publicising a mission statement, perhaps because it has learnt that one statement cannot sum up the driving forces behind a whole, complex business.

For those that do use mission statements, the model shown in Figure 51.2 gives a clear sense of their purpose. To develop a strong mission statement it is necessary to link each of the four elements of the model so that they reinforce one another.

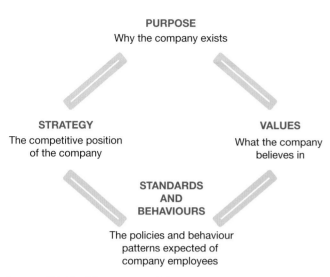

PURPOSE
Why the company exists

STRATEGY
The competitive position
of the company

VALUES
What the company
believes in

**STANDARDS
AND
BEHAVIOURS**
The policies and behaviour
patterns expected of
company employees

Figure 51.2 Mission model
Source: Campbell et al. (1990)

In turn, each element suggests the following.

- *Purpose (i.e. the reason why the company exists)*. This is clearly shown by the Nike **mission**, which emphasises the desire to provide innovative products for athletes. In fact a sceptic could point out that Nike builds much of its branding around advertising, imagery and visual design rather than product innovation. Nike's brilliance has been to keep everyone sure that the company cares about supporting athletes, rather than exploiting them.

- *Values (i.e. what the company believes in)*. In the case of Pret A Manger, it is not just that it believes in natural, fresh food, but also that the business has always:
  - used packaging that is made from recycled materials and can be recycled in future
  - taken care to source its products from suppliers that treat staff fairly
  - wanted to push customers to try new things, especially from sustainable sources.

  The values of the business are a key part of its culture, and should also include the way staff are treated and other ethical considerations.

- *Standards and behaviours (i.e. the standards set by managers and the behaviour expected from staff)*. In 2006, Cambridge graduate Polly Courtney told *The Observer* about her experiences as a highly paid banker in the City. The work culture meant that people would send emails at 2.00 in the morning to show how late they worked, and Polly found sexism rooted in a 'lads' culture in which nights out ended at the strip club. As the only woman in an office of 21, she was treated like a secretary and bypassed for

the more important jobs. Polly wrote a book about her experiences, whereas others have successfully sued merchant banks on grounds of sex discrimination. Clearly the managements are wholly at fault in allowing such a situation to develop.

- *Strategy (i.e. the medium- to long-term plans adopted by the business to make the aims and mission achievable)*. This is dealt with in Unit 50.

How valuable are mission statements?

As an example of the possible downsides of mission statements, it is interesting to look back at companies' former mission statements. For example, Coca-Cola used to say: 'Our mission is to get more people to drink Coke than water.' Today that seems quite a shocking idea. Clearly it would mean a dramatic worsening of the obesity problem that affects most of the developed world. Yet Coca-Cola had this as its mission statement up until ten years ago. The fact that it has dropped this statement in favour of the socially more acceptable 'to refresh the world' raises the question of whether mission statements are little more than public relations exercises.

Even more serious is the possibility that mission statements are a substitute for the real thing. They may be a bureaucratic management's attempt to provide a sense of purpose in a business that has none. If so, this would be the wrong way to approach the problem. If staff lack inspiration, the starting point is to find a real sense of purpose, probably through the staff themselves. For example, doctors and nurses used to be hugely proud to work for the NHS; now they are more likely to moan about its shortcomings. Writing a mission statement would be treated with derision by the staff. Far more important is to find out from staff what they dislike about the current management and discuss how to restore staff pride in the service.

51.4 Culture

Culture can be described as 'the way we do things round here'. In other words, it's the attitudes and behaviours shown within the workplace. This will be built up over many years as a result of:

- the aims or mission of the business – if the aim is to be innovative, this should affect the business culture

- the behaviour of the company directors and other senior staff – if they pay themselves huge bonuses and jump at chances to fly business class to questionable conferences, staff will pick up the idea that 'me, me, me' is at the heart of the business culture

- the attitude of senior management to enterprise and risk – if a failed new product launch leads to the dismissal of the manager leading the project, this will send out a message to all staff to beware of taking on responsibility, which could be very damaging in the long term

- the recruitment and training procedures – research has shown that dynamic companies have a mixture of different types of staff – some who are very organised, some who are creative but perhaps chaotic, some who are argumentative and so on; some HR departments use psychometric tests to recruit 'our type of person' and screen out potential 'troublemakers'; the culture could become quite passive – safe but dull – if new recruits are always the same type of efficient but uninspired people.

The culture of the business has many aspects that are fundamental to its success or failure. First are the business values. An organisation's mission statement provides an opportunity to shape this business culture. The challenge is to develop a set of values that employees can feel proud of. It should also motivate them to work towards the organisation's objectives. This may be difficult to achieve, particularly in large companies where each different department of the firm may have its own culture. In this case there may be no dominant corporate culture.

The business culture will show through in many ways, including those described below.

- The team versus the individual: some organisations work in a 'dog-eat-dog' fashion in which individuals are climbing up the career ladder partly through their ability to cut the rungs away from their rivals; in others, an individual's effectiveness when working with a team is especially highly prized.

- Attitude to hard work: in some businesses, as in some schools, the group norm is to laugh at those who work hard – they may be referred to as 'crawlers' (or worse). To survive, such a business must have a protected, perhaps monopoly, position. At the other extreme are organisations where working 12- to 15-hour days is regarded as a proper sign of commitment, such as in some City merchant banks. Perhaps the ideal is a boss who expects people to give their best throughout the day, but encourages everyone to go home at 5.30.

- Customer-centred or focused inwards? This is crucial, as many organisations allow staff to develop a 'them and us' attitude to customers. Customers can be viewed as the inconvenient people who disrupt the day-to-day life of the staff. One of Britain's main exam boards set up a call centre so that teachers could no longer phone staff directly, thereby 'distracting them from getting on with their jobs'. Yet what is an exam board for other than to serve its customers: teachers?

- Attitude to risk: as mentioned above, the key thing here is whether the business establishes an enterprising, risk-taking culture – as at Apple, Nintendo, Innocent and Toyota – or a bureaucratic culture in which risks are eliminated by layer after layer of managers who never seem to make decisions. (Career advice: make sure to avoid working for such a frustrating business.)

- Ethical stance: the culture will help staff know how to deal with difficult decisions, such as 'Should I accept this invite for a chat with our main competitor about prices?' or 'Should I accept this Christmas present from our main supplier?' In the best-run companies, staff will know that the business and all its employees are never to cut moral corners, even if profits are hit as a result.

A-grade application
Reckitt Benckiser

Reckitt Benckiser is the company behind Cillit Bang, Lemsip, Dettol, Strepsils and many other household brands. It's a big business, with annual profits of £1 billion, but it competes with two giants: Unilever and Procter & Gamble. Reckitt's chief executive, Bart Becht, says that the group's culture is 'the number one driver of success – no question. It is our only sustainable advantage. Everything else can be copied, but it's close to impossible to copy culture.'

A key target for Reckitt is that at least 40% of sales should come from products launched within the past three years. Therefore the business culture involves swift decision making, innovation and risk-taking. Those joining the company can find the culture a bit of a shock, as it is fast-paced and quite aggressive. The low managerial labour turnover (10%), though, makes it clear that staff enjoy the achievement-focused culture. A recent recruit from rival Procter & Gamble describes the culture as 'much leaner, much more informal, much more individualistic' than that of his previous employer.

It is clear that Reckitt's 'strong' culture is needed for the number three business competing with two giants. It provides the strength, and the speed of thought and action that keeps the company successful.

Issues For Analysis

In order to analyse the aims of an organisation there are a number of key issues that should be considered. These include the following.

- Are employees aware of what the organisation is trying to achieve? Is it necessary to write down these aims? Ideally an understanding of the purpose of the business should be embedded so deeply in staff that it influences their actions without them realising it.

- If the aims are clear, is there really any need to repackage them as a mission statement? It may be that the process of devising a mission statement is a worthwhile one, especially if all staff are involved. Yet the final text may be no more than a statement of the obvious, or may be so over the top that no one can take it seriously.

- Another key question for analysis is whether the aims of the organisation are reflected in its culture. For example, what is the underlying attitude towards risk-taking, sharing information and evenly distributing rewards in the firm? If the culture is strong and positive, it will not matter whether a new mission statement has been produced.

Key terms

Aims: a generalised statement of where the business is heading.

Ethos: the distinguishing character of a group of people.

Mission: an aim expressed in a particularly inspiring way.

Mission statement: a short passage of text that sums up the organisation's mission. This may get displayed on walls throughout the business and placed prominently on the website.

Further reading

Campbell, A., Devine M. and Young, D. (1990) *A Sense of Mission*. Economist Books/Hutchinson.

51.5 Corporate aims, mission and culture
an evaluation

Good evaluation is based upon a questioning approach to the subject matter. This should apply to the case material being looked at, and to the underlying theory. This section of the course provides huge scope for careful questioning; this should *not* be in the form of blanket cynicism ('all mission statements are rubbish'), but by carefully considering the evidence. Is a new boss genuinely trying to improve the motivation and behaviour of staff for the benefit of customers and the business as a whole? If so, perhaps a mission statement is a valuable centrepiece to a whole process of culture change.

At other times, though, the case material may present a new mission statement as no more than a sticking plaster on a diseased wound. Genuine problems need genuine solutions, not slogans. You need to make judgements about which situation is which, then justify your views with evidence from the case and drawn from the theory set out in this unit.

Exercises

A. Revision questions

(35 marks; 35 minutes)

1 Why do clear aims help people or businesses achieve their goals? (3)

2 Why may a formal statement of aims be unnecessary in a small business with a limited number of employees? (3)

3 Outline the difference between the workplace culture at *The Sun* and that of John Lewis. (3)

4a What is the purpose of a mission statement? (3)

4b Identify the four elements that make up the 'mission model'. (4)

5 Explain why poor recruitment could lead to an ineffective business culture. (4)

6 Briefly explain whether you think *two* of the following businesses would be likely to have an entrepreneurial or a bureaucratic business culture (i.e. you choose two from four):
   (a) Marks & Spencer
   (b) Facebook
   (c) L'Oréal
   (d) Ryanair. (6)

7 Look again at Coca-Cola's new mission compared with its old one. Explain why it might be difficult to persuade staff to believe in a changed 'mission' such as this. (4)

8 Why are mission statements often criticised for being ineffective in practice? (5)

B. Revision exercises

B1 Data response

In 1994 a 30-year-old New Yorker called Jeff Bezos read about the internet. He moved to California and in a year had set up an internet bookshop. When orders came in, he packed and posted the books from his garage. By February 1999, Bezos employed 1600 people and his shares were worth $2500 million. In February 2008 there were more than 15,000 employees and sales of over $10,000 million. Jeff Bezos is the founder and 40% shareholder in Amazon.com, the world's biggest internet retailer.

What are the aims that helped guide him to become one of the first internet billionaires? His workforce mission is to 'Change the world in an important and fundamental way. Our motto is: Work hard, have fun, make history.' In the 2006 accounts Bezos included a copy of the letter he sent with the 1997 annual report, to show that the entrepreneurial culture of the business was unchanged: the aim in relation to customers is to 'provide the best customer experience … That means we have to have the biggest selection! The easiest to use website! The lowest prices! And the best purchase decision information!'

Asked about his huge wealth, Bezos replied: 'I don't think it matters much. The biggest change is that I don't have to look at menu prices any more.'

Questions

(40 marks; 50 minutes)

1 Distinguish between aims and mission with reference to this case. (6)

2a What is meant by an 'entrepreneurial culture'? (2)

2b Why may it be harder to maintain this culture in a large business than in a small one? (6)

3 What evidence is there in the text that business people are not motivated only by money? (6)

4 Outline four factors that might lead to a change in Amazon.com's aims in future. (8)

5 Discuss whether Mr Bezos was successful because of his aims or because his success allowed him to adopt such aims? Explain your answer. (12)

B2 Case study

The John Lewis culture

Very few bosses of public limited companies rose to their position via a job in personnel or human resources. Most have had a career in finance, marketing or operations. The John Lewis boss, Andy Street, is an exception. It may be his background as Personnel Director that makes him so focused upon his staff. Or perhaps it is simply a result of the John Lewis **ethos**.

What makes John Lewis unusual is that, in 1929, its founder put all the company's shares into an employee-owned trust. In other words, the shares went to the staff instead of to Lewis's children. Today, nearly 70,000 John Lewis 'partners' work for a business that has no conventional shareholders. Nor does it have a profit motive, other than to provide an annual bonus to the staff and to provide the finance for the growth of the enterprise.

If anyone doubts whether this can work, take a look at the accounts at www.johnlewispartnership.co.uk. In 2008 the accounts showed a sales revenue of nearly £7 billion and an operating profit of nearly £400 million. This profit margin is very similar to that of Tesco.

Andy Street visits his 28 John Lewis and 180 Waitrose stores regularly and says that he can tell within minutes if a store's culture is not right: 'It's about the extent to which we manage to bring that dream alive of having motivated partners giving excellent customer service.'

The John Lewis culture is especially strong because labour turnover is exceptionally low. Many staff have worked at John Lewis since school or university (including Andy Street). The other factor is the John Lewis mission, which emphasises the need to satisfy staff in order to satisfy customers. This, of course, is due to the partnership approach (i.e. that the owners of the business are its staff). The uniqueness can be seen in the way the business describes its culture on its website:

> What unites all of us is our behaviour, which is based on our powerful and distinctive partnership culture. You can work in a company where you can be honest, give respect, recognise others, show

enterprise, work together and achieve more, as well as being a co-owner.

Some other retailers like to refer to John Lewis as halfway to working for the civil service. But the partnership's success at building market share and profitability makes it seem more than just a big bureaucracy. On Boxing Day 2007, the first day of the John Lewis sale, Andy Street was at his local John Lewis branch to help serve the rush of customers. Being this down to earth should help him ensure that staff remain clear that, ultimately, it is the customer that matters.

Source: Adapted from *Observer*, 30 December 2007 and www.johnlewispartnership.co.uk

Questions

(40 marks; 50 minutes)

1 Outline two distinctive features of the business aims of the John Lewis Partnership. (6)

2a Calculate the profit margin at John Lewis. (3)

2b Outline two actions the business could take to improve its profit margin. (8)

3 Based on the text, explain in your own words the workplace culture of John Lewis. (8)

4 On the basis of the evidence provided, discuss whether you would want to work for John Lewis. Explain your answer. (15)

C. Essay questions

(40 marks each)

1 With reference to any organisation with which you are familiar (football club, school, part-time employer, etc.) discuss the importance of its aims in determining the actions and decisions it takes.

2 'If a business feels the need to write out a mission statement, it has no mission.' Discuss.

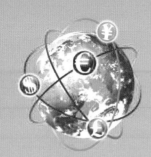
FUNCTIONAL OBJECTIVES AND STRATEGY

52.1 Introduction

Each of the four functional departments within a business (marketing, finance, operations and people) has its own objectives. Together, the four sets of objectives must match the organisation's own corporate objectives. Each of the four must fit together to make the overall targets reachable.

For example Hamleys' corporate objective of increasing internet sales from £3 million to £50 million by 2011 would require action by each of the four functions.

1 The marketing director might set objectives such as 'to boost customer recognition of the Hamleys website from 8% to 60% within three years'.

2 The finance director might set an objective of 'to increase the available budget for internet development from £1 million to £5 million a year'.

3 The operations director might set the objective of 'to increase the capacity of our internet stock and distribution warehouse from £5 million to £60 million worth of sales by 2010'.

4 The personnel director might set the objective of: 'Switching our graduate recruitment focus so that 50% of our graduate intake have IT degrees by 2010'.

If all four directors succeed in their own objectives, the business will be in a good position to achieve its overall goal.

52.2 Corporate objectives

This topic is covered in Unit 50. For now, the key is to understand why and how different firms have different objectives. The mistake to avoid is the assumption that all businesses are driven by the desire for profit. Many are, but not all. Among many possible objectives, the following are the most common (see also Table 52.1, overleaf).

● *Growth:* the only explanation for Tesco's actions in the past 15 years has been that the business has been pursuing a growth objective. Originally this was to become Britain's number one, outstripping Sainsbury's (see Figure 52.1). After that was achieved, Tesco developed its business in eastern Europe, South East Asia and now America – becoming the world's third biggest supermarket business. This is a wonderful objective for staff (lots of career openings), for managers and potentially shareholders, as long as profits improve as well. In fact, Tesco is also one of the world's most profitable supermarket chains too.

● *Profit optimisation (i.e. making the 'right' amount of profit, not the maximum possible):* most large firms

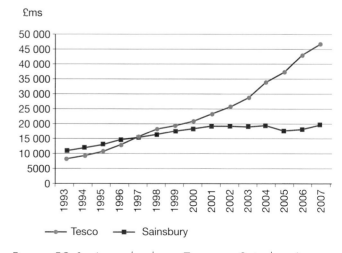

Figure 52.1 Annual sales – Tesco vs Sainsbury's

Table 52.1 Business objectives

Type of objective	Example of objectives
● Growth	● To become Britain's number one ● To achieve a £1 billion turnover by 2012
● Profit optimisation	● To achieve profit growth of 10–12% a year for the next four years ● To return profit margins to the 8% level achieved two years ago
● Profit maximisation	● To drive profit up by at least 50% this year ● To become Britain's most profitable window replacement business
● Not-for-profit	● To become Britain's bank of choice for those concerned ethically about how their money is used (Co-op Bank) ● To finance and build one water pump a day (One Water)

want their profits to rise as smoothly as Tesco's sales line in Figure 52.1. So even if they know that a sudden rush for one of their brands could allow them to increase the price and make huge profits, few would be tempted. They do not want to risk alienating customers who may blog about being 'ripped off'; and they do not want profits to soar this year but slide next. Shareholders love to see steady profit growth.

● *Profit maximisation:* this objective means making as much profit as possible, with the implication that it should be made in as short a time as possible. This is most likely to be the objective for a small to medium-sized business run by individuals with little regard for their customers or for the long-term reputation of their business. 'Cowboy' builders maximise their profit by charging high prices for shoddy work. They do not rely on repeat purchase, but on finding another unsuspecting customer victim. Few large plcs deliberately pursue profit maximisation, though executives with huge share options might take decisions that maximise profit this year at the possible expense of the future.

● A *not-for-profit motive:* the owner of the One Water business, Duncan Goose, has a very unusual business objective. At present his charitable water business funds one new water well in Africa every eight to ten days. His objective is one a day. To achieve this he needs growth in the sales and in the profits made by selling bottles of One Water in the UK. Other businesses, such as John Lewis Partnership and the Co-op Bank, need profit to survive and to grow, but also have not-for-profit objectives.

52.3 Functional objectives

Functional objectives are the targets of the individual business departments (functions). They will stem from the corporate objectives and are either set by the chief executive or may be the result of discussion between directors.

Having set the company's objectives, the key is to take care over each department's objectives. They must work separately and together, so that the overall goal can be achieved. For the 2012 London Olympics, the operations function must ensure that the stadium is built, while the marketing department sets ambitious targets for selling the millions of tickets to fill it to capacity. If one succeeds while the other fails, the London organisers will be laughed at by the world's media.

Success requires that the leaders within each department/function do the following.

● *Coordinate what they are doing:* what, when and how. Timing will be crucial, such as having the right amount of stock to cope with the demand expected on the launch day. So marketing, operations and personnel must be acting together, perhaps using **network analysis** software to make sure that the whole project is kept on track.

● *Make sure that all within their own department know the overall objective* as well as the functional one, and that all are motivated towards achieving it. In 2007 and 2008 the BBC worked on a plan to switch production from London to Manchester; it was clear from the start that many staff in London were unhappy with this and tried to sabotage the move.

● *Work together to achieve a common goal:* this may seem obvious, but in many organisations managers and even directors are jostling for promotions or positions, not really working together (just think of Roman Abramovich and Jose Mourinho at Chelsea), so the marketing director might be happy to see the operations director humiliated.

A-grade application

iPhone

At precisely 6.02 on the Friday evening of 10 November 2007 the iPhone was launched in the UK. That evening the first TV advertisements appeared and, by the following Monday, 100,000 iPhones had been sold. The brilliance of the exercise was making sure that there were enough iPhones in stock to cope with the demand. The coordination of this was a result of superb organisation by the Apple management. As Sony has shown on many occasions, it is easy to run short of stock on a hot new product.

52.4 Functional strategies

A strategy is a medium- to long-term plan for meeting objectives. This should come about from a careful process of thought and discussion throughout the business, though key decisions will almost always be made at the top. To make the right decision about strategy, a useful approach is known as the 'scientific decision-making model' (Figure 52.2). It shows that strategy decisions must:

1 be based on clear objectives

2 be based on firm evidence of the market and the problem/opportunity, including as much factual, quantitative evidence as possible (e.g. trends in market size, data on costs, sales forecasts)

3 look for options (i.e. alternative theories – hypotheses – as to which would be the best approach); for example, to meet an objective of higher market share we could either launch a new product or put all our energies and cash behind our Rising Star existing product

4 be based on as scientific a test of the alternatives as possible (e.g. a test market of the new product in the Bristol area, while doubling advertising spending on the Rising Star in the north-east – then comparing which approach provided the bigger market share gains)

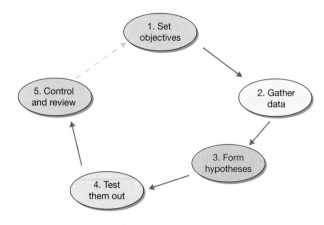

Figure 52.2 Scientific decision-making model

5 control the approach decided upon – the final stage (e.g. if it's a new product launch, to manage the quality and timing of every aspect of production, sales, advertising and delivery) – then review, to learn from any mistakes or unexpected successes before (the dotted line on the diagram) starting again with a new objective and a new strategy.

Within this process, the single most important thing is that the business should make sure that the functional strategies are all part of one overall strategy (and match the overall objective). For many years the objective of the Apple Corporation was to succeed by being more customer-friendly that its then only rival, Microsoft.

Table 52.2 Apple iPod strategy

Functional areas	Actual strategy in the early iPod years
Marketing strategy	Quirky poster advertisements emphasising street style rather than the product
Operations strategy	Design a great-looking product with distinctive headphones (the white wires) and a great interface
People strategy	Hire free-thinking people and give them the space and environment to be creative (don't over-manage or over-control them)
Financial strategy	Provide all the finance needed for product development, and don't over-control later decisions (e.g. the Nano launched while the original Shuffle model was still in its growth phase)

The strategy for achieving this was to be one step ahead in design rather than technology. This strategy focus on design became the beginnings of a goldmine with the 2001 launch of the iPod. Table 52.2 describes what this meant for each functional area.

Issues For Analysis

Top firms unite behind a single strategy based on clear objectives. Therefore, when analysing case material about any business, it is wise to ask the following questions.

- How clear is the overall company objective? Is it precisely stated, with a timescale, thereby making it easy to measure success or failure? This is often called a **SMART objective** (i.e. Specific, Measurable, Achievable, Realistic, Timebound).

- Having considered the overall objective, what are the functional objectives agreed by the directors? Is each one also SMART? Or does HR, for example, have only vague targets because the importance of the human element has been overlooked?

- Then comes the overall strategy, for which each of the functions should be contributing its own crucial part. In November 2007 Sony announced gleefully that sales of its PS3 had doubled because Nintendo had run out of pre-Christmas supplies of its Wii games console. Nintendo's superb marketing had been let down by mistakes in its operations (production) function.

As with every aspect of business, success comes from working together towards a common goal.

Figure 52.3 Clothing retailer Next

the problem more collective, due to poor communications within a department or (much more likely) between the functional areas?

Alternatively, it is sometimes the case that no one deserves blame (or praise for success). After more than ten years of sales and profit growth, Next and French Connection both struggled in the period 2006–2008. The recovery of Marks & Spencer, and the rapid growth of Primark, Topshop and Zara meant the market became far tougher. For sales at Next to be falling by 2.5% a year was not necessarily a disgrace; just as, years earlier, managers at Next did not really deserve the huge praise they received when sales were rising at 6% a year. They were largely benefiting from the period when women lost confidence in the ability of Marks & Spencer to provide affordable, wearable clothes.

The key judgement, then, is whether a firm's success is entirely down to its own good management. A better explanation might be that external factors were largely the reason. In which case managers deserve credit for taking advantage of favourable circumstances; but they should beware of jumping to the conclusion that they have the magic touch.

Functional objectives and strategies

Having analysed the business situation, judgements have to be made. If a business hits problems, is one department (function) to blame (e.g. the marketing department let the side down because of a poor advertising campaign)? Are there specific staff who lack ability or motivation? Or was

Key terms

Network analysis: a way of planning that minimises the duration of a project by ensuring that everyone knows the latest completion time for every activity within the project.

SMART objectives: these are more likely to lead to successful outcomes because they are Specific, Measurable, Achievable, Realistic and Timebound.

Exercises

A. Revision questions

(25 marks; 25 minutes)

1 What is meant by the term 'functional areas'? (2)

2 Why is it important that objectives should be:
  (a) measurable (2)
  (b) timebound? (2)

3 Are the following good or bad corporate objectives? Briefly explain your reasoning.
  (a) To boost our share of the fruit juice market from its current level of 22.3%. (4)
  (b) To become the best pizza restaurant business in Britain. (4)

4 What might be a successful overall objective for:
  (a) the charity Oxfam, which focuses on preventing and relieving famine (2)
  (b) the Conservative Party? (2)

5 Explain in your own words why it is important that the different business functions should work together to achieve the corporate (overall) objective. (4)

6 Explain the difference between an objective and a strategy. (3)

B. Revision exercises

B1 Data response

In August 2006 Claude and Claire Bosi put their Hibiscus restaurant up for sale. This was a surprise because it had two Michelin stars, making it one of Britain's top ten restaurants. The couple decided that, while still young, they must move from Ludlow in rural Shropshire to the challenges of opening in London. Could Claude Bosi's cooking stand out in London, when in competition with Gordon Ramsay, Jamie Oliver and many Michelin-starred restaurants?

They sold the restaurant for £250,000 and moved to London to look for a good site. Famously, business success in restaurants depends not only on great cooking but also on location, location, location. After several months they found a site in Mayfair that could be turned into a 60-seat restaurant, though the site, the building work and the equipment would cost 'around £1 million'. The finance would come from their own £250,000 plus share capital from a wealthy Ludlow customer and two of his friends.

The objective of the couple is to establish in London a restaurant as successful as the one in Ludlow. Clearly, London offers far greater potential, both financially and in terms of personal recognition. To recreate Hibiscus in London, Bosi persuaded most of his staff to move to London and has a menu that is largely made up of the dishes developed in Ludlow. He even buys many of his supplies from farms in Shropshire.

The restaurant opened in London in November 2007 and, as nearly 40% of new restaurants close within three years, the success or failure of this business decision is likely to be clear by the end of 2008. Apart from the quality of cooking, an important issue will be pricing. The couple have decided to charge the same price for three courses as they charged in Ludlow: £45. This may seem high, but is nothing like as expensive as restaurants such as Gordon Ramsay's, which would be twice the price.

Questions

(20 marks; 35 minutes)

1 Explain what you believe to be the business objectives being pursued by Claude and Claire Bosi. (5)

2 From the text, how SMART do the couple's objectives seem to be? (6)

3 Use Google to check on the progress of the business. You will find restaurant reviews and, at www.hibiscusrestaurant.co.uk, the restaurant's latest prices and marketing messages. Then comment on whether the couple seem to be succeeding in achieving their business objectives. (9)

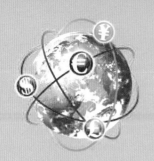

RESPONSIBILITIES TO STAKEHOLDERS AND SOCIETY

53.1 Introduction

All firms come into contact on a daily basis with suppliers, customers, the local community and employees. Each of these groups has an impact on the firm's success and at the same time is likely to be affected by any change in its activities. If, for example, the managers decide to expand the business, this may lead to:

- overtime for employees

- more orders for suppliers

- a wider range of products for consumers

- more traffic for the local community.

Groups such as suppliers, employees and the community are known as the firm's **stakeholder** groups because of their links with the organisation. A stakeholder group both has an effect on and is affected by the decisions of the firm. Each stakeholder group will have its own objectives. The managers of a firm must decide on the extent to which they should change their behaviour to meet these objectives. Some managers believe it is very important to focus on the needs of all the different stakeholder groups. Others believe that a organisation's sole duty is to its investors (i.e. that decisions should be made in the best interests of **shareholders** alone).

This is known as the 'shareholder concept'. The logic is clear: the shareholders employ managers to run the company on their behalf and so everything the managers do should be in the direct interests of shareholders. The managers should not take the needs or objectives of any other group into consideration. If the owners want short-run profit, for example, this is what the managers should provide. If the owners want expansion, then this is what the managers should aim

for. According to this view, the only consideration managers should have when making any decision is to meet their owners' objectives. Generally, this means maximising **shareholder value** (e.g. increasing the share price and the dividends paid to shareholders).

The alternative view places emphasis on the need to meet the objectives of a wider group. This is known as 'the stakeholder concept' as opposed to 'the shareholder concept'. The stakeholder approach suggests that managers should take into account their responsibilities to other groups, not just to the owners, when making decisions. The belief is that a firm can benefit significantly from cooperating with its stakeholder groups and incorporating their needs into the decision-making process. Examples include:

- improving the working life of employees through more challenging work, better pay and greater responsibilities, so that the business benefits from a more motivated and committed workforce

- giving something back to the community to ensure greater cooperation from local inhabitants whenever the business needs their help – for example, when seeking planning permission for expansion

- treating suppliers with respect and involving them in its plans so that the firm builds up a long-term relationship; this should lead to better-quality supplies and a better all-round service; if, for example, your supplier has limited availability of an item, it is more likely you would still get supplied because of the way you have treated the supplier in the past.

The stakeholder approach is, therefore, based on an inclusive view in which the various groups that the firm affects are included in its decision making rather than ignored. This, it is argued, can lead to significant advantages for the firm.

A-grade application
Stakeholders: Northern Wreck

In 2007 customers of the Northern Rock bank lost confidence in the business. They queued to withdraw their money in the first 'run' on a British bank for more than 50 years. More than £50 billion of taxpayers' money was risked in supporting Northern Rock before, in February 2008, it was taken into state ownership.

The bank's collapse occurred because of the excessively risky way in which it had financed its rapid expansion. During the good times, from 2001 to early 2007, this meant huge profits and – importantly – multi-million-pound bonuses for its key directors. During the growth period, staff enjoyed the increasing promotion opportunities, but when the bank collapsed they were left with very uncertain future prospects. The directors had already been able to cash in their bonuses, and were free of financial worries. The real problems were faced by shareholders, staff and the general public. Without having even been asked, every taxpayer in the country ended up lending £1000 to the failing bank. One stakeholder group – the directors – had damaged the interests of all other groups.

53.2 What are the gains of the stakeholding approach?

There are numerous gains that might result from the stakeholding approach. For example, existing employees might be more willing to stay with the firm. It may also attract people to work for the organisation. Employees are increasingly concerned about the ethical behaviour of the organisation they work for. Firms that put the shareholders above all else may deter some people from applying or accepting a job with them. The stakeholder approach is also increasingly popular with investors. There are a growing number of financial institutions that specifically seek to invest in organisations that follow the stakeholder approach, in the belief that it will lead to long-term rewards. A firm can also gain from better relations with the community, suppliers and distributors, and more favourable media coverage. By working with other groups rather than against them a firm is also less likely to be targeted by a **pressure group**.

However, while this approach may seem attractive in theory there are a number of problems in practice. First,

the owners may insist that the managers serve their interests and no one else's. Many shareholders of public limited companies, for example, demand short-term rewards and may take some convincing that the firm should be paying attention to the needs of other groups. After all, it is their money that is invested in the business. Second, the managers may not be able to meet all their potential responsibilities to these various groups and may have to make some decisions regarding priorities. They may also have to decide between what they regard as their obligations to society and what is commercially viable.

Society's interest in the responsibilities of business seems to grow each year. This means people are expecting firms to take a much broader view of their activities than in the past. In 2007 the clothes retailer Gap was criticised for allegedly using suppliers who used child labour to make its clothes. Although Gap was not directly employing these children and had clear policies to try to ensure its suppliers did not either, it was still held responsible for the failings of others.

53.3 Corporate social responsibility (CSR)

In recent years there has been a great deal of interest in corporate social responsibility (CSR). CSR refers to the extent to which a business accepts obligations to society over and above the legal requirements. This obviously refers to how it treats its stakeholder groups. Investors, customers, employees and the media regularly examine the way in which a business is treating various stakeholders. What is it doing to reduce its impact on the environment? To what extent is it protecting its employees and improving the quality of their working lives? How is it helping the local community?

When considering CSR, it is important to be cautious. Is it a reflection of a genuine concern by the business for its customers, staff and society? Or is it part of a public relations campaign to improve the firm's image? In March 2008, Jamie Oliver fronted a TV campaign for Sainsbury's associating the supermarket with a fun-run athletics event. It proudly boasted that 25p would be given to support the event for every bag of penne (one shape of pasta among many) sold at Sainsbury's stores. Hundreds of thousands of pounds spent on advertising, yet sponsorship money coming just from one shape of pasta? This is CSR as an arm of marketing, not a meaningful commitment towards healthier lifestyles.

A-grade application

BT and social auditing

A number of companies now undertake a social audit. This means they have an external assessment of the impact of their activities on society. This is to help them understand the effect of their actions so that they can take appropriate steps and can be seen to be concerned about such issues. The telecommunications business, BT, for example, produces an annual social audit that examines its relationship with the six groups that it believes are crucial to its success, namely:

1 customers
2 employees
3 suppliers
4 shareholders
5 partners
6 community.

According to BT, 'Our vision is to be dedicated to helping customers thrive in a changing world. Doing this in a responsible way is what our corporate social responsibility (CSR) work is all about.' The indicators it measures include customer satisfaction, employee engagement with the business, ethical performance, CO_2 emissions, waste recycling and investment in the community.

53.4 Are the stakeholder concept and CSR really new?

In recent years people have come to expect more from business organisations. In the past they were just expected to provide good-quality goods. Now many consumers want to know exactly how the goods are produced, what the company does for the environment and how it treats its employees. Stories about the exploitation of staff, the sale of goods to a military regime or the pollution of the environment can be very damaging to firms. This has probably resulted in more public companies adopting the stakeholder approach.

However, there are a number of companies, such as the John Lewis Partnership, that pioneered this approach long before the term 'stakeholder' was even thought of. Many of the origins of this approach go back to the paternalistic style of companies such as Rowntree and Cadbury in the nineteenth century. These family companies were the major employers in an area, and built a reputation for treating customers, employees and suppliers with great respect.

53.5 Can a firm satisfy all stakeholder groups?

According to the shareholder concept a firm's responsibilities to other groups directly conflict with its responsibilities to shareholders. If the firm tried to help the local community, for example, this would take funds away from the shareholders. Similarly, more rewards for the owners would mean fewer resources for employees. In the shareholder view, all these different groups are competing for a fixed set of rewards. If one group has a larger slice of the profits that leaves less for others.

Under the stakeholder approach, however, it is believed that all groups can benefit at the same time. By working with its various stakeholder groups the firm can generate more profit. Imagine, for example, that more rewards are given to employees out of profits. In the short run this may reduce rewards for the shareholder, but in the long run it may generate more rewards for everyone. Better-quality work can lead to improved customer loyalty and therefore less marketing expenditure to achieve the same level of sales. Similarly, by building up better relations with suppliers the firm can produce better-quality goods leading to more orders and more business for both parties. However, at any moment managers are likely to have to decide which group(s) are most important. This will depend on the values of the owners and managers, the interests of different stakeholders and their power to bring about change. If, for example, stakeholders organise themselves into an effective pressure group they may be able to change a firm's behaviour through actions such as demonstrations and boycotts.

Issues For Analysis

When answering a case study or essay question it may be useful to consider the following points.

● An increasing number of firms claim to be adopting the stakeholder approach. They recognise their responsibilities to groups other than the shareholders and are taking their views into account when making decisions. Claims made by firms, though, may largely be for public relations reasons. Companies should be judged on what they do, not what they say.

● Even firms that genuinely mean to change will find many managers stuck in the previous culture of profit/shareholder first. Changing to more of a stakeholder culture will take years.

● The stakeholder approach can lead to many benefits for organisations, such as attracting new customers, attracting and keeping employees, and building a strong long-term corporate image. However, the business may not be able to fulfil the objectives of all groups. Meeting the needs of one group may conflict with the needs of others.

● The stakeholder approach may prove to be a fad. When the profits of firms fall, for example, they sometimes decide that short-term profit is much more important than obligations to other groups. So a sharp recession would be likely to make every business more profit/shareholder focused.

It may not be possible to meet the needs of all interest groups, however. Firms must decide on the extent to which they take stakeholders into account. Given their limited resources and other obligations, managers must decide on their priorities. In difficult times it may well be that the need for short-term profit overcomes the demands of various stakeholder groups. It would be naive to ignore the fact that TV consumer programmes such as the BBC's *Watchdog* keep exposing business malpractice. Even if progress is being made in general, there are still many firms that persist in seeing short-term profit as the sole business objective.

Key terms

Pressure group: a group of people with a common interest who try to further that interest (e.g. Greenpeace).

Shareholder: an owner of a company.

Shareholder value: a term widely used by company chairmen and chairwomen, which means little more than the attempt to maximise the company's share price.

Social responsibilities: duties towards stakeholder groups, which the firm may or may not accept.

Stakeholder: an individual or group that affects and is affected by an organisation.

53.6 Responsibilities to stakeholders and society

an evaluation

In recent years there has been much greater interest in the idea that firms should pay attention to their **social responsibilities**. Increasingly, firms are being asked to consider and justify their actions towards a wide range of groups rather than just their shareholders. Managers are expected to take into account the interests and opinions of numerous internal and external groups before they make a decision. This social responsibility often makes good business sense. If you ignore your stakeholder groups you are vulnerable to pressure group action and may well lose employees and investors. If, however, you build your social responsibility into your marketing this can create new customers and save you money through activities such as recycling.

Exercises

A. Revision questions

(40 marks; 40 minutes)

1 What is meant by a 'stakeholder'? (2)

2 Distinguish between the 'shareholder concept' and the 'stakeholder concept'. (3)

3 Some people believe that an increasing number of firms are now trying to meet their social responsibilities. Explain why this might be the case. (3)

4 Outline two responsibilities a firm may have to:
   (a) its employees (4)
   (b) its customers (4)
   (c) the local community. (4)

5 Explain how a firm might damage its profits in the pursuit of meeting its shareholder responsibilities. (4)

6 Explain why a firm's profit may fall by meeting its stakeholder responsibilities. (4)

7 Some managers reject the idea of stakeholding. They believe a company's duty is purely to its shareholders. Outline two points in favour and two points against this opinion. (8)

8 What factors are likely to determine whether a firm accepts its responsibilities to a particular stakeholder group? (4)

B. Revision exercises

B1 Data response

Sandler plc produces a range of paints that are sold in the major DIY stores in the UK under the brand name Lifestyles. The company has had a very successful few years and expects demand to be much higher than capacity in the next few years. The company has considered two options:

1 extending capacity at its existing site, or

2 moving to a new purpose-built factory 60 miles away.

Although the second option is more expensive initially, building a completely new factory is estimated to be more profitable in the long run.

The problem is that the chosen site is close to an Area of Outstanding Natural Beauty (AONB) and the firm is concerned that protesters might object to it building there. Also, the closure of the existing factory at Headington will lead to serious job losses in the area. The company has been based at Headington for over 50 years and has worked well with the community. Telling the workforce and local authorities will not be easy. On the other hand, it will be creating jobs at the new location, which is an area of high unemployment, whereas Headington is booming at the moment.

Questions

(40 marks; 45 minutes)

1 Identify four stakeholder groups that may be affected if Sandler closes its Headington factory. Explain briefly how each would be affected. (8)

2 Should Sandler plc close its Headington factory? Fully justify your answer. (12)

3 If the firm decides to close its Headington factory, should it tell the employees immediately or wait until nearer the time? Explain your reasoning. (10)

4 Outline the difficulties Sandler might face with stakeholders other than the workforce if the decision is taken to move to the new site. (10)

B2 Data response

Stakeholders vs shareholders

In a recent poll, 72% of UK business leaders said shareholders were served best if the company concentrated on customers, suppliers and other stakeholders. Only 17% thought focusing on shareholders was the only way to succeed. This represents a marked change from five years ago, when the stakeholding idea was widely ignored.

However, not everyone agrees with the stakeholder view. According to two UK writers, Shiv Mathur and Alfred Kenyon, the stakeholder view 'mistakes the essential nature of a business. A business is not a moral agent at all. It is an investment project . . . Its raison d'être is financial.'

Others believe the stakeholder and shareholder views do not necessarily conflict with each other. For example, the US consultant James Knight writes:

Managing a company for value requires delivering maximum return to the investors while balancing the interests of the other important constituents, including customers and employees. Companies that consistently deliver value for investors have learned this lesson.

Source: adapted from the *Financial Times*

Questions

(30 marks; 35 minutes)

1 Distinguish between shareholders and stakeholders. (4)

2 Analyse the possible reasons for the growth in popularity of the stakeholder view in recent years. (8)

3 Examine the factors which might influence whether a firm adopts the stakeholder or the shareholder approach. (8)

4 Discuss the view that the interests of shareholders and stakeholders necessarily conflict. (10)

B3 Case study

BP: shareholder or stakeholder approach?

On 23 March 2005, a huge explosion at BP's Texas oil refinery killed 15 people and injured more than 180. Most were its own staff. The refinery, America's third largest, had suffered safety problems before. In 2004, two workers died when scalded by super-heated water that escaped from a high-pressure pipe.

In Texas, the local media were outraged by 'yet another' safety scandal involving BP. Yet, in Britain, BP's reputation remained largely unaffected. It remained a media darling for its constant references to global warming,

sustainability and social responsibility. Journalists were used to praising BP for its ethical standards. Its website used – and uses – lots of green colours to communicate its message: BP is a socially responsible, ethical company.

From BP's website ('About Us'):

'Our business is run on the principles of strong corporate governance, a clear system of delegating accountability and a set of values and policies that guide our behaviour.'

Figure 53.1 The destruction caused by the Texas explosion in which 15 people died

In 2006, more bad headlines came from another part of America. In January BP was fined $1.42 million for safety violations at its Prudhoe Bay oilfield in Alaska. Two months later, a hole in an oil pipeline leaked more than 1.2 million litres of oil, creating an environmental 'catastrophe'. BP had failed to maintain the pipeline properly.

In November 2006 an official US report made it clear that BP managers had known of 'significant safety problems' at the Texas refinery long before the deadly explosion. The US Chemical Safety Board (CSB) found numerous internal BP reports setting out maintenance backlogs and poor, ageing equipment. Late in October 2006 the CSB Chairwoman blamed the explosion on 'ageing infrastructure, overzealous cost-cutting, inadequate design and risk blindness'.

She went on to say that 'BP implemented a 25% cut on fixed costs from 1998 to 2000 that adversely impacted maintenance expenditures at the refinery'. The report stated that 'BP's global management' (i.e. British head office) 'was aware of problems with maintenance spending and infrastructure well before March 2005' – yet they did nothing about it. The Chairwoman delivered the final critique:

Every successful corporation must contain its costs. But at an ageing facility like Texas City, it is not responsible to cut budgets related to safety and maintenance without thoroughly examining the impact on the risk of a catastrophic accident.

BP confirmed that its own internal investigation had findings 'generally consistent with those of the CSB'.

Questions

(40 marks; 50 minutes)

1 Explain two possible reasons why BP went wrong in its attitude to human and environmental safety in its US operations. (6)

2 Given the evidence in the case, comment briefly on the statement in the box taken from BP's website: 'About Us'. (4)

3 Discuss whether BP was carrying out a 'shareholder' or a stakeholder' approach to its decision making during the period covered by the text. (15)

4 Is it time for stronger government controls on business activities? (15)

C. Essay questions

(40 marks each)

1 'Meeting the objectives of different stakeholder groups may be desirable but it is rarely profitable.' Discuss.

2 Consider whether the objectives of the different stakeholder groups necessarily conflict.

3 'A manager's responsibility should be to the shareholders alone.' Critically assess this view.

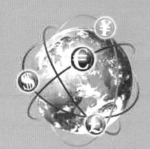

FINANCIAL OBJECTIVES AND CONSTRAINTS

54.1 Types of financial objective

It is generally assumed that all businesses operate in order to maximise profit. This is of course true to a certain extent – why would people invest in a business if not to make profit? However, within this there are many other considerations, as outlined below.

● *Ownership vs management:* in a small business the management and the owners are often the same people. In large companies such as a **public limited company (plc)** the management (the directors) and the owners (the shareholders) are usually separate. The shareholders will want to see a healthy and immediate return on their investments but the directors may have other aims: they may be looking for growth or diversification, or may be content to just keep the business ticking along (satisficing). An increasing trend is for the bonuses of company directors to be related to the achievement of the financial objectives. Directors may therefore have an interest in setting targets that are achievable rather than challenging.

● *Short term vs long term:* some business goals, such as growth or diversification, will need investment. This may mean a reduction in short-term profits with the hope of increasing returns in the future. If a business is in difficulty it will need to focus much more on survival, so increasing profitability will be a definite short-term goal.

● *Stakeholders vs shareholders:* in some businesses the pursuit of profit may cause conflict between the different groups with an interest in the business, as in the following examples.

– The rise of interest in the environment has meant that costs have increased for many firms and therefore profit has been reduced. However, many firms have also discovered that they can make huge savings, such as by limiting waste.

– Some firms, most notably supermarket chains, are accused of driving the prices of their suppliers to the lowest possible level. Low supply costs increase profits. Businesses need to ensure that there is a balance between keeping costs low and maintaining the quality of the supplies. In the food chain, tough bargaining by supermarkets may cause unacceptable welfare conditions for animals such as chickens and piglets; this, in turn, may backfire on the retailer's reputation.

A-grade application
Royal Bank of Scotland

Sir Fred Goodwin, the chief executive of Royal Bank of Scotland, looks set to miss out on a bonus worth almost £1 million, as a result of the bank's diving share price. Details buried in the bank's last **annual report** reveal that Goodwin is in line for a £1.7 million bonus from his medium-term bonus plan – in addition to his salary and other bonuses. But RBS's dismal return to shareholders over the past three years will ensure most of the bonus does not pay out.

RBS has generated a total shareholder return of minus 11% over the three-year period linked to the bonus, according to analysts. The European banking sector has generated total returns of 54% over the same period, leaving RBS's performance well below that of many peers.

Source: The Business, *27 December 2007*

– Taxation may be a consideration. Large multinational companies may deliberately reduce profit in one country in order to pay less tax, and increase profit in another where profits are taxed at a lower level. They are able to do this by charging differential prices between subsidiaries in different countries.

– Public image: a firm may choose to spend money on charitable concerns or sponsorship; this as a cost will reduce profit. However, it may well get a return on its investment through creating a better brand image or good public relations.

Profit is a major objective

Whether it is long or short term it is safe to say that, for most businesses, high and rising profits are a major objective. However, just stating that the firm wants to increase profit is a very general objective. Most companies will be more specific in defining their financial objectives. They may look to increase gross or net profit. They may also use other measures, such as return on capital employed (ROCE). The measurements of profitability are interlinked. Firms that have a high gross profit margin will find it easier to finance high spending on research and development, marketing or investing in assets. Firms that have better control of costs are going to be more profitable than other firms in their sector. Businesses that generate high profits are going to have contented shareholders.

Revenue targets

The directors may set an overall aim, such as to increase revenue by 10% or more. This approach will be especially important for a business in the early stages of a growth market. For example, in the early days of Innocent Drinks, the key thing for the business was to grow rapidly in order to gain market domination before rival PJ Smoothies (owned by the massive PepsiCo) could get fully established.

Cash flow targets

All businesses need to keep a healthy **cash flow**. The level of cash flow should be carefully managed. A company that is cash short will have difficulty with the day-to-day management of its liabilities. It may find it difficult to pay **creditors**. It may also miss opportunities to develop the business. A new order may have to be refused if it has insufficient cash available. A business that has cash reserves that are too high will be missing out on opportunities to use that cash to generate additional business. The 'right' level of cash will depend on the nature of the business. The business may set itself a target of keeping cash at a percentage of turnover or as a stated amount.

A-grade application

Dolcis

In January 2008 the 145-year-old shoe chain Dolcis fell into administration. It had simply run out of cash and was unable to pay £2.5 million of rent demands. Some 600 people lost their jobs straight away and 89 shops were closed. During 2007 the company had taken on a lot of debt, creating interest payments that could not be covered during a poor Christmas trading period. Short of cash, the business had to close.

Cost minimisation

A business may concentrate on minimising costs. Lowering costs will increase profitability. This may be a general overall aim, such as reducing fixed costs by 5%, or it may be more specific such as reduce wastage in the factory and therefore reduce material costs by 4%. A strategy of cost minimisation may be necessary when times are hard. In early 2008 the furniture retailer Land of Leather reported than its sales had fallen by more than 16%. At times such as these, cost-cutting may be the only wise response (see Table 54.1).

Table 54.1 Cost-cutting strategies

To cut fixed costs	To cut variable costs
● Consider closing loss-making branches or factories ● Consider moving the head office or main factory to a lower-cost location ● Consider carefully whether a layer of management could be removed to reduce staffing costs	● Renegotiate with existing suppliers to try to agree lower prices ● Look for new suppliers, perhaps from a low-cost country such as China ● Redesign the goods to make them simpler and therefore quicker and cheaper to produce

Return on capital employed (ROCE)

This is a measure of how well the company is using its assets to create profit. It is calculated by taking net profit or operating profit as a percentage of capital employed. (see Unit 57 on ratio analysis).

Capital employed is all the long-term finance used to operate the business. Although this is a measure of profitability it concentrates on the use the business is making of its assets. Obviously, the business will want the highest possible return. It is important that the business should achieve a ROCE of more than the rate of interest that it is paying on borrowed funds. The ROCE can be improved by reducing capital employed or by increasing net profit.

Shareholder returns

These can be expressed in terms of the dividend payments that will be given to shareholders or in terms of maintaining or adding value to the share price. Shareholders hope to gain from their investment in the business in two ways.

1   Any increase in the value of their shares will mean that they can sell their shares at a higher price than they were bought at. This is a capital return.

2   Shareholders receive income on their shares through the payment of dividends by the business. Yearly profit made by the business can either be kept in the business for development (retained profit) or distributed to shareholders as dividends. These dividends are the income that the shareholders receive as a return on their investment. If the company is making insufficient profit to satisfy shareholders then shareholders will sell their shares and invest elsewhere. This is turn will cause the share price to fall.

A business that is seen as a poor investment by shareholders will find it very difficult to attract investment. It is therefore important that the level of profit and the level of dividends are kept at a level that satisfies shareholders. This in turn keeps the value of the share price high. Balancing the retained profit and dividend distribution is a difficult decision. If the business wants to expand or diversify it may wish to retain more profit and therefore risk upsetting shareholders by paying low dividends.

Figure 54.1 Cadbury Schweppes aims to consistently deliver superior shareholder return

54.2 How are financial objectives set?

Financial objectives are determined by taking into account the overall company aims. They express the financial aspects of the overall company plan. They will be decided like any other business objective, by taking into account the internal position of the business and the external business environment. The internal aspects of the business, such as what the business is currently doing and what resources it has available, will determine what the business can achieve. This has to be put into the perspective of the external environment. The external environment will affect how easy it is to carry out the plans. An increase in sales is unlikely to be achieved in an economy that is going into recession.

What makes a good financial objective?

As with any other business objective, financial objectives should be SMART:

- *Specific* – they should be clearly defined so that all staff know and understand the aims

- *Measurable* – if the objective can be measured then it is possible to see if the target has been achieved

- *Achievable* – a good objective is challenging but it must be achievable; to set a target that is impossible is demoralising for staff – it could also create poor shareholder and public confidence if objectives are not met

- *Realistic* – any objective should make good business sense

- *Timebound* – financial targets usually relate to the company's financial year; they can also look further into the future.

54.3 Internal and external influences on financial objectives

There are many factors that will influence the way a firm sets its financial objectives. These can be categorised as internal and external constraints.

Internal constraints

- *Financial:* although it may seem strange to talk about internal finance as a constraint on financial objectives it can play an important part. The pursuit of higher profit might be constrained by lack of cash flow, especially at a time of rising or even booming demand.

- *Labour force:* any business activity requires the cooperation of the workforce. It is also important that the business has the manpower with the necessary skills.

- *Type of business:* new or young businesses may set themselves financial objectives but because of inexperience or the difficulty in assessing a new market they may set unrealistic targets. Larger, more established businesses will find it easier to set and achieve their objectives because of the experience that they have. PLCs may be more constrained in their objectives, as they will have to satisfy the shareholders as well as the management.

- *Operational:* a firm that is close to **full capacity** may find that it has fewer opportunities for improving the profitability of the business, unless it has the confidence and the resources to increase capacity, perhaps by moving to bigger premises.

External constraints

- *Competitive environment:* the plans of almost every business can be affected by the behaviour and reaction of competitors. A plan to increase profit margins by increasing prices may be destroyed if competitors react by reducing prices or by advertising their lower prices.

- *Economic environment:* the state of the economy plays a vital part in how well businesses can achieve their financial targets. A booming economy will help businesses to improve sales. However, high interest rates would reduce customers' disposable income and therefore spending, so financial targets may not be met. The effect will depend on the business. Supermarket own-brand producers may do better, whereas branded goods may suffer.

- *Government:* a firm may find its financial objectives limited by regulatory or legislative activity. Consumer watchdogs such as the Office of Fair Trading (OFT) have powers to fine businesses that they believe are not acting in the best interests of consumers. Legislation may also be introduced that increases business costs. A recent European Union environmental policy has forced producers of goods such as refrigerators to pay for their disposal when consumers have finished with them.

Building in the constraints

Good business planning involves being aware of the possible constraints. The internal constraints are easier to evaluate. External constraints will always be subject to more uncertainty as they are outside the power of the business. It is therefore important when setting financial objectives that the business includes a series of 'what if' scenarios when setting the objectives.

A-grade application

Thousands of football fans win 'rip-off' replica shirt refunds

High-street sportswear chain JJB Sports is to pay compensation to shoppers for the 'rip-off' prices of replica England and Manchester United football shirts. In what is seen as the first example of American-style consumer justice in Britain, 1000 people who joined the test case brought by Which?, the consumer watchdog, will each receive £20 from the company. The shirts went on sale with prices fixed by a cartel that included Allsports, Blacks Leisure Group, Manchester United, Sports Soccer, JD Sports and Umbro Holdings. JJB has paid more than £16 million in fines to the Treasury. The OFT proved that price fixing had taken place between 2000 and 2001.

Ms Prince also called on other companies caught out in price-rigging scandals to compensate consumers. She said: 'Corporate responsibility is the buzzword in every boardroom the length and breadth of Britain. Well, I say come on, when you've been found out and admitted price fixing then do the right thing and compensate your customers.'

Source: adapted from an article by Valerie Elliot, The Times, 10 January 2008

Key terms

Annual report: the annual financial statement showing the financial results for the business; for any limited company this is a statutory requirement.

Cash flow: the flow of cash into and out of the business.

Creditors: people who are owed money by the business.

Full capacity: when the business is fully utilising all its assets.

Public limited company (plc): a company with limited liability and shares that are available to the public. Its shares are quoted on the stock exchange.

Issues For Analysis

When analysing financial objectives the key issues are as follows.

- How have the objectives been determined? Any consideration of the firm's objectives must be put into the context of the business and its external environment. Think about the type of business and who the objectives are aiming to please.

- You will need to have an understanding of the different measures used to define financial objectives. It is especially important to ask whether a firm is setting the 'right' objectives: is it pursuing revenue growth when a focus on profit would be more appropriate?

- Are the objectives realistic? A challenging objective may look good in the annual report but is it achievable?

- When looking at why a business has failed to meet or has exceeded its financial objectives you need to consider the part played by both the internal and the external constraints, and the extent to which these are important.

54.4 Financial objectives and constraints
an evaluation

There are advantages and disadvantages to setting tight financial objectives. Some people consider that objectives are vital to give direction to the business. A good set of objectives will enable plans for each sector of the business to be developed. Each individual within the organisation will then know the role that they are to play. Without objectives, the business may drift aimlessly.

Other people consider that objectives can stifle entrepreneurship and initiative. They feel that managers operate to satisfy the objectives but do not go beyond them. They also feel that they dampen risk-taking, which may prevent a business from taking the kind of leaps forward shown by Apple (iPod, iPhone) and Nintendo (Wii) in 2007 and 2008.

Exercises

A. Revision questions

(40 marks; 40 minutes)

1 What is meant by financial objectives? (2)

2 Why is improving or maintaining profit likely to be the most important financial objective? (4)

3 Give two examples of how stakeholder interests might affect the setting of business objectives. (6)

4 What is meant by 'retained profit'? (2)

5 List two likely results for shareholders if profits fall? (4)

6 Explain the term 'return on capital employed'. (4)

7 List and explain two possible internal constraints on achieving financial objectives. (6)

8 Discuss two external constraints that should be taken into account when financial objectives are set by *one* of the following businesses:
   (a) Innocent Drinks
   (b) Game (software retailer)
   (c) Versace clothing. (8)

9 What government activity might act as a constraint on businesses achieving their financial objectives? Give an example. (4)

B. Revision exercises

B1 Data response

Manchester United profit doubles

Manchester United says its annual pre-tax profit doubled on increased sponsorship after it expanded its stadium and won the League title. Pre-tax profit in the 12 months to 30 June 2007 rose to £59.6 million from £30.8 million in the year-earlier period, the club said on Friday.

The 2006–2007 Premiership-winning club, owned by US billionaire Malcolm Glazer, said annual revenue surged 27% to £210 million from £165 million. Interest in the world's richest soccer league and new sponsorship will keep pushing income higher, Chief Executive David

Gill said. 'I am confident that the uplift in the Premier League television deal, together with our new sponsorship sales structure will enable the club to continue to increase its revenues and profitability,' Gill said in a statement.

Britain's Barclays Premier League is followed in more than 200 countries as fans in Africa or Asia want to see stars such as Wayne Rooney and Christiano Ronaldo, both at United.

More seats at Manchester United's Old Trafford stadium helped the club lift its match-day revenue by 30% to £92.6 million, the club said. Reaching the semi-finals of the lucrative UEFA Champions League competition and the final of the domestic FA Cup helped the Reds increase their media revenues by more than a third, to £61.5 million.

Replica shirts, shirt sponsorship by American International Group and other commercial revenues rose 15% to £56 million. The club said it has about 333 million followers around the world.

At a time of soaring players' salaries, the club managed to cut its wages-to-turnover ratio to 43.6% from 51.6%. By contrast, players' agents were paid more: £2.1 million last season from £1.8 million during the previous one.

Source: article by Elena Moya, 11 January 2008 Reuters London

Questions

(40 marks; 45 minutes)

1 What was the percentage rise in pre-tax profits for the year up to June 2007? (4)

2 Explain why the rise in pre-tax profits and the rise in revenue are not the same. (8)

3 What is meant by 'the club managed to cut its wages-to-turnover ratio'? (4)

4 What factors would the club have to take into account when setting financial objectives for the next financial year? (10)

5 Discuss whether it is sensible for a business like a football club to set financial objectives. (14)

B2 Case study

Sitting uncomfortably

In January 2008 Specialist sofa retailer ScS Upholstery announced that its annual results for the financial year were likely to be at the lower end of market expectations after 'disappointing' trading over the first three weeks of the Boxing Day and January sale period.

Gross margins have been maintained, but like-for-like sales order intake over that period was down by 16%. Total sales order intake is down by 12% for the comparable period.

'We see no relief from the credit squeeze and pressures on consumers' disposable income for the remainder of the financial year and although our comparable numbers are softer, it is unlikely that we will see any significant improvement on our year to date like-for-like sales performance,' said the group.

Due to the circumstances, the board will not be recommending the payment of a dividend this year. Until trading conditions improve, it has also deferred the current expansion programme, with only one store likely to open before the end of the financial year.

Questions

(35 marks; 40 minutes)

1 What does the company mean when it says that 'its annual results are likely to be at the lower end of market expectations'? (4)

2 What, according to the company, has caused its current problems? (8)

3 How will the non-payment of a dividend affect shareholders? (8)

4 Evaluate the decision to defer the expansion programme. (15)

C. Essay questions

(40 marks each)

1 Financial objectives are only there to please shareholders. Discuss

2 Setting financial objectives is a waste of management time. Discuss.

3 Financial objectives are more important for large organisations. Discuss.

DEFINITION

An income statement is an accounting statement showing a firm's sales revenue over a trading period and all the relevant costs generated to earn that revenue. Public limited companies use the term income statements, whereas small firms refer to the profit and loss account (sometimes abbreviated to 'the P&L').

55.1 Introduction

The function of accounting is to provide information to various stakeholder groups on how a particular business has performed during a given period. The groups include shareholders, managers and creditors. The period in question is usually one year. The key financial documents from which this information can be drawn are balance sheets and income statements. This unit focuses on the income statement; the balance sheet is covered in Unit 56.

The income statement records all a business's costs within a given trading period. Income statements constitute a vital piece of evidence for those with interests in a company. For many stakeholders, profit is a major criterion by which to judge the success of a business:

- shareholders are an obvious example of those assessing profitability

- government agencies such as the HM Revenue & Customs require data on profits or losses in order to be able to calculate the liability of a business to **corporation tax**

- suppliers to a business also need to know the financial position of the companies they trade with in order to establish their reliability, stability and creditworthiness

- potential shareholders and bankers will also want to assess the financial position of the company before committing their funds to the business.

For all these groups the income statement provides important information.

Making a profit is one of the most significant objectives for business organisations. It is this profit motive that encourages many people to establish their own business or expand an existing one. Without the potential for making a profit, why should individuals and companies commit time and resources to what may be a risky venture?

Despite the importance of the profit motive, a number of organisations exist that pursue objectives other than profits. Charities seek to assist those who are in need; their task is to redistribute resources rather than make profits. But even charities must seek to generate revenues to at least match their expenditure, otherwise they cannot survive. Therefore the income statement is as important to a charity as it is to a company.

55.2 The uses of income statements

The information yielded by an income statement can be used for a number of purposes:

- it can measure the success of a business compared with previous years or other businesses

- the calculation of profit can assess the actual performance of the business compared with expectations

- it can help in obtaining loans from banks or other lending institutions (creditors would want some proof that the business was capable of repaying any loans)

- it enables the owners and managers of a business to plan ahead – for example, for future investment in the company.

55.3 Measuring profit

Profit is what remains from **revenue** once costs have been deducted. However, the word 'profit' on its own means little to an accountant. Profit is such an important indicator of company performance that it is broken down into different types. This enables more detailed comparisons and analyses to be made.

The main types of profit are described below.

Gross profit

This is the measure of the difference between income (sales revenue) and the cost of manufacturing or purchasing the products that have been sold. It measures the amount of profit made on trading activities alone (i.e. the amount of profit made on buying and selling activities).

gross profit = revenue − cost of goods sold

Gross profit is calculated without taking costs, which could be classified as expenses (administration, advertising) or overheads (rent, rates), into account. This is a useful measure as, if a company is making a lower level of gross profit than a competitor, it is clear that the company must look very closely at its trading position. It may be that the business should attempt to find a cheaper supplier, or may need to put its prices up.

Net profit

This is found by subtracting expenses and overheads from gross profit. It is often termed **operating profit**.

net profit = gross profit − (expenses + overheads)

Net (operating) profit is a more important measure than gross profit, because it takes into account all the operating costs including overheads. A business may find itself making a healthy gross profit but a very small net profit in comparison to competitors. The business may not be controlling costs such as salaries and distribution as effectively as it might. The calculation of both gross and net profit allows owners, managers and other interested parties to make a more detailed and informed assessment of a business's performance.

Profit quality

It is not just the amount of profit that a business makes that is important, but also the likelihood of this profit source continuing for some time. If a profit has arisen as a result of a one-off circumstance (such as selling assets for more than their expected value), its quality is said to be low because it is unlikely to continue into the future. On the other hand, high-quality profit is trading profit that is expected to last for a number of years. For instance, the annual operating profit Arsenal makes through its turnstiles is high quality, whereas a transfer profit made by buying a player for £2 million and selling for £10 million is regarded as low quality.

55.4 Determining profit

Businesses calculate their profit or loss at regular intervals during a trading period. This supplies managers with important information to assist in the running of the business. At the end of the trading period the final calculation is made, which will form a major element of the published accounts.

Since 2005 there have been significant changes to the way that public companies in the UK present their accounts. A European Union regulation required public companies to prepare financial statements complying with the International Financial Reporting Standards (IFRS) after 1 January 2005. This requirement has not yet been extended to **private limited companies**, though this may happen in the future. This move is intended to

		£m
	Revenue	26.0
less	Cost of Sales	17.0
gives	Gross profit	9.0
less	Overheads	4.0
gives	Operating profit	5.0
less	Financing costs	1.5*
gives	Profit before taxation	6.5
less	Tax	2.0
gives	Profit after taxation for the year	4.5

*In this case more interest was earned than paid out

Figure 55.1 The basic structure of a profit and loss account

bring about greater similarities between the ways in which companies in different countries report on their performance. Differences still remain between European and American systems, but they will be brought into a single format in future. Consistent standards make it easier to compare the financial performances of companies in different countries; this will make it easier for companies (and individuals) to invest across national boundaries. This section considers income statements in a structure that meets international (IFRS) requirements, therefore it matches the approach used by all Britain's public limited companies (plcs).

Figure 55.1 sets out the basic structure of an income statement. Although this is the format adopted by a large number of firms, there is some variation according to the type of business.

The income statement comprises four main stages, as outlined below.

1 First, 'gross profit' is calculated. This is the difference between the income (this can also be called sales revenue) and the cost of the goods that have been sold. The latter is normally expressed simply as 'cost of goods'.

2 Second, 'operating profit is calculated'. This is done by deducting the main types of overhead, such as distribution costs and administration costs.

3 Next, profit before taxation is calculated, which is arrived at by the inclusion of interest received by the business and interest paid by it. These are normally shown together as a net figure labelled 'financing costs'.

4 The final stage of the income statement is to calculate profit after taxation. This is arrived at by deducting the amount of tax payable for the year and shows the net amount that has been earned for the shareholders.

Calculating gross profit

This element of the income statement shows how much revenue has been earned from sales less the **cost of goods sold**. In other words, it calculates gross profit.

income (revenue) − cost of goods sold = gross profit

When calculating revenue, taxes on sales such as VAT are also excluded. Although customers pay taxes to the business as part of the purchase price, the business has to pass this on to HM Revenue & Customs. The business does not, therefore, receive any part of this revenue and so it is excluded from the sales figure.

The next stage in calculating gross profit requires businesses to deduct cost of sales from the sales figure.

cost of goods sold = opening stock + purchases − closing stock

Cost of goods sold shows the expenses incurred in making or buying the products that have been sold in the current financial period. In most cases, companies will actually start a financial period selling stock that was made or bought in the previous financial period. The cost of these stocks is therefore brought into this period as this is when it is going to be sold. To this is added the purchase of goods made within the period.

Finally in the calculation of cost of sales, closing stock is deducted. These leftover stocks (closing stocks) need to be subtracted from the cost of goods sold, as they have not been sold. Their cost will be accounted for in the following trading period.

Logically, the closing stocks at the end of one financial period become opening stocks for the next period.

These calculations provide a value for the total cost of goods sold during the period in question. An example of a trading account is shown below.

H Baker Ltd: Gross profit for the period ended 30 May

	£	£
Revenue		47,800
Less cost of goods sold		
Opening stocks	4,700	
add Purchases	24,000	
less Closing stocks	6,000	22,700
Gross profit		25,100

If cost of goods sold exceeds income, a loss is made.

Calculating operating profit

The next stage of the income statement sets out the net operating profit, or net operating loss, made by the business. The gross profit figure is necessary to calculate operating profit so this naturally follows on from calculating gross profit.

An important relationship to remember is that operating profit equals gross profit less expenses.

Expenses

Expenses are payments for something that is of immediate use to the business. These payments include cash expenditures on labour and fuel, as well as non-cash items such as depreciation.

A-grade application

Shell sets UK profits record

The Anglo-Dutch oil firm Royal Dutch Shell reported annual profits of £13,900 million in 2007, a record for a UK-listed company. Much of this rise in profits has been attributed to rising oil prices, which nearly doubled during the financial year. Jeroen van der Veer, the company's chief executive, described the profits as 'satisfactory'.

However, some groups have been critical of the size of the company's profits at a time when consumers and businesses are suffering from the effects of high oil prices. The joint general secretary of the trade union Unite described the level of profits in the oil industry as 'quite frankly, obscene'.

Examples of overhead expenses include:

- wages and salaries
- rent and rates
- heating, lighting and insurance
- distribution costs.

Operating profit

Deducting expenses from gross profit leads to operating profit. Most firms regard this as the key test of their trading performance for the year. At the very least a firm would want operating profit to be:

- up by at least the rate of inflation compared with the previous year
- a higher percentage of the capital employed in the business than the cost of that capital (e.g. the interest rate)
- at least as high a percentage of capital employed as that achieved by rival companies
- high enough to ensure that shareholders can be paid a satisfactory dividend but still have money left to reinvest in the future of the business.

Financing costs

Financing costs can add to or subtract from the operating profit of a business. Most companies have relatively high borrowings and therefore can have to pay out a large proportion of their profit in interest charges.

Japanese and German companies like to have substantial bank deposits earning interest, so this item can be a positive figure.

Profit before and after taxation

All businesses pay tax on their profits. Companies pay corporation tax on profits. At the time of writing (spring 2008) the rate of corporation tax paid by larger companies on profits has just been cut from 30% to 28%. Once tax has been deducted, the final figure on the income statement is profit after taxation for the year. This figure is also known as the company's 'earnings'.

Using profits

'Earnings' can be used in two main ways: it can either be distributed or retained. Usually businesses retain some profits and distribute the remainder. The balance between these two uses is influenced by a number of factors.

- *Distributed profit*: the company directors will decide on the amount to be paid out to shareholders in the form of dividends; if the shareholders are unhappy with the sum paid out, they can vote against the dividend at the Annual General Meeting.

- *Retained profit*: any prudent owner or manager of a business will use some of the profit made by the business to reinvest in the business for the future.

A complete income statement for a private limited company is shown below.

H Baker Ltd: Income statement for the period ended 30 May

	£	£
Revenue		47,800
Less cost of goods sold		
Opening stocks	4,700	
add Purchases	24,000	
less Closing stocks	6,000	22,700
Gross profit		**25,100**
Less expenses		
Wages and salaries	8,100	
Distribution	1,850	
Advertising	2,300	
Rent and other bills	3,550	
Depreciation	1,200	17,000
Operating profit		**8,100**
Financing costs		500
Profit before taxation		**7,600**
Taxation		2,128
Profit after taxation for the year		**5,472**

55.5 Examining income statements

The first thing to do when studying a profit and loss account is to look at the title. The title will always give the following information:

● business name

● income statement for the year ended

● DD/MM/YYYY.

The title provides some important information. First, the business name shows whether the firm has unlimited or limited liability. If the latter, it shows whether it is a small private company (Ltd) or a larger public limited company (plc).

The year-end date is also an important factor to take into consideration when comparing company accounts. Many types of businesses and markets suffer from trends and fashions as well as seasonal fluctuations in demand. The dates of the financial year can affect what the accounts will show. If the income statement covers a period of less than one year's trading it is worth noting whether it covers key selling periods such as December.

Most income statements record the appropriate information for at least two years' trading. This assists stakeholders in identifying trends. For example, it is possible to look at the increase, if any, in revenue, expenses or operating profit. This helps to make a judgement about the financial well-being of the business.

55.6 Public limited companies

Public limited companies (plcs) are required by law to publish their accounts. This means that they are available for scrutiny not only by the owners (shareholders), potential investors and bankers, but also by competitors.

When a company draws up its income statement for external publication it will include as little information as possible. Public limited companies usually supply no more detail than is required by law. This format is illustrated below, for Tesco.

55.7 Income statements and the law

The legal requirements relating to income statements are set out in the Companies Act 2006. This legislation demands the production of financial statements including an income statement. It also specifies the information to be included in these accounts.

The income statement does not have to detail every expense incurred by the firm, but summarises the main items under standard headings. The Act sets out acceptable formats for presentation of the relevant data. A summarised form of one of these is shown below, for Tesco.

Summarised group income statement for Tesco plc
(year ended 24 February 2007)

	2007 (£m)	2006 (£m)
Revenue (sales excluding VAT)	42,641	39,454
Cost of sales	39,178	36,426
Gross profit	**3,463**	**3,028**
Administrative & other expenses	815	748
Operating profit	**2,648**	**2,280**
Finance income	221	196
Finance costs	(216)	(241)
Profit before tax	**2,653**	**2,235**
Taxation	772	649
Profit for the year from continuing operations	**1,881**	**1,586**
Profit/(loss) for the year from discontinued operation	18	(10)
Profit for the year	**1,899**	**1,576**

The notes to the income statements must disclose details of:

● auditor's fees

● depreciation amounts

● the total of directors' emoluments (pay and fringe benefits)

● the average number of employees, together with details of cost of wages and salaries, together with National Insurance and pensions.

Companies must disclose the following information.

● *Exceptional items*: these are large (usually one-off) financial transactions arising from ordinary trading activities. However, they are so large as to risk distorting the company's trading account. An example of exceptional items took place when the high-street banks incurred unusually large bad debt charges.

● *Extraordinary items:* these are large transactions outside the normal trading activities of a company. As a result they are not expected to recur. A typical example is the closure of a factory or division of a business. Once a factory is closed down, the costs of closure cannot arise again in future years.

A-grade application

Ford takes action following loss

Ford, the global car manufacturer, announced a record loss of £6350 million ($12,700 million) in November 2007. The company has taken immediate action to cut its costs in the wake of this huge loss. It has conducted negotiations with unions in America with the intention of cutting employment and its costs in relation to pensions and health insurance as well as wages. It is thought that the company will shed between 8000 and 10,000 jobs, although no announcement has been made.

Simultaneously the company is seeking an injection of cash from the sale of two iconic British car manufacturing brands: Land Rover and Jaguar. The company is expected to sell these two businesses to the burgeoning Indian car manufacturer Tata.

Issues For Analysis

● The income statement provides an insight into the performance of a business. Identifying trends in revenue can provide evidence about the success of a company within the marketplace. Is revenue rising after allowing for inflation? If so, this could be a healthy sign. If Tesco's UK sales are rising by 6%, but Morrisons at 9%, Tesco's shareholders will want answers from the company's chief executive.

● The income statement also gives details of how well the company is controlling its costs. Analysing the trends in gross and operating profits can be of value. For example, a rising figure for gross profits alongside a falling operating profit figure suggests that a promising business is not controlling its expenses.

● The key to analysing an income statement is to look at the performance of the business over a number of years. This may involve comparing various elements of the income statement to gain a further insight into the business. This approach is followed up in Unit 57.

55.8 Income statements (profit and loss accounts)
an evaluation

Two evaluative themes can be considered in relation to income statements. It is easy to make the assumption that a rising level of operating profit is evidence of a company that is performing well. There are a number of factors that need to be considered when making such a judgement. Has a new management pushed up prices, boosting profit for a year or so, but at the cost of damaged market share in the future? Is a company that pollutes the environment, uses materials from unsustainable sources, but makes a large profit, a successful business? Is profit necessarily the best measure of the performance of a business?

Even if we assume current profits are a good indication of how a company is performing, a number of other factors need to be taken into account. Is the market growing or declining? Are new competitors coming onto the scene? To what extent is the business achieving its corporate objectives? Is the profit earned likely to be sustained into the future – that is, is the profit of good quality? Information such as this is vital if a meaningful judgement is to be made about business success.

Key terms

Corporation tax: a tax levied as a percentage of a company's profits (e.g. 25%).

Cost of goods sold: calculation of the direct costs involved in making the goods actually sold in that period.

Gross profit: revenue less cost of goods sold; profit made on trading activities.

Operating profit: gross profit minus expenses.

Private limited company: a business with limited liability whose shares are not available to the public.

Revenue: sales revenue (i.e. the value of sales made); also known as income.

Stock exchange: a market for stocks and shares; it supervises the issuing of shares by companies and is also a second-hand market for stocks and shares.

Exercises

A. Revision questions

(40 marks; 40 minutes)

1 Give two possible reasons why a firm's bank would want to see its income statement. (2)

2 Outline two ways in which employees might benefit from looking at the income statement of their employer. (4)

3 List the elements necessary to calculate cost of sales. (4)

4 Distinguish between gross and operating profit. (4)

5 Last year Bandex plc made an operating profit of £25 million. £20 million of this came from the sale of its London training centre. The previous year the business made a profit of £15 million. Use the concept of 'profit quality' to decide whether last year was successful or unsuccessful for the business. (6)

6 Explain why even a charity such as Oxfam might want to make a profit. (4)

7 Explain what might be included under the heading 'financing costs'? (4)

8 Give one example each of exceptional and extraordinary items that might appear on the income statement of a business. Briefly explain each one. (4)

9 Look at the Tesco income statement on page 381.
   (a) Calculate the % increase in its 2007 income and its profit before tax. (4)
   (b) Explain one conclusion that can be drawn from those findings. (4)

B. Revision exercises

B1 Data response

The chairman of Thurton plc has come under some pressure lately. Shareholders have complained about the firm's lacklustre performance. Today, though, he is creating favourable headlines. The *Sunday Press* has announced that 'Thurton drives forward'. In the

Financial Guardian the chairman is quoted as saying: 'This is a great day for Thurton. Profit before tax is up by more than 50% and we have been able to double our dividends to shareholders. I am confident we will be able to maintain or increase this dividend next year.'

Income statement for Thurton plc

	This year (£m)	Last year (£m)
Revenue	24.5	25.8
Cost of sales	10.0	9.6
Expenses	12.4	11.1
Operating profit	?	?
Extraordinary item	6.4	–
Finance income	0.5	0.4
Finance expenses	0.9	0.9
Profit before taxation	?	?
Taxation	2.4	1.4
Profit after taxation for the year	**5.7**	**3.2**

Questions

(25 marks; 30 minutes)

1 Calculate Thurton plc's operating profit and profit before taxation for this year and last. (4)

2 Analyse Thurton plc's profit performance this year, by comparing it with last year. Within your answer, consider the quality of the profit made by Thurton this year. (9)

3 Use your analysis to comment on the accuracy of the chairman's statement. (12)

B2 Data response

Reckitt Benckiser plc is one of the world's leading manufacturers of cleaning products, and a member of the FTSE 100 Index of the largest companies traded on the London **Stock Exchange**. The company was formed by a merger between Britain's Reckitt & Colman and the Dutch company Benckiser NV in December 1999. Reckitt Benckiser has operations in more than 60 countries and sells its products in more than 180 countries. The company focuses on high-margin products and has shown strong growth in earnings per share in recent years.

Reckitt Benckiser group income statement (summarised)

	Six months to 30/06/2007 £m	Six months to 30/06/2006 £m
Revenue	2,560	2,386
Cost of sales	?	?
Gross profit	**1,475**	**1,328**
Operating expenses	965	961
Operating profit	**510**	**367**
Finance income	10	10
Finance expenditure	(26)	(27)
Profit before taxation	**494**	**350**
Taxation	(99)	(89)
Profit after taxation for six months	**395**	**261**

Source: Reckitt Benckiser Interim Report, 2007

Questions

(40 marks; 50 minutes)

1a Calculate Reckitt Benckiser's cost of sales for both periods. (5)

1b Calculate each figure as a percentage of the company's revenue for the corresponding period. (4)

1c Comment on your findings. (6)

2a Calculate the percentage increase Reckitt Benckiser achieved in 2006 compared with 2007 in:
(i) revenue (3)
(ii) operating profit. (3)

2b Analyse the data to suggest why the percentage increase in operating profit was greater than the increase in turnover. (8)

3 Why may it be unfair to judge a firm such as Reckitt Benckiser on its profit performance over a six-month period? (11)

B3 Data response

AstraZeneca

AstraZeneca plc, a large Anglo-Swedish pharmaceutical company, was formed on 6 April 1999 by the merger of Swedish Astra AB and British Zeneca Group plc. AstraZeneca develops, manufactures and sells pharmaceuticals to treat a range of mental and physical disorders in humans.

Its corporate headquarters are in London, England; its the research and development (R&D) headquarters are in Södertälje, Sweden. The company's main R&D centres are located in the United States, United Kingdom, Sweden and India.

Source: www.astrazeneca-annualreports.com/annualreport2007/financial_statements

Questions

(30 marks; 35 minutes)

1 Explain the meaning of the following terms:
(a) cost of sales
(b) finance income. (4)

2 Outline two uses to which the following data might be put. (4)

3a Identify three key trends in the data. (3)

3b Analyse the possible causes of the trends you have identified. (8)

4 Evaluate the usefulness of this data to an investor considering purchasing shares in AstraZeneca. (11)

AstraZeneca Group income statement for the year ended 31 December 2007

	2007 $m	2006 $m	2005 $m
Revenue	29,559	26,475	23,950
Cost of sales	(6,419)	(5,559)	(5,356)
Gross profit	**23,140**	**20,916**	**18,594**
Distribution expenses	(248)	(226)	(211)
Research & development expenses	(5,162)	(3,902)	(3,379)
Selling, general and administrative expenses	(10,364)	(9,096)	(8,695)
Other operating income and expenses	728	524	193
Total expenses	(15,046)	(12,700)	(12,092)
Operating profit	**8,094**	**8,216**	**6,502**
Finance income	959	888	665
Finance expenses	(1,070)	(561)	(500)
Profit before tax	**7,983**	**8,543**	**6,667**
Taxation	(2,356)	(2,480)	(1,943)
Profit for the period	**5,627**	**6,063**	**4,724**

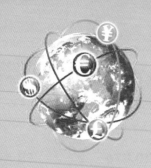

BALANCE SHEETS

The balance sheet is an accounting statement that shows an organisation's assets and liabilities at a precise point in time, usually the last day of the accounting year. Assets are resources owned by the organisation that have a monetary value. Liabilities are debts owed by the organisation to others.

56.1 Introduction

Unit 55 explained how an income statement provides information on how a business has performed over a given period of time, such as a year. It is the business equivalent to the question: 'How much did you earn last year?'

This unit focuses on the balance sheet. This accounting document looks at a different question: 'How rich are you?' To find out how rich someone is, you would need to find out what they own and what they owe on a particular day. The balance sheet does this for a business, with the particular day being the last day of the financial year. Balance sheets provide the means whereby owners, managers, financiers and other stakeholders can obtain information about an organisation that is not available on the income statement.

Since 2005 public limited companies have had to comply with new rules about presenting accounts. They must follow the International Financial Reporting Standards (IFRS), which, in truth, make accounts much more complicated to read. This requirement has not yet been extended to private limited companies. This chapter will start by examining the pre-IFRS approach, looking at private limited companies, before contrasting this later with how public companies present their balance sheets.

The balance sheet shows where a business has obtained its finances – its liabilities. It also lists the assets purchased with these funds. Therefore the balance sheet shows what the business owns and what it owes. For many finan... ...is of vital importance when ...cidin... ...to:

- invest in a business
- lend it some money
- buy the organisation outright.

A balance sheet enables the various stakeholders to make decisions as to that company's stability, its ability to pay debts and its ability to expand. A balance sheet therefore shows how secure a business is and what the potential for profit may be. It shows the asset strength built up in a business over all its years of trading. In effect, therefore, it shows the wealth of the business at a point in time.

How a business is financed and the resources it owns are of vital importance when making business plans and decisions. For example, if an organisation wanted to buy an expensive piece of equipment, how should it do it?

- *Buy it outright using cash from its bank account?* Yes, if there are sufficient funds to do so. But may the business be left short of money to meet future needs like paying bills and wages, or buying new stock?

- *Get a loan from the bank?* Again, this is a reasonable method of finance provided the business does not already have a lot of loans. Existing debt levels are shown on the balance sheet and can be examined to avoid the firm becoming dangerously indebted.

- *Attract new investors?* An organisation can take a partner or attract new shareholders. With the new funds invested it can purchase the equipment outright, therefore incurring no monthly payments or interest. However, new investors will receive a share of company profits and may want a say in the running of the business.

There is no single correct answer to the above. It depends on many factors, including the individual company's current circumstances. Some organisations may have a very healthy bank balance, whereas others may be struggling. It is the balance sheet that shows the current circumstances of the business. By analysing this information, decisions can be made to match the source of finance to the business needs.

56.2 The composition of the balance sheet

The balance sheet of a business is a 'snapshot' showing the position of a company at a given point in time. It shows only what the business owns and owes on the date the balance sheet was compiled – in other words, the balance sheet is a picture of an organisation's assets and liabilities at that date.

The main classifications that are used in balance sheets for most private limited companies are described below. We shall see later that similar categories are used for public limited companies, but that different terminology is used.

Assets

- *Fixed assets:* **fixed assets** are those items of a monetary value that have a long-term function and can be used repeatedly, such as vehicles or machinery. These are assets the business plans to hold for a year or more, and are not intended for immediate resale.

- *Current assets:* these are items of a monetary value that are likely to be turned into cash before the next balance sheet date. These include stocks, debtors and cash. Debtors and cash are often called liquid assets.

- *Other assets:* assets that do not fall into either of the above categories (e.g. investments in other businesses).

Liabilities

- *Owners' capital:* money or resources invested by the owners; called 'capital' for sole traders or partnerships and 'share capital' for limited companies.

- *Long-term liabilities:* money owed by the business that has to be paid in more than one year's time.

- *Current liabilities:* money owed by the business that has to be paid in less than one year's time. Examples include overdrafts, trade **creditors** (suppliers) and unpaid tax.

56.3 The structure of the balance sheet

The vertical balance sheet is the one most widely used in business today. By law, all public limited companies must publish their accounts in this form. Therefore it is the format focused upon in this unit.

The foundations of the balance sheet (at the bottom) consist of the firm's capital. This may have come from shareholders, bankers or from reinvested profit. If Spark Ltd has £400,000 of capital invested, it follows that it must have £400,000 of assets. The top section shows the type of assets bought. The table below shows a summarised and simplified version of this position.

Spark Ltd: Simplified vertical balance sheet

	£
Long-term (fixed) assets	300,000
Short-term (current) assets	100,000
Total assets	400,000
Total capital	400,000

Assets on the vertical balance sheet

Fixed assets are long-term assets, including the following.

Tangible assets:

- land and buildings – property owned by the business, either freehold or leasehold

- plant/machinery/equipment – anything from specialised machinery used in manufacturing to computers or even furniture

- vehicles – all types.

Intangible assets:

- goodwill – the prestige a business enjoys, which adds value over and above the value of its physical assets

- patents/copyright – exclusive rights to make or sell a particular invention.

Current assets include stock, debtors and cash. In balance sheets, these assets are treated differently from fixed assets. This is because they change on a daily basis as bills come in, stock is sold and cash comes into the shop tills. The sudden arrival of £20,000 of stock from a supplier adds to current assets. But if the company now owes £20,000 to that supplier, it is clearly no better off. Thus current liabilities such as this are deducted from current assets to give a total called net current assets (also known as **working capital**).

Spark Ltd: Fuller version of the firm's balance sheet

	£	£
Property	180,000	
Machinery and vehicles	120,000	300,000
Stock	80,000	
Debtors and cash	60,000	
Current liabilities	(40,000)	
Net current assets		100,000
Assets employed		400,000
Total capital		400,000

Notes

● The two-column format allows individual items to be shown on the left, leaving the 'big picture' totals to be seen clearly on the right.

● Current liabilities of £40,000 have been deducted from the £140,000 of current assets to show net current assets (or working capital) of £100,000.

● Assets employed of £400,000 still balances with the capital employed (total capital).

Capital on the balance sheet

Companies have three main sources of long-term capital: shareholders (share capital), banks (loan capital) and reinvested profits (reserves). Loan capital carries interest charges that must be repaid, as must the loan itself. Share capital and reserves are both owed to the shareholders, but do not have to be repaid. Therefore they are treated separately. Share capital and reserves are known as shareholders' funds.

Assuming Spark Ltd's capital came from £50,000 of share capital, £250,000 of loan capital and £100,000 of accumulated, retained profits, the final version of the vertical balance sheet would look like this:

Spark Ltd: Balance sheet for 31 December last year

	£	£
Property	180,000	
Machinery and vehicles	120,000	300,000
Stock	80,000	
Debtors and cash	60,000	
Current liabilities	(40,000)	
Net current assets		100,000
Total assets less current liabilities		400,000
Loan capital		(250,000)
Net assets		150,000
Share capital	50,000	
Reserves	100,000	
Shareholders' funds		150,000

The concept of capital as a liability

It is hard to see why money invested by the owners should be treated as a **liability**. This is due to a concept in accounting called 'business entity'. This states that a business and its owners are two separate legal entities. From the point of view of the business, therefore, any money paid to it by the shareholders is a liability because the firm owes it back to them. In reality, capital invested by the owners is likely to be paid back only in the event of the business ceasing to trade.

56.4 More detail on balance sheet calculations

Working capital

Current liabilities need to be repaid in the near future, ideally using current assets. Taking the former away from the latter gives a figure called working capital. This shows an organisation's ability or inability to pay its short-term debts.

If current assets exceed current liabilities the business has enough short-term assets to pay short-term debts. It has positive working capital and should therefore have enough money for its day-to-day needs.

In Figure 56.1, Ted Baker plc has plenty of working capital, because its £26 million of short-term (current) liabilities are easily covered by its £57 million of current assets.

If current assets are less than current liabilities the business does not have enough short-term assets to pay short-term debts. Working capital is negative (e.g.

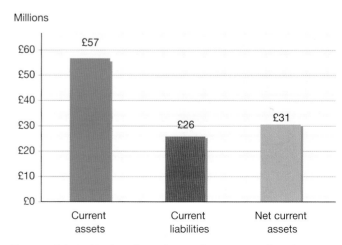

Figure 56.1 Ted Baker plc working capital, 28 January 2008

current assets are £50,000 but current liabilities are £70,000, so working capital is −£20,000). This may mean a day-to-day struggle to pay the bills. In this case the figure on the balance sheet may be called net current liabilities.

The balance between current assets and liabilities is a very important figure. Suppliers and banks expect to be paid when debts are due. At the very least, the failure to pay on time will mean a worsening in relations. At worst, it may result in court action.

The effect of making a net loss on the balance sheet

In the event that a business makes a net loss rather than a net profit over a financial year, then the layout of the balance sheet remains completely unchanged. The only effect is that the loss reduces the reserves figure and therefore cuts the shareholders' funds. This will be balanced in the accounts by a reduction in the net current assets.

This reflects that if a business has made a loss over the financial period, expenses have exceeded revenues received. Therefore the overall value of the business will have fallen and so must the value of the owners' funds invested.

56.5 The published accounts of public limited companies

Since January 2005 the implementation of International Financial Reporting Standards (IFRS) has required that listed public companies present their balance sheets in a format slightly different from that set out above. There are a number of differences in the terminology used on the IFRS balance sheet, as outlined below.

- Fixed assets are called non-current assets but continue to include tangible and non-tangible assets.

- There are two changes within the current assets section of the balance sheet: stocks are renamed as inventories and debtors are now termed 'trade and other receivables'.

- Under current liabilities creditors are referred to as 'trade and other payables'.

- Long-term liabilities are renamed 'non-current liabilities'.

- Reserves in the final section of the balance sheet are

supplemented by 'retained earnings'. Retained earnings are profits that a company has generated that have not been paid out to shareholders.

- Shareholders' funds are termed 'total equity' or 'total shareholders' equity'.

The overall structure of the balance sheet is the same, even though the terminology varies. The two figures that balance are the net assets of the business (simply all its assets less its total liabilities) and the total equity figure (which is share capital invested plus reserves and retained earnings from past trading). The reason for balancing the figures in this way is to enable shareholders to see at a glance what the balance sheet suggests the business is 'worth' – that is, the bottom line of the balance sheet (total equity).

The implications of the changes introduced by IFRS rules are greater than just changes in terminology, but are not within the scope of this book. The main reason is to allow greater comparability between the performances of companies in different countries. It is hoped that this will increase investors' confidence and therefore encourage international investment flows.

Below is a summary of a recent balance sheet for JD Wetherspoon. This follows the IFRS format for listed companies, though a few minor differences exist between the formats of balance sheets for different public companies. However, it is common for two years to be shown side by side. This is to help financial interpretation of the accounts and the analysis of trends.

Balance sheet for JD Wetherspoon as at 29 July 2007

	2007 £m	2006 £m
Non-current assets	794	759
Inventories	19	14
Receivables & cash	31	31
Total assets	844	804
Current liabilities	(129)	(129)
Net current assets	(79)	(84)
Non-current liabilities	(542)	(473)
Net assets	173	202
Share capital	144	139
Reserves & retained earnings	29	63
Total shareholders' equity	173	202

Source: adapted from annual accounts for JD Wetherspoon, 2007

Key conclusions to be drawn from JD Wetherspoon's balance sheets over the two years include:

- the company's long-term borrowing (non-current liabilities) has increased significantly between the two years

- current liabilities outweigh current assets, causing net current assets to be strongly negative

- Total shareholders' equity fell during the year. This was the result of a deliberate strategy on the part of the firm to buy back more than 13 million of its own shares to return capital to shareholders.

JD Wetherspoon's balance sheet shows a growth in assets, though non-current liabilities have grown more rapidly. Some shareholders may be concerned by this. However, the company's short-term financial position (as shown by the fall in its net current liabilities) has improved slightly.

A-grade application

HBOS balance sheet hit by 'credit crunch'

HBOS, the UK's fourth-largest bank, has said it will reduce the value of its assets on the company's balance sheet by £180 million following the much-publicised 'credit crunch' in world financial markets.

The bank stated that it expected its financial statements to show a 'good full year outcome' despite difficulties in global financial markets. It said that it was reducing the value of some of the financial assets that it holds and that the loss of value had not been caused by difficulties in the American 'sub-prime' mortgage market. The bank said that investments in the American mortgage market were less than 0.1% of the value of its balance sheet.

56.6 Window dressing accounts

Window dressing means presenting company accounts in such a manner as to flatter the financial position of the company.

Window dressing is a form of creative accounting that is concerned with making modest adjustments to sales, debtors and stock items when preparing end-of-year financial reports. There is a fine dividing line between flattery and fraud.

In many cases, window dressing is simply a matter of tidying up the accounts and is not misleading. Two important methods of window dressing are as follows.

1 Massaging profit figures: surprisingly, it is possible to 'adjust' a business's cost and revenue figures. At the end of a poor year, managers may be asked to bring forward as many invoices and deliveries as possible. The intention is to inflate, as much as possible, the revenue earned by the business in the final month of trading.

2 Hiding a deteriorating **liquidity** position: this allows businesses to present balance sheets that look sound to potential investors. A business may execute a sale and leaseback deal just prior to accounts being published. This increases the amount of cash within the business and makes it look a more attractive proposition.

It is important to remember that, although window dressing happens, the overwhelming majority of companies present their accounts as fairly and straightforwardly as possible.

Issues For Analysis

- The balance sheet is an important statement full of information for anyone with an interest in a business. Analysis of the balance sheet can provide the reader with an insight into the strengths and weaknesses of a business, its potential for growth, its stability and how it is financed.

- The balance sheet gives details as to where and how an organisation has obtained its finance, alongside information as to what this finance has been spent on. This allows judgements to be made about the financial performance of the business in question.

- Examining individual balance sheets can be interesting and provides the reader with a great deal of information. However, it must be remembered that a balance sheet is only a 'snapshot' of a business on one day out of 365, and that for a meaningful analysis to take place it must be compared to previous balance sheets, to see what changes or trends can be identified. The primary method of balance sheet analysis is through accounting ratios. These are explained in Unit 57.

Balance sheets
an evaluation

Several key areas can be considered with regard to balance sheets. The first is the assumption that just because a company possesses thousands or millions of pounds' worth of assets it is doing well. It is how the company has financed these assets that counts. A company could look in quite a stable position, but what would be the effect of a rise in interest rates if most of the company is financed by debt?

Similarly, equal importance must be placed on the short-term asset structure of the company. Many profitable companies close down or go into liquidation, not through lack of sales or customers but through poor short-term asset management (i.e. management of working capital).

As with all financial data and decisions, it is not sufficient just to consider the numerical information. External considerations such as the state of the market or economy must be taken into account. Comparisons with similar-sized organisations in the same industry must be used. Any worthwhile judgement requires an investigation into the non-financial aspects of the business. A company could have millions of pounds of assets, a healthy bank account, a good profit record and be financed mainly by share capital. However, all this means little if the workforce is about to go on strike for three months or its products are becoming obsolete.

Key terms

Creditors: those to whom a firm owes money (e.g. suppliers or bankers); these may also be called payables.

Fixed assets: items of value the business plans to hold in the medium to long term, such as vehicles or property.

Liability: a debt (i.e. a bill that has not been paid or a loan that has not been repaid).

Liquidity: a measurement of a firm's ability to pay its short-term bills.

Working capital: day-to-day finance for running the business (current assets − current liabilities).

Exercises

A. Revision questions

(30 marks; 30 minutes)

1 Define the term 'balance sheet'. (2)

2 Distinguish between non-current and current assets. (4)

3 Explain why it is that the two parts of a balance sheet will always balance. (2)

4 What are the main reasons for presenting a balance sheet in vertical format? (3)

5 How would you calculate working capital? (2)

6 Why is it important for a supplier to check on the liquidity of a potential customer? (4)

7 Explain what is meant by the term 'window dressing'. (4)

8 Describe two ways in which a business might window dress its accounts. (4)

9 What is the difference between an intangible and a tangible non-current asset? (3)

10 State two items that may be listed as current liabilities. (2)

B. Revision exercises

B1 Data response

D Parton Ltd balance sheet for year ended 31 December 2007

		£000
	Property	600
	Stock	120
	Machinery (at cost)*	240
	Creditors	100
	Cash	170
	Reserves	350
less	Debtors	280
	Tax due	140
	Assets employed	(200)
	Net current assets	760
	Overdraft	200
	Share capital	500
	Capital employed	760

*Book value: £120,000

Questions

(20 marks; 25 minutes)

1 Identify ten mistakes in the balance sheet above. (10)

1b Draw up the balance sheet correctly. (10)

B2 Stimulus question

The balance sheet shown below is taken from Marks & Spencer's 2007 annual report and accounts. Marks & Spencer is one of Britain's best-known and largest retailers, selling clothing, food and household durables. In 2006–2007 the company's sales turnover rose to £8588 million, from £7798 million in 2005–2006. In the 2006–2007 financial year the company's operating profit rose by 22% to £1044 million.

Marks & Spencer plc balance sheet as at 31 March 2007

	2007 £m	2006 £m
Intangible non-current assets	194.1	163.5
Tangible non-current assets	4,340.5	3953.3
Inventories	426.3	374.3
Receivables and cash	420.1	767.8
Total assets	5,381.0	5,258.9
Current liabilities	1,606.2	2,017.0
Net current liabilities	(759.8)	(874.9)
Non-current liabilities	(2,126.6)	(2,038.2)
Total liabilities	(3,732.8)	(4,055.2)
Net assets	**1,648.2**	**1,203.7**
Share capital	629.2	582.9
Reserves & retained earnings	1,019.0	620.8
Total equity	**1,648.2**	**1,203.7**

Questions

(30 marks; 40 minutes)

1 Explain the meaning of the following terms:
(a) balance sheet
(b) net assets. (4)

2 Describe two external users of financial information, and explain why they might analyse a balance sheet. (6)

3a Identify three key trends in this data. (3)

3b Analyse the possible causes and implications of the trends you have identified. (6)

4 Evaluate the usefulness of this data to an investor considering purchasing shares in Marks & Spencer. (11)

B3 Case study

Imperial Tobacco is the world's fourth-largest international tobacco company; it manufactures, markets and sells a comprehensive range of cigarettes, tobaccos and cigars. The company grew significantly during the 2006–2007 financial year, principally as a result of buying up other companies.

Balance sheet for Imperial Tobacco plc as at 30 September 2007

	2007 £m	2006 £m
Non-current assets	6,255	4,982
Inventories	998	789
Trade and other receivables	1,254	1,067
Cash & equivalents	501	305
Total assets	9,008	?
Current liabilities	(3,172)	(3,002)
Net current assets/(liabilities)	?	(841)
Non-current liabilities	(4,695)	(3,543)
Net assets	1,141	598
Total equity	1,141	?

Questions

(40 marks; 50 minutes)

1 Distinguish between net current assets and net current liabilities. (3)

2a Complete Imperial Tobacco's balance sheet by inserting the missing figures. (3)

2b Explain one way in which Imperial Tobacco plc might have window dressed its accounts to make them look as favourable as possible. (4)

3 Imperial Tobacco is expanding by buying other companies. Analyse whether its balance sheet is strong enough to encourage banks to lend it further capital to finance its plans. (12)

4 To what extent can you judge the performance of Imperial Tobacco plc over the period 2006–2007 from the information included in the company's balance sheet? (18)

C. Essay questions

(40 marks each)

1 'Balance sheets can only measure the financial worth of a business. The real worth depends upon far more.' In relation to any business with which you are familiar, discuss how important a balance sheet is, then, in judging whether a firm is well managed.

2 With reference to any business with which you are familiar, consider whether its balance sheet is more useful than its cash flow forecast, or vice versa.

3 'Balance sheet evaluation is the key to making successful long-term investment decisions.' With reference to any real-world business, consider the extent to which you believe this to be true.

RATIO ANALYSIS

DEFINITION

Ratio analysis is an examination of accounting data by relating one figure to another. This approach allows more meaningful interpretation of the data and the identification of trends.

57.1 Introduction

The function of accounting is to provide information to stakeholders on how a business has performed over a given period. But how is performance to be judged? Is an annual profit of £1 million good or bad? Very good if the firm is a small family business; woeful if the business is Carphone Warehouse and annual revenue is more than £3991 million. What is needed is to compare this information to something else. This can provide a way of judging a firm's financial performance in relation to its size and in relation to the performance of its competitors. The technique used to do this is called ratio analysis.

Financial accounts, such as the income statement and the balance sheet, are used for three main purposes:

1 financial control

2 planning

3 accountability.

Ratio analysis can assist in achieving these objectives. It can help the different users of financial information to answer some of the questions they are interested in. It may also raise several new questions, such as:

● Is this company/my job safe?

● Should I stop selling goods to this firm on credit?

● Should I invest in this business?

● Is my money safe in this bank?

● Just how much profit is ESSO making out of high petrol prices?

57.2 Interpreting final accounts: the investigation process

To analyse company accounts, a well-ordered and structured process needs to be followed. This should ensure that the analysis is relevant to the question being looked at. The seven-point approach shown below and in Table 57.1 is helpful.

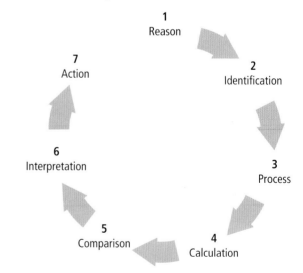

Figure 57.1 Seven-point approach to ratio analysis

57.3 Types of ratio

The main classifications of ratios are as follows.

● *Profitability ratios*: measure the relationship between gross/net profit and revenue, assets and capital employed. They are sometimes referred to as performance ratios.

● *Activity ratios*: these measure how efficiently an organisation uses its resources, such as inventories or total assets.

- *Liquidity ratios:* these investigate the short-term financial stability of a firm by examining whether there are sufficient short-term assets to meet the short-term liabilities (debts); the 2007/08 credit squeeze showed that even banks can run out of the cash they need to keep operating.

- *Gearing:* examines the extent to which the business is dependent upon borrowed money; it is concerned with the long-term financial position of the company.

- *Shareholder ratios:* this group of ratios is concerned with analysing the returns for shareholders. They examine the relationship between the number of shares issued, dividend paid, value of the shares and company profits.

The following sections look at each classification of ratios in more detail.

Table 57.1 Seven-point approach to ratio analysis

The investigation process		
Step 1	Reason	The starting point for interpreting financial accounts is establishing why you are doing so. If you are considering supplying a company with a large order of goods, you want to try to establish its financial stability and ability to pay.
Step 2	Identification	Identify the relevant figures from the financial accounts.
Step 3	Process	Decide what method(s) of analysis will provide you with the most useful and meaningful results.
Step 4	Calculation	Make a comparison between data by calculating one figure as a ratio of another. Such as profit as a percentage of sales revenue or borrowings as a proportion of total capital.
Step 5	Comparison	Compare the figures from this period with the results from the last period, those of your competitors or other companies under investigation.
Step 6	Interpretation	Look at the results obtained and interpret them in relation to values that would be considered poor, average or good.
Step 7	Action	If certain results are worrying, initiate further investigation (maybe into areas which are not covered in the financial accounts), or take corrective action.

57.4 Profitability ratios

For private businesses, a key objective is to make a profit. But how much profit? Consider the following example.

Example

Companies A and B operate in the same market. At the end of the year they report profits as follows:

	Company A	Company B
Profit	£100,000	£1 million

Which is the more successful company? Company B, surely. However, take into account the following additional information.

	Company A	Company B
Profit	£100,000	£1 million
Capital invested	£200,000	£10 million

This shows that company A has done very well compared with the capital invested in the business. Much better, in fact, than company B. Profitability ratios allow comparisons such as this to be made in detail. The figures can be compared in percentage terms. This makes comparison easier.

	Company A	Company B
Profit £	100,000	£1 million
Divided by	£200,000	£10 million
X 100 (to get a percentage)	50%	10%

Company A's success can now be seen much more clearly.

Unit 55 distinguished between various types of profit. Because of the different types of profit, there are a number of different profit ratios. The net profit margin was looked at as part of Unit 18. There are two other profitability ratios to consider.

Gross profit margin

This ratio examines the relationship between the profit made before allowing for overhead costs (gross profit) and the level of revenue. It is given by the formula:

$$\text{gross profit margin} = \frac{\text{gross profit}}{\text{revenue}} \times 100$$

For example, a furniture shop buys sofas for £200 and sells them for £500 each, making a gross profit of £300 per sofa. In a week it sells ten, so its gross profit is £3000 and its revenue from sales is £5000. The gross profit margin is therefore:

$$= \frac{\text{gross profit}}{\text{revenue}} = \frac{£3000}{£5000} \times 100 = 60\%$$

Note that although this sounds a terrific profit margin, no allowance has yet been made for all the overhead costs of the business, such as rent, rates, staff costs, advertising and much more.

Interpretation

Obviously, the higher the profit margin a business makes the better. However, the level of gross profit margin will vary considerably between different markets. For example, the amount of gross profit percentage on clothes (especially fashion items) is far higher than on food. Any result gained must be looked at in the context of the industry in which the firm operates. It will always be possible to make comparisons with previous years' figures. This will establish whether or not the firm's trading position has become more or less profitable.

Altering the ratio

The gross profit margin can be improved by:

● raising sales revenue while keeping the cost of sales the same, or

● reducing the cost of sales made while maintaining the same level of sales revenue.

Return on capital employed (ROCE)

This is sometimes referred to as being the primary efficiency ratio and is perhaps the most important ratio of all. It measures the efficiency with which the firm generates profit from the funds invested in the business. It answers the key question anyone would ask before investing or saving: 'What annual percentage return will I get on my capital?'

$$\text{ROCE} = \frac{\text{operating profit}}{\text{capital employed}} \times 100$$

Operating profit is profit after all operating costs and overheads have been deducted. It is, however, profit before interest and taxation are paid. Capital employed is long-term loans (non-current assets) plus total equity (shareholders' funds).

Interpretation

The higher the value of this ratio the better. Where there is a good and increasing ROCE it is possible to conclude that the management of the business is using its resources effectively. ROCE measures profitability and no shareholder will complain at huge returns. The figure needs to be compared with previous years and that of other companies to determine whether this year's result is satisfactory or not.

A firm's ROCE can also be compared with the percentage return offered by interest-bearing accounts at banks and building societies. If bank interest rates are 6%, what is the point of a sole trader investing money in his or her business, working very hard all year and making a return on capital employed of 4%? S/he would be better off keeping the money in the bank, taking little risk and staying at home.

Table 57.2 The return on capital employed (ROCE) achieved by a selection of public limited companies in 2007

Company	Annual operating profit	Capital employed	ROCE
Burberry (clothing)	£157,000,000	£419,300,000	37.44%
BP (oil extraction and refining, retailing)	$32,352,000,000	$158,845,000,000	20.37%
Tesco (retailing)	£2,648,000,000	£16,655,000,000	15.90%
Cadbury Schweppes (confectionery and soft drinks)	£796,000,000	£6,706,000,000	11.87%

So what is the *right* level of ROCE? There is no clear answer, but most companies would regard a 20% ROCE as very satisfactory. The returns achieved by a selection of public companies in 2007 are shown in Table 57.2.

Altering the ratio

The return on capital employed can be improved by:

- increasing the level of profit generated by the same level of capital invested, or

- maintaining the level of profits generated but decreasing the amount of capital it takes to do so.

57.5 Financial efficiency ratios

These four ratios are concerned with how well an organisation manages its resources. Three of them investigate how well the management controls the current situation of the firm. They consider stock, debtors and creditors. This area of ratios is linked, therefore, with the management of working capital. The fourth ratio looks at the position of the whole business: how well it is generating sales income from the investment it has made in assets. This important ratio is called asset turnover.

Stock (or inventory) turnover

This ratio measures the number of times a year a business sells and replaces its stock – on plc balance sheets stock is termed 'inventories', but for the purpose of this ratio we will use the term stock. For example, if a market stall trader bought stock from wholesalers every morning and sold all the stock by the end of the afternoon, replacing the stock daily would mean a stock turnover of 365 times per year. The formula for stock turnover is:

$$\text{stock turnover} = \frac{\text{cost of goods sold}}{\text{stock}}$$

expressed as times per year.

Interpretation

This ratio can only really be interpreted with knowledge of the industry in which the firm operates. For example, we would expect a greengrocer to turn over stock virtually every day, as the goods have to be fresh. Therefore, we would expect to see a result for stock turnover of approximately 250 to 300 times per year. This allows for closures and holidays and the fact that some produce will last longer than one day. A second-hand car sales business might take an average of a month to sell the cars; therefore the stock turnover would be 12 times.

It is possible to convert this ratio from showing the number of times an organisation turns over stock to showing the average number of days stock is held. It is given by the formula:

$$\text{stock turnover} = \frac{365}{\text{number of times}}$$

expressed as days (e.g. 'the company holds 7 days' worth of stock').

Altering the ratio

The stock turnover ratio can be improved by:

- reducing the average level of stocks held, without losing sales, or

- increasing the rate of sales without raising the level of stocks.

Note that the stock turnover ratio has little meaning for service industries as they do not buy or sell stocks of goods.

Debtor days

This particular ratio is designed to show how long, on average, it takes the company to collect debts owed by customers. Customers who are granted credit are called debtors. On public companies' balance sheets they are called 'trade receivables', but we will use the term debtors for this ratio. The formula for this ratio is:

Table 57.3 Information from the Ted Baker accounts: debtor position

	Annual income	Debtors	Debtor days
Year to 27 January 2007	£125.6m	£11.8m	34.3 days
Year to 28 January 2008	£142.2m	£14.1m	36.2 days

$$\text{debtor days} = \frac{\text{debtors}}{\text{annual income}} \times 365$$

expressed as days.

The accounts for the fashion clothing business Ted Baker plc make it possible to calculate the following debtor days' position (see Table 57.3).

Interpretation

In other words, the average Ted Baker customer took 34 days to pay in 2007 and 36 days to pay in 2008. This slippage in collecting its money would have (very slightly) worsened Ted Baker's cash position. Better to have the cash than to be waiting for it.

Altering the ratio

The debtors' collection period can be improved by reducing the amount of time for which credit is offered (e.g. from 90 to 60 days) or offering incentives for clients to pay on time (e.g. cash discounts or stepping up the efficiency of the credit control department). A common approach is **aged debtors analysis**; this means sorting debtors into the age of their debts to you – oldest first. This helps focus upon collecting debts from the slowest payers. It may also encourage a firm to refuse to supply a persistent slow payer in future.

Creditor days

This particular ratio is designed to show how many days, on average, it takes the company to pay its suppliers. Creditors are people and organisations that are owed money by the business. On public companies' balance sheets they are called 'trade payables', but we will use the term creditors for this ratio. The formula for this ratio is:

$$\text{creditor days} = \frac{\text{creditors}}{\text{cost of sales}} \times 365$$

The accounts for the fashion clothing business Ted Baker plc make it possible to calculate the following creditor days' position (Table 57.4).

Interpretation

In other words, the average Ted Baker supplier had to wait 142 days to be paid in 2007 and 133 days in 2008. Ted Baker is getting slightly better, but from a very poor starting point. This would be important to know if your business was considering supplying Ted Baker for the first time (it's a long wait!). From Ted Baker's point of view, though, it's great to be able to hold onto the cash for ages before paying.

It is valuable to compare creditor and debtor days for a given business as it provides some information on the business's cash position. If a business has a lower figure for creditor days than debtor days, then it is settling its own debts more quickly than it is receiving money from its debtors. This could place pressure on its cash flow position. Alternatively, a higher figure for creditor days is likely to strengthen a business's cash position.

Altering the ratio

Creditor days can be reduced by paying bills more promptly. This might actually worsen a business's cash position but could improve its corporate image.

Asset turnover ratio

The asset turnover ratio measures how many pounds' worth of sales a company can generate from its net assets. Net assets are non-current assets plus net current assets less non-current liabilities. In other words, they equal total equity. Company directors often use the phrase 'make the assets sweat' – in other words, make the assets work hard. If there is a period in the year when a factory is quiet, an active company director might want to find a source of extra business. In this way the company could keep generating sales from its existing assets. This would push up the value of the asset turnover ratio.

Table 57.4 Information from the Ted Baker accounts: creditor position

	Cost of sales	**Creditors**	**Creditor days**
Year to 27 January 2007	£52.0m	£20.2m	141.8 days
Year to 28 January 2008	£59.6m	£21.8m	133.5 days

Table 57.5 Information from the Burberry accounts: asset turnover figures

Year	Sales revenue £m	Assets employed £m	Asset turnover
2006	742.90	386.6	1.92 times
2007	850.30	396.9	2.14 times

Source: www.advfn.com/p.php?pid5ukfinancials&symbol5LSE%3ABRBY

$$\text{asset turnover} = \frac{\text{annual income}}{\text{assets employed}}$$

expressed as times per year.

The fashion clothing and accessories company, Burberry, had the asset turnover figures in 2006 and 2007 shown in Table 57.5.

In 2007, the asset turnover ratio for Burberry rose compared with the previous year. This figure represented a significant increase on the asset turnover figures achieved by the company a few years earlier (for example, it was 1.57 in 2004). This trend suggests that the company's efficiency is increasing as the management team makes more effective use of the company's assets.

Interpretation

Some companies pursue a policy of high profit margins, perhaps at the cost of high sales. An antiques shop in an expensive part of town may be beautifully laid out but never seem to have any customers. Its asset turnover will be low because it generates low sales from its high asset base. Fortunately for the firm, its profit margins may be so high that the occasional sale generates enough profit to keep the business going.

Other companies may follow a low-price, high-sales approach. Tesco used to call this 'pile them high, sell them cheap'. Here profit margins may be low, but the asset turnover so high that lots and lots of small profits add up to a healthy profit total. Asset turnover, then, should be looked at in relation to (net) profit margins. If net profit margins are multiplied by asset turnover, the result is the company's ROCE. So boosting asset turnover is as helpful to a firm as boosting its profit margins.

Altering the ratio

To increase asset turnover there are two options. Either work at increasing sales from the existing asset base (making the assets 'sweat'). Or sell off under-utilised assets, so that the sales figure is divided by a lower asset total. Either approach would then have the effect of boosting a company's ROCE.

57.6 Liquidity ratios

These ratios are concerned with the short-term financial health of a business. They are concerned with the organisation's working capital and whether or not it is being managed effectively. Too little working capital and the company may not be able to pay all its debts. Too much and it may not be making the most efficient use of its financial resources.

Current ratio (also known as the liquidity ratio)

This ratio looks at the relationship between current assets and current liabilities. It examines the **liquidity** position of the firm. It is given by the formula:

$$\text{current ratio} = \frac{\text{current assets}}{\text{current liabilities}}$$

This is expressed as a ratio – for example, 2:1 or 3:1.

Example

Bannam Ltd has current assets of £30,000 and current liabilities of £10,000:

$$\begin{aligned}
\text{current ratio} &= \text{current assets} &:& \text{ current liabilities} \\
&= \text{£30,000} &:& \text{ £10,000} \\
&= 3 &:& \text{ 1} \\
\text{current ratio} &= 3
\end{aligned}$$

Interpretation

From the above worked example the result shows that Bannam Ltd has three times as many current assets as

Table 57.6 *The current ratios of a selection of public companies in 2007*

Company	Balance sheet date	Current assets	Current liabilities	Current ratio
Tate & Lyle	31/03/2007	£1,480,000,000	£933.000.000	1.59
Burberry	31/03/2007	£423,700,000	£330,400,000	1.28
BP	31/12/2007	£78,916,000,000	£77,068,000,000	1.02
Imperial Tobacco	30/09/2007	£2,753,000,000	£3,172,000,000	0.87
Tesco	24/02/2007	£4,576,000,000	£8,152,000,000	0.56

current liabilities. This means that, for every £1 of short-term debts owed, it has £3 of assets to pay them. This is a comfortable position.

Accountants suggest the 'ideal' current ratio should be approximately 1.5:1 (i.e. £1.50 of assets for every £1 of debt). Any higher than this and the organisation has too many resources tied up in unproductive assets; these could be invested more profitably (or the cash should be handed back to shareholders). A low current ratio means a business may not be able to pay its debts. It is possible that the result may well be something like 0.8:1. This shows the firm has only 80p of current assets to pay every £1 it owes.

The current ratios of a selection of public companies in 2007 are shown in Table 57.6. As this table shows, it would be wrong to panic about a liquidity ratio of less than 1. Very successful firms such as Tesco have often had spells when their liquidity levels were less than 1.

Altering the ratio

If the ratio is so low that it is becoming hard to pay the bills, the company will have to try to bring more cash into the balance sheet. This could be done by:

● selling under-used fixed assets

● raising more share capital

● increasing long-term borrowings

● postponing planned investments.

Acid test ratio

This ratio is sometimes also called the quick ratio or even the liquid ratio. It examines the business's liquidity position by comparing current assets and liabilities, but it omits stock (or inventories) from the total of current assets. The reason for this is that stock is the most illiquid current asset (i.e. it is the hardest to turn into cash without a loss in its value). It can take a long time to convert stock into cash. Furthermore, stock may be old or obsolete and thus unsellable.

By omitting stock, the ratio directly relates cash and near cash (cash, bank and debtors – known as liquid assets) to short-term debts. This provides a tighter measure of a firm's liquidity. It is given by the formula:

$$\text{acid test ratio} = \frac{(\text{current assets} - \text{stock})}{\text{current liabilities}}$$

Again, it is expressed in the form of a ratio, such as 2:1.

Interpretation

Accountants recommend that an 'ideal' result for this ratio should be approximately 1:1, thus showing that the organisation has £1 of short-term assets for every £1 of short-term debt. A result below this (e.g. 0.5:1) indicates that the firm may well have difficulties meeting short-term payments. However, some businesses are able to operate with a very low level of liquidity – supermarkets, for example, who have much of their current assets tied up in stock.

Table 57.7 The acid test ratios of a selection of public companies in 2007

Company	Balance sheet date	Current assets – stock (inventories)	Current liabilities	Current ratio
Tate & Lyle	31/03/2007	£977,000,000	£933.000.000	1.05
BP	31/12/2007	£52,362,000,000	£77,068,000,000	0.68
Thomas Cook	31/10/2007	£2,275,800,000	£3,737,900,000	0.61
Imperial Tobacco	30/09/2007	£1,755,000,000	£3,172,000,000	0.55
Tesco	24/02/2007	£2,645,000,000	£8,152,000,000	0.32

The acid test ratios of a selection of public companies in 2007 are shown in Table 57.7.

57.7 Gearing

Gearing is one of the main measures of the financial health of a business. Quite simply, it measures the firm's level of debt. This shines a light onto the long-term financial stability of an organisation.

Gearing measures long-term loans as a proportion of a firm's capital employed. It shows how reliant the firm is upon borrowed money. In turn, that indicates how vulnerable the firm is to financial setbacks. The Americans call gearing 'leverage'. In boom times, banks and investors find leverage (debt) very attractive; but high gearing always means high risk.

Highly geared companies can suffer badly in recessions, because even when times are hard they still have to keep paying high interest payments to the bank.

The formula for gearing is:

$$\text{gearing} = \frac{\text{long-term loans}}{\text{capital employed}} \times 100$$

This is expressed as a percentage.

Interpretation

The gearing ratio shows how risky an investment a company is. If loans represent more than 50% of capital employed, the company is said to be highly geared. Such a company has to pay substantial interest charges on its

Table 57.8 The gearing ratios of a selection of companies in 2007

Company	Balance sheet date	Non-current liabilities (long-term loans)	Capital employed	Gearing
Tate & Lyle	31/03/2007	£1,134,000,000	£2,129,000,000	53.26%
John Lewis	27/01/2007	£1,046,500,000	£2,689,200,000	38.91%
Tesco	24/02/2007	£6,084,000,000	£16,655.000.000	36.53%
ITV plc	31/12/2007	£1,528,000,000	£4,767,000,000	32.05%
Morrisons	29/07/2007	£1,532,000,000	£5,616,600,000	27.28%

Carlyle Capital Corporation

In early March 2008 a US blogger with the fabulous name of Postman Patel warned that the Carlyle Capital Corporation (an American investment fund) was unable to pay its bills. Within a week it had collapsed, owing over $16 billion. It emerged that Carlyle Capital had a gearing level of 97%. In other words, only 3% of the money it invested was its own money; all the rest was borrowed. When times were good its shares were worth $20 each. Now they were worth nothing. High gearing means high risk. Ridiculously high gearing means ridiculously high risk.

borrowings before it can pay dividends to shareholders or retain profits for reinvestment. The higher the gearing, the higher the degree of risk. Low-geared companies provide a lower-risk investment; therefore they can negotiate loans more easily and at lower cost than a highly geared company.

Banks would be especially reluctant to lend to a firm with poor liquidity and high gearing. It is useful, therefore, to look at the gearing for some of the same firms whose liquidity was investigated earlier. This is shown in Table 57.8.

Tate & Lyle (which supplies sugar and cereal-based products to retailers and industrial customers) has a high gearing level. The company might experience difficulties if interest rates rose, or if it encountered a really poor period of trading. However, if its markets have growth potential, the company probably has the resources to benefit from it.

In contrast, ITV, and especially the supermarket chain Morrisons, have fairly low gearing levels. This could be a weakness if the economy was expanding rapidly. Their management teams could be judged as timid as the companies are not in a position to benefit from rapid growth. An investment in a firm with a low gearing could be regarded as safe, but dull.

Altering the ratio

The gearing ratio can be altered in several ways, depending on whether the organisation wishes to raise or lower its gearing figure.

Raising gearing	Reducing gearing
Buy back ordinary shares	Issue more ordinary shares
Issue more preference shares	Buy back debentures (redeeming)
Issue more debentures	Retain more profits
Obtain more loans	Repay loans

Manchester United reliant on success to pay debt interest

Manchester United is the most successful UK football club in financial terms, having announced a record sales revenue for 2006/07 of £245 million, a 27% increase on the previous financial year. At the same time the club's holding company announced that its profits before tax had risen 93% to £59.6 million. The company's strong financial performance was, in part, due to the football club winning the Premier League title in the 2006/07 season.

However, the holding company that owns Manchester United has borrowed heavily – it had to raise £790 million in 2005 when it bought the club. In May 2007 the company's annual interest payment was £62 million, at which time a club spokesman said that the debts continued 'to be comfortably serviced by the business'. Analysts say that banks will be supportive to the company so long as its revenue is sufficient to service the debts. However, if the club's fortunes on the pitch were to decline, serving the huge debts could become more difficult.

57.8 Shareholder ratios

Investing in shares provides two potential sources of financial return. The share price might rise, providing a capital gain. In addition, firms pay annual dividends to shareholders. The size of the dividends depends upon the level of profits made in the year. Shareholder ratios provide a way of judging whether the shares are expensive or inexpensive, and whether the dividends are high enough. They do, however, put some pressure on companies to achieve short-term profits and to pay out high dividends. This may damage the interests of the company's stakeholders in the long term.

Earnings per share (EPS)

This ratio measures the company's **earnings** (profit after tax) divided by the number of ordinary shares it has issued. This can be used to measure a company's profit performance over time. It is shown on the income statements of public limited companies. The EPS also shows the potential for paying out a dividend to shareholders. It is given by the formula:

$$\text{earnings per share} = \frac{\text{profit after tax}}{\text{number of ordinary shares}}$$

usually expressed in pence.

Interpretation

Earnings per share is relatively meaningless if analysed on its own, although the higher the result the better for shareholders. Meaning can only be established by comparisons with previous years' results. A rising EPS is likely to please shareholders.

Altering the ratio

This ratio can only really be improved by increasing the level of profits made. This may cause the pressure for short-term profits mentioned earlier.

Dividend per share (DPS)

This ratio is calculated by dividing the total dividend to be paid to the shareholders by the number of shares issued. Thus:

$$\text{dividend per share} = \frac{\text{total dividends}}{\text{shares issued}}$$

The result of this ratio is normally expressed in pence.

Interpretation

The result of this ratio does not provide much insight into the company's performance as it means little without comparison to the current share price for the company concerned. The ratio below (dividend yield) completes this calculation.

Altering the ratio

This can be done in two ways. The directors can announce that a larger proportion of the company's profits will be distributed to shareholders as dividends or the number of shares that are issued by the company can be reduced through a buy-back scheme.

Dividend yield

This ratio directly relates the amount of dividend actually received to the market value of the share. It shows the shareholders' annual dividends as a percentage of the sum invested. It is given by the formula:

$$\text{dividend yield} = \frac{\text{ordinary share dividend}}{\text{market price}} \text{ (pence)} \times 100$$

Interpretation

Again, the higher the result the better. However, it would need to be compared against previous years and the results of competitors.

Altering the ratio

As this ratio is based partly on the market price of ordinary shares, anything that affects this value will impact on the ratio. A higher result can be obtained by either making greater profits or making a greater proportion of profit available for distribution as dividend.

Issues For Analysis

- There are many more areas of ratio analysis than those outlined within this unit. Specialist ratios exist for all types of organisation, especially those in the public or voluntary sector where profits and capital are not so readily determined.

- Another aspect that needs discussion is that the analysis and interpretation of financial statements is really only the first step in a lengthy process. The data gathered from this exercise must be presented to and understood by those who will then go on to make decisions based upon it. Also consider the validity of making long-term decisions based upon findings from an income statement and balance sheet that may be several months out of date. As well as conducting ratio analysis, other information contained within the annual reports should also be used, such as the chairman's report.

- As a final point for further investigation, the accuracy of ratio analysis itself is often called into question. Factors such as the effect of inflation on accounts from one year to the next, differences in accounting policies and the effect of economic change may have a significant effect on the ratios.

57.9 Ratio analysis
an evaluation

Ratio analysis is a powerful tool in the interpretation of financial accounts. It can allow for **inter-firm comparisons**, appraisal of financial performance and the identification of trends. It can therefore be of great help in financial planning and decision making.

However, because of its usefulness and the range of possible applications, there is a tendency to attach too much importance to the results gained from this analysis. Other types of analysis exist, and there are sometimes more important issues at stake than just financial performance.

Many financial analysts are now using the concept of 'added value' to see if shareholder value has been increased. Consideration must also be given to the fact that often stakeholders are not fluent in financial and business terminology, and that the use of ratio analysis may be a case of 'blinding them with science'. Also, a changing society has seen a change in focus away from pure financial performance towards consideration of social and ethical factors. Although ratio analysis is useful, it is limited in the area it investigates.

Key terms

Aged debtors analysis: listing debtors in age order, to identify the slowest payers.

Earnings: for a company, earnings means profit after tax.

Inter-firm comparisons: comparisons of financial performance between firms; to be valuable, these comparisons should be with a firm of similar size within the same market.

Liquidity: the ability of a firm to meet its short-term debts; liquidity can also be understood as being the availability of cash or assets that can easily be converted into cash.

Exercises

A. Revision questions

(40 marks; 40 minutes)

1 List four groups of people who may be interested in the results of ratio analysis. (4)

2 State the key stages in conducting an analysis of company accounts using ratios. (7)

3 Briefly explain the difference between financial efficiency ratios and profitability ratios. (4)

4 Explain why the return on capital employed (ROCE) is regarded as one of the most important ratios. (3)

5 Why might the managers of a company be pleased if its stock (inventory) turnover ratio were falling? (4)

6 What might the figure for debtor days tell you about the way in which a business controls its finances? (4)

7 Outline the difference between the current ratio and the acid test ratio. (2)

8 Why might a small investor be particularly interested in the dividend yield ratio? (4)

9 Outline two problems a company might experience if its gearing ratio rose significantly. (4)

10 Explain one reason why investors might treat the results of ratio analysis with caution. (4)

B. Revision exercises

B1 Practice exercises

(75 marks; 90 minutes)

1 J Orr Ltd makes garden gnomes. When analysing J Orr's annual accounts, state and explain which three ratios you think would be of most use to:
(a) a firm wondering whether to supply J Orr with materials on credit (6)
(b) the trade union representative of J Orr's workforce (6)
(c) a pensioner, wondering whether J Orr will be a good investment (6)
(d) the management of J Orr's main rival, Gnometastic Ltd (6)

(e) J Orr's main customer, Blooms of Broadway garden centre. (6)

2 A garden furniture producer wants to buy a garden centre. It has identified two possible businesses and conducted some ratio analysis to help it decide which one to focus on. Look at the ratios for each business in the table below, and decide which one you would recommend and why. (10)

	Blooms of Broadway	Cotswold Carnations
Gross profit margin	60%	45%
Return on capital	15.2%	14.6%
Stock turnover	18 times	24 times
Gearing	52%	35%
Sales growth (last 3 years)	13.5% per year	14.8% per year

3 **Balance sheet for GrowMax Co as at 31 December**

	£000
Fixed assets	860
Stock	85
Debtors	180
Cash	15
Current liabilities	200
Loans	360
Share capital	160
Reserves	420

(a) Calculate the firm's net current assets and capital employed. (4)
(b) Last year's revenue was £1,460,000 and operating margin was 10%. Comment on the firm's profitability. (10)
(c) GrowMax's main rival offers its customers 30 days' credit.
  (i) How does this compare with GrowMax? (4)
  (ii) Outline two further questions the GrowMax management should want answered before deciding whether their customer credit policy should be revised. (8)

(d) Outline three difficulties with drawing firm conclusions from comparisons between the ratios of two rival companies. (9)

B2 Data response

Since the beginning of the year, Phones4Kids has enjoyed rapid growth as a result of booming exports to America. Financing the increased production has required an extra £80,000 of working capital, and now the production manager has put in an urgent request for £240,000 of new capital investment.

The firm's managing director doubts that he can find the extra capital without giving up control of the business (he currently holds 54% of the shares). The finance director is more optimistic. He suggests that: 'Our balance sheet is in pretty good shape and the mobile phone business is booming. I'm confident we can get and afford a loan.' So it came as a huge blow to hear that Barclays had turned the company down. It wondered what it had done wrong …

Phones4Kids balance sheet as at 31 December

	£000	£000
Fixed assets[1]	420	
Inventories	250	
Debtors[2]	140	
Cash	130	520
Current liabilities		380
Non-current liabilities		200
Net assets	360	
Share capital	50	
Reserves	310	
Total equity		360

[1]Depreciated straight line over 10 years
[2]Including a £15,000 debtors item 12 months overdue

Questions

(35 marks; 45 minutes)

1 Analyse why the bank manager might have turned the request down? (10)

2 Recommend how the expansion might be financed, showing the effect of your plan upon key indicators of the firm's financial health. (10)

3 Given your answers to 1 and 2, discuss whether the firm should proceed with its expansion plan. (15)

B3 Data response

The Whitbread Group plc operates a range of brands in the hospitality industry. The company has interests in hotels, restaurants and health and fitness clubs, including Premier Inn, Brewers Fayre, Beefeater and Costa Coffee. Whitbread is listed on the London Stock Exchange and is a part of the FTSE 100 Index. The company was founded as a brewery in 1742 but no longer has any interests in brewing.

The company sold two major businesses during the two-year period reviewed below (Marriott Hotels and Pizza Hut UK), which explains in part the profits from 'discontinued operations'.

Whitbread plc: Extract from 2007 Annual Report & Accounts

Summary Consolidated (Group) Income Statement

	2007 £m	2006 £m
Revenue	1,410.8	1,491.9
Gross profit	**1,211.8**	**1,217.2**
Expenses	(995.1)	(1,027.9)
Operating profit	216.7	189.3
Extraordinary items	196.6	(8.7)
Profit before financing and tax	**413.3**	**180.6**
Net finance (income-expense)	(38.1)	(88.3)
Profit before tax	**375.2**	**92.3**
Taxation	(145.8)	(44.2)
Profit from discontinued operations	52.1	216.3
Profit for the year	**281.5**	**264.4**

Balance sheet, 1 March 2007

	2007 £m	2006 £m
Non-current assets	2,626.0	2,876.0
Inventories (stocks)	12.8	17.5
Trade & other receivables	67.5	119.0
Cash & cash equivalents	70.5	49.6
Other current assets	74.5	333.8
Current liabilities	379.6	423.8
Non-current liabilities	1,412.6	1,425.6
Net assets	**1,059.1**	**1,546.5**
Share capital	190.3	190.0
Reserves	868.8	1,356.5
Total equity	**1059.1**	**1,546.5**

Source: adapted from Whitbread plc Annual Review and Summary Report 2006/07

Questions

(50 marks; 60 minutes)

1 State Whitbread plc's working capital in 2006 and 2007. (4)

2 Calculate Whitbread plc's:
   (a) 2007 cost of sales (2)
   (b) 2006 and 2007 gearing. (4)

3a Assess the company's profitability in 2007 compared with 2006. (10)

3b What further information would be needed in order to make a full assessment of the effectiveness of the company's management at generating profit in 1997? (4)

4a What are Whitbread plc's current ratios for 2006 and 2007? (4)

4b Briefly analyse the possible implications of these figures for the managers of the business. (6)

5 A major insurance company is considering buying a large number of shares in Whitbread plc as part of its investment portfolio. Assess the strengths and weaknesses for outsiders of using this company's accounts to decide on such a major decision. (16)

C. Essay questions

(40 marks each)

1 'Ratios are of little to no use to a person intending to make a small investment.' Comment on the accuracy of this statement.

2 'The ability to assess the long- and short-term financial stability of an organisation is vital to every stakeholder.' To what extent do you agree with this statement?

3 With the economy entering a recession, an investor wants to reassess her share portfolio. Examine which ratios she should focus upon, given the economic circumstances.

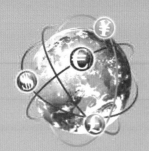
LIMITATIONS OF ACCOUNTS

'True and fair view' is the phrase used by auditors when checking a firm's accounts, to confirm that they are accurate within the terms of the accounting practices used to draw them up.

58.1 Introduction: giving a true and fair view?

The final accounts of a business are usually the first point of reference for anyone interested in analysing its value or performance over a period of time. For instance, the revenue and expenses generated over a period of time are reported in a firm's profit and loss account. The balance sheet gives us information needed to calculate its book value (i.e. the difference between its total assets and any liabilities it may have). Together these statements allow ratio analysis to be carried out. However, all this information gives an incomplete and possibly misleading view of what a business may actually be worth.

58.2 What accounts leave out

- *Focus on quantitative data:* money acts as the language of accounting, allowing business transactions to be measured, compared and added together. This means that accounts focus on items that can be given a financial value. Yet a successful business depends on a lot more than the price paid for property and equipment, or the size of its outstanding debt. For example, a firm's culture and its attitude to risk-taking will be at the heart of its performance. Similarly, a highly skilled, loyal and motivated workforce, a commitment to behaving in an ethical and environmentally friendly manner or a reputation for excellent customer service can increase a firm's ability to compete against rivals. These aspects of a business are likely to make it worth more, both to existing owners and potential buyers. However, such features are difficult to express in numerical terms and are, therefore, usually ignored by the main accounting statements

- *Using profit as a performance indicator:* profit is generally regarded as one of the most important indicators of performance. Yet the long-term success of a business may depend on a firm's willingness to sacrifice profits, in the short term at least. It may be useful, therefore, to also consider other indicators, such as growth in revenue and market share or investment in research and development and new product success. For example, the massive Reckitt Benckiser plc (Cillit Bang, Air Wick fresheners, etc. – see the A-grade application) has a target that at least 35% of its sales should come from products launched in the past three years.

Figure 58.1 Air Wick Freshmatic, produced by Dutch firm Reckitt Benckiser

The state of the market: the nature of accounts means that they are historical (i.e. they reflect what has happened in the past, rather than commenting on the present or looking ahead to the future). No business can assume that the environment in which it operates will remain the same. The conditions that contributed to past performance, however recent, are bound to change at some point. For example, the number of competitors in a market may increase, or a healthy economy may suddenly descend into recession. Although most large companies produce a chairman's statement, which may speculate on future prospects, this document is not, strictly speaking, part of the accounts and may be deliberately written to create an overly favourable impression.

A-grade application
Reckitt Benckiser

Dutch firm Reckitt Benckiser is the world's largest manufacturer of cleaning products and is responsible for a number of famous brands, including Air Wick, Cillit Bang and Vanish. The company's chief executive, Bart Becht, claims that its success in maintaining sales growth and profit margins in recent years comes from its commitment to innovation. According to Becht, over £2 billion of the company's total revenue of £5.3 billion generated in 2007 came from products launched in the previous three years.

58.3 Problems interpreting accounts

Although the purpose of a firm's accounts is to assign a value to the items contained within them, there are a number of reasons why such values should be treated with caution.

Land and buildings: the accounting convention of valuing assets at historic (or original) cost is likely to mean that any figures for land or property owned by a business are unlikely to reflect their current market value. Such fixed assets tend to appreciate in value over time, meaning they are effectively undervalued. This could mean that the business might struggle to raise loan finance, due to an apparent lack of collateral. Moreover, it could make it vulnerable to a hostile takeover from other firms keen to benefit from disposing of undervalued assets in order to generate funds.

Intangible assets: these include intellectual property such as patents, copyright and brand names. Such assets may well have a role in generating sales and profits for a business, especially for service-based firms that trade on image and reputation. However, estimating the monetary value of **intangible assets** can be very difficult. For example, the importance of even a well-known brand to a firm's success can quickly diminish – perhaps as a result of negative publicity or a change in fashion. **Goodwill** is a concept that may arise when one business is bought by another. It refers to the value placed on the business by the buyer, over and above its book value, in recognition of its good reputation and established customer base. This may mean the business is worth more as a **going concern** than the value of its parts, but the buyer may end up overstating its value.

Debtors: firms are usually content to sell goods on credit to customers in order to generate sales – any outstanding payments are recorded as a current asset on the balance sheet. However, this figure tells us very little about the nature of the debtors themselves. Does the overall debtors figure consist of regular customers who can be relied upon to pay on time, or long overdue amounts that are unlikely to ever be received? A high proportion of debtors made up of **bad debts** will result in an overvaluation of a firm's current assets on the balance sheet, increasing the chances of liquidity problems.

Stock: the value of stock at the end of a trading period affects both the value of the business due to its inclusion on the balance sheet (under current assets) and the value of profit (due to its effect on cost of goods sold in the trading account). But, given that stock is the least liquid of a firm's current assets, how reliable is the value attached to it? The value of stock can change rapidly, especially in industries subject to frequent changes in customer tastes. The traditional accounting practice is to value stock at cost or **net realisable value**, whichever is the lower. This means that the value of stock that will not sell is potentially zero!

Profit quality: the ability to generate profit is generally accepted as a key indicator of success. However, it is also worth checking the source of this profit in order to assess the likelihood of such profits continuing into the future. Selling off a piece of machinery at a price above its book value will generate a surplus, but this can only happen once and is, therefore, described as being of low **profit quality**. It is important that a firm's accounts separate 'one-off' low-quality profit from the high-quality profit that results from its normal trading activities.

A-grade application

Valuing global brands

Brand consultancy Interbrand produces a list of the top 100 global brands every year. The purpose of the list is to underline the importance of brands as business assets. Each brand in the list is given a dollar value that, according to Interbrand, represents the net present value (NPV) of its future earnings. In 2007, the top ten global brands were as follows.

Brand	Brand value ($m)
1. Coca-Cola	65,324
2. Microsoft	58,709
3. IBM	57,091
4. GE	51,569
5. Nokia	33,696
6. Toyota	32,070
7. Intel	30,954
8. McDonald's	29,398
9. Disney	29,210
10. Mercedes	23,568

The British brand that made it highest up the list for 2007 was HSBC, ranked at number 23. The only other British brands to make the list were Reuters (76), BP (84), Smirnoff (91), Shell (93) and Burberry (95).

Source: Brand Republic

58.4 Manipulating the published accounts

There are a number of reasons why a business may decide to manipulate its accounts in order to flatter its financial position at a particular point in time. Such practices, known as **window dressing** or creative accounting, do not necessarily mean that fraud has been committed, but may nevertheless result in the users of accounts being misled. There are a number of reasons why a firm might window dress its accounts – creating the impression that a business is financially stronger than it actually is can help to secure loans or support the sale of new shares. Common methods of window dressing include the following.

- *Sale and leaseback of fixed assets*: this allows a business to continue to use assets but disguise a poor or deteriorating liquidity position by generating a sudden injection of cash

- *Bringing forward sales*: a sale is recognised (and included in profit calculations) when an order is made, rather than when payment is received. Encouraging customers to place orders earlier than usual will mean that they are included at the end of one financial period rather than at the start of the next, giving an apparent boost to revenue and profit.

- *A change in approach to depreciation*: for example, increasing the expected life of a fixed asset will reduce the annual depreciation charge, increasing the level of reported profit as well as increasing the asset value on the balance sheet. Presenting a more favourable set of accounts may attract more investment or help fight off a hostile takeover bid.

- *Writing off bad debts*: the decision to treat a customer's unpaid bill as a bad debt will mean that the figure has to be charged to the profit and loss account as an expense. This will reduce the firm's net profit figure, reducing the level of corporation tax paid.

The Companies Act 1985 places a legal obligation on companies to provide accounts that are audited and give a true and fair view of their financial position. In addition, the Accounting Standards Board has the responsibility of providing a regulatory framework in order to create greater uniformity in the way company accounts are drawn up. Despite this, the pressure on businesses to not only perform well but to be seen to do so is likely to mean that window dressing practices will persist.

Issues For Analysis

Opportunities for analysis are likely to focus on the following areas:

- the problems of relying on financial data to analyse a firm's financial position and performance

- the difficulties of trying to get an accurate measure of the value of a business

- the consequences of failing to provide an accurate value of a business

- the reasons why a firm might attempt to window dress its financial position.

Limitations of accounts
an evaluation

Accounting information plays a key role in assessing the value and performance of a business. However, using such information alone, and failing to consider other relevant factors, will give an incomplete picture of a firm's current position and future potential. The quality of the workforce, investment in new technology and the state of the market in which it operates may be difficult to quantify but may be more accurate indicators of a firm's long-term success than an impressive set of final accounts.

Key terms

Bad debts: when a firm decides that amounts outstanding as a result of credit sales are unlikely to be recovered, perhaps because the customer concerned has gone into liquidation.

Going concern: the accounting assumption that, in the absence of any evidence to the contrary, a business will continue to operate for the foreseeable future.

Goodwill: arises when a business is sold and the buyer pays more than its book value in recognition of the good reputation and customer base that is being obtained. This amount is shown as an intangible asset on the firm's balance sheet.

Intangible assets: these are assets that have no physical existence, such as plant and machinery, but contribute to sales and profits. Examples include patents, copyright, brand names and goodwill.

Net realisable value: this is the value given to an asset (usually stock) on the balance sheet if it is expected to be sold for less than its historic cost.

Profit quality: this assesses the likelihood of the source of the profit made by a business continuing in the future. High-quality profit is usually that which is generated by a firm's usual trading activities, whereas low-quality profit comes from a one-off source.

Window dressing: the practice of presenting a firm's accounts in a way that flatters its financial position (e.g. selling and leasing back assets in order to generate cash and disguise a poor liquidity position).

Exercises

A. Revision questions

(35 marks; 35 minutes)

1 What is meant by the phrase 'a true and fair view' in the context of accounting? (3)

2 Identify three aspects of a business that may increase its value but are unlikely to be included in its accounts. (3)

3 Describe two problems that a firm might experience from understating the value of land or property that it might own. (6)

4 Analyse one reason for and one reason against attempting to include a value for a firm's intangible assets on its balance sheet. (6)

5 Explain the difference between a debtor and a bad debt. (4)

6 What is meant by the term 'window dressing'? (3)

7 Describe two reasons why a firm might window dress its accounts. (4)

8 Outline three ways in which a business might attempt to window dress its accounts. (6)

B. Revision exercises

B1 Data response

Valuing global brands

Diageo is the world's leading producer of alcoholic drinks. Its portfolio includes a number of market-leading brands, including Guinness, Baileys, Johnnie Walker whisky and Tanqueray gin. The company is also responsible for Smirnoff vodka, was ranked at number 91 in the 2007 Interbrand top 100 brands list. Diageo's global sales for the half-year to 31 December 2007 were £5.667 billion, an increase of nearly 6% on the previous year. The company's operating profits for the same period amounted to £1.414 billion, up from £4.022 billion in 2006.

Questions

(30 marks; 30 minutes)

1 Outline two influences on the value of a brand. (10)

2 Calculate the percentage change in Diageo's half-year operating profits between 2006 and 2007. (4)

3 Analyse the main arguments for and against Diageo including its brand names in the company's balance sheet. (16)

B2 Case study

$100 billion of window dressing

During the last quarter of their 2006/07 financial year, America's largest companies boosted their working capital by $100 billion. This was in time for the annual scrutiny of their accounts by the media, Wall Street analysts and shareholders. During the following quarter (the first quarter of the 2007/08 year), the same companies had a working capital decrease of $122 billion. Here, for the first time, was evidence of the scale of window-dressing by public companies.

The findings by the US financial consultancy REL were reported on by the *Financial Times* on 1 November 2007. The paper went on to explain that the main ways to achieve the window-dressing were:

● discounting products (to turn stocks into cash)

● halting purchases of supplies

● accelerating the collection of bills due (see the effect in Figure 58.2 overleaf)

● delaying necessary investments until the new financial year

● overproducing – running at full capacity to produce the appearance of lower unit costs

● delaying payments to suppliers.

From this list it can be concluded that the main two ratios that would be affected by this window dressing would be the acid test and the return on capital ratios.

58.6 Workbook

REL's report went on to say that 'It is clear that year-end gamesmanship is akin to binge dieting, where an unreal and unsustainable illusion of beauty is created for the purpose of meeting the expectations of others.' Further comment came from a former chairman of a key Wall Street committee, who said that 'Efforts to bolster year-end earnings are part of a syndrome of short-termism . . . The net result is that too many companies postpone necessary investments and capital expenditure.'

The newspaper also pointed out that 'executives have an added incentive because their compensation [pay] is often linked to the company's yearly performance.'

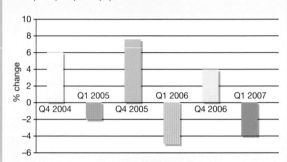

Figure 58.2 *Well-dressed sales figures (% change)*
Source: REL

Questions

(35 marks; 40 minutes)

1a Explain the meaning of the term 'window dressing'. (3)

1b Examine one motive managers may have to window dress their accounts. (5)

1c Explain the possible impact of window-dressing on one of the company stakeholders mentioned in the text. (6)

2 Examine whether the bar chart in Figure 58.2 supports the argument put forward in the text. (6)

3 To what extent should short-termism be regarded as the enemy of successful business strategy? (15)

FINANCIAL STRATEGIES AND ACCOUNTS

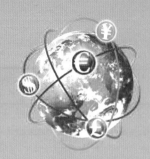

DEFINITION

Financial strategy aims to structure and manage an organisation's finances effectively, in order to support the achievement of its medium- and long-term objectives.

59.1 Introduction

In 2007–08, banks throughout the world struggled to cope with wave after wave of 'restatements' of their financial position. Many that had been claiming to be highly profitable (and paying top staff huge bonuses) were having to admit huge 'write-offs'. In other words, their day-to-day accounting had failed to pick up huge potential losses, so these losses were suddenly being acknowledged. HSBC, for example, wrote off $11.7 billion of losses in the US mortgage market (the so-called 'sub-prime loans').

Maintaining or improving the financial health of an organisation is vital if it is to continue to survive and develop in the long term. This requires not only profitable trading and careful cost controls, but also a sound financial structure. Financial health can be measured by a firm's gearing. An apparently profitable firm could be particularly vulnerable to changing economic conditions if the bulk of its capital comes from debt finance. In addition, the firm will need to maintain a healthy liquidity position to ensure that sufficient cash is available when it is needed.

Once established, some businesses may choose to continue to operate on a relatively small scale, perhaps in order to maintain an entrepreneurial culture. Most firms, however, see growth as a major objective. Operating on a larger scale offers a number of potential benefits to businesses, including the opportunity to benefit from economies of scale, and to spread risk by increasing product range or selling in new markets. Such growth will also need to be managed carefully in order to minimise risks and maximise the chances of success.

59.2 Raising finance

Unit 16 looked at the **external sources of finance** available to businesses at start-up. These – such as overdrafts, loans and venture capital – are also potential sources of finance for established businesses. There are also some additional ways for an established business to secure external finance. For example, suppliers may be prepared to offer generous trade credit arrangements in order to win the custom of growing firms with a proven track record of paying on time. Rapidly growing firms may also choose to ease cash-flow problems by **factoring** invoices. This involves selling them to a company that will pay a percentage of the invoice value in advance and then recover the outstanding amount, in exchange for a fee. Hire purchase and leasing offer firms a means of obtaining the use of assets without having to pay out large sums of money straight away. For limited companies, long-term finance can be obtained from equity or share capital, possibly via a **rights issue**, giving existing shareholders the opportunity to buy more shares at a price below the current market price, in order to raise finance relatively cheaply. Equity finance has the advantage of not having to be repaid. Unlike loan repayments, there are no interest charges and dividends to shareholders do not have to be paid if the company fails to make a profit.

Once a business has been operating for some time, it should also be able to rely on **internal sources of finance** (i.e. those generated from within the business itself). These will include those described below.

● *Retained profit*: trading profitably will create a source of funds that can be reinvested back into the business in order to buy new stock, replace worn out fixed assets or expand operations. This **retained profit** is an important source of long-term finance as it does not need to be paid back. The level of finance available from this source depends on the performance of the business and the rate of dividends expected by the firm's owners. Around 60% of all long-term capital comes from this source (which is also sometimes known as ploughed-back profits).

● *Sale of assets*: established firms own fixed assets, such as premises and machinery, which have been purchased to be used as part of its operations. Ideally, a firm can use redundant assets to do this (i.e. those that are no longer required as part of the production process). It may be possible to raise finance using assets that are still required, via **sale and leaseback**, by paying rent or a fee to the new owner.

● *Managing working capital more effectively*: established firms may grow complacent when it comes to managing **working capital**. Stocks may begin to build up and outstanding customer invoices may go unnoticed. Squeezing working capital (i.e. managing it more effectively) can create more finance for a firm's day-to-day activities, easing pressure on cashflow. This could involve running down stocks or chasing up debtors. Relationships developed with suppliers over time may also mean that longer credit periods can be negotiated.

A-grade application
Tesco goes Stateside

In February 2006, UK supermarket giant Tesco announced its intention to enter the US grocery market. The company's strategy focused on establishing a number of relatively small convenience stores, based on its highly successful Express format, beginning on the US West Coast from 2007. Initial planned capital expenditure was £250 million per year for the next five years. The chief executive was confident that this huge sum could be financed from Tesco's own cash resources.
Source: www.tesco.com

59.3 Finance: is it adequate?

Adequate finance means having access to sufficient levels of funding to meet the firm's needs, as and when they occur. Established firms will need to pay workers, suppliers and other expenses on time, regardless of whether enough cash has been generated from sales to cover such expenses. They will also need to replace equipment and machinery when it wears out or becomes obsolete. Few businesses are faced with totally predictable demand. Therefore, adequate resources (including finance) should be available to respond successfully to a unexpected upsurge in orders, as well as allowing a firm to cope with an unexpected fall in sales.

Ensuring access to adequate funding is equally important for those firms looking to expand. Not only will such firms require capital for the purchase of new assets, but also to cover additional working capital requirements in the form of increased materials, wages and fuel. **Overtrading** refers to the situation where a business expands at a rate that cannot be sustained by its capital base. A sudden surge in orders may tempt firms to buy additional stocks on credit. However, a significant gap between having to pay for these stocks and receiving payment from customers could lead to liquidity problems. Inadequate funding is one of the most common reasons why apparently successful businesses with rapidly growing sales end up failing.

59.4 Finance: is it appropriate?

Appropriate finance means ensuring that the type of finance matches its intended use. An overdraft may provide a much-needed bridge between having to pay suppliers once month and being paid by customers the next. Yet it would be an expensive method of borrowing to finance asset purchase, unless it could be repaid quickly. There are a number of factors that will determine the most appropriate source(s) of finance for established businesses to use in any given situation. These include the following.

● *The type of business*: expanding businesses may decide to become limited companies in order to raise finance more easily and offer owners the protection of limited liability. However, private limited companies may still struggle to find sufficient shareholders as their shares are not openly available to the general public. Therefore the business may seek a public flotation on the stock market – opening up the possibility of ownership being spread widely among the public, as with a business such as Marks & Spencer plc, which has 250,000 different shareholders.

● *The level of success enjoyed by the business*: it is often said that 'success breeds success', and this is usually the case with finance. Highly profitable firms are able to generate internal finance but are also likely to attract outside investors and creditors. Firms with low or falling profits may struggle to raise the finance needed to improve performance because they are seen as too risky. A well-worn business phrase is that 'banks don't deal with people who need them'.

- *The use of funds:* a business looking to raise finance for working capital would normally use short-term finance (i.e. repaid within one year). On the other hand, capital expenditure on an expensive piece of machinery used within the business for a number of years is likely to require long-term finance (i.e. that required for much longer periods, usually over five years).

- *The attitude of the owners/shareholders of the business:* there are a number of reasons why the owners of a business may have an influence on the choice of finance. Some may prefer not to use loan finance, because of the risk of not being able to meet repayments on time. Others may avoid bringing in new shareholders or involving venture capitalists, in order to prevent their control of the business from being diluted (watered down). There may also be a conflict of interest between shareholders, who view profit as a source of dividend income, and managers, who would prefer to pay lower dividends in order to retain profits to finance expansion.

- *The state of the economy:* firms may be reluctant to borrow when economic conditions are deteriorating and sales are predicted to fall. A more buoyant economy may increase business confidence and encourage firms to take greater risks.

59.5 Allocating capital expenditure

Capital expenditure refers to money spent by a firm in order to support its long-term operations. The purchase of fixed assets, such as premises and machinery, is clearly an example of capital expenditure, as they are bought with the intention of using them over a number of years. Funds used to take over other businesses can also be regarded as capital expenditure, even if the assets acquired are subsequently sold off. It could be argued that firms should also regard spending on research and development as an item of capital expenditure, given that it is likely to provide benefits over a lengthy period of time.

The first issue to consider with capital expenditure is the amount needed to maintain a firm's operations in a healthy, efficient state. For example, Network Rail allocates about £2.5 billion a year to maintaining Britain's railway system. This includes replacing ageing trains with new ones, updating tired stations, and so forth. This expenditure can be regarded as essential. Without it, the business will start to go downhill. To switch examples, in 2007 the average age of British Airways' aircraft was ten years; contrast that with Singapore Airlines, which has an objective of having a fleet with an average age of three years.

Once enough capital is allocated to maintaining a healthy business, the key financial decision is how much to allocate to growth. During the 1990s, McDonald's poured $billions into opening up more stores worldwide. Only in 2004/05, when profits started to sag, did the business switch from quantity to quality. Starbucks had a similar experience, though in its case the decision to slow down the growth rate came only in 2007/08.

Any business, regardless of size, will have more potential uses of funds than the amount of finance available, so the allocation of capital expenditure will depend on corporate objectives and market conditions.

59.6 Implementing profit centres in a business

Profit centres are distinct sections within a business that can be regarded as self-contained, and therefore measured for their own profitability. In effect, a profit centre becomes a firm within a firm, which can help

Table 59.1 Short-term vs long-term finance: some examples

	Short term	Long term
Internal	Squeezing working capital	Sale (and leaseback) of assets Retained profit
External	Trade credit Debt factoring Overdrafts	Bank loans Share (rights) issue Venture capital

Table 59.2 *Advantages and disadvantages of profit centres*

Advantages of profit centres	Disadvantages of profit centres
• The success – or otherwise – of individual areas of the business can be identified more easily	• Not all of the costs or revenues of a business can easily be associated with specific areas of operation
• The delegation of control over local operations may increase motivation	• Areas of the business may end up competing against each other, damaging overall performance
• Decision making will be localised, making it quicker and better suited to local conditions	• The good or bad performance of one profit centre may be the result of external changes beyond its control (cutting the link between the performance of the group members and the results of the group activities)
• When they work well, they are a perfect antidote to big-business bureaucracy that results in diseconomies of scale	

motivate the relatively small number of staff within the section. It is hard to feel important as one person among 250,000 other Tesco staff; but one person among 16 at an individual store can see the impact of their efforts.

The basis for establishing profit centres is very much dependent on the individual circumstances of the firm in question and may be based on:

- a person – individual employees within a business may be responsible for generating revenues and incurring costs
- a product – a multi-product business may be able to distinguish the separate revenues earned and costs incurred by individual product lines
- a department – areas within a business that perform certain functions may generate both costs and revenues
- a location – a business, such as a bank or retailer that is spread geographically, may choose to use each branch or division as a profit centre.

Establishing profit centres can provide valuable information to a business to help it enhance its financial performance, perhaps enabling it to identify unprofitable areas that may need to be closed down. The responsibility delegated to managers of individual profit centres may also inject a degree of motivation. However, there are a number of potential problems in attempting to implement profit centres. For example, it may prove difficult to choose an accurate method of allocating a firm's overheads to each profit centre. It may also lead to a situation where individual profit

centres compete against each other, to the detriment of the business as a whole.

59.7 Cost minimisation

One way that firms can achieve a competitive advantage over their rivals is by pursuing a strategy of cost minimisation. Firms operating in fiercely competitive markets may have little control over the prices they charge but can still make acceptable profits by pushing down unit costs as low as possible. In theory, cost minimisation is straightforward enough. For example, firms may be tempted to switch to the cheapest supplier or cut out staff training in order to offer the lowest prices possible. However, this is likely to lead to a loss of competitiveness in the longer term, as poor-quality and poorly trained employees result in customer dissatisfaction.

The key to implementing this strategy successfully is to charge prices that are close to but below the market average, to avoid arousing customer suspicions, and reduce average costs without compromising operations. Lower unit costs can be generated by producing standardised products in large volumes, in order to benefit from economies of scale, and finding ways of keeping overheads as low as possible. Examples of businesses that have been particularly successful at pursuing cost-minimisation strategies include Aldi, Ryanair, EasyJet and Primark. Focusing on price alone can lead to problems, however, if an even lower-cost competitor enters the market.

A-grade application

Ryanair: a model of cost minimisation

The establishment of Ryanair as Europe's leading low-fares scheduled passenger airline has been the result of a strategy of cost minimisation adopted in the early 1990s, following the appointment of chief executive Michael O'Leary. By targeting price-conscious leisure and business passengers, the airline has experienced phenomenal growth – from under a quarter of a million passengers in 1990 to over 40 million in 2007. The company's success has largely been the result of its ability to contain costs and achieve a number of operational efficiencies, without compromising customer service. These have included the following.

- *Frequent short-haul flights:* eliminating the need to provide passengers with 'frills' services, such as complimentary meals and drinks, which add to variable costs.
- *Using the internet for flight reservations:* the airline's system accounted for 97% of flight bookings in 2007, helping to keep labour costs down.
- *Favouring secondary routes:* e.g. flying to Girona rather than Barcelona in Spain. These less congested destinations mean faster turnaround times, fewer terminal delays and lower handling costs.
- *Minimising aircraft costs:* initially, this was achieved by the purchase of second-hand aeroplanes of a single type; however, in response to a recent shortage of such aircraft, the company has resorted to purchasing from a single supplier in order to limit training and maintenance costs, as well as the purchase and storage of spare parts.
- *Personnel productivity:* Ryanair controls its labour costs by paying highly competitive salaries to pilots and cabin crew but demanding much higher productivity levels than its competitors.

Source: www.ryanair.com

Figure 59.1 Ryanair is Europe's leading low-fares carrier

Issues For Analysis

Opportunities for analysis are likely to focus on the following areas.

- The benefits and drawbacks of using different forms of finance in different circumstances (e.g. seeing that there are costs and risks involved in using an overdraft to finance long-term commitments).

- The need to think about financial strategy in relation to the overall strategy; for example, if the business has a bold, quite risky, marketing strategy (based, perhaps, on new product launches into short product life cycle markets) it is wise to have a cautious financial strategy (e.g. low gearing and high liquidity); this is the approach taken by firms such as Nintendo and L'Oréal.

- The advantages and disadvantages of adopting cost minimisation as a financial strategy and seeing its essentially close links with marketing, operational and personnel strategies. This is shown effectively in the A-grade application on Ryanair.

59.8 Financial strategies and accounts
an evaluation

Choosing an appropriate financial strategy is crucial to an organisation's continuing success, regardless of its size or its objectives. A business may need to raise finance for a variety of reasons – this finance will need to be both adequate and appropriate to its needs in order to be effective. Financial strategy is also very much concerned with how funds are used to support the development of the business. This involves making choices as to how expenditure is to be allocated between competing capital projects and controlling ongoing costs in order to ensure the firm's long-term financial health.

The most important judgements, though, are about getting the right balance between risk and safety. The 2007 collapse of Northern Rock was due to a faulty (foolish, even) financial strategy. Yet if managers are too cautious, they are likely to find their business left behind as rivals sweep past them. Greed is never good, but neither is it right to be *too* careful. Good chief executives find a way to be bold but sensible.

Key terms

Capital expenditure: spending on fixed assets (e.g. premises and machinery).

External sources of finance: funds generated from sources outside an organisation (e.g. bank loans, venture capital).

Factoring: passing a copy of a customer invoice to your bank, which then credits you with 80% of the invoiced sum within 24 hours, then collects the debt for you (for a fee of perhaps 4%).

Internal sources of finance: funds generated from an organisation's own resources (e.g. retained profit, sale of assets).

Overtrading: this refers to the liquidity problems experienced by a firm that expands without securing the finance required to support it – for example, to bridge the gap between paying suppliers and receiving payment from customers.

Profit centre: a part of a business for which a separate profit and loss account can be drawn up.

Retained profit: profit left over after all the deductions (and additions) have been made to sales revenue, including cost of sales, overheads, tax and dividends.

Rights issue: giving existing shareholders the right to buy extra shares in the business before allowing outsiders that right to buy; a rights issue usually offers the shares at a discount to the existing market price. It is likely to be cheaper to raise finance by this method than a full public issue.

Sale and leaseback: a method of raising finance by selling an asset but paying to continue to use it.

Working capital: the day-to-day finances needed to run a business – generally seen as the difference between the value of a firm's current assets and its current liabilities.

Exercises

A. Revision questions

(45 marks; 45 minutes)

1 State two reasons why an established firm might wish to raise finance. (2)

2 Describe two influences on a firm's choice of finance. (4)

3 Outline two ways in which a firm could raise finance to buy the additional stock needed to meet an unexpected order. (4)

4 Analyse two appropriate sources of finance available to a private limited company looking to set up a production facility in Poland. (6)

5 Use numerical examples to explain how a firm's gearing and liquidity position would affect its choice of finance. (6)

6 Explain why a rapidly expanding firm might suffer from overtrading. (4)

7 Using examples, briefly explain the difference between capital expenditure for maintenance and capital expenditure for growth. (4)

8 Explain what is meant by the term 'profit centre'. (3)

9 Analyse one benefit and one drawback for coffee retailer Starbucks from choosing to operate its outlets as individual profit centres. (6)

10 Examine one advantage and one disadvantage for a company such as Ryanair of adopting a strategy of cost minimisation. (6)

B. Revision exercises

B1 Data response

Can Lara Croft's creators fight back?

In February 2008, SCi Entertainment, the company behind *Tomb Raider* and Lara Croft, claimed it needed £55 million in order to avoid collapse. The announcement came after the Wimbledon-based company revealed half-year losses of £81.4 million, on top of a loss of £17.9 million the previous year. SCi said it was in talks with its bank, Lloyds TSB, to extend its current overdraft of £20 million. However, the company's chief executive, Phil Rogers, indicated that he preferred to raise new equity, via a rights issue. At the time, Rogers said, 'the right thing, right now, is to move quickly – and the right thing, right now, is to go and talk to our shareholders'. Earlier in 2007, US media group, Time Warner, bought a 10% stake in the business for 504p a share. SCi's share price fell to just 39p after the loss announcement, valuing the company at £34 million. Rogers announced a major financial overhaul, aimed at keeping the company afloat, including abandoning the development of 14 new games and reducing the size of the workforce by 25% to 800, leading to cost savings of £14 million.

As Britain's only sizeable games group, SCi generated sales turnover of £73 million in the six months to the end of December 2007, slightly below the figure for the previous year of £74.5 million, despite worldwide sales of 1.4 million copies of its latest game, *Kane & Lynch*, over Christmas 2007.

Source: Adapted from www.guardian.co.uk

Questions

(30 marks; 35 minutes)

1a Calculate the % loss made by Time Warner by buying shares that had fallen to 39p within a year. (3)

1b Outline two possible reasons that might have been behind Time Warner's purchase of SCi shares. (4)

2 To what extent do you agree with Phil Rogers' view that a rights issue is the most appropriate means of financing SCi's rescue plan? (11)

3 Discuss the other key factors that may determine whether SCi is successful in tackling its financial problems. (12)

B2 Data response

Cost minimisation means success at Aldi

Privately owned German supermarket Aldi opened its first UK store in 1990 and now has over 300 outlets across the country. Although its share of the fiercely competitive UK grocery market was just 3% at the beginning of 2008, its reputation as a quality discounter has led to a steady growth in popularity, particularly among the country's affluent middle-class. Indeed, this success led to supermarket giant Tesco launching a range of 300 'no frills' products, as well as a March 2008 claim to match Aldi's prices on over 2000 items.

According to Aldi, its success is down to its 'less is more' approach to retailing, with all decisions aimed at guaranteeing a 'low-cost shop' for its customers. Aldi's operations are designed around the key objective of minimising costs without compromising quality. This objective is achieved in a number of ways, as described below.

- Offering customers a limited range of its most frequently purchased own brand grocery and household products, rather than branded goods, allows the retailer to buy in bulk from suppliers. Many of these suppliers are well-known food manufacturers who are prepared to sell to Aldi at lower prices because of the large volumes involved. (Although Aldi is small in Britain, it is huge in Germany and across Europe.)

- Aldi has a no-frills in-store approach, where products are often sold straight from boxes rather than shelves and staff levels are kept to a minimum; this keeps overheads down. Customers have to pay for carrier bags and the use of a shopping trolley requires a £1 deposit, to encourage its return.

Despite its low prices, Aldi insists that it does not compromise when it comes to quality – indeed, the retailer emerged as a key winner, alongside Waitrose, at the 2007 Quality Foods Awards.

Source: www.aldi.co.uk; www.telegraph.co.uk

Questions

(25 marks; 30 minutes)

1a Analyse the main ways in which Aldi's operations are successful in minimising costs.
(10)

2 To what extent do you believe that Aldi can continue to increase its share of the UK grocery market?
(15)

INVESTMENT APPRAISAL

Making investment decisions on the basis of quantitative and qualitative criteria.

60.1 Introduction

Every day managers make decisions, such as how to deal with a furious customer or whether a cheeky worker needs a disciplinary chat. These decisions can be regarded as tactical (i.e. **tactical decisions**) because they are short-term responses to events. Investment appraisal applies to decisions that concern strategy rather than tactics (i.e. the medium–long term). As they are significant in the longer term, they are worth taking a bit of time over – ideally, by calculating whether or not the potential profits are high enough to justify the initial outlay (the sum invested).

To carry out a full investment appraisal might take a manager several weeks, even months. Not because the maths is so complex, but in order to find accurate data

to analyse. For example, if trying to choose whether to launch new product A or B, a sales forecast will be essential. Carrying out primary market research might take several weeks until the results are received and analysed. Only then could the investment appraisal begin. Yet what is the alternative? To take an important decision without proper evidence and information? Table 60.1 gives an idea of the data required to take effective decisions using investment appraisal.

Quantitative methods of investment appraisal

Having gathered all the necessary facts and figures, a firm can analyse the data to answer two main questions.

Table 60.1 *The data required to take effective decisions using investment appraisal*

Decisions requiring investment appraisal	Information needed to make the decision
Should we launch new product A or B?	Sales forecasts, pricing decisions, and data on fixed, variable and start-up costs
Should we make a takeover bid for Sainsbury's?	Forecast of future cash flows into and out of Sainsbury's; compare the results with the purchase price
Should we relocate our factory from London to Prague?	Estimate of fixed and variable costs there compared with here, plus the initial cost of the move
Shall we expand capacity by running a night shift?	Forecast of the extra costs compared with extra revenues

1 How long will it take until we get our money back? If we invest £400,000, can we expect to get that money back within the first year, or might it take four years?

2 How profitable will the investment be? What profit will be generated per year by the investment?

To answer these two questions there are three methods that can be used:

1 payback period

2 average rate of return

3 discounted cash flows.

Two of these (methods 1 and 2) need to be used together; the third can answer both questions simultaneously. All three methods require the same starting point: a table showing the expected cash flows on the investment over time.

An example would be an investment of £60,000 in a machine that will cost £10,000 per year to run and should generate £30,000 a year of cash. The machine is expected to last for five years. The cash flow table would look like the one shown in Table 60.2.

Exam papers might present this information in the form of a graph. The graph in Figure 60.1 shows the **cumulative cash** total based on the table figures.

These figures will be used to explain the workings of each of the three methods listed above, which we will now look at in more detail.

Table 60.2 Example cash flow table

	Cash in	**Cash out**	**Net cash flow**	**Cumulative cash total**
NOW*	–	£60,000	(£60,000)	(£60,000)
Year 1	£30,000	£10,000	£20,000	(£40,000)
Year 2	£30,000	£10,000	£20,000	(£20,000)
Year 3	£30,000	£10,000	£20,000	–
Year 4	£30,000	£10,000	£20,000	£20,000
Year 5	£30,000	£10,000	£20,000	£40,000

*NOW is the moment the £60,000 is spent; can also be called the initial outlay or the sum invested

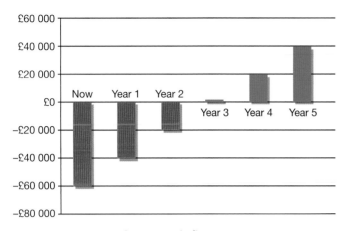

Figure 60.1 Cumulative cash flows on an investment of £60,000

60.2 Payback period

Calculation

This method focuses on one issue alone: how long does it take to get your money back. In the above case, the £60,000 investment takes exactly three years to get back, as can be seen in the right-hand column: the cumulative cash total. All the £60,000 is recovered in three years because the business is generating £20,000 of cash per year.

If the annual net cash flows are constant over time, a formula can be used to calculate the payback period:

$$payback: \frac{\text{sum invested}}{\text{net cash per time period}}$$

$$\text{e.g.} \quad \frac{£60,000}{£20,000 \text{ a year}} = 3 \text{ years}$$

What if the cash flows aren't constant over time?

This can make it a little harder to work out a precise answer, though the principles are the same. For example, take the investment of £40,000 shown in Table 60.3.

In this case, payback has not yet occurred by the end of Year 2 (there's still £5000 outstanding). Yet the end of Year 3 is well beyond the payback period. So payback occurred in two years and x months. To find how many months, the following formula will work:

$$\frac{\text{outlay outstanding}}{\text{monthly cash in year of payback}}$$

$$\text{e.g.} \quad \frac{£5000}{£12,000/12\text{m}} = 5 \text{ months}$$

In this case, then, the payback period was two years and five months.

Interpretation of payback period

The word investment suggests spending money now in the hope of making money later. Therefore every investment means putting money at risk while waiting for the profit. The payback period is the length of time the money is at risk. It follows that every business would like an investment to have as short a payback period as possible. Company directors may tell their managers to suggest an investment only if its payback is less than 18 months. This yardstick is known as a **criterion level**.

It is important to bear in mind the risks involved in investment. Even if well-researched sales estimates have led to well-considered cash flow forecasts, things can go wrong. For a new house-building business, an

Table 60.3

	Cash in	Cash out	Net cash flow	Cumulative cash total
NOW	–	£40,000	(£40,000)	(£40,000)
Year 1	£20,000	£5,000	£15,000	(£25,000)
Year 2	£30,000	£10,000	£20,000	(£5,000)
Year 3	£36,000	£24,000	£12,000	£7,000

unexpected rise in interest rates may lead cash inflows to dry up, as buyers hesitate. Or a new 'AllFresh' restaurant may find that food wastage levels are much higher than expected, causing cash outflows to be disturbingly high. Getting beyond the payback period is therefore always a crucial phase.

Although managers like a quick payback, it is important to beware of **short-termism**. If directors demand too short a payback period, it may be impossible for managers to plan effectively for the long-term future of the business. Quick paybacks imply easy decisions, such as for Primark to expand its store chain by opening its first store in Plymouth. A much tougher, longer-term decision would be whether Primark should open up stores in France. This might prove a clever move in the longer term, but the high costs of getting to grips with French retailing might lead to a minimum of a three-year payback.

A-grade application
The opposite of short-termism

In November 2007, Tesco opened its first 'fresh&easy' stores in America. Getting to this stage had taken three years of careful research in America, and the commitment of an investment level of £250 million by the British supermarket giant. At the outset, Tesco boss Terry Leahy cannot have expected a payback period of anything less than five years, yet he decided to go ahead because he believed that this move could lead eventually to 5000 Tesco fresh&easy stores in America – and a significant share of America's £350 billion grocery market.

Figure 60.2 A Tesco Fresh & Easy shop

Table 60.4 The advantages and disadvantages of payback

Advantages of payback	Disadvantages of payback
Easy to calculate and understand	Provides no insight into profitability
May be more accurate than other measures, because it ignores longer-term forecasts (the ones beyond the payback period)	Ignores what happens after the payback period
Takes into account the timing of cash flows	May encourage a short-termist attitude
Especially important for a business with weak cash flow; it may be willing to invest only in projects with a quick payback	Is not very useful on its own (because it ignores profit), therefore is used together with ARR or NPV (see below)

60.3 Average rate of return

This method compares the average annual profit generated by an investment with the amount of money invested in it. In this way, two or more potential projects can be compared to find out which has the 'best' return for the amount of money being put into it in the first place.

Calculation

Average rate of return (ARR) is calculated by the formula:

$$\frac{\text{average annual return}}{\text{initial outlay}} \times 100$$

There are three steps in calculating ARR, as follows.

1 Calculate the total profit over the lifetime of the investment (total net cash flows minus the investment outlay).

Table 60.5 Figures for BJ Carpets

Year	Net cash flow	Cumulative cash flow
0	(£20,000)	(£20,000)
1	+£5,000	(£15,000)
2	+£11,000	(£4,000)
3	+£10,000	+£6,000
4	+£10,000	+£16,000

2 Divide by the number of years of the investment project, to give the average annual profit.

3 Apply the formula: average annual profit/initial outlay×100.

For example, BJ Carpets is considering whether to invest £20,000 in a labour-saving wrapping machine. The company policy is to invest in projects only if they deliver a profit of 15+% a year (see Table 60.5).

Here, the £20,000 investment generates £36,000 of net cash flows in the four years. That represents a lifetime profit of £16,000 (see bottom right-hand corner of Table 60.5). To apply the three steps, then, proceed as indicated in Table 60.6.

BJ Carpets can therefore proceed with this investment, as the ARR of 20% is comfortably above its requirement of a minimum ARR criterion level of 15%.

Interpretation of ARR

The strength of ARR is that it is easy to interpret the result. Clearly firms want as high a rate of profit as possible, so the higher the ARR the better. This makes it easy to choose between two investment options, as long as profit is the key decision-making factor. (It might not be, because some firms are pursuing objectives such as growth or diversification.)

How do you interpret an ARR result, though, if there is only one investment to consider? For example is 12% a good rate of return? In this case the key is to analyse the **reward for risk**. This compares the ARR result with the only way to achieve a safe rate of return – by keeping your money on deposit at a bank.

Reward for risk

If an ARR result comes out at 12%, ask yourself what the current rate of interest is. If it is 5.75%, for example, a business could receive a 5.75% annual income at zero risk and by doing nothing. So, why invest? Well, in this case, the reward for investing would be the 12% ARR *minus* the 5.75% interest rate, meaning that the investment yields a 6.25% annual reward for taking a business risk. Clearly if the reward for risk was small, or even negative (5% ARR when interest rates are 5.75%),

Table 60.6 BJ Carpets: applying the three steps

Step 1	Identify lifetime profit	£16,000
Step 2	Divide by number of years (4)	£4,000
Step 3	Calculate annual profit as a % of initial outlay	$\frac{£4,000}{£20,000} * 100 = 20\%$

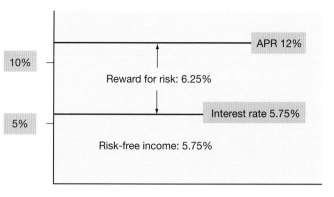

Figure 60.3 *Diagram to show reward for risk*

it would seem crazy to invest. Note that an implication here is that the higher the interest rate, the less attractive it becomes to invest. In an exam, the key is to interpret the ARR through the reward for risk, then make a judgement about how risky the investment

seems. A 6.25% reward for risk, for example, would seem very low for a brand new restaurant, as 40% of new restaurants fold within three years of starting up. (See Figure 60.3.)

The average rate of return (ARR) method takes account of all the cash flows throughout the life of a project, and focuses on the key decision-making factor: profitability. However, it ignores *when* the cash flows occur, which can have a significant bearing on the risks of a project. Look at the example of the *average* rate of return on two investments, both of £10,000, in Table 60.7.

Investments A and B come out with the same average profitability. Yet Investment A's quick, one-year payback makes it greatly preferable to Investment B. After all, it is much easier to forecast one year ahead than three years. So Investment B's crucial year 3 might prove much worse than expected. Meaning the ARR proves much lower in reality than the 30% expected at the start.

Table 60.7 *Example of the average rate of return on two investments*

Year	Investment A net cash flows	Investment B net cash flows
0	(£10,000)	(£10,000)
1	+£10,000	+£3,000
2	+£6,000	+£6,000
3	+£3,000	+£10,000
Average rate of return	30%	30%

Table 60.8 *The advantages and disadvantages of average rate of return*

Advantages of average rate of return	Disadvantages of average rate of return
Uses all the cash flows over the project's life …	… but, because later years are included, the results will not prove as accurate as payback
Focuses upon profitability	Ignores the timing of the cash flows
Easy to compare % returns on different investments, to help make a decision	Ignores the time value (opportunity cost) of the money invested

60.4 Discounted cash flows

Useful though payback and ARR can be, they can work effectively only when used together. ARR provides information on average profitability, while payback tells you about the timing of the cash flows. Better, surely, to have one method that incorporates profits and time. This is the third method of investment appraisal, which is based on 'discounted cash flows'.

Discounted cash flow (DCF) is a method that is rooted in opportunity cost. If a firm invests £10,000 in computer software, it is important not only to ask 'What is the rate of return on my investment of £10,000?', but also 'What opportunities am I having to give up as a result of this investment?' At its simplest, £10,000 tied up in software prevents the firm from enjoying a 5.75% return on its money in the bank (when interest rates are 5.75%).

From the idea of opportunity cost, businesses want to know the implication of the timing of cash flows on different projects. If one investment generates +£40,000 in year 1, while another provides that inflow in year 4, the firm must consider what it is missing out on by waiting four years.

In short, it is always preferable to have money now than the promise of the same quantity of money in the future. This is because money held at the present time has a greater value than the same quantity of money received in the future. In other words, £100 received in a year's time is worth less to a firm than £100 in the bank today. How much less? Well, if interest rates are 10%, £100 in the bank for a year would become £110. So £100 in a year's time is worth 10% less than £100 today.

When considering potential capital investments on the basis of predicted future cash flows, it makes sense to ask, 'What will the money we receive in the future really be worth in today's terms?' These **present values** are calculated using a method called 'discounting'.

To discount a future cash flow, it is necessary to know:

● how many years into the future we are looking, since the greater the length of time involved, the smaller the present or discounted value of money will be

● what the prevailing rate of interest will be.

Table 60.9 Extract from a discount table

Table of selected discount factors						
Years ahead	4%	6%	8%	10%	12%	15%
0	1.00	1.00	1.00	1.00	1.00	1.00
1	0.96	0.94	0.93	0.91	0.89	0.87
2	0.92	0.89	0.86	0.83	0.80	0.76
3	0.89	0.84	0.79	0.75	0.71	0.66
4	0.85	0.79	0.74	0.68	0.64	0.57
5	0.82	0.75	0.68	0.62	0.57	0.50

Once these have been determined, the relevant discount factor can be found. This can be done by calculation, or looked up in 'discount tables'. An extract from a discount table is given in Table 60.9.

The future cash flows are then multiplied by the appropriate discount factor to find the present value. For example, the present value of £100 received in five years' time, if the expected rate of interest is 10%, would be:

$$£100 \times 0.62 = £62$$

The higher the rate of interest expected, and the longer the time to wait for the money to come in, the less that money is actually worth in today's terms.

So how does a firm decide which discount factor to choose? There are two main ways.

1 The discount factor can be based on the current rate of interest, or the rate expected over the coming years.

2 A firm may base the factor on its own criteria, such as that it wants every investment to make at least 15%; therefore it expects future returns to be positive even with a 15% discount rate.

This A-level includes just one technique of discounting future cash flows to find their present value; this is the net present value method.

Net present value (NPV)

Calculation

This method calculates the present values of all the money coming in from the project in the future, then sets these against the money being spent on the project today. The result is known as the net present value (NPV) of the project. It can be compared with other projects to find which has the highest return in real terms, and should therefore be chosen.

The technique can also be used to see if *any* of the projects are worth undertaking. All the investments might have a negative NPV. In other words, the present value of the money being spent is greater than the present value of the money being received. If so, the firm would be better off putting the money in the bank and earning the current rate of interest. Projects are only worth carrying out if the NPV is positive.

For example, a firm is faced with two alternative proposals for investment: Project Z and Project Y (see Table 60.10). Both cost £250,000, but have different patterns of future cash flows over their projected lives. The rate of interest over the period is anticipated to average around 10%. The calculation would be as shown in the table.

Despite the fact that both projects have the same initial cost, and they bring in the same quantity of money over their lives, there is a large difference in their net present values. Project Y, with most of its income coming in the early years, gives a much greater present value than Project Z.

Table 60.10 Project Z vs Project Y

Year	Cash flow	Discount factor	Discounted cash flow (£s)		Cash flow	Discount factor	Discounted cash flow (£s)
		Project Z				**Project Y**	
0	(£250,000)	1.00	(£250,000)		(£250,000)	1.00	(£250,000)
1	+£50,000	0.91	£45,500		+£200,000	0.91	+£182,000
2	+£100,000	0.83	£83,000		+£100,000	0.83	+£83,000
3	+£200,000	0.75	£150,000		+£50,000	0.75	+£37,500
		NPV =	+£28,500			NPV =	+£52,500

Table 60.11 *The advantages and disadvantages of NPV*

Advantages of NPV	Disadvantages of NPV
Takes the opportunity cost of money into account	Complex to calculate and communicate
A single measure that takes the amount and timing of cash flows into account	The meaning of the result is often misunderstood
Can consider different scenarios	Only comparable between projects if the initial investment is the same

Interpretation

This method of appraising investment opportunities has an in-built advantage over the previous techniques. It pays close attention to the timing of cash flows and their values in relation to the value of money today. It is also relatively simple to use the technique as a form of 'what if?' scenario planning. Different calculations can be made to see what returns will be obtained at different interest rates or with different cash flows to reflect different expectations. The results, however, are not directly comparable between different projects when the initial investments differ.

60.5 Qualitative factors in investment appraisal

Once the numbers have been calculated there are decisions to be made. On the face of it, the numbers point to the answer, but they are only part of the decision-making process. For example, perhaps a board of directors can afford no more than £2 million for investment and must choose between the two alternatives shown in Table 60.12.

Investment B is clearly superior on all three quantitative methods of appraisal. Yet there may be reasons why the board may reject it. Some of these are outlined below.

- *Company objectives*: if the business is pursuing an objective of long-term growth, the directors might feel that a relaunch of a declining brand is too short-termist; they may prefer an investment that could keep boosting the business long beyond the next five years.

- *Company strategy*: if the business has been suffering from low-priced imported competition, it may seek higher value-added, differentiated products. Its goal may be to become more innovative and therefore the board may opt for Investment A.

- *Company finances*: if the £2 million investment capital is intended to be borrowed, the company's balance sheet is an important issue. If the business is highly geared, it may be reluctant to proceed with either of these investments, as neither generates an irresistible ARR.

- *Confidence in the data*: the directors will ask questions about how the forecasts were made, who made the

Table 60.12 *Investment A vs Investment B*

	Investment A	Investment B
Type of investment	New R&D laboratory	Relaunching an existing product with flagging sales
Investment outlay	£2 million	£2 million
Payback period	4.5 years	1 year
Average rate of return (over next five years)	8.2%	14.2%
Net present value	£32,000	£280,000

forecasts and what was the evidence behind them. If the Investment B data came from the manager in charge of the product with flagging sales, may they be biased? (S/he may have been over-optimistic in interpreting the findings of small-scale market research.) Ideally, data used in investment appraisal should come from an independent source and be based on large enough sample sizes to be statistically valid.

- *Social responsibilities*: investing in recycling or energy-saving schemes may generate very low ARRs, but the firm may still wish to proceed for public relations reasons, to boost morale among staff or just because the directors think it is ethically right.

Issues For Analysis

- Having mastered the mathematics of investment appraisal, the next key factor is to be able to interpret the results effectively. If the business has a payback criterion level of 18 months, is this holding it back in any way? Is there evidence that the firm is *too* focused on the short term? Of course, if the firm's cash flow or liquidity positions are weak, it is understandable if there is a great emphasis on speed of payback. Yet, in some cases, businesses are short-term focused for less acceptable reasons – for example, multi-million-pound short-term profit bonuses for directors may be leading them to ignore the long-term future of the business.

- Always ask yourself about the reliability of the data provided – how were they gathered; who gathered them; what variables were taken into account?

- Decisions should always be based on a mixture of quantitative and qualitative data. Beware of placing too great an emphasis on numbers on the basis that they are somehow more concrete and therefore more reliable. Qualitative factors may be more important, such as considering the environmental impact of a decision. Today's profits can turn into tomorrow's public relations disaster if stakeholders discover unacceptable side-effects of your approach to production.

60.6 Investment appraisal

Investment appraisal methods will often give conflicting advice to managers, who must be willing to make decisions based on a trade-off between risks and profit. This must be taken alongside the objectives of the business, which could well dictate which of the criteria involved is of most importance to the firm.

The size of the firm will also have an impact. Small firms will often have neither the time nor the resources to undertake a scientific approach to investment appraisal. They will often rely on past experience or the owner's hunches in making decisions such as these. In larger firms, however, the issue of accountability will often lead managers to rely heavily on the projected figures. In this way, should anything go wrong, they can prove they were making the best decision possible at the time, given the information available.

Key terms

Criterion level: a yardstick set by directors to enable managers to judge whether investment ideas are worth pursuing (e.g. ARR must be 15%1 or payback must be a maximum of 12 months).

Cumulative cash: the build-up of cash over several time periods; for example, if cash flow is +£20,000 for three years in a row, cumulative cash in year 3 is +£60,000.

Present values: the discounting of future cash flows to make them comparable with today's cash. This takes into account the opportunity cost of waiting for the cash to arrive.

Reward for risk: calculating the difference between the forecast ARR and the actual rate of interest, to help decide whether the ARR is high enough given the risks involved in the project.

Short-termism: making decisions on the basis of the immediate future and therefore ignoring the long-term future of the business.

Tactical decisions: those that are day-to-day events and therefore do not require a lengthy decision-making process.

Exercises

A. Revision questions

(40 marks; 40 minutes)

1 Distinguish between qualitative and quantitative investment appraisal. (4)

2 Why should forecast cash flow figures be treated with caution? (4)

3 How useful is payback period as the sole method for making an investment decision? (3)

4 Briefly outline the circumstances in which:
   (a) payback period might be the most important appraisal method for a firm (4)
   (b) average rate of return might be more important than payback for a firm. (4)

5 How are criterion levels applied to investment appraisal? (3)

6 Explain the purpose of discounting cash flows. (4)

7 Using only qualitative analysis, would you prefer £100 now or £105 in one year's time, at an interest rate of 10%? (3)

8 Outline two possible drawbacks to setting a payback criterion level of 12 months. (4)

9 What qualitative issues might a firm take into account when deciding whether to invest in a new fleet of lorries? (4)

10 Why is it important to ask for the source before accepting investment appraisal data? (3)

Calculate the payback and the average rate of return. (6)

2 The board of Burford Ltd is meeting to decide whether to invest £500,000 in an automated packing machine or in a new customer service centre. The production manager has estimated the cash flows from the two investments to calculate the following table:

	Packing machine	Service centre
Payback	1.75 years	3.5 years
NPV	+£28,500	+£25,600

   (a) On purely quantitative grounds, which would you choose and why? (6)

   (b) Outline three other factors the board should consider before making a final decision. (6)

3 The cash flows on two alternative projects are estimated to be:

	Project A		Project B	
	Cash in	Cash out	Cash in	Cash out
Year 0	–	£50,000	–	£50,000
Year 1	£60,000	£30,000	£10,000	£10,000
Year 2	£80,000	£40,000	£40,000	£20,000
Year 3	£40,000	£24,000	£60,000	£30,000
Year 4	£20,000	£20,000	£84,000	£40,000

Carry out a full investment appraisal to decide which (if either) of the projects should be undertaken. Interest rates are currently 8%. (12)

B1 Data response

Questions

(30 marks; 30 minutes)

1 Net annual cash flows on an investment are forecast to be:

	£000
NOW	(600)
End of year 1	100
End of year 2	400
End of year 3	400
End of year 4	180

B2 Data response

Dowton's new finance director has decided that capital investments will be approved only if they meet the following criteria:

Payback	30 months
Average rate of return	18%
Net present value	10% of the investment outlay

The assembly department has proposed the purchase of a £600,000 machine that will be more productive and produce to a higher-quality finish. The department estimates that the output gains should yield the following cash flow benefits during the expected four-year life of the machine:

Year 0	−£600,000
Year 1	+£130,000
Year 2	+£260,000
Year 3	+£360,000
Year 4	+£230,000

In addition:

1 the machine should have a resale value of £100,000 at the end of its life

2 the relevant discount factors are – end year 1 0.91; year 2 0.83; year 3 0.75; year 4 0.68.

Questions

(30 marks; 35 minutes)

1 Conduct a full investment appraisal, then consider whether Dowton's should go ahead with the investment on the basis of the quantitative information provided. (16)

2 Outline any other information it might be useful to obtain before making a final decision. (8)

3 Explain two sources of finance that might be appropriate for an investment such as this. (6)

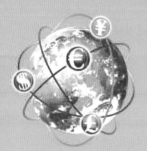
INTEGRATED FINANCE

61.1 Finance: an overview

Finance is an area of the syllabus people either love or hate. Many students worry about the maths involved and so tend to avoid finance when possible. The maths is not all that complicated, though, and it is worth putting some effort into learning how to do the financial calculations. A correct financial calculation can get you full marks – much harder to obtain with a written answer.

The calculations in themselves are only a means to an end. Businesses do financial calculations to help them manage the business; in both coursework and examinations you should treat the figures the same way. When answering questions on finance, and even when revising, ask yourself the following questions.

● What do they show?

● What do they not show?

● What other information would help to explain the situation?

It is always worth considering that the finance answer is only part of the information needed to make an assessment of the situation. Remember that, in a business, finance does not stand alone. It is always connected with other aspects of the business, such as marketing or production. Controlling costs is not just important for profit – it also contributes to the marketing effort by enabling competitive pricing. If the business is to stay ahead, sufficient funds need to be generated, both through profit and external finance raising.

61.2 Why study finance?

Finance is about managing the business. It is about the management of money in the business. The management techniques perform several functions.

● Some tell managers how the business is performing. These include profit and loss accounts and balance sheets.

● Some help managers to make decisions. Investment appraisal, break-even, cost and contribution analyses are included here.

● Some help managers to control the business. These include cash flow, budgeting and cost accounting.

● Some, such as accounting ratios, help managers to compare their business with other businesses, or to look at how business performance is changing.

Finance is pretty fundamental to the whole business. A successful company will be profitable, so satisfying its shareholders. It will have sufficient day-to-day funds, so it will be able to pay its creditors and its workers. It will be able to access funding for expansion and development. It will be able to achieve its financial objectives.

Who is concerned about finance?

Finance is very much an internal activity. Unlike marketing, there is no direct interaction with the consumer. However, external groups are interested in and affected by the financial health of the business. All stakeholders have a vested interest, as outlined below.

● Workers rely on the viability of the business to ensure that their jobs continue and their wages remain competitive.

● Customers will look to the business to provide good-quality goods at reasonable prices. This means that the company must remain financially viable so that it can invest in R&D and new machinery.

● Controlling costs will enable the business to control prices. Continuing viability is also important to the customer who needs aftercare or continuity of supply.

● Investors will be looking for a return on their capital and will want to know that the business is being financially well managed.

● Prospective investors will be interested in the past performance of the business and its potential in the future.

- The government will want the business to succeed, both as a source of employment and as a tax payer.
- The local community will also benefit from having a viable business in its midst.

So a well-managed business will have a wide impact. Finance as a tool for good management will play its part. Financial decisions will impact on other aspects of the business and therefore are, indirectly, a part of the relationship with the customers and other external groups.

61.3 A-grade finance

A-grade finance depends upon understanding, not just memory. Getting the sums right is obviously the first requirement for the A-grade finance answer. However, getting higher grades requires more than just being able to do the calculations – it also requires an understanding of what the figures mean, where they came from and how reliable they are. This will help in two ways.

1 If the numbers you are given to make the calculation are not exactly the ones you are used to, you will be able to get back to the figures you need. For example, investment appraisal calculations are normally based on net cash flow figures. An understanding of how net cash flow is calculated will enable you to do the calculation if you are given cost and revenue figures.

2 If you understand where the figures came from you will be able to make some assessment of their validity. Are the basic figures actual or estimated? Knowing this will help you to comment sensibly on the results. A cash flow forecast will nearly always be based on estimated figures. However, the revenue figures may be contractually agreed with the customer and will therefore be much more reliable than best guesses.

Another important consideration is understanding what is included in the figures and what is not. The figures may not tell the whole story. An A-grade student will know that the figures may be only part of the picture, and will look for other information. Two businesses may have identical sales this year but what about future prospects? One may be facing fierce competition from a new rival or experiencing a period of labour unrest. The other may have no threats and so faces a much more healthy outlook. So the A-grade student will put the figures into the wider perspective before commenting on the results. This is particularly important in case study and report papers, and is necessary to demonstrate an understanding of the integrative nature of business.

61.4 Issues in finance

There are several recurrent themes in finance. Being able to discuss these will often help to give a deeper, more evaluative, answer to a finance question.

Issue 1: the importance of profit

Profit is clearly important to a business. It is necessary for the business to continue and an essential requirement for growth. However, it does not have to be the overriding consideration, and many businesses balance other objectives with the profit motive. Some small businesses may fulfil a personal need to survive financially with other personal needs such as enjoying work. Larger businesses may balance the profit made with the requirement to maintain good public relations. Businesses may forego immediate profit in order to put in place strategies for growth or survival, or increased profit in the future.

Neither does profit have to be continuous. Many new businesses take some time to become profitable. Many existing businesses may have periods when they make no profit, and may even show losses. As long as liquidity is maintained the business will be able to survive making a loss, at least in the short term.

Issue 2: the ethics of profitability

Newspapers contain much discussion about the ethics of profitability. Businesses need profit, but how much and at what cost? What balance should be achieved between profit and issues such as the environment or exploitation of workers? Answering this question will require a balancing of the various interests involved. When answering a question involving ethics it is important to look at all sides of the issue and to avoid becoming emotionally involved with one point of view. This may be very difficult if you have strong beliefs about an issue such as animal welfare. By all means express your views but remember to balance them with the other side of the case. Animal welfare is important, but what about the jobs of people in the industries? What about increased costs passed on to consumers who may not be able to afford to pay more? Should the views of one small group change things for everyone?

Issue 3: the importance of liquidity

Understanding this issue requires an understanding of

the difference between liquidity and profit. Liquidity is about having access to sufficient cash on a day-to-day basis to meet the business's commitments. Even if the cash is not available within the business, all is not lost if it is able to generate the required cash from external sources. Poor liquidity is not just a short-term problem. Unless the business is properly funded, the problem will keep returning. It is essential that the business has sufficient working capital for its short- and long-term needs.

Issue 4: is financial management only for large businesses?

While larger companies have the resources to employ financial experts, good financial management is essential for all businesses. Many new businesses fail because of poor financial management. This is the most common cause of early business failure. Smaller businesses may well need tighter financial management. They will not have the resources to buffer the business if mistakes are made. They are also less likely to have access to outside funding to bail them out in difficult times. Small firms may also have a smaller product range, which means financial risks are more concentrated. However, as the business grows there will be a widening gap between ownership and control. Financial management systems will be necessary to keep control of this growing business. Financial analysis will enable the business to evaluate new developments and ensure that they contribute positively to the business.

Issue 5: financial information cannot be trusted

Many people suspect that the published accounts of large firms are manipulated: they show what the company wants the outside world to see. To some extent this is true. Firms can 'massage' the figures to a certain extent to make liquidity or profitability look more or less favourable. They may wish to do this to even out profitability over several years in order to minimise the tax payable. They may wish to convince outsiders that the company is in a better position than it really is. However, the scope for this window dressing is limited. Businesses have to legally conform to certain financial reporting requirements. All limited company reports must be audited by an independent accountant. This generally ensures that the figures are accurate and a true representation of the company's position. However, there may be situations where the auditors are unaware of questionable business activities. As auditors are outside agencies, they depend on the company giving them correct information; their scope for investigation is limited. Although this was the defence given by Arthur Andersen when blamed for the collapse of Enron in 2001/02, few were willing to accept it. These days, accounting statements must be right.

Exercises

A. Revision questions

(60 marks; 60 minutes)

1 List three uses for company accounts. (3)

2 Why is profit important to a business? (2)

3 What is the difference between profit and cash flow? (3)

4 How can an understanding of contribution help a business? (4)

5 List two methods of investment appraisal. (2)

6 Describe the differences between the two methods. (4)

7 Name an accounting ratio that measures liquidity. (1)

8 Why is liquidity vital to a business? (2)

9 List two likely sources of finance for a new business. (2)

10 List and discuss two ways in which a business could finance expansion? (6)

11 What does a cash flow forecast show? (2)

12 How can cash flow forecasts help a business? (4)

13 Identify and discuss two ways in which a firm can deal with a predicted future cash flow shortage. (6)

14 What does break-even analysis show? (3)

15 Distinguish between fixed and variable costs. (2)

16 How do you calculate unit contribution? (2)

17 What is the purpose of budgeting? (2)

18 What is a cost centre? (1)

19 Why is window dressing a cause for concern? (3)

20 Explain two ways a firm could reduce its gearing level. (6)

B. Revision exercises

B1 Data response

Massey Boots

Massey Boots produces boots for working men but has recently begun selling its boots for general wear. It has been surprised by the interest shown by teenagers and young adults. At the moment it produces three types of boot, but increased demand has placed considerable strain on the production facilities. The production manager believes that if the company only produced two types of boot, the production facilities could be used more efficiently, then some of the problems it is facing at the moment could be reduced. It has decided to cut the range to two types and needs to decide which to continue producing. It is confident of selling all the boots it makes. The machinery and labour force can be used to manufacture any of the boots without the need for additional expenditure. The maximum number of boots that can be produced is 300,000 pairs. The finance department has produced the figures shown in the table below.

Type of boot:	Toughman	Rough-neck	Cruncher
Sales per year	150,000	80,000	70,000
Selling price	£45	£40	£60
Costs:			
Direct materials per boot	£12	£8	£18
Direct labour per boot	£13	£10	£12

Total fixed costs are £600,000.

Questions

(20 marks; 25 minutes)

1 Calculate the unit and total contribution for each type of boot. (6)

2 If the factory made only one type of boot calculate the break-even level of production for each of the three types. (6)

3 Using the calculations, comment on the production manager's suggestion. (8)

B2 Case study

Simon's gift shop

Five years ago Simon started a sole trader business. He was made redundant and used his redundancy payment, together with a loan of £30,000, to start up a gift shop in a suburb of Oldtown. Oldtown is a large town that used to be very prosperous but has suffered from the closure of a large factory in the last year. Simon's venture is doing well, however. His turnover has been rising steadily and last year he made a net profit of £42,000. Two years ago he took out another loan of £35,000 to expand and redecorate the shop. He has also been ploughing back some of the profits in the business, and the total capital employed is now £130,000.

Simon feels that the time is right to start a second shop. Rents have fallen in the town following the closure of the factory and there are premises available. He has identified three possibilities. These are:

1 a large shop in another suburb – this is a fairly new, prosperous residential area
2 a shop in the centre of town close to the major chain stores – this is a busy area with plenty of passing trade but there are other gift shops in the area
3 a small shop in the redeveloped Docks area – this is some distance away but is a successful tourist area.

All three shops have five-year leases available. Simon has estimated the costs and expected profit for each shop. These are shown in the table below.

	Suburb	Town centre	Docks area
Initial outlay	£80,000	£105,000	£116,000
Expected annual profit	£25,000	£35,000	£40,000

Simon will have to pay 10% interest on any borrowed money. The discount factors at 10% are:

- end year 1   0.91
- end year 2   0.83
- end year 3   0.75
- end year 4   0.68
- end year 5   0.62

Simon will need to go to the bank for a loan. The role play (see below) will involve preparing and presenting the case for the loan to the bank manager.

Preparation

1 Review each of the sites using investment appraisal techniques.
2 Evaluate the project.
3 Decide the course of action you think Simon should take.

Role play

Acting as Simon, make a presentation, suitable for a bank manager, applying for a loan to finance the investment.

B3 Case study

The Yummy Biscuit Company

The Yummy Biscuit Company has been operating for about ten years. It was started by two friends and was so successful that, eight years ago, the owners convinced friends and family to invest in the business. It converted to a private limited company. With the new expansion it was able to lease a factory on a new industrial estate and purchase new machinery. Business has been booming and it is now at full capacity. Production continues day and night, which is placing considerable strain on resources.

The company has now reached the point where the managers need to make some hard decisions. They feel there are two choices: to expand or to cut back sales to a slightly lower level. The latter option will take some of the pressure out of the system so that each machine breakdown does not cause a crisis. If the company is to expand it will need to raise about £200,000. This will pay for the new machinery, new premises and vehicles, and the recruitment and training of new staff as well as the cost of the move. Sales last year were £250,000 and overheads amounted to £150,000. Variable costs are 25% of turnover. If the company expands, the managers anticipate they can easily double sales and that overheads could be reduced to 50% of turnover.

The balance sheet at the end of the last financial year looked like this:

	£
Fixed assets	265,000
Current assets	115,000
less Current liabilities	30,000
= Working capital	85,000
Assets employed	350,000

	£
Financed by:	
Loan	80,000
Share capital	250,000
Retained profit	20,000
Capital employed	350,000

Questions

(25 marks; 40 minutes)

1 If the business decides to expand, discuss how it might raise the necessary funding. (6)

2 Calculate the actual profit for last year and the anticipated profit for next year, assuming that the company expands. (5)

3 In addition to the financial information, what else should the business consider before making the decision? (4)

4 Write a report to the company managers advising them whether or not to expand. (10)

B4 Integrated case study

Whitbread

A company that started life in 1742 is bound to have seen some changes throughout its life. When Samuel Whitbread started brewing beer in London he could not have envisaged how his company would develop. Especially surprising might be the fact that it is coffee (through the Costa Coffee chain), not beer, that is now contributing to company profits.

The company became a limited company in 1889 and became a public limited company (plc) only in 1948. During the recession of the 1970s the company came very close to bankruptcy. It managed to survive, helped perhaps by the good public image of the brand. As it recovered it began a major expansion through mergers and acquisitions of other businesses. This started with the takeovers of several breweries but, in the 1970s, the company began a policy of diversification; several of its brewing enterprises were closed down. This included the original brewery in Chiswell Street in London. It built up a wine and spirits division using Threshers, which it had previously acquired as its retail outlet. Its brands included Beefeater Gin and Long John Scotch whisky. It also manufactured and sold Heineken lager and Stella Artois under licence agreements. These moves reflected the change in the market as beer consumption fell and demand shifted towards lager and wine. In 1974 the first Beefeater restaurant and pub was opened. This was followed in 1979 by the opening of the Brewers Fayre chain of pubs and restaurants. The company also entered into the hotel industry with its Travel Inn chain of budget hotels.

This move into food continued with a joint venture with PepsiCo and the opening of a chain of Pizza Hut restaurants. Later, TGI Friday's was added to the company's portfolio. One big factor in the decline of the brewing sector was the ruling by the Monopolies & Mergers Commission that brewers were not allowed to operate more than 200 tied pubs. (These are pubs that are owned or leased by the brewery and only sell the company's products.) This meant that Whitbread had to dispose of more than 200 pubs. With too many pubs on the market and a fall in the value of property the result meant that the business had little capital for further expansion of its other activities and a planned expansion into Europe had to be shelved.

As things began to improve, and helped by a £300 million capital injection from the sale of its regional brewing interests, the company again started to expand. Among its acquisitions were:

- the German Maredo steak restaurant chain
- 16 Marriott hotels
- David Lloyd Leisure, which owned 20 fitness clubs and 24 Gatehouse nursery schools
- the Costa Coffee chain
- the Pelican group, which ran the Café Rouge, Dome and Mamma Amalfi outlets
- the Bright Reasons group, whose outlets included Bella Pasta.

By the end of 1999 the brewing sector generated only around 12% of the total business profits. A huge shift from its roots.

This change of emphasis continued at the beginning of the twenty-first century, with the company selling off its pubs and breweries. The sale of the pubs raised over £1 billion. Part of this was used to reduce debt and some was returned to shareholders as a special dividend. The company development included selling off some of it restaurant chains, such as Café Rouge, renovating and upgrading many of its underperforming outlets and investing heavily in the David Lloyd fitness and leisure businesses.

Further rationalisation occurred in 2007, with the sale of the Lloyd fitness clubs, the company's 50% stake in Pizza Hut and the TGI Friday's chain raising £925 million. When questioned about these sales, CEO Alan Parker said: 'We wanted to follow a well thought out strategy of exiting from the low returning and limited opportunity businesses – particularly those where we didn't own the brands – into the three businesses we have at the moment, where we believe there is a tremendous opportunity for expansion and good returns to be made.'

Whitbread now consists of the budget hotel chain Premier Inn, the Costa Coffee shops, and the Brewers Fayre and Beefeater pub restaurants.

Premier Inn is the biggest hotel chain in Britain. It has 5% market share, which the company hopes to double. It is looking at each town in Britain to determine where there is a demand for budget rooms, either for the business community or people taking part in leisure activities or visiting relatives, such as students at university. It is also planning to expand overseas. It first hotel opens in Dubai in 2008, where it is looking to provide a budget alternative to luxury hotels. It also plans to expand into India, where it sees the growing middle-class as an opportunity and has plans to

slot in between the five-star hotels and the backpacker hostels.

Whitbread is also planning to expand the Costa Coffee chain. Expansion continues in the UK and the overseas expansion is also set to continue with ventures into Russia and China.

Questions

(70 marks; 80 minutes)

1 Using the figures given in Table B, calculate the percentage change in net profit from 2005/06 to 2006/07 for each of the business sectors. (9)

2a What is a special dividend? (3)

2b Do you think the shareholders should be happy with the way the business is being run? (8)

3 Diversification is a risky strategy. How do you think a business should go about making its decision to take over another business? (8)

4 How might a firm raise funding for expansion? (8)

5 What do you think Whitbread CEO Alan Parker meant when he said 'We wanted to follow a well thought out strategy of exiting from the low returning and limited opportunity businesses – particularly those where we didn't own the brands – into the three businesses we have at the moment, where we believe there is a tremendous opportunity for expansion and good returns to be made'? (10)

6 What financial risks are involved when a company expands overseas? (8)

7 Using the figures in Tables A and B and the information in the text, evaluate the business performance. (16)

Table A

	2002/03	2003/04	2004/05	2005/06	2006/07
Group turnover £m	1,794.1	1,788.2	1,450.5	1,584.0	1,410.8
Profit before tax £m	202.4	211.7	222.8	303.6	434.8
Ordinary dividends per share (pence)	19.87	22.30	25.25	27.30	30.25
Average number of employees	55,315	52,437	53,483	34,419	31,703

Table B

		2006/07 £m	2005/06 £m
Costa	Revenue	175.1	143
	Net profit	18.1	13.3
Restaurants	Revenue	518.9	619.9
	Net profit	52.3	74.9
Premier Inns	Revenue	458.5	392.9
	Net profit	156.2	129.8

Source: Whitbread.co.uk

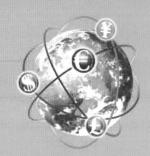

UNDERSTANDING MARKETING OBJECTIVES

62.1 How are marketing objectives set?

At a very senior level in the company

In most firms, marketing is central to board-level strategic decisions. Not marketing in the sense of price cuts and promotions, but marketing in the sense of analysing growth trends and the competitive struggle within the firm's existing markets, and decisions about which markets the firm wishes to develop in future. For example, the chief executive of Asda announced in February 2007 that 'Our primary objective this year is to grow our core business ... through increases in like-for-like sales.' To achieve this, Asda had to cut its prices to keep them below the level of those of market leader Tesco. As a result, by the end of 2007, Asda's market share had risen, keeping it ahead of Sainsbury's as Britain's second-biggest grocery chain.

Rooted in the company's vision of its future (its mission)

A **vision** is a company's projection of what it wants to achieve in the future. It should be ambitious, relevant,

Table 62.1 Vision: six requirements for success

Requirement	Comment
1. Provides future direction	As shown in the examples of *Microsoft* and *Chrysler*
2. Expresses a consumer benefit	e.g. *Pret A Manger*: 'Our mission is to sell handmade extremely fresh food ...'
3. Realistic	Realistic? *Innocent Drinks* 2007: 'To be the most talent-rich company in Europe'
4. Motivating	*Body Shop*: 'Tirelessly work to narrow the gap between principle and practice, whilst making fun, passion and care part of our daily lives.'
5. Fully communicated	Easy to achieve if it's as simple as *Kwik Fit*'s: 'To get customers back on the road speedily, achieving 100% customer delight.'
6. Consistently followed in practice	A company might claim to be at the leading edge of technology; it will lose all credibility if it reacts to the next recession by cutting spending on research and development.

Source: Davidson (1997)

easy to communicate and capable of motivating staff – or even inspiring them. Bill Gates' 1980s vision for Microsoft was 'a computer on every desk and in every home'. Today, that seems uninspiring, even obvious. In the 1980s it seemed extraordinary.

A firm's marketing objectives need to reflect its long-term aims/mission. The American car company Chrysler's mission statement says: 'Our purpose is to produce cars and trucks that people will want to buy, will enjoy driving, and will want to buy again.' This sets the background for marketing objectives that focus on developing new, probably niche market, exciting rather than ordinary cars, and promoting them in ways that emphasise fun rather than safety or family.

In his book *Even More Offensive Marketing*, Hugh Davidson suggests that there are six requirements for a successful company vision. These are listed in Table 62.1.

By striking a balance between what is achievable and what is challenging

Objectives work best when they are clear, achievable, challenging and – above all else – when staff believe in them. To fit all these criteria, the firm must root the objectives in market realities. In 2008, Guinness set out to convert drinkers to Guinness Red. This new product was more like a lager than the traditional Guinness, but it still looked dark and therefore heavy. After ten years of sales decline, the Guinness management hoped that £2.5 million put behind Red would turn things around. The chances seem extremely slim.

Figure 62.1 *Guinness Red*

Marketing objectives should not be set until the decision makers have a clear view of current customer behaviour and attitudes. This will probably require a lot of market research into customer usage and attitudes to the different products they buy and don't buy.

Once the marketplace and financial factors have been considered, objectives can be decided that stretch people, but do not make them snap. Cadbury has had a 30% share of the UK chocolate market for decades. Setting a target of 35% for two years' time would be implausible. After all, will Mars or Nestlé just sit and watch? A wise marketing director might accept the challenge of 32% in two years' time, but would warn everyone that it might be very difficult to achieve this. (Note: each 1% of the chocolate market represents over £20 million of sales, so these matters are not trivial.)

A-grade application
Marketing objectives can fail

In early 1997, the business giant Unilever (Walls, Persil, Birds Eye, CK One and much else) set its sights on obtaining one-third of its worldwide sales from Asian markets by 2001. This company objective was based upon observation of the rapid growth rates in economies such as China. It planned to achieve this by launching new products tailored to local tastes and needs. In fact, in 2001 only 22% of its sales came from Asia, which was only just up on the figure for 1997. Even by 2007 the figure of 33% had not been achieved. Its objective was clear, but probably too ambitious. In business there is no magic formula that says objectives + strategy = success.

62.2 Types of marketing objective

There are four main types of marketing objective:

1 increasing product differentiation

2 growth

3 continuity

4 innovation.

Increasing product differentiation

Product differentiation is the extent to which consumers see your product as different from the rest. It is the key to ensuring that customers buy you because they want you, not because you're the cheapest. It is a major influence on the value added and therefore profit margins achieved by the product.

To increase product differentiation requires a fully integrated marketing programme. Objectives must be set that separate your product from its rivals. These include:

- distinctive design and display

- unusual distribution channels – avoiding supermarkets, perhaps

- advertising based on image building, not sales boosting (e.g. television and cinema advertising rather than blockbuster sales promotions or competitions)

- an integrated marketing programme focused solely upon the relevant age group or type of person.

Growth

Some firms see growth as their main purpose and their main security blanket. They may reason that once they are number one, no one else will be able to catch them. So they set sales or market share targets that encourage staff to push hard for greater success.

This is understandable, but may prove self-defeating. A school or college pushing hard for rapid growth in student numbers would risk damaging its reputation. Class sizes would rise, hastily recruited new staff may be ineffective, middle management would be overstretched and quality standards would be at risk.

From a marketing point of view there is also the threat of 'cannibalisation'. This occurs when the sales of a newly launched product come largely from the company's existing products. This would have been the case when Cadbury launched a new 'Double Choc'

version of its classic Dairy Milk bar. The bigger a firm builds its market share, the bigger the problem becomes. For example, if Wrigley launches a new chewing gum, sales will largely come from other Wrigley brands, as the company holds an astonishing 85% market share.

Cannibalisation has been a major problem in recent years for three giant businesses. In its pursuit of growth, McDonald's built up more than 100,000 stores worldwide before realising that its new stores were taking mainly from existing ones. Starbucks found the same thing in 2007, and it's arguable that Marks & Spencer has the same problem: every time it opens a Simply Food store at a railway station or motorway, it's robbing sales from existing large M&S stores.

Of course, the pursuit of growth may be essential. When social networking became the hottest property on the web, Facebook was right to rush to satisfy this demand. If it had not grown rapidly, others, such as Bebo, would have done so. Therefore the company's objective of rapid growth was very sensible. Too slow would have become too late.

Continuity for the long term

The companies that own major brands, such as Levi's, Bacardi or Cadbury, know that true success comes from taking a very long-term view. Unilever even tells its brand managers that their key role is to hand over a stronger brand to their successor. In other words, they must think ten years or so ahead.

Doubtless Bacardi could boost sales and profits this year by running price promotions with the major supermarkets and off-licences. Or next year, by launching Bacardi iced lollies or bubble gum. But where would the brand's reputation be in a few years' time? Would it still be a classy drink to ask for at a bar?

Large firms think a great deal about their corporate image and the image of the brands they produce. They

Table 62.2 Businesses where innovation is especially important

Business category	Business sector
Fashion-related	Music business Clothing and footwear Entertainment (e.g. eating out)
Technology-related	Consumer electronics and IT Cars and aircraft Medicines and cosmetics

may try to stretch their brands a little, to attract new customers. Yet Cadbury must always mean chocolate, not just snack products. Levi's must always mean jeans, not just clothes. Only in this way can the brands continue to add value for the long term.

Innovation

In certain major sectors of the economy, a key to long-term competitive success is innovation – in other words, bringing new product or service ideas to the marketplace. Two main categories of business where innovation is likely to be crucial are fashion-related and technology-related, as shown in Table 62.2.

There are two key elements to innovation: get it right and get in first. Which is the more important? This is not possible to answer, as past cases have given contradictory results. The originator of the filled ice cream cone was Lyons Maid (now Nestlé), with a product called King Cone. Walls came into the market second with Cornetto. In this case, getting it right proved more important than getting in first. In many other cases, though, the firm in first proved dominant for ever. Coca-Cola ('the real thing'); Cadbury's chocolate (in Britain) or Hershey's (in the USA); even the humble Findus Crispy Pancake (with its 80% market share); all have built long-term success on the back of getting in first.

62.3 Turning objectives into targets

The purpose of objectives is to set out exactly what the business wants to achieve. To ensure success, it is helpful to set more limited targets – staging posts en route to the destination. For example, a firm pursuing the objective of innovation may want at least 40% of sales to come from products launched within the past five years. If, at present, only 30% of sales come from this source, a jump to 40% will not be easy. The targets listed in Table 62.3 may help, especially if – as below – they are linked with the strategy for achieving them.

Targets such as these:

● ensure that all the marketing staff know what to aim for

● provide a sound basis for cooperation with other departments (such as R&D and operations management)

● provide an early warning of when the strategy is failing to meet the objectives – should it be re-thought? Or backed with more resources?

● help psychologically; just as an end-of-year exam can concentrate the mind of a student, so a target can motivate a manager to give of her best.

These benefits hinge on a key issue: have the targets been communicated effectively to the staff? This is an obvious point, but vital nonetheless. If the entire marketing department is based in one large office, it would be astonishing if anyone was unaware of new objectives. But what if it is a retail business and there are 400 branches around the country? Then a head office initiative can fall down at the local level, when a local manager thinks s/he knows best. Expertly considered **marketing targets** may fail unless they are communicated effectively to all relevant staff.

Table 62.3 Targets and strategies for meeting them

Timescale	Target (% of sales from products launched in past five years)	Strategy for meeting target
First year	32%	One national new product launch plus another in test market
Second year	35%	One national new product launch and two others in test market
Third year	40%	Two national new product launches

62.4 Marketing objectives and the small firm

Do small firms set aside time to consider, set and write down objectives and targets? Very rarely. If you interviewed a dozen small business proprietors, you might find none who finds the time and several who would regard such time as wasted.

There are two issues here.

1 In a very small firm, with all business decisions taken by the proprietor, the marketing objectives may be clear in the mind of the boss, even though they are not written down. That may work satisfactorily. When the firm gets 15 or more staff, however, it may have to change.

2 The bosses of small firms often find themselves swamped by day-to-day detail. Customers expect to speak to them personally, staff check every decision and may wait around for their next 'orders'. Only if such bosses learn to delegate will they find the time to think carefully about future objectives and strategy.

There are some bright, young entrepreneurs, however, who apply a more thoughtful approach. Julian Richer identified a gap in the hi-fi market for high-quality equipment sold by music enthusiasts at discount prices. This was intended to appeal to younger, more streetwise buyers. The target image was 'fun'. In the summer, customers at Richer Sounds receive free ice lollies; at Christmas, mince pies. The public face of Richer Sounds is that 'We have a laugh. We don't take ourselves seriously, but we do take our customers seriously.' Behind the scenes, though, careful target setting for stores and sales staff helped Richer Sounds achieve a *Guinness Book of Records* entry for the highest sales per square foot of any store in the UK.

62.5 Constraints on meeting marketing objectives

However well conceived, objectives do not automatically lead to success. Various factors may occur that restrict the chances of the objectives succeeding. These are known as **constraints**. They may occur within the firm (internal constraints) or may be outside its control (external constraints).

Internal influences

- *Financial influences affect virtually every aspect of every organisation.* Even Manchester United has a budget for players, which the manager must keep within. A marketing objective might be set that is unrealistic given the firm's limited resources. That is an error of judgement. Or the firm may have the finance in place at the start, but setbacks to the firm may cause budget cuts that make the objectives impossible to reach.

- *Personnel constraints may be important.* The objective of diversifying may be appealing, but the firm may lack expertise in the new market. A recruitment campaign may fail to find the right person at a salary the business can afford. This may result in the project being delayed, scrapped or – worst of all – carried on by second-rate staff.

- *Market standing:* the marketing objectives may be constrained most severely by the firm's own market position. The big growth sector in food retailing has been in chilled, prepared meals. So why no activity from the food giant Heinz? The answer lies in its success at establishing itself as *the* producer of canned soup, and bottled salad cream and ketchup. The Heinz market image (its key marketing asset) constrains it from competing effectively in chilled foods.

External influences

- *Competition is usually the main constraint outside the firm's control.* It is the factor that prevents *The Sun* from charging 50p a copy. It is also the factor that makes it so hard to plan ahead in business. You may set the objective of gaining an extra 1% market share, only to be hit by a price war launched by a rival.

- *Consumer taste is also important.* If fashion moves against you, there may be little or nothing you can do to stop it. A logical approach is to anticipate the problem by never seeking fashionability. In 2002/04 no clothing business was hotter than French Connection, with its powerful FCUK logo. When this joke wore thin, though, sales collapsed as customers steered clear of yesterday's brand.

- *The economy can also cause huge problems when setting medium- to long-term objectives.* This year's economic boom becomes next year's recession. Sales targets have to be discarded and a move upmarket comes to seem very foolish.

62.6 Marketing decision making: the marketing model

Successful marketing is not just about thinking. It is about decisions and action. Marketing decisions are particularly hard to make, because there are so many uncertainties. The procedure shown in Figure 62.2 is one of the most effective ways of ensuring a decision is well thought through.

Figure 62.2 Marketing decision-making

The intention is to ensure that the strategy decided upon is the most effective at achieving the marketing objectives. In this process, market research is likely to be very important. It is crucial for finding out the background data and again for testing the hypotheses. Test marketing may also be used. This is a way of checking whether the market research results are accurate, before finally committing the firm to an expensive national marketing campaign.

The **marketing model** is the way to decide how to turn a marketing objective into a strategy.

Key terms

Constraints: factors that limit a firm's ability to achieve its objectives.

Marketing model: a procedure for making marketing decisions in a scientific manner.

Marketing targets: specific, measurable goals to be achieved within a relatively limited timescale.

Vision: conceiving where the business wants to be in the future; the term implies something ambitious.

Issues For Analysis

● Marketing objectives are the basis for all marketing strategy. Therefore they will be central to almost every substantial exam question on marketing. For example, pricing decisions will depend upon the objectives. A firm pursuing growth might price a new product relatively cheaply, to ensure high market share and to discourage competition. Objectives will also affect the advertising approach: aimed at encouraging loyalty from existing users, or developing a new image/customer base.

● To understand objectives fully, it is vital to be able to distinguish them from strategy. It is also important to remember that the setting of objectives cannot be done in isolation. The managers have to bear in mind the market situation, findings from market research, and the financial resources and personnel the firm has available. Coca-Cola's objective of moving into the UK water market foundered when it launched Dasani bottled water in 2004. On paper the objective may have looked fine, but in practice it became a classic marketing failure.

62.7 Understanding marketing objectives
an evaluation

What career are you aiming for? If you have a definite answer to that question, you probably have a clear idea how to achieve it. You are also likely to be very well motivated towards the qualifications you need. Most A-level students have little idea of what they want to do. In other words, they have no objectives. As a result, they have no plan and may struggle to find the motivation to succeed at A-levels.

Marketing objectives are just as important. They allow a clear strategy to be devised, a plan to be set, and give the motivation to succeed. Therefore they are the single most important element of marketing.

Further reading

Davidson, H. (1997) *Even More Offensive Marketing.* Penguin.

Exercises

A. Revision questions

(45 marks; 45 minutes)

1 Explain why it is important for a business to have clear marketing objectives. (3)

2 What do businesses mean by the term 'vision'? (3)

3 Why is it important that marketing objectives should be rooted in thorough market research? (4)

4a State the four main types of marketing objective. (4)

4b Briefly explain which objective is most likely to be important for **one** of the following:
(a) Coca-Cola
(b) Bebo
(c) Subway. (3)

5 Why might a firm seek to increase the product differentiation of one of its brands? (3)

6 What problems might a firm face if it focuses solely upon short-term objectives? (5)

7 Is it essential that marketing objectives should be written down in detail? Explain your answer. (4)

8 Explain the meaning of the following terms:
(a) internal influences (3)
(b) external influences. (3)

9 Outline two external constraints that might affect car sales over the coming months. (4)

10 Identify and explain two problems a firm might face if it makes marketing decisions without using a decision-making framework such as the marketing model. (6)

B. Revision exercises

B1 Data response

Beanz meanz roublz?

Figure 62.3 Heinz Baked Beans
Source: Google images

In Spring 1997 Heinz made its first move into the Russian food market. Although the economy was growing at that time, average wage levels were still very low – typically under £25 per week. Yet Heinz chose to price its Baked Beans at around 50p per can – the equivalent of charging £5 in Britain.

Heinz had set its sights on the long-term objective of building a prestigious brand name. When the famous beans first came to Britain in 1901 they were sold by Fortnum & Mason for £1.50 per can. Now Heinz was aiming to pull off the same trick again – nearly 100 years later.

Its target sales figure for year 1 was 12 million cans in Russia. This compared with 450 million cans in the UK each year. If the company's strategy was successful, Heinz Beans might become trendy among Russia's growing middle classes. Even before the move by Heinz, its products were available on the black market, gaining it the status accorded to other western products such as Coca-Cola and Levi's.

Soon after launching in Russia, in August 1998, there was a virtual meltdown of the Russian economy that cut living standards sharply. To its credit, Heinz withstood this external constraint and persisted in this new market. By 2007 the Heinz annual report singled out Russia as one of its fastest-growing markets and one of its most profitable. Will beanz mean more and more roublz? That remainz to be seen.

Questions

(30 marks; 35 minutes)

1 Identify Heinz's marketing objective for its beans in Russia. (3)

2 State the target Heinz set as the test of whether its objective was met. (3)

3a Explain the strategy Heinz chose to meet its objectives. (4)

3b Suggest and explain an alternative strategy it might have adopted. (6)

4a Outline the external constraints faced by Heinz. (5)

4b Discuss how a business might react to changed external constraints, if it was determined to achieve its marketing objectives. (9)

B2 Case study

Hoshil and Sunil's business started in rather dubious circumstances. While students they built up their capital by trading in 'second-hand' mobile phones. Now they were planning to open a nightclub aimed at young Asians. It would have two dance floors, one for Indian music and one for western pop music. One of the bars would be alcohol-free, have pool tables and music soft enough to allow people to chat. It would still be a nightclub, but with some of the benefits of a pub. The vision was clear: to provide a thriving social facility for young Asian men and women.

The investment outlay would be £150,000. Hoshil and Sunil put in £25,000 each and were fortunate that Hoshil's wealthy brother Satyam was able to put in the other £100,000. They would soon be ready to start.

Sunil and Satyam sat down to plan their marketing strategy. The objective was to maximise takings from day one – they needed to pay back their borrowings as soon as possible. After carrying out market research at their local community centre, the boys decided to focus on better-off 16–24 year olds. Prices would be kept relatively high, as there was no competition in the area. The location would be in the centre of Croydon, as the Tramlink service would bring people by public transport from a long way away.

Despite the agreement to focus on the better-off, when there was only a week until the opening night, Sunil panicked. Would there be enough people to create a good atmosphere? He printed 2000 leaflets saying 'Half Price Drinks For All The First Week!' and distributed them through the local newsagents. The opening night went very well and on the following Saturday it was impossible to move. By the second week, though, the numbers were dropping away. When research was carried out it showed that customers thought the drinks were expensive.

It took about six months to establish a really strong reputation as a top club. Large profits were being made and Hoshil's skills as a host were becoming well known. The national paper, the *Daily Jang*, ran a whole feature on him. He was very happy, while Sunil and Satyam were enjoying the large dividends on their investments.

Questions

(50 marks; 60 minutes)

1 Outline the business importance of the following terms.

(a) marketing strategy (5)

(b) market research (5)

2 How important to the success of the club was the clear vision and objectives? Explain your answer. (10)

3 Examine which of the four types of marketing objective were involved in this business success. (8)

4 How serious a risk did Sunil take by carrying out a marketing campaign that was at odds with the overall strategy? (10)

5 What do you consider to be the most important aspects of marketing for a small business? (12)

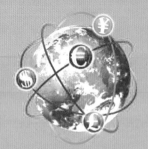
DEFINITION

When businesses refer to the market for their products, they mean the customers: how many there are, whether the number is rising or falling, what their purchasing habits are, and much else. Successful marketing relies on a complete understanding of 'the market'.

63.1 What market are we in?

This sounds a daft question, but the marketing guru Theodore Levitt considers it vital. Is Liverpool FC in the football business, the sports business or the leisure business? Tottenham Hotspur nearly went into liquidation in the 1980s because of an unsuccessful diversification towards leisure clothing. The management thought it was in the leisure business, but its skills and the club's reputation stretched no further than football.

Long ago, Nintendo was Japan's number one producer of playing cards. It decided that its market was the broader games business and experimented with electronic games in the 1970s. Today it is a fabulously profitable producer of games consoles and software (its 2007 profit of £1 billion was more than that of the massive Sony Corporation). Sales of playing cards represent less than 1% of the modern Nintendo.

So Tottenham and Nintendo asked themselves the same question, came up with the same answer, but Nintendo made it work while Spurs flopped. Market analysis is never easy.

63.2 The purpose of market analysis

Managers tend to get caught up in the day-to-day needs of the business. A photo of Keira Knightley wearing a silk scarf might make sales leap ahead, forcing clothes store managers to focus 100% on how to find extra stocks of scarves. Market analysis should be a cooler, more thoughtful look at the market's longer-term trends. In 2006 Dixons Stores Group made the brave decision to rename the shops Currys.digital and to emphasise that online sales were as welcome as sales through the shops. The company had looked ahead and seen the huge threat from the internet. It acted sensibly to prevent the whole business from sliding back in future years.

Other clever pieces of market analysis include:

● Tesco spotting the opportunities in Hungary and Poland before other western retailers

● Danone seeing the opportunity for 'functional foods' (i.e. foods bought because they are believed to be good for you), such as Activia yoghurt, then putting more money behind its brands than anyone else; it showed huge confidence in its understanding of the market

Figure 63.1 A Nintendo games console

Harvey Nichols (classic London posh shop) seeing the opportunity for a branch in Leeds, in an era when there was plenty of money in the north; when it made the move, other retailers doubted whether Leeds would be posh enough – it was and it is.

All these examples have one thing in common: they are the result of careful analysis of trends within a market, backed by an ability to take bold decisions (and get them right).

63.3 Consumer usage and attitudes

Market analysis is rooted in a deep understanding of customers. Why do they buy Coca-Cola, not Pepsi? Yet they prefer Tropicana (made by Pepsi) to Minute Maid (made by Coke). And who are the key decision makers? Purchasers (perhaps parents buying a multipack in Tesco) or the users (perhaps young teenage children slumped in front of the television)? Is the brand decision a result of child pester power, or parental belief in the product's superiority? Knowledge of such subtleties is essential. Only then can the firm know whether to focus marketing effort on the parent or the child.

To acquire the necessary knowledge about usage and attitudes, firms adopt several approaches. The starting point is usually qualitative research such as group discussions. Run by psychologists, these informal discussions help pinpoint consumers' underlying motives and behaviour. For example, it is important to learn whether KitKat buyers enjoy nibbling the chocolate before eating the wafer biscuit – in other words, to discover whether playing with confectionery is an important part of the enjoyment. This type of information can influence future product development.

The major multinational Unilever has appointed a Head of Knowledge Management and Development (David Smith) to ensure that insights such as this can be spread around the business. As he says, 'The company's collective knowledge is potentially a great competitive advantage.' By encouraging improved communication and networking, Unilever believes it is benefiting from:

- improved decision making
- fewer mistakes
- reduced duplication
- converting new knowledge more quickly into added value to the business.

Among the other ways to gather information on customer usage and attitudes are quantitative research and obtaining feedback from staff who deal directly with customers. An example of the latter would be bank staff whose task is to sell services such as insurance. Customer doubts about a brochure or a product feature, if fed back to head office, might lead to important improvements.

Quantitative research is also used to monitor customer usage and attitudes. Many firms conduct surveys every month, to track any changes over time in brand awareness or image. This procedure may reveal that a TV commercial has had an unintended side-effect in making the brand image rather too upmarket, or that customers within a market are becoming more concerned about whether the packaging can be recycled.

63.4 Consumer profiles

Marketing decisions are very hard to make without a clear picture of your customers. Who are they? Young? Outgoing? Affluent? Or not. From product and packaging design, through to pricing, promotion and distribution – all these aspects of marketing hinge on knowing your **target market**.

A consumer profile is a statistical breakdown of the people who buy a particular product or brand (e.g. what percentage of consumers are women aged 16–25)? The main categories analysed within a consumer profile are customers' age, gender, social class, income level and region. Profile information is used mainly for:

- setting quotas for research surveys
- segmenting a market
- deciding in which media to advertise (*Vogue* or *The Sun*?).

A large consumer goods firm will make sure to obtain a profile of consumers throughout the market as well as for its own brand(s). This may be very revealing. It may show that the age profile of its own customers is becoming older than for the market as a whole. This may force a complete rethink of the marketing strategy. The company may have been trying to give the brand a classier image, but may end up attracting older customers.

63.5 Market mapping

Having analysed consumer attitudes and consumer profiles, it is possible to create a market map. This is done by selecting the key variables that differentiate the

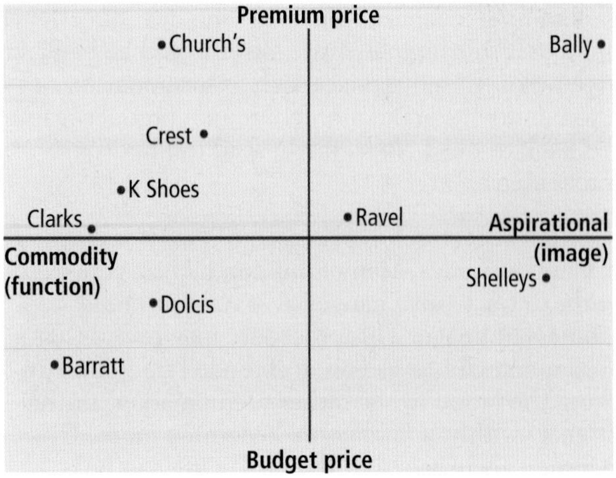

Figure 63.2 Market mapping
Source: author's estimates

brands within a market, then plotting the position of each one. Usually this is done on a two-dimensional diagram as in Figure 63.2. Here, the image of shoe shops has been plotted against the key criteria of price (premium–budget) and purpose (aspirational–commodity). For example, Bally shoes are expensive and are bought to impress others. Church's are expensive but bought because their buyers believe they are a top-quality product.

Market mapping enables a firm to identify any gaps or niches in the market that are unfilled. They also help monitor existing brands in a process known as **product positioning**. Is their image becoming too young and trendy? If so, booming sales in the short term might be followed by longer-term disappointment. By monitoring

A-grade application

The Dualit toaster

Founded in 1945, Dualit built up a reputation for its toasters and kettles. Fierce competition from multinational electrical goods firms in the 1960s and 1970s forced it out of the consumer market. Instead of giving up, the company redesigned its products to aim for the catering trade. Dualit stainless steel, extra-durable toasters became the norm in cafés and hotel kitchens. Dualit's founder has explained that: 'I spotted a gap in the market and started to cater for the smaller demand in what was a niche area.' Remarkably, the elegant and robust design of the Dualit toaster has made it fashionable again in the past ten years. Today Dualit makes DAB digital radios as well as a host of kitchen appliances, including a special edition Marmite toaster – in 'Marmite colours, for those who love the stuff'.

Source: various, including www.dualit.com

the position of their brands on the market map, firms can see more easily when a repositioning exercise is required. This may involve a relaunch with a slightly different product, a new pack design and a new advertising campaign.

Issues For Analysis

Among the main issues raised by this chapter are the following.

● The importance to a firm of constantly measuring and rethinking its position in the market: this is why expenditure on market research needs to be regular; not just related to the latest new project.

● Given the importance of market knowledge, how can new firms break into a market? The answer is: with difficulty. Super-rich Microsoft launched Xbox in Britain in 2002, having to compete with the established Nintendo and Sony consoles. By 2008, despite the higher market share achieved by the Xbox 360, Microsoft was still many $billions down on the Xbox experience.

● If all companies follow similar techniques for market analysis, why don't they all come up with the same answers? Fortunately, there remains huge scope for initiative and intuition. Two different managers reading the same market research report may come up with quite different conclusions. The Apple iPod was the inspiration of just a few people at Apple and its suppliers. The Wii was also a very individual achievement by a select few at Nintendo.

63.6 Analysing the market
an evaluation

Market analysis is at the heart of successful marketing. All the great marketing decisions are rooted in a deep understanding of what customers really want – from the marketing of the Spice Girls through to the sustained success of the (incredibly pricey) Chanel No. 5 perfume. These successes were rooted in an understanding of the consumer. The clever market stall trader acquires this understanding through daily contact with customers. Large companies need the help of market research to provide a comparable feel. Techniques such as market mapping then help clarify the picture.

Having learnt what the customer really wants from a product, perhaps helped by psychological insights from qualitative research, it is relatively easy to put the strategy into practice. If the marketing insight is powerful enough, the practical details of the marketing mix should not matter too much. The Nintendo Wii was a brilliant piece of marketing, but few commentators had anything good to say about the brand's advertising or packaging. The genius came earlier in the process.

> ## Key terms
>
> **Product positioning:** deciding on the image and target market you want for your own product or brand.
>
> **Target market:** the type of customer your product or service is aimed at. For example the target market for Cherry Coke is 10–16 year olds of both sexes.

Exercises

A. Revision questions

(35 marks; 35 minutes)

1 Re-read Section 63.1 and ask yourself 'What if Nintendo had not decided to define its market more widely? What would the business be like today?' (3)

2 Explain why Tesco's market analysis in Hungary and Poland can be described as 'clever'. (3)

3 Explain two reasons why it might be important to distinguish 'purchasers' from 'users'. (4)

4 Explain how qualitative research could be used helpfully when analysing a market. (4)

5 When *Look* magazine was launched in 2007 it announced that its target market was '24-year-old women'. Explain two ways it could make use of this very precise consumer profile. (4)

6 Explain how market mapping might be helpful to *two* of the following:
   (a) an entrepreneur looking at opening up a new driving school
   (b) the brand manager of Werther's Original sweets, worried about falling market share
   (c) a private school thinking of opening its first branch in China. (8)

7 Why does market research need to be carried out regularly, not just related to a new product? (3)

8 Explain the importance of market research in achieving effective market analysis. (6)

B. Revision exercises

B1 Data response

What business is Cadbury in? For the first 100 years of the firm's life, the answer would have been chocolate. But in 1989 it bought the Trebor and Bassetts brands, to form a large sugar confectionery unit. With Wrigley enjoying uninterrupted growth in chewing gum, Cadbury then bought Adams – a major US gum producer (for £2.7 billion). It followed this up with purchases of other chewing gum producers, in countries such as Turkey.

In 2007, Cadbury launched the Trident gum brand in Britain. This was bold because Wrigley enjoyed a market share of more than 90% in the UK. By March 2008 Cadbury was able to announce that 'an astounding £38 million of extra sales value has been added to the gum category, with 75% of this growth delivered by Trident'. Research showed that 2 million customers were buying chewing gum in 2007 for the first time. Wrigley replied by saying that 'Wrigley currently has an 88.6% share of [the £278 million gum market] . . . while our nearest competitor accounts for just 7.6%.'

UK confectionery market 2007

Chocolate	£2750m
Sugar confectionery	£1470m
Chewing gum	£280m
Total market	£4500m

Questions

(30 marks; 35 minutes)

1 Explain why companies such as Cadbury need to ask themselves, 'What market am I in?' (6)

2a What is meant by the term 'market share'? (2)

2b Why might Cadbury have been worried about tackling a business with 'a market share of more than 90%'? (5)

3 How might Cadbury have used effective product positioning to enable the Trident launch to attract 2 million new customers to the chewing gum market? (5)

4a Calculate the sales achieved by Trident in 2007, its launch year. (3)

4b Discuss whether Cadbury or Wrigley should feel the more pleased about its position in the 2007 market for chewing gum. (9)

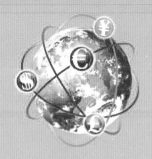

Unit 64 Measuring and forecasting trends

DEFINITION

Forecasting involves estimating future consumer tastes, actions and behaviour.

64.1 Introduction

It is very important for managers to look ahead. They need to think about what is likely to happen in their industry and prepare accordingly in all areas of the business. One of the most important forecasts that needs to be made is the **sales forecast**. This forms the basis of most of the other plans within the organisation. For example:

- the human resource plan will need to be based on the expected level of sales; a growth in sales may require more staff

- the cash flow forecast will depend on projected sales and the payment period

- the profit and loss forecasts will depend on the level of revenue predicted

- the production scheduling will depend on what output is required

- stock levels will depend on the likely production and demand over a period.

The sales forecast therefore drives many of the other plans within the business and is an essential element of effective management planning.

When a business starts up, it is extremely difficult to interpret its sales data. An ice cream parlour that starts up in April may find that sales double in May, again in June and again in July. Excited by the business success the entrepreneurs may rush to open a second outlet. Yet a wet August may see sales knocked back followed by a sales slump in the autumn. The business may be overstretched and in liquidation by February.

As long as a business can survive the first year or two, managers can start to interpret its sales data. Above all else, managers want to understand the **trend** in product sales and compare it to trends in the market as a whole.

64.2 Moving averages

A useful way to show trends is by using a moving average. This is helpful in two main circumstances:

1. where there are strong seasonal influences on sales, such as in the ice cream parlour example

2. when sales are erratic for no obvious reason; wild ups and downs may make it hard to see the underlying situation.

The first column in Table 64.1 shows the 'raw data' for a small supermarket (i.e. monthly sales figures). As you can see, they jump around, forming no obvious pattern.

Table 64.1 Example of a moving average

	Raw data (monthly sales) £	Centred three-month total £	Centred three-month average £
Jan.	48,000		
Feb.	57,000		52,000
March	51,000	156,000	49,000
April	39,000	147,000	47,700
May	53,000	143,000	46,300
June	47,000	138,000	45,300
July	36,000	136,000	44,700
Aug.	51,000	134,000	

To find the moving average of the data:

● the first step is to calculate a moving total, in this case a three-month total – in other words, the January–March figures are totalled, then the February–April figures, and so on.

● the third column shows the centred average (i.e. the January–March total of 156,000 is divided by 3 to make 52,000); this monthly average sales figure for January–March is centred to February, because that is the 'average' of January–March.

Note how well the three-month moving average clarifies the data, revealing the (awful) underlying trend. The graph (Figure 64.1) simply plots column 1 and column 3 to show the value of the technique.

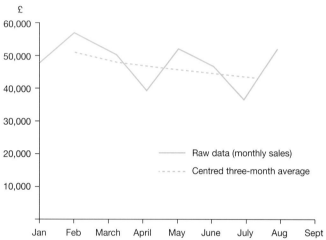

Figure 64.1 How moving averages reveal underlying trends

64.3 Forecasting sales using extrapolation

The simplest way of predicting the future is to assume it will be just like the past. For the immediate future this may be realistic. It is unlikely (though not impossible) that the economy or demand will change dramatically tomorrow – an assumption that the pattern of sales will continue to follow recent trends may therefore be reasonable. If demand for your product has been rising over the past few months it may not be illogical to assume it will continue in the foreseeable future. The process of predicting based on what has happened before is known as extrapolation. Extrapolation can often be done by drawing a line by eye to extend the trend on a graph (see Figure 64.2).

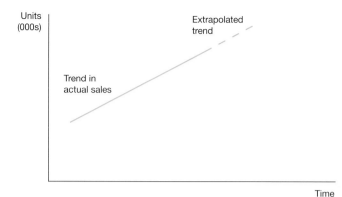

Figure 64.2 An extrapolated sales trend

Here a very steady upward trend over a long period may well continue and be predicted to continue. However, such stability and predictability are rare. The values of data plotted over time, called time-series analysis, can vary because of **seasonal variations**/influences and also because of genuinely random factors, which can never be predicted. For example, another outbreak of foot and mouth disease would lead to a sudden collapse in the sales of meat. Or a revaluation of the Chinese currency might lead to a huge wave of new tourists coming to London (1300 million?). Despite the uncertainties, predicting sales based on extrapolated trends is the most widely used method.

As with every business technique, there is also a need for judgement. Look at Figure 64.3. Based upon the

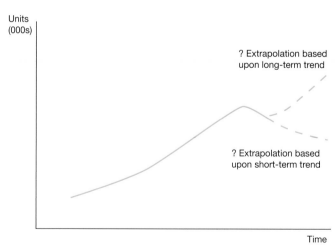

Figure 64.3 Requirement for judgement when extrapolating trends

longer-term trend, you might believe that the recent downturn is temporary (as with UK house prices, perhaps). Or it might be that you believe that the recent figures have established the likely trend for the future. It is never wise to simply use a calculator, a computer or graph paper without thinking carefully about what makes the most sense.

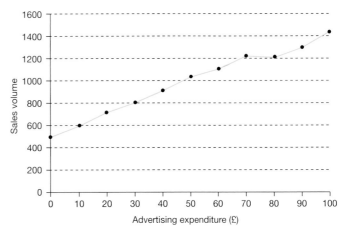

Figure 64.4 *Strong positive correlation between advertising expenditure and sales*

A-grade application

Sales Forecasting Manager
Fast-moving consumer goods industry (fmcg)

Location: Merseyside
Salary: £35,000–£40,000

We require a Sales Forecasting Manager for a large fmcg business. Reporting to the Supply Chain Manager, you will be responsible for producing sales forecasts, monitoring performance and detecting any deviations from plan to evaluate and make corrective action in order to drive and maintain high performance levels.

Who we're looking for:
We require someone with an excellent forecasting background who has the proven ability to monitor actual targets against forecasts and to take action when needed. As Forecasting Manager you will have a proven background and ability to improve accuracy to required standards. You must also possess excellent communication skills, excellent IT skills, be able to work as part of a team and also able to use your own initiative.

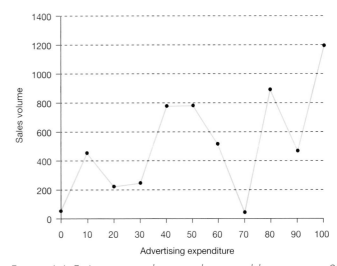

Figure 64.5 *Loose correlation: other variables important?*

64.4 Correlation

Businesses are always keen to learn about the effect on sales of marketing strategies such as TV advertising, sales promotion or direct mailshots. Often researchers will compare sales volume and advertising expenditure. A good way to do this is on a graph. In Figure 64.4 there is clearly a strong relationship, or correlation, between the two. The correlation is positive: as one increases so does the other. It is important to realise that each point correlating the two variables represents one observation covering a period of time.

In Figure 64.5, however, there is not so much linkage as the diagram is little more than a collection of randomly dispersed points on the diagram. In this case there is low correlation between advertising and sales, suggesting that the firm should stop wasting its money until it has

found a way to make its advertising work more effectively.

What the researcher is looking for is cause and effect, namely evidence that the advertising has caused the increase in sales. Now correlation by itself does not indicate cause and effect. The rising of the sun in the morning may be strongly correlated with the delivery time of newspapers to letterboxes but it does not cause them to be delivered. Strong correlation is evidence that cause and effect *may* be present. Further evidence is needed to know how the variables are affecting each other. Clearly, the purpose of advertising is to generate sales, so it is highly likely that cause and effect may be at work. But managers know there are many variables at work all the time in markets. The sales of a product could rise because of cheaper credit terms, the disappearance of a competitor, or even unusual weather, and not just advertising. In cases like that presented in Figure 64.5, where there is weak correlation, researchers clearly should be considering other variables as well as advertising.

A-grade application

Correlation

The government-owned Met Office offers businesses a service, charging a fee for predicting the sales of products ranging from lemonade to cat food. It uses correlation analysis to predict how demand will vary according to the time of year and the prevailing weather. It has found that lemonade sales rise in the summer, but tail away if the weather is very hot (presumably consumers switch to non-fizzy drinks or to ice lollies). More surprisingly, cat food is weather-affected. Rainy days boost demand (the cats don't go out) while, if it's hot, cats eat less.

In March 2008 the website www.metoffice.gov.uk featured a producer of hot ready meals that used the Met Office's correlation software to find out that it lost £70,000 of sales for every 1 degree of temperature increase above 20°C. Needless to say, using a weather forecast could enable the business to forecast sales more accurately, and therefore reduce stock losses on its perishable goods.

64.5 Alternative methods of forecasting

The moving averages technique of forecasting has some limitations. The points calculated for the trend will always be less than the number of points in the actual raw data. This technique is most appropriate in stable circumstances when elements of the business environment, such as competition, are not expected to change very much. It is less useful in periods of change or instability.

Test markets

If a market or industry is undergoing major change or if you do not have past data to help you forecast sales then you may need to make use of experts' opinions or market research. By testing a product out in a small representative market, for example, you may be able to gather data from which you can estimate sales when you roll out the product on a bigger scale. Alternatively, you might ask experts who know the industry well to help you estimate likely sales.

The Delphi technique

One method of gathering expert opinion is known as the Delphi technique. This involves using experts who are asked for their opinions individually. Their comments are then summarised anonymously and circulated to the contributors, who are then invited to comment again in the light of the previous feedback. Each time the findings are circulated for a given number of times, or until a consensus is reached.

Scenario planning

Some businesses also use scenario planning. This process involves an analysis of particular scenarios in the future. Rather than simply estimating sales, for example, experts try to anticipate what market conditions will be and what will be happening in the market as a whole. For example, a business might try to consider the market in a position of fast growth or steady growth, and the impact of this on a range of business decisions.

The oil giant Shell is known for its use of scenario planning. For example, it will consider what the year 2015 might be like if oil prices had risen to $250 per barrel, or fallen to $50.

64.6 Other variables to consider when forecasting

When considering your sales forecast you will want to take into account any internal or external changes that you know are about to happen. External changes could include:

- new entrants into the market
- population changes
- climate changes or changes in weather conditions
- legal changes (e.g. limiting particular forms of promotion or increasing taxation)
- internal factors that you know may affect sales; this could include changes in the salesforce, changes in

the amount of spending on promotion or the way that the money is being spent, or the launch of a new product.

In most cases the actual sales forecast will not be absolutely accurate. However, this does not make forecasting a waste of time – as long as it can provide an estimate that is approximately correct it will have helped the firm plan its staffing, funding and production. Better to plan and be approximately right than not plan at all and be unprepared. However, it is always important to review your sales forecasts and compare this with what actually happened; this can help the firm to improve its forecasting techniques and provide better estimates in the future.

A-grade application
Retail sales in China

In 2007, retail sales in China were growing at a rate 15.5% faster than the official forecast. The growth in sales was boosted by the expanding Chinese middle classes, who have greater disposable income. Government initiatives to encourage spending by lowering taxes, especially in rural areas, have also increased spending. Annual sales of building and decoration materials were increasing by 31.5%, while annual sales of jewellery were increasing by 30.8%.

Issues For Analysis

- Forecasting is an important element of business planning.

- The sales forecast forms the foundation of many other of the business plans, such as cash flow and workforce planning.

- Sales forecasts are often based on past data, but must also take into account seasonal factors and changes in internal or external factors that are known about.

64.7 Measuring and forecasting trends
an evaluation

Sales forecasts can be very important to a business because so many other plans rely on them. They can determine how many people to employ, how much to produce and the likely dividends for investors. They may not always be accurate, but they can provide important guidelines for planning.

A badly run business will find itself in a crisis because its precisely forecast future turns out to be surprisingly different in reality. An intelligent manager tries hard to predict with precision, but thinks about the effect of sales being unexpectedly high or low. Nothing demoralises staff more than a sudden lurch by management (hiring one minute, firing the next). So the future needs thinking through carefully.

Key terms

Sales forecast: a method of predicting future sales using statistical methods.

Seasonal variation: change in the value of a variable (e.g. sales) that is related to the seasons.

Trend: the general path a series of values (e.g. sales) follows over time, disregarding variations or random fluctuations.

Exercises

A. Revision questions

(35 marks; 35 minutes)

1 What is a sales forecast? (2)

2 Explain how you can show the trend in a series of data. (4)

3 Explain how two of the following Heinz managers could be helped by two weeks' warning that sales are forecast to rise by 15%:
 (a) the operations manager
 (b) the marketing manager, Heinz Beans
 (c) the personnel manager
 (d) the chief accountant. (8)

4 What do you understanding by the term 'extrapolation'? How is it used to make a sales forecast? (5)

5 Explain how Coca-Cola might be helped by checking for correlations between the following factors:
 (a) sales and the daily temperature
 (b) staff absence levels and the leadership style of individual supervisors. (6)

6 Explain why it is risky to assume cause and effect when looking at factors that are correlated. (4)

7 What is the Delphi technique? (2)

8 Explain briefly how the 2012 Olympic Committee might make use of scenario planning ? (4)

B. Revision exercises

B1 Data response

The US aircraft manufacturer, Boeing, has predicted an increase in demand from airlines for smaller aircraft, but large jumbo jet sales are expected to be lower than expected over the next 20 years. Boeing raised its projected sales of commercial jets by all manufacturers by $200 billion to $2.8 trillion (£1.4 trillion) in the next two decades. Regional, single-aisle and twin-aisle jets for non-stop routes would prove more popular than expected, it said. However, it

reduced its forecast for jumbos carrying more than 400 people. Boeing now expects that the market will buy 960 of the bigger craft, down from the 990 it set out in last year's forecast.

20-year industry forecast:

- 17,650 single-aisle aeroplanes seating 90–240 passengers
- 6290 twin-aisle jets seating 200–400 passengers
- 3700 regional jets with no more than 90 seats, up from 3450 forecast last year
- 960 jumbo jets seating more than 400 passengers.

According to Boeing, passenger numbers would rise about 5% a year, while cargo traffic would increase 6.1%. Emerging markets are crucial for future sales, with about one-third of the demand coming from the Asia-Pacific region.

Boeing believes its success is secure thanks to its relatively small 787 plane. It believes this will take sales from its rival Airbus. Twin-engined but with a long range, it will be able to fly direct to far more of the world's airports. This means that passengers will not need to make a connecting flight first to travel long distance.

Questions

(30 marks; 35 minutes)

1 Analyse the ways in which Boeing might have produced its industry sales forecasts. (10)

2 Discuss the possible consequences for Boeing of the findings of its research. (20)

C. Essay questions

(40 marks each)

1 'Since we can never know the future, it is pointless trying to forecast it.' Discuss.

2 'Quantitative sales forecasting techniques have only limited use. Qualitative judgements are needed in a constantly changing world.' Evaluate this statement.

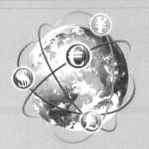

SELECTING MARKETING STRATEGIES

DEFINITION

Marketing strategies are carefully evaluated plans for future marketing activity that balance company objectives, available resources and market opportunities.

65.1 What are the keys to a successful marketing strategy?

A strategy is the plan of the medium-to-long term actions required to achieve the company goals or targets. Selecting the best marketing strategy means finding a fit between the company objectives, customer requirements and the activities of competitors.

The aim of this planning is to shape the company's activities and products to generate the best returns for the business. Marketing strategy is about adding value. It takes advantage of any unique selling points. It helps the business to identify the right mix between design, function, image and service.

Strategy is about the future

The term 'strategy' implies looking to the future. It is important not to look at what is working well now but at what future prospects are. Toyota recognised that there was a growing interest in environmental issues. It started to invest in the production of hybrid cars. Although requiring significant investment with no sure return, Toyota executives felt that this was the way forward. The move was highly successful, with demand for the Prius surprising everyone by outstripping supply.

Strategy must be achievable

Strategy is concerned with what is possible, not just desirable. It must take into account market potential and company resources. The company needs to recognise its own limitations and potential. It also needs

to consider economic and social circumstances. If the world economy is weakening, firms will be much more cautious about entering new export markets. If the home market is stagnating, businesses may well concentrate on lower-priced 'value' products.

Strategy is company specific

Each company will have a different marketing strategy. The strategy selected will reflect the individual circumstances of the business. Different companies within the same industry may be pursuing different goals. The strategies that they select will reflect those different goals. Within the same industry, one company may be aiming to increase market share while another looks for cost reductions in order to compete on price. The tyre industry is a good example of this. The market leaders were faced with increasing price competition from developing countries. They had to develop new marketing strategies. Their responses differed: Goodyear reduced costs; Michelin put its effort into innovation and widened its product range; Pirelli decided to concentrate on the market for luxury and speed.

Marketing strategy is the marketing plan of action that:

- contributes to the achievement of company objectives
- finds the best fit between company objectives, available resources and market possibilities
- looks to the future
- is carefully thought out
- is realistic
- sets out exactly what marketing activities will be carried out, and when.

A-grade application
Travel with a smile

The travel company Thomson has been the market leader in the UK for many years but it has now been forced to adapt. The business has been forced to change its strategy as it has been hit by several changes in the marketplace. These include the following:

- The growth of the internet, which has allowed:
  - the rise of online travel businesses, such as Expedia.co.uk and Lastminute.com
  - the customer to book flights, hotels and so on direct.
- The growth of low-cost airlines.

In 2006, the company ran a campaign with the slogan 'Web prices on the high street'. This was the beginning of its shift from the traditional discounted package tour operator to its flexible online and high-street holiday shops. In September 2007, it launched the second phase of its campaign to reposition the brand away from its traditional 'package holiday' image. The campaign aims to reinforce that the company now offers customers the flexibility to book separate products such as flights, hotels and car hire, as well as promoting its modern and upmarket approach with products such as its Premier Collection of hotels.

Thomson's advertising manager Zoe Dark said: 'Consumers have changed with the onset of the internet, so we have also had to move with the times and offer what they expect: a wider range of services.' Analysts think that if Thomson can combine the personal service of a tour operator with the ease and flexibility offered by online booking then it should be able to successfully reposition itself.

Failure to make this strategy work will raise questions about the long-term survival of the business.

65.2 Strategy versus tactics

Strategy is not the same as tactics (see Table 65.1). Strategy is an overall plan for the medium to long term. Tactics are individual responses to short-term opportunities or threats. The marketing strategy may be to increase sales by developing a new market segment. One of the tactics used may be to undercut a competitor on price in a price-sensitive segment of the market.

65.3 Types of strategy

A useful way to look at marketing strategy is to follow the approach taken by Igor Ansoff, who developed 'Ansoff's matrix'. Before explaining this approach, it is helpful to look at Ansoff's view of 'strategy'. In his 1965 book *Corporate Strategy*, Ansoff described strategy as a decision of medium- to long-term significance that is made in 'conditions of partial ignorance'. This 'ignorance' stems partly from the timescale involved. If you look three years ahead there are huge risks that

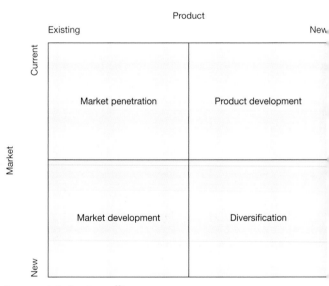

Figure 65.1 Ansoff's matrix

Table 65.1 Strategy vs tactics

Marketing strategies	Marketing tactics
Keep the main message consistent over time (e.g. BMW – 'The ultimate driving machine')	Offer everyone who comes onto the Confused.com website a chance in a £1 million prize draw
Make sure that every message to the consumer shouts low prices – as Ryanair has done consistently for ten years	Run a midweek special – 'All You Can Eat for a Tenner' during the winter months

marketplace changes will make your plans and forecasts look foolish. Such decisions are usually discussed and decided at board level.

Ansoff's matrix (Figure 65.1) is constructed to illustrate the risks involved in strategic decisions. These risks relate to the firm's level of knowledge and certainty about the market, the competition and customer behaviour – both now and in the future. The key issue is that risk becomes ever greater the further a firm strays from its core of existing products/existing customers (i.e. the top left-hand corner of the matrix).

Ansoff identified four types of strategy within his matrix; these are described below.

Market penetration

This is about increasing market share by concentrating on existing products within the existing market. It is the most common and safest strategy because it does not stray from what the company knows best. If Tesco has opened 400 stores in towns all over Britain, and all are profitable, it is a simple matter of market penetration to open store 401 in a good-sized town that has not yet got its first Tesco.

Market penetration opportunities arise by:

- finding new customers – perhaps by widening the product's appeal to attract additional buyers

- taking customers from competitors – this may be achieved by aggressive pricing or by offering additional incentives to the customer

- persuading existing customers to increase usage – many food companies give recipes with their products to suggest additional ways of using the product; shampoo manufacturers introduced a frequent-wash shampoo to boost product usage.

Market development

This is about finding new markets for existing products. It is more risky because the company must step into the unknown. For Cadbury to start selling chocolate in Chile would require a huge effort to learn to understand the Chilean consumer, yet it may still fail because customer psychology is complex and ever-changing.

Market development can be carried out by the following means.

- **Repositioning** the product: this will target a different market segment. This could be done by broadening

the product's appeal to a new customer base. Land Rover's traditional market was farming and military use; it has now repositioned the product to appeal to town dwellers.

- Moving into new markets: many British retailers have opened up outlets abroad. Some, such as Tesco and Laura Ashley, have opened up their own outlets. Others have entered into joint ventures or have taken over a similar operation in another country.

Moving Tesco into Hungary and Poland was a major market development decision taken in the late 1990s. So far it has proved very successful. Yet the hugely successful sandwich chain Pret A Manger hit problems when opening up in New York and Japan. Even the mighty Gordon Ramsay had an embarrassment when he took a London restaurant concept to Glasgow, and it went bust.

Why the difficulty? Surely market research can reveal whether customers in Glasgow want the same things as those in London? Up to a point, perhaps. But the skill with market research is knowing exactly what questions to ask and how to interpret the answers. This requires a degree of market knowledge that cannot always cross county boundaries, let alone national ones. This was why, over 80 years ago, the Ford Motor Company chose to set up a factory and offices in Britain, instead of relying on exporting from America. The rush of US firms that followed (e.g. Heinz, Gillette, General Motors/Vauxhall) was followed much later by Japanese companies such as Sony, Hitachi and Honda. All took huge risks at the start, but believed they would only succeed in the long term by getting a deep understanding of local habits and needs. Famously, Sony budgeted for a 15-year payback period when it started up in Britain.

Product development

Product development means launching new products into your existing market (e.g. L'Oréal launching a new haircare product). Hard though market development can be, it could be argued that product development is even harder. It is generally accepted that only one in five new products succeeds – and that is a figure derived from the large businesses that launch new products through advertising agencies. In other words, despite their huge resources and expertise, heavy spending on R&D and market research, plus huge launch advertising budgets, companies such as Birds Eye, Walls, L'Oréal and McVitie's suffer four flops for every success.

In highly competitive markets, companies use product development to keep one step ahead of the competition. Strategies may include those listed below.

● *Changing an existing product:* this may be to keep the products attractive. Washing powders and shampoos are good examples of this. The manufacturers are continually repackaging or offering some 'essential' new ingredient.

● *Developing new products:* the iPod is a fantastic example of a new and successful product development, taking Apple from the computer business into the music business

Diversification

If it is accepted that market development and product development are both risky, how much more difficult is the ultimate challenge: a new product in a new market, or **diversification** in Ansoff's terminology. This is the ultimate business risk as it forces a business to operate completely outside its range of knowledge and experience. Virgin flopped totally with cosmetics and clothing, WH Smith had a dreadful experience in the DIY market with Do It All, and Heinz had a failed attempt to market a vinegar-based household cleaning product.

Yet diversification is not only the most risky strategy, it can also lead to the most extraordinary business successes. Nintendo was the Japanese equivalent of John Waddington, producing playing cards, until its new, young chief executive decided in the early 1970s to invest in the unknown idea of electronic games. From being a printer of paper cards, Nintendo became a giant of arcade games, then games consoles such as the Wii.

Even Nintendo's diversification success is dwarfed by that of Nokia, which once made car tyres and toilet rolls. Its transformation into the world's number one mobile phone maker would have been remarkable no matter what, but the fact that it came from tiny Finland makes it an incredible success. Ansoff emphasised the risks of diversification, but never intended to suggest that firms should fight shy of those risks. Risks are well worth taking as long as the potential rewards are high enough.

65.4 Marketing strategy in international markets

Entering into international markets carries the extra risk identified by Ansoff as market development. Naturally, the extent of the risk will depend on just how different the new market is from the firm's home country. For Green & Black's to start selling chocolate in France may not be too much of a stretch. French tastes are different

and the distribution systems are very different from those in Britain, but there are many similarities in climate and affluence. But what about selling organic chocolate to Saudi Arabia? Or China? Or Sierra Leone? Figure 65.2 shows the way Ansoff would indicate the increasing level of risk involved.

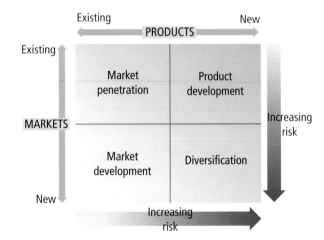

Figure 65.2 Ansoff's matrix

It is also possible that the product will need to be modified in order to be successful in the new market. International markets are littered with products and businesses that tried to shift their existing products and business models into overseas markets but failed. Even the best marketing strategies can fail. Some common causes of failure are:

● language/interpretation problems

● misunderstanding the culture

● mistiming – this can be economic or even political.

All these can be minimised by careful research to ensure that there is a good understanding of the new market before the company attempts to do business.

Some of the most successful ventures into international markets involve working in cooperation with existing firms in local markets.

65.5 Marketing strategy: a continual process

Once the strategy has been developed, it needs to be constantly reviewed. An idea that looks good on paper will not necessarily work in reality. There may need to be some testing of strategies, especially if they are risky. Market research and monitoring are necessary to ensure that the actions are producing the desired results. Evaluation of results will feed back into the system and in turn contribute to the development of revised objectives and strategies. This ongoing cycle is known as the strategic cycle (see Figure 65.3).

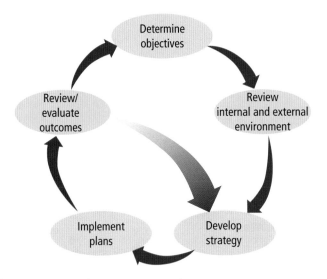

Figure 65.3 The strategic cycle

A company's marketing strategy does not exist in a vacuum. It may provoke responses from competitors. Market opportunities will be changing constantly. If the company is to be successful, it needs to be responsive and to adjust the strategy to cope with any changes in the environment or within the company. For example, the giant Heinz company found that its approach to global marketing was ineffective – it shifted strategy to become more local. Only in Britain were baked beans an important seller, so the baked bean pizza was developed for the UK alone. In Korea, people love to pour ketchup on pizza, so a deal with Pizza Hut put a Heinz bottle on every table.

65.6 Assessing the effectiveness of marketing strategies

An effective marketing strategy achieves the marketing objectives; but is there more to it than that? Could a strategy be too successful? Perhaps yes, as in the case of Magners Cider (see the A-grade application).

More often, the issue will be how to judge a marketing strategy that has under-performed. It may have achieved certain targets, yet failed in the most important: sales.

A-grade application
Magners

In the first half of 2006, sales of Magners were 264% up on the previous year. Hot weather plus the 'over ice' advertising pushed aside the market leader, Bulmers. Magners' management spent £135 million expanding its Irish product site. Yet, one year later, Bulmers was spending as heavily as Magners on TV advertisements promoting the idea of cider and ice, and Magners sales fell by 'high single digits', while its 2007 profits fell by 33%.

When launching a completely new product, companies know that there are four stages consumers must go through before they purchase (known by the acronym **AIDA**):

- *Awareness:* in July 2007 57% of adults had heard of the still-quite-new Moneysupermarket.com; by September awareness had risen to 74%

- *Interest:* 'perhaps I'll have a look at the site'

- *Desire:* this might be conscious – 'If I can find that Kate Moss dress in my size I'm buying it' – or subconscious (i.e. you only realise you wanted that new Malteser chocolate bar when you find you've bought it when buying a magazine)

- *Action:* the actual moment of purchase; though it is important to remember that, for the advertiser, that is only the start; few products survive on single sales; success comes from repeat purchase and brand loyalty.

To assess the effectiveness of the marketing, it is sensible to measure performance at each of these stages. High brand awareness is useless if the brand image is too poor to create interest and then desire (at the time of writing, the Glade Flameless Candle has achieved this doubtful honour in the author's household). The single most important factor, however, is the 'conversion rate' from product trial to product loyalty. If that figure is low, the game is up and the marketing strategy has failed.

Possible reasons for a marketing strategy that fails to meet its sales objectives are:

- the objectives may have been unrealistic

● the budget (the total amount available to spend on the strategy) may have proved inadequate for the task

● competitors may have reacted unexpectedly fiercely to your launch, making it very difficult to succeed – for example when Rupert Murdoch launched the free *thelondonpaper*, the owners of the 50p *Evening Standard* launched the free *London Lite* to stop Murdoch's paper taking a grip on the capital; this fierce response will cost both companies tens of millions before one gives way

● one element of the mix may have proved a disappointment (e.g. promised media coverage (PR) never quite happened, or the distribution levels were lower than planned, or the advertising never had the impact that everyone expected).

As is clear, several of these are to do with poor performance by one or more members of the marketing team, but some are out of the company's control.

Issues For Analysis

Issues that may need to be considered in response to case study or essay questions are:

● the relative importance of strategic market planning in different types of business – can small firms possibly devote the time, thought and resources to strategy that would be spent by firms such as Heinz?

● the added risk and uncertainty of moving into international markets – firms need to ensure that the market is thoroughly researched; this can be difficult for all firms, but particularly for smaller enterprises

● the extent to which it is possible to develop clear strategies in a constantly changing marketplace

● the influence of individuals may be important – the degree of risk in a firm's strategy may depend partly on the personality of the key decision maker; an entrepreneurial marketing director may achieve breakthroughs (or disasters) that a more cautious person would avoid.

● how businesses find a balance between what is desirable and what is achievable – in some firms, the balance is determined at the top (by directors who may not understand fully the market conditions); others adopt a more participative style, in which directors consult junior executives to get a clear idea of what can be achieved.

65.7 Selecting marketing strategies
an evaluation

It would be nice to think that businesses carefully evaluate the marketing environment and then devise a strategy that fits in with overall company objectives. In reality, the strategy may be imposed by management, shareholders or even circumstances. In some instances, the only business objective may be survival. Strategy may then be reduced to crisis management. The other reality is that the business environment is not always clear and logical, so it may be very difficult to generate realistic and effective strategies.

Key terms

AIDA: a useful way to remember the stages in getting someone to try a new product – Awareness, Interest, Desire, Action.

Diversification: when a company expands its activities outside its normal range. This may be done to reduce risk or to expand possible markets.

Repositioning: changing the product or its promotion to appeal to a different market segment.

Further reading

Ansoff, I. (1965) *Corporate Strategy*. New York: McGraw-Hill.

Exercises

A. Revision questions

(40 marks; 40 minutes)

1 What is marketing strategy? (2)

2 What is a unique selling point? Give two examples. (4)

3 What is meant by product differentiation? (3)

4 What are the four steps in developing a marketing strategy? (4)

5 Why is it important for a firm to examine its internal resources before deciding on a strategy? (3)

6 What is the difference between market development and product development? (4)

7 How does marketing strategy relate to the objectives of a business? (4)

8 Why is market research an important part of marketing strategy? (4)

9 Why is market development more risky than market penetration? (4)

10 Apply the AIDA model to the recent launch of any new product or service. Explain how well the business has done at each stage. (8)

B. Revision exercises

B1 Data response

Apple's cash machine

The Apple iPod was launched in 2001, into a market dominated by Sony. For a company based on computers, the move into personal music appeared risky. As the graph in Figure 65.4 shows, sales grew slowly; iTunes was launched in 2002 but only in late 2004 did iPod sales move ahead dramatically. This was partly due to the launch of the iPod Mini, but also coincided with the start of the brilliant 'silhouette' advertising campaign. In fact, Apple has handled iPod's marketing strategy very cleverly.

iPod marketing mix

● *Product:* quick product development, from iPod 2001 to iPod Mini 2003, iPod Photo 2004 to iPod Shuffle 2005, and the iPod Touch in late 2007. As with all its competitors, the iPod is made (very cheaply) in China, so the key to its success is the stylish design, not high-quality manufacture.

● *Price:* always startlingly high; at launch, the iPod was over £200; even today the iPod Mini 2 is £139, whereas other MP3 players can cost as little as £20. Apple has managed the business dream of achieving market penetration at prices that skim the market.

● *Place:* nothing new here; Apple has distributed the iPod through the normal mixture of department stores, electrical shops and online retailers.

● *Promotion:* brilliant and lavish use of posters and TV, featuring one of the all-time great images, the 'silhouette'.

The key to the strategy has always been to achieve high credibility through brilliant design and a non-corporate image. Consumers have tended not to notice that the iPod is an amazing cash machine. In 2007, the revenues generated by iPod and iTunes exceeded $10,000 million.

Questions

(40 marks; 50 minutes)

1a What is meant by the term 'product life cycle'? (2)

1b Explain what Figure 65.4 shows about iPod's product life cycle in the period up to the end of 2007. (5)

2a Explain briefly how Ansoff would have interpreted Apple's move into the personal music market. (2)

2b Explain why Ansoff would have considered this move to be risky. (4)

3 Discuss which of the elements of iPod's marketing mix have been the most important in its sales success. (12)

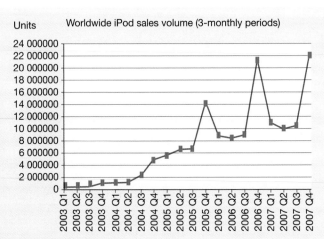

Figure 65.4 A real product life cycle graph – showing sales over three-month periods
Source of data: Apple Corp's quarterly financial accounts. Apple accounts started to mention the iPod only in the fourth quarter of 2003; before that it was regarded as too trivial to be worth mentioning to shareholders.

4 Given the business's success with the iPod (and iPhone), discuss whether Apple should now make a move towards the games console business, competing with Nintendo, Sony and Microsoft.   (15)

B2 Data Response

DIY no longer does it for trendy B&Q

B&Q, the 320-store retail giant, will this week ditch its iconic 'You Can Do It' strapline, which it has used in some form since the mid-1980s, as part of the biggest repositioning in the chain's 38-year history.

In an attempt to move beyond its DIY roots, the Kingfisher-owned chain will take on John Lewis and Habitat with the launch of 4000 new upmarket furnishing, wallpaper and paint lines. It has also signed tie-up deals with high-end brands such as Monsoon, the fashion and homewares group, and Fired Earth, a paint label and the maker of ceramic tiles. The changes are part of an effort by B&Q to appeal to female shoppers and tap into the £60 billion market for fashionable home decoration, which is worth three times the traditional DIY market. Trendy wallpaper and curtain lines also command higher margins than DIY products such as boxes of screws, planks of wood and garden tools.

B&Q's shift in emphasis will be reflected in a new multi-million-pound TV and print ad campaign. The ads will showcase a new slogan – 'Let's Do It' – and feature families relaxing in homes decorated with B&Q products. The campaign is a radical departure from B&Q's traditional ads, which showed employees holding up paint tins.

Chief Executive Ian Cheshire said that home improvement retailing is becoming increasingly like fashion retailing, with shoppers updating their homes with the latest trends regularly. 'In the same way that fashion retailing went from one or two shopping trips a year to "fast fashion", we think that people will be doing "fast fashion" for the home,' he said. 'What was good enough in 1995 is no longer good enough now.'

The chain is currently undergoing a massive store refurbishment programme. One-third of its 115 large stores will be revamped by the end of the year at the cost of £2.5 million per store. Kingfisher is targeting a 25% uplift in sales per square foot in revamped stores. The retailer is this week expected to say that first-half pre-tax profit rose to £183 million, up from £178.5 million last year. Like-for-like sales are expected to have grown by 2% over the period.

Source: The business.co.uk, 16 September 2007

Questions

(50 marks; 60 minutes)

1a What is meant by 'the biggest repositioning in the firm's history'? (4)

1b Using the data given, calculate the cost to B&Q of the store refurbishment. (6)

1c What effect does B&Q expect this to have? (2)

2 Why is B&Q moving away from the DIY market? (6)

3 Explain how you think B&Q has arrived at this new strategy. (6)

4 Analyse the actions that B&Q is taking to implement this new strategy. (10)

5 Consider how a firm might alter its marketing strategy if market research showed a considerable change to customer buying habits. (16)

C. Essay questions

(40 marks each)

1 How useful is Ansoff's matrix in evaluating the risk involved in new marketing strategies?

2 'Only large companies need and can afford to have a marketing strategy.' Discuss this statement.

3 'Marketing strategy can be successful only if a firm has set the right objectives.' Discuss.

4 'Marketing strategy is the key to business success.' Discuss.

Developing and implementing marketing plans

66.1 The marketing plan

The marketing plan puts the company's marketing strategy into action. It explains the background to the planned marketing activity. It describes the marketing strategy and explains how it contributes to the overall corporate objectives. The marketing strategy is broken down into action plans. These are the individual activities that put the strategy into practice. In effect, the marketing plan shows how the marketing budget is to be spent.

The purpose of the marketing plan is to ensure that staff understand the actions that will be taken, the reasons behind the actions and the timing of the actions. For example, it is important that the production department knows when an advertising campaign will be run. It can ensure stocks are high enough to cover the boost to demand.

What does a marketing plan look like?

For smaller businesses the **marketing plan** may be an informal document. Larger companies will formalise the plans in report format. Typically it will have the contents shown in Table 66.1.

Why is marketing planning important?

If I had eight hours to chop down a tree I'd spend six sharpening my axe. (*Abraham Lincoln*)

A properly developed marketing plan is important because:

Table 66.1 Typical contents of a marketing plan

Introduction	Gives an overview of the plan, and the economic and competitive background to it
Corporate and marketing objectives	States the overall business aims and the relevant marketing objectives
Marketing strategy	Outlines the strategy that will be used to achieve the objectives
Action plans	Details the individual marketing activities used to carry out the strategy, including media advertising and sales promotions, plus detailed timings
Detailed budgets	Breakdown of expected revenue and costs by product or department or marketing activity
Control tools	Details of how the budgets and plans will be monitored

- it helps to ensure that marketing activity is properly focused and integrated

- it enables everyone in the organisation to know exactly what will happen, and when

- it enables the business to take advantage of market opportunities

- it helps to ensure that the business remains healthy by preparing for possible problems

- it puts the business in a better position to react to unexpected events.

66.2 How is the marketing plan determined?

Once the marketing strategy has been agreed it needs to be put into action. The strategy will have been determined taking into account all the internal and external issues that affect the business. For example, if the strategy is to increase the market share of a product, the competitive situation will help decide whether to cut price or to launch a new product.

The plan must be realistic and take into account the internal situation of the business. It needs to consider, for instance, if there are enough staff with the right skills to carry out the plans.

The most important considerations are those listed below.

- *Finance:* the amount of finance that is available to spend on marketing will obviously be important. A business cannot plan a national advertising campaign if the finance available will only fund a local mail shot. However, even if funding is available, the plan should take into account the return on expenditure. The results of the marketing must be monitored to measure the effectiveness of the expenditure.

- *Operational issues:* the marketing plan should take into account whether the organisation can cope with the increased demand that may result from any marketing campaign. This may be in production or people terms. Boosting demand that cannot be satisfied by available stocks is a waste of time, effort and money. It may even backfire as ill will is created among retailers and consumers.

- *Competitors' actions:* any marketing effort is likely to promote a response from competitors. This needs to be considered at all stages of the planning process. A price reduction that produces a price war will do nothing except reduce margins for all concerned.

A-grade application
Nintendo Wii

2007 was the year of the Nintendo Wii. In the period April to December, sales jumped from 3.2 million units in 2006 to 14.3 million in 2007 (an increase of 350%). Yet from August 2007 it was clear that Nintendo was struggling to keep up with worldwide demand. So it was surprising that the company ran a huge advertising campaign in December 2007 in Britain. The result was predictable. Shops ran out of stock, and Sony enjoyed an unexpected boost to its sales of the PS3! Nintendo may be the best at games console innovation, but the company has a thing or two to learn about marketing.

Once these three issues have been considered, the plans can be developed. The type of marketing activity that is used will be determined in different ways in different businesses. Some businesses will just continue to do what they did the previous year: 'It seemed to work, so let's carry on.' Others will take a more sophisticated approach. This will involve analysis of what has worked well in the past. Which aspects of the marketing mix are more appropriate? Are there any areas that could be improved? What are the current issues that concern consumers? With the growth of environmental considerations many businesses are putting green issues at the heart of their marketing approach.

66.3 Marketing expenditure

The marketing department will have to work within the constraints of the allocated finance. One of the most difficult questions facing the marketing manager is how to spend the available resources. It is a common error to equate marketing expenditure with the cost of advertising. Many other costs are associated with marketing the product. Among the most important are the design and development of the packaging, thorough and independent market research and the achievement of good distribution.

How the available money is spent will depend on many factors. These include those listed below.

- *The likely return from the expenditure:* any marketing expenditure should produce a return. It should be evaluated in the same way as any investment in the business.

- *Type of product:* some products are supported by very high levels of spending while others are not. The level of spending may be related to how easy the product is to differentiate in the market. In markets where there is little difference between competing products, businesses will want to use marketing to give their product a competitive edge – to make it seem different. It is only possible to afford high marketing budgets, though, if the value added is high. Cosmetics, cars and washing powder are examples of this. Each is supported by high levels of promotional spending.

● *Product life cycle*: for most products the highest levels of expenditure will be in the launch and growth stages. From time to time the product may need to be supported with additional spending. This will happen when the product is given additional support as part of an extension strategy.

● *Type of customer*: companies selling consumer goods and services will tend to have higher levels of marketing expenditure than those supplying industrial customers.

66.4 Marketing budgets

A very important aspect of the marketing plan is the **marketing budget**. Once a plan has been developed it needs to be put into action. It is also important that the plan is monitored so that the business can see if the plan is being achieved and if it is being effective. A marketing budget must be set to both implement and control the firm's marketing expenditure.

In everyday language a budget is the amount available for spending. In business a budget is not only an expenditure target but also a target for achievement. The marketing budget is the quantified plan for the marketing department. It shows the marketing objectives in numerical terms, such as market share or distribution targets. It is usually produced as an annual budget, but for the purpose of control will often be broken down into monthly figures.

For example, the marketing objective may be to increase sales by 10%. The budget will give monthly sales targets that will deliver that annual figure. Alongside the sales figures, targets for expenditure will be given. So if the additional sales are to be generated by a new advertising campaign, the budget will include expenditure targets for that advertising.

Measuring performance against budget

If performance is to be measured effectively then it is important that there is a range of data available. The management accounting system will produce some figures, such as sales and costs. It may need to be developed to produce other information to measure marketing effectiveness. Competitive information will be important. Car manufacturers look at market share figures based on new car registrations as a key measure of performance. If Ford's market share figures are slipping behind the targets, the company will step up its marketing effort (including price cutting) to regain its intended levels.

Issues For Analysis

There are several issues that are likely to be important when looking at marketing plans.

● Consideration should be given to the usefulness or otherwise of the plans. Do they really help the business to manage its marketing effort or does the process constrain real marketing initiatives? Quite often this will depend on other factors in the business, such as management style. Are staff encouraged to stick rigidly to the plan or is initiative rewarded?

● When considering how the plans are developed it is important to put the plans in the context of the business and its competitive environment. Consideration of how well a plan will work for this particular business must take these factors into account.

● A key factor for businesses is setting the right level of marketing budget. In 2008 Nestlé launched KitKat Senses, effectively a 'me-too' (copy) of Kinder Bueno and Mars Delight. Perhaps because it would be hard to achieve high sales against established competition, the UK launch marketing budget was set at £7 million (a very high figure for the chocolate business). Time will tell whether this generous budget proves sensible.

Developing and implementing marketing plans

The two most important aspects of marketing plans are getting the right level of marketing budget, then finding the right balance between a fixed plan and a flexible one. In a well-run business, the budget will be set after discussion between key managers and set at a level that takes into account the objectives and the difficulty in achieving them. If a new product is being launched into a fiercely competitive market, there should be no halfway house between setting a high budget or scrapping the whole idea. A compromise may be the worst of all worlds.

After the budget is set, and decisions have been made about how and when to spend it, junior staff can put the plan into practice. TV commercials can be written and filmed; commercial breaks can be booked. If circumstances change within the year, though, it may be wise to make adjustments. A TV campaign planned for October might be brought forward to September if a rival is bringing out a new product. Every plan needs a degree of flexibility.

Figure 66.1 KitKat Senses

Key terms

Marketing budget: the sum allowed for spending on marketing a particular product or brand.

Marketing plan: a document detailing how and when the marketing budget will be spent.

Exercises

A. Revision questions

(30 marks; 30 minutes)

Read the unit, then answer:

1 What is a marketing plan? (2)

2 List four topics that you would expect to be included in a marketing plan. (4)

3 Outline two reasons why firms prepare marketing plans. (4)

4 Why is company finance an important factor when preparing marketing plans? (5)

5 Why is it important that operational issues are taken into account when determining a marketing plan? (4)

6 How does the competitive environment influence marketing planning? (4)

7 What is a marketing budget? (2)

8 How can a marketing budget help to control marketing expenditure? (5)

B. Revision exercises

B1 Data response

Marketing plans show shift to internet marketing for business-to-business firms

A recent survey, undertaken by a business-to-business online magazine, discovered that, in spite of economic problems, businesses were planning to increase their levels of marketing expenditure. The survey also showed that online marketing expenditure would be the main focus of this increase. The survey, which was conducted online, had 250 responses; 60% of the respondents said that their firms planned to increase their marketing budgets, but 80% of them planned to increase their online marketing budgets. This was up from 70% in the previous year's survey. Only 10% of replies indicated that their marketing expenditure would be reduced;

70% of the businesses were planning to launch a new advertising campaign in the coming year and nearly half planned to increase the number of staff employed in marketing.

The main marketing goals identified by the survey were:

- getting new customers – 60%
- increasing brand awareness – 20%
- retaining customers – 15%.

Approximately a third of marketing budgets would be spent on online marketing. This is a 10% increase over last year's levels. This expenditure would be for:

- website development
- direct email marketing
- search engine marketing
- video webcasting
- sponsorship.

The other main results from the survey were:

- a large rise in the number of businesses planning to use event marketing
- a reduction in the amount of advertising in newspapers and magazines
- continuing growth in the use of direct mailing.

Questions

(35 marks; 40 minutes)

1 What is meant by 'business to business'? (2)

2 Why might the results of this survey not give a true picture of marketing plans for all businesses? (8)

3 Why do you think there might be a trend for businesses to increase their marketing activity online? (5)

4 Why do you think that firms may be considering moving away from newspaper and magazine advertising and towards direct mailing? (8)

5 Discuss whether or not a business such as Marks & Spencer should spend a third of its marketing budget on online marketing. (12)

B2 Case study

Ewans Motor Company is a car dealer based in the Midlands. It has two outlets. One has the franchise for a range of small family cars. The other offers larger luxury cars.

Business has been steady over the past few years, but has seen no real growth in total sales or profitability. The business is facing increased local competition from another garage offering a similar range of family cars. There is also the threat of an economic downturn in the area as one of the largest employers is threatening to cut staff as a result of lower export sales due to the stronger pound.

The owner, Peter Ewans, has brought in a new marketing manager with the hope that the business can cope with these challenges and hopefully increase profitability. The new marketing manager, Sharon Crisp, agreed to join the business providing the marketing budget was increased from its current 1% of turnover. She feels that in the highly competitive climate of the small car business, the budget needs to be slightly more than doubled. Sharon is sure that she can justify this additional expenditure by raising profitability. She also introduced the

concept of a marketing budget that she feels is long overdue. Previously, expenditure has been on a rather ad hoc basis and there have been no targets set for sales or profitability. There has also been little or no monitoring of the results.

After analysing both the market situation and the figures for the business for the last few years, Sharon produced the marketing budget figures shown below.

Sharon felt that there was going to be a need to use some price discounting on the smaller cars to combat the increased competition in the area. Her plan was to allow the salespeople to discount the price by as much as they felt was necessary to ensure the sale. She allowed an average of £100 for each small car for this. To support the salespeople Sharon planned to double the mail shots. These would inform customers of special offers and also invite them to special family days. These days would be very child orientated, offering family entertainment and gifts for children; all the slightly increased promotional budget would be spent on this. She also planned to support the family days with additional advertising in the local press. The sponsorship of sporting activities in local schools fitted into the plan, so this would also be continued.

Budget	Last year	This year
Sales: small cars	1600	2000
Sales: luxury cars	800	950
Average selling price: small cars	£12,000	£11,900
Average selling price: luxury cars	£25,000	£25,000
Average contribution per small car	£840	£740
Average contribution per luxury car	£3000	£3000
Total marketing expenditure	£392,000	£800,000
Breakdown of marketing expenditure:		
Price discounting	0	£200,000
Direct mailing	£100,000	£200,000
Advertising	£150,000	£250,000
Promotional offers	£92,000	£100,000
Sponsorship	£50,000	£50,000

Industry reports suggested that the luxury car business would grow at about 6% in this year so Sharon decided to do very little except for mail shots to support this sector of the market.

At the end of the year the actual figures were as shown in the table at right:

After analysing the results, Sharon feels that both the marketing plan and the budgeting exercise have been successful.

Questions

(50 marks; 60 minutes)

1 Do you think that the marketing plan was appropriate for the business in its present circumstances? (10)

2 Why did Sharon Crisp feel that a marketing budget was long overdue? (4)

3 What advantages and disadvantages might there be for the business in introducing a marketing budgeting system? (8)

4 Calculate the variances between the budgeted and actual figures. (8)

5 Why do you think the more significant variances might have occurred? (8)

6 Using the figures and other information in the case study, comment on Sharon Crisp's assertion that the marketing plan and the budgeting exercise were successful. (12)

	Actual
Sales: small cars	1800
Sales: luxury cars	800
Average selling price: small cars	£11,800
Average selling price: luxury cars	£25,000
Average contribution per small car	£640
Average contribution per luxury car	£3000
Total marketing expenditure	£960,000
Breakdown of marketing expenditure:	
Price discounting	£360,000
Direct mailing	£180,000
Advertising	£250,000
Promotional offers	£120,000
Sponsorship	£50,000

C. Essay questions

(40 marks each)

1 Some businesses do not have formalised marketing plans. Discuss the arguments for and against a formal marketing planning system.

2 Many firms are moving away from the 'last year plus a bit' approach to producing marketing budgets. Discuss two alternative approaches and explain why the firm might use these methods.

INTEGRATED MARKETING

67.1 Marketing: an overview

Which is more important to a firm – revenue or costs? You might say that they are equally important. Or you might say that a firm must have revenue – therefore revenue is the key. Yet students revise costs (finance and accounting) far more thoroughly than revenue (marketing). This is partly because they feel weaker at finance and wish to improve; also, they underestimate the analytic demands (and importance) of marketing.

Firms can have many different objectives, but profit making is clearly a vital aspect of business activity. The most important formula in this subject is the one for profit:

profit = total revenue − total costs

or, to use the expanded form:

profit = (price × quantity) − ([variable cost × quantity] + fixed costs)

Marketing decisions have a direct influence upon:

- the price and quantity of goods sold

- the variable cost per unit (as bulk-buying discounts are affected by sales volume)

- fixed costs, as they include marketing expenditures such as advertising and promotions.

In other words, marketing influences every aspect of the profit formula.

67.2 What is marketing?

- Is it about responding to consumers or persuading them?

- Is it about creating competition or attempting to avoid it?

- Is it ethical or unethical?

Every textbook has its own definition. A definition such as 'to fulfil consumer needs, profitably' suggests that marketing is about identifying and meeting needs, and is therefore serving the consumer's best interests. Is this true? Always? Do consumers need a Snickers chocolate bar or a smoothie?

Marketing today is seen as the all-embracing function that acts as the focal point of business activity. Top business consultant Richard Schonberger described the best modern firms as those that 'build a chain of customers'. In other words, marketing forms the link between the firm and its customers. It therefore determines the type and quantity of goods to be designed and produced.

67.3 A-grade marketing

Marketing consists of a series of concepts and themes (such as the marketing mix). All good students know these; better ones can group them together and relate them to one another. They can be grouped as follows.

- *An understanding of markets*: the price mechanism, price elasticity, market segmentation and competitive tactics.

- *An understanding of consumer behaviour*: psychological factors in product pricing and image, brand loyalty, consumer resistance.

- *Product portfolio analysis*: product life cycle, Boston Matrix.

- *Marketing decision making*: the marketing model, market and sales research and analysis, the need to anticipate, not just reflect, consumer taste.

- *Marketing strategy*: both in theory and in practice through the marketing mix/four Ps; an understanding of risk through Ansoff's matrix.

- *Marketing planning*: how marketing plans are used and developed, and the importance of marketing budgets in implementing and controlling the plans. The usefulness of budgets and variance analysis in reacting to changes in the marketing and business environment.

A-grade marketing requires a grasp of big underlying issues such as those discussed below. These are areas of discussion, which should lead you to draw conclusions in answers or case studies. They represent ways of evaluating the wider significance of concepts such as the product life cycle.

Issue 1: Is marketing an art or a science?

Is marketing about judgement and creativity, or scientific decision making? If it is a science, the numerate information provided by market research would lead to a 100% success rate with new products. The reality, of course, is different. Coca-Cola researched Coke Vanilla heavily – and spent millions advertising a flop. While Baileys Irish Cream became a worldwide best-seller even though research said women would not buy a whisky-based liqueur; and the iPod had very little market research before launch (partly to keep its design a secret).

Marketing relies upon anticipating consumer behaviour. Research can help enormously, but the final decision on strategy is a judgement. Therefore individual flair and luck play an important part.

Issue 2: Does marketing respond to needs or create wants?

It is easy to see the importance of marketing to the firm. But what are its effects upon the consumer/general public? Is it just a way of encouraging people to want things they do not need?

Health issues are important in this debate. You may be 'Lovin' McDonald's, but is it what your stomach needs? And is it right that children should pester their parents for McCain Oven Chips, when a baked potato is much cheaper and much more nutritious? You must form some views on these questions. You may feel that marketers' pursuit of new products, flavours, trends and glitz makes life fun. Or you may feel that marketing can manipulate people, and that its most persuasive arm (TV advertising) needs to be controlled. The government's recent decision to ban fast food advertising during children's TV programmes implies that it favours control.

Issue 3: Has market orientation gone too far in Britain?

The trend towards a market-led approach was good for companies that produced the same products in the same way, year after year. Market orientation brought in new ideas and more attractive product design.

However, it also encouraged Ford to focus too much on the styling and imagery of its cars, while BMW and Honda concentrated on their production quality and reliability; and Toyota thought ahead with new, greener technology. Money that had once been spent on research and development was now spent on market research. The number of engineering graduates declined as the numbers on marketing and accounting courses ballooned. Manufacturing industry depends upon high-quality engineers and a skilled workforce. Marketing alone is not enough.

Exercises

A. Revision questions

(50 marks; 60 minutes)

1 Why is a reduction in price unlikely to benefit a firm whose products are price inelastic? (2)

2 Distinguish between primary and secondary research. (2)

3 Why might a firm's long-term pricing policy differ from its short-term one? (3)

4 Explain the term 'product differentiation'. (2)

5 Give two reasons why a firm may sell, for a limited period of time, part of its product range for a loss. (2)

6 List three factors a firm should consider when determining the price of a new product. (3)

7 Give two ways in which decisions made within the marketing department might affect activities in the personnel department. (2)

8 Distinguish between marketing objectives and marketing strategy. (3)

9 Identify three factors that are likely to influence the choice of distribution channel for a product. (3)

10 Give two examples of ethical dilemmas a marketing manager might face. (2)

11 Distinguish between product orientation and market orientation. (3)

12 A business decides to reduce the price elasticity of its product from £3.00 to £2.75. As a result, sales rise from 2500 to 3000 units. Calculate the price elasticity of demand for its product. (3)

13 Explain what is meant by 'negative income elasticity'. (2)

14 State two business objectives, other than profit maximisation, that will influence a firm's marketing strategies. (2)

15 The price of a good is 100p, of which 40p is the contribution. If the price is cut by 30%, how much extra must be sold to maintain the same total contribution? (3)

16 Only one in five new product launches is successful. Why? Give three reasons. (3)

17 State three ways of segmenting a market. (3)

18 What is a marketing budget? (2)

19 Suggest three possible extension strategies for a brand of bottled lager for which sales have levelled out. (3)

20 State two approaches a firm might take to defend itself if a price war broke out. (2)

B. Revision exercises

B1 Data response

A manufacturer of footballs has sales of 100,000 units a month and fixed costs of £240,000 a month. Raw materials are £3.00 per unit and the pricing method is a 100% mark-up on variable costs. When it last increased its prices, price elasticity proved to be about 0.6. Now it is thinking of a further 10% price rise.

Questions

(15 marks; 15 minutes)

1 Calculate the effect on profit of this 10% rise. State your assumptions. (8)

2 What factors may have caused the price elasticity to have changed since the time it was measured at 0.6? (7)

B2 Report writing

You are product development manager of a new tinned cat food called Leno. Its consumer USP (unique selling point) is 'a low-fat, high-fibre food for superfit cats'. Market research has convinced you that demand will be sizeable. Your marketing director wants to be satisfied on four key issues before giving the go-ahead to launch:

(a) that you have considered three pricing

methods, and can now make a recommendation on a suitable pricing policy

(b) that you can explain the research you conducted and how it has helped you make your sales forecast

(c) that you can explain the method you will use to set an advertising budget

(d) that you have considered carefully three of the most likely responses by existing competitors to the launch of Leno.

Questions

(20 marks; 25 minutes)

1 Write a report to the marketing director covering these points. (20)

B3 Business simulation

Should Schweppes launch this new product?

Appendix A: Briefing document

Sparkler is a brand new, sparkling, exotic fruit drink. It is aimed at the mass market and will sell to shops at the same price as Coca-Cola (35p). Schweppes has developed the product, registered the trademark and is about to hold a meeting to decide whether or not to launch it.

Assess the information provided below and, as joint marketing directors:

1 decide what you recommend and why

2 prepare a PowerPoint presentation to explain your views.

Appendix B: Market research findings

Regular drinkers of:

	Pepsi	Coke	Sparkling orange	Other fruit flavours	TOTAL
Sample size	80	340	170	50	640
Will definitely try	24%	21%	32%	39%	26%
Will probably try	36%	37%	39%	38%	37.5%

Following product trial:

	Pepsi	Coke	Sparkling orange	Other fruit flavours	TOTAL
Will definitely buy regularly	21%	17%	35%	47%	27%
Will probably buy regularly	37%	31%	32%	36%	32%

Source: adapted from Gallup Poll Research Company

Appendix C: Cost data

	Production of cans per week		
	Up to 99,000	100,000–499,000	500,000+
Sparkler production cost per can	3.3p	3.0p	2.8p
Sparkler delivery cost per can	2.7p	2.0p	1.2p
Weekly fixed costs:			
Salaries and administration	£20,000		
Marketing costs	£40,000		
Other expenses	£10,000		

Appendix D: Market size and share data

	Market size	Coca-Cola	Pepsi	Orange	Other fruit flavours
3 years ago	£2.5 bn	23.4%	8.9%	7.4%	4.6%
2 years ago	£2.7 bn	23.9%	8.7%	7.7%	4.9%
Last year	£3.1 bn	24.1%	8.6%	7.9%	5.3%

Appendix E: Sales information

Forecast sales volume	If research is positive	If research is negative
Year 1	400,000 pw	200,000 pw
Year 2	600,000 pw	300,000 pw
Year 3	700,000 pw	280,000 pw
Year 4	750,000 pw	200,000 pw

B4 Integrated case study

Emirates

To build a brand is difficult in any circumstances, but to build a strong global brand in under 20 years is a great marketing achievement. Emirates airlines, which operates out of Dubai, started flights in 1985. It has grown at around 20% each year since then and is now one of the world's best-known and most profitable international airlines. It flies to over 90 destinations in 59 countries and has a fleet of over 100 aircraft. This expansion is due to continue. The airline's expansion will support the Dubai government's commitment to bring 15 million visitors a year to the emirate.

Even if you do not fly with the airline the name is difficult to miss. The Emirates Stadium, which is Arsenal's home ground, and its sponsorship of numerous world-class sporting events such as the 2006 FIFA World Cup are just two examples of how the Emirates name has been promoted.

Emirates has been able to take advantage of its geographical location but nevertheless growth of 20% a year needs to be supported by strong marketing.

So how has Emirates managed to do this? The company does not talk about marketing, but about brand management. Tim Clark, president of Emirates Airlines, explains: 'We know how we want to project ourselves. It covers sponsorships, advertising, media relations – everything about how we control and portray our brand. Call it what you like – it's brand management.'

Spending on sports sponsorship is backed up by advertising, which the airline hopes will convert awareness of the brand into sales. Its approach to advertising is also different. Instead of developing advertising campaigns in-house or having one agency to do the advertising, it has a global network of agencies. The general outline of a campaign is sent out to all its agencies, which are then invited to submit their ideas for the campaign. This is all done through an extranet link. In this way, the airline believes that it has a global approach to its promotion.

Another difference for the airline is that its marketing budget is much higher than those of its rivals in the airline industry (4% of revenue). Clark defends this: 'Others kind of play around the edges,' he says. 'But if you want to be a big player you need to think high. Our aim is to be a premium global brand and to do this you have to go after these big ones. Eventually you judge them as being affordable because of the return on investment.'

Source: adapted from an article by David Knibb, www.airlinebusiness.com; August 2006 Airline Strategy awards

Questions

(50 marks; 60 minutes)

1 What is meant by sponsorship? (4)

2 What is meant by brand management? (4)

3 How might sponsorship work to improve brand awareness? (6)

4 How do you think having a global network of advertising and promotional agencies helps Emirates? (8)

5 Analyse how developing a global marketing plan might differ from a marketing plan for a local market. (14)

6 Discuss the importance, when planning a marketing campaign, to be aware of the return on investment. (14)

C. Essay questions

(40 marks each)

1 'Marketing is the most important activity in the business.' Discuss this statement.

2 Do you agree that good-quality goods sell themselves?

3 Do you think that marketers ought to be concerned about encouraging people to spend money when it increases their debt?

UNDERSTANDING HRM OBJECTIVES AND STRATEGY

DEFINITION

HR is a common term for the personnel function within a business. HR professionals like to see their role as being central to the overall goals and policies of the business.

68.1 Introduction

People are a resource of the business. Like any other resource they have to be managed. In fact, many organisations claim their people are the most important of all their resources and that the management of them makes a significant difference to business success. In this unit we examine the activities involved in human resource management (HRM), typical HR objectives and different approaches to HRM.

68.2 The management of people

The management of people (otherwise known as human resource management) involves a wide range of activities. These begin with identifying the workforce requirements of the organisation in the future so that the appropriate plans can then be developed; for example, more staff may need to be recruited, existing staff may need training or redeployment, or in some cases redundancies may be needed. Planning ahead for these changes is known as **workforce planning**. Workforce planning involves an examination of the organisation's future needs, a consideration of the existing labour supply and then the development of plans to match the supply of people and skills to the demand.

Of course, people management is not just about the flow of people into and out of the organisation. It also involves managing people when they are part of the business.

This will involve activities such as those listed below.

Designing the jobs that people do: this can have a big effect on their motivation and also their effectiveness; poor job design may be demotivating and fail to build on or develop individuals' skills.

Developing appropriate reward systems: this will have a big impact on how employees behave. For example, a commission-based system is likely to push employees to make sales, but staff may be unwilling to do tasks that do not directly lead to a sale.

Developing appropriate training programmes: these can serve a variety of purposes, such as informing employees of future developments within the business, developing employees' skills to do an existing job or helping them gain the skills needed to take on new tasks.

Developing effective communication systems: these may include bulletins from managers, newsletters, systems of meetings or consultation with employee representatives. The communication systems will be designed to inform employees and at the same time achieve a desired level of consultation with staff.

The decisions taken by the human resource function will be linked to the overall business objectives and strategy. For example:

● if the business is growing the HRM function may need to recruit more staff; if it is expanding abroad it will recruit staff with language skills

● if the business is changing the nature of its operations the HRM function may need to invest more in training to ensure employees have the right skills; alternatively it may mean some jobs are lost and others are created

● if the business is trying to reduce its costs then the HR function will be looking for ways of helping to bring this about; for example, combining jobs, removing a layer of management or reducing the training budget.

The activities and objectives of the human resource function should, therefore, be integrated with the corporate plans and should contribute to the achievement of the corporate objectives.

At the same time, corporate planning needs to take account of a firm's human resource strengths and constraints. Expansion may not be possible in the short run, for example, if the firm does not have and cannot easily get the staff available. On the other hand, if employees have particular experience of and insight into a market sector this may make a business consider expanding into this segment.

A-grade application

Job advertisement for kidsunlimited nurseries

We are looking for a qualified Nursery Nurse to join our team of dedicated care professionals to support and enhance the care and development of our children.

What can we offer you?

We believe that our staff are our greatest asset and therefore reward staff by offering an excellent employment package that includes:

- competitive salary
- 28 days' annual leave, increasing to 33 days
- flexible hours of work
- bespoke employee benefits package
- contributory pension
- discounted childcare
- comprehensive induction on commencement of employment
- range of further training and career opportunities to support your own development
- nationally recognised professional qualifications that include NVQs.

What can you offer us?

Applicants must be able to demonstrate the ability to provide and sustain an environment that is caring, welcoming and stimulating, and reflective of the kidsunlimited ethos and philosophy. Applicants must have minimum NVQ Level 2 or equivalent in Childcare and Early Years Education, and previous nursery experience is preferred.

Source: www.kidsunlimited.co.uk

68.3 Who is responsible for human resource management?

The responsibilities for human resource management may well lie with **line managers**. This means that the marketing manager may be responsible for managing her marketing team and dealing with all the 'people issues' that come with this. These might include recruitment, training and setting appropriate reward rates within an overall budget. Similarly, the operations manager may look after all the operations employees. This approach to HRM is quite common, particularly in smaller businesses where it may be felt that it is not financially viable (or indeed necessary) to employ a HR specialist.

However, in other organisations (often where there are more people to manage and therefore more people issues to resolve or plan for) there will be a specialist HRM department. People working within this department will act as advisers to the line managers, keeping them informed of the legal requirements affecting employing people, advising them on best practice and supporting them in HR issues. The final decisions are usually made by the line managers (after all, it is their team of staff), but the systems, procedures and approaches they use may well be developed by HR specialists.

68.4 HRM objectives

The overall aim of managing people is to maximise the contribution of employees on an individual and group level to the organisation's overall objectives. To do this, specific objectives need to be met. These HRM objectives, like all functional objectives, will be derived from the targets of the business as a whole.

An organisation's objectives for its people might focus on the following aspects.

- *The desired level of staffing and skills:* organisations are continually changing in terms of the work being done and the way it is done. This reshaping requires changes in the human resource input. For example, it may require more people, greater flexibility or different skills. The human resource function is responsible for making sure the business has the right number of people at the right time, with the right skills and attitudes. This, of course, has a big impact on the ability of the business to meet its customer needs. A lack of appropriate staff can lead to delays for customers, rushed and poor-quality work, and an inability to accept some contracts. By comparison, if the human resource requirements are met, a business may be able to provide a high-quality service and fulfil the expectations of customers. Achieving the right number of staff may be relatively easy if, for example, you can simply recruit more people when you need them. However, it can also be a very long-term process that involves enormous planning. In the case of the health service, for example, the training period for doctors and surgeons is several years. The NHS has to plan years in advance for the number of doctors it wants in relation to the number likely to be available.

● *Productivity*: this measures the output per employee. This can be measured in many different ways, depending on the business. It could be the number of products made by each employee (or team), such as the cars produced per day. It could be the number of telephone calls answered in a call centre, the number of meals served in a fast-food restaurant or the number of claims processed in an insurance office. While the productivity of employees will depend on many factors, such as the level of investment in technology, it can be affected enormously by the way in which people are managed. Effective people management will lead to more motivated staff, a better organised workflow and employees who have the necessary skills. By increasing productivity a business may become more efficient. This is because if each employee produces more output the labour cost per unit is reduced. This can help to boost profit margins or enable the business to be more price competitive. Given that markets are getting very competitive and customers are continually looking for better value for money there is constant pressure on firms to increase their efficiency. This in turn puts pressure on businesses to increase their productivity, which is why this is a common HRM target.

● *Cost targets*: like all the functions, HRM must work within budgets. You cannot simply spend whatever you want because the money may not be there. All businesses work within constraints, and decisions must be made within these restrictions. However, this does not mean to say that employees are all paid the minimum wage or that staffing levels are always kept to the bare minimum – this all depends on the strategy being adopted. In the case of the budget airlines such as easyJet and Ryanair, for example, the focus is on tightly controlling costs; staff are expected to work a lot of hours for their money and undertake a wide range of tasks. Staffing levels are relatively low. However, in the case of Harrods, the upmarket department store, staffing levels are quite generous. In the case of investment banks such as Casenove and Goldman Sachs, staff are paid very well to reflect the amount they earn for the business and the value

of their skills. Organisations will therefore monitor their spending on human resources and set targets to ensure they get value for money in all aspects of the process (such as recruitment or training).

● *Employer/ee relations*: the relations between managers and employees depend on the quality of communications and the trust between them. This in turn will depend on what communications mechanisms exist within the business, the extent to which employees are involved in making decisions and the way in which staff are treated. Are they listened to? And do they have the opportunity to influence the business policy? The nature of the relations between employers and employees will affect employees' commitment, their motivation and their readiness to work. You can tell when relations break down when employees and managers fail to cooperate effectively; this can even result in a strike. The quality of these relationships will affect employees':
  – openness to change – the business environment is very dynamic, with internal and external change occurring all the time; employees' attitude to change and their willingness to cope with or embrace change will depend on the way they are managed and how well they get on with their managers
  – levels of motivation, their commitment to a job and willingness to provide a quality service – this is particularly important in the service sector, where the willingness of staff to help, to provide advice and to listen to customers can be an important differentiating factor
  – willingness to contribute ideas and innovate – if relations are good, employees will feel part of the business and strive harder to improve it.

Many of these specific areas of human resource management, such as workforce planning and employer–employee relations, are dealt with in more detail in later units.

68.5 HR strategies: soft and hard HRM

Hard HRM

While all organisations undertake the various activities involved in managing human resources (such as recruitment, selection and training) the attitude and approach of managers towards employees can differ significantly. At one extreme we have what is called **hard HRM**. This basically regards employees as a necessary if unwelcome cost; people are an input that is required to get the job done, but it is believed that they add little to the overall value created by the business. With this approach managers see themselves as the 'thinkers'; they develop the best way of doing things and employees are expected to get on with it. This fits with the approach of F. W. Taylor, which you may have studied at AS-level (see Unit 26).

Hard HRM usually adopts a top-down management style in which employees are directed and controlled. Employees are expected to fit in with the design of the organisation; managers and supervisors instruct them and then monitor their actions. Jobs tend to be broken down into relatively small units so that one person does not have much control over the process and a replacement can easily be recruited, selected and trained. This type of approach can often be seen in call centres, where the work of operatives is very closely monitored, or in highly controlled outlets such as McDonald's.

The hard approach to HRM has many benefits such as:

- the outcomes should be predictable because employees do as they are told

- employees should be easily replaceable

- managers retain control for decision making and so this reduces the risk of major errors being made.

However, the disadvantages of this approach include:

- a possible failure to build on the skills, experiences and insights of the employees; this can lead to dissatisfied employees and low morale

- a danger that the organisation as a whole is at risk because it relies so heavily on the senior managers; if they make mistakes the business as a whole could fail because there is no input from lower levels.

The hard HRM approach sees the business as a machine and employees are cogs within that machine. This may work well provided the machine is designed effectively and is fit for purpose, but the approach does not encourage change and flexibility. As the environment changes managers may not spot these developments at ground level and employees may not be able to cope with new demands being made on them.

Soft HRM

By comparison, the **soft HRM** approach takes the view that employees can add a great deal of value to an organisation, and the business should develop, enhance and build on their interests, skills and abilities. Under a

soft approach managers see themselves more as facilitators. They are there to coach and help employees to do their job properly perhaps by ensuring sufficient training is provided and that the employee can develop in his or her career. This approach fits with McGregor's Theory Y style of leadership (see box).

The advantages of a soft approach to HRM are that:

- the organisation is building on the skills and experiences of their employees; this may enable the business to be more creative, more innovative and differentiated from the competition

- the organisation may be able to keep and develop highly skilled employees with expectations of a career with the business

- individuals throughout the business are encouraged to contribute, which may make the organisation

---

Douglas McGregor's Theory X and Theory Y

McGregor's book, *The Human Side of Enterprise* (1960), popularised his view that managers can be grouped into two types: Theory X and Theory Y. McGregor had researched into the attitudes of managers towards their staff. He found that most managers assumed their employees were work-shy and motivated primarily by money; he termed this type of manager Theory X. The alternative view was from managers who thought that underperforming staff were victims of poor management. Theory Y managers think that as long as people are given the opportunity to show initiative and involvement, they will do so.

Figure 68.1 Douglas McGregor

more flexible and adaptable to changing market conditions.

The disadvantages of a soft HRM approach may be that:

- time is taken in discussion and consultation rather than 'getting the job' done

- employees may not have the ability or inclination to get involved; they may just want to be told what to do and be rewarded for it; in this case a soft approach to HRM may be inappropriate and ineffective.

Which is the right strategy: hard or soft?

The attitude of managers towards their employees can be influenced by many different factors, such as those listed below.

- *Their own experience:* if you have taken an encouraging approach towards staff in the past and been let down then you may be reluctant to try this again.

- *The nature of the employees:* the skills, attitudes and expectations of employees will influence the way in which you manage them. If they are able, engaged and eager to progress then a soft approach is more likely.

- *The nature of the task:* if the task is simple, routine and repetitive then a hard approach is likely to be adopted. If there is little room for creativity or innovation because the task is standardised then the directive approach with clear instructions may well be the most efficient.

However, in general in the UK in recent years there has been a greater expectation by employees that they are involved in decision making and that managers take account of their welfare and skills development. The workforce is, on average, better educated than it was 20 years ago, employees are clearer about their rights (and there is more legal protection than before) and expect more in terms of their careers. Furthermore, we now have a 'knowledge economy', whereby many jobs require innovative thinking, independent decision making and the ability to 'think outside the box' (think of design work, software development, advertising, the music industry). As a result, a soft approach may be more suitable because it encourages individuals' contributions.

Issues For Analysis

- There are two valuable lines of analysis built into this chapter. The first is the question of who is responsible for the key HR decisions. The answer is often **not** the HR department. Most shop-floor workers are trained, managed and appraised by their supervisor. Similarly, most executives deal with their line manager, not their HR manager. In an accountancy department, then, it may be that the manager has little or no skill in people management; yet s/he may make all the most important decisions about the future of junior staff. HR departments can be little more than administration functions; all the key decisions about people are made elsewhere.

- The second issue is 'hard' versus 'soft' HR. This is also important, as it provides a useful analytic comparison. It encourages a view of HR that is questioning rather than flattering. In a world in which large companies worsen the pension rights of their own staff, it is right to be sceptical about whether modern HR methods are truly in the best interests of staff.

68.6 Understanding HRM objectives and strategy
an evaluation

Human resource management is one of the functions of a business. The overall approach to HRM (e.g. soft vs hard) and specific HRM decisions (e.g. to recruit or train) will be linked to the objectives and strategy of the business as a whole. A decision by a business to downsize or to expand abroad, for example, will have major implications for the HRM function. At the same time, the HRM resources of a business will influence the strategies a business adopts.

Key terms

Hard HRM: when managers treat the human resource in the same way they would treat any other resource (e.g. ordering more one week, and less the next); in such a climate, employee relations are likely to be strained and staff may see the need for trades union involvement.

Line managers: staff with responsibility for achieving specific business objectives, and with the resources to get things done.

Soft HRM: when managers treat the workforce as a special strength of the business and therefore make sure that staff welfare and motivation are always top priorities.

Workforce planning: checking on how future workforce needs compare with an audit of staff today, then planning how to turn the skills of today's employees into the skills required from tomorrow's staff.

Further reading

McGregor, D. (1960) *The Human Side of Enterprise*. McGraw-Hill Higher Education.

Price, A. (2004) *Human Resource Management*. Thompson Learning.

Exercises

A. Revision questions

(30 marks; 30 minutes)

1 What might be the effects of managing human resources in the same way as all the other resources used by a business? (4)

2 Identify three important features of the job of a human resource manager. (3)

3 Some people think that schools should stop teaching French and instead teach Mandarin (Chinese). If a school decided to do this, outline two implications for its workforce planning. (4)

4 A fast-growing small business might not have a human resources manager. The tasks may be left up to the line managers. Examine two reasons in favour of creating a human resources management post within such a business. (6)

5 Outline two ways in which a human resources manager might be able to help increase productivity at a clothes shop. (4)

6 Briefly discuss whether a Theory Y manager would ever adopt a 'hard HRM' approach? (9)

B. Revision exercises

B1 Data response

Extract from *Human Resource Management* (Price, 2004)

Storey (1989) has distinguished between hard and soft forms of HRM. 'Hard' HRM focuses on the resource side of human resources. It emphasizes costs in the form of 'headcounts' and places control firmly in the hands of management. Their role is to manage numbers effectively, keeping the workforce closely matched with requirements in terms of both bodies and behaviour. 'Soft' HRM, on the other hand, stresses the 'human' aspects of HRM. Its concerns are with communication and motivation. People are led rather than managed. They are involved in determining and realising strategic objectives.

Questions

(25 marks; 30 minutes)

1 The passage explains that hard HRM emphasises 'headcounts' and managing numbers effectively. Outline one strength and one weakness of this type of approach to managing people. (6)

2 Explain what the author means by the phrase 'people are led rather than managed'. (8)

3 Discuss whether staff at a car factory such as Honda's plant in Swindon are likely to want to be 'involved in determining and realising strategic objectives'. (11)

B2 Data response

A British private equity company has called in one of the leading US union-busters to stop workers at one of the country's best-known upmarket crisp producers, Kettle Chips, joining a trades union.

The California-based Burke Group has been engaged by Lion Capital, owners of Kettle Foods, to dissuade the 340 workers at its Norwich factory from joining Unite, the country's largest union.

Workers are balloting today on whether to join. Some 40% of the workers are migrants from eastern Europe.

The company makes upmarket and organic crisps and snacks, supplying supermarkets such as Waitrose and Tesco; it also manufactures own-brand products for Marks & Spencer.

It says it has had to seek advice from 'a number of sources' to fight what it considers are union experts in organising recognition campaigns. It did not comment directly on employing Omega Training, part of the Burke Group. The company does not want to recognise a union. It said: 'We are very proud of our workforce and continue to believe passionately that direct engagement with employees in the spirit of mutuality is in the best interests of our employees and shareholders.'

A spokesman added: 'All our employees enjoy a

secure salary (the lowest of which is 25% above the minimum wage); we have a 38-hour week with 25 days' paid holiday per annum increasing with service, and we offer a blue-chip benefits package that includes 100% sick pay ... and a profit-sharing bonus that is open to all employees. We're not sure what Unite the union wishes to do for our employees.'

The union is baffled why the company is so determined to block recognition. Miles Hubbard, Unite's eastern region organiser, said: 'They are a good company with a decent record so we cannot understand why they are being so aggressive about union activity. We were called in by the workers when they did not receive annualised payments for overtime.'

Source: www.guardian.co.uk (this article appeared in the *Guardian* on Monday 1 October 2007 on p. 27 of the 'Financial' section. It was last updated on 26 November 2007)

Questions

(25 marks; 30 minutes)

1 What is meant by the term 'trades union'? (2)

2 A characteristic of a 'hard HRM' approach would be to resist trades unions in the workplace.

   (a) Why might a workforce be interested in being represented by a trades union? (5)

   (b) Why might a 'hard HR' management want to resist trades union recognition? (6)

3 The Kettle Chip staff voted to keep the union out. Discuss why they might have decided to vote against. (12)

C. Essay questions

(40 marks each)

1 Discuss whether a 'hard HRM' approach is the right way to run a supermarket branch where 50% of the staff are part-time students.

2 After announcing developments in India and Poland, in 2008 Marks & Spencer announced its intention to 'generate 20% of group revenues from international operations within five years'. To what extent will the success or failure of this objective depend upon a successful HR strategy?

WORKFORCE PLANNING

DEFINITION

A workforce plan is developed to ensure a business always has the right number and skills of employees to meet the people requirements of the organisation.

69.1 Introduction

Managing a firm's human resources is a key element of business success. This includes ensuring the business always has the number and skills of employees that it requires. This is the purpose of workforce planning. The process of workforce planning includes recruitment and selection, training and development, and appraisal.

69.2 Recruitment and selection

The purpose of the recruitment and selection process is to acquire a suitable number of employees with the appropriate skills and attitudes, in order to meet the people requirements of the organisation. It is in the interests of the business to achieve this goal at a minimum cost in terms of both time and resources.

There are three stages to this process:

1. determining the human resource requirements of the organisation

2. attracting suitable candidates for the vacancy

3. selecting the most appropriate candidate.

Determining the human resource requirements of the organisation

Recruitment and **selection procedures** need to fit in with the overall workforce plan. **Workforce planning** starts by auditing the current employees. How many will be retiring over the next 18 months? What are their skills? And how many are prepared to take on new tasks or challenges? This information must be compared with an estimate of the future workforce needs, based on the firm's overall corporate strategy for the next year or two. A sales push into Europe, for example, might require more French or Spanish speakers; planned factory closures may require redundancies and redeployments. The workforce plan must then show how the business can move staff from where they are now, to where they need to be later on. With firms regularly reviewing their overall strategies their workforce plans need to be updated frequently as well.

Effective workforce planning requires managers to question the existing employment structure at every opportunity. Changes can occur when:

- an individual leaves the business because of retirement or finding alternative employment

- an employee is promoted within the business, creating a vacancy

- an increase in workload occurs

- the development of a new product, or an emerging technology, which means that the organisation requires employees with additional skills

- a change in the business strategy such as an expansion or downsizing, changing the overall people needs of the organisation.

Many businesses fill vacancies automatically with no analysis of alternative actions. However, it may be more effective to consider reorganisation of job responsibilities. For example, if someone has retired, you might consider whether the job should be redesigned. A good human resource manager will look ahead to the future needs of a department before just advertising for a replacement. Should the new job holder be able to speak a foreign language? Is a full-time employee needed? Should the business opt for increased flexibility by shifting to the use of part-time employees? Or should the tasks be contracted out to a specialist firm?

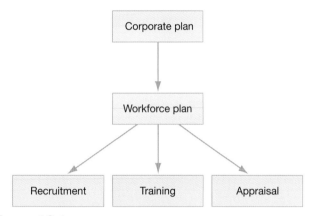

Figure 69.1

Attracting suitable candidates for a vacancy

Once the firm's human resource provision has been considered and the need for a new recruit is established, it is necessary to find a method of attracting suitable candidates.

The first step in this process is to develop a 'job description'. This will usually consist of:

- a job title

- a statement outlining how the job fits into the overall structure of the organisation

- details of the job's content, such as the tasks that must be performed and the responsibilities involved

- an indication of the working conditions the job holder can expect; this includes details of pay, hours of work and holiday entitlement.

Many firms will then choose to produce a person specification. This details the qualities of the ideal candidate, such as 'highly numerate', 'graduate' and 'good teamworker'. This should help to identify the criteria to use to shortlist and then select the best candidates from those who apply.

At this point the business must decide if the post will be filled from within the company or from outside it. 'Internal recruitment' (i.e. recruiting from within the business) ensures that the abilities of candidates will be known. In addition, other employees may be motivated by the evidence of promotion prospects within the firm. However, external recruitment will provide a wider pool of applicants from which to select. It can also introduce new thinking to the organisation.

The recruitment process can be expensive. It includes not only the cost of the advertising, but also the administration of, perhaps, hundreds of applications. Then there is the management time spent in the shortlisting and interviewing phases. The insurance giant Standard Life spends over £500,000 a year to recruit 50 management trainees. That's over £10,000 each!

The successful management of human resources demands that the effectiveness of recruitment advertising should be monitored. The most common method adopted is to calculate the cost of attracting each new employee. The appropriateness of recruits is also a concern. This can be judged by keeping a record of the proportion of candidates recruited by the firm who remain in employment six months and then one year, two years and even five years later. Standard Life is rightly proud that 99% of the graduate trainees it employs are still with the company two years later.

Selecting the right person for the job

The selection process involves assessing candidates against the criteria set out in the person specification. The most frequently employed selection process is to:

- shortlist a small number of applicants based on their application forms

- ask for a reference from their previous employers/teachers

- call for interview those individuals whose references are favourable.

The choice of who will be offered the job is made by the interview panel, based on which candidate they feel most closely matches the person specification for the post. Research suggests that the use of interviews is not a very reliable indicator of how well an individual will perform in a job. This is largely because interviewers are too easily swayed by appearance, personal charm and the interview technique of applicants. A number of other selection techniques have therefore been developed to complement, or replace, the use of this selection procedure.

Testing

There are two types of test. Aptitude tests measure how good the applicant is at a particular skill, such as typing or arithmetic. Psychometric tests measure the personality, attitudes and character of an applicant. They can give an indication of whether the applicant will be a team player or a loner, passive or assertive, questioning or accepting, and so on. The firm can make a selection judgement on the appropriate type of person from experience, and from the specific requirements of the job. This approach is particularly common in management and graduate recruitment.

Many doubts have been raised about the accuracy and validity of psychometric tests. Do they give an unfair advantage to certain people? Certainly the questions must be checked to remove social, sex or racial bias. There is also concern about whether firms are right to want all their managers to have similar characteristics. A wide range of personalities may lead to a more interesting, sparky atmosphere with livelier debates and better decisions.

Assessment centres

Assessment centres are a means of establishing the performance of job candidates in a range of circumstances. A group of similar applicants are invited to a centre, often for a number of days, for an in-depth assessment. They will be asked to perform tasks under scrutiny, such as role playing crisis situations. This is a good way to assess leadership qualities.

Research suggests this approach is the most effective selection technique for predicting successful job performance. Although the use of these centres is growing they are expensive and time consuming. Only large firms can afford to use this recruitment strategy and it is appropriate only for individuals who will potentially fill senior positions within a firm in the future.

Whichever selection procedure is adopted, a growing number of organisations are encouraging line managers to become involved in the recruitment decision. The role of the human resource department is increasingly one of providing support to functional departments rather than driving the recruitment process itself. Line managers are more aware of the key requirements of a post because they see it being carried out from day to day.

69.3 Training and development

Training is the process of instructing an individual about how to carry out tasks directly related to his or her current job.

A-grade application
Shell seeks the right qualities

Dutch-owned oil giant, Shell, believes it knows the qualities required for management success. It has researched carefully among its own high-flyers and come up with a list. When recruiting management trainees it uses a variety of tests to see which applicant best matches the required qualities. These include the ability to explore problems about which they had little previous knowledge, to see long-term implications and to cope better with the unknown. The specific attributes Shell looks for include: problem analysis; creativity and judgement; drive, resilience and empathy (seeing other people's point of view); and the action qualities of organising and implementing.

Figure 69.2 Employee training

Development involves helping an individual to realise his or her full potential. This concerns general growth, and is not related specifically to the employee's existing post.

An organisation that introduces a training and development programme does so in order to ensure the best possible return on its investment in people.

The four key objectives of training and development are as follows.

1 To help a new employee reach the level of performance expected from an experienced worker. This initial preparation upon first taking up a post is known as 'induction' training. It often contains information dealing with the precise nature of the job, layout of the firm's operating facility, health and safety measures, and security systems. An attempt may also be made to introduce the individual to key employees and give an impression of the culture of the organisation. The firm's induction training should aim to drive each employee along their own personal learning curve as quickly as possible (see Figure 69.3).

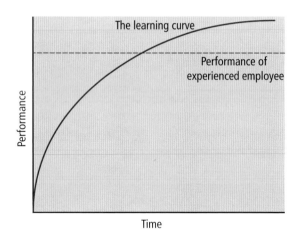

Figure 69.3 Objective of induction training

2 To provide a wide pool of skills available to the organisation, both at present and in the future (see Figure 69.4).

3 To develop a knowledgeable and committed workforce.

4 To deliver high-quality products or services.

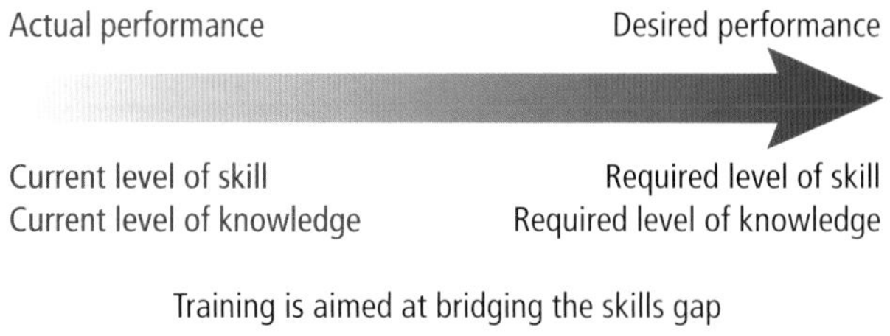

Actual performance   Desired performance

Current level of skill   Required level of skill
Current level of knowledge   Required level of knowledge

Training is aimed at bridging the skills gap

Figure 69.4 The training gap

Types of training

On-the-job training involves instructing employees at their place of work on how a particular task should be carried out. This may be done by an experienced worker demonstrating the correct way of performing a task, or by a supervisor coaching an employee by talking them through the job stage by stage. Job rotation involves switching an employee around a range of tasks in order to develop their skills in more than one area.

Off-the-job training is any form of instruction that takes place away from the immediate workplace. The firm itself may organise an internal programme based within on-site facilities, or send employees to a local college or university for an external development scheme. This approach to training is more likely to include more general skills and knowledge useful at work, rather than job-specific content.

The cost of not training

If an organisation chooses not to train its workforce it will be faced with additional recruitment costs. This is because when new skills are required existing employees will have to be made redundant and new people employed who have the right skills or experience.

Untrained staff will not be as productive, or as well motivated, as those who are trained. They will be unable to deal with change because their skills are specific only to the present situation. There may also be more accidents in the workplace if the workforce is unskilled. In addition, employees are less likely to know and work towards achieving, the organisation's aims and objectives.

Training in practice

A wide range of research has indicated that organisations in the UK, both in the private and public sector, fail to invest appropriately in training and development. Many organisations view training only as a cost and therefore fail to consider the long-term benefits it can bring.

Rather than planning for the future by anticipating the firm's knowledge and skill requirements, many businesses develop training programmes only as an answer to existing problems. This is reactive rather than proactive. The UK government responded to the reactive nature of training by launching the Investors In People (IIP) campaign. This encourages firms to develop a more strategic view of training and development. An organisation can gain IIP accredited status if it analyses its training and development needs, plans and implements a programme in response, and evaluates the effectiveness of its provision.

A-grade application

Investors In People

Over ten years ago, business at the 62-bedroom Park Hotel in Liverpool was poor. Profit had fallen to £60,000 and the occupancy rate was only 30%. Ron Jones, general manager, decided that the fundamental problem was lack of repeat and recommended (word-of-mouth) business. The cause of this seemed to be the lukewarm efforts of staff.

He responded by bringing in an expert to retrain staff and build morale, and then went for the Investors In People (IIP) award. The first step was to devise a SWOT analysis in conjunction with staff. Then heads of department explained their objectives and the staff skills required to achieve it. Every member of staff had a personal development plan drawn up and was given the training they required.

By the time of receiving the IIP award, the hotel had already gained in many ways. Labour turnover fell to 5% (compared with 35% for the industry nationally). Occupancy rose to 72% and the profit was in excess of £500,000 on turnover, which had doubled to £1.4 million.

The hotel's general manager, June Matthews, is certain that Investors In People stimulated higher participation and more positive attitudes among staff: 'Without a shadow of doubt it was worth it.'

69.4 Appraisal of performance

Appraisal is a formal assessment of the performance of a member of staff. It involves establishing clear objectives for each employee and evaluating actual performance in the light of these goals. The most important element of an appraisal system is usually a one-to-one discussion between an individual and his or her manager. This can be held frequently, but usually happens once a year. The discussion may consider specific performance measures such as individual output, or involve a more general review of the contribution the employee makes to the smooth running of the business.

The main objectives of an appraisal system are:

- to improve the performance of the employee
- to provide feedback to the individual about his or her performance
- to recognise the future training needs of the individual
- to consider the development of the individual's career
- to identify employees in the organisation who have potential for advancement.

An appraisal system provides information that allows the business to plan and develop its human resource provision.

Appraisal in practice

Research suggests that approximately 80% of UK organisations have some form of appraisal system. The current trend is to extend schemes beyond managers and supervisors to clerical and shop-floor workers. This is being partly driven by the Investors In People initiative discussed above. This demands that all employees must be involved in, or have the option of joining, an appraisal system if it is to be recognised by the project.

The use of appraisal does not seem to be limited to large firms. Evidence suggests that the majority of firms employing fewer than 500 people have in place some form of appraisal system. There is some evidence, however, that linking appraisal with pay can cause disharmony in the workplace. This is because employees may not discuss their performance openly if they think this leads directly to a pay award.

Redundancies

In some cases the corporate plan may involve restructuring and cost cutting. This may involve job losses as the scale or nature of the firm's operations change. Perhaps jobs are redesigned, offices are closed or operations are outsourced. In all these cases jobs may no longer exist and redundancies may have to be made. A redundancy occurs when there is a closure of all or part of the business. When they are made redundant employees are entitled to some financial payment (linked to the number of years they have worked at the business and their age); some firms will also work closely with employees to help them find alternative employment.

A-grade application
GlaxoSmithKline

In 2007 GlaxoSmithKline (GSK), the global pharmaceutical company, announced job cuts as part of a strategy to cut costs by £1.5 billion following poor sales results for its diabetes treatment Avandia. The company employs more than 100,000 people globally, including 22,000 in the UK at sites in Ware, Temple Hill in Dartford, Maidenhead and Worthing. This announcement came after its rival AstraZeneca said it would axe 7600 jobs worldwide as part of a cost-cutting plan earlier in the year.

Sales of Avandia fell by 38% in the quarter to £225 million as GSK reported a 7% fall in third-quarter profits.

The chief executive at GSK, said: 'GSK is also constantly seeking ways to adapt its operations and its cost base to remain competitive. We regret that job reductions will be a necessary part of this programme. We will do everything we can to support those employees who are affected.'

The labour market

The workforce plan is not only influenced by the firm's own strategy. It is affected by the state of the labour market. If there is a skills shortage in the UK, for example, the firm may have to look to recruit from overseas. Alternatively there may be a large supply of relatively cheap labour available that makes expansion easier or makes it viable to use more labour rather than invest in capital equipment. In recent years the UK has experienced a major inflow of labour from central and eastern Europe (following the expansion of the EU in 2004). This has provided a relatively low-wage source of labour for many UK firms.

Changes in external labour markets, such as an increase in the minimum wage or a change in the age structure, will influence a firm's workforce plan.

A-grade application
Migrant workers

The graph in Figure 69.5 shows the nationality of migrant workers into the UK in the three years after the 2004 EU enlargement, and Figure 69.6 shows the sectors of the economy where they are now working.

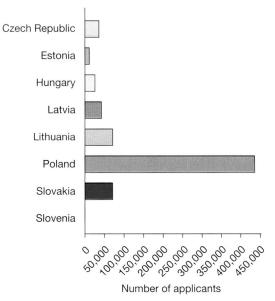

Figure 69.5

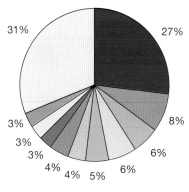

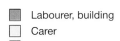

Figure 69.6

Workforce planning and business success

People play a vital role in the success of most business organisations. The creatives at the Saatchi & Saatchi advertising agency, the programmers at Google, the coaches and players at Chelsea are all essential to the organisation's success. Having the right people, with the right skills, is therefore critical to business planning. Without them you may not be able to expand, you may not be able to deliver the level of service offered and you may not make the profits you expect. Staffing shortages can mean you cannot meet customer orders; skills shortages may mean you lack the flexibility you need to compete effectively. Planning your human resource requirements and reviewing the workforce plan is therefore a major contributor to the overall performance of a business.

Issues For Analysis

When analysing a firm's workforce plan be aware of the following aspects.

- Check that the workforce plan is closely linked to the overall corporate plan. Expansion is likely to mean recruitment; relocation may mean transfers or even redundancies. Effective human resource management means the business is planning ahead to identify its future workforce requirements, rather than merely responding to short-term events and allowing these to shape human resource policy?

- Effective recruitment and selection usually involves preparing job descriptions and person specifications in order to ensure the recruitment process selects individuals with the most appropriate skills for the vacant post.

- A business should try to use a range of selection techniques and be wary of relying on interviews alone.

- Training can help individuals have the skills and knowledge they need to perform to a better standard.

- A business should have an employee appraisal system; this can help to develop individuals.

69.5 Workforce planning
an evaluation

Managing people effectively is the single most common factor that links successful organisations. This involves planning the human resource requirements very carefully when there are changes in the business strategy or the external environment.

The success of a workforce plan will depend on how well it anticipates the demands for and supply of labour, and how well the corporate and workforce plan is implemented.

Businesses today understand the important contribution employees make towards competitiveness. This has made workforce planning a central topic, even though planning itself has become more difficult as the rate of change has increased.

Key terms

Off-the-job training: any form of training not immediately linked to a specific task. It may take place within the firm – perhaps in conference facilities – or away from it – for example, at a local technical college.

On-the-job training: the process of instructing employees at their place of work on how a particular job should be carried out. This usually involves watching an experienced operative carry out a task, or actually undertaking the activity and being guided as to appropriate technique.

Selection procedure: the process by which organisations choose to differentiate between the applicants for a specific job in order to pick out the most appropriate candidate. The most commonly used technique is interview, but a range of different approaches (e.g. personality testing) are being used more frequently in order to complement traditional methods.

Workforce planning: the process of anticipating in advance the human resource requirements of the organisation, both in terms of the number of individuals required and the appropriate skill mix. Recruitment and training policies are devised with a long-term focus, in order to ensure the business is able to operate without being limited by a shortage of appropriate labour.

Exercises

A. Revision questions

(35 marks; 35 minutes)

1 Why is it important that an organisation challenges its existing employment structure each time an opportunity to do so emerges? (4)

2 Why do 'job descriptions' and 'person specifications' play an important part in the selection of appropriate personnel? (4)

3 What advantages does the process of internal recruitment offer to the business over the appointment of individuals from outside the organisation? (4)

4 Identify three benefits to a firm of using assessment centres in selecting key staff. (3)

5 What might be the costs of not training:
 (a) new supermarket checkout operators (4)
 (b) crowd stewards at Manchester United. (4)

6 What kinds of non-financial rewards might be offered to employees? (4)

7 What is the main purpose of 'induction' training? (4)

8 What benefits might a firm derive from achieving an Investors In People award? (4)

B. Revision exercises

B1 Case study

Human resource development at Prest Ltd

Three years ago Prest Ltd, manufacturer of electronic components, closed three factories and concentrated its operations on a single site. At the same time it reorganised the remaining plant to cut costs and improve product quality. Before modernisation, 50% of the machinery being used at the site had been over 15 years old. This was replaced with the latest equipment. The new production line was designed to run continuously, with operators being expected to take 'first level' decisions at the point of production to keep it

functioning. As a result, tasks such as fault finding and machine maintenance became an important part of the job of each worker.

The modernisation of the plant signalled a shift to team working, in order to encourage employee flexibility. Multi-skilled operators were needed with a deeper understanding of the production system. The employees needed to know how the new machinery could best be used to ensure consistently high levels of production quality. These changes had clear implications for the human resource department at Prest. Recruitment would have to focus on a new type of employee, and existing employees would need to be retrained.

The human resource manager conducted a feasibility analysis in order to review the strengths and weaknesses of the company's existing workforce and its ability to handle the new situation. This concluded that both shop-floor supervision and the engineering section needed strengthening. In response, 15 new engineers were recruited and five staff redeployed to improve production supervision.

As an answer to the immediate need for greater skill levels, a comprehensive training programme in quality control was introduced for all staff. Machine operators were encouraged to mix with engineers during this exercise, helping to break down barriers between the two groups. For many individuals this was the first formal company training they had ever received. The development initiative was successful enough to stimulate requests for further learning opportunities. As a result, Prest created a link with a local technical college to provide more extensive instruction for those who wished to learn more about modern production techniques.

Although the benefits of the training were clear, three problems emerged that Prest had not anticipated. The greater knowledge of the operators made them anxious to put their acquired skills into practice. After nine months the new production line had reached only 80% efficiency. Senior managers believed employees were losing interest when machinery was functioning normally. In addition, some workers felt the extensive training they had received was not reflected in enough increased responsibility. Their expectations of a more interesting job had been raised, but the reality seemed little different than before. Finally, 12 newly trained staff left the company because they could now apply for more highly paid posts at other firms in the area.

Prest also considered the long-term human resource implications of the move to a more sophisticated form of production. The workforce knew little about new production technology, so the firm's training school ran a course on robotics. The decision was also taken to provide a sponsorship scheme to encourage new recruits to study on an engineering degree course at university. The firm wished to ensure it did not face a shortage of talent in the long term.

Questions

(40 marks; 45 minutes)

1 Analyse the possible implications for human resource managers following the introduction of new technology and different working practices at Prest Ltd. (8)

2 Discuss the human resource issues that might emerge as a result of the feasibility study conducted at Prest Ltd. (12)

3 Analyse the appropriateness of the development programme introduced by Prest Ltd in the light of the problems identified by the feasibility study. (8)

4 Consider whether the difficulties experienced after staff training at Prest Ltd suggest that employees can receive too much training. (12)

C. Essay questions

(40 marks each)

1 Johnson Engineering plc is suffering from a lack of skilled engineers. Consider how its human resource department might set about solving this problem.

2 In order to establish a competitive advantage, a business must make sure its selection, appraisal, development and reward of employees each 'fit' together in order to form a single human resource policy approach. Discuss how this might be achieved and the difficulties that may be encountered.

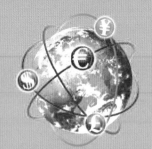

FLEXIBILITY AND INSECURITY

70.1 The need for a more flexible approach

The rise and rise of Toyota and its model of lean production has taught many firms many things. Above all else, it showed that mass production systems lack the flexibility needed for today's markets. When oil prices leap from $25 to $100 within a couple of years, whole model ranges have to change. In early 2008, with sales of its Hummer 'beasts on wheels' down by 25%, General Motors needed to switch to smaller, more environmentally friendly cars. It needed a more **flexible approach**. But if you have forced an employee to work at the same job day in day out for 15 years, it may be very difficult to retrain them.

Today's businesses need a more flexible approach within their operations. The need has arisen for a number of reasons.

● Increasing competition means that the marketplace is subject to frequent and often rapid change. Firms need to be able to anticipate these changes and respond to them quickly in order to maintain a competitive edge.

● Many consumers want more customised goods and services (i.e. better tailored to smaller segments of the population); firms have to adapt the production process in order to meet demand, while still operating efficiently and keeping costs down.

● Increasing competition, especially from overseas firms, has forced businesses faced with fluctuating or seasonal demand to introduce greater operational flexibility, in order to eliminate any unnecessary costs.

To succeed in modern markets that are often fragmented into relatively small niches, and where customer tastes are ever changing, many firms have adopted lean production. This approach implies the use of machinery that can quickly be reprogrammed to carry out a range of tasks, and the creation of a multi-skilled and flexible workforce that can quickly adapt – and be adapted – to meet a firm's changing requirements.

A-grade application
Benefits of flexible working

British businesses need to modernise their working practices if they are to succeed in competing in global markets, according to Sir Digby Jones, former leader of the CBI. Sir Digby made his claims in a speech at the beginning of Work Wise Week 2007 – an initiative set up to raise awareness of the benefits of flexible working. According to him, 'The impact of the wider adoption of new smarter working practices will be profound . . . Not only will there be improvements in productivity and competitiveness, but also in the well-being of staff, which in turn impacts positively on employee relations. It is not about working harder but more cleverly.'

Source: Work Wise UK

70.2 Achieving greater flexibility within the workforce

There are a number of ways in which firms can attempt to increase the level of workforce flexibility, some of which are described below.

Functional flexibility

This occurs when workers become multi-skilled (i.e. they are given the scope and ability to carry out a variety of tasks (functions), rather than specialising in completion of one particular area). This can be encouraged through the use of job rotation, in which workers carry out an increased number of tasks at the same level of difficulty. In a hotel, for instance, the people who are usually on reception could spend time organising wedding receptions – giving them a wider understanding of the business. In Japan this is known as horizontal promotion, as it implies that the company has enough faith in the individual to invest time and money in training him/her for an extra job.

Increasing the level of functional flexibility should, in theory, mean that a firm's human resources can be used more effectively. Keeping workers fully occupied should lead to improved productivity. It should also mean that employees are equipped with the skills needed to cover for staff absences, minimising any disruption or loss of production that this may otherwise have caused. Individual workers may respond positively to the increased variety and new challenges provided, improving motivation and increasing productivity further. However, firms may be unwilling to bear the costs of additional training unless the benefits of adopting a new approach are obvious and immediate.

Table 70.1 Creating functional flexibility: benefits and drawbacks

Benefits	Drawbacks
Increases in productivity from greater utilisation of employees	Potential loss of production as workers switch between different tasks
Reduction in disruption to production caused by staff absence	Greater training requirements as individual workers need to acquire a wider range of skills, increasing costs
Greater employee motivation created by more varied and challenging tasks at work	Workers may be reluctant to acquire new skills, especially if there is no corresponding increase in pay

Numerical flexibility

All firms face the problem of having enough workers to respond to increases in customer demand, without having to bear the cost of employing unnecessary staff

should sales decline temporarily. Increasing the level of numerical flexibility involves a firm using alternatives to the traditional approach of employing staff on permanent, full-time contracts. These alternatives include the use of temporary contracts, agency staff, and **subcontracting** or **outsourcing** certain operations to other firms. Flexible temporary staff enable firms to respond to a sudden rise in sales by increasing the workforce quickly – and then reducing its size just as quickly, should the sales increase prove to be temporary. However, while a reliance on temporary staff and external organisations may help to reduce costs and improve reaction to change, productivity may be harmed by a lack of expertise and worker loyalty to the firm.

Time flexibility

Greater flexibility can also be created by moving away from the traditional 9 to 5 working day and 38-hour working week in order to respond more effectively to customer demands. There are a number of methods used by firms to vary the pattern of working, including the use of part-time work, job sharing, annualised hours contracts and flexitime. For example, banks, insurance companies and mobile phone operators make extensive use of flexitime systems to provide 24-hour employee cover via the telephone and internet, in order to provide customers with greater convenience. Introducing greater time flexibility can also have a number of benefits for employees who may have family or other commitments during normal working hours. Providing staff with more flexible working arrangements

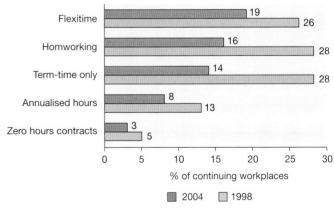

Figure 70.1 Changes in flexible working arrangements in the UK

can help to improve recruitment, increase motivation and reduce labour turnover, leading to reduced costs and boosts to productivity.

70.3 A model of the flexible firm

The flexible firm is able to change its own structure in response to changing needs. This means creating a structure that allows quick changes to take place. In order to achieve this, firms have tended to identify a 'core', which forms the basis for all its operations, and a 'periphery', which consists of all the other tasks needed to run the firm but that are not central to the business.

For a firm producing household goods such as washing machines, **core workers** might comprise designers, the market research team and workers on the production line, among others. The canteen and cleaning staff, and even advertising campaign staff may be seen as being less central to the firm, and so may be employed on a part-time basis, or even brought in at specific times to undertake a specific task; these are known as **peripheral workers** (see Table 70.2).

Table 70.2 Core and peripheral workers

Core workers	Peripheral workers
Full-time employees	Part-time, temporary or self-employed
Do tasks central to the business	Perform less critical, or less permanent, tasks
Secure jobs	Insecure jobs
Committed to the firm's goals	Committed to self-interest

The benefit of being a flexible firm, of course, is that the periphery can be increased quickly when needed to meet a particular change in the market place.

In his book *The Age of Unreason*, Professor Charles Handy suggested that instead of firms comprising two elements, the core and periphery, there were actually three parts to modern firms; he called this idea the 'Shamrock Organisation', as illustrated in Figure 70.2. The first leaf of the shamrock represents the professional core, made up of qualified professionals, technicians and managers. The second leaf, called the contractual fringe, is for the work that has been contracted out to someone else because it is not central to the firm. Professor Handy notes that many firms that used to be manufacturers now do little more than assemble parts bought in from suppliers. As much as 80% of a firm's work may be done outside the business itself. The third and final leaf is the flexible labour force, made up of temporary and part-time workers. In effect, Handy has split the periphery into an internal periphery (the flexible labour force) and an external periphery (the contractual fringe).

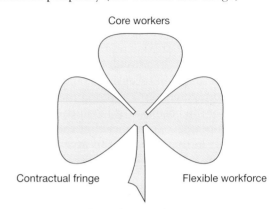

Figure 70.2 Handy's Shamrock Organisation

A particular type of flexible worker is the homeworker. This is someone who works at home, probably on a laptop connected permanently to the main office. In some cases it can be that a full-time employee does two days a week at home – with fewer distractions from the phone, from meetings and from gossipy staff. In other cases, the business may want as few people as possible at head office, to keep overhead costs down, so they encourage staff to work at home, and perhaps occasionally come in and '**hot-desk**'.

Some really enjoy this arrangement, whereas it makes others feel insecure. Ideally, an employee would have this as an option; it would be much less satisfactory if it were forced upon the worker.

A-grade application
Homeworking eases stress

Working from home reduces stress in office workers, but leads to fears about career progression, according to research. A survey of 749 staff in managerial or professional positions conducted by Durham Business School showed that homeworkers worried about missing out on 'water-cooler networking' – where potential opportunities for moving up the ladder are discussed informally in the office.

Despite these concerns, the study also found that working from home generally had a positive effect on an employee's work/life balance, giving them more time with the family, and leading to less stress and less chance of burnout.

Four in ten respondents who worked more than 20 hours per week at home reported feeling a great deal of stress because of their job compared with 65% of employees who worked solely in the office.

Source: www.PersonnelToday.com, 5 April 2008

70.4 Flexible operations and 'hard' HRM

Whether or not flexibility was necessary for a firm's success, 'hard HR' managers saw scope for increasing their control over staff. Full-time, permanent staff who were resistant to changes put forward by management might find themselves threatened with being 'outsourced'. Outsourcing is when a firm uses sources outside the business to undertake functions that used to be done internally by a section of the business itself. Tasks such as designing new products or undertaking market research can be bought in by the firm as and when needed. In effect, it turns what used to be a fixed cost (a staff salary) into a variable cost – a cost that need only be incurred when there is demand for it.

Although that may sound logical, it has some serious potential downsides. Outside contractors have no loyalty to the business and no reason to contribute anything that is not being paid for (such as an idea for doing things more efficiently). So firms that shrink their core workforce too much (see Figure 70.3) can find that the organisation is like a Polo – all outside and no heart.

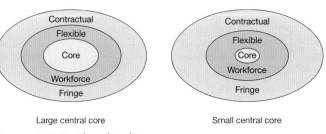

Large central core   Small central core

Figure 70.3 The shrinking core

70.5 Insecurity

The increasing desire for firms to increase their flexibility has generated a number of concerns – in particular, in terms of loss of job security for workers. While those employees in core roles have continued to enjoy a great deal of job security, peripheral workers have experienced a growing sense of insecurity as the use of temporary contracts and the threat of insecurity has increased. An increasing number of workers have also had to overcome an instinctive resistance to change by having to repeatedly retrain in order to carry out new job roles. However, some would argue that demands for increasing flexibility within the workplace have created new opportunities and challenges, including opportunities to learn new skills and diversify into new career paths, rather than ending up 'stuck in a rut'.

Issues For Analysis

Opportunities for analysis may arise when asking the following questions.

● What is the pressure behind a change in production system from inflexible (mass) to flexible (lean)? If the reasons are positive, it may be easy to convince staff of the benefits. Unfortunately the move to 'lean' can also be a move to 'mean' (i.e. increased flexibility may be at the cost of increased insecurity). Always, the question of trust is crucial. Does the workforce trust the management?

● What are the reasons behind a firm's decision to choose a more flexible approach to staffing? Is it to be more helpful to staff, perhaps especially those with small children? Or is it a way of maximising management control over staff, and minimising labour costs?

70.6 Flexibility and insecurity
an evaluation

The adoption of a more flexible workforce can, in principle, be an attractive prospect for any modern business, offering a number of benefits, including reduced costs and an increased ability to respond to changing customer demands. The separation of employees into a highly valued core and an easily dispensable periphery may allow a business to 'pick and mix' skills and obtain the exact combination required within the market at that particular moment in time.

However, it can also lead to a number of problems in the long term, especially if it creates insecurity among peripheral workers that leads to high levels of staff turnover. The ability to cut labour costs quickly and easily in the face of a downturn in the market has obvious attractions. However, in the long term, the establishment of a multi-skilled and loyal workforce, able to adapt and diversify into new markets, may lead to even greater success.

Key terms

Core workers: employees who are essential to the operations of a business, supporting whatever makes it distinctive or unique. Such workers are likely to receive attractive salaries and working conditions, and enjoy a high degree of job security.

Flexible approach: an approach to operations that implies a move away from mass production to batch production, the use of machinery that can be quickly reprogrammed to carry out a range of tasks, and the creation of a multi-skilled and flexible workforce that can quickly adapt to meet a firm's changing requirements.

Hot-desk: an approach that provides a temporary desk for homeworkers to use when they come to the main office; they are not allowed to leave any of their own possessions there.

Outsourcing: involves a firm finding an external business to carry out part of the production process, in order to cut costs or achieve a better level of service. For example, it might involve hiring cleaning or catering services from other businesses.

Peripheral workers: those workers who are not seen as being central to a firm's operations. They may carry out necessary tasks, but may be required only on a temporary basis and be easily replaced.

Subcontracting: where another business is used to perform or supply certain aspects of a firm's operations (see *outsourcing*).

Further reading

Handy, C. (1989) *The Age of Unreason*. Hutchinson.

Exercises

A. Revision questions

(40 marks; 40 minutes)

1 Why might increased market change have an effect on the way people are employed today? (3)

2 Outline two reasons why firms may have chosen to adopt a more flexible approach to workforce arrangements. (4)

3 Briefly explain what is meant by the term lean production. (3)

4 Explain, using examples, what is meant by the term functional flexibility. (4)

5 Outline one advantage and one disadvantage for a small textiles manufacturer of trying to increase the degree of functional flexibility among its workforce. (6)

6 Explain what is meant by numerical flexibility in respect of a firm's workforce. (3)

7 State two ways in which a bank offering telephone and internet services to customers would benefit from introducing greater time flexibility. (4)

8 Explain the idea of the 'Shamrock Organisation'. (3)

9 Outline two reasons why a firm's employees might welcome the decision to move towards increased labour flexibility. (4)

10 Examine two reasons why the move towards greater flexibility might lead to increased insecurity within the workforce. (6)

B. Revision exercises

B1 Data response

Flexible working at First Direct

First Direct is one of the UK's leading commercial banks, providing a wide range of financial services via telephone and the internet to over 1.2 million customers. When it launched in 1989, banks opened only between 9am and 3pm, Monday to Friday. However, the company set out to create a different business model, based on the customer need for greater convenience. Since its establishment, First Direct's reputation has rested on the fact that it is the bank that never closes and ignores weekends and bank holidays. Operators in the company's call centres handle approximately 235,000 calls each week, more than 13,000 of which each day are outside normal working hours, and with more than 500 coming from overseas.

The company's operations have required it to develop a working culture that is very different from the traditional model. This has included longer shifts, a high proportion of part-time and home-based workers, and reliance on so-called 'mushrooming' – a term used to describe workers employed to work night-time shifts.

According to Jane Hanson, head of human resources at First Direct, 'It's about making life convenient . . . We have people phoning us while they're on holiday or in the middle of the night because they wake up worrying that they haven't paid their Visa bill.'

First Direct appears to have succeeded on a number of levels. The quality of its customer service has resulted in high rates of customer retention. Employees also appear to approve of the company's approach to flexible working – the company claims to have very good rates of staff retention, claiming, for example, that 90% of female staff return to their jobs after maternity leave.

Source: Work Wise UK

Questions

(20 marks; 25 minutes)

1 Identify two examples of flexible working practices used by First Direct. (2)

2 Analyse two possible benefits for a business such as First Direct of creating a more flexible workforce. (8)

3 To what extent is the creation of a more flexible workforce crucial to the continuing success of a company such as First Direct? (10)

70.7 Workbook

B2 Data response

UK employees lead in terms of insecurity

Workers in the UK suffer from a major sense of insecurity, according to a survey carried out by Right Management Consultants in 2005. The survey measured overall confidence levels of workers from 18 of the world's leading economies, based on criteria that included job security and ability to find replacement work. Over 24% of British workers felt it 'very probable' or 'somewhat probable' that they would lose their jobs in the next 12 months. Furthermore, 71% of them felt they would struggle to find alternative work if they did lose their jobs.

Table 71.3 Overall confidence table

1	Japan	68.6%
2.	South Korea	67.0%
3.	Norway	63.6%
4.	Denmark	62.9%
5.	Spain	61.4%
6.	Ireland	60.0%
7.	Sweden	58.2%
8.	Australia	54.9%
9.	Italy	53.1%
10.	Hong Kong	52.5%
11.	Canada	51.7%
12.	Netherlands	51.0%
13.	UK	50.3%
14.	France	49.3%
15.	Belgium	48.2%
16.	USA	47.3%
17.	Switzerland	44.1%
18.	Germany	43.4%

Source: www.bbc.co.uk

Questions

(15 marks; 20 minutes)

1 Explain two reasons why UK workers might suffer from greater levels of job insecurity than workers in other countries. (6)

2 Discuss the key implications of the findings of the survey carried out by Right Management Consultants for UK businesses. (9)

C. Essay questions

(40 marks each)

1 To what extent do you agree with the view that UK manufacturing firms can survive only by adopting 'hard HRM' methods?

2 Assess the possible impact of adopting more flexible working practices on the international competitiveness of a UK firm such as Cadbury.

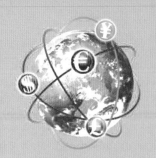

EMPLOYEE PARTICIPATION AND TEAM WORKING

71.1 Participation in practice

As early as 1918 Cadbury pioneered elected works councils in its Bourneville factory. Ten years later, Elton Mayo showed that morale and productivity can be boosted if staff feel involved and therefore respected. The main risk is that participation can become a three-monthly chore rather than part of the business culture. Effective participation is part of daily life, not postponed for a meeting. Nearly a century after Cadbury's initiative, employee participation remains patchy.

Figure 71.1 Employees at Cadbury's Bourneville factory early in the 20th century

Many managers realise that workers have a tremendous amount to offer in terms of ideas and insight into solving problems. Involving the people who do the work on a daily basis enables managers to learn how the job could be done more effectively. This reveals specific problems faced by the employees in a particular work area.

The importance of managers actually listening to their employees and paying attention to their social needs was highlighted in Mayo's study of the Hawthorne plant. When employees were asked for their opinions their productivity rose, simply because managers were paying them attention and showing that they were valued. Greater participation has been shown to have tangible results in many companies, such as higher motivation, more innovation and lower labour turnover. This means that developing more effective employee participation can be an important element of business success. It involves using one of your resources more effectively (and the human resource is the only one that can decide to walk out of the door and not return).

There are, of course, problems involved in participation. Involving more people may slow up decision making, although even this can be a good thing as it forces managers to discuss their ideas and listen to employees' comments. This may help to avoid hasty decisions, which are later regretted. However, there are some situations, such as a crisis, where a quick decision is important and where any delay may prove damaging. In this situation too much discussion could cause problems.

Participation can also prove frustrating. When people attend a meeting, for example, they often have very different ideas of what they are trying to get out of it. They may well hope to achieve one thing but become irritated when it becomes clear that others are trying to achieve something else. Managers may resent the fact that their ideas are being challenged by workers in meetings and may wish they did not have to discuss things at all. Employees may also be unhappy because they may expect more power than they are actually given. Having become involved in decision making they may well want more information or more control over issues than management is willing to allow.

Simply announcing that employees will be invited to participate more in decision making does not in itself necessarily improve the performance of the business. The process needs to be planned (e.g. who is to participate and how), employees need to be consulted so they understand the benefits and do not feel they are being exploited (i.e. being asked to give ideas in return for nothing) and the process managed (i.e. a regular review of what works and what does not).

A-grade application

Partnership

Everyone who works at John Lewis is an owner of the organisation and is called a 'partner'. The fact that partners have a stake in the business means that they have the right to expect managers to explain their decisions to them.

At store level, local managers meet with partners on a regular basis. They provide information on how their part of the business is doing and brief staff on issues concerning the organisation as a whole. Partners have the right to question any decision and receive an explanation. Managers in John Lewis are, therefore, far more accountable to staff than they are in most other organisations.

At the end of each financial year, a percentage of the profits is paid out to each partner. It is often as high as 20% of a partner's annual salary. John Lewis and its sister company, Waitrose, have been successful, growing businesses for many years. This demonstrates that employee participation has the potential to be a successful, profitable approach.

71.2 How do employees participate in decisions?

There are numerous mechanisms to increase the amount of employee participation within a firm. These occur at different levels within the organisation and deal with different types of issues. They include those described below.

Kaizen groups

Devised in Japan by firms such as Toyota and Nissan, these have become popular throughout the west. *Kaizen*

means 'continuous improvement', so the idea is to meet regularly and keep coming up with ways to do things better (or to tackle niggling faults). For example, workers may meet to solve problems of high wastage levels in one part of the factory. Employees are usually paid for their time in meetings and are expected to present their findings to management.

Works councils

A **works council** is a committee of employer and employee representatives that meets to discuss company wide issues. Works councils have worked well in some countries, such as Germany, but have not been so popular in the UK. A works council will usually discuss issues such as training, investment and working practices that affect the whole workforce. It will not cover issues such as pay, which are generally dealt with in discussions with trades union representatives.

Autonomous work groups

An autonomous work group consists of a team of people who are given a high level of responsibility for their own work. These responsibilities might include the scheduling of the work and decisions over the allocation of their tasks (they might choose to use job rotation). To be really effective, such teams should be invited to join recruitment panels for new staff and be given the capital budget necessary to buy new machinery when it is needed.

Employee shareholders

An increasingly common way to develop a common sense of purpose is to give employees shares in the business. For example, employees at Innocent Drinks and at Tesco have the opportunity to buy shares in the company. This should mean they become more interested in the overall performance of the firm as well their own personal performance. If they can think of it as 'their' company rather than a company, job done.

Other methods

Other methods of encouraging employee participation include suggestion schemes and a more democratic style of management.

When deciding on how to improve participation in the business managers must therefore consider the options

nd decide which are most appropriate. The speed and
method of introduction must also be considered to
nsure that they are accepted and that employees value
hem as much as managers.

A-grade application

The world's most successful car producer is Toyota. For
the past 50 years it has made its suggestion scheme a
fundamental part of the business. It receives over 1
million staff suggestions a year for workplace
improvement. It has always reported that the keys to a
successful scheme are filtering, implementation and the
promise of no redundancies. Filtering means checking
ideas out on other staff to weed out bad or unpopular
ones. The rate of implementation has to be high to keep
staff bothering to come up with new ideas. And the
promise of no redundancies is critical (e.g. when an
employee first suggested that robots should take over the
job of painting car bodies, to save the lungs of staff;
'paint shop' staff were retrained for jobs elsewhere in
the factory).

71.3 European directives

n most European countries the works council (which
onsists of elected representatives) is an integral part of
mployee participation within the firm. It is consulted
whenever management plans to do anything that is
kely to affect the majority of employees, such as
hanging employment terms and conditions or staffing
evels. Up until recently, works councils have been very
are in the UK. However the EU's European Works
Council directive is forcing some large UK firms to
hange their approach to employee participation and
ntroduce works councils.

hese works councils will have information and
onsultation rights in relation to company performance
nd strategic planning. In effect, there should be
onsultation and a dialogue on any proposed actions by
he employer that could affect employees' jobs.

Consultation is defined in the regulations as 'the
xchange of views and establishment of dialogue'
etween the employer and employees or employee
epresentatives.

71.4 Teamwork

Many organisations now expect employees to undertake
their work in teams. This is because they believe that
team working leads to more efficient and effective
production. People often respond positively to working
with others because this satisfies their social needs
(Mayo). The fact that managers are willing to delegate
responsibility to teams also meets employees' ego and
self-actualisation needs. Teams also allow individuals to
gain from the strengths of others. There may be some
areas in which you are relatively weak but someone else
is strong, and vice versa. Imagine you are trying to solve
a crossword, for example. It is usually much quicker and
more fun sharing the task with others. Working in
teams also allows individuals to change jobs, which can
provide some variety at work.

However, some people do not particularly enjoy working
in teams. This may be because of their personality or
because they think their own performance would be
better than that of the other members of the team –
they are worried about being dragged down. Teamwork
can also bring with it various problems: decision making
can be slow and there may be serious disagreements
between the members of the group.

Figure 71.2 Teamwork can lead to greater efficiency

A-grade application

Semco

Richard Semler is world famous for his belief that people and companies perform best when they are left to themselves without management interference. Semler took over the family business, Semco, from his father and immediately started to dismantle the old structure. Employees were no longer searched when they left the factory; clocking in was ended and then all controls on working hours were removed. Employees wear what they want. One-third of them even set their own salaries; the rest are discussed within business units according to performance. All meetings are open to everyone. There are no receptionists and no secretaries. Managers are elected by their subordinates and their performance is reviewed by subordinates every six months. Those who have not performed satisfactorily will be moved to another position. Management decisions are taken by a 'committee of counsellors'. Even though Semler owns 90% of the company his ideas are often rejected.

Richard Semler recognises that this approach may not be an easy one to imitate (indeed he called his book about the company *Maverick*!), yet he stresses the need to involve people in decision making to a much greater extent than in the past. According to Semler, genuine participative management is possible only when managers give up decision making and let employees govern themselves. While other managers watch the Semco approach with interest, few have been willing to imitate Semler's ideas. Many are still sceptical about its impact on performance in the long run.

(To find out more about Semler's ideas, see the 'Further reading' section on page 511.)

71.5 Employee participation, team working and business success

Employees are an important resource of a business. They provide ideas for new products and new ways of doing things, they solve problems and they move the business forward. Utilising this resource effectively is therefore one of the many challenges of managers. As part of the process of human resource management managers must decide on the level and method of employee participation. They must weigh up some of the potential problems (such as the time and cost) with the benefits (such as more views and insights into problems).

It is not realistic, or even desirable, for everyone to participate in every decision. This would make for a very unwieldy organisation that is slow to react. So managers must decide who should be involved in various decisions. Teams and committees can help managers to cut across departments, divisions and products to improve communication and the sharing of information. They can provide a diversity of views, which is often essential in a business operating in global markets, and they can share a range of skills and talents. They also build employees' level of commitment and understanding of the firm's values and strategy. All of which makes participation (when done correctly) very important to business success. The benefits of participation can be seen in better decisions, fewer mistakes, higher levels of satisfaction and innovation, and greater effectiveness.

Issues For Analysis

When analysing employee participation within an organisation you might find it useful to consider the following points.

- Approaches to participation are all rooted in the theories of Mayo, Maslow and Herzberg. Analysis can be enriched by making and explaining the connections between theory and practice.

- Greater participation by employees may provide the business with a competitive advantage. It may provide more ideas, greater motivation, greater efficiency and greater commitment from the workforce. This makes change easier, and – in the service sector – has a direct effect upon customer image.

- There is every reason to suppose that employees today need more opportunities for participation; nowadays employees are generally better educated and have a higher standard of living, and therefore want to be involved to a greater extent.

- Despite this, some researchers argue that many managers have become more authoritarian in recent years. Consequently, participation may have reduced in many organisations. This is especially true in the public sector, where staff in professions such as medicine or teaching find themselves less involved and less often consulted than in the past.

71.6 Employee participation and team working
an evaluation

Managed effectively, employees can provide better-quality and more innovative work at a lower cost and a faster rate. To achieve such improvements in performance employees must be involved. They must have the ability to contribute and feel they are listened to. Greater participation can help a firm to gain a competitive advantage. This is why managers in all kinds of successful organisations claim that their success is due to their people. However, despite the potential gains from participation this does not mean every manager has embraced the idea. After all, the more employees participate in decisions, the more managers have to explain their actions to them. Some managers find this change difficult to cope with.

Participation can also slow up the decision-making process and, if handled incorrectly, can lead to conflict. Greater participation must be part of a general movement involving greater trust and mutual respect between managers and workers. Employees cannot be expected to participate positively if, at the same time, their conditions and rewards are poor. Successful participation is part of an overall approach in which employees are given responsibility and treated fairly.

Managers must also consider the most effective method and the most appropriate degree of participation for their organisation. This will depend on the culture of the organisation, the pace of change, and the attitude and training of both managers and workers. Despite the growth of participation in the UK, employee representation is still relatively low – especially when compared with countries such as Germany, where employees are often represented at a senior level. However, although this system appears to work well in Germany this does not necessarily mean it will work as effectively in the UK because of the two countries' different traditions and cultures.

Key terms

Industrial democracy: an industrial democracy occurs when employees have the opportunity to be involved in decision making. In its most extreme form each employee would have a vote. When examining a business you should consider the extent to which employees are involved in decision making.
Teamwork: individuals work in groups rather than being given highly specialised, individual jobs.
Works council: a committee of management and workers that meets to discuss company-wide issues such as training, investment and expansion.

Further reading

Herzberg, F. (1959) *The Motivation to Work*. Wiley International.

Maslow, A. H. (1987) *Motivation and Personality*. HarperCollins (1st edn 1954).

Mayo, E. (1975) *The Social Problems of Industrial Civilisation*. Routledge (1st edn 1949).

Semler, S. (2001) *Maverick*. Random House.

Semler, S. (2003) *The End of the Weekend*. Century.

Exercises

A. Revision questions

(40 marks; 40 minutes)

1 Explain the possible benefits to a firm of greater employee participation. (5)

2 Why do some managers resist greater participation? (4)

3 Why do some workers resist greater participation? (4)

4 Examine two possible problems of involving employees more in decision making in a business such as Tesco plc. (6)

5 Consider the advantages and disadvantages to a Europe-wide business such as Coca-Cola of having a works council covering staff from all its factories across Europe. (6)

6 Outline two benefits of teamwork. (4)

7 How would team working be viewed by a motivational theorist of your choice? (5)

8 Examine the possible impact on a firm's profit of a move towards the use of autonomous work groups in the workplace. (6)

B. Revision exercises

B1 Data response

John Lewis Partnership

John Lewis is one of the world's biggest employee-owned businesses. As all staff are 'partners' with a profit share and voting rights, it should have exceptionally impressive employee participation. In many ways it does. It has employee councils that meet regularly, to provide insights from the shop floor and to involve staff in decision making. And all staff can attend the Annual General Meeting.

As not everyone likes speaking in public, there is also a staff survey, answered by more than 90% of the 69,000 staff (in most businesses, a 40% response rate would be impressive). In 2007, the survey showed good results on the following four factors: 'be honest', 'show respect', 'recognise others' and 'work together'. Results were less impressive on two other criteria: 'show enterprise' and 'achieve more'. Now the key thing will be how senior managers respond to this information. Only if they can find ways to encourage staff to show more enterprise and gain more sense of achievement can the participation be said to be a success.

Questions

(25 marks; 30 minutes)

1 **(a)** Identify two forms of **industrial democracy** used at John Lewis. (2)

  (b) Examine how one of the two might affect staff motivation. (4)

2 John Lewis provides the right structures for participation, but may fail to sufficiently encourage day-to-day consultation between managers and staff. Explain why that might undermine the effectiveness of its workplace democracy. (8)

3 Discuss how senior John Lewis managers might set about improving their staff's ability to 'show enterprise' at work. (11)

B2 Case study

The Old Hen

'I don't know why I bother,' said Nina Burke, the manageress of the Old Hen pub in Oxford. She had just had one of the weekly staff meetings and all she had heard was one complaint after another. 'They want more money, they want shorter working hours, they want free food, they don't like the T-shirts they have to wear, they don't like the shift arrangements. Honestly, I don't know why any of them even turns up to work, the amount they complain. They even seem to resent being asked for their ideas,' said Nina to her husband.

Nina began to wonder whether she was running these meetings effectively. The previous landlord had never really held staff meetings and had certainly not asked employees for their opinions. When she took over, he had said: 'Half of them will be moving on to new jobs anyway within a few weeks or are just doing this as a part-time job, so what's the point? Tell them what to do and then make sure they get on with it.' Nina began to think he may be right although she had been very enthusiastic when she first had the idea of asking employees for their input.

She had noticed that staff in this pub seemed to leave very frequently and were generally pretty miserable. They seemed much less motivated than at her previous pub (where she was deputy manager). The money was not good but no worse than anywhere else. She decided it must be because they were not involved in decision making at all. In her last job everyone had felt able to give an opinion (even if their ideas were then ignored!) and were often asked what they thought about how the pub was run. It was a good atmosphere and Nina had enjoyed working there. She hoped she could recreate the same feeling here but was losing confidence that it would ever be possible.

Questions

(50 marks; 60 minutes)

1 How might Nina's experience at the Old Hen be explained by:
   (a) a Theory X manager
   (b) a Theory Y manager? (10)

2 Consider whether Nina is right to try to introduce greater employee participation at the Old Hen. (10)

3 According to many motivational theorists, employees should respond positively to greater participation. Discuss the possible reasons why Nina's schemes seem ineffective. (15)

4 An increasing number of managers claim to be encouraging employee participation. Consider why greater participation might be regarded as particularly valuable today. (15)

C. Essay questions

(40 marks each)

1 'Greater competitiveness and higher profits in the future will depend upon much more employee participation than in the past.' Critically assess this statement.

2 'Managers are appointed to make decisions. Workers are hired to do the job they are told. Employee participation simply wastes time and money.' Critically assess this view.

3 'Teamwork brings with it more problems than benefits.' Discuss.

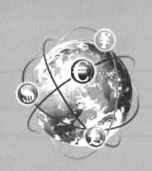

EFFECTIVE EMPLOYER/ EMPLOYEE RELATIONS

DEFINITION

Are staff and management able to work together for the good of the business, or is there friction and inefficiency? Motivation can be undermined by poor employer/employee relations.

72.1 Introduction

The relations between bosses and workers would be effective if communications were good and there was a sensible amount of give-and-take between them. They would be bad if there was a lack of trust, leading to restricted communication ('information is power') and

A-grade application
ACAS

ACAS (the Advisory Conciliation and Arbitration Service) is Britain's most important, independent voice on the workplace. Over more than 30 years it has developed a view of what it thinks is the 'model workplace'. The ACAS model includes the following six themes:

1 ambitions, goals and plans that employees know about and understand
2 managers who genuinely listen to and consider their employees' views, so everyone is actively involved in making important decisions
3 people to feel valued so they can talk confidently about their work, and learn from both successes and mistakes
4 work organised so that it encourages initiative, innovation and working together
5 a good working relationship between management and employee representatives that in turn helps build trust throughout the business
6 formal procedures for dealing with disciplinary matters, grievances and disputes that managers and employees know about and use fairly.

Source: www.acas.org.uk

the tendency to make demands rather than conduct conversations. In a perfect world, adults would behave in an adult manner towards each other. But just as no family is perfect, neither is any individual business organisation. The key is not to be perfect, but to be better than most.

There are three main areas to consider within the heading 'effective employer/employee relations':

1 good communications
2 methods of employee representation
3 the causes and solutions to industrial disputes.

72.2 Good communications

The importance of effective communication

Effective communication is essential for organisations. Without it, employees do not know what they are supposed to do, why they are supposed to do it, how to do it or when to do it by. Similarly, managers have little idea of how the business is performing, what people are actually doing or what their customers think. Communication links the activities of all the various parts of the organisation. It ensures that everyone is working towards a common goal and enables **feedback** on performance. Imagine studying for an exam if you were not told by the teacher what you were supposed to do and had no idea of your standard. Then you can appreciate how important good communication is. By communicating effectively the management is able to explain the objectives of the organisation and employee can have an input into the decisions that are made.

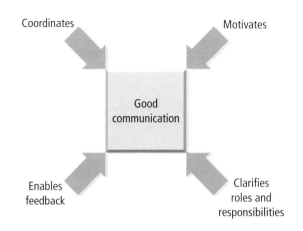

Figure 72.1 Communication

Effective communication is also vital for successful decision making. To make good decisions managers need high-quality information. If they do not know what is happening in the market, for example, they are less likely to be successful. If, however, their market knowledge is good they are more likely to develop an appropriate marketing plan. Effective communication provides managers with the information they need, in a form they can use, when they need it.

Good-quality information should be:

- easily accessible
- up to date
- cost effective.

Good communication is also extremely important to motivate employees. People need to know how they are getting on, what they are doing right and in which areas they could improve. Working on your own without any kind of feedback at all is extremely difficult. It is much easier if someone is taking an interest and providing support. Interestingly, nearly all staff surveys reveal that employees do not feel that management communicate with them very effectively. So there is clearly a need for managers to improve in this area.

To ensure that communication is motivating, managers need to ensure that employees:

- understand the objectives of the organisation as a whole
- understand why their job is important and how it contributes to the overall success of the firm
- know how the job should be completed
- know how they are performing.

The importance of communication in employee/employer relations

If the key to employer/employee relations is trust, then good communication is a vital factor. Watching the BBC TV series *The Apprentice* is interesting for this. Individual potential apprentices are, in turn, required to lead teams in a challenge such as devising, producing and selling a new snack food. The team might have six people in it, who might be split into two groups, to get things done more quickly. Can the team leader manage both groups effectively? Partly it depends on whether the team members believe that their leader has both the talent and the desire to win the task. Or might the team leader be distracted by some other motive, such as shining brilliantly *despite* the team? If the team members do not trust the leader, they will start discussing things secretly and may not provide all the information the leader needs. Once staff start withholding information, serious problems are inevitable.

In a well-run organisation with effective delegation and consultation, good communication will flow from the top and to the top. The overall business leader can do many things to help, as outlined below.

- Have a chat with every new member of staff; this may be impossible for the boss of Tesco's 250,000 employees, but is perfectly possible in most cases.

- Take regular initiatives to meet with staff; some retail bosses go out every Friday to two or three different stores to discuss problems with shop-floor staff; this is bound to encourage communication not only then, but also later, if an issue arises that an individual feels very strongly about, such as sex discrimination.

- Treat every piece of communication from staff as being as important as if it were from a friend or a big shareholder. If staff know their complaints or suggestions are being addressed, they will be happy to keep contributing their thoughts. Most staff want their workplace to be efficient, to allow them to do as good a job as possible; inefficiency is frustrating for all. Toyota reports that its Japanese staff alone make 500,000 suggestions a year for workplace improvement; this is perhaps because the company implements a high proportion of all the ideas put forward.

If the leader can get communications right, there is every chance that staff will do the same. Unfortunately there are some serious barriers to effective communication. The first is that middle managers may not want staff communicating over their heads to senior staff. If they insist that communications should filter up through the management layers, there is a chance at every stage that the message will be suppressed. Middle managers may not want their bosses to receive grumbles, complaints or suggestions. After all, they could be seen as criticism of the middle layers of management. Bosses have to make a special effort, therefore, to make sure that staff really do feel that they can communicate one to one with the business leader.

If communications are well managed, the impact on employer/employee relations can be huge. The many benefits to the business include those described below.

- Staff that understand the difficulties faced by the organisation, and therefore can seek to help management rather than criticise it. In 2007 the high value of the Euro against the US dollar made it incredibly hard for European Airbus aircraft manufacturing to compete with Boeing. Keeping staff aware of the problems helped encourage them to cooperate, even when job cuts were called for.

- If **vertical communications** are weak, frustrated staff may look for a trades union to represent their views to management. If the company is reluctant to recognise a union as the representative of staff, employer/employee relations may become very difficult. In 2006 Asda and the GMB union had a bitter dispute over union recognition for lorry drivers; a planned five-day strike was averted only when Asda backed down, granting recognition to the union.

- Ineffective communication, by comparison, leaves employees frustrated and dissatisfied. Poor communication makes people uncertain about their role or duties. They become unsure of what they are supposed to be doing. It can also lead to rumours going around the firm. This can cause problems if people get worried about things that are not actually true, or resent the fact that they have heard something before being officially told.

Communication and size

As a firm grows it tends to introduce more layers of hierarchy. This makes communication more difficult as vertical communications (from the top to the bottom) have to go through more people. This slows down decision making. It also introduces a greater risk that the message will get distorted. Instead of communicating directly to the person you want to talk to, you have to contact someone else, who then gets in touch with someone else, and so on. In the end your message can become rather confused.

Another problem is that as the number of people involved in an organisation increases, the use of written communication rises even faster. Instead of a quick conversation to sort something out you can end up passing numerous messages backwards and forwards. This can lead to a tremendous amount of paperwork and is often far less effective than face-to-face communication. When you are actually talking to someone you can get immediate feedback and can see if they do not fully understand something. You can then talk it through until you are happy they have understood what you mean. When you send them a written message, however, you are never quite sure how they will interpret it. What you think you have said and what they think you have said can be very different.

Communication problems can also occur because of different business cultures within the firm. This is usually more of a problem in large firms than in small ones. If there are only a few people working in an office they tend to share the same approaches to work and the same values about what is and what is not acceptable business behaviour. If anyone new joins the group they soon learn the way that everyone else works and the newcomer will usually fit in quite quickly. In large organisations, however, it is much more difficult to develop a common approach. People tend to develop their own little groups within the firm so that the mood, attitudes and values of employees can vary tremendously in different parts of the firm. The marketing department, for example, may have a different view from the production department of what the business is trying to achieve and how it wants to conduct its business.

72.3 Methods of employee representation

Intelligent bosses realise that success depends on the full participation of as many staff as possible. Football managers typically use the club captain as the representative of the players. Small firms might have an informal group consisting of one person from each department; monthly meetings are used as a way to raise issues and problems, and discuss future plans. In larger firms, more formal methods are used to ensure that there is a structure to allow an element of workplace democracy. These include those listed below.

- *Works council:* a works council is a committee of employer and employee representatives that meets to discuss company-wide issues. Although works councils have worked well in Germany they have not been so popular in the UK. However, under European Union legislation larger companies that operate in two or more EU countries must now set up a Europe-wide works council. Works councils will usually discuss issues such as training, investment and working practices. They will not cover issues such as pay, which are generally dealt with in discussions with trades union representatives.

● *Employee groups, organised by the business but with representatives elected by the staff:* these may be little different from a works council, but the fact that they are purely the invention of the business (i.e. the management) may mean that they lack real credibility. Staff may know that management frown upon those who raise critical issues. They may be seen as little more than a talking shop that provides a veneer of democratic respectability. In a similar way, some school councils are vibrant and meaningful, while others are largely ignored by the school management.

● *Employee cooperatives:* these range from huge organisations such as the John Lewis Partnership to the 150 staff at Suma (see the A-grade application). Because all staff are part-owners of the business, all have a right to have their voices heard at every stage in the decision-making process. Inevitably, the board of directors includes representatives from ordinary shop-floor workers, ensuring that everyone's voice is heard.

A-grade application

Suma

Suma was born in 1975 when Reg Taylor started a wholefoods wholesaling cooperative in Leeds. Its purpose was to allow small independent health food shops to be able to buy together in bulk. Although Reg started it in his back bedroom, within a year a tiny two-storey warehouse had been bought in Leeds. Suma was one of the pioneers of organic foods, and has benefited greatly from the growing consumer interest in chemical-free food. This has caused its own pressures, as the cooperative has had to cope with employee growth from seven members in 1980 to over 150 today. All staff receive the same pay, no matter what their responsibilities may be, and all have an equal say in how the business should be run. The high level of staff motivation and participation has allowed Suma to become the number one organic foods wholesaler in the north of England.

For further information on Suma, go to www.suma.co.uk.

72.4 Trades unions

What is a trades union?

A trades union is an organisation that employees pay to join in order to gain greater power and security at work. The phrase 'unity is strength' is part of the trades union tradition. One individual worker has little or no power when discussing pay or pensions with his/her employer; union membership provides greater influence collectively in relations with employers than workers have as separate individuals.

Some people assume that union membership is only for people in low-status jobs. In fact, although trades unions are in decline in Britain, some powerful groups of 'workers' remain committed to membership. For example, the PFA (Professional Footballers' Association) includes almost all Premiership players, and the airline pilots remain loyal to their union BALPA. At the time of writing, Hollywood script writers are on strike; they think the film studios are being unfair in not sharing the revenues from sales of DVDs and computer games based on Hollywood films.

Traditionally, unions concerned themselves solely with obtaining satisfactory rates of pay for a fair amount of work in reasonable and safe working conditions. Today the most important aspect of the work of a trades union is protecting workers' rights under the law. Far more time is spent on health and safety, on discrimination and bullying, on unfair dismissal and other legal matters than on pay negotiations. One other important matter today is negotiations over pension rights. Since 2001 many companies have cut back on the pension benefits available to staff; the unions fight these cutbacks as hard as they can.

Traditionally, the key function of a union was 'collective bargaining'. This means that the union bargains with the employers on behalf of all the workers (e.g. that all nurses should get a 4% pay rise). The 2008 industrial dispute between Virgin Atlantic and its cabin crew was a good example of this. Virgin staff wanted a substantial pay rise to match the wages earned by British Airways' staff. They pressed their union to threaten strike action to achieve their objectives.

Union recognition

'Recognition' is fundamental to the legal position of a trades union. In other words, management must recognise a union's right to bargain on behalf of its members. Without management recognition, any actions taken by a union are illegal. This would leave the union open to being sued. Until recently, even if all staff joined a union, the management did not have to recognise it. Why, then, would any company bother to recognise a union?

● Generally it can be helpful for managers to have a small representative group to consult and negotiate with. Collective bargaining removes the need to bargain with every employee individually.

● It may ease cases of possible difficulty, such as relocation or renegotiation of employment conditions and contracts. Trades union officials can be consulted at an early stage about causes, procedure and objectives. This may give the workforce the confidence that management are acting properly and thoughtfully. It also gives the opportunity for the trades union to offer advice or objection at an early stage. It promotes consultation rather than conflict.

● Trades unions provide a channel of upward communication that has not been filtered by middle managers. Senior managers can expect straight talking about worker opinions or grievances.

Today, employers with 21-plus staff members must give union recognition if more than 50% of the workforce vote for it in a secret ballot (and at least 40% of the workforce takes part in the vote). This government policy has helped unions to recruit more members at a time when membership is generally falling.

72.5 Methods of avoiding and resolving industrial disputes

It is only natural that there will be disagreements between management and staff. Clearly, staff want as high a pay rise as possible, whereas the bosses have a duty to their shareholders to keep costs down (and profits up). Usually, companies and unions are able to resolve their differences by compromising (i.e. give and take). Staff may 'demand' 8%, but only be offered 2%. After much wrangling, a compromise of 4% may be agreed. In some cases, though, a build-up of mistrust and hostility over time may mean that compromise is not seen as acceptable. Then an industrial dispute may occur, which may lead to industrial action, such as a strike.

When an industrial dispute occurs, it is up to the management and unions to resolve it. Sometimes, however, there seems to be no compromise that is acceptable to both sides. The result might be a strike – in other words, workers refusing to work and therefore giving up their pay. The inevitable consequence of a strike is that both the company and the employees lose money, therefore there will soon be pressure for a way to resolve the dispute. Often, one or both sides will suggest bringing ACAS in to help. ACAS stands for the Advisory Conciliation and Arbitration Service; it is government-financed, but acts independently of government and politicians.

Founded in 1975, the mission statement of ACAS is:

to improve the performance and effectiveness of organisations by providing an independent and impartial service to prevent and resolve disputes and to build harmonious relationships at work.

ACAS seeks to:

● prevent and resolve employment disputes

● conciliate in actual or potential complaints to industrial tribunals

● provide information and advice

● promote good practice.

ACAS can be used by employers and employees to help them work together to resolve industrial relations disputes before they develop into confrontation. Where there is a collective dispute between management and workforce, either or both may contact ACAS. Before acting, ACAS will want to see that union officials are involved and that the organisation's disputes procedure has been followed. ACAS can also be used to offer **conciliation** to the parties in a dispute, assuming their own procedures have been exhausted, to avoid damaging industrial action. Such conciliation is entirely voluntary and ACAS has no powers to impose a settlement.

If conciliation is unsuccessful, ACAS can offer **arbitration**, by providing an independent arbitrator who can examine the case for each side and then judge the right outcome to the dispute. If both sides agree in advance, the arbitrator's decision can be legally binding on both sides. Occasionally, ACAS is asked to provide mediator who can act as an intermediary suggesting the basis for further discussion.

Issues For Analysis

- When analysing employer/employee relations it is good to start with a clear understanding of the vision and objectives of the business. The vision at Cadbury Schweppes plc is 'working together to create brands people love'. As long as the company's decisions are in line with that vision, it is easy to see that it could be the basis of close cooperation between employees and their employers.

- Yet Virgin Atlantic boasts that 'our vision is to build a profitable airline where people love to fly and where people love to work'. This did nothing to prevent the 2008 industrial dispute between cabin crew and management. So successful employer/employee relations is about much more than saying the right thing.

- When analysing a business situation, look beyond what managements say and see how they are actually treating their staff. Are they really showing respect by listening to what staff say and acting on their views. That, after all, is how Toyota became the world's number one car maker.

72.6 Effective employer/ employee relations

an evaluation

Good relations are built on shared goals, on trust and on good communications. Yet they are always fragile. One instance of hypocrisy can ruin years of relationship-building. A boss may claim to be acting for the good of all the staff, yet switch production from Britain to Asia (James Dyson), or cut pension benefits to staff while keeping them intact for directors. In the long term, some firms really stick by the view that 'our people are our greatest asset', while others just pretend they believe that. Staff will learn which is which. Where they find they cannot trust their bosses, joining a trades union becomes a sensible way to get greater protection and greater negotiating power. Union representation will make the employer/employee relationship more formal, and occasionally more fractious. Yet, as Tesco has shown, trades union representation can help move a business forward. So it would be wrong to jump to the conclusion that unions are 'trouble'. Real trouble comes when employers and employees have no relationship at all.

Exercises

A. Revision questions

(35 marks; 35 minutes)

1 Explain why good communications within a firm are important. (3)

2 Explain why feedback is important for successful communications. (3)

3 State three actions a firm could take in order to improve the effectiveness of communication. (3)

4 Identify three reasons why communications may be poorer in large firms than in small ones. (3)

5 Explain why good communication is an important part of motivating employees. (4)

6 How might a business benefit from a successful works council? (4)

7 Why might an employee cooperative have better employer/employee relations than a public company? (4)

8 Why is it so important to a union to gain recognition from employers? (4)

9 Outline the role of ACAS. (4)

10 Distinguish 'conciliation' from 'arbitration'. (3)

B. Revision exercises

B1 Data response

Employee communication

Faced with intensifying competition and an accelerating pace of change, companies are seeing effective communication with employees as an ever more important part of organisational efficiency. It is also a constructive way to harness employees' commitment, enthusiasm and ideas. However, companies tend to place considerable emphasis on communicating big but vague messages about change and company performance. It is highly debatable whether such messages are relevant to employees or easily understood by them. Employee attitude surveys consistently highlight communication as a major source of staff dissatisfaction.

While managers tend to use communication channels that send general messages downwards, employees place more importance on mechanisms that communicate immediate and applicable information. For example, around 40% of staff found one-to-one meetings with their manager very useful while less than 5% gave business television the same rating. Too many businesses try to tell staff too much, leading to communications overload. Successful communication methods involved discussion and feedback, whereas business TV or company newsletters provided purely one-way messages.

Questions

(30 marks; 35 minutes)

1 Outline the possible value to staff of a 'one-to-one meeting with their manager'? (5)

2 Explain why communication is more than just 'the provision of information'. (5)

3 Explain why staff disliked business TV or company newsletters. (4)

4 Examine the importance of good communication within *either* a McDonald's restaurant *or* a supermarket. (7)

5 Discuss the problems that can occur when employees are dissatisfied. (9)

B2 Case study

Industrial disputes at Express

In January 2007 strike action at Express newspapers was narrowly averted. Hours before the journalists were to go on strike the Express management compromised their redundancy plans. The paper group had wanted to axe 35 permanent jobs and 'outsource' the City department (financial news) and the travel desk. The members of the National Union of Journalists (NUJ) voted to strike unless managers backed down on the threat of compulsory redundancies.

The final agreement that prevented the strike included:

- no compulsory redundancies
- redundancy pay cap lifted from £30,000 to £40,000 per employee
- the union to be consulted about any further outsourcing plans.

In December 2007, Express was back in the headlines as its journalists voted to strike over a 3% pay offer from Express management. The union said, 'The 3% offer is way out of line with other current Fleet Street pay offers, including 4.8% at *The Guardian* and 4.5% at the *Financial Times*.' The union offered to take the dispute to arbitration at ACAS, but management refused.

A key factor underpinning these disputes is that Richard Desmond, the owner of the Express group, is known to pay himself more than £40 million a year, making him one of Britain's highest earners. The journalists find it hard to square these riches with their own struggles.

Questions

(40 marks; 45 minutes)

1 From the article, explain the purpose of belonging to a trades union from the journalists' point of view. (5)

2 (a) Examine the state of employer/employee relations at the Express group. (8)

   (b) How might these relations be affected by Mr Desmond's earnings? (4)

3 Explain why a management might refuse to take a dispute to ACAS for independent arbitration. (8)

4 Discuss whether it would be right for a future government to remove the right to union recognition (i.e. to allow employers to refuse to recognise a union such as the NUJ). (15)

C. Essay questions

(40 marks each)

1 Consider the view that effective communications is at the heart of successful operations management.

2 'Greater competitiveness and higher profits in the future will depend upon much more employee participation than in the past.' Critically assess this statement.

3 'Good managers welcome trades unions as a way of improving workplace performance.' Discuss.

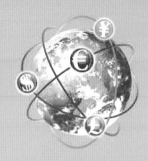

INTEGRATED PEOPLE IN ORGANISATIONS

73.1 Human resources strategy: an overview

Some writers like to suggest that modern managers have a more enlightened view of staff than did their counterparts in the past. Sadly, there is little evidence of this. For every well-run firm with motivated staff there are businesses with staff who are frustrated or resentful. Good management of staff remains the single best way to succeed as a business. Yet it remains difficult.

As is clear from the Terminal 5 case study (see exercise B2 in the Workbook section), the management of staff at British Airways has long been unsatisfactory. There has always been a 'them and us' culture that creates a barrier between management and the workforce. Many hospitals and colleges would say the same thing.

The underlying problem remains what Douglas McGregor (nearly 50 years ago) called Theory X and Y. Too many managers view their own staff with suspicion. This leads them to adopt 'hard HRM' practices such as incentive schemes, temporary contracts, and the regular setting and monitoring of targets. Most staff want to be trusted, involved, respected and paid a regular (and 'good') salary. Hard HR managers assume that everyone is motivated by money, and that without careful monitoring they may be too lazy to achieve anything.

Managing human resources successfully involves a delicate and continuous balancing between meeting the various needs and aspirations of employees and meeting the objectives of the business itself. Clearly, day-to-day personnel functions such as recruitment, training and appraisal still need to be carried out. However, any human resources strategy needs to be integrated into a firm's overall corporate planning if it is to develop and utilise its employees effectively. Firms also need to recognise that human resource strategies cannot be 'written in stone' but will be constantly evolving, shaped by events within the firm and also those in the external environment.

Issue 1: human resources holds the key to achieving competitive advantage

For most companies, long-term success relies not on screwing costs down to the last penny, but on constantl finding better ways to do things. Motivated marketing managers can find opportunities for new products, and can identify innovative ways to promote them. Operations staff who really care about what they are doing take pride in running trains on time or on delivering a truckload of biscuits on time to Asda. Better still, if you have a bright, enthusiastic staff, not only do your customers tend to notice (especially for service businesses) but also you find better and better people applying for jobs with you.

The better you can handle your people, the better able the firm will be to fight or beat the competition.

Issue 2: downsizing, delayering and outsourcing

Whenever the economy moves sideways or backwards instead of forwards, cost pressures can pile up. The driv to remain competitive increases the desire to create businesses that are as lean and flexible as possible. Suddenly firms start using terms such as 'downsizing' an 'delayering' as more elegant ways of saying that they are reducing staff numbers in order to cut costs. Downsizing means cutting staff throughout the business; delayering means cutting overhead costs by removing a complete management layer from the hierarchy. This would force senior staff to delegate more, as it will increase the span of control within which they have been working.

However, cost-cutting exercises produce one-off results that cannot be repeated year after year. Furthermore, firms may experience problems in meeting customer requirements due to skills shortages and quality shortfalls. This has led to a recognition that firms need to strike a balance between financial viability, on the one hand, and effective workforce planning on the other.

Exercises

A. Revision questions

(80 marks; 80 minutes)

1 Explain what is meant by the term labour productivity. (3)

2 Outline two reasons why a firm would aim to increase labour productivity. (4)

3 Identify two possible human resource objectives for a mobile phone operator embarking on a programme of rapid expansion in order to keep up with increasing demand. (4)

4 Explain the difference between 'hard' and 'soft' human resources management. (5)

5 Identify three factors that might have an influence on the way a firm manages its human resources. (3)

6 Outline two benefits to a firm from developing a human resources strategy. (4)

7 What is the main purpose of workforce planning? (3)

8 Identify and briefly explain one internal and one external influence on the process of workforce planning. (4)

9 Explain what is meant by the term 'delayering'. (3)

10 Examine one advantage and one disadvantage to a firm from creating a flatter organisational structure. (6)

11 Briefly explain the meaning of the term 'centralised organisational structure'. (3)

12 Suggest two reasons why a business might adopt a centralised approach. (2)

13 Outline two implications for a firm moving from a centralised to a more decentralised structure. (4)

14 Briefly explain, using examples, what is meant by the term 'flexible workforce'. (3)

15 Analyse one potential benefit and one potential problem resulting from a firm attempting to create a more flexible workforce. (6)

16 Explain why maintaining effective communication with employees is important to a rapidly expanding business. (3)

17 Outline two benefits to a firm of increased employee participation in decision making. (4)

18 Outline three methods that a business could adopt to increase the level of employee participation. (6)

19 Examine one advantage and one disadvantage to an employer of collective bargaining. (6)

20 Describe two reasons why a car manufacturer such as PSA Peugeot Citroën would set up works councils. (4)

B. Revision exercises

B1 Data response

The end of 'nine to five' in the UK?

Britain is moving away from the traditional pattern of the nine-to-five working day according to a recent report. The findings of a survey, carried out by the Centre of Economics and Business Research (CEBR) and released in May 2007, claimed that one-third of UK workers carry out their jobs outside of standard hours. The report also found that such working practices were no longer concentrated in areas such as the leisure, entertainment, hotel and catering industries, with 36% of managers, half of trades people and 58% of manufacturing employees now working at least some of their time between 5 pm and 9 am.

Possible reasons for the adoption of more flexible working practices include increasing consumer demands for around-the-clock services, and the need for employees to fit work around family and other responsibilities. However, other commentators, including trades unions, claim that the changes have resulted from workers being pressurised into working longer hours by employers, often in the form of unpaid overtime.

Full-time UK employees work the longest average hours in Europe. Research carried out by the TUC in 2007 found that the average working week in the UK is 43.5 hours, as opposed to 39.9 hours in Germany and 38.2 hours in France. Despite this, labour productivity levels in both Germany and France are higher than those in the UK. Furthermore, 4 million people in the UK work an average of more than 48 hours a week, despite the UK's adoption in 1998 of the EU working time directive, which places restrictions on working hours beyond this level. According to the TUC, the average British worker completes unpaid overtime worth £4800 each year, amounting to £23 billion per year in total.

Source: www.bbc.co.uk; www.thisismoney.co.uk

Questions

(25 marks; 30 minutes)

1 Examine the main benefits to businesses of adopting more flexible working practices. (10)

2 Discuss the key implications of the TUC's findings on working practices in the UK. (15)

B2 Case study

BA's Terminal 5 fiasco

On the morning of 27 March 2008, every UK national newspaper carried articles on the wonderful new terminal opening at Heathrow that morning. BAA (the airport's operator) was proud that it had been finished on time and on budget. British Airways, with sole use of Terminal 5, looked forward to its huge advantage over every other airline – as they were all stuck in the scruffy, over-used terminals 1–4. Everything was set for a public relations triumph.

But no one told the staff.

Baggage handlers from Terminals 1–3 arrived for their 4 o'clock shift to find insufficient parking, tough new security systems and huge changes to their working practices. The real chaos began when the new baggage-handling system started up. Many of the 400 British Airways' handlers were not only unable to find their workstations but were also unfamiliar with the new system: 'Only 50 or so of 400 baggage handlers had been fully trained when the terminal opened'.* Quickly overwhelmed, chaos struck as aircraft left

without luggage and a baggage mountain of 25,000 items soon built up. Day after day of chaos followed, with flights being cancelled to allow the still fragile baggage systems to work.

How could this happen? After all, even a new system in an existing workplace can be hard to bed in. Here, three separate workforces were being uprooted and put into a brand new workplace, with brand new systems. Surely, with effective training and trialling, it should be possible?

When difficulties strike a business, the key thing is to have committed, involved staff with the power to make the necessary changes. At British Airways there has been a long history of suspicion between management and the workforce. The *Financial Times* reported that, 'While goodwill and staff flexibility are vital to any company experiencing the kind of minute-by-minute difficulties that have hit Terminal 5, they are often in short supply.'

On 5 April, the *Financial Times* ran an article reflecting on the chaos. It interviewed (anonymously) many senior managers at British Airways and BAA. Although there were elements of bad luck involved, the main message involved the culture of the workplace and the style of leadership. The paper said of British Airways:

Its failure to prepare staff for the move was compounded by a management culture that left them reluctant to raise concerns with the airline's abrasive boss, Willie Walsh . . . A number of insiders said that he expected to be brought solutions rather than problems: 'He will have been told what he wanted to hear.'

* *Financial Times*, 5 April 2008, p. 5

Figure 73.1 Terminal 5 at Heathrow

Questions

(30 marks; 35 minutes)

1 Examine two key failures of human resource management in British Airways' move to Terminal 5. (8)

2 Outline two possible explanations of why 'only 50 or so of 400 baggage handlers had been fully trained' by British Airways. (4)

3 Explain the importance within a business of 'management culture'. (3)

4 To what extent should responsibility for a failure such as this be put at the door of chief executive Willie Walsh? (15)

B3 Case study

UK job losses as Peugeot moves east

In January 2007, European car manufacturer, PSA Peugeot Citroën, closed down its assembly plant in Ryton, near Coventry. The final closure took place six months earlier than original announcements had indicated, provoking angry reactions from the unions representing remaining workers who, they claimed, had been denied the chance to look for alternative work. However, Peugeot claimed the decision to advance the closure of the factory, responsible for the production of its 206 model, had come after requests from increasing numbers of the remaining workforce to leave in order to take up jobs elsewhere.

The announcement of the closure in April 2006 had been followed by a move from a double to a single shift system in August of that year, and a reduction in the workforce from 2300 to 800. A Peugeot spokeswoman claimed at the time that requests to leave from a quarter of the remaining workers had meant that the company had been forced to take on temporary staff in order to continue production. According to Peugeot, workers received redundancy payments of between £20,000 and £25,000 – the equivalent of between one and three years' salary – requiring the company to set aside £227 million against the plant's closure.

According to Peugeot, the decision to close the Coventry plant was based on high production and logistical costs, rather than productivity figures. Figures produced by the Cardiff Business School showed that, in 2003, Ryton produced 67 cars per worker, compared to 69 at its best-performing factory at Vigo, Spain, and 54 at its factory in Poissy, France. However, the company claimed that Ryton was the most expensive factory within the group, costing €415 more to make a car there than at Poissy. Car production planned to take place at Ryton was switched to the company's new state-of-the-art assembly plant on the outskirts of Trnava, Slovakia.

In June 2006, workers at Ryton voted against a proposal from the TGWU to go on strike in response to the closure decision. Instead, the union went ahead with a £1 million joint campaign of national action with Amicus, which included a series of national newspaper adverts encouraging people to boycott sales of Peugeot cars. Union members also staged a number of protests, leafleting outside Peugeot dealers and the London Motor Show in July 2006.

Source: www.bbc.co.uk

Questions

(25 marks; 30 minutes)

1 What is meant by the following terms:
(a) productivity
(b) redundancy. (4)

2 Examine the reasons why Peugeot decided to close down its Ryton plant. (8)

3 Assess the key factors that may have influenced the outcome of the union's campaign to save the Ryton plant. (13)

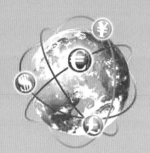
UNDERSTANDING OPERATIONAL OBJECTIVES

74.1 Introduction

All organisations share common operational objectives, regardless of their size and the sector in which they operate. Ensuring that these objectives are met is vital in order to satisfy customer needs and compete effectively within the marketplace. All firms will attempt to produce goods and services that are 'fit for purpose', delivered quickly and on time. They will also aim to produce the right number of goods as cheaply as possible, bearing in mind the overall strategy.

If, like Ryanair, your target is to be the lowest-cost airline in Europe, every cost will be shaved to the minimum. If your business strategy is to be the highest-rated airline in the world (such as Singapore Airlines), you may accept costs that will seem high to other airlines. The crucial thing is that a firm's operational objectives must be fully in line with its objectives regarding marketing and its management of its people.

Finally, there needs to be enough flexibility within operations to allow activities to be varied or adapted quickly in order to accommodate changes in demand.

74.2 Key operational objectives

The key operational objectives are shown in Figure 74.1 and described below.

Cost

All firms are concerned with keeping costs down, particularly those that compete directly on price. Not

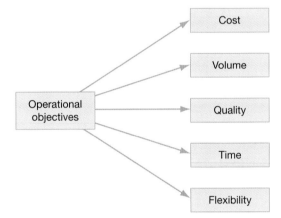

Figure 74.1 The key operational objectives

only do costs determine what is charged to the customer – and, therefore, a firm's ability to compete – but also the profits that can be generated. Costs are determined by the **efficiency** of a business. This can be measured in a number of ways – for example, wastage rates or the **productivity** of the workforce.

Volume

Ensuring that goods and services are made available in the right quantities may seem obvious but, in reality, this will require a firm to make decisions and commit resources now based on predictions of future demand. Overestimating the volume required is likely to lead to wasted goods, increased stock-holding costs and price cutting. On the other hand, underestimating the amount of products required will mean missed sales opportunities and customer dissatisfaction.

Quality

The exact meaning of quality for any individual organisation will depend to some extent on the nature of its operations. Put simply, quality is about getting things 'right' by meeting or beating customer expectations over and over again. Quality has a crucial role to play in guaranteeing customer satisfaction. Not only should firms aim to produce goods or services that are 'fit for purpose', they also need to create a sense of dependability by ensuring that products are ready when customers expect them. Failure to do so is likely to create customer dissatisfaction and encourage customers to switch to rival products. A high degree of quality and dependability is also required within the organisation. Managers need to ensure that quality standards are being met. They also need to synchronise production so that products pass smoothly from one stage to the next. This will help to reduce production time and costs, meaning that goods are ready for dispatch to customers sooner.

A-grade application

From public relations triumph to disaster

Before British Airways opened its Heathrow Terminal 5 in March 2008, it boasted to the press and public about a fabulous new travelling experience. Publicity used words and phrases such as 'stress-free', 'luxury' and 'the service busy travellers deserve'. Unfortunately, through shockingly bad operations (and human resource) management, Terminal 5 opened to scenes of chaos, creating a baggage mountain that was publicised worldwide. From public relations triumph to disaster. When interviewed, a former head of public affairs at BA said, 'With projects such as this, expectations should be managed downwards. Management should then try to exceed them.'

Time

This factor is important in many ways, both to the consumer and the producer. Many consumers are 'money-rich, time-poor' as they rush from a well-paid job to pick up the kids, eat, then go out. So operations that can save time for the customer can be very successful (e.g. Tesco online grocery shopping, pizza delivery). Time-based management is also important to firms in product development. Stung by the success of the Toyota Prius, General Motors is desperate to get the first mass-market electric-only car out by 2010. If it can develop a successful pollution-free car before anyone else, it is sure it will regain its position as the world's number one car producer. Also the firm that is first to market is able to charge higher prices than its slower rivals. Speed is also important within the business. The faster items pass through the production process, the lower the costs of warehousing materials and work-in-progress.

Flexibility

Firms need to be able to vary the volume of production relatively easily, in order to respond effectively to unexpected increases or decreases in demand. The ability to adapt or modify a standard product range allows a firm to appear to be offering customised products that meet customer needs more precisely, but still benefit from high volume production, keeping costs down. This flexible approach to production is a form of **lean production** that has been used successfully by a number of companies, including computer manufacturer Dell.

A-grade application

Lean production reaches sportswear

Nike became the first sportswear manufacturer to embrace the concept of lean production when it established a new online design facility in 2000. Nike iD allows customers to create their own versions of a range of footwear and clothing. Customers follow a step-by-step customisation process, picking from a choice of colours and materials, and adding logos, names and personalised messages in order to create a 'unique' product. The customised goods are manufactured and delivered within four weeks of an order being placed. A 'teamlocker' version of the service also exists, offering the facility to sports teams and groups. The success of the concept has been followed up with the opening of a number of Nike iD Studios around the world, including London's Oxford Street in November 2007. Each studio has a team of qualified design consultants on hand to help customers make their choices.

Source: www.nike.com

74.3 The importance of innovation

Innovation means more than merely inventing a new product or process – it involves turning a new idea into a commercial success. Innovation within operations is crucial to the long-term survival and growth of a firm, allowing it to keep ahead of the competition. New products will often require new production methods and machinery. New processes for producing existing goods or delivering services can help to reduce costs and improve the quality and speed of production.

In 2003, stung by the success of the European Airbus project, Boeing announced a new 'Dreamliner' plane that would fly 250 passengers longer distances non-stop than ever before. It would also be 20% more fuel-efficient than ever before because of a series of innovations. Up to 50% of the plane would be made from super-strong, but super-light 'composite' materials instead of traditional aluminium. And by getting suppliers to produce a one-piece fuselage (instead of the traditional two-pieces-then-weld) 1500 aluminium sheets and 40,000–50,000 fasteners are eliminated from each plane. With 900 firm orders for this $150 million plane by mid-2008, it has become the most successful product launch in aviation history. (By the way, 900 × $150 million is $135,000 million!)

Figure 74.2 Boeing's 'Dreamliner' plane

74.4 The impact on operations of environmental objectives

The adoption of environmental policies by a firm will have a number of implications for its operations. For instance, it may mean that the business will need to change its supplies of materials to those that come from replenishable or recycled sources. It may need to adopt new processes that are more energy efficient, and produce less waste and pollution. Even the methods of transportation used to bring in materials and deliver goods to customers may need to be investigated in an attempt to reduce congestion. Furthermore, staff will need appropriate training in order to ensure that these policies achieve their objectives.

74.5 Influences on operational objectives

● *The nature of the product:* the product is at the heart of any firm's operations, so its nature will obviously dictate operational objectives. For example, car manufacturers such as BMW and Mercedes have a long-established reputation for high standards of quality, which must be taken into account when developing new models.

● *Demand:* the level and nature of demand will act as a major influence on operational objectives. A business must attempt to predict sales volumes and any likely fluctuations, in order to ensure that customer expectations are met in a cost-effective manner.

● *Availability of resources:* a lack of availability of the right level and quality of resources, including human resources, can act as a major constraint in attempting to achieve operational objectives. For example, skills shortages in a number of industries in the UK, including healthcare, has led to a reliance on workers from abroad. Similarly, a shortage of financial resources will act as a constraint on the achievement of operational objectives.

● *Competitors' behaviour:* few firms have the luxury of operating alone in a market and no firm, however successful, can afford to become complacent. Rival firms will strive to increase their market share, and their activities are likely to have a major influence on operational objectives.

Issues For Analysis

Opportunities for analysis are likely to focus on the following areas:

- considering the factors likely to permit or prevent a business from achieving its operational objectives

- examining the implications for a given business of repeatedly achieving key operations

- analysing the potential consequences for a business of failing to meet key operational objectives.

Key terms

Efficiency: refers to how effectively a firm uses its resources. It can be measured in a number of ways, including labour productivity and wastage rates.

Innovation: this means taking an idea for a new product or process and turning it into a commercial success.

Lean production: instead of mass producing, it produces goods to order and therefore satisfies the customer while helping the firm avoid stockpiles of unsold stock.

Productivity: measures how efficiently a firm turns inputs into the production process into output. The most commonly used measure is labour productivity, which looks at output per worker.

Understanding operational objectives

The effective management of operations is central to the success of any business, regardless of its size or the sector in which it operates. The key to this is a clear understanding of what the business is attempting to achieve. The establishment and communication of appropriate operational objectives is, therefore, vital in order to develop the strategies required to deliver this success.

Exercises

A. Revision questions

(45 marks; 45 minutes)

1 Explain what is meant by the term 'operational objectives'. (3)

2 Outline two reasons why it is important for a business to keep its costs as low as possible. (4)

3 Analyse the main consequences for a firm of failing to accurately forecast the volume of production required to meet demand. (6)

4 Briefly explain what is meant by quality for a car manufacturer such as Mercedes. (4)

5 Choose one of the following businesses. Outline two possible ways in which it delivers quality to its customers.
(a) electronics manufacturer Sony
(b) luxury hotel chain Malmaison
(c) discount retailer, Lidl (6)

6 Examine two key benefits for a firm that develops a reputation for quality. (6)

7 Give two reasons why a firm might aim to achieve a high degree of flexibility in its operations. (2)

8 Explain, using examples, what is meant by the term lean production. (4)

9 Analyse two ways in which a business can benefit from a commitment to innovation. (6)

10 Outline one advantage and one disadvantage for a business from establishing environmental objectives. (4)

B. Revision exercises

B1 Data response

Distribution problems at Sainsbury's

UK supermarket chain Sainsbury's reported its first ever loss in 2004, after an attempt to update its distribution and IT systems left many stores with bare shelves. The retailer had outsourced part of its IT to consultants Accenture in 2000. This was part of a £1.8 billion seven-year contract aimed at reviving its fortunes and achieving an advantage over its competitors in an efficient and cost-effective manner. However, Sainsbury's was forced to write down £140 million in IT assets and £120 million in automated distribution after prolonged supply chain problems created serious stock shortages. Some 3000 staff were employed to stock shelves by the company in an attempt to rectify the situation.

Sainsbury's share of the UK market fell to 15.3% in September 2004, down from 15.9% a year earlier. This pushed the business down to number three in the UK grocery market, behind Asda. It had been overtaken as market leader by Tesco in 1995.

Source: www.bbc.co.uk; www.silicon.com

Questions

(20 marks; 25 minutes)

1 Analyse the likely consequences of the distribution problems experienced by Sainsbury's. (8)

2 Re-read Section 75.2, then discuss the key operational objectives for a business such as Sainsbury's, operating in a highly competitive market. (12)

B2 Case study

Renault targets the cheap mass market

In 2004, car manufacturer Renault launched a new model aimed at the super-budget segment of the market, in an attempt to fight off increasing competition from the fast-growing car industries in China and India. The no-frills Logan saloon has a price tag of the equivalent of around £5000, while the Logan estate, launched in 2007, sells for the equivalent of £6000. Both models are targeted at customers who would normally opt to buy second-hand, rather than a brand new car. Three new models are being planned for launch in the near future.

The cars are made at Renault's Dacia plant in Romania, which was taken over by the company in 1999. The Logan was originally intended to be sold in Romania only, but proved to be a huge success in both France and Germany, with waiting lists of customers eager to get hold of the car. The company plans to increase annual output from 200,000 in 2006 to 350,000 by 2008. Although workers at the Dacia plant are highly skilled, the production process is low-tech. However, the main reason behind the car's cheap price is low labour costs – a Romanian car worker gets paid an average of £170 per month, an eighth of the pay of equivalent workers in France.

Source: BBC News

Questions

(20 marks; 25 minutes)

1 Examine Renault's operational objectives in launching its Logan car range. (8)
2 To what extent do you agree that the other major car manufacturers will be forced to follow Renault and target the low-cost segment of the market? (12)

ECONOMIES AND DISECONOMIES OF SCALE

DEFINITION

Economies of scale are factors that cause average unit costs to fall as the scale of output increases in the long-run. Diseconomies of scale are factors causing average costs to rise as the scale of output increases in the long run.

75.1 Two ways firms can grow

1 *Internal growth* occurs when a firm expands its own sales and output. Firms growing in this manner must invest in new machinery and usually take on extra labour too. Firms that are successful in achieving internal growth have to be competitive. Companies like Ryanair and Nike have grown rapidly by taking market share from their less efficient competitors.

2 *External growth* is created by takeover and merger activity. In October 2007 Carlsberg and Heineken announced that they were considering making a takeover bid for another brewer, Scottish & Newcastle. The takeover would enable Carlsberg and Heineken to gain access to Russian beer brands such as Baltika that sell very well in eastern European beer markets, which are growing at a faster rate than markets in western Europe.

The trend towards increased industrial concentration has largely been due to external growth. There are many reasons why firms may wish to grow by takeover or merger. One of the most significant is that many managers believe growth will create cost savings for their firms. They anticipate benefiting from economies of scale. Unfortunately, this is not always true. Many mergers and takeovers actually reduce efficiency; any economies of scale prove to be outweighed by diseconomies. Research has shown consistently that, on average, takeovers and mergers fail to improve efficiency.

75.2 Economies of scale

When a firm grows there are some things it can do more efficiently. The group term given to these factors is 'economies of scale'. When firms experience economies of scale their unit costs fall. For example, a pottery that could produce 100 vases at £5 each may be able to produce 1000 vases at £4.50 per unit. The total cost rises (from £500 to £4500) but the cost per unit falls. Assuming the firm sells the vases for £6 each, the profit margin rises from £1 per vase to £1.50. Economies of scale are, in effect, the benefits of being big. Therefore, for small firms, they represent a threat. If a large-scale producer of televisions can sell them for £99 and still make a profit, there may be no chance for the small guy. There are five main economies of scale. These are discussed below.

Bulk-buying economies

As a firm grows larger it will have to order more raw materials and components. This is likely to mean an increase in the average order size that a firm places with its suppliers. Large orders are more profitable to the supplier. Both the buyer and the potential suppliers are aware of this. Consequently, firms who can place large orders have significant market power. The larger the order, the larger the opportunity cost of losing it. Therefore the supplier has a big incentive to offer a discount. Big multinational manufacturers like Volkswagen have been relentless in demanding larger discounts from their component suppliers. This has helped Volkswagen reduce its variable costs per car.

The $3000 million discount

How much would you be willing to pay for a brand new 150-seater Airbus 319? Film stars such as John Travolta strip out the seats and furnish the interior luxuriously. The list price for an Airbus 319 is $50 million. Yet in October 2002 easyJet struck a deal to buy 120 of these aircraft at a 50% discount. Aircraft priced at $6000 million were bought for just $3000 million. This bulk-buying benefit helped to justify easyJet's boldness in taking over rival discount airline Go. Together, the purchasing power of easyJet plus Go made it far easier to pressure the European makers of Airbus, and thereby benefit from purchasing economies of scale.

Technical economies of scale

When supplying a product or service there is usually more than one production method that could be used. As a firm grows it will usually have a greater desire and a greater ability to invest in new technology. Using more machinery and less labour will usually generate cost savings. Second, the new machinery may well be less wasteful. Reducing the quantity of raw materials being wasted will cut the firm's variable costs.

Such cost savings may not be available to smaller firms. They may lack the financial resources required to purchase the machinery. Even if the firm did have the

The Airbus A380

The Airbus A380 is a true giant of the skies. As the size of a structure increases, the surface area to volume ratio falls. In the case of an aircraft this ratio is very important. Fuel costs are heavily influenced by drag, therefore so long as an aircraft can fly it makes sense to minimise surface area, because this will also minimise drag too. The double-decker layout of the A380 has created an aircraft with a relatively low surface area to volume ratio. The unique design of the A380 means that the aircraft offers 50% more floor area than its main rival: the Boeing 747-400. Airbus estimates that the operating costs of its aircraft will be at least 15% lower than those of its rivals – a considerable economy of scale that is likely to become increasingly important as the price of oil and plane fuel increases.

money it may still not invest. Technology becomes viable to use only if the firm has a long enough production run to spread out the fixed costs of the equipment. For example, a small company may wish to buy a new computer. As the firm is small it may end up using it for only two days a week. The total cost of the computer will be the same whether the firm uses it one day or five days per week. So the average cost of each job done will be high as the small firm is unable to make full use of its investment. **Capital investment** becomes more viable as a firm grows, because capital costs per unit fall as usage rises.

Specialisation

When firms grow there is greater potential for managers to specialise in particular tasks. For instance, large firms will probably have enough financial work to warrant employing a full-time accountant. In many small firms the owner has to make numerous decisions, some of which he or she may have little knowledge of – for example, accounting. This means the quality of decision making in large firms could be better than in small firms. If fewer mistakes are made, large firms should gain a cost advantage (see Figure 75.1).

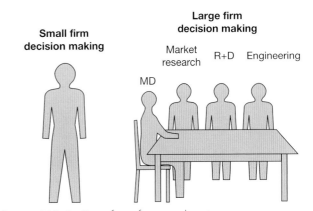

Figure 75.1 Benefits of specialisation

Financial economies of scale

Many small firms find it difficult to obtain finance. Even if banks are willing to lend they will tend to charge very high rates of interest. This is because logic and experience show that lending to small (especially new) firms is more risky; they are more likely to go into liquidation than large firms. There are two main reasons for this.

1 Successful small firms grow into large firms. Consequently, large firms tend to have more established products and have experienced teams of managers.

2 Small firms are often over-reliant on one product or one customer; larger firms' risks are more widely spread.

The result of all this is that it is far easier for large firms to find potential lenders. Second, they also pay lower rates of interest.

Marketing economies of scale

Every aspect of marketing is expensive. Probably the most expensive, though, is the salesforce. These are the people who visit wholesale and retail outlets to try to persuade them to stock the firm's goods. To cover the country, nothing less than six sales staff would be realistic. Yet that would cost a firm around £200,000 per year. For a small firm with sales of under £1 million a year, this would be a crippling cost. Larger firms can spread the costs over multi-million sales, cutting the costs per unit.

75.3 Other benefits of size

Apart from achieving cost-reducing economies of scale there are some other benefits attached to size.

Reduced risk

If a firm grows by diversifying into new markets the firm will now be less dependent on one product. A recession might cause sales in one area of a business to fall. However, if the firm also manufactures products that sell strongly in recessions, the overall turnover of the organisation may change little. In recent years a high percentage of takeovers and mergers have involved firms operating in totally different industries. When Volvo bought out Procordia, a firm in the processed food business, Volvo was seeking a wider product base; this helps the company avoid the risk inherent in 'having all your eggs in one basket'.

Increased capacity utilisation

Some firms may wish to grow in order to increase their **capacity utilisation**. This measures the firm's current output as a percentage of the maximum the firm can produce. Increasing capacity utilisation will spread the fixed costs over more units of output. This lowers the total cost per unit.

So if a fall in demand for chocolate meant that Cadbury's factories were under-utilised, it might be tempted to launch a new product to try to get better use of its factory space.

75.4 Diseconomies of scale

When firms grow, costs rise. But why should costs *per unit* rise? This is because growth can also create diseconomies of scale. Diseconomies of scale are factors that tend to push unit costs up. Large organisations face three main types of diseconomy of scale, as discussed below.

Poor employee motivation

When firms grow, staff may have less personal contact with management. In large organisations there is often a sense of alienation. If staff believe that their efforts are going unnoticed, a sense of despondency may spread. A falling level of work effort will increase the firm's costs. Poor motivation will make staff work less hard when they are actually at work. Absenteeism is also a consequence of poor motivation. This means that the firm may have to employ more staff to cover for the staff they expect to be absent on any given day. In both cases output per worker will fall. As a result, labour costs per unit will rise.

Poor communication

Communication can be a significant problem when a firm grows. First, effective communication is dependent on high levels of motivation. Communication is effective only if the person being communicated with is willing to listen. If growth has left the workforce with a feeling of alienation, communication can deteriorate alongside productivity. A second reason for poor communication in large organisations is that the methods chosen to communicate may be less effective. As a firm grows it may become necessary to use written forms of communication more frequently. Unlike verbal communication, written communication is less personal and therefore less motivating. Written messages are easier to ignore and provide less feedback. Relying too much on written forms of communication could result in an increase in the number of expensive mistakes being made.

Poor managerial coordination

In a small firm coordination is easy. The boss decides what the goals are, and who is doing what. As firms row, it becomes harder for the person at the top to control and coordinate effectively. The leader who refuses to **delegate** 'drowns' under the weight of work. The leader who delegates finds (later) that manager A is heading in a slightly different direction from manager B. Regular meetings are arranged to try to keep everyone focused on the same goals through the same strategy. But not only are such meetings expensive, they are also often poorly attended and lead to grumbles rather than insight. Coordination works well and cheaply in a small firm, but is expensive and often ineffective in large corporations.

75.5 Combining economies and diseconomies of scale

It is important to realise that growth normally creates both economies and diseconomies of scale. If growth creates more economies than diseconomies then unit costs will fall. On the other hand, if the growth creates more diseconomies, the opposite will happen (see Figure 75.2).

Normally, when a firm is small, initial bouts of growth will create more economies of scale than diseconomies. So growth pushes average costs down.

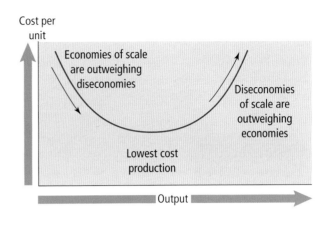

Figure 75.2 Production costs and production scale

What can managers do about diseconomies of scale?

Diseconomies of scale are to a certain extent inevitable. However, this does not mean that managers should just accept them. With careful planning, many diseconomies may be minimised or avoided completely. They key point is that diseconomies are more likely to arise either when growth is unplanned or when it is too rapid. When a firm embarks on a programme of growth it is vital that managers recognise the need to change and adapt.

Table 75.1 Actions required to correct diseconomies of scale

Diseconomies of scale	Corrective action required
Poor motivation	Delegate decision-making power Job enrichment Split the business up by using the following: ● profit centres ● autonomous work groups
Poor communication	Improve employee motivation as above Send managers on attitudinal training courses Create new communication structures such as works councils
Poor coordination	Decentralise Empowerment Wider spans of control

Issues For Analysis

'Economies of scale' is a concept used frequently by students in examinations. When using it to analyse a business situation, the following points should be considered.

● In most business circumstances, a rise in demand cuts average costs because of improved capacity utilisation. In other words, if a half-used factory gets a big order, unit costs fall because the fixed overheads are spread over more output. This is great, but should not be referred to as an economy of scale. It is simply an increase in capacity utilisation. The term 'economies of scale' refers to increases in the scale of operation (e.g. when a firm moves to new, bigger premises).

● The cost advantages from bulk buying can be considerable, but are often exaggerated. A medium-sized builder can buy bricks at much the same cost per brick as a multinational construction company. It should also be remembered that materials and components form quite a low proportion of the total costs for many products. For cosmetics or pharmaceuticals, bought-in materials would usually cost less than one-tenth of the selling price of the product. So lively minds dreaming up new products will count for far more than minor savings from bulk buying.

● Traditionally, managers of growing or merging companies have tended to predict economies of scale with confidence, but to turn a blind eye to diseconomies. In the medium to long term, though, managerial problems of coping with huge organisations have tended to create more diseconomies than economies of scale.

75.6 Economies and diseconomies of scale
an evaluation

Three important issues should be considered.

1 *If diseconomies are all people problems, why can't they be better managed?* Most diseconomies of scale are caused by an inability to manage people effectively. When firms grow managers must be willing to delegate power in an attempt to avoid the problems caused by alienation. Some types of manager might find it hard to accept the need for delegation. If the manager has strong status needs and has **Theory X** attitudes, he or she may find it difficult to cope. Enriching jobs and running training courses is expensive in the short term. These costs are also easy to quantify financially. The benefits of job enrichment and training are more long term. Second, they are harder to quantify financially. This means that it can be quite hard for the managers of a company to push through the changes required to minimise the damage created by diseconomies of scale. Public limited companies may find this a particular problem. Their shares can be bought freely and sold on the stock market. This means that considerable pressure is put on the managers to achieve consistently good financial results. The penalty for investing too much in any one year could be a falling share price and an increased risk of takeover.

2 *Do economies of scale make it impossible for small firms to survive?* In highly competitive markets it is difficult for small firms to compete with large established businesses, especially if they try to compete with them in the mass market. In this situation the small firm will lose out nine times out of ten. The small firm will not be able to achieve the same economies of scale. As a result, its prices will have to be higher to compensate for its higher costs. To a degree this view is correct. However, the fact that the majority of firms within the economy have fewer than 200 employees proves that small firms do find ways of surviving, despite the existence of economies of scale.

3 *The importance of being unimportant.* Many small firms do not need economies of scale to survive. They rely upon the fact that they do not compete head on with their larger competitors. Small firms often produce a highly specialised product. These products are well differentiated. This means the small firm can charge higher prices. So even though they have higher costs their profit margins can be healthy. The larger firms in the industry are frequently not interested in launching their own specialist products. They believe there is more money to be made from the much larger mass market. By operating in these smaller so-called niche markets, many small firms not only survive but often prosper. By being small and by operating in tiny market segments they are not seen as a threat to the larger firms. As a consequence they are ignored because large firms see them as unimportant.

Key terms

Capacity utilisation: actual output as a proportion of maximum capacity.
Capital investment: expenditure on fixed assets such as machinery.
Delegate: to hand power down the hierarchy to junior managers or workers.
Theory X: Douglas McGregor's category for managers who think of workers as lazy and money-focused.

Exercises

A. Revision questions

(40 marks; 40 minutes)

1 Identify three managerial motives for growth. (3)

2 State two possible benefits from specialisation. (2)

3 Explain why large companies are frequently able to command larger discounts from their suppliers than are smaller firms. (4)

4 Outline two diseconomies of scale that might harm the profitability of a nightclub that opens a chain of 12 nightclubs. (4)

5 Explain the likely consequences for a large firm of a failure to control and coordinate the business effectively. (4)

6 Many car manufacturers, like Nissan, are attempting to reduce the complexity of their designs by using fewer parts in different models. With reference to the concept of economies of scale, explain why this is happening. (4)

7 Give three reasons why employee morale can deteriorate as a consequence of growth. (3)

8 Outline three ways in which managers could tackle these morale problems. (6)

9 Explain how economies of scale could give a firm such as Ryanair a considerable marketing advantage. (5)

10 Explain 'the importance of being unimportant' to a small producer of luxury ice cream that competes locally with Ben & Jerry's (owned by the giant Unilever, which also owns Walls). (5)

B. Revision exercises

B1 Data response

Geoff Horsfield and his sister Alex are worried about whether they can compete effectively with their big local competitor, Bracewell plc. Alex believes that Bracewell's economies of scale mean that Horsfield Trading cannot compete with

it head on. Therefore she wants to switch the company's marketing approach away from the mass market towards smaller niches.

Geoff is not sure about this. He knows that Bracewell has a more up-to-date manufacturing technique, but has heard of inefficiencies in its warehousing and office staff. He doubts that Bracewell is as efficient as Alex supposes. Therefore he argues that Horsfield Trading can still compete in the mass market.

Fortunately the employment of an accountant from Bracewell plc has enabled direct comparisons to be made. These figures, shown in the table below, should help Geoff and Alex decide on Horsfield's future strategy.

	Horsfield Trading Ltd	Bracewell plc
Capital investment	£240,000	£880,000
Factory employees	28	49
Other employees	7	21
Guarantee claims per 100 sales	1.2	2.1
Output per employee (units per day)	21	23

Questions

(30 marks; 35 minutes)

1 Calculate the capital investment per employee at each company. What do the figures tell you? (6)

2 Outline the probable reasons for Alex's wish to aim at smaller market niches. (5)

3 (a) What explanations may there be for the differences between the guarantee claims of each business? (8)

(b) What may be the short- and long-term effects of these differences? (6)

4 Outline any other evidence in the case of diseconomies of scale at Bracewell plc. (5)

B2 Case study

Burgers: big or small?

Despite concerns about obesity, the UK market for fast food is still growing. The market leader in the UK remains McDonald's, which has 1225 UK outlets. The sheer scale of McDonald's UK operation creates significant economies of scale. For example, by rolling out the brand across the UK, McDonald's has managed to create substantial marketing economies of scale. Economies of scale enjoyed by large dominant companies can make life extremely tough for smaller companies battling to make headway in the same market.

A new entrant to the UK fast-food market dominated by McDonald's is the Gourmet Burger Kitchen (GBK). The business was set up by three ex-pat New Zealanders who spotted a gap in the market for premium-quality gourmet burgers, freshly prepared to order. In addition to a standard burger and chips, the GBK menu also includes more esoteric menu items such as a chorizo spicy Spanish burger and a hot chicken satay sandwich. On average, a burger at GBK costs nearly £8.

In 2007, GBK had just 28 restaurants in the UK, most of which were located in the Greater London area. The company has already won several 'Best Burger' and 'Best Eats' awards in the capital. The management of GBK has set an objective of growth. In five years' time they want to have 350 restaurants in the UK.

Business analysts believe that GBK's programme of growth could yield substantially more economies of scale than diseconomies of scale.

Figure 75.3 Gourmet Burger Kitchen

Questions

(35 marks; 40 minutes)

1 What is meant by the term 'economies of scale?' (2)

2 Explain why economies of scale are important to companies such as McDonald's and GBK? (7)

3 **(a)** What are marketing economies of scale? (2)

   (b) Explain two reasons why McDonald's will be able to achieve more marketing economies of scale than GBK. (4)

4 Identify and explain two additional economies of scale that GBK might be able to benefit from if it manages to achieve its objective of having 350 UK outlets. (6)

5 Explain two diseconomies of scale that could affect GBK if it manages to achieve its growth targets. (6)

6 Examine one strategy that a small company such as GBK could use to compete effectively against a larger firm, such as McDonald's. (8)

B2 Case study

The drugs deal that went wrong

In 2000 Glaxo and SmithKline, two giants of the pharmaceutical industry, merged. The goal was to create cost-saving economies of scale that, it was hoped, would boost profitability. City analysts claimed that the deal might create economies of scale worth as much as £1.8 billion. It was also hoped that the merger would create a dominant and innovative industry goliath, that would be able to generate new products at a rate the competition could not match.

Unfortunately, GlaxoSmithKline discovered that in business size does matter, but not in the way it had hoped. Bigger does not always equate to better because growth can create problems that, if not tackled, will push costs up. Like many companies before it, GlaxoSmithKline forgot that growth creates both economies and diseconomies of scale.

By 2002 these diseconomies began to emerge. Poor profitability, the loss of patents on top-selling products and the loss of key skilled personnel led to a halving of the share price. The rumour on the stock market was that the new company was struggling to adjust to its new scale of operation. Overheads soared following the merger. A good example was the new head office, which was so big that it required a permanent team of window cleaners. There were many corporate luxuries for the staff at head office. In addition to cafés and shops, staff had the pleasure of a river that ran through the middle of the site.

The growth created by the merger also led to a change in organisational culture. Prior to the merger both companies were known for their innovative and entrepreneurial approach. This culture began to wane in the new organisation, as the company became progressively more and more bureaucratic. For example, staff selection for crucial middle-management positions began to favour those with strong organisational skills over those possessing the qualities of vision and inspiration.

Growth also created coordination and control problems for the London-based management. Their centralised business empire now consisted of 104 manufacturing sites in 40 countries, and a further 24 research and development centres in seven countries. With an organisation this large, attempts to monitor the performance of every division proved unsuccessful. Underperforming overseas divisions were not spotted fast enough, so corrective action was sometimes taken too late to prevent losses.

Questions

(30 marks; 40 minutes)

1 State what is meant by the term 'diseconomies of scale'. (2)

2 Outline the diseconomies of scale that came about as a result of the GlaxoSmithKline merger. (8)

3 Analyse two economies of scale that senior managers would have expected from the merger between Glaxo and SmithKline. (6)

4 Most business theorists believe that diseconomies of scale are not inevitable. Discuss the actions GlaxoSmithKline should have taken in order to minimise potential diseconomies of scale. (14)

C. Essay questions

(40 marks each)

1 Small firms are often said to have better internal communications than larger organisations. Does this mean that growth will always create communication problems? If so what can be done about these difficulties?

2 MHK plc is a large manufacturer of semiconductors. Discuss the opportunities and problems it may face if it decides on a strategy of growth through centralising production.

3 Given the existence of economies of scale, how do small firms manage to survive?

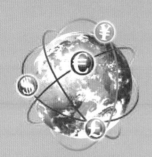

INNOVATION AND RESEARCH AND DEVELOPMENT

76.1 Introduction to innovation

New ideas and inventions are not the only job for the R&D department. The idea must be developed into a usable process or a marketable product. Not only will the R&D specialists need to be involved in this process, but also the other main functional areas of the business will need to help out too.

Innovation and finance

Invention, innovation and design all require significant amounts of long-term investment. Innovation takes time, and that time is spent by highly paid researchers. The result is that firms who are unwilling to accept long payback periods are unlikely to be innovators. Short-termist companies are far more likely to copy other firms' successes. In fact, much of the money spent by firms on invention and innovation provides no direct payback. Ideas are researched and developed before discovering that they will not succeed in the marketplace. The result is that innovation is something of a hit-and-miss process. There are no guaranteed rewards, but the possibility of a brand new, market-changing product. It is these successes that can radically alter the competitive conditions within a marketplace, allowing an innovative company to claim a dominant position.

Innovation and people

Inventors are sometimes caricatured as 'mad scientists' working alone in laboratories with bubbling test tubes.

This is far from the truth. For many years, firms have realised that team working provides many of the most successful innovations. As a result, research teams are encouraged to share their breakthroughs on a regular basis in the hope that the team can put their ideas together to create a successful product. These research teams are often created by taking specialists in various different fields of operation, from different departments within an organisation. This means that a team may consist of several scientists, an accountant, a production specialist and someone from the marketing department. This blend of expertise will enable the team to identify cost-effective, marketable new ideas that can be produced by the company, without the need for the new idea to be passed around the different departments within an organisation.

Many management gurus, such as Tom Peters, believe that in the future, innovation will be the responsibility of everyone within an organisation. In this way, the organisation can harness the creative power of an even wider range of specialists. In theory, this idea is excellent. The problems arise in the practical implementation of such a system.

Invention, innovation and production

As mentioned previously, invention and innovation are not limited to finished products. New production processes can be invented or developed. These can lead to more efficient, cheaper or higher-quality production. Furthermore, new products often need new machinery and processes to be developed for their manufacture. Design is also important in production. The process needs to be thought through clearly so that every machine and activity has a logical place in the production system.

Innovation and marketing

Many would argue that the most important element of the marketing mix is the product itself. Successful product development keeps a firm one step ahead of the competition. This usually means keeping one step ahead in pricing as well. Whether you are introducing a new drug such as Viagra or a new football management computer game, you have the opportunity to charge a premium price. Innovative new products are also very likely to get good distribution. Tesco is very reluctant to find space on its shelves for just another ('me-too') cola or toothpaste, but if the new product is truly innovative, the space will be found.

Research and development is carried out by companies in order to develop new products or improve existing products. Larger firms, particularly multinational companies, will tend to have separate research and development facilities. These will be staffed by highly trained scientists, usually working towards developing products to a specific brief.

Product-orientated firms are likely to focus on areas of scientific expertise and push their researchers to produce the most technically advanced product possible. For market-orientated firms, the research brief will largely be influenced by the needs of consumers and any gaps identified in the market. However, it is important to note that R&D is *not* market research.

As can be seen from Table 76.1, some industries see particularly heavy R&D spending. One in particular is the pharmaceutical industry. These companies spend vast quantities of money, researching new drugs or cures for diseases. Developing a new product in this market can generate £millions of revenue for many years.

76.2 Protecting new ideas

There are three main avenues open to firms whose R&D produces useful outcomes.

1 *Patents:* a patent is the exclusive right to use an invention. Patents can last for up to 20 years. Patents are a commodity that can be bought, sold, hired or licensed.

2 *Registered designs:* designs can be protected in two ways. Design right gives a weaker form of protection than a patent, but registered designs can be used only by the firm or individual holding the registration. The registration can last for up to 25 years and, just like a patent, can be bought or sold.

3 *Trademarks:* a trademark allows a firm to differentiate itself, or its products, from its competitors. Most trademarks are words or symbols, or a combination, but sounds and smells can be registered as trademarks too. Registration of a trademark is denoted by the symbol ®.

76.3 Benefits of successful R&D

- *Monopoly:* successful innovation, assuming it is protected by a patent, creates a monopoly. Such a situation, in which there is only one supplier of a

Table 76.1 *R&D as a percentage of sales in some UK manufacturing industry sectors*

	1995	**2000**	**2001**	**2002**	**2003**	**2004**	**2005**
Pharmaceuticals	28.0	35.9	35.0	36.1	32.5	34.2	33.3
Aerospace	11.3	8.5	10.7	11.8	14.1	16.9	22.2
Electrical machinery	3.6	3.8	4.1	4.8	4.7	4.3	4.2
Chemicals	2.5	2.6	2.0	2.4	2.4	2.3	2.6
Motor vehicles	2.5	3.2	8.4	2.9	3.4	2.5	2.0
Mechanical engineering	1.6	1.7	2.3	na	na	na	na
Other manufacturing	0.5	0.6	0.6	0.5	0.7	0.5	0.4

Source: Science, Engineering & Technology Statistics (DTI); http://www.abpi.org.uk

particular type or product, offers huge benefits to the successful innovator.

- *High price:* with no competition, selling price can be set high to cream off revenue from customers who want the product. This pricing strategy of skimming the market allows the firm to reduce its prices as it anticipates competitors arriving, perhaps as a result of finding an alternative way to make the product, or the expiry of the patent.

- *Reputation:* innovators tend to have a positive reputation in the minds of consumers. Sony's development of the first ever personal stereo occurred over 20 years ago, yet it has maintained the impetus that this innovation bought by continuing to develop 'cutting edge' products and kept the benefit of being seen as a pacesetter in the consumer electronics market.

76.4 Unsuccessful R&D

The problem with spending huge amounts of money on research and development is that it carries no guaranteed return. New scientific developments may prove to be unusable in the market. Perhaps the idea is one that nobody actually wants or, alternatively, the firm may not be able to find a way to put its new idea into large-scale production at a viable cost. It is this problem that explains perhaps the major stumbling block to R&D budgets: very few firms are willing to invest when there is not a measurable return. The nature of R&D requires substantial sums to pay for the scientific expertise and equipment needed and, therefore, the only firms willing and able to invest in R&D are likely to be very large firms that also have a management team committed to long-term, rather than short-term, success.

R&D and international competitiveness

Innovation is a crucial factor in determining the international competitiveness of a country's businesses. A country whose companies invest heavily in R&D is likely to find its economy healthy as its firms find success in export markets and have the innovative products needed to stave off import competition in their home market. It may therefore come as something of a worry to UK readers to see the UK in 11th place in the world league of R&D shown in Table 76.2. The implications of this are far reaching and serious for the UK. With higher costs of manufacturing than many countries,

allied with a failure to innovate, the UK may struggle to find a genuine competitive advantage in the twenty-first century's global marketplace. This could spell economic stagnation.

Table 76.2 Selected countries' R&D as a % of GDP, 2006

1	Sweden	3.8%
2	Finland	3.5%
3	Japan	3.1%
4	Korea, Republic of (South Korea)	2.6%
5	Switzerland	2.6%
6	United States	2.5%
7	Germany	2.5%
8	Denmark	2.4%
8	Austria	2.4%
9	France	2.1%
10	Canada	1.9%
11	United Kingdom	1.8%

Source: UNDP (2008) *Human Development Report 2008*

Issues For Analysis

- Invention should not be confused with innovation. The British have a proud record as inventors. Hovercraft, television, penicillin, Viagra and many more products were British inventions. In recent years, however, there has been less success in this country with innovation. The Japanese have been the great innovators in electronics, the Americans in computers and the Swiss in watches. British firms have failed to invest sufficiently to develop ranges of really innovative new products.

- Major innovation can completely change a firm's competitive environment. The market shares of leading companies may change little for years, then an innovation comes along that changes everything. The firm that has not prepared for such change can be swept aside. This has happened to music stores that have not established a major presence on the internet.

- Good management means looking ahead, not only to the next hill but the one after that. Anticipation makes change manageable. It may even ensure that your own firm becomes market leader due to the far-sightedness of your own innovation. In turn, that would ensure high product differentiation and allow relatively high prices to be charged.

- Innovation can happen in management procedures, attitudes and styles. A management that is progressive and adventurous might well find that an empowered workforce is generating the new ideas that seemed lacking before. It would not be wise to assume that invention and innovation is all about scientists and engineering. It is about people.

Figure 76.1 The Hovercraft, a British invention

76.5 Innovation and research and development

an evaluation

The fundamental theme for evaluating any question involving invention and innovation is long- and short-term thinking. Invention and innovation are long-term activities. Companies whose objective is short-term profit maximisation are unlikely to spend heavily on innovation. However, a firm with objectives directly related to producing innovative products is likely to spend heavily on research. GlaxoSmithKline, Britain's highest spender on R&D (just under £3.5 billion in 2006), is an excellent example.

Most British companies do not have a particularly impressive record in invention and innovation. Table 77.2 shows that a comparison of international R&D spending places Britain outside the top ten. The conclusion must be that short-termism is a particular problem in Britain. An unhealthy focus on success in the short term does not fit in with a commitment to expensive R&D, designed to ensure long-term growth. As a result, British firms have a tendency to please their shareholders with high dividend payments, rather than retaining profits for investment in R&D.

Selling innovative products is not the only way to build a successful business. Many firms carve out a successful segment of their market based on selling copycat products at lower prices and their ability to cut costs to the bone, maintaining a satisfactory profit margin. However, these low-cost firms tend to be based in countries with lower labour costs than the UK. Other costs in the UK, such as property and business services, are also high relative to international rivals and, therefore, this low-cost strategy is unlikely to work for many UK firms trying to compete internationally. As a result, it seems likely that the continued survival of major UK multinationals is dependent on producing innovative products based on successful R&D.

Exercises

A. Revision questions

(40 marks; 40 minutes)

1 Distinguish between product and process innovation. (3)

2 Why is it 'vital' to patent an invention? (3)

3 Explain why R&D has an opportunity cost. (2)

4 Briefly explain the role of each of the following departments in the process of successfully bringing a new product to market:
   (a) marketing
   (b) finance
   (c) HR. (12)

5 Why might product-orientated firms produce more inventions than market-orientated ones? (4)

6 How are the concepts of short-termism and innovation linked? (4)

7 What effect would a lack of innovation have on a company's product portfolio? (4)

8 Many businesses are concerned at the fall in the number of students taking science A-levels. How might this affect firms in the long term? (4)

9 Explain how a firm may try to market a brand new type of product developed from successful R&D. (4)

B. Revision exercises

B1 Case study

Mach 3: at the cutting edge of technology

Gillette's UK research and development facility is located just outside Reading. Men in white coats test revolutionary shaving technologies – all searching for the perfect shaving experience. From its position of UK market dominance (57% market share), which has been based on innovation, including the launch in 1971 of the world's first twin-bladed razor, Gillette is pushing forward the frontiers of shaving technology. The newest model to have been developed by

Gillette is the Mach 3. The new product has been described as the 'Porsche of the shaving world', with its sleek design, and its hefty price tag of £4.99 for the handle and two cartridges. The Mach 3 was advertised in America as the 'billion-dollar blade'. However, this was probably an underestimate of the costs incurred during the razor's seven-year development:

- $750 million (£440 million) on building the production system for the razor

- $300 million on the launch marketing

- $200 per year on research and development.

Gillette expects to sell 1.2 billion units of the Mach 3 per year.

The testing regime for Gillette's new products involves a product evaluation group of more than 3000 men throughout the UK, who are supplied with Gillette products and provide feedback on the level of quality consistency, in addition to testing experimental products. Among these guinea pigs are the mysterious men who turn up at the research facility in Reading every morning – paid for the shaving risks they take there and performing the role of test pilots – sworn to secrecy on the new technology they are using.

The building, an old jam factory, is kitted out with the latest CAD technology. Research focuses on computer models of human skin – a substance that Gillette has found very tough to model accurately. However, its current modelling is the most accurate it has ever used and skin irritation is measured using the same laser technology as that employed in police radar guns. The jam factory was the birthplace of the Mach 3, a birth heralded by success in the long-running attempt to add a third blade without causing blood loss. With sales of the Mach 3 starting off at encouraging levels, the old jam factory appears to have turned out another winning idea.

Questions

(40 marks; 50 minutes)

1 Using examples from the text, suggest what marketing advantages arise from successful innovation. (8)

2 Describe the pre-launch testing methods used by Gillette, and explain why these are so vital to success. (9)

3 Why might the research laboratories for a product as ordinary as a razor be shrouded in secrecy? (6)

4 Using examples from the Gillette story, explain why successful innovation requires input from all departments within a firm, not just the research and development department. (12)

5 Given the information in the text, how long will it take Gillette to recover the research, development and launch costs of the Mach 3, if running costs average out to £2.99 per unit. (5)

B2 Case study

R&D in pottery

Josiah Wedgwood & Sons Ltd is part of the huge Waterford Wedgwood company formed by the takeover of ceramics firm Wedgwood by the Irish glass manufacturer Waterford Crystal. Despite a history dating back hundreds of years, Wedgwood still needs to carry our R&D to maintain its position in a hugely competitive global market. As is so common for many major British brands, Wedgwood can survive in the global market only by offering top-quality products at reasonable prices. In the push to bring costs down without sacrificing quality of design, Wedgwood has developed a brand new piece of machinery that is able to print intricate designs on non-flat surfaces (i.e. cups). Previously, patterns were applied to cups by hand as decals (stickers). New decals took around four weeks to produce, while the application of the decals pushed the lead time for a new design up to 16 weeks. The machine has enabled direct printing onto cups and therefore reduced lead times to just one week for new designs. In addition to far quicker delivery to customers, the machine has significantly reduced material and labour costs while maintaining high-

quality products. Wedgwood identified three key factors in the success of the machine's development:

1 management commitment was critical to a potentially high-impact yet risky project in which each machine cost over 0.5 million euros

2 development engineers with the experience to develop radical new approaches and machinery

3 collaboration between technical, production and engineering departments.

Source: Adapted from www.manufacturingfoundation.org.uk

Questions

(30 marks; 35 minutes)

1 Analyse the financial benefits that Wedgwood will receive as a result of the new machine. (8)

2 Briefly explain how the new machines should provide marketing benefits. (4)

3 Analyse the likely reaction of staff to the development of the new machine. (6)

4 Consider how the case demonstrates the need for collaboration of different departments in successful R&D. (12)

C. Essay questions

(40 marks each)

1 To what extent does an innovative product guarantee success?

2 'Any business has two, and only two, basic functions. Marketing and innovation.' Discuss whether there is value in this statement by Peter Drucker.

3 'Luck is the most important factor in successful innovation.' Discuss the validity of this statement.

4 'Spending on research and development is wasted money since many firms find success through copying other firms' products.' Discuss this statement.

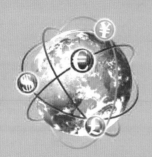

INDUSTRIAL AND INTERNATIONAL LOCATION

DEFINITION

The site(s) where a firm decides to carry out its operations.

77.1 The location decision

Unit 7 covered 'location factors for a business start-up'. It included an overview of many of the basic issues involved, such as the cost of land and the need for space to expand. This chapter looks at the expansion or relocation of a business, including decisions relating to international location.

The choice of location for a business is crucial to its success. Opting for the 'right' location can help keep costs of production low and, at the same time, generate higher revenue from sales than alternative sites. For instance, costs can be reduced by opting for cheaper premises, closer proximity to suppliers or locating in an area with effective transport links. High-street locations make retailers more visible to customers and are more likely to attract sales.

Once a firm is established, there are two main reasons why managers may be faced with making a location decision.

1 It may be the result, for example, of a decision to expand operations by operating as a multi-site organisation, acquiring additional factories, offices or outlets. This can help to increase capacity and sales, and it may also help the business to recognise and respond to local market conditions more effectively. However, the business may require a new structure in order to continue to perform effectively, and a duplication of certain functions and job roles – especially at management level – can lead to increased overheads.

2 It may also result from a decision to relocate operations to a new site – one that may be in a position to attract more customers, offer better opportunities for modernisation or lead to a reduction in operating costs. Before going ahead, however, the business needs to consider the costs of relocation as well as the benefits. For example, will existing employees accept the move or leave the firm, leading to increased recruitment costs and a los of expertise?

77.2 Making the choice: quantitative methods

If Boeing wants to set up its first aircraft factory in Europe, it is clear that there are some key issues to do with numbers. It will need a massive site, which might have a cost ranging from £50–£300 million, depending where it is. Then there are wages, which might range from £300–£1500 per person per month, depending on whether the location is eastern Poland or western Germany.

Given its importance to the success of a business, it is vital that the location decision is based on accurate data. There are a number of quantitative decision-making techniques that can be used, including those discussed below.

Investment appraisal

This refers to a set of techniques that can be used to assess the viability of a project (i.e. will the expected returns from the relocation site meet or exceed corporate targets?). Alternatively, they can be used to help choose between two or more sites for expansion or relocation that are under consideration. For example:

● *payback* provides information on how quickly the investment costs of a project will be recovered from expected revenues or cost savings

● *average rate of return (ARR)* calculates the average annual profit generated by a project, expressed as a percentage of the sum invested.

Ideally, the results of any analysis using **investment**

ppraisal techniques would present a business with the cation that enjoyed the quickest payback period and ighest ARR. This is unlikely in reality, so the choice ill be based on the individual firm's circumstances. A m faced with liquidity problems, for example, is likely go for the option with the quickest payback. (See nit 60 for more information on investment appraisal.)

reak-even analysis

alculating the break-even point tells a firm how much needs to produce and sell in order to avoid making a ss, given its current level of fixed costs and ontribution per unit. Fixed costs will include rent on remises (or the interest charged on loans for land rchase), business rates and staff salaries, whereas the ost of raw materials and transportation may be regarded variable. A prime location that improves image or the vel of convenience offered may mean that products n be sold at higher prices. Clearly, differences in these osts between locations are likely to have a significant fect on a firm's break-even level of output and sales d, therefore, the overall profitability of a project. (See nit 14 for a reminder of break-even analysis.)

ormula reminder:

$$\text{reak-even point} = \frac{\text{fixed costs}}{\text{contribution per unit}}$$

77.3 Qualitative factors

here are a number of other factors that, although less sy to measure in terms of their impact on costs and ofitability, can have an important influence on the ventual choice of location for a business. Many ntrepreneurs may have chosen to locate near to where ey live and remain there, despite the potential nancial benefits of relocating elsewhere. Many borough uncils and regional development agencies aim to mpt businesses into relocating by offering a better ıality of life for owners and employees.

he reputation of a particular location and its sociation with a particular industry may continue to t as an incentive, encouraging new firms to locate ere. This may continue even after the original reasons r doing so are no longer significant (known as **dustrial inertia**). The concentration of an industry in particular area may lead to a number of **external conomies of scale**, including the availability of suitably illed workers and locally based suppliers.

77.4 Making the optimal decision

Every manager faced with a decision hopes to make the best decision in the circumstances. With location, however, it is impossible to know what is the 'best'. Honda established its Swindon factory in Britain in the 1990s, intending it to be its base for selling cars throughout Europe. It was a sensible decision at the time, but then (a) Britain chose not to join the euro and (b) the £ spent the years from 1996–2006 grossly overvalued against the euro (making Honda's exports from the UK unprofitable).

All a manager can hope to do is make the most sensible decision in the circumstances, accepting that it might be five or twenty years before anyone really knows whether it was the right thing to do. This is known as an 'optimal decision'; it means it is a sensible balance between varying pressures. It might be, for example, that instead of choosing the lowest-cost location in eastern Poland, or the location with the highest availability of skilled staff (in Germany), the optimal decision is to strike a balance, choosing a location in Portugal.

An optimal decision will bear in mind quantitative and qualitative factors, and probably be based on careful and detailed research, but also consultation with managers and workers.

A firm's location decision is likely to be influenced by several factors. Some can be quantified but many cannot. The factors may include:

A-grade application
The 'Cinderella' highroad

MPs and industry chiefs have called on the government to make improvements to the transport network in Moray, Speyside. The area is the centre of Scotland's multi-million-pound whisky industry. MSP David Stewart described the A95, the road at the heart of the network, as a 'Cinderella' road, claiming that it was not 'fit for purpose'. According to Mr Stewart, 'There are so many heavy lorries using the road there is a safety issue and a cost issue to the companies because the road is so slow.' The road acts as a vital link between the highland distilleries and packaging plants further south.

In 2007, drinks manufacturer Diageo announced its decision to open the first new distillery in Moray for 40 years. The company already has 17 of its 27 existing Scottish distilleries in the area.

Source: *Northern Scot*, December 2007

- the cost and suitability of the site
- access to customers
- access to supplies
- access to workers – either highly skilled or low-cost, or some combination of the two
- quality of the area's infrastructure
- availability of government assistance.

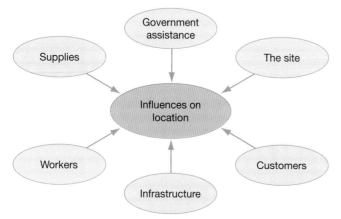

Figure 77.1 *Influences on a firm's location*

77.5 International location

A **multinational** organisation is a business with production facilities in a number of different countries. There are a number of ways in which a firm's operations may develop an international dimension. These include the following.

- *To exploit new markets:* a firm operating in a slow-growth or saturated domestic market might decide to target foreign customers in order to generate new sales. Alternatively, developing a number of overseas markets should protect a business to some extent from recession and falling demand at home. Either way, locating closer to overseas customers will help firms to recognise and understand differing tastes and requirements.

- *To benefit from greater economies of scale:* an increase in a firm's scale of production may lead to a reduction in unit costs, perhaps as a result of receiving discounts for buying larger quantities of raw materials. Lower average costs should lead to an improvement in competitiveness by allowing firms to lower prices or generate funds for new product development. However, the extent to which a firm may benefit from economies of scale depends on whether it can produce standardised products to meet

demand across a range of markets, or whether differences in tastes require significant modifications.

- *To benefit from cheaper labour costs:* taking advantage of large pools of cheap, unskilled labour is a long-established practice of UK manufacturers relocating low-skill production processes to developing countries in order to reduce costs. However, the growing supply of young, well-educated workers in low-wage economies, especially in Asia, has stimulated the relocation of many industries in both the secondary and service sectors (see Table 77.1). Moreover, the latest expansions of the European Union (EU) in 2005 and 2007 have given UK firms access to relatively low-cost locations in Poland, Hungary and the Czech Republic, with the additional protection of a common legal system.

- *To benefit from cheaper land and reduced transportation costs:* cheaper land and taxes (as well as fewer legal restrictions on issues such as health and safety and employment law) in other countries may permit a firm to reduce its fixed costs. These may be offered as an inducement to attract foreign investment by national governments. In addition, there may be further significant cost savings to be enjoyed by relocating overseas, in order to be closer to either suppliers or customers. The economies gained by being closer to key suppliers in the Far East and new markets in Japan and Australia was one of the main reasons given by James Dyson for the relocation of his company's production activities from Malmesbury, Wiltshire, to Malaysia in 2002/03.

Figure 77.2 *The Dyson factory near Malmesbury, Wiltshire*

- *To minimise the impact of exchange rate fluctuations:* the revenue and costs of firms producing in the UK and exporting to or importing from overseas will be subject to exchange rate fluctuations. For example, an appreciation in the value of sterling against the euro is likely to lead to a loss of sales for UK exporters to markets within the eurozone. This is because the increased euro price will lead to a fall in demand. Alternatively, a cut in the euro price in order to maintain demand will lead to a reduction in revenue per unit sold. Moving production to a location within the eurozone would offer protection from such fluctuations.

To overcome trade barriers: national governments and international trading blocs use a number of measures to protect domestic industries and markets from competition from foreign firms. These may include **quotas**, **tariffs** or **non-tariff barriers**. For example, the European Union uses a range of protectionist measures against goods from outside the area that act to increase prices and reduce demand. Companies from non-member states can, however, overcome these trade barriers and gain free access to EU markets by locating production facilities within its boundaries.

77.6 Offshoring

In the last few years, the practice of **offshoring**, where firms transfer aspects of their operations from high-cost to low-cost countries, has become a controversial issue in the UK. In particular, concerns about the number of jobs lost from the domestic economy have generated a great deal of media coverage and trades union campaigning. The majority of the activities 'offshored' to date have included call centres and software development, as well as **business process outsourcing** (BPO) of tasks such as payroll processing. However, the trend is increasingly towards the transfer of higher-value jobs, such as those in research and development (R&D) and financial services. These activities are either carried out in company-owned facilities or outsourced to separate firms based in low-cost countries. Currently, the main offshore bases include India, China, Poland, Russia, South Africa and Brazil. India has proved to be a particularly attractive destination for UK businesses looking to offshore activities, producing over 2 million English-speaking graduates every year.

77.7 Potential problems of international location

Although expansion or relocation of operations into overseas markets can offer a number of benefits, firms must also be aware of the potential problems that can arise, including those described below.

- *Language and cultural differences*: given that barriers to communication can exist within firms employing workers that speak the same language, it is not difficult to imagine the potential problems and costs associated with managing an international, multilingual workforce. UK firms have benefited from the fact that English is commonly spoken around the world and remains the language of business. However, there are a number of differences in working practices between countries, including the length of the working week and number of public holidays, which can impact on performance and productivity.

- *Economic and political instability*: the dynamic nature of the business environment means that firms need to be able to adjust to a certain level of change if they are to enjoy long-term success. However, rapid and unforeseen changes can pose serious challenges to survival. Because of this, firms are more likely to opt for international locations with a history of economic and political stability.

- *Impact on public image*: a number of UK companies have attracted media attention over allegations of worker exploitation in low-cost economies, in order to keep costs down and offer cheap prices to consumers. In December 2006, a report published by War on Want claimed that workers from Bangladesh were paid less than 5p an hour (less than £80 per

Table 77.1 *Comparative pay rates between India and the UK*

Occupation	Salary in India	% of UK salary
Call centre operator	60p to £1.25 per hour	13–20%
HSBC average	£2500	14%
Software engineer	£5000 to £15,000	15–17%

Source: The Work Foundation, January 2004

month) to produce clothes for UK retailers Tesco, Asda and Primark, despite all three companies being signed up to an initiative designed to provide such workers with an accepted living wage and improved living conditions.

Issues For Analysis

Opportunities for analysis using this topic are likely to focus on the following areas:

- examining the advantages and disadvantages to a firm of relocating

- comparing quantitative and/or qualitative aspects of different location sites

- calculating and commenting upon the most profitable location for a firm

- analysing the factors that a business would take into account before establishing production facilities overseas.

77.8 Industrial and international location

an evaluation

Location is a key aspect of all business operations. Even in the most footloose of industries, firms cannot afford to ignore the need for sufficient quantities of appropriately skilled workers or effective transport and communications networks. The optimum location is the one that allows a business to keep costs down while maximising revenue opportunities. Once made, incorrect location decisions can be costly to put right, and can lead to customer inconvenience and dissatisfaction. However, in a dynamic and increasingly competitive environment, the pressure on firms' costs is relentless. Therefore, firms need to regularly assess the suitability of their location in order to ensure that their operational strategy continues to be effective.

Key terms

Business process outsourcing: moving administrative tasks, such as accounting and human resources management, to an external firm.

External economies of scale: cost advantages enjoyed by a firm as a result of the growth of the industry in which it is located (e.g. close proximity of a network of suppliers).

Industrial inertia: when firms continue to locate in a particular area or region even after the original advantages of doing so have disappeared.

Investment appraisal: a range of quantitative decision-making techniques used to assess investment projects, including payback, average rate of return and net present value.

Multinational: a business with productive bases – either manufacturing or assembly – in more than one country.

Non-tariff barriers: hidden barriers put in place by governments to restrict international trade without appearing to do so (e.g. insisting on technical standards that it is difficult for foreign firms to meet).

Offshoring: the relocation of one or more business processes – either production or services – from one country to another.

Outsourcing: moving business functions from internal departments to external firms.

Quota: a trade barrier that places restrictions on the number of foreign goods that can be sold within a market in a given period of time.

Tariff: a tax placed on imports in order to increase their price and therefore discourage demand.

Exercises

A. Revision questions

(40 marks; 40 minutes)

1 Outline two reasons why a business might choose to relocate its operations. (4)

2 Identify four factors that might influence a firm's location decision. (4)

3 Examine one advantage and one disadvantage for an estate agent that locates on a town's main high street. (6)

4 Briefly outline two quantitative methods that could be used to help a business decide between two location sites. (4)

5 What is meant by the term industrial inertia? (2)

6 Describe one external economy of scale that might result from the concentration of an industry in a particular area. (3)

7 In September 2006, fashion group Burberry announced its decision to relocate production from its factory in Treorchy, Wales, to a site in Spain, Portugal, Poland or China. Examine two reasons why Burberry may have decided to relocate production overseas. (6)

8 Explain the difference between **outsourcing** and offshoring. (5)

9 Analyse two problems that a bank might experience as a result of relocating some of its business processes to the Philippines. (6)

B. Revision exercises

B1 Data response

Has offshore had its day?

An increasing number of UK companies have reversed decisions to set up call centres in low-cost countries, following negative feedback from customers. Well-known UK companies, such as HSBC, Lloyds TSB, Royal Sun Alliance and Norwich Union, have transferred call centre operations to Asia in recent years, in the hope of achieving significant cost reductions. However, the experiment has failed to live up to expectations in some cases and several businesses, including Powergen and insurance firm esure, have transferred operations back to the UK.

A number of companies, such as the Royal Bank of Scotland, the Halifax and the Co-operative made commitments from the outset to continuing to operate from within the UK. Some have gone further, by choosing to incorporate the decision within their marketing strategies. For example, NatWest based a recent advertising campaign around its claim that its customers were guaranteed to speak to staff in Barnsley or Cardiff, rather than Bombay or Calcutta.

The decision to remain 'onshore' has been backed up by market research findings. In 2004, a survey carried out by ContactBabel claimed that 75% of people felt negatively about companies that route their enquiries abroad. According to the report, more than a quarter of a million customers changed banks in 2003 as a direct result of customer service offshoring. In a more recent survey carried out by YouGov, over half of those asked said that their biggest problem using a call centre was having to deal with staff outside the UK.

Over-50s holiday and insurance company Saga has refused to move its call centre out of the UK, despite claiming this could result in an average saving of 65p per call. Its decision to do so is supported by ContactBabel's research. The firm calculated that the cost savings for a bank transferring 1000 of its call centre workers from the UK to India would be around £9.26 million a year. However, the effect on revenues from a reduction of less than 0.35% of its customers as a result of the move would cancel out any cost savings made.

Questions

(25 marks; 30 minutes)

1 Explain what is meant by the term offshoring. (3)

2 Examine the main benefits for an insurance company from transferring some of its business processes from the UK to India. (8)

3 Discuss whether it is likely that the recent trend for UK firms to relocate operations from the UK to other countries has come to an end. (14)

B2 Case study

Relocating production at Blueberry Fashions Ltd

'It's the decision that no one wanted to face, but we have no choice.' The words of Blueberry Fashions managing director, Susanne Burrell, gradually sank into the other members of the board. Despite 12 months of a high-profile campaign that had included a number of local celebrities, the company had just announced its decision to go ahead with the closure of one of its three factories in the UK in a little over a year's time, resulting in the loss of over 350 jobs. Despite the firm's success in maintaining its reputation as one of the UK's most successful global brands in recent years, there was no escaping the fact that many of its designer items could be made at a higher quality and a significantly lower cost elsewhere in Europe. Sites in a number of locations were under consideration but the board had yet to reach a decision.

Questions

(20 marks; 25 minutes)

1 On the basis of the evidence provided, evaluate the relocation options available to Blueberry Fashions. (20)

C. Essay questions

(40 marks each)

1 Lord Sieff, former head of UK retailer Marks & Spencer, is reported to have once said, 'There are three important things in retailing: location, location, location.' To what extent do you agree with this view?

2 Discuss the implications for UK service-sector firms that have offshored IT or administrative functions to low-cost economies, such as India.

Appendix A: Comparative figures, 2007

	Poland	Slovakia	Romania
Forecast cost of expansion (€m)	4.	5.1	3.9
Unemployment rates %	12.8	8.6	4.1
Growth rates %	6.5	8.8	5.9

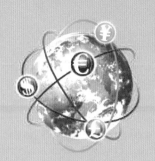
PLANNING OPERATIONS (INCLUDING CPA)

DEFINITION

Planning how a project will be carried out to ensure that it is completed quickly, cost-efficiently and on time. A network diagram helps identify the critical path, which shows the activities that require the most careful management scrutiny.

78.1 Operational planning

Operations management involves many considerations, including location, quality, stock control and information technology. Well-run firms will bring all these aspects into a single strategic plan. This should then be turned into a day-by-day plan to show supervisors and workers exactly what they should be doing. What, when and how. This kind of planning and control is fundamental to effective management. A useful model for planning an operational project is network analysis. It provides the basis for monitoring and controlling actual progress compared with the plan.

78.2 Network analysis

Network analysis is a way of showing how a complex project can be completed in the shortest possible time. It identifies the activities that must be completed on time to avoid delaying the whole project (the 'critical path'). Management effort can be concentrated on ensuring that these key activities are completed on time. This leaves greater flexibility in timing the non-critical items. The objectives are to ensure customer satisfaction through good timekeeping and to minimise the wastage of resources, thereby boosting the profitability of the project.

Have you ever tried to put together some flatpack furniture? Piece of wood A has to be fitted into piece B and then screwed into C. Meanwhile, someone else can be gluing D and E together. Then ABC can be slotted into DE. (And on and on until worker/parent A is screaming at worker/parent B.) The manufacturer's instructions follow the exact logic of network analysis.

This would work well, were it not that the instructions are usually set out poorly, and the 'workforce' is untrained. In business it is easier to make the technique work effectively.

A **network** shows:

● the order in which each task must be undertaken

● how long each stage should take

● the earliest date at which the later stages can start.

If a house-building firm can predict with confidence that it will be ready to put roof beams in place 80 days after the start of a project, a crane can be hired and the beams delivered for exactly that time. This minimises costs, as the crane need only be hired for the day it is needed, and improves cash flow by delaying the arrival of materials (and invoices) until they are really required.

A network consists of two components.

1 An 'activity' is part of a project that requires time and/or resources. Therefore waiting for delivery of parts is an 'activity', as is production. Activities are shown as arrows running from left to right. Their length has no significance.

2 A 'node' is the start or finish of an activity and is represented by a circle. All network diagrams start and end on a single node.

As an example, the flatpack furniture example given earlier would look as shown in Figure 78.1.

How long should it take to complete this little project? Although A, B and C can be completed in 8 minutes, D and E take 12, so the final 4-minute activity can occur only after the 12th minute. Therefore the project duration is 16 minutes.

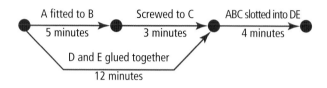

Figure 78.1 Flatpack network

78.3 Rules for drawing networks

1 The network must start and end on a single node.

2 No lines should cross each other.

3 When drawing an activity, do not add the end node straight away; wait until you have checked which activity follows.

4 There must be no lines that are not activities.

5 Due to the need to write figures in the nodes, it is helpful to draw networks with large circles and short lines.

78.4 Case example: the need for networks

A chocolate producer decides to run a '3p off' price promotion next February. Any need for network analysis? Surely not. What could be easier? Yet the risk of upsetting customers is massive with any promotion. What if a huge order from Tesco meant that Sainsbury's could not receive all the supplies it wanted?

Think for a moment about the activities needed to make this promotion work smoothly. It would be necessary to:

● tell the salesforce

● sell the stock into shops

● design the 'flash' packs

● estimate the sales volume for one month at 3p off

● get 'flash' packs printed

● order extra raw materials (e.g. a double order of cocoa)

● step up production

● arrange overtime for factory staff

● deliver promotional packs to shops ...

... and much, much more.

An efficient manager thinks about all the activities needed, and puts them in the correct time sequence. Then a network can easily be drawn up (see Figure 78.2).

Once the manager has found how long each activity is likely to take, s/he can work backwards to find out when the work must start. Here, the work must start 70 days before 1 February. This is because the longest path through to the end of the project is 70 (14 + 28 + 21 + 7).

Having drawn a network, the next stage is to identify more precisely the times when particular activities can or must begin and end. To do this, it is helpful to number the nodes that connect the activities. It also

A-grade application
Delays can cost billions

The first commercial flight of the massive Airbus A380 took place in November 2007. This was eight years after the new plane was announced and more than two and a half years after the plane's first test flight. Singapore Airlines had been expecting to fly its first 'Superjumbo' in April 2006, and therefore had been waiting for more than 18 months.

The problem arose because the plane's designers had failed to think through the production implications of installing 300 miles of electric wiring (per plane) with 100% accuracy! The direct cost to Airbus has been estimated at more than £5000 million. The indirect effects are no less severe. Before Airbus admitted that its project was behind schedule, the company had sold more than 150 planes at £150 million each. After the embarrassment became public, orders dried up and rival Boeing enjoyed a sales bonanza.

When the wiring problem became the critical one for Airbus, management failed to find a successful way of coping. In this case, poor critical path analysis cost Airbus £billions.

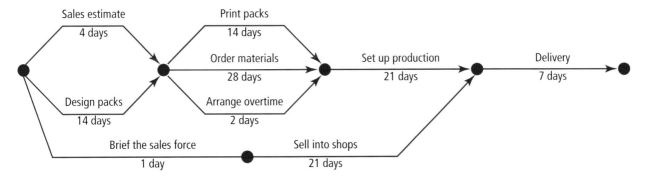

Figure 78.2 '3p off' network (1)

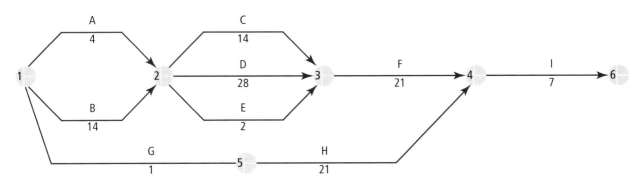

Figure 78.3 '3p off' network (2)

makes it easier to follow if there is not too much writing on the activities. Figure 78.3 shows the 3p off example with the activities represented by letters and the nodes numbered.

78.5 Earliest start times and latest finish times

Space has also been left in the nodes in Figure 78.3 for two more numbers: the earliest start time (EST) and the latest finish time (LFT). The EST shows the earliest time at which following activities can be started. On Figure 78.3, activities C, D and E can begin only after 14 days. Because, although A takes only four days, C, D and E need both A and B to be complete before they can be started. So the EST at node 2 is the longest path through to that node (i.e. activity B's 14 days).

Figure 78.4 shows the complete network, including all the ESTs. Note that the start of a project is always taken as 0 rather than 1. Therefore activities C, D and E can start on day 0 + 14 = 14. Activity F can start on 0 + 14 + 28 = 42. And the earliest the project can be completed is by day 0 + 14 + 28 + 21 + 7 = 70.

Calculating the ESTs provides two key pieces of information:

1 the earliest date certain resources will be needed, such as skilled workers, raw materials or machinery; this avoids tying up working capital unnecessarily, for instance by buying stocks today that will not be used until next month at the earliest

2 the earliest completion date for the whole project (this is the EST on the final node).

The EST on the final node shows the earliest date at which the project can be completed. So when is the latest completion date that a manager would find acceptable? As time is money, and customers want deliveries as fast as possible, if next Wednesday is possible, the manager will set it as the latest acceptable date. This is known as the latest finish time (LFT).

The LFT shows the time by which an activity must be completed. These times are recorded in the bottom right-hand section of the nodes. The LFT shows the latest finish time of preceding activities. The number 42 in the bottom right-hand section of node 5 (Figure 78.5) shows that activity G must be finished by day 42 in order to give activities H and I time to be completed by day 70.

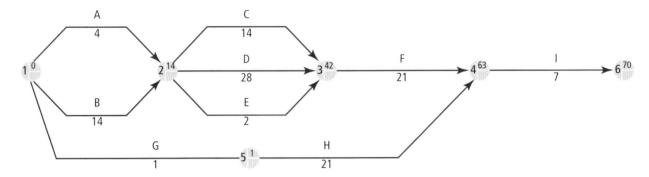

Figure 78.4 '3p off' network (3)

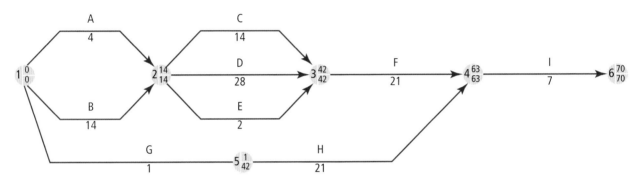

Figure 78.5 '3p off' network (4)

The LFTs on activities are calculated from right to left. In node 6 the LFT is 70, because that is the latest a manager would want the project to finish. Node 4 shows the LFT for activities F and H. Both must be finished by day 63, to leave seven days for activity I to be completed. Working back through the nodes:

● node 5 – LFT = 42, because 63 − 21 = 42; therefore activity G must be finished by day 42

● node 3 – LFT = 42, because 63 − 21 = 42; therefore activities C, D and E must be finished by day 42

● node 2 – LFT = 14, because unless A and B are finished by day 14, there will not be enough time for D to be completed by day 42; therefore to calculate the LFT at node 2 you must find the longest path back to that node (42 − 28 = 14)

● node 1 – LFT = 0 because the longest path back is 14 − 14 = 0.

Calculating the LFTs provides three main pieces of information:

1   it provides the deadlines that *must* be met in order for the project to be completed on time

2   it helps to identify the activities that have 'float time' – in other words, some slack between the EST and the LFT; activity H can be started on day 1 and must be finished by day 63, but takes only 21 days to complete; so there is no rush to complete it

3   it identifies the critical path.

78.6 The critical path

The **critical path** comprises the activities that take longest to complete. They determine the length of the whole project. In this case it is activities B, D, F and I. These are the activities that must not be delayed by even one day. For then the whole project will be late. With C a delay would not matter. There are 28 days to complete a task that takes only 14. But D is on the critical path, so this 28-day activity must be completed in no more than 28 days.

Identifying the critical path allows managers to apply **management by exception** – in other words, focusing on exceptionally important tasks, rather than spreading their efforts thinly. Of the nine activities within the 3p off network, only the four critical ones need absorb management time. The others need far less supervision.

f a supervisor sees a possibility that an activity on the critical path might overrun, s/he can consider shifting labour or machinery across from a non-critical task. In this way the project completion date can be kept intact.

To identify the critical path, the two key points are:

1 it will be on activities where the nodes show the EST and LFT to be the same

2 it is the longest path through those nodes.

When drawing a network, the critical path is identified by striking two short lines across the critical activities (see Figure 78.6).

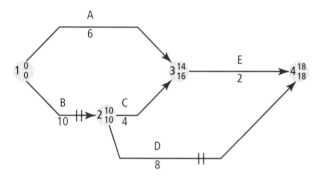

Figure 78.6 Indicating the critical path

Any activity that is not on the critical path is non-critical. Even if there is a delay to a non-critical activity, it may be that the project can be completed on time. A non-critical activity has some slack (e.g. it takes two days to complete, yet there are five days in the schedule between its earliest start time and its latest finish time); these three days of slack are known as 'float time'.

A firm might take the opportunity to get the job done straight away, then switch staff to other activities. Or the managers may give staff the extra time to give more thought to the activity. For example, designing a new logo may need only two days, but it may well be that a better logo could be designed in five.

Advantages

● It requires careful planning of the order in which events need to occur, and the length of time each one should take. This should improve the smooth operation of an important project such as a new product launch.

● By identifying events that can be carried out simultaneously, it shortens the length of time taken to complete a project. This is an important element in the modern business focus upon time-based management. For example, if a law is passed that allows 14 year olds to ride motorbikes with engines of less than 40cc, the first company to design and launch a suitable product would do extremely well.

● The resources needed for each activity can be ordered/hired no earlier than their scheduled EST. Just such a focus upon careful planning of when stocks are needed is the heart of just-in-time production systems. In this way cash outflows are postponed as long as possible, and the working capital tied up in the project is minimised.

● If the completion of an activity is delayed for some reason, the network diagram is a good starting point for working out the implications and deciding on appropriate courses of action.

Disadvantages

● A complex project (such as the construction of the Olympic village) entails so many activities that a drawing becomes unmanageable. Fortunately, computers can zoom in and out of drawings, enabling small parts of the network to be magnified and examined.

● Drawing a diagram does not, in itself, ensure the effective management of a project. Network analysis provides a plan, but can only be as successful as the staff's commitment to it. This suggests that staff should be consulted about the schedule and the likely duration of the activities.

- The value of the network diagram is reduced slightly because the activity lines are not in proportion to the duration of the activities.

Issues For Analysis

Issues for analysis in relation to networks include the following.

- That critical path analysis (CPA) allows a business to translate strategies into plans of action – enabling each member of staff to know what has to be achieved by when; practical techniques such as this are needed to enable delegation to be effective.

- Drawing networks is a valuable skill, but at least as important is interpreting diagrams that have already been drawn; this can be made easier by asking 'What if?' questions about different scenarios. What if a critical activity is delayed? What if critical activity B can be bought in from an outside supplier who promises to take half the time?

- The need for a technique such as CPA to enable just-in-time to work in practice; care over timing and meticulous organisation are the essentials in both systems.

- Networks are a crucial way to organise resources so that working capital usage is minimised; this is especially important in long-term projects such as construction work or new product development.

78.9 Planning operations (including CPA) an evaluation

The cliché 'time is money' has been around for years. Only recently, though, have systems such as just-in-time focused clearly on time-based management. Time is vital not only because it affects costs, but also because it can provide a crucial marketing edge. Primark's key advantage over Next is that it is much quicker at getting catwalk fashions into high-street shops. So time can add value. Careful production planning can also help to get a firm's new product to the market before the opposition.

Network analysis is a valuable practical tool for taking time seriously. It involves careful planning and can be used as a way of monitoring progress. If critical activities are falling behind schedule, action can be taken quickly. This serves as a reminder that successful business management is not just about clever strategic thinking. Ultimately, success depends upon what happens at the workplace or at the construction site. Network analysis is a helpful way to ensure that strategies become plans that can be carried through effectively. Nevertheless, they guarantee nothing. Ensuring that the paper network becomes reality will remain in the hands of the managers, supervisors and staff on the job. So effective personnel management and motivation will remain as important as ever.

Key terms

Critical path: the activities that must be completed on time for the project to finish on time. In other words, they have no float time at all.

Management by exception: the principle that because managers cannot supervise every activity within the organisation, they should focus their energies on the most important issues.

Network: a diagram showing all the activities needed to complete a project, the order in which they must be completed and the critical path.

Network analysis: breaking a project down into its component parts, to identify the sequence of activities involved.

Exercises

A. Revision questions

(35 marks; 35 minutes)

1 Explain the business importance of operational planning. (3)

2 Identify two objectives of network analysis. (2)

3 Distinguish between an activity and a project. (3)

4 State three key rules for drawing networks. (3)

5 Explain how to calculate the earliest start time for an activity. (4)

6 Why is it important to calculate the latest finish time on an activity? (4)

7 What is meant by 'the critical path' and how do you identify it? (4)

8 Explain why it would be useful to know which activities have float times available. (3)

9 Analyse the value of network analysis for a small firm in financial difficulties. (4)

10 Explain how the use of critical path analysis could help a firm's time-based management. (5)

B. Revision exercises

B1 Data response

(40 marks; 45 minutes)

Activity	Preceded by	Duration (weeks)
A	–	6
B	–	4
C	–	10
D	A & B	5
E	A & B	7
F	D	3

1 **(a)** Construct a network from the above information. (6)

(b) Number the nodes and put in the earliest start times. (4)

2 **(a)** Draw the following network:

Activity A and B start the project. C and D follow A. E follows all other jobs. (6)

(b) Work out the earliest start times of the activities and put them in the nodes if, in the above question, A lasts 2 days, B = 9 days, C = 3, D = 4, E = 7. (4)

3 **(a)** Use the following information to construct a fully labelled network showing ESTs, LFTs and the critical path. (12)

Activity	Preceded by	Duration
A	–	3
B	–	9
C	–	2
D	A	5
E	C	3
F	B, D, E	5
G	C	9

(b) If the firm was offered a £2000 bonus for completing the project in 12 days, which activity should managers focus upon? Explain why. (8)

B2 Case study

Every Friday needs managing

Last Friday had been a washout. Claire, Bren, Alliyah and Ruth had dithered over what to wear, where to go and how to get there, and ended up watching a rotten DVD in Bren's bedroom. This week was going to be different. Bren had just been taught critical path analysis and she was determined to use it to 'project manage' Friday night. As it was Bren's birthday on Friday, the others had to agree.

They sat down on Tuesday to agree all the activities needed for a great night out. They started by focusing on the activities:

Alliyah: We have the best nights when we start at Harry's Bar for a couple of hours, then on to the Orchid at about midnight.

Claire: I like Harry's but prefer RSVP; no argument, though, we should go to the Orchid.

After half an hour back and forth, the agreement was Harry's at 9.00 and Orchid at 12.00.

Then they realised that there was a lot more to it than that. It would take half an hour to get to Harry's and they'd have to get ready beforehand: bath, hair, nails, make-up. And what about the preceding activities? Shopping for a new top . . . and shoes . . . and earrings . . . and getting some highlights done.

They argued about which comes first, a top and then shoes and earrings to match? Or the other way round? It was time for Bren to set it all out:

Activity	Preceded by	Duration
A Booking a hair and nails appointment	–	1 minute
B Clothes shopping	–	4 hours
C Shopping for shoes	–	3 hours
D Shopping for earrings	B, C	1 hour
E Hair and nails appointment	A	2 hours
F Bath	D, E	1 hour
G Make-up and get dressed	F	1 hour
H Constant phone conversations	–	24/7

Questions

(20 marks; 25 minutes)

1 Draw up Bren's network, to help plan her birthday. (8)

2 How much float time is there on activities E and D? (2)

3 Explain why workers on a building site could benefit as much or more from critical path analysis as Bren and her friends. (10)

B3 Data response

Davey & Prior Building is a struggling partnership. Three of its last four jobs have been completed late and have therefore incurred cost penalties. Jim Davey blames the suppliers but Anne Prior is convinced that Jim's poor organisation is the real cause. Now Anne has persuaded Jim to plan the next project using a network analysis software program.

Activity	Preceded by	Duration (weeks)
A	–	6
B	A	2
C	A	4
D	–	8
E	B	12
F	B, C, D	6
G	B, C, D	9
H	D	10
J	F, G	5

Questions

(25 marks; 30 minutes)

1 Explain the circumstances in which network analysis is useful to firms such as Davey & Prior. (5)

2 Jim has broken the next project down into the following activities:

(a) Draw the network, complete with full labelling. (10)

(b) Indicate and state the critical path. (4)

(c) If a machinery failure delays the completion of activity E by three weeks, what effects would this have on the project? What might Anne and Jim do about it? (6)

C. Essay questions

(40 marks each)

1 Your uncle is a builder who dislikes 'paperwork and planning'. You have heard that he is about to embark on his biggest ever project, building four two-storey houses. Attempt to persuade him to adopt network analysis to help him plan and control the work. Make sure your arguments are relevant to the building industry and are solid enough to persuade a doubter.

2 'Using network analysis to manage projects is as important to the finances and marketing of a business as it is to operations management.' Discuss.

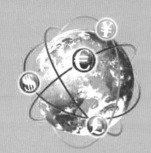

79 Unit

KAIZEN (CONTINUOUS IMPROVEMENT)

DEFINITION

Kaizen is a Japanese term meaning continuous improvement. Staff at firms such as Toyota generate thousands of new ideas each year – each aimed at improving productivity or quality. Over time, these small steps forward add up to significant improvements in competitiveness.

79.1 Introduction

If a man has not been seen for three days his friends should take a good look at him to see what changes have befallen him.

This ancient Japanese saying seems to sum up *kaizen* quite nicely. Continuous improvement, or **kaizen**, is a philosophy of ongoing improvement based around small changes involving everyone – managers and workers alike. There are two key elements to *kaizen*.

1 Most *kaizen* improvements are based around people and their ideas rather than investment in new technology.

2 Each change on its own may be of little importance. However, if hundreds of small changes are made, the cumulative effects can be substantial.

A-grade application

A *kaizen* improvement at Barclaycard

An example of a *kaizen* improvement comes from Barclaycard. In processing billions of pounds of credit card transactions per year, a major problem is fraud. An employee suggested a way of analysing bogus calls to the company's authorisation department. This has saved Barclaycard over £100,000 a year. The precise method is secret, but it works by blocking the credit card numbers of callers trying to buy goods fraudulently. It can also trace the callers, resulting in the arrest of the fraudsters involved.

In the early 1990s, the term *kaizen* was virtually unknown outside Japan. Research carried out in Britain in early 2007 showed that over 75% of private-sector businesses say they use strategies for continuous improvement.

79.2 The components of the *kaizen* philosophy

Describing *kaizen* as just 'continuous improvement' is simplistic. To work effectively, *kaizen* requires a commitment from management to establish a special, positive **business culture** within the organisation. This culture must be communicated and accepted by all those working at the company. It must permeate the whole organisation. What are the characteristics of this culture or philosophy?

One employee, two jobs

According to the *Kaizen* Institute the goal of any *kaizen* programme should be to convince all employees that they have two jobs to do – doing the job and then looking for ways of improving it. The *kaizen* culture is based on the belief that the production line worker is the real expert. The worker on the assembly line does the job day in day out. This means knowing more about the causes of problems and their solutions than the highly qualified engineer who sits in an office. The *kaizen* philosophy recognises the fact that any company's greatest resource is its staff.

Team working

To operate *kaizen* successfully employees cannot be allowed to work as isolated individuals. Team working is vital to the process of continuous improvement. These teams are composed of employees who work on the same section of the production line as a self-contained unit. Each team is often referred to as a 'cell'. The members of a cell are responsible for the quality of the work in their section. Over time the cell becomes expert about the processes within its section of the production line. *Kaizen* attempts to tap into this knowledge by organising each cell into a quality circle. The members of each cell meet regularly to discuss problems cropping up within their section. The circle then puts forward solutions and recommendations for management to consider.

A-grade application
Tesco: 'Every Little Helps'

How would you react if Lidl or Aldi announced the intention of becoming Britain's number one, high-quality grocery chain? The better you know the stores, the more you would laugh at the thought. Yet that was largely the position of Tesco when it decided to move upmarket in the early 1980s. It had been famous for being a cheap, low-cost, low-quality alternative to Sainsbury's.

Over the following two decades it had a mountain to climb, yet stumbled upon the slogan 'Every Little Helps'. This not only became the clever advertising line when introducing initiatives such as its Clubcard and 'Only One in the Q' (i.e. or we'll open another aisle). It also became vital behind the scenes, as staff started to realise that small steps forward were appreciated by management.

Using its 'Every Little Helps' approach has led Tesco to the situation in which, by 2007, its annual profit of £2650 million dwarfed Sainsbury's £477 million.

Empowerment

Empowerment is essential to any *kaizen* programme. Empowerment involves giving employees the right to make decisions that affect the quality of their working lives. Empowerment enables good shop-floor ideas to be implemented quickly.

Once the necessary *kaizen* apparatus is in place, good ideas and the resulting improvements should keep coming. The number of suggestions made each month should improve over time once employees see the effects of their own solutions. However, if quality circles and team working are to be truly effective, employees must be given real decision-making power. If good ideas are constantly being ignored by management they will eventually dry up as the employees become disillusioned with the whole process.

A-grade application
Using team working to create *kaizen* customer service benefits

Julian Richer is a strong believer in the merits of team working and *kaizen*. He is the owner of a highly innovative and successful hi-fi retailing chain called Richer Sounds. Apart from offering excellent value for money Richer has utilised the creative ideas of his staff to create customer service with a difference. For the benefit of every Richer Sounds customer each outlet is equipped with its own free coffee and mint dispensing machine. Each shop has its own mirror that says 'You are looking at the most important person in this shop', and a bell that customers can ring if they feel that they have received excellent service. Many of these innovations have come from Richer's own style of quality circle. Once a month staff at each outlet are encouraged to talk to each other about new ideas. To lubricate this process, Richer gives each of his staff £5. This is because at Richer Sounds they hold their *kaizen* discussions at the pub!

Kaizen/continuous improvement: famous sayings

'Continuous improvement is better than delayed perfection.' *Mark Twain, famous American writer*

'If there's a way to do it better . . . find it.' *Thomas Edison, inventor*

'If you're not making progress all the time, you're slipping backwards.' *Sir John Harvey Jones, former chief of ICI*

'I believe that there is hardly a single operation in the making of our car that is the same as when we made our first car of the present model. That is why we make them so cheaply.' *Henry Ford, legendary car maker*

'Our company has, indeed, stumbled onto some of its new products. But never forget that you can only stumble if you're moving.' *Richard Carlton, former head of American giant 3M*

'Be not afraid of going slowly; be only afraid of standing still.' *Chinese proverb*

Source: Stuart Crainer (1997) *The Ultimate Book of Business Quotations*, Capstone Publishing

79.3 Potential problems of implementing a successful *kaizen* programme

Culture

In order for *kaizen* to really work, employees must be proud to contribute their ideas to the company. Japanese companies do not offer financial rewards in return for suggestions. Their attitude is that employees are told when they are recruited that *kaizen* is part of company policy. For them, employee commitment to *kaizen* is gained via genuine staff motivation rather than by financial bonuses. Creating the right organisational culture is therefore vital for success. Resistance can come from two quarters.

1 *Management resistance:* managers with autocratic tendencies may be unwilling to pass decision-making power down the hierarchy.

2 *Employee resistance:* a history of poor industrial relations and a climate of mistrust can create resistance to change among the staff. Employees may see the 'new empowerment programme' as a cynical attempt to get more out of the staff for less. The result? Reluctant cooperation at best, but little in terms of real motivation.

A-grade application

Hans Rissmann emigrated from Germany to Scotland 13 years ago to manage the Edinburgh International Conference Centre (EICC). When Mr Rissmann was appointed he immediately set up an employee **suggestion scheme** despite being warned of the 'wee Jimmy scenario'. A firm in Scotland had started a *kaizen* scheme for its workers. An employee working on the shop floor made a suggestion that saved the business £165,000 a year. The boss quickly summoned him to his office, congratulated him, said he was in line for a bonus, and then asked him how long he had been with the business. The answer came back: 'Seventeen years, sir.' 'And how long have you had this idea?' he asked. 'Seven years, sir.' 'So why didn't you tell us before?' asked his boss. 'Because nobody asked me.'

Despite being warned about the 'wee Jimmy scenario', Rissmann pushed ahead with his plans to introduce *kaizen*, but not before he introduced a new German-style flat management culture combined with a less formal more open approach to communication. Rissmann's approach has paid dividends. In 2006 the EICC made profits of £395,000, up from £177,000 in 2003.

Source: adapted from an article published in the *Scotsman*, 20 August 2007

Training costs

Mistakes made by managers in the past can have severe long-term effects. Changing an organisation's culture is difficult as it involves changing attitudes. The training required to change attitudes tends to be expensive. It can also take a very long time to change attitudes. Consequently, the costs are likely to be great.

Justifying the cost of *kaizen*

The training cost and the opportunity cost of lost output is easy to quantify. It may be harder to identify and prove the financial benefits of a *kaizen* programme. Managers can quite easily produce financial estimates of the benefits of capital investment. It is much harder to assess programmes designed to develop the stock of human capital within the company. Consequently, in firms dominated by the accountant, it can be very difficult to win budgets for *kaizen* programmes.

79.4 The limitations of *kaizen*

Diminishing returns

Some managers argue that the improvements created through a *kaizen* programme will invariably fall as time goes on. The logic is that the organisation will seek ways of solving the most important problems first. So by implication the problems that remain will become progressively less important. If this is the case it might prove to be difficult to maintain staff enthusiasm. However, supporters of *kaizen* would reject this criticism on the grounds that there is no such thing as a perfect system. According to them, even the best system is capable of being improved. A former chief executive of Cadbury Schweppes was asked which management theory was the most overrated. He replied, 'If it ain't broke don't fix it. Everything can be improved.' This is a perfect statement in favour of *kaizen*.

Radical solutions

Sometimes radical solutions implemented quickly are necessary in order to tackle radical problems. *Kaizen* may not be appropriate in all situations. The solution might have to be more dramatic than yet another change to an old system. It may be time to throw out all the old and replace it with something totally new. This is usually the case in industries facing radical changes brought on by a rapid surge in technology.

A perfect example is the telecoms giant Motorola. In 2005 Motorola's range of Razr mobile phones was hot. Market share was won from Nokia and annual profits topped $4.5 billion. Two years later the picture was transformed, with sales sliding and profits collapsing to a loss-making position. In March 2008 Motorola announced that its design centre in Birmingham would lose 50% of its staff and may have to close altogether. Times of crisis are not times for gradual, continuous improvement.

Figure 79.1 Motorola's Razr mobile phone

79.5 Kaizen (continuous improvement)

an evaluation

Does the *kaizen* approach encourage bureaucracy? In the global market of the twenty-first century, managers have come to realise that an ability to adapt and change is vital if the firm is to survive. However, many managers and many businesses have great problems with change management. The main issue is that many individuals are frightened of the uncertainty that usually goes hand in hand with change. Some managers seek security, stability and predictability in their own working lives.

In the circumstances it is not surprising that those who are afraid of anything too radical choose *kaizen*. This is because each improvement is relatively small. In summary, when those with bureaucratic tendencies embrace *kaizen* the result can be very little in terms of meaningful change.

Are *kaizen* and radical change mutually exclusive? It is possible to use both approaches. Even in Japan *kaizen* is not used exclusively. The Japanese even have their own word, *kaikaku*, which roughly translated means 'a radical redesign'. In practice, many Japanese firms use *kaikaku* as a source of a major breakthrough when one is required. They then follow this up with a *kaizen* programme in order to perfect and then adapt this new system to suit new conditions as they emerge.

Issues For Analysis

- *Kaizen* is not a process that can simply be imposed on reluctant staff. It has to be part of a workplace culture that is based upon respect for staff. *Kaizen* originated in Japanese car factories such as Toyota and Nissan, where staff would often be well-paid university graduates. If managers hire minimum-wage staff and boss them around, it would be absurd to expect them to contribute positively to a *kaizen* programme.

- *Kaizen* improvements to a product are more likely to be effective in the earlier stages of a product's life cycle. If the *kaizen* programme is started too late it may only slow down the rate of decline rather than reverse it.

Key terms

Business culture: the attitudes prevailing within a business.
Kaizen: continuous improvement.
Suggestion scheme: a formal method of obtaining written employee suggestions about improvements in the workplace.

Exercises

A. Revision questions

(35 marks; 35 minutes)

1 Give three reasons why *kaizen* improvements can prove to be cheaper than improvements gained via business process re-engineering. (3)

2 State three limitations of the *kaizen* philosophy. (3)

3 Explain why a re-engineering programme can lead to a deterioration in employee morale within the organisation being re-engineered. (3)

4 Why might some managers find it harder than others to implement *kaizen*? (4)

5 Give three reasons why it is vital to involve both management and shop-floor staff in any programme of continuous improvement. (3)

6 To be truly effective why must *kaizen* programmes be ongoing? (3)

7 Why is it important to set and monitor performance targets when attempting to operate *kaizen*? (4)

8 Explain how *kaizen* can help to create a better-motivated workforce. (4)

9 Why might some managers believe that *kaizen* brings diminishing returns over time? (4)

10 Explain how 'Every Little Helps' has helped turn Tesco into Britain's number one retailer. (4)

B. Revision exercises

B1 Data response

Hail the Star!

Julian Hails was once a star player in lower league football teams such as Southend. He believed in teamwork, in training and in continuous improvement. He joined Star Electronics as a sales manager, but became managing director after just three years – promoted over the head of the chairman's son, Richard Star. His enthusiasm was infectious, and his *kaizen* programme soon bore fruit. This was fortunate because a slump in Star's sector of the electronics market caused a decline in market size.

At the latest board meeting, Julian presented figures recording the impact of the company's *kaizen* programme. Young Richard Star took the opportunity to snipe at Julian's achievements, saying: 'So after this programme of continuous upheaval, I see our total costs per unit are higher than they were two years ago.'

Questions

(30 marks; 35 minutes)

1 Explain the links between 'teamwork' and 'continuous improvement'. (4)

2 Analyse the data provided overleaf to evaluate the key successes of Julian's policies. (12)

3 Explain what Richard Star meant by his use of the term 'continuous upheaval'? (6)

4 What further information is needed to assess the validity of Richard Star's claim? (8)

	Two years ago	Last year	This year
Rejects per unit of output	7.8	6.8	6.2
Assembly time (minutes)	46	43	39
Stock value per unit of output	£145	£128	£111
Direct costs per unit	£42.50	£39	£36.50
Overhead costs per unit	£64	£67	£72

B2 Case study

Toyota

Toyota's main factory in Japan is located in Toyota City (20 km away from Nagoya), a sprawling conurbation that is home to 250,000 people, 80% of whom work for the company, the Tsutsumi plant turns out two cars a minute. Its two heavily automated lines produce nine models, any colour you like. Ageing robots weld a stream of different models, instructed by computers. Meanwhile, assembly workers dodge into car bodies, attaching wiring, dashboards and air-conditioning. They have to run to keep up.

It is one of the largest Japanese plants, employing 4500 people, and among the most productive. It is, says general manager Hiroshi Nakagawa, a combination of the 'Toyota Way' and another well-known Japanese buzzword kaizen – listening to employees – that has driven the company over the decades. Workers said picking up bolts was difficult wearing gloves. A contraption called 'the chameleon' now does it for them.

While Toyota's history was built on refinement of production, its future, says Watanabe, is to develop tomorrow's cars. In Toyota's paradoxical style, it claims it is ahead of the game, while being threatened by competition at the same time. Environmental cars have swallowed a lot of investment. It launched its Prius hybrid car (powered by battery motor and petrol engine) in 1997, and now leads the market, along with Honda, selling 300,000 a year. Getting investment in the right products is the key. According to Toyota, 4–5% of revenue is spent on research. Toyota has long been a heavy investor. In addition to kaizen, Toyota's management believes in the virtues of jidoka – harnessing the productivity of machinery with

human innovation. But, spending a fixed proportion of revenues can hurt the bottom line – as it did last year. Toyota insists it is the right course. Some technologies will not work, like Toyota's ill-fated dual cycle engine, developed in the 1980s. Others could. In 30 years we might know the answer. In the meantime, as Toyota says, 'Experience of failure results in improvement.'

Source: Adapted from an article in The Guardian, April 2006

Questions

(20 marks; 25 minutes)

1 In 2008 Toyota will overtake General Motors to become the biggest producer of cars in the world, producing nearly 9 million cars per year. Explain how kaizen might have helped Toyota to steal market share from rivals such as General Motors. (6)

2 Explain why Japanese companies, such as Toyota, seem to be able to operate kaizen programmes more effectively than companies such as General Motors and Ford. (5)

3 Discuss whether Toyota is right to spend 4–5% of its revenue on research and development. (9)

C. Essay questions

(40 marks each)

1 Two years ago the management team at Lynx Engineering commissioned a benchmarking survey to assess its relative position within the marketplace. To their horror the managers discovered that they were lagging behind the competition in terms of both cost and product quality. In an attempt to rectify the situation, a massive £2 million re-engineering programme was announced. Two years later things have still not improved. Assess what could have gone wrong. What should the company do next?

2 How might a firm set about improving its efficiency? What factors are likely to affect the success of any strategy designed to achieve this goal?

3 'It has been proven time and time again that, in order to survive, firms must be willing to initiate change successfully within their own organisations. Firms that are afraid of change will fail because those that are more adventurous will always leave them behind.' To what extent do you agree or disagree with this statement?

80.1 Operations management

Operations involves the management and control of the processes within an organisation that convert inputs into output and then delivery. Traditionally this activity was called 'production'. Now, with more than 70% of all jobs in Britain based within the service sector, it seems wrong to use such an old-fashioned term. Operations management is as important within a service business as in manufacturing. In both cases, a satisfied customer is one that gets exactly what they want at the time they want it. Customers are likely to want this to be achieved with as little effort on their own part as possible (e.g. one click of a mouse button leads to an on-time delivery of piping-hot 12-inch pepperoni pizza).

In order to achieve that one-click magic, managements establish appropriate operational objectives, and then design and implement strategies in order to achieve success. They need to consider:

- the purpose and implications of innovation: some managers take innovation to mean 'launching new or novel products', such as the ludicrous Lemon Yoghurt KitKat chocolate bar (which flopped); the important innovation may be to create the most user-friendly website.

- that because every business is unique, the factors influencing location are unique to that firm; one pizza place might need an expensive high-street location, whereas another will thrive in a cheaper side street (especially if online ordering forms part of its strategy)

- the positive and negative implications for a firm from implementing lean production techniques

- how businesses decide on their scale of production, the benefits of getting the decision right and the problems caused by getting the decision wrong.

In order to achieve a good A-level grade, it is vital to move beyond an understanding of the new terms and concepts introduced and to consider the possible implications for the business involved. Two of the key issues underpinning operations management are considered below.

Issue 1: the link between operations management and the other business functions

A firm's operations are central to the business – without a product there would be no business. However, successful operations management cannot be achieved independently of a firm's finance, human resources and marketing functions. Effective operations will depend on the existence of sufficient numbers of appropriately skilled and motivated employees, yet the techniques used within operations can make a significant contribution to the motivation (or otherwise) of the workforce. Similarly, investment in suitable machinery, and the development of innovative products and processes will be possible only if sufficient finance can be made available, while new products and increased productivity can improve a firm's financial position. In other words, changes in operations need to be considered in the wider context of the business as a whole.

Issue 2: the link between operations management and competitiveness

Efficient operations have always held the key to a firm's ability to continue to prosper in a competitive environment. If, on a sunny day, a trip to a sweetshop reveals an empty ice cream fridge, the customer will go elsewhere next time. In a world where there is a fine line between success and failure, this can be very important. The fine line can best be seen by taking a Wednesday-evening walk down a street full of restaurants. Some are empty and some are frantic. Rents are very high in such areas, so today's empty restaurant is tomorrow's business closure.

The importance of effective operations can only grow in importance as the degree of competition intensifies.

Two EU enlargements in 2004 and 2007 have created a number of opportunities and threats for UK businesses. The increased labour pool through an influx of migrant workers is good news for business, but there are also increases in the volume of imports from firms based in the lower-cost economies of central and eastern Europe. The rapid growth of the Chinese and Indian economies has increased competitive pressures still further, leading to a large number of businesses offshoring part of their operations, or relocating completely.

Does this mean that production – and in particular, manufacturing – is doomed in the UK? Perhaps not, but only those firms that are successful in supplying high-quality, differentiated products are likely to succeed in the long term.

Exercises

A. Revision questions

(80 marks; 80 minutes)

1   What is meant by operations management? (2)

2   Using examples, briefly explain the difference between an operational objective and an operational strategy. (4)

3   Identify two possible operational objectives that a business might have. (2)

4   Outline two ways in which operations management can affect a firm's competitiveness. (4)

5   Explain why Terry, an A-level student, was wrong to write that 'economies of scale mean that production costs are falling'. (5)

6   Outline two economies of scale that might be enjoyed by an expanding sports shop business. (4)

7   Explain what is meant by the term diseconomies of scale. (3)

8   Why might the growth of a business from five staff to 400 lead to a loss in employee motivation? (4)

9   Analyse two consequences of deteriorating communications within a rapidly expanding business. (4)

10   Suggest two ways in which a firm could attempt to ensure coordination within the business as it grows. (4)

11   Outline one advantage and one disadvantage to a manufacturer of wool jackets when switching from a labour-intensive to a more capital-intensive system of production. (6)

12   Explain the difference between product and process innovation. (4)

13   Examine two possible consequences of a cut in expenditure on research and development at games console and software manufacturer Nintendo. (4)

14   Outline two factors that might affect the location of a call centre for an insurance company. (4)

15   Briefly explain two reasons why a UK manufacturer of electrical goods might choose to switch its operations to an overseas location. (6)

16   Analyse two ways in which a building firm operating in a period of falling property prices could benefit from the use of critical path analysis. (6)

17   Outline the main purpose of lean production. (3)

18   Identify three possible causes of waste for a car manufacturer. (3)

19   Describe one potential benefit and one potential drawback for a firm deciding to adopt a system of just-in-time production. (4)

20   Explain why worker empowerment is essential to the successful implementation of a *kaizen* programme. (4)

B. Revision exercises

B1 Case study

GM adopts lean production to regain global top spot

In 1998, it took US firm General Motors – then the world's largest car manufacturer – 50% more hours to produce a car than Japanese rival, Toyota. The difference was significant enough to mean that GM failed to generate a profit on any of its models. Unsurprisingly, by the beginning of 2007, Toyota claimed to have taken the global number one spot, selling 2.348 million cars worldwide in the first three months of the year, as opposed to an estimated 2.26 million by GM in the same period.

Most commentators agree that the Japanese car maker's ability to produce cars more cheaply and at a higher quality than its rivals has come from its system of lean production. GM's attempts to secure its survival and close the productivity gap have focused on the introduction of a global manufacturing system that incorporates the key features of the philosophy. Like Toyota, the aim of GM's new system was to use the same methods to produce the same cars in all its 178 plants located across 33 countries. Each plant is able to adapt the specification of the car models produced in response to local market conditions.

Toyota's lean production system was responsible for pioneering the just-in-time approach. For example, at the company's plant in Georgetown, Kentucky, the company's 300 suppliers (most of which are located within half a day's drive) are notified electronically when parts are needed, sometimes resulting in several deliveries each day. Lean production has also allowed Toyota to respond quickly to changes in customer tastes. It takes the Japanese company 18 months to develop a new model, compared to three years at GM.

Source: www.bbc.co.uk

Questions

(20 marks; 25 minutes)

1 Identify and briefly explain two features of lean production, other than just-in-time. (6)

2 Examine the main benefits for a company such as General Motors of adopting a system of lean production. (14)

B2 Case study

Made in England – still!

It would be easy to sympathise with any UK textiles manufacturer, faced with a seemingly unstoppable flood of cheap imports from Asia, that decided to ring the factory bell for the last time and relocate abroad. However, luxury knitwear manufacturer John Smedley remains firmly rooted to the Derbyshire location where the business was established over 200 years ago. In fact, according to the company, its heritage is an important part of the 'indefinable quality' of its products. The company, whose fine-knit wool and cotton sweaters, tops and cardigans are favoured by celebrities such as Victoria Beckham and Madonna, has a workforce of 450 and generated sales of £13 million in 2007.

The company's survival strategy is based on targeting a low-volume niche, competing on grounds of quality rather than price. The average

Figure 80.1 John Smedley's Derbyshire factory

retail price of a John Smedley piece of knitwear is £100. Around 70% of the company's production is exported, mostly to Japan. A highly skilled workforce, carefully sourced materials and a rigorous system of quality control are vital ingredients in the manufacturing process.

The company has been faced with a number of challenges in the past. It was forced to close its spinning division, resulting in a significant number of redundancies, after making losses in 2002 and 2003, and continues to struggle with the problems caused by rising raw material and energy costs. A rise in the value of the pound against the yen over the last few years has made the company's products 20% more expensive in Japanese markets. However, the company rejected proposals to offshore production to China after discovering that this would result in an average price reduction of only £8 per garment.

One of the main constraints facing John Smedley is a chronic shortage of suitably skilled workers. The company's staff receive between six months' and two years' training, and are paid between £300 and £400 per week. Many existing employees are close to retirement as the firm has been unsuccessful in recruiting younger workers. In an attempt to deal with this, it has introduced a number of Japanese knitting machines, at a cost of £125,000 each, able to produce a whole garment in around one hour.

Source: Adapted from BBC News

Questions

(30 marks; 35 minutes)

1 Examine the key influences on the operational objectives of John Smedley. (6)

2 Assess the main implications of the company's decision to move to a more capital-intensive method of production. (12)

3 To what extent do you agree with the company's decision to keep production at its Derbyshire factory? (12)

B3 Case study

Efficient operations support expansion at BareFruit Juice

When BareFruit Juice was established by Col Marafko in 2005, its aim was to transform the negative image of fast food by establishing the first genuinely healthy juice bar chain in the UK. Since then the business has expanded rapidly nationwide and has ambitions to become a major international brand. According to Col, the company's market penetration has been achieved by offering 'a better product at more competitive prices' than rivals. The smoothies and juices on sale contain no colourings, preservatives, flavourings, sugar concentrates or pasteurised ingredients, and are prepared to order in front of customers.

The key operational objectives set by the firm focus on the provision of a quality service. For a 'fast food' chain, a quality service has to mean a speedy service – the company has a demanding three-minute service time target, and staff are trained to acknowledge customers and take their orders as quickly as possible. The taste experience is at the forefront of product development and depends on the sourcing of quality ingredients from reputable suppliers using traceable supply chains. Stocks have a very limited shelf life – one day in the case of fresh fruit and up to one week for frozen ingredients. Stock management is the responsibility of each store manager and an average of between three and four days' supply of frozen ingredients is held as a buffer. However, sales are heavily influenced by the weather and can fluctuate dramatically, emphasising the importance of good relationships with suppliers.

Visibility – the extent to which a firm's operations are exposed to customers – is an important part of customer service at BareFruit. The genuine and honest use of ingredients is a core principle for the business. Ingredients are freshly squeezed and blended to order, in front of customers. Visibility also has an important influence on the location of the juice bars. The firm's research suggests that 40% of people eat or drink something while out shopping, and a large number of customers buy on impulse. Current BareFruit bars are all located in large covered shopping centres, such as Manchester's Arndale Centre and Merry Hill near Dudley in the West Midlands.

The company uses footfall data to choose units in the busiest areas, rather than within dedicated eating areas. Such locations mean that BareFruit's overheads are high – the cost of premises is the company's single biggest cost, with rents and business taxes accounting for nearly 45% of total costs. Keeping variable costs down is, therefore, crucially important and the control of waste is a key feature of the company's training programmes.

A culture of continuous improvement (*kaizen*) has been firmly established within the business, and all staff are encouraged to put forward ideas on how to improve service and enhance the customer experience. The core offer of a range of classic smoothies has been gradually extended to include sandwiches, soups and other healthy snacks. For an extra 50p, customers can upgrade their smoothie with the addition of a booster. BareFruit has also confirmed its commitment to the environment by ensuring that over 95% of the drinks packaging used by the company is fully biodegradable.

Source: BareFruit Juice

Questions

(40 marks; 50 minutes)

1 Describe three ways in which BareFruit attempts to deliver a quality service to its customers. (6)

2 Examine the importance of quality to a company such as BareFruit. (8)

3 Identify the key influences on the location of BareFruit juice bars. (8)

4 Analyse two ways in which BareFruit might have benefited from establishing a culture of *kaizen* within the business. (6)

5 Discuss two changes that BareFruit could make in order to reduce operating costs. Explain which of the two you would recommend, and why. (12)

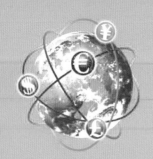

INTRODUCTION TO EXTERNAL INFLUENCES

DEFINITION

An external influence is a factor beyond a firm's control that can affect its performance. Examples include: changes in consumer tastes, laws and regulations, and economic factors such as the level of spending in the economy as a whole.

81.1 The impact of external influences on firms

Some external influences have a favourable effect on firms. Saga specialises in providing holidays targeted at the older generation. A good example of a beneficial external influence for Saga holidays might be rising life expectancy. An ageing population will enlarge Saga's target market, giving the company a good opportunity to increase its revenue and profit. As shown in Figure 81.1, the number of over-60s is set to boom over the coming years.

On the other hand, other external influences can have adverse effects on firms. In 2008 Transport for London announced an increase in the London congestion charge for 4x4 cars to £25 per day. Less-polluting vehicles with smaller engines pay only £8 per day. This change is unlikely to affect dealers selling brand new 4x4s such as the BMW X5 (retail price: £50,000). However, the change in regulation could definitely reduce the profit of a second-hand car dealer specialising in selling used 4x4s to more price-sensitive customers.

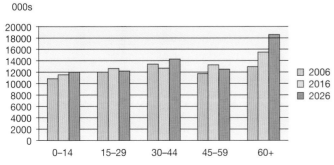

Figure 81.1 Ageing UK population

New laws and regulations

Changes in the law can have a dramatic effect on a business. A good example is the regulation changes to child car seats, which came into effect in September 2006. They forced all motorists to provide 'seat restraints' for children sitting in the back of a car. For example, every child under 12 must not only wear a sea belt, but must also be sitting on a 'booster seat'. Younger children and babies must have their own special car sea

Overnight this regulation created a huge boost for businesses such as Britax (a car seat manufacturer) and Halfords (the main motor supplies retailer). From a business point of view, this is a marvellous type of external change, because the government announced the change in early 2005, giving the companies involved plenty of time to build production capacity an stock levels.

Demographic factors

Demography refers to changes to the size, growth and age distribution of the population. **Demographic** changes can create opportunities for some firms. However, for others, the same demographic trend migh create a threat.

In recent times one of the most important demographic changes to impact upon Britain is immigration. In 2004 the European Union expanded by admitting ten new member states: Poland, Czech Republic, Hungary, Slovakia, Slovenia, Estonia, Lithuania, Cyprus, Malta and Latvia. Britain, along with Sweden and Ireland, granted the citizens of the new 'EU 10' the immediate right to live and work in Britain. In 2004 wages in eastern Europe were far below the wages offered to

British workers. Since then, according to the BBC, more than 800,000 eastern Europeans have registered to work in the UK. Firms that have undoubtedly benefited from this external influence include those discussed below.

JD Wetherspoon

Immigration helps to keep wages in check. Pub chains like JD Wetherspoon have benefited from a plentiful supply of workers provided by inward migration into the UK. Most migrants from eastern Europe are hard working and easily possess the skills needed to work behind a bar. JD Wetherspoon continues to expand. Without immigration JD Wetherspoon might have struggled to attract the additional labour required to expand. In the absence of immigrants the company may have been forced into raising its wage rates for bar staff, adversely affecting its profits. Wetherspoon's has also capitalised on the increasing number of Poles living in Britain by stocking a wide range of Polish bottled beers, which have helped to boost the company's profits.

Property developers

Most eastern European immigrants to Britain cannot afford to purchase property, so they rent instead. The increase in the number of people looking to rent has helped property developers who buy houses to rent out. Britain is now home to over a million landlords. The boom in buy-to let property investing has helped house prices in the UK to double since 2000, creating capital gains for property development companies. Without immigration from eastern Europe it is unlikely that this opportunity for property development would have existed.

On the other hand, immigration from eastern Europe has disadvantaged some UK businesses. For example, as a direct consequence of immigration, many UK plumbing firms have been forced into cutting their prices. In the past there was an acute shortage of plumbers in the UK. Unsurprisingly, given the lack of competition, plumbers could charge customers pretty much whatever they liked. Today the situation is very different. The influx of Polish plumbers into Britain has forced prices down and standards up. This is good news for British homeowners with blocked sinks, but bad news for British plumbers who were able to enjoy high income levels until the competition arrived.

Technological factors

Technological change can also create opportunities and threats for firms. Before the advent of digital technology, ITV had only two competitors: the BBC and Channel 4.

Today the situation is completely different. Technological advances now mean that ITV has to compete against the hundreds of channels provided by Sky and cable TV providers such as Virgin and Telewest. Advances in internet technology have opened up new entertainment possibilities (such as YouTube and Bebo) that compete head on with conventional TV. These technological advances threaten ITV's ability to generate revenue from selling advertising slots in between its free-to-air programmes. On the other hand, these same technological advances have created opportunities for entrepreneurs with vision, such as Larry Page and Sergey Brin, the founders of internet search engine Google.

Commodity prices

Commodities are internationally traded goods such as oil, copper, wheat and cocoa. Commodities are normally bought by firms as a raw material. For example, as Figure 81.2 shows, the price of oil rocketed between 2004 and 2008.

The price of oil is an important external influence for most firms. Oil prices affect the cost of transportation because petrol, diesel and kerosene all come from crude oil.

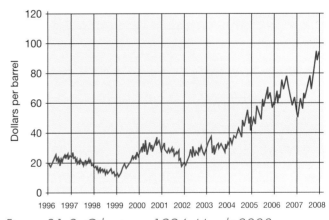

Figure 81.2 Oil prices, 1994–March 2008

Oil is also a very important raw material. Even companies such as Apple will be affected by rising oil prices because it will cost Apple more to buy in the plastic pellets needed to produce the casings for its laptop computers, iPods and mobile telephones. The price of oil is determined by the relative strength of the world supply and the world demand for oil. The world oil price is beyond the control of any single firm, making it an excellent example of an external influence.

A-grade application
Ryanair and rising oil prices

Companies such as the airline Ryanair have been adversely affected by soaring oil prices, which have pushed up their operating costs. Ryanair operates on slender profit margins, so it has been forced into responding to rising oil prices by passing most of this cost increase on to its consumers by way of higher fares. Unfortunately, most of Ryanair's customers are likely to be quite price sensitive because they travel for leisure, rather than for business reasons. If the price elasticity of demand for Ryanair flights is elastic the airline will lose revenue when fares are raised. Evidence arrived in February 2008 when Ryanair announced that its profits were 27% down on the year before.

Economic factors

Individual firms have no influence over economy-wide factors such as the rate of economic growth, the level of unemployment and the rate of inflation. However, these factors will definitely affect firms. Firms will also be affected by government fiscal and monetary policy responses. For more details see Unit 84.

81.2 What can firms do about external influences?

Make the most of favourable external influences while they last

Luck can play an important role in determining whether a business flourishes or not, especially in the short run. However, over time good and bad luck has a habit of levelling out. The key to success, then, is to make the most of any favourable external influence while it lasts. For example, interest rates were relatively low between 1993 and 2007. This encouraged a debt-fuelled consumer spending boom that greatly assisted companies supplying luxury goods and services.

However, these firms should never have relied on low interest rates for their success because it is a factor over which they have no control. They should have made the best of the situation while it lasted, but also asked themselves a series of **'What if?' questions**. In this case, 'What if interest rates were suddenly increased?', 'How would this change affect our business?', 'How would we respond to a sudden drop in demand for our product if the commercial banks withdrew cheap and easy credit?'

Minimise the impact of unfavourable external influences

When faced with adverse external influences, successful firms make compensating internal changes to their business to offset the external constraint. Ryanair can do nothing about rising oil prices, however it can attempt to cut other costs within the business to compensate for the rising oil price. If Ryanair can improve its internal efficiency the impact of the adverse external influence can be minimised. Successful businesses try, as far as it is possible, to internalise external constraints.

Issues For Analysis

- Most firms, most of the time, hold their fate in their own hands. Most have built up regular customers who keep coming back, and therefore have reasonably predictable sales. Poor managers may drive some customers away, but it may take a long time before the cracks start to show. As long as the poor managers are replaced before too long, the business can be brought back on track. This situation has occurred with Marks & Spencer, Sainsbury's, Tottenham Hotspur FC and perhaps every other sports club.

- Just sometimes, though, a company's whole existence can be thrown into question by an external factor. Barratt Homes spent £2.2 billion in 2007 buying out a competitor, and was soon afterwards hit by the credit crunch and property price collapse. Circumstances such as these are a huge test of the management. For other companies, changing technology, new competition or changes in the law may be every bit as significant. The good student spots the big issues and starts to think how to handle them.

Introduction to external influences
an evaluation

An important aspect of any evaluation of external factors is to distinguish between external change that was predictable and change that was not. For example, the 2007 ban on smoking in pubs was known about for more than a year before it occurred. Therefore every pub had the time to think through a new strategy for appealing to customers. Contrast this with the complete unpredictability of events such as the collapse in transatlantic travel that followed the terrorist attack on New York's World Trade Center in September 2001.

Managers that fail to deal with predictable events are exceptionally weak. Those that succeed in unexpected situations are especially impressive.

Key terms

Demographic: factors relating to the population, such as changes in the number of older people or in the level of immigration.

'What if?' questions: hypothetical questions (i.e. they are used to test out different possibilities or theories).

Exercises

A. Revision questions

(25 marks; 25 minutes)

1 What is an external influence? (2)

2 Explain how a company such as Cadbury might be affected by a decision by Britain to withdraw from the European Union. (6)

3 Give examples of the types of firms that have probably benefited from the invasion and the military occupation of Iraq. (4)

4 In 2008 Scottish & Newcastle announced plans to close its brewery in Reading. Give examples of firms in and around Reading that might be adversely affected by this decision. (4)

5 Record companies find it increasingly difficult to generate revenue because of internet file-sharing sites that enable music lovers to illegally download music. What actions should record companies take to minimise this external constraint? (4)

6 British Airways suffered a worldwide humiliation with its 'bag mountain' at the launch of Terminal 5 in March 2008. Can the management put problems such as this down to bad luck? (5)

B. Revision exercises

B1 Case study

Soaring pay lures Poles back home

Polish graphic designer Barbara Wasik has seen her wages triple in two years, not as a result of moving to the UK, but of returning to Poland. Barbara moved back at the end of last year, to the job she left in 2005, working for the same employer, in the same town. The only difference is her pay packet.

Wages in Poland are rising strongly as the economy expands. Last year wages grew by 6.5%. By comparison pay in France and Germany grew 2%. As living standards in Poland improve, life in the UK has become less attractive.

Barbara worked 12-hour shifts from Monday to Friday for a high street sports retailer. "Life in the UK was just work. I had no time for myself. Back here I have time for my friends, time for leisure, time to party," she said. Barbara does not regret her time in the UK, but is happy about coming home. "I used to live in Luton, renting a room with my ex-boyfriend. Here I rent a flat for myself for the same money."

It is difficult to accurately measure the numbers of people returning to Poland, although those moving do so because of rising wages and changes in the currency market.

As Poland's economy grows, its currency, the zloty, has strengthened against the pound. When Poland joined the EU, the pound was worth almost seven zloty. That has now fallen to just 4.5 zloty, making UK wages less alluring.

Source: Adapted from BBC News

Questions

(30 marks; 35 minutes)

1 Explain two reasons why Polish workers such as Barbara Wasik have returned home. (4)

2 In recent years many British firms have come to rely on relatively cheap, well-qualified staff from eastern Europe. If Poles and other immigrants from eastern Europe opt to leave Britain, how will this trend affect UK companies such as the company that previously employed Barbara Wasik? (6)

3 Describe two actions that UK companies could take to help reduce the worst effects of Polish workers leaving Britain. (6)

4 JD Wetherspoon purchases Polish beer for its pubs from brewers such as Tyskie.
   (a) Explain how the fall in the value of the pound against the Polish zloty might affect JD Wetherspoon. (5)
   (b) Examine how JD Wetherspoon might react to this change in the exchange rate. (9)

B2 Case study

Britain's Monster Credit Binge

At the beginning of 2008 Britain had not suffered from a recession for well over a decade. During that time interest rates were historically low. These low interest rates led to many consumers in Britain taking on steadily higher levels of debt. So what was the money spent on?

TV property shows such as *Location, Location, Location* encouraged many people to borrow huge sums of money to purchase property for investment purposes. Property was seen as a safe bet. At the time many people believed that 'house prices only ever go up'. The result was a speculative bubble in UK property. Banks also helped to provide the fuel for rampant house price inflation by relaxing lending standards. As house prices rose, many households took the opportunity to spend the profit locked up in their homes by remortgaging. The equity released was mostly spent on imported luxuries. Britain was living beyond its collective means.

The collapse of the Northern Rock bank in the autumn of 2007, and the resulting credit crunch, signalled the beginning of the end. Commercial rates of interest rose steadily as banks became more cautious about their lending. As the availability of credit dried up, house prices began to fall. Consumer confidence nosedived. The boom was over.

The problem with debt is that it has to be paid back. By April 2008 it was payback time, but by then total UK personal debt stood at £1421 billion, more than the entire country's GDP.

Questions

(35 marks; 40 minutes)

1. What is a recession? (2)
2. Explain how businesses such as restaurants and gyms benefited from cheap and easy credit. (5)
3. Explain three examples of firms that benefited from the UK's house price boom. (6)
4. **(a)** What is consumer confidence and why is it important to firms? (5)
   (b) How might falling UK house prices affect consumer confidence? (5)
5. Discuss the actions that a private school might take in order to prepare for a recession. (12)

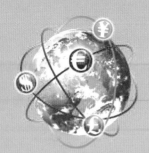

IMPACT ON FIRMS OF ECONOMIC FACTORS

'Economic factors' can sometimes be described as 'macroeconomic factors' (i.e. affecting the whole economy), such as a change in interest rates.

82.1 Economic growth and the business cycle

What is economic growth and why does it matter?

Over time the economy tends to grow. This means that the output of goods and services produced by the country increases compared with the year before. Economic growth is caused by productivity advances, perhaps due to technological innovation. This means that more goods and services can be produced with the same population. Economic growth is important to a country because it improves the standard of living. If the UK economy produces more goods and services there will be more goods and services for UK citizens to consume. Economic growth in Britain has tended to average 2.5% per year. This makes the average level of affluence double every 25–30 years.

Economic growth is very important to firms. A growing economy creates more opportunities for British firms. It is easier to set up or expand a business in a country that has a rapidly growing economy. New gaps emerge in the market, creating more opportunities for budding entrepreneurs.

The economic growth rate of other countries will also be a concern for British firms. For example, the rapid growth in China has led to rising demand for Rolls Royce cars. To cope with the extra orders Rolls-Royce might have to take on extra staff. It will also have to buy in more components. This will benefit Rolls-Royce suppliers, who will also have to increase output and probably employment. The UK is a relatively small country. This means that UK domestic market is also quite small: 90% of the cars Rolls-Royce sells are for export. UK firms like Rolls-Royce, that want to grow, depend partially upon the economic growth rate in other countries.

The business (trade) cycle

Unfortunately, the economy does not grow at an even rate over time. History shows that the British economy has experienced periods when it has grown rapidly; these periods are called booms. Booms are usually followed by recessions; during a recession, economic growth grinds to a halt. Technically, a recession is defined as 'two successive quarters of falling output', but even a slowdown can be called a 'growth recession'. If matters do not improve the economy could end up in a slump. A slump is a sustained period of negative economic growth. The Japanese economy experienced

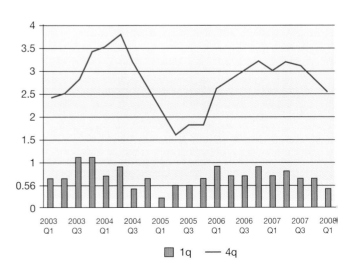

Figure 82.1 UK GDP growth 2002–2007

Table 82.1 The phases of the trade cycle

	Boom	**Recession**	**Slump**	**Recovery**
Consumer and business confidence	● Optimistic	● Doubts emerging	● Pessimistic	● Gradually returning
Consumer spending	● High ● Low levels of saving ● Spending supplemented by credit	● Falling ● Spending financed by credit starts to fall	● Falling ● Consumers save to pay off debts built up during the boom	● Rising ● Debts have now been paid off
Economic growth	● Strongly positive	● GDP begins to fall	● GDP growth might now be strongly	negative
Unemployment	● Weak, but slowly improving	● Close to zero	● Low, but starting to rise	● High
Inflation	● High, but starting to fall	● High, and possibly accelerating	● Still positive, but falling ● Firms now start to think twice about raising prices	● Stable prices, or even some deflation (falling prices) is possible
Number of firms failing	● Price stability	● Low	● Low, but rising	● High
Business investment	● Falling	● Firms are optimistic about the future ● Investment takes place for both replacement and expansion	purposes	● Falling ● Expansion programmes may be postponed

this situation during the period 1990–2003. At the time of writing, commentators are wondering whether the same sustained slump might hit the US economy from 2008 onwards.

The impacts of the trade cycle

The trade cycle will affect different firms in different ways according to the type of good or service that the firm sells. In general, businesses like Ferrari that produce luxury goods will benefit most from economic booms.

On the other hand, firms like Lidl may struggle during economic booms because consumers will probably respond to a boom by 'trading up' to more expensive alternatives such as Waitrose.

Managers must be expert at predicting the future state of the economy. It takes time to plan and introduce changes. Firms that react to economic changes once they have already happened usually struggle to compete.

What actions should a producer of luxury goods take today if it predicts a recession in the near future?

Business objectives

During a recession, a producer of luxury goods might need to change their corporate objective from growth or profit maximisation to one of survival. During a recession, revenue is bound to fall. The key to survival is to minimise losses; this strategy can be achieved by introducing a package of cost-saving measures. Some of these changes might permanently damage the competitiveness of the business. For example, cutting back on expensive new product development will leave the product with an ageing product range in the future. However, if the firm does not cut costs now the business might not have a future to worry about! In a recession managers usually have to make difficult and unpopular decisions.

Marketing

Some businesses react to a recession by changing their marketing strategy to emphasise value for money in an attempt to hold up revenue at a time when the market might be shrinking. Some companies might consider reacting to a recession by cutting prices to help boost sales. However, this might be risky because a price cut might cheapen the brand's image, resulting in a loss of sales once the economy recovers.

Production

Sales of luxury goods fall during a recession. To prepare, producers of such goods should aim to cut production sooner rather than later. Cutting production cannot be achieved overnight, however. For example, suppliers of raw materials and components will probably have minimum notice periods written into their contracts. If the firm waits until sales start falling before cutting production the result is likely to be a build-up of stock. Stock is expensive to store and it also ties up cash. During recessions expansion plans tend to be shelved because the extra capacity created by expansion will not be needed at a time when sales are expected to fall.

Human resource management

During a recession a manufacturer of luxury goods might not need as many staff because not as many goods are being sold. One way of slimming down a workforce is via compulsory redundancy. Getting rid of staff because they are not needed any more is expensive, may create negative publicity and is bad for staff morale. A better alternative may be to reduce your wage bill via **natural wastage**. This

involves suspending recruitment. By not replacing employees who leave or retire, workforce numbers will fall naturally without the need for redundancies.

Some firms use the job insecurity created by a recession to force through changes in working practices that are designed to reduce costs. During a recession, job opportunities elsewhere tend to be scarce; ruthless managers might use this to their advantage. They would argue that the whole business will be leaner and fitter as a result.

Finance

Firms fail when they run out of cash (creditors with unpaid bills take them to court). During recessions producers of luxury goods leak cash because of low demand. Logically, the best chance of survival is for those businesses that started the period of recession with healthy balance sheets, low borrowing levels and high liquidity. To conserve cash during an unprofitable period of trading, a business could:

- carry out a programme of zero budgeting throughout the organisation to trim any waste from departmental budgets

- restrict the credit given to customers and chase up debtors who currently owe the firm money.

- rationalise – sell off any under-utilised fixed assets such as machinery and property; this will bring cash into the business.

- attempt to refinance the business by taking on additional loan capital; unfortunately, during recessions the availability of credit tends to dry up as banks reassess their attitude towards risk; if a firm can persuade a bank to grant loan capital it will normally be lent only at a penalty rate of interest.

Evaluation

Recessions do not last for ever. Firms should aim to survive so that they can benefit when the economy recovers. Not all firms suffer during a recession – companies selling essentials may even gain ground. However, during a boom these same companies will probably have to take cost-cutting measures in order to survive.

Firms can do nothing about booms or recessions; they are external factors that are beyond the firm's control. However, managers need to make offsetting internal changes to the business – cutting costs, for example – to minimise the worst effects of the recession. The challenge for management is to have a long-term strategy that can keep the business healthy in good times and bad.

But what if there is a boom? What should a firm do with the windfall profits it may be able to make? In the UK the threat of takeover might encourage public limited companies to increase their dividend payments to shareholders. Unfortunately, paying increased dividends will do nothing to improve the firm's long-term competitiveness. Managers running companies owned by long-termist shareholders will be able to use the profits made possible by an economic boom to increase their investment in new products and production methods that will make their business more competitive in the long run. Businesses owned or run by more conservative owners might decide to set aside some of the profits made by the boom as a cash reserve that will improve the firm's chances of surviving the next recession, when it arrives.

Most banks react to economic booms by relaxing their lending standards. As a result firms that wish to expand will normally find that it is easier and cheaper to borrow the funds they need to finance the expansion. Banks also tend to be more willing to lend to customers that want credit. A surge in the availability and the price of consumer credit will obviously help car manufacturers and other firms that produce expensive 'big ticket items' that consumers typically purchase using credit. Spread across the economy, these actions can lead to rising **inflation**.

82.2 The effects of inflation on a firm's financial position

Introduction: what is inflation?

Inflation measures the percentage annual rise in the average price level. Inflation reduces the purchasing power of money within an economy. For consumers, inflation increases the cost of living. At the same time, inflation usually leads to rising wages, so households are not necessarily any worse off. Most people's **real wages** may be unchanged in value, so consumer spending in the shops need not be affected.

The impacts of inflation on a firm's finances are mixed.

Advantages of inflation to a business

- Inflation makes real assets become worth more. For example, the value of any property or stock that the firm might own will increase if prices are going up. A firm with more valuable assets will have a more impressive balance sheet. As a result the firm might

find it easier to raise long-term finance from banks and shareholders because the business now looks more secure.

- Firms with large loans also benefit from inflation because it erodes the real value of the money owed. Firms with high borrowings find that the fixed repayments on their long-term borrowings become more easily covered by rising income and profits. A £1 million loan may be worth only £0.75 million by the time the borrower repays the loan (after, say, five years). In the same way, some householders have trivial mortgage payments because they took out the loan to help buy a house valued then at £40,000 (and perhaps worth £240,000 today).

Drawbacks of inflation

- Inflation can damage profitability, especially for firms that have fixed-price contracts that take a long time to complete. For example, a local building company might agree a £5 million price for an extension to a local school, which is expected to take three years to finish. If inflation is higher than expected, profit might be wiped out by the unexpectedly high cost increases created by the inflation. Even if there were an agreement for the school to pay an inflation allowance on top of the price, the producer would have to fund the unexpectedly high cash outflows.

- Inflation can also tend to damage cash flow because it will also push up the price of machinery. Consequently, inflation tends to penalise manufacturing companies like Ford, which need to replace their machinery regularly in order to stay internationally competitive.

- Inflation can also damage industrial relations (i.e. the relationship between the business and its staff). When making pay claims for the year ahead, staff representatives (perhaps a trades union) will estimate what the inflation rate is likely to be in the future. This estimate may be higher than that expected by management. Differences in inflationary expectations have the potential to cause costly industrial disputes that may damage a firm's reputation.

> **Evaluation**
>
> Inflation will impact upon different firms in different ways according to the type of product they sell, the production methods (and lead times) used, and whether or not the firm has loans. For example, inflation might benefit a hairdresser but severely damage a company engaged in heavy manufacturing such as aeroplane maker Airbus Industrie.

82.3 Unemployment

Unemployment is created when the demand for labour has fallen relative to the available supply of labour. Rising unemployment tends to be associated with recessions. During economic booms unemployment usually falls. In addition to the demand for labour, unemployment can also be affected by factors such as emigration and immigration, which affect the supply of labour. Unemployment can be measured as a total or as a rate (the percentage of those of working age who are not in work and who would like a job) (see Figure 83.2). In the period 2006–2007 unemployment decreased in the UK, indicating that the demand for labour grew at a faster rate than the supply of labour.

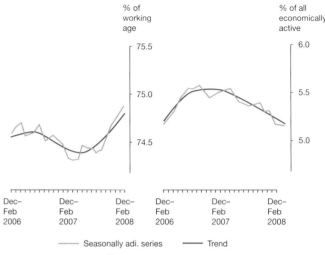

Figure 82.2 Employment rate increases to 74.9%
Source: www.statistics.gov.uk/cci/nugget.asp?id=12

The impacts of unemployment on firms

Unemployment can have both positive and negative impacts on firms (see Table 82.2).

Table 82.2 The benefits and drawbacks of unemployment

Benefits created by unemployment	Costs/problems created by unemployment
(i) Theory X managers might use the fear created by unemployment and the potential for redundancies to force through cost-saving changes in working practices	(i) Unemployment can create insecurity, which could sap morale within the business
(ii) When unemployment is high most employees choose to stay where they are as job vacancies begin to dry up. Labour turnover falls when unemployment is high. Low rates of labour turnover save the firm money on recruitment, selection and training. Over time, if the rate of labour turnover falls, productivity could rise as the workforce gains experience	(ii) Unemployment can affect consumer spending, which in turn can affect a firm's revenue and profit. For example, the credit crunch of 2007/08 caused banks and other financial institutions in the City of London to lay off staff. As a result, local service-sector businesses in the area, such as dry cleaners and sandwich shops, suffered from a drop-off in business
(iii) Recruitment should become a lot easier. When unemployment is high the firm should receive plenty of applications for any vacant position. The quality of applications should improve too. For example, during a period of high unemployment it may be possible to hire a graduate for a non-graduate post	(iii) In areas where unemployment remains high in the long term, firms can be adversely affected by crime and other social problems created by unemployment. Structural unemployment (unemployment caused by a declining industry) can also result in a situation where the unemployed do not possess the 'right' skills

Evaluation

Theory X managers are unlikely to worry too much about making redundancies at a time when unemployment might already be high. They view employees as tools for making a profit. Theory Y managers are more people-orientated. During recessions, they will try their best to avoid redundancies, even if this is at the expense of short-run profit. Japanese companies with a paternalistic culture, such as Mitsubishi, react to structural unemployment by diversifying. They move out of markets that are in decline, such as coal mining and ship building, and invest in markets with better long-term prospects (e.g. computer software and nuclear power). They then retrain staff to move them from their old jobs to new ones.

82.4 Exchange rates

n Britain goods and services are sold in our currency, he pound. In America goods and services are sold in dollars. The exchange rate measures the quantity of foreign currency that can be bought with one unit of another currency (e.g. £1 buys $2). Movements in the exchange rate can dramatically affect profitability because the exchange rate affects both the price of imported and exported goods. Firms cannot influence he exchange rate. For example, the pound's rate of exchange against the US dollar is determined by the supply and demand for the pound on international currency markets. An individual firm is too small to affect the exchange rate; it is a good example of an external constraint that is beyond the control of any one manager. Exchange rates affect firms in different ways.

The impacts of a high exchange rate

On firms with large export markets

UK firms, such as Wedgwood pottery and Morgan cars, which sell a high proportion of their output overseas, will prefer a low exchange rate (i.e. a weak pound).

Why is this so? The best way of explaining is via a numerical example.

America is an important export market for Morgan cars. Morgan charges its UK customers £18,000 for a basic two-seater Roadster. To achieve the same profit margin in America Morgan will have to charge a price in US dollars that will convert into £18,000. At the beginning of 2007 the exchange rate against the US dollar was £1:$1.90. To obtain the £18,000 it needs, Morgan will have to charge its American customers: £18,000 × $1.90 = $34,200.

By November 2007 the exchange rate had gone up to £1:$2.10. To generate the same £18,000 of export revenue per car sold, Morgan will now have to charge its American consumers: £18,000 × $2.10 = $37,800. In other words, Morgan will have to increase the price of its car in America by $3600 to maintain the current profit made on each car sold in the USA. If Morgan does decide to react to a rising pound by putting up its prices in the States, demand for the two-seater Roadster will almost certainly drop, causing Morgan's profitability to fall. On the other hand, if Morgan decides against raising its prices in America, it will have to accept a lower profit on each car sold there; either way Morgan loses out as a result of a high exchange rate.

On firms that import most of their raw materials or stock

Firms such as Tesco that import most of their stock will prefer a high exchange rate. A high exchange rate reduces the cost of buying goods from abroad. For example, Jack Daniel's whiskey is a popular product with Tesco's British consumers. However, Tesco has to import this product from the American firm that produces it. If the price of a case of Jack Daniel's is $50 the price paid by Tesco will be as follows.

- If the exchange rate is £1:$1.90, the case will cost Tesco $50/1.90 = £26.32.

- However, if the exchange rate goes up to £1:$2.10 the same case of Jack Daniel's will now cost Tesco £23.80 ($50/2.10 = £23.80). A high exchange rate will benefit Tesco because it will now be able to make more profit on each bottle of Jack Daniel's that it sells to UK customers.

A-grade application
Exchange rate woes for Airbus

One of Europe's most successful manufacturing businesses is Airbus Industrie. Ten years ago Boeing was the undisputed leader of aircraft manufacture worldwide. By 2008 Airbus and Boeing were neck and neck. Although the world's airlines buy planes priced in US dollars, the Europeans were able to compete. This was until the euro strengthened sharply against the dollar. Between 2005 and early 2008 the euro rose 50% against the dollar. This raised the possibility that Airbus planes would have to be priced far above those of its Boeing competitors.

The impact on Airbus was awful. It had to price its planes in dollars, but almost all its costs were in euros. This led, in March 2008, to a very unusual announcement: Airbus would insist on paying all its European suppliers in dollars in future. This would pass the exchange rate risks onto those suppliers. Before, a rise in the euro would make it harder to afford to pay the European suppliers. Now, a rise in the euro would be offset slightly by the cheaper prices for supplies. The suppliers (such as Britain's Rolls-Royce engines) complained bitterly, but they had little choice but to accept.

The impacts of a low exchange rate

The impacts of a weak exchange rate are the reverse of the impacts of a strong exchange rate. Firms such as Wedgwood and Morgan, which were damaged by a strong currency, find life easier when the exchange rate falls. A weak pound makes their exports seem cheaper to foreign consumers, so Morgan should be able to sell more of its cars in America.

On the other hand, firms such as Tesco will be damaged by a low exchange rate because it will now cost Tesco more in pounds sterling to buy in its imported stock. If Tesco reacts to the falling exchange rate by raising its prices the company could lose customers. If it does nothing it will make less profit on each unit of imported stock sold.

Evaluation: what can firms do about the economy and the exchange rate?

- A weak pound might benefit Morgan and Wedgwood. However, both companies would be unwise to rely on a weak pound for their profitability because the exchange rate can change.
- Economic booms will also benefit Morgan and Wedgwood because both companies sell luxury goods that have a positive income elasticity of demand that is well above 1. Sales will tend to grow at a faster rate than the general economy. Unfortunately, despite politicians' assurances, economic booms are not permanent. So it would also be unwise for either company to rely on a favourable external business environment for its profitability.
- Successful firms are able to predict adverse economic trends that will depress profitability before they arrive. Firms can do nothing about the exchange rate and the economy. However, they can make internal changes to their businesses that are designed to minimise the worst effects of a forthcoming economic calamity. For example, if Morgan believes that the pound will carry on appreciating against the US dollar the company could attempt to cut its costs by automating production. If Morgan can cut its unit costs it can maintain its profit margins, despite the fact that it now receives a lower sterling revenue on each car sold in the USA. In short, Morgan should aim to internalise external constraints.

Key terms

Inflation: although often defined as the rate of rise in the average price level, inflation is better understood as a fall in the value of money.

Natural wastage: allowing staffing levels to fall naturally, by not replacing staff members who leave.

Real wages: changes in money wages minus the rate of change in prices (inflation) – for example, if your pay packet is up 6% but prices are up 4%, your real wage has risen by 2%.

Issues For Analysis

There are two main ways to consider businesses and economic change.

- The more obvious is how a business should respond (e.g. to a rise in interest rates). It may anticipate a rise in customer demand and therefore increase production; it may rethink its marketing strategy.

- The second issue is tougher: what strategies should a firm carry out to protect itself from unknown economic changes in the future. By definition this will be difficult, as how can one anticipate the unknown? Yet, for a house-building firm or a bank in early 2007, was it so difficult to anticipate the problems that might arise in future? The problem, often, is that directors of plcs have such huge financial incentives to achieve profit increases that they ignore actions to protect the business from possible downturns. In a family-run (Ltd) business there is much greater reason to think about the next ten years rather than the next ten months.

Impact on firms of economic factors

Businesses are sometimes badly run, leaving them exposed to potential collapse if interest rates rise or a recession occurs. In other cases bad luck may be a factor (e.g. a well-run café has to close because the factory nearby closes down). In an ideal world every business would anticipate every risk facing it, and devise a relevant survival strategy. This may not always be possible.

One of the best judgements a director can make is to ensure that a firm is always equipped financially for any future economic change. If the business keeps its borrowings relatively low and its liquidity relatively high, it will survive almost any problem. The sudden collapse of Northern Rock and Bear Stearns in 2007/08 showed the level of risk that exists among firms that lack that judgement.

Exercises

A. Revision questions

(35 marks; 40 minutes)

1 What is the business cycle? (2)

2 Explain why a business such as Chessington World of Adventures might be affected by a recession in America. (4)

3 Define the term the trade cycle. (2)

4 Explain two typical features of a recession. (6)

5 Give an example of a firm that might benefit from a recession in the UK. (1)

6 What is trading down and why does it occur? (4)

7 Why might a firm respond to the threat of a recession by suspending recruitment, even before the recession actually arrives? (4)

8 What are inflationary expectations and why are they important? (5)

9 How might inflation benefit a small one-stop convenience store? (3)

10 Explain two reasons why staff morale can plummet during a recession. (4)

B. Revision exercises

B1 Case study

Airbus hit by the dollar's collapse

In 2003 the euro and the US dollar were at parity (i.e. the dollar/euro exchange rate was €1:$1). A weak euro helped the European aircraft manufacturer Airbus sell more planes to US airlines. At the time, Airbus used a weak euro to steal market share from its American rival, Boeing. In the same year the company announced record profits of €152 million, an increase of 8% on the previous year.

Unfortunately for Airbus this situation did not last, and by November 2007 the company was at breaking point. From 2003 to 2007, as Figure 82.4 on page 589 demonstrates, the euro rose almost continually against the US dollar.

As the dollar fell, Airbus found it increasingly hard to compete against Boeing. To hold up sales Airbus embarked upon a programme of cost cutting, which included 10,000 job losses. However, Airbus found it difficult to cut its costs as fast as the dollar was falling. At the end of 2007 the chief executive of Airbus, Tom Enders, made headlines by announcing that: 'The dollar's rapid decline is life-threatening for Airbus' and that 'The dollar exchange rate has gone beyond the pain barrier.'

Questions

(25 marks; 30 minutes)

1 What is the exchange rate? (2)

2 The catalogue price of an Airbus A320 is approximately €65 million. To generate the same profit margin from its sales to US airlines how much would Airbus have to charge in US dollars at:
   (a) the euro/dollar exchange rate as it was in 2003? (2)
   (b) the euro/dollar exchange rate as it was in 2007? (3)

3 Explain the actions that Airbus has taken to offset the problem of a weak dollar. (3)

4 So far, a weak dollar has damaged Airbus's profits. Explain one action that Airbus could take to turn a weak dollar from a weakness into a strength. (3)

5 Discuss whether Tom Enders is correct to claim that 'the dollar's rapid decline is life-threatening for Airbus'. (12)

Figure 82.4 *The value of the Euro against the US dollar*

B2 Data response

Exchange rate movements and business

Xavi moved to London from Spain in 2004. After many months working as a waiter, he started to look at business opportunities. The most promising seemed to be to link up with an older brother in New York. The plan would be to buy leather (cheaply) from Spain, get it made into belts and jackets, then sell the products on to New York.

The business started life as XL Ltd in January 2006, at a time when £1 = $1.77 and £1 = €1.46. For each jacket Xavi, bought in 51.10 euros (€) worth of leather, paid £20 of labour costs in east London, £12 per jacket in delivery costs to New York, then sold the jackets to US shops for $177. The jackets used high-quality leather, were stylishly cut and sold like hot cakes. In the first year of operation, with strong sales and costs remaining very stable, the business made more than £80,000 of net profit.

In response to exchange rate changes plus the high demand from New York, Xavi put his US prices up by 20% in April 2007. His New York sales slipped back by 5%, but still allowed the business to run profitably. The autumn was much less comfortable, however. By November his profits were being squeezed in two directions. He put his dollar prices up by a further 10%, but the retail situation had changed dramatically since April. New York shoppers were worried about recession and more resistant to price changes. Price elasticities on products such as his had risen to around −2.

On the weekend of 1/2 March 2008, with the pound at an all-time record low of €1.30, Xavi thought about putting his business into liquidation. Monthly operating profits since November 2007 had been negative and he didn't want all the accumulated cash in the business to be eaten away by constant losses. He had to decide: keep going or close down?

Questions

(40 marks; 45 minutes)

1 Calculate the profit per jacket (in £s) when the business started up in January 2006.   (6)

2 (a) Describe the exchange rate movements of the £ against the euro in the period from January 2006 to February 2008.   (4)

(b) From your observations of the £ vs € exchange rates, why were Xavi's 'costs remaining very stable' in the first year of XL Ltd's operation?   (3)

3 (a) Calculate the price elasticity of Xavi's products in New York in April 2007. (3)

(b) Calculate the effect of the November 2007 price rise on the sales volumes of Xavi's leather jackets.   (3)

4 Explain the effect on Xavi's business of the 2006–2008 movements of the £ against the $.   (6)

5 Discuss whether Xavi should continue the business or close it down?   (15)

Figure 82.5 Monthly average exchange rates, July 2003–1 March 2008

B3 Case study

Antonia Dyball-Jamieson is worried. She is the founder and managing director of Emporium, an upmarket chain of clothes shops located in prosperous market towns in Surrey such as Reigate and Guildford. Emporium stocks aspirational high-fashion brands such as Jack Wills and Abercrombie & Fitch that sell at premium prices (e.g. £70 for a logo T-shirt). The business serves a target market made up of privately educated teenagers whose expenditure is largely funded by their high income earning parents who work, mostly, in financial services in the City of London. The high prices that Antonia is currently able to charge ensure that each of her stores operates with a low break-even point and a healthy safety margin.

Over the last seven years the business has taken advantage of a favourable economic climate and has expanded steadily: on average Antonia manages to open a new branch every year. On average, on a like-for-like basis, Emporium has managed to increase its sales by 7% annually. During the boom years the business has found it relatively easy to raise the additional loan capital required to enlarge the business.

Over the last couple of months, however, Antonia has become increasingly concerned about the state of the economy. Her favourite economic guru, Evan Davis, the BBC's economics editor, recently predicted that economic growth could grind to a halt next year. Even more alarmingly, Vicky, Antonia's old friend from university, warned that investment banks, such as Goldman Sachs, were planning large-scale redundancies. Vicky also complained that she had been told by her boss that her bonus this year would be that she would be keeping her job; last year she received £120,000 in addition to her basic

salary of £75,000. 'How will I cope without my bonus!' wailed Vicky.

In the next week Antonia has some big decisions to make. She has found an excellent potential location for her next branch of Emporium in prosperous Godalming, which will cost £5000 a year to lease. In addition, £20,000 will have to be spent fitting out the new site, and five new members of staff will have to be hired and trained. Antonia's Dad, Sebastian, believes that she should not postpone her expansion plans. According to him David Smith, the economics correspondent for *The Times*, believes that the economy will continue to grow because interest rates will stay low for the foreseeable future.

Questions

(26 marks; 30 minutes)

1 Calculate the income elasticity of the products sold by Emporium assuming that, on average, incomes in Surrey have risen by approximately 2% per annum over the past seven years. (4)

2 Explain why businesses such as Emporium are particularly sensitive to movements in the trade cycle. (4)

3 Describe three actions that Antonia could take to help prepare her business for a downturn in the trade cycle. (6)

4 Should Antonia go ahead with her plans to open a new Emporium store in Godalming? Discuss the arguments for and against. (6)

5 Using the case study as a starting point, discuss whether it is essential that managers such as Antonia have a good understanding of economic theory in order to make effective long-run decisions. (6)

B4 Case study

British economy statistics

Questions

(20 marks; 20 minutes)

1 Plot the data shown in the table onto a graph designed to illustrate trends in the UK's economic growth rate, inflation rate and unemployment rate over the period 1980–2007. (6)

2 Can you identify any boom or slump years? (4)

3 Compare and contrast the characteristics of a boom with the characteristics of a recession. (8)

4 What is the main limitation of this data for managers? (2)

Year	Economic growth rate %	Inflation % (RPI)	Unemployment rate % (based on the claimant count measure of unemployment)
1980	−2.5	17.8	6.0
1981	−1.2	12	9.4
1982	1.6	8.6	10.9
1983	3.3	4.5	10.8
1984	2.6	5.0	11.0
1985	3.8	6.0	10.9
1986	4.3	3.4	11.2
1987	4.8	4.1	10.0
1988	5	4.9	8.1
1989	2.2	7.8	6.3
1990	0.4	9.5	5.9
1991	−2.2	5.9	8.1
1992	−0.5	3.7	9.9
1993	2.5	1.6	10.4
1994	4.3	2.5	9.2
1995	2.8	3.3	7.9
1996	3.4	2.9	7.2
1997	2.7	2.8	5.4
1998	2.7	3.3	4.6
1999	2.7	2.4	4.3
2000	3.0	3.0	3.6
2001	2.4	1.8	3.2
2002	1.8	1.7	3.1
2003	2.5	2.9	3.0
2004	3.2	3.0	2.7
2005	2.1	2.8	2.7
2006	2.6	3.2	3.0
2007	3.2*	4.1*	2.6*

* 2007 figures based on annualised data collected during September of that year
Source: www.statistics.gov.uk/

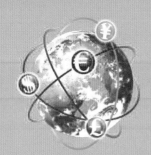

Unit 83

GLOBALISATION AND DEVELOPMENT

83.1 Introduction

Globalisation is by no means a new force. In 1900 a quarter of the world's population lived under a British flag, bringing with it a 'culture' of tea, cricket and – from 1902 – Marmite. In the 1920s, American companies such as Ford and Coca-Cola started their moves to multinational status. By the 1960s Mickey Mouse, US films and British pop music were global forces. Yet the term globalisation only really started to stick in the 1980s. It was in this period that the huge growth of McDonald's, Levi's jeans and Coca-Cola made people start to question whether the world was becoming a suburb of America. The 1990s growth of Microsoft and Starbucks brought the question further into focus. Figure 83.1 gives a sense of the extraordinary growth in world trade, but lends little support to any view that globalisation 'arrived in the 1990s'.

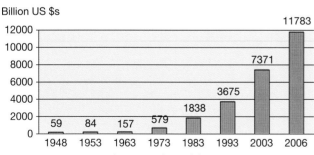

Figure 83.1 Growth in total world exports, 1948–2006 ($)

The term globalisation encompasses many issues. Some are based on cultural questions, such as whether a language such as French can survive the onslaught of (American) English. Some are based on ethical questions that seem much more stark when a rich western company is getting its supplies from Cambodian labour paid 30p an hour. Others are more focused on the economic question 'Are global giants wiping out national producers and restricting consumer choice?' Clearly these are all massive questions in a Business A-level course.

83.2 Government efforts to increase world trade

Trade between countries had been growing for centuries until the 1929 Wall Street crash led to increasing **protectionism** worldwide. The political changes in Germany and Japan in the 1930s (which led to the 50 million deaths in the Second World War) were partly due to these two countries' concern at being excluded from export markets. With the lessons learned from this governments since 1945 have tried hard to make it easier for countries to do business with each other.

Following marathon negotiations lasting from 1986 to 1994, the World Trade Organization (WTO) was established in 1995. Overnight the value of tariff-free imports went from 20% to 44% of the worldwide total. Today it is over 50%. In other words, only in a minority of cases are taxes placed on imported goods. The development of the WTO was boosted further when China joined in 2001.

The WTO tries to ensure that there is **free trade** between countries, but that the trade is based upon common rules. For example, all WTO member countries should provide legal protection for the **intellectual property** of companies and individuals.

Many people argue that WTO rules favour rich countries against poorer ones. There is a strong case for saying that free trade is the ideal form of trade for countries and companies at a similar stage of

evelopment (because it encourages competition). But
ss developed countries would surely benefit from
rotection of their **infant industries** until they have
eveloped a scale of production that enables them to
ompete with multinational giants. In the early days of
he motor industry in Japan and China, local car
ompanies were protected by huge tariff barriers (import
x rates of around 40%). In both countries there is no
onger any need for import tariffs as the industries are
ficient and competitive.

lthough the WTO can be criticised for the extent to
hich policy-making is dominated by America and
urope, there is no doubt that the substantial economic
owth of the 1998–2008 period has spread increased
rosperity far and wide around the world. Very sadly,
he child mortality figures for Nigeria (see Table 83.1)
ow there is still a long way to go.

83.3

The case for globalisation

seph Stiglitz, in his book *Globalization and its Discontents*
2002), became the word's most famous critic of
obalisation. Yet he identifies many important benefits
om increasingly open world trade. To him, the biggest
ep forward by far is the increase in the number of people
less developed countries whose lives have been
nproved. He mentions the opening up of the Jamaican
ilk market (allowing US competition in) as a huge benefit
poor children in Jamaica, even if it hurt the profits of the
cal farmers. It is also important to bear in mind that,
owever awful the figures may be for infant deaths before
e age of one, they are incomparably better than they were
), 40 or 50 years ago. Globalisation of healthcare is as
nportant here as the globalisation of the economy.

mong the main advantages of globalisation are:

- increased competition forces local producers to be
  efficient, thereby cutting prices and increasing
  standards of living (people's income goes further)

- providing the opportunity for the best ideas to be
  spread across the globe (e.g. AIDS medicines, water
  irrigation and mobile phones)

- if multinational companies open up within a country,
  this may provide opportunities for employment and
  training, and allow local entrepreneurs to learn from
  the experience of the more established businesses

- providing outlets for exports, which can allow a
  country to boost its standards of living by reducing

dependence on subsistence farming (growing just
enough to feed the family)

- it has provided the opportunity for a series of
  countries (e.g. Egypt, Mexico, China and India) to
  break away from poverty; for example, average living
  standards in China rose by 800% between 1990 and
  2008; Table 83.1 shows the impact economic growth
  can have on infant mortality; sadly the benefits have
  not shown through in all cases – Nigerian standards
  of living have not risen since 1990, so the death rate
  among under-5s remains shocking

Table 83.1 *Infant mortality (deaths per 000 under-5s)*

	1990	**2006**
Egypt	104	33
Mexico	46	27
China	49	27
India	123	74
Nigeria	230	194
Great Britain (for comparison)	10	6

Source: UNICEF statistics, February 2008

A-grade application

Bangladesh

In the 20 years until 1990, the annual growth rate in
Bangladesh* was an extremely low 0.6%. This left its
under-5 mortality rate at 149 per 1000 in 1990. Each
year, more under-5s died in Bangladesh than all the
under-5s living in Britain. By 1990 Bangladesh was
developing a clothing industry based upon very low-
wage labour, targeting western companies. In the period
1990–2006 the growth rate rose to 2.9% per person,
helping the infant mortality rate to halve to 73 per 1000.

Bangladesh has by no means become a wealthy
country. Fewer than half of all households have access
to clean water and, by 2005, only 5% of the
population had a phone. But economic progress has
made an impact, and should continue to do so.

* Bangladesh, with 150 million people, is the world's seventh most
populated country

83.4 The case against globalisation

The economic case against

Critics suggest that globalisation has made it harder for local firms to create local opportunities. In 2002 virtually no overseas car producer had a factory in India; but, with the growth of the Indian economy, by 2008 Hyundai, Suzuki and BMW were present, with Toyota and Honda announcing new factories by 2010. Although the local Tata Motors has announced the production of the world's cheapest new car (at £1250 each), it may be that the middle of the car market will be captured by the big European and Far Eastern car producers.

There is also concern that new production in a country does not necessarily mean new wealth. Some multinational firms establish a factory locally, but use it in a way that could be called exploitation. In India there are many clothing factories that supply companies such as Gap, Primark and Asda. Wage rates are extremely low by western standards, and working conditions are poor. Little of the value created by the sale of a £20 jumper in a London Gap outlet may seep back to India. If the clothing design, the branding and the packaging are all done in the west, all that is left is labour-intensive, low-paid factory work.

The social and cultural case against

In 2002, a French farmer made the headlines worldwide by bulldozing a McDonald's outlet. He was protesting about the Americanisation of France. Remarkably, even the French cosmetics powerhouse L'Oréal is inclined to show English-language television commercials in France. The increasing number of US outlets in French high streets was the farmer's main concern: KFC, McDonald's, Subway, Gap, Starbucks, and so on. Around the world, many agreed that their high streets were starting to look like those in America; they probably discussed it on their Moto phone while also listening to Britney Spears on their iPod. Globalisation started to be criticised for making our lives less interesting by reducing the differences between countries and cities.

Among the main disadvantages of globalisation are:

● that everywhere starts to look like everywhere else

● that globalisation is built on exploitation – the strong exploiting the weak

● that it may make it hard for local producers to build and grow in a way that is suited to local needs.

A-grade application

Nigeria

There is probably no country in the world that has under-achieved as severely as Nigeria. In the 20 years to 1990 its economy shrank by an average of 1.4% a year. Its 1990 child mortality of 230 per 1000 was among the world's worst. Since then, growth has been no higher than an average of 0.7% a year. This despite the fact that Nigeria is oil rich. Over the past 15 years more than £50 billion of oil has been exported from the country. This has been good for BP and Shell, but the people of Nigeria have little benefit to show for all this wealth. Corruption has been an important problem, but many Nigerians would point to the oil multinationals as well as their own leaders. The benefits of globalisation have passed them by.

83.5 Globalisation and the British economy

Britain should probably have benefited more from the growth of world trade, given the country's 10% share of world exports in 1950. Since then, though, there has been a process of **deindustrialisation** in Britain, as industries such as textiles, ship building and car production wilted under foreign competition. Figure 83.2 shows Britain's dramatic decline in the years between 1948 and 1973. Since then there has been a further, steady reduction in Britain's share of 'merchandise exports'.

Fortunately for the economy, Britain has kept its strong position in sales of services to countries around the world. In 2006, Britain was second only to the United States in its share of the market for internationally traded services. Whereas the 2006 share of world trade in goods was 3.8%, Britain's share of 'invisible' exports was nearly 10%.

It is also important to remember that the increase in world trade of the past ten years has brought a significant increase in living standards in Britain. On average, those in work are very much better off than ten years ago, with items such as clothes, cars, furniture and household electronics down sharply in price. Cheap imports from China and Cambodia are not only enjoyable, but are also vital in keeping UK inflation low. Low prices help our money to go further, making us all better-off.

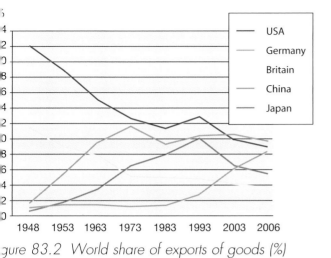

Figure 83.2 World share of exports of goods (%)

83.6 Development

The most important thing is to realise that development happens. In 1981, 40% of the world's population lived on less than $1 a day (about 60p). By 2001 the figure had nearly halved to 21% (the figures are a true comparison, because changes in prices have been allowed for). By 2015, the World Bank estimates that the figure will have fallen to about 15%. Let's be clear, here, that 15% of a 6.6 billion world population means that 1000 million people are living on extremely low incomes. That, in itself, is a disgrace in a world where there is so much wealth. But it is wrong to treat the issue of development with a shrug of the shoulders.

There are hopeful signs. Table 83.2 shows the economic performance of a selection of less developed countries. Despite the figures in the right-hand column, the two central columns show that improvements are definitely occurring.

In the period since 1981, the big development wins have been achieved in China, in South East Asia more generally, and in South America. Without exception, these gains have come about as a result of economic development. In other words, poverty has not been reduced because rich Chinese have given more to poor Chinese; this has come about because the Chinese economy has been able to produce more wealth for all.

Does economic aid have much to do with this relative success? Not really, as governments and charities rarely do enough to make much impact throughout a country. For countries such as China, India and Mexico, the key factors have been:

- greater willingness to accept inward investment from multinational or other big, wealthy companies from the west or Japan

- greater enterprise on the part of the local business population

- more stable government than before, especially in India and Mexico

- easier access for exports to countries such as Britain, America and the rest of Europe, partly thanks to the World Trade Organization.

Table 83.2 Economic performance of selected countries

	GDP at PPP 2007*	Average annual growth in GDP per head 1970–1990	Average annual growth in GDP per head 1990–2005	% of population below $1 a day 1994–2004
Bangladesh	£700	0.6	2.9	36%
Benin	£750	0	1.4	31%
China	£2650	6.6	8.8	17%
India	£1350	2.2	4.2	35%
Nicaragua	£1600	−3.8	1.5	45%
Nigeria	£1100	−1.4	0.7	71%

Source: CIA Factbook; assuming £1 = $2

Issues For Analysis

Globalisation needs to be seen as a catch-all term that may mean different things to different people. It is assumed to be a very new thing (which is arguable) and is assumed by many to be a bad thing. When analysing issues to do with globalisation it helps to:

- be clear about the definition you are using and the limits you are placing on that definition (e.g. 'economic globalisation' but not 'cultural globalisation' – though you might later want to explore whether this separation is artificial)

- be calm, measured and balanced; whatever the strength of your views, push yourself to consider a different perspective – for instance, many people feel strongly about 'sweatshop' work for low pay in countries such as Vietnam, but it may be that Vietnamese workers would prefer a factory job to a job in the fields; we cannot jump to conclusions about other people's lives

- avoid slipping into too small-scale a viewpoint; globalisation is at least as much about increasing competition between big western companies as it is between the west and the developing world; unarguably, Volkswagen versus Renault versus Toyota is global rivalry we all benefit from.

Key terms

Deindustrialisation: the steady decline in manufacturing output and employment that changed Britain from being an industrial powerhouse to a service-sector economy.

Free trade: imports and exports being allowed into different countries without taxation, limits or obstruction. This ensures that companies from different countries compete fairly with each other.

Infant industries: new, young industries in a developing country that may need extra, but temporary, protection until they have grown big and strong enough to compete with global giants (e.g. a new Zambian factory producing instant coffee, trying to compete with the global number one – Nestlé/Nescafé).

Intellectual property: legal protection for the rights of the originator of new written, visual or technical material (e.g. protected by copyright, trademarks or patents).

Protectionism: government actions to protect home producers from competition from overseas (e.g. by setting import taxes – 'tariffs' – or imposing import quotas that place a cap on the number of goods that can enter a country).

Further reading

Stiglitz, J. (2002) *Globalization and its Discontents.* Norton.

83.7 Globalisation and development

an evaluation

The judgements involved in this area need to be especially subtle. Beware of poorly justified judgements that may suggest intolerance towards others, or ignorance of the extreme disparities between incomes in rich and poor countries. The more you read about different countries' successes and failures, the better rooted your judgements will be.

It is also valuable to take a critical look at all the evidence provided, questioning whether the claims made by businesses about their motives is the truth or just public relations. The same sceptical approach should be taken to any other form of evidence, whether from pressure groups such as Greenpeace or from government ministers or officials. Globalisation is a topic in which opinions are often clearer than facts.

Exercises

A. Revision questions

(40 marks; 40 minutes)

1 Re-read the definition of globalisation at the start of the unit. Outline one advantage and one disadvantage of the world 'becoming one market'. (4)

2 Please refer to figure 83.1

   (a) Calculate the % increases in world exports in the following periods:
   (i) 1973–1983
   (ii) 1983–1993
   (iii) 1993–2003. (5)

   (b) How well do these figures support the idea that globalisation 'arrived in the 1990s'? (2)

3 Outline two reasons why consumers might suffer as a result of a government policy of import protectionism. (4)

4 Examine one reason why a new car factory in Nigeria might benefit if the Nigerian government used the infant industries argument to protect it. (4)

5 Outline two other factors that might affect a country's infant mortality, apart from economic development. (4)

6 Use Figure 83.2 to describe three major changes that have happened in the world economy between 1948 and 2006. (6)

7 Should wealthy countries increase the rates of tax on their own populations in order to finance greater help to people living on less than $1 a day? (5)

8 Outline three possible reasons that might explain why China's growth rate is so much higher than that of Nigeria or India. (6)

B. Revision exercises

B1 Case study

Starbucks agrees to Ethiopian coffee branding

CSRwire.com reports that Starbucks and Ethiopia recently signed a distribution, marketing and licensing agreement that should help Ethiopian coffee farmers reap value from the intellectual property of their distinctive, deluxe coffees:

Eight months ago Oxfam began working to raise awareness of Ethiopians' efforts to gain control over their fine coffee brands. Today, Starbucks has honored its commitments to Ethiopian coffee farmers by becoming one of the first in the industry to join the innovative Ethiopian trademarking initiative.

We covered this story last winter, looking at how Oxfam threw the weight of its powerful nonprofit brand behind the cause of poor Ethiopian coffee farmers. At stake were the Sidamo, Harrar, and Yirgacheffe varietals, thought to be among the best in the world. Policy Innovations raises its mug to this multi-stakeholder cooperation.

Source: fairerglobalization.blogspot.com

Questions

(25 marks; 30 minutes)

1 Explain what 'intellectual property' there can be in Ethiopian coffee. (4)

2 Explain how Ethiopian farmers might benefit from this initiative. (6)

3 Discuss the possible reasons why Starbucks may have decided to sign this deal with the Ethiopian coffee producers. (10)

4 Explain what the author means by the phrase 'this multi-stakeholder cooperation'. (5)

B2 Case study

Channel 4 cleared over Tesco child labour story

A Tesco complaint about a *Channel 4 News* item on child labour has been rejected by media regulator Ofcom. The *Channel 4 News* story alleged that child labour was being used by suppliers in Bangladesh in the production of clothes for Tesco stores.

Tesco complained that the report, which featured a 'little boy who looks no more than eight' and other allegedly underage workers, was unfair. The supermarket company, represented by solicitors Carter-Ruck, said the boy was in fact 12 years old and claimed the 'child' workers featured were aged 18 or over. But Ofcom said the secretly filmed report – made by independent producer Evolve Television for *Channel 4 News* – was 'properly supported' and put in 'fair context'. Ofcom also said Tesco had been given an appropriate amount of time to respond to the allegations.

The media regulator, in its ruling published today, said *Channel 4 News* had not been unfair in its treatment of the supermarket. Ofcom added that the *Channel 4 News* report, which aired on 10 October 2006, had 'questioned Tesco's ability to ensure its ethical standards are met throughout the supply chain'.*

'The report did not allege that Tesco was deliberately or knowingly using child labour to produce its clothing,' the regulator said. 'Rather, it showed that companies supplying Tesco were employing workers who were below the legal age limit in Bangladesh (i.e. aged under 14) and that some of these workers were producing clothes for Tesco.'

Tesco had claimed the boy who was described as looking 'no more than eight' was in fact 12.

The company said he had no connection with the factory and was delivering lunch to his cousin. But *Channel 4 News*, in its response, said Tesco's claim was 'directly at odds' with what its film-makers had seen, 'namely that the boy was sewing creases into denim trousers as part of the production process'.

Channel 4 News editor, Jim Gray, added: '*Channel 4 News*'s reputation is founded upon its track record for delivering high-quality original journalism through thorough, rigorous and accurate investigation. This report possessed all of these qualities and investigative journalism remains at the heart of everything we do.'

Ofcom's Fairness Committee, its most senior decision-making body, made a provisional finding rejecting Tesco's complaint. The supermarket then requested a review of the provisional finding on the grounds that it was flawed. It was also not upheld.

* The supply chain is the network of suppliers that takes a product through all the stages from raw materials through to the retail store

Source: guardian.co.uk, 25 February 2008

Questions

(30 marks; 35 minutes)

1 Explain why it would be difficult for Tesco to 'ensure its ethical standards are met throughout the supply chain'. (8)

2 Discuss the probable reasons why Tesco decided to make this public complaint against Channel 4. (10)

3 Discuss whether Tesco should now withdraw all its clothing production from Bangladesh. (12)

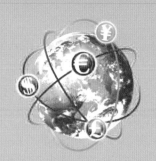

IMPACT OF GOVERNMENT ECONOMIC POLICY

Economic policy is the grouping of actions taken by the Chancellor of the Exchequer to try to achieve the government's economic objectives.

84.1 Government economic objectives

The most important goal of any politician is re-election. Electors make their voting choices partly on the competence of the government at managing the economy. Therefore any government will try hard to achieve its economic objectives, which typically include the following.

- *Economic growth*: economic growth occurs when the total value of all goods and services produced within the economy in a year increases. If the government can increase the rate of economic growth the material standard of living within the country should increase, helping to boost the government's popularity. Economic growth is also beneficial to businesses. If average incomes rise consumers will have more money to spend, creating larger markets and additional opportunities for UK firms. As the British economy has tended, in the long term, to grow at 2.25–2.5% a year, any government would be thrilled to have achieved a higher growth rate.

- *Low inflation*: inflation is the percentage annual change in the average price level. Price stability will make it easier for UK firms to compete against their foreign rivals, both at home and abroad. The stability created by low inflation also encourages investment, leading to stronger economic growth.

- *Low unemployment*: if the government can reduce the number of people in the country who are without work, the country's output should increase. Spending levels should also increase because those previously unemployed will now have a wage to live off, rather than unemployment benefit. Higher levels of spending will again help firms to expand and grow.

- A *favourable current account balance*: the UK receives income from selling exports abroad. On the other hand, UK citizens also spend money on imported goods and services. The **current account** measures the difference between export income and import expenditure. In general the government would like to avoid a current account deficit, a situation where import expenditure exceeds export income. Current account deficits are financed by a general increase in borrowing, or asset sales, across the economy, leading to a fall in society's collective net worth.

- A *stable exchange rate*: the exchange rate measures the volume or amount of foreign currency that can be bought with one unit of domestic currency (e.g. £1:$2.10 means that one pound can buy two dollars ten cents). A stable exchange rate helps firms to forecast how much profit, or loss, they stand to make from exporting or importing. If firms can forecast the future with greater confidence they will be more likely to go ahead and trade with foreign firms, boosting UK economic activity.

84.2 Government economic policies

The government uses economic policies to achieve its economic objectives. As a Business Studies student the key for you is to understand how these policies affect different types of business. The economic policies that you will need to know about are discussed below.

Fiscal policy

Fiscal policy refers to the government's budget. The

budget concerns the government's tax and spending plans for the year ahead. The main areas of government expenditure for 2007 were as shown in Figure 84.1.

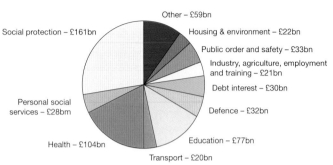

Total managed expenditure: £587 billion

Other – £59bn
Housing & environment – £22bn
Social protection – £161bn
Public order and safety – £33bn
Industry, agriculture, employment and training – £21bn
Debt interest – £30bn
Personal social services – £28bm
Defence – £32bn
Health – £104bn
Education – £77bn
Transport – £20bn

Figure 84.1 The main areas of UK government expenditure for 2007
Source: UK Treasury budget documents

How does government expenditure affect firms?

● In general, an increase in government spending will increase the total level of spending within the economy, causing most markets to grow. For example, if the government awards above-inflation pay rises for nurses, this could help businesses such as Asda or Ryanair that target ordinary working people. Nurses are likely to spend the bulk of any pay rise they receive (e.g. on a European holiday).

● About 40% of the UK economy revolves around government spending; firms such as construction companies (road and school building), publishers (textbooks) and computer suppliers are all hugely dependent upon government spending (see Figure 84.2).

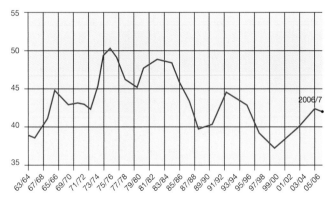

Figure 84.2 Long-term government spending
Source: HM Treasury

● The war in Iraq has increased the amount the government spends on the armed services. According to the October 2007 government spending review, total defence spending is anticipated to rise by £2.9 billion by 2011. Manufacturers of military aircraft,

tanks and bullets will benefit from this additional spending.

● Increased spending on the NHS will increase the turnover of the construction companies that win the contracts to build new hospitals. There will be multiplier effects too. For example, firms that supply the construction companies with the concrete, brick and steel, and so on, will also benefit from additional government expenditure on the NHS. The same point also applies to drug manufacturers, and firms that produce medical equipment such as MRI scanners and hospital beds.

The main sources of tax income for 2007 were as shown in Figure 84.3.

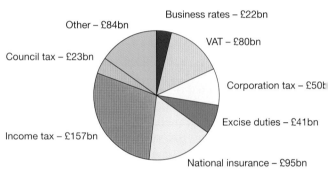

Total receipts: £553 bilion

Other – £84bn
Business rates – £22bn
Council tax – £23bn
VAT – £80bn
Corporation tax – £50b
Excise duties – £41bn
Income tax – £157bn
National insurance – £95bn

Figure 84.3 The main sources of UK tax income for 200
Source: UK Treasury budget documents

How does taxation affect firms?

● The largest component of the UK government's income comes from income tax. Income tax tends to reduce consumer spending because higher income ta rates widen the gap between gross (before tax) and net (after tax) pay. At times the government is forced into collecting more income tax in order to finance increases in public expenditure. This tends not to be a popular policy. Most firms do not benefit If more money is collected through income tax, demand for products and services may shrink as consumer spending falls. The UK income tax system is mildly 'progressive'. This means that those earning lower incomes pay a smaller percentage of their income in tax than those earning higher salaries. Changes to the income tax system can affect some firms more than others. For example, if the government decided to increase the top rate of income tax from 40% to 50% this change would hit BMW car dealerships, but might have no effect on sales of bicycles.

● Value added tax (VAT) is added to the retail price c a product. It is an example of an indirect tax (i.e. a tax levied on expenditure, rather than on income).

At present the UK government charges a standard rate of VAT of 17.5%, apart from food, newspapers, books and clothes for children, which are zero rated. VAT makes goods more expensive. Changes in VAT rules can affect businesses. If the government decided to extend VAT to newspapers the price of newspapers would be forced up, leading to a fall in the volume of newspapers bought and sold.

Excise duties are indirect taxes levied, in addition to VAT, on a wide range of products including petrol, cigarettes and alcohol. The impact of excise duties on a market is very much influenced by consumer price sensitivity. For example, petrol retailers such as Shell tend not to be too badly affected by increases in petrol duty because the demand for petrol in the UK tends to be price inelastic. In other words, the price increase created by the increase in fuel duty has a minimal effect on the volume of petrol that Shell sells. Oil companies find it relatively easy to pass on any increase in petrol duty to the motorist by raising petrol prices. Increasing excise duty rates on a price-inelastic product also benefits the government because it will raise more in taxation from this market.

Corporation tax is a tax levied on a company's profits. In 2007 the UK government cut the corporation tax rate from 30% to 28%. A fall in the corporation tax rate will give firms an increased opportunity to invest because, all other things being equal, the less paid in corporation tax the greater the level of retained profit.

Types of fiscal policy
- *Expansionary fiscal policy:* the government runs an expansionary fiscal policy when planned government spending for the year ahead exceeds planned tax income. Expansionary fiscal policy tends to benefit most firms in the short run because the total level of spending in the economy will rise.
- *Contractionary fiscal policy:* the government runs a contractionary fiscal policy when planned expenditure is less than planned tax income. Contractionary fiscal policy tends to depress the total level of spending within the economy.
- *Neutral fiscal policy:* if planned tax income equals planned government spending the government's budget is said to be 'balanced'.

Monetary policy

Monetary policy concerns the availability and price of credit. In the UK, monetary policy is implemented by the Bank of England. The Bank of England's Monetary Policy Committee (MPC) meets every month to set the interest rate. The interest rate is the price of borrowed money. An increase in interest rates makes borrowing more expensive. On the other hand, saving becomes a more attractive proposition when interest rates rise. Interest rates are a powerful economic policy instrument because they can simultaneously affect a firm's revenue and costs.

Monetary policy can be tightened or slackened according to the economic circumstances. Recessions are caused by a lack of spending. If the economy is in recession the Central Bank will normally cut the interest rate because lower interest rates encourage people to spend more. Lower interest rates will encourage more borrowing and less saving.

On the other hand, during a boom demand is normally high and this can cause inflation. To reduce this threat the Central Bank normally reacts by 'tightening' monetary policy. This involves increasing interest rates. An increase in interest rates reduces borrowing and increases saving. As a result of the interest rate rise, total spending falls and the threat of inflation reduces.

The impacts of interest rates on firms

The interest rate is a good example of an external constraint; it is a factor that is beyond the firm's control. However, changes in the rate of interest can affect a firm's costs and revenues

Impacts on cost

Loan capital is an important source of finance for many businesses. The main benefit of a loan is that, unlike retained profit, it can enable a firm to expand rapidly. However, unlike share capital, taking on additional loan capital does not compromise ownership. Highly geared firms, whose share capital is made up mostly of loan capital, can be highly vulnerable to interest rate changes, particularly if they have not borrowed at a fixed rate. A sudden increase in the interest rate will increase their fixed costs, leading to lower profits.

Impacts on revenue

Interest rates influence spending in a variety of different ways. During the period from September 2006 to July 2007, the UK base rate of interest rose on five separate occasions, from 4.5% to 5.75%. Rising interest rates tend to depress consumer spending for the following reasons. First, they cut into disposable incomes.

Disposable income measures the amount of income a person has to spend once taxes, pensions and other fixed outgoings have been subtracted from gross pay. There are several reasons why an increase in interest rates leads to lower disposable incomes.

Mortgage repayments

Most houses are bought using a mortgage – a loan that is secured against the value of the property. If interest rates go up the person owning the mortgage will now have to pay back more to the bank each month in interest, cutting into their disposable income.

Figure 84.4 Most homes in the UK are bought using a mortgage

Consumer credit

The UK is addicted to credit. According to the pressure group Credit Action, total UK personal debt at the end of August 2007 stood at **£1363 billion**. The growth rate increased to 9.9% for the previous 12 months, which equates to an increase of £115 billion. If interest rates go up, those with large personal debts will find their monthly disposable incomes being cut. If interest rates stay high firms selling products such as cars and furniture, which are typically bought using a form of consumer credit, will probably suffer from falling sales.

Impacts on investment

The rate of interest can affect investment decisions. If interest rates rise, the cost of funding an investment project will also increase if the project is financed using borrowed money. For firms with cash in the bank that do not need to borrow, the interest rate can still affect investment decision making because the interest rate also affects the opportunity cost of investing. Interest rates also affect the reward for risk – the difference between an investment's expected profitability (its ARR) and the prevailing interest rate. So the higher the rate of interest the lower the level of investment spending by businesses.

Impacts on the exchange rate

A change in the interest rate tends to affect the exchange rate. If UK interest rates go up, wealthy foreign investors will be attracted to the pound: they will buy British pounds to take advantage of the high rates of interest that we offer. On the other hand, the reverse is also true. If the Bank of England decides to cut interest rates, the pound is likely to fall. The exchange rate is important for many businesses because it affects the price of imports and exports.

Evaluation

Interest rates changes are mostly likely to affect:

- firms that want to expand quickly, but that lack the retained profit to fund the expansion internally
- highly geared firms that need to borrow heavily to invest in the latest technology in order to remain competitive
- businesses that sell luxury goods or discretionary items that are typically bought on credit.

A sudden rise in interest rates can be a disaster, especially for a company that has just borrowed heavily in order to expand. An increase in the interest rate causes costs to rise and revenues to fall simultaneously. Watch those profits fall! Many firms have been surprised by a sudden unanticipated rise in interest rates and have been forced into liquidation as a result.

84.3 Supply-side policies

The government uses supply-side policies to increase the economy's productive capacity. In other words, it is an attempt to make it easier for UK firms to supply UK customers with the goods and services they require. For example, opening up postal deliveries to private-sector business was intended to force the state-owned Post Office to become more efficient.

Types of supply-side policy
Privatisation

This is the selling off of state-owned organisations to private-sector owners. Firms in the private sector have to make a profit to survive. In order to make a profit in competitive market firms must be efficient. Public-sector organisations do not have to make a profit to survive. Instead, their role is to provide public services. If a public-sector organisation is inefficient its survival is not normally threatened. This lack of fear of closure due to inefficiency arguably leads to low productivity and inefficient management. **Laissez-faire** economists that favour the free market believe that the private sector will always be more efficient than the public sector. Unfortunately this could only be true in circumstances where there is effective competition. The privatisation of the railways, for example, simply established a series of railway monopolies that have been free to push rail fares to among the highest in the world.

Deregulation

Deregulation involves removing legal barriers to entering an industry. Deregulation therefore can make markets more competitive. An increase in competition should lead to an increase in efficiency. The greater rivalry between firms will force all firms to find ways of cutting costs so that they can survive by cutting prices. Until recently the air travel market between the UK and America was highly regulated. To operate on this route, airlines had to apply to the UK and the American governments for take-off and landing 'slots'. In the past, 'slots' were granted only to a limited number of American and British airlines. This acted as a barrier to entry, limiting competition on this route. Arguably, these regulations encouraged inefficiency and high prices. In 2007, the UK and the American governments deregulated this market in a so-called 'open skies agreement'. Today, any airline can now fly on this route.

Increase the incentive to work

Unemployment benefits and other social security benefits could be reduced. Benefit entitlement rules could also be tightened. For example, only those that are prepared to attend job interviews will receive their benefits. Income tax rates could also be cut. The personal tax allowance could be increased, which will increase the financial benefit of taking a low-paid job compared to remaining unemployed and living off benefits. An increased incentive to work will help firms that need extra labour to expand. Wage rates may also fall.

Flexible labour market legislation

A **flexible labour market** is a labour market that favours the employer rather than the employee. The labour market can be made more flexible by passing laws that do the following.

- Enable employers to dismiss workers with few legal formalities (e.g. the employee receives no compensation and is not entitled to notice of dismissal). It could be argued that this situation encourages employers to take on new staff when they wish to grow because the same staff can be released quickly and at little cost in a downturn.

- Reduce non-wage labour costs for the employer (e.g. in the UK employers pay minimal maternity pay for six months). In Sweden working mothers receive two years' pay. It could be argued that low non-wage labour costs encourage UK firms to hire labour because it's cheaper to do so. The productive capacity of the economy should increase.

The UK labour market is a mixture of flexible and inflexible. The national minimum wage places an effective floor under wage rates. In America, the minimum wage is much lower than in Britain, providing lots of flexibility at the cost of lots of poverty.

Immigration

An influx of labour into a country will increase that country's labour supply, lifting the economy's productive capacity. Immigration can also help to ease skill shortages.

Education and training

If the government can increase the effectiveness of education and training within the economy, productivity (output per employee) should increase, which will help to lower costs. If the standard of education improves, the profitability of private-sector business investments should also increase. If it becomes more profitable for private businesses to invest they should respond, out of self-interest, by upping their investment levels. This will benefit the economy in general.

Transport infrastructure

If the government spends more money on upgrading Britain's road and rail networks, businesses should benefit. At present millions of pounds are lost each year because our roads are congested, and our railways are slow and antiquated. Like education, transport infrastructure is a form of complementary capital used by firms. If the quality of this infrastructure can be improved, the costs of operating a business in the UK will fall, increasing both the profitability and the desirability of investing in the UK.

Issues For Analysis

It is important to have an idea about the impact the Chancellor's decisions can have on businesses, but high marks for analysis will come from the ability to use economics to explain the impact on business. The starting point will be to think with care about the business itself. Is it affected by exchange rates? (Topshop definitely is, but *The Sun* newspaper is hardly affected at all.) In this topic area, there is a close overlap between application and analysis. A sharp increase in National Insurance charges would have a fierce impact on a labour-intensive business, but not on a capital-intensive one. The analysis depends on the circumstances.

84.4 Impact of government economic policy
an evaluation

There is an age-old story about the boy who cried 'wolf' so often that no one believed him when a real wolf arrived. Business lobby groups are like this. Disgracefully, BP spent years warning that a move to lead-free petrol would be a serious mistake. Similarly, lobby groups warned of a huge rise in unemployment if the government brought in a minimum wage; this proved untrue. Exam papers often feature new proposals by government – often opposed bitterly by business groups. No one should ever assume that business groups are unbiased in what they say. History shows that they argue their case fiercely, warning of dire consequences, and then keep quiet when the change proves absolutely fine. Governments have to make decisions, and cannot always rely on businesses to be open and supportive of change.

Key terms

Current account: the country's accounts, when subtracting the value of imports from the total value of exports. If exports > imports, the account is in surplus.
Flexible labour market: a labour market with light regulation, making it easy for employers to pay what they want, and hire and fire as they see fit.
Laissez-faire: literally, 'let it be'. In economics it means leaving private-sector businesses to operate free from government intervention.

Exercises

A. Revision questions

(40 marks; 40 minutes)

1 Distinguish between government economic objectives and economic policies. (4)

2 Explain why low inflation is an important government objective. (3)

3 Define the term fiscal policy. (3)

4 Explain two examples of businesses that could benefit from increased UK government spending on pensions. (4)

5 Show two ways in which Tesco might be affected by an increase in the UK's rate of corporation tax. (4)

6 Define the term monetary policy. (2)

7 Explain two reasons why the turnover of a posh French restaurant might be expected to fall following an increase in interest rates. (4)

8 Explain how a sharp increase in interest rates might affect a rapidly growing company such as Innocent Drinks. (6)

9 What are supply-side policies? (2)

10 Define the term privatisation. (2)

11 What is deregulation? (2)

12 Outline two reasons why the quality of education provided by the UK government might affect the profitability of Marks & Spencer. (4)

B. Revision exercises

B1 Data response

Campaign for better transport slams government plans for 'traffic hell'

The government predicts we will have to contend with 5.7 million more cars on our roads by 2031, a growth of 21%. Simply parking these cars would fill a 52-lane motorway all the way from Edinburgh to London. Worryingly, because we are also driving more, government forecasts show that traffic will increase even more – up 31% by 2025. The result will be 'traffic hell', warns Campaign for Better Transport: more traffic jams, longer journeys, more pollution and more stress. The organisation, formerly known as Transport 2000, is today outlining a better way forward for traffic.

Executive Director Stephen Joseph says, 'We can't go on like this – traffic is destroying our communities, our health and our environment. The Government must stop catering for all this traffic and instead give people and businesses good alternatives to driving. Campaign for Better Transport will continue the organisation's long-standing role of coming up with practical solutions to transport problems.'

Source: Campaign for Better Transport press release September 2007

Questions

(25 marks; 30 minutes)

1 The government predicts that there will be 5.7 million more cars on our roads by 2031. Outline two likely reasons that might explain why there might be more cars on our roads in the future. (4)

2 Give two examples of UK businesses that might benefit from greater car ownership. (2)

3 Identify and explain three costs of traffic congestion to a business of your choice. (6)

4 Motoring organisations such as the RAC and AA argue that the government should respond to the threat of growing congestion on the roads by building more roads and motorways. Examine two businesses in the UK that would gain greatly if the UK government decided to increase the amount of money spent on new building roads? (4)

5 Discuss whether UK manufacturers should consider factors such as pollution and stress when making decisions concerning how they should distribute their goods. (9)

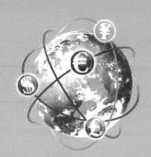

GOVERNMENT POLICIES AFFECTING BUSINESS

DEFINITION

The government policies covered in this unit are those that exclude economic policy – about which you have just read a whole unit. These government policies fall into two main categories: government initiatives to pass laws affecting business operations and government foreign policy towards international trade.

85.1 The European Union

Britain is a member of the European Union. The European Union is a community of countries that form a single market as a result of laws centred on the free movement of people, goods, services and capital between all member countries.

Tracing its roots back to the 1950s, the EU has undergone a series of expansions where extra countries joined the community, to a point where, at the time of writing, there are 27 member countries, creating a market including nearly 500 million people that generates over 30% of the world's economic activity. The map in Figure 85.1 shows the member countries, along with those countries hoping to join the EU at some point in the future.

EU Expansion

British governments of recent years have tended to be broadly supportive of EU expansion. There are strong economic arguments for the UK to support an expansion of the single European market, based upon two major factors.

1   EU enlargement means an increased size of market for UK exporters to other EU countries. Since a UK firm can sell its products in any other EU country without having to worry about paying import taxes or customs duties, membership of the EU provides UK firms with a 'home' market consisting not only of the 60 million or so who live in the UK, but the 500 million EU consumers. This can be contrasted with a similar situation for a US company with a home market of just over 300 million people. This larger

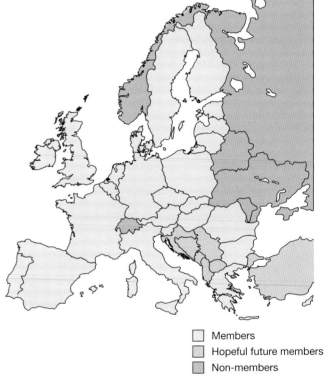

Members
Hopeful future members
Non-members

Figure 85.1 European Union membership

'home' market should give UK firms a competitive advantage over their US rivals.

2   Freedom of movement of people creates a source of cheap, often skilled labour for British firms, especially from newer EU members such as Poland and Romania. The issue of immigration is a controversial one, not just in the UK, but in most other western European countries. Extra workers put downward pressure on wage rates, which helps to prevent wage inflation. It also helps the economy to grow faster than its long-term trend growth rate. Unfortunately,

the benefit to business and to shoppers is not shared by British workers, some of whom will have their pay pushed down to minimum wage rate by the competition for jobs.

A-grade application

Immigrants run the UK economy

A 2006 Bank of England report on the effect of immigrant workers on the UK economy came up with some interesting findings. Relative to UK-born workers, immigrant workers are over-represented in low-paid sectors such as hotels, restaurants and unskilled jobs. Yet they are also over-represented in high-paid occupations (managers and professionals) and high-paid industries (finance, property and business activities). In general, immigrant workers are younger, better educated and work longer hours than those born in the UK. The report suggests that overall productivity within the UK could increase, with those in lower-paid occupations prepared to work harder, with higher skills levels, for less money. Good news for their UK employers!

Source: Bank of England Report ('The economic characteristics of immigrants and their impact on supply')

85.2 A single European currency

One political issue on which the UK has failed to join its European partners is that of the single currency, the euro. The UK government shows little sign of considering adopting the euro as the UK's currency. This means that UK firms lose the advantages that the single currency brings about. The central benefit is the ability to carry out international transactions without the need to worry about exchange rate fluctuations. At the time of writing (spring 2008) the pound has fallen by 15% against the euro within the past six months. This is potentially very costly to anyone (such as Majestic Wine) that imports a lot from euro countries such as France.

The UK government's view is that the UK's economy is not currently suited to adopting the euro. The concern is that any country that uses the euro has its monetary policy decided by the European Central Bank. It has to set one interest rate that is correct for all the economies that use the euro. If Germany needs high interest rates at a time when Britain needs low rates, will Britain's needs be taken fully into account? It may be many years before a UK government takes the plunge and starts the process of adopting the single currency, a process that

many feel should begin with a referendum of the whole UK electorate.

Table 85.1 EU members who use the single European currency (the euro)

Austria	Belgium	Cyprus
Finland	France	Germany
Greece	Ireland	Italy
Luxembourg	Malta	The Netherlands
Portugal	Slovenia	Spain

85.3 Free trade

The World Trade Organization (WTO), is an international organisation that seeks to promote free trade between nations, by creating agreements governing the way in which global trading is conducted. The ultimate goal of free trade would mean an end to all import taxes (tariffs), and physical limits on the amount of goods that can be imported to any country (quotas).

Though not all countries in the world have signed all the WTO's agreements, all major economies are members or are in the process of securing membership. The WTO also acts as a judge in disputes between countries where one feels another has broken free trade agreements. An example of this role is the WTO's investigation into the aircraft makers Airbus (Europe) and America's Boeing (both private-sector companies). The WTO is looking into whether each business has received illegal government subsidies to help them compete.

Free trade is a noble goal – the chance for the world economy to become truly efficient as those companies that do things best are able to offer their services globally. This would eliminate smaller, less efficient local rivals and improve the living standards of consumers around the world.

A government may be keen to protect jobs in its own country, by using trade barriers to discourage foreign competitors from entering the home market. For example, before the European Union, France 'protected' its wine makers from competition from Spain by placing an import tax on Spanish wines. Protectionist measures such as this give home producers a cost advantage. Governments may be keen to provide this protection to encourage the development of an industry that is new to a country. Other governments may be keen to protect certain industries to avoid job losses that might lead to an election defeat.

In every presidential election in America the candidates make speeches about 'protecting American jobs'. The World Trade Organization's job is to stop an election promise in America leading to job losses in Sheffield or Cairo.

A-grade application
The EU and USA at war

Despite generally cordial relations in many fields, there has long been a rather uneasy trading relationship between the EU and the USA. One recent row arose when the EU banned imports of US beef due to the overuse of growth hormone in 90% of US beef production. The US countered this threat by announcing that it was considering imposing 100% tariffs (effectively doubling the selling price) on a range of EU products, including Danish ham, French truffles and Belgian chocolates. At the same time, the two powers were still fighting a trade war based around bananas, with the USA claiming that the EU had provided unfair subsidies to non-US banana producers. The USA, in retaliation, had imposed quotas (physical limits on the volume of imports) on EU products including Scottish cashmere sweaters and French handbags. Eventually the storm was sorted out at the WTO. In the short term, though, things were very uncomfortable for the companies that produce the goods in the firing line.

85.4 Legislation

UK businesses are subject to laws (legislation) passed by both the UK parliament and also the European parliament. Since both UK and EU law are passed by parliaments, housing members of political parties, laws are affected by party politics.

Traditionally, it has been safe to assume that Conservative governments try to interfere as little as possible with the workings of business. In other words, the tendency is to take a laissez-faire approach. This means trusting businesses to do their best for their customers and employees – in other words, let the market regulate business activities.

Labour governments are more likely to be suspicious that businesses may act in their shareholders' interests, not those of their customers. Therefore there is a greater temptation to bring in laws to regulate business activity. Before the Labour government established the National Minimum Wage in 1999, employers could, and did, pay as little as £3 an hour. The October 2008 rate of £5.73 per hour is not riches, but provides some protection for the lower paid.

There are four main areas in which the law affects businesses:

1 employment

2 consumer protection

3 environmental protection

4 health and safety.

Employment legislation

Employment law sets out, and aims to protect, the rights of employees at work. These rights include the right to fair pay, sick leave, maternity and paternity leave, employment contracts being honoured, relationships with trades unions, the ability of employers to shed staff and the responsibilities of employers who make staff redundant.

As a general rule, businesses like to have minimal legal constraints on their activities. A business craves flexibility in the way it deals with its staff; legislation tends to impose certain restrictions on how staff are dealt with. UK business leaders argue that more employment legislation makes them uncompetitive relative to their international rivals. Yet UK employment legislation is not as tight as that in major rivals such as France and Germany.

Consumer protection legislation

Consumer protection law is designed to ensure that consumers are treated fairly by the companies from which they buy. This area of the law covers issues such as whether a product does what it claims to do, whether products are correctly labelled and measured out, levels of safety required from products, and the rights of the consumers after purchase for refunds or exchanges of faulty goods. Consumer protection legislation should ensure that no firms can gain an unfair competitive advantage by taking short-cuts in how their products are made. If all products and services must meet a minimum legal standard, this ensures against unscrupulous companies using unsafe and cheaper materials to gain a competitive edge.

Table 85.2 Implications of employment legislation

Key area of employment law	Possible implications for firms
Minimum wage	Increased labour costs, which may lead to increased automation in the longer term and increased unemployment; on the plus side, employees may be more motivated by a fair wage satisfying basic needs
Right to a contract of employment	Meets employees' security needs but can reduce employers' flexibility in how they use their staff
Increased right to sick, maternity and paternity leave	Increased cost of paying for cover for these staff; however, staff may feel more valued as they feel well treated by employers, reducing staff turnover levels, which saves the costs of recruiting new staff
Redundancy	Reducing capacity becomes expensive due to statutory payments to staff made redundant; this can mean that closing a factory or office has a negative impact on cash flow in the short term
Trades union rights	Employers can be forced to deal with a trades union if enough staff are members; this can bring both benefits and drawbacks.

Environmental protection legislation

Laws governing the impact of business on the environment are a key area today, given the increased acceptance of the need to legislate to protect the environment. A wide range of laws governs issues as diverse as the materials that firms must use for certain products, the processes firms are allowed to use in manufacturing and the extent to which firms must ensure their products are recyclable at the end of their lives. Environmental protection laws, perhaps more than any others, seem to most firms to be a source of additional cost without much of an upside. Firms in the UK are also subject to EU laws; this is an area in which several EU directives have led to increased expectations of businesses in terms of the ability to recycle their products at the end of their lives (see below). Of course, all these firms feel a sense of injustice that they are competing against firms in other countries with less stringent environmental laws, feeling that their international rivals have an unfair advantage when not having to meet the extra costs involved in abiding by environmental protection laws.

A-grade application

Recycling 8 million cars

The EU End-of-Life Vehicles (ELV) Directive became operational in 2002, stating that all car manufacturers are responsible for the disposal of any new vehicles sold after that time. Britain's Society of Motor Manufacturers and Traders (SMMT) estimated the cost to the UK car industry alone as £300 million per year.

Figures provided by Friends of the Earth show the scale of the issue. With over 8 million vehicles scrapped every year within Europe, cars are a major source of waste. Of the 8 million tons or so of waste generated, three-quarters is already recycled, however, 2 million tons is still an awfully large hole in the ground to try to dig every year.

However, by 2007, the UK was struggling to cope with the demands of the directive, with only around one-third of scrapped vehicle owners completing the correct procedures for ensuring that the disposal of their vehicle adheres to the ELV Directive. Media commentators were blaming the UK government for failing to establish an effective system for enforcing the directive.

Health and safety legislation

Health and safety legislation is designed to ensure the safety of employees and customers within the workplace. The Health & Safety at Work Act 1974 places the major burden on employers. They have to provide a safe working environment for their staff. The main areas covered by the legislation include the physical conditions in which staff are required to work, precautions that firms are required to take when planning their work and the way in which hazardous substances must be treated in the workplace.

Despite the tight laws in Britain, there are still a worrying number of deaths at work, as shown in Table 85.3. Even more striking is that there are as many as 200,000 workplace injuries a year. Health and Safety cannot be taken for granted.

Table 85.3 Deaths at work, 2006–2007

Industry sector	Number of workers killed
Agriculture, forestry and fishing	34
Manufacturing	35
Construction	77
Service industries	85
Extractive and utility supply	10
Overall	241

Source: Health & Safety Commission

Issues For Analysis

● One major argument relating to government policies revolves around the UK's possible future adoption of the single European currency (the euro). A vast array of arguments have been put forward both in favour of and against the UK adopting the euro. Many arguments are economic, while others tend to be more overtly political, relating to issues of political sovereignty and loss of independence as a nation. The arguments that will concern you will be those that have a direct impact on UK businesses, such as the stability of the exchange rate. As more than half of Britain's exports are to EU countries, joining the euro would remove a significant source of uncertainty for British firms.

● Many exam questions debate the need for laws to govern the activities of businesses – in other words, laissez-faire versus government intervention. It will be helpful to have thought about the extent to which businesses can be trusted to look after the best interests of their customers and employees.

85.5 Government policies affecting business

an evaluation

There is a danger of making an unchallenged assumption that all trade is good, so free trade is a must. This assumption can – and indeed should – be challenged in several ways. Nevertheless, the British have grown wealthy on an economic system that seems to work, so it is understandable that we urge other countries to follow our approach. This allows large businesses to be allowed to do many good things, but also many less good ones. Worst, perhaps, is the avoidance of tax. This robs the country of the income required to improve public services.

Legislation seeks to ensure that all firms compete on a 'level playing field'. This is a noble goal, yet with increased international trade, there are circumstances where one country's tough legislation is the reason why a company from that country fails to gain an international contract that is won by a company producing in a country with fewer laws affecting the cost they can offer the customer. The ultimate level playing field for businesses is one in which all countries have identical laws governing how businesses operate – and this is not going to happen in your lifetime.

For those who argue that laws are unnecessary because market forces will drive unscrupulous firms out of business, there is a disappointing lack of evidence to suggest that this argument holds water. Though plenty of businesses are convicted of breaking the law, it is a real challenge to find just one example of a firm that has been forced to close as a result of doing so. Is the incentive to avoid prosecution strong enough?

Exercises

A. Revision questions

(25 marks; 25 minutes)

1 What is the name of the international organisation that seeks to regulate trade between nations? (1)

2 Explain the benefits that businesses gain from being based in an EU country. (5)

3 Briefly describe the main aims of the following legislation:
   (a) employment laws
   (b) consumer protection law
   (c) environmental protection law
   (d) health and safety law. (8)

4 Explain two possible consequences of a tightening of environmental protection laws for one of the following:
   (a) a supermarket
   (b) a chemical manufacturer
   (c) a bank. (6)

5 Briefly explain why many firms would welcome a relaxation of employment laws affecting the rights of part-time staff. (5)

B. Revision exercises

B1 Case study

The success of Cheapotels had caught analysts by surprise. There had seemed to be little demand in the UK for really cheap hotel accommodation until charismatic entrepreneur Rob Doyle launched the first five Cheapotels on an unsuspecting UK market three years ago. Since then, Rob has barely been out of the tabloids, pulling off all manner of publicity stunts to keep the brand in the public eye. He has also managed to open in another 13 locations across the UK.

Based on what Rob describes as a hardcore version of the 'no frills' philosophy that brought easyGroup success in the 1990s airline market,

Cheapotel buys up cheap property in poor parts of major UK cities and offers a bare room with a bed and washbasin at a flat cost of £20 per room per night. Targeting young consumers has allowed Cheapotel to build a customer base around nightclubbers, stag and hen parties, and students coming out of late-night gigs.

Much of the firm's success has been attributed to Rob's marketing wizardry; however, deeper below the surface lies a clever extension of a well-known fact about the UK hotel market: a vast proportion of UK hotel workers are from other EU countries, working in the UK at minimum wage level. A total of 95% of Rob's staff are from eastern European EU countries and Rob himself admits that wages are low. In addition, staffing levels are tiny relative to other hotels, with a minimal cleaning staff and just one receptionist/manager on duty in each location at any one time.

Contrary to all expectations, Cheapotel is profitable after just three years' trading, and despite very low profit margins, Rob is confident that this profitability can continue. He is confident enough to be planning to open in another 20 locations within the next 18 months, including Cheapotels in Prague, Krakow, Budapest and Bucharest.

Questions

(30 marks; 30 minutes)

1 Analyse the reasons why Rob Doyle is likely to support further EU expansion. (8)

2 Explain why the case of Cheapotel can be used to illustrate the need for employment protection law. (6)

3 The front page of today's *Sun* features photos of a Cheapotel corridor with three rats running through it. Use the case study to discuss whether consumer protection law is necessary or whether market forces can be relied upon to ensure that customers receive a decent service. (16)

B2 Case study

Maintaining a legal factory is a lot harder than you might expect – just ask Dave Maisey, managing director of Forbes Bricks Ltd. Forbes is one of a handful of bespoke brick makers left in the UK. It can tailor-make any shape, size, colour or material of brick – a feature that explains its enduring popularity among those looking for masonry to restore or maintain older properties. A medium-sized firm, Forbes owns a single factory, in Kent, with a loyal workforce of skilled and semi-skilled staff. Dave, however, has the look of a tired man. Charged with managing most aspects of the business, Dave is also ultimately responsible for the firm's compliance with the legislation affecting the business. His biggest headache, he says, is health and safety legislation: 'They just don't seem to understand that making bricks is a dusty business. You can't make bricks without dust, and the inspector we had round the other week was measuring dust levels all round the shop floor, tutting as she went.'

The inspector from the HSE (Health & Safety Executive) was at the plant to measure the level of dust particles in the air and to assess the measures taken by the firm to ensure that staff suffered no long-term respiratory damage from the dusty working conditions.

Dave continued: 'I'd only just finished a full risk assessment on the new kiln we've bought, so luckily I managed to impress her with that. The inspector went over the accident record book, and our whole Health & Safety manual. I spent the whole day with her, time I could have spent out on the road finding new business, or working with the boys in the materials in section to find a better solution to some of the stock-holding issues we've had recently.'

Two weeks after the inspector's visit, Dave called a meeting of the firm's directors to discuss the recommendation from the HSE: to spend an extra £105,000 on extractor units to reduce the dust levels in the air to standards acceptable under UK and EU law. Dave was also dreading the opportunity to see what Purchasing Director Andy Hemmings had discovered when he had visited a similar factory in China the previous month. Dave feared that Andy may have found a factory with poor working conditions, paying well below Forbes' rates to staff and offering similar bricks at half the price.

Questions

(35 marks; 40 minutes)

1 Analyse three reasons why Dave seems unhappy about the legislation affecting Forbes Bricks Ltd. (9)

2 Outline Dave's general responsibilities to his staff according to UK Health & Safety law. (6)

3 To what extent does the case study illustrate the problems of different countries adopting different legal standards in a world encouraging free trade? (20)

C. Essay questions

(40 marks each)

1 'Businesses will continue to infringe the law until the penalties they face are strong enough to hurt the individuals running those businesses.' To what extent is this statement accurate?

2 'Further expansion of the EU represents a great opportunity for large UK companies wishing to become global players.' Discuss why this may or may not be the case.

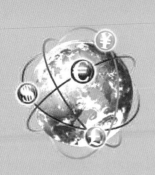

HOW FIRMS RESPOND TO POTENTIAL AND ACTUAL CHANGES

DEFINITION

Potential changes are those that may be needed in future; actual changes are those that have really happened.

86.1 What changes need to be addressed?

Operating in a changing environment is an inescapable reality for businesses. Business success depends on how firms respond to both potential and actual changes. The list of changes below suggests the major external causes of changes to which firms will need to find a response. All the changes are covered elsewhere in this book, so the rest of this unit will focus on the following responses to these external changes.

- Economic factors and trends in economic variables – Unit 82 deals with the impact on firms of the major economic variables:
  - the business cycle and economic growth
  - interest rates
  - exchanges rates
  - unemployment
  - inflation.

- Globalisation of markets – covered in Unit 84.

- Emerging markets – the growth of China and India is covered in Unit 92, while other emerging markets are covered in Units 83 and 85 (government policies affecting business).

Responses to change

Responses to change will vary from short-term actions to major changes in the firm's long-term plans. Short-term changes are known as tactical responses, while a long-term change to the firm's overall plans is considered to be a strategic change.

The rest of this unit will consider strategic changes, rather than tactical measures.

86.2 Marketing strategy

Product portfolio

Changes to the products made by the firm may represent a sensible response to external change. The basic choice is likely to be between expansion or reduction of the product portfolio. Should the firm launch new products to exploit a newly created opportunity? A firm expecting an economic downturn may consider the option of producing a low-cost version of a best-selling product that is likely to appeal in times when money is tighter. Alternatively, the chance to break into a new market, offered by political change, may result in the need to add a brand new product to the portfolio, specifically designed to cater to the needs of that market. For instance, in 2008 India still refused to allow large foreign retail companies to operate in the country. Tesco and others would love to have a presence in the world's second most populous country (1100 million and rising). As yet they cannot. If and when the Indian government changes its mind, there will be a mad rush to be the first supermarket chain into India. The clever ones have already got their plans in place.

Reduction of the product portfolio may also make sense in some cases. External change may make some existing products poor sellers overnight, in which case a firm may decide to drop these immediately.

Image shift

Some external changes may prompt a shift in corporate image. A UK company suffering from increased global competition may find that it can gain a competitive advantage by pushing the 'Britishness' of the brand. Not only could this boost UK sales, but other markets may be keen to buy into a brand that plays on its Britishness, such as Burberry or Aston Martin.

Figure 86.1 Burberry has used 'Britishness' to gain a competitive advantage

86.3 Financial strategy

Sources of finance

Responding to changes usually requires cash. Whether launching a new product or laying off staff, some cash outlay will be involved. Therefore financially a firm needs to consider carefully the sources of finance it uses. Increased interest rates make borrowing more expensive and therefore less attractive as a means of raising capital. On the other hand, a booming stock market would mean that expected dividend payments may make share capital more expensive than loan capital. Careful assessment of the gearing ratio in the light of the external change will be the major analysis that needs to be conducted prior to deciding on an appropriate source of finance.

Returning cash to shareholders

At times, external changes lead to rationalisation, ranging from the sale of fixed assets to the sale of an entire subsidiary company. This will generate cash for the business. In some cases, firms may seek to protect their return on capital by buying back shares or returning cash to shareholders. This takes the cash off their balance sheet and therefore out of their capital employed. The result is that, without increasing operating profit, the firm's ROCE will be boosted.

86.4 Operations strategy

Update facilities

External change may be the stimulus behind a firm's decisions to upgrade its production facilities. Upgrading should boost efficiency and mean that the firm either gains a competitive edge or simply keeps up with competitors who are taking advantage of the same opportunity.

Consider a new location

Changes that are likely to lead to increased demand may well prompt the construction of new facilities. This will allow the firm to increase its capacity in anticipation of increased levels of sales. It is important to consider how long it will take to make these new facilities operational. Major new construction projects – perhaps a new, state-of-the-art factory for a manufacturer – may well take in excess of a year. If the firm needs to react more quickly, there is another option available: subcontracting.

Subcontracting

Contracting another firm to carry out work for you is a far quicker way of increasing overall capacity. In the case of sudden change this may be a useful alternative to building brand new facilities. Firms such as Nike and Gap tend to use subcontracting for most if not all of their production, since it offers greater flexibility. However, the experience of these firms, most notably criticism for poor treatment of workers in their subcontractors' plants, reveals a major problem. The business is losing control over the day-to-day operational side of its own production. This may lead to quality control problems or raise doubts on the part of customers. In 2007, the 'Norfolk turkey' business Bernard Matthews lost credibility because it became clear that many of its turkeys actually came from eastern Europe.

Close facilities

Firms that decide demand is falling in the long term may decide to close some of their facilities permanently. These decisions, taken at the very highest level of the organisation, will be expensive, with redundancy payments and decommissioning costs to cover. However, in the long run they will allow a firm to

duce its fixed cost base to a level that makes break-
en easier to achieve. In some cases, closure may in
ct be a relocation – with a firm closing an operation in
ne country in order to shift operations to another,
ually in search of lower costs.

A-grade application

Ford

Ford US has suffered from problems of overcapacity
since Honda, Toyota and Volkswagen started chipping
away at its market share. For several years Ford tried to
find marketing solutions to rebuild its market share. Faced
with losses measured in billions of dollars in 2007, Ford
decided to start a programme of factory closures,
beginning in 2008; 16 plants were to be closed, with
30,000 jobs lost. The board would have been unlikely
to take such a drastic step without accepting that the firm
faced no other option. In effect, Ford is admitting that it
has lost the market share permanently.

36.5 HR strategy

orkforce planning is designed to incorporate the
anges the firm expects into its management of its
ople. Really good workforce planning will anticipate
ange and will already have started to respond to the
plications of the change in ensuring that the firm has
e right number of staff, with the right skills in the right
aces within the organisation. This will be achieved
rough a mix of a long-term approach to recruiting
ff, using training to equip staff with the skills needed
lowing the change, and perhaps also carefully
edding staff who will no longer be required. This is far
s painful if achieved over the long run, through
tural wastage, than a quick hit of redundancies.

A-grade application

Workforce planning at BMW

BMW announced in early 2008 that it was to reduce
its German-based production staff by 2500, around 3%
of the total workforce. At the same time, the firm
announced a new training initiative to equip staff with
the skills required for the company's new products.
Elsewhere, the firm is planning to raise production levels
in the USA (to overcome the problem of the weak dollar)
and China (to take advantage of its booming car
market). BMW also opened a new factory in India in
2007. Careful workforce planning ensured that all
2500 redundancies would be voluntary, with new jobs
on offer to many of the staff.

Retraining

Firms that value the loyalty and experience of their staff
may be able to adapt to change by retraining their
existing staff. This would be a major undertaking for the
HR department and would be likely to require a
substantial investment. However, in return, the firm
would maintain the flexibility that people offer over
machinery, while it would also hope to benefit from
continued high levels of motivation within a workforce
that feels valued.

Flexibility

In itself, creating a more flexible workforce may be an
appropriate response to a change, or indeed an
increasing rate of change. Workforce flexibility can be
achieved through two fundamental routes. Building a
staff that possess adaptable skills and are keen to
embrace changes can allow a firm to maintain the agility
needed to cope with change. Alternatively, a firm may
choose to follow a model suggested by management
thinker Charles Handy. He suggests keeping a small
permanent ('core') staff whose major role is to
coordinate specialist contractors hired on fixed-term
contracts to fit the particular need faced by the firm at
the time. The latter are the 'peripheral' workers.

Table 86.1 Summary of common responses to change

Marketing	Finance	Operations	HR
New products	Raise extra finance	Update facilities	Workforce planning
Ditch existing products	Return cash to shareholders	Close facilities	Recruit
Image shift	When change is rapid, check variance against budget	Subcontract	Shed staff
Use Boston Matrix to appraise portfolio	Consider actions to lower fixed costs and therefore break even	Build new plants or consider relocation	Retraining to increase flexibility

Issues For Analysis

- A crucial analytical question is suggested by this unit's title. Potential and actual changes will provoke differing responses from different firms. Those whose culture is more accepting of change are more likely to think about, discuss and plan for potential change. Other businesses are more likely to hope that change does not happen. Of course, anticipating changes might look foolish if the expected changes do not occur. On the other hand, slower-moving firms, with bureaucratic cultures, are unlikely to respond to change until after it has occurred. Though seemingly safer, such an approach may lead to failure in the long term as the firm ends up falling far behind its more flexible rivals.

- Responses to change will also offer the opportunity to consider several options. Breaking down a firm's choices, and assessing the pros and cons of each choice of action is exactly the analytical approach that Business Studies seeks to promote. Rest assured that any large firm considering how it should respond to change will go through a process similar to that which you should expect to demonstrate in an exam.

86.6 How firms respond to potential and actual changes an evaluation

Judging the correct response to potential or actual changes is an area where evaluation is likely to be needed. Straightforward judgements as to the best possible response to change will be enhanced if they are clearly rooted in the context being considered. A firm with limited finances, operating on a national scale and seeking merely to survive will probably respond in a very different way to a successful multinational firm. Answers showing an awareness of the impact of a firm's current position on its response to change will be better rewarded.

However, it is worth reflecting carefully on any changes to which a response is required. Some firms may actually be better off not responding, or at least waiting to see what happens – the dotcom boom of 2001 drove many firms out of business as a result of their eagerness to respond rapidly to a perceived change that they had misjudged. On the other hand, external changes could be the right time to make bold strategic moves such as a switch to an entirely different market. Above all else, though, be aware of the possibilities of failing to effectively 'read' the effects of the change appropriately. No business can forecast exactly how the future will turn out, and those that respond with flexibility may be better equipped to deal with the unexpected.

Exercises

A. Revision questions

(48 marks; 50 minutes)

1 (a) Identify three recent changes that may
       have affected major oil companies such
       as Shell and BP.   (3)

   (b) Explain how *one* of those changes may
       have affected Shell or BP.   (4)

   (c) Analyse the likely response of the oil
       company to the change explained in
       part b.   (5)

2 Analyse two ways in which a confectionery
   manufacturer might respond to a tightening of
   the laws governing the advertising of unhealthy
   foods.   (8)

3 Explain why workforce planning should help
   firms to respond effectively to *one* of the
   following potential changes:
   (a) the opening up of India's retail market to
       western supermarkets   (6)
   (b) a severe US recession that is hitting
       consumer confidence in Britain.   (6)

4 Analyse two possible responses by British Airways
   to the arrival of competition from budget airlines
   on the profitable London–New York route.   (8)

5 Analyse two possible marketing responses by a
   UK manufacturer of premium ice cream to a
   general worsening of the state of the UK's
   economy.   (8)

B. Revision exercises

B1 Case study

G & A McInnes Ltd is a major manufacturer of
mobile phone accessories. Though well
established in the mobile phone market, it has
only been around for 15 years. It has enjoyed a
spectacular rise from market stall to UK's number
one supplier of mobile accessories. The
company's growth has been very hard to
manage for brothers Gary and Adam. However,
through a mixture of clever management and a

heavy dose of luck, the firm evolved from a
Glasgow market stall into a company employing
248 head office and sales staff. By 2007, new
designs were being created weekly at head
office, sent to trusted Chinese manufacturers and
shipped back to regional distribution centres in
Europe. From these, the firm delivers direct to the
retailers that stock the low-priced product range.
Having started out in the UK, the company now
sells in every EU market. The firm currently sells
only in European markets.

As the new year dawned, Gary and Adam
talked over the changes facing the firm. A
summary of the major issues is shown below:

- changes in economic growth rates in both the
  UK and EU
- increased flak from pressure groups over the
  plastics used to manufacture the products,
  many of which are perceived by consumers
  as disposable
- handset manufacturers are broadening their
  own ranges of accessories, and adding more
  to the original phone bundles.

Gary had gathered a variety of numerical data
that he considered relevant to the decision-
making process they faced. Adam was
particularly keen on breaking away from the
firm's reliance on the European market. He felt
that the time was right to expand geographically.
He wanted to look into the possibilities offered
by the rapidly developing Brazilian economy. He
had brought his own data to the meeting to help
to convince Gary that the firm's immediate future
lay in South America. The weakening pound
suggested to Adam that the firm may be better off
operating from its existing facilities in Europe and
simply exporting to Brazil. He did not, however,
rule out the possibility of building a distribution
centre in Brazil that could accept deliveries
straight from its Far Eastern suppliers.

The brothers had plenty to discuss. Gary was
unconvinced of the need for further expansion.
He was concerned that the firm's growth had
been too rapid and that they had allowed costs
to spiral out of control. Perhaps they should
spend the next few years consolidating the firm's
position and boosting profitability by seeking to

reduce cost levels without any focus on boosting turnover.

Strategic options:

1 consolidation – stay put, boost profits by cutting costs

2 export to Brazil – products still delivered to EU distribution centres, then sent directly to Brazilian retailers

3 build facilities in Brazil – construct a new distribution centre in Brazil that can accept products directly from China.

Questions

(70 marks; 80 minutes)

1 Analyse the possible implications for the firm of the following changes in the case study.

(a) The forecast changes in economic growth in both the UK and EU. (10)

(b) Increased criticism from pressure groups over the plastics used to manufacture the products, many of which are perceived by consumers as disposable. (10)

(c) Handset manufacturers are broadening their own ranges of accessories, and adding more to the original phone bundles. (10)

2 Make a fully justified recommendation to the firm on which of the three strategic options to pursue. (40)

Table 86.2 Slowdown in EU markets

	This year	**Next year**	**2 years' time**	**3 years' time**
UK GDP growth (%)	2.1	2.0	2.2	2.7
EU GDP growth (%)	1.4	1.1	1.0	1.4
World GDP growth (%)	3.2	2.5	2.9	3.6

Table 86.3 Data for Brazil

	This year	**Next year**	**2 years' time**	**3 years' time**
GDP growth (%)	5.3	5.0	5.1	5.4
Mobile phones per 1000 people	636	662	686	695
% houses with broadband	2.3	4.6	7.2	9.3

B2 Case study

Altria Inc. is one of the world's largest firms. Its best-known brand, Marlboro, became increasingly socially unacceptable during the late twentieth century. Yet the firm generates healthy, multi-billion-dollar profits each year.

Altria was the new name selected by the owners of the Phillip Morris group of companies – a group whose success was founded on its portfolio of cigarette brands, headed by Marlboro. Founded in 1860 in London, the company moved to the USA by the start of the twentieth century and, until 1970, was a highly successful cigarette manufacturer. In 1970 it acquired the Miller Brewing Company, adding beer to cigarettes.

By the 1980s the health dangers of smoking had become clear and social pressures had increased. Increasingly tough legislation on the advertising and sale of cigarettes led to the start of the long-term decline in smoking in the developed world. Therefore, in 1988, the company bought Kraft Foods, to add to a smaller food company taken over three years earlier. By 2000, the group had extended its food portfolio still further, acquiring Jacobs Suchard and Nabisco. This diversified portfolio, along with a healthy US economy in the 1990s, brought the firm great success.

The twenty-first century saw Altria's strategy reversed. Instead of acquiring new businesses, the management began to sell off divisions. Kraft Foods was sold in 2007, while 2008 was expected to see the firm sell off the international division of its cigarette manufacturing operation. The sell-offs were primarily designed to boost earnings per share, as the divisions being sold were less profitable than the remaining divisions. At the same time, the firm was making substantial lay-offs at its US tobacco manufacturing facilities, designed to reduce overheads. This would enable the firm to keep stock markets happier with its financial performance at a time when the major western economies were beginning to see an economic slowdown.

Questions

(40 marks; 50 minutes)

1 Discuss whether the company's acquisitions between 1970 and 2001 represented a wise strategy given the social and market changes outlined in the case. (15)

2 Examine the possible impact of the two sell-offs of 2007 and 2008 on the company's financial performance. (5)

3 To what extent does the fact that 'the twenty-first century saw Altria's strategy reversed' prove that it was the wrong strategy in the first place? (20)

C. Essay questions

(40 marks each)

1 To what extent is the ability to respond effectively to external changes the key to success in the modern global marketplace?

2 Discuss the possible strategic responses available to a UK high-street music retailer faced with a steady increase in the amount of music and film downloads from online retailers.

3 'There is a danger in responding too rapidly to potential changes.' Discuss the truth of this statement in the context of a car manufacturer.

BUSINESS ETHICS

87.1 What are business ethics?

Ethics can be defined as a code of behaviour considered morally correct. Our individual ethics are shaped by a number of factors, including the values and behaviour of our parents or guardians, those of our religion, our peers, and the society in which we live and work.

Business ethics can provide moral guidelines for the conduct of business affairs. This is based on some assertion of what is right and what is wrong. An ethical decision means doing what is morally right. It is not a matter of scientifically calculating costs, benefit and profit. Most actions and activities in the business world have an ethical dimension. This has been highlighted recently in relation to whole industries (such as the alcohol industry) and to businesses that use cheap labour in less developed countries.

Two major influences shape the moral behaviour of businesses. First, an organisation is composed of individuals, who all have their own moral codes, values and principles. Naturally they bring these to bear on the decisions that they have to make as a part of their working lives. Second, businesses have cultures that shape corporate ethical standards. These two factors combine to determine the behaviour of businesses in a variety of circumstances having an ethical dimension.

The extract below illustrates a situation in which the corporate culture may well be dominant. Texas Instruments prepares its employees to take ethical decisions at all levels within the organisation. If unsure, employees are urged to seek advice from their line manager rather than make a decision that may be unethical.

Figure 87.1
The Values and Ethics of TI

Ethics at Texas Instruments (TI)

The booklet, *The Values and Ethics of TI*, defines the culture of ethics within the company and is now in its eighth revision since 1961. All TI's employees are given this booklet to guide them in making decisions that are ethical.

TI's board of directors established an ethics office in 1987 and appointed the company's first ethics director. Its ethics director and staff have three primary functions:

1 ensure that business policies and practices are continuously aligned with ethical principles
2 clearly communicate ethical expectations
3 provide multiple channels for feedback, through which stakeholders may ask questions, voice concerns and seek resolution of ethical issues.

The TI ethics director reports to the Audit Committee of the board of directors and serves on an oversight group, the TI Ethics and Compliance Committee. The ethics director is also responsible for updating the TI Ethics and Compliance Committee, the Audit Committee of the board of directors and the president and CEO on a regular basis.

There are things at TI that haven't changed, and we're working hard to make sure they don't change. We've had values and principles that have guided us very well through 75 years. I have learned first-hand the level of ethics at TI and how much a leadership position it is for us. *(David Reid, TI's Vice President and Director of Ethics)*

Source: www.ti.com/corp/docs/csr/downloads/corp_citz_reports/csr_corpcitz_rpt_2006.pdf, pp. 45, 46

87.2 Business ethics and business objectives

A useful starting point may be to consider business objectives in relation to ethical behaviour. We can pose the question 'Why do businesses exist?' For many businesses the answer would be 'to make the maximum profit possible in order to satisfy the owners of the business'.

Some notable academics support this view. Milton Friedman, a famous American economist, held the view that all businesses should use the resources available to them as efficiently as possible. Friedman argued that making the highest possible profit creates the maximum possible wealth, to the benefit of the whole society.

Friedman's view, however, ignores the fact that many individuals and groups – the stakeholders – have an interest in each and every business. We could argue that to meet the demands of stakeholders means that a business has to take morally correct decisions. The following scenarios illustrate circumstances in which maximising profits conflicts with **stakeholder interests**.

Scenario 1

Tobacco companies have responded to declining sales in the western world by increasing production and sales in Asia and Latin America. Consumers in these countries are less knowledgeable about the dangers of smoking and more likely to purchase potentially harmful products.

Oxford University Professors Richard Peto and Rory Colins have monitored death rates from tobacco in several developing countries, including China. Their research has revealed that worldwide deaths from tobacco are likely to increase from about 4 million per year at present to about 10 million per year by the 2040s. An estimated 70% of these deaths will be in developing countries.

A-grade application

The tobacco industry's response to the advertising ban in the UK: subverting the science

The tobacco industry continues to promote its products aggressively, especially to young people and those in developing countries.

Evidence shows that the industry has sought to cast doubt on good-quality scientific research that demonstrates the causal link between tobacco and disease, and especially the link between passive smoking and lung cancer.

The tobacco industry has been known to recruit scientists and doctors to express views favourable to the industry. In 'Project Whitecoat', tobacco consultants were found to have infiltrated a select committee of the House of Commons, *The Lancet* and the International Agency for Research into Cancer (IARC), among others.

The tobacco industry has also commissioned studies designed to discredit accepted scientific principles, such as reviews casting doubt on epidemiological findings, especially in relation to passive smoking.

Studies funded by the tobacco industry have purported to identify other risk factors behind the ill-health of smokers' partners, such as low intake of vegetables. These carefully orchestrated studies often receive prominence in the media and, although refuted by sound health experts, send out damaging messages that smokers use to falsely reassure themselves of the health risks of their habit.

Source: Cancer Research UK (http://info.cancerresearchuk.org/publicpolicy/briefings/prevention/tobaccocontrol/industrystactics/?a=5441)

Scenario 2

Should a retailer seek to sell alcohol (which has potential to damage health if excessive quantities are consumed) at very low prices and possibly at a loss? This loss leader pricing strategy is designed to attract consumers into a particular shop in the hope that they will also buy full-price (and profitable) products as well. Are profits more important than the health of consumers, or are people able to make informed decisions about their own spending behaviour?

Shop alcohol offers 'unethical'

Alcohol charities and doctors' leaders have criticised supermarkets for offering "unethical" cut-price deals on drink over the festive season.

Alcohol Focus Scotland and the British Medical Association (BMA) in Scotland said "deep discounting" by major retailers leads to binge drinking and the Scottish Government has said it would ban "irresponsible" off-sales deals.

The Wine and Spirit Trade Association (WSTA) said the price of alcohol is not a major factor in consumption levels.

Gillian Bell, from the charity Alcohol Focus Scotland, said: "Alcohol's never been more affordable – it's 62% cheaper now than it was in 1980.

"Supermarkets, particularly at this time year, enter price wars and as soon as you enter the shops, you see a variety of drinks stacked up – all on special offer – that's something we're really concerned about.

"When you can buy beer cheaper than water, that's a major problem and it's not surprising that we're seeing spiralling liver disease rates and alcohol-related deaths."

Source: Adapted from BBC News, December 2007
(http://news.bbc.co.uk/1/hi/scotland/7155825.stm)

87.3 The developing ethical environment

A number of high-profile accidents in the late 1980s led to calls for businesses to act in more socially responsible ways and to put moral considerations before profits. Incidents such as the disastrous fire on the North Sea oil rig *Piper Alpha* in 1988 prompted demands for greater ethical accountability. The pressures on UK businesses increased as a series of investigations exposed fraudulent activities at a number of high-profile companies, including the Bank of Credit and Commerce International (BCCI) and Guinness.

This move towards changing corporate cultures was strengthened as a result of the report of the Cadbury Committee in 1992. One of the recommendations of the Committee was to reinforce the role of non-executive directors. It was hoped that these independent directors would encourage a more ethical culture in corporate decision making. Non-executive directors do not take an active role in the management of the company and are well placed to control unethical practices.

Figure 87.2 A fire on the Piper Alpha North Sea oil rig in 1988

Changing corporate cultures is not easy to achieve even when external pressures are encouraging such change. Texas Instruments (profiled earlier) took the view that ethical behaviour began at the grassroots of the company. Its management contended that, for a business to behave ethically, all its employees must behave ethically. The quote below highlights one of the ways in which the management team at Texas Instruments endeavours to create an ethical culture within the business.

> Is the action legal?
> Does it comply with our values?
> If you do it, will you feel bad?
> How will it look in the newspaper?
> If you know it's wrong, don't do it.
> If you are not sure, ask.
> Keep asking until you get an answer.

Source: Texas Instruments website (www.ti.com)

Texas Instruments issues this advice to all employees on a business card.

By attempting to ensure that all staff within the organisation behave in an agreed ethical manner, companies seek to avoid the potential conflict of ethics and delegation. In organisations where the culture of ethical behaviour does not extend beyond senior (and perhaps middle) managers, delegation brings risks. Delegation in such circumstances may result in junior staff taking decisions that may be regarded as immoral or unethical.

Other companies have operated on ethical principles since their inception. Innocent Drinks is well known for its strong ethical stance. The extract below, taken from the company's website, summarises Innocent's position.

Our ethics
We sure aren't perfect, but we're trying to do the right thing

It might make us sound a bit like a Miss World contestant, but we want to leave things a little bit better

than we find them. We strive to do business in a more enlightened way, where we take responsibility for the impact of our business on society and the environment, and move these impacts from negative to neutral, or better still, positive. It's part of our quest to become a truly sustainable business, where we have a net positive effect on the wonderful world around us.

One of the most significant developments in corporate ethical behaviour in recent years has been the move towards sustainability. Sustainable production means that a business seeks to supply its products in such a way as not to compromise the lives of future generations by, for example, damaging the environment or depleting non-renewable resources. A common feature of this aspect of ethical behaviour is the desire to reduce the company's 'carbon footprint' or even to become a carbon-neutral business. Some businesses find this an easier stance to adopt than others. In 2005, HSBC, one of the world's largest banks with 10,000 offices in 76 countries, announced that it was to become carbon neutral. The bank estimated the cost in the first year of carbon-neutral trading would be under £4 million. Other businesses have found it more difficult to reduce or eliminate their carbon footprints, especially those in the manufacturing sector. However, a wide range of businesses in the UK have recognised the marketing benefits of taking this kind of ethical stance. The Eurostar story in the A-grade application illustrates the importance of sustainability in the transport industry. It also shows how Eurostar can use it as a competitive weapon against rivals such as easyJet and other budget airlines.

A-grade application
Eurostar goes carbon neutral

All Eurostar journeys from the new St Pancras International Station will be carbon neutral thanks to offsetting, recycling – and fuller carriages.

From November 2007, all Eurostar journeys will be completely carbon neutral, making it the world's first footprint-free method of mass transport. The impact of rail travel between London and Paris or Brussels had always been at least ten times lighter than the equivalent journey by plane, a traveller generating 11 kilograms of carbon dioxide compared with 122 by his or her counterpart on the plane. It is, the company says, the difference between enough CO_2 to fill a Mini and the amount needed to fill a double-decker bus.

Figure 87.3 New Eurostar journeys will be carbon neutral

But by making a raft of new changes across the business – from installing energy meters on all trains to tightening up on recycling and making 'train capacity efficiencies' (filling every seat, in other words) – the operator is lightening its environmental load. In addition, it has set itself a new target of reducing its carbon dioxide emissions per passenger by a quarter by 2012.

Source: *Daily Telegraph*
(www.telegraph.co.uk/travel/eurostar/738814/Eurostar-the-eco-express.html)

87.4 Ethical codes of practice

An example of an ethical code of practice is:

> To meaningfully contribute to local, national and international communities in which we trade by adopting a code of conduct that ensures care, honesty, fairness and respect.

As a response to consumer expectations and competitive pressures, businesses have introduced **ethical codes** of practice. These are intended to improve the behaviour and image of a business. The box below, about the Institute of Business Ethics (IBE), highlights the extent to which UK businesses have appreciated the importance of being seen to behave ethically. Furthermore, the very existence of the IBE is evidence of the growing importance of this aspect of business behaviour.

The Institute of Business Ethics (IBE)

The IBE was established in 1986 to encourage high standards of business behaviour based on ethical values. Its vision: 'To lead the dissemination of knowledge and good practice in business ethics.'

The IBE raises public awareness of the importance of doing business ethically, and collaborates with other UK and international organisations with interests and expertise in business ethics.

It helps businesses to strengthen their ethics culture and encourage high standards of business behaviour based on ethical values. It assists in the development, implementation and embedding of effective and relevant ethics and corporate responsibility policies and programmes. It helps organisations to provide guidance to staff and build relationships of trust with their principal stakeholders.

IBE research

In 2003, IBE research found that companies with a code of ethics financially outperformed those without. Now, most firms (85 of the FTSE100) have codes of ethics and so having a code is no longer a clear sign of being 'more ethical'; it is not sufficient to act as a unique selling point (USP). A commitment to embedding ethical values into business practice through a training programme differentiates companies from those that simply declare a commitment to ethical values.

The results of the IBE's research reveal that companies with a demonstrable ethics programme benefit from the confidence that is instilled in their stakeholders. This helps to build the company's reputation, enhances relations with bankers and investors, assists firms in attracting better employees, increases goodwill, leaves the firms better prepared for external changes, turbulence and crisis, and generally helps the firm run better.

Source: Institute of Business Ethics
(http://www.ibe.org.uk/DBEP%20Revisited.pdf)

An ethical code of practice is a document setting out the way a business believes its employees should respond to situations that challenge their integrity or social responsibility.

The precise focus of the code will depend on the business concerned. Banks may concentrate on honesty, and chemical firms on pollution control. It has proved difficult to produce meaningful, comprehensive codes. The National Westminster Bank, for example, took two years to produce its ten-page document. A typical code might include sections on:

- personal integrity – in dealings with suppliers and in handling the firm's resources

- corporate integrity – such as forbidding collusion with competitors and forbidding predatory pricing

- **environmental responsibility** – highlighting a duty to minimise pollution emissions and maximise recycling

- social responsibility – to provide products of genuine value that are promoted with honesty and dignity.

A common feature of ethical codes of practice is that companies publicise them. This is because they believe that being seen to behave ethically is an important element of the marketing strategy of many businesses.

Critics of ethical codes believe them to be public relations exercises rather than genuine attempts to change business behaviour. What is not in doubt is that the proof of their effectiveness can be measured only by how firms actually behave, not by what they write or say.

Ethical training

The research conducted by the IBE (see above) has shown that operating ethical codes of conduct may not be sufficient to act as a USP. This is possibly truer for larger businesses than smaller ones. However, many larger and highly competitive businesses are taking ethical behaviour a step further and engaging in training employees in ethical behaviour on a systematic basis. This approach helps to transfer ethical actions from a corporate to an individual level. Ethical training offers the opportunity to reinforce ethical behaviour, to provide positive publicity for the business and to help to attract high-calibre employees to apply for jobs within the organisation.

There has been a major increase in the number of British companies training their staff in business ethics, according to a report published by the IBE. The IBE surveys UK companies every three years on the use of their codes of ethics. The 2007 survey showed that 71% of businesses now provide training on codes, compared to 47% in 2004.

Ethical training involves providing employees at all levels within an organisation with the skills and knowledge to take ethical decisions and to make ethical behaviour normal working practice. Training can relate to issues from all functions within a business, such as:

- protecting the environment through actions such as the use of sustainable sources of raw materials

- dealing with bullying, harassment and discrimination within the organisation

- the provision of accurate financial and other numerical information

- anti-competitive practices

- testing products on animals and similar production issues

- whistleblowing on unethical practices within the business.

87.5 Pressure groups and ethics

The activities of **pressure groups** affect all types of businesses and most aspects of their behaviour. Most of the high-profile pressure groups are multi-cause and operate internationally. Greenpeace is one of the best-known pressure groups; it lobbies businesses to restrict behaviour that might adversely affect the environment. Other single-cause pressure groups exist to control the activities of businesses in one particular sphere of operations.

- Action on Smoking and Health (ASH) is an international organisation established to oppose the production and smoking of tobacco. It publicises actions of tobacco companies that may be considered to be unethical. ASH frequently focuses on the long-term effects of tobacco on consumers of the product.

- Compassion in World Farming is a UK-based pressure group campaigning specifically for an end to the factory farming of animals. The group engages in political lobbying and high-profile publicity campaigns in an attempt to end the suffering endured by many farm animals.

A-grade application

Supermarket giant makes huge commitment to chicken welfare

Sainsbury's has made a commitment to improve the lives of 70 million chickens a year by moving away from the most intensively farmed chickens in a decision that is heralded as a 'huge step forward' by leading farm animal welfare charity, Compassion in World Farming.

The supermarket giant has announced a move away from stocking poor-welfare factory-farmed chickens across all the chicken it sells and will instead adopt the Freedom Food standard, or equivalent, as the minimum.

Dr Lesley Lambert, Director of Food Policy, welcomed the move, saying, 'This will dramatically improve the lives of 70 million chickens every year and is one of the most significant moves in farm animal welfare in the UK.'

Freedom Food or equivalent standards ensure more space, slower-growing birds with fewer welfare problems, and environmental enrichment such as straw bales, which allow for more natural behaviour.

'By reaching the equivalent of Freedom Food standards, Sainsbury's is leading the way among the big four supermarkets on chicken welfare, joining M&S and Waitrose as pioneers in this area. This is a huge step forward. We urge consumers to support higher welfare for chickens through the power of their purse and preferably choose free range,' continued Dr Lambert.

Source: Compassion in World Farming press release, January 2008 (http://www.ciwf.org.uk/publications/prs/NR0308.pdf)

87.6 The ethical balance sheet

Advantages of ethical behaviour

Companies receive many benefits from behaving, or being seen to behave, in an ethical manner. These are discussed below.

Marketing advantages

Many modern consumers expect to purchase goods and services from organisations that operate in ways that they consider morally correct. Some consumers are unwilling to buy products from businesses that behave in any other way. This trend has been accelerated by the rise of consumerism. This has meant that consumers have become increasingly well informed and are prepared to think carefully before spending their money.

Some companies have developed their ethical behaviour into a unique selling point (USP). They base their marketing campaigns on these perceived differences. An example of a high-profile company adopting this strategy is the Body Shop International.

A key point is that not only does the company seek to support relatively poor communities in the less developed world, but it publicises these actions. By creating a caring image through its marketing the Body Shop hopes to gain increased sales.

Marketing advantages

Companies also gain considerable public relations advantages from ethical behaviour. Once again this can help enhance the image of the business, with positive implications for sales and profits.

In 2006, the Co-operative Group announced a 12% increase in pre-tax profits to £107.5 million, while confirming the maintenance of its ethical principles. Its Trading Group operating profits before significant items was up 29.2% to £275 million, an increase of £62 million. In part this is due to the business's strong ethical stance. The Co-operative Retail Society is a strong supporter of ethical products and sells, for example, a high proportion of Fairtrade products.

Positive effects on the workforce

Firms that adopt ethical practices may experience benefits in relation to their workforce. They may expect to recruit staff who are better qualified and motivated. Employees can be expected to respond positively to working for a business with a positive ethical image and this can lead to greater competition for employment

A-grade application

Cafédirect: strong numbers in a challenging year

Cafédirect plc, the UK's largest and longest-running Fairtrade hot drinks company, announced pre-tax profits for the year ended 30 September 2007 of £705,000. These rose from £48,000 in 2006. The company's performance was buoyed by its best year ever in the out-of-home sector (restaurants, cafés, businesses, venues), which at £4.6 million grew by 33% compared with 2006 and now represents over 20% of the company's total revenues.

Total turnover grew 3% to £22.3 million for the financial year ended 30 September 2007. In the retail sector, although Cafédirect's sales slowed 4% to £17.0 million, distribution reached an all-time high, and the company's market share for hot drinks equates to 34%, 32% and 14% respectively of the UK's Fairtrade coffee, tea and drinking chocolate markets.

Financial returns are only part of Cafédirect's impact, however. The company works directly with 39 grower organisations across 13 developing countries, directly benefiting the lives of 1.4 million people. In the same financial year, the amount paid to coffee, tea and cocoa growers over and above the market price totalled nearly £1 million, bringing the total for the past three years to more than £4.3 million.

Source: Adapted from Cafédirect press release, February 2008 (http://www.cafedirect.co.uk/pdf/press/2008_feb_5_onward_and_upward.pdf)

with such companies. Innocent Drinks has 187 employees and has had only 201 different permanent members of staff on its payroll since its creation in 1999. This is a very high rate of retention of staff and has meant that the company has reduced employment costs associated with recruitment, selection and training. Creating an ethical culture within a business can also improve employee motivation. This may be part of a wider policy towards employee empowerment.

Disadvantages of ethical behaviour

Inevitably, a number of disadvantages can result from businesses adopting ethical policies.

Reduced profitability

It is likely that any business adopting an ethical policy will face higher costs. It may also be that the company has to turn down the opportunity to invest in projects offering potentially high returns. Exploiting cheap labour in less developed countries may be immoral but it can be very profitable. Equally, the Body Shop International's commitment to purchasing its supplies from sustainable sources means that it incurs higher costs than if it purchased raw materials without regard to the environment.

Businesses adopting an ethical policy may also incur additional costs in training their staff to behave ethically in their decision making. Similarly, adapting production processes to protect the environment may result in increased costs of production.

It is possible to argue that, depending on the nature of the business and its market, profits may not be reduced as a consequence of adopting an ethical policy. A premium price may be possible, or new niche markets may be uncovered by a business marketing itself as ethical.

Conflict with existing policies

Introducing an ethical policy can create internal divisions within the business. A business with a tradition of delegation and empowerment might experience problems introducing an ethical policy. Staff may perceive the implementation as autocratic and a move towards centralisation. They could argue that such a concept conflicts with the philosophy of delegation. As a consequence they may resist the policy.

A company may also experience difficulty in spreading the message in a company that is decentralised. Even if employees view an ethical policy favourably, it may be difficult to implement it into everyday activities. Almost certainly, considerable training will be required.

87.7 Ethical behaviour: future developments

t has been suggested that most of the interest in business ethics and its development has been in universities and colleges. However, there is increasing evidence available to suggest that ethical awareness is becoming more firmly rooted in business practice. A number of arguments can be set out to support the view that ethics will be of increasing importance to businesses throughout the world.

The adoption of ethical practices

By 2007 over 80% of the major businesses in the UK had implemented an ethical code of practice. Over 70% of chief executives see ethical practices and behaviour as their responsibility. Although everyone in a business needs to conform to an ethical code of practice, it is only senior managers who have the power to bring about the necessary changes in corporate culture.

The commercial success of high-profile 'ethical' companies

Companies that are seen to have high ethical standards have enjoyed considerable commercial success over recent years. Innocent Drinks has been a stunning financial success since its inception in 1999. In the 2006/07 financial year the company's sales grew by 40% to £96.2 million. Similarly, Toyota has benefited financially from its commitment to sustainable methods of production. The company's environmentally friendly hybrid car, the Prius, has been highly successful in global markets.

The 'not-for-profit' Charity Bank was launched in 2002 and provides cheap loans to charities with no access to mainstream lending facilities. Investors in the new bank receive a flat rate of interest of 2% and the bank uses any surpluses to support charities. The Charity Bank works to increase the long-term viability of community organisations, supporting those working in areas that typically can't get access to finance through commercial lenders. By December 2007 it had agreed loans of more than £55 million for more than 500 charitable organisations, over 60% of which targeted less privileged people in the UK.

Public expectations

The success of the 'ethical' companies mentioned above is evidence that the public respond favourably to a positive ethical stance. Consumers are likely to become better informed and better educated about products, processes and companies. They will demand products and services that do not pollute, exploit, harm or waste. Successful companies will need to respond positively to the demands of the 'new' consumer.

Issues For Analysis

- Cynics might well argue that many businesses may adopt so-called ethical practices simply to project a good public image. Such organisations would produce an ethical code of practice and derive positive publicity from a small number of 'token' ethical actions, while their underlying **business culture** remained unchanged. Such businesses, it is argued, would not alter the way in which the majority of their employees behaved, and decisions would continue to be taken with profits (rather than morals) in mind.

- This may be a realistic scenario for a number of businesses. But it is also a dangerous strategy in a society where increasing numbers of people have access to information. Certainly the media would be looking to publicise any breaches in a business's ethical code of practice. Being revealed as hypocritical is always a difficult position to defend.

- Among the key issues for analysis are the following.
  - What is the underlying intent? If a decision has been made on the basis of profit, it is not truly ethical. An ethical decision is made on the basis of what is morally correct.
  - What are the circumstances? A profit-focused decision that might be considered questionable in good times might be justifiable when times are hard. For example, a firm threatened with closure would be more justified in spending the minimum possible on pollution controls.
  - What are the trade-offs? In many cases the key ethical question is profit versus morality. In others, though, the trade-offs are more complex. Making a coal mine close to 100% safe for the workers would be so expensive as to make the mine uneconomic, thereby costing the miners their jobs.

87.8 Business ethics
an evaluation

Evaluation involves making some sort of informed judgement. Businesses are required to make a judgement about the benefits of ethical behaviour. Their key question may well be whether ethics are profitable or not.

In this unit, convincing arguments have been put together as to why this might be the case. For example, ethical behaviour can give a clear competitive advantage on which marketing activities can be based. However, disadvantages may lurk behind an ethical approach. The policy can be the cause of conflict and may be expected to reduce profits.

Operating an ethical policy gives a USP if none of your competitors has taken the plunge. Being first may result in gaining market share before others catch up. In these circumstances an ethical code may enhance profitability. It can also be an attractive option in a market where businesses and products are virtually indistinguishable. In these circumstances a USP can be most valuable.

Ethical policies may add to profits if additional costs are relatively small. Thus for a financial institution to adopt an ethical policy may be less costly than for a chemical manufacturer. Clearly companies need to weigh increased costs against the marketing (and revenue) benefits that might result.

Ethical policies are more likely to be profitable if consumers are informed and concerned about ethical issues. It may be that businesses can develop new niche markets as a result of an ethical stance.

Key terms

Business culture: the culture of an organisation is the (perhaps unwritten) code that affects the attitudes, decision making and management style of its staff.

Environmental responsibility: this involves businesses choosing to adopt processes and procedures that minimise harmful effects on the environment – for example, placing filters on coal-fired power stations to reduce emissions.

Ethical code: document setting out the way a company believes its employees should respond to situations that challenge their integrity or social responsibility.

Pressure groups: groups of people with common interests who act together to further that interest.

Stakeholder interests: stakeholders are groups such as shareholders and consumers who have a direct interest in a business. These interests frequently cause conflict – for example, shareholders may want higher profits while consumers want environmentally friendly products, which are more costly.

Voluntary codes of practice: methods of working recommended by appropriate committees and approved by the government. They have no legal authority – for example, much advertising is controlled by voluntary codes of practice.

Exercises

A. Revision questions

(40 marks; 40 minutes)

1 Define the term 'business ethics'. (2)

2 State two factors that may shape the moral behaviour of businesses. (2)

3 Outline one circumstance in which a company might face an ethical dilemma. (3)

4 Explain the difference between a business behaving legally and a business behaving ethically. (4)

5 Why might decisions made upon the basis of a moral code (ethics) conflict with profit? (5)

6 Look at each of the following business actions and decide whether they were motivated by ethical considerations. Briefly explain your reasoning each time.
   (a) an advertising agency refusing to accept business from cigarette producers (2)
   (b) a private hospital refusing to accept an ill elderly person whose only income is the state pension (2)
   (c) a small baker refusing to accept supplies of genetically modified flour (2)
   (d) a small baker refusing to deliver to a restaurant known locally as a racist employer (2)

7 Why might a policy of delegation make it more difficult for a business to behave ethically? (4)

8 Give two reasons why a business might introduce an ethical code of practice. (2)

9 Why might a business agree to abide by a **voluntary code of practice**, when the code has no legal authority? (5)

10 Outline the positive effects the adoption of an ethical policy may have on a business's workforce. (5)

B. Revision exercises

B1 Stimulus questions

Saudi Arabia has agreed to buy 72 Eurofighter Typhoon jets from BAE Systems. The deal is worth about £4400 million but contracts for maintenance and training are expected to take the bill to £20,000 million. In addition to the price paid for the planes, there is also expected to be a lucrative deal for the munitions that go with them.

BAE Systems is Britain's largest exporter of defence equipment and has publicly adopted a more ethical approach to its operations in recent years. BAE Systems said it welcomed 'this important milestone in its strategy to continue to develop Saudi Arabia as a key home market with substantial employment and investment in future in-Kingdom industrial capability'.

The negotiations had been overshadowed by a UK inquiry into allegations Saudi Arabia took bribes from BAE under a military-plane deal struck between the two nations two decades ago. Britain's Serious Fraud Office last year investigated BAE Systems' £43 billion Al-Yamamah deal in 1985, which provided Hawk and Tornado jets plus other military equipment to Saudi Arabia. However, the investigation was pulled by the British government in December 2006 in a move supported by then Prime Minister Tony Blair amid statements about the UK's national interests.

Questions

(30 marks; 35 minutes)

1 Explain the phrase 'a more ethical approach'. (3)

2 Explain the ethical dilemma that British Aerospace might face in exporting fighter aircraft to Saudi Arabia. (6)

3 British Aerospace presents itself as a very moral company. Analyse the factors that might shape a moral business culture. (9)

4 Some business analysts have observed that the company's ethical policy will make it less profitable. Discuss whether this is likely to be true. (12)

B2 Case study

Vivien's bank under fire

Vivien's appointment as chief executive was front-page news. She was the first woman to lead one of Britain's 'big four' banks. Her predecessor, Malcolm Stanton, had been fired due to the bank's poor profit performance. The board made it clear to Vivien that a significant profit improvement was needed within 18 months.

Vivien's approach to management was broadly Theory Y. She trusted that people would give their best as long as the goals were clear. The manager of the bank's overseas section was delighted to be told there would no longer be a monthly review of performance; in future, an annual meeting with Vivien would be sufficient. The target of a 40% profit increase was more of a shock, but after discussion Vivien relaxed it to 33%.

At the half-year stage, Vivien was delighted to see that overseas profits were up by more than 30%. Her delegation programme had worked. The first sign that anything was going wrong came from an article in *Private Eye* magazine. Its headline, 'Vivien's bank under fire!', was followed by an article suggesting that the bank was the main financier of the arms trade in war-torn Central America. Within a fortnight the national papers had dredged up more scandal. The bank was accused of involvement with an environmental disaster in Brazil and a corruption case in the Far East.

Interviewed on BBC Radio 4's *Today* programme, Vivien defended herself by assuring the audience that, 'Neither I nor any board member has any knowledge of any of these cases. I have put in hand a thorough inquiry that will look into every aspect of these rumours. This bank has an ethical code that we take very seriously. I am confident that these stories will prove to be just that. Stories.'

Questions

(50 marks; 60 minutes)

1 Analyse the business benefits Vivien would have been expecting to gain from her policy of delegation. (10)

2 Why might her approach to delegation have created a situation in which unethical practices were adopted by the overseas section of the bank? (12)

3 Consider why the bank's ethical code may have been ineffective in this case. (12)

4 Business ethics are strongly influenced by the culture of the workplace.
   (a) What is meant by the term 'culture'? (3)
   (b) Discuss the approaches Vivien might take to influence the ethical culture of the bank in future. (13)

C. Essay questions

(40 marks each)

1 'A modern, democratically led company with an empowered workforce would be the type of organisation that would be expected to operate an ethical policy.' To what extent do you agree with this statement?

2 Discuss the view that few businesses take truly moral decisions and that most implement ethical policies to gain a competitive advantage.

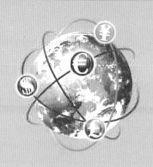

BUSINESS AND THE ENVIRONMENT

DEFINITION

Environmental issues are those relating to pollution, global warming, sustainable development and other elements of the 'green' agenda. Businesses today are making more effort to measure and publicise their performance through environmental audits.

88.1 Introduction

This is not a unit on the environment. You do not need scientific understanding of the processes involved in climate change. This unit outlines the ways in which environmental issues act as an external constraint on the operation of business. Successful businesses need to consider the effects of their activities on the environment, whether positive or negative.

Many companies, especially large public limited companies, already have environmental policies. These may be designed to minimise any damage their activities may cause to the environment; or they may be to minimise the chances of damage to the reputation of the business. These policies usually cover production issues, but may be used as a positive aspect in the companies' marketing activities. There is little doubt that the importance of the environment as an issue for businesses has grown over the last 20 years. However, environmental legislation is imperfect in the UK and throughout the EU.

88.2 The environmental issues affecting business

Pollution

As societies become wealthier, consumers start to think less about money and more about their quality of life. Factory smoke becomes unacceptable, as does the inconvenience and pollution caused by traffic jams. Voters put pressure on government to pass stronger laws. Firms find that 'fish die in river pollution disaster' is front-page news, so most try to prevent bad publicity by looking carefully at their noise, air and water emissions. Some firms even go so far as to pursue zero emissions.

Recycling

From Brazilian rainforests to South African gold mines, the extraction of natural resources is expensive and often environmentally damaging. Higher levels of **recycling** can reduce the need to extract more raw materials. It also reduces the amount of waste material that needs to be dumped or incinerated. Firms today are proud to display the recycling logo that tells the customer that they are trying to minimise their use of primary materials.

Sustainable development

Key building blocks of modern life include oil, coal and wood. If modern economies use these commodities excessively there must be a threat that, in the long term, the resources will run out. This has already started to happen with stocks of cod in the North Sea. Many businesses now try to ensure that they use replaceable natural resources. It is now hard to find greetings cards that are not made from paper from sustainable forests.

Global warming or climate change

Excessive production of carbon dioxide is believed to be a primary cause of climate change. This largely comes from burning fossil fuels such as coal and oil in order to produce electricity. Firms able to help counter climate change could expect excellent publicity. A recent development has been increased use of the term 'carbon footprint'. A carbon footprint is a term used to describe the amount of carbon dioxide produced by the operations of a person, business or process. The size of a company's carbon footprint can be reduced by using energy-saving measures along with taking steps to positively take carbon dioxide out of the environment (offsetting) – for example, planting extra forests.

A-grade application

Cheese and onion carbon footprints

Walkers was one of the first firms in the UK to add a carbon footprint label to its packaging. Figure 88.1 shows the breakdown of the 75g of carbon dioxide created in making a bag of crisps.

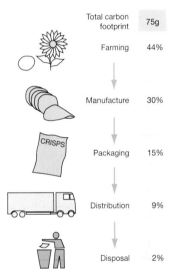

Total carbon footprint	75g
Farming	44%
Manufacture	30%
Packaging	15%
Distribution	9%
Disposal	2%

Figure 88.1 Carbon footprint of a packet of Walker's crisps
Source: Walkers

Coca-Cola, Boots, Cadbury and Innocent Drinks are also promising to introduce carbon footprint labelling.

88.3 International environmental standards

In 1997, 176 of the world's governments gathered in the Japanese city of Kyoto to agree targets for reducing emissions of harmful gasses. The major weakness of the agreement was that the world's largest polluter, the USA, failed to sign up. President Bush rejected the Kyoto Protocol because it excluded fast-growing developing countries such as China.

In the same way that quality standards exist to certify excellence in quality control, there are similar certifications to highlight good environmental practice. The International Standards Organization (ISO) has an environmental certification (ISO 14001) that is mainly applicable to manufacturing industry.

88.4 Environmental auditing

An **environmental audit** is an independent check on the pollution emission levels, wastage levels and recycling practices of a firm. If the results are published annually, there is a clear incentive for the business to try to do better. After all, if its wastage levels rise, newspapers will inevitably point this out to their readers. Therefore firms that carry out (and publish) environmental audits annually should be more willing invest in ways to improve their environmental practice. The Body Shop, ICI and IBM have all been publishing annual environmental audits for a number of years, however there is no legal obligation to do so. As a result, firms who perform poorly in this area are unlikely to publish the results of any audit. An EU proposal of the early 1990s recommended compulsory environmental auditing in certain key industries. This proposal was watered down as a result of pressure from industrialists and environmental audits remain voluntary.

Figure 88.2 The Body Shop publishers on annual environmental audit

88.5 The environment and marketing

There are a number of environmental issues that may have a bearing on the marketing decisions taken by firms. A number of firms have emerged that are prepared to actively use environmental friendliness as a marketing tool. A good reputation can act as a positive encouragement to certain consumers to choose one brand over another. So firms have spent time and money building up a 'green' image as an integral part of their marketing strategy. Examples include the Co-operative Bank and BP.

If a firm is successful in creating a green image, a number of advantages may follow. In addition to increased sales and possibly stronger brand loyalty, a 'green' firm may well be in a position to charge a price premium for its products. Many different products, from shampoos to banks, trade on the environment as a unique selling point. Many analysts suggest that this trend may continue until a 'green' image is no longer unique, but a requirement for all products.

A positive image in relation to the environment can help a firm's marketing activities. It is important to remember, however, that there is an opposite – and often much stronger – reaction to those who damage the environment. Bad publicity for firms who cause damage to the environment can result in significant marketing problems. One example is the airline Ryanair, which found bookings hit in early 2007 because of concerns over the carbon footprint of low-cost airlines.

88.6 The environment and production

There are three stages of production in which environmental issues may have an important effect. These are illustrated in Figure 88.3.

The materials used to manufacture a product may be finite or replenishable. Materials such as oil or coal, once used up, cannot be replaced. These are materials of which the Earth has a limited supply.

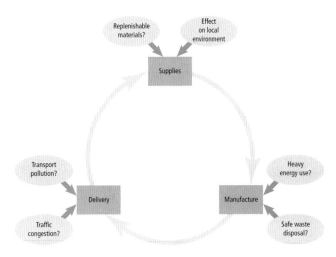

Figure 88.3 Environmental effects of production

Other materials may be replaceable, such as wood. If trees are planted to replace those that are cut down, the supply of wood can continue indefinitely. In some circumstances, firms may be able to choose whether to use finite or renewable resources to manufacture their products. Often the finite resource may be cheaper. The firm must then face a straight choice: cheap or environmentally sound.

2 The processes used to manufacture products may be more or less harmful to the environment. The key issue here is energy. Some processes require more energy than others and energy is a problem. The main sources of energy generation on earth are oil and coal – both finite resources. Furthermore, burning coal and oil to generate energy gives off harmful emissions that damage the environment. There are more environmentally friendly energy sources, such as wind power, but energy generated in this way tends to be more expensive. Again, firms are faced with the same choice: cheap or environmentally friendly.

3 Directly harmful pollution emissions can also cause immediate environmental damage. In 2004, environmental pressure group Friends of the Earth, reported the major pollution incidences in the UK listed in Table 88.1 overleaf.

Table 88.1 Major pollution incidences in the UK, 2004

Company	Location	What leaked	Why it's bad	How much got out	Where did it go?
AES Drax	Selby	Nitrogen oxides	Linked to acid rain	49,600 tonnes	To air
BP Oil	Coryton Refinery	Copper	May affect soil micro-organisms	15.5 tonnes	To water
Carpenter	Glossop	Dichloromethane	May cause cancer and genetic damage	513 tonnes	To air
Esso	Southampton	Phenols	Water pollutant	23.4 tonnes	To water
Glaxo	Ulverston	Dichloromethane	May cause cancer and genetic damage	64.9 tonnes	To water
Huntsman	Redcar	BTEX	Water pollutant	36.7 tonnes	To water
INEOS CHLOR	Runcorn	Trichloroethylene	May cause cancer and genetic damage	138 tonnes	To air
INEOS CHLOR	Runcorn	Trichloromethane	May cause cancer	41.9 tonnes	To air
INEOS CHLOR	Runcorn	Dichloroethane	May cause cancer and genetic damage	714 tonnes	To air
Magnesium Elektron	Manchester	Sulphur hexafluoride	A potent greenhouse gas	31.6 tonnes	To air
Sevalco	Bristol	Hydrogen cyanide	Very toxic at certain concentrations	50 tonnes	To air
Talisman Energy	Stromness	Benzene	May cause cancer	295 tonnes	To air

Issues For Analysis

- The main issue for analysis is to consider whether the motives of organisations are strong enough to achieve actual environmental improvements rather than pretend ones. Today almost every piece of packaging has an environmentally based claim (e.g. recyclable, from renewable sources or made from recycled paper). But is it any different from before, or have the producers simply found a label they can attach without needing to change anything?

- In 2000, BP started proclaiming itself to be 'Beyond Petroleum'. It portrayed itself as the greenest of the oil companies. In fact pollution disasters and industrial accidents at BP in 2005 and 2006 revealed that this was just hot air. Nor are consumers much better than companies. Many talk about recycling and fuel savings, then drive off to the airport in their gas-guzzling cars.

Another factor when analysing questions on this subject is to be sure to consider both costs and benefits. A course of action with environmental benefits may also have other social costs, such as unemployment. Is it right to make 200 workers redundant because the factory they work in is polluting the environment? It is important to consider all sides of every argument.

Many environmentalists believe that the most important step that business and consumers need to take is to move away from the so-called 'disposable society'. This is where products are used once and then thrown away. There may be a need to return to a more traditional situation where products are designed to last for a long time, in order to avoid the need to replace them frequently. This, however, might threaten to reduce levels of production, and presumably profit. This is therefore unlikely to happen as a result of decisions taken by businesses. Perhaps the only way is for consumers to act on what they say they believe about the environment. If people refuse to fly on holiday, airlines will cut flights and therefore cut pollution. Without real action, it is unfair to blame firms for carrying on largely as normal.

> ### Key terms
>
> **Environmental audit:** an independent check on the pollution emission levels, wastage levels and recycling practices of a firm.
>
> **Recycling:** dismantling and/or sorting products so that they can be collected and reused. This reduces the need for fresh raw materials to be used.

8.7 Business and the environment
an evaluation

dgement can often be shown by looking for the underlying use of a problem – in this context, the root cause of the vironmental problems faced or caused by business. hough production activities may damage the environment, e bulk of environmental harm is actually caused by the nsumption of products. Many firms are actually quite good producing in an environmentally friendly way. However, eir products may cause more harm to the environment nen they have been consumed. This may be the result of e need to dispose of the consumed product or its ckaging, or because the product is designed to be used ly once, thus encouraging further consumption and erefore production.

Exercises

A. Revision questions

(20 marks; 20 minutes)

1 What aspects of a firm's activities will be covered by an environmental policy? (3)

2 What is meant by the term 'sustainable development'? (3)

3 What marketing advantages may come from an 'environmentally friendly' image? (4)

4 'Environmentally friendly' firms may find various aspects of people management easier as a result of their image. Why might this be so? (4)

5 How can recycling lead to cost reductions? (4)

6 Why would longer-lasting products cause less harm to the environment? (2)

B. Revision exercises

B1 Case study

Surprised by green success

The Toyota Prius is undoubtedly the standard bearer for green motoring. The Prius is a hybrid car, powered by an electric motor, backed up by a traditional petrol engine. The car's success followed its adoption by a number of environmentally conscious Hollywood stars, including Leonardo DiCaprio, Billy Crystal, Harrison Ford and Susan Sarandon. The level of success took Toyota by surprise – it failed to meet demand in 2004. Since then, production capacity has been increased to cope with steadily rising global demand.

Toyota's rivals were caught out even more – without rival hybrid models. As a result, Toyota gained a significant 'first-mover advantage' in the hybrid car market. Given the nature of the product, this early market success was vital, with new car models taking years, rather than months, to develop. The result has been a comfortable period with no competition for Toyota, allowing the Japanese company to further develop both the product and the Prius brand. UK sales in

2007 were over 10,000, well behind mass-market models such as the Volkswagen Golf and the Ford Focus, but strong enough to indicate the existence of a healthy 'green' niche within the UK car market.

Questions

(25 marks; 30 minutes)

1 Briefly explain the benefits of gaining first-mover advantage. (4)

2 Analyse the possible problems that Toyota may have experienced as a result of failing to meet demand for the Prius in 2004. (8)

3 Discuss the view that the secret of environmentally friendly business is huge investment in research and development. (13)

B2 Case study

Plan A for Marks & Spencer

In 2007, Marks & Spencer committed itself to becoming a carbon-neutral business within five years. In a strategy referred to as Plan A, M&S Chief Executive Stuart Rose vowed to cut energy consumption, stop using landfill sites and sell more products made from recycled materials. Certainly the firm seemed serious in its commitment to reducing the carbon dioxide emissions that could be traced back to its activities. However, critics were concerned that the firm would rely on 'offsetting' – the practice involving compensating for carbon emissions by planting lots of trees, suggesting that trees take a long while to actually offset the damage immediately caused to the environment through CO_2 emissions. However, M&S claims that it will use offsetting only as a last resort, and aims to ensure that none of its packaging or clothing products need to be thrown away – instead ensuring that they are recyclable.

Extracts from Marks & Spencer's Plan A are shown below.

Combating climate change

As one of Britain's largest retailers, our carbon

footprint is a large one: the combined result of our own UK and Irish operations, our suppliers' activities and the CO_2 that's emitted whenever you shop with us and use our products.

One of our five top priorities is to shrink it right down. Because if big businesses like ours take action with individuals like you, we can do our bit to tackle climate change.

Climate change is a complex area and we don't claim to have all the answers. But we do know that we need to act fast. That's why our goal is to make our operations carbon neutral in the next five years and help you and our suppliers cut CO_2 emissions too.

Reducing energy use

In the last four years, we've already reduced our CO_2 emissions by 30% per square foot in our UK and Irish stores. And even though we've opened another 130 UK stores, we've also reduced CO_2 emissions from our lorries by 25%. Building on this, we want to:

- reduce the amount of energy we use in our UK and Irish stores by a further 25%
- achieve a 20% improvement in fuel efficiency and in energy use in our UK warehouses
- open model 'green' stores in Pollok, Bournemouth and two Simply Food stores this year
- open a model 'green' clothing factory with one of our suppliers.

Using green energy

At the same time as we reduce the energy we use, we will begin switching to 'green' alternatives. We want to:

- power all our UK and Irish shops and other buildings with green energy from a variety of sources, including 'anaerobic digestion' – energy generated by waste from our stores and from farms
- make sure all our lorries run on at least 50% bio-diesel
- buy carbon offsets only as a last resort where no green alternative exists yet – as with airplane fuel, for example
- offset all our home furniture deliveries.

Tackling food miles

The issue of food miles is one we know we need to work particularly hard on. That's why we aim to:

- source as much food from Britain and Ireland as we can – for example, continuing to sell 100% British/Irish fresh poultry, eggs, milk, beef, pork and salmon
- double regional food sourcing within 12 months and grow our local supply networks
- work with growers over the next three years to extend British growing seasons through new varieties and growing techniques
- continue to research our food's carbon footprint with the Carbon Trust, and set targets to reduce it over the next year
- set targets to reduce the amount of food we import by air
- offset our remaining CO_2 emissions from air-freighted food within 12 months
- label all air-freighted foods as 'flown' within six months.

Helping you cut carbon

To support you and our suppliers in cutting carbon emissions, we plan to:

- through our M&S Supplier Exchange, help suppliers find ways to reduce emissions significantly
- open a model green clothing factory with one of our suppliers
- develop and sell ranges of low-carbon products
- launch campaigns with the Women's Institute and the Climate Group to help you work out and reduce your carbon footprint
- help customers to reduce their carbon emissions by encouraging them to wash clothing at 30°C by printing the message 'Think Climate – Wash at 30°C' on the garment care labels of our clothing.

Source: www.marksandspencer.com

Questions

(60 marks; 70 minutes)

1 Analyse two main benefits that M&S might receive as a result of committing to becoming carbon neutral. (8)

2 If Marks & Spencer's main target group is middle-income consumers, explain why it might be more likely to commit to environmental action than other firms targeting lower-income consumers or those who mainly supply other businesses. (8)

3 Discuss whether Marks & Spencer's move is

driven only by the desire to generate favourable publicity. (14)

4 To what extent are gestures such as that made by Marks & Spencer possible only for companies that are in a strong financial position? (14)

5 'Significant environmental progress is possible only if major firms such as Marks & Spencer take bold steps forward.' To what extent do you agree with this view? (16)

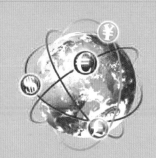

BUSINESS AND THE TECHNOLOGICAL ENVIRONMENT

The technological environment involves developments both in terms of what is being produced and how it is being made.

89.1 Introduction

Technology is changing at an extremely fast rate. New products and new processes are being developed all the time. In markets such as computers and mobile phones hundreds of new products are being launched every month. The minute you buy the latest Blu-ray player, PC, phone or digital camera you know it is about to be outdated. Firms face similar problems. The welding robot bought last month is already less efficient than the model announced for next month, probably at a lower price. Whatever you buy, whatever technology you use, the chances are someone somewhere is working on an improved version.

This rate of change is getting ever faster. Product development times are getting quicker and, consequently, more products are getting to the market in less time. The result is that the typical product life cycle is getting shorter. Naturally this creates serious problems for firms. With more and more products being developed, the chances of any one product succeeding are reduced. For many years research showed that only one in five new products succeeds in the marketplace. Today the figure is one in seven – in other words, six out of seven fail. Even if a new product succeeds, its life cycle is likely to be relatively short. Given the ever higher quality demanded by customers, firms are having to spend more on developing products but have less time to recoup their investment.

One of the main reasons for the rapid growth of technology is actually technology itself. The development of **computer-aided design (CAD)** and **computer-aided manufacture (CAM)** has enabled even faster development of new products and processes. Technology feeds off itself and generates even more ideas and innovations. This rapid rate of change creates both threats and opportunities for firms. The threats are clear:

- firms that do not adopt competitive technology will struggle to keep their unit costs down …

- … or provide goods or services of sufficient quality relative to their competitors.

Technology can certainly make life a great deal easier for firms. Just think of how slow it would be to work out all of a large company's accounts by hand instead of using a computer spreadsheet. If one company avoids the latest technology while its rivals adopt it, it is likely to suffer real problems with competitiveness. The rivals may be able to offer lower prices or substantially better or faster service standards.

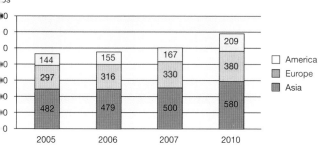

	America	Europe	Asia
2005	144	297	482
2006	155	316	479
2007	167	330	500
2010	209	380	580

Figure 89.1 The growth in industrial robots

A-grade application

GM to take on Toyota

General Motors, still reeling from Toyota's attack on the US market headed by its Prius hybrid car, plans to outflank Toyota's technology by 2010. Its Chevy Volt is intended to be a plug-in hybrid (electric engine plus petrol engine) that can run for 40 miles on the electric battery alone. Then, on getting the car back to your garage, you plug it in to recharge the battery. In this way someone with a short daily commuting drive would never need the petrol engine at all (saving fuel bills and eliminating carbon monoxide and carbon dioxide exhaust emissions).

The Volt will also have other new technology features such as dashboard controls modelled on the iTouch phone. General Motors is investing many hundreds of millions of dollars into the Chevy Volt and is determined to make it a success. Toyota (a far richer company than General Motors) is keeping quiet about its own plans for a new, higher-technology Prius.

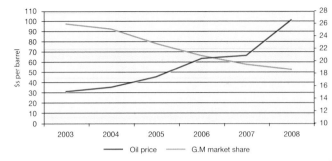

Figure 89.2 The effect of rising oil prices on General Motors
*2008 figures are estimates

89.2 Assessing the effects of technological change

Unfortunately, because of the costs involved, it is not always possible for a firm to acquire the technology it wants. New technology can represent a significant investment for a firm and cannot be always be undertaken as and when the managers feel like it. This is particularly true when technology is changing at such a rate that any investment may be out of date very rapidly. The difficulty is knowing when to buy. Buy too late and you may well have lost the competitive advantage – your rivals will already be producing better-quality, more cost-competitive work.

As mentioned above, Toyota's high-tech, environmentally friendly Prius has made General Motors (GM) suffer. Because GM decided not to invest in greener technology in the 1990s, it made itself over-reliant on gas-guzzling cars and vans (such as the Hummer). As oil prices soared, Toyota boosted market share from 10% to 16%, leaving GM trailing badly (see Figure 89.2).

A key technological change is the arrival of internet-driven services such as online shopping. In 2008, online grocery shopping accounted for 3% of the £120 billion grocery market. By 2012 it is expected that 12% of grocery sales will be online, making sales worth more than £14 billion. This will be a bonanza for a specialist online grocer such as Ocado, but will start to take a

serious chunk out of the sales of the traditional stores. Any grocery business planning ahead needs to build in the expectation that high-street sales will soon be leaking away to the internet.

In other sectors the situation is even more serious. Electronic delivery of music has brought many record shops to their knees; books and travel are also switching away from retail sales. In 2002, almost all British Airways' sales were through travel agents; today the great majority of bookings are made online through the BA website.

To assess the effects of these changes, a business needs first to rethink its own position in the marketplace. For example, if standard, heavy grocery items such as potatoes, milk and washing powder are increasingly likely to be bought online, grocery stores must rethink what they are offering. They will need to increase the number of in-store tastings and make their displays more interesting. Good marketing will be a matter of finding reasons to get the shopper into the store.

The existence of online competition should make all tertiary businesses (such as shops) think even harder about successful customer service. Customers have always hated finding that a shop is out of stock of the exact product they wanted to buy; with the growth of the internet, this will become increasingly unacceptable. An unhappy shopper will not return; they may simply switch to Ocado's online retail supply.

There is also the possibility of unhappiness within the business, if staff come to feel that technological change is taking place too abruptly. The spring 2008 opening of Heathrow's Terminal 5 showed the potential pitfalls of introducing new technology among unhappy, untrained staff. In many cases, however, people object to change because they are scared by it or do not understand why it is needed. The management of technological change, therefore, needs careful handling. The process must be done at the right pace and employees must be involved wherever possible.

resistance to change will come from:

- people who do not understand why it is necessary

- people who will be worse off (e.g. they no longer have the right skills)

- people who are worried unnecessarily about its effects

- people who disagree with it (i.e. they understand it, but are convinced it is a bad idea).

39.3 The response of businesses to technological change

Technological change can provide enormous opportunities for firms. There is a tendency to think of technology as a potential problem for businesses (e.g. something that may lead to unemployment). In fact it is an aid to us all. Imagine what life would be like without televisions, phones, cashpoints, CDs or credit cards, for example. Similarly, technology makes working life considerably easier: routine jobs can be replaced, work can generally be speeded up and problem solving made easier. Just think what it would be like solving some of your business problems without a calculator.

Technology also creates new markets. Telephone banking, computer games and email are all relatively recent developments that we now take for granted. These markets create great opportunities for firms able to exploit them and for employees with skills that are in demand.

As with any change, technological developments create potential gains and potential threats. Whether a particular firm wins or loses depends on its ability to predict this change and its ability to react. When it launched Vista in 2007, Microsoft was convinced it was a winner. Yet its new-technology features failed to catch on. Not all new technology is commercial magic. Therefore it is hard to anticipate the impact of changes in technology.

Key terms

Computer-aided design (CAD): uses a software package to help draw and store new designs in digital form.
Computer-aided manufacture (CAM): uses software to specify speeds, accuracy and quantity to an automated production system.

Issues For Analysis

When answering questions about new technology, bear in mind that:

- technology creates both opportunities and threats; it both destroys and creates new markets; it can provide a firm with a competitive advantage or make its product or service obsolete

- the introduction of technology needs to be carefully managed; managers have to consider issues such as the compatibility of the technology, the financial implications and how best to introduce it

- new technology can place additional stress on employees who might be worried about their ability to cope.

39.4 Business and the technological environment

Whether new technology provides an opportunity or a threat for an organisation depends on the technology itself, the resources of the firm and the management's attitude to change. Used effectively, new technology can reduce costs, increase flexibility and speed up the firm's response time. In all areas of the firm, from marketing to operations, technology can increase productivity, reduce wastage, and lead to better-quality goods and services.

However, it may not always be possible for a firm to adopt the most appropriate technology (perhaps because it does not have the necessary finance). Even if it does adopt new technology the firm needs to ensure that the change is managed effectively. People are often suspicious or worried by new technology, and managers must think carefully about the speed of the change and the method of introduction. Organisations must also monitor the technology of their competitors. If they fail to keep up they may find they cannot match their competitors' quality standards. However, they may be limited by their ability to afford the technology. Typically, managers will be faced with an almost constant set of demands for new technology from employees. Nearly everyone can think of some machine or gadget they would like in an ideal world. Managers must decide on priorities given their limited resources, and also look for the gains that can be achieved with existing equipment. As the *kaizen* approach shows, success sometimes comes from gradual improvements rather than dramatic technological change.

Exercises

A. Revision questions

(35 marks; 40 minutes)

1 What is meant by the term 'technology'? (3)

2 Explain how improved technology can improve a firm's performance. (4)

3 What benefits might a firm derive from linking CAD to CAM? (3)

4 Examine three possible problems of introducing new technology. (6)

5 Explain how technological change has helped in the following areas:
   (a) retailing (3)
   (b) stock control (3)
   (c) car production. (3)

6 Outline two factors that might explain why there are relatively few robots in the UK. (4)

7 Why may technology be an important factor in a firm's international competitiveness? (3)

8 How may staff benefit from the introduction of new technology? (3)

B. Revision exercises

B1 Case study

Coal 'can be clean and reliable'

A UK think-tank report says that new technology can make coal a clean and secure source of energy.

Coal has traditionally been seen as dirty fuel because it is high in carbon emissions – a key factor causing climate change. But a report by the Centre for Policies Studies, published advance of the UK Energy White Paper, expected in May, says the environmental damage can be reduced. Coal can also be stored and provided on demand, unlike some renewable energy.

"New clean technologies are being developed around the world which can reduce the

environmental impact of coal-fired generation," the report said. These new techniques are "proven", the study added.

It said Powerfuel's new development at Hatfield in Yorkshire was an example of how a new clean coal plant can be developed in practice. The site, near Doncaster, was reopened in 2006, as part of plans to revamp the colliery and develop a clean coal power station.

The report argues that developing clean coal in the UK would not only be good for the domestic market, but would also set an example for developing economies, including China and India, in how to take advantage of coal reserves in an environmentally acceptable way.

However, the think-tank said clear political support to encourage investors and systematic planning rules for coal sites were needed. The government should also provide the same degree of subsidy as it does for renewable energy, it added.

It said the combination of more reliable energy and cheaper electricity for the consumer which would result from the use of the new technologies ought to be attractive to all policy-makers.

Source: Adapted from BBC News, 17 May 2007

Questions

(25 marks; 30 minutes)

1 The article states that 'New clean technologies . . . can reduce the environmental impact of coal-fired generation [of electricity]'. If that is true:
   (a) outline two possible effects on competitor suppliers of fuel – gas and oil (6)
   (b) outline two ways in which the global environment could benefit from cleaner technology. (6)

2 Discuss whether or not it's a good thing to have a new technology that provides 'cheaper electricity for the consumer'. (13)

B2 Case study

Brooks

Last Monday the management of Brooks plc announced the purchase of new equipment that would radically improve productivity levels. The investment would lead to some job losses, the management explained, but there was no doubt it was in the best interests of the company as a whole. Employees had not been consulted because management felt they had more than enough information to make the decision. Consultation would simply slow up the process. In the long run, the new equipment should increase the firm's competitiveness and the purchase was an expensive necessity. Working practices would, of course, have to be altered and employees would certainly have to learn new skills. The managers promised to provide the necessary training although they could not guarantee everyone a job if they could not adapt successfully.

Following the announcement, the employees were furious and considered taking industrial action. Hearing the rumours of possible strikes the management admitted that it might not have handled the issue in the best way possible but would not reconsider the decision.

Questions

(40 marks; 45 minutes)

1 What factors may have made the management of Brooks plc decide to invest in new technology? (8)

2 Do you think the employees at Brooks plc would be justified in taking industrial action? Explain your answer. (10)

3 Analyse the factors that the managers at Brooks plc might have taken into account before acquiring the new equipment. (10)

4 The management of Brooks plc admitted that they may not have handled the issue in the best possible way. In your opinion, how should they have handled it? Justify your answer. (12)

C. Essay questions

(40 marks each)

1 'Technology is something to be feared rather than welcomed.' Consider this view.

2 To what extent should a firm make introducing new technology a priority?

3 'The key to better performance is better management not more technology.' Critically assess this view.

IMPACT OF COMPETITIVE AND MARKET STRUCTURE

DEFINITION

Competitiveness measures a firm's ability to compete (i.e. compares its consumer offer to the offers made by its rivals).

90.1 Introduction: what is a competitive market?

In the past, markets were physical places where buyers and sellers met in person to exchange goods. Street markets are still like that. Today, some buyers and sellers never meet each other, such as those that transact on eBay.

Some markets are more competitive than others. In general, a competitive market could be described as one where there is intense rivalry between producers of a similar good or service. The number of firms operating within a market influences the intensity of competition; the more firms there are, the greater the level of competition. However, the respective size of the firms operating in the market should also be taken into account. A market consisting of 50 firms may not be particularly competitive if one of the firms holds a 60% market share and the 40% is shared between the other 49. Similarly, a market comprising just four firms could be quite competitive because the firms operating within this market are of a fairly similar size.

Consumers enjoy competitive markets. However, the reverse is true for the firms that operate in these markets. In competitive markets, prices and profit margins tend to be squeezed. As a result, firms operating in competitive markets try hard to minimise competition, perhaps by creating a unique selling point (USP) or using **predatory pricing**.

It could be argued that marketing is vital no matter what the level of competition is within the market. Firms that fail to produce goods and services that satisfy the needs of the consumers that make up their target market will find it hard to succeed in the long term. Ultimately, consumers will not choose to waste their hard-earned cash on products that fail to meet their needs.

90.2 The degree of competition within a market

One dominant business

Some markets are dominated by one large business. Economists use the word 'monopoly' to describe a market where there is a single supplier, and therefore no competition. In practice, pure textbook monopolies rarely exist; even Microsoft does not have a 100% share of the office software market (though it does have a 90% share). The UK government's definition of a monopoly is somewhat looser. According to the Competition Commission a monopoly is a firm that has a market share of 25% and above.

Monopolies are bad for consumers. They restrict choice and tend to drive prices upwards. For that reason most governments regulate against monopolies and near monopolies that exploit consumers by abusing their dominant market position.

Deciding whether or not a firm has a monopoly is far from being a straightforward task. First of all, the market itself has to be accurately defined. For example, Camelot has been granted a monopoly to run the National Lottery. However, it could be argued that Camelot does not have a dominant market position because there are other forms of gambling, such as horse racing and the football pools, available to consumers in the UK. Second, national market share figures should not be used in isolation because some firms enjoy local monopolies. In 2007 the Competition Commission accused Tesco of abusing its market position in towns such as Inverness and Slough by occupying sites previously occupied by its rivals. In both towns consumers had to travel more than 15 minutes by car to reach another supermarket chain.

irms implement their marketing strategy through the marketing mix. In markets dominated by a single large business firms do not need to spend heavily on promotion because consumers are, to a degree, captive. Prices can be pushed upwards and the product element of the marketing mix should be focused on creating innovations that make it harder for new entrants to break into the market. Apple spends millions of dollars in research and development in order to produce cutting-edge products such as the iPod Touch. Apple is still the market leader in MP3 players with a 60%-plus share of the massive US market. To ensure that Apple maintains its dominant market position new product launches are patented to prevent me-too imitations being launched by the competition.

igure 90.1 iPod Touch

Competition among a few giants

The UK supermarket industry is a good example of a market that is dominated by a handful of very large companies. Economists call markets like this **oligopolistic**. The rivalry that exists within such markets can be very intense. Firms know that any gains in market share will be at the expense of their rivals. The actions taken by one firm affect the profits made by the other firms that compete within the same market.

In markets made up of a few giants, firms tend to focus on **non-price competition** when designing the marketing mix. Firms in these markets tend to be reluctant to compete by cutting price. They fear that the other firms in the industry will respond by cutting their prices too, creating a costly price war where no firm wins.

The fiercely competitive market

Fiercely competitive markets tend to be fragmented – made up of hundreds of relatively small firms that compete actively against one another. In some of these markets competition is amplified by the fact that firms sell near identical products called commodities. Commodities are products such as flour, sugar or blank DVDs that are hard to differentiate. Rivalry in commodity markets tends to be intense. In markets such as this firms have to manage their production costs very carefully because the retail price is the most important factor in determining whether the firm's product sells or not. If a firm cannot cut its costs it will not be able to cut its prices without cutting into profit margins. Without price cuts, market share is likely to be lost.

In fiercely competitive markets firms will try, where possible, to create product differentiation. For example, the restaurant market in Croydon, Surrey, is extremely competitive. There are over 70 outlets within a two-mile radius of the town centre. To survive without having to compete solely on price, firms in markets like this must find new innovations regularly because points of differentiation are quickly copied.

A-grade application
Market saturation

The pattern of growth shown in Table 91.1 gives an idea of how competition can transform the way businesses operate. In 1970 there would only have been one Indian restaurant in any town or district. By 1990 there would often be two or three. Therefore, to be successful, there had to either be competition on price, or a move to more differentiation of menu and cooking style. Today, in a saturated market, a new Indian restaurant will have to offer something very special to get established.

Table 90.1 Number of Indian restaurants in the UK

Year	No. of restaurants	Market growth rate
1960	500	
1970	1200	140%
1980	3000	150%
1990	5100	70%
2000	7940	56%
2004	8750	10%
2008	8800	1%

90.3 Changes in competitive structure

New competitors

The number of firms operating within a market can change over time. If new competitors enter a market the market concerned will become more competitive. New entrants are usually lured into a move into a new market by the high profits or rapid growth achieved by the existing firms. These high profits are usually created by a rapidly growing market and/or high prices. A good example is the market for smoothies. Although second into the market (behind PJ), Innocent Drinks has been able to enjoy a near-monopoly combined with exceptionally rapid growth. Only in 2008 did PepsiCo (owner of Tropicana) start to take the market seriously. Once Innocent's turnover had broken the £100 million mark, PepsiCo launched Tropicana Smoothies, to try to break into Innocent's profitable market.

In markets that are suffering from low or negative profitability, firms tend to exit, leaving the market concerned less competitive than it was. A good example is the UK mortgage market. In 2008, many UK lenders reduced the number of home loans available because of falling profitability caused by crashing property prices and an increase in the number of homes being repossessed. As the number of banks operating in the market declined, prices within the market (i.e. mortgage interest rates) went up, reflecting a market that had suddenly become less competitive.

The emergence of dominant businesses

A dominant business is one that has a high market share. Markets that are dominated by a single business or a small number of businesses tend to be less competitive than markets that are less concentrated. Businesses that dominate their respective markets often possess the ability to set prices for all other smaller firms that operate within the same market. For example, the UK chocolate market is dominated by three companies: Cadbury, Nestlé and Mars. If a smaller firm, such as Finland's Fazer, wanted to try to enter the UK market it probably would be wise for Fazer to set its prices below those of the 'big three' in order to stimulate trial purchase.

Dominant businesses can emerge naturally over a long period of time due to organic growth. Organic growth occurs when a firm grows bigger because it has increased production and/or opened up new factories or branches. In the long run, organic growth usually reflects a change in consumer preferences in favour of the firm that has achieved the growth. Organic growth requires customer support. Firms that sell products that consumers like will tend to grow naturally over time. A good example is the UK supermarket chain, Tesco. For many years Tesco was number two in the market, behind its main rival, Sainsbury's. Gradually, Tesco, through its superior efficiency, managed to grow its market share by offering UK consumers lower prices and better quality than its main rivals. In 2008, Tesco dominates the UK supermarket industry, holding a market share of 31.4%. Sainsbury's, Tesco's closest rival, has a market share of just 16.4%.

Dominant businesses can also emerge via takeover or merger. If two firms in the same industry and at the same stage of production integrate, the result will be an increase in market concentration and a corresponding fall in competition. In 2007 the Irish airline, Ryanair, tried to buy out its main Irish rival, Aer Lingus. The proposed takeover would have given Ryanair a near monopoly over the supply of air travel between the UK and the Irish Republic. Fortunately for the travelling public, the European Commission blocked the takeover on competition grounds. According to a European Commission spokesman, 'there are only two international airlines operating from Dublin; if a takeover were allowed to go through there would only be one'. In other words, the proposed takeover would have strengthened Ryanair's dominance of the market to an unacceptable level.

Changes in the buying power of customers

Changes in the state of the economy can affect consumer spending levels and, at the same time, the level of competition within most markets. For example, during recessions, when national income is falling and unemployment is rising, many consumers opt to spend less. The markets for luxury goods and services are likely to contract. When the American economy was under pressure in early 2008, sales of the iconic (and very expensive) Harley-Davidson motorbikes fell by 12%. As the market shrinks, rivalry increases because the same number of firms now have to fight for a falling number of customers. To maintain its sales in a shrinking market, each motorbike manufacturer wants to increase its market share. This usually means price cutting and may lead to a price war.

On the other hand, if consumer buying power is increasing, markets tend to grow quite rapidly, especially or luxury goods that have an income-elastic demand. During economic booms when incomes are growing rapidly most markets normally become less competitive, especially in the short run. In the longer term, the additional profits created by additional consumer spending power tend to attract new entrants into a market, making the market concerned more competitive again.

Between 1993 and 2007 consumer spending power in the UK was supported by an abundant supply of cheap and easy credit. This credit-fuelled consumer boom created market growth in sectors such as building, banking and air travel. The credit crunch, which started in 2007, partially shut off the supply of cheap credit. This threatened to make the price competition in the airline market even more fierce, with Ryanair offering millions of flights in early 2008 for 1p (plus taxes).

Changes in the selling power of suppliers

In addition to demand, the level of competition within a market is also determined by market supply. If market supply decreases, but market demand does not, competition will increase. One factor that affects the selling power of suppliers is raw material costs. In recent times the price of oil has rocketed. Oil is a very important raw material. For example, even companies such as Apple will be affected by the price of oil. Plastic is made from oil. If the price of oil increases, Apple will need to pay more for the plastic pellets needed to produce casings for its iPods, iPhones and iMacs. If the price of raw materials goes up, firms will tend to supply less because the profit generated from each unit supplied will fall. The selling power of suppliers also depends upon other factors, such as wage rates and taxes. Wages are a day-to-day expense that consume working capital. If wages go up firms may be forced to cut output because they lack the working capital needed to maintain their current output level.

On the other hand, if profits are soaring and firms have plenty of working capital, supply is likely to grow.

Market sharing agreements

The level of competition within a market can change over time if established firms elect to set up a cartel. A cartel is a group of companies that operate in the same market that decide to cooperate, rather than compete, with each other. The members of the cartel collectively restrict market supply by agreeing to production quotas. Cartels lead to a less competitive market. A market with

several firms apparently competing against each other may effectively be a monopoly.

A-grade application
Construction company collusion

On 17 April 2008, the Office of Fair Trading announced a probe into 112 construction companies. They were accused of **collusion**, meaning getting together to agree who would win contracts in supposedly competitive situations. For example, an NHS hospital might ask five building firms to bid for a £40 million contract to build a new hospital ward. Instead of putting forward an honest 'best price', the five would get together and agree to submit four falsely high bids, leaving one to get the business. Next time around, a different one of the five would get the contract.

Even though 40 of the building firms admitted to price fixing, the industry association claimed that no one had been overcharged. The Office of Fair Trading disagreed, stating that: 'Cartel activity of the type alleged today harms the economy by distorting competition and keeping prices artificially high.'

Key quotations

'People of the same trade seldom meet together, even for merriment and diversion, but the conversation ends in a conspiracy against the public, or in some contrivance to raise prices.' *Adam Smith*, The Wealth of Nations, *1776*

'Competition is not only the basis of protection to the consumer, but is the incentive to progress.' *Herbert Hoover, US President, 1929–33*

'Like many businessmen of genius he learned that free competition was wasteful, monopoly efficient. And so he simply set about achieving that efficient monopoly.' *Mario Puzo*, The Godfather, *1969*

90.4 Responses of businesses to a changing competitive environment

In a market that has become more competitive firms might be forced into the following actions in order to defend market share.

Price cutting

Many firms attempt to fight off a competitor by cutting price. If the competition can be undercut, consumers will hopefully remain loyal to the company that has cut its prices. Firms that use price cutting as a way of fighting off the competition will normally try to cut their costs in line with the price cut in an attempt to preserve profit margins. If profit margins are already tight and costs have already been cut to the bone it probably will not be possible to respond to a new competitor by cutting prices.

Increase product differentiation

Product differentiation is the degree to which consumers perceive a brand to be different, and in some way superior to, other brands of the same type of product. Some firms might be apprehensive about responding to a competitive threat by cutting price because the long-term result could be a deteriorating brand image that could hinder, rather than help, sales. Many consumers still associate price with product quality. If product differentiation can be increased, consumers will be less likely to switch to products supplied by the competition. To a degree, differentiation helps a firm to insulate itself from competitive pressure. Firms that want to increase differentiation can do so by the following means.

Design

An eye-catching design that is aesthetically pleasing can help a firm to survive in a competitive market. By using design as a unique selling point British manufacturers can compete on quality rather than price, making them less vulnerable to competition from China and India. Good-looking design can add value to a product. For example, the BMW Mini relies upon its retro 1960s styling to command its price premium within the small car market.

Brand image

Many products rely very heavily on their brand image to sell. When products, such as Jack Wills clothes and BMW 4x4 cars, are purchased the consumer hopes to share some of the brand's personality. The consumer believes that some of the brand's image will rub off on them. They hope that others will notice too. Public consumption of a brand tells others something about you. Purchasing famous brands, which are then publicly consumed, effectively amounts to purchasing elements of personal identity. In many markets brand image is crucial. A strong brand image can help a firm to fight off its competitors without having to resort to price cuts.

Unique product features

In markets that are highly competitive some firms react by redesigning their products to ensure that they possess the latest must-have feature. For example, in the car market, Toyota's hybrid drive technology has appealed to consumers that are interested in buying an environmentally friendly car with very low emissions.

Superior quality

Some firms try to fight off new competition by improving the quality of the products they sell. If product quality can be improved, consumers should stay loyal. A good example of a firm that has reacted to competition by improving product quality is Rolls-Royce, which hopes to fight off its competitors by offering consumers a bespoke service for its new Phantom model. Consumers can choose special features such as a 24-carat gold Spirit of Ecstasy, or the customer's initials embroidered into the seat headrests.

Find new markets

If a market suddenly becomes more competitive because new firms have entered it, some firms react by trying to find new markets overseas that are less competitive. Even companies such as Tesco find it easier to build sales by opening superstores in eastern Europe, rather than trying to grow sales by taking yet more market share away from its UK rivals.

Takeover

Some large dominant firms react to a new successful competitor by trying to take them over. Among many examples are the purchase by Cadbury of Green & Black's organic chocolate and the purchase by Google of YouTube in 2006 (Google paid $1.65 billion for a business that was only 20 months old). Although governments are supposed to stop takeovers that crush competition, their record is not impressive.

Predatory pricing

If it is not possible to reduce competition by taking over a competitor, some firms might be tempted to use predatory pricing. Predatory pricing occurs when a firm cuts its prices in a deliberate attempt to undercut a rival so that it goes out of business. The prices charged are very low, so losses are made. Predatory pricing tends to be used by large dominant companies against smaller new entrants. These smaller firms tend not to have as much cash as the firm that started the price war. As a sult, the smaller firm will be forced to close down way efore the large firm runs out of money. Predatory ricing is illegal. However, it is still very common ecause the potential rewards that come from using redatory pricing greatly outweigh any fines imposed by ie Competition Commission.

Issues For Analysis

usiness guru Michael Porter has suggested that there re five forces that determine a firm's ability to compete ffectively. These are: the number of direct substitutes; ie ability of new firms to enter the market; the argaining power of buyers (e.g. Tesco buying over 30% f all Britain's groceries); the bargaining power of uppliers (e.g. a sweetshop buying chewing gum from Vrigley, with its 85% market share); and the policies nd actions of competitors. Any firm's competitive osition can be analysed in this way. For example, in 008 China protested loudly when the world's biggest iining company (BHP Billiton) offered nearly $150 illion to buy the world's number three, Rio Tinto Zinc. China was worried that the huge size of this supplier of iinerals such as iron and copper would put the ompany in too strong a position when negotiating with uyers such as China. Changes in the buying power of ustomers or suppliers can affect a company, or perhaps ven a country.

Impact of competitive and market structure

As has always been the case, the best way a business can ensure its survival in a competitive world is to find something it is good at, and stick with it. Cadbury is great when it concentrates on making chocolate; Heinz is brilliant at making and marketing baked beans. Even if the massive Hershey Corporation brings its chocolate from America, Cadbury need not fear. Similarly the launch of Branston Beans made little impact on Heinz.

Sometimes, though, big judgements have to be considered, such as to risk launching a new product in a new country. When Tesco did this in 2007, launching fresh&easy stores in America, the questions were (a) 'Did it need to?', and (b) 'Was it looking in the right direction?' (Wouldn't China or India have made more sense?) All too often, business leaders take actions that seem more to do with ego than logic. Models such as Porter's five forces are based on an assumption that business is about reacting to pressures, whereas a great deal of business decision making is about choices and judgements.

Key terms

Collusion: when managers from different firms get together to discuss ways to work together to restrict supply and/or raise prices. (See the Adam Smith quotation on page 648.)

Non-price competition: competing on any basis other than price (e.g. image, product design, quality of service).

Oligopolistic: competition among a few big firms, such as the UK chocolate market, dominated by Cadbury, Mars and Nestlé.

Predatory pricing: when a financially strong company prices its products so low that it threatens to force weaker competitors out of business.

Exercises

A. Revision questions

(40 marks; 40 minutes)

1 What is a monopoly? (2)

2 Explain two reasons why monopolies exist. (4)

3 How might an increase in competition within the UK banking market affect shareholders of banks such as NatWest and HSBC? (3)

4 Analyse two factors that could decrease the level of competition within the car market. (6)

5 Which stakeholder group benefits most from new entrants joining a market? (2)

6 Explain why some companies decide not to respond to additional competition by cutting price. (4)

7 Outline two reasons why a supermarket such as Waitrose might be concerned if Mars and Cadbury merged into one business. (6)

8 How might product differentiation help a firm adjust to a more competitive market? (3)

9 Explain why many large firms prefer to buy out smaller rivals, rather than competing against them head to head. (4)

10 Discuss whether it is right for some firms to use tactics such as predatory pricing to influence market structure. (6)

B. Revision exercises

B1 Data response

Economists like competitive markets and they encourage governments to pursue policies that are designed to make markets more competitive. One such policy is deregulation. Markets are deregulated when the government removes legal barriers to entry. A good example of a market that has been deregulated is air travel. In 2007, the UK and the US governments signed an 'open skies agreement' that was designed to deregulate air travel between the two countries. Prior to the agreement, the USA and UK allowed only four airlines to operate direct scheduled services between the two countries.

On 30 March 2008, the new legislation came into force and the market for direct scheduled services between the USA and the UK suddenly became more competitive. Airlines such as British Airways and Virgin Atlantic now had to compete against new entrants such as Air France, Delta, Northwest and Continental Airlines. According to Bob Schumacher of Continental, 'We can finally take them [BA and Virgin] on their own turf. They've been living in a protected commercial environment for many years and at long last we can fly our flag next to theirs and the customer can choose.'

When the European air travel market was deregulated in the 1990s, new entrants, such as Ryanair and easyJet, piled into the market and fares dropped sharply as a result. Can consumers expect to pay less in the future for their flights between the UK and the USA? The answer is probably yes. British Airways and Virgin currently charge over £3000 for a business-class return ticket. New entrants like Delta and Northwest will probably try to steal customers away from BA and Virgin by undercutting these prices. A new airline called Zoom has been set up offering travellers a no-frills Ryanair-style service between Gatwick and New York for just £129 one-way.

Questions

(30 marks; 35 minutes)

1 Define the term deregulation. (2)

2 Deregulation will enable Air France to steal market share away from BA on the London–New York route. Following deregulation, examine two actions British Airways could take in order to take advantage of deregulated air travel between America and Europe? (6)

3 Deregulation has already made the market for air travel between the USA and the UK more competitive.

(a) Explain why Virgin might be reluctant to

react to the additional competition created by deregulation by reducing its business-class prices. (6)

(b) Outline two tactics other than price that Virgin could use to fight off the additional competition created by deregulation. (6)

4 Discuss the possible implications of the 'open skies agreement' for the various stakeholders in British Airways. (10)

B2 Data response

In April 2007 Dutch brewers including Heineken and Grolsch were fined £185 million by the European Commission for price fixing. The move followed a lengthy inquiry by the Commission into sales of beer to Dutch bars and restaurants in the late 1990s. Competition Commissioner Neelie Kroes said the brewers had 'carved up' the market between them, adding that such behaviour was 'unacceptable'. She said that board members and senior executives at the companies concerned had either participated or been aware of the actions and done nothing to stop them. 'The highest management of these companies knew very well that their behaviour was illegal but they went ahead anyway and tried to cover their tracks,' she said

The Commission said individual consumers may now seek compensation in the Dutch courts against the firms concerned. A trade association representing Dutch hotels and restaurants said it would seek financial redress in the form of discounts on future beer purchases, and possibly compensation.

The Commission has already taken action against brewers in Belgium, France and Luxembourg for similar offences. It formally accused the three brewers and smaller firm Bavaria of unfair trading practices in 2005, having launched its investigation several years earlier. They were alleged to have colluded in setting the price of beer sales in the Netherlands, keeping prices artificially high.

The Netherlands is one of Europe's largest beer-drinking markets although sales have fallen in recent years as older consumers tend to favour wine.

Source: Adapted from bbc.co.uk

Questions

(25 marks; 30 minutes)

1 What is price-fixing? (2)

2 Explain why firms like Heineken and Grolsch might enter into market sharing agreements that are designed to 'fix prices' within a market. (6)

3 Explain why many Dutch pubs may decide to sue Heineken and Grolsch. (4)

4 What factors might the European Commission have taken into account when deciding upon the scale of fine to impose on the brewers that carried out the price fixing? (4)

5 The article states that older consumers now favour wine over beer. Examine how this trend might affect the level of competition in the Dutch beer market in the short and long run. (9)

B3 Case study

Tesco's £9 toaster

The prices of consumer electronics, such as toasters, satellite TV set-top boxes and MP3 players, have tumbled in recent years. Supermarket chains such as Tesco now sell DVD players that previously cost hundreds of pounds for less than £10. So, why have the prices of these goods fallen? In part, the price falls reflect the falling price of the components that go into consumer electronics. Low prices also reflect the fact that there is now more competition in the market. In the past consumers typically bought items such as TVs and computers from specialist retailers such as Currys and Comet. Today, the situation is somewhat different; in addition to these specialist retailers consumers can now buy electrical goods over the internet and from supermarkets. Some industry analysts also believe that some of the supermarket chains are using set-top boxes and DVD players as loss leaders.

In today's ultra-competitive environment, manufacturers of consumer electronics face intense pressure from retailers to cut costs so that retail prices can be cut without any loss of profit margin. To cut prices without compromising product quality, manufacturers such as the Dutch giant Phillips have transferred production from Holland to low-cost locations such as China.

Questions

(40 marks; 50 minutes)

1 Describe three characteristics of a highly competitive market. (6)

2 Explain why the market for consumer electronics has become more competitive. (5)

3 Examine three factors that would affect the competitiveness of a manufacturer of MP3 players. (9)

4 **(a)** Use a dictionary or A–Z to find out the meaning of the term 'loss leader'. (3)

   (b) Why do supermarkets use this tactic? (3)

5 Discuss whether, in today's competitive market for consumer electronics, firms must constantly cut costs and prices if they are to survive. (14)

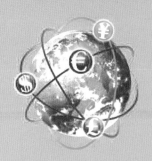

CHANGES IN OWNERSHIP AND COMPETITIVE STRUCTURE

DEFINITION

Growth can occur as a result of naturally increasing sales levels. This is called organic, or internal, growth. Growth may also be the result of changes in business ownership – mergers and takeovers. Takeovers occur when one firm buys a majority of the shares in another and therefore has full management control.

91.1 Organic growth

Organic growth is a safer, but slower method of growth than takeover. Its safety comes from the avoidance of the culture clashes involved in mergers or takeovers. Steady growth also avoids the need to add debt to a company's balance sheet, since finance is more likely to come from retained profits. However, a reliance on organic growth could lead firms to miss out on surges of growth in their industry if they fail to develop sufficient capacity to cope with the potential demand. For example, when Cadbury saw the increasing consumer interest in organic chocolate, it chose to buy up Green & Black's instead of developing its own organic brand.

A-grade application
Rapid organic growth

In late 2007, John Lewis announced plans to build an extra 24 department stores over the next ten years to add to its current 24 stores. The stores are to be built in areas not currently covered by existing stores. The rationale behind the expansion is straightforward: John Lewis believes it has a winning department store formula that is currently available to only some of the UK population. By building new stores in new areas, customers who would like access to John Lewis products will be able to switch from stores they currently use to the John Lewis stores, which, the firm hopes, will be more attractive stores in those areas. Although the expansion is dramatic in size, the chain will hope to be able to ensure that new staff can be inducted into the John Lewis culture in a new job, rather than taking over other stores that have closed down and attempting to change a previous culture.

Despite the appeal of takeovers to achieve rapid growth, the low success rate of takeovers and mergers encourages some businesses to aim for rapid organic growth. This is challenging, but can be achieved. Between its start in 1999 and 2007, Innocent Drinks' turnover grew from £0.4 million to £130 million, entirely organically (i.e. without buying up other companies). (That's a total growth of 32,400%!)

91.2 Mergers and takeovers: an introduction

Every time a company's shares are bought or sold on the stock exchange, there is a change in the ownership of that company. However, the significant changes occur when a majority of shares is bought by an individual or company. Any individual or organisation that owns 51% of a company's shares has effective control over

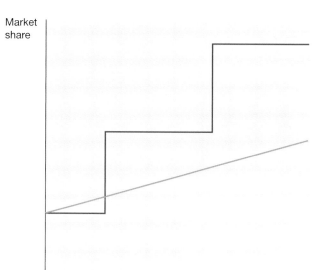

Figure 91.1 Organic vs. external growth
Blue = organic
Red = external

that company. To successfully take over a company, a firm (or individual) must therefore buy 51% of the shares. In America, this process is called mergers and acquisitions (M&A), acquisitions being another word for purchasing.

Why do firms merge with or take over other companies?

Growth

The fastest way for any firm to achieve significant growth is to merge with, or take over, another company. The motives behind the objective of growth may be based on any of the reasons outlined below. However, as a basic motive behind mergers and takeovers, growth is often the overriding factor.

Cost synergies

Cost savings are often used as a primary argument for corporate integration. It is suggested that **economies of scale** will arise from operating on a larger scale. If two businesses merge, output will increase. As a result, they are more likely to benefit from economies of scale, such as cheaper bulk purchasing of supplies. Synergies are the benefits from two things coming together. In this context, it is that the two firms together will have lower costs (and higher profits) than the two firms separately. In effect, **synergy** means that $2 + 2 = 5$.

Diversification

This means entering different markets in order to reduce dependence upon current products and customers. Diversification is a way of reducing the risk faced by a company. Selling a range of different products to different groups of consumers will mean that, if any one product fails, sales of the other products should keep the business healthy. The simplest way to diversify is to merge with or take over another company. This saves time and money spent developing new products for markets in which the firm may have no expertise.

Market power

When two competitors in the same market merge, the combined business will have an increased level of power in the market. It may be possible that this increased power can be used to reduce the overall competitiveness within the market. If prices can be increased a little, then margins will increase and the market will become more profitable.

Table 91.1 *Reasons for takeovers, and some examples*

Reasons for takeovers	Examples
Growth	• Royal Bank of Scotland beats Barclays to buy ABN Amro (Dutch) bank for £49 billion in October 2007 • Procter & Gamble buys Gillette for £32 billion in 2005
Cost synergies	• Morrisons taking over Safeway for £3 billion in 2004 • Co-op taking over Somerfield (it bid £1.7 billion in 2008)
Diversification	• Tesco buying Dobbies Garden Centres in 2007 • The Glazer family (owners of Tampa Bay American football team) buying Manchester United FC for £790 million in 2005
Market power	• Indian car producer Tata (producers of the world's cheapest new car) buys Jaguar and Land Rover in 2008 • In 2006 Ryanair bid £1 billion for Irish airline Aer Lingus; the bid was rejected as 'designed to

91.3 Types of business integration

here are four main types of merger or takeover (see igure 91.2), as discussed below.

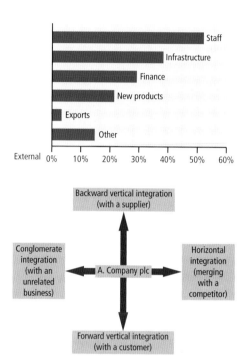

Figure 91.2 Vertical and horizontal integration

ertical integration

ertical integration occurs when one firm takes over or erges with another at a different stage in the oduction process, but within the same industry.

ckward vertical integration occurs when a firm buys t a supplier. In March 2008 Boeing announced the rchase of a key supplier to its 787 airplane. Boeing d it hopes this will enable it to overcome production oblems that have delayed the delivery of the plane to itish Airways and Virgin. The key benefit of a ckward vertical takeover is security of supply.

rward vertical integration means buying out a stomer, such as the purchase of retailer Body Shop by smetics producer L'Oréal. This shows the major nefit of forward vertical integration – guaranteed tlets for your products.

ble 91.2 explains the major advantages and sadvantages of backward and forward vertical tegration for three important stakeholders: the mpany (and its shareholders), the workforce and the stomers.

A-grade application

Vertically integrated entertainment

When video recorders were first available, Sony was horrified to find that its high-quality Betamax player was swept aside by the inferior VHS system. Toshiba, the originator of the VHS, had persuaded Hollywood film studios to use the VHS system for the film rental market. Sony decided: never again. The Japanese company chose (in the face of great hostility from America) to buy its way into the Hollywood studios. It bought Columbia Pictures and several other studios. At first it lost $billions, as Sony struggled to manage a Hollywood studio effectively.

The huge reward came in early 2008. In an exact parallel of the earlier video wars, Sony had pitched its Blu-ray HD disk against Toshiba's (and Microsoft's) preferred HD DVD. Using its power in Hollywood, Sony persuaded key businesses such as Disney to go for the Blu-ray format. In future, high-definition DVD will mean buying Blu-ray from Sony.

Horizontal integration

Horizontal integration occurs when one firm buys out another in the same industry at the same stage of the supply chain – for example, the 2008 purchase of Somerfield by the Co-op. In effect, this means buying a competitor. In the UK, if the market share of the combined companies is greater than 25%, the Competition Commission is likely to investigate before the integration will be allowed.

Of the four types of takeover, the most common by far is horizontal integration with a competitor. Typical examples include:

- Adidas buying Reebok

- mining giant BHP Billiton's $140 billion bid for rival Rio Tinto Zinc

- Mercedes buying the US car giant Chrysler.

For the purchaser, there are three major attractions:

1 huge scope for cost cutting by eliminating duplication of salesforce, distribution and marketing overheads, and by improved capacity utilisation

2 opportunities for major economies of scale

3 a reduction in competition should enable prices to be pushed up.

Table 91.2

	Backward vertical integration	**Forward vertical integration**
Advantages to the company	■ Closer links with suppliers aid new product development and give more control over the quality and timing of supplies ■ Absorbing the suppliers' profit margins may cut supply costs	■ Control of competition in own retail outlets: prominent display of own brands ■ Firm put in direct contact with end users/consumers
Disadvantages to the company	■ Supplier division may become complacent if there is no need to compete for customers ■ Costs might rise, therefore, and delivery and quality become slack	■ Consumers may resent the dominance of one firm's products in retail outlets, causing sales to decline ■ Worries about image may obstruct the outlet, e.g. Levi Stores rarely offer discounted prices
Advantages to the workforce	■ Secure customer for the suppliers may increase job security ■ Larger scale of the combined organization may lead to enhanced benefits such as pension or career opportunities	■ Increased control over the market may increase job security ■ Designers can now influence not only how the products look, but also how they are displayed
Disadvantages to the workforce	■ Becoming part of a large firm may affect the sense of team morale built up at the supplier ■ Job losses may result from attempts to cut out duplication of support roles such as in personnel and accounting	■ Staff in retail outlets may find themselves deskilled. Owner may dictate exactly what products to stock and how to display them. This would be demotivating
Advantages to the consumer	■ Better coordination between company and supplier may lead to more innovative new product ideas ■ Ownership of the whole supply process may make the business more conscious of product and service quality	■ With luxury products, customers like to see perfect displays and be served by expert staff, e.g. at perfume counters in department stores ■ Prices may fall if a large retail margin is absorbed by the supplier
Disadvantages to the consumer	■ The firm's control over one supplier may in fact reduce the variety of goods available ■ Supplier complacency may lead to rising costs, passed on to customers as higher prices	■ Increased power within the market could lead to price rises ■ If the outlet only supplies the parent company's products, consumer choice will be hit, as in brewery owned clubs or pubs

Of course, no purchaser states publicly that the plan is to push prices up. But if you owned four consecutive motorway service stations covering over 190 km of driving, would you not be tempted to charge a bit more?

As horizontal mergers have particular implications for competition, they are likely to be looked at by the Office of Fair Trading. If there is believed to be a threat to competition, the Competition Commission will be asked to investigate. The Competition Commission has the power to recommend that the Office of Fair Trading refuse to allow the integration, or recommend changes before it can go through. For example, if Unilever (which produces Walls ice cream and much else) made a bid for Mars, the Competition Commission would probably let the takeover through, on the condition that the Mars ice cream business was sold off.

Conglomerate integration

Conglomerate integration occurs when one firm buys out another with no clear connection to its own line of business. An example was the purchase by the household goods giant Procter & Gamble of the Gillette shaving products business. Conglomerate integration is likely to be prompted by the desire to diversify or to achieve rapid growth. It might also be for purely financial motives such as asset stripping (breaking the business up and selling off all its key assets).

Although the achievement of successful diversification helps to spread risk, research shows that conglomerate mergers are the ones least likely to succeed. This is largely because the managers of the purchasing company have, by definition, little knowledge of the marketplace of the company that has been bought.

Retrenchment and demergers

Sometimes firms will decide that they have grown too large to be controlled effectively. This is likely to be the case when diseconomies of scale are causing huge reductions in efficiency. In such cases, Directors may pursue a policy of **retrenchment** – deliberately shrinking in size.

Meanwhile, there has been growing scepticism about the benefits of mergers and takeovers. Recent research has shown that the majority of takeovers are unsuccessful, as measured by criteria such as profits, market share or the share price. This has resulted in a growing trend in the past few years towards the **demerger**. This occurs when a company is split into two or more parts, either by selling off separate divisions or by floating them separately on the stock exchange. Demergers are often the result of unsuccessful takeovers. Once a firm has seen that the economies of scale it expected are not happening, it will seek to sell off the business it originally bought.

A-grade application

In 1998, Mercedes of Germany bought the US Chrysler car business for $38 billion. What followed was one of the most disastrous takeovers of all time. Not only did Chrysler lose $billions in operating losses, but the German leadership's focus on America led to a downturn at Mercedes. Engineering and quality standards dropped alarmingly in 2003–2005, and Mercedes' reputation for quality has only just recovered. In 2007, Mercedes finally accepted its failure and sold Chrysler for $7 billion. By early 2008 the demerger was completed. Some analysts have suggested that the total losses to Mercedes from its ten-year US nightmare might be as high as $100 billion.

Another common situation leading to demergers is the desire of a company to reduce interest payments in times of economic downturn. Since many takeovers are financed heavily by borrowed capital, selling off recently acquired businesses will generate cash to pay back those loans.

Some firms, however, may simply decide to concentrate on core activities due to a change in their overall strategy. This might be caused by a change in economic circumstances or just because a new chief executive has been appointed. Having identified the core activities they will sell off others, even if they are profitable.

91.4 Private equity and gearing

Takeovers have always taken place between trading companies – for example, BP buying the US oil giant Amoco. By 2005, though, a new force had emerged in takeovers. Half the money spent on takeovers in the UK was coming from 'private equity', not from 'ordinary' companies. That year, private equity had snapped up Travelex, the Tussauds Group and Kwik-Fit. By 2007 private equity deals for firms as huge as Boots were going through (for £11 billion).

Private equity is a management group backed by sufficient bank finance to make a takeover – usually of a public limited company. Usually the financing of these takeovers is hugely reliant upon bank loans. In other words, the gearing can be as high as 90%. If the business is doing well (perhaps because the economy is in an upturn), the high gearing can boost the profits made by the investors. Unfortunately, if there is an economic downturn, trading losses will quickly eat away the small shareholders' funds within the business, pushing it into liquidation.

Private equity is the latest term for what were once known as leveraged buy-outs (LBOs) in America and **management buy-outs (MBOs)** in Britain. All share a common characteristic – extremely high gearing. This creates a situation of highly questionable business ethics – broadly 'heads I win, tails you lose'. If all goes well, the few private equity shareholders can make fabulous profits. If it goes wrong they can make staff redundant to cut costs and, if things continue to go wrong, pay themselves off before closing the business down. A 2008 report presented to the Davos forum of world leaders showed that private equity businesses cut 7% of staff within two years and have a significantly higher failure rate than ordinary businesses.

Debenhams store group has been a classic example of private equity. Taken private in 2004, the stores were re-floated on the stock market in 2006, creating enormous personal profits for the key directors. Since the 2006 flotation, the stores have lost market share and the shares have lost two-thirds of their value. The business itself was in significant difficulties by spring 2008.

A serious criticism of a business such as Boots 'going private' is that it no longer has to provide the accounting information demanded from a public company. The people who felt like stakeholders in the old public company (staff, customers and, of course, shareholders) no longer have access to the accounts.

Nor can they question the directors personally, as you can at a plc's **annual general meeting**.

91.5 Takeover decisions and Ansoff's matrix

A useful way to analyse the risks and rewards from a takeover is to apply Ansoff's matrix (see Unit 65). This considers the extent to which a business is keeping close to its core business (and knowledge/experience) or whether it is moving into new territory. For example, in February 2007 the US retail giant Wal-Mart paid $1 billion to buy a Chinese business with 101 hypermarkets in China. Does Wal-Mart know enough about Chinese grocery shopping to make a success of this takeover? Only time will tell. On Ansoff's matrix, this radical move into a new market would be represented as a major, high-risk move. If Wal-Mart bought a store chain in Canada (or Britain, where it owns Asda), it would be much safer.

The same type of analysis could work for considering the risks involved in ITV's 2006 purchase of the social network (for oldies) site, Friends Reunited. What did a television channel understand about running a website? Not a lot, which may explain why this takeover is widely considered to have been a flop. It could be debated whether this takeover was an example of product development or diversification. Either way it pushed ITV's management too far away from its area of expertise. It is a tough job running any business; it is often only arrogance that leads business leaders to believe they can run two different businesses at the same time.

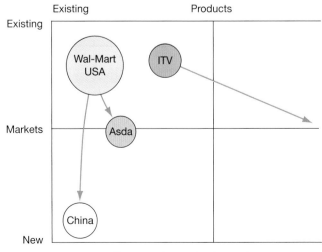

Figure 91.3 Ansoff's matrix applied to takeovers

Issues For Analysis

- The key theme for analysis when considering any question on mergers and takeovers is the identification of advantages and disadvantages. These are outlined briefly above, for each type of transaction. It is important to consider which advantages and disadvantages are likely to be relevant in the particular situation being considered. For example, a sugar producer that buys a soft drink manufacturer will not have any significant degree of control over the way its products are sold by retailer. In this case, one of the most significant advantages of forward integration disappears.

- Never forget that a merger or takeover will bring disadvantages as well as advantages. Research in America and Britain has shown consistently that the majority of takeovers fail to improve business performance. This is largely because managers anticipate the economies of scale from integration, yet they overlook the diseconomies from problems such as communication and coordination.

- Another important analytical theme is the differing effects upon different stakeholder groups. Many questions will offer marks for analysing the effects on consumers, or the workforce, rather than simply focusing on the effects on the firm as a whole.

91.6 Changes in ownership and competitive structure
an evaluation

A key judgement that is required is to see through the public relations 'hype' that surrounds takeover bids. Company leader A makes a bid for Company B, claiming that 'synergies will lead to better service and lower prices to our customers'. Really? Or will it mean factory closures, the elimination of small niche brands and – later – higher prices for all? Similarly, the leader may claim that the reason for a takeover is very businesslike, such as 'creating a world-leading company'. Yet the high failure rate of takeovers must imply that many claimed business benefits are a fig leaf. The real reason for many takeovers is arrogance, and perhaps greed, on the part of the executives concerned.

An explanation for the problems firms may encounter after a merger or takeover is resistance to change. This will be especially true if the business cultures are widely different and

e two companies. One may be go-getting and
ntrepreneurial; the other may be cautious and bureaucratic.
dgement is again required to consider whether a takeover
especially vulnerable to a clash of culture when the firms
ome together.

he other key issue raised in this unit is that of diversification.
aditionally, diversification was perceived as a good thing.
heorists such as Ansoff, Tom Peters and Bob Waterman
ave raised serious doubts. The management of the original
ompany may know little about the industry within which the
ew business operates. This means that those making major
rategic decisions may be doing so from a position of
norance. The advice in recent years has been to 'stick to
e knitting' – in other words, concentrate on doing what
ou do best.

Key terms

Annual general meeting: the once-yearly meeting at
which shareholders have the opportunity to question the
chairperson and to vote new directors to the board.

Demerger: this occurs when a firm is split into two or
more different companies.

Economies of scale: the factors that cause average
costs to be lower in large-scale operations than small ones.

Management buy-out (MBO): a specialised form of
takeover where the managers of a business buy out the
shareholders, thereby buying ownership and control of the
firm.

Organic: growth from within the business (e.g. getting
better sales from existing brands, or launching new ones).

Retrenchment: a deliberate policy of cutbacks, perhaps
to lower a firm's break-even point.

Synergy: this occurs when the whole is greater than the
sum of the parts $(2 + 2 = 5)$. It is often the reason given
for mergers or takeovers occurring.

Exercises

A. Revision questions

(30 marks; 30 minutes)

1 What is horizontal integration? (2)

2 For what reasons might a manufacturer take over one of its suppliers? (4)

3 Outline two reasons for each why Nokia might like to make a takeover of:
   (a) Motorola (4)
   (b) Vodafone. (4)

4 Why might a firm decide to carry out a demerger? (3)

5 Why may takeovers be riskier when financed by 'private equity'? (3)

6 Why might diversification be a bad idea for a growing firm? (3)

7 Explain the meaning of the word 'synergy'. (3)

8 Explain why businesses should consider Ansoff's matrix before making a takeover bid. (4)

B. Revision exercises

B1 Data response

Body Shop: because you're worth it

2006 saw the purchase of the Body Shop by French cosmetics giant L'Oréal. The deal was controversial because Body Shop shareholders and customers were concerned that L'Oréal would fail to maintain Body Shop's unique culture of socially responsible business. However, Body Shop was eventually sold for around £500 million, enabling L'Oréal to add another brand to its portfolio of products including Ambre Solaire, Lancôme, Elvive, Studio Line and Plenitude. L'Oréal's plan was to run Body Shop as a self-contained business, in an attempt to retain the firm's image, its major selling point among a loyal band of customers that undoubtedly makes up a significant niche within the beauty market.

Questions

(35 marks; 40 minutes)

1 Explain the possible motives behind L'Oréal's purchase of Body Shop. (6)

2 Analyse the possible difficulties that L'Oréal may encounter within Body Shop following the takeover. (8)

3 Explain why Body Shop will add to L'Oréal's product portfolio, without cannibalising existing brands. (6)

4 To what extent is L'Oréal's plan to run Body Shop as a separate business a sensible choice? (15)

B2 Data response

The 30%/70% rule.

On 15 May 2007, a £9 billion merger was concluded between the publisher Thomson and the news service Reuters. During this period of merger-mania, most corporate bosses have hardly bothered to justify the strategic logic behind the bid. Even though research shows that most mergers fail, rising share prices point to the love stock market investors currently have for takeovers.

The Thomson–Reuters merger took place in a week when Daimler (Mercedes) sold off the American business Chrysler after suffering losses of more than £20 billion since buying Chrysler in 1998. If Mercedes can't run a car company, what hope is there for any takeover bidder?

After announcing the merger, senior executives from Reuters and Thomson were interviewed by the *Financial Times*. They acknowledged that academics estimate that 70% of mergers fail, but Chief Executive Tom Glocer argued that Thomson Reuters should be 'firmly in the 30% camp'. He continued: 'It's important to look at why they fail. A lot comes down to culture. This has been an unusually warm and close transaction.'

The senior executives seem to assume that, because they can work together, all the staff will get along with each other. This remains to be seen. Tom Glocer is right to identify culture as a critical issue, but naive to think it is easy to manage.

When talking about the merger in practice, Glocer outlined the £250 million of cost-saving 'synergies' they hoped to benefit from. He emphasised, though, that staff should not be concerned. Another executive pointed out that: 'The hardest integrations are when you are consolidating. We're not consolidating, we're growing.' (Consolidating means the same as rationalising – that is, usually it amounts to cutbacks in jobs and in the variety of product ranges.)

The big hope is that the merger will boost revenues rather than cut costs. The new chairman said that: 'The strategic fit is about as compelling as can be. Reuters is strong in Europe and Asia and Thomson in North America'.

In 1998 the claims made about Daimler and Chrysler were equally optimistic. The strategy was Mercedes in Europe and Asia, Chrysler in the USA. The failure of that 'merger' was all down to problems in management, notably the inability to create a new common culture. In five years or so it will be clear whether Tom Glocer was right to put Thomson–Reuters 'firmly in the 30% camp'.

Questions

(30 marks; 35 minutes)

1 Explain the meaning of the following terms:
  (a) synergies (3)
  (b) strategic fit. (3)

2 Discuss whether Tom Glocer is wise to assume that this merger should be 'firmly in the 30% camp'. (12)

3 Examine why it can be hard to motivate middle managers within a newly merged business such as Thomson–Reuters. (12)

B3 Case study

The £9 billion computer games merger

In late 2007, two major computer games manufacturers announced plans to merge in a deal worth £9.15 billion. Activision, formed in 1979, is a major player in the console games market, producing titles such as the *Tony Hawk* series and the *Guitar Hero* games. It produces games for all major consoles, notably the PS3, Xbox 360 and Nintendo Wii, owning the rights to produce games for movie franchises such as *Spider-Man* and *X-Men*. Blizzard, previously owned by French entertainment firm Vivendi, is the world's largest online gaming company, producing, among others, the *World of Warcraft* game, played by over 9 million people. Geographically, Blizzard's strengths are in the Asian market, where online gaming is most popular, while Activision has traditionally been strongest in Europe and the USA.

The new company formed will be called Activision Blizzard and will become a global leader in the games market. Those behind the deal are hopeful that the coming together of two companies with contrasting strengths will enable the new firm to share the expertise of both staffs, while avoiding some of the more common problems associated with mergers, such as clash of cultures. Above all, the new company hopes to be in a stronger position than its smaller rivals to cope with continued troubled times for games developers, who have been struggling to cope with falling profits in an increasingly turbulent marketplace.

Questions

(35 marks; 40 minutes)

1 Explain why having contrasting strengths will benefit the newly merged company. (6)

2 Analyse two possible internal problems that may result from this merger. (8)

3 Explain why the merger may help the company to survive in 'an increasingly turbulent marketplace'. (6)

4 To what extent is a merger less likely to experience the problems of rapid growth than a takeover? (15)

C. Essay questions

(40 marks each)

1 Discuss the people management problems that may arise within a firm that has been taken over.

2 'The high level of takeover activity in the UK leads to short-termism'. Explain why this is so and discuss the implications for UK firms.

3 Synergy is often quoted as the reason for mergers and takeovers.
   (a) What is synergy?
   (b) To what extent is synergy a myth?

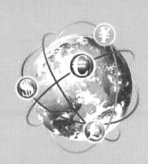

CHINA VS INDIA

92.1 China?

In 2001, investment banks coined the phrase BRICs to sum up the huge growth potential of Brazil, Russia, India and China. In fact the growth in China and India is far, far more significant than in the other two countries. In Brazil a growth rate of 3.7% is applauded; China sees a growth rate of 10% as a disappointment.

In 1997 the streets of every Chinese city were dominated by bicycles. The private car was still quite rare. Fewer than four households in a thousand owned a car. In 2006 China overtook Japan to become the world's second biggest car market (after the USA). In just that year, the Chinese car market grew by 25% and sales of Rolls-Royces rose by 60%. Volkswagen sells more cars in China than in Germany. The boom in China is incredible.

For more than 15 years the Chinese economy has grown by around 10% a year. That is faster than any other major economy in history. Even in Britain's Industrial Revolution the economy only grew at around 2–2.5% a year. And, of course, China is not only remarkable for its rate of growth, but also its population size. This is a country with nearly a quarter of the world's population. If 1300 million people have economic wealth, even the United States will have to step back. China is set to become the world's superpower. Or is it …?

92.2 Or India?

Some argue that India is in an even more powerful position. Although far behind China, its accelerating growth and population might make it the dark horse that eventually wins the prize. India has long been one of the world's poorest countries, yet one of the most populous. At 1100 million, its position as the world's second-most populated country puts it way ahead of America (in third place with 'only' 300 million).

In the last three years, the growth rate in India has risen to 8–9% – a huge increase on the 2–3% of ten years ago. Furthermore, its population has two features that China cannot match: it is rising and it is very young. Over the next 20 years there will be far more keen 20 year olds entering the Indian job market than in China. This is because China has made huge efforts over the past 25 years to curb population growth by pressing its people to have only one child per family. Due to this policy, only 20% of the Chinese population is 14 or under. In India the figure is 30%.

The Indian economy is also remarkable for its dynamic technology sector. This means that although India is a relatively undeveloped economy, it can compete with Britain and America in IT – one of the world's fastest-growing sectors.

Table 92.1 China and India: population figures

	China	India
Population growth	0.6% a year	1.4% a year
Population level 2007	1.32 billion	1.13 billion
Population level 2026 (est.)	1.46 billion	1.45 billion
Population 14 and under (2007)	274 million	337 million*
Population aged 20–30 in 2026 (est.)	190 million	240 million

*Note that the number of under-5s in India is greater than the whole UK population

92.3 Which has been growing faster?

Here the answer is clear. As shown in Figure 92.1, since 1991 the Chinese economy has completely outstripped that of India and managed to overtake Britain. This has largely been due to massive increases in 'fixed capital formation'. In the early 1990s the Chinese government started investing heavily in the economy, and started to encourage western companies to invest as well.

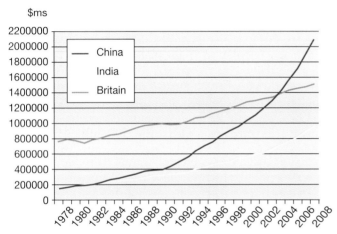

Figure 92.1 Growth in the size of the total economy: China, India and Britain
Source: National Bureau of Statistics of China; Government of India Ministry of Statistics; CIA and author's estimates for 2008 (China 10%, India 8%, Britain 2%)

Typically, the western companies invested by building factories (taking advantage of extremely low-cost labour), while the government started building dams (for water and electricity), roads and other forms of **infrastructure**. Today that government investment is going into housing, railways, schools and hospitals. China is gearing up for continuing success. Figure 92.2

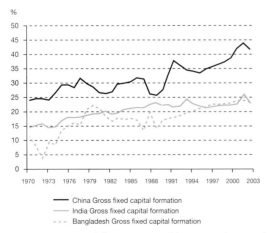

Figure 92.2 Capital formation: China, India and Bangladesh 1970–2005

shows that China is now spending more than 40% of it annual output on investing in its future (fixed capital formation). By comparison, India's spending is no higher, relatively, than in the less successful Bangladesl

China's long-term success has largely been built on export growth. In 2007, China's exports were six times higher by value than India's. Look, though, at Figure 92.3 and you can see how India's recent performance matches China's. India has important clothing exports and it now also exports steel. At the heart of its commercial success, though, are '**invisible exports**' such as software engineering and running English-speaking call centres. India has two important advantages over China: good English (the global language) and an education system that is excellent at the top end – so it produces many excellent managers and software experts

The big question now is whether India can sustain her recent success.

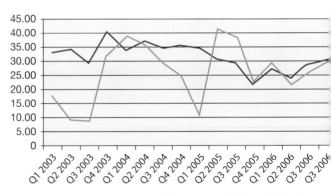

Figure 92.3 Export growth 2003–2006 (US 12m ag

92.4 Can India grow rapidly and consistently?

India has three key weaknesses in its attempts to keep up with China.

1 *Its poor infrastructure*: under-investment means that the road system lags behind China's – especially in motorway construction. It is possible that the reason is political. In China the government can dictate to the people that 40% of spending will be on investment. In India, there is a democratically elected government, and it may be that the public is unwilling to cut back too severely on today's spending in order to invest in the country's future.

2 *The narrow education system*: whereas the literacy level in China is 91%, in India it is only 58% (i.e. 42% of the population cannot read or write). Therefore if the growth rate led to job opportunities for a wider range of people, many

would be unable to take up the jobs due to illiteracy.

International trade: whereas in 2006 China had a current account surplus (more exports than imports) of $179 billion, India had a deficit of $26 billion. The deficit has been growing rapidly as Indian consumers have increased their spending on everything from cars to aircraft. Big deficits would make it hard for India to keep growing without a sharp, inflationary, fall in the value of the rupee.

nevitable overheating?

his is not an issue of global warming, but of economic erformance. In the past, accelerations in industrial oduction seem to have triggered rises in inflation. This is made the Bank of India respond by pushing up terest rates. From 6% in 2006 they reached 7.75% in pril 2007. Table 92.2 shows the apparent effect of erly rapid growth on India's inflation levels. This is a assic sign of overheating. The result of the Bank of dia's action on interest rates was to cut manufacturing owth back to +9% in April–September 2007. This ows the doubt there must be about India's ability to atch China's remarkable growth rates.

92.5 Can China outstrip America?

Some have expressed doubts about the sustainability of China's growth. They suggest that export growth must flatten out as Chinese wage rates start to rise. At present McDonald's pays its part-time staff in China about 30p per hour, so there is some way to go! In any case, this view assumes that China will remain a producer of low-cost items. In fact, China's exports of passenger cars rose by 100% in 2007 compared with 2006. Within five years China expects to be selling millions of cars in Europe and America. It does not need to rely on tiny wages. Nevertheless, it is true to say that China will lose some low-cost production. For example, at the moment minimum wage rates in India are slightly below £1 a day (i.e. about 12p per hour). So India can already undercut China.

ible 92.2 *India: manufacturing growth and inflation levels*

	Manufacturing growth	**Inflation**
May/June 2004	6.6%	3.6%
February 2005	8.7%	4.4%
February 2006	9.1%	4.8%
February 2007	11.3%	6.7%

urce: Indian government statistics, 2007

Table 92.3 Global carbon dioxide emissions

	Tonnes of CO_2 per head p.a.	Total CO_2 mn tonnes
India	1.0	1100
China	3.5	4700
UK	9.6	540
USA	20.2	5800
Russia	10.5	1500
World	4.2	26,000

Source: Energy Information Administration, 2004

Others believe that China is an environmental disaster, on the edge of collapse. There is no doubt that pollution is dreadful in industrial towns such as Linfen. Overall, though, China is investing heavily in cleaning up its rivers and air, and the country makes a relatively modest contribution to greenhouse gases. Table 92.3 shows the major contributors to CO_2 emissions. Generally, the richer the country, the higher the CO_2 emissions, though there are some exceptions, such as Russia. For some reason, Russia seems to escape criticism for its environmental record, whereas America is desperate to paint China as the 'bad guy'.

As China grows, its emissions will rise as well. This is why emissions in developed countries will have to be cut if there is to be a chance of stopping the global figure from growing further.

92.6 What opportunities are there for British business?

Every director of every public company knows that s/he must have a strategy for China and India. Tesco has its investment in Chinese superstores and has made clear its desire to get into India (foreign retail chains are not allowed to invest at the moment, for fear that millions of small local shops will be wiped out). Kingfisher owns a successful chain of DIY shops in China.

Yet these are examples of British firms buying their way in to China. What about actually selling to them (i.e. competing directly)? Here, Britain has made a very bad start. Today, the value of German exports to China is more than six times the value of Britain's; even France outsells Britain 2:1. Of all China's imports, Britain supplies less than 1%. And whereas imports to China rose 168% between 2002 and 2006, Chinese imports from Britain rose by just 57% – in other words, Britain's market share is small and getting rapidly smaller.

What about India? Britain ran India (as a colony) for 150 years, so there must be trade links remaining. Indeed in 2002 the British share of Indian imports was 4.96% (about in line with Britain's share of world trade). By 2006, however, the British share had fallen t 3.56%. Despite this decline, Britain still has distinct advantages over France, Italy and even Germany. The need is for British businesses to commit themselves to an effective strategy for India.

Issues For Analysis

- A2 exams are based on corporate (company-wide) objectives and strategy. Not, 'Should we put the price up/run a BOGOF promotion?' but 'Should we focus our efforts on India or China?' As few firms ca afford to do everything all at once, choices have to be made. Therefore it is vital to have some understanding about the future potential of differen countries and their economies. America will remain the richest place to live for years to come, but the growth rate and huge population of China make it inevitable that it will overtake America in the (relatively near) future. Will businesses be ready for this?

- It is interesting to wonder why Britain has done so badly in China. Is it because of a lack of initiative o far-sightedness by our business leaders? Or is it just a temporary problem at a time when the products China wants are not the ones we produce (e.g. cars) If so, perhaps there will be a future boom period when China starts buying the banking, media, creative and design service skills that generate such lot of our wealth at the moment.

72.7 China vs India

an evaluation

China has been growing at 9–10% for 15 years and looks capable of doing the same in the future. It may be short of younger people, but it has over 400 million people working on the land, many of whom would be pleased to earn higher wages in a factory. India also has good prospects, though it is less clear that it will be able to deliver high growth year in year out. It needs huge investments in education and infrastructure, but the Indian government is unwilling, or unable, to provide this. In this two-horse race, the one to back is China.

Nevertheless, for an individual business India may be the better bet. For a young British company lacking export experience, it would probably be easier to break into India than China, if only because there are fewer language and cultural barriers. Above all else, India lacks an effective manufacturing sector, so it may be a perfect place for British manufacturing exports or for setting up new factories. As always, each business case is different.

Key terms

Infrastructure the name given to the road, rail and air links, sewage and other basic utilities that provide a network that benefits business and the community.

Invisible export: the sale of a service to an overseas customer.

Exercises

A. Revision questions

(30 marks; 30 minutes)

1 Outline two reasons why China's growth prospects may be greater than India's. (4)

2 Outline two reasons why India's growth prospects may be greater than China's. (4)

3 Explain the significance of the figures shown for 'capital formation' in Figure 92.2. (6)

4 Explain what is meant by 'overheating', as shown in the text and the data in Table 92.2. (5)

5 Outline two reasons why a British retail firm such as Next might choose to invest in China rather than India. (4)

6 Look at Table 92.3 and answer the following questions.
   (a) Why is Russia criticised in the text given that its total carbon emissions are 'only' 1500 million tonnes? (2)
   (b) America regularly criticises China for its impact on global warming. Analyse this view based on the data provided. (5)

B. Revision exercises

B1 Case study

Exporting to China

Coventry-based Oleo International is a British company that has built up successful exports to China. In 2004 the Chinese government announced a £100 billion investment in its railways, including the construction of its own, Chinese-built 'bullet' trains. By 2020 China plans on building more new track than in Europe and America combined.

Oleo – a world leader in energy absorption equipment – saw its chance. It makes very advanced shock absorbers for railway carriages. These enable passenger trains to start up and stop with minimal bumping of passengers.

In 2004 Oleo, helped by the government's 'UK Trade & Investment', set up an office in Shanghai and invited Chinese officials to come and visit the Coventry factory. China was building its own track and trains, but still valued the British company's design and engineering expertise.

Oleo managed to obtain over £1 million of sales in 2005, its first trading year in China. Since then things have gone from strength to strength, encouraging the company to open its second sales office on the Chinese mainland. For any engineering business, China is quite simply the biggest opportunity in the world.

Questions

(40 marks; 45 minutes)

1 Outline two entrepreneurial skills shown by Oleo's management in this case. (6)

2 Explain the Oleo story in terms of its aims, objectives and strategy. (10)

3 Is it right that British taxpayers' money should be spent supporting companies such as Oleo to set up in China? Explain your view. (10)

4 One analyst has said that 'any engineering company that ignores China is signing its own death warrant'. To what extent do you agree with this statement? (14)

B2 Data response

China's about toys and plastics, isn't it?

In 1985, the value of exports from China amounted to $27 billion. Much of this was in the form of plastic products or cheap metal items such as toy cars. They were unsophisticated products from an undeveloped country. By 2007 the total value of Chinese exports had grown to $1220 billion, while the total value of its imports amounted to $920 billion. More interesting, perhaps, were the types of products exported by China in 2007 (first nine months only):

Rank	Category	Value (bn)	% change since 2006
1.	Mechanical and electrical products	$562	+28%
2.	High-tech products	$278	+25%
3.	Clothing and textiles	$141	+19%
5.	Shoes	$21	+16%
6.	Plastic products	$12	+9%
8.	Toys	$7	+37%

Source: China International Business, January 2008

Questions

(25 marks; 30 minutes)

1 Look at the figures above. Outline the changes in the types of export China is selling in 2007 compared to 1985. (6)

2 With reference to the same figures, what conclusions can you draw from the % changes in exports that have taken place since 2006? (6)

3 In 2007, 21% of China's exports went to America and 7.5% of its imports came from America.
(a) Calculate the balance of exports–imports between China and America in 2007. (5)
(b) Explain why American people and politicians might be reluctant to see this situation continue. (8)

B3 Case study

Growth vs inflation in India

NEW DELHI – India's economy will likely grow almost 9% this fiscal year, but rising inflation is a cause for concern according to the country's Finance Minister. He said he also worries that some industries are persistently underperforming despite the buoyancy of the broader economy.

India's economy expanded at a 9.1% rate in the first half of the fiscal year that ends in March 2008, and the Minister says he expects full-year growth to be almost 9%. That would put India's economic expansion — averaging more than 8% a year the past three years — close to the rate in China. The record for growth in the Indian economy was 10.5% in the fiscal year ended in March 1989. The economy grew 8.4% last year.

'We look back with considerable satisfaction at what has been achieved in the past year . . . [but] the only dark cloud as the year came to close was rising inflation,' he told business leaders at the annual meeting of the Federation of Indian Chambers of Commerce & Industry. India's inflation climbed to a rate of 5.5% the week ended 23 December, despite falling fuel and raw material prices in recent weeks.

The Finance Minister said the latest upturn in inflation was mostly driven by a rise in prices of some manufactured products. 'Even 4% inflation is unacceptable,' he said, warning that rising inflation could push up interest rates and slow economic growth in coming years. India's central bank has already increased some key rates, and commercial banks have increased their lending and deposit rates by a half to a full percentage point in recent months.

He said he was also concerned over the uneven spread of growth in the manufacturing sector. While overall manufacturing output is growing, several industries showed contraction. Those industries included food processing, paper, leather, chemicals and basic metals. He asked business leaders to look into why production was slackening in these sectors. Some of these industries are labour-intensive and a contraction could fuel unemployment.

Source: adapted from Rajesh Mahapatra, Associated Press, 1 September 2007

Questions

(30 marks; 40 minutes)

1 The Minister seems very gloomy. Outline one reason why he should be very pleased, given the information provided. (5)

2 Explain, in your own words, the Minister's reasons for saying that 'even 4% inflation is unacceptable'. (5)

3 What might be the consequence for Indian firms of the statement that 'India's central bank has already increased some key [interest] rates'? (8)

4 Taking the whole article into account, discuss the extent to which it supports the argument in the chapter that: 'This shows the doubt there must be about India's ability to match China's remarkable growth rates'. (12)

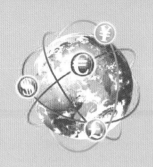
93.1 Introduction

ome 90% of the time most businesses can be successful y just focusing on themselves. Are we more efficient han a year ago? Is our staff well motivated and well -ained? Yet the other 10% can be critical. McDonald's ent straight ahead into a terrible storm when it ¡nored the rising tide of criticism about its menu and s advertising focus on children. Northern Rock hit the uffers when the US credit crunch took away its short--rm funding.

ong-term business success is achieved when 1anagement is able to delegate short-term issues to 1iddle managers who understand the long-term plan. 'hen the senior managers can make sure to think about 1e changing external influences on the business, witching focus when necessary. easyJet started as a irect cost-focused rival to Ryanair. Seeing the growth 1 affluence of the middle-market customers in the eriod 2000–2007, the management repositioned the usiness. It would no longer be the discount airline but he everyday airline: better value than British Airways nd better service than Ryanair.

ome businesses are naturally insulated from external ifficulties. Supermarkets such as Sainsbury's can

Figure 93.1 Supermarkets such as Sainsbury's can ary their product ranges to cope with changes in lemand

increase their range of posh products when the economy is in a boom period, and boost their value range when recession looms. For a business such as Land of Leather, though, economic conditions are critical. In the boom times people are happy to sign up to three years' credit terms on a gleaming leather sofa or two. When the credit crisis hit Britain in early 2008, though, sales at Land of Leather fell by 16%. Why not keep the old sofa for a while longer? It's not too bad, really. (Yet, in the same period, market leader DFS managed to keep its sofa sales unchanged.) Every business is unique in its sensitivity to external factors. Every generalisation is a mistake.

A useful way to look at each firm's sensitivity to external factors is to conduct a PEST analysis. All this means is to look at the company's vulnerability to Political, Economic, Social and Technological factors. A PEST analysis is a way of assessing changes in the major external influences on a business in the present and the future.

PEST analysis
Purpose

When a firm is considering its future, it will want a full assessment of its current and future situation. In addition to assessing the internal strengths and weaknesses of the company, the planners will need to assess the external environment in which the firm operates. The PEST framework offers a checklist of the major factors. Current and expected future factors can be listed under the appropriate heading in an attempt to ensure that foreseeable events or risks are considered in the strategic planning process. These factors are likely to fall into one of two categories: threats or opportunities. Threats represent possible or actual constraints on a firm's ability to achieve its objectives. An opportunity is a positive external chance for development that a firm may decide to pursue.

Political factors

Government policies can affect businesses both directly and indirectly. The effects may be direct, such as tax incentives designed to encourage R&D expenditure. Or they may be indirect, such as sales of car audio equipment being hit by new environmental laws designed to reduce car use.

Table 93.1 *The effects of government policies*

Possible government policies	Possible effects on firms
Laws on environment	Reduced sales or increased costs for some, while opportunities may arise for others
Health and safety law	Increased costs to comply with the laws (e.g. spending on training and equipment)
Employment law	Possibly less workforce flexibility, though this might force firms to behave more responsibly towards their staff
Competition policy	Constraint on possible merger or takeover strategy – though that may save businesses from an unwise merger
Smoking ban	Businesses fought hard to stop the regulation banning smoking in public places; now most (apart from the tobacco companies) would wonder why they bothered
Foreign policy (e.g. war in Afghanistan)	Britain is a major arms manufacturer; war means higher demand for guns, bombs and bullets
Sanctions against certain countries	May remove possible export markets

A-grade application

The smoking ban

On 1 July 2007, smoking was banned in all public places, including pubs and restaurants. The effect of the ban hit manufacturers such as Imperial Tobacco, directly, with Imperial reporting a 4% decline in sales over just the first three months of the ban. However, others affected include pubs and restaurants, which have seen the effects of smokers staying away. The effect of public smoking bans in other countries, such as Ireland, have shown a mellowing over time. Irish pubs and restaurants report that sales recovered within two years of corresponding bans, with more customers enjoying a smoke-free environment.

Political factors in overseas markets can also have an impact on business strategy. Installation of governments that are unfriendly to 'the West' may make trading harder with those countries. Meanwhile other markets, such as China, begin to open up as both a supply source and an export market as internal political change encourages international trade. Within Europe, the enlargement of the EU has provided huge opportunities for businesses such as Cadbury (which now produces much of its chocolate in Poland, and has enjoyed booming demand for its products in eastern Europe).

Economic factors

Variations in the overall level of consumer demand in an economy, perhaps caused by the trade cycle, affect some firms more than others. Well-run businesses have a good idea of how their sales respond to economic change. Sales of jewellery can easily fall by 10% if the economy dips by 2%. Careful planning ahead is vital in a business where stocks are so expensive to finance and to insure.

Individual economic variables, such as interest rates, inflation and exchange rates, will have an impact on many firms, but the trouble with assessing economic changes is that it is easy with hindsight but difficult to forecast! In 2005, BP's planning assumption for 2008 was that the oil price would be less than $50 a barrel. In fact, in May 2008 it was $130. If an oil company cannot forecast oil prices, it is hardly surprising that it is hard to estimate future changes across the whole economy.

The hardest economic variable to forecast is the exchange rate. None of the City's highly paid 'analysts' forecast the sharp drop in the pound's value against the euro in 2008 (down 15% from €1.45 to €1.23 within ight months). The key for businesses, then, is to be prepared for all possibilities. They should look ahead and wonder: what if the pound rises by 10% or 20%? And what if it falls by the same amount? The skill in strategic analysis comes in interpreting the likely effects on the business of the possible scenarios. This is called **scenario planning** by Shell, and is the company's favoured way of planning ahead.

Social factors

Changes in society can have a profound effect on a business. Businesses as diverse as Nike, Danone and Innocent have surfed the wave of western fascination with healthy lifestyles. Coca-Cola, McDonald's and Cadbury have had to fight against the same forces to avoid being hit hard.

Table 93.2 shows just a few current issues within the UK and the possible impact on the strategic planning of a business.

Technological (and environmental) factors

As scientific research allows the development of new technologies, the external environment in which firms operate can shift. The rate of technological change can represent a major external factor affecting business strategy. Technological change is likely to have two major impacts on businesses.

1 Production methods and materials can be enhanced, offering major cost advantages through increasingly efficient methods of production. Such a cost advantage may provide a major marketplace advantage with the ability to cut selling prices without accepting a loss of margin. Meanwhile, new methods may bring increased quality of products, which may become a key feature of a company's marketing. Those firms that fail to take advantage of any technological advances in production methods are likely to struggle in a competitive market.

2 Products may become obsolete as a result of technological change. (VCRs, for example, have been entirely superseded by DVD players in a very short space of time.) Such examples mean that PEST analysis plays a vital role in identifying as early as possible any technological changes that will damage the sales of existing products. Of course, such changes can also represent an opportunity to those firms that are able to produce brand new products that rely on new technologies. Such opportunities can bring high margins, market leadership and a strong reputation as an innovator for years to come, if the potential use for the technological change can be spotted early enough.

Table 93.2 *Social factors and their possible impact on strategic planning*

Social change	Explanation	Possible impact
Ageing UK population	Lower birth rates and longer life expectancy in the UK are contributing to a population that consists of a growing proportion of pensioners	Increased focus on niche markets catering to older consumers – anything from holidays to car insurance (and, of course, stairlifts)
Increased power of the 'pink pound'	Increasing acceptance of homosexuality has led to the growth of niches in many markets aimed specifically at the pink pound	Another opportunity to exploit a clearly definable and growing niche market leads to the creation of new brands, shops, pubs and clubs aimed squarely at the pink pound
Childhood obesity	Growing social concern over levels of childhood obesity, caused by a mix of poor diet and lack of exercise	Need to adjust product portfolio, introducing healthier children's food, and accept government pressure to stop advertising fatty foods in children's TV programmes
Healthy lifestyles	Increased awareness of the need to lead a healthy lifestyle in order to live longer has changed spending patterns	Need to adjust product element of the marketing mix, perhaps using only organic ingredients; health clubs move into the mass market, away from the traditional young adult niche

A-grade application
New types of TV

Glass-makers in Wales whose major business was manufacturing traditional TV screens suffered heavily in 2005 as a result of failing to adjust early enough to technological change. Three factories in South Wales made staff redundant as plasma and flat-screen TVs replaced traditional TVs in living rooms throughout Europe. Both Sony and NEG announced that, as a result of falling sales of traditional TVs, they were either closing their factories or making staff redundant in order to reduce running costs. Such technological changes are often sweeping – destroying the markets for some products completely within just a few years. The job losses experienced at these factories could have been avoided if the changes had been spotted early enough to allow a strategic overhaul to take place that converted these factories to production of flat screens or plasma screens.

Increasingly, technological change is becoming interwoven with environmental issues. Having seen the rise and rise of the hybrid Toyota Prius, US car makers are desperate to be first with the next great step forward in greener motoring: the electric car. Whichever company is first to market with a credible electric car will have huge sales potential – and gain the green glow currently worn (smugly) by Toyota.

Weaknesses

There are of course weaknesses to this type of formal analysis. The external environment is, by its very nature, unpredictable. PEST analysis is therefore, to a certain extent a mixture of guesswork, experience and hunch. Not only will some external events catch firms by surprise, but also the effects of external factors may be hard to figure out in advance. Something that had seemed an opportunity may in fact turn out to be a threat.

This leads to the second possible weakness of PEST analysis. There is a danger that a full and thorough PEST analysis, perhaps carried out once a year, will lead a firm to be complacent until the next major PEST review.

In 2006, the best-selling business author Nicholas Taleb wrote a book called *The Black Swan*. The point of the title is that everyone in Europe thought swans could only be white, until the first travellers to Australia told of **black swans**. Taleb's point was that people's ideas are fixed, based on their experience to date. Taleb warned

of the likelihood that the economic, financial and housing boom would explode unexpectedly. As his book was published, in 2007, the markets duly exploded. PEST analysis should always include some thought about how well the business could cope with a completely unexpected disaster.

Issues For Analysis

● Breaking down a firm's external influences into the PEST categories can help to separate key from peripheral issues. Then a consideration of the implications of each external factor allows the construction of analytical chains of cause and effect. This is especially important because some factors may have only an indirect influence on an organisation.

● Another issue to consider is the timeframe of a PEST analysis. How far into the future is the analysis trying to examine? Predicting external changes over the next year or two may be relatively straightforward in some industries, but very tough in others. Just consider the impact of 2007's credit crunch on the banking and building industries. Other firms have inevitably to look decades ahead. For example, if BAA wants to build a third runway at Heathrow, it will take at least ten years (Terminal 5 at Heathrow took nearly 20 years from the first plans to its April 2008 opening).

93.2 Integrated external influences on business strategy
an evaluation

Judgement may come in the form of deciding which issues are most likely to occur and which are likely to have the most impact on the firm, then weighing them up to prioritise which issues need to come to the top of the strategic agenda following a PEST analysis. This is indeed the kind of risk assessment-based approach that many firms take when allocating resources to deal with PEST factors. Most resources go to dealing with those issues that are most likely to happen, with the greatest potential impact on the company.

Successful interpretation of a PEST analysis is more likely to be achieved by those with a gift for interpreting market data and the experience required to really understand what the analysis means for a particular firm.

final point to note is that effective management relies on
n awareness of what is not foreseeable – those who stick
gidly to the strategies constructed on the basis of a one-off
EST analysis are likely to be slow in reacting to
nforeseeable changes.

> **Key terms**
>
> **Black swan:** an event that could not be forecast
> because it is outside past experience.
> **Scenario planning:** thinking of a range of possible
> future outcomes, both economic and social, then
> considering how the business should respond to those
> situations.

Further reading

Taleb, N. (2007) The *Black Swan*. Allen Lane.

Exercises

A. Revision questions

(30 marks; 30 minutes)

1 Briefly explain why a firm such as British Airways needs to consider the external environment when planning its future strategy. (5)

2 Analyse the possible positive effects of an economic upturn on a manufacturer of luxury goods. (5)

3 Outline how two firms of your choice might be affected by a sharp increase in food prices as a result of global warming. (4)

4 PEST factors tend to provide both opportunities and threats to a business. If a strategy is to address both, explain how it might include the following:
   (a) opportunities
   (b) threats. (6)

5 Briefly explain two possible weaknesses of using PEST analysis. (6)

6 Outline two ways in which a firm's financial strategy might be affected by the idea of a black swan (i.e. that unpredictable events do happen). (4)

B. Revision exercises

B1 Data response

Fopp flops

Fopp, a UK music retailer, went into administration in summer 2007. Despite a good reputation with customers, Fopp simply failed to cope with the external influences affecting music retailing in the UK. Shortly after the firm's closure, a industry source announced that UK CD sales were down 10% in the first half of 2007. Much of this slump, part of an ongoing trend, was the result of increasing numbers of online music downloads, and was affecting other retailers too. Soon afterwards, HMV announced that its profits had halved for the first part of 2007. Fopp's other major problem was competition from online

retailers and supermarkets selling CDs and DVDs at cheaper prices than traditional high-street retailers. Other analysts suggested that Fopp had also struggled to maintain cash flow as a result of its purchase of 67 stores from failed competitor Music Zone. Whatever the cause, the end result was several hundred redundant staff, many creditors seeking payment for the debts the company owed and the loss for many of a popular high-street brand.

Questions

(35 marks; 40 minutes)

1 Although Fopp had set up a website offering online CD sales, the site never gained the popularity enjoyed by other online retailers. Examine the possible reasons for this. (8)

2 To what extent could a formal PEST analysis have helped the firm avoid the problems it encountered? (15)

3 To what extent should a company's senior management be blamed when a collapse happens, as at Fopp? (12)

B2 Case study

Simpsons & Sons Ltd is a long-established IT hardware supplier, specialising in providing interactive whiteboard technology to schools and colleges throughout the UK. The firm has seen huge success over the past five years as government has made funds available to schools specifically to purchase interactive whiteboards.

Ian Simpson, the Chief Executive, believes that the market has another five years of rapid growth until it reaches saturation – a point at which every classroom in the UK has an interactive board. Simpsons needs to make some strategic decisions about how to prepare to make the most of the next five years. Joe Simpson, the marketing director, has commissioned market research that indicates that Simpsons' products are considered reasonably priced and of excellent quality.

This is good news to purchasing manager Sam, who pushed through the decision to use a

Chinese subcontractor to manufacture the boards. Operations manager Molly needs to work with HR Director Nikki to decide whether to hire more sales engineers (they install the whiteboards and provide after-sales service). Sam is keen to know whether the Chinese supplier can be encouraged to maintain production at current high levels in order to keep unit costs low. At a board meeting, the only non-family director, Stefan Sansom, has provided the following information.

- The UK government is planning to pass a new law requiring all IT hardware providers to test their wireless networking components for health issues.
- Economic forecasts suggest that the UK is expected to enter a recession next year that could last for up to three years.
- Scientists have issued a new report that links the use of wireless networks to behaviour problems in the under-20s.
- An independent think-tank publishes a report claiming that students who use interactive whiteboards see a significant increase in their achievement while at school.
- *The Sun* is running a campaign to ban wireless networks in schools due to fears of brain damage.
- UK government policy will shortly specify the need to use interactive whiteboards in every UK classroom.

Questions

(35 marks; 45 minutes)

1 Under which heading of PEST analysis should the external factors listed in the case be placed? Explain when you think a factor could be listed under more than one heading. (10)

2 Analyse the possible impact on Simpsons of the following:
   (a) the independent think-tank report (5)
   (b) the new law on testing wireless equipment. (5)

3 Write a report to the directors explaining, with examples from the case, how a PEST analysis could help them to develop a strategy for the next five years. (15)

C. Essay questions

(40 marks each)

1 'In rapidly changing markets such as that for consumer electronics products, regular use of PEST analysis is an absolute necessity.' To what extent is this statement true?

2 Using a pre-set and limited framework such as PEST to analyse the external factors affecting a business inevitably leads to oversights. Discuss whether this undermines the usefulness of the technique.

CAUSES OF AND PLANNING FOR CHANGE

DEFINITION

Change is a constant feature of business activity. The key issues are whether it has been foreseen by the company – and therefore planned for – and whether it is within the company's control.

94.1 Internal and external causes of change

Change arises as a result of various internal and external causes. The internal ones (such as a change in objectives) should at least be planned for. External causes may be unexpected, which makes them far harder to manage. Table 95.1 sets out some possible internal and external causes of change.

Of all the issues relating to change, none is more crucial than when a business is having to cope with a period of rapid growth. For example, in the first stage in the rapid growth of Bebo (the social networking site launched in 2005, which sold for $850 million in 2008), the number of employees rose from one to twenty-eight within nine months.

94.2 Business effects of forecast rapid growth

In certain circumstances managers can anticipate a period of rapid **organic growth**. This may be temporary (such as the effect of a change in the law) or may seem likely to be permanent (such as the growth in demand for a hot website). The most successful firms will be those that devise a plan that is detailed enough to help in a practical way, but flexible enough to allow for the differences between forecasts and reality.

When rapid growth has been forecast, firms can:

- compare the sales estimate with the available production capacity

- budget for any necessary increases in capacity and staffing

- produce a cash flow forecast to anticipate any short-term financing shortfall

- discuss how to raise any extra capital needed.

Timescales remain important, though. The forecast ma▾

Table 94.1 *Examples of internal and external causes of change*

Internal causes	External causes
• New growth objectives set by management • New boss is appointed • Decision to open up new export markets • A decision to increase the shareholders' dividend makes it difficult to find the capital to invest in the business	• Rising consumer demand/the product becomes fashionable • Economic boom benefits a luxury product • Closure/fire/strike hits competitor, boosting your sales • New laws favour your product (e.g. new safety laws boost sales of first aid kits)

over the next three months, but increasing capacity may involve building a factory extension, which will take eight months. In which case there may be five months of excess demand to cope with (perhaps by subcontracting).

Smooth though all this sounds, there remains a lot of scope for error. The starting point is the increased workload on staff. Extra sales may put pressure on the accounting system, the warehouse manager and the delivery drivers. With everyone being kept busy, things can occasionally start to go wrong. Invoices are sent out a little later, unpaid bills are not chased as quickly and stock deliveries are not checked as carefully. Suddenly the cash flow position worsens and costs start to rise. A strong, effective manager could retrieve this, but many are weak and woolly. Once they start to go wrong, plans are hard to sort out.

94.3 Management reorganisation during growth

Problem of adjustment from boss to leader/manager

The typical creator of a successful new business is lively, energetic, creative, often impatient and always a risk-taker. Such a person will have a strong personality, and quite possibly an autocratic though charismatic leadership style. When the business started, their own speed of decision making, attention to detail and hard work were fundamental to the firm's success.

With success comes a problem. How to cope with the additional workload? At first the boss works ever harder; then s/he takes on more junior staff. Then comes the crunch. Is s/he willing to appoint a senior manager with real decision-making power? Or will a weak manager be appointed who always has to check decisions with the boss?

Staff will always find it hard to accept a new manager because everyone will know that it is really the boss's business. It is said that, ten years after Walt Disney died, 'managers were still rejecting ideas on the basis that Walt wouldn't have done it that way.' How much harder if the founder is still there: James Dyson at Dyson, Bill Gates at Microsoft, and Larry Page and Sergey Brin at Google.

The boss must make the break, however. No longer should s/he attend every key meeting or demand regular reports on day-to-day matters. Delegation is necessary.

In other words, authority should be passed down the hierarchy to middle managers without interference from above. And instead of looking for the next great opportunity the boss may have to focus on getting the right management structure to ensure a smooth-running business.

Even if the founder of the company *is* able to adjust to managing a large organisation, there remains the problem of motivation. Will the new staff be as 'hungry' as the small team that built the business? Usually the answer is no. The drinks giant Diageo thinks it has a solution, though. It is a business with annual profits of over £2000 million, based on brands such as Smirnoff, Baileys and Guinness. To keep staff hungry, the chief executive gives managers a 'HAT': a Hairy Audacious Target. In other words, a bold, challenging goal. Achieving these HATs will give each manager the chance to make huge bonuses. The chief executive believes HATs can stretch 'our people's imaginations to achieve these aggressive targets'.

Change in management structure/hierarchy

As a business grows, the management structure has not only to grow too, but also to change. New layers of management may be needed and completely new departments may be founded, such as personnel or public relations. And all the time, as the business grows, new staff are being recruited, inducted and trained. So there is constant change in personnel and their responsibilities. This can be disconcerting for customers and suppliers. Strong relationships are hard to build, making customer loyalty tough to achieve.

Even more important, though, is the internal effect of these personnel changes. With new staff appearing frequently, and managerial changes occurring regularly, team spirit may be hard to achieve. Junior and middle managers may spend too much of their time looking upwards to the promotion prospects instead of concentrating on their own departments. The potential for inefficiency, or even chaos, is clear. Too many new staff may mean too many mistakes. If customer relations are relatively weak, the result could easily be loss of business.

These unpleasant possibilities can largely be set aside if a good example is set from the top. If the founder of the business continues to be involved – especially on customer service – all may still be well. The leader needs to make sure staff keep sight of the qualities that brought the business its success in the first place. If new management structures threaten to create communications barriers, the leader should set an example by visiting staff, chatting to them and acting on their advice. The leader must fight against being cut off from the grassroots – the staff and the customers.

Risk of loss of direction and control

Each year, Templeton College Oxford produces data on what it calls the Fast Track 100. These are the fastest-growing 100 small companies in Britain. The December 2007 survey showed that the average growth rate of the top 10 of these firms was:

- sales turnover +180% per year
- employees +150% per year.

The typical Fast Track 100 firm had gone from 25 staff to 136 staff in the past three years. No wonder, then, that rapidly growing small firms can struggle to cope. The same survey showed that the key challenges faced by these companies were staff and infrastructure (source: www.fasttrack.co.uk).

The **entrepreneurs** who get swamped by the success of the business are those whose firms will fail to sustain their growth. They may become side-tracked by the attractions of expense account living. Or – the other extreme – become so excited by their own success that they start opening up several different businesses. They assume that their golden touch will ensure success in whatever they do. Instead, just as their core business becomes harder to handle, they are looking at a different venture altogether. Problems may then hit from several directions at once.

The key message is, therefore: focus on what you are good at.

94.4 Problems of transition in size

From private to public

At certain points in a firm's life there will be critical decisions to be made regarding growth. Few are more fundamental than the decision to 'go public'. A private limited company is a family business, often dominated by the shareholdings of one person – probably the founder. Although its accounts must be published, it is still able to maintain a substantial veil over its activities. Its private status minimises the pressures upon the management. A year of poor trading may disappoint the family, but there is no publicly quoted share price to embarrass the firm or to threaten it with a hostile takeover. This protection from outside pressures enables private companies to take a long-term view of what they want to achieve and how.

Switching from private to public company status is not in itself, a difficult or expensive process. The big change comes when a firm floats its shares on the stock market. Only public companies are allowed to do this. From the protected world of the private company, the firm will enter the glare of public scrutiny. Before floating, the firm must issue a **prospectus** that sets out every detail of the firm's business, its financial record, its expectations and its key personnel. Newspapers and analysts will scrutinise this fully, and carry on writing about the firm when every set of financial results comes out.

The purpose of going public is usually to achieve a substantial increase in share capital. This can enable a highly geared private firm to achieve a more balanced capital structure, as shown in Table 94.2.

Table 94.2 Cutting gearing by going public

Sharps Ltd (before going public)		Sharps plc (after raising £4m on the stock market)	
Loan capital	£4m	Loan capital	£4m
Share capital	£1m	Share capital	£5m
Reserves	£3m	Reserves	£3m
Capital employed	**£8m**	**Capital employed**	**£12m**
Gearing level:	50%	Gearing level:	33%

the case of Sharps plc, the addition of 50% more
capital (from £8 million to £12 million) will give a huge
opportunity for major expansion. Indeed, if the
management act slowly, the purchasers of the £4 million
extra shares may get restless. So the managers will be
inclined to make a big move. Perhaps they will make a
takeover bid. Or perhaps a diversification, by launching
a new product range. Either way, the risks are
substantial. Does this business have the expertise to
succeed with either approach? What it needs is the
confidence to keep focused upon what the management
is good at. But the public pressure to make a big step
forward may encourage the management to take a step
too far.

Retrenchment

Just as big steps forward can lead to problems, so can
steps backward. Yet few firms will keep growing without
the occasional sharp setback. Retrenchment means
cutting back. This may be achieved through a general
reduction in staffing, or perhaps only a halt on
recruitment. Most often, though, it will imply a
rationalisation in which there are significant changes to
the organisational structure and/or to the capacity level
of the business.

In 2008, there were major worldwide rationalisations by
giants such as Ford, General Motors, Kodak and
Lehman Brothers (investment bank). In all cases, the
key factor is to ensure that retrenchment does not cause
lasting damage to morale, relationships and trust.
Therefore it is vital to be honest, open, fair and as
generous as possible to anyone who is losing a job.

When forced to cut back, firms have many options, as
outlined in Table 94.3.

94.5 Planning for change

For managers who can foresee significant change, a
strategic plan is needed. This should help in managing
the change process, ensuring that the business has the
personnel and the financial resources to cope. The
strategic planning process is undertaken by an
organisation's senior managers. The first decision they
face is: 'How do we turn this change to our own
advantage?'

Having established the strategic direction the
organisation will adopt, the senior managers must next
set the boundaries within which middle and junior
management will take day-to-day decisions. A series of

Table 94.3 *The benefits and drawbacks of different types of retrenchment*

Type of retrenchment	Advantages	Disadvantages
Freeze on recruitment and/or offering voluntary redundancy	• not threatening; should not cause problems of job insecurity • viewed by staff as fair	• no chance to reshape the business • good people are always leaving, so they need to be replaced
Delayering (i.e. removing a whole management layer)	• should not affect direct operations (such as staff on the shop floor) • may empower/enrich remaining jobs	• may over-intensify the work of other managers, causing stress • risk of losing a generation of managers • loss of promotion prospects for those who remain
Closure of a division or factory, or a number of loss-making outlets	• sharp reduction in fixed overhead costs will reduce break-even point • capacity utilisation may rise in the firm's other factories	• once closed, the capacity is unlikely to be available for the next economic upturn • loss of many good staff
Targeted cutbacks and redundancies in divisions throughout the business	• can reshape the business to meet future needs (e.g. no cutbacks among IT staff) • by keeping good staff, their average quality level may rise	• huge problems of perceived fairness (unless there is a high degree of trust) • job security may be hit ('Will it be me next?')

integrated actions must be set out. These will have the purpose of moving the organisation forward in the identified strategic direction. This plan will be introduced over a period of time known as a 'planning horizon'. This will commonly be between one and three years, but may vary depending on how stable the organisation's competitive environment is. The greater the stability, the longer the planning horizon will be.

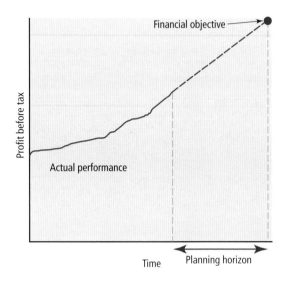

Figure 94.1 Financial objectives

Strategic planning is only necessary because firms operate in a changing environment. If this was not the case then a single strategy, once designed, would bring success to the business on a permanent basis. However, changes in key variables such as technology, consumer tastes and communications make planning strategy increasingly important. The pace of change is intensifying, creating shorter product life cycles and encouraging increased competition. It is change that creates the '**strategic gap**' that must be closed by the second phase of the planning process.

Organisations that seek to achieve objectives such as the maximisation of long-term profits will set themselves financial targets. These will be influenced by shareholders' expectations and the personal and business ambitions of the company directors. These expectations will determine the financial objectives of the organisation over the forthcoming planning period.

The difference between the profit objective and the forecast performance of the business, is known as a strategic gap (see Figure 94.2).

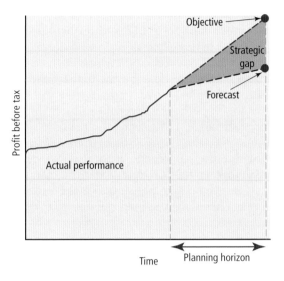

Figure 94.2 A strategic gap

Closing a strategic gap

Once a strategic gap has been identified it is necessary to devise a series of strategies to close it.

It may be possible to achieve this to some extent by performing existing operations more efficiently, in order to reduce costs and boost profit. However, this is unlikely to solve the whole problem. Only careful strategic planning can develop the means by which the organisation can increase its effectiveness in order to meet its financial objective.

The analysis of the strategic gap should reveal how difficult it will be to cope with the change. The future may look bright, such as for an organic farmer in a period of change towards more care and thought over healthy eating. Or it may look bleak, such as for a house-building business in 2008 in the wake of sharp falls in house prices. Whether the gap is upwards or downwards (forcing the business to retrench), a careful planning process should make the transition easier.

Contingency planning

A strategic plan should outline the critical assumptions that have been made about the future competitive environment. If the success of the project depends on these judgements a 'fallback' position, or **contingency plan**, should be developed in case they prove wrong. As part of the planning process, 'What if?' questions should be asked. For example, a manufacturer of bicycles, thrilled about the sales boom in 2006–2008 should ask the question: 'What if a sharp US recession forces oil

rices back down again?' Lower oil prices would get
eople back into their cars, forcing demand down for
les of new bicycles. Contingency planning allows the
rm to consider what action it will take if particular
pportunities or threats emerge as a strategy is
nplemented.

Issues For Analysis

/hen tackling questions about the causes of – and plans
or – change, the following lines of analysis are helpful.

- If the business faces rapid growth, is it planned
  (internal) or unplanned (external)?

- Is the business leader's management style capable of
  changing as the business develops?

- Does the firm have the financial resources to cope
  with the need for capital during a time of change?

- How well does the firm cope with growth shocks,
  such as a stock market flotation? Can the
  management keep focused upon the strategy and the
  strengths of the business.

- Would managers who have handled growth well be
  equally good at handling retrenchment? Only if they
  have and deserve the trust of the staff.

Key terms

Contingency plan: a Plan B in case Plan A goes
wrong.
Entrepreneur: an individual with a flair for business
opportunities and risk-taking. The term is often used to
describe a person with the entrepreneurial spirit to set up a
new business.
Organic growth: growth from within the business (e.g.
sales growing rapidly because a product is riding a wave of
consumer popularity).
Prospectus: a document that companies have to produce
when they go public (i.e. are quoted on the stock
exchange); it gives details about the company's activities
and anticipated future profits.
Rationalisation: reorganising to increase efficiency. The
term is mainly used when cutbacks in overhead costs are
needed in order to reduce an organisation's break-even
point.
Strategic gap: the difference between where the
business is and where it plans to be.

74.6 Causes of and planning for change
an evaluation

hange is normal, not abnormal. Therefore firms need to be
ert to causes of change and quick to devise a strategic
an for coping. Many successful businesses do not have a
rmal strategic planning process. This does not mean that
e issues raised here are not relevant to these organisations.
e same problems must be dealt with when strategy
merges over time as when it is planned more
stematically. The advantage of explicitly setting aside time
r strategic planning is that managers' minds are
oncentrated on the key questions facing the firm in the
ture. Then the actions decided upon can be more closely
tegrated.

Exercises

A. Revision questions

(50 marks; 50 minutes)

1 Explain why rapid growth can cause problems for a company's:
   (a) cash flow (2)
   (b) management control. (2)

2 Distinguish between internal and external causes of growth, using examples. (5)

3 Why may there be a problem in adjusting from 'boss' to 'leader/manager'? (4)

4 Identify three problems for a fast-growing firm caused by changes in the management structure. (3)

5 Outline two strengths and two potential weaknesses of stock market flotation for a rapidly growing business. (8)

6 Explain the possible problems (and benefits) to a small computer software firm of changing status from private to public limited company. (4)

7 Explain in your own words the idea of the planning horizon. (4)

8 Explain why it might be hard for young, inexperienced managers of a successful business start-up to cope effectively with an unexpected, dramatic change. (5)

9 (a) Explain the meaning of the term 'retrenchment'. (3)
   (b) Outline two suitable methods of retrenchment for an airline that is losing market share. (4)

10 Explain why it may be hard for a struggling jewellery business to fill its strategic gap. (6)

B. Revision exercises

B1 Data response

From Google to Facebook

Sheryl Sandberg wants to bring to Facebook what she brought to Google: discipline and inventiveness to foster rapid growth. Two weeks into her job as Facebook's Chief Operating Officer (COO), the 38-year-old executive, second in command to 23-year-old CEO Mark Zuckerberg, is rolling out new management and operations procedures. Among these are guidelines for employee performance reviews, processes for identifying and recruiting new employees, and management-training programmes.

Ms Sandberg's experience expanding operations and building talent is just what the social networking site may need as it aims for a big expansion. 'Facebook is a different space than Google, with tremendous potential to connect people, but it needs scale, it needs systems and processes to have impact, and I can do that,' she says.

The social networking site, which allows users to create personal profiles to share with friends, had more than 100 million visitors in January, a fourfold increase from the year-earlier period. But it's still burning up more cash than it is generating in revenues, according to people familiar with the company's finances.

At Facebook, which is privately held, Ms Sandberg is in charge of sales, business development, public policy and communications. One immediate focus is on international growth. Until a few months ago, Facebook was only for English speakers. Now it's available in French, German and Spanish, and within the next few months the site will be translated into 21 additional languages.

Meanwhile, Ms Sandberg must rally Facebook's 550 employees, who work at several offices in downtown Palo Alto, to embrace change. Many are recent college graduates who wear flip-flops and jeans to work, and scrawl graffiti on the office walls. At a company meeting two weeks ago, she addressed the concern among some employees that Facebook's close-knit culture will disappear as it grows.

'Scaling up is hard and it's not as much fun not to know everyone you work with,' she told employees. 'But if we get to work on things that affect hundreds of millions of people instead of tens of millions, that's a trade-off worth making.'

Mr Zuckerberg had been looking for a COO who could create a new business model, build a management team, ramp up operations and expand internationally – all of which Ms Sandberg had done at Google. She joined Google in 2001 without knowing exactly what her job would be. Over the following six years, she built Google's global online sales unit into the company's biggest revenue producer and expanded her staff from four to four thousand.

She developed a reputation for being a charismatic executive. She describes herself as a 'tough-love leader', who aims to 'mentor and demand at the same time, and make it safe to make mistakes,' she says.

Source: adapted from Carol Hymowitz, *Wall Street Journal*

Questions

(30 marks; 35 minutes)

1 Outline two problems that might arise when a 38 year old is appointed as number two to a 23 year old. (6)

2 Discuss whether Ms Sandberg's speech to Facebook's employees is likely to have overcome staff concerns about whether 'Facebook's close-knit culture will disappear as it grows'. (10)

3 From the extract as a whole, discuss whether Ms Sandberg's ideas are likely to help or hinder Facebook in the dramatic growth that is forcing huge changes on the business. (14)

C. Essay questions

(40 marks each)

1 Dell Computers has grown at a rate of 50% per year for nearly a decade. Outline the problems this might cause. What might be the most effective way for management to tackle them?

2 Discuss whether corporate plans are an effective way of dealing with unexpected changes such as the sudden collapse in confidence in the housing market that occurred in 2007/2008.

ORGANISATIONAL CULTURE

Organisational culture sums up the spirit, the attitudes, the behaviours and the ethos of 'the organisation'. It is embodied in the people who work within the organisation, though traditions may have built up over time that seem part of the fabric of the buildings.

95.1 Introduction

Unit 51 covered the key elements of business culture, such as:

● entrepreneurial versus **bureaucratic**

● purposeful versus purposeless

● ethical versus profit-driven

● focused on customers versus focused inwards.

In this unit the issues of business culture are developed in three main ways:

1 looking at Professor Charles Handy's famous analysis of types of culture

2 considering how to change an organisation's culture

3 assessing the importance of culture.

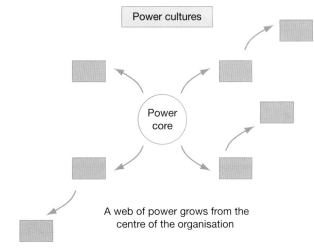

Figure 95.1 Power cultures

95.2 Handy's four types of culture

In his book *Gods of Management* Charles Handy developed four ways of classifying business culture. These are discussed below and can be used to analyse business culture in more depth.

Power cultures

Power cultures are found in organisations in which there is one or a small group of power holders. Pleasing the boss can become the driving force behind the daily actions of staff. There are likely to be few rules or procedures and most communication will be by personal contact. This encourages flexibility among employees. Decision making is not limited by any code of practice. This can result in questionable, perhaps unethical, actions being taken in an attempt to please the boss. The leadership style in such a situation is clearly autocratic, and has been displayed in recent times by leaders such as Tony Blair (British Prime Minister) and Sir Alan Sugar (boss of Amstrad and notorious as the central character in BBC TV's *The Apprentice*).

Role culture

Role cultures are found in established organisations that have developed a lot of formal rules as they have grown. Power depends on the position an individual

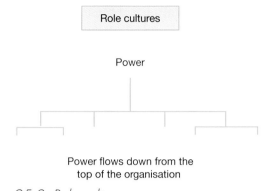

Power flows down from the
top of the organisation

Figure 95.2 Role cultures

...lds in the business, rather than the qualities of the
...rson themselves. All employees are expected to
...nform to rules and procedures, and promotion follows
...predictable pattern. This culture is bureaucratic,
...utious and focused on the avoidance of mistakes. It
...ay be appropriate when the competitive environment
...stable – for example, in industries with long product
...e cycles. However, if the pace of change becomes
...ore rapid, staff will struggle to adapt to new market
...nditions. This is the approach taken in businesses
...ch as Microsoft, where the key thing is to preserve its
...ge share of the software market. The leadership style
...uld be autocratic or paternalistic.

...sk cultures

...sk cultures have no single power source. Senior
...anagers allocate projects to teams of employees made
...of representatives from different functional
...partments. Each group is formed for the purpose of a
...gle undertaking and is then disbanded. Power within
...e team lies in the expertise of each individual and is
...t dependent upon status or role. This culture can be
...ective in dealing with rapidly changing competitive
...vironments because it is flexible – for example, in
...rkets with short product life cycles. However, project
...ms may develop their own objectives independent of
...e firm. The approach to leadership in such
...ganisations is a mixture of paternalistic and
...mocratic.

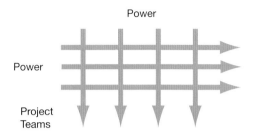

Power flows down from the functional departments at the top
of the matrix, but also lies horizontally within project teams

Figure 95.3 Task cultures

Person cultures

Person cultures are developed when individuals with
similar training and backgrounds form groups to
enhance their expertise and share knowledge. This type
of culture is most often found within functional
departments of large, complex organisations, or among
professionals such as lawyers or accountants. It is largely
associated with democratic leadership.

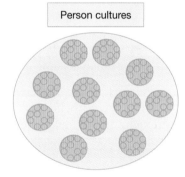

Power lies within each group of individuals flowing
from their common knowledge and skills

Figure 95.4 Person cultures

95.3 Changing the culture

When a new chief executive joins a business, her first impressions will be of the culture. Is the customer embraced by the business, or kept at arm's length by voicemail and answerphone messages? Do staff enjoy Monday morning or only Friday afternoon?

If the new chief exec is unhappy about the culture, achieving change is unlikely to come easily. After all, some staff may have been working at the same place for 15 years, and will find it very difficult to change. Even more problematic is that staff collectively have a set of attitudes that may be tough to overcome. A manufacturing business may be dominated by middle-aged engineers who are sure they know best how to make a car or a caramel. Switching to a more market-orientated business may be very difficult.

The key to success in this process will be to ensure that all staff believe that the change is genuinely going to happen (and, preferably, that the change is the right one). There will be middle managers who are crucial to making things happen (e.g. human resource managers or the finance staff who supervise the budget-setting process). If these people believe that the change is only skin-deep, they will hold back from supporting it. The engineers are likely to resist the change and perhaps they will prove right. Perhaps the new chief executive will be pushed aside by a board of directors who start to worry about whether a mistake is being made.

The key to cultural change, then, is to have a clear, consistent message. If everyone believes that the change is to be pushed through, they are far more likely to support it.

95.4 Assessing the importance of culture

In the years 2004–2007 banks turned their backs on tradition and turned themselves into casinos. For centuries, a culture of caution had been at the heart of banking. The successful banker was one who went through a career without making any awful mistakes. Now this approach was considered old-fashioned. The focus was no longer on building a career, it was on building a bonus. As that bonus might be from £100,000 to £10,000,000 (a year!), who would look any further ahead than the coming months?

Nor was it difficult to make the profits required to get the bonuses. With plentiful cheap money (low interest rates) the clever thing was to borrow lots and lend it out as fast as possible. Why check on whether 'sub-prime' borrowers were likely to default in a year or two, if this year's bonus could be boosted to £500,000?

The collapse of this house of cards in August 2007 led to a predictable collapse into huge losses (estimated by the World Bank at $1 trillion). The culture of recklessness and greed had been created by a crazy bonus system that gave people (non-returnable) rewards based on the short term. In the longer term, the shareholders, the bank customers and governments had to pay the bills.

This example shows that culture is at the heart (or is the heart) of every organisation. Unusually, the banking example shows that culture can be transformed quite quickly, in certain circumstances. More often, businesses find that 'the way we do things round here' is very resistant to change. In 2007 Newcastle United FC appointed the hugely successful Bolton manager Sam Allardyce to transform its underperforming stars. He brought his own results-orientated approach to St James's Park and soon found himself swamped by the supporters' fury at his boring football. The 'Newcastle way' (the culture) is for bright, attacking, flair football. Big Sam did not last long.

Every organisation has its own culture. One school will have a staff room that is buzzing 40 minutes before the start of the day; another's staff car park will still be almost empty. One clothes shop will have staff who take their time helping customers, while another's staff play and joke with each other. And one charity will be focused entirely on the people it is set up to help, while another will behave as if the charity itself is more important than its 'customers'.

Distinguishing between healthy and unhealthy cultures is not difficult. It can be summed up in the following:

- focus on the customer versus focus on the staff (though senior management should appreciate that only a well-motivated staff will serve customers effectively)

- an attitude of 'can-do' rather than of 'must we?'

- a real feeling for the organisation as 'us', as a long-term commitment

- a conviction among staff that the organisation is a force for good (i.e. not just a money-making machine).

95.5 Is change always better?

Not all cultural changes prove a success. Sometimes new leaders assume that a change in culture is essential, because they do not take the time to understand the strengths of the existing one. The Conservative governments of the 1980s and 1990s swept away the tradition of NHS hospital wards being run by an all-powerful 'matron'. A failure to clean the ward properly would have meant risking the wrath of matron; cleaners cleaned. The new approach was to award contracts to outside cleaning companies, then check that agreed targets had been met. The matrons were pushed aside in favour of professional, 'can-do' managers. The managers were supportive of the new cleaning businesses; unfortunately the cleaners were not so committed to cleaning. The later wave of MRSA-bug bacterial problems in hospitals can be put down to a management change based on inadequate understanding.

Issues For Analysis

- Professor Charles Handy's four types of culture are quite hard to understand, but that can make them especially impressive as a tool to use within an analysis of a firm's culture. The analysis becomes all the more effective if you can relate the types of culture to the leadership style shown within the organisation.

- Yet culture goes far beyond Handy's approach, involving as it does the ethics of the organisation and the staff within it. In April 2008, the Office of Fair Trading accused 112 UK construction companies of rigging prices when bidding for public-sector contracts such as building schools. The scale of this (illegal) practice suggests that the culture within much of this business sector has been corrupted. To be able to identify this issue of ethics as an issue of culture is a vital skill. Analysis requires arguments that can show how one thing relates to another.

95.6 Organisational culture
an evaluation

Business leaders make many claims about the culture among their staff. They enjoy using words such as 'positive', 'can-do' and 'entrepreneurial'. Does the fact that the leader says these things mean that they are true? Clearly not. The leader cannot admit in public that the culture is 'lazy', 'negative' or 'bureaucratic'.

A well-judged answer to a question about culture will look beyond claims and public relations, and look for the evidence. Is there evidence that staff suggestions are welcomed and that they make an important contribution to the business? Is there evidence that mistakes are treated as learning experiences, rather than as reasons to be fired. And, perhaps most important of all, is there evidence that staff love their jobs and look forward to coming to work? All these things are tests of an organisation's culture.

Key terms

Bureaucratic: an organisation in which initiative is stifled by paperwork and excessive checking and re-checking of decisions and actions.

Person culture: where power comes from groups of people with the professional expertise to dominate and therefore create the culture, e.g. a group of professors dominating a university, enabling each, as individuals, to have influence but also independence.

Power culture: where the dominance of the leader (and his/her immediate circle of friends or advisers) overrides systems and conventional hierarchy. (This was the exact culture of Nazi Germany, where relatively junior staff could have power if they had access to Hitler.)

Role culture: where each individual has a tightly defined role that must be stuck to. Such an organisation will be bureaucratic and therefore highly frustrating for an individual with initiative. The culture will be dominated by the avoidance of risks.

Task culture: where groups of employees are delegated the power and resources to tackle tasks and projects, probably in a cross-functional way (so-called 'matrix management'). This is highly motivating, such as for the Nintendo development team that came up with the Wii.

Further reading

Handy, C. (1995) *Gods of Management*. Arrow.

Exercises

A. Revision questions

(30 marks; 30 minutes)

1 Explain why it is unlikely that a task culture could exist in a business with an authoritarian leadership. (4)

2 Explain why a role culture would be inappropriate for a new software company seeking to be more innovative than Google. (4)

3 Sir Alex Ferguson became manager of Manchester United in November 1986. When he retires, the new manager must either fit in with the culture created by Ferguson, or must change it. Examine two problems in changing the culture at an organisation dominated by one person, as at Manchester United. (8)

4 To what extent does the example of the UK banking sector in 2004–2007 suggest that an entrepreneurial culture is not always a good thing? (6)

5 In April 2008, a former quantity surveyor told the BBC that he had left the construction industry because he was so disillusioned by the problem of price fixing. Discuss how a new leader of a construction firm might try to change the culture to one of honest dealing. (8)

B. Revision exercises

B1 Data response

The top job advertisement

Company: Topshop/Topman
Post: Area Trainer
Location: Oxford Circus, West London, Middlesex
Salary: circa £21–23K + excellent benefits

Working for Topshop and Topman is not like working for other fashion retailers. The size of the business, the culture of the company, the quality of training and direction of the business all combine to offer exciting and challenging careers. We currently have an exciting opportunity to join us an Area Trainer within our London flagship store, the world's largest fashion store. With over 1000 employees on site, you will be responsible for the delivery of leading training solutions that directly support the key business objectives.

Source: Myjobsearch.com website

Questions

(30 marks; 35 minutes)

1 Examine two ways in which the culture of Topshop might be different from that of other clothing retailers. (6)

2 This particular job is at 'the world's largest fashion store' (the Oxford Circus branch of Topshop). Use Handy's four types of culture to discuss how the culture might differ in this Topshop outlet compared with a small Topshop branch employing perhaps 12 people. (12)

3 Discuss whether or not this job as Area Trainer would be one that you would like to get within the next five years. (12)

B2 Case study

Bakery culture

Gianni Falcone had built his Italian bakery up over a 40-year period in Britain. He came to escape a life dominated in the 1960s by the Sicilian Mafia, and started a bakery in south London. For the first ten years his life had been hard and very poor. Baking just white rolls and white bread, he had to keep his prices low to compete with local supermarkets. Up at 1.30 am every day to get the bread prepared then baked, his working day would end 12 hours later. With a young family of four, he could not get to bed until 8.30 in the evening. In five hours' time he would be back to work.

Eventually he started to see ways of adding value to his dough. A half kilo loaf of bread with 30p of ingredients would sell for 80p, but roll it flat, smear tomato, cheese and herbs on it (cost: 25p) and it became a £3 pizza. A series of value-added initiatives came through, all adding both to the popularity of the shop and to its profitability. By 2000 the queues on a Saturday morning were legendary. Gianni was able to finance houses for all his family and he was starting to dream of owning a Ferrari.

By 2005 the business employed all the family members plus six extra staff. All worked the Gianni way. All knew the principles behind the business: ingredients should be as natural as possible and of as high a quality as possible. The customer is not always right (rowdy schoolchildren will be thrown out if necessary) but the customer must always be treated with respect. A slightly over-baked loaf will be sold at half price and day-old currant buns are given away to regular customers. Above all else, Gianni wanted to be honest with customers; they knew that all the baked goods were baked freshly on the premises.

Then, in 2007, Gianni was taken ill. The problem was with his lungs; quite simply, 40 years of flour in the bakery air had taken its toll. He had to retire. As none of his family wanted to take on the commitment to the awful working hours, he had to sell up. The only person with the inclination and the money to buy was an experienced baker from Malta, Trevi Malone. He bought the business for £250,000. Gianni was able to retire to the substantial home he had built in Sicily (now relatively Mafia-free).

From the start, Malone's approach was dramatically different. While Gianni had been ill, all the baking had been done by his bakery assistant Carol. She had worked miracles by herself, so that the shelves were full every morning. Now, from the first morning, Malone showed his distaste for her ways of working. Why did she use organic yeast when there were perfectly good, cheaper ones? Why did she 'knead' the dough in batches of 5 kilos when it would be better to do it by machine in 20-kilo quantities. And when she suggested that it would be good to start making hot cross buns, Malone snapped: 'This crazy place already makes too many different lines; just concentrate on what you're doing.' In the past, Carol's ideas had led to successful new products such as a top-selling apricot doughnut. Now she was to be silenced.

In the shop, Malone's approach was also quite different. Instead of casual clothes, everyone

would wear uniforms; customers would be addressed as 'Sir' or 'Madam', and every order must be followed by an 'upselling' suggestion. The person who bought only a loaf of bread should be asked 'Would you like any doughnuts or cakes today?' The sales staff thought this was a daft idea, because – with so many regular customers – people would soon tire of being asked to spend more money. But they had quickly picked up the idea that Malone was not interested in discussion – he knew best.

Over the coming weeks things were changed steadily. The ham used on the meat pizza was changed from 'Italian baked ham' at £10 a kilo to a much cheaper Danish one (with 20% added water). As Malone said to Carol, 'Our customers don't see the ingredients label, so who's to know?' Malone noticed that doughnuts took longer to prepare than was justified by their 60p price tag, so he started to buy them in from a wholesale baker. Outsourcing was the sensible approach.

Within two months Carol was looking for a new job. She found it in another bakery, but soon left that as well, and went to college to retrain for a new career. Other staff steadily left, including all of Gianni's family. The newly recruited staff were accepting of Malone's rules, but none seemed particularly keen on the work. Perhaps that was fortunate, because sales started to slip after two months, and then fell at an increasingly rapid pace. Staff who left were not replaced, as they were no longer needed. Even more fortunate was that Gianni was not well enough to travel back to England. He never knew how quickly 40 years of work fell apart.

Questions

(40 marks; 50 minutes)

1 Use the example of Gianni's bakery to discuss whether it is right to say that value added is at the heart of all business activity.
(15)

2 Examine why outsourcing the doughnuts may not have been 'a sensible approach' for Malone. (10)

3 Malone paid £250,000 for a business that steadily went downhill. To what extent was the problem due to the change in culture within the workplace? (15)

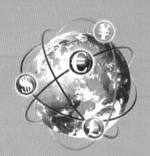

MAKING STRATEGIC DECISIONS

96.1 Introduction

The word 'strategy' means a plan for meeting your objectives. It is therefore subordinate to objectives. Typically, directors set objectives and managers carry out the strategy. Yet the term 'strategic' means a lot more than this. Businesses refer to it in two ways: strategic thinking and strategic decisions.

Strategic thinking involves visualising what you hope to achieve within coming years (given consumer tastes and lifestyles, plus the competition you face), assessing the strengths of your business in relation to those aims, then identifying an approach that can enable you to get there. This process should be carried out with a wide range of senior – and, ideally, some junior – staff, in order to get a wide range of views and a real consensus.

After this process of strategic thinking takes place, new objectives can be identified and a new strategic plan put into action.

Strategic decisions, then, are the result of strategic thinking. In 1990 the chairman of car tyre maker Nokia decided to stake the future of the business on a then still trivial business – the mobile phone. In the period 2001–2007 the directors of Northern Rock decided to change from being a sleepy building society based in the English north-east to become a major national bank. Both were hugely important **strategic decisions** and these two examples highlight that big decisions are not necessarily correct ones. Table 96.1 shows some examples of strategic decisions, contrasting them with smaller-scale day-to-day **tactical decisions** faced by managers.

Table 96.1 Examples of strategic and tactical decisions

Strategic decisions	**Tactical decisions**
• Should we relocate our factory from Slough to Sri Lanka?	• Should we replace our CCTV system as our current pictures are too fuzzy?
• Should we close down our out-of-town stores and concentrate more on online sales?	• Should we mark down the prices on this Christmas stock today (23 December), rather than wait until the January sales?
• Should we focus all our investment capital for the next two years on building a sizeable operation in India?	• Our labour turnover has been rising steadily, so should we conduct a staff questionnaire to find out what's wrong?
• Should we move from Anfield to a new, multi-million-pound, bigger stadium nearby?	• Should we switch our Sunday opening from 11.00–5.00 to 12.00–6.00?

96.2 Important influences on strategic decision making

Relative power of stakeholders

The 1990s had been very kind to Arsenal FC, as trophies kept coming and the club rivalled Manchester United as Britain's top football team. The supporters loved the club, the manager and the ground – Highbury – and felt sure the good times would keep coming. Arsenal's directors were not so sure. Highbury could hold only 38,000 people, while Old Trafford was steadily being expanded to take twice that number. If the Manchester club could generate twice the income, how could Arsenal continue to compete in the long term? So the directors took a £400 million gamble on moving the club to the 60,000-seater Emirates stadium. As the shares in the football club were held by a few wealthy people, this gamble was possible. If the shares had been held by the general public, there would have been much less willingness to such a chance. Directors can take bold strategic decisions only if they are supported by the shareholders. This may be easier in a business that is not a public limited company.

Available resources

Arsenal's £400 million gamble was very difficult to finance, but it proved possible. In other cases, a business may have a brilliant idea that has huge potential, yet it may be unable to secure the necessary finance. It may lack the internal finance and find it impossible to persuade outsiders of the attractions of the proposal. In some years banks seem willing to offer finance to very unattractive propositions; in other years they refuse to finance rock-solid ideas.

Top companies try to make sure that they always have enough cash to be able to put strategic decisions into practice. On 29 December 2007, Apple had $16 billion of cash and cash investments on its balance sheet – to provide the liquidity to take advantage of any opportunity. Tesco plc also has a hugely strong financial position, allowing it to declare in 2007 that in the five years until 2012 it would be investing £250 million a year in building Tesco stores in America.

Ethical position

In the 1990s the term business ethics meant little.

Today it is a significant part of boardroom discussion in plcs and other businesses. The question remains, however, 'Are the discussions about how to operate ethically, or are they about how to be thought to be operating ethically?' In others words, is it genuine or is it for show? In fact, company directors can be forgiven for being quite cynical about ethics, because consumers are often as hypocritical as companies. People talk about animal welfare, but can't resist two chickens for a fiver; and they talk about global warming as they're driving down to the shops.

There is no doubt, though, that if consumers believe a business is a force for good, there can be financial benefits. Innocent Drinks has, in reality, done relatively little to deserve its reputation as an ethical business. Its high prices hardly imply a social desire to promote healthy living. Yet people accept its story that it is a pure little company with a big heart. The fact that this is working so well (sales are rising beyond £150 million a year) has ensured that Innocent took the strategic decision to maintain its socially conscious image by switching to fully recyclable packaging and giving 10% of profits to social causes.

96.3 Different approaches to strategic decisions

There are always two alternative methods to making a decision: evidence-based (scientific) or hunch. It is important to realise that either method may be successful, or unsuccessful. There is no evidence that one is better than the other.

In 2007 senior management at Whitbread plc went through a detailed analysis of the four operating divisions of its business. It decided that it had two rising stars, one dog and one cash cow. It decided that the correct strategy would be to sell the latter two divisions in order to generate more cash to finance the growth of the two stars. Understandably, the 'dog' (the restaurants division, including Beefeater) was difficult to sell, but cash cow David Lloyd Leisure was sold for £925 million. In this case the strategic decision was based on evidence of the financial performance of the different parts of the business. Therefore it was logical – scientific even.

Also in 2007, in the wake of the Northern Rock banking collapse, Richard Branson put himself forward as the bank's possible saviour. He did this long before there was clear understanding of the extent of the bank's difficulties. He was acting purely on hunch. Doubtless he would get his accountants to check the figures before signing up to anything, but his strategic decision was to place himself at the centre of the

Northern Rock affair. At the time of writing it is not clear why, but despite a few mistakes in his career, Branson's reliance on hunch has been hugely successful overall.

96.4 The significance of information management

The bosses of most plcs make their decisions on the basis of data, not hunch. Therefore information management is crucial. The first critical issue is to have full knowledge of your own business. This might seem obvious, but in January 2008 a major French bank found that one of its own employees had been gambling with €50 billion of the bank's money. Sorting out the mess cost more than £3000 million. A huge bank that, one week, was considering plans for its long-term future, was – the next week – fighting for its short-term survival.

Few businesses have such problems, but there are others that find out only much too late that sales have been worse than expected. Good companies have good, up-to-date information about themselves. This requires IT systems that show instantly how the business is doing, so that the senior directors can think quickly about whether current strategies are working. If they are not, it may be time for a radical rethink.

A-grade application

Greggs

For Greggs, Britain's biggest bakery chain, 2007 was destined to be a dreadful year. All its key variable costs had shot ahead in price: wheat by nearly 100% and butter and cheese by 50%. Its IT systems were feeding back disappointing daily sales to head office, so the management made significant changes to its marketing strategy. Greggs brought in the no-nonsense comedian Paddy McGuinness to be the public face of the brand, and started using YouTube and Facebook as media for its advertising messages. By the end of 2007 there were 12 Facebook 'Greggs Appreciation Societies'! Halfway through its 2007 financial year Greggs was able to report a 5.8% sales increase.

Issues For Analysis

These days chief executives of plcs are paid huge sums (literally, £millions) to run large businesses on behalf of the shareholders. The only reason to pay such high sum is to attract people who can get the key strategic decisions right. Tesco's Sir Terry Leahy has successfully steered the company into eastern Europe and the Far East, so shareholders trust his 2007 decision to spend £1250 million moving Tesco into America. Although Sir Terry will have gathered as much information about the US grocery market as possible, ultimately the decision will have been made as much on the basis of hunch (backed by huge experience) as on the basis of scientific evidence.

When studying a business situation – perhaps in the exam room – these are the key questions:

● Has the business done all it reasonably can to gather data such as primary research?

● Has the business made effective use of relevant asset (including the expertise within its staff)?

● Does the leadership have the experience, the enthusiasm and the wisdom to make a sound judgement – and then ensure that the new approach is carried through effectively?

● Has the business the financial and human resources to turn the right idea into the right strategy?

96.5 Making strategic decisions
an evaluation

Strategic thinking should be radical, innovative and free from internal constraints such as 'that's not how we do thing round here'. The traditions and culture of an organisation should always be taken into account, but cannot be allowe to act as an absolute constraint. Careful discussion with a wide range of staff should help bring insight to the process and assist in the process of communicating the need for a new approach.

the strategic thinking is right, the strategic decisions should
also be right. Sometimes, though, the pressures upon the
decision makers lead to mistaken compromises.
Shareholders who are unhappy about short-term profitability
may not be willing to back a strategic decision that has a
five-year timeframe. Short-term cost-cutting may be the only
language the shareholders understand. It is the job of the
highly paid chief executives to find the right balance
between what is right and what is acceptable.

Key terms

Strategic decision: one that is made in circumstances
of uncertainty and where the outcome will have a major
impact on the medium- to long-term future of the
organisation.

Tactical decision: deciding what to do in circumstances
that are immediate (short term) and where a mistake is
unlikely to have a major impact on the business.

Exercises

A. Revision questions

(35 marks; 35 minutes)

1 Explain the difference between 'strategy' and 'strategic'. (4)

2 Outline two qualities you would want in a manager who has to take strategic decisions. (4)

3 Look at Table 96.1. Explain why relocation from Slough to Sri Lanka would be regarded as a strategic, not a tactical, decision. (5)

4 Apart from shareholders, explain why two other stakeholder groups might be interested in the strategic decision to 'close down our out-of-town stores and concentrate more on online sales'. (6)

5 Briefly consider how well each of the following businesses could cope with a strategic decision that would require a major capital investment.
(a) Business A has a current ratio of 0.95 and a gearing ratio of 55% (5)
(b) Business B has an acid test ratio of 1.05 and would need to increase staffing levels by 12% to be able to produce the extra goods required by the strategy (5)

6 Should business ethics ever be a matter of tactics, or should they always be part of the strategic thinking behind strategic decisions? (6)

B. Revision exercises

B1 Data response

Damaged Wolseley is in need of urgent repairs

The foundations shook at Wolseley, the plumbing and building materials group, as £600 million of value was wiped off within seconds of the first shares changing hands. The group warned that profits for the five months to the end of December are likely to be down by almost one-third. The slump in US housing demand is to blame. The crisis is also spreading to Europe.

Wolseley is carrying out urgent repair work on its overheads but it may not be enough to stop the roof falling in again. The group admits present market conditions are likely to worsen. Dearer mortgages and tougher lending policies are bringing home sales to a near standstill, while the commercial building market remains fragile.

The conditions may throw up opportunities, however. Wolseley made ten bolt-on acquisitions worth £170 million during the spell, and tougher trading means smaller rivals might fall into its lap. But this is scant consolation for retrenchment on an epic scale. Around 3000 jobs have been cut, saving £60 million a year, and further action is not being ruled out. Trading profits in the USA are down 40%. Europe has not suffered so badly – yet – with profits up 1% on revenue 17% higher, but some markets, such as Italy, France and Austria, are weak.

The shares have lost 45% of their value in the past year. By the close, they had clawed back one-third of yesterday's initial falls. Brokers are expecting profits to fall 20% this year, but at this stage accurate forecasting is impossible.

Source: *Independent*, 26 January 2008

Questions

(30 marks; 40 minutes)

1 The article suggests that Wolesley's sliding profits came as a shock at the end of the year. Examine how a firm such as Woleseley can use information management to ensure that managers are regularly updated on how well or badly the business is doing. (5)

2 During 2007 it was well known that the US housing market had slumped. To what extent can a business such as Woleseley be expected to buck a trend such as this? (12)

3 Discuss the implications for strategic decision making within a business such as Woleseley of the phrase 'at this stage accurate forecasting is impossible'. (13)

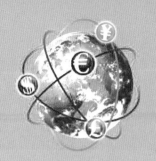

IMPLEMENTING AND MANAGING CHANGE

Change management involves controlling the activities required to move an organisation from its current position to a new one.

97.1 Identifying the need for change

Change is an unavoidable part of life, both for individuals and organisations. Existing markets decline and new products are developed. Experienced workers retire or leave, and are replaced by new employees with fresh ideas. According to research published by the Chartered Institute of Personnel Development (CIPD) in 2007, organisations undergo major change once every three years on average, with smaller changes taking place almost continually.

The need for change can result from influences within and outside the business. Change is an inevitable part of business growth. For a firm that grows organically, this change may be relatively slow and steady, occurring over a prolonged period of time. However, managers will still need to have the skills and expertise required to anticipate and manage this change effectively. Change resulting from merger or takeover will be more sudden, and may be followed by a painful period of adjustment, unless effective planning has taken place beforehand.

Change may be anticipated, such as the introduction of a new marketing strategy, or unanticipated – for example, the collapse of an important supplier or a sudden deterioration in customer satisfaction. Changes may well be beyond the control of individual businesses, such as the introduction of a national minimum wage or a ban on advertising during children's television programmes. A successful firm will see change as an opportunity to re-examine its operations and market conditions or, better still, anticipate changes before they occur and develop a competitive advantage over rivals.

97.2 Organisational barriers to successful change

No matter how much time and how many resources are put into the planning stage, a number of organisational issues may arise that a have a negative impact on the implementation of changes within a business. These include the following.

- *A lack of effective leadership and project management*: the failure to coordinate projects effectively can lead to missed deadlines and wasted resources, affecting a firm's performance.

- *A lack of effective training*: a business must ensure that all those involved in implementing change initiatives have the expertise required to do so, including project management and leadership skills.

- *Poor communication*: effective two-way communication must be established between all the individuals and groups affected.

Figure 97.1 Causes of organisational change

97.3 Resistance to change

Resistance to change may be defined as 'an individual or group engaging in acts to block or disrupt an attempt to introduce change' (CIPD, 2007). Workers within an organisation may resist change for a number of reasons. For example, people may be concerned about a loss of control or status, feel vulnerable to the threat of redundancy or resent the break-up of social groups within the workplace. Resistance may be directed at the change itself, perhaps because it seems to go against the prevailing culture (e.g. introducing an extra management layer to a business with an entrepreneurial culture).

Resistance can also come in different forms. Active resistance occurs when opposition is clearly stated, such as if workers decide to take industrial action. Passive resistance might include actions such as failing to attend meetings or respond to messages. Although more subtle, passive resistance can be just as (if not more) effective in blocking successful change, especially as its existence is less likely to be detected.

Dealing with negative responses and resistance to change requires a great deal of skill by managers. Such responses may well result from rational and reasonable concerns and, therefore, need to be handled calmly and sympathetically, if a way forward is to be found and a situation of stalemate avoided.

To overcome resistance, key factors will be as follows.

● Starting with objectives that are clear to all, and are accepted as necessary or desirable by the great majority of staff.

● For senior management to have provided adequate resources to enable the change to be effected efficiently; these include financial resources, human resources, and the right operational and technological back-up.

● Paramount among the resources would be training; this can be expensive, but not as expensive as the alternative – not training. The difficulty is that unmotivated or sceptical staff can be very critical of what they see as second-rate training. Poorly run training sessions can set the change process back; training must be excellent to be adequate. Therefore it needs to be planned and carried out by an important figure within the change process, such as the **project champion** (see below).

A-grade application

No product champion for Terminal 5

In March 2008 the new British Airways Heathrow Terminal 5 opened after 19 years of planning. The new terminal was trumpeted as a customer service breakthrough, with its high-tech new systems, such as that for baggage handling. Yet its opening proved a humiliating fiasco. The key problem was with the baggage-handling systems, leading to chaos as bags piled up.

It later emerged that staff who had been working at Terminals 1, 2 and 3 had received far less training than had been planned on the new technology system. Only 50 of the 400 baggage handlers had received the planned four days of training at Terminal 5. BA Chief Executive Willie Walsh had not delegated effectively to a project champion who could make sure that this big change worked effectively.

97.4 Implementing change successfully

Despite the individual circumstances and the particular changes faced by any given business, there are a number of key factors that should be considered in order to develop a programme that will incorporate change and overcome any resistance effectively. These factors include those listed below.

● *Ensuring that the objectives and details of any changes are communicated as clearly and as quickly as possible to employees:* leaving staff in the dark can lead to rumours and speculation about the changes that, once established, can be difficult to challenge. Far better to keep everyone informed of the objective and the plans.

● *Appointing a project champion:* it is easy for new ideas to be stifled by the bureaucracy within middle management; a project champion should have the power and the passion to push the change through and to persuade staff that the new methods will be more successful than the old.

● *Involving staff rather than imposing change:* unless there is a need for confidentiality, involving staff in the change process can lead to a number of benefits. Consulting staff regularly or setting up **project groups**, taking members from different functional departments, to work on particular areas should help to generate a wider range of ideas, but also help to combat anxieties and increase commitment by creating a sense of ownership.

● *Ensuring appropriate leadership:* no particular leadership style is most effective at dealing with change. The most appropriate style will depend on the circumstances of the particular organisation and the nature of the changes it faces. However, all leaders will need to provide their subordinates with the vision and rationale for change required to make the process a success.

● *Creating a culture for change:* a 'learning organisation' is one where change-orientated thinking has been embodied in all employees, so that change is seen as an opportunity rather than a threat. Such organisations are likely to be more receptive and to adapt more quickly to changes, even those that are unexpected. Over the years the England football team has been very resistant to any change in tactics; this can be contrasted with the huge fluidity of a team such as Manchester United, who accept the manager's decisions without a quibble.

97.5 Managing change

Once the process of change has been implemented, it needs to be managed effectively. This involves two stages.

● *Control:* this involves taking steps to ensure that the final outcome of the change process is as close as possible to the objectives identified at the planning stage. Regular checks will allow the firm to detect problems quickly and deal with them promptly, in order to avoid delays and wasting resources. This will only be possible if the business has set measurable goals (i.e. quantifiable targets against which performance can be compared). However, even the SMARTest objectives are subject to influences beyond the control of the organisations that set them. **Contingency planning** encourages firms to attempt to identify what might go wrong and develop strategies to deal with these problems in order to get back on course. For example, training may prove to be inadequate – in which case, new courses need to be made available to remedy the situation quickly.

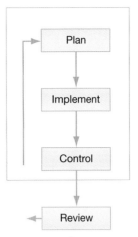

Figure 97.2 The process of managing change

2 *Review:* once change has been implemented and objectives achieved, the organisation needs to consider the 'What next?' scenario. This may seem strange, given the upheaval created by attempting to adjust to recent changes. However, the nature of business is to keep in touch with its marketplace. Increased competition, changes in technology and customer requirements mean that no business can afford to stand still for long.

97.6 Radical vs continuous change

Business process re-engineering (BPR) is an approach requiring an organisation to totally rethink its approach to its current operations. BPR focuses on the processes undertaken within the organisation, rather than its structure. This requires a clear idea of the specific roles of workers within the organisation and how they relate to customers. Once the aims and objectives have been established, the organisation is completely redesigned from scratch.

A key advantage of BPR is that it considers the efficiency of the organisation as a whole, in terms of meeting customer requirements, rather than simply focusing on individual parts. However, an organisation is unlikely to undergo such radical change unless it is faced with a crisis threatening its very survival, given the upheaval that it is likely to create. In most situations, businesses are more likely to prefer a *kaizen* approach (i.e. a process of continuous improvement).

Issues For Analysis

Opportunities for analysis may arise in the following areas.

- A consideration of the benefits and problems of introducing a programme of change; this should take into account the crucial question of whether 'do nothing' is an acceptable alternative. The fiasco of British Airways' change to Heathrow Terminal 5 does not mean that it did the wrong thing; it just did it in the wrong way.

- Many managements see change as an operational issue. For example, many government departments have wasted £billions in trying to establish new IT systems that proved unusable. They saw the change as a technical, operational issue, driven forward by independent management consultants; later investigations showed that the mistake was ignoring the importance of staff and the knowledge they have of how the systems really work. There is huge scope for analysing whether the correct way forward is via staff or via operations management (and the ideal is an effective combination of the two).

- An analysis of the consequences of resistance to change within an organisation.

97.7 Implementing and managing change
an evaluation

All organisations need to accept and face up to the need for change and, in the modern business environment, the pace of change appears to show no signs of slowing down. Any business that is unwilling or unable to adapt to the ever increasing pace of change appears to be doomed to become less and less competitive. Yet there are always exceptions to every rule. In business, every generalisation proves a mistake. For every nine businesses that need change to survive, there will be one that thrives on remaining unchanged, from a traditional private school to a producer of handcrafted British sports cars (such as Morgan or handmade wedding dresses.

It is easy for managers to neglect existing customers or suppliers in an attempt to demonstrate their change management skills, but the resulting damage may cancel out the benefits of change. However, change requires the support of the employees within an organisation – without the support of employees, change is unlikely to succeed. The ability to establish trust between management and workers in the face of change appears to be the way forward in managing the process of change successfully.

Key terms

Business process re-engineering (BPR): a radical approach to changing an organisation, in which it is completely redesigned in order to meet the needs of customers more effectively.
Contingency planning: preparing for unlikely and unwanted possibilities, such as the onset of recession, or the collapse of a major supplier or customer.
Kaizen: the Japanese term for continuous improvement.
Project champion: an individual appointed from within an organisation to support the process of change.
Project group: where members of different departments within an organisation are put together (temporarily) to generate ideas, to put the plan into practice and maintain good communications between departments.

Exercises

A. Revision questions

(40 marks; 40 minutes)

1 Outline two causes of change that might be generated from within a business. (4)

2 Describe two causes of change that are likely to be outside a firm's control. (4)

3 Examine the main consequences to a fashion clothing business of failing to identify and respond to changes in the external environment. (6)

4 Identify two reasons why a firm might encounter resistance to change from within the workforce. (2)

5 Use examples to explain the difference between active and passive resistance. (4)

6 Examine one way in which a business could attempt to successfully tackle resistance to change. (4)

7 Briefly explain the importance to effective change of a 'project champion'. (4)

8 Analyse one benefit of creating a culture of change within an organisation. (4)

9 Examine one potential benefit and one potential drawback to a business from adopting a programme of business process engineering. (4)

10 Outline the role that human resources managers can play in the change management process. (4)

B. Revision exercises

B1 Case study

Managing change at M&S

When Stuart Rose was appointed as CEO of Marks & Spencer in May 2004, it was clear that change within the company was long overdue. The high-street retailer's recovery between 2000 and 2002, after years of dwindling sales, had proved to be short-lived. Profits and share prices were falling and the company was faced with a £9.1 billion takeover bid from retail entrepreneur Philip Green. Marks & Spencer stood accused of having developed a culture of arrogance and of losing touch with its core customers.

Rose's three-year recovery plan for a Marks & Spencer revival focused on its 11 million core customers – mainly women in the 35–55 age range. It would concentrate on cutting costs and product lines, reducing bureaucracy and streamlining buying practices by making suppliers accept tighter deals. The programme began with the company's board of directors. A number of executives were dismissed and replaced with a core team of people that Rose had worked with and trusted.

The next step involved getting the message across to all those involved in the recovery plans. Rose refused to put forward a lengthy and detailed strategy for the company's renewal – even objecting to the use of the word strategy because of its 'complicated' undertones. Instead, he provided a statement that was simple to communicate but sufficiently specific to get across the changes needed and to focus effort in the direction required: 'improve the product, improve the stores and improve the service'.

In order to reinforce the message internally, the company's 56,000-strong workforce was put through a series of motivational training sessions, focusing on teamwork and customer service. Incentive structures within the business were adjusted to reward service performance rather than seniority. Rose's approach resulted in an impressive turnaround for the company. Like-for-like sales increased by 8.2% between 2005 and 2006, and pre-tax profits rose from £505.1 million to £745.7 million over the same period. The company's share price rose to 750p in January 2007, from 360p at the time of Rose's appointment. In the same year, staff benefited from pay-outs of between £1000 and £45,000 from the Marks & Spencer employee share-save plan.

Source: Adapted from In Business; BBC News

97.8 Workbook

Questions

(25 marks; 30 minutes)

1 Analyse two benefits to a company such as Marks & Spencer from training staff during a programme of change. (10)

2 Assess the contribution of the changes introduced by Stuart Rose to the improved performance of Marks & Spencer since 2004. (15)

C. Essay questions

(40 marks each)

1 'The problem of change is people.' Discuss.

2 After 20 years as a full-service restaurant, Luigi Ristorante is to change to a self-service format. Discuss the key aspects of change that Luigi should tackle to ensure that this new plan proves a success.

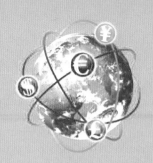

98.1 Introduction: change in the current business environment

ost business commentators agree that the greatest allenge facing managers currently is how to deal ffectively with change. They are probably right in this, it underestimate the extent to which this has always en true (and always will be). There is not one single ange today that compares with the arrival of steam wer (and therefore the railways and electricity) or the rival of motor transport. In every aspect of Business udies, a broad perspective is essential.

espite this plea for perspective, it is true to say that the ce of change appears to be speeding up. An creasingly competitive environment and the balisation of markets has required firms to adopt a ore innovative approach to their products and their oduction processes. Changes in economic conditions yond the influence of individual organisations, such as change rate fluctuations or a reduction in the ailability of credit, can force a complete strategic think.

ie need for change may also come from within an ganisation, perhaps as a result of the development of w products. The changes required may be structural, quiring a business to reorganise its activities and sources, or may be cultural, altering established itudes and norms. Change may be incremental or olutionary, over a relatively long period of time, or volutionary, such as the decision to transfer a firm's tire operations overseas. Finally, while some change n be anticipated and planned for, unforeseen events ll still need to be managed effected if any negative nsequences are to be minimised. Ultimately, while noring change or its significance to an organisation ay be tempting for managers, the long-term nsequences of doing so can be very costly indeed.

iange is a key concept within Business Studies. udents need to have an awareness of the variety of fluences that might create a need for change, cluding economic, social, political, legal and technical

factors, as well as the competitive structure of the markets in which firms operate. More important, though, will be to understand the managerial and cultural issues involved in making change an opportunity rather than a threat.

While the impact of and response to change need to be considered on an individual business basis, there are a number of common issues that underpin the successful management of change.

98.2 Three key issues in dealing effectively with change

Issue 1: planning change effectively

In order to succeed, programmes of change need detailed and thorough planning. An essential part of the planning process is to formulate clear objectives for change (i.e. the corporate aims that set out where the business wants to be). However, the business will also need to carry out an honest assessment of its current situation – 'where it is now' – in order to establish the 'strategic gap' in terms of the changes that are needed and the capabilities and resources required to achieve them. The planning process may also involve the need to prioritise. Too many changes introduced in short succession can lead to 'change overload' among staff, leading to increased stress and demotivation. Managers may, therefore, be required to make important choices regarding the areas where change is most urgently required.

Issue 2: managing change requires effective leadership

Leaders and managers have a critical role to play in managing the change process within an organisation. Although the stimulus for change can come from a variety of sources, managers are required to act as 'change agents'. They must provide clear vision, develop and monitor policies, and mobilise those involved by communicating and justifying the need for change. Failure to do so could lead to mistakes, delays and even resistance to change, reducing the effectiveness of the change initiative.

Issue 3: coping with change requires a suitable culture

The creation of a 'culture for change' would appear to be the most effective way of coping successfully with the demands of the modern business environment. An organisation where change-orientated thinking is an approach adopted by all individuals, rather than just senior management, is likely to be better equipped to react to even radical change more effectively. Furthermore, a firm that develops a positive approach is more likely to be able to anticipate and manage change more effectively than a firm that sees every change as a crisis.

Exercises

A. Revision questions

(80 marks; 80 minutes)

1 Identify two characteristics of a power culture. (2)

2 Analyse one benefit and one drawback for a business adopting a role culture. (6)

3 Explain why a task culture might be most appropriate for a company designing games software. (5)

4 Examine two problems that managers might face in attempting to move from a role culture to a task culture within the business. (6)

5 Explain the difference between a tactical and a strategic decision. (4)

6 Outline three possible effects on Walkers of a decision by government to ban the advertising of potato crisps and other fatty snack foods. (6)

7 Examine one external change that might have a serious effect on British Airways. (4)

8 Using examples, explain why the 'correct' management style is dependent on an organisation's individual circumstances. (4)

9 State the four phases involved in managing change. (4)

10 Explain what is meant by scientific decision making (3)

11 Identify one benefit and one drawback of adopting a scientific approach to decision making. (4)

12 Briefly explain what is meant by a corporate plan. (3)

13 Outline two factors that could influence a firm's corporate plan. (4)

14 Outline two possible reasons why brands such as Marmite are able to last for more than 100 years with very little change in the product. (4)

15 State two possible internal causes and two external causes of change within an organisation. (4)

16 Outline the role of leadership in the process of managing change. (3)

17 Outline two changes that a company might consider making after merging with a competitor. (4)

18 Identify the key stages involved in the process of managing change. (3)

19 Explain what is meant by contingency planning. (3)

20 Examine one advantage and one disadvantage for a firm that adopts a *kaizen* approach to implementing change. (4)

B. Revision exercises

B1 Data response

Nokia is top for developing leaders

Nokia was named as the number one company in Europe for developing leaders in 2007. The study, part of research involving 540 companies worldwide, used criteria such as leadership culture, values and practices, as well as company reputation and business performance to rank the companies. According to Mark Hoyal of Hewitt Associates, one of the sponsors of the research, 'In this increasingly complex and global marketplace, companies must build leadership practices that have consistency throughout the world if they want to be successful.'

Within Nokia, this sense of direction and consistent behaviour is provided by the 'Nokia Way', a set of core values, developed from extensive employee involvement, that act as a foundation for the company's evolving culture. These core values are adapted by managers around the world to reflect local conditions. There is an emphasis on personal growth through self-leadership, with all employees being encouraged to take responsibility for their own development. Staff are also encouraged to criticise, and even the most senior leaders are expected to make changes if better ideas are put forward.

Questions

(30 marks; 35 minutes)

1 Identify three characteristics of an effective leader. (3)

2 Examine two reasons why senior managers at Nokia may have involved employees extensively in the development of the Nokia Way. (8)

3 Assess the role that leaders within a business such as Nokia can play in coping with a rapidly changing environment. (7)

4 To what extent do you agree with the view that modern management is more about empowering employees rather than leading them? (12)

Table 98.1 *Europe's top ten companies for developing leaders, 2007*

Company	Headquarters	Sector	Employees
1 Nokia	Finland	Telecommunications	68,400
2 BBVA	Spain	Financial services	95,000
3 Inditex	Spain	Fashion distribution	70,000
4 GlaxoSmithKline	UK	Healthcare	100,000
5 L'Oréal	France	Cosmetics	60,000
6 Randstad Holding	Netherlands	Personnel services	44,000
7 Deutsche Lufthansa	Germany	Air transport	94,500
8 UBS	Switzerland	Financial services	69,500
9 SAP	Germany	Software	35,800
10 BMW	Germany	Automobile	107,500

Source: *Personnel Today; HR Director;* Nokia website (www.nokia.com)

B2 Case study

Creating an effective organisational culture at Carphone Warehouse

Since opening its first store in London in 1989, Carphone Warehouse (CPW) has enjoyed significant growth. The mobile phone retailer now has over 1400 stores spread across the UK and nine other European countries, and has expanded into a number of related sectors. In 2003, CPW launched its fixed-line telecommunications brand, Talk Talk, followed by the introduction of a lifelong free broadband offer to customers in 2006. The buy-out of rival AOL in October 2006 increased the company's customer base to 2.7 million users, making it the third largest internet service provider (ISP) in the

UK, behind BT and Virgin Media. By April 2008, rumours had begun to emerge that CPW was considering taking over fourth-placed Tiscali, a move that would make the company the UK's largest ISP.

In 2008, six companies controlled 95% of the UK's increasingly mature ISP market, making competition fierce between rivals. CPW recognised the importance of customer service in such an environment, and the vital role played here by the company's employees. According to Cristina Jauregui, head of compensation and benefits at CPW, despite offering a relatively low starting salary, the company's organisational culture and benefits package help it recruit and retain staff with the right skills. She describes CPW as still having a 'small company mentality' and being 'a fun place to work'. It has made a point of retaining a number of features introduced when the business was first established These include the 'beer bust', when it pays for drinks for employees at all of its sites on the last Friday of every month, and the annual employee ball. The company also operates a number of financial incentive schemes, including share option plans, in order to motivate staff and create an element of competition between store managers. The performances of all shops are measured against one another and, at the end of the year, managers of the top 25% of stores receive an extra 50% of shares – the bottom 25% have the same amount taken away!

Questions

(30 marks; 35 minutes)

1 Describe three features of an entrepreneurial culture. (6)

2 Analyse the key advantages and disadvantages of the organisational culture created at Carphone Warehouse. (10)

3 To what extent to you believe that CPW will be able to continue to maintain a 'small company mentality' as it continues to grow? (14)

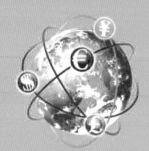

99 Unit

HOW TO WRITE AN ESSAY

99.1 Introduction

Some people believe that essays require a plan. Others favour spider diagrams. In fact, there is no evidence on exam papers that essay plans lead to better essays. Good essays are far more likely to come from practice.

So what are the skills that need practice? The single most important one is the ability to build an argument. Take this essay question from a past A-level exam: 'A crisis has led to a dramatic loss of confidence among the customers of a medium-sized company. Consider the effects this may have on the organisation and how it may respond.'

Many answers to a title such as this will include six, seven, perhaps twelve points. As a result, each point will be developed through no more than four or five lines of writing. In effect, a point will be made and then given a sentence or two of development. This approach can never develop the depth of analysis required for essay success. A far more successful approach is to tackle only two or three themes (not points), then develop each one into a lengthy (perhaps half-page) paragraph. Acquiring the skill of writing developed prose proves equally important in case study work as well.

Having completed your analysis of key themes to answer the question, it is time to write a fully reasoned conclusion. This should be focused upon the question, making judgements on the issues you have analysed. A conclusion is usually worth about one-third of the marks for an essay, so it is worth devoting plenty of time to it. Certainly no less than ten minutes.

99.2 Ten golden rules for writing a good essay

To help you write a good essay, here are ten golden rules you should follow.

1. There is no such thing as an essay about a topic

An essay is a response to a specific title. At A-level, the title is usually worded so that it cannot be answered by repeating paragraphs from your notes. Hence there is no such thing as 'the communications essay', because every answer should depend upon the title, not the topic. A past A-level essay question read 'When selling a good, price is the single most important factor. Evaluate this statement.' This popular question was widely misinterpreted and yielded low marks to candidates. The reason was that few students focused upon the words 'single most important'. They chose, instead, to consider price in relation to the remainder of the marketing mix. Therefore they failed to weigh up the market, economic or corporate factors that could lead price to become the single most important factor (or not, as the case may be).

2. There is no such thing as a one-sided essay

If the title asks you to consider that 'Change is inevitable' (as on a past question), do not fall into the trap of assuming that the examiner just wants you to prove it. If there was only one side to an answer, the question would not be worth asking. The only questions A-level examiners set are ones that can provoke differing viewpoints. Therefore, after developing a strong argument in one direction, write 'On the other hand, it could be argued that ...', so that you assess the opposite viewpoint.

3. All essays have the same answer

With few exceptions, A-level essay questions can be answered in two words: 'It depends.' Put another way, the cause or solution to a business problem or opportunity usually depends upon a series of factors such as the company's objectives and the internal and external constraints it faces. Often, then, your main task

planning the essay is to consider what the answer
depends upon.

. Essays need a structure

When marking essays it is awful to feel you have no idea
where the answer is leading. Some structure is needed. If
you do not jot down a plan, at least tackle an essay that
asks you to 'Discuss the factors . . .' by stating that
'There are three main factors . . .'. A useful trick is to
leave the number blank until you have finished the
essay – by which time you will have found out how
many factors you think there are!

. Most candidates have forgotten the title by the second page

As set out in points 1 and 2 above, the key to a good
answer is the wording of the title. Discipline yourself to
refer back to the question regularly – probably at the
end of every paragraph.

. Every paragraph should answer the question set

A good paragraph is one that answers a specific aspect of
the question in enough depth to impress the reader.
Read over one or two of your essays and ask yourself
whether *every* paragraph is directed at the question set.
You will probably find that several are sidetracks or
simple repetition of your notes/a textbook. In an exam,
such paragraphs gain virtually no marks. The examiner
is interested only in material that answers the precise
wording of the question.

. Content

Good marks come from the breadth of your knowledge
and the clarity of understanding you have shown.
Generally, if you *analyse* the question with care you will
pick up most of the content marks in passing. For
example, in the essay mentioned in point 1 above,
analysis of the circumstances in which price might not
be the most important factor would have led to
discussion of distribution, promotion and the product
itself. There was no need for a paragraph of description
of the marketing mix.

8. Analysis

How well can you apply yourself to the question set?
Can you break the material down in a way that helps
reveal the issues involved? Can you think your way into
the context outlined by the question? For example, an
investment appraisal question set in the context of a
stable market such as chocolate should read differently
to one set in a frantic market such as for computer
games software. Can you use relevant concepts to
explore the causes and effects? Analysis means using
business concepts to answer the question with precision
and depth.

9. Evaluation: the key to high essay marks

Evaluation means judgement. For good marks you need
to:

- show the ability to examine arguments critically, and
  to highlight differing opinions

- distinguish between fact, well-supported argument
  and opinion

- weigh up the strength of different factors or
  arguments, in order to show which you believe to be
  the most important and why

- show how the topic fits into wider business, social,
  political or economic issues.

10. Play the game

Examiners love to read business concepts and
terminology used appropriately. They hate streetwise
language ('They're all on the fiddle') and any
implication that the issues are simple ('It is obvious that
. . .'). Keep your work concise, businesslike and relevant,
making sure that you leave long enough to write a
thoughtful conclusion.

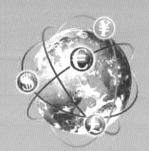
Studies have shown that good revision can add as much as two grades to a student's result at A-level. The aim of this unit is to help you to appreciate what makes up a quality revision programme.

100.1 Aims and objectives

A good revision programme should be aimed at achieving specific targets that will maximise your chances of success in the exam. How should these targets be set?

The basis for setting revision targets can be found in three places:

1 the specification (syllabus)

2 past papers

3 examiner's reports.

The specification

The content of the course will be outlined in some detail in the specification. Since the questions in the exam will be based closely on this document, you must ensure that you have sufficient knowledge of each area.

The specification will tell you what skills the examiner will be looking for. As well as basic factual recall as appropriate to the case being discussed, there will be a range of other skills you must demonstrate if you are to score highly.

Knowing what skills the examiner is looking for will help you produce better-quality answers in an exam. However, like all skills these can be developed only through practice. So it is important to start your revision early and not leave it until the end. In fact you should try to review your work every few weeks to make sure there are no gaps in your notes and that your files are well organised. This way it becomes easier to revise at the end of the course because everything is in place.

Definitions of higher academic skills

Analysis (breaking down):

● identification of cause, effect and interrelationships

● the appropriate use of theory or business cases/practice to investigate the question set

● breaking the material down to show underlying causes or problems

● use of appropriate techniques to analyse data.

Analysis involves a chain of argument linking ideas and concepts, and showing the relationship between them. You might be analysing why something happened or the consequence of something occurring.

Look back at previous answers you have written and try to find examples of how you could extend your responses. Were there any occasions when you could have used business theory such as elasticity, motivation or break-even to strengthen your arguments and provided a higher level of analysis?

Synthesis (bringing together):

● building the points/themes within the answer into a connected whole

● logical sequencing of argument

● clarity through summarising an argument.

This skill is particularly important when you have a piece of extended writing such as a report or an essay. In a good essay, for example, each paragraph will have a clear purpose. The arguments will be well organised and lead to a logical conclusion that builds on the earlier analysis. In some exams the synthesis marks may be awarded separately; in others, they will be part of an overall mark for an answer.

Evaluation (judgement):

● judgement shown in weighing up the relative importance of different points or sides of an argument, in order to reach a conclusion

● informed comment on the reliability of evidence

● distinguishing between fact and opinion

judgement of the wider issues and implications

conclusions drawn from the evidence presented

selectivity – identifying the material that is most relevant to the question.

Past papers

Previous exam papers are very important in helping you prepare for your exam. They will show you exactly what sort of questions you will face and the number of marks available. They will also give you a feel for the type of words used in the question. It goes without saying that exam questions must be read carefully. However, there will be key words used in the questions that tell you how to answer them. There is, for example, a great difference in the answers expected for the following two questions.

Analyse the key elements of ABC plc's marketing strategy.

Evaluate the key elements of ABC plc's marketing strategy.

Unless you know what is expected from these two questions, you are unlikely to know how much detail is required or how your answer ought to be structured.

Examiner's reports

These are available for each examination and can be found on the relevant exam board's website (e.g. www.aqa.org.uk). They are written by the principal examiner of each exam and provide an insight into what he found worked well or was not so successful. By looking at these reports you will get a good sense of the weak areas of candidates and common issues they had when interpreting questions. This provides another useful input when it comes to revising and knowing where to focus your efforts.

100.2 Resources

The following list contains items that will be of enormous value in preparing for an exam. They should all be familiar to you before you begin revising, and should have played a constant part in your studies throughout the course.

Class notes

A copy of the specification

3 Past exam papers, mark schemes and examiners' reports

4 A revision plan

5 Newspapers/cuttings files of relevant stories

6 A good textbook

7 Access to your teacher

8 Other students

Class notes

Since these are the product of your work and a record of your activities, they will form a vital part of your understanding of the subject. They should contain past work you have done on exam-style questions and model answers that will help prepare you for the exam. As you make notes try to make sure these will be legible and useful later on in your revision. Make sure you keep them in the right order as you go – having to sort them out later is much more of a challenge.

A copy of the specification

The specification tells you several important things:

● what knowledge you could be tested on

● what skills the examiner will be looking for

● how the marks will be allocated

● what you will be expected to do in each exam paper you sit.

Past exam papers, mark schemes and examiners' reports

By working from past papers you will develop a feel for the type of question you will be asked and the sorts of responses you will be expected to give. Examiners' reports will give you an insight into what they thought worked well and what surprised them in terms of the responses. This in turn will give you some idea of how and what they want to assess in the future.

A revision plan

As described in the previous section. This will help keep you on target to achieve everything that you need to cover before the exam.

Newspapers/cuttings files

Since Business Studies is a real-life subject, the ability to bring in relevant examples will boost your answers and grades. By studying what is happening in the business world you will be able to apply your answers much more effectively – this is because you will develop a better understanding of the key issues in different markets and industries. It will also help you to draw comparisons between different types of business, which can lead to good evaluation. Keeping some form of 'business diary', where you track at least one story a week, is a good way of keeping up to date with what is happening. When making notes about your story try to highlight the underlying business issues and relate it to theory rather than just describe it. This will help you to analyse cases and business situations.

A good textbook

Choose one that will help clarify any points that you are still unsure about (this one we hope!).

Access to your teacher

Asking your teacher for help is vital. S/he is able to give you useful advice and insights, to quell sudden panics and suggest ways to improve your performance. Don't hold back – ask! Whenever you get a piece of work back where the mark is disappointing make sure you know what you need to do differently next time. Read any comments on your work and try to improve in the specific areas mentioned in the next piece of work. Remember, the journey to success is full of small improvements (this is, of course, the philosophy of *kaizen*).

Other students

Talk to other students to help discuss points and clarify ideas. Learning from each other is a very powerful way of revising. Studies often show that you remember something much more when you have to explain it to someone else. Why not agree as a group to revise some topics? Study them individually then get together to test each other's understanding. This works very well. Remember you can all get A*s if you are good enough, so there is no problem helping others to improve their performance (as long as it is all their own work in the exam) and you will almost certainly benefit yourself from working with others.

100.3 Learning the language of the subject

Clear definitions of business terms are essential for exam success. They count for much more than the odd 2-mark question here or there. By showing the examiner that you understand what a term means you are reassuring her that your knowledge is sound; this is likely to help your marks for other skills as well. If the examiner is not convinced you understand what a concept actually means then they are less likely to reward the other skills at a high level. Even on very high-mark questions it is important to define your terms.

For revising business definitions you could use:

- definition cards
- past papers
- crosswords/word games
- brainteasers.

There are many possible sources of good definitions of business terms. In this book, key terms have been highlighted and given clear and concise definitions. Your definitions should be written without using the word in question. ('Market growth is the growth in the market' is not a very good definition, for example!)

It is important, then, that you can produce high-quality definitions in an exam. This can be done only through learning and practice. Possible ways to achieve this are as follows.

Definition cards

Take a pack of index cards or postcards, or similar-sized pieces of thick paper. On each one, write a particular term or phrase that you can find in the specification document. Remember to include things like motivation theories where a clear definition/description can give an excellent overview. It is extremely unlikely that you will be asked to know a precise definition for any term that is not specifically in the specification.

On the back of each card write an appropriate definition. This could come from your class notes, a textbook or a dictionary such as *The Complete A–Z Business Studies Handbook* (see the 'Further reading' section at the end of the unit for details). Make sure that the definition you write:

- is concise

is clear

does not use the word being defined in the definition.

arn them by continual repetition. Put a tick or cross
each card to show whether or not you came up with
acceptable effort. Over time, you should see the
mber of ticks growing.

uffle the cards occasionally so that you are not being
ven clues to some definitions because of the words or
rases preceding them.

y doing the exercise 'back to front', by looking at the
finitions and then applying the correct word or
rase.

ast papers

using as many past papers as possible you can find out
actly what type of definition questions are asked.
ore importantly, you can see how many marks are
ailable for them, which will tell you exactly how
ich detail you need to go into in your answer.

possible, get hold of examiners' mark schemes. These
ll again give you a clear idea of what is being looked
r from your answer.

usiness crosswords and brainteasers

ou will be able to find many examples of word games
magazines such as *Business Review* (see the 'Further
ading' section at the end of the unit for details). By
mpleting these you are developing your business
ocabulary and linking words with their meanings.

r a fuller, alphabetical source of exercises such as
ese, Ian Marcousé's *A–Z Business Studies Worksheets*
ee 'Further reading') is very helpful. It contains
erally thousands of questions – all with answers in the
ck of the book.

00.4 Numbers

ll business courses contain aspects of number work,
nich can be specifically tested in exams. It must be
membered, however, that there are two clear aspects
numbers:

calculation

interpretation.

ne calculation aspects of business courses are one area

where practice is by far the best approach. Each
numerical element has its own techniques that you will
be expected to be able to demonstrate. The techniques
can be learnt, and by working through many examples
they can become second nature. Even if mathematics is
not your strong point, the calculations ought not to
cause problems to an A-level student. Something that at
first sight appears complex, such as investment appraisal,
requires only simple techniques such as multiplying,
adding and subtracting. Going through the 'Workbook'
sections of this book will provide invaluable practice.
Ask your teacher for a photocopy of the answers
available in the *Teacher's Guide*.

Once calculated, all business numbers need to be used.
It is all very well to calculate the accounting ratios, for
example, but if the numbers are then unused the
exercise has been wasted. You must attempt to follow
each calculation by stating what the numbers are saying
and their implications for the business.

100.5 General tips for revision

1 Start early.

2 Know the purpose of your revision.

3 Work more on weaker areas.

4 Use past papers as far as is possible.

5 Keep a clear perspective.

Finally, do no more revision on the night before the
exam – it won't help and can only cause you anxiety.
Eat well and get a good night's sleep. That way you will
be in good physical shape to perform to the best of your
abilities in the exam.

Further reading

Business Review (available from Philip Allan Publishers,
see www.philipallan.co.uk).

Lines, D., Marcousé, I. and Martin, B. (2006) *The
Complete A–Z Business Studies Handbook* (5th edn),
Hodder Education.

Marcousé, I. (2008) *A–Z Business Studies Worksheets*,
www.a-zbusinesstraining.com.

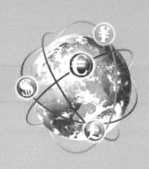
To achieve an A grade requires far more than simply knowing all the subject matter – you need to be able to weave ideas together to generate mature analysis from which judgements (evaluation) can be made. You need concepts that enable your answers to rise above those of the majority. There are two categories of 'A grade' concept: those that are transferable and those that are naturally analytic.

101.1 Transferable concepts

A transferable concept is one that can be used to answer a wide variety of questions. You may have been taught the concept in relation to one issue, but the A-grade student sees the scope for using it more often. At AS-level, the main transferable concepts are:

● opportunity cost

● objectives

● strategy

● risk.

Table 101.1 Using opportunity cost in exam answers

The opportunity cost answer

Actions taken will have an opportunity cost (e.g. cutting staff levels will cut costs but may reduce customer service and hit the ability to develop new products)

Could redesign jobs to enrich them, but this may mean missing out on the opportunity to improve productivity (e.g. by automation)

This will mean missing out on the opportunity to develop good design links with suppliers, and will make it harder to respond quickly to fashion change (which is why Zara gets supplies only from Europe)

Opportunity cost

This is the cost of missing out on the next best alternative when making a decision. This appears in Unit 9, placing opportunity cost in the context of new business start-ups. This is fine, but you need to see the many other ways in which the concept can be used. Literally any answer to a question about decisions or strategies would benefit from consideration of opportunity cost. Table 101.1 shows the scope that exists.

The rule is simple: every decision and every action has a opportunity cost, because there is a limited amount of time and money. Always think about what a business misses out on when making a decision.

Objectives

These are the goals set (or agreed) by the business, b the department or by the individual. Exam answers o decision making are usually rooted in profit (i.e. they assume that the business will do whatever generates the highest revenue or lowest cost). In fact, business decisions are based on the overall or personal objectives. A manager with a £400,000 budget for advertising will spend it all, even if the last £100,000 is not really useful, because spending the budget is th manager's objective. This might sound daft but it is absolutely true (and one of the weaknesses of a strict system of budgets). A business with the objective of growing to become the market leader will charge lower prices than one attempting to maximise its profits.

The rule: business decisions (good and bad) are based o **corporate** and personal goals. These may be focused on profit, but may also be focused on growth, or on surviva or on a social goal such as improving the environment. A good exam answer is based on the circumstances of the specific business; in this case, what exactly are its objectives?

Strategy

The creation of a medium- to long-term plan for meeting the objectives. Clearly this will be successful only if (a) the plan is a good one and (b) managers put it into practice effectively.

The key to an A-grade answer is to see the differences between strategy and tactics. Tactics are short-term responses to opportunities or threats. For example, Burger King might choose to cut its prices sharply in August in Scunthorpe because a new McDonald's Drive-thru is opening; meanwhile in August in Bournemouth it pushes prices up because so many holidaymakers arrive. Overall, though, Burger King's long-term pricing strategy has been to charge higher prices than McDonald's.

Any question on objectives must lead through to strategy; after all, objectives mean nothing without a plan to make them happen. Beware, though, of straying away from strategy into tactics. Questions about how to achieve marketing objectives are often answered with reference to BOGOF (buy one get one free) or other short-term tactical sales promotions.

The rule: strategy is medium to long term; tactics are short term.

Risk

This covers the chance elements within a decision that need to be assessed before carrying on. Second-rate managers in second-rate organisations may have a long career without ever doing anything risky. If bosses hate 'mistakes' they will hate decisions involving risk. Yet no decision worthy of the name is risk-free. Just because launching new products is risky this should not mean that no new products are launched; clearly that would sign the death certificate of the business.

Entrepreneurs are, by definition, willing to accept risk as part of the decision-making process – so are good managers in good companies. One of the world's biggest companies is Unilever. Up until 2005 its chairman was Niall Fitzgerald. Before being promoted to chairman, Fitzgerald had been responsible for an awful new product flop called Persil Power. Appointing Fitzgerald sent a very positive message to all staff: 'We know that if you take risks some won't come off; but the odd failure won't stop you getting to the top.'

The rule: risk is part of business because the future cannot be known. Good entrepreneurs and good businesses take risk in their stride; it is just part of a calculation about the positives versus the negatives when making a decision.

These are ideas that are quite complex, but if you can master them you can show a quality level that sets you apart from other exam candidates. At A2-level there are many, but at AS-level there are really only three:

1 distinguishing between cash flow and profit (re-read Unit 20, then tackle Data response B1, below)

2 competitiveness

3 the business context.

Competitiveness

Competitiveness is the ability of a business to compete effectively against its rivals. This term is invaluable. It has two aspects: the ability to compete on price and the ability to compete in other ways.

Price competitiveness is based on costs. In the long term you can compete with Ryanair on price only if you can keep your costs as low as Ryanair's. Look at the extraordinary staff cost comparisons for 2007 shown in Table 101.2, overleaf.

These figures show that British Airways' wage bill is 12.9 times more than that of Ryanair per passenger.

Non-price factors

Fortunately for British Airways, there are other ways to stay competitive. Its most profitable route is Heathrow to New York. Here it has managed to stay among the leaders for offering a great business-class service (at prices of up to £4000 return). Its quality of service helps it to remain competitive in a sector that is less concerned by price.

Key **non-price factors** that can make customers willing to pay high prices include:

- great design

- prestige brand names

- high-quality production

- terrific personal service and after-sales service

- a satisfied glow (e.g. organic, environmentally sound).

The rule: if a business has no strategy for competitiveness it may not be around for long. Directors must decide whether to aim for price competitiveness or

Table 101.2 Staff cost comparisons, 2007

	Passengers flown	**Wage bill**	**Wage cost per passenger**
Ryanair	42.5 million	£226.5m	£5.33
British Airways	33.0 million	£2,277m	£69.00

Source: data from British Airways and Ryanair annual accounts, year ending 31 March 2007

Figure 101.1 New York, a British Airways destination

to stand out from rivals using one or more of the non-price factors.

The business context

A-grade answers show real understanding of the specific business situation set by the examiner. This is not announced in advance, so the 400 words of text have to provide all the clues needed for success. For an A-grade student it should not matter what the context is. All the key information is in the text. Among the key things to look for are those listed below.

● *Is it a manufacturing or a service business?* Usually service businesses have direct customer contact, so staff motivation is critical to the brand image. Also, manufacturing firms are more likely to face direct competition from low-cost producers such as China, so they have more serious competitiveness issues than service firms.

● *Is it a recent start-up or an established business?* Even if the firm is small, a few years of success can make it quite easy to cope with a difficult period; the finances might be quite strong and a loyal customer base may exist. For brand new companies, even a temporary problem, such as flooding, may wreck the business

plan. Every new firm needs a bit of luck, or at least the absence of bad luck.

● *What is the external context for the business?* The economy may be strong, with confident consumers – or weak, with worried customers keeping their hands in their pockets. The market for your product might be trendy and booming or tired and slipping. Competition may be fierce, and perhaps from big well-financed firms; or it may be quite mild, with many small firms keeping to their local area.

The rule: never start answering a business question until you have given yourself the time to ask 'What's special about this particular business?' Its unique features will give you the scope for developing those A-grade answers.

Key terms

Competitiveness: the ability to compete (i.e. highly competitive means in a great position to beat the competition).
Corporate: the company as a whole, so corporate objectives affect the whole business.
Non-price factors: all the factors affecting consumer demand for a product other than price, e.g. brand image and product quality.

Exercises

A. Revision questions

(35 marks; 35 minutes)

1 Why is it better to spend revision time on transferable concepts than any other? (2)

2 Outline the opportunity cost to Innocent Drinks of spending £2 million to buy up a German producer of smoothies. (4)

3 Identify whether each of the following is an objective, a strategy or a tactic:
   (a) to run a 'blue cross day', with 25% off all stock this Sunday
   (b) to become the first carbon-neutral car manufacturer
   (c) to boost sales by 20% within the next two years
   (d) to concentrate our advertising spending on TV
   (e) to give a huge office party to celebrate winning a big order. (5)

4 Outline three risks faced by a school-leaver who borrows £5000 to start an online auction site specialising in Manchester United football programmes. (6)

5 Explain one key factor in making each of these companies competitive:
   (a) Mercedes cars
   (b) Primark
   (c) L'Oréal cosmetics. (6)

6 (a) Outline two important features of the UK economy over the past six months. (4)
   (b) Explain the effect that each of these trends might have on a business start-up focusing on loft extensions and other costly building work. (8)

B. Revision exercises

B1 Data response

The Furniture Shop

(40 marks; 50 minutes)

Section 1

A furniture shop has been operating for six months with regular income of £100,000 in monthly sales. Its monthly fixed costs are £50,000 and it sets its prices by doubling the variable costs of buying supplies in from the manufacturers (i.e. variable costs are half the sales revenue).

1a Calculate the monthly profit/loss being made. (3)

A bright young manager carries out some research and finds that sales can be doubled by making an offer of 'buy now, get interest free credit for 3 months'.

1b Calculate the new monthly profit/loss when sales double. (3)

Section 2

The business decides to go ahead with this offer, and plans to introduce it on 1 February. This will boost profit, but what will it do to the firm's cash flow? Copy out the grid on page 718 and fill it in carefully (in pencil, preferably). Note that the business has £50,000 in the bank at the start of January.

2 Fill in the January–June cash flow table. (12)

Section 3

After running the interest-free offer for five months, it is decided that the offer will be closed at the end of June. Draw up the cash flow position for the business from July–October.

3 Fill in the cash flow table below. (8)

Section 4

Now that the offer is over, it is possible to see the difference between profit and cash flow.

4 Draw a line graph to show cumulative cash and cumulative profit over the period January to October. Label the graph carefully, then shade in the area that indicates the difference between profit and cash flow. (14)

All figures in £000s

	Jan	Feb	Mar	Apr	May	June
Cash at start	50					
Cash in						
Cash out						
Net cash						
Accumulated Cash						−300

(Keep trying this until you get *minus* £300,000 in the bottom right-hand corner.)

All figures in £000s

	July	August	September	October
Cash at start	−300			
Cash in				
Cash out				
Net cash				
Accumulated cash				+300

(Keep trying this until you get *plus* £300,000 in the bottom right-hand corner.)

B2 Data response

The Sustainable Farm

In 2005 Ben and Charlotte Hollins' father died. He had been a pioneer of organic farming, keeping his Fordhall Farm free of chemicals for 65 years. But he had never owned it. The Hollins family had worked as tenant farmers on this land for 700 years.

The freehold owners of the land gave Ben and Charlotte a year to raise £800,000 to buy the land, otherwise they would sell it to developers. As Ben and Charlotte were 22 and 24 respectively, this looked an impossible task. Yet certain things were in their favour. Britain was in the middle of an organic food boom, with demand growing at 30% a year; and the story of young Ben and Charlotte was bound to sell newspapers. Best of all, the economy was in its 12th year of growth, making people feel quite comfortable about spending their money freely.

Helped by the Soil Association and, later, Sting and Prince Charles, a huge wave of publicity put forward the Fordhall Community Land Initiative as a great way to support organic farming. People were invited to buy £50 shares in the farm, and the money poured in. By August 2006, over £500,000 had been invested by ordinary members of the public. Ben and Charlotte then put out an appeal for a further £100,000 of five-year interest-free loans, and again the public provided the money. A £200,000 bank loan completed the financing.

Now Ben and Charlotte have to deliver. In the short term they need to make enough money to repay the loans. Further into the future, the key thing will be to make the farm sustainable financially as well as environmentally. Judging by the information given on their website (www.fordhallfarm.com) things are going very well.

Questions

(25 marks; 30 minutes)

1 How would you sum up Ben and Charlotte's objectives? (4)

2 Outline the role of opportunity cost in this case. (4)

3 Ben and Charlotte must now make sure that the farm is sufficiently competitive to survive. Examine two ways they might do this. (A look at the website will help answer this question.) (8)

4 To what extent is this form of financing unique to the circumstances outlined in the text? (9)

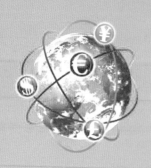

A-level examiners love a candidate who understands how to get the marks – it makes their life easier! Getting those marks is, on the face of it, quite simple. All you have to do when answering a question is to:

● define any key terms (show that you know what you're talking about)

● use them to examine the specific business context (the case material you're dealing with)

● analyse the question using theory when necessary, and with reference to the case

● make a judgement when you're asked to do so – and justify it.

The truth is that it is not that easy. Many students are poor at showing these skills in a classroom. Add in the pressure of the exam room and many students' ability to think goes out of the window. It's replaced by one thing alone: the ability to remember. In the exam room, the examiner is trying to tap into the student's brain (have a look around; decide whether it knows enough and is clever enough to be worth an A). But many students are pushing the examiner away ('No, I think you've asked me the wrong question, dear examiner; what you should have asked me is this – look, I prepared it especially for you …').

To the examiner, the pyramid below is the basis of all exam marking. It forms a pyramid because at the base is the foundation of every good answer: knowledge. If the question is on opportunity cost and you don't know what that is, no amount of waffle will dig you out of the hole. What the pyramid also shows, though, is that no matter how much knowledge you have, you cannot get more than 30% of the marks available, and that is never enough for a pass. Therefore it is essential that you master the other skills too.

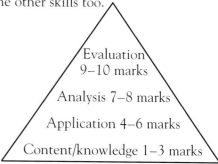

Evaluation
9–10 marks

Analysis 7–8 marks

Application 4–6 marks

Content/knowledge 1–3 marks

At AS-level, the key skills are knowledge and application. Between them they account for 60% of the marks and therefore can enable you to achieve a grade B. At A2, the keys are analysis and evaluation, though it is important to remember that analysis is dependent on knowledge, and evaluation relies on good application.

Table 102.1 Assessment objectives for all A-level Business Studies specifications from 2008

Skills	AS	A2	A-level
Evaluation	20%	30%	25%
Analysis	20%	30%	25%
Application	30%	20%	25%
Knowledge	30%	20%	25%

102.1 Mastering each of the assessment objectives

Knowledge

Business Studies isn't Chemistry. In Chemistry you either know what happens when iodine is mixed with sulphuric acid or you don't. The same is true in some aspects of business. For example, do you know what happens when a business with cash flow problems turns to factoring? (Yes, it should improve the cash flow position.)

Yet in many other cases it is not obvious that technical knowledge is required. Many questions use words that anyone has access to, whether they have attended lessons or not. Here are a few examples:

Discuss how XYZ Ltd should improve the motivation of its workforce.

Examine the possible effects on XYZ Ltd of a rise in consumer spending.

Explain two ways in which XYZ Ltd could increase its profit.

In each of these three cases, a student with weak knowledge can write plenty and probably come out of the exam feeling great. Their result will be a great disappointment, however. This is because the examiner will see many of this candidate's answers as waffle.

Examiners are actually very generous – they want to give marks. But their great fear is giving a high mark to well-written waffle that, on a second reading, proves to be empty of business knowledge. So help them: start your answer with a precise definition that will convince them that you're a good student who attended lessons, did your homework and bothered to revise.

Your opening sentences in answer to the above three questions might be as follows.

Motivation, according to Professor Herzberg, is 'people doing something because they want to, not because they have to'.

Rising consumer spending will increase the sales of most products, boost sharply the sales of luxury products (and services), but cut the sales of 'inferior products' such as Tesco Value Beans.

Profit is revenue minus costs, therefore it can be increased by boosting revenue or cutting costs (fixed or variable).

Examiner tips on revising knowledge

1 Four weeks before the exam, make lists of all the key terms within the section of the specification being examined. Use the official exam board specification for this.

2 Write a definition for each of the terms, ideally based either on this book or classroom notes or the *Complete A–Z Business Studies Handbook* (5th edn, Hodder Education, 2006). Beware of Googled definitions, because most will be American and their business terminology is not quite the same as Britain's, and many will be aimed at university, not A-level, students.

3 Keep trying again to write the definitions from your own memory and from your understanding of the topic. For example, the explanation of profit given above is something that you would not memorise, but that you should 'know'.

4 Don't spent time trying to remember lots of advantages and disadvantages of things; this will distract you from the key matter: what is it (i.e. the definition).

Application

Application marks are given for your ability to think your way into the specific business situation facing you in the exam. This might be a context you know quite well (the launch of the Nintendo Wii) or might be one you have never heard of before (Tesco's unsuccessful first attempt at operating in America). In fact, it doesn't matter. The text will contain all you need to develop your answers to the questions. Unit 103 gives a very full account of how to get the most out of data when tackling an exam question.

To get OK marks at application, you need to use the material in the text effectively. Not just repeating the company name, but being able to incorporate factors such as Tesco's challenge in building up supply lines in America (i.e. making good deals with US suppliers).

To get full marks at application, you need not only to be able to use the context, but also to see its significance. For example, showing that you see the importance of Tesco deciding to halt its US expansion at 50 stores, when it had originally talked of building 200.

Every business is unique. It is also true to say that every year is unique for every business. The more you master the specific issues that relate to the specific company or industry, the better your marks at application.

Examiner tips on revising application

1   Throughout the course, take every opportunity to read *Business Review* articles, to read business stories in newspapers, to watch business TV (e.g. *The Apprentice, Dragons' Den*) and take note of relevant news items.

2   Three weeks before the exam, start working on the B1 and B2 exercises within this book. Read the text and write short notes on the key business aspects of that unique business. If possible, do this with a friend, so that you can swap ideas. It is helpful to debate which (of all the points you've identified) is the single most important feature of that business.

3   One week before the exam, start going through past papers. Identify the key features of that unique business and think about how they can be connected to the questions set.

Analysis

Analysis is shown in two main ways. The first is through the build-up of argument, in which you are showing an ever deeper understanding of issues, causes and consequences. This can also be called 'sequences of logic'. In other words, 'if that happens, this will be the consequence'.

It is quite easy to practise sequences of logic using the 'analysis framework' shown in the table below.

Note that the key to analysis marks is not getting the initial points (cut its prices, hold prices, find a new niche), it's the ability to think each point through to its logical conclusion.

Examiner tips on revising analysis

1   Throughout the course, ask your tutor two questions 'Why is that the case?' and 'What would be the effect of that?'

2   Two weeks before the exam, use the above model to think through any of the major topics in the specification (the ones on the left-hand side of the document).

3   One week before the exam, go through past papers, using the analysis framework on any question that carries more than 8 marks.

Evaluation

Evaluation means judgement. In other words, it's about you making a judgement and giving your reasons (i.e. justifying it). Each Friday, Messrs Ferguson and Wenger must make their decisions on team selection. They will talk through their judgements with their closest advisers, explaining their thoughts. The advisers (Assistant Manager and Head Coach) may argue or may agree. The managers' decision, of course, is final. In an exam, the ideal answer would give the judgement and explain it (in terms of tactics, the strength of the opposition, which players are on form, which are needed for next Tuesday's game against Barcelona, and so on).

In a business exam, you might be asked to recommend whether the firm should, or should not, launch a new product. You must decide on the basis of the evidence, then explain which aspects of the evidence pushed you

1   What might be the effect on the XY Co of a major new competitor arriving?

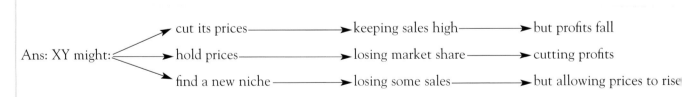

2   What might be the effect on the XY Co of a rise in its labour turnover?

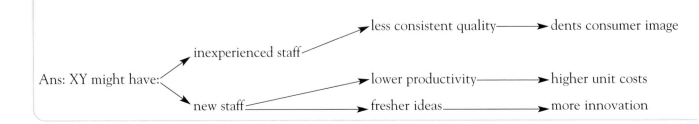

owards your decision. You might also reflect on how
onfident you are of the decision. Is it a 'no-brainer'? Or
 it finely balanced?

Other questions are more frustrating because they
equire you to invent your own evaluation (e.g. 'Discuss
he advantages to XYZ Ltd of using the Boston Matrix').
This style of question gives you nothing real to evaluate,
ut needs you to seize any opportunities available to
ou. For instance, the accompanying text might tell you
hat XYZ Ltd's sales have been slipping a bit, recently.
This might enable you to suggest that, 'The most
mportant benefit to XYZ would be the possibility that
sing the Boston Matrix will help the business identify
nd support one or more Rising Stars. This could enable
he company to turn around its poor sales performance.'

1 Practise making judgements. For example, when you
see a new restaurant opening up in your high street,
do you think it will succeed? Do you think it will
fail? Why do you think that? Then keep an eye on it
to see how it's going.

2 Two to three weeks before the exam, start going
through the two exam papers in Unit 104, focusing
on the judgements required, e.g. questions 2b and 2c
of the Unit 1 exam. Then start going through past
exam questions.

3 On the day of the exam, make sure to leave yourself
long enough to write a conclusion to any question
that starts with trigger words such as 'Discuss',
'Evaluate' or 'To what extent'. Then, before starting
to write the conclusion, ask yourself 'What do I
really think about the answer to this question in this
situation?' Then write your explanation for the
judgement you have made.

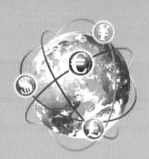
TACKLING DATA RESPONSE QUESTIONS

103.1 Introduction

A data response question requires you to do three things simultaneously:

1 understand and use the data (perhaps an article)

2 keep in mind the classroom/textbook theory

3 answer the precise terms of the question set.

It would not be crazy to suggest that most human beings can do only one thing at a time; two at a push. But three? That is why data response papers are harder than they look.

For students who revise at the last minute, the problem is especially acute. The cramming blocks out the other two factors, making the answers one-dimensional. The examiner can see the knowledge, and may admire it, but the marks for application, analysis and evaluation are few and far between.

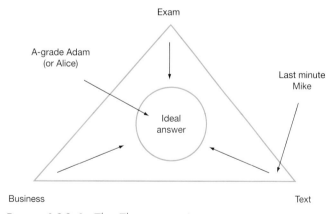

Figure 103.1 The Three-way Answer

103.2 Using the data

The key is to find a way to get the guts out of the short passage of text – to find the real business bits that matter. Many students use a highlighter pen, but seem to mark up too much, turning it from a white page to a lurid pink one. That achieves little. It's better to jot down the key points as you go. These amount to:

● key points about the business context – competitors, consumer fashions, and so on

● key points about the business – its products, its image, its efficiency, and so on

● key points about the people running it – their experience, their enthusiasm, their judgement, and so on.

Below is a short piece of text on PD Ltd. Identify at least three key points that you could use to enrich the application within exam answers. Give yourself a few minutes, then look at the suggestions given at the end of the unit.

> **PD Ltd**
> Den and girlfriend Pam started PD Ltd with £15,000 borrowed from a friend and £15,000 from HSBC. Both keen surfers, their plan was to open the first surfing school in north-east England, on the coast above Newcastle. They were confident that they could persuade the Geordies to take up surfing, despite the cold weather.

This exercise shows the enormous importance of readin the text with great care.

When in the exam room, you can make use of every subtlety built into the text, but some of the more common issues worth looking out for are listed in Table 103.1.

Table 103.1 *Some common issues to look out for*

Topic or issue	From one extreme ...	... to the other
Seasonal sales	70% of the whole year's sales occur in the three-week run-in to Christmas (e.g. toys, posh perfume)	Sales vary little month by month (e.g. toilet paper)
Degree of competition	Fiercely competitive market in which customers care greatly about price	Few competitors, and they focus on giving high service levels to their own customers
Product life cycle	Very short product life cycles; a brand's sales can be ended by a technological breakthrough by another	Long life cycles protected by the conservatism of consumers (e.g. Heinz Ketchup – people won't try another)
Risk	A sole trader has started a new restaurant using borrowings secured against the family home	Tim started a limited company to run a small education business offering maths tutoring

103.3 Using numerical data

Quite often, data response questions include numerical data such as budget statements or cash flow forecasts. These are very helpful. The reason is that they offer a quick and easy method for getting high marks.

The valuable thing about numbers is that they:

- give you a starting point for building an argument (to get analysis marks) while ...

- ... forcing the examiner to give you extra marks for application (because if you use the specific numbers given in the exam, your answer is automatically applied to the specific context).

So an answer that uses the numbers effectively is automatically getting double marks. It can also be argued that numbers provide a good student with the opportunity to show both their knowledge of the course and provide a basis for making judgements. In other words, it can generate every one of the assessment objectives.

With numerical data (such as sales figures) it will always be valid to ask yourself certain questions (see Table 103.2).

Table 103.2 *Questions to ask yourself about numerical data*

Valid questions about data	Example of good data	Example of bad data
Is the data actual or forecast?	Actual data on weekly sales over the last 18 months	A forecast of next year's sales made by a businessman wanting a loan
Is it based on a valid sample?	Based on a quota sample of 600, carried out by Gallup, an independent research company	Based on research carried out by the sales department
Is there a valid way to make comparisons?	The figures show sales of all our brands compared with the same period last year and the year before	The figures show the huge success of Brand P, which has seen a 70% sales increase in the past two months

103.4 Bringing it all together

The amount of data provided in a data response exam question may be quite substantial. It cannot, therefore, all be used to answer every question. Don't worry: the important thing is *not* to 'know it all'; the key is to have picked out enough key features to show that you're really trying to think for yourself while in the exam room. Examiners are giving you the opportunity to break away from your teacher and show that you're far from just being a puppet, with your teacher pulling the strings.

Having read the text and thought about the numbers, make sure to jot down the key points. If you don't, there's a risk that you'll forget the details by the time you tackle your third question. Every answer requires the context (i.e. an effective analysis of the case being looked at).

Application points: PD Ltd

Things to look out for include the following.

- *The 'first' surfing school in north-east England*. This may mean that there is a fortune to be made, but it also suggests high risk (whereas being the 15th surfing school in Newquay, Cornwall, would probably not be a total disaster).
- *'They were confident that . . .'* The key here is what it does *not* say. It does *not* say: 'They'd done some market research, which gave them confidence that . . .'. Their confidence may mean nothing. Anyone who watches *The Apprentice* has seen no end of people with confidence but startlingly little ability. The key requirement in this case is evidence not confidence.
- *'£15,000 borrowed from a friend and £15,000 from HSBC'*. No bank would lend unless it has seen the owners invest at least half the start-up capital, so Den and Pam have probably not told the bank that they have borrowed it all. Having such high debts (relatively) must increase the riskiness of the investment.

Other possibilities include: the importance of the Ltd status (protection from unlimited liability); the importance of seasonality (especially in the north-east); the possible significance of the boyfriend/girlfriend relationship – how long have they been together?

this exam you must answer *all* the questions. You will
ed up to ten minutes to skim-read and then re-read
e text, making brief notes in the margin. That leaves a
ark a minute for answering the questions, and five
inutes to check your work.

he quality of your English will be assessed in your
swers to questions 2b and 2c. Be careful to write fully
veloped prose (i.e. avoid bullet points and
breviations) and make sure to check your written
rk carefully.

would be best to tackle this mock exam in timed
nditions, even if you are doing it at home.

Mock exam: Unit 1

(60 marks; 75 minutes)

Dream Holidays Ltd

wo years ago, Karl and Natalia took up parachuting.
hey both worked at a solicitor's, Natalia as the office
anager and Karl as the accountant. Soon their week's
ork was purely a filler between the important thing in
e: the parachuting. Then Natalia had an idea.

'hy not start a holiday business focusing on
arachuting? The modern, adventure-seeking traveller
uld love a parachute drop in a beautiful part of mid-
'ales, with a group leader who would then have to
ide the group – on foot – to the nearest town. The
ext day, they would move on to another part of Wales.
day Wales, tomorrow Austria or Brazil.

hey talked to other parachuters and to friends who
ent on diving and other active holidays. All loved the
ea. One said: 'I've never bothered with parachuting
cause I thought it would always be into the same dull
·ld. This would definitely get me interested.' And what
uld people expect to pay for a parachuting holiday in
'ales? Or in Brazil? Broadly, the answer was £1500 and
·500 respectively.

Natalia did some research into hiring planes in Wales –
not as expensive as she had thought – and the cost of
three-star hotels. Assuming a group size of 12, it was quite
easy to see that a profit could be made. Weekly fixed costs
came out at £8000, variable costs at £500 per person and
the price would be £1500. Natalia said with confidence:
'If we just run one parachute holiday per week in Wales
in the six months May–October, there's still enough
profit to make a good living. And if one of us is the group
leader and the other one the emergency back-up, we'll
have free parachuting all summer long.' They also
discussed taking on extra staff to run more courses.

Karl's worry was about how to build up to the necessary
numbers of customers: twelve customers a week would
be great, but what if there were only six? He carried out
some research by dropping in to eight adventure-travel
agencies in Manchester and Birmingham. After that he
felt much more comfortable; as one agent said: 'That
price won't put off people in the segment you're
targeting. You'll soon have rich City boys wanting to
spend their bonuses with you on £10,000 trips
parachuting onto Caribbean islands'.

Reassured by this, Karl started work on a cash flow
forecast (Figure 104.1). They thought about an internet-
only operation, but decided customers would like the

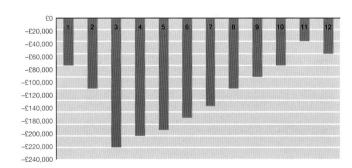

*Figure 104.1 Cumulative cash balance for XDream
Holidays Ltd (months 1–12)*

reassurance of a proper office to come and visit. Now
the remaining hurdle was raising finance; their £20,000
in savings would be nothing like enough to get the

business going. In preparation, Natalia went to Companies House to establish XDream Holidays Ltd. Karl started to think about giving notice to quit their jobs. The dream was starting to come true.

See Unit 106 for exam answers plus an examiner's commentary.

Questions

Question 1

1a Natalia spotted the parachute business opportunity through her personal experience. State two other ways of identifying a business opportunity. (2)

1b Briefly explain whether you would regard Karl's research among travel agents as qualitative or quantitative. (2)

1c What is meant in the case by the term 'segment'? (2)

1d Calculate the break-even point for XDream Holidays in Wales. (4)

1e What profit per week can Karl and Natalia expect if they achieve their target of 12 customers? (4)

1f Explain two possible reasons for setting up the business as a Ltd organisation. (

Question 2

2a Examine the factors Karl and Natalia should consider when deciding where to locate their new business. (1

2b Discuss whether Karl or Natalia showed the most enterprise. (1.

2c Karl and Natalia have not yet undertaken a formal business plan. Discuss whether completing a business plan would guarantee the success of the start-up of XDream Holidays Ltd. (1.

MOCK EXAM FOR UNIT 2

This exam is based on unseen material (i.e. neither the candidates nor the teachers know in advance what the text will be about). There are two sets of questions, each based on text that is about 300–400 words long. The exam lasts 90 minutes and the mark total is 80. Therefore there are 10 minutes for reading and a minute per mark when answering the questions (2-mark question = 2-minute answer; 12-mark question = 12-minute answer).

Usually, one set of questions will be based on a newspaper article about a real business situation, and the other questions on a made-up case study. Candidates need to be used to reading articles from newspapers such as *The Guardian*, *The Times*, the *Daily Telegraph* and the *Financial Times*.

The following mock exam follows the exact style of the AQA exam.

Mock exam: Unit 2

(80 marks; 90 minutes)

Answer all questions.

Question 1

Read the article below, then answer the questions that follow.

What sort of boss gives a monkey's about his staff?
Simon Caulkin, The Observer, 28 January 2007

A survey by a management consultancy found that three-quarters of senior executives would do an annual cutback of their workforce to boost productivity and performance. One in six think they could get rid of 20% of employees without damaging performance or morale; nearly half reckon firing up to 5% a year would be a good thing.

Even though only 4% actually carry out this threat, it is still a revealing finding. This is what executives really think of their 'most valued asset'. Not only that, it utterly ignores their own contribution to their employees' underperformance, raising so many questions it's hard to know where to begin.

But let's try. In another survey, the Chartered Institute of Personnel and Development (CIPD) noted that if Britain at work was a marriage, it was 'a marriage under stress, characterised by poor communications and low levels of trust'. Only 38% of employees feel senior managers and directors treat them with respect, and 66% don't trust them. Around a quarter of employees rarely or never look forward to going to work, and almost half are leaving or trying to. 'The findings suggest many managers aren't doing enough to keep their staff interested,' said the CIPD's Mike Emmott. The result: underperformance, low productivity and high staff turnover.

The last UK survey for Gallup's Employee Engagement Index makes similarly grim reading. In 2005 just 16% of UK employees were 'positively engaged' – loyal and committed to the organisation. The rest were unengaged or actively disengaged – physically present but psychologically absent. And it is getting worse: since 2001 the proportion of engaged employees has fallen, while those actively disengaged have increased to 24%.

Gallup puts the cost to the economy of active disengagement at £40 billion, as employees express their disenchantment by going sick, not trying, leaving, or threatening strikes. The culprit, says Gallup, is poor management. 'Workers say they don't know what is expected of them, managers don't care about them as people, their jobs aren't a good fit for their talents and their views count for little.'

Source: adapted from *The Observer*, 28 January 2007. For the full article, go to http://www.guardian.co.uk/business/2007/jan/28/theobserver.observerbusiness4

Questions

1a Explain how an annual cutback of a workforce could 'boost productivity'. (4)

1b Use a motivation theory of your choosing to analyse the methods and attitudes of the senior executives/senior managers highlighted in this article. (9)

1c The article blames managers for the poor performance of staff. Discuss how organisational structure might affect the performance of a large business. (12)

1d Some business experts believe that poor staff morale and performance can undermine a firm's ability to develop effective customer service and quality management. To what extent do you agree with this view? (15)

Question 2

Read the case material below then answer the questions that follow.

Coney Cycles

Ten years ago 19-year-old Dean Coney inherited a bicycle shop when his father died. It was located in Ealing, west London. The business had barely broken even for years, so Dean thought about closing it down. He didn't, largely because of his own passion for racing bikes. He worked hard at modernising the shop, but for the first four years it was a struggle to take any pay out of the business.

Then the shop started to get busy. Commuters were turning to bikes to avoid the London congestion charge and the overcrowding on public transport. Furthermore the increasing focus on personal health and fitness was turning whole families towards bikes. Between 2002 and 2007 the use of bikes doubled in London. All Dean had to do was to take his share of the growing market.

A threat, though, was that Halfords saw the same opportunity. It used heavy TV advertising to promote the expanded cycling sections in its 400 stores, and opened a new Superstore a mile away. After buying and reading a couple of business books, Dean decided to start marketing his shop actively. He bought long-term contracts on poster sites in Ealing High Road and started the 'Coney Cycling Club', organising 'Sunday Cycles' in the country. On summer Sundays there were often 50 to 60 people taking their bikes by train or minivan, with Dean taking the opportunity to talk bikes and biking with his customers. No one would turn up on a Sunday with their latest bike from Halfords, so people were hooked in to staying with Coney Cycles. Dean's bikes were never going to be cheaper than at Halfords, but he made sure to stock high-quality makes to match the high prices.

Over the past year a further issue has been staffing. When he started, he could run the shop on his own. Now he needed two full-time staff and four part-timers for hectic spring Saturdays and for the run-up to Christmas. He chose to recruit only those with a clear love of bikes, then he trained them carefully on different brands. All newcomers were taken to the Brompton Bicycle factory in west London, to see the manufacturing process. The close links formed with suppliers such as Brompton was a key part of Dean's approach to the business.

Coney Cycles: forecasts for July–September this year

Sales	1000 bikes at an average of £250 each
Variable costs	£150 per bike
Total costs	£220,000
Net cash flow	(£40,000)

Now, for the first time, Dean feels in a position to open a second bicycle shop, about three miles away in Acton. He is confident that the finances of the business are strong enough to take the strain.

See Unit 106 for exam answers plus an examiner's commentary.

Questions

2a(i) Calculate Coney Cycles' forecast fixed costs for July–September.

(ii) Calculate the forecast % net profit margin in the July–September period.

(iii) Analyse two actions Dean could take to try to increase this % profit margin.

2b(i) Calculate the difference between Coney Cycle's profit and its net cash flow for the period July–September.

(ii) Discuss what the reasons may be for this difference (1

2c A former member of Dean's staff was overheard saying that 'he hasn't a clue about marketing; Halfords will steamroller him into the ground within five years'. To what extent do you agree with this view? (1

That is the end of the exam.

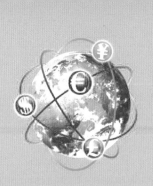
106.1 Mock exam Unit 1 (for full exam paper see Unit 105)

After you have looked carefully at the specimen exam paper in Unit 105, look at the suggested answers (on the right) and the examiner advice (on the left).

Examiner's Advice	Possible Answers
1a Natalia spotted the parachute business opportunity through her personal experience. State two other ways of identifying a business opportunity. **(2)**	
Brief answers are fine here	Carry out primary market research Analyse market data
1b Briefly explain whether you would regard Karl's research among travel agents as qualitative or quantitative. **(2)**	
Just a 2-mark question so don't write too much.	It was qualitative because it was small scale and impressionistic, not a large scale sample survey using questionnaires and data analysis.
1c What is meant in the case by the term 'segment'? **(2)**	
This is a bit long, but nicely applied to the holiday context.	A way of looking at a market – in this case for holidays. Holiday-makers have differing needs. One segment wants cheap sea and sun; Xdream's segment wants adventure even if it costs more.
1d Calculate the break-even point for XDream Holidays in Wales. **(4)**	
Showing your workings (especially the formula) helps your marks. Under exam pressure mistakes happen, so it's wise to help the examiner give you marks even if the final answer's wrong.	Break-even $= \dfrac{\text{Fixed costs}}{\text{Contribution per unit}}$ **(1)** $= \dfrac{£8,000}{£1,000}$ **(1)** $= 8$ (1) people per week (1)
1e What profit per week can Karl and Natalia expect if they achieve their target of 12 customers? **(4)**	
	Profit = Revenue − Total costs (1) Revenue: 12 x £1,500 = £18,000 (1) Costs: (£500 x 12) + £8,000 = £14,000 (1) Profit = £4000 per week (1)

Examiner's Advice	**Possible Answers**

1f Explain two possible reasons for setting up the business as a Ltd organisation. (6)

A 6 mark question requires quite a detailed answer. In this case the two answers use the context (XDream) quite well. A weaker student would just say 'to avoid being personally responsible for company debts'.	To avoid being personally responsible for company debts; this is a high-risk business start-up, therefore the dangers of unlimited liability must be avoided To give people more confidence that they are dealing with a 'real' business, i.e. XDream Holidays Ltd may sound more permanent and better established than XDream Holidays.

2a Examine the factors Karl and Natalia should consider when deciding where to locate their new business. (10)

The attempt to define 'location' is important here. It is rare to see definitions of terms as 'obvious' as location or marketing, but if there are lots of marks at stake, it is very worthwhile.	Choosing a business location combines quantitative factors such as costs, plus qualitative ones such as image. The people Karl and Natalia want to sell to are likely to be relatively well off and relatively young so their location should match. It could be in a city centre, near banks and offices, or in a university town but not on a scruffy back street. They will have to consider whether the rent is affordable. And the surrounding businesses, e.g. it might help to be near shops selling adventure gear or the sort of clothes parachutists wear (known as complementary goods). Judging by the £220,000 negative cash flow (month 3) it is critical that the cost of the location should not be too high, yet the text suggests that the posh clients may want to be reassured by the location, so there will be a tension between cost and 'classiness'.

2b Discuss whether Karl or Natalia showed the most enterprise. (15)

Start with definition ...	Enterprise means showing the initiative and drive to turn an idea into a reality.
Build a case for one	The case for Karl is that he was the one who took his research out to the people who knew the market – the adventure travel agents. He also took the initiative to draw up a cash flow forecast.
... then consider the other	Natalia's most obvious contribution was spotting the gap in the market; hers was the initial idea; she then kept on turning the idea into reality, e.g. by researching into hiring planes and by (with Karl) talking to other parachuters and friends about the idea. She also went to Companies House to establish the Ltd company.
... then make and justify your judgement/verdict	On balance, they shared the activities and actions, but Natalia's original idea tips the balance in saying she was the more enterprising.

Examiner's Advice	Possible Answers
2c Karl and Natalia have not yet undertaken a formal business plan. Discuss whether completing a business plan would guarantee the success of the start-up of XDream Holidays Ltd. (15)	
This starts with a fair definition ...	A business plan sets out in detail the idea, the goals, the financing and the plan for how to achieve success.
... but then turns into an ill-structured series of points; the suggestion is clear that the student is running out of time.	No plan can guarantee success, but not having a plan might lead to failure.
Note that it's better to build one solid paragraph than to jump around in this way.	They would need a plan to get a bank loan.
	It would help them to keep a check on their progress as time goes on. Are they on target? Have they reached break even?

106.2 Mock exam Unit 2 (for full exam paper see Unit 105).

After you have looked carefully at the specimen exam paper in Unit 105, look at the suggested answers (on the right) and the examiner advice (on the left).

Examiner's advice	Answer (in note form)
1a Explain how an annual cutback of a workforce could 'boost productivity'. (4)	
Start with a definition ...	Productivity is efficiency, measured as output per worker ...
... then move to explanation	Fewer staff will boost productivity as long as they can produce as much as before, or perhaps slightly less.
1b Use a motivation theory of your choosing to analyse the methods and attitudes of the senior executives/senior managers highlighted in this article. (9)	
Choose a relevant motivation theory (e.g. Mayo or Herzberg), then define it ...	In these circumstances, an appropriate theorist is Professor Herzberg. His two-factor theory separated factors causing motivation from those causing demotivation. Herzberg would have focused on the idea of 'physically present but psychologically absent', emphasizing the exact fit with his view that hygiene factors achieve 'a fair day's work', but that people can give much, much more if they are positively motivated.
... then look first at methods ...	Herzberg said that job enrichment (the way to achieve motivation) required good, direct communications, whereas the text says that workplaces are 'characterised by poor communications'; he would also have echoed Mayo by condemning a situation where workers 'views count for little'
... then on to attitudes	Herzberg would also echo the idea that senior executives should look at themselves. If 66% of staff believe their bosses don't trust them, this suggests that senior executives are locked into negative thoughts that will undermine key motivators such as recognition for achievement.
Note that there is no need to draw a conclusion as the question did not ask for a discussion/evaluation	

Examiner's advice	Answer (in note form)
1c The article blames managers for the poor performance of staff. Discuss how organisational structure might affect the performance of a large business. (12	
Start with definition ...	Organisational structure is the formal design of how the business is to be managed, set out in a hierarchy diagram.
... then establish that you are thinking about a **large** business	Whereas a small firm can operate informally, with no clear structure, this would be chaotic in a big business. Staff need to know who they are answerable to, and what the objectives are fo the part of the business they work for. They also need to know the formal communication channels. A clear structure should help the efficiency of the business, as people are clear about what they should do, and can feel motivated by the clear career ladder that exists above them.
... before showing that your views are two-sided (note the value of the phrase 'on the other hand').	On the other hand, the structure may impose rigidities and attitudes that stifle workforce initiative and motivation. The structure may have too narrow a span of control, leading to over-supervision and too little room for staff decision-making and creativity. This might stifle innovation, condemning the company to stand still as the market moves ahead.
Then finish off with a judgemental conclusion	The organizational structure has to be right for the circumstances of the business. In a fast-moving market where innovation is critica (mobile phones; pop music; fashion clothing) the structure needs sufficient flexibility to allow staff to be enterprising. So the spans of control need to be wide. In a slow-moving, mature business such as canned food it may matter less if the spans of control are narrow. Many business leaders would claim, though, that all modern markets need constant innovation, so perhaps all firms should free up their staff by giving them wider spans of control and therefore more responsibility.

Examiner's advice	Answer (in note form)

d Some business experts believe that poor staff morale and performance can undermine a firm's ability to develop effective customer service and quality management. To what extent do you agree with this view? (15)

Examiner's advice	Answer (in note form)
Again, start with a definition (or two)	Staff morale will be poor if the workforce is lacking motivation and confidence. This would be likely to affect customer service, which is the practical and psychological impact on the customer of the shopping experience they have had. A bright, friendly and efficient shop assistant can make shopping fun.
Carry on with the argument:	If morale is high, staff are likely to have low absenteeism, low levels of lateness and high levels of productivity and − as the article puts it − 'engagement'. High productivity may help profits, but it is engagement that makes an impact on customers. Feeling cared for is a wonderful aspect of customer service, be it for a student in a school or a passenger on a plane. This relates directly to quality management, because customer service is a vital part of quality from the customer viewpoint.
Then counter it:	On the other hand it would be easy, but wrong, to overstate the link between morale and customer service. This is because many staff make no contact at all with customers. As a passenger, do I care if the train driver's morale is high, as long as s/he is efficient at the job? As I make no contact with the driver I cannot know or care. Performance is different, though, because poor performance can hurt me as a passenger, either because of poor driving (jerky braking or scary speeds) or because of absenteeism (cancelled trains).
Before drawing a conclusion	Overall, I agree that the experts are making a sound point. There may be exceptions to the rule, as suggested in relation to the train driver's morale, but there will usually be a strong correlation between low morale and poor customer service/poor quality. This highlights the importance of taking care over workforce motivation.

Examiner's advice	Answer (in note form)

a(i) Calculate Coney Cycles' forecast fixed costs for July–September. (2)

Examiner's advice	Answer (in note form)
Don't panic! In the pressure of an exam you might not realise that the figure can easily be worked out	Fixed costs are part of total costs. If total costs are £220,000 and the variable costs are 1,000 x £150 = £150,000, then the fixed costs must be the balance, i.e. £70,000.

ii) Calculate the forecast % net profit margin in the July–September period. (3)

Examiner's advice	Answer (in note form)
Make sure to explain what you're doing. Don't just scribble down lots of numbers.	Net profit is profit after deducting variable and fixed costs, i.e. £250,000 − £220,000 = £30,000 % net profit margin = £30,000/£250,000 x 100 = 12%

Examiner's advice	**Answer (in note form)**
(iii) Analyse two actions Dean could take to try to increase this % profit margin.	**(8**
Make sure to develop each point, explaining in detail why each action could increase the profit margin. A numerical example can help.	One way to increase the net profit margin is to increase sales. This will spread the fixed costs over more units of output and therefore reduce the fixed costs per unit (which, in turn, increases the profit margin). For example, when selling 1,000 bikes, the £70,000 fixed costs amount to £70 per bike. If sales could be doubled to 2,000, the £70,000 fixed costs would only account for £35 per bike.
Note that the second point does not need to be as detailed as the first.	A second way to increase the margin is to cut the costs, as long a the cut doesn't affect the customer too badly. There may be staff who are under-worked and could be 'let go', or part of the costs might be caused by theft of the bikes, so a sharper focus on security among the staff may be a great help.

2b(i) Calculate the difference between Coney Cycle's profit and its net cash flow for the period July – September.	**(2**
	Profit is forecast to be £30,000, yet the cash flow is forecast at −£40,000, i.e. there is a £70,000 cash flow shortfall.

(ii) Discuss what the reasons may be for this difference.	**(11**
Start by defining terms	Profit is a calculation of the difference between revenue and costs based on a series of assumptions, e.g. that customers will pay in full for today's credit sales. Cash flow simply measures the difference between what goes into the bank account and how much comes out.
Then apply the theory to the reality of this case ...	Even though Coney Cycles' summer may be profitable, there are still reasons why cash flow may be £70,000 adrift. The text make clear that Dean was working on opening a second outlet. The investment cost for that (e.g. buying a lease on shop premises) would hit cash flow yet leave profit unaltered. There are also many other possible start-up costs such as fitting out the shop; because these are one-off investment costs they do not count towards profit, yet can be costly in terms of cash-flow. Just as cash flow is seriously negative in the early days of a brand new business, so the same will occur when opening a second outlet.
	On the other hand there may be less favourable reasons. Cash flow can dip because of over-stocking, i.e. buying more bikes from the suppliers than you are able to sell to customers. In this case the weak cash flow could be a worry. The July-September 'profits' may disappear in January when a huge sale is needed to get rid of unwanted stock.
... and draw a conclusion	The text does not provide enough information to be sure whether the difference is a worry or whether it is a normal result of expansion. Dean should certainly investigate to satisfy himself tha the business is running as it should.

Examiner's advice	Answer (in note form)
c A former member of Dean's staff was overheard saying that 'he hasn't a clue about marketing; Halfords will steamroller him into the ground within 5 years'. To what extent do you agree with this view? (14)	
can be risky to start with 'a conclusion/verdict', but ere it is well handled. Both paragraphs are substantial, with the second one showing clear understanding of marketing. The whole answer is evaluative and it justifies he clear conclusion.	I would not agree at all. Dean has been realistic about his place in the market and recognised that he can not compete on Halford's terms. He has gone for the more specialised segment of the market – with expensive, more profitable bikes and employing knowledgeable staff. He has booked long term advertising and been enterprising in starting a cycle club. This is not Halford's market sector. If anything, his greatest threat would come from someone else starting up another independent cycle shop nearby.
An unusual approach but a successful one.	It sounds as if the former staff member doesn't understand what marketing really is. Dean has shown his ability to get close to his customers and to serve them effectively; that's superb marketing. It does not matter whether he knows how to write a TV commercial because his small business could never afford a serious advertising budget.
	As said at the start, I disagree entirely with the view expressed.